Praise for
THE TRAGEDY
OF RUSSIA'S REFORMS

"The Tragedy of Russia's Reforms is destined to become the most authoritative analysis of Russia's first postcommunist decade. Incisive and impeccably well researched, the book avoids the clichés, the wishful thinking, and the sheer blindness of most Western commentary on the Yeltsin era with its false dichotomy between 'reformers' and 'hard-liners.' Instead, the authors describe the ideology of the Yeltsin elite and the 'Washington Consensus' that backed it as 'market bolshevism.' . . . As a leading scholar of the movement for human rights in the Soviet period, Reddaway is free of all nostalgia for the Soviet record but equally free of self-deception about Russia's postcommunist reality. There were—and still are— alternatives to market bolshevism, and this excellent book explains them."

—JONATHAN STEELE
Assistant editor of The Guardian *and author of* Eternal Russia:
Yeltsin, Gorbachev, and the Mirage of Democracy

"This spirited and highly controversial study will predictably serve as a stimulus for renewed debate concerning the Gorbachev and Yeltsin periods and the economic 'reforms' associated with them. This book should be read for its well-documented discussion of the bottomless pit of crime and corruption that opened up in postcommunist Russia."

—JOHN B. DUNLOP
Hoover Institution

"An erudite and provocative analysis of Russia's troubled efforts to transform its economy and society in the 1990s. Well worth reading for its insights—even for readers who may not agree with the authors' perspectives and conclusions."

—ROSE BRADY
Author of Kapitalizm: Russia's Struggle to Free Its Economy

"A monumental book, unsurpassed in sophistication and insight. *The Tragedy of Russia's Reforms* is a must-read for anyone struggling to understand Russia's past, present, and future. Reddaway and Glinski provide a much-needed service in alerting us to missed alternatives and important lessons to be learned."

—DAVID JOHNSON
Johnson's Russia List

"The Tragedy of Russia's Reforms is nothing less than a tour de force. Russia's collapse in the 1990s shattered many cherished political and economic models, but this book makes sense of the catastrophe, relying on an impressive command of the facts and setting it firmly in the context of Russian history and political science theory."

—PAUL KLEBNIKOV
S*enior editor for* Forbes *magazine and author of* Godfather of the Kremlin: Boris Berezovsky and the Looting of Russia

THE
TRAGEDY OF
RUSSIA'S REFORMS

THE TRAGEDY OF RUSSIA'S REFORMS

MARKET BOLSHEVISM AGAINST DEMOCRACY

PETER REDDAWAY
& DMITRI GLINSKI

UNITED STATES INSTITUTE OF PEACE PRESS
WASHINGTON, D.C.

UNITED STATES INSTITUTE OF PEACE
1200 17th Street NW, Suite 200
Washington, DC 20036-3011

First published 2001

Printed in the United States of America

The paper used in this publication meets the minimum requirements of American National Standard for Information Sciences—Permanence of Paper for Printed Library Materials, ANSI Z39.48-1984.

Library of Congress Cataloging-in-Publication Data
Reddaway, Peter.
 The tragedy of Russia's reforms : market bolshevism against democracy / Peter Reddaway and Dmitri Glinski.
  p. cm.
 Includes bibliographical references and index.
 ISBN 1-929223-07-2 (cloth) — ISBN 1-929223-06-4
 1. Russia (Federation)—Politics and government—1991– 2. Post-communism—Russia (Federation) 3. Russia (Federation)—Social conditions—1991– 4. Russia (Federation)—Social policy. 5. Russia (Federation)—Economic conditions—1991– 6. Russia (Federation)—Economic policy—1991– I. Glinski, Dmitri, 1971–

DK510.763 .R43 2001
947.086—dc21

00-020482

CONTENTS

PREFACE

IN THIS BOOK, we attempt to employ the perspectives of political science and contemporary history to explain some rather complex social phenomena. These two disciplines typically converge in the academic field of area studies, in which scholars who devote themselves to studying entire regions and their countries from a variety of perspectives endeavor to isolate and explain the interrelationships among a country's broad social movements, the distribution of its national resources, and its political institutions. This task, weighty in its own right, is complicated when it comes to isolating a particular set of policies that have strongly affected almost all of these institutions in a country whose political system and language have seemed rather distant—literally and figuratively—and somewhat ineffable to even the most engaged observers in the West. The task is further complicated when the scholar seeks to convey the implications of these policies during and after a profound transformation of the country's political, social, and economic systems.

In all their various branches, disciplines, and subdisciplines, the social scientists who study particular countries try to employ standard methodologies and terms of reference that will sharpen existing analysis and refine the accumulated knowledge about the country. When scholars attempt to convey that knowledge to those outside the discipline—be they students, policymakers, or simply those who have a general curiosity or concern about the subject—selecting language to communicate concepts and examples that are familiar to both their colleagues and nonspecialists can be quite difficult. Hence our purpose in this preface is twofold: First, we seek to provide a frame of reference for the names of the people, political movements, and institutions addressed in this book. The second and related purpose is to provide some background about terminology that we hope will orient the lay reader to the frenetic period of the Soviet Union's dissolution and the re-emergence of the Russian state—a truly historic, kaleidoscopic period. To our academic colleagues who are well acquainted with what follows, we beg your indulgence for a few pages.

Many lay readers will likely encounter in this book Russian names and terms that strike a familiar chord, despite the variations in the translations and transliterations adopted by various Western media outlets and publishers. Because we have wanted to convey the themes and actors in this book to as wide an audience as possible, we have departed from the Library of Congress system of transliterating Russian names, using instead the kind of spellings that lay readers may have encountered in the major Western media. Inevitably this has led to

ix

some minor problems, especially regarding the standardization of spellings used in the text and the bibliographic references. For ease of reference, we have used, in most cases, abbreviations drawn from our own translations of the names of Russian political parties and government agencies.

Regarding the problem of how best to render in English the terms that Russians use to categorize, for example, politicians and political movements, we have tried to avoid straight translation and use words that best convey the meaning to Western readers. Complications arise, however, because of the variety of labels applied to different tendencies within a single broad category. For example, the term "national-patriots" is used by Russians for the broad category of nationalistically minded conservatives; because the latter phrase is clumsy, we usually use the term "national-conservatives." Then, however, there are variants within this category which we render, for example, as "left-wing conservatives" because, like Gennadi Zyuganov, they are both socially conservative and in some degree socialist; or as "right-wing conservatives" because, as with Aleksandr Lebed and Vladimir Zhirinovsky, their conservatism is combined with economic views not so different from those found in Western conservative parties; or as "radical imperialist conservatives" because, for them, restoring the USSR in a new form is the first priority; or as "conservative traditionalists" because, like Aleksandr Solzhenitsyn, they are neither radically imperialist, nor particularly left- or right-wing, but focus mostly on reviving what they see as the traditional virtues of the Russian people.

Returning to the broader level, we have decided to categorize informal mass-based political groups with lower-case spellings. This practice reflects the categorization found in much of the Russian (and, to some extent, Western) media at the time. Thus Soviet and Russian "democrats" comprise all segments of the body politic that sought an end to one-party rule and the establishment of more representative political institutions. Similarly, "communists" range from those who have desired a return to the Soviet political order, with its specific institutional apparatus, to those whose values could be described as traditional, social-democratic, or conservative—descriptors that easily can be applied to many members of, notably, the Agrarian Party to the Russian Communist Party to the Communist Party of the Russian Federation (CPRF). Conversely, for the period up to about 1989, we sometimes refer to the Communist Party of the Soviet Union (CPSU) simply as "the Party," thus reflecting the dominance of this political institution during much of the period we cover. When we refer to "Communist(s)," we have in mind specific parties or members of specific parties.

Because this book covers a period during which three different sets of political institutions existed in Russia, readers who are not experts will find the changing terms rather confusing. We therefore spell out here, in simplified form, when and how the changes took place, and how the names changed.

To begin, the Union of Soviet Socialist Republics (USSR) was a "socialist federation" consisting of fifteen union republics, of which the Russian republic (the Russian Soviet Federated Socialist Republic, or RSFSR) was its largest constituent member; the RSFSR was further divided into regular regions (*oblasti*) and nominally autonomous, ethnically defined administrative units, as was also the case to a limited extent within other union republics. The latter republics (in Soviet parlance, Soviet Socialist Republics, or SSRs) included those along the Baltic coast (Lithuania, Latvia, and Estonia); the western republics of Ukraine, Byelorussia (Belarus), and Moldova; the republics straddling the Caucasus mountains to Russia's south—Armenia, Azerbaijan, and Georgia; and, across the Caspian Sea, the Central Asian republics of Kazakhstan, Kirghizia (Kyrgyzstan), Tajikistan, Turkmenistan, and Uzbekistan.

Beneath this territorial division, the "classic" Soviet administrative model that existed until 1989 was based on two exactly parallel hierarchies—that of the state and that of the Party—whose structures were replicated in each of the union republics but were controlled by the federal organs in Moscow. The state hierarchy, which was politically weak but conducted most of the administration, consisted of a pyramid of legislative councils, or soviets, the members of which had been "popularly elected" after running unopposed. Theoretically—and, from 1989, to a considerable extent in practice—the executive governments at each administrative level answered to these councils. At the highest level of the union, the legislature was called the USSR Supreme Soviet; the executive branch consisted of the Council of Ministers, headed by a prime minister, and the ministries that were subordinate to it. Many of the latter ran entire industries, including their various branches in the republics.

However, parallel to these state structures was the exactly parallel and politically much more powerful Party hierarchy, headed by its general secretary; the holders of this position in the post-Stalin era were Nikita Khrushchev, Leonid Brezhnev, Yuri Andropov, Konstantin Chernenko, and, finally, Mikhail Gorbachev. At the top of this hierarchy stood the Party's Central Committee and its two main decision-making bodies, the Secretariat and the Political Bureau (Politburo).

In order to make sure that the central government's decisions were implemented throughout the fifteen republics that made up the theoretically voluntary union, this Party hierarchy prescribed all the basic policies to be adopted by the hierarchy of soviets. It then monitored how well or badly the hierarchy of soviets passed the relevant laws and implemented them. Where necessary, the Party intervened; through its apparatus of trusted officials, it could do this easily because, first, membership of the party apparatus and the legislative/executive hierarchy overlapped heavily and, second, the main job of the committees that made up the party apparatus was to steer and monitor, though not actually administer, the different branches of government.

By the time of Gorbachev's ascension to the post of general secretary, enough of a consensus had formed in the Soviet leadership that the accumulation of economic and social problems (which visibly manifested themselves during the Brezhnev period's "stagnation") was reaching the point of systemic crisis.

Gorbachev and his associates decided that this system was too bureaucratic and inert to "get the Soviet Union moving again." Hence in early 1989, they began to create a new system in which the party apparatus would largely disengage itself from government (and focus on ideological and strategic planning issues), and the hierarchy of soviets would start to take full responsibility for governing the country.

To launch this new system, first the old Supreme Soviet was abolished, and then two-thirds of the members of a new superlegislature called the Congress of People's Deputies (CPD) were popularly elected—with a real choice of candidates, in many cases—and a third were nominated by big organizations, such as the CPSU and the trade unions. The 2,250 members of the unwieldy CPD parliament had sessions twice a year and elected a much smaller working parliament called the Supreme Soviet, to which the Council of Ministers was in certain ways democratically accountable. In 1990, the same set of institutions was set up in each of the union's fifteen republics, including the RSFSR.

At this point, the problem of dual power started to arise, partly because the RSFSR had a population more than half that of the whole country and therefore possessed potentially enormous political weight. Sitting in the same city as the union's government, Moscow, Russia's government duly began to assert its autonomy under Boris Yeltsin: first, Yeltsin was the leader of Russia's parliament; then, from June 1991, he was its president. Which parts of Moscow were under the RSFSR's jurisdiction, which parts under the union's? What happened if Russia did not hand over to the union government all the tax and other revenues the union thought were its due? The answers were not clear.

What was clear, though, was that Russia had parallel governments—the Soviet Union's and Russia's—competing for authority on a poorly demarcated field. As Yeltsin's popularity rose and Gorbachev's declined, Russia's government gradually got the upper hand, and the personal antagonism between the two men sharpened. When the hard-line coup of August 1991 aimed to restore full union control over all the republics, and ignominiously failed, the USSR was virtually doomed. Four months later, the presidents of Russia, Ukraine, and Belarus secretly initiated a process that quickly led to the splintering of the Soviet Union on December 25. Its fifteen federated republics became fifteen independent countries, even though most of them were far from ready for independence.

In Russia, opposition to the Yeltsin government's economic policies of "shock therapy," which were launched on January 2, 1992, quickly became focused in the country's legislature—the Russian CPD and Supreme Soviet. A year and a half of unceasing conflict between the executive and legislative branches—caused at first by the former repeatedly trying to impose its policies on an unwilling parliament, and exacerbated by the unsuitability of the Soviet-era constitution, which was constantly amended—ended in October 1993, when the Yeltsinites dispersed the parliament by armed force. They then rammed through (in an apparently rigged referendum) a new constitution that created the "Russian Federation" and gave extensive powers to the executive—especially the president—and few to the new parliament. The latter, elected in December, was made up of a lower house (the Duma) of 450 members, who represented voters largely through their parliamentary factions, and an upper house (the Council of the Federation), whose members, much like the United States Senate, represented Russia's eighty-nine "subjects of the federation"—its regions and ethnically designated republics and other units—each of which had two deputies. The Duma's powers differed from those of the Federation Council and, in general, caused the government more problems.

In October 1993, Yeltsin also dissolved by decree the regional and lower levels of Russia's soviets and then replaced them with unicameral counterparts of the federal legislative institutions. The chief executives of most of the regions were now called governors, but the twenty autonomous republics (for example, Chechnya and Tatarstan) continued to have presidents.

P. R.

Acknowledgments

M ANY PEOPLE have contributed to this book. We would like to thank, first of all, those colleagues and friends who generously read the manuscript in whole or in part at various stages and in various forms, and gave us the benefit of their critical comments: Robert Otto, John Dunlop, Joan Urban, Priscilla McMillan, James Millar, George Breslauer, Blair Ruble, Stephen Cohen, David Johnson, Bruce Parrott, Janine Wedel, and two publisher's reviewers who have remained anonymous. We also express profound appreciation to Bob Otto for his untiring help in locating sources, as well as for debating at length most of the book's issues. We are also indebted to Catherine Dale, Andrei Tsygankov, Webster Tarpley, Thomas Buck, Katrina Elledge, Alexander Pankov, and Andrew Knight, who made substantial contributions as resourceful and friendly research, editorial, and, in Tarpley's case, writing assistants, thanks mostly to funding from George Washington University's Institute for Russian, European, and Eurasian Studies, directed by James Millar. Catherine Dale was also a talented co-author for the writing up of some public opinion research we refer to, which, in addition, she helped to plan and conduct. Further, we appreciate the comments on earlier drafts of chapter 1 and the epilogue, which were published in, respectively, *Demokratizatsiya* 6, no. 3 (Summer 1998) and *Journal of Democracy* 10, no. 2 (April 1999).

Peter Reddaway is also specially grateful to John Dunlop and Martin Dewhirst for bibliographic advice and assistance; and to Constance Barrett and Susanne Sternthal for translation and editing work, respectively. He also owes a particular debt to the United States Institute of Peace, which gave him a fellowship in 1993–94 and sponsored a research trip to Russia. He would like to thank in particular the head of its Jennings Randolph Fellowship Program, Joe Klaits, for his help and encouragement during and since that time, as also Dan Snodderly and Kay Hechler of the Institute's Press. Most of all, he is grateful to Peter Pavilionis, who has been the hardest-working, most supportive, and most unflappable book editor he has been lucky enough to work with.

He also owes major debts to the Smith Richardson Foundation for two research grants, to the National Council for Soviet and East European Research for a grant for public opinion research, and to Stanford University's Hoover Institution for a summer fellowship.

In less direct but still important ways, he is indebted to numerous discussions and debates over the years on the themes of this book with colleagues who are not mentioned above, especially Wayne Allensworth, Keith Bush, Richard

Dobson, Dmitri Furman, Paul Goble, James Goldgeier, Thomas Graham, Steven Grant, Stefan Hedlund, Paul Henze, Eugene Huskey, Anne Jablonski, Donald Jensen, Igor Klyamkin, Amy Knight, Anatol Lieven, Dominic Lieven, Edward Lucas, Michael McFaul, Rajan Menon, William Odom, Robert Orttung, Aleksandr Prokhanov, Peter Rutland, Viktor Sheinis, Louise Shelley, Lilia Shevtsova, Valery Solovei, Jack Sontag, Peter Stavrakis, William Taubman, Vladimir Toumanoff, Mikhail Tsypkin, Michael Urban, Anne Williamson, Enders Wimbush, and Vyacheslav Zhitenev.

For their forbearance, he is grateful to his son Chris and his daughter Becky, and above all to his wife Betsy.

Dmitri Glinski is most grateful to Bruce Parrott, Florence Rotz, and Johns Hopkins University's Paul H. Nitze School of Advanced International Studies for their understanding and supportive attitude. Also, he expresses his biggest, and perhaps irredeemable, debt to his mother.

Finally, while the text of this book has gone through many revisions and editings, we note that each of us bears the primary responsibility for those sections for which he developed the initial draft.

INTRODUCTION

F̲EW WOULD DISPUTE that the events of 1989–91 that originated in Moscow and culminated in the disappearance of the Soviet Union and the emergence of Russia as its main successor state marked a watershed in recent world history. Yet the true meaning and consequences of these events are subjects for a world-wide debate that is only beginning to unfold. While many Western observers—and a few fortunately positioned Russians—exulted in these changes and in the glowing prospects they saw for a new world order, Russia from at least 1990 has been sinking—from the socioeconomic, demographic, cultural, and moral points of view—into turmoil and decay. From late 1991–early 1992, a period marked by the first application of the medicine of radical deregulation, privatization, and an economic austerity regime prescribed by the International Monetary Fund (IMF)—a course of "treatment" that was known, perhaps for lack of a better term, as "shock therapy"—the country's disease became markedly more severe. Whether the eventual bottoming out and upturn in the economy of 1999–2000 can be sustained remains to be seen.

The amount of destruction has exceeded that of the comparable American experience during the Great Depression and the industrial loss inflicted on the Soviet Union in 1941–45 by World War II. To give but a few figures: from 1991 to 1998, Russia's gross domestic product (GDP) declined by 43.3 percent; in particular, industrial production fell by 56 percent, and the agricultural decline was even larger.[1] (For comparison, from 1929 to 1933, U.S. GDP shrank by 30.5 percent; between 1941 and 1945, the Soviet GDP declined by 24 percent.[2]) Meanwhile, capital investment in the Russian economy fell by a spectacular 78 percent between 1991 and 1995, and this decline has continued ever since. Of all the country's economic activities, its high-technology industries—which are strategically important for the economic development and survival of major industrial nations—suffered the worst. Thus, for example, production in electronics fell by 78 percent between 1991 and 1995. Closely related to this collapse of domestic production, imports in 1997 made up half of the Russian consumer market until the ruble's 1998 collapse reversed the trend. Inflation, which soared to 1,354 percent in 1992, was gradually but never fully tamed—declining to 11 percent in 1997, but rising sharply again in 1998 to 84 percent, and then declining again. It cut the average real incomes of working Russians by 46 percent in 1992; incomes managed to improve until 1998; but in 1998–99, the population's real disposable income dropped by a third.[3]

Behind these figures lurk qualitative changes in Russia's identity and its place in the world. Thus Russia has been precipitously losing its status as an intellectual great power—a status it enjoyed for a much longer time, and with much more benefit for itself and the rest of the world, than it enjoyed its status as a military giant. The number of Russian scientists (who once accounted for one-fourth of the world's total) has shrunk from 3.4 million to 1.3 million from the late 1980s to the present. Although Russia's economic reformers may believe that they saved money by cutting the funding for academia to one-twelfth of what it was in 1985, Russia's net financial loss from the decline of its science amounts, by some estimates, to $500–600 billion annually.[4] For the first time in recent world history, one of the major industrial nations with a highly educated society has dismantled the results of several decades of economic development— however tortuous, costly, and often misdirected it may have been—and slipped into the ranks of countries that are conventionally categorized as "Third World." To make this experience even more dramatic, this comprehensive national collapse occurred at the same time as the nation's leaders and some of their allies in the West promised Russians that they were just about to join the family of democratic and prosperous nations.

The consequences of this disastrous experience will not disappear in the foreseeable future. Moreover, some of them have dynamics of their own and are spreading fast across Russian borders. The major threat is that the Russian state may well become weakened beyond repair, while its core functions are being privatized by illegitimate and unaccountable forces, including corrupt officials and organized crime. According to estimates by the Russian State Statistics Committee, unregistered and untaxed economic activity accounts for some 25 percent of the national economy, while the Ministry of Interior estimates the sum at no less than 40 percent—figures surpassing the boldest dreams of the most fervent advocates of laissez faire.[5] A report from the Center for Strategic and International Studies (CSIS) maintains that organized crime syndicates and criminal capital flight originating in Russia "constitute a direct threat to the national security interests" of the United States. The CSIS experts may have been somewhat alarmist, but they concluded that Russia may in certain respects be evolving into a "criminal-syndicalist state."[6] A survey of Western business executives conducted by Control Risks Group in November 1997 identified Russia as the world's most corrupt country, while surveys by Transparency International rate it only slightly better.[7]

Yet numerous critical observers inside and outside Russia fail to perceive that many of the roots of these unwelcome developments can be found in the reform policies designed and carried out from 1991 on—policies that the leading Western participants hailed and fostered with enthusiasm.

THE PURPOSE OF THIS BOOK

This book has several aims. The first and most basic is to share with the reader our understanding of how and why the rulers of postcommunist Russia (with the aid of their Western advisers and supporters) have taken their country in a direction that—predictably, in our view—led to tragic consequences for the country and its people. Believing that alternative courses existed and are still available—even though they would require more and more strenuous efforts of reason and will to achieve, given the continuing decay of the Russian state and society—we will draw attention on occasion to alternatives advocated by some Russians and Westerners at various stages of the "reforms." Thus we will also offer the reader some analysis and evaluation of those diverse opposition forces that expressed and advanced these alternatives on the Russian political stage, both within the so-called reform movement and in the camp that is usually viewed as "hostile" to reform.

The anti-Yeltsin opposition, which has often been dismissed in the West as "dark forces," issued timely warnings about the perils of these reforms. Recently, Western observers have become increasingly aware of this fact. Yet one of the main riddles of the Yeltsin period (especially for those Western readers who fully or partly share our critique of shock therapy) has been the striking helplessness of the opposition of all stripes—its chronic inability or unwillingness to take advantage of the Kremlin's obvious failures and to mobilize its resources in order to replace the regime or at least to make a durable and constructive impact on the government's policies. Among all the European countries of the former Soviet bloc, Russia remains the last where the initial postcommunist regime is still hanging on—despite the fact that it is responsible for brutal economic and social disruptions on a scale that most nations in this group have managed to avoid. An enigma of contemporary Russian history has been the Yeltsin's regime's tenacity, even as the condition of nation, society, polity, and economy have deteriorated.

We will try to shed light on this paradox in the pages of this book. We will discuss how and why the "nationalist" (or, in Russian parlance, "patriotic") opposition failed to establish itself as an influential force, despite many painful blows to the national feelings of most Russians, while the ruling elite and establishment media successfully appropriated most of its rhetoric; and why Gennadi Zyuganov's Communist Party of the Russian Federation (CPRF), rather than any of the more principled and forward-looking political forces, filled the niche of opposition party No. 1 and thus fuelled a "Red Scare" in Russia and abroad. In conclusion, we will discuss what developments we think are likely to occur in the future, and consider the relevance of Russia's recent experiment with reforms for the international community as a whole.

Let us say a few words about what not to expect from this book. It makes little sense for us to debate at length—though we will on occasion—with those Western experts and officials of governments and international financial institutions who still believe that the dynamic of postcommunist Russian development has been positive and that Russian society is more healthy and "advanced" today than it was during the last years of the Soviet Union. We will refrain from this mainly because the pitiful condition in which today's Russia finds itself is a starting point for our analysis. Moreover, this condition has in fact become well known to the Russian and Western publics through the mass media and academic writings, and we assume it to be evident to most observers. To a large extent, Western sources—except for those coming, until recently, from international financial institutions and former Western advisers to the Kremlin such as Jeffrey Sachs and Anders Aslund—agree with one another in describing the symptoms of the disease now afflicting Russian government and society.[8] The key disagreements begin when discussion moves on to the diagnosis of and possible cures for the sickness. It is at this stage of the debate that a meaningful discussion becomes possible.

By emphasizing and exploring counterfactual opportunities that Russia has missed, we want to distance ourselves from those who express extreme and indiscriminate pessimism about Russia's ability to improve its lot. This sense of hopelessness—a mirror image of the missionary zeal and optimism projected by some Western enthusiasts of reform—is currently more widespread in Russia itself than elsewhere. The Russian mind, especially in today's conditions, strongly inclines toward a fatalistic view of history that sees the present ordeal through the grim lens of desperation and disbelief that any economic or moral betterment is possible. According to a January 2000 poll by the Public Opinion Foundation in Moscow, 77 percent of respondents characterized the Russian economy as "crisis-ridden," while only 15 percent believed it to be "normal."[9] According to a joint survey conducted by Michigan State University and the Institute of Sociology in Moscow, a content analysis of the whole spectrum of the Russian media has demonstrated that more than 80 percent of the authors of relevant articles incline toward the most pessimistic outlooks concerning both the short- and long-term futures.[10]

Even occupants of the highest seats of power in Russia, including those who figured among the initiators of the ill-fated reforms, have been on a par with most Western observers and Russian citizens in their dark assessments of what is going on in the country. Strikingly gloomy comments on the regime's performance were regularly issued by none other than Boris Yeltsin, who in his address to the Russian parliament in March 1997, after six years as president, stated that the situation in the country was "on the brink" and that "people have reached the limits of their patience."[11] "Bandit capitalism" is the definition of the newly created social system in Russia offered by former first deputy prime minister Boris Nemtsov, one of those who embraced early on the radical "transition to the market."[12] In one of his books, the father of Russian shock therapy, Yegor Gaidar, acknowledges in his usual aloof manner that postreform Russian society is oligarchical and that "Unfortunately, the combination of imperial rhetoric, economic adventurism, and large-scale theft seem likely to become the long-term determinants of Russian realities."[13] The speaker of the lower house of parliament (the State Duma), Gennadi Seleznev—until recently, a relatively clear-headed politician of the opposition camp—commented in the wake of the scandalous Sviazinvest auction that Russia has become a "bandit state."[14]

But if the immobilizing sense that the present course of events is preordained and irreversible is not surprising to find among the broad masses of the population, who with minor exceptions have no levers of influence on the ruling elite, the profession of helplessness by senior officials is a far more ominous sign, suggesting a paralysis of will and a chronic lack of the qualities required for national leadership. "We wanted to make things better, but they've turned out the same as always"—this utterance by Viktor Chernomyrdin, which slipped out amid the conflagration of the Chechen war and has now entered popular folklore, epitomizes the extraordinary feeling of impotence of the prime minister of a nation with a thousand years of history that remained at the time an influential player in the modern world. A similar intonation of obediently accepting one's lot as a plaything of incomprehensible and ungovernable historical forces is also characteristic for a wide range of established opposition figures. This worldview seems to us one of the major reasons for the flabbiness of the regime's opponents and for the profound demoralization of their rank-and-file followers. We address this issue in subsequent chapters.

Yet as events have shown, both the missionary fervor of Western pro-Yeltsin radicals and the hopeless resignation of people being led like cattle to the slaughter (which is now typical for large segments of the Russian elite and society) are symptoms of a dangerous decline of analytical reasoning and a failure to learn from historical experience. This is why the lessons to be learned from the early stages of reform seem to have enlightened neither the lackluster opponents of the regime, nor the rulers of the country, nor their influential supporters in the West.

The present work is addressed to those people inside and outside Russia who share our conviction that Russia's recent decline into economic and social degradation and the squandering of its human capital can and should be reversed. This in turn requires the development of an enlightened international public opinion that would be able to exercise influence on governments and legislatures in major countries on which Russia is currently dependent. We hope that opinion groups will earnestly try to influene those governments and international financial institutions that were involved in the direct and indirect sponsorship of Russia's corrupt regime and its crony capitalists. Most of these organizations have roles to play in Russia's future relations with the outside world, relations that may have the potential for mutual advantage.

We believe that such a course would promise strategic benefits to the United States and Western Europe from the standpoint of their national interests. A future Russian government that was no longer under humiliating and ineffective Western tutelage from the IMF and a multitude of foreign creditors and took full responsibility for its actions should have a much better chance than its predecessors to undercut organized crime in its citadel, to head off a mass exodus of refugees caused by worsening conditions in Russia, and to avoid further alienation between the West and the silent majority of Russians (which probably includes future Russian leaders). Also, such a course would improve the chances that the former Soviet space would be anchored by a more stable Russia. This in turn would provide better hope both for the development of viable regional and global security arrangements and for the evolution of less tense, more cooperative relations between Russia and many key international organizations.

The strategy proposed here requires joint actions by responsible Russians and democratically minded Westerners, based on a qualitatively new and better informed grasp of what has happened in Russia over the past decade and of why the euphoric hopes of 1991 have yielded to such abrupt and painful disillusionment. It is in hope of advancing a thorough reevaluation of Russia's reforms and of the related stereotypes governing Western policy that we have written this book.

OUR DISCIPLINE AND ITS METHOD

Let us briefly describe our approach to the subject matter and the research methods employed for the present work. Earlier in this century, the study of politics as a sphere of inquiry remained for several decades a terrain of controversy where the practitioners of disciplines that claimed to be more advanced—primarily historians and economists—crossed swords over the right to define the rules and criteria of the most appropriate methodology. The banner of victory changed hands periodically, reflecting shifts in dominant trends and intellectual fashions in Western social thought, which in their turn shaped the professional careers of those students of modernity who bound themselves to one or another methodology imported from a neighboring discipline. In the late 1960s, during a major methodological debate and partly under the impact of Karl Popper's assault on the principles of historicism, economics seemed to assert itself finally and irreversibly as the law-giver and fashion-setter in all spheres of social knowledge. Among the factors behind this triumph of economic reductionism were the prevailing assumptions of the neopositivist worldview, according to which every sphere of knowledge is worth the honorable title of science only to the extent that its methods promise to achieve the certainty and predictability of the Newtonian universe. In its extreme form, this uniform standard required a formal quantification of the results of each and every piece of scientifically significant research and their definitive insertion in the iron chain of cause and effect.

Let us remark in passing that these formal, neopositivist criteria came to dominate the social sciences and even the humanities precisely at the time when they were being subjected to the most radical critique and revision in the citadel of positivism—in the epistemology of the "hard" sciences themselves.[15] These considerations notwithstanding, quantitative methodologies borrowed from natural science via economics have remained, despite all powerful intellectual challenges, the mainstream of Western social science and the standard of scientific validity in many institutions and colleges that feature textbooks of statistics and econometrics as the required catechisms for students of society and politics.

With its epistemological criteria of validity, this dominance of economic reductionism has undoubtedly played some positive role by protecting empirical knowledge against the perils of abstract metaphysics and opinionated journalism. However, it is increasingly evident that this approach exhausted its usefulness long ago, and that its persistence as a universal standard will harm the further advance of our knowledge about society. Among the deplorable legacies of the undisputed rule of formal "natural science" methodology is a certain inferiority complex in the social sciences and humanities, which, despite every exertion, have failed to conform to such artificially imposed criteria of truth. This set of methodological conventions was closely linked with the theories of rational choice, game theory models, and similar antihistorical constructs imported from economics, which treated society as a mechanistic sum total of individual consumers with a given and uniform system of "innate" and "rational" preferences and values. This framework, characterized by neglect for cultural and psychological factors and for the diversity of values within societies right down to the level of individuals, deprived social inquiry of its human dimension, paradoxically fostering the convergence of some major trends in Western social sciences with the species of Marxist sociology that even in the Soviet Union was often characterized as "vulgar."

Yet this perception of social reality turned out to be particularly seductive for a number of intellectuals East and West, in part because it generated euphoric illusions about the ease with which social engineering experiments could be carried out on entire nations. These assumptions and patterns of thought were shared by, among others, the theorists of Russia's economic transition and some "transitologists" who had been prominent in major universities and international financial institutions. Not unlike proponents of human cloning, they believed that the genes of Western economic agents that had taken shape under special historical conditions over centuries could be surgically transferred into the womb of a different social organism without producing a monster. It was their advice, touted as the latest fashion among advanced Western scholars, that the inexperienced and morally disoriented leaders of the postcommunist regimes rushed to put into action. The bitter harvest of these fallacies has been reaped by Russia and some of its East European neighbors. True, other such neighbors fared better. Poland, for example, eventually came through the pain of transition with relative success, but only after the basic elements of shock therapy and radical monetarism were either abandoned or diluted in a different program of structural reforms sponsored by the European Union that left considerable room for government intervention, including protectionism and industrial policies. Yet even in Poland, 61 percent of respondents expressed dissatisfaction with the outcomes of the transition process, a figure that points to more fundamental problems with the design of transition than purely economic failures. All this raises the question of whether or not there are some profound and paradoxical dissimilarities between Russia and Poland at this "metahistorical" level.[16]

We believe that in the context of the ongoing reassessment of some of the classical axioms of economic rationality, and of the growing awareness of their limited scope of applicability, a return to history and to historicist conceptual frameworks of development and continuity has become an acute necessity for the social sciences. By this we do not imply that we subscribe to any "iron laws" about the irreversible and linear development of societies (as described by some of the opponents of historicism). *Homo historicus* is neither backward nor crippled by its past, as economists tend to imply. In reality, key turning points of history require human choices among a large if not infinite number of alternatives, whose character and limits have been conditioned by all the antecedent historical experience of a given society.[17] Choosing among these alternatives, and the very awareness that they exist, is contingent upon the material, intellectual, and moral resources of the protagonists, their ideological preferences, their psychology and culture, and last but not least, the availability of leadership and willpower in the ruling group and in major social forces.[18]

In addition to what has been said so far, our understanding of the historical method implies a reliance upon empirical data and a careful examination of primary sources. Unfortunately, the predominant trend among political analysts in the West who analyze contemporary Russian politics is a one-sided reliance on those sources, which in their opinion express the dominant or mainstream attitudes. Often, this entails an excessive dependence on government documents, mass-circulation periodicals, and the writings of the most influential political groupings—to the detriment of evidence and sources that seem to be marginal, at least regarding the short term. One of us has already asserted the importance of taking into account the writings of social, political, and cultural forces that operate underground and seemingly lack serious prospects.[19] As things turned out later, it was precisely the dissident movements and their intellectual offspring in the Gorbachev era, with all their faded and dog-eared mimeographed leaflets, that played a substantial—if not decisive—role in the history of the last decades of the Soviet regime and in preparing the ground for the attempt at a democratic revolution in 1988–1991.

However, we do not intend to ignore other trends and approaches of recent decades, including those of postmodernist scholars who, on the basis of their own worldview, also came to challenge neopositivism. In particular, we share with many of these schools of thought the simple, yet often neglected, idea that students of modern society are themselves an integral part of their subject matter; their analytical tools are part and parcel of the evidence about their society and the Zeitgeist with all its intellectual and other prejudices. In the same way, most of the so-called hard facts are not theory-neutral: The way they are selected and described betrays underlying assumptions, whatever standards of objectivity and personal detachment the researcher uses in treating empirical data. In scientific arguments it is often not the new facts that disprove an old theory, but, rather, facts discovered (or described anew) in the light of an innovative theory that confront an old theory based on a different set of facts.[20] Thus in social science, the careful interpretation of survey or election results depends on one's own theoretical assumptions about the nature of human preferences and opinions, about individual responses to external stimuli, about the limits of freedom and rationality of choice, about the meanings to different people of words in a questionnaire, and so on.[21] Most of the so-called positive (or "value-free") descriptions or explanations of social reality are bound to reflect the value premises of their author and thus carry ethical and normative implications, even if these implications are not obvious at first glance to the scholars themselves.

These and similar insights stand behind the renewed quest for a more honest social science, where the value premises are made explicit in various fields of our discipline, as expressed by Johann Galtung and other scholars. It should be kept in mind that these challenges to mainstream sociology, with its positivist theory of knowledge, are not limited to the innovations of postmodernism (as much prevailing opinion holds). They have a far longer pedigree, perhaps as long as the life span of positivism itself and of the Weberian criteria of objectivity in social science. (Consider in particular the antipositivist treatise of the founding father of modern Russian philosophy, Vladimir Solovyov.[22])

However, many of the extreme conclusions developed under postmodernist influence cannot but evoke a cautious response. In particular, we do not share the tendency to perceive nations and cultures as isolated and mutually impenetrable units—a tendency represented most strikingly, if not exclusively, in the once fashionable deconstructionist theories. This tendency also reverberates at the opposite end of the intellectual spectrum in Huntington's theory about an unavoidable "clash of civilizations." Such views hold that basic ideas about freedom and justice, democracy and human dignity, which have been developed by Western and other cultures, are a priori alien to the Russian and other mentalities. In our view, this theory is unconvincing. Moreover, its practical application may produce unfortunate and perhaps unintended results, such as new Iron Curtains that artificially insulate races and cultures.

We also do not believe that social theory is walled off from political reality and from practical attempts to improve this reality. This position does not need to be strongly defended in Russia, where traditionally (due to the manifest inclination of Russian intellectuals to conceive the world in its totality and interconnectedness) the constructs of social thought and theoretical interpretations of reality have immediately generated programs of action for the most thorough transformations of this reality. Twice in this century, determined and ruthless attempts to implement one or another set of prescriptions deduced from abstract theories in Russia via revolution from above—namely, Marxism in 1917 and neoclassical macroeconomics in 1991–92—have generated a wave of enthusiastic expectations among the masses which were followed by human suffering on a large scale. Yet for an audience in the West (where abstract theories also guide policymaking, but more often indirectly and unconsciously) the link between social thought and practical policies is not so obvious—partly because of that narrow specialization that leads to barely surmountable professional barriers between theorists and practitioners in social fields. For them, Russia's recent experience of putting fashionable economic theories into practice may hopefully provide an enlightening lesson.

A Brief Summary of This Work

In the layout of this work we intend to combine chronology with an issue-centered analysis. Following this introduction's presentation of the book's main themes, chapter 1 summarizes the cycles of Russian and Soviet history, with their common strands of reform and reaction. Chapter 2 gives a review and interpretation of some major developments in Western social theory of the twentieth century as they relate to the Russian case. We find most useful and relevant to our analysis the insights of major theorists that are focused on the issue of legitimacy and legitimation of power; the conflictual relationship between democratic and capitalist development in the general framework of the modernization paradigm, as well as the limitations of the paradigm itself; the problems of institutional choice between specific forms of government, such as presidential versus parliamentary; the various existing forms of nationalism in their relation to Russian national consciousness; theories of dependency in international relations; and, last but not least, the consequences of economic globalization for dependency and democracy.

Chapter 3 provides the immediate historical background to our subject by analyzing the rule of Mikhail Gorbachev as the prelude to Yeltsin's reforms. The focus of this chapter is on the various forms of a grassroots anti-establishment movement—of both the democratic and the conservative-nationalist tendencies. We conclude that the democratic wing of this movement, despite its numerous flaws and inner tensions, constituted the leading—if not the only—force of reform able to accomplish a comprehensive transformation from the bottom up and with a meaningful participation of the majority. We will discuss the strengths and weaknesses of the major anti-establishment groups, whose strategic deficiency stemmed from the fact that the democratic development of society lagged behind the capitalist development of the *nomenklatura,* the privileged top echelon of Communist Party members. The anti-establishment movement, and particularly its democratic branch, overlapped with but was by no means identical to the Democratic Russia (DR) movement that coalesced around Boris Yeltsin—a man who showed great skill as a populist leader, but had little commitment to democracy, the national interest, or the economic development of his nation. Among Yeltsin's following, genuine democratic idealists were thoroughly mixed with anarchic-libertarian enemies of any government presence, whether democratic or not; with commercialized nomenklatura elements; and with virtual criminals.

Chapter 4 presents our analysis of the logic and development of the August 1991 events culminating in the attempted hard-line coup against Soviet president Gorbachev. By focusing on this historic episode in some detail, we hope to

convey the texture of Russian politics in a major crisis. The failure of the perpetrators of the coup to mobilize the country's hard-line forces (including anti-
establishment and reform-minded nationalists, who were opposed to the destruction of the Soviet Union and to a brutal imposition of nomenklatura capitalism)
revealed the extent of weakness, social polarization, and lack of a viable political
vision on the part of the hard-liners. For their part, ordinary people inspired by
democratic ideals showed more cohesion by pouring into the streets of major
cities in the thousands and confronting the plotters with the threat of a bloodbath,
thus playing a substantial part in the defeat of the coup. This was the last moment
when the democratic movement, if endowed with a more cohesive, far-sighted,
and principled leadership, could have become the dominant force, established a
contract with Yeltsin and his team, and defined the substance of the future reforms. Yet in the world of Russia's Byzantine shadow politics, where Yeltsin and
elites of various political stripes struggled over their survival and the realloca-
tion of power and wealth, the democrats—just like their ideological opposite
numbers but social twins, the conservative nationalists—were manipulated like
puppets on a stage, only with more contempt. Yeltsin's skilful maneuvering,
which permitted him to stage a countercoup and to prevent Gorbachev from returning to power, owed more to his grasp of how elite politics worked than to any
systematic mobilization of the democratic movement.

Chapter 5 examines the background, development, and concomitants of the
shock therapy strategy that Boris Yeltsin adopted in October 1991 and that continued the Russian historical pattern of revolutions from above. The theory of
shock therapy was promoted with crusading fervor by Yeltsin's freelance advisers,
by a number of scholars, and by the functionaries of the IMF, with uneven support from top U.S. government officials. The essence of this theory was the
administrative imposition of standards of economic development considered to be
"Western" and universally applicable, ignoring the historical, cultural, and value
differences between nations. We do not intend to evaluate Yeltsin's entire economic course on the grounds of economic theory as such; yet from political,
social, and moral grounds it was clearly a disaster for both the nation and the
state, and therefore for the purpose of economic development itself.

In the political and social context of 1991–92, Yeltsin's economic revolution
helped to stave off the potential civic democratic revolution against the nomenklatura, which had threatened to erupt beyond the control of Yeltsin and his associates. The "free market" revolution from above and the democratic-populist
revolution from below represented the two basic political and social alternatives,
both of which implied a redistribution of power and property. As for the specific economic programs, although they obviously made some difference, each
of them would serve primarily as a tool for the implementation of one of these
major alternatives.

It cannot be denied that by late 1991 the limits of Yeltsin's choice in economic policy had become extremely narrow—primarily because of Yeltsin's own

previous policies of financial subversion of the Union government, a course that resulted in an acute dependency of the new regime on foreign loans and subsidies. The choice to be made in October 1991 was by no means between a bloody revolution and gradual reform (as later claimed by Yeltsin, Gaidar, and others), but only between various types of painful and disruptive structural change, with various degrees of mass participation. The type of transformation path ultimately chosen by Yeltsin hinged upon his choice of allies in society at large and coalition partners. After August 1991, such a choice was far from pre-ordained, as both the democrats and the nomenklatura were deeply divided (the latter split roughly into conservative rent-seekers in the raw materials sector, financiers, and trade middlemen, and growth-oriented managers in high-tech and other advanced industries). As we will see, the choice was made in favor of the commercialized nomenklatura and of its sympathizers in the West, at the expense of the middle class and of the democrats, putting the new Russia on the road toward a kind of liberal market authoritarianism—or, as we call it, market bolshevism. Although a different choice would have required a lot of moral force and statesmanship that were in short supply, we do believe that such a choice, along the lines sketched out in chapter 5, would have helped Russia to avoid the ominous course it has taken and would have given it better prospects for development than it has today.

Chapter 6 focuses on the rise of the first wave of opposition to Yeltsin's policies, which germinated within the democratic movement as early as 1990 and took its final shape in 1992–93, on the eve of the movement's collapse. These were the years when the democrats splintered between those who supported market authoritarianism, the disbanding of the Union, and shock therapy, and those who did not. The latter had a variety of complexions. Some attacked the government from the left, while others convincingly argued that Yeltsin's shock therapy had little to do with a genuine free market but amounted to a top-down expropriation and redistribution in disguise, in the Bolshevik style. A notable contingent of anti-Yeltsin democrats moved into the disunited camp of the nationalists and spearheaded the creation and activities of the National Salvation Front. What was common to them all was their inability to unite in a coalition. By late 1993, most of Yeltsin's democratic opponents—and an entire generation of talented and idealistic would-be leaders of Russia's body politic and civil society—had been pushed off the political stage, along with the democratic movement as a whole.[23]

Their place was gradually filled by the forces of conservative, elitist, and sometimes antidemocratic opposition that had emerged from the Soviet nomenklatura and was therefore more moderate and more acceptable to the Kremlin; its most prominent element has been the Zyuganov-Podberezkin group that in 1993 gained control of the only mass-based national party after the collapse of Democratic Russia—the Communist Party of the Russian Federation. In fact, this was less an opposition to the Yeltsin regime than to the influence of the democrats and to the remaining democratic elements in government. Without dropping the word "communist," which was attractive to the legions of elderly pensioners, they thoroughly revamped the party's ideology to make it conservative-traditionalist in content and only residually socialist. The overwhelming beneficiary of all this was the Yeltsin administration.

In chapter 7, we look in some detail at the crisis of September–October 1993 and its antecedents, which were in some ways a reiteration and a logical development of the events of August 1991. The crisis of 1993, which stopped just short of unleashing a civil war with an unpredictable outcome, exposed the glaring weaknesses of Russia's institutions, as well as the personalistic nature of power in the country. By 1993, the failures of shock therapy and the growing ability of the opposition forces to cooperate and to draw lessons from their mistakes created an executive-legislative impasse, which Yeltsin ended on September 21, 1993, by illegally suspending the constitution and dissolving the Russian parliament.

As the parliament itself had no credible leadership and no clear alternative set of policies, the majority of citizens kept neutral in this strife, which enabled Yeltsin to prevail by a mixture of cunning and force, given his initial advantage. In this effort, he secured neutrality and even some support from such would-be opposition figures as Zyuganov, Vladimir Zhirinovsky, and some centrists, who had well-grounded hopes for a strong representation in the future parliament once the previous opposition was wiped out. When regional leaders and authoritative centrist politicians were about to step in as arbiters, and when uncritical support for Yeltsin in the West began to come under pressure from public opinion, Yeltsin's security services quickly and skillfully staged a provocation that unleashed violence on the part of the opposition, thus giving Yeltsin a pretext to proceed with a bloody crackdown on the parliament and the introduction of an authoritarian police regime.

These policies backfired on December 12, 1993, with the thumping defeat of the progovernment parties in the elections for the new parliament; in addition, as some evidence suggests, the regime had to resort to outright fraud in the referendum for the new Russian constitution to declare it valid. However, the election's winner, Zhirinovsky, having started his career in 1990 as a politician covertly funded by the Soviet government to divide the opposition, was not too dangerous or unpredictable for the Kremlin. He even strengthened international support for Yeltsin by raising much anxiety in the West, where he was mistaken for a leader of the radical opposition. Again, as in August 1991, a combination of roles was played by the Westerners involved: While the support for Yeltsin's parliamentary coup (on the part of the Clinton administration and like-minded officials in other Western governments) encouraged him to go ahead and destroy the parliament, the Kremlin's fear of Western public opinion compelled the regime to preserve the basic formal features of a democratic constitutional order, including an elected parliament, with which Yeltsin, under different circumstances, seemingly would have been happy to dispense.

The events of late 1993 put an end to this revolutionary stage in Russia's most recent history. In this period, so rich in unfulfilled potentialities, a far-reaching transformation of the system from the bottom up, based on cooperation between society and government, might have been achieved. After the demise of both democratic and nationalist rivals of the nomenklatura and the dispersal of the parliament and most regional and local representative assemblies, the new oligarchical-criminal order could evolve with few if any constraints.

Chapter 8 covers a relatively long period—from late 1993 through Yeltsin's re-election in July 1996—when the country was by and large marking time. The central paradox of this period was Yeltsin's re-election for a second term as president, despite his ignominious defeat in the brutal two-year war against the Russian constituent republic of Chechnya, and despite his steady single-digit approval rating at the beginning of the re-election campaign in February 1996. Yeltsin's electoral "triumph" of 54 percent became possible thanks only to the breaking of the law on a spectacular scale (by exceeding the legal maximum spending limit many times over), to direct and indirect financing from abroad, to extreme monopolization of the mass media by a group of banks loyal to him, and to successful efforts to ward off the dangerous specter of a coalition between major opposition candidates.

Having isolated its rivals, the regime used the "Red Scare" tactic, forecasting civil war and a return of the Gulag if Yeltsin was not re-elected. Thus Russia yet again missed its chance to set a precedent for a democratic and orderly presidential succession (if Yeltsin had yielded power in case of his defeat). Zyuganov's potential victory would not have been a threat to democracy, because his political weakness and lack of foreign support would have compelled him to cooperate with some of his opponents among the democratic reformers and to govern by coalition—something that was not to be expected from Yeltsin.

In the same chapter, we also explore the following themes that were central to this period: how the system of court politics actually functioned; the ways in which parliament, opposition groups, and the rule of law were largely marginalized by this sort of politics; the rise to a position of great power of Boris Berezovsky and other "oligarchs"; the worrying development of corruption and criminality; and the role of the Chechnya war in deepening the alienation of the military and society and provoking the emergence of a military protest movement.

In chapter 9 we will analyze and interpret the second round of shock therapy, which was conducted in 1997–98 by the government team of Anatoly Chubais and Boris Nemtsov. We will examine how they tried to address some of the vices of the crony capitalism that had developed thanks to Chubais's Faustian bargain with the oligarchs in 1995, but were defeated by the oligarchs' power and also by the major financial crisis of 1997–98 that resulted from excessive Kremlin borrowing and from the plundering of the state treasury by Russia's ruling class.

In this chapter, we also examine Yeltsin's impulsive removal of his long-serving premier Chernomyrdin in March 1998 and the search for a successor who would not only carry on Yeltsin's legacy but also, more important, shield the president from prosecution upon his leaving office. After a contentious succession of candidates, Yeltsin finally found the right man in Vladimir Putin.

Fearful that progovernment parties would do poorly in the Duma elections of December 1999, and intent on building up Putin so that he could win the presidency, the Kremlin engineered a new war against the Chechens. Putin's star rose fast, and the Kremlin's supporters performed adequately in the parliamentary contest. After Yeltsin resigned on New Year's Eve and was instantly granted immunity from prosecution, Putin succeeded him. In March 2000, he became president with 54 percent of the vote. However, it was not clear how much change Putin wanted, nor whether he could build enough power to implement serious change. Clear signs suggested, though, that Putin and part of the ruling class wised to establish a stronger, more repressive authoritarian order.

Finally, we conclude this work with an epilogue, which will provide a balance sheet of the Yeltsin era, using some theoretical criteria drawn from chapter 2, re-examine the issue of missed alternatives, and briefly discuss possible scenarios for the foreseeable future.

1

REFORM OR REACTION? THE YELTSIN ERA IN A MILLENNIUM OF RUSSIAN HISTORY

Peter the Great was the first Bolshevik.

—*Maximilian Voloshin*

IN RUSSIAN AND WESTERN DEBATES about developments in the post-Soviet world, the term "reforms" has become a kind of magic fetish. The mere mention of reforms, like a shamanistic incantation, unleashes a storm of passions across the spectrum of public opinion. However, the specific meanings of the term are often as murky and diverse as the interests and goals of those who invoke it. Profound and substantive differences exist over what is meant by "Russia's reforms"—differences between Russians and Westerners, as well as between various intellectual and political camps in Russia itself. Thus, in the view of most present-day Western observers, as well as old-style Westernizers inside Russia (including most of the orthodox Marxists in the early twentieth century), reform has been deterministically linked to the idea of modernization, and more generally to a belief in the linear progress of humanity. In this conception of history, all nations are perceived as developing, perhaps at different speeds, in the direction of a single universal standard. One of the popularizations of this doctrine was the much advertised essay by Francis Fukuyama on "the end of history."[1]

However, it is clear enough that in late Soviet and post-Soviet Russia the number of orthodox proponents of the optimistic view of modernization and a linear perception of history has been shrinking. By contrast, an increasing number of Russian historians and social scientists have embraced variations of the cyclical paradigm of change. The roots of this approach go back to Heraclitus and, in modern times, to Giambattista Vico, whose teaching about the *corsi e ricorsi,* the ebbs and flows of history, was the first in modern Western thought to challenge the doctrine of universal and irreversible historical progress. While few serious scholars would interpret the historical cycles as mere repetition without development, establishing parallels between distant periods of Russian history has long been an ingrained mode of thinking characteristic of Russians' view of their past, present, and even future. It is worth noting that such a cyclical interpretation of a nation's history is, although a specially prominent feature of Russian culture, not unique to Russia and has parallels even in such dissimilar historical experiences as that of the United States. Therefore, it does not need to deny the idea of progress, nor to imply perennial backwardness on the part of a nation.[2]

The cyclical conception of Russian history was elaborated most eloquently by a wide-ranging intellectual of the Silver Age, Maximilian Voloshin (1877–1932). To him belongs the reconceptualization of Bolshevism as an extemporal idea that generalizes the whole pattern of leaps toward "modernization" via coercive revolutions from above, as first done in Russia by Peter the Great. In our times, variations of the cyclical paradigm were adopted even by such unambiguous Westernizers as Aleksandr Yanov and Natan Eidelman. The latter, in his *Revoliutsiia sverkhu v Rossii* (Revolution from Above in Russia), saw the series of "revolutions from above" as a progressive spiral.

To use a popular and easily recognizable metaphor, Russian history is often presented as a pendulum swinging back and forth—between progress and conservative backlash, between despotic, bloody police regimes and the anarchic

"Times of Troubles" that have periodically brought the country to the brink of disintegration and virtually destroyed the state. The initial impulse for the pendulum swings—both to the right (in the direction of dictatorship) and then to the left (toward the weakening of the state)—is often seen to be the recurrent attempts of Russian rulers to carry out a radical, top-down transformation of society.

The figure shown on the next pages does not claim to present an established pattern of cause and effect that has remained immutable in the course of Russia's historical experience. For it goes without saying that throughout five centuries of Russian history the major problems facing the various reformers, the correlation of social forces around the different reformist programs, the international context, and many other factors have changed substantially. And yet, certain essential similarities common to reformist attempts across the centuries—similarities of methods and style of action, of ideological and cognitive parameters—suggest a clear cultural, institutional, and psychological continuity that can be seen as the reformers' "path dependence," as every new round of reforms was shaped by memory of the past and comparisons with similar previous experience. This provides a fertile ground for typological comparisons across time, notwithstanding our awareness that the comparisons are bound to be incomplete and in many ways one-sided.

What was common to many reformist programs was the initial impulse: a crisis of governmental revenues, the inability to secure the necessary fiscal base for political power—not only for long-term investment projects, but sometimes even for resolving immediate tasks and fulfilling the government's daily functions.[3] This recurrent illness has dogged the Russian state at the major turning points of its history. But it has surfaced in its most painful forms during foreign policy crises. At these times, the inability to feed the army properly and to ensure the necessary or desirable level of military buildup has presented immediate threats to national security and thus pushed the usually complacent oligarchy toward modernization and reform. If reform was delayed, the government often yielded to the temptation of printing money, thus triggering inflation and serious disruptions in the economy. (This practice has been especially true in recent times, when Russia's monetary system has become extremely vulnerable to the pressures of international financial markets and institutions.) The consequent worsening of the revenue crisis, coupled with increased social tensions, exacerbated the security threat by widening the social gap between the officer corps and their troops. In turn, this led to the demoralization of the army, to public rejection of the elite's foreign policy goals, and then to humiliating military defeats (for example, Ivan the Terrible's Livonian War, the start of the Northern War under Peter the Great, the Crimean War of 1853–56, the Russo-Japanese War of 1904–05, World War I in 1915–17, and the Afghan War of 1979–88). In such cases, fiscal bankruptcy and social upheaval, combined with military failure, threatened to paralyze state power, and in some cases brought the state itself to the brink of demise (and, in 1917, beyond that). Sooner or later, awareness of

Figure 1. The cycles of state repression and instability in Russian/Soviet history.

◀— authoritarian police state   reforms, instability, breakdown —▶

Reforms of Ivan IV (1547–60)

Ivan IV (the Terrible), oprichnina (1564–72)

Reforms of Boris Godunov (1598–1605)

"Time of Troubles" (1604–13)
Polish invasion

Reforms of Prince Vassili Golovin (1680s)

Rebellion of the Archers
(1698)

Reforms of Peter the Great (1698–1725)

Reforms of Catherine II (the Great) (1760s)

Emergence of underground
opposition
(Novikov, Radishchev)

Pugachev's rebellion
(1771–74)

Paul I (1796–1801)

Reforms of Mikhail Speranski et al. (1801–12)

Arakcheev (1812–25)   Decembrist movement

Nicholas I (1825–55)   Decembrist rebellion (1825)

First Polish rebellion (1830)

**Alexander II's Great Reforms
(1857–66, 1879–81)**

Second Polish rebellion (1863)

Figure 1. (continued)

◄— authoritarian police state   reforms, instability, breakdown —►

Narodnaya Volya
(People's Will) terrorism.
Other populist groups

Counterreforms, 1880s–90s
(K. Pobedonostsev, D. Tolstoi et al.)

Count Witte's industrialization

Reforms of Witte, D. Svyatopolk-Mirski (1903–04)

Revolution of 1905–07

Reforms of Stolypin (1906–11)

Antiparliamentary coup, June 3, 1907

Revolution of 1917

"Military Communism" (1918–21)

Lenin's "New Economic Policy"
(1921–28): agrarians vs. industrialists
and other factional Party feuds

Stalin's "Revolution from Above" (1929–37)

Khrushchev's thaw (1953–65)

Dissident movement

"Real socialism," or "stagnation" (1966–84)
in USSR and Eastern Europe

Andropov's crackdown on dissent

Gorbachev's perestroika (1986–90)

Collapse of the USSR (1989–91)

---

the depth and systemic nature of the crisis paved the way to power for proponents of radical change.

Meanwhile, partly because of the lack of natural barriers along Russia's often changing and ill-protected western border, "the West"—too often misperceived as a monolith with fixed boundaries and without internal contradictions—remained a major source of psychological insecurity, an object that the Russian elites simultaneously wanted to imitate and compete against.[4] This competition with "the West" in general, rather than with any specific country, imposed on the nation a burden of security concerns that was excessive and often unbearable for the Russian population and for the organizational capacities of the state. In addition, it was to Western experience that Russia's rulers always turned in times of confusion, surprised as they were by the ability of Western governments to transform the economic activity of their citizens into a steady and reliable source of revenue for the treasury. At the same time, the mainstream opposition groups also turned to the West for inspiration and support in their desire for a radical transformation of society—be it in the era of the Muscovy tsars (Prince Andrei Kurbski, Grigori Kotoshikhin), under the St. Petersburg empire (from Novikov and Radishchev to the Constitutional Democrats and socialists of the early twentieth century), or under Bolshevik rule (from the rebels of Kronstadt to the activists of the democratic movement of the 1960s to 1980s).

The antagonism (often more emotional than substantive) between Slavophiles and Westernizers that runs through Russian intellectual and political history has often led observers to perceive "reform" as a partisan slogan monopolized by the Westernizers—despite the fact that many of the reforms (or at least the most successful ones, such as the Great Reforms of 1857–66) contained a mixture of Westernizing and native ingredients.[5]

But even if we accept this narrow understanding of reforms as "turning toward the West" and attempts to "embrace Western values," we are bound to discover that the understanding of "Western values" in Russian history is multifaceted and riven with inner tensions. For different reformers and at various points in time, "Western values" could mean a high level of technological development, efficiency of government administration, the existence of autonomous economic actors (both private and collective), respect for human rights, social guarantees for the poor and dispossessed, and development of democratic institutions of governance. Even within Western civilization, the relationships between these features of modernity are sometimes contradictory. And much more so in Russia, where almost every historically significant reformist strategy has implicitly contained an "either-or" choice—at times leading to a violent clash—between diverse aspects of "Westernization" and development, some of which were targeted as the major goal of reforms at the expense of others.

In particular, the meaning of Westernization and reform was with rare exceptions a matter of profound disagreement between most of the ruling elite and most of the educated part of Russian society. In both strategic and value terms, the keystone of each developmental breakthrough involved a choice between a strong state and a strong society as the end-point of reform—which was once reflected in Lenin's somewhat simplistic but famous formula as a choice between the "Prussian" and "American" models of development. The first option implied that the paralyzing fiscal crisis was to be overcome by a coercive extortion of revenues from the most vulnerable social groups, as occurred under Russia's authoritarian rulers from Ivan the Terrible to Joseph Stalin. It also aimed to create a powerful, privileged layer of committed supporters of the regime, which would supplant the inefficient or disloyal elites of the past and systematically carry out the confiscations and extortions on behalf of the authorities. In the alternative case (as in Russia's Great Reforms of the 1860s), the efforts of reformers were directed toward stimulating the social and economic activity of the underprivileged, middle-income layers of the population—in the hope that their confidence in the government, generated by its liberal policies, would help achieve the economic goals of the elite in a more "natural," noncoercive way. Thus, two basic patterns of reform were established and institutionalized in Russian political culture: a violent, "Bolshevik" *transformation* of society from above versus the political and intellectual *awakening* of society. In the latter case, the liberal impulse, though still emanating from the elite, moves society by careful pushes toward self-organization and a more active participation (within historically contingent limits) in defining the priorities of national development.

Undoubtedly, to fulfill its developmental tasks, Russia has required both efficient and authoritative bureaucratic administration and a vibrant, economically active and politically influential civil society. Only a strong and legitimate government, endowed with a revenue base whose stability rested on the foundation of mutual trust and reciprocal cooperation with society, could sustain a long-term effort to create the infrastructure required for economic development of the largest country in the world. Only such a symphony of state and society could allow the necessary redistribution of financial and other material resources in accordance with the nation's developmental priorities.

However, Russia's perennial problem has been that the modernizing activity of the state and the self-organization of society have as a rule proceeded in inverse proportion to each other. The reformist programs, which had as their cornerstone accelerated modernization, plus military and technological catching up in a real or imaginary race with the West (the reforms of Peter the Great, to a lesser extent those of Prime Minister Pyotr Stolypin, and especially Stalin's revolution from above), were carried out through authoritarianism and coercion. They often involved brutal crackdowns on the "counterreformist" or "counterrevolutionary" opposition, the wiping out of those social forms and ways of life that would not adapt to the new system, and the comprehensive unification and regulation of social relationships; and, vice versa, the emancipation and the increased autonomous activity of the unprivileged layers of society often tended to go hand in hand with a decline in the state's administrative capacity under the assault of radicalism of all kinds, and on some occasions with the deepening of the systemic crisis that had triggered the reforms in the first place. The historical memory of these patterns, deeply ingrained and institutionalized in Russian political culture, has shaped the elites' perception of the entire set of issues related to the modernization and development of Russia, in the spirit of a zero-sum game between state and society.

The causes of this recurrent conflict between the two prime movers of national development could be the subject of a separate inquiry that would greatly exceed the scope of these historical prolegomena to the study of the latest "reforms." Let us just note here that the Achilles' heel of many modernization projects was the inability—or unwillingness—of "revolutionaries from above" to build on pre-existing social structures (beyond the limits of a narrow, self-appointed elite) and to reach a common understanding with the most politically organized and active forces of society on the goals, means, and priorities of national development. On the other side of the coin, there was exorbitant radicalism, impatience, and intolerance on the part of the advocates of a bottom-up transformation from within society. The famous Russian *mnogoukladnost'* or "many-layeredness"—the perennial coexistence of highly diverse economic forms and ways of life that have often been incongruent with each other and developed at different speeds and sometimes in different directions—manifested itself, in particular, in the existence of a political and cultural counterelite made up of an enlightened and self-confident, but often socially inexperienced, "vanguard" minority. This group consisted of the educated clergy and the junior bureaucrats of the *prikazy,* or ministries, in pre-Petrine Russia; of the gentry and free professional intelligentsia in the eighteenth and nineteenth centuries; and of the Soviet-era intelligentsia, which preserved the core value system of their predecessors with minor adjustments through all the disruptions and terror of communist rule.

The majority of this counterelite was not simply far better prepared to undertake a modernizing leap than the rest of the country's population. As a rule, the counterelite had already advanced the cause of reforms for decades, notwithstanding repression, having acquired its heroes and martyrs in the process. As a result, by the time the top-down reforms actually started, they were seen as "too little too late" and even meaningless in comparison with the expectations, the actual needs, and the sacrifices borne for so long by the counterelite. For the counterelite, the old order had long ago become a brake on its self-fulfillment and development, and had lost the last vestiges of legitimacy. Thus the counterelite now viewed the reforms primarily as a springboard for more comprehensive changes; instead of constructively cooperating with the reformist government, it acted to erode the very ground under the feet of the reformers by fomenting revolutionary tensions in society.

Another factor worth mentioning was the traditionally weak sense of identification of key parts of society with the national state. Some of the most educated and active groups of the population viewed the tasks of development and the nation's mission, if any, as disconnected from, or even incompatible with, the existing institutions of government. The incongruity, or even split, between the nation and the government (which in fact precluded the full development of a European-type nation-state) had become a fixture in public consciousness as early as the 1820s, when the publication of Nikolai Karamzin's classic, *The History of the Russian State,* was followed by the polemical counterhistory written by Nikolai Polevoy, *The History of the Russian People.*

In connection with this people-state dichotomy, most of the reform strategies put forward by the counterelite on behalf of unprivileged classes were only partly related to the Russian state as such, and typically included a much broader international or even universalist agenda. The latter could take the form of Russia's embracing Western civilization to the point of almost dissolving itself into it (as advocated by the mainstream Westernizers of the nineteenth century, to a lesser extent by Aleksandr Herzen, and more recently by the Sakharov wing of the democratic movement) or, alternatively, of radically reshaping Western and even global civilization (Vladimir Solovyov with his ecumenical utopia, the Tolstoyans, the Russian Marxists of the early twentieth century, and Aleksandr Solzhenitsyn in his 1978 Harvard speech criticizing Western materialism). Striving for these global supergoals often led the reformist counterelite to neglect the requirements of an efficient government and national security, or even (as in 1917) the imperative of the state's survival. No wonder that whenever a foreign policy conflict came on top of a domestic crisis, the reform-minded counterelite was suspected by the authorities (and by all Russians concerned with the declining ability of the state to perform its functions) of being a tool of foreign interests allegedly seeking to weaken or undermine Russia.

Meanwhile, at the other end of the spectrum, the patriotic and state-oriented parts of society found themselves identified as "foes of change" or "dark forces" in the eyes of the public opinion shaped by the counterelite. If they had come from the ranks of the intelligentsia, they were treated as "splitters" and forced to the sidelines of public life by the proponents of radical change. This was the fate of such leading writers and public figures as Dostoevsky, Leskov, Konstantin Leontiev, and Vasily Rozanov in the nineteenth century, and many more in recent times. Ultimately, the tension between the two archenemies—a reform-minded government trying to secure the survival and protection of the state, and a reform-minded counterelite dreaming of rebuilding the state from scratch in accordance with its own program—ended in a clash, with either the government abandoning reform and resorting to a crackdown or (as in 1917) the comprehensive obliteration of the status quo and of the Russian state as it had previously existed.

THE SOVIET INTERLUDE

The social order erected by the Bolsheviks and designated as "communist" or "socialist" (even though it is easy to argue that it was just as dissimilar from the teachings of Marx or, indeed, from the professed goals of the Communists themselves as the current state of the Russian economy is different from the lofty ideals of liberal market reformers) was based on government seizure of all revenue-generating property and the regulation of all economic activity, with the simultaneous subordination of government itself to the dictatorship of the Communist Party elite—the nomenklatura—and its vigilant security services. Despite substantial differences from the past, the Soviet system and political culture inherited a number of genetic traits from its predecessors. Among these birthmarks was the much exacerbated conflict between the developmental functions of the central bureaucracy in promoting modernization, and the autonomous initiative of unprivileged social groups.

The situation was complicated by the fact that the Bolshevik regime gradually set for itself an extremely high standard for its own legitimation. By the 1950s, its declared goals included building the most just and equitable system in the world, a system that would at the same time be able to satisfy consumer demands and—in addition—sustain the Union of Soviet Socialist Republics (USSR) as a military superpower. Contrary to the tenets of the once powerful totalitarian model, which viewed the Soviet system as based entirely on coercion and fear, the regime was obliged to aim for a high level of legitimacy: Given the negligible material rewards offered by the state to its employees (that is, almost the whole workforce of the country) and the low efficiency of convict labor, the accelerated modernization undertaken by the Communist Party depended on the enthusiastic support of the strategically important urban strata. This support in turn was contingent on the attainability of the goals the Party had proclaimed. In the eyes of millions both in Russia and abroad, it was this teleological dream that provided the major (if not the only) justification for the abject poverty, the discrimination and outright terror, and the recurrent expropriations that the Soviet regime imposed on most of its citizens.[6]

During the Soviet period, the centuries-old reform pendulum kept swinging back and forth. When the regime needed to stimulate initiative from below to avoid stagnation, it was repeatedly forced to stage "thaws" (that is, the partial or comprehensive liberalization of repressive policies). One of the goals of such thaws was to stir up ministerial bureaucracies and other agents of the command economy, such as the nomenklatura managers of state companies, by encouraging limited public criticism of the system's shortcomings.[7] But almost every liberalization produced unintended side effects, as long-suppressed tensions threatened to blow the lid off the kettle and called into question whatever legitimation of the system had been so painfully achieved.

Among these unwelcome by-products were social conflicts between urban and rural dwellers (from the 1920s onward), between the authorities and the unprivileged intelligentsia (on a recurrent basis), among various ethnic groups, between all of these groups and the central government (also on a recurrent basis), and, finally, between the nomenklatura and the lower classes (at least from the 1960s on). Each of these crises exposed the failure of the nomenklatura system to satisfy the demanding criteria for its legitimation. Yet attempts made by Soviet rulers and ideologues to replace these criteria with less exigent ones—based either on the imperial idea, ethnic Russian nationalism, or pragmatism of the "social contract" variety—did not succeed for various reasons. After the overthrow of Nikita Khrushchev in 1964 and the gradual and tacit abandonment of the communist ideal by his oligarchic Party successors, the ideological basis of the Soviet system's legitimacy rapidly eroded, together with the system's economic and administrative efficiency. By the 1970s, the rapid economic and technological growth of Khrushchev's thaw, which had so impressed the West, had markedly slowed, yielding to low growth and then stagnation.

THE SOVIET MIDDLE CLASS

At this point, we need to address a central issue in the sociological analysis of the Soviet system—the nature and character of the middle class and how much this class was divided regarding its goals and values. So far we have spoken about the nomenklatura and the rest (the latter being an unstructured mass of urban workers and peasants), with not much in between. While this simple pyramidal model of Soviet society may have been more or less adequate for the age of Stalinism, the system became substantially more complex, at least from the 1960s onward.

Most important, the last decades of rule of the Communist Party of the Soviet Union (CPSU) featured the upward social mobility of urban professionals, a development that was convincingly used to help explain the Gorbachev phenomenon.[8] Some rigorous sociologists may question whether "middle class" is an appropriate term for this group, as it did not fulfill some economic criteria used in the West to define the middle class—such as entrepreneurial activity and the ownership of income-generating capital or property. On this basis, the shock therapists and radical reformers of the past decade asserted that a middle class had to be created from scratch by means of social engineering.

However, the contemporary notion of the middle class in Western countries stretches beyond the confines of economic reductionism. Evidence suggests that modern Western professionals, such as employees of corporate and government bureaucracies, are not defined by entrepreneurship or property ownership, as was the middle class in the age of Marxism and Weberian sociology, and in many cases now may altogether lack an independent economic base.[9] These professionals are nevertheless categorized as a part of today's middle class, being typologically similar to their nineteenth-century predecessors in their mentality, expectations, and sense of personal identity.

Clearly, the Soviet middle class (as we will call it from now on, with all those caveats in mind) consisted of wage earners in the all-encompassing public sector, who typically had no source of income that was autonomous from the state;

possessed very little private property in strictly legal terms; and was propor-
tionally much smaller to the rest of society and less affluent than its Western
counterpart.[10] Still, it was a new and important presence in late Soviet history.
Moreover, by the late 1980s, it had become more numerous, and therefore potentially more powerful, than what could be called the middle class—the medium
and small-size property owners and entrepreneurs, plus the intelligentsia—in
late imperial Russia. To summarize, their economic situation and their ethic of
contempt for the establishment had close to nothing in common with what is
typically seen as middle class in the West, but their political and economic expectations and the standards of personal accomplishment put them as close to the
"ideal type" of middle class as was feasible in the historical conditions of late
Soviet Russia.

While this middle class included the lower levels of the government bureaucracy, highly skilled workers in certain sectors of the economy, and a layer of
semiprivate and for the most part illegal entrepreneurs, its predominant core
was made up of the intelligentsia in the broad Russian meaning of the term—
from people in academia and the arts and humanities to engineers, teachers,
and physicians. While it would be an exaggeration to speak about a single ethos
or esprit de corps for the intelligentsia as a whole, its politically radical core did
inherit the mentality and value system of a self-conscious counterelite from its
nineteenth-century predecessors.[11] Even though only a tiny minority of this broad
layer opted out of the Soviet system and into the various branches of dissent, its
intellectual and political activities reverberated all the way through the system,
and by the mid-1980s millions of people were at least tangentially involved in
the illegal and semi-underground civil society. Indeed, discontent with the system
was rapidly spreading beyond intelligentsia circles—thus 40 percent of those
arrested from 1976 to 1983 for dissident activities were employed in manual
labor.[12] In light of all this, the democratic as well as nationalist groups in the anti-
establishment movement that coalesced in the Gorbachev era should be viewed
in the context of these middle-class stratas' quest for political representation.

Having said this, we should note that the middle class was clearly not immune
to inner tensions, such as those between the entrepreneurial proclivities of
some better-off urbanites engaged in the shadow economy and the intrinsically
egalitarian ethos of always siding with the poor and oppressed that defined the
ideal type of the traditional intelligentsia. Further, the intelligentsia itself was
riven with income and status inequalities, often as a direct consequence of long-
term policies designed to divide the stratum whose members were traditionally
seen as the most dangerous opponent of the authorities. Thus the major cities'
cultural elite, which enjoyed connections abroad and was considered a strategically important group by the regime, was gradually included in the informal
networks of nomenklatura privileges. At the same time, in the economy at large,
wage premiums for those with education and skills were miserable, and professionals in such sectors as education and health on average had lower living

standards than some groups of manual workers. Overall, 20 percent of the trained people with university education belonged in the lower part of the Soviet wage scale.[13] Yet, while this significant part of the Soviet intelligentsia often lived below the average middle-class level in material terms, it was more reform-minded and imbued with modernizing attitudes than most "liberals" in the Soviet establishment.

On the economic side, the Soviet middle class used the relatively prosperous and stable 1960s and 1970s to amass a considerable amount of personal savings in government bank accounts. In the Gorbachev era, when denationalization and deregulation of the economy came on the agenda, these middle-class savings were ripe to be channeled toward productive investment in industry, which in a broader framework of reasonable reform policies could have led to internally generated and sustainable growth along the lines of the postwar Japanese miracle. These savings also could have been used to acquire pieces of denationalized property and to set up private businesses. Yet the opposite happened—shock therapy and the hyperinflation triggered by Gorbachev's and Yeltsin's economic policies (since 1991, under more or less vigilant IMF guidance) wiped out these savings and polarized and ultimately destroyed the economic and political fortunes of the middle class.[14]

GORBACHEV AND THE COLLAPSE OF THE SYSTEM: AN OVERVIEW

By the time Gorbachev assumed the Kremlin throne, people in the most diverse strata of Soviet society were eagerly, even anxiously, hoping for a new swing of the reform pendulum. All the traditional features of systemic crisis mentioned above were plain to see. The informal "social contract" between regime and society—which had embodied a tacit joint understanding of the system's main goals and the ways to achieve them, and had underlain the rapid economic development of the past—had fallen apart in full view of every attentive observer. The suppression of dissent and the discrediting of the reformist optimism of the 1960s had created an atmosphere of civic apathy in which people increasingly dropped out of the official system; in fact, the system was quietly sabotaged at every level except the summit of the bureaucracy. The decline of the work ethic and the mass escape into private life with its material concerns were stimulated by the increasingly conspicuous self-enrichment of specific groups in oligarchic circles and of their clients in the shadow economy. The stagnation of productivity, in the absence of either material or idealistic motivations for conscientious work in the public sector, led to mounting concerns about treasury revenues. A number of tasks in the development of basic infrastructure (transportation, housing, health care, and so forth) left over from the Stalin-Khrushchev period remained unfinished and desperately required top-priority government expenditure.

However, the moneyed nomenklatura, consumption-oriented and obsessed with Western luxury merchandise, and its numerous clients in the large cities mounted formidable pressures on the state-controlled market for goods and services and on the black market for scarce imported goods. To satisfy these demands, the regime was compelled to divert resources away from infrastructure and basic industries and toward purchasing more and more imports. Meanwhile, smaller cities were already experiencing severe shortages of basic goods, and their authorities increasingly resorted to food rationing. Inequalities of distribution and the pervasiveness of numerous perquisites for the nomenklatura fueled the sentiment of mutual mistrust in society, while the inability of the regime to provide Western consumer living standards caused resentment and grumbling among the voracious Moscow elites and their clients. The widening gaps in the official distribution system were rapidly filled by the black market, which was created and often controlled through close cooperation between the criminal underworld and the commercialized segments of the ruling nomenklatura.[15]

In the meantime, the Kremlin gerontocracy of the early 1980s, hopelessly bogged down with a demoralized army in the Afghan quagmire and haunted by the specter of the Reagan administration's Strategic Defense Initiative, was plagued with increasing worry about lagging behind in the military, technological, and propaganda contest with the West—a competition that traditionally served as the main barometer of security and self-confidence for Soviet oligarchs. Military expenditures, coupled with the consumer addiction of the elite, predictably forced inflationary recourse to monetary expansion in both cash and credit circuits, leading to incremental devaluation of private savings and the heating up of social tensions.[16] The increased reliance on the export of natural resources in chasing hard currency for short-term spending revealed the growing dependency of the Soviet economy (which lacked flexible adaptability) on the fluctuations of global markets.

The historical memory of earlier cycles of reforms and their blind alleys of authoritarianism and anarchy was apparently on the mind of Gorbachev and his associates: Upon assuming power in 1985, they undertook a new shift toward modernization and reform. These lessons of history most likely contributed to Gorbachev's design of his political "seesaw," which involved a delicate balancing act between an authoritarian mobilization of the bureaucracy in pursuit of change and the spurring of the radical intelligentsia and the unprivileged classes of society to take autonomous action at the grassroots level. Gorbachev understood that he also needed the cooperation of a third party—the state-minded, liberal-patriotic forces in society. With the cooperation of all three entities, he hoped he could transform the system radically enough to implement the outstanding developmental tasks, to ensure the renewal of the system's legitimacy, and to bridge the gap between the elite and society—without completely destroying the basic social order. These seesaw tactics and the need to engage the moderate part of the counterelite (the liberal patriots) were manifest in the Andropov-style inauguration of Gorbachev's reforms; in the conservative-patriotic and moralistic rhetoric of his closest associate, Yegor Ligachev; in the official campaign against privileges and corruption; and in the overtures of both men to the "village prose" writers and the circle of thinkers around the journal *Novy mir.*

Yet it turned out that the reforms Gorbachev had started were seen as belated, the path he had to walk between irreconcilably inimical social forces was too narrow, and the resources of legitimacy of the post-1917 order were exhausted. All this, combined with escalating social and ethnic clashes, contributed to the swelling of antisystemic poles on his right and left that finally submerged the middle ground he sought to occupy. Most important, the tensions between the get-rich-quick nomenklatura and the unprivileged layers of society were so strong that a radical transformation of the system—in the interests of either one or the other opposing camps—and thus profound change in the political makeup of the system apparently proved to be unavoidable.

Thus perestroika seemed to reproduce the well-known (and, in the view of many Russians, inevitable) pattern of a zero-sum game that was deeply entrenched in Russian history between the government and society. Ultimately, Gorbachev's seesaw tactics had to yield to feverish maneuvering between the Scylla of anarchy and the Charybdis of dictatorship. On discovering that he had been fatally misled in his hopes for generous aid on the scale of the Marshall Plan from the West, Gorbachev in August 1991 willingly or unwillingly encouraged actions leading to that month's abortive hard-line putsch. Soon after its failure, the curtain was pulled down on both Gorbachev's presidency and the history of the Soviet state.

YELTSIN AS A REFORMER IN THE CONTEXT OF RUSSIAN HISTORY

Although strictly speaking, Boris Yeltsin became head of a sovereign state only on December 12, 1991, when the Russian Supreme Soviet ratified the Belaya Vezha Agreements on the dissolution of the USSR, in reality the Yeltsin era started in the summer of 1990, when Gorbachev's perestroika found itself in a blind alley. The election of Yeltsin as chairman of the Russian Supreme Soviet on May 29, 1990, his stature as the most popular and trusted politician in the country, and the mass grassroots movement standing behind him at that time— all this under conditions of chaos in the legal system and near-paralysis in the all-Union government—made Yeltsin the only legitimate national leader and the focus of diverse hopes and expectations among the most disparate social groups. Soon there was not a single political action of any consequence that could be carried out in Moscow without Yeltsin's consent. Given the unpopularity and ineptitude of the Soviet authorities and the pivotal role of Russia in the Union, it was Yeltsin who, from the middle of 1990, bore the lion's share of responsibility for the fate of the country and its choice of direction. After being sworn in on July 10, 1991, as the first democratically elected president of Russia, he shared this responsibility with Russia's Congress of People's Deputies (CPD) and Supreme Soviet, the only institutions that could have provided a counterweight to the rapid consolidation of one-man rule. But this lasted for only four months, until November 5, 1991, when the parliament—swayed by the "personality cult" that was built up around Yeltsin in the wake of the August coup—eagerly abdicated its share of responsibility by almost unconditionally transferring to Yeltsin a large part of its constitutional powers, formally for a one-year "emergency period," but, as things turned out, indefinitely.

It would be premature and foolhardy to deliver a clear-cut historical verdict on Yeltsin as a personality. When future historians assemble his portrait, they will blend (in ways incomprehensible to us today) the seemingly heroic figure standing on the tank in front of the Russian legislature's White House who surprised the world with his apparent courage when resisting the August coup with the "Tsar Boris" of 1995–99, a man at the mercy of the pettiest passions; who poorly controlled himself, not to mention his country, while in office; and who became the butt of thinly veiled mockery and contempt from domestic and foreign spectators during the final years of his presidency. What follows here is but a preliminary attempt to contextualize the drama of Yeltsin's policies—in spite of all their apparent inconsistencies and inner tensions—within the structural paradigm of Russian reforms sketched above.

Yeltsin's instinct for political survival, plus his entourage's awareness about the failure of previous reform efforts in Russian history, seemed to suggest to him from the beginning the need for a calibrated mixture of liberalization and centralization, of society-oriented and state-oriented ingredients in his reform strategy. He arrived in power in 1990–91 equipped with a program for, on the one hand, dismantling the decrepit Union center and removing the rotten nomenklatura establishment while, on the other hand, asserting and strengthening the new Russian democratic state, which, although still in its infancy, was already endowed with a legal-rational and also moral legitimacy that was unprecedented in Russian history. Yeltsin's inner circle viewed the realization of the state-building program primarily along the lines of setting up a rigid top-down executive chain of command, firmly attached to the authoritarian charismatic person of the president. Yeltsin's problem—unique, given the specific conditions of the time, but typologically similar to that of most Russian reformers—was how to forge a viable coalition of social forces that would be able to fulfill simultaneously the equally important tasks of dismantling the outdated system and building and consolidating the new one, while also avoiding the perilous extremes of excessive centralization and loss of governability. The resolution of this dilemma depended on the Yeltsinists' choice of allies and "prime movers" of change among the mutually hostile strata and institutions of the crumbling Soviet order.

In the political and institutional vacuum that emerged after the collapse of the CPSU in August 1991, there were two forces (in addition to the authority of Yeltsin and the Russian Congress) that defined the social and political landscape. One was the newborn civil society, made up mainly by members of the middle class and united around the democratic-"populist" anti-establishment movement. (Within the latter, the Democratic Russia movement was the most visible and vocal, but not exactly the most representative, component.) The other force was the Party, Komsomol (or Young Communist League), and managerial nomenklatura, some segments of which were openly or covertly allied with the burgeoning underground empires of the shadow economy.

The correlation between these two forces had been in unstable equilibrium, but in August 1991 the balance abruptly shifted in favor of the anti-nomenklatura democrats. The latter, to whom Yeltsin in large measure owed his ascent to power—and, even more, his legitimacy—could develop or be steered in two different directions. On the one hand, they had destructive antistate potential, because most of them were indifferent to the prospect that the USSR might disintegrate and that the government in Russia itself might be weakened, while some even welcomed this prospect. On the other hand, they also had social reformist energy that potentially enabled the Russian leadership to sideline the most decadent elements in the natural alliance between the Communist Party nomenklatura and the shadow-economy entrepreneurs. In the latter case, the genuine reformers and modernizers in the new Russian government could have then redistributed the national resources appropriated by that alliance to be used in the new stage of national economic development.

However, if the ruling elite were to be replaced and the radical reform program of the anti-establishment movement were to be carried out, the political influence of this new movement undoubtedly would grow. Such a scenario would threaten Yeltsin and his entourage by turning them into transitional figures for whom competition with rising politicians from outside the nomenklatura could end in their own weakening or even in their retreat from the political stage. In particular, the impending emergence of new all-Union–caliber leaders out of this anti-nomenklatura movement who would be sufficiently sensitive to the concerns of the Union's non-Russian citizens in order to consolidate and strengthen the legitimacy of the federal institutions would create new hurdles for Yeltsin in his drive to amass and consolidate power in the Kremlin. Therefore, from the very moment that Yeltsin came to share de facto power with Gorbachev (in the summer and fall of 1990), he found it in his interest to use the democratic movement not as a tool of creative social reform but as a tool of destruction, primarily to weaken the all-Union institutions that were propping up Gorbachev. In this way, instead of a profound social transformation that might have enabled the Union to be kept together, Yeltsin opted for dismantling the Union state while preserving the basic social structures of the nomenklatura system and pursuing policies that even widened the gap between elite and society.

As could have been expected, the use of the disoriented and credulous leaders and activists of the Russian democratic movement as a battering ram aimed at the destruction of the Union (with all the ensuing disarray of the economy and disruptions of daily life) utterly discredited this movement, primarily in the eyes of its own rank-and-file followers. This led to its rapid disintegration and disappearance from the political stage in 1992–93. Thus, by using the democratic momentum for destructive purposes, the new Russian rulers squandered powerful social energies that could have been channeled toward rebuilding and fortifying state institutions from the bottom up (starting from local self-government, as advocated by, among others, Aleksandr Solzhenitsyn).

In the meantime, Yeltsin and his inner circle cultivated intimate relations with those groups in the Soviet elite that had amassed wealth through corruption and abuse of power in the institutions of the state and the Party. Wanting to safeguard monopoly positions for themselves in newly created markets, they sought the fastest possible transition to a "capitalist" system. It was the dialogue and interaction with these groups that shaped the Yeltsin-Gaidar shock therapy plan of transition to the market. The plan presupposed the creation of a new class of entrepreneurs not on the basis of the existing middle class (with its modest and legally earned savings) but, rather, on that of the commercialized Party-Komsomol elite and the networks of the shadow economy, which included organized crime. The legalization of the black market was openly put on the reform agenda by many representatives of the anarchic-libertarian strand among the "reformers," such as Vitaly Naishul' and Lev Timofeyev. Besides removing legal barriers and speeding up the redistribution of state property among the nomenklatura (which had so far proceeded covertly), this line of action entailed economically subverting and marginalizing those social strata that constituted the core of the democratic anti-nomenklatura movement. The key steps included the transfer of price-setting authority from state bureaucracies to semi-governmental trade monopolies (in the so-called price liberalization of January 1992); the confiscatory freezing and devaluation of personal savings accounts in the State Savings Bank belonging mostly to the middle class; the issuing to all citizens of transferable vouchers for the privatization of property that were subsequently bought up by a secondary market of well-funded consortia; and the imposition on most companies of a privatization scheme with a complex system of ownership that allowed the morally bankrupt managerial bureaucracy to become de facto private owners of most of the capital without taking full responsibility for the enterprises' performance and leaving little access to shares for most of the employees or for outside bidders. Seen against the background of the democrats' aspirations for social change from the bottom up, Yeltsin's economic policies represented reaction—or, in terms of the cyclical paradigm of Russian history, a *counterreform*. In short, Yeltsin was trying to create a market economy by top-down, "Bolshevik" methods; hence his strategy was, in our term, "market bolshevism."

By pursuing this line of action, Yeltsin, Gaidar, and their associates apparently hoped that in place of the radical grassroots movement (with its inconvenient pretensions to a policymaking role and reformist idealism) they could acquire a more powerful and reliable social base among the new entrepreneurs, who would help them to consolidate the new regime and to build new state institutions. Here again Yeltsin followed the old Bolshevik pattern of reforms applied by Ivan the Terrible, Peter the Great, and Joseph Stalin: He tried to create a privileged class of committed supporters of the regime by rapidly redistributing national resources in their favor at the expense of the majority of Russians and also of the state treasury.

As the preliminary balance sheet of Yeltsin's rule indicates, that solution turned out to be self-defeating. The new capitalist class—both the small-scale voucher traders and speculators of 1991–93 vintage, and the financial oligarchy that dominated from 1994 on—proved to be unreliable allies; in some cases, they became outright foes of Yeltsin's attempts to strengthen the administrative capacity of the government. Meanwhile, with the demise of the democratic movement, the deluded and disoriented participants in the aborted social revolution found themselves thrown back to the Brezhnev era—with its bizarre blend of adaptive-conformist and nihilistic attitudes; with a sense of mistrust and enmity toward the powers that be; and with silent resentment against the appeals and wishful proclamations from above about economic growth, timely payment of taxes, and the preservation of law and order.

Driven by his desire for more and more power (as well as by the interests of his new allies), Yeltsin did not try to achieve a modus vivendi with the parliamentary opposition that coalesced in late 1991 and early 1992 to protest against, first, the dismantling of the Union that had been accomplished in a surreptitious and undemocratic way and, second, shock therapy. This opposition, consisting mostly of his former allies in the democratic movement, favored with few exceptions a strong state with increased administrative capacity and institutions based on a politically neutral civil service; thus, it could have been turned into a loyal support base for Yeltsin's putative policy of state building. But Yeltsin preferred to bully the opposition and finally to throw it aside in 1993 by sending tanks to destroy the parliament. He then attempted to carry out major elements of the opposition's program in the area of centralization and state-building, relying not on the state-oriented forces of society inside and outside the parliament, but on the police, army, and security establishment, as well as on courtiers personally loyal to him (namely, presidential security chief Aleksandr Korzhakov, Defense Minister Pavel Grachev, Deputy Prime Minister Oleg Soskovets, Federal Counterintelligence Service Chairman Sergei Stepashin, and others). From 1993 to 1996, the country repeatedly found itself on the brink of becoming an authoritarian police state.

However, these armed agencies lacked the resources to establish a full-scale dictatorship—not least because the Yeltsin regime, having tied itself to the predatory interests of the rejuvenated nomenklatura, could not offer society any constructive program capable of justifying and legitimizing its authoritarian scenario of state building. By early 1995, when the Grachev-Korzhakov clique bogged Russia down in the morass of the Chechnya war, nationalist rhetoric (together with the ideology of centralization and state building) became just as widely discredited among Russians by Yeltsin's misuse of it as the slogans of the democratic movement had become by 1992. This misuse of nationalist ideals and human capital by the Yeltsin regime became indisputably clear when Russia's nascent nationalist political movements lost many of their supporters and slumped to defeat in the State Duma elections of December 1995. Finally, in June 1996, under the pressure of a financial cartel (the "Seven Bankers" group of oligarchs) and the Western and pro-Western advisers who were running his re-election campaign, Yeltsin purged from the Kremlin the entire group of military and security chiefs who in 1993 had ensured his triumph in the armed assault on the parliament.

The outcome of this zigzag evolution of the Yeltsin's first term along the lines of Russia's historical zero-sum game between state and society was twofold: We saw, on the one hand, an extremely debilitated system of state power that lacked genuine legitimacy and a reliable social base; and, on the other hand, an equally weak and disorganized society existing in an intellectual void and deprived of adequate representation of its interests. In other words, if the Yeltsin reforms were initially targeted to resolve at least one of the two perennial problems of Russia (either state building or social development), they failed on both counts.

For its part, the privileged class of "New Russians" created through the social engineering of shock therapy and privatization has proved to be neither a defense nor a support for the regime against the mirages of conspiracy by irreconcilable enemies of reform. Rather, it has revealed itself as the direct heir to the old Soviet elite. Perhaps the single core difference between the two was that the New Russians, unlike the old nomenklatura, were not restrained even by those largely ritual limits of ideological "correctness" that until the late 1980s governed social interaction and made possible the communication of values among various layers of Soviet society. This mutual understanding, however tenuous, allowed the rulers of the USSR to set in motion the forces necessary for at least a partial attainment of national goals. By contrast, in today's Russia, which is torn apart by "information wars" between media-controlling financiers and Kremlin officials, the communication between the government and the economic elites it has engendered looks more like bargaining between the envoys of foreign powers. Even in this kind of relationship, as in international politics, the factor of interdependence obviously applies. The Kremlin and the business magnates in finance and foreign trade, from Boris Berezovsky to Vladimir Gusinsky, still unite and mobilize in the face of common threats, such as the specter of an electoral victory by the opposition—even though the leading opposition forces, especially the Communist Party and, to a lesser extent, Yabloko, have been largely integrated into the system already. Yet, as the experience of the mid- to late 1990s fully demonstrates, the two sides are unable to reach a long-term agreement on the priorities of national development and on joint actions to achieve them. Thus, in the absence of major external shocks, it is likely that the state-centralizing and institution-building needs of the Kremlin, as well as the imperative to provide for a sustainable revenue base, will diverge from the interests of the plutocratic clans more and more.

In the meantime, the government has found itself—certainly under Yeltsin and potentially under Vladimir Putin as well—not only without sustainable support in society but also without a recruiting ground from which to staff its bureaucracy with reliable personnel. As in the decades before Gorbachev, government service is widely viewed as an unworthy and even somewhat ignominious occupation for educated professionals. At the same time, the tenure in government of such quintessential New Russians as "oligarchs" Vladimir Potanin and Berezovsky (and, more recently, Berezovsky's proxies, such as presidential chief of staff Aleksandr Voloshin) was marked by innumerable conflicts of interest and earned few positive comments even from within their own camp.

It is increasingly likely that Yeltsin's successors, in their search for an exit from the systemic crisis that has paralyzed the country, will be compelled to seek understanding and support from those same social strata that were the driving force of the abortive anti-establishment revolution of 1988–91. In that case, the future leaders of Russia will have to reassemble piece by piece the social and human capital that was dissipated by the Yeltsin regime in 1992–93 and later. For their part, the heirs of the civic movement of the 1980s will hopefully, unlike their predecessors, be more mindful of the perils of a weakened state unable to fulfill its basic functions. But such mutual understanding and cooperation between state authorities and the representatives of social movements will be possible only if and when both sides draw the appropriate lessons from the disastrous experience of the past and the present. This will require clear and widespread awareness of the fact that the Yeltsin regime and its allies in Russia and the West bear full responsibility for the imposition of an experiment that has been destructive for most Russians and that has negated the original developmental goals of Russia's reform movement and the Yeltsin regime itself.

In the next chapter we survey the various political and developmental theories that both we and scholars with whom we disagree have considered useful for better understanding Russia's exit from communism and the possible paths it might then take. What was the pedigree of these theories, and how did they divide political scientists and economists in both Russia and the West? Also, how well have they measured up to the task at hand?

2

RUSSIAN POSTCOMMUNISM IN THE MIRROR OF SOCIAL THEORY

We aimed at communism—but we hit Russia.

—*Aleksandr Zinoviev*

T HE MULTIFACETED AND UNPRECEDENTED CHANGES that were thrust upon Russian society between 1987 and 1993 have provided voluminous material for exploration by social science and political theory. The transformation of the Soviet political order, the economic changes, and the events referred to as "the collapse of empire" were interdependent processes, confronting both observers and participants with a wide range of issues that cut across disciplinary boundaries of the social sciences and political thought. These issues include the following:

- The nature of democracy as a social order and the probability of its taking root and bearing fruit if transplanted to different nations and cultures.
- The nature and structure of the existing global order and the chances for a newcomer like Russia to join it without compromising its sovereignty, national security, and legitimate interests.
- The notion of national consciousness as an aspect of individual and collective identity.
- The relationships between national/ethnic identities and the values of modern civilization.
- The role of agents of change in the political order, economy, culture, and process of nation building, and the interrelationship among these elements of a society.
- Russia's particular place in world history, given its receptivity to mutually contradictory foreign influences in its eternal quest to create a unique national identity.
- The meaning and implications of Russia's whole experience, as viewed in the global context of modernity.

These, and other issues to follow, relate to different fields and levels of analysis in the social sciences and the humanities. Usually, ontological inquiry into the basic nature of democracy, markets, the nation-state, and the like falls within the boundaries of philosophy and inevitably entails normative value judgments. In contrast, social science and political theory often, explicitly or implicitly, accept as given a set of assumptions about knowledge and the ontological interpretation of a subject (even though both may prove arbitrary or inappropriate). So the questions they ask are more instrumental than substantive—not "what?" and "whence?" but "why?" "under what conditions?" and "whither?" Modelbuilders, in turn, follow in the footsteps of theorists and typically do not bother with meanings and questions of ontology but, rather, focus on explaining *how* the subject under investigation evolved from one historical condition to another or made a transition from point A to point B.

In reality, the boundaries between these approaches are fluid and contingent, though the utility of one over the other clearly depends on the nature of the query. Russian social and political thought, unlike most Western approaches, has a propensity to integrate knowledge and other types of experience holistically; in its best moments, it has blurred the barriers among various disciplines.

Major Russian thinkers based their philosophical systems on wide-ranging empirical analysis of national and world history; while for many sociologists, historians, and essayists, basic ontological issues were open to scrutiny. Although similar examples can be found among Anglo-American thinkers, the very paradigm of Western epistemology is based on sharp interdisciplinary boundaries, at least as a frame of reference.

The prevalent response of both Western and Russian mainstream theorists to the events of the late and post-Soviet periods in Russia has been strikingly one-sided. The most vigorous activity was displayed by model makers, especially transitologists and macroeconomists such as those discussed below. Many of them hurried into the ruins of the Soviet system, treating the aftermath as a new and promising testing ground that was suitable for demonstrating how the sequence of transition was supposed to work on the basis of established theories. Some of them went further, prescribing the proper direction and timing of democratization, marketization, and so forth. The approach of these academics—some of whom became advisers to post-Soviet governments—can be described, metaphorically, as a kind of social cloning. On the basis of their beliefs, they persuaded their audiences that the successes of Western countries could be replicated by "fixing" those social and cultural genes they felt resulted from an unfortunate error of historical evolution.

In short, pondering the proper direction of "transition" and the inherent potential for damage—which required considering, first, whether the Western developmental model was really applicable outside Euroatlantic terrain and, second, whether it would be welcomed by Russians—lagged seriously behind the hurried charting of maps that focused on "how to get there." Meanwhile, the deeper theoretical inquiry into the nature of Russia's dizzying changes and their place in world history is only just beginning. Both Western and Russian social and political philosophy, which produced such profound and diverse responses to the rise and triumph of Soviet Bolshevism, have so far been almost mute in the face of its collapse.

At least one of the reasons for this inadequacy has been the intellectual seclusion of most of Sovietology from major trends in neighboring disciplines, an isolation that has been noticed with regret by a number of observers inside and outside the field.[1] Like many other area studies, Sovietology tended to insist upon the exceptional nature of its subject. This insularity, together with the "strategic" nature of the field, effectively shut off many Sovietologists (although never without exception) from interdisciplinary communication with such related fields as the theory of international relations or social psychology and from comparative study of more accessible regions and cultures, such as Latin America or, for that matter, the United States. Although this incarceration was not (and could not be) absolute, it often resulted in the acceptance of the most convenient theories as given and exempted practitioners in the field from too much reflection and scrutiny of their unspoken underlying assumptions.

Although Sovietology itself has left a problematic legacy, other branches of contemporary Western social thought provide us with insights into the ontology of Russia's reforms and concomitant national breakdown. Most of these insights have been achieved thanks to the theorists' increased awareness of their underlying assumptions about society, assumptions that tend to be defined by their time and place. This chapter reviews some of these promising approaches—hopefully moving them a step forward—and outlines fruitful contexts in which Russia's experience has been and most likely will be examined by Western theorists. It begins with a cursory review and interpretation of some basic concepts and themes, most of which may be familiar to a Western audience. However, given Russians' intimate relationship with many Western theories and modes of thought —from Marxism to neoclassical economics—we believe that an examination of the same topics in the Russian literature and their possible interpretations is crucial for an adequate grasp of Russia's current state of affairs and of its often invisible but painstaking search for an exit from the nadir of the 1990s.

LEGITIMACY AND LEGITIMATION OF POWER

The issue of why some people should govern and others should obey is among the fundamental questions of history and one of the pivotal themes in every philosophical and religious system. Although the bedrock of conservative wisdom—expressed in this century by Walter Lippmann's phrase that "people need to be governed," even if a particular government is not up to the task—has been challenged only at the margins of intellectual inquiry (that is, by anarchists), the quest for the ethical justification, or legitimation, of the reality that certain people wield power over others in specific ways has been central to most modern societies and thus to political thought. In contrast to premodern times (when power was routinely based on the application of direct violence, and the passive obedience of the populace was sufficient for the stability of their rulers), bureaucratic centralization and expansion has required the public's sustained and conscious cooperation with the state and other power-wielding bureaucracies for these institutions to function and survive. Consequently, the legitimation of political, economic, and other types of power has become more and more complex and demanding.[2]

From the point of view of positivist methodology, with its orientation toward the natural sciences, the concept of legitimacy is murky and elusive. It does not yield to quantification, and the degree of its presence or absence cannot be unambiguously determined on the basis of empirical data. It can only be inferred from people's beliefs and actions; yet even elections and polls, though necessary, are insufficient indicators of legitimacy. The fact that a large portion of the electorate does not vote, or that many voters simply choose "the lesser evil" when the choice of candidates is limited, can cast doubt on the legitimacy of even democratically elected rulers. The legitimacy of an entire social or political system is even more tricky to determine, given the composite nature of such systems and the fact that some social groups will always regard certain subsystems or even the whole system as lacking legitimacy. In addition, given the diversity of people's beliefs, the legitimacy of a single authority in any one society can be built on the support of a variety of groups, each of which sees different and sometimes—objectively speaking—mutually exclusive virtues in the same authority. Such a case was Peter the Great, whom some saw as a bold revolutionary and others as a traditional ruler who brought despotism to perfection.

Nevertheless, although it lacks an agreed-upon intersubjective meaning, the concept of legitimacy has clear-cut objective dimensions. Its presence or absence can be strikingly manifest, evidenced by either enthusiastic commitment of the general public to the powers that be or by the paralysis and collapse of their authority. Thus the passive acquiescence of most Soviet citizens, including powerful elites, to the demise of the Soviet system and state in 1991 attested to the fact that both had irretrievably lost their legitimacy.

In the 1970s and 1980s, the issue of the legitimation crisis as a central issue of modernity came to the fore in profound debates across the intellectual spectrum. Although Jurgen Habermas, whose work set the tone for discussion (primarily among scholars on the left), initially applied it to "late capitalism," the concept of legitimation crisis soon was stretched to encompass most social systems and the hierarchical relations of modern civilization as a whole.[3] Meanwhile, as passions in the Western debate were receding, theories about legitimation crises proved to be particularly apposite for analyzing the so-called socialist or communist states, whose ruling elites were conspicuously losing their "mandate of heaven." The works of T. H. Rigby and Leslie Holmes substantially enlarged the conceptual framework of the legitimation problem.[4] In particular, Rigby expanded the concept of rational legitimation, pioneered by sociologist Max Weber, beyond its purely legal confines to include the important notion of an instrumental or teleological (goal-oriented) legitimacy, which can obtain when rulers and key sectors of society concur in their aspirations and efforts to achieve desired goals of political and social development—be they the "building" of communism, capitalism, or democracy; catching up with the West or with the East; or merely balancing the budget.

Clearly, this mode of legitimation hinges upon the linear view of history as having, if not a clear-cut end, then at least a preferable direction and purpose, and it implies that the rulers should be seen as sincerely committed to their goals and fit to lead the nation in the pursuit of the stated aim. The elements of goal-oriented legitimacy are ubiquitous, and where a goal is not in sight, it often has to be invented. However, it rarely becomes as vital to a political system as it did in the Soviet Union, with its virtual absence of either traditional or legal modes of legitimation for its rulers. The finite objective of establishing a just and equitable society became the justification for mass suffering and deprivation, as well as the major (perhaps the only) source of legitimation for the Communist Party's monopoly on all forms of power. Consequently, it was the failure to approximate this objective and increasingly obvious deviations from this path that undermined the legitimacy of the Soviet system, leading to its degeneration and decay.

Holmes, whose legitimacy-oriented theory of the Soviet collapse is as fruitful as it is conducive to sweeping and divergent interpretations, further expands the Weberian taxonomy. He identifies no less than ten modes of legitimation of power (some of which, however, are easily reducible into other modes), and he deserves much credit for his sophisticated distinction between various versions of instrumental legitimacy.[5] In addition to a teleological, future-oriented version of legitimacy, another is a version based on the populace's expectation that the system will provide for consumer needs either directly, as in primitive distribution systems, or via the rational and smooth operation of the market economy. In emphasizing the growing importance over time of consumer-based legitimation in the countries of the Soviet bloc, Holmes sums up the observations of Western analysts who studied economic reforms in these countries from the 1950s onward. These reforms were not geared toward a social ideal of a utopian order, but toward satisfying the short-term material demands of the establishment and its clients—demands that were skyrocketing under the pressure of media-created "demonstration effects" of allegedly universal and unproblematic consumer affluence in Western countries. These developments indicated the extent of the Soviet bloc's latent integration into the U.S.-dominated global economic order, integration that occurred at least at the level of elites and of those mass beliefs about economic welfare that the elites had shaped. Thus it was plain to see how the leaders of the East had been converging toward the West in their views on the importance of ensuring the material well-being of influential social groups to secure the legitimacy of their governmental authority.[6]

Whatever the case, the shift of emphasis to a consumer-based legitimacy, which had apparently occurred in the minds of the Soviet elites and public by the mid-1960s, did not help stave off the growing legitimation crisis, as the promise of bringing the Soviet standard of living in line with prevailing images of Western societies failed to be realized. To make things worse for the Soviet ruling class, the abandonment of the ideal of distributive justice and the acceptance of Western consumer standards gradually exposed the USSR's urban centers to those components of the contemporary global economy that were viewed as repulsive and harmful by most ordinary citizens—from social pathologies, such as pornography, drugs, and organized crime to the vagaries of currency markets and uncontrolled capital flows. In the 1970s and 1980s, these elements of Western life penetrated Soviet society through holes in the Iron Curtain drilled by corrupt nomenklatura oligarchs, black-market dealers, and the criminal underworld. What did not seep through from the West were its salutary social elements, such as civil society and the rule of law. The outcome of such developments is aptly described by Holmes:

[A]s the process unfolded, it appeared to many citizens and even officials in the Communist world that they were being increasingly subjected to all the negative aspects of both capitalism and Communism . . . at the same time as the positive aspects of both . . . seemed in many cases at least as distant as they had ever been. In short, Communism . . . appeared more and more to represent the worst of all worlds, rather than the best.[7]

While accepting Holmes's general framework of analysis, we cannot avoid taking issue with his view that the anticorruption campaigns of the 1980s represented a decisive shift to legal rationality as the basis of the regime's claim to legitimacy. While Soviet leaders had repeatedly expressed their intention to move toward the rule of law from 1953 (the year of Stalin's death) onward, the mounting anticorruption campaigns of the 1980s were probably a response to the visible public discontent with those new features of the system that were seen as inequitable and unjust, and thus in violation of the system's stated purpose. Therefore, while the ruling nomenklatura and other affluent strata quietly dispensed with the teleological claim to legitimacy, a large part of Soviet society did not. Indeed, the more obviously the behavior of the ruling establishment and its urban clients deviated from the fundamentals of the system, including its official pledge to promote social justice, the more the general public grew anxious and disgruntled.

This discontent developed in the late Soviet era, despite the evidence that by the 1980s, the notion of communism was no longer taken seriously by the vast majority of Communist Party members—not to speak of the rest of educated Soviet society—and the scientific reputation of Marx and Lenin's writings as a guideline for the betterment of society was thoroughly undermined even among members of the Politburo. Nevertheless, the demand for a more just social order endured, especially among the unprivileged but educated and socially active strata of the population, and strategically minded Soviet leaders such as Andropov and, later, Gorbachev were compelled to take it into account. Apparently, these ideals were deeply ingrained in the national culture, and the manifest unwillingness of the nomenklatura to pursue them even as distant goals undermined the legitimacy of the system without discrediting the norm. Neither were these goals pursued, nor did the Kremlin provide any viable replacement for them.[8] The problem lay in the absence of a clear-cut and authoritative alternative to official Marxism that could chart the road to a more acceptable economic system. Meanwhile, the dissidents who made up the counterelite sought an alternative developmental strategy mostly in political and moral (not socioeconomic) terms. Yet even among them, there was no consensus at all on the most desirable national strategy. The most comprehensive political alternative—that outlined by Aleksandr Solzhenitsyn over two decades in works such as *Letter to the Soviet Leaders* to *Rebuilding Russia*—was too disturbing for the opposition mainstream of liberal Westernizers.

To be sure, in the late 1980s the set of public beliefs in the Soviet Union about legitimacy was a complex blend of the most diverse ingredients. While the longing for "equality and brotherhood" was probably the most widespread (and emanated from below), it competed and coexisted with other goals, such as the "return to world civilization" (which was equated with the West and, specifically, with "advanced industrial countries") and the more or less traditional slogan calling for "national rebirth." "Building the rule of law" was also important, as were the expectations of consumer affluence and the charisma of political leaders. In this context, the outcome of the power struggles in the late 1980s depended on which group of politicians was better able to present itself as the embodiment of the most relevant types of legitimacy. Regarding the most significant of these power struggles, although Gorbachev drew his legitimacy from such important factors as tradition, legal rationality, Western support, and his considerable charisma, he fell seriously behind Yeltsin in 1989–90 as a credible advocate of moral and distributive justice.

The evidence suggests that, in distinction to Gorbachev's revamped Soviet polity, Russia's newly emerging political institutions of the 1990–91 vintage— like those of most of the first postcommunist governments in the former Soviet bloc—enjoyed a high degree of legitimacy that was unprecedented at least since 1945 and was at least on a par with that of most Western governments of the time. This can be inferred from the high turnouts (compared with those in the West) for the spate of elections and referenda that accompanied the USSR's dissolution, as well as from the enthusiastic involvement of many thousands of rank-and-file citizens in civic organizations and mass actions. The latter overwhelmingly expressed their support for most of the new leaders and institutions and, more broadly, for the promise of a new social order that these leaders and institutions claimed to embody. In this brief period of great authority, with August 1991 as its pinnacle, Yeltsin's regime (which was still widely viewed as the government of the "democrats") appeared to have mastered the range of relevant modes of legitimation: legal rationality; leadership charisma (as personified by Yeltsin); appeal to the pre-Bolshevik tradition of statehood (with the slogan of "national rebirth"), as well as to the early soviet tradition of class-conscious democracy (with the slogan of "All power to the soviets!"); public support for the tasks of national development (however vaguely conceived); and, not least, high material expectations on the part of many urban dwellers. All these factors worked in favor of the new authorities—President Yeltsin; the parliament that had brought him to power; local and regional soviets (or governing councils); and the only mass-based national proto-party, Democratic Russia. While the social and economic status quo (the bureaucratic supermonopoly called "socialism," which was quietly evolving into criminal-nomenklatura "capitalism") was vehemently rejected by the majority, the new political regime was widely and sincerely perceived as an ally of the public in its desire to dismantle that system.

It is against this background that one must trace the dramatic evolution of the post-Soviet Russian political order that ran the gamut from the glorious start of 1991 to the mass alienation, fatalistic sense of powerlessness, and contempt for the authorities that have characterized the public mood since late 1993, when Yeltsin dispatched the army's tanks to attack an allegedly "antidemocratic" parliament. In March 1996, the presidential elections were on the verge of being canceled; in the summer, Boris Yeltsin, the triumphant winner of the 1989–91 elections and referenda, had to use all the legal and illegal means at his disposal to cajole the majority of active voters into believing that he, rather than his opponent, represented "the lesser evil."[9] (The "lesser evil" argument was made explicitly on behalf of the leader himself as the regime's last resort in a legitimacy crisis and may serve as an idiosyncratic contribution of the Yeltsin regime to the existing typologies of political legitimacy.)

As for the legitimation of a democratic order in Russia, this is a separate issue in terms of theory. From 1992 on, Yeltsin and his entourage visibly distanced themselves from their original democratic rhetoric and from "the democrats" as the movement that embodied it. And yet, as evidence presented in subsequent chapters of this work will suggest, in Yeltsin's Russia the legitimacy of democracy as a system of rule also gradually became a matter of dispute. Western observers have widely missed the fact that the democratic idea was attacked most forcefully, in both theory and practice, by the very figures they touted as liberals and reformers. Even though democracy has not yet been tried in Russia as a regular and functioning system, it also became discredited among a significant segment of ordinary Russians—not least under the impact of those liberals and reformers who worried that the Russian understanding of democracy as popular rule could very well create dangerous obstacles for the administrative redistribution of state property away from the public sector.

As we will see, although the legitimation crises of the Yeltsin regime and of the democratic idea are tightly linked, each had its own logic and separate dynamic. A closer review of various approaches to democracy by some twentieth-century Western theorists will help to shed light on this distinction.

The Democratic Idea in Western Social Thought

Whatever definition of democracy we accept, it is plain to see that the concept is not immanent in Western political culture. Since well before the Socratic era, democracy was under political and philosophical assault from various corners, and the critics periodically prevailed—often for centuries. It is worth recalling that as recently as 1941, only three European nations qualified as democracies.

A decade ago, after the global "third wave" of democratization (whose epicenter was in the former Soviet bloc) spilled over into the field of political theory, some theorists began to claim with unwarranted optimism that democracy has become the only legitimate system of rule in the world and does not have any plausible alternatives.[10] Indeed, the earlier spread of democratic institutions to

Latin America, southern and Eastern Europe, and then to some of the Asian and African countries seemed to confirm that democracy was not limited to the confines of European civilization, but had become a truly universal phenomenon. Before long, though, there were aspects of this democratic upsurge that began to look undesirable and even disturbing to many observers West and East. As a result, critics resumed the offensive by vigorously denouncing various "illiberal" democracies and their rulers, who were diverging from familiar democratic standards.[11]

The present work accepts as its starting point the declared intent of Soviet and Russian reformers of the late 1980s to move in the direction of democracy. If the promise of democratization turned sour, as many Russia-watchers agree, it was clearly not because of the explicit resistance of some antidemocratic "dark forces" but, rather, because of a profound but rarely recognized discord among the different—and occasionally irreconcilable—views of democracy in Russia. The most telling example was the near–civil war of 1993 between the Kremlin and the parliament, in which prominent figures on each side saw themselves as righteous defenders of democracy—each, of course, with his own interpretation. This clash of interpretations of democracy in political practice has echoed much older disagreements and tensions within Western democratic theory.

Joseph Schumpeter defined democracy as "an institutional arrangement . . . in which individuals acquire power to decide by means of a competitive struggle for the people's vote," and this became a reference point for other currents of democratic theory.[12] Schumpeter's concept of democracy, which focused on forms and procedure, was shaped by the conditions of those years when democracy in continental Europe seemed to have little future and when the fate of the world and its almost exclusively Anglo-Saxon democratic minority was being decided on the Eastern front of World War II in a struggle between two despotic regimes. Schumpeter's intent was to preserve some space for democracy by showing it to be harmless for, and compatible with, the centrally organized social systems that pessimists believed would dominate the world in the foreseeable future. With this purpose in mind, Schumpeter labored to disentangle democracy from its alliance with free market capitalism, Anglo-American individualism, and middle-class values, presenting this form of government as a purely neutral decision-making procedure that did not predetermine the content of policy decisions and was thus equally acceptable for any economic system and culture. In so doing, he tried to restore the legitimacy of procedural democracy that had been debased and discredited among many of his European contemporaries, who viewed it as a tool of particular social and national interests directed against unprivileged social strata and nations.

Soon, however, democracy seemed to defy the prophets of its doom, becoming the trademark of the Allies' victory in World War II and the establishment of the Euroatlantic political and economic architecture designed to protect Europe from communism. In the optimistic and missionary mood of postwar Western thought about democracy, Schumpeter's cautious minimalism yielded the intellectual center stage to various versions of the modernization paradigm closely identified with major interpreters of Weber in the Anglo-American world, such as Talcott Parsons and Seymour Martin Lipset.[13] The modernization theorists' notion of democracy was firmly anchored in their linear, unidirectional view of history, in which nations were moving along a single axis of development; accordingly, democracy was the ultimate result of progress in other realms, such as economy and culture.

This belief in the inexorable logic of preconditions and scientific regularities, such as the rise of the middle class and labor unions, exhibited a paradoxical affinity with the "vulgar" brand of Marxist sociology in that both agreed—despite their seemingly irreconcilable political antagonism—that the industrial-capitalist base supported the democratic "superstructure." The principal difference between the two was that for the modernization theorists it was the Anglo-American system of liberal-democratic capitalism, rather than Soviet Communism, that served as the shining pinnacle of history, the common goal for all societies. Modernization theorists fervently shared with Marxists the same Enlightenment axiom that world history was rationally organized in stages and that the logic of modernization was inescapable. They were confident (like some of America's foreign-policy makers of their time) that industrialized capitalism, the Protestant work ethic, and democratic institutions were bound to expand to new frontiers by wiping out or marginalizing traditional values, cultures, and habitual ways of life. Some of the more discerning thinkers among the modernization theorists, such as Barrington Moore, saw universal development as being far from devoid of conflict, but even those social strata and nations that chose to defy some attributes of modernity (such as India) were seen as unable to alter fundamentally the course of progress. Thus, any major rebellion against the logic of modernity would effectively push the rebellious nation or force of antimodernity to the margins of history's highway.

In the first decades after World War II, versions of this approach became the dominant paradigm in comparative politics, thus elevating particular historically contingent Western ways of life and governmental systems as the standard to which the rest of humanity could aspire. Promulgators of the modernization approach focused on identifying and classifying necessary and sufficient preconditions for the democratic system to emerge and stabilize. The works from Lipset's school examined the social and economic premises that included capitalist industrialization, the rise of a well-to-do middle class, a social safety net for the lower classes, education, urbanization, and cross-cutting divisions among workers and the subsequent erosion of their class consciousness. Following in the tracks of Talcott Parsons, theorists of "civic culture" ascribed the stability of democratic institutions in the Anglo-Saxon world to these countries' superior culture, which managed to produce in society a properly calibrated blend of "citizen" and "subject" attitudes such as participation and willing conformism, respectively. In comparison, even countries such as Germany and Italy were regarded as being poorly equipped for self-sustaining democracy, the former because of citizens' overly zealous loyalty to the state, and the latter because of the excessively turbulent involvement of its citizenry in the affairs of the state, allegedly dooming it to continuous anarchy and turmoil.[14]

This line of reasoning represented a partial return to the interwar, pre-Schumpeterian mindset, in which true democracy was defined by reference to a single culture and economic system. Although Weber himself saw the vocation of a social scientist infused with dispassionate objectivity, the Weberians and quasi-Weberians of postwar academia shared the sincere belief of elites in their countries (and of many dissidents on the other side of the Iron Curtain) in the Anglo-American system's special mission as the custodian and messenger of genuine democracy. Deductive theories and Western political practice suggested to them that, in the absence of the required socioeconomic and cultural "preconditions," the only way to spread democracy was by exporting those preconditions. In extreme cases, these attributes of democracy could be imposed through military occupation, as happened in Germany, Italy, and Japan.

It was this purportedly universal but actually rather ethnocentric version of democracy that was vigorously offered to Soviet society by Western cultural diplomacy and broadcast media after the fall of the Iron Curtain, and it was accepted by Soviet and post-Soviet oligarchs, anxious to sustain themselves in power with the help of their newly acquired teachers and patrons. Although some of the nomenklatura reformers loudly proclaimed themselves democrats, they embraced the modernization paradigm primarily because it rationalized their intention to place the top-down economic and cultural transformation of Russia ahead of the political participation the rest of society demanded. They were not disturbed by the evidence that Russia in many ways had already been modernized from above (even if in a brutal and largely misguided way) under Stalin and that the cultural and political effects of this modernization largely explained why a growing number of citizens, especially among the relatively better-off middle strata, became so acutely aware of disparities in power and wealth between the nomenklatura and the dispossessed majority of society.

It is clear that the modernization doctrines of democracy, representing just an episode in the twenty-five hundred years of the democratic idea's evolution, are inadequate to account for the history of Athens and Rome or for the democratic communes in medieval Europe. Nor can they explain why the most advanced and democratic political systems in the contemporary period feature certain forms of power that are exercised in undemocratic ways, such as corporate decision making. While a set of basic procedural norms has remained the universal currency of democracy, the word has always had a variety of substantive meanings and implications, as can be inferred from the pervasive use of qualifiers in such phrases as "liberal" and "social" democracy; "Christian" and "Islamic" democracy; "direct," "representative," and "participatory" democracy;

and so on. Throughout their histories, the British and American systems (to cite only these two countries) have always contained a tension between the tendency to leave the interpretation of the voters' will to their elected representatives (forcefully advocated by Edmund Burke) and the divergent tendency to have representatives closely accountable to the electorate. The inherent deficiencies of representative democracy in a modern mass society have often been acknowledged and reflected in appeals for grassroots civic intervention in politics, as well as in mass-based populist movements.[15] The "economic theories" of democracy, which envisioned politics as a marketplace and voting as a shopper's visit to a supermarket to select among given alternatives on the basis of rational self-interest informed by advertisement,[16] have been aptly rebuked by those who view democracy as a way for citizens to participate in the formation of alternative—something that has no equivalent in the marketplace.

In addition, some assumptions of modernization theorists about the most advanced forms of democracy have been countered with convincing empirical evidence. The sociocultural analysis of British society, for example, has called into question the strength of the so-called preconditions for democracy, revealing some elements of social psychology that did not fit into the "citizen-subject" framework of civic culture and had no outlet within liberal democracy.[17] A study of witch-hunting campaigns in American history orchestrated by various factions within the establishment brought to light a significant reservoir of intolerance and "archaic" impulses that have coexisted with democracy.[18] Most recently, the illuminating study of Italian regional history by Robert Putnam demonstrated how the stability and success of democratic institutions are intrinsically linked to the culture of horizontal relations within a society that are not a product of capitalist development but, rather, date back to pre-industrial times.[19]

Ironic as it may be, the fall of the Iron Curtain and the cascade of democratic transformations in the former Soviet bloc plunged the traditional mainstream of democratic theory into a severe state of crisis. On the one hand, the failure of Gorbachev's vision of a socialist democracy and the rhetorical flamboyance of the new rulers across Eastern Europe, zealously swearing their allegiance to both democracy and markets simultaneously, did not bode well for Schumpeter's assumption that democracy could coexist with any kind of economic or social system. Instead, they seemed to confirm the intuitions of conservative and other thinkers who insisted on democracy's inextricable link with private entrepreneurship, a free market, and individualist values. In light of these developments, the lead article in a symposium that evaluated Schumpeter's magnum opus on democratic theory states matter of factly that "almost every one of its main propositions has been empirically falsified."[20] On the other hand, the widespread legitimation of democratic values and norms, and the considerable popularity of democratic institutions in countries as bereft of economic and sociocultural "preconditions" as Mongolia, cast serious doubt on the rigid cause-and-effect framework of the modernization school. Even its patriarch, Lipset, acknowledged major discrepancies between the established developmental paradigm and new evidence, a fact that attests to his intellectual honesty.[21]

In the later years of the Soviet Union, Western messages about modernization and democracy fell upon fertile ground. Even though brief and distant in time, Russia's own experience with at least some elements of democracy had been enlightening and left recognizable imprints on its national memory. Dating back to the medieval city-states of Novgorod and Pskov, whose republican systems of rule were destroyed by Moscow autocrats, and to the Assemblies of the Land in the sixteenth and seventeenth centuries (an analog to France's Estates General), democratic institutions and norms were resurrected in modern times after the Great Reforms of Alexander II in the 1860s—first in the form of local self-government (the *zemstvo* system), then in brief experiments with parliamentary democracy from 1905 to 1918, and finally in the multiparty Soviets of Workers' and Peasants' Deputies before these became finally subjugated to the dictatorship of the Communist Party in 1920–21.

Let us single out four specific features of the Russian democratic tradition that in our view made it much different from the premises and expectations of Western theorists. First, Russian democracy, as shaped by its national history, tended to be *participatory and egalitarian,* not least because Russia had more experience with grassroots movements and local forms of "direct democracy" than with modern procedural parliamentarism. (This radical interpretation of democracy as governance directly by and for the people was not exclusive to Russia. As David Held observed, "Within the history of democratic theory lies a deeply rooted conflict about whether democracy should mean some kind of popular power . . . or an aid to decision-making."[22] It is the "popular power" concept, with all its intrinsic egalitarianism, that one usually finds at the historical origins of most democratic systems). The archetypes of Russian democracy, the Novgorod and Pskov city-states, were governed by a *veche,* a popular assembly summoned at the ringing of church bells, not unlike town meetings in medieval England and elsewhere in Europe.[23]

The second characteristic of the Russian democratic tradition was that democratic institutions tended to be built around the *representation of collective interests,* based on either estates (as in the 1905–17 Duma) or class structure (as in the original democratic soviets), rather than around the Western system of one person–one vote.

The third feature—and perhaps the most important for the purposes of this book—was that, rather than organically growing out of modernization, democracy in Russia had a track record of *clashing with centralized and coercive "revolutions from above"* that claimed to be moving the nation toward the common denominator of European modernity ("one size fits all"), as perceived by the envious and inferiority-haunted elite. Thus, the city-states of northern Russia fell prey to the first great Russian modernizer, Grand Duke Ivan III of Moscow, and were completely devastated by his grandson, Russia's first tsar, Ivan the Terrible;

Assemblies of the Land were quietly discontinued by Tsar Alexis, the bureaucratic reformer of the Orthodox Church, while the latter's political autonomy and right to choose its supreme hierarchs were terminated by Alexis's son, Peter the Great. Communal forms of local self-government and the independence of the Duma were undercut by the free-market reformer, Pyotr Stolypin. And the most recent "great modernization," directed by Stalin, quickly did away with the soviets' timid claims to be relatively independent from the Communist Party.

Finally, Russia's intellectual tradition of *narodovlastie* (that is, democracy understood as people's rule) was built almost entirely on *defiance of materialistic determinism* as manifested in Nikolai Karamzin's and the Decembrists' romanticizing of the medieval Novgorod and Pskov, in the political ideals of the early democratic Slavophiles, and in the virtually unanimous disdain for material development and enrichment on the part of Russia's democratic mainstream—Herzen, Mikhailovsky, and the Populists, as well as a large segment of Soviet-era dissidents. This attitude was not unrelated to the fact that, given Russia's poverty and the administrative, top-down provenance of most of its capitalist entrepreneurship, the supposedly iron logic of cause and effect—a logic that was emblematic of both Marxist and Western positivist economic reasoning—left little chance for democratic development on Russian soil.

It is now easier to see that the wholesale import in the late 1980s of mainstream Anglo-American assumptions about democracy that had been tailored to fit specific political needs gave rise to inner tensions when combined with the grassroots democratic impulses of Russians themselves. An imitation of purely procedural and electoral democracy, with limited participation from and responsiveness to the general public, could only lead to rapid disenchantment. This did not bode well for democracy and ultimately for Russia, especially in view of the fact that a basic consensus on the legitimacy of the new economic and social order had not been achieved. More specifically, a narrow emphasis on proceduralism was often seen as an attempt to "expropriate" democracy from the people. No wonder that 48 percent of Russians polled in July 1994 opined that voting as such did not give them a say in the political process, and 80 percent of respondents in a survey sponsored by the United States Information Agency agreed that elected officials did not care much about what they thought.[24]

This mixture of transplanted concepts and the historically conditioned beliefs of the Russian public was made more incendiary by the fact that the purported "transition to democracy" of the 1990s coincided with what many saw—and continue to see—as a "transition to capitalism" accompanied by only minimal democracy. This view was conditioned by a traditional Russian tendency to see democracy and capitalism in the Russian experience as being in conflict with each other. In the West, the degree of this conflict has been lower but has still given rise to a profound and long-standing debate. This debate is worth examining because it sheds light on Russia's current predicament.

ARE DEMOCRACY AND THE FREE MARKET TWINS?

For many American students of non-Western economies, all good things come in a package, and capitalism is "an essential requisite for political freedom."[25] Not surprisingly, the most zealous crusaders for an unbridled global market have come from the ranks of these writers and theorists. Even if the objectives of democracy and capitalism may clash as a consequence of rapid modernization, these conflicts are bound to disappear at a higher stage of development, as they allegedly did in the Anglo-American world. Meanwhile, a more reflective and critical analysis of the West itself, undertaken by Robert Dahl, Charles Lindblom, and their followers, reveals a fundamental and permanent tension between the market and democracy in societies that claim to have reached a high stage of development on both counts.

Dahl and Lindblom developed and sharpened the pluralist model of Western society into a theoretical framework of polyarchy. The traditional notion of power attached to politics, and the idea of "separation of powers" included only those forms of power that had a clear-cut legal and constitutional base. By contrast, the pluralist model, as it evolved over time, views contemporary Western societies as prone to a fluctuating and at times chaotic dispersal of power, both within and beyond the confines of a legally established separation of powers. This idea is explicitly developed in Lindblom's work, in which the free market is conceptualized as an arena of power that features power-wielding corporations constituting mini-states in their own right, with their own bureaucratic chain of command, their own "electorate," their own foreign policies, and so forth. While these new sources of power are connected with traditional and legally established institutions of governance via direct and indirect pressure groups, they are nonetheless positioned outside of the constitutional separation of powers and usually beyond the reach of democratic norms.[26]

The systematic elaboration of the pluralist model led its proponents to conclude that in the contemporary Western world, democracy serves primarily as a political *norm*, a reference point to evaluate reality; this does not imply, however, that any country incarnates democracy in the rigorous meaning of the word. Market capitalism is the key limiting factor, because according to Dahl, it "is persistently at odds with values of equity, fairness, political equality . . . and democracy."[27] Or, as a thoughtful analyst of democracy and global markets observed, "Market relations are themselves power relations that constrain the democratic process."[28]

Leaving democracy aside for normative purposes, Lindblom and Dahl introduced the notion of polyarchy as more suitable for a practical, descriptive analysis of power relations in more complex political-economic systems. The major distinctive trait of polyarchy is that power is thinly spread across different groups and organizations—both formal and informal, constitutional and civic—that compete with one another to attain their goals and to increase their power. This environment restricts the possibilities of any one power-holder, including one elected or appointed within the democratic and constitutional framework, to make effective decisions or achieve its goals on its own.[29] In this system, both democracy and capitalism act as a brake on each other. In the late 1980s, when Western terminology was randomly borrowed without much thought given to the meaning of terms, "pluralism" was used as an attribute of or even a synonym for democracy in Russia. Yet, as we have seen, such major exponents of the theory as Dahl and Lindblom regard the plurality of the sources of power as serving—for better or worse—to constrain democracy. In the example of Russia, one can only wonder to what degree the naive or intentional confusion of concepts such as "pluralism" and "democracy," which had been taken out of their original context, resulted in fatal distortions of the end product of "democratization." In any case, the result by the end of the 1990s is that Russia has achieved neither democracy as aspired to by democrats East and West, nor pluralism, because most of the political and economic power in the country is monopolized by extraconstitutional authorities in and around the Kremlin.

Taking the contradiction between the absolute norm of democracy and the polyarchical realities of corporate capitalism a step further, some scholars have discovered the coexistence of two distinct types of social consciousness with rather different value systems whose bearers can be identified (with inevitable simplification) as "marketeers" and "democrats." Indeed, as Lindblom implies, the often tense coexistence and potential conflict between the two may be seen as lying at the core of contemporary Western and global political culture. This hypothesis has received empirical corroboration from surveys of American public opinion, which indicated to the researchers that "those most firmly attached to democratic values exhibit least support for capitalism, and those most firmly attached to capitalist values exhibit least support for democracy."[30] The same opinion polls suggest that democratic values enjoy comparatively greater support among Americans. With necessary adjustments for the differences in culture and history of the United States and Russia, this evidence and the conclusions drawn from it are strikingly similar to the analysis of public opinion in the Soviet Union based on information from Soviet surveys conducted in 1989: The majority of those surveyed supported democratic reforms, yet they favored preserving the social guarantees and obligations provided by the government.[31]

A comparison of these results attests again to the inadequacy of traditional clichés such as "West is West, East is East" when used to describe fundamental human aspirations. It is not surprising, though, that the tensions between democracy and markets are much more pronounced in a transition period, when a new social order is in its infancy and when democracy tends to be equated with people's power, at least in a normative sense. As the transitologist John Loewenhardt observed, "the project of developing both democracy *and* capitalism at the same time is ridden with a basic internal conflict: that between fostering equality in the political sphere and inequality in the economic sphere."[32] Thus Russians' hopes in 1989–91 of embracing simultaneously democracy and free markets could be implemented only with an emphasis on one or the other goal. The Yeltsinites soon opted for capitalism, and they obscured the fact that their understanding of both capitalism and democracy differed profoundly from the popular understanding. For them, democracy could not interfere with their quest for economic power.

In this light, one has to admit that tensions between democracy and markets assume a different shape in each and every society, and that the manifestations of those tensions can contribute to either healthy development or stagnation and breakdown. The outcome depends on the political and cultural traditions of a given country; the specific alignment of social forces at a given moment in history; and, not least, the position of the country in the structure of the world economy. For many reasons, in most Western societies the tensions between "marketeers" and "democrats" remain low key and do not translate into the kind of irreconcilable hostility that would threaten the stability and the functioning of the system. One of the possible explanations for this, advanced by Lindblom, posits that in a typical Western society neither value rules the roost; governments provide democracy (in election campaigns, which give the people's support to one or another elite group) and also considerable freedom for markets (limited by the rule of law, by the clear borderline between the public and private sectors, and by the social safety net). Perhaps most revolutionary societies that enter a period of stabilization are likely to achieve such a peaceful cohabitation between the two. In the Russian transition period, however, they were virtually bound to clash. In absolute terms, Russia's choice between 1990 and 1992 came down to either radical democratic egalitarianism reminiscent of the medieval *veche* and the early soviets, or to an unbridled capitalism whose era had passed in the West with the Industrial Revolution and which in the Russian case was historically prone to striking an alliance with archaic traditions of autocracy. *Therefore, the choice of the ruling elite and its Western allies for an abrupt marketization, privatization, and deregulation led very rapidly—and with full awareness on the part of key Russian participants like Yeltsin and Gaidar—to the abandonment of the democratic road to reforms.*

In practice, the conflict between democratization and marketization came to the surface in the increasingly overt antagonism between the two most influential and active proreform groups that defined the agenda in the twilight years of the Soviet Union: the urban middle class and the commercialized wing of the ruling elite. Democratic values were most widespread among the former, large segments of which had viewed the Western-minded intelligentsia as their spiritual leaders. The "free market" values—or, more precisely, the "black market" values (because the Soviet economic experience made the free market and the black market virtually synonymous for most Soviet citizens)—were more deeply entrenched in the commercialized elite, which had managed to integrate itself into the global economy during the détente era and obsessively looked to the West for its standards of consumption, credits, and access to imported goods.

This commercialized wing of the Soviet establishment, also known to average Soviet citizens as the *Mafiya,* had equipped itself with clients at various levels of society, from the voraciously corrupt foreign trade bureaucracies down to the networks of illegal traders in big cities. All the partners in this formidable coalition were able to enrich themselves conspicuously at the expense of most of the country's population, thanks to the numerous breaches in the rusty Iron Curtain that they had turned into private channels for profitable trading.

The tension between the unprivileged strata of society and the black market–oriented Mafiya-elite alliance manifested itself in the form of antagonism between the anti-nomenklatura movement of the middle class and the antidemocratic measures of the Soviet establishment. Yet the conceptual core of this social conflict was largely unacknowledged. Indeed, it could not be otherwise because, first, most of the political debate had been conducted in Aesopian language; second, the study of Western and Russian political thought was limited by censorship; and, third, the governmental media served every imaginable purpose except that of collecting and providing information to the public. Even Mikhail Gorbachev, with his access to information and his professional expertise on Soviet agricultural policies, was woefully incompetent in dealing with the national economy as a whole and international economic issues, and the emerging democratic politicians and thinkers were little better. Most of them, though visibly unhappy with the existing injustices, did not trouble to think through an economic strategy or devise a blueprint for a desirable economic order. Some simply satisfied themselves with the vague notion of convergence between socialism and capitalism, as understood in Russia through Andrei Sakharov's loose interpretation in 1968 of John Kenneth Galbraith's ideas, which were increasingly seen from both sides as wishful thinking.[33]

At that time, many authentic democrats fiercely opposed the monopoly of power exercised by the nomenklatura in politics and fell prey to the hypnotic effects of a bipolar vision of the world in which every component of the Soviet system of rule had to be immediately replaced with whatever seemed to qualify as the opposite. Brainwashed by this vision and the propaganda of the commercialized nomenklatura, as well as by some of the more aggressive elements of the West's Cold War establishment, many of these democrats ended up sincerely believing that a consumer paradise could be created in Russia, if not overnight then in five hundred days at the latest, once the Western entrepreneurial spirit and Protestant ethic were transplanted to Russian soil. Meanwhile, members of this nomenklatura, and especially its "golden youth" in the Komsomol and the junior ranks of the security services, abandoned their governmental positions and prospects for a bureaucratic career with seeming equanimity, thereby creating an illusion of political victory among the democratic intelligentsia. In reality, the nomenklatura simply pulled back to their covertly prepared positions in the monopolistic and restricted "private" sector, while at the same time debilitating and undermining the emerging democratic institutions of governance—a task greatly facilitated by the antibureaucratic and antistatist mood of the democrats themselves. These and other developments (to be discussed in more detail in subsequent chapters) negated the vast majority of the nascent democratic achievements in the legal and constitutional sphere. They also cleared the path for the nomenklatura and their Mafiya allies to exert wide-ranging oligarchical powers by buying off or simply ignoring governmental agencies.

In this situation, it was vitally important to articulate clearly the differences between the democrats and the "freemarketeers" (whose particular laissez-faire ideology we examine in chapter 5) within the reform movement and let the voters judge. However, such an open philosophical debate was made more difficult by the attitude of the reformers' Western allies, whom both the democrats and the nomenklatura "marketeers" perceived to be their strategic partners in their struggle for change. The foreign policy of the Reagan-Bush era (described by Ken Jowitt as "America's democratic Zhdanovism"[34]), together with some of the mainstream democratic theories discussed previously, conveyed to the audience inside the Soviet Union that an exemplary country should become simultaneously and rapidly liberal, democratic, capitalist, pro-Western, and open to global markets. In the image of the world that the most active Western missionaries projected to Soviet citizens, democracy and free-market capitalism were firmly intertwined, no conflicts between them were to be expected, and the intrinsic tensions and trade-offs between them, existing even in the West, were obscured.

To be sure, this interpretation does not imply in any way that the basic principles of democracy and free markets are predestined to remain in conflict forever on Russian soil, or that their contradictions might not be reconciled and overcome to a considerable extent under a different scenario of reforms; any such conclusion would be premature and highly speculative. Rather, under the specific conditions of Soviet decay, in which burgeoning private economic activities were for the most part the privilege of the nomenklatura and criminals, and democratic activism was severely repressed until 1988–89, the interests of democrats and freemarketeers became—often unbeknownst to the former—antagonistic to each other in the reform movement. The outcome of this struggle depended in significant ways on the West, for whose material and moral support both sides implicitly competed. As we shall see in later chapters, the preference the West gave to its and Russia's IMF-style marketeers, coupled with a much cooler attitude toward the democratic movement as a whole, helped unleash the bacchanalia of shock therapy and privatization of the state. This preference contributed heavily to the defeat of democrats and democratic values at the present stage of Russian history.

THE LURE OF AUTHORITARIAN MODERNIZATION

In 1989–90, when Marxism was widely derided and a stream of radical-reformist rhetoric poured daily from most Soviet media, it seemed nearly impossible to imagine a slogan that might serve as a viable alternative to democracy among Russian intellectuals. Everything suggested that those Russians who favored the free market more than democracy and had few outstanding intellectuals in their ranks had no political theory at all on their side. However, without a theory, they would have been doomed to lose. In Russia, political actions, however selfish, are unlikely to succeed without an elaborate and scientifically formulated doctrine to justify them, preferably one with an established Western pedigree. Likewise, the commercialized nomenklatura and the Mafiya would not have been successful in exerting pressure on democratic institutions short of direct violence, and would have failed in their attempts to privatize major government agencies if no intellectual counterweight to the democrats' egalitarianism had been proffered. Such an antidote was found in the theory of authoritarian modernization.

A number of Western scholars developed different brands of this theory and promoted them with various degrees of intensity, but it is most closely associated with Samuel Huntington.[35] If for Max Weber the legitimacy of power was the central issue of modern politics, for Huntington it was stability and order that were the highest virtues of the state, almost regardless of the extent of their legitimation and whether order was built with popular participation or imposed from above. In focusing his attention on countries of the Third World and on those societies bent on catching up with the West, Huntington concluded that "accelerated modernization" required a reformist pro-Western elite to concentrate and mobilize national resources by authoritarian means. From this perspective, the democratic institutions and traditions of these countries (often associated with agrarian communal culture and ways of life) were viewed as a hindrance for the big leap into the bright and rationally organized industrial future. Huntington's own writings (before the advent of the "third wave" of democratization) took a gloomy view of the viability of democracy in countries outside the West. He even praised communists on occasion for being able to secure the order and stability that Third World democratic populists were prone to undermine.[36]

The theory's premises and practical implications were transparent. In its derisive attitude toward democracy as "people's power," it converged with the classical theory of elites (from Mosca, Pareto, and Michels), which questioned the ontological foundations of the "democratic myth" and was sometimes placed among the intellectual harbingers of fascism.[37] If taken outside this political context, however, Huntington's theory was strikingly bold in addressing a problem to which most of the mainstream modernization theorists had been blind: the contradictions between democracy, with its intrinsic egalitarianism and lack of predictability, and the requirements of accelerated industrial development in most of the poor countries of the contemporary world.

Huntington's theory did not come out of the blue. It was the result of synthesizing the most diverse examples of history—from Hitler's Germany and Stalin's USSR to the "Asian Tiger" economies, where the entrepreneurial "miracle" solidly relied on the mobilization of cheap labor through restricted political freedoms, rubber-stamp parliaments, little social legislation, and ruthlessly suppressed trade unions. The theory may have served as an instruction manual for those modernizers in Latin America and elsewhere who were frustrated by the impediments of civic institutions and disobedient parliaments and political parties. The theory certainly received a new lease on life during the 1970s and 1980s, when it appeared to have been validated by economic growth and the success of foreign investors in apartheid South Africa and Pinochet's Chile.

Given the disturbing implications of this theory for the liberal idealist tenets of American foreign policy, even those policy analysts and advisers who embraced it preferred to serve it to their consumers in a mixture with more mainstream modernization theories. This eclectic blend usually postulated that an authoritarian regime could play a positive role in the relatively short formative period during which major social forces would be permitted to establish a civil society that was populated primarily by private entrepreneurs and a middle class. This sector of society, however, would soon begin to seek political representation and, as it gained strength, would take the necessary steps toward establishing democracy, gradually extending it to the lower reaches of society.[38] Although this version of the theory appears to have been proved correct in a number of cases, it did not address the issue that may well be its ethical litmus test—whether this type of modernization, for all its alleged benefits, was worth the amount of repression and human suffering that it inevitably entailed.

Let us digress from this theme to remark that the theory of authoritarian modernization, which evoked much bitter argument in Western academia, did not have anything substantially new to offer for Russian intellectuals. Over the centuries, Russian autocrats relentlessly exerted themselves to "overtake and surpass" whatever happened to be viewed at the time as the most advanced standard of modernity. Whether under Ivan the Terrible, Peter the Great, or Stalin, signs of democratic life from ringing church bells in the city-states of Novgorod and Pskov to intraparty factions, semi-independent soviets, and labor unions were all perceived as impediments to be ruthlessly wiped out so that slave labor of various types could toil without distraction in the service of the millenarian dream of modernization. The most recent of these leaps into the future—the one engineered by Lenin and his cohorts—elevated "Bolshevism" into a generic term for the syndrome of authoritarian modernization, pursued at whatever the cost to ordinary citizens. "Peter the Great was the first Bolshevik"—the previously quoted words of Maximilian Voloshin—is a good example of this motif in Russian history. Beginning with Pushkin's "Bronze Horseman," Russian writers and philosophers of history have repeatedly examined this phenomenon, exploring it in more depth than their colleagues in other cultures—not least because in Russia the most gifted and best-educated people fell victim to violent modernization and "Westernization" campaigns on a bigger scale than elsewhere. The response of the Russian humanistic tradition translated into the language of contemporary social science would probably sound like this: *The losses of human and social capital and the blackouts of memory about one's own identity incurred in the course of the "big push" not only dwarf the most spectacular achievements of this type of modernization (a fact that may be irrelevant to the modernizers themselves), but also negate the very purposes of this effort and may often throw society backward, forcing the nation to start from the beginning and to travel the same path over and over again.*

Yet, paradoxical as it may seem in light of Russia's own experience, the idea of authoritarian modernization evoked an enthusiastic response in an important segment of Moscow's intellectual establishment. From 1989 on, the works of Huntington and his cothinkers began to be deferentially discussed in Soviet journals and newspapers—precisely at the time Gorbachev's authority among Soviet citizens went into free fall and the unwieldy thousand-member parliament that he created was becoming increasingly unpredictable. A staunch advocate of authoritarian modernization has been Andranik Migranyan, who established himself as an influential columnist and prolific writer in the heyday of perestroika.[39] The Huntington school did not apply its theory systematically to the Russian and Soviet experience, and Migranyan did not quote directly from their works. Hence, the Russian version of this doctrine, though clearly derived from a foreign source, could safely be called "Migranyan's theory." Followed by political sociologist Igor Klyamkin and others, Migranyan borrowed the Cold War–era distinction between totalitarian and authoritarian systems from Western theorists and argued that Russia should move from totalitarianism to authoritarianism and the market, and that introducing elements of a full-fledged democracy would amount to a voluntaristic "skipping of a stage." If Russia were successfully to embrace Western-style economic freedoms, with their inevitable dislocations and social inequalities, full-fledged democracy might be an impediment.

Paradoxically, Migranyan believed that reforming the Soviet system by means of authoritarian modernization was suitable for the purpose of eliminating the damage incurred under the previous bout of coercive modernization carried out by Lenin and Stalin. Moreover, his totalitarian-authoritarian dichotomy neglected the fact that the Soviet Union already had its market—albeit a monopolistic and distorted one that accounted for 20 percent of the economy—as well as widespread inequalities, and therefore could already be described as *a market-bureaucratic oligarchy* rather than a totalitarian or authoritarian system. (This critique of Migranyan's approach to Russia's internal reform problems is not meant to diminish his achievements as a leading theorist of Russia's foreign policy and one of the most astute thinkers about the place of Russia in the international system.)

While these views initially raised quite a few eyebrows in the reform-minded circles of society, they were received with great interest in those politically hard-line but economically liberal segments of the elite that wanted to restore equilibrium to society without yielding power. Migranyan, along with his arguments borrowed from Western theorists, became part of the back-room deliberations that, in March 1990, resulted in the establishment of a Soviet presidency bent on continuously expanding its powers at the expense of parliament. Because Gorbachev was inherently incapable of acting as a dictator, the authoritarian drift of his entourage during the fall and winter of 1990–91 was bound to remain but a parody of Chile, even though both regimes claimed their victims. After Gorbachev's half-hearted authoritarianism had stumbled over eighteen casualties in the streets of Vilnius and Riga and ran out of steam in March 1991, the authoritarian modernization doctrine was offered to the team of Boris Yeltsin. Within the Russian republic, the circulation of Migranyan's ideas facilitated the precipitous and irreversible transfer of constitutional powers from parliament to the executive branch from March 1991 on, as well as the emasculation of municipal representative bodies, starting from Moscow under a local authoritarian privatizer, Mayor Gavriil Popov. All this culminated in Yeltsin's October 1993 coup against the parliament and in the establishment of a regime that claimed to pursue a qualitatively new type of modernization but continuously fell back on the familiar pattern of "Bolshevism." In defiance of the Huntington-Migranyan theory, not only did this regime fail to be a better modernizer than its predecessors, but according to many economic, social, and demographic indicators, it has turned back the clock of history in crucial areas of national development. Indeed, there is much truth in Stephen Cohen's observation that the end product of the present cycle of reforms has been a far-reaching "demodernization and deindustrialization" of Russia. Nevertheless, in 1996 the old recipes of authoritarian modernization were eagerly recycled by Russian and Western political consultants, who this time supplied them to Aleksandr Lebed, a new contender for the prestigious role of authoritarian modernizer.

MODERNIZATION AND MODERNISM AMIDST THE CRISIS OF MODERNITY

The recent fascination of many Russian intellectuals with theories of modernization, a fascination spurred by their musings about "centuries-old Russian backwardness" and the need to "catch up with civilization," deepened the nervous and oppressive atmosphere that permeated the Soviet elite and society in the twilight years of the USSR. This stressful and exhausting mood—appropriate for a commuter dashing for a moving train or a would-be star pupil who has just failed an exam—was only partly justified by the fact that strategically important sectors of the Soviet economy were indeed lagging behind leading industrial powers in the worldwide transition to a new technological level of development. To no small degree, this sudden awakening of the national inferiority complex was caused by the conspicuous consumption now paraded by the Westernized nomenklatura and its Mafiya clients. This affluence, which resulted mostly from corruption, large-scale theft, and the desire of the newly rich to acquire the atypical opulence displayed by Western elites when entertaining high-level Soviet guests, created the delusional image of Western societies as the incarnation of that millenarian dream about the world in which everything is available but nobody has to work too hard. Clearly, these worries about backwardness were driven more by consumer envy than by genuine concerns about national economic development or by the desire for cultural self-improvement. As such, they spelled nothing but trouble for the national psyche. On top of that, such sentiments prevailed in the East just at the time when Western social thought was contemplating a crisis of basic values and goals associated with modernity, as well as a mounting sense of longing for something that had been lost along the way.[40]

The consideration of tradition and modernity, as well as of the uncertain postmodernist epoch that has so far been unable to define itself in positive terms, goes far beyond the limits of social and political theory. It constitutes a boundless field of quasi-academic speculation, in which a lack of methodological clarity and the elusiveness of underlying assumptions coexist with the most sweeping generalizations that claim to have universal validity. Nevertheless, these issues are relevant to the interpretation of recent Russian history because they underscore the inherently controversial nature of and the multiplicity of meanings behind the powerful spell of modernization theory. From today's vantage point, the question of the morally dubious means used in coercive modernization, particularly in the contemporary Russian experience, appears secondary to the question of whether the goal itself is rational, unambiguous, and adequately thought out.

It is easy to see that, even within this century, the notion of modernity has fluctuated, depending on its cultural and historical context. Thus many reformers in the late Soviet Union viewed the socialist elements in their system as a manifestation of their own backwardness, even as the major hurdle to be overcome before the final leap into the open arms of "modern civilization." On the other hand, some in the West considered the socialist system (in its abstract form, as a Weberian ideal type, but not in its Soviet incarnation) to be among the most integrated expressions of the values and goals of the Modern Age—especially the goal of rationalizing societal relationships and restraining the primordial chaos of unbridled individualism. As Holmes puts it, at least some of the founders and defenders of that system "were pursuing *ideal* modern values which were too extreme and too pure for the real world"[41] (a view that may suggest the crisis of modernity dates back as far as 1917, when the practical flaws of these "ideal modern values" were revealed to many Westerners in the example of Russia).

Whatever the case, the world that emerged after the fall of the Iron Curtain displays some widespread traits that are manifestly at odds with the values and premises generally associated with modernity, traits such as the waning strength of rationalist political ideologies and values inherited from the Enlightenment (liberalism, socialism, and even democracy); the "withering away" (in a sad travesty of Marx) of the strong centralized state, with its traditional obligations to its citizenry; mounting problems of government corruption, international crime, and nuclear safety; the explosion of ethnic and tribal consciousness and of primitive superstitions and fatalism; the reappearance of pre-industrial, unregulated capitalism; and biological experiments threatening the identity of human beings and, perhaps, civilization as a whole (such as genetic engineering and cloning). Judging by these indicators, the countries of the former Soviet Union and other underdeveloped areas of the world (such as the "failed states" of sub-Saharan Africa) may not be the caboose of historical development. In fact, they may be the vanguard, showing us the most alarming manifestations of postmodernity, whose destructive force has so far been blocked—or merely retarded—by the institutional safeguards of Western societies.

It is important at this stage to differentiate between modernization and development. The critique of the modernization paradigm, with its "one-size-fits-all" and "ends-justify-the-means" approaches, does not need to imply that all development must lead to degeneration and decay, or to endorse the uncritical glorification of the ways of life of peasant communities that were damaged by industrialization (a path taken by, among others, theorists of moral economy[42]).To state the obvious yet often neglected fact, development occurs even in those nations whose theorists proudly think about them as "developed," and it does not need to reduce Leibniz's "infinite potentiality" of life to a common denominator. Yet it is open to debate whether all nations would be developing in the same direction and going through roughly the same stages unless international forces were trying to enforce a standard of modernization and, in various ways, punishing those nations that deviate from an exogenously imposed itinerary.[43]

"THE GOAL IS NOTHING, MOVEMENT IS EVERYTHING": LESSONS IN TRANSITOLOGY

The science of "transitology" was another influential offspring of the modernization paradigm, and at one time it aspired to become a separate discipline.[44] It was born at Princeton University's Woodrow Wilson Center in the mid-1980s as a result of joint efforts by students of transitions from authoritarianism to democracy that took place after 1974 in several countries of southern Europe and Latin America. Transitologists loved to tinker with models and had little concern for underlying assumptions about history or the nature of democracy and dictatorship. That said, they deserve credit for escaping from the iron cage of determinism (where most modernization theorists are trapped), thanks to their abandoning the search for "preconditions" for democracy, whose limited explanatory power was plain to see. But the growing brouhaha about the "end of history" impaired their ability to reassess critically their own assumptions about the purpose and direction of the type of development they were studying. Instead, they preferred to focus their attention on the processes and techniques of "transition" and "consolidation." As Ken Jowitt aptly remarked, "The 'transitology/consolidology' perspective emphasizes political mechanics and voluntarism at the expense of persistent sociocultural realities."[45] Liberal idealism aside, the boom in transitology often reflected a genuine, pragmatic interest by international political consultants in the instrumental technologies of mass manipulation and top-down social engineering.

The transitologists' reluctance to think through the deeper theoretical foundations of their models fostered an eclectic and at times indiscriminate use of disparate elements from diverse scholarly paradigms and schools of thought. Some, like Giuseppe di Palma, demonstrated affinity with radical and even revolutionary trends of democratic theory, emphasizing the grassroots forces of civil society as the prime movers of change.[46] More often, however, transitologists viewed democratization through the prism of elite theory, as a sequence of conflicts and settlements among the shifting interests of "old" and "new" elites, in which the general public was afforded the privilege of legitimizing at the ballot box a set of compromises that had been predetermined from above.[47] Some of the transitologists borrowed insights from the social science versions of von Neumann's and Morgenstern's game theory and from the more-or-less sophisticated brands of rational choice and social choice frameworks. Both of these theories are based on *homo economicus*—an abstract human being who is unreflecting, endowed with absolute infallible rationality, fully informed, and relentlessly in pursuit of short-term material interests within a rigorous and uncontradictory payoff matrix. In the mechanistic and one-dimensional world of *homo economicus,* the past is irrelevant, as are any circumstances beyond the immediate context of the problem at hand. All this creates the illusion of an absolute freedom of choice with no inherent constraints on the "maximization of utility." (This peculiar view of human beings is also shared by radical free market theorists who have assisted with various degrees of success and failure in typologically similar attempts to tailor the behavior of Bolivians, Poles, Yugloslavs, Russians, Ukrainians, and other nations to their doctrine via the implementation of shock therapy.)

The limitations of transitology with respect to the former Soviet Union have been so clearly and repeatedly debated that a cursory review of some basic criticisms will suffice.[48] Transitologists tended to neglect the fact that the multifaceted character of change in the former Soviet bloc—the political and economic transformations and the demise of empire—was an extraordinary event that required a framework of analysis substantially different from the one that might have been adequate for understanding the change of political systems in Spain or Argentina. Even within the Soviet bloc itself, there appear to be few similarities between the comprehensive changes that occurred in Poland and the state of affairs in Russia (the latter being more likely to represent the final stages of degeneration and decay of the pre-existing oligarchical order than an accomplished transition to something qualitatively new). Although transitologists identified the democratization of the 1970s and 1980s as an international phenomenon, they did not inquire about the role of international forces, particularly those of global economic structures and institutions, that may have fostered or hindered the transition to democracy in specific countries. Last but not least, for these theorists the meaning of democracy was unambiguous. This undifferentiated view precluded them from seeing that the beliefs and expectations about democracy espoused by elites and by the general public were widely divergent and, at times, even opposite to each other.

The transitologists' unshakable faith in the capabilities of farsighted elites and strong-willed reformers to lead the masses toward a bright future was very much in tune with the utopian worldview of many radical democrats in postcommunist countries, including Russia before the onset of shock therapy. Most of them would have agreed with di Palma that democracy was going to be established and accepted simply because there were no credible alternatives. They also largely shared his view that the legitimation of the democratic order would hinge exclusively on the spread of its values, and that former dissidents and opposition leaders would smoothly evolve into "normal" and thriving politicians under the democratic system of rule.

It is plain to see that most of these aspirations, however noble and sincere, turned out to be wishful thinking, at least in the case of Russia. As Loewenhardt remarked, theorists like di Palma simply "confused the initiation of transition with its successful completion."[49] In much of the Eastern Bloc and in the republics of the former Soviet Union, particularly Russia, most democrats and dissidents who played central roles in bringing down the *ancien régime* (with a few exceptions) were forced into purely ceremonial roles or onto the sidelines of politics, and leadership positions were filled by either nationalist-authoritarian leaders or former nomenklatura bosses with the gift of mimicry. Those distinguished figures of the dissident movement who dared to oppose this course of events—people like Michnik and Dubcek, or, in the Russian case, Solzhenitsyn and Sinyavsky—were ostracized by the market authoritarians. In places like Russia, any tangible benefits of transition fade when one takes stock of the crippled and stunted political organisms that evolved in the place of the healthy civil society that was expected to emerge. And yet, the fact that the cocksure theorists and politicians failed, by and large, to deliver the results they had promised does not justify succumbing to fatalism or advising a new generation of Russian democrats to put their agenda on hold for another century until the preconditions have been fulfilled. Instead, the shortcomings of transitology serve as a warning about the fallibility of the most benevolent of political intentions if they are not accompanied by wisdom and tenacity. Democracy may hardly be an "organic" development akin to biological evolution, but the crafting of democracy requires more sophisticated tools and a more comprehensive design that takes into account both national history and the international landscape and does not mistake the democratic-liberal-capitalist trinity for an ecumenical creed.

CHOOSING A CONSTITUTIONAL DESIGN: DILEMMAS AND CONSEQUENCES

The transitologists' strong interest in the process of codifying the political "rules of the game" prompted them to explore the pluses and minuses of various political systems, electoral laws, and constitutional mechanisms providing checks and balances and the separation of powers. What was common to this research was the pervasive assumption that the "rules of the game" can serve as an unambiguous and generally acceptable frame of reference in any country. Little attention was given to the history of conflicts among different constitutional traditions and political cultures, the wide disparities in resources and differences in basic values among major political forces, and the changing identities of political personas.

By the early 1990s, it became evident that in most countries of the former Soviet Bloc (unlike in Greece or Spain in the mid-1970s, the initial objects of transitology studies), the postcommunist elites had made their constitutional choice in favor of presidents with extensive powers elected by direct popular vote. If some countries managed to counterbalance a strong presidency with an assertive parliament and a vigilant judicial branch, in Russia (as in the Soviet successor states of Central Asia), the imperial presidency of Boris Yeltsin and his government occupied center stage, pushing the parliament, the Constitutional Court, and the political parties into the shadowy margins of national politics.

The first alarm in the West about the tendency of the framers of postcommunist constitutions to imitate the American and French systems was voiced by the distinguished transitologist Juan Linz.[50] As Linz argued, a strong and popularly elected presidency can easily doom a country to confrontational election campaigns that turn into a zero-sum game, while the rigidity of the fixed presidential term leaves little room for political maneuver in times of crisis. Echoing the transitologists' common belief in the importance of an elite consensus achieved through bargaining and coalition-building, Linz viewed presidentialism as a hindrance to this goal and cautioned new democracies against this type of constitutional design.

Linz's article triggered a fierce debate in the *Journal of Democracy* and in some academic periodicals.[51] Some authors, apparently with the French model in mind, pointed to strong parliamentary parties as a perfect antidote to the excesses of presidentialism. Others, such as Arend Lijphart, remarked that the ability of parties and parliament to serve as a counterweight to the executive hinged upon the choice in election laws between the winner-take-all and proportional systems. Still others, such as Highley and Gunther, wisely observed that the constitutional design itself had a secondary role in shaping the course and outcomes of the political process; more important were the distribution of social forces at a given time, the type of problems the country was facing, and the traditions and norms of elite behavior. The most sober conclusion to come out of these discussions was that the "profound lack of consensus among political scientists . . . would seem to call for extreme restraint in advising particular systems of rule to countries in transition from autocracy."[52]

At first glance, in light of Russia's experience with a strong presidency, Linz's arguments would appear fairly convincing and farsighted. The introduction of the Russian presidency in March 1991 laid the groundwork for a continuous expansion of the authority of a single man who came to wield, formally speaking, no less power than the last Russian autocrat before the 1917 revolution. Under Yeltsin, the Russian-style imperial presidency was distinguished by aggressive confrontation and posturing, sordid acts of personal ambition, and a conspiratorial style of decision-making. As a result, the image projected by Yeltsin to the outside world became a negative advertisement for Russia.

On the other hand, a purely parliamentary system of a British or German type would most likely be unworkable in Russia, and in the conditions of late 1991 —given the ambitions of some local leaders—might have doomed Russia to follow the Soviet Union's example, if in less drastic ways, and partially fragment. The fact that most alternative constitutional projects drafted in 1993 by Yeltsin's opponents featured a powerful presidency also suggests caution in blaming presidentialism for the failures of the Russian transition. It seems that the degeneration of the democratic presidency into a pitifully inept authoritarianism hobbled by special interests was not determined primarily by constitutional choices or election laws. Instead, it appears to have resulted from such deeply ingrained structural features of Russian politics as the mutual convertibility of power and wealth; from the weakness and disorientation of civil society in the wake of shock therapy; from the ideological and social content of Yeltsin's peculiar type of rule; and, not least, from the personal qualities and behavior of major figures across the political spectrum.

With the advent of Vladimir Putin to power, it appeared that the weak, inept authoritarianism of the Yeltsin regime might be evolving into an authoritarianism that was less weak and inept, and somewhat different. In 2000, the Putin administration began "rationalizing" Russia's governmental institutions to address the deep changes in societal relations of the 1990s. For example, they started taming the Duma more effectively; they also began to co-opt civil society as a whole more systematically and, where that proved difficult, to intimidate it. In addition, the security ministries favored by Putin were imbued with new confidence and were used, among other purposes, to harass selected regional governors and also certain oligarchs—primarily, perhaps, to help rival oligarchs, but conceivably also as an initial attempt to curb oligarchic power in toto.

If the transitologists' writings helped to lay the foundation for a new domestic political and economic order in Russia, we should note that they also indirectly served to undermine Russia's inchoate sovereignty and, thus, to bolster the national-conservative political agenda at the expense of other, more constructive opposition parties. How did this come about?

NATIONALISM AND NATIONAL CONSCIOUSNESS IN THEORY AND PRACTICE

As alluded to earlier, nationalism as an intellectual and political force has been a somewhat ghostly and anemic presence in late twentieth-century Russia despite frequent attempts to use it as a bogeyman both within and outside the country. This requires explanation, especially because nationalism has gained the status of a major legitimizing ideology on a par with democracy in many parts of the world, and particularly so in the countries along Russia's periphery that emerged from the ruins of the former USSR.[53] Although Russian nationalism and national consciousness are not the central focus of this book, the striking weakness of both (which we analyze later, especially in chapter 6) has been an important factor in the survival of the market bolshevik regime, as well as in the radical reshaping of the international system that the United States and its allies in the North Atlantic Treaty Organization (NATO) have brought about with little concern for the opinion of other major nations, notably Russia. In sum, Russia's rapid decline as a world power, caused by this reshaping, by market bolshevism, and initially by the collapse of the USSR, warrants an overview of some of the relevant Western ideas and concepts of nationalism and international relations.

In discussing the issue of national identity and its relationship to reform, development, or democracy, it is important to make clear the level of analysis and the social entity that is under consideration. The following discussion aims to do that. Until quite recently, both social science and political practice were built on the assumption that nation-states are the building blocks of the international realm and, as such, are its ultimate units of analysis. In the framework of the modernization paradigm, the nation-state (whose political, civic, and cultural boundaries were mostly expected to coincide) was seen as an organic and inevitable product of the universal transition from agrarian to industrial society, from local forms of governance to bureaucratic centralization, and from social relations based on personal networks to the uniform regularity of impersonal rules of the game.[54] In the course of modernization, nationalism as the ideology of state-building, fostered and maintained by the ruling elite, played a beneficial role. Most important, it helped to forge an unwritten contract between rulers and ruled that produced homogeneous, fluid, standardized societies of interchangeable human beings, amenable to uniform standards. This mainstream theory of modern nationalism is exemplified, among others, by the writings of Ernest Gellner.[55]

Most Western scholarship in this field goes back again to Max Weber, who counterposed his theoretical framework centered on the state to Marxist class-based sociology. In the Weberian, or "Realist" view of the world, nation-states were often reified as self-conscious entities that had monopolized violence on behalf of and with the tacit consent of society, possessed an unequivocal and purposeful will, controlled their territory and economic resources, and spread the sense of cohesiveness among their populaces by the use of nationalist ideology.[56] Mirroring the early Marxist view of classes (and mainstream economists' belief in "rational utility maximizers"), nation-states strutted on the Realist stage almost like classical heroes, thrilling the audience with their endless striving for power and *Lebensraum.* Realists themselves would not dispute that this image of statehood was, in Weber's own words, only an ideal type. Germany itself, once a role model for statists everywhere, obviously lost many of the attributes of this absolute sovereignty as a result of its defeat in World War I. However, for a Realist it would be unthinkable that a nation might willfully relinquish some of its sovereignty without a major defeat or an unfavorable shift in the balance of power. In a world defined by this type of rationality, nations do not sacrifice themselves, they do not voluntarily submit to destruction, they do not commit suicide.

Judging by these Realist standards, not only the Soviet Union of 1989–91 but even the Russia of 1999 did not fit the definition of sovereignty. Some of Russia's deficiencies as a sovereign power could possibly be explained within the Realist framework as a logical result of the USSR's defeat in the Cold War. And yet the evidence suggests that, in contrast to Weimar Germany, Russia lacked some essential elements of sovereignty (in the classical meaning of the term) that the Soviet Union unquestionably possessed and that its Cold War rival apparently had no intention of taking away. Western observers became increasingly alarmed by the fact that the Russian state surrendered its monopoly on the use of force on its own territory (not only to organized and disorganized crime but also increasingly to legally established private armies of big businesses). It also lost its ability to defend its territorial integrity (as demonstrated by the unilateral secession of Chechnya and, potentially, other parts of the North Caucasus), to formulate a coherent and univocal foreign policy, and to have even residual control over many of the activities of regional and corporate barons. There was no consensus on what Russia's national borders should be; nor was there a distinct national consciousness, nor a definable chain of command in the institutions of government.[57] The amorphous condition of Russian statehood was even more striking after nearly a decade of Yeltsin's intermittent and largely unsuccessful attempts at an authoritarian concentration of power. Whether Putin will achieve that goal, and, if so, at what cost to society, are questions for the future.

Yet it is possible to argue that the erosion of sovereignty in the case of Russia and some of its neighbors, however extreme and dangerous for a nuclear power, may be by no means exceptional. Many modern nations—not only in the Third World, but also among the economically developed Western powers—fail to meet the standards usually assumed by Realists for a nation-state (that is, unified will, rationality, self-control, and a set of undisputed values and beliefs about legitimacy). Pluralist or polyarchical models appear to be more realistic depictions of modern polities than those of Realism. At the empirical, if not perhaps at the normative level, structural limitations on the classical notion of sovereignty have been discovered and recognized over the past decades. These include the conflicting interests and loyalties of decision-making elites, the autonomy and feudal fragmentation of government bureaucracies, the pressure of domestic interest groups (including foreign lobbies), the activity of transnational corporations and global economic actors, international flows of private capital, and the workings of international crime syndicates and private intelligence services.

Thus, for example, institutions like the International Monetary Fund and the Bank for International Settlements have entered the domain of national economic policy and in many cases severely circumscribed national sovereignty with their conditionalities. As a result, the nation-state is caught between the newly powerful private interests acting from below as centrifugal forces, and the international structures, such as NATO, the Group of Seven (G-7), the IMF, and others, exerting their pressures from outside the state's borders. These phenomena may be seen as a kind of atavistic reversion to the age of the Holy Roman Empire and the Holy Alliance. The intellectual response to such dyadic pressure has been a general shift of focus, at least in theories of international politics, away from nation-states to lower (down to individual) and higher (up to global) levels of analysis.[58]

In this new environment, the state—the only institution of modern world politics that is normatively based on the equal rights of all citizens and the democratic representation of its *individual* constituents—has become but one of many actors (and, in a number of instances, not the most powerful one) both internationally and even within its own territory. This progressive diffusion of sovereignty, this shifting of decision-making authority to international, supranational, and domestic (bureaucratic, corporate, and regional) levels, was reflected in the words of a traditional Realist who defined the post-modern international system as "a neo-medieval form of universal political order."[59]

The tangible erosion of state sovereignty and the resulting feeling of a cultural and psychological void have caused flare-ups in West and East of a new nationalism, whose characteristics set it apart from the classical modernizing nationalism portrayed by Gellner. In many cases, this new self-styled nationalism is a protest against features of modernity and a plea for local autarky with the aim of warding off the dehumanizing and impersonal forces associated with both the global order and national government. (This has become visible in some of the European movements against the European Union: in the politics of France's National Front, Italy's Northern League, and to some extent Austria's Freedom

Party; and in the growing antigovernmental and antiglobalistic sentiment in various parts of the United States that is common to opponents of the North American Free Trade Agreement, activists of the Perot and Buchanan presidential campaigns, and members of mushrooming militia organizations and similar groups.) However vague and poorly articulated, this universal trend may well contain in embryonic form that "creatively destructive ideology . . . appropriated by an institutionally innovative social force," in the absence of which Ken Jowitt has blamed the current stagnation that he identifies in global politics.[60]

Several "national liberation" movements in Eastern Europe, some of which have discarded their democratic facade soon after getting their hands on power, have likewise been viewed by their own compatriots as movements of protest against the impersonal culture, secularity, rationalistic reasoning, and liberal ideology associated with modernization and globalism, which are all increasingly seen as having deprived life of its deeper values.[61] This primordial sentiment, along with "enlightened" democratic nationalism, has clearly played a significant role in breaking up the modernizing multiethnic states of the Soviet Union, Yugoslavia, and Czechoslovakia, and has evolved into a sort of neotribalism by legitimizing the abuse of civil and political rights of ethnic minorities in Latvia, Estonia, Romania, Croatia, Serbia, and several other countries. All this has renewed scholarly interest in various types of nationalism and their implications, and in tracing the fuzzy boundary between a sense of national identity as a universal norm and nationalism as a political ideology.

It follows that ideologically motivated nationalism is a fairly ambiguous concept that can assume the most diverse incarnations and serve a multitude of contradictory purposes. It can be used to legitimize imperial conquests or an antiimperial struggle for national self-determination. It can be associated with both oppression and the quest for freedom. A single theory of nationalism is improbable because "only with reference to a concrete historical context can we say what the term actually does or should signify." In the final analysis, Peter Alter comes to the paradoxical but well-grounded conclusion that "nationalism does not exist as such, but a multitude of manifestations of nationalism do."[62]

Classical nationalism (using this qualifier for lack of a better word) was unquestionably a product of the nineteenth century, and each of its major versions had either a French or German intellectual pedigree. The French tradition emphasized the rationalist and voluntaristic aspect of national identity, expressed most forcefully in the famous definition by Ernest Renan that "the existence of a nation . . . is an everyday plebiscite."[63] In further developing this view of national identification as a product of subjective will, modern left-wing theorists have suggested that national consciousness comes into being only through collective political action. Thus, for Karl Deutsch, a nation is a politically mobilized people that has its own state at its disposal.[64] It is difficult, however, to think of more than a handful of nations that would match such a stringent definition. Perhaps the logically natural development of this radically voluntaristic approach is found in the deconstructionist proposition that nations and national sentiment are just one more product of collective imagination in a long line of political myths.[65]

The German approach, originating in the writings of Schelling and early Romanticism (which heavily influenced the ideology of the first generation of Slavophiles), tended to view national consciousness as immanent, ideally or structurally given—an eternal beauty waiting to be awakened by artists, philosophers, and national political leaders. A more realistic school, however, taking its inspiration from Herder's historicism, differentiated between the nation and the state. It viewed political self-identification and the existence of a national government as merely one of the possible external manifestations testifying to the existence of a nation. For these authors, nations that have their distinct cultures but are not nation-states (*Kulturnationen*, in Hans Kohn's parlance) are no less significant realities of history than *Staatsnationen*, which may be more numerous but in some cases have a poorly developed cultural identity.[66]

In the latter case, states may arise out of purely extraneous circumstances or by the decision of elites (as happened with some decolonized countries of the Third World and some of the former Soviet republics). "We have created Italy," said Risorgimento leader Massimo d'Azeglio in somewhat different circumstances—"Our next task is to create Italians."[67] This may have been a provocative exaggeration, and yet the discrepancy between the ethnocultural community and the state that was supposed to represent it has been a much more widespread historical phenomenon than it may seem. Although the most explicit case of a cultural nation were the Jews before the creation of the state of Israel, this dichotomy has also manifested itself in Russia. The long-standing Russian split between the nation and the state (identified and discussed in the previous chapter) has led to the emergence of two distinct identifications of Russians—as an ethnic entity with a clear-cut cultural dimension (*russkie*) and as citizens of what was supposed to become a nation-state (*rossiyane*).

In cases of such a discrepancy between the ethnocultural nation and the state, nationalism more often than not becomes a political artifact that is consciously and purposefully created. The recognition of this fairly common "reality" was reflected in a sort of convergence between the initial German and French perspectives in much of the contemporary writing on nationalism. As Gellner commented, "Having a nation is not an inherent attribute of humanity, but it has now come to appear as such. . . . Nations, like states, are a contingency, and not a universal necessity . . . [they are] the artifacts of men's convictions and loyalties and solidarities. . . . It is nationalism which engenders nations, and not the other way round."[68] Veljko Vujacic, concluding from his research on his native Serbia, sees national sentiment as "a field of contested and contestable possibilities, constantly remade by ideologists and politicians."[69]

If one accepts the influential view of nationalism as created by elites for the purpose of mass mobilization, this begs the question about the relationship between nationalism and democracy. Here again, different intellectual traditions and cultures are in dispute. In the liberal-democratic creed prevailing in Anglo-Saxon thought and in smaller countries of western Europe—where democracy is tightly bound to individualist values—the collectivist dimension of nationalism places it in an uneasy and sometimes antagonistic relation to democracy.[70] In contrast, the Realist line of reasoning, with its "black box" model of a world consisting of mutually impenetrable nation-states, reconciles an outward-oriented nationalism with democracy at home by establishing a barrier between foreign policy and domestic policy.

While working from within the Weberian paradigm, Vujacic has made further steps to reconcile and integrate both concepts by outlining his theory of *democratic nationalism.* Vujacic's study of Eastern Europe enabled him to perceive the egalitarian side of nationalism that manifests itself with particular strength in conditions of a patriotic war and that "inverts traditional, peace-time social hierarchies."[71] Vujacic praises this type of nationalism as a potentially strong democratic force that gives the poor "the only form of status superiority" that is available to them. Vujacic's democratic nationalism is akin to the type of national sentiment that is depicted in Tolstoy's *War and Peace,* but qualitatively different from the elite-engineered nationalist ideology of a Count Uvarov or the chauvinism that dominated France during the period of the Dreyfus trial.

Vujacic's theory has a heuristic usefulness that enables it to explain the mixture of nationalist and democratic components in some of the "national liberation" movements of the Third World. It can also serve as an analytical tool for those cases where a small army, with much room for upward mobility, fights against a clearly identifiable external foe (as happened, in Vujacic's case, in the former Yugoslavia). In these conditions, democratic nationalism helps to build an important bridge between soldiers and generals, which may impart a decisive psychological advantage against an army that is socially divided and lacks a unifying set of beliefs and values. One should note, however, that the democratism of an "army-state" invariably turns out to be short-lived. In most cases, it is not translated into a peacetime democratic system of rule. On the contrary, with the end of a heroic period, the former leaders of democratic nationalism often resort to witch-hunting, xenophobia, and outright authoritarianism to retain and expand their power.

The opposition to Boris Yeltsin's policies over the past years featured significant elements of the type of democratic nationalism found in the national liberation movements of the Third World. In fact, these democratic nationalists were an important presence in Yeltsin's original coalition of 1990–91 and later formed the mainstream of the early anti-Yeltsin opposition—up until the rise of the renovated Communist Party. As we will see, some of the democratic nationalists (Sergei Baburin, Ilya Konstantinov, Vladimir Isakov, Oleg Rumyantsev, and others) constituted the most active part of the parliamentary resistance to Yeltsin's autocratic drift that ended in the 1993 coup against the parliament. Had they not been defeated in Yeltsin's parliamentary tank assault, they might have become an enlightened alternative to the ruinous policies of market bolshevism. In any case, their sense of nationhood was qualitatively different from the paranoid xenophobia of the Black Hundred or the elite-centered ideology of national corporatism developed by Yeltsin's own courtiers and cronies.

And yet, one has to admit that prior to Putin's advent, neither the democratic nationalist trend in the early opposition, nor any other form of nationalism, acquired widespread and active support among Russians. As opinion polls showed, the votes cast for those who were viewed as nationalists between 1993 and 1997 (which never amounted to an absolute majority) reflected public disaffection with the ruling elite, corruption, and criminal capitalism, rather than some clearly formulated nationalist sentiment against an external opponent. It is particularly revealing that Zyuganov's CPRF, whose image in the pro-Yeltsin media was painted in political tones of "red and brown," finished first in the 1995 parliamentary vote after being one of the most vocal opponents of the Chechnya war, and garnered a lot of votes and frequently won majorities in the ethnically non-Russian territories.[72] In our opinion, Zyuganov lost his presidential bid half a year later not least because he reverted to conservative nationalism.

Even the nationwide anti-NATO sentiment that gathered steam in the course of the debate over the alliance's expansion in the mid-1990s and transformed itself into a national defensive consensus in the wake of the NATO war on the Federal Republic of Yugoslavia (FRY) in March 1999 can hardly be classified as nationalist in the traditional sense of the term. Although a range of Western observers attempted to fit the Russian reaction to the war into a "nationalist" box by referring to the mythical idea of "Slavic" or "Orthodox Christian" brotherhood, these premodern sentiments were a marginal ingredient in the negative reaction to the war, a reaction that came largely from the urban, educated, and rational-minded parts of Russian society. What caused the most outrage in Russia was the unilateral redefinition of international law and the disregard of the FRY's sovereignty by NATO's leaders.

In sum, the absence of a strong political force that was ethnically nationalist or externally expansionist was perhaps the only clear-cut political plus of the Yeltsin era—even though this obtained in spite, not because, of Kremlin policies. For the outside observer, the absence was even more striking, given Russia's huge loss of territory, economic potential, and international status during and after the collapse of the Soviet Union. This has prompted some Western analysts who feel sympathy for Russia in its present plight to speak of the "underdevelopment" of the Russian national consciousness and of a crisis of national identity. With some regret, Vujacic concludes that Russians are "unavailable" for mobilization around a national idea as such. But in the same work, he offers an insightful explanation of this paradox: In contrast to the Serbs' view of themselves, the Russian self-definition was, and remains, not centered on an ethnic identity, a state, or a religion; rather, it is *outward oriented,* and its creators are engaged in a constant, though sometimes invisible, search for universal, integrative solutions to the injustices of the international system, solutions that would be applicable on a global scale.[73]

In Russia, the "national idea" in its aggressively nationalistic understanding never enjoyed support beyond a close-knit circle of elites. The very word *natsionalizm* in Russian is negatively charged by virtue of its association with ethnic intolerance and with Nazism, Russia's great enemy in the twentieth century. Few of the most radical Russian politicians are eager to use it openly in public. This is probably a major reason that Russia, in contrast to Yugoslavia, avoided civil war in the course of the Soviet collapse, and that the poorly thought out Chechen venture ended in the defeat of the Yeltsin regime. In a nation where the first known literary work, *Povest Vremennykh Let* (The Tale of Years Past), began with a description of humanity as a unified family of peoples, and whose modern philosophy, founded by Vladimir Solovyov, was built on the idea of universality *(vseedinstvo)* and the mutual responsibilities of individuals, nationalism was, and is likely to remain, an imported ideology. It is equally possible that the "never accomplished" national consciousness of Russians, with their profound alienation from the temporal forms of the state and their openness to all sorts of universalist messages, may enable Russia to come up with a more generous and far-reaching response to the glaring deformities of globalization than the parochial nationalisms of ethnic exclusivity, with their pursuit of ostrich-style autarky, that abound in the Balkans and elsewhere.

These insights help us to perceive why Russia (perhaps not unlike the United States) is one of the few major countries of the world where nationalists pure and simple, whether democratic or not, simply have never had a broad-based popular appeal. It may be precisely that the sequence of events that enabled the national conservatives to rise to the top of the anti-Yeltsin opposition and to appear as the only realistic alternative to his regime made it impossible for any kind of opposition to win power. A more detailed analysis of these developments, and of the Kremlin's own contributions to the cause of the national conservatives who pretended to be its opponents, belongs to subsequent chapters.

THE INTERNATIONAL CONTEXT OF REFORMS: DEPENDENCY, GLOBALIZATION, AND DEMOCRACY

The observation has been made with regard to earlier revolutions of the Modern Age that "the outcomes of social revolutions have always been powerfully conditioned not only by international politics but also by the world-economic constraints and opportunities faced by emergent new regimes."[74] And yet, both traditional-style Sovietologists and, more strikingly, analysts of post-Soviet "transitions" have tended until recently to treat the international dimension of Russian reforms as entirely exogenous and, moreover, an immutable and uncontroversial aspect of reality.[75]

Methodologically, this attitude stemmed from the aforementioned autarky that has been typical of most subfields of Western social science. The inner development of a society and the system of international relations were assumed to need fundamentally different types of analysis with clearly identifiable boundaries. If the study of a country's domestic politics used the Aristotelian inventory of political forms of government (such as democracy, absolute monarchy, and the like) for both descriptive and normative purposes, in the international realm, according to the traditional school of Realism, the natural state of affairs was anarchy.[76] Nation-states were viewed as closed systems that collided with each other like billiard balls and used force, cunning, or a mixture of both to address and resolve mutual concerns; they could exert only a marginal influence, if any, on each other's will and internal arrangements, and not much more on the international system. Liberal internationalists, while disputing the Realists' skepticism about the possibility of rationally organizing the international system, typically did not contest very strongly the core normative assumption of Realism, which held that nations were endowed with a single will, and that no nation-state could be infiltrated by another except through deliberate subversion.

Starting around World War II, the revolution in communications sharpened the temptation for governments to apply different standards at home and abroad. It created a means to subvert unfriendly or enemy governments not directly, but indirectly, through radio broadcasts aimed at their citizens. Later it spawned additional means: television broadcasts, the Internet, and electronic ways of impacting other countries' economies through manipulation of capital flows and foreign-exchange rates. In other words, globalization created instruments for what "victim governments" perceived as cultural and economic imperialism and political subversion. At the same time, because technology itself has no values, the same instruments could carry cultural enlightenment, education about human rights and democracy, humanitarian assistance, and political goodwill.

So globalization is morally ambiguous. A dissident in a country with an authoritarian government will welcome a radio program on human rights, while the government will view it as subversive. Governments can combine propagation of their own values and precepts with the calculated pursuit of self-interest and even territorial claims against any particular country. Through the long decades of the Cold War, both sides took this approach—the West promoting freedom and democracy, the USSR social justice and equality. The danger for both sides was that exploiting these universalistic ideals to advance their own military, economic, and political purposes could easily corrupt and discredit the values that were being promoted.

Against this background, the international outlook of most Russian democrats and reformers (and of their Eastern European cousins) was strikingly at odds with the typical distinction made by governments between their domestic and their international behavior. In contrast with Russia's post-1991 economic policies, which very soon came to be shaped by the senior and junior members of the nomenklatura, the foreign policy of Yeltsin's Russia was dominated by liberal-democratic idealism until as late as 1993. To use Ken Jowitt's analogy from a different context, Russian democrats brought to the "Protestant" world of international Realism (with its clear-cut division between "domestic" and "foreign") an all-embracing "Catholic" belief in the integrity and openness of civilization as a whole. For Russia's democrats, "the family of nations" and Gorbachev's "common European home" were not rhetorical devices but actual images of the world, both normative and descriptive. They took the democratic and free-market propaganda emanating from the West at face value and extrapolated it to the level of international relations, thus betraying their lack of familiarity with the workings of world politics. They also attempted to translate parliamentary procedures and etiquette into the international realm and overestimated the impact of international law, as well as the authority and benevolence of those international organizations, such as the IMF, the G-7, the World Trade Organization, and even NATO, that they initially rushed to join.

In the meantime, driven by a sense of guilt because of the Realist foreign policies of the now deceased "evil empire," and eager to prove their own moral credentials, Russian democrats and reformers voluntarily and hastily renounced most of the characteristic expressions of world power status that still remained in Russia's hands after the demise of the Union, such as the clear articulation and pursuit of national interests at the global level. We should note in passing that their Western interlocutors did little to correct such misperceptions but, rather, responded with similar rhetoric—while at the same time quite rationally reaping the fruits of the Russian elite's own blunders, such as Yeltsin and Foreign Minister Andrei Kozyrev's initially permissive attitude toward NATO expansion, their mindlessly confrontational posture toward the Muslim world, and their tendency to manipulate Russia's weaker and poorer neighbors.

Not surprisingly, the brief period of illusion soon yielded to a bitter awakening. Utopian hopes about global democracy were disappointed, conspiracy theories gained currency, and a sense of nostalgia for the past and of shame caused by unthinking self-harm slowly spread across the intellectual and political spectrum. By 1994, even though Kozyrev was still hanging on as the titular chief of Russian diplomacy, the setting of the foreign policy agenda, with few exceptions, was transferred to the conservative and state-oriented wing of the old Soviet establishment, a shift that unfortunately excluded Russia's relations with international financial institutions, specifically the IMF. Deeply distrustful of the "democratic Comintern," the new set of foreign-policy makers around the Ministry of Defense and other "armed agencies" of the government found a golden key to all international issues in the worldview of traditional geopolitics.[77]

By its pedigree, geopolitics is a quintessential antagonist of all brands of historicism. The vague and fluid core of present-day geopolitics in Russia features a perennial enmity—political, military, psychological, and cultural—between "oceanic" and "continental" powers and their allies. It also devotes considerable attention to ethnic and religious tensions, viewing them for the most part as eternal and insurmountable. Thus some strains of this scholarship embrace the recently fashionable belief in an impending "clash of civilizations." In the past few years, the Russian intellectual market has been inundated with geopolitical treatises, from those written for popular consumption to those for academic audiences. Insights and assumptions from the theory of geopolitics permeate the work of various authors, from Gennadi Zyuganov to the *enfants terribles* of Russian postmodernism, Eduard Limonov and Aleksandr Dugin.[78]

Perhaps the only common feature of American Realism, Russian democratic utopianism, and geopolitics has been their failure to account in a systematic and uncontradictory way for the phenomenon of national economic dependency, a notion that is critical for understanding the logic of the Yeltsin-era reforms and their predictable failure in the context of a global political economy. Western academics have focused attention on such concepts as universal interdependence, globalization, and international flows of information and capital. These concepts reveal more about the international context of Russia's reforms than other approaches mentioned previously and are typically characterized by the systems approach to international relations, which views nations and states as—for better or worse—inherently open systems and finds many explanatory cues for modern politics in the fluid realm between domestic and international affairs. These currents of thought have not enjoyed wide circulation in Yeltsin's Russia, not least for the fact that they have been associated (rightly or wrongly) with neo-Marxist approaches.

Theories of dependency sought a better understanding of development problems in Third World countries, and for some time they were viewed with suspicion by the Anglo-American academic mainstream until their insights were incorporated into broader and more middle-of-the-road writings about interdependence.[79] One of the most parsimonious structural models of dependency theories' "patron-client relations" on the international scale was developed by Johan Galtung, who provided a basic outline for future, more complex endeavors.[80] In this seemingly very simple model, the world consists of Center nations and Periphery nations, with each nation having its own domestic center (elite) and periphery (the peasantry, underdeveloped regions, and so on). In addition to material inequalities between the center and the periphery, information is distributed unequally, given the differences of history, culture, education, and technology between the periphery and the center. Thus those who possess a larger amount of information are in a position to control (or at least heavily influence) the conscience and behavior of "junior brothers," whose ability to perceive and act upon their interests is constrained from the start; hence, assumptions about economic rationality do not apply to them. Within a Periphery nation, the disparity between its center and its own periphery tends to be greater, a tendency that enables the center to grow faster than its periphery by serving as a transit point for wealth. In addition, the model helps us to see how the control and channeling of information flows work so that "alliance formation between the two peripheries is avoided, while the Center nation becomes more, and the Periphery nation less, cohesive and hence less able to develop long-term strategies."[81] All of this is perfectly applicable to Yeltsin's Russia.

Jowitt made a notable contribution by applying this sort of "patron-client" model of international relations to Eastern Europe and to Russia in particular. His daring though somewhat contradictory research interpreted the Bolshevik Revolution as an attempt to escape from Russia's dependent position in the international system.[82] Although rigorous historical methodology may cast doubt on Jowitt's attempts to stretch the notion of dependency back to the early twentieth century, his theoretical formulations and analysis provide an interesting view of the modern international system and of Russia's position in it. In Jowitt's model of the world, consisting of "modern" and "traditional" societies (regardless of his theoretical radicalism, he clings to the terminology of the modernization paradigm), the elite in a traditional society seeks out a modern society to be its patron. The resulting international relationship is then hierarchical in the same way that the elite-mass relationship is hierarchical inside the traditional society. Jowitt also formulates three key elements of cultural dependency: "1) a moral and psychological chasm between the oligarchic, bureaucratic elite and the lower classes; 2) mechanical transfer of liberal institutional facades from the West; 3) external power as an ideological-cultural referent and patron for the local elite." Although his attempt to find these traits in the sociopolitical landscape of Russia under Nicholas II is not entirely convincing, his definition of dependency more fully applies to present-day Russia and its relationship to the West.

In the course of the 1980s, with growing awareness of and concerns about globalization, the notion of dependency, which had been ushered out of the door of mainstream political theory, came back in through the window. As mentioned previously, it was absorbed by liberal modernizers of the traditional Realist approach, who made wide use of the concept of "global interdependence." Much of this writing treated the concept positively, often suggesting that interdependence would restrain the self-serving and aggressive aspirations of national leaders who might otherwise end up as victims of their own internationally destabilizing activity.[83]

Some of these ideas influenced Gorbachev's team as it was laying the groundwork for his doctrine of "new thinking" in foreign policy. Evidence suggests that either Gorbachev or his speechwriters genuinely believed that "interdependence" operated uniformly across the planet, with the result that Western governments did have a major stake in the success or failure of Gorbachev's domestic reform policies. This idealistic aberration inspired Gorbachev with excessive self-confidence in bargaining for Western material aid and in his belief that the mechanics of interdependence would force Western elites to help him in his domestic troubles. Subsequent events demonstrated, however, that even if such a factor existed, it did not work in the Soviet Union's favor, and that (paraphrasing Orwell) everybody was interdependent, but some were more interdependent than others. Galtung's and Jowitt's analyses would have helped Soviet and Russian leaders to better grasp their predicament, but for various reasons (not least because the Soviet educated class shunned any thinking that smacked of "leftism") the conceptual void left after the demise of Gorbachev's "new thinking" was rapidly filled by the quasi-science of geopolitics.

What does democratic theory tell us about the consequences of globalization and the world's uneven "interdependence" for domestic politics? So far, relatively little work has been done on this sensitive subject, but a rather comprehensive analysis does appear in a recent work by David Held.[84] Held proceeds from the Lindblom-Dahl analysis of tensions between democracy and markets as modes of power, extending the polyarchical model of a nation-state to the global level, while incorporating the insights of dependency and interdependence theorists. His reconstruction of the international body politic presents a systematic alternative to the convenient Realist myth that the international system is anarchic because it has no hierarchy. In this schema, the ways in which the international economy and politics are managed are subject to the same analytical tools used to understand governance within a nation-state; thus international order can be sustained and modified in a similar way to the domestic realm. At their best, Held's writings resurrect the integrity of the social universe and are permeated with messages *urbi et orbi* that do not attempt to conceal their own idealism—something that is today unusual in his field. His work is all the more noteworthy for providing a non-Marxist, but radically democratic, critique of Western realities from the standpoint of the ideals and norms of Western civilization itself—thus continuing the tradition exemplified by Immanuel Kant's *Zum ewigen Frieden* (his 1795 treatise on perpetual peace) and John Rawls's *A Theory of Justice*. Held's approach would certainly strike a chord among thinkers belonging to the reflective and critical branch of today's Russian Westernizers.

Held's earlier work had expanded the notion of dependency as a generic characteristic of the modern nation-state, both rich and poor, whose room for maneuver is shrinking under the mounting pressure of nongovernmental and non-democratic institutions.[85] A by-product of this development is the devaluation and decreasing impact of democratic values and norms, as democratic procedures carry less weight in comparison with the forces of the global political economy. In Held's own words, the most dramatic historical paradox of the 1990s is that "more and more nations and groups are championing the idea of 'the rule of the people' . . . just when the very efficacy of democracy as a national form of political organization appears open to question. As substantial areas of human activity are progressively organized on a global level, the fate of democracy . . . is fraught with difficulty."[86] Thus the pivotal problem of present-day world politics lies in a dangerous incongruity between the will of democratic constituencies, which is constrained by the boundaries of their nation-states, and the international private and corporate actors that often exercise power over the former while staying largely beyond the reach of democratic institutions (and sometimes, as in the case of transnational corporations, financial markets, and global flows of capital, outside of any public control whatsoever). This unresolved contradiction, according to Held, creates a chasm "between the idea of a political community determining its own future and the dynamics of the contemporary world economy."[87]

Therefore, the power of international players and the rules of the game that they craft and help to sustain circumscribe (for better or worse) a country's ability to choose its economic strategies on the basis of democratic deliberation (as has become clear in the case of Russia's shock therapy and, again, in the Asian financial crisis of 1997–98). In particular, the productive resources of the real economy, primarily industrial capital, which are for the most part firmly tied to a given territory, are at a permanent disadvantage relative to financial and speculative capital (which nowadays circles the globe at the push of a button). Global financial markets react capriciously to the smallest variations of policy by destabilizing capital flows. In such a way, capital flows exercise "an effective veto" over the kinds of democratic policy choices that financial institutions or even single individuals in the market find objectionable.[88] This imposes increasingly severe limits on strategic decision making about national development in all countries, including the leading Western democracies. In this context, even such organizations as the IMF, which was established in 1946 as an intergovernmental agency to administer an international monetary system that broke up a quarter of a century ago, can sometimes be used by powerful governments as enforcement tools that benefit the private interests of financial groups operating in foreign countries at the expense of the taxpayers and national treasuries in those groups' home countries.

RUSSIAN HISTORY AS A CONTEST OF MEANINGS

In 1946 George Orwell, with a sense of bitterness, wrote in a letter to a friend:

> The words *democracy, socialism, freedom, patriotic, realistic, justice* have each of them several meanings which cannot be reconciled with one another. In the case of a word like *democracy,* not only is there no agreed definition, but the attempt to make one is resisted from all sides. It is almost universally felt that when we call a country democratic we are praising it: consequently the defenders of every kind of regime claim that it is a democracy, and fear that they might have to stop using the word if it were tied down to any one meaning. Words of this kind are often used in a consciously dishonest way. That is, the person who uses them has his own private definition, but allows his hearer to think he means something quite different.[89]

Orwell's words, although directed against the media and propaganda of his age, apply equally to the fate of various basic political and philosophical concepts.

In Russia, the banners of democracy, Westernization, or nationalism often have been carried simultaneously by mutually alienated and even antagonistic forces. Most recently, the pageantry and pomp of the "transition to postcommunism" have made many observers blind to what we perceive as a major theme of the period: the hidden struggle in the reform camp among those labeled or claiming to be "Westernizers," "democrats," and "reformers"—that is, the vast majority of Russians politically active from 1988 to 1993—over the divergent and sometimes irreconcilable meanings of these terms. Thus, for example, if democracy as a set of procedures for competing for power was widely upheld as a common currency, it was predictably not sufficient for many genuine democrats, who articulated and promoted substantive definitions of democracy that were normatively acceptable or simply advantageous and convenient for their own ideal or material purposes, or both.

Likewise, the authors of this book subscribe to notions of democracy and reform (implicit and sometimes explicit in our argumentation) that we do not claim to be immune from value judgments or superior to others in an absolute sense. Nor do we view as a tragedy the fact that Russia's current rulers champion an idea of reform that is very different and in some ways opposite to ours. The real tragedy is that the culture of Bolshevism espoused by the Russian elite and its Western supporters, together with some of the global factors discussed previously, precluded an open and equitable comparison and contest among these interpretations of reform and enabled a few of the reformers to prevail by obscuring, suppressing, or destroying the bearers of alternative interpretations.

In Russian culture's formative period, an intensely mystical brand of Christianity coexisted with four centuries of peasant slavery and with alternations between despotism and chaotic turbulence. This combination engendered a special type of social mentality and attitude toward authority. Let us call it *anarchical absolutism*. In this composite, the content of absolutism is twofold: It denotes the aspiration for a maximum fulfillment of ideal or material goals and a rejection of a fragmented vision of the world as a number of special, sui generis units. In other words, it has an intense longing for and desire to regain an integrity of the universe—both cosmic and social—that is felt to have been lost. The eagerness to expand each newly discovered higher principle indiscriminately resulted in the pursuit of universal utopias—religious, artistic, philosophical, and also political. Some of the political utopias, such as pan-Slavism and Bolshevik Marxism, pushed Russia onto a path of expansion; others, like the liberal-democratic-capitalist utopia of the last decade, propelled it toward self-destruction. In each case, this absolutist upsurge provided rare moments of unity and confidence among the vast majority of Russians and their ruling elites, and made a constructive contribution in general to the advancement and enlightenment of the nation. Yet as soon as it became clear that the ultimate telos or goals of universal integration and happiness were beyond reach, the pendulum began to swing backward, from mass enthusiasm and consolidation toward social entropy, atomization, and strife. This reverse side of Russian absolutism prompts us to qualify it as anarchical.

The antagonism of absolutes (the latter often disguised under a single term, as in the previous examples) made it at best problematic for intermediate political forms based on compromise—be they constitutional monarchy, parliamentarism, or social democracy—to put down deep roots in Russian soil. Thus the incipient liberal constitutionalism of 1879–81 was squeezed and destroyed in the clash between an all-consuming autocracy and the radical-democratic populism of the group Narodnaya Volya. This anarchic Russian tradition, seemingly a fatal handicap by Western standards, always found a way to win in the longer term. Having lost the battle in the open field, it retreated into the underground, beyond the reach of the state. As it involved more and more people, this parallel "shadow" reality became pervasive, depriving the official government of its feedback from society and paving the way for its partial surrender or demise.

From 1988 to 1992, democracy, Westernization, and reform were but the aliases of the latest incarnation of Russia's absolutist, teleological dream. The battle over the meaning of these concepts, in which not only the Russian elites and masses, but also their Western fellow travelers were engaged (even if they did not see it that way), ended in complete defeat for the definitions of democracy and reform espoused by the majority of those actively involved. This defeat was conditioned by, among other things, the forces of globalization and dependency that were part of the reason for Yeltsin's embrace of shock therapy and IMF loans and that were, in turn, strengthened by Yeltsin's policies. In this way, a leap forward in "Westernization" in terms of private economic initiative incurred the cost of a grave setback for "Westernization" regarding the development of civil society and representative institutions; the integrity and efficiency of public administration; and the safeguarding of the social safety net, education and health, and freedom of the press. On all of these indicators, the "postreform" era has performed much worse than the preceding Gorbachev period; on some of them, it does not withstand comparison even with earlier periods of Soviet rule.

As for democracy, the formal test for a minimalist, procedural democracy, defined as regulated competition for power, was only barely passed in both July 1996 and March 2000. But a substantive understanding of democracy—as informed by Russian cultural traditions—was severely discredited and debased because the Yeltsinites consistently abused the term. In addition, as we show in subsequent chapters, the Yeltsin regime refrained from encroaching on the procedural bases of democracy only as long as they exerted negligible influence on decision making related to the fate of the country and the position of its elites. From the point of view of content, Yeltsin's system of rule was an amorphous type of *pluralist autocracy,* where the power of the president was nothing more than a pathetic parody of authoritarianism, despite the dearth of credible rivals. The ostentatiously autocratic decisions emanating from the Kremlin were sabotaged on a daily basis, while the feudalization of the bureaucracy, the bacchanalia of special interests, and the general lawlessness revealed the increasing impotence of a state that was deprived of national roots and ignored or rejected by much of society.

It would be premature to interpret this mass disdain for the government and the disregard for its laws by its own bureaucrats and citizens as a sign that the Russian mind has irrevocably abandoned the quest for a just and legitimate authority, a quest that has been part of its national creed throughout modern history. Rather, this pervasive anarchic sentiment in Russia (as, perhaps, in some other parts of the world) reflects the hazy feeling that the modern state as we know it today—formalized, mechanistic, impersonal and aloof, disconnected from the daily life of its constituents, and, in some cases, privatized by the elite—has proved unable to approximate the normative values of both freedom and justice that have been the foundation of political legitimacy since the era of the Enlightenment. In those countries where an "organic" view of the state is culturally ingrained—Russia is but one characteristic example—a longing for more personal and caring authorities united with the citizens by a set of common purposes contributed indirectly to the unwelcome growth of mafias (as discussed in chapter 3, the term is derived from the Italian word for "family"). The distorted and destabilizing character of such growths, in both Russia and other countries, cannot negate the fact that they fulfill an essential function neglected by modern governments and does not mean that a more creative and enlightened alternative is inconceivable in the future.

Likewise, there are no grounds to assert that the Russian mind has quenched its thirst for universalist projects and solutions and reconciled itself to the fragmentation of the world. The integrative bent of the Russian national psyche reveals itself in the country's submissive acceptance of the market fetishism of the shock therapists, who managed to convince many Russians that their theory and policies embody the universal laws of capitalist development. In 1991–92, many Russians selflessly acquiesced to these policies, even though they were detrimental to their material interests and prospects for survival. But even as the myth of largely unregulated markets that had been mistaken for a universal standard of modernity gradually lost its magic in the following years, Russia did not opt to consider itself a special case, as the appearance of a powerful isolationist movement would have implied. Adverse international conditions, such as the often protectionist economic policies of the European Union and the United States, and sudden blows, such as NATO expansion and the U.S.-led NATO war against the Federal Republic of Yugoslavia, would seem sufficient to push Russia toward a nationalist backlash. Yet only in 2000 did nationalists finally win power, and then only in large part by contriving a new war in Chechnya. However, they too refrained from considering Russia a special case.

Today, judging by almost all the official media and academic periodicals, Russia may be one of the most conservative major nations in the world. The narrowness of the range of acceptable intellectual paradigms and the tight

boundaries of political correctness, which have been internalized by both supporters of the regime and most of the legal opposition, recall the kind of intolerance of the McCarthy era in the United States. In Russia's own history, they
evoke the reign of Nicholas I, who on the eve of 1848 was proud to see his
absolutism as the solitary rock undisturbed by the worldwide sea of change.
Much of the present Moscow elite espouses the politically correct views of "world
society," including the top-down approach to global politics. In a world replete
with confrontations between the strong and the weak, where the legitimacy of
privileged clubs is constantly in dispute, the rulers of Russia, so arrogant toward
their own subjects, have been ready to embrace any humiliation in order to obtain
a semblance of insider status with the privileged club of the Group of Seven.

Yet the eventful year of 1999 and anecdotal evidence gleaned from everyday
Russians point to new forces that lurk underneath this thin and fragile surface.
While the Yeltsinites deliberately ignored their deepest feelings and the Putinites
clearly distrust them, Russia appears to confirm—and sometimes anticipate—
the most far-reaching theoretical insights of Western and Russian thought.
Once again it claims, as it did at the beginning of the twentieth century, the role
of "the weakest link in the chain" of the global status quo. The hidden intellectual and moral work that goes on in the depths of society, the growing awareness
of the alien and ephemeral character of the post-1993 arrangements, Russia's
underlying openness to integrative ideas and trends—these and other developments portended, as the decade of turbulent stagnation wound to a close, a search
for some new recipe for salvation, very possibly conceived in the absolutist
terms explored in this chapter. The magnetic force of this incipient new upsurge
may or may not lead to a genuine national revival and does not promise the sort
of definitive happy ending that history, in any event, cannot offer; yet it may
have the potential to fill the global void with a "creatively destructive ideology."[90] Enlightened observers, who will have recognized the first portents of
this trend, will be wise enough to refrain from exhibitions of joy or grief. For,
through the great peaks and valleys of Russian history, spiritual achievement is
often associated with physical and moral suffering. In accordance with Karl
Jaspers's words, breakup and failure reveal the true nature of things.

Finally, before we turn to a close analysis of the Gorbachev years and the resurgence of Russia's democratic tradition, we express the hope that those bold
theorists and their pupils who may soon be tempted to apply their assumptions and
findings on the fertile terrain of post-Yeltsin Russia will do nothing that might,
even indirectly, increase the already excessive suffering of ordinary people.

3

POPULISTS, THE ESTABLISHMENT, AND THE SOVIET DECLINE

Perestroika would not have faltered . . . had
  Gorbachev been able to force himself to renounce
privileged access to goods. . . . Everything could
    have gone in a different way, for people would
not have lost their faith in the declared slogans. . . .
  But when people know about flagrant social
inequality and see that the leader is doing nothing
  to fix this shameless expropriation of goods by the
  top brass of the Party, then the last droplets of
faith evaporate. . . . As long as we are so poor and
wretched . . . I cannot eat sturgeon and take away
  its taste with caviar . . . I cannot swallow special
imported medicine, knowing that the woman next
  door has no aspirin for her kid. Because I would
be ashamed.

—*Boris N. Yeltsin,* Ispoved' na zadannuyu temu
(translation by the authors)

WHAT WAS THE COMBINATION OF DEVELOPMENTS that set in motion the Gorbachev reforms and the subsequent demise of the Soviet system? Scores of books and articles have been written on this subject, invoking various domestic and international, proximate and underlying, causes of the Soviet collapse. Some have assigned the definitive role to pressures from the international system, particularly to the offensive strategy of the Reagan administration in the years 1981–86, which disoriented and broke the will of the Soviet leadership.[1] Others have pointed to the effects of the Soviet Union's "imperial overreach." Still others have emphasized the internal dynamics of economic decay, alleging the inherent unworkability of adding ill-considered market elements to a centrally planned economy.[2] A few, captivated by the "great men" vision of history dating back to Plutarch, have given most of the credit for the Soviet collapse to the supposedly altruistic idealism of Gorbachev and his inner circle of advisers.[3]

While each of these explanations does contain at least a grain of truth, one driving force of the Soviet decline has so far received less attention than it deserves, to say nothing of a comprehensive explanation and analysis—popular, grassroots mass discontent with the system. There are compelling reasons to address this subject, even before one can authoritatively speak about the impact that it had in comparison with that of other "prime vectors" on the downfall of the Soviet system. Specifically, discontented Soviet citizens represented a force—in contrast to foreign actors and institutions—that might have been expected to strive to make the inevitable changes in the Soviet Union as organic and painless as possible. Unlike the impersonal factors at work in the Soviet economy, most reform-minded Russians were endowed with a clear will and intentions (even if they often cannot be treated as "rational" in the narrow, scholastic sense of the word), as well as with a loose set of common understandings about the nature of the Soviet system's profound problems. Finally, given that the call for a "transition to democracy" was the unifying battle cry for many Soviet citizens unhappy with their system, there is every reason to inquire as to what extent their initial strivings and concerns were actually reflected in the policies of the first democratically elected ruler of the country, Boris Yeltsin, and of the self-proclaimed democrats who surrounded him in 1989–91. To put it simply, the goal of this historical analysis is to evaluate the legitimacy of the Yeltsin government when it claimed from 1991 on to speak on behalf of the disgruntled citizens who were numerically the largest, if perhaps not the most powerful force (compared with the West's Cold War machine) behind the dismantling of the Soviet political system.

To achieve this explanatory goal, this chapter will first examine the extent of popular discontent in the Soviet Union by the mid-1980s and review the main points of contention. We conclude that dissent was widespread, concerned most of all with the gulf between rulers and ruled, and with obtaining social justice more than curbing, let alone dismantling, the socialist economy. Our survey leads us to a comparison of this type of mass discontent with similar periods in

Russian history and even with the American experience, and we identify the strand running through all these periods as a type of progressive populism. To shed light on this populism, we examine the roots of late Soviet populism in Tsarist Russia, in the early Soviet years, in the populist strand of Khrushchev's policies, and in Aleksandr Tvardovsky's journal *Novy mir.*

We also analyze the main three intellectual theories in the USSR of the late 1980s regarding the principal reason why the Soviet system created popular alienation. Leftists favored the view that the nomenklatura was concerned only with its own power. It had confused and deceived the people by abolishing free speech, manipulating Marxist-Leninist ideology, and creating a great divide between itself and the masses. Salvation lay in removing the nomenklatura and establishing a people-based democracy. Other liberals, including libertarians, put the main emphasis on the suffocatingly bureaucratic nature of the whole system and saw salvation in sweeping the bureaucracy away, cutting the power of the state in all spheres, and giving citizens maximum economic and other freedoms. And third, nationalists ("national-patriots," or, as we call them, "national-conservatives") tended to believe that a foreign ideology, Marxism, had been imposed on Russia, mainly by Jews, Balts, and Transcaucasians. According to this view, salvation required above all the removal of non-Russians, Marxist ideology, and Marxism's cousin, liberalism, from the political scene.

From this analysis we conclude that adherents (conscious and unconscious) of all three theories had enough in common with one another that most of them could, given the skill, be mobilized behind a single populist leader. This was first achieved in 1986–88 by Mikhail Gorbachev, and then, when Gorbachev's centrist balancing act started to fail in 1988, by Boris Yeltsin.

Before turning to the USSR's collapse and Yeltsin's emerging strategy of 1990–91, we examine a crucial factor in both these phenomena, the rise of the so-called *Mafiya.* We look at the Mafiya's roots in the penal colonies and exile settlements of the tsars and then examine its manifestation in Soviet society, from a brief flirtation with the new regime to the deep alienation of its "thieves in the law" from the state. We also trace the growth of its commercial relationships with the increasingly corrupt nomenklatura of the Brezhnev years, its blossoming as the USSR entered terminal decline under Gorbachev, and its forging of a strategic partnership with Yeltsin and the economic libertarians on whom he came to rely in 1991.

In charting Yeltsin's ascent from 1985, one of our main concerns is to gauge how much it was based on ambition and opportunism, as opposed to ideological conviction, and how much it depended on the Gorbachevites' miscalculations, as they constantly attempted to manipulate political forces. We show, for example, how Gorbachev at times facilitated Yeltsin's advance to intimidate conservative forces in the CPSU and at other times curbed it to prevent him from becoming too powerful.

Meanwhile, Gorbachev underestimated the potential force of nationalism in the minority republics and failed to build a strong coalition for promoting reform in ways that would preserve the Union. As a result, the collapse of communism in Eastern Europe in 1989, followed by parliamentary elections in the Soviet republics in February–March 1990, unleashed Baltic, Russian, and other nationalisms. This gave the opportunistic Yeltsin, who had courted nationalists since 1987, the opening he needed—the chance to build an extensive power base in the Russian Soviet Federated Socialist Republic (RSFSR). Equally important, though, this interlude also gave Yeltsin the temptation—not finally embraced until after the coup attempt of August 1991—to break up the Union and secure his own power in Russia for the long term by clamping down on (and soon emasculating) the democratic revolution that he himself had led.

Popular Discontent in Soviet Russia: A Belated Discovery

As is now clear to most observers, latent resistance to the Soviet authorities never died out among their subjects, neither in Russia nor in other countries and territories that had fallen under Soviet rule. Contrary to what the totalitarian model of Soviet society suggests, even repeated waves of Stalin's Great Terror in 1929–33, 1936–38, and 1946–53, with many millions of victims, were not enough to wipe out dissent completely. Indeed, it was the experience of Stalin's terror itself, after its extent was gradually revealed to the public, that resulted in a thorough rethinking and critique of the very foundations of the system in those social strata (first and foremost, the intelligentsia and urban labor) that had been the loyal power base for the Communist Party. The relevant evidence was also available to Western observers willing to search for it. As early as 1958, Merle Fainsod, who had studied documents from the Smolensk archives of the local Soviet government that had reached the West via Germany during World War II, found in them "unimpeachable evidence of widespread mass discontent with Soviet rule" in the prewar period, at least in that particular locality (even though his study did not devote much investigation to the deeper issues behind the evidence).[4] Further voluminous information on the mounting tensions in Soviet society came to the West from the dissident movement, as well as from polls and surveys among Soviet emigrants.[5]

While this evidence, like any other, had to be scrutinized for bias and exaggeration, such a critical analysis was too often hampered by pervasive neglect or distrust on the part of many practitioners in Soviet studies with regard to information from unofficial sources about Soviet society. Some of this negative attitude probably stemmed from the belief that discontent and the desire to emigrate were a peculiar trait of marginal social groups. There was also an overoptimistic belief that a country where three revolutions had occurred in a twelve-year span between 1905 and 1917 would have already changed its system of governance if public discontent had been as widespread as the dissidents alleged. In other cases, lack of interest in these nonofficial sources may have reflected political sympathy for the Soviet regime, or simply anxiety that the use of such sources might jeopardize future entry visas to visit the USSR or high-level contacts with the Soviet establishment. Not unlike the portrayals in official Soviet propaganda, the views of many Western scholars regarding discontented Soviet citizens tended to classify them as defectors from the socialist camp whose observations were distorted by their alleged right-wing bias. As a consequence, even émigré Soviet scholars seeking academic careers in the West often found a more attentive audience among the political and security establishment than in intellectual circles. (This Western attitude to Soviet dissidents has been mirrored by almost all Soviet and now by Russian Americanists, whose attention has been fixated on what they consider, rightly or wrongly, "the mainstream" of American society and politics, to the neglect of those phenomena that appear "marginal.")

The Soviet authorities, by contrast, always took actual or potential eruptions of dissidence quite seriously. The evidence on political repression, once scattered and circumstantial, has become more statistically rigorous now that parts of the official Soviet archives have been declassified. Thus between 1958 and 1986, the total number of prosecutions under the two most explicitly political statutes of the Criminal Code—Articles 70 (anti-Soviet agitation and propaganda) and 190-1 (defamation of the Soviet political and social system)—was approximately six thousand.[6] The annual number of cases ranged from as many as 1,416 in 1958 to just 56 in the "calm" year of 1978. In addition to direct legal action, between 1967 and 1974 a remarkable total of 69,984 individuals were formally warned (warnings that the KGB reports classify as "prophylactic measures") that they were on the verge of being charged under Article 70, the graver of the two.[7] In this way, as the Committee for State Security (KGB) chairman proudly reported, between 1971 and 1974, "through prophylaxis alone, 1,839 anti-Soviet groups were put out of action at the point where they were in the process of being formed."[8]

Apart from the comparatively rare cases of open public attacks on the authorities, angry citizens resorted to anonymous protests against various specific features of the Soviet system, protests that came to the KGB's attention in the form of letters or leaflets. The annual number of such "protests" handled by the KGB ranged between the low of 8,723, recorded at the 1987 peak of Gorbachev's perestroika, and 22,502 in 1981. The number of authors of anonymous material the KGB thought it had identified ranged from 1,376 in 1985 to 2,088 in 1977 (the year when the new Brezhnev-era Soviet Constitution was ratified). Because the KGB went to great lengths to identify and punish those responsible, writing and distributing leaflets was very risky and could have appealed only to a tiny minority of discontented citizens. For the years 1975–79 and 1981–88 for which data are available, the KGB reported that 849 (or 5 percent) out of a total of 17,593 alleged authors were jailed, and a further 2,438 (or 14 percent) were committed to mental hospitals.[9]

Given the breadth of such dissident expression, it is clear that public disaffection had many different roots—socioeconomic, moral and psychological, ideological, and political among them—and was nourished by diverse normative conceptions of a better society. Over time, the diversity of opposition sentiment only increased, especially in the Gorbachev era, when the vast majority of the public was suddenly exposed to a cacophony of disturbing information about Soviet society and to competing ideas and programs of both Russian and Western origins. An investigation of all the dissident groups and movements from the 1960s to 1985, when they were the only outlet for public discontent and its transmitter to the outside world, can yield only partial answers. Although the dissidents were successful in providing verbal expression and a rational framework for much of this sentiment, their pronouncements were only one important element in the broader landscape of public opinion. Many Soviet citizens, who were profoundly resentful or suspicious of the authorities, simply did not consider this dissident type of behavior as a rational or a feasible response to the perversities of the system.

WHAT PUBLIC DISCONTENT WAS NOT

Before looking at the varieties of political activism and offering an analytical framework in which to view the popular, grassroots movement of discontent that peaked in 1988–91, it is helpful to identify the generic, "structural" foundations that unified all movement participants, irrespective of ideology. Here, many outside observers have understandably fallen prey to a *post hoc, ergo propter hoc* fallacy: Seeing that the final outcome of the events of 1988–91 featured the collapse of the Communist Party and the promulgation of democracy and market reforms by the new regime, some have tended to conclude that the popular sentiment behind these events was anticommunist, "reformist," pro-Western, and geared toward democracy and free markets in the Western meaning of these words.[10] Although each of these labels does fit some social stratum or organization that helped to bring down the Soviet system, it is easy to show that none of them reflected the common traits of the popular movement as a whole.

While the word "reform" became, in defiance of common sense, the trademark of the stagnation of the Yeltsin era, talk of reform could be heard very rarely, if at all, in the opposition groups of the 1988–90 period. "Revolution" was much more in vogue, with "peaceful" or "nonviolent" as obligatory qualifiers for those who wanted to show circumspection and political correctness. Both "reform" and "revolution" appeared in Gorbachev's official pronouncements, for he and his closest associates had a penchant for revolutionary phraseology. (This rhetoric later became a target for Yeltsin and the post-1991 elite, who excoriated all talk of revolution and purged the term from their political lexicon.) The first major organization of "reformers," as opposed to "revolutionaries"—

the Movement for Democratic Reforms, set up in July 1991 by such unpopular establishment figures as Gavriil Popov and Arkady Volsky—was bitterly opposed by most mainstream democrats as a tool designed to slow down or even to subvert the grassroots transformation of society.

It would plainly be wrong to say that all discontented Russians were pro-Western. The national-patriotic wing of public opinion—from widely respected intellectuals and writers of the "village prose" school all the way to the notorious Pamyat' Society—was hardly pro-Western, although it reflected a profound disaffection with the status quo. Many moderate nationalists, deeply resentful of the intrusion of Western thought and pop culture into the USSR, allied themselves at various stages with both Gorbachev and Yeltsin. On his first foreign trips to the United States and France (1989–91), Yeltsin was snubbed by Western admirers of Gorbachev (from George Bush to socialists in the European parliament) and came back with mixed feelings about Western elites, feelings that shaped his subsequent behavior. About his visit to the European parliament in early 1991, he wrote, "I was blasted in Strasbourg with a cold—I would say even icy—shower. . . . The Western reaction was a terrible blow for me."[11] This sentiment seemed to echo those of many Russian Westernizers who saw their own idealism of the dissident era crushed by international Realpolitik. And, as discussed in the previous chapter, even those among the opposition in 1988–91 who shared a belief in Russia's imperative need to join the Western "family of nations" diverged widely in their views about which features of social organization were indispensably "Western" and which were not.

It seems safer to call most activists who opposed the existing system "modernizers." Indeed, they overwhelmingly agreed in their objective to catch up with what they viewed as developed countries of the world in spheres where the Soviet Union was obviously lagging, such as in the use of advanced industrial technologies. Yet this sentiment was intertwined with retrospective utopias calling for a return to some blessed past that had allegedly existed before the modernization drives launched under communism. Thus, loyal Gorbachevians invoked the positive example of the New Economic Policy (NEP) of the early 1920s; radical democrats aspired to undo the results of the October 1917 "coup"; and many conservative patriots, following Aleksandr Solzhenitsyn, insisted that Russia had been diverted from the path of righteousness by the February 1917 overthrow of the monarchy that, in turn, had been caused by Russia's foolhardy entry into World War I under the auspices of the Triple Entente. In sum, most politically engaged citizens were as concerned with rewriting modern Russian history from scratch as they were about moving forward.

In narrower partisan terms, Soviet public discontent has been treated as anticommunist and, therefore, promarket. This is a simplistic attempt to fit the story into the obsolete "right-versus-left" political framework, which has limited usefulness when analyzing Western societies and is completely inadequate for the Russian case. First, it must be kept in mind that after Khrushchev fell in

1964, the leaders of the CPSU gradually dropped from their speeches and documents references to communism as an attainable goal. By 1985, indeed, the more opportunistic and adaptive groups among the privileged Soviet elite acknowledged, accepted, and welcomed elements of convergence between Soviet and Western economic systems, at least so far as this convergence helped to raise the elite's living standards. Second, orthodox Communists and liberal Marxists were a visible presence among the broad spectrum of critics of the Soviet system in 1986–89. Even the most radical dissident group, the Democratic Union, which constituted itself as the first political party in May 1988, contained a Eurocommunist faction alongside liberals and Christian Democrats. Third, it was commonly held that the CPSU was not a political party at all, but, rather, a governing institution that in practice no longer required a commitment to Marxism-Leninism. Thus it was no surprise to see rank-and-file members of the CPSU rallying jointly with Democratic Russia to denounce the Party leadership and the existing system of power.[12]

The spirit of public protests was neither "promarket" nor "procapitalist," especially if those loose terms designate an abrupt abolition of the government's price-setting and property-ownership functions of the type that occurred in 1991–92. An overwhelming majority of the economic programs put forward by the opposition in 1988–91 advocated a mixed economy, or *mnogoukladnost,* with state, collective, and private companies competing on equal terms—a characteristic of the Russian economy under NEP before Stalin conducted his *Gleichschaltung,* or total standardization of society. It is true that most of these groups believed that private business was vital for the development of a regular civil society and should be encouraged by the government, whose responsibility they believed was to ensure a level playing field in legal and political terms. But virtually nobody would have suggested that the Soviet managerial class and the black-market dealers should be allowed to evolve smoothly into private owners of most of the nation's economic assets—as was allowed to occur under Yeltsin's rule. On the contrary, much of the grassroots indignation of the 1980s was directed against the creeping transformation of the Mafiya and parts of the party nomenklatura into legally propertied "capitalists."

Finally, the word "democratic" is often applied to the popular movement (the present work is no exception). There are compelling arguments for this usage. An overwhelming majority of opposition groups (including all the influential ones) advocated competitive elections and, from 1988 on, worked diligently to advance their aims by electoral and parliamentary means. Those that stayed away from the elections, such as the Pamyat' Society and the Democratic Union, were treated as fringe groups and rapidly marginalized—unlike Lenin's Bolsheviks, who boycotted the 1906 elections to the First Duma but nevertheless managed to stay afloat. Nobody except a few orthodox Stalinists spoke about abolishing popular elections to the legislature and the highest executive offices. Such a position did not emerge until 1993, when it was first aired in periodicals run by radical Yeltsinists and shock therapy advocates, and when Yeltsin announced on March 20 that he was introducing presidential rule and suspending the powers of parliament.

These pervasive democratic attitudes might be dismissed as sometimes opportunistic, especially regarding the often successful performance of many members of the party establishment in the 1989–90 elections. But such suspicions could cast doubts on the sincerity of even the most committed democrats; after all, only words and actions, not thoughts, can be analyzed empirically. We believe it fair to define almost all opposition groups of the Gorbachev period (including mainstream nationalists and Marxists disaffected with the Soviet system) as democrats in the minimalist, Schumpeterian meaning of this term. At the same time, we should note that most of these democrats professed expanded understandings of democracy that were often mutually incompatible, as discussed later in this work.

Yet there are practical problems with calling all of these groups democrats. In Russia the term—with and without quotation marks—came to acquire a far narrower meaning, applying to those who emphatically called themselves "democrats" while denying everybody else the right to this self-definition. Ultimately, many of their opponents, wanting to avoid identification with them, yielded them the term and applied to themselves other labels, such as "liberal." In the most exclusionary use of the term, it applied to members of Democratic Russia and its constituent groups, the electoral coalition that was the core of Yeltsin's support in the 1990–93 parliament, though steadily shrinking, and remained on his side until it disappeared in the flames of the political system it helped Yeltsin to destroy in September–October 1993. As Democratic Russia became steadily smaller, more sectarian, and more rigidly organized, a rapidly increasing number of supporters of democracy who had stayed outside Democratic Russia or disagreed with its leadership were labeled by the Kremlin-loyal media as nondemocrats, and even as enemies of democracy. (This kind of classification was not unlike what happened in previous decades, when Soviet patriots and Westerners who criticized the Communist Party were labeled "anti-Soviet," even if they favored giving the elected soviets the real power they were denied under the Bolshevik dictatorship.) This appropriation of democratic credentials had by 1992 made "democracy" a narrowly partisan concept, discredited in the eyes of millions of Russians who had plenty of reasons to mistrust the self-styled democrats. Another reason this term cannot be applied to the entire movement of public discontent is that it would exclude people like Gorbachev and his associates, who evolved toward democracy but were clearly the major targets of the popular movement's hostility.

WHY THE SOVIET SYSTEM MADE PEOPLE UNHAPPY

There is little direct evidence for a sociologically authoritative judgment as to what common set of grievances motivated people of the most diverse convictions to reject the late-Soviet status quo in favor of an uncertain alternative. To our knowledge, no polls were conducted among rank-and-file activists across the spectrum. Some insights can be gained, however, from methodologically rigorous studies of at least one identifiable group of angry citizens—Soviet emigrants. Contrary to widely held prejudice, the mere fact of leaving the USSR was not inherently linked to any specific ideological bias. Many people left the country for economic and personal reasons, although the formidable obstacles to emigration often compelled them to assume a political pose that, if acted out convincingly, would provide them with the necessary foreign contacts and with leverage to bargain with the authorities over their exit visas.

The seminal work on the subject was conducted by participants in the Harvard Project on the Soviet Social System, launched in 1950. This research is particularly valuable because it covered emigrants of the so-called "Second Wave"— mostly persons displaced by World War II whose emigration was often not of their own making and who, therefore, were the least politicized generation of emigrants. In fact, this amounted to an almost random sample of the 1941–44 inhabitants of the German-occupied European part of the Soviet Union.

In brief, the study revealed a deeply ingrained view of Soviet society as divided into a privileged class of Party personnel and the rest of the nation. Ninety-five percent of those questioned felt that the Party establishment had received more than its fair share from society, that its interests were in conflict with those of other classes, and that it was "foremost in having done them harm."[13] These findings were even more significant given the fact that those surveyed displayed only a rather vague class consciousness with respect to other social groups (even though most were inclined to see the intelligentsia as marginally better off and more egotistical than workers, peasants, or government employees). Overall, the study demonstrated much resentment toward those features of the Soviet system that fit a broad notion of injustice—in social, as well as in legal and moral terms. It is important to add that this intense dislike for the Communist Party and its political domination coincided with much more supportive attitudes toward the key features of the Soviet socialist system, such as government ownership of heavy industry.[14]

Later surveys were somewhat less representative because they focused on the predominantly Jewish emigrants of the "Third Wave," for almost all of whom emigration was a conscious choice and involved painstaking efforts that alienated them from the rest of society. With that caveat, it was still significant that emigrant dissatisfaction with perceived disparities in wealth and status among Soviet citizens had only increased over the intervening generation. Overall, the survey data yielded remarkable continuity with respect to the Harvard project: the Brezhnev-era emigrants blamed and praised many of the same features of Soviet reality that their Stalin-era predecessors did.[15]

These findings and similar sociological data, together with the previously formulated understanding of what the Gorbachev-era discontent was not, bring us closer to grasping what it actually was. As we have seen, this discontent was not directed against Marxist, Leninist, or Stalinist ideology, nor was it based on a particular dislike of key features of the socialist system, such as extensive welfare entitlements, free education and health care, and government ownership of strategic sectors of the economy. On the other hand, this sentiment was not markedly *in favor* of the dominant ideology: Not many angry citizens, to say nothing of dissidents or emigrants, expressed their resentment in rigorous Leninist terms; it would be fair to say that they held widely different views, ranging from extreme right to extreme left on the conventional Western spectrum of political beliefs. Nor did they tend to blame any particular leader for the plight of their nation. What ignited their resentment was the unjust and unwarranted distribution of power in favor of the Party establishment.

Like the opinion polls among Soviet emigrants of the 1950s and 1980s, the writings and pronouncements of opposition activists in the Gorbachev era convey the image of a horizontal split between the rulers and the ruled and express an acute sense of injustice and illegitimacy. This single idea united all political groups outside the Communist establishment. "The alienation of the majority of society from politics, from power, from decision making has become obvious," announced a 1988 manifesto from the moderate reformist intellectuals of the Perestroika Club. "The apparatus of administration has replaced the communities of citizens as political actor."[16] "We must break through the artificial barrier between the 'high' and the 'low'!" declaimed the ultranationalists of Pamyat' in 1987.[17] The Inter-Regional Association of Democratic Organizations, which belonged to the radical-democratic mainstream, stated in 1989 that "for almost three-quarters of a century the fate of hundreds of millions of citizens was determined not by them, but by a narrow circle of individuals belonging to the top USSR leadership. . . . Now is the first time in the history of the Soviet Union that the citizens have a real opportunity to take their destiny into their own hands."[18] The socialist protoparty led by Boris Kagarlitsky expressed its dissatisfaction with the role of a "traditional political opposition that reflects and safeguards the division of societies into the rulers and the ruled."[19] "Power to the People!" was the eloquent headline chosen in 1989 by the most respectable opposition democrats, the Inter-Regional Group of Deputies of the USSR Congress of People's Deputies.[20] This slogan evoked the label "populism," which was used by a host of columnists and Soviet officials in the perestroika years to berate radical opposition groups, especially the grassroots followers of Boris Yeltsin, as he rose from disgrace and oblivion to take center stage in national politics in 1988–90.

POPULISM AS A DEMOCRATIC FORCE

To understand better the views and motivations of these groups, a brief historical summary of the evolution of Russian populism is helpful. The widespread pejorative use of the term, in Russia as elsewhere, is strikingly inconsistent not only with the momentous role that the original Populists and their descendants have played in Russian history, but also with the valuable contribution of the American populists to U.S. history.

In the American experience, the term "populism" owes its origin to the People's Party, founded in Cincinnati, Ohio, on May 19, 1891, which desperately fought for the presidency of the United States in elections held between 1892 and 1912, trying to break the monopoly of Republicans and Democrats on presidential politics. The name of the party and the term "populism" were coined by educated farmers (akin to the "Latin farmers" who had played a prominent role in the revolutionary events in Massachusetts in 1775–76); the founders of the party were mindful of the *pars popularis,* the Popular Party in the Roman Republic, which under the leadership of Tiberius and Caius Gracchus had been the archetypal agrarian reform movement in European history.[21]

In the vein of this tradition, American Populism was a powerful grassroots agrarian movement of protest against the growing price disparity between farm production and industrial goods that threatened the immiseration of farmers. The Populists, some of whom had split off from the Democratic Party, scorned both major parties as being dominated by the plutocratic interests of Northeast financial and industrial circles. They argued that the formal procedures of democracy existing in their time were inadequate, and that a more direct representation of the public interest was required. Their main focus was on economics, where they advocated the nationalization of railroads to drive down the cost of transporting their crops, federal loans to help keep excess crops off the market, government intervention in the financial sector to reduce interest rates, measures to curb the excessive profits of commercial middlemen, and a program of government-funded public works to reduce unemployment. Their major target was the monetary and financial system based on the gold standard (the "Cross of Gold," in the classic words of William Jennings Bryan).

The Populists also championed such issues as the graduated income tax, the filling of the Senate seats by direct elections instead of through state legislatures, grassroots self-organizing in the form of cooperatives, and the use of such tools of direct democracy as local initiatives and referenda. As acknowledged by Richard Hofstadter, one of populism's harshest critics, "populism was the first modern political movement of practical importance in the United States to insist that the federal government has some importance for the common weal; indeed, it was the first such movement to attack seriously the problems created by industrialism."[22] Hofstadter also noted that the Populist movement of the 1890s was merely "a heightened expression" of a sentiment that is "endemic in American political culture."[23] Although the Populists never won—and perhaps never could have won—the presidency, their advocacy had a progressive and long-lasting impact on the national agenda: Most of the Populist issues found their place in the progressive reformism of the twentieth century, from Theodore Roosevelt to the New Deal. Significant parts of their program were enacted over the following decades, including the direct election of senators, initiatives and referenda, recall of officials from office, taxation according to the size of income, parity prices, interstate commerce regulations, a federal farm credit system, postal savings banks, and government regulation of working conditions. Absent Populist influence, the American republic might not have become the worldwide standard-bearer of democracy and justice that it became in the twentieth century.

With such a cross-cutting agenda, the Populists defy classification according to the usual left-right scheme. While some of their demands may seem to coincide with those of the traditional political left, one cannot ignore their uneasiness with key elements of the modernization ethos of Western social reformism. They cherished the family farm as the most effective unit of production and culture, based on the values of mutual responsibility. They also discerned a looming threat to these organic patterns from the rise of modern financial and industrial institutions, of an impersonal bureaucratic state beyond the reach of citizens, and of an international system that tended to counterbalance or negate the democratic will of a national constituency. Accordingly, many of them viewed the progressive social policies advocated by liberals at the national level as yet another exercise in top-down manipulation and social engineering.[24] Although many features of the Populist movement were historically unique and peculiar to American culture, some of its basic elements are found in the modern histories of a number of different nations.

In Russian, the literal translation for "Populists" is *narodniki,* the name coined to describe the members of the underground opposition movement in Russia in the 1860s–1880s and their numerous sympathizers across the country.[25] This movement emerged on the wave of protest against the compromises and inconsistencies of the agricultural reforms of Alexander II, often called the Tsar-Liberator for his role in abolishing serfdom in 1861. In stark contrast to the American Populists, the *narodniki* movement consisted overwhelmingly of dispossessed intellectuals who roamed around the country for years in a desperate search for grassroots support among a peasantry they idealized and aspired to empower. The paramount concern of the Russian Populists was to preserve the peasant *mir,* the autonomous agrarian communes, with their egalitarianism and mutual aid, family networks, and unique ways of life, against the dehumanizing intrusion of bureaucratic governments and markets. With such a concern, the *narodniki* showed themselves to be the intellectual heirs of the Slavophile opposition of the 1840s. They blamed the Great Reforms of 1857–64 for their administrative imposition of "progress" on the countryside and for not protecting rural life against the incursions of greedy urbanites driven by commercial interests. They were particularly hostile to Alexander II's decision to emancipate the serfs as individuals, forced to redeem their plots of land from their past owners through payments in cash or labor. This compromise, the result of intricate bargaining among imperial bureaucrats and the landed gentry, was for the Populists the most infamous example of a top-down, inhuman "progressivism" that left the peasants more destitute than before and transformed most of them into rural or urban proletarians.

Along with their attempts to stir up a nationwide peasant insurrection that proved futile, the Populists resorted to terrorism, which culminated in the murder of Alexander II in March 1881. His son and heir, Alexander III, administered a brutal crackdown on the movement, although it managed to sustain itself by turning to local, small-scale educational and other activities. Its nationwide political organization was resurrected in December 1905 amid the turbulence of Russia's first democratic revolution, when the veterans of the movement founded the Party of Socialist Revolutionaries (SRs), whose radical faction staged high-profile killings of repressive tsarist officials, and whose moderate wing managed to secure representation in the Duma. Over time, the SR party grew more nationalist and successfully competed for support among radicalized layers of society against a new brand of top-down urban modernizers—the Marxists of the Russian Social Democratic Labor Party, which had already split into Bolsheviks and Mensheviks. These years witnessed the fulfillment of the early Populists' dream: The SRs acquired an enthusiastic mass following in the Russian countryside (while also solidifying their support among the urban intelligentsia).

Though it would be wrong to idealize the SRs, whose organization, like all other opposition parties at the time, was infiltrated and influenced in various ways by the police and intelligence services, their program did express the interests and moral beliefs of Russia's huge peasant majority. A hypothetical coalition government of the SRs with other socialist and progressive parties, including democratic elements among the Bolsheviks, may have offered Russia a path to a less traumatic and more organic transition to modernity, especially if the country had obtained a democratic government before its disastrously ill-conceived entry into World War I. By the summer of 1917, the SRs had emerged as the leading force in Russia's first republican government and the most popular party in the country. In November 1917, two weeks after the Bolshevik coup that toppled the SR-led Provisional Government, they garnered 40 percent of the national vote and more than half the seats in the first and last fully democratic elections in pre-Bolshevik Russia—the elections to the Constituent Assembly. They might well have become the ruling party of a democratic and moderately nationalist Russia, somewhat along the lines of the Kuomintang Party in China. In any event, Lenin's Bolsheviks exploited the split between the right and the left wings of the SR party to paralyze its resistance to the October coup and to destroy the Constituent Assembly. By the early 1920s, most SR leaders and activists were exiled or imprisoned, and the party itself was outlawed and ceased to exist.

POPULISM IN SOVIET POLITICAL CULTURE

Even though its organizational forms were brutally destroyed, the spirit and the ethic of Russian Populism never died, but quietly made their way into the

Communist Party, bypassing the rigid and self-confident elitism of Lenin, Stalin, and their cohorts, who viewed themselves as an anointed "vanguard force" of the backward masses. In the minds of yesterday's peasants now joining the Party through their service in the Red Army, the vision of an organic and harmonious community made up of autonomous self-regulating units continued to smolder under a thin veneer of Bolshevist indoctrination. With the advent of Nikita Khrushchev and his famous Thaw, this deeply hidden peasant spontaneity and sense of moral justice rose from the middle ranks of the party to its apex and helped to break the ice of Stalinism. The early years of Khrushchev's rule have often been described as the era of the "second emancipation" for the Russian peasantry. The universal elements of the populist ethos were echoed in Khrushchev's antibureaucratic rhetoric, his insistence that the CPSU must be "a party of *all* the people," and his blunt hostility to arcane diplomatic maneuvering. He irritated the establishment by setting up economic soviets *(soviety narodnogo khozyaistva)*, territorial self-management units that were intended to bring planning closer to the people and to counter the rigid bureaucratism of the party and sectoral planning bureaucracies. His concern over the underdog position of the peasantry and the urban-rural price disparity was an important factor behind the notorious price hike on foodstuffs in 1962, which set off riots of urban workers in Novocherkassk and became one of the key factors behind Khrushchev's demise in October 1964 by a nomenklatura yearning for "stability." Most of his innovations were soon dismantled by the coalition of urban bureaucratic interests that succeeded him and quickly reinstalled the rusty hierarchy of administrative command forged by Stalin's terror.

Over recent decades, "populism" has often been used quite indiscriminately in academic and journalistic contexts to describe all sorts of unconventional movements and policies, from those of Juan Perón in Argentina to Kim Dae-Jung in South Korea. The term often has a pejorative overtone, making it almost synonymous with demagoguery. Such an association has little to do with historical populism; in fact, as a generic notion, populism has indeed become a universal phenomenon and a powerful presence in modern politics at various times in different countries. Its diverse national incarnations share a number of common structural features, such as poignant memories of an organic agrarian lifestyle, retrospective utopias glorifying the justice and morality of family-based productive communities, mistrust of top-down social engineering by a bureaucratic or moneyed elite, and a teleological vision of a self-regulating polity based on direct participation by its members. The cultural and cognitive basis of this worldview, especially with regard to countries of the Third World, has engaged the interest of Western scholars, leading to the emergence of a formidable body of socioeconomic writings known as "moral economy" studies.[26]

While the history of the Russian Populists constitutes a prodigious amount of scholarly writing, the place and significance of populist sentiment in the social and political developments that led to the Soviet demise remain to be studied. Even though the limited available evidence about the decades of discontent among Soviet citizens has not been analyzed with proper methodological rigor, even a cursory comparison of that discontented citizenry with other politically motivated groups across time and space suggests that the overwhelming majority of mass-oriented opposition groups in the Gorbachev era carried generic traits of populism as a worldwide phenomenon with adjustments dictated by the specific context of Russian culture. Moreover, populist sentiment was perhaps the single common denominator that united phenomena as ideologically disparate as the ethnocratic nationalism of Pamyat' and the anarchic hostility to the state expressed by some radical groups in the democratic movement.

This should not be surprising, given the fact that the major social force of discontent over decades was the emerging middle class, which consisted to a large extent of first-generation urbanites.[27] These were people with conflicting identities, for whom the trauma inflicted by the violent collectivization and virtual disenfranchisement of the peasantry under Stalin was the central formative experience of their extended families. Like Khrushchev, most of them believed in the fundamental virtues of the Soviet system but often understood them in a radically different way—not according to official Leninism, but through the moralistic prism inherited from communal culture. One big difference between the Soviet official culture and that of the discontented first-generation urbanites was the latter's rejection of the fundamental Leninist dichotomy between ways and means: Although they were forced to pay lip service to this ideology, they were never able to accept the idea that a "temporary" injustice can serve as an indispensable tool for building a just society.

This simple idea, in its innumerable variations, served as a focal point for what became the first legal base of "semi-opposition" in Soviet society—the journal *Novy mir,* with its circle of widely acclaimed writers and columnists. Few would now dispute the fact that *Novy mir* under Aleksandr Tvardovsky (its editor-in-chief, 1950–54 and 1958–70), with its attacks on the bureaucracy, denunciations of Stalinism, and thinly veiled implications that the regime and society had gravely abused the peasantry, was an important precursor of perestroika. *Novy mir* was by far the most popular Soviet periodical among the '60s generation; for many Soviet readers, its muzzling by the authorities and Tvardovsky's resignation in 1970 signaled the definitive end of an epoch and the cultural triumph of neo-Stalinism.

It is important to note for the sake of our argument that the *Novy mir* circle was united more by its rebellious populistic spirit than by any identifiable ideological affiliation. This spirit was not the result of a clever marketing strategy designed to maximize the journal's audience; quite the contrary, it captured an inherent populist mentality for which the moral and cultural divisions of society carried more weight than differences along the conventional right-left spectrum. This feature of *Novy mir* was reflected in the subsequent careers of its authors. The intellectual offspring of the journal ranged from the spiritual leaders of the dissident movement, such as Aleksandr Solzhenitsyn, to the "village prose" writers who became a distinguished part of the Soviet literary establishment. In terms of their political philosophy, the authors who had started their careers at *Novy mir* varied from xenophobic nationalists, such as Vasily Belov, to left-liberal Westernizers and humanists of the Sakharov vintage, such as Yuri Burtin. Each of these authors had his or her own identifiable audience with its clear-cut ideological sympathies. Yet there was a core set of beliefs and sentiments that all these readers shared, notably a profound mistrust toward official politics and the actual, as opposed to the declared, intentions of the rulers. What divided this educated and critical part of the middle class was the specific diagnoses they offered for society's ills, diagnoses that, in their turn, implied widely different methods of treatment.

WHO WAS TO BLAME? THREE PERSPECTIVES FROM THE INSIDE

As we have seen, the clear-cut division between rulers and ruled was the key structural element of Soviet citizens' perception of their society. Insofar as the Soviet system of governance—at least in the post-Stalin era—was widely seen by Soviet people as a form of oligarchy in the basic classical meaning of the term, the negative sentiment against it, as well as the broad-based protest movement of the late 1980s that grew out of this sentiment, can be described as *prima facie* anti-oligarchical. This label, in our view, is valid for all currents of the movement and reflects its fundamental, generic features better than any of the other labels ("anticommunist," "reformative," "Westernizing," and so forth) considered above. But who were the oligarchs in such a highly complex and modern society as the Soviet Union? Opposition intellectuals advanced three distinctive theories, outlined below, which roughly correspond with and help shed light on the subsequent evolution of the three major currents of rebellion against the Soviet system. Representatives of these currents identified themselves respectively as the democrats, the freemarketeers, and the national-patriots.

1. *The Nomenklatura Theory.* Of unmistakably Marxist origin, this theory postulated that Soviet society was ruled by a new exploitative class of party and state nomenklatura. The theory, in its general form, originated from Milovan Djilas's work *The New Class,* which in turn was inspired by the anti-Stalinist treatises of Lev Trotsky.[28] The theory was applied to late Soviet society with the implacable rigor of Marxist sociology by Mikhail Voslensky, a nomenklatura insider who was stripped of Soviet citizenship in 1977 and became a West German Social Democrat.[29] For discontented Soviet citizens, the major advantage of this theory was its cognitive consistency with the Holy Writ of official doctrine: It exposed the duplicity of the actual Soviet system and provided a scientific justification for hating the ruling class without casting doubt on Marxist ideological fundamentals such as economic determinism, the overarching impact of

property relations on the development of society, and the notion of history's linear progress. Intellectuals' attraction to the nomenklatura theory suggested the persistence of an underlying teleological vision of an alternative, just, and classless society. Yet the tone of moral indignation attested to the theory's populist provenance: In Djilas's and Voslensky's writings, the nomenklatura class was portrayed as more vicious and reactionary than that of Western capitalists because it had somehow conspired to conceal from the general public its true interests and intentions in exploiting society. It was not so much the exploitation per se, but the double-talk and the enormous power of deception that allegedly made the nomenklatura the consummate evil of the modern world. In pursuing this line of reasoning, Voslensky charged the demoralized Soviet gerontocrats of the Brezhnev era with an ill-concealed ambition for global hegemony. Thus leftist exponents of the nomenklatura theory found themselves in certain respects allied, paradoxically enough, with the most resolute of the Western Cold Warriors.

All this explains why the nomenklatura theory found enthusiastic support among the democrats and Westernizers of the Gorbachev era, for example in Sakharov's circles. To be precise, its analysis of divisions in Soviet society was not rigidly bound to the Marxist paradigm, just as Marxism has no intellectual patent on the notion of classes. The nomenklatura theory was espoused by a wide variety of critics of the Soviet system, most of whom did not subscribe to the sociological orthodoxy of Trotsky, Djilas, or Voslensky. Removing the nomenklatura from power was a rallying cry for most of the opposition groups that coalesced both outside and inside the CPSU in 1988–90. A telling, although by no means exceptional, example of this radical-democratic populism can be found in the documents of the Popular Front in the city of Penza: "Elimination of the nomenklatura as a class through election of economic managers and other leaders is the only way to get out of an acute crisis comparable to that of 1917."[30]

Indeed, the nomenklatura analysis was a powerful analytical tool regarding Soviet society, and the present work is in tune with some elements of the approach (although we tend to see the nomenklatura as both a sociological and a cultural entity). However, the adherents of the nomenklatura theory had little if any clarity about what social structure would replace the nomenklatura system, whether there was any single antagonistic class or alliance of classes that would be able to unseat the nomenklatura, and how this sociopolitical change was to occur. Nor did they pay enough attention to the growing rifts within the nomenklatura itself—between the holders of political and of economic power; between "party soldiers" and "party merchants"; between company managers and bureaucratic planners; among production executives, traders, and financiers; between all these and labor union officials; and so forth. Many democrats tended to seek the solution along purely political lines, arguing what has turned out to be the rather simplistic view that democratic elections and stripping the CPSU of its political power would simultaneously deprive the nomenklatura of all other kinds of power. This exclusive focus on politics seemed dubious to other critics of the system, and this dissatisfaction gave rise to alternative theories and recipes for change.

2. *Theory of the Administrative Command System.* This perspective, which assumed multiple forms and variations, was given its clearest shape in 1987 by Gavriil Popov, an establishment academic and very moderate reformer from Gorbachev's inner circle, who put the term "administrative command system" into colloquial use.[31] Put simply, the approach viewed the government-party bureaucracy as the ruler of the country and thus solely responsible for stifling the freedom and initiative of firms, local governments, and rank-and-file citizens. Accordingly, if the proponents of the nomenklatura theory advocated giving more power to democratically elected governmental bodies, the antibureaucratic approach implied the need to reduce the scope of all government administration, whether democratic or not. In retrospect, it seems quite natural that this view inspired the future freemarketeers, led by Gaidar, Anatoly Chubais, and Popov himself, whose purposes and policies were bound to diverge quite radically from those of the anti-nomenklatura democrats.

However, if the trade-offs between increasing the power of a democratic government and decreasing the scope of government as such—or, more broadly, between order, justice, and freedom—may be quite obvious for someone living in a modern capitalist society, it was anything but obvious for Soviet intellectuals and everyday citizens. Indeed, the foes of the nomenklatura and the foes of bureaucracy saw almost no discrepancies between their views until shock therapy began, but their lack of experience with markets and democracy was only part of the reason. What united them was an influential stream of Russian Populist thought that aspired to a classless *and* a stateless society, and originated in the writings of Mikhail Bakunin, the founding father of Russian anarchism.

While some may consider Bakunin's teachings as belonging to the fringe of political thought, his writings are actually much closer to the mainstream of Russian philosophy and social theory than they may seem.[32] His point of convergence with Slavophiles and most of the *narodniki* was in the glorification of the Russian peasant commune as a uniquely organic social body built on mutual aid and trust. It was the communal experience that, in the view of these thinkers, might have enabled Russia to transcend the class and administrative-hierarchical divisions between rulers and ruled that ran through Western history and to skip the oppressive and dehumanizing capitalist "stage" of modernization's allegedly linear development, thereby avoiding the negative effects of both government bureaucracies and private corporations on the creative development of individuals. Most of these writers would have agreed that the structure of modern mass societies made the highest ideals of democracy and justice unattainable in practice. Hence, in the robust tradition of the Russian intelligentsia, most of them came down in favor of the ideals and contemplated in various ways the dismantling of the bureaucratic monolith of the Russian state into local, self-regulated social and economic entities approximating, to the extent possible, the communal states of medieval Russia (as well as those of more distant times and places).

Because the writings of Bakunin, fellow anarchist Prince Pyotr Kropotkin, and their followers were not publishable under CPSU rule, rank-and-file critics of the system usually had no first-hand knowledge of their ideas. However, their views were transmitted and interpreted with varying degrees of accuracy by intellectual leaders of the opposition, and they struck a chord with persistent elements of political culture. The daily experience of ordinary citizens, as elsewhere in the world, fueled animosity toward bureaucracy of all sorts, and this sentiment was bound to influence the popular expectations aroused by perestroika. As was the case with the nomenklatura, the differences between the upper and lower echelons, between federal and regional levels of bureaucracy, and among agencies supervising the production and distribution of public and private goods were blurred.[33]

Given the cultural legacy of populist hostility to the state, it should not be surprising that the liberal and the anarchic elements of the antibureaucratic tendency went hand in hand. In fact, in this part of the opposition, the dominant worldview was libertarian rather than liberal in the usual Western sense. The social base of the future freemarketeers within the populist anti-oligarchical movement was more receptive to the metaphysical speculations about absolute freedom, exemplified by Friedrich von Hayek and Robert Nozick, than to the disciplinary rigor and circumspection of regular free-market economists. At the early stage of the movement, the anarchic element was fairly influential, while advocacy of free-market capitalism was barely visible at all. The Commune Club, later transformed into the Confederation of Anarcho-Syndicalists, was among the most visible of opposition groups from 1987 to 1989. In 1989–90, when the transition to the market became a major issue, the Confederation fragmented and gradually disappeared, with some of its activists joining the anti-nomenklatura forces in denouncing the rigged rules of the market transition, while others took a more positive view of the government's retreat from the economy.[34]

3. *The Sect Theory.* The third explanation of the rift between rulers and ruled, in terms congenial to most self-described national-patriots (national-conservatives), was presented in its most comprehensive form by Igor Shafarevich, a famous mathematician and dissident who had been a fearless human rights campaigner alongside Andrei Sakharov during the 1970s.[35] Yet the views forcefully expounded by Shafarevich and his followers, even though they shared a common cognitive basis with populist culture, turned out to be so disturbing for most other opponents of the Soviet system that Shafarevich soon found himself separated from the rest of the movement by a kind of intellectual barbed wire.

The starting point for Shafarevich was his visceral abhorrence not only of socialism and Marxism, but of any kind of social revolution. His reflections on the Russian revolutionary experience in the twentieth century have much in common with the passionate conservatism of Edmund Burke. Accordingly, his assault on modernity goes as far back as the French Revolution. However, the immediate source of his perspective on this event was not Burke, but the French historian Augustin Cochin (1876–1916), who introduced the notion of *"le petit peuple"* or "sect" as a synonym for the *"Nation Jacobine,"* a cultural community within the French nation whose value system and ideals, in his opinion, radically diverged from those of the majority of Frenchmen.[36] In Shafarevich's interpretation of Cochin, the "sect," using propaganda to manipulate public opinion, borrows foreign social models and tries to impose them in a uniform and supposedly rational way on the majority of the nation, thus destroying society's uniqueness and complexity. In Russia "the sect" designated by Shafarevich as the "Russophobes" is a foreign body in the Russian nation, pursuing a destructive critique of the historical foundations of society. In October 1917, the "sect" emerged, according to Shafarevich, as the rulers of Soviet Russia.

But who made up "the sect" and where did they come from? For Cochin, they were an ideological bloc that had formed around the late–eighteenth century philosophical and political clubs called the *sociétés de pensée,* which he studied at length. But on this question, Shafarevich turned uncharacteristically vague. In some instances he put the blame for the Bolshevik experiment on the turn-of-the-century cosmopolitan and Western-oriented intelligentsia, infatuated as it was with Marxist ideology and social engineering. Elsewhere, he viewed with alarm what he saw as the hyperactivity of ethnic minorities in the 1917 Revolution. In several cases, he pointed in no uncertain terms to the Jews, and even indulged in numerical calculations of the proportion of Jewish membership in revolutionary parties. To the detriment of his own case, he found a "solid majority" of Jews only in the leadership of the Socialist Revolutionary Party.[37] This discovery was quite ironic, for, as we have seen, the SRs were the most Russophile party in the revolutionary camp—they won electoral support from the majority of illiterate peasants and were, after all, the big loser in the October 1917 revolution. Yet Shafarevich, apparently not discouraged by this inconsistency, extended his search for a special role of the Jews, and ethnic minorities more generally, into the period of Soviet decline. In his own intellectual and dissident environment, he found an overblown attention to the problems of minorities, such as the right to emigrate, and more concern "for the fate of the Crimean Tatars than for the fate of the Ukrainians, more for the Ukrainians than for the Russians."[38]

Shafarevich's writings deserve serious attention as the most thorough exposition of mainstream national-conservative ideology as it has survived, with minor adjustments, until the present day.[39] Taken analytically, they contain two distinct claims, one cultural and one ethnic. Shafarevich provided a deeper insight than other authors into one of the flaws of the Soviet system by identifying the cultural gulf that did indeed separate the founders and rulers of the Bolshevik state from most of their subjects. Anyone who had been exposed to official Soviet pronouncements could clearly see that the language of CPSU propaganda required a special ability to read between the lines to find the real meaning of the words. However, the cultural rift between the elite and the masses did not originate with the Communists, but had been a persistent fixture of Russian national consciousness since at least Peter the Great. Yet it is true that the rift was more acutely felt under the Bolsheviks, for whom daily communication with the public was an essential tool of legitimation and governance. The arrogant elitism of Lenin and his cohorts, which became the hallmark of Communist rule, deemed that censorship, lies, threats, and the manipulation of conscience were appropriate and necessary means for transforming a backward populace into exemplary builders of a modern and rational society.

As we will see, the ruling establishment carried this vanguard mentality and contempt for the average person without much alteration into the post-1991 democratic-capitalist age. It was also possible to argue that the kernel of this arrogance was contained in the rationalist outlook of the Western-oriented intellectuals, in their cult of modernization and their hypercritical attitude toward the rest of the population, regardless of whether they belonged to the revolutionary or the conservative camp.[40] (At times, this hypercriticism has damaged Russia in the eyes of the world, and continues to do so by assisting those foreign groups for whom a negative image of Russia and its people may suit some economic or geopolitical purpose.)

However, Shafarevich might have gained a more profound insight into the nature of these problems if he had given impartial consideration to the alternative hypothesis—namely, that this pessimistic attitude toward the Russian people originated not from ethnically alien sources or from the margins of society but, rather, from the depths of the national identity itself. It is hard to find a leading Russian writer among both Westernizers and those critical of the West who did not reserve some bitter words for the motherland. "What a devil's idea it was for me to be born in Russia, having some brain and talent!" exclaimed none other than Aleksandr Pushkin in one of his letters. "The unwashed . . . land of slaves, the land of masters," wrote Mikhail Lermontov in a farewell poem before leaving the Russian heartland for the Caucasus. Applying Shafarevich's test to Russian literature and philosophy, one would have to describe many of its masterpieces as "Russophobic," or inspired by the sinister "sect."

This hypothesis about national pessimism, whether founded or not, finds solid support in present-day public opinion polls. As for the role of the intelligentsia and ethnic minorities in the great upheavals of the early twentieth century, it was significant. But both groups were underprivileged and, in the case of the non-Russians, severely harassed in prerevolutionary Russia; it was only natural for them to defend their interests by seeking political representation. In sum, while Shafarevich's insightful remarks on the cultural alienation of the establishment from the people were on target, they were discredited by his misguided attribution of responsibility for Russians' own assessments of their country's gloomy past and present to some evil outside conspiracy. The relentless pursuit of this theme by Shafarevich and his followers drove them into the blind alley of ethnic and cultural intolerance, relegating the national-patriotic brand of populism to a marginal role in the universalistic mainstream of Russian political culture.

The three approaches outlined above had fairly distinct pedigrees and led to different practical conclusions; however, in the political context of 1988–91, they were by no means incompatible. Indeed, none of the major authors and politicians, from Sakharov and Solzhenitsyn to Yeltsin and Communist leader Gennadi Zyuganov, fits neatly into any one category, and over the past decade most political initiatives of any importance have emerged from the interstices of these outlooks. The resulting ideological hybrids became possible not least because the populist wave of the 1980s was not inspired by a specific ideology or set of political goals, but because it was chiefly a sociopolitical and cultural revolt against the duplicity, incompetence, and caste-like exclusivity of the rulers. The crisis of confidence between the highly organized "top" and the disorganized "bottom" of society, each of which had lost contact with the other, was acute. As Andropov bravely admitted during his brief reign, "We (the elite) have not yet studied properly the society in which we live and work. . . . Therefore, we are forced to act . . . in a quite irrational manner of trial and error."[41] Thus distrust of government permeated the daily life of Soviet citizens and was much more tangible than the abstract political notions of right and left. In the colloquial language of the 1980s, all those who were against the existing elite qualified as "the left," regardless of whether their target was the privileges of the nomenklatura or the bureaucratic abuses practiced by the government.

In this context, two alternative political strategies could be pursued. If genuine democratic reforms were the main goals, then a radical revamping of state institutions was required to assert the public interest. If, however, the prime aim was the abrupt dismantling of the state, its property would have to be given mostly to the existing elite, and social differentiation would sharpen. This dilemma meant that reformers were compelled, sooner or later, to choose their strategic allies either from within the bureaucracy or from within the nomenklatura. Unfortunately, the imminence and tremendous significance of this choice escaped the public's notice. No wonder the coalition that brought Boris Yeltsin to power and helped him destroy the Soviet state included anti-nomenklatura democrats along with antibureaucratic liberals and anarchists (who later ripened into radical freemarketeers).

THE MAFIYA: A TRADITION OF LIBERTARIAN ANARCHISM IN RUSSIA'S CULTURAL HISTORY

So far we have made little mention of yet another powerful and pervasive force in late Soviet society and politics—the one widely known as the Mafiya. It is scarcely mentioned in most textbooks and scholarly research, its nature and activities are difficult to document, and rather few efforts have been made so far to define and explain this increasingly influential presence in Russia and many other contemporary societies. And yet, the explosive global spread of the Soviet-born Mafiya over the years of so-called reforms suggests that it was a crucial player in the historical drama referred to as the collapse of communism.

Although a lengthy analysis of this subject is beyond the scope of the present work, a brief discussion of it is important because the Mafiya played a crucial role not just in dooming the USSR, but also in determining the direction taken by Yeltsin's government in 1991–92.[42] In everyday speech, "Mafia" designates clandestine networks that unite government officials with organized crime. Yet "Mafia" is neither a legal notion nor the equivalent of organized crime; indeed, the Soviet and Russian *Mafiya* has had its own aristocracy that performs important regulatory functions but in many cases does not participate in criminal actions and may not even have any knowledge of them. Nor is "Mafia" an economic term, synonymous with the black market, an institution which involves many disconnected individuals and companies acting on their own; although the black market often intersects with the Mafia, it is not a part of it. Considering the origin of the word from the Italian *famiglia* (family), it is more precise to define the Mafia as a form of social bond, an institution with its own unique organization and culture.

In this context, the family is implicitly counterposed to the state, just as an organic cell of society is contrasted with a mechanical construction dealing with atomized and uniform individuals, a *Gemeinschaft* with a *Gesellschaft.* In modern Italy, the rapid industrial development of the north dragged the "backward" south behind it; only later did the northerners discover that the Mafia as a type of social organization and form of protest had negated many of the effects of the change they had tried to impose from the top down. In other countries, the Mafia also grew in response to an elitist "imposition" of so-called progress accompanied by the dissolution of traditional communities. Thus the Mafia has often been a vehicle for the underground survival of direct personal relations and familial networks in the face of impersonal and merciless rules that are seen as unjust and illegitimate. Intellectually purchased as such, this type of social organization has a distant historical similarity to the populist eruptions described above, although it has evolved in a quite different direction and its ultimate purposes have in most cases become irreconcilably antagonistic to those of grassroots reformers. While the populists usually wanted to transform the state by making it more accessible and responsive, one of the results of Mafia operations was to make the state irrelevant and, in the final analysis, to hijack its basic functions.

It is sometimes argued that the Russian *Mafiya* was an unwanted offspring of the Communist regime. Nothing could be farther from the truth. Although various starting points could be chosen, perhaps the most appropriate is the massive increase in the convict population of the Russian Empire that followed Alexander II's emancipation of the peasantry—a comprehensive attempt to stimulate "industrial revolution" by forcing peasants into the urban labor market.

With the stroke of a pen, the Emperor's Manifesto of February 19, 1861, made most of yesterday's serfs into a huge mass of rural proletarians who had little or no means of buying land from their erstwhile owners. A sizeable number of these people had to leave the countryside for the cities, where they often ended up jobless and turned to crime, as large-scale industry and industrial infrastructure were still in their infancy. The subsequent erosion of the peasant commune was completed by Interior Minister Pyotr Stolypin's reforms of 1907–11, which set off another skyrocketing wave of crime.

The inmates of Russian prisons and Siberian penal colonies shared in large measure a set of attitudes toward the status quo. Their basic view was that the social system had reneged on its centuries-old obligation to provide subsistence and paternalistic care to the destitute, and thus had stripped itself of its basic legitimacy. For these people, the state and its laws had therefore become a totally external and hostile element of nature, both incomprehensible and immoral— not unlike the long and harsh Siberian winter that engulfed them. The only way to make it through the winter was to band together in a brotherhood of the wretched, to create a state within a state, with its own language, hierarchy, pageantry, and unwritten laws; this inmate community was called *blatnoy mir* — "Thieves' world."[43]

In the godforsaken universe of Siberian prisoners, all wealth was the result of someone's looting someone else; to steal it back again was a righteous way to survive in an unjust life. Among the convicts of the tsarist era, political prisoners or exiles (like Lenin and his comrades) were a tiny minority, and they were inevitably exposed to the cultural diffusion of *blat*. It was most probably this culture, rather than Proudhon's abstract writings on the topic, that suggested to them the famous slogan, "Expropriate the expropriators!" While Lenin himself did not have to wonder where his next meal was coming from, among the rank-and-file "professional revolutionaries" the boundary between political theorizing and violent methods of procurement was not that clear.[44] For its part, the underworld "aristocracy" was often literate enough to debate Marx, although most of its members probably preferred the teachings of Bakunin and Kropotkin. In Russia, the granting of a comprehensive amnesty had historically become the hallmark of a genuine change of regime, thus organized crime was likely to be particularly interested in the overthrow of the monarchy, although no reliable documentary records of financial support for the Bolsheviks from current or former fellow convicts have surfaced so far. However, it is well known that a number of ex-convicts embarked on impressive careers in Soviet institutions, including the army and especially the secret police, at the dawn of the bright new era; their expertise was used in such Stalinist-era ventures as the manufacturing of counterfeit foreign currencies.[45]

The history of the Mafiya's rise in Soviet times remains to be written. Clearly, though, the relationship between the authorities and the criminal underworld was ambiguous. Stalin's mad rush to industrialize required the use of convict labor, so the population of penal colonies steadily grew. At the same time, the Bolshevik elite had reasons to expect gratitude from the criminal underworld, primarily in the form of unconditional loyalty to the status quo, plus assistance in exposing and suppressing political dissent among the educated strata. Indeed, many criminals cooperated with the "organs" of repression and were rewarded with privileged positions and perquisites in the convict communities. However, as the Soviet order naturally fell short of what the criminal world viewed as its anarchical or communitarian promises, and even imposed additional regulations and greater disparities in wealth, cooperation with the authorities came to be seen as a shameful betrayal. If an informant was exposed while in prison, he or she was stigmatized as a *suka* (bitch) and excluded from the criminal community. A convict who had been anointed as a "thief-in-law"—the Russian equivalent of a Mafia don or *capo*—in recognition of his fearless defiance of the system, and had been awarded a "pension" by the other criminals, always risked the loss of these privileges (and even murder) if he was judged guilty of informing.[46]

However, most of the Mafiya's relationships with the authorities evolved in the opposite direction. The world of thieves often managed to gain indirect access through corrupt officials to government institutions concerned with resources, finance, and trade.[47] The Mafiya reached the pinnacle of its influence in the late Brezhnev era, when the leadership vacuum in the Kremlin created a propitious climate for it to flourish. Earlier, the similar vacuums created by the death of Stalin and the departure of Khrushchev suggested to Russians acquainted with their history that the current stage of the historical cycle unavoidably pointed toward anarchy, and the Mafiya was the most organized expression of the anarchic-libertarian spirit in Russian history. Thus, gradually, some segments of society became more open to it as an inevitable evil. In addition, the ethic of *blat* struck a chord with the disillusioned generation of the 1970s, which treated official ideology as an empty shell but was equally skeptical about the chance to reform the system in a rational and humanistic way—after all, that had been tried in vain by the "people of the '60s." The more self-conscious part of this new generation admired itself as being more radical than its predecessors because instead of tinkering with an unreformable state, they were outsmarting or ignoring it. This liberal-anarchist mindset welcomed the Mafiya code of behavior. Later, in the early 1990s, this generational and cultural group would provide strong and decisive support for radical market reforms and shock therapy.

In the 1970s, the shadowy Mafiya kingpins sought to secure indirect political representation for their interests and recognition as a legitimate force in society. Their success was reflected in the extensive penetration of convict jargon into the daily argot of educated society. In the process, some terms changed their meaning—*blat,* for example, no longer referred to convict networks but, rather, to lucrative connections or bureaucratic graft. The Mafiya overtures to the ruling establishment were duly appreciated, especially in the Interior Ministry (MVD): Soviet law enforcement officials claimed that cooperating with organized crime and upholding the underground authority of established thieves-in-law would help reduce random youth crime because expert criminals had better information and stronger deterrence methods for policing their younger cohorts than did the government. This innovative theory fueled the rapid interpenetration of police units and organized crime during the tenure of Brezhnev's favorite, Nikolai Shchelokov, as minister of the interior.[48] These ideas remained in vogue until the onset of the "Great Criminal Revolution" (Stanislav Govorukhin's phrase) of the shock-therapy era, whose revolutionaries brazenly brushed aside the allegedly unshakable authority of the senior gangsters and made commonplace many atrocities that underworld veterans characterized as senseless and outrageous. Only then was the peculiar theory of an "elite settlement" or top-level deal between the government and the Mafiya apparently discarded.[49]

The chief joint venture run by the Mafiya and corrupt Soviet bureaucrats was the shadow economy. Because most economic issues belong to chapter 5, we will merely note here that increasing commodity shortages—stemming in part from the inefficiency of Soviet planning and in part from manipulation by special interests in the trade sector—fragmented the national economy into a multitude of specialized illegal markets in which the procurement of each specific commodity or service required a separate *blat* relationship with the authorities or the criminals. This system permitted the charging of high monopolistic prices for scarce goods. But it also required political stability in the country, because any major reshuffling of official personnel in the administrative chain of command would upset the intimate relationships between the bureaucracy and the Mafiya, and make all the arrangements subject to renegotiation on a case-by-case basis.

However, in the late 1970s this stability became increasingly shakier, because the interests of the Mafiya and its allies among the acquisitive junior layers of the establishment were frequently at odds with the strategic concerns of Brezhnev's potential successors. We will not rehearse the Byzantine maneuvers of the Kremlin gerontocracy in the twilight of the Brezhnev era, extensive analysis of which has already been conducted by historians of this period.[50] Suffice it to say that these years witnessed the coalescence of a powerful political bloc consisting of leaders of the security services and the military command, the agrarian reformers, and ideological conservatives alarmed by the Soviet decline and the alienation of the citizenry. Many of them tended to view the Mafiya-bureaucracy alliance as a major source of societal ills. The point man of this soon-to-be ruling coalition was Yuri Andropov, KGB chairman (1967–82) and Brezhnev's successor as the CPSU's general secretary on November 13, 1982.

THE MAFIYA THREAT AND THE ANDROPOV GAMBLE: A MISSED CHANCE FOR THE KREMLIN AND THE POPULISTS

The significance of Andropov's brief tenure for the initial design of perestroika and the formation of the Gorbachev team has been illustrated by a broad range of insiders, including Gorbachev himself.[51] What concerns us here, however, is one of Andropov's endeavors that regrettably was *not* carried out by his successors —namely, his attempts to initiate a genuine war against corruption and organized crime. Andropov's strong determination to curb the Mafiya's efforts to dictate the rules of the game to the Soviet establishment stands in striking contrast to the purely rhetorical nature of both Gorbachev's and Yeltsin's anticorruption campaigns. Nowadays, when Russian organized crime has become a global security concern, one can safely predict that the legacy of Andropov, whose record as an uncompromising Cold Warrior evoked no appreciation in the West, is likely to come under more dispassionate scrutiny by both Russian and Western historians.

Andropov's hostility to the Mafiya stemmed not only from ideological and economic concerns, it also contained a thinly veiled political overture to society at large. Andropov's unparalleled intelligence resources provided him with ample evidence about the scale and dangerous dynamics of grassroots discontent. As we have seen, much of this discontent was unfocused and aimed at a whole range of targets. But the Mafiya and its nomenklatura clients were blamed almost unanimously by society for shortages, corruption, rampant social inequalities, and the chaotic distribution of much-needed goods. The outrage was especially vocal among the intelligentsia and the middle class in general, which faced a painful choice between becoming customers of the Mafiya-dominated market to meet their urgent needs and preserving their rigidly defined social and cultural identities as standard bearers of higher moral principles.

The mobilization of support among members of these groups was strategically important for Andropov and his associates, who were banking on the hard-sciences and engineering intelligentsia for technological breakthroughs to rival the West in the accelerating arms race. Andropov was apparently looking for ways to channel the vague anti-oligarchical sentiment into an attack on the Mafiya and evidently saw no risk that such a campaign might turn into a political insurgency. As potential leaders of such a campaign, the dissidents had been imprisoned or exiled and in any case seemed to be completely irrelevant to the down-to-earth materialism of the younger generation of urbanites fascinated with the cynical attitudes of America's young urban professionals. Thus, Andropov's anti-Mafiya campaign was a unique chance to forge an alliance between the top national leadership and the most active discontented citizens against a common foe. However, Andropov realized that he could not win credibility unless the Mafiya's channels of influence to the top of the ruling establishment were promptly and publicly exposed and shut down.[52]

The first shots in the campaign were fired while Brezhnev was still alive. January 1982 was marked by the arrest of a prominent jewelry smuggler directly linked to Galina Brezhneva, the daughter of the general secretary, who was notorious for her conspicuously affluent and depraved lifestyle. (Brezhneva had been smuggling diamonds out of the country on such a scale as to threaten the world diamond cartel arrangements presided over by DeBeers Consolidated Mines.) The detention of her associate was followed by the mysterious suicide of Semyon Tsvigun, Brezhnev's man at the KGB, who had sabotaged Andropov's investigatory activities; within several days, Brezhneva herself was summoned to KGB headquarters. Although the limits of political correctness ruled out open media coverage of the case, leaks were spread rapidly by informal channels. Those leaks helped boost Andropov's stature both within and outside the establishment and probably played a crucial role in his informal recognition as the heir apparent, a status that was seemingly confirmed at the CPSU Central Committee Plenum in May 1982.[53] The case of Brezhneva and her companions was quietly laid to rest—but the Mafiya campaign was not. Thus in October 1982, Moscow was aroused by the arrest of several top managers of the upscale Yeliseevski municipal food store, a front for Mafiya dealings; its chief manager received a death sentence.

Some Russian and Western analysts, including Peter Schweizer, are inclined to doubt whether Brezhnev's death on November 10, 1982, occurred from natural causes, although such speculation is hard to substantiate.[54] Whatever the case, Andropov's ascent to power was immediately followed by the ouster and arrest of Interior Minister Shchelokov. Shchelokov later committed suicide, while his deputy (and Brezhnev's son-in-law) Yuri Churbanov, who was reportedly a friend of the highly connected Mafiya kingpin Vyacheslav Ivankov, was tried and convicted for corruption.[55] This was the denouement of the decades-long turf war between Soviet police and intelligence services, in which Andropov's KGB prevailed with the support of Dmitri Ustinov's Defense Ministry. The new head of the MVD, lifelong KGB careerist Vitaly Fedorchuk, subjected the MVD to a drastic personnel purge. In a Soviet-style demonstration of their resolve to revive the declining work ethic, Andropov and Fedorchuk also staged a street operation to detain truant government employees in December 1982. Meanwhile, the Moscow trade Mafiya was also hit hard: Investigations in the case of the Yeliseevski gourmet store exposed the misdeeds of Nikolai Tregubov, Moscow's top retail administrator and a close ally of the Moscow city party boss, Viktor Grishin. In 1983, the Moscow retail store bureaucracy lost dozens of officials to arrests and suicides.[56]

However, the effects of this campaign on public opinion were bound to remain limited, because the media censorship so deeply entrenched in Soviet political culture made open and direct communication between the leaders and the discontented masses on such inflammatory issues virtually impossible. Andropov himself, an experienced dissident-hunter, probably felt that full glasnost' on the high-level corruption in Moscow would breed destabilization and trouble.[57]

Yet he desperately needed a high-profile case to give him political traction. He wanted this campaign to create new popular heroes for the new Andropov era—heroes sufficiently distant from the establishment to project credibility, and yet loyal enough to steer public discontent and desire for change in the proper direction by serving as mediators between the populist mass and the Kremlin. It was probably for this purpose that the Andropov team picked Tel'man Gdlyan, a modest, forty-two-year-old Armenian-born prosecutor, and chose the strategically important Soviet republic of Uzbekistan as a proving ground for this new and risky stage of the struggle against the Mafiya. Soon the Uzbek affair turned out to be the most fateful battle of the entire campaign, and its reckless handling doomed Andropov's strategy.

The "Uzbek case," which quickly became intertwined with and absorbed into the "Gdlyan case," is replete with contradictory evidence. Most available sources can be traced back to participants in the scandal and therefore have limited credibility.[58] What follows is an outline of what has become widely known. The arrests of corrupt officials in Uzbekistan, spearheaded by the Uzbek branch of the KGB, started in February 1983 with a probe of the republican interior ministry's department for combating theft of state property; by the end of the year, the interior minister had resigned in disgrace. The subsequent wave of indictments and exposures culminated with the apparent suicide of the Uzbek party boss and prominent CPSU Central Committee member, Sharaf Rashidov, on October 31, 1983, although the exact connection between his death and Gdlyan's mission has not been clearly established. Already after Andropov's death, the Uzbek Communist leadership had undergone a comprehensive reshuffling in June 1984 under the supervision of a tough enforcer sent from Moscow, Yegor Ligachev. Yet only in August 1984 was the first prominent member of the Uzbek party nomenklatura arrested on corruption charges—first secretary of the Bukhara regional party committee, A. Karimov. As correctly noted by Gdlyan himself, who takes much credit for this investigation, "This arrest set a very important precedent—this was the first indictment in decades of such a high-ranking party official."[59] Karimov's confiscated assets amounted to six million rubles, mostly in gold coins, the equivalent of $10 million at the official rate of exchange, or about $2–3 million at the black market rate.[60]

It seems quite plausible that Andropov and his faction deliberately limited the anticorruption campaign among high-level party officials to targets in far-off republics and jailed them only after they had been forced out of their posts. Perhaps this restriction was a temporary tactical ploy not to upset the overall fragile equilibrium that rested on the special privileges and immunity of the party elite. But Gdlyan and his associates, endowed with semiformal extraordinary powers by the KGB, conceived their task more broadly. As the funerals of Andropov and his immediate successor Konstantin Chernenko and the emergence of new figures at the top made the situation in Moscow increasingly unpredictable, they gradually began to act as independent figures.

Possessing a considerable gift for passionate stump speeches, Gdlyan knew how to navigate carefully in the prevailing climate of suspicion and mistrust between various groups in Soviet society—or at least he thought he did. He skillfully sought publicity and often proved more anxious to target a prominent Uzbek affiliate of the nomenklatura than to corroborate his case with convincing evidence. It must be said in his defense that his investigations inevitably required more intricate information than any one team could assemble. The Mafiya and the party bosses were far from identical; despite their symbiosis, both groups were fragmented into clans that competed for wealth and influence. The evidence needed to convict some thugs could often be obtained only by cooperating with even more malign characters. Gdlyan, who began to feel disoriented by the extreme complexity of the groups he was investigating, probably did abuse some of his suspects to extort confessions, as they later complained. In other cases, he fell prey to the convenient black-and-white distinctions increasingly dominant in the public consciousness that simplistically equated the conservative nomenklatura with the Mafiya. Like many populists, Gdlyan missed the point that some true believers in the system could be uncompromising enemies of corruption, while some of the liberal reformers could be soft on the Mafiya or even lobby for its interests.

The sunset of Gdlyan's investigative career came in 1988, when he publicly accused several high-ranking Party members—Ligachev among them—of being the godfathers of the Uzbek Mafiya. Given Ligachev's credentials as a conservative puritan and a fervent believer in the socialist moral code, the accusation struck the informed public as implausible. A special Party commission chaired by the democrat and erstwhile dissident Roy Medvedev essentially repudiated Gdlyan's allegations, while bringing to light some of his prosecutorial misconduct. Gdlyan's blunders severely undermined the entire anti-Mafiya cause and paved the way for a subsequent backlash: Some cases were reopened and the verdicts overturned, while former prisoners and suspects in the crackdown were honored as national heroes in Uzbekistan. Later, during the shock-therapy era, some Russian media portrayed the anticorruption drive of the 1980s as the last attempt of the "totalitarian communist state" to repress the acquisitive instinct allegedly inherent in human nature.

Yet even before Gdlyan's missteps were revealed, the Uzbek case had caused second thoughts among the Soviet leadership and was removed from the agenda for much more serious reasons. The Andropov design, it was realized, had been flawed from the outset—it had neglected the vast national and cultural differences among the Soviet republics. Among these, Uzbekistan was a thoroughly traditional, paternalistic society, as ill-suited for a zealous application of an alien legalistic framework as Russia was for shock therapy, or as America would have been for central planning. Thus Gdlyan and his team unavoidably careened into an all-out war against traditional ways of life that centered on clan relationships and personal connections outside the informal networks of republican party organizations—a fact that the top CPSU officials either failed to factor into the Andropov design or viewed as a pernicious consequence of affirmative action in republican party branches. In any event, the Uzbek campaign led to mass arrests of ordinary citizens—a fact that Gdlyan and his associates themselves later had to admit ruefully, although they tried to blame their Moscow superiors for their policy of using an undiscriminating dragnet.[61] When all this was brought to light in 1989–90, it ignited much legitimate resentment in Uzbekistan, whose elites now display on average the most anti-Russian attitudes in Central Asia.

Such was the price Andropov paid for the risk-averse strategy that prompted him to transfer the war on corruption from the Russian heartland to the Soviet colonial periphery. The Uzbek case also alerted the conservative Communist establishment in other Central Asian republics, whose leaders managed to block Gorbachev's initial attempts to continue Andropov's campaign. The critical test came on December 17, 1986, when Gorbachev dismissed the veteran Party boss of Kazakhstan, Dinmukhamed Kunayev, and replaced him with a Russian, Gennadi Kolbin, thus signaling the possibility of criminal investigations against the thoroughly corrupt Kazakh establishment. The Kazakh bosses responded by covertly mobilizing in the streets of Alma-Ata a huge crowd of young people, many of them intoxicated, who staged the first mass-scale anti-Russian protest in decades, thus awakening ethnic passions elsewhere across the Soviet Union.[62] Although the rally was crushed, from then on even a pale copy of the Uzbek investigations was politically out of the question. The riots left Kolbin a lame duck, and within two years he had to yield his seat to a native Kazakh, Nursultan Nazarbayev.

GORBACHEV THE POPULIST, 1985–1989: RIDING THE UNTAMED TIGER

The failure or unwillingness of the post-Andropov leadership to mobilize public discontent and channel it toward fighting corruption and the Mafiya opened the final, revolutionary stage of Soviet decline, during which the Kremlin soon had to face mass-based, intransigent opposition to its policies—an opposition that could not be diverted any more against the Mafiya, because the latter was now squarely identified with the ruling elites itself. The major credit—or blame, depending on one's perspective—for the abrupt transition to this stage has been almost unanimously assigned to Mikhail Gorbachev, who by the time of Andropov's death in February 1984 was numbered among the top handful of Soviet leaders and emerged as master of the Kremlin on March 11, 1985, after thirteen months of Chernenko's uncertain tenure.

Although Gorbachev had enjoyed Andropov's protection and had aligned himself politically with the Andropov team, his background and modus operandi made him profoundly different from his late patron. Most important for our purposes, Gorbachev was a first-generation urbanite, whose major focus throughout his political career had been agriculture. This single fact establishes a direct parallel with Khrushchev, the only CPSU general secretary whose outlook and policies were conditioned to a similar extent by his original rural mentality.[63] Yet, unlike Khrushchev in the last decade of Stalin's rule, Gorbachev prior to 1984 had had very little experience in dealing with policy issues of nationwide concern. The same, even more emphatically, was true about most other members of the new generation of leadership, such as Ligachev, Nikolai Ryzhkov, Eduard Shevardnadze, and others, each of whom served as regional or republican party secretaries or enterprise managers and brought to the Kremlin some sectoral, institutional, or regional bias that hampered an overall systemic grasp of the domestic and international predicament of their country.

In the absence of democratic deliberation and a political class of the Western type, such a systemic, integrative approach to national development was almost exclusively confined to a few closeted institutions (much to the misfortune of the Soviet system), such as the KGB and the Ministries of Defense and Foreign Affairs, historically known up to the present day as the "power ministries."[64] It was in their analytical departments that the original design of perestroika was elaborated. But owing to their bunker mentality and (especially in the case of the KGB) their bloody historical record, they were widely seen by society, by the West, and even by many ill-informed members of the Soviet establishment as the most reactionary of administrative organizations. In reality, analysts and senior officials of these three agencies were well positioned to perceive the inchoate legitimation crisis of the entire system; however, they also were aware that any hypothetical attempt to seize control of the situation in their own name would undermine the credibility of even the best-designed reforms in the eyes of both Western and domestic observers—even though Andropov became the regime's leader, he still regarded the credibility gap as being far too wide for a move of such boldness.

If the domestic aspect of the brewing crisis was arguably not yet so pressing, the foreign policy front was so beset by the unrelenting pressure of the Reagan administration that a new leader with a dovish face had already become the absolute condition for the successful launching of reforms. This is one plausible explanation for the fact that, after Andropov's death, neither Defense Minister Ustinov nor Foreign Minister Andrei Gromyko claimed the highest office for himself but supported Chernenko as a temporary solution and Gorbachev as his anointed successor in line. As it soon turned out, the specific worldview of Gorbachev himself and his closest associates drastically altered the design and implementation of systemic reforms, which departed from what had originally been planned inside the power ministries.

If Andropov treated populist grassroots sentiment as a part of objective reality that had to be addressed and steered in the desired direction, Gorbachev behaved as if he identified himself with much of this discontent and even internalized it. Devoid of the secret intelligence mentality that had constrained

Andropov, Gorbachev spent much of his first years in office touring the country and parading his convoluted, self-confident rhetoric before crowds to "shake up society" and to "pull it out of hibernation." At least until 1988, this behavior was spectacularly successful, momentarily making him the most popular national leader in decades (despite his imprudent promotion of his wife, Raisa, which aroused a somewhat irrational hostility among his audiences). Yet the Achilles' heel of Gorbachev's eloquence was the random, unfocused character of the "shake-up" he demanded. To judge from his pronouncements, almost every area of Soviet reality was to be reformed at once, while the ordering and sequence of the Kremlin's actual priorities were clouded in uncertainty.

Although the goal of quantitative "acceleration" in the Soviet machine-tool building industry—a leftover from Andropov's industrial projects—still figured for some time as a development target in the speeches and reports of the leadership, it was most probably marginal to Gorbachev's mindset. Influenced by his career experience, Gorbachev tended to pay more attention to the organizational forms of management at the microeconomic level, at the expense of strategic nationwide planning and structural change.[65] Many of his economic as well as political pronouncements betrayed his fixation on the operating principles of local production units, such as a collective farm or industrial enterprise, each of which he saw as being self-contained. He argued at great length and with much conviction in favor of increasing the autonomy of such units and tended to view larger parts of the national economy as unstructured agglomerations of such autonomous entities. In Gorbachev's intellectual worldview, this remarkable emphasis on *local* initiative is characteristically complemented by the most ambitious and utopian *international* projects, with very few coherent and consequential ideas at the intermediate, or *national,* level. He also became infatuated with the model of participatory democracy, extolling his ideal of "wholehearted, active participation by the whole community in all of society's affairs," and of democracy as a means of "self-regulation by society."[66]

This was the typical outlook of a Russian communitarian populist. More specifically, Gorbachev's views were anchored in the liberal-anarchic tradition of populism, even though the existing rules of the game left him with no choice but to abide in his rhetoric by the Holy Writ of Marxism, and he probably had never read Bakunin or Kropotkin anyway. Antibureaucratic sentiment and the devolution of power from the Moscow federal "center" all the way down to companies and local administrations were the main thrusts of perestroika's ideology. In most Western countries, this ideology would appear to be congenial to the Anglo-American conception of a radical free market (and indeed, it turned out as such in the longer run, with the growing exposure of Soviet society to economic globalization). Yet it had quite a different connotation in Russian culture, where the retrospective ideal of self-sufficient communal self-government remained a vivid alternative to both the state and private sectors.

In such a light, it is easy to understand why Gorbachev's antibureaucratic exhortations initially found such an enthusiastic response among the unprivileged strata of Soviet society, well beyond the tiny layer of intellectuals and artists in Moscow who were quickly enticed by the sudden granting of individual liberties and perks into becoming the vocal solid core of Gorbachev's supporters outside the government. And yet already by 1987–88, despite the initial improvement of economic indicators and advances in foreign policy, the development of the domestic debate he had initiated made Gorbachev feel increasingly insecure in his populist saddle; the emergence of influential forces of protest that were either indifferent or openly hostile to him attested to his fundamental lack of credibility as a populist leader.

To account for this, a number of explanations are needed. The most basic is that Gorbachev himself was seen as a part of the machine that he aspired to reconstruct and make more efficient. He had incrementally risen to power inside the system; as the party helmsman, he was the foremost bureaucrat in the country—even though he ostentatiously delayed assuming the ceremonial office of chief of state until 1988 and therefore held no formal position in the government (he was probably the only person who considered this as a show of respect for the principle of separation of powers). Second, he encouraged ordinary citizens to demand justice and reform from the bureaucracy but gave them neither weapons for the struggle nor protection from retaliation by the bureaucrats. This made Gorbachev's "shaking up" sound irresponsible and provocative, especially because scores of Soviet citizens had already sacrificed their careers and social status for antibureaucratic crusades and "truth-seeking" over the past decades.

In addition, Gorbachev's liberal arguments, coupled with his implicit assertion that a harmony of interests existed among nations and also among social strata, were widely seen as a deliberate attempt to obscure the irreconcilable social and cultural antagonisms between the rulers and the ruled, as well as within specific groups of Soviet citizens. As a consummate nomenklatura *apparatchik* (Party or state bureaucrat), Gorbachev was perceived to be on the other side of the barricades that separated the elite from the rest of society. Moreover, he had no credible response to the national and racial hatreds that were fueled by vast disparities in social development and living standards among the regions and ethnic groups that populated the Union. As tensions mounted, the elite groups that had sponsored Gorbachev's launching of perestroika became aware that he had reached the limits of his ability to mediate between the ruling establishment and the general public.[67]

A New Job for the Apparatchiks: Manufacturing Opposition to Themselves

Gorbachev's efforts to "lead from the front" by using his populist charisma failed in part because the political engineering designed to create a bandwagon of focused political support for his goals soon backfired. Shortly after perestroika began, various groups within the Soviet leadership came to the conclusion that the alienation of the populace and its indifference to appeals emanating from above were a major obstacle to achieving significant changes. Some new and more efficient form of communication between the elite and the masses was needed to replace the rent "transmission belts" inherited from the Stalin era. In 1985–86, with the publication of several provocative articles and a few previously forbidden authors in leading official periodicals, the Gorbachevians started the cautious and carefully calibrated process of fostering political debate and differentiation in the government-controlled media. In 1986, Gorbachev's inner circle also adopted a position of benign neutrality and even tacit encouragement toward the first unofficial public groups "in support of perestroika" (such as the Club for Social Initiatives, led by a group of young moderate leftists).[68]

The ultimate result of these efforts was aptly described by the leading mastermind of Gorbachev's public relations and "architect of perestroika," Aleksandr Yakovlev: "We created an opposition to ourselves."[69] Few would disagree with Yakovlev's starting point that "perestroika was launched by a very small group of party and government leaders." Their decision was not prompted by a movement of mass protest, as in Poland, and there was no alternative political elite ready to compete for power, as in Hungary. Anyone remotely resembling an autonomous public politician was either in exile or in jail; prominent dissidents had been deported from the USSR or compelled to emigrate. Because any overtures to these hostile elements would have been politically explosive, new transmission belts to (and from) an alienated society, such as political and semipolitical associations, had to be created among the more loyal groups of the Soviet middle class. While Yakovlev's ideological department of the Central Committee was busy designing and anticipating various "informal" activities and publications on the liberal, pro-Western flank, Yegor Ligachev and his apparatchiks labored to complement and counterbalance that initiative by manufacturing conservative clubs and public events. Scores of officials at the lower levels of the bureaucracy were involved on both sides. An indispensable role in this process was assigned to the Moscow party machine (from December 1985, presided over by Boris Yeltsin). The would-be independent organizers badly needed offices, staffers, telephones, faxes, copying machines, and so forth. Once the decision to help had been taken at the top, the delivery of these goods was administered by municipal apparatchiks.

This contrived origin of the Gorbachev-era opposition, both reformist and conservative, left a recognizable imprint on its further development—and ultimately on the identity and mode of operation of almost all the politicians of the Yeltsin era. One of the consequences of this contrived origin was the persistent disconnect in the 1990s between the interests and aspirations of the discontented but disorganized citizenry on the one hand and, on the other hand, the predominantly artificial nature of nongovernmental organizations and political parties created on its behalf with open or covert input from the authorities.

After decades of deliberate and thorough atomization of Soviet society, the nomenklatura and its intelligence apparatus possessed a monopoly of organizational culture and managerial skills. Thus, even if would-be organizers did not belong to the nomenklatura, they had to master its networking and administrative practices or risk quick failure. No wonder that many nongovernmental organizations of the Gorbachev period (including the latest, largest, and most promising of all, Democratic Russia) were characterized by a cultural gap between the leaders and their following. The latter were suspicious of what they correctly perceived as elements of nomenklatura culture, which in their view might make the organization into a tool for nomenklatura interests. But the disgruntled followers inside the organization had insufficient skills to challenge their administrators without risking the destruction of the organization itself. Thus Gorbachev's policies of nurturing the future opposition inadvertently expanded the scope of conflict over issues real and imaginary between the nomenklatura and everybody else, fueling increased disenchantment, fatalistic resignation, and unfocused rage on the part of the populace.

THE AGE OF THE MEDIA CRUSADES

Gorbachev and his associates viewed the liberalization of the media as the major channel of feedback between the elite and society. While virtually all institutions of the Soviet system (for example, the Communist Party, Komsomol, official labor unions, and power ministries) had lost their credibility and were viewed as inhuman and self-centered bureaucratic-oligarchical monsters, the newspapers and "thick" literary journals continued to attract vast audiences. Reading between the lines to get the truth about Soviet society had become the favorite pastime of the educated middle class. Knowing this, the Gorbachev team maintained close relations with the most outspoken editors and authors of popular periodicals. These journalists were expected to filter and articulate the popular discontent emanating from below, while at the same time explaining both the announced and hidden intentions of perestroika's leaders in simple and straightforward language understandable to the masses.

All this sharpened the existing political differentiation in the media outlets and the literary establishment that controlled them. In the early Gorbachev years, the central role was allocated to the influential group of rurally oriented village writers and columnists known as the *derevenshchiki* and to their vehicles among the thick journals—above all *Novy mir,* whose new editor, Sergei Zalygin, aspired to restore the journal to the central position it had enjoyed among the advocates of change in the 1960s. The "village group" displayed a broad variety of political views, from the intense ethnocratic nationalism of Vasily Belov and, sometimes, Viktor Astafiev, to the sophisticated conservatism of Valentin Rasputin and Zalygin himself, to liberal denunciations of bureaucratic violence against the peasantry by Vasily Selyunin and Yuri Chernichenko. All of them were united in their initially Aesopian-style censure of Stalin's brutal collectivization of the peasantry, their eloquent laments over the decline of the countryside, their complaints about the moral relativism and depravity of the urbanites, and their adherence to the environmental theme, which they framed in terms of man's gratuitous violence against Mother Nature. This mindset was an easily recognizable mix of antibureaucratic and cultural populism; historically, it was identified with the *pochvenniki,* the worshippers of the soil, a current dating back to Dostoevsky. Much of the village group's agenda converged with Western social conservatism, and their moral preaching was reflected in the Gorbachev-Ligachev alcohol prohibition policies.[70]

For quite some time the village authors, either willingly or not, had functioned as a vigorous lobbying force on the side of the government's agricultural bureaucracy, which used their writings and pronouncements in its behind-the-scenes struggle for a favorable share of the budget. No wonder Gorbachev, a veteran of agricultural politics, felt a special affinity with the village writers. In addition, he seemed to be strongly impressed by their vision of an impending environmental catastrophe, an issue that became pivotal to his "new political thinking." The environmental theme expanded the ranks of Gorbachev's coterie of fans among the European Greens and such fashionable prophets of doom as Alvin Toffler.

The influence of the village authors peaked in 1985–86, when they managed to rally a broad and diverse informal coalition of resistance to the project for diverting the course of the great Siberian rivers to the south, an idea originally advanced by a lowly water transportation ministry. Although in theory the project would have benefited the infrastructural development of parched southern Siberia and Central Asia, it appeared to be unfeasible without risking potentially devastating environmental consequences. Soon the project's opponents managed to politicize it. Neighboring countries such as Turkey and China successfully carried out similar projects at the time, but radical environmentalists portrayed the river diversion as yet another form of violence against nature, on a par with Stalin's crimes against the peasantry. In the wake of the fateful explosion at the Chernobyl nuclear plant in April 1986, the cause of the radical environmentalists seemed virtually beyond dispute, and support for it became overwhelming, especially among those poorly informed about the nuts and bolts of the problem. The project was soon canceled at the highest political level. The first open civic campaign in decades, waged under the antibureaucratic populist banner and tolerated by the authorities, ended in victory. In implicit recognition of this fact, a major novel by a leader of the campaign, Valentin Rasputin, was honored with the most prestigious USSR State Prize.[71]

But times were changing fast. The severe revenue crisis of 1986, sharpened by U.S.-Saudi collusion to lower prices on the world oil market,[72] the renewed flare-up of the Afghan War, and the scare over Reagan's Strategic Defense Initiative, put Soviet relations with the West on the front burner. The Politburo was divided between the advocates of redoubled efforts to catch up in the military-industrial and technological race and the U.S.-oriented group led by Foreign Minister Eduard Shevardnadze and Yakovlev. Addressing themselves to the managerial elite and the urban intelligentsia, both sides had little sympathy for the Slavophile communitarian utopianism of the village writers.

By early 1987, the intensifying debates in the Kremlin spilled over into the media, where the tones of acrimonious conflict were increasingly heard. The newly appointed editors of the periodicals in Yakovlev's "sphere of influence," such as *Ogonyok, Moscow News,* and *Argumenty i fakty,* launched a wave of articles denouncing much of the Soviet past and present. These salvos were answered by the neo-Stalinist mouthpieces of the military-industrial sector, such as *Sovetskaya Rossiya* and *Molodaya gvardiya.* The middle-of-the-road village group could not keep its base: *Novy mir* lost much of its readership to more radical publications on both sides, while *Nash sovremennik,* another village group monthly, slid into ethnocratic nationalism and closed ranks on most issues with the radical nationalist right. In particular, a watershed was marked by Viktor Astafiev's novel, *The Sad Detective,* whose thinly veiled attacks on Jews and Georgians shocked the liberal public. For its part, the Stalinist wing of the establishment feared that Russian nationalism would undermine the cohesion of the Soviet Union by encouraging ethnic intolerance in non-Russian territories and covertly blamed Gorbachev for his flirtation with the neo-Slavophiles. Some village authors, such as Selyunin and Chernichenko, joined the radical pro-Western camp, while the erosion of the liberal-patriotic center left Gorbachev balancing above a disappearing political base in 1986–87.[73] Meanwhile, as Sakharov and other dissidents were brought back from exile and prison, semilegal associations and clubs tolerated or encouraged by the establishment shifted the emphasis to direct action and deprived the media of their role as surrogates for political organization.[74]

The unraveling of Gorbachev's moderate-populist coalition sent waves of frustration and radicalism through those segments of Soviet society that had responded enthusiastically to perestroika's initial promises. Behind the bitter debates in the media, astute readers perceived muscle flexing by narrow interest groups, none of which addressed the broad issues behind public unrest. The literary establishment fragmented along partisan lines, and its factions launched a no-holds-barred competition for the privilege of being the officially certified interpreter of the Kremlin's murky strategies. The self-styled April Group tried to assert itself as Gorbachev's political and literary base on the radical-liberal flank, but the morally dubious reputation of its leaders, such as Yevgeny Yevtushenko, who claimed to speak on behalf of the entire '60s generation, undermined its credibility among potential followers. Their opposite numbers, the literary lobbyists for military and expansionist causes, such as Yuri Bondarev and Aleksandr Prokhanov (the latter dubbed by his detractors as "the nightingale of the General Staff"), who had their stronghold in the secretariat of the RSFSR Union of Writers, had little more to offer.[75] The bickering among literary factions was increasingly focused not on social or philosophical issues but, rather, on carving up the property of the foundering Union of Soviet Writers, with its magazines and publishing houses, luxurious headquarters, dachas and sanitariums, foreign travel assignments, and lucrative state prizes. From this point on, the political opinions of many literary and artistic luminaries began to shift wildly as they positioned themselves around newly emerging sources of perks and booty. For their rank-and-file public, this feverish organizational activity worked as a negative advertisement for the looming era of corrupt public politics ("Welcome to the age of the Big Grab!" would have been an apt slogan), and many of them recoiled from such an unsavory picture.

THE RISE AND DEMISE OF PAMYAT', 1987–88

To illuminate both the artificial elements in much of the politics of 1987–88 and also a significant episode in the rise of Yeltsin, we now turn to a brief case study. For a populist movement to be credible, it must appear to have emerged spontaneously. This was initially the case with the notorious Pamyat' (Memory) Society, which paraded onto Moscow squares and the front pages of the leading periodicals in mid-1987. Before long, Pamyat' had become almost synonymous with the emerging Russian nationalist movement—much to the detriment of the latter. Historically, Pamyat' was the first and paradigmatic attempt to set up a mass populist organization under the banner of ethnocratic Russian nationalism.

The inordinate attention that Pamyat' enjoyed in the media was out of all proportion to its actual impact and number of followers. Walter Laqueur's estimate that "for every member of Pamyat' there has been an article in the Russian and Western press" was probably not far off the mark.[76] Nonetheless, the glory days of Pamyat' were over in little more than a year. It started in May 1987 with a much-advertised rally in downtown Moscow, followed by an audience granted to its leaders by Moscow party boss Boris Yeltsin—an unprecedented step for a Soviet official, given the fact that Gorbachev himself had not yet met with Sakharov or any other democratic dissenter. By May 1988, when a prosecutorial warning issued to Pamyat' leaders for igniting national discord was published by *Argumenty i fakty,* the plight of Pamyat' failed to capture much public attention or to evoke sympathy from prominent nationalists. Soon afterward, Pamyat' fell apart into a dozen rival groups on the margins of public life, while its ideological niche was taken over by other previously unknown figures, who winced and threw up their hands at the mere mention of Pamyat'.[77]

The group's short-lived fame tended to confirm the belief of knowledgeable observers that this had never been an authentic grassroots phenomenon but, rather, was the product of covert maneuvers at the higher levels of society. In retrospect, Pamyat' fits the pattern of a manufactured and disposable opposition, a pattern that has persisted throughout the whole era of perestroika and Yeltsin's reforms, and whose instrumental role was later revealed by such political engineers as Yakovlev.[78] While conservative figures of the establishment may have hoped that Pamyat' would serve as a vehicle for their prospective careers in the era of public politics, liberal reformers of the Yakovlev type seemed interested in inflating its importance to stigmatize the entire camp of their conservative opponents by association with the radical ethnocrats from Pamyat', a strategy that to a considerable extent worked.

A detailed history of Pamyat' is beyond the scope of this inquiry, but suffice it to say that the central role in its creation was played by a group of Stalin-worshipping journalists and novelists who were affiliated with the power ministries, including Dmitri Zhukov, Feliks Chuyev, Vladimir Chivilikhin (whose posthumously published book was entitled *Memory*), and Marshal Vasily Chuykov, a prominent veteran of World War II. A host of theories have been spun around the initial purposes of its creators and sponsors, but at this stage they largely defy documentation. Putting aside the most conspiratorial versions, one can see Pamyat' as a ramified grassroots extension of several official government organizations, including the Bibliophile Societies (which by the late 1980s were pretty much under control of the conservative literary establishment); VOOPIK (the All-Union Society for the Protection of Historical and Cultural Monuments); and DOSAAF, a semi-educational network of amateur sports clubs affiliated with the Ministry of Defense. In the twilight years of the Soviet era, these agencies were suffering from declining public support and had to be politically innovative to get their piece of the shrinking budgetary pie. Pamyat' was for them a useful front, especially because of its recreational profile, which was untainted by visible connections with the nomenklatura or the government bureaucracy. Over time, the group's activities acquired a romantic semiclandestine aura, which appealed to the younger generation and produced a moderate increase in its gate receipts.

Whether plausible or not, this analysis can hardly account for the boisterous performance of Pamyat' in public politics in 1987–88, something for which the reclusive bureaucrats of the party and state agencies had neither the qualifications nor the fortitude. As in similar obscure cases, it is often tempting to bring the KGB into the picture, like a *deus ex machina* in an ancient drama. Thus, in a study of otherwise superior quality, the KGB is alleged to have simultaneously controlled and encouraged the activities of Pamyat' to: (a) discredit Russian nationalism through the erratic behavior of Pamyat' leaders, (b) set up a bogeyman to boost support for the Gorbachev regime as the lesser evil, and (c) provide a counterweight to the emerging democratic movement. The same research maintains that the KGB also engineered splits within Pamyat' to prevent the emergence of a united opposition.[79] For this interpretation to be coherent, one has to assume either that the KGB was in the business of outsmarting itself, or that the KGB had become a host of independent agents, all doing their own thing.

While some input from the KGB and similar institutions is quite conceivable, let us spell out another interpretation, based on the well-established historical fact of Boris Yeltsin's official encounter with Pamyat' activists in the wake of their first rally. Given what is known about Yeltsin, it is doubtful that he would have reacted so promptly if he had not been prepared. Keep in mind that this meeting took place only five months before his momentous anti-Gorbachev speech of October 21, 1987. For quite some time in 1986–87, Yeltsin had been positioning himself to assume the high-risk role of independent populist leader, and he was looking around for a prospective organizational base. Not long before, he had instructed the Moscow city soviet to liberalize its regulations on public rallies. It is quite conceivable that Yeltsin and his associates may have encouraged or even masterminded the first rally of Pamyat', seeing in it a potentially beneficial political event. This hypothesis finds support in the curious fact that Yeltsin, throughout his subsequent career and even in the heyday of his cooperation with the democratic internationalists from 1989 to 1992, never came out against Pamyat' and once even defended it against the charge of anti-Semitism.[80] Likewise, the group's leaders never attacked Yeltsin, not even for his role in the demise of the Soviet Union or in shock therapy. In 1993, they were in the ranks of those nationalists, alongside Zhirinovsky, who welcomed the dispersal of the parliament and Yeltsin's semi-autocratic constitution.

Whatever Yeltsin's personal attitude to the ethnocratic messages of Pamyat' might have been, his direct experience with the group must have discouraged him from attempts at further cooperation. While Pamyat' seemed valuable for its ability to stir public controversy and to destabilize Gorbachev, it was unlikely to sustain itself as a political force: In the tense atmosphere of Soviet interethnic relations, the group's agenda was too divisive, and its members, while infatuated with its underground counterculture, had neither the skills nor the enthusiasm needed for regular politics. If anything attracted people to Pamyat' rallies, it was not its nationalist stance but its anti-establishment cultural message, something it shared with other less fortunate or less advertised unofficial organizations at the time.

Meanwhile, the destructive capacity of Pamyat' soon came into full view, as its rallies and pronouncements prompted an anti-Russian backlash in the minority republics of the Soviet Union. The group's debut on May 6, 1987, which was intended to commemorate the Victory Day of 1945, created a precedent that made it easier for clubs of Baltic nationalists to stage their own protest rallies on August 23 to mark the anniversary of the 1939 Molotov-Ribbentrop Pact between the USSR and Germany. Any attempt by the government authorities to break up these demonstrations would have created a double standard, flying in the face of Gorbachev's proclaimed internationalism. By mid-1988, with mounting ethnic hostilities in the Caucasus and tensions brewing elsewhere, Pamyat' was generating nothing but embarrassment for both liberals and conservatives in the Kremlin, all of whom were anxious about the potential fragmentation of the Soviet Union. On top of that, the scandalous international publicity given to Pamyat' was threatening to crowd Gorbachev's reforms off the pages of the Western media.

The far-out pronouncements and clownish antics of Pamyat' made it an easy target for both the radical-reformist and the official mainstream media. An anti-Pamyat' campaign soon engulfed the entire nationalist-conservative camp, with the more enlightened and sophisticated patriots finding it impossible to disassociate themselves from Pamyat'.[81] The turning point in Kremlin policy toward Pamyat' came in mid-1988, when Gorbachev was preparing for the politically delicate governmental celebrations of the millennium of Russian Orthodox Christendom. In the highly charged ethnic and political situation, such a major boost for the Orthodox clerics and the Russian nationalists required a counterbalancing display by the government to distance itself from extreme Russian nationalism. This was achieved by the expulsion from the CPSU of prominent Pamyat' activist Kim Andreyev, as well as by widely publicized threats of criminal prosecution against other Pamyat' leaders.

However, the authorities realized that actual trials could have an adverse effect on public opinion, both in the USSR and abroad.[82] Instead of resorting to the Soviet Criminal Code, they used time-tested techniques to dismember the organization and deflect media attention to more pressing issues. A tiny group of hard-core Pamyat' activists were rewarded for their loyalty with a government grant of farmland, and they settled down as communal landowners on their "Yaroslavl kibbutz." Their rare public statements evolved from pledges of loyalty to perestroika and the CPSU to militant anticommunism and monarchism, remarkably in tune with the permutations of Yeltsin's political line. The radical-nationalist flank that Pamyat' had vacated was rapidly filled by minuscule parties, movements, and fronts that ceaselessly multiplied by fission and whose influence could only hope to be felt in some future historical directory.

YELTSIN IN OCTOBER 1987: REBEL WITHOUT A CAUSE

The encounter with Pamyat' made Yeltsin the most controversial figure in the top Soviet leadership. He became the first Party boss to shake hands with political activists outside the CPSU; on top of that, he seemed to have privately encouraged them. This was seen as an open bid for leadership in the dialogue with society, which the Party nomenklatura needed so badly and which other leaders of the country were poorly equipped to conduct.

It is not our intent to reconstruct here Yeltsin's political biography. We merely offer a reinterpretation of certain widely known facts and of Yeltsin's confessions in his 1990 autobiography (compiled on his behalf by his future chief of staff, Valentin Yumashev).[83] His unexpected transfer from the seat of first secretary of the party province committee in the major industrial city of Sverdlovsk to Moscow in April 1985, just one month after Gorbachev's ascent to power, was ironically the product of vigorous lobbying by Ligachev, the Politburo's outspoken conservative populist and indefatigable anti-vodka campaigner. After eight months of being vetted in a low-key post as head of the CPSU Central Committee's Construction Department, Yeltsin was nominated by the Politburo to take the job of one of the notoriously corrupt and retrograde Kremlin elders, Viktor Grishin, the first secretary of the Party's Moscow city committee.

Such a rapid promotion to one of the key positions in the ruling elite, while facilitated by Yeltsin's organizational ability and other personal assets, was designed to serve the special interests of an increasingly assertive group of regional barons. The nomenklatura of the Urals and western Siberia, which was aligned behind Ligachev in 1985, was characterized by a peculiar subculture that set it apart from other clans and regional alliances in the Byzantine world of Soviet politics.[84] Although this group controlled strategically important industrial and academic centers of the country, it had lingered too long on the sidelines of national politics and felt mistreated by two other groups in the Soviet establishment, the permanent Moscow insiders and the officials from the southern republics, which it considered inordinately depraved and corrupt. The Ligachev cadres had reason to believe that the Muscovites and the elites in the non-Russian republics and their clients were getting a bigger slice of the national pie than they deserved, mostly because the loyalty and stability of their realms were more important to the Kremlin than anything going on in the remote Russian heartland. This sentiment was shared by their local constituents, whose brewing discontent had vaguely regionalist and nativist overtones.[85] Party bosses from the Urals and Siberia embraced perestroika as an opportunity to take revenge on the more fortunately positioned clans of the establishment. In this context, Yeltsin's Moscow appointment was seen as the prelude to a thorough purge of municipal agencies and appointments to the lucrative freed-up positions of candidates from the provinces, all under the banner of an all-out war on the Mafiya, corruption, and privileges.

Yeltsin did not betray these expectations. Of the Party's thirty-three ward bosses in Moscow, twenty-three were kicked out during his brief tenure. In a major assault on the deeply entrenched trade Mafiya—the embryo of the new Russian capitalist class—eight hundred people were put on trial in slightly more than a year.[86] By dint of his determination, the new Moscow boss gained much respect among ordinary citizens. He scored even more points by his overtly populist gestures, such as riding on overcrowded buses in the early morning rush hour to listen to the complaints of angry citizens, or showing up at food stores to inspect the availability of merchandise and to expose financial abuses. Rumors about Yeltsin roaming across Moscow in pursuit of evil bureaucrats and profiteers raised his stature to the level of a mythic hero, the fighter for justice of Russian fairy tales. To top it off, he made a strikingly sincere speech at the Twenty-Sixth Party Congress in February 1986, where he took himself to task for his lack of "sufficient courage" and his failure to resist Brezhnevite "stagnation."[87]

While this image won Yeltsin the sympathy of significant groups in the middle and lower classes, as well as of Moscow newcomers, the upper layer of the intelligentsia in the capital remained wary and apprehensive. Over decades, Moscow academics, professionals, and cultural figures had forged client relationships with the ruling establishment and accepted much of the nomenklatura culture, along with a fair amount of snobbery and social egoism, as their trademark. They cherished their allegedly unique role as masters of public opinion and felt uneasy about the looming populist alternative that threatened to disturb their influence over mass consciousness.

It was this metropolitan cultural elite (or in Soviet terms "creative intelligentsia") that by early 1987, craving political clout and captivated by Western consumer culture, had supplanted the backward-looking and politically inexperienced agrarian populists of the village prose group as the major bulwark of ideological support for Gorbachev's policies. Because Soviet foreign policy problems were becoming more acute, Gorbachev heeded the advice of his U.S.-oriented adviser Aleksandr Yakovlev and sought an alliance with this cultural establishment, expecting these media celebrities to advertise perestroika in the West and mobilize its Western sympathizers as an antidote to Reagan's anti-Soviet rhetoric; this was one of the functions of the new glasnost policy.

The most vocal mouthpieces for the Yakovlev line were *Ogonyok* and *Moscow News,* whose editors were Vitaly Korotich and Yegor Yakovlev, respectively. They denounced Stalin's crimes and rehabilitated "anti-Sovietists," from the poet Nikolai Gumilev (executed in 1921) to present-day dissidents and political emigrants. The authors and columnists rallying around these radical periodicals under Aleksandr Yakovlev's umbrella soon acquired the privileged status of what were known as "superintendents of perestroika." While leaving them ample room for verbal bravery, Gorbachev simultaneously hedged his bets by nurturing the ideological ambitions of the conservative and nationalist-leaning Ligachev, who patronized the military propagandists of *Molodaya gvardiya,* the orthodox Communist zealots of *Sovetskaya Rossiya,* and the village writers-turned-ethnocrats of *Nash sovremennik.*[88] Gorbachev's balancing at the fulcrum of this ideological seesaw encouraged a confrontational posture on both sides, but such maneuvering also turned counterproductive for Gorbachev himself, as his actual intentions became more enigmatic, and each side blamed him for the climate of risk and uncertainty. The seesaw dynamic locked public debate into an either-or conflict between radicals and conservatives, leaving no room for compromise between the two or the emergence of a third force.

Yeltsin behaved as if he were not aware of this pseudo-bipartisan arrangement; his actions and pronouncements did not fit within either camp. He kept to his habit of reaching out to ordinary people, seeking to find and fix their problems, even though Gorbachev and Ligachev were already winding down their regular provincial trips and stump speeches. Yakovlev's highbrow superintendents now had the floor, and they were advocating Western blueprints to transform the Soviet Union into a liberal, consumer-oriented society. Yeltsin's heavy-handed authoritarian style, repulsive for Moscow liberals, and his peculiar regional brand of patriotism appeared to have been designed to win over Ligachev's constituents and to reframe their traditionalist causes in a radical and subversive way, thus upsetting the seesaw system.

The Pamyat' case marked a turning point in Yeltsin's career. It broke the unspoken ban on ethnic Russian nationalism that had been imposed to avoid roiling the ethnic groups along the Soviet periphery and to assist Gorbachev's campaign for a new détente with the U.S. government. A month later, Ligachev (who had already clashed with Yeltsin when he demanded that Yeltsin shut down a Moscow brewery) dressed Yeltsin down behind the closed doors of the June 1987 CPSU Central Committee Plenum for having amended city regulations on holding rallies to permit the Pamyat' spectacle. Apparently the fact that Gorbachev had gone on vacation without trying to restore the balance, plus Yakovlev's hands-off attitude, suggested to Yeltsin that a high-level collegial decision had been made to throw him to the wolves of public opinion by framing him as a nationalist.[89]

It was most probably at this point that Yeltsin decided to act. If he was about to be dumped, it was better to launch a preemptive strike that would make him a celebrity and leave the door open for a future comeback on a wave of public support. He also needed to broaden his political base quickly so as not to get stuck with a Pamyat' label. With this purpose in view, he encouraged several semilegal political clubs, recently founded and poorly connected to one another, to organize a joint conference that was openly held under the sponsorship of the Moscow party committee in late August 1987.[90] Participants in the conference were skillfully filtered to exclude most dissidents and open anticommunists. Perhaps the only organizer who had taken part in the dissident movement was Vyacheslav Igrunov (now a leader of Yabloko, the main party of the democratic opposition in the Duma). Igrunov brought to the conference a well thought-out project that seemed to neutralize Yeltsin's association with Pamyat'. He called for the creation of a new group called Memorial, which he projected as an all-Russian civic committee to honor and preserve the memory of Stalin's victims. (Memorial was founded in 1988 and grew into a broad movement and a moral force involving all layers of society, in which Yeltsin's followers would find their place alongside the radical intelligentsia and nomenklatura reformers.) The August 1987 conference adopted a rather moderate package of declarations, and a number of groups loyal to Yeltsin coalesced into a Federation of Socialist Public Clubs (FSOK). Before long, FSOK would pay dividends on this investment by staging a rally in Yeltsin's support in the wake of his ouster from the Moscow party committee.

The stage was set for a decisive move. Two weeks later, on September 10, with Gorbachev still at the Black Sea, Yeltsin drew up an angry letter to the general secretary (which he would later republish in his memoirs).[91] The letter illustrated Yeltsin's inability to come up with a substantive, conceptual critique of any Gorbachev policies. Rather, it was an emotional statement of protest over Ligachev's interference in what Yeltsin saw as his exclusive responsibilities, complaining in particular about the recent creation of a special party commission to investigate the state of affairs in Moscow (Yeltsin had clashed again with Ligachev over nomenklatura privileges at a Politburo session). Although the letter ended with a plea to be relieved of his duties, Yeltsin in his subsequent memoirs admitted that he was uncertain whether he would be ousted, especially given the support he had mustered in the city. He hoped that a dramatic tendering of his resignation would actually strengthen his position in his struggle with Ligachev.

Gorbachev's usual evasiveness and his unwillingness to resolve the feud with Ligachev fueled Yeltsin's discontent. Yeltsin hated uncertainty and, once embroiled in a conflict, preferred to raise the stakes to make the outcome of the crisis, whatever it might be, more meaningful and consequential. At another Politburo session, he dared to infringe upon Gorbachev's own turf by delivering critical comments on his draft report for the seventieth anniversary of the 1917 Revolution. Gorbachev exploded in rage.[92] The big crisis seemed to be imminent, but for no clear reasons the issue of Yeltsin's resignation was never raised. It was as if someone were goading Yeltsin into more and more inflammatory moves, moves Gorbachev or others needed to break the stalemated confrontation between the conservatives and the radicals in the Party leadership.

On October 21, at a Central Committee Plenum, Gorbachev delivered his report on the anniversary of the Revolution with a soul-searching reassessment of the most critical stages of Soviet history. The rest of the session went behind closed doors. As soon as Gorbachev left the podium, Yeltsin raised his hand to take the floor. According to the minutes of the session, published in 1989, acting chairman Ligachev tried to ignore the demand and close the Plenum, but Gorbachev twice insisted that "Comrade Yeltsin" had something to say, as if he were impatient to let the steam out of the kettle.

Yeltsin's speech, as contained in the stenographic record and later republished by Yeltsin himself in his memoirs, strikes the reader as incoherent and rambling. Yeltsin himself writes that he did not prepare his statement in any systematic way.[93] He started by reiterating his well-known critique of Ligachev and his management style in the Central Committee Secretariat, which was nothing new after Yeltsin's earlier swipes at Ligachev in June and September. Next, he questioned the timetable of perestroika, noting that people had become disillusioned by the lack of visible results and that longer-term targets were required. The climax of his speech was a personal attack on Gorbachev, which contained a thinly veiled hint about an emergent "personality cult" of a neo-Stalinist type. Although the proceedings of the Plenum were secret, this part of the speech was designed for wide public circulation, and it soon spread across the country in rumors. Although short on argumentation, it scored points for Yeltsin's popularity: A frontal attack against the sitting general secretary from within the Party seemed to be a thrilling deed of unprecedented courage. Among all of Yeltsin's complaints and allegations, this was the easiest to understand for the unsophisticated public that he was targeting, and it raised him at once to the level of Gorbachev's rival—that is, the de facto No. 2 man in the country, way ahead of his obedient colleagues in the Politburo.

As a final touch, in his speech Yeltsin resigned as candidate member of the Politburo but, relying perhaps too much on his power base in Moscow, he did not repeat his offer to step down as Moscow party boss. He announced cryptically that his Moscow tenure was a separate issue to be decided upon by the municipal party committee.

The die was cast: Yeltsin's oversized personal ambitions were plain to see. The absence of any substantive policy issue in his remarks (he had hardly any major policy opinions to defend at that stage) made it easy for Gorbachev to turn the entire discussion toward personality issues. Predictably, nobody came forward in Yeltsin's defense, and a final resolution censuring his "politically erroneous" statement, along with what amounted to a binding recommendation to the Moscow party committee to dismiss Yeltsin, was passed by a unanimous vote.

Within a week, the transcript of the Plenum had been leaked to the Western media and thence, through radio and rumors, to the Soviet audience. Yeltsin's rebellion, so confidently launched and yet unsupported by any conceivable group of interests within the Party leadership and identified with no specific ideological message, made him a fascinating enigma for outside observers. His revolt against Gorbachev got the sympathetic attention of many people, from party-liners to radical reformers who had grown frustrated with Gorbachev's intricate maneuvering and unwillingness to tackle issues head-on. During the November 7 celebration in Moscow, Yeltsin even got unusually warm hugs from Fidel Castro and Polish president General Wojciech Jaruzelski as they were taking seats on top of the Lenin Mausoleum in Red Square.

Although the story of Yeltsin's noisy ouster as Moscow party boss on November 13, 1987, was widely published on the following day, it still contains an unresolved mystery regarding Yeltsin's illness. In his 1990 book, Yeltsin writes that he collapsed with a headache and chest pains on November 9, was treated for an unspecified reason with tranquilizers, and was then brutally ordered by Gorbachev to leave his hospital bed to attend a full day of the Moscow party conference devoted entirely to savaging him. He admits that the treatment he was receiving left him physically and psychologically unable to respond to the accusations leveled against him. He does not, however, voice any suspicions about his physicians and does not mention the possibility that they drugged him on orders from the Kremlin. Whatever the actual drama behind Yeltsin's loss of self-control on that day, it was the first nationally registered case in a long series of his "sick" appearances that clearly had more to do with the state of his mind than with the state of his body.

Yeltsin's demotion proved to be slower and more gradual than could be expected under normal circumstances. He was soon appointed deputy chair of the State Committee on Construction, a post that was upgraded to ministerial rank just for him—a strange way to silence a political opponent in a country where the ousted prime minister Georgi Malenkov was sent to be the manager of a Siberian hydroelectric dam in the mid-1950s. Yeltsin was allowed to give interviews to the foreign media—and only to the most important media, carefully selected for him by the authorities. He was quietly deprived of his Politburo candidacy in February 1988, but was never evicted from the Central Committee and was even elected a delegate to the Nineteenth All-Union CPSU Conference of June 1988, where he was permitted to take the floor at a crucial moment to enunciate his political platform. In his first book of memoirs, he admits that his so-called disgrace, on which he capitalized in his later election campaigns to sell himself as a victim of political abuse, was never complete. The obvious incongruity between the media attacks on Yeltsin and the benign tolerance for his highly visible presence in Moscow raised some eyebrows. Yeltsin's own explanation is that Gorbachev "needed" him as a "scourge" of the overly complacent Party establishment and as a way to buttress the seesaw system: "There is the conservative Ligachev, who plays the villain; there is Yeltsin, the bully boy, the madcap radical; and the wise, omniscient hero is Gorbachev himself."[94]

While Yeltsin's insight is not to be disputed, it seems to have been only a part of the story. Our analysis of elite-mass relations presented so far suggests that *the Kremlin badly needed Yeltsin as a credible populist leader, a unique transmission belt to the discontented and underprivileged (who would keep them more or less behind Gorbachev), differentiated from the rest of the nomenklatura by his status as a punished "truth teller"—and yet not so alienated as to become unmanageable in the future.* His participation in big Party meetings put him under tight control and prevented him from joining ranks with some would-be radical opposition force, or from creating one himself. His social circle remained very much the same, and some of his former associates offered their friendship and support "for free"—including Yeltsin's bodyguard and perpetual shadow, KGB Major (demoted to Captain in 1987) Aleksandr Korzhakov. Let us note in passing the benevolent interest of many KGB cadres, who saw the unraveling of the perestroika plan they had helped to design, in the resumption and development of Yeltsin's public career. In his book, Yeltsin frankly admits that he is "after all, familiar with this agency" and that "the KGB guys" treated him "not badly." This is surely an understatement, given the fact that after he had been stricken from the list of speakers for the Nineteenth CPSU Conference, the KGB guards took it upon themselves to let him through the door that led to the conference rostrum—and beyond that, to three years of campaigning, bargaining, and maneuvering in his struggle for the keys to the Kremlin.[95]

For Gorbachev, Yeltsin's excessive ambitions had upset his plans and dangerously raised the political temperature. Events were starting to slip out of his control. And worse was soon to come.

STORMS ROCK THE SEESAW: ANDREYEVA AND OTHERS, 1988

In early 1988, changes snowballed: media rhetoric grew more strident; the ethnic and social conflicts in the Baltic republics, the Caucasus, and Central Asia multiplied; and the first blood was spilled in Azerbaijan in an Azeri pogrom against Armenians at Sumgait. While Gorbachev's popularity was skyrocketing in the West, the Soviet establishment and many ordinary citizens already saw him as an indecisive, transitional figure. The seesaw he had set in motion was teetering wildly, as self-styled leftists and rightists began to derive pleasure and benefits from the game and threw their weight around with reckless abandon. Their bitter and inconclusive media debates about history and politics were tinged with crusading zeal and venom, as if the superpower animosities of the Cold War suddenly had been shifted from the battlefield of international politics to the core of Soviet society. A new Time of Troubles was looming large.

On March 13, 1988, the fragile stability was shaken by a letter entitled "I Cannot Forsake My Principles" that appeared in the orthodox Communist daily *Sovetskaya Rossiya* and was signed by Nina Andreyeva, an obscure chemistry teacher from Leningrad.[96] Andreyeva's manifesto protested the debunking of Soviet history and preached an almost full return to Stalinism in its expansionist, National Bolshevik variant of 1946–53 vintage (in other words, laced with a heavy dose of anti-Semitism). While Andreyeva sternly censured the mainstream conservative nationalists of the village group for their "misunderstanding" of the Soviet historical experience, her program was a blueprint for what was soon to be known as "red-brown" ideology. In different proportions, and in a slightly modernized form, this ideological effluvium was taken over by the more influential wing of the present-day Communist Party and by the writings of its leader, Gennadi Zyuganov. Back in 1988, the unsolicited manifesto was widely seen as a desperate attempt by the conservative wing of the Party to anchor vague populist sentiment in traditionalist Soviet values.

If this was the case, Andreyeva's essay failed to achieve its goals. After three weeks of tense uncertainty, it was rebuffed on March 5 by an unsigned anti-Stalinist article (actually drafted by Aleksandr Yakovlev) in *Pravda*. Andreyeva's essay did little to advance the conservative cause, thus testifying to the unattractiveness of a nostalgic, backward-looking alternative, even to those who resented the ill-conceived and chaotic gyrations of Gorbachev's perestroika. Many conservatives either were assailed by Andreyeva or distanced themselves from her manifesto. This result strikingly exposed the sectarian fragmentation of the conservative wing of the Soviet elite, which was now divided among factions and interest groups, including neo-Stalinists (military industrialists), ethnic nationalists (agrarians), and orthodox Leninists (representing the interests of the Party bureaucracy and its clients in academia). However inconsequential in the short run, the Andreyeva case appears in retrospect to have established a pattern that was to reappear in the 1990s in the public's reaction to the so-called red-brown type of conservatism. This reaction involved the Kremlin's painting its opponents as communists and extreme nationalists ("red-browns") who wanted to bring back the nightmare of Stalinism, whenever this image was needed to swing public opinion behind those portrayed as radical reformers, no matter how dubious the latter's current policies were on their merits. As we shall see in chapter 8, Yeltsin did this on a grand scale when running for re-election in 1996.

The radical backlash against Andreyeva's letter produced mass rallies in major cities in favor of democratic reforms, thus enabling Gorbachev to obtain a loyal majority at the June 1988 Nineteenth Party Conference. This majority pushed through his agenda of multicandidate elections and empowerment of the soviets, similar to the widely popular agenda of 1917–18, which was emasculated by the Party in the first months of Bolshevik rule and discarded completely before long. In retrospect, the June conference stands as one of Gorbachev's major domestic achievements. It also produced a new challenge for him: a semi-opposition of economic technocrats who held that Gorbachev's politically motivated fiscal laxity, his devolution of economic decision making to companies or low-level bureaucratic agencies, and his destabilizing media rhetoric were responsible for the mounting inflationary pressures in the economy. A gloomy forecast was delivered from the conference rostrum by the authoritative economist Leonid Abalkin, and Gorbachev's agitated and incompetent rebuke only convinced the public that Abalkin had a point.

From the opposite flank, a concerted denigration campaign against Ligachev by the radicals, spearheaded by Yeltsin and Tel'man Gdlyan, facilitated Gorbachev's decimation of the power of Ligachev and the Central Committee apparatus three months later. By autumn, the seesaw mechanism was badly out of kilter. Gorbachev was under fire from all sides, pilloried by radicals as being too sluggish and by conservatives as being a revolutionary in disguise. Having apparently lost hope of bringing the intramural party debate to a constructive conclusion without a major push from outside the Party, Gorbachev pinned his hopes on the plans he unveiled at the Party conference for a quasi-parliament, the Congress of People's Deputies, whose intricate multilayered construction his advisers designed, and which he expected to produce a cohesive and cooperative majority to help him push through future reforms.

MAKING A CROWD INTO A SOCIETY: PARTIES, ELECTIONS, OPPOSITION

As just mentioned, the Andreyeva controversy and the June 1988 Party conference were marked by the first mass opposition rallies, in which a mixed bag of activists turned out to demonstrate for loosely defined radical causes. Among those present were highbrow Party intellectuals (such as the maverick historian Yuri Afanasiev and the economist Gavriil Popov); the anti-nomenklatura and antibureaucratic fans of Yeltsin and Gdlyan; veteran dissidents and human rights campaigners (epitomized by Andrei Sakharov); young professionals seeking a meteoric career in the newly opening field of public politics (such as Sergei Stankevich and Ilya Zaslavsky); plus ethnic and religious minority activists with agendas ranging from restoring destroyed houses of worship to eventual secession from the Soviet Union. With them were thousands of ordinary people from various parts of the country. This unlikely coalition seized the initiative in the media debates and the squares of big cities and determined the political climate in the major urban and suburban areas of the European part of the USSR on the eve of the March 1989 elections to the Congress of People's Deputies.[97]

Needless to say, this type of coalition was possible only in the absence of anything resembling a positive program. Swearing an oath to democracy was the indispensable rite of induction; in practice, democracy could mean anything, or, to be precise, anything diametrically opposite to the realities of the Soviet past and present. Given the enormity of this desired transformation, building democracy was a longer-term issue and was pre-empted by more urgent interests and goals, some of them controversial and potentially conflicting (such as getting rid of bureaucracy wherever possible, on the one hand, and making more equitable the government-administered distribution of goods, on the other hand). Meanwhile, for many self-anointed leaders of the movement, democracy as a formal procedure was nothing more than a cover for pursuing these partisan goals. Besides, the rules of the game were uncertain and the legitimacy of existing laws and regulations was heavily disputed; little imagination and effort were needed to doctor the rules and procedures to get an outcome that would reflect the existing correlation of power.

For attentive observers, the cleavages within this embryonic coalition were plain to see. The populists and the intellectuals tended to suspect each other of collusion with the establishment. Some liberal intellectuals thought that the elite had deliberately ignited populism to take attention away from the issues of political freedom and Westernization, while the populists mistrusted the intelligentsia as being soft on crime, corruption, and special privileges. Among the educated and ideologically astute core of the opposition, Yeltsin and Gdlyan were questionable both as democrats and as genuine populists. On the other hand, cautious pro-Western modernizers from the Gorbachev team, such as Gavriil Popov, treated the whole process of democratic transition as a kind of intra-elite bargaining over the new rules of the game (along the lines of the transitological school discussed in chapter 2). Popov and his followers regarded the social energy represented by the grassroots as an instrument to be manipulated and saw Yeltsin as a destabilizing force that would mess up the elite's deal making.[98]

Either way, not much could be done about Yeltsin. The cause of fair and equitable distribution that he claimed to advance had much wider support than bland doctrinaire liberalism or issues identified by the general public with narrow special interests, such as the right to emigration or religious freedom. Even worse for the democratic elitists, populist themes resonated with their rank-and-file base in the middle class. A poll conducted by the moderate Moscow Perestroika Club in April 1988 highlighted social justice as a paramount value, supported by 70 percent of its respondents. In a broader sample from the All-Union Center for the Study of Public Opinion (VTsIOM), almost 57 percent of those polled deplored the lack of material prosperity, and less than 15 percent gave precedence to political rights.[99] Under these circumstances, if the new democratic rules were to be taken at face value, the intellectuals either had to take the populist predominance as a given and fight to influence the populist majority by weaving their democratic message into a broader-based agenda or else bow out of the coalition. In this situation, dissident intellectuals were grudgingly forced to yield the command of rallies to blunt populist leaders like Yeltsin.

There was also a marked difference in organizational patterns. Opposition intellectuals, the carriers of the dissident legacy, assumed that a political organization should fit into a specific part of the Western ideological spectrum with a well-defined program and elected leaders. In comparison, the mass-based Popular Fronts and similar formations had a vague and diffuse set of goals; paid more attention to local or special-interest issues than to nationwide politics; and defied the right-left classification, often gravitating around a leader, such as Yeltsin, who was not a member and did not have any clear obligations to the rank and file. Yet before long, the larger groups sucked in the membership of the intellectual clubs, together with their relatively sophisticated ideas and programs. This brought a more respectable and recognizable cachet to the larger political groups.

However, just as in Eastern Europe, the first steps toward institutionalizing political opposition were made by dissident intellectuals. In June 1988, about a hundred ex-dissidents and former political prisoners, mostly from the Westernizer wing of the Dissident movement, gathered in a Moscow apartment to form the Democratic Union (DU), a self-proclaimed opposition party.[100] This "constituent congress" was ruthlessly dispersed by a police raid, and some participants were briefly detained; others resumed their session at Sergei Grigoryants's dacha in the Moscow academic suburb of Kratovo. The party organizers—Dmitri Starikov, Valeria Novodvorskaya, Eduard Molchanov, Viktor Kuzin, Andrei Gryaznov, Aleksandr Eliovich, Aleksandr Lukashov, and others—were united by a set of moral and cultural principles and by their rejection of the Soviet system, but they had little else in common. A wide array of ideological platforms coexisted within the party; however, with the exception of the leaders, most party members had no ideological affiliation. The organization was infiltrated from the outset by KGB operatives and by people with totally extraneous interests and goals; however absurd it may seem, the party featured an obscure lawyer, Vladimir Zhirinovsky, and some of his future associates among its founding members.

DU staged dozens of high-profile rallies in major cities, acquiring a membership of about two thousand and receiving considerable publicity in the official media controlled by Yakovlev. But the fervent idealism of its leaders, which was poorly connected to the interests of specific social groups, trapped DU in the delusional world of an urban intelligentsia that still took its traditional position in the public sector for granted. For this reason, DU was not afraid to try to destabilize the government, which it saw as a hostile and omnipotent totalitarian monolith that was to be harassed with protests and demands, not addressed with a coherent program for national development. DU entered into dubious alliances, such as with ethnocratic nationalists and secessionist movements in the constituent republics of the USSR, often serving the undemocratic intentions and local economic interests of the nomenklatura in these republics. For many months, DU leaflets served as the major source of inflammatory antigovernment rhetoric: slogans such as "Down with the CPSU!" and words like "criminal" and "totalitarian" soon became the common currency of democratic and revolutionary parlance, spoken and understood by destitute Yeltsin admirers, by the reform-minded wing of the nomenklatura, and by the semiclandestine entrepreneurs eager to loosen the government's grip on the black market. By contrast, the DU activists and leaders themselves never became integrated into the system or acceptable to it. As principled and incorrigible idealists, with their desire for martyrdom, they were impossible partners for the mimicry-prone elite.

While their demands and slogans were plagiarized by the phalanxes of newly converted Democrats deserting the Communist Party, DU itself waned into near-oblivion. However misguided their extreme (but nonviolent) antigovernmental actions and pronouncements might seem in hindsight, the core of DU activists and leaders consisted of uniquely creative and indomitable personalities who adamantly believed in the intelligentsia's mission to serve as a moral counterelite. Despite their radical pro-Western bias, which on occasion subordinated Russia's vital interests to the crusading fervor of global democratic messianism, they were classic products of mainstream Russian culture. During shock therapy, most DU veterans were driven out of public life by acute poverty. Only Valeria Novodvorskaya managed to remain in the limelight as a commentator and journalist, owing to her remarkable gift for exhibitionism, which she had refined during long stays in overcrowded Soviet prison cells and psychiatric hospitals. Her largest collection of writings, entitled *Beyond Despair,* is an unusually well-written book (albeit thoroughly misanthropic) full of profound cultural and psychological insights about Russian politics.[101] Her profile, both exhibitionist and tragic, epitomizes the fate of this first wave of modern Russian democrats.

The more cautious and pragmatic groups of the urban intelligentsia, such as the Perestroika Club, Commune, and Civic Dignity, refrained from defining themselves as oppositionist so as not to scare off prospective followers. Most of their members tried to replicate the Western ideological spectrum and Western styles of action, but proved unable to shed the image of elitist clubs. The Popular Fronts fared better, sprouting at the municipal and regional levels on more down-to-earth issues, such as a fairer and more transparent budgetary process in the soviets. The largest and most vocal of them was the Leningrad People's Front, dominated by attractive public speakers and organizers: radical populists as well as democrats, such as Marina Salye, Ilya Konstantinov, and Vitaly Skoybeda. The Moscow People's Front (MPF), administered by young straight-arrow academics, was smaller and less influential, and by 1989 was already riven by conflicts between right-wing freemarketeers and social-democrats, when most of the country's political activists had not yet learned about this distinction. However, the MPF leaders managed to mount a campaign for the Moscow city soviet elections in 1990, and one of them, Sergei Stankevich, became deputy chairman of the city soviet under Gavriil Popov. Although the Popular Fronts had the greatest potential for growing into a nationwide political movement, they stubbornly clung to their local issues and special concerns, thus fostering the political fragmentation of the country. An attempt to unite all of them under a single umbrella (in August 1988 in Leningrad) ended in failure.[102]

Meanwhile, inside the CPSU, reformists of various stripes cautiously began to set up clubs to debate and advance their interests and programmatic views, some of them simultaneously positioning themselves around juicy pieces of the fragmenting government sector that would soon be privatized. Here, the ideological distinctions were much better appreciated. Their discussions later gave rise to the large Democratic Platform group on the right (which became the cradle for a host of postcommunist parties) and the tiny Marxist Platform on the left. Yet another type of semi-official organization was represented by the elitist clubs of the intellectual establishment, which attracted veterans of the dissident movement seeking a shortcut to political influence, reform-minded academics from the upper layer of the party, and progressive columnists. Foremost among these clubs was Moscow Tribune, set up in October 1988. Although Sakharov, Afanasiev, and other committed democrats were among its founders and served as figurehead members of its board, Moscow Tribune soon assumed an exclusionist and paternalistic posture toward the civil society that was struggling to be born. Its weekly sessions were used for setting a consensus line for liberal commentary on various issues and as an informal admissions committee for those aspiring to a career in the "democratic movement." The board of Moscow

Tribune invited selected activists of the Popular Fronts and the minuscule intellectual clubs and parties to address their sessions, and hand picked the most promising among them, such as Stankevich or Oleg Rumyantsev, giving them a green light to the front pages of mass-circulation periodicals and offering useful connections for subsequent electoral campaigns. Gorbachev and his liberal associates, such as Aleksandr Yakovlev, who were fearful of showing up at mass rallies because of the latter's anti-nomenklatura hostility, regarded Moscow Tribune as a comfortable halfway house in the communication channel between Pushkin Square (Moscow's analogue to London's Hyde Park Corner) and Old Square, where the CPSU Central Committee was headquartered.

In December 1988, Gorbachev pushed through the USSR Supreme Soviet constitutional amendments and election laws to establish the Congress of People's Deputies (hereafter, "the Congress"), an oversized quasi-parliament of 2,250 members that was reminiscent of the medieval Assemblies of the Land *(zemskie sobory)*. To minimize risks, only two-thirds of the seats were to be elected by a democratic multicandidate vote, while one-third of the seats were assigned to the appointed delegates of various established national organizations (including one hundred deputies chosen by the Communist Party). The Congress itself was to elect a permanent standing legislature, the Supreme Soviet. The elections for the Congress, set for March 1989, created an opportunity for cooperation among Popular Fronts, informal cabals inside the CPSU, kitchen clubs, and "parties" with only a handful of members. The civic space was filled with mushrooming voters' clubs that coalesced around specific candidates, whom they helped to run the bureaucratic gauntlet of nomination and registration in election committees, often by exerting pressure on those regional and local barons who meddled in the work of the committees and in the electoral process. Although voters' clubs emerged in widely separated parts of the country, they followed strikingly similar organizational patterns. In a number of cases, they were set up by visiting democratic celebrities from Moscow who toured select regions and passed judgment on local activists and prospective deputies who were championing a democratic or a populist cause.

In the final analysis, thanks to the hectic work of local activists and the enthusiasm of thousands of volunteers, as well as thinly veiled support from the Gorbachev team, a small but strongly motivated group of diverse individuals carrying the banners of democracy and social justice captured the vote in the largest urban and suburban centers and gained seats in the Congress. In Western terms, most of them would have qualified as liberals and leftists. They viewed all types of Russian nationalism as an artifact of dark forces and identified even moderate nationalists with Pamyat'. Thus the beginnings of civil society in Russia, in many ways a by-product of Gorbachev's seesaw technique, had a heavily partisan skew to the left. But at the same time, the Moscow democrats threw their support to the ethnocratic nationalists fielded by the local nomenklatura in the Baltic republics, western Ukraine, Georgia, and Armenia.

Meanwhile, Russian nationalists were demoralized by the relentless media onslaught on the part of the radical internationalists and virtually abandoned hope of setting up an electoral machine of their own. If they had tried to create one, they would have received little government assistance. Virtually none of the nationalists risked running in their own districts. The most famous nationalists happened to be Muscovites by birth or by choice, but Moscow was already under the tight grip of the radicals. At the last moment, some conservative authors and columnists were given slots in the deputies list of the Writers' Union; and Rasputin and Belov were inserted by Gorbachev himself among the hundred CPSU deputies nominated by the Central Committee. One of the few candidates who dared to campaign under the nationalist banner in a regular district was a still obscure Afghan War veteran, Colonel Aleksandr Rutskoi, who lost his race despite his considerable gift for incendiary rhetoric.[103]

YELTSIN ON THE CAMPAIGN TRAIL: GREEN LIGHT FOR THE RADICAL OPPOSITIONIST

Perhaps the most predictable result of the 1989 vote was Yeltsin's landslide victory in the premier district of the country, the "national-territorial" district of Moscow, something like an "at-large" seat for the whole capital area. The authorities did virtually nothing to prevent him from running, and there was no competition to speak of; the only opposing candidate was the unpretentious managing director of the ZIL automobile company. Furthermore, the campaign waged by Yeltsin's detractors was inept and counterproductive. In his first volume of memoirs, Yeltsin recalls being asked whether the municipal authorities (the Moscow city party boss was by now the military-industrial bureaucrat and Politburo member Lev Zaikov) were on the payroll of his campaign headquarters. It is likely that a decision had been made at the top to make no effort to block Yeltsin, although Gorbachev also may have seen that any clumsy moves against him would have only boosted his chances. Once he entered the race, his victory was a foregone conclusion, barring a challenge by some famous democrat with a distinct agenda of his or her own. Looking ahead, let us remark that the fatalistic myth about Yeltsin as a pre-anointed winner was carefully re-created around him by his team in each of his subsequent campaigns, and he always skillfully managed to exploit it. Yeltsin captured Moscow with no fewer than five million votes, or 89 percent—a result that, he later conceded, could not have been expected under "civilized" conditions.[104]

These results were even more remarkable because they occurred in Moscow, the most privileged and tightly controlled city in the country, where the issues of social justice, corruption, and nomenklatura privileges were traditionally less prominent among the discontented than the mainstream liberal values of political, economic, and cultural freedom. This indicates that grassroots support

was neither the only nor the most relevant factor (as compared to covert support from high-level factions) behind Yeltsin's success. This was especially true,
given the fact that several prominent democrats and reformers, running in smaller,
"administrative-territorial" districts of Moscow had been carefully filtered off
the ballot by election committees. For instance, this happened with *Ogonyok*
editor-in-chief Vitaly Korotich, who had become an unabashedly pro-Western
liberal and had flirted with the Democratic Union. He had distanced himself on
several occasions from Yeltsin's populism, and his high-circulation magazine
had raised doubts about Yeltsin's democratic credentials. In Moscow's Dzerzhin-
ski district, Korotich was thrown off the ballot by the electoral committee, and
mass public protests did not restore him. The democrats in the district vowed to
boycott the election to make it invalid and start the nomination process all over
again. In any event, the voting was declared to have been valid, with slightly over
50 percent of the electorate turning out (thanks to a mysterious last-minute
increase in the number of registered voters). The seat was captured virtually
without competition by Yuri Skokov, an obscure manager of a military-industrial
plant without progressive credentials but with family ties in the Politburo. He
was an obvious client of Zaikov and was soon to become the closest conservative associate of Yeltsin.[105]

In sum, it looked as though the waning Gorbachev-Yakovlev group of highbrow liberals had lost Moscow in advance of the actual vote, thanks to all the
Byzantine manipulation, while a certain part of the ruling oligarchy either did
not oppose, or even welcomed, Yeltsin's electoral triumph in the capital. Yeltsin
entered the Kremlin Palace of Congresses as the anointed leader of whatever opposition to Gorbachev might emerge, far better positioned than any self-made
democrat. In contrast to most of them, Yeltsin was not a member of a Popular
Front, or a proto-party, or even a CPSU platform group, and thus had no obligations to anyone. Quite the contrary, scores of organizations, mistreated by the
media and suffering from low name recognition, were ferociously competing
for at least some sort of symbolic association with Yeltsin.

During the first meeting of the Congress, under Gorbachev's chairmanship,
members of the tiny opposition minority had to fight hard to make a single remark
at the microphone in the back of the hall—but Yeltsin was given the floor
twice, without much struggle on his part. In Yeltsin's big speech, he identified
the major issue of the moment as "the question of power, which must justifiably
belong to the people." The injustice and illegitimacy of the existing social order
was the central theme of his thundering invectives:

> The stratification of society on the basis of wealth is intensifying. The principles
> of social justice and social equality are not being implemented. The number of
> poor people is growing and the faith of the Soviet people in the real results of
> perestroika is declining. . . . [T]he broadest possible popular masses have not
> truly become involved in the management of the state. Our press . . . remains under
> the control of a group of individuals and does not reflect the entire variety of

opinions of the members of our society. . . . There is every reason to speak of the existence of a system of elitism in our society. . . . *(Applause.)* Why is it that in the country there are dozens of millions of people living below any kind of poverty line while others are swimming in luxury?. . . Perhaps we should begin . . . by eliminating all illegal privileges from the nomenklatura and, in general, remove from our vocabulary the word "nomenklatura." *(Applause.)* This would enhance the moral condition of society.[106]

The democrats and liberals who had looked askance at Yeltsin's radical populism (honed by his image-makers) and scorned him for deluding the poorly educated strata now had to resign themselves to sharing with him the mantle of the progressive opposition. Moreover, as they discovered in the back rooms of the Congress, Yeltsin's populist charisma commanded solid support among regional deputies, including those of the nomenklatura who respected him for having humiliated and tamed the capital's establishment during his tenure at the Moscow party committee. Most remarkably, Yeltsin's pronouncements won him support from the provincial intellectuals in whom the Moscow liberals had invested so much hope, but who, unlike them, were not scared off by populism. His candidacy was consecutively proposed for the posts of chairman of the Supreme Soviet, deputy speaker of the House of Nationalities, and chairman of the People's Control Committee (which had been designed to oversee the actions of the executive and offered a perfect springboard for someone who would commit himself to a systematic onslaught against corruption). In all three cases, he withdrew his candidacy. Yet after Yeltsin failed to make the cut in the Congress's vote for membership in the Supreme Soviet, a law professor from Omsk, Aleksei Kazannik, yielded his own seat in Yeltsin's favor. The rules were quickly adjusted to make this valid, and before long Yeltsin had joined the presidium of the Congress as the chairman of the Committee on Construction and Architecture.[107]

Meanwhile, from the very first days of the Congress it became obvious that the ideologically committed radicals on both the conservative and populist-democratic sides were but a tiny minority in the huge assembly. The pre-election illusion that the country had divided into powerful ideological camps and was thus ready for a multiparty system resulted from a distorted picture created by the Moscow media. In the Supreme Soviet, both ideological extremes got even more meager representation. The main bulk of the deputies consisted of a mass of local party bosses and their clients, indifferent to ideology and organizationally pulverized but seething with emotional hostility toward the alien and incomprehensible forces that had upset their traditional way of life. Yuri Afanasiev's comment about the "aggressively obedient majority" remains the most succinct and accurate description of the major group in this parliament, which was also known as "the swamp." The inarticulate rage that many deputies brought from their districts was unleashed against any obvious target that presented itself. Most often the target became the democrats, especially Andrei Sakharov and, of course, Gorbachev himself, who often lost control over the deliberations of the Congress. Before long, Gorbachev became visibly appalled at the destructive power of this 2,250-member legislature and turned his back on it, as he had already turned his back on the Party.[108] While Gorbachev and his associates were busy crafting the new institution of the presidency, the management of the Congress fell into the hands of Anatoly Lukyanov, a skillful manipulator of crowds and a committed enemy of the populist-democratic opposition.

Given that democrats and liberals taken together commanded an insignificant fraction of the Congress seats, they had to take what they could get. For that reason, Gavriil Popov, Gorbachev's favorite opposition figure, had to drop his dreams of becoming the sole leader of the quasi-opposition Inter-Regional Deputies' Group (IDG) that he was about to set up. In the elections of the five IDG co-chairmen in July 1989, Yeltsin was the big winner, with 97 percent of the votes. Sakharov, the most committed democratic opposition spokesman, came in fifth, with less than 50 percent of the votes. Sakharov evoked a subliminal sense of guilt among the newly minted democrats who had been enjoying life in the Party's service while he had been cut off from the world in his Gorki exile, but he never got more than lukewarm support among these Johnny-come-latelies. Indeed, Sakharov was probably allowed into the IDG leadership mostly because of his international prestige. In addition to Yeltsin and Sakharov, the other co-chairmen were Popov; Yuri Afanasiev (the rector of the Institute of History and Archives and a Sorbonne-trained expert on the French Revolution, whose worldview was rapidly evolving toward Sakharov-style democratic internationalism); and Viktor Palm, an Estonian professor representing the opposition from the USSR's non-Russian republics.[109]

DEMOCRACY AND REFORMS ON BOARD THE TITANIC

While Russian democrats, liberals, populists, and moderate party reformers were busily defining themselves in relation to one another, the Soviet Bloc entered the final phase of its existence. It was no coincidence that the explosion of anti-Soviet and anti-Russian sentiment along Russia's periphery, including some of the Union's republics, occurred in sync with the deterioration of the Soviet economy and the entire Comecon system.[110] In our view, the disintegration of the Soviet Bloc perhaps might have been averted or at least delayed by launching around 1987 a comprehensive program of economic restructuring and development for the Comecon countries as a whole, along with democratic reforms to ensure a reasonably fair and legitimate distribution of benefits. Had Gorbachev and his economic advisers presented a coherent development strategy with realistic short-term targets, perhaps along the lines of the import-substitution policies of postwar Japan and the Asian Tigers, they might have been able to guide the region's burgeoning civil societies toward constructive goals, with specific and tangible measures of achievement. Instead, Gorbachev kept tinkering with microeconomic experiments at the organizational level, which gave a pretext for the nomenklatura of the regions and republics to tailor or simply disregard the federal laws for their own benefit. This only sharpened the frustration and discontent of the populace because everybody saw that Gorbachev's airy theorizing about local initiative and his communitarian brand of populism led, in practice, to the abrogation of the Kremlin's basic responsibilities to the citizenry, and to the devolution of authority to feudal barons who were often more corrupt, oppressive, and incompetent than the federal bureaucracy. Meanwhile, the government of Prime Minister Nikolai Ryzhkov, dominated by sectoral and regional parochialism, was intrinsically unable to produce a systemic vision of the situation and needs of the country as a whole in the late 1980s, let alone an economic strategy for Comecon.

It is hard to identify the precise moment when the doom of the Soviet bloc was sealed. Certainly, though, the glacier began to move in the spring of 1989, with the election defeats of the nomenklatura in Poland and Hungary. The events of 1989 revealed the true nature of Gorbachev the liberal anarchist, shuttling between Moscow, Prague, and Beijing, sending his envoys, quietly encouraging the rebels, and urging the governments to exercise moderation in response. This appears to have been an attempt to break out of the Soviet domestic stalemate by establishing pro-Gorbachev reformist regimes in the satellite countries. If so, it was an ill-conceived operation, betraying the Kremlin's overconfidence in its manipulative abilities and its overestimation of dependent nations' gratitude toward what appeared to be a deliberately self-destroying patron state. Gorbachev would have been better advised to compare himself with his predecessors in the Kremlin, who thought that presumed gratitude for extensive welfare provisions would prevent their subjects from rebelling, and who later discovered they were wrong. In any case, the socialist reformers installed with Gorbachev's support, like Karoly Grosz in Hungary, either were washed overboard by the tidal wave of democratic and undemocratic nationalism, or soon turned their backs on Moscow.

On the domestic front, from early 1989 Gorbachev's authority went into precipitous decline. He had proved unable to muster a reliable base of support in the Congress and Supreme Soviet or to maintain the loyalty of the Party. By now, these institutions had only a vague sense of unifying purpose, so they started fragmenting along social and ethnic lines, driven apart by special interests. If there was one thing in common among the democratic and conservative minorities and "the swamp" of local party bosses in these institutions, it was their mistrust and hostility toward Gorbachev. The political situation of the time was defined by the abundance and diversity of opposition forces, while the ruling force in the country was increasingly hard to identify.

The seesaw equilibrium between the right and the left was now a thing of the past. If the self-styled democrats were able to attract a broad audience and

present themselves as being on the winning side of history in the light of the
East European developments, they had no conservative counterweight of any
size and credibility. After the tidal wave of anticommunist publications, the orthodox Marxist circles in the Party were disoriented. Advocates of preserving the
Union, like Ligachev, were discredited by their alleged association with ethnic
Russian imperialism or fascism. They had no charismatic leaders, and their antag-
onists were too elusive: every important democrat or nationalist leader in the
major republics vigorously repudiated the goal of breaking up the USSR. Indeed,
some of them, such as the leader of the future Lithuanian secessionist movement
Sajudis, Vytautas Landsbergis, argued ardently in 1989 in favor of renegotiat-
ing the Union Treaty (which defined Soviet federalism) among the republics.
Thus if the empire was fragmenting, there was virtually no one to blame except
Stalin, who had been too brutal in his attitude toward ethnic minorities, and Gorbachev, who had been too permissive. Behind the imminent collapse, people
saw the invisible hand of fate, and to resist it would have been foolish.

Even if isolated voices of enlightened and forward-looking conservatism were
occasionally heard, they were drowned out by the main conservative force of
the day, the disoriented but aggressive nomenklatura-bureaucratic majority in
the Congress and the regional barons. Their ideological commitments were diffuse, although hundreds of Congress deputies sprang to their feet in ecstatic
approval when Sergei Chervonopiski, an Afghan War veteran from Ukraine,
lashed out at Sakharov in defense of the war, shouting the magic formula,
"Great Power, Motherland, Communism!" which was vaguely reminiscent
of Count Uvarov's "Autocracy, Orthodoxy, National Spirit!" of a century and a
half earlier.[111]

Attempts to re-create a conservative-populist alliance were unsuccessful.
New conservative and nationalist organizations were set up in spades, such as
Veniamin Yarin's United Workers' Front, which later became the organizational base for Viktor Anpilov's Russian Communist Workers' Party, and the
International Fronts (Interfronts), which emerged among Russian speakers to
resist the nationalists in the secessionist republics of the Union. But they were a
weak conservative reaction to radical initiatives, and therefore in each case they
failed to create a momentum of their own.[112]

In mid-1989, mass labor strikes became the hot topic of the season. The major
driving force of this new crisis were the coal miners in Siberia's Kuzbass region,
in the Ukrainian Donbass, and in the mining center of Vorkuta near the Arctic
Circle. In Vorkuta, the protesters soon shifted from economic complaints to
openly political demands, including multiparty elections and the resignation of
the government. Soon, this city became a major stronghold of the radical democratic labor movement. In several towns, especially in the Kuzbass, workers' committees seized local power and took control of the distribution of goods, curbing the trade Mafiya and sidelining the inept municipal authorities. The miners'
agenda, even though it was not yet articulated with great clarity, was much

more than a list of vague populist demands focusing on immediate redistribution of national wealth. The miners demanded that the Ryzhkov government immediately present a blueprint for economic transition to what was called at the time a "regulated market." But the program the government produced was poorly conceived, with heavy input from the financial and trade bureaucracies. Its most clearly understandable ingredient was an across-the-board price hike. Within a few days of its announcement, panicky consumers emptied the shelves in the stores.[113]

A characteristic feature of the new labor activism was that it cut across the borders of the republics—the strikers advanced identical or very similar demands, whether in Byelorussia, the Baltics, or the Russian heartland. If the labor movement that was born out of this strike wave had had more time to develop, it might have constituted in our view a major internationalist force that could have helped to achieve the desired social change at the level of the Soviet Union as a whole. No wonder the democratic internationalists, such as Andrei Sakharov and Yuri Afanasiev, extended whatever moral and political support they could give to the strikers and the budding independent labor unions (while Yeltsin showed little interest). Labor militancy under democratic banners spurred the formation of grassroots structures to support the Inter-Regional Deputies' Group; these included the USSR-wide Inter-Regional Association of Democratic Organizations, put together through the efforts of the Leningrad People's Front. It was perhaps at this point that the opposition came closest to forming a nationwide democratic movement along the lines of Poland's Solidarity, which—if republic secessionism had been headed off by urgent renegotiation of the Union Treaty —might have been able to oust the discredited nomenklatura while preserving the country's territorial integrity.

In early December 1989, a group of radically minded leaders of the democratic opposition, including Sakharov and Afanasiev, issued a public appeal for an open-ended general strike to force the resignation of the incompetent Ryzhkov cabinet. The authors of the appeal were savagely attacked by both conservative and liberal media. Some of the co-signers, such as Yuri Chernichenko, were secretly induced to disavow their signatures and to join the attacks on the initiators of the appeal. A few days later, on December 14, 1989, Andrei Sakharov was found dead in his apartment. His funeral brought huge crowds of mourners into the streets, and the nationwide general strike was quietly relegated to the back burner, having lost one of its prospective political leaders.

As 1990 drew near, the Western world was joyfully celebrating the demise of the Berlin Wall and the democratic revolutions across Eastern Europe. In contrast, the politically active minority of Soviet citizens was once again plagued by the paralyzing obsession of falling behind the locomotive of historical progress. Instead of a mass democratic mobilization, the general mood across the country was characterized by an emotional crisis and disorientation in the rapidly changing global and historical landscape. Rational motivations increasingly yielded to the unfocused rage of those who felt besieged by the new and unfamiliar. The air was filled with a growing sense of misfortune, collapse of the social order, rapid decay in living standards, and fear of an unpredictable future. This pervasive anxiety repeatedly boiled over with rumors of impending price hikes, ruble devaluation, or the confiscation of savings accounts, all of which led to protracted bouts of consumer panic. The free hand allowed to secessionists in the Baltics, Georgia, and western Ukraine triggered a backlash in Russia itself. Amid growing ethnic tensions and suspicion toward outsiders, many regional and municipal authorities imposed a ban on the sale of various goods to non-residents, and their neighbors retaliated in kind. The Soviet Union was swept by what was called "the war of laws": republics, regions, and even cities were adopting new laws and regulations that blatantly violated the federal constitution, but there was no authoritative arbiter to prohibit them from doing so.[114]

On December 31, 1989, the shock waves from the nationalist revolutions in Eastern Europe tipped over the first domino of the Soviet edifice. To boost its chances in the upcoming elections to the parliament in Vilnius, the Lithuanian Communist Party, led by Algirdas Brazauskas, announced its separation from the CPSU. Gorbachev's trip to Vilnius to cajole the Lithuanians to rescind their decision became an additional sign of impotence. The driver's seat was empty, and people looked around impatiently for a strong hand to rapidly finish the business of destruction and then to restore a minimum of order. Someone was needed who could burst onto the stage, sort out conflicting emotions, and direct them toward an identifiable goal.

It was this mood of irrationality and despair that spurred Yeltsin and his associates into action. In all probability, they must have felt that if Yeltsin were not to assume this consolidating role, someone else would show up to claim it before long.

SCUTTLING THE UNION: PARLIAMENTARY ELECTIONS IN THE REPUBLICS, 1990

If Mikhail Gorbachev had ever dared to assume responsibility for direct action designed to preserve the Soviet Union, his last chance would have been canceling or postponing the elections to the republican legislatures that, according to the Soviet-era schedule, were due and in fact held in February and March 1990. Bearing in mind all the risks of speculative hypotheses about what might have been, we still regard them as an essential antidote to deterministic or fatalistic beliefs that what happened was bound to happen. If Gorbachev had seized on the developing labor movement in the fall of 1989 to make it the bearer of a major program of reforms based upon cooperation between the Kremlin and the citizenry, he would have found a sympathetic audience in the democratic and progressive-minded circles of society that wanted the Soviet Union to follow the East European path of democratic revolution. Then he would have been able to win a campaign for direct election as president of the Union. Had he run on a clear platform of social reformism, he probably would have been able to beat back a potential challenge from Yeltsin, especially because the latter would have had trouble mustering support in the Union's non-Russian republics. After launching the presidential race, together with the campaigns for local and municipal soviets, Gorbachev then would have had little trouble convincing the majority of Soviet citizens to accept the postponement of elections at the republic level— not only for the sake of preserving the Union, but using a more convincing argument that a strong federal authority together with local self-government were the most essential carriers of reforms and the indispensable counterweights to the arbitrary rule of the republican elites. Gorbachev could have pointed out that simultaneous elections to the republican parliaments, before the authority of the new democratic institutions at the federal and the local level had had enough time to solidify, would trigger an uncontrolled devolution of power to the republics' Communist nomenklatura (as in fact happened).

Instead, after having allowed a new, stringent standard of democratic legitimacy to be established, Gorbachev refused to submit himself to this standard by running in unionwide elections. He also did not delay elections in the constituent republics, even though the first ones were going to be held in Lithuania, where opinion polls already showed the secessionists with a majority. It was clear that a secessionist victory in Lithuania's parliament would be a negative advertisement for the Union and would set a precedent, fomenting breakaway movements even in those republics where advocates of independence had only marginal support. It was equally clear that the nomenklatura in the republics was preparing to play the radical nationalist card decisively, thus strengthening secessionist forces and even creating them where none had existed previously. This gambit would furnish the ideal pretext to stop paying taxes to the Union treasury and to appropriate whatever resources or Soviet property they coveted.

For Russian democrats, the 1990 elections were an unfamiliar experience. It was the first time that they had been obliged to deal with the RSFSR as not merely an administrative entity, but a political one as well. The very existence of the Russian Republic within the Union had always been soft-pedaled, and virtually nobody, irrespective of political affiliation, had ever equated it with historic Russia. But if these elections were to become as meaningful as the simultaneous elections in other republics, then the RSFSR had to be conceived of as the real Russia, or at least presented as such to the electorate. This meant *ipso facto* that territories once carved out of historic Russia and made into quasi-autonomous republics by Stalin's cartographers had to be counted once and for all as non-Russian.

These controversies caused a lot of soul-searching among democrats, who had to sort out their conflicting identities as citizens of the RSFSR, the Soviet Union, and the world. No wonder the democratic movement as a whole, or even the Inter-Regional Deputies' Group and its followers, failed to come up with an agreed-upon solution. Quite a few of them, including Gavriil Popov, Anatoly Sobchak, Sergei Stankevich, Ilya Zaslavsky, and others, who had already become celebrities as deputies of the Union Congress, ducked the problem by running for local soviets in "democratic" cities and districts where they were sure to win control over important local administrations. Others, most notably Yuri Afanasiev and his team of radical anti-establishment intellectuals with social-democratic convictions, opted to ignore the elections because of what they saw as the powerless parliament of a phantom republic. They bet all their chips on the possibility that the 1989 East European revolutionary scenario would be replayed on the scale of the USSR. This would have meant a tidal wave of mass demonstrations and strikes, followed by roundtable negotiations between the regime and the opposition forces, which would lead to an agreement on early elections for a new, more democratic legislature. According to this scenario, the Inter-Regional Deputies' Group was to remain the rallying point of the democratic opposition and snatch up the reins of power after they had slipped from Gorbachev's hands. For these radical democrats, elections in the republics were an unwelcome distraction, diverting resources from the major tasks at hand. Besides, they were almost all committed internationalists and Westernizers: like Sakharov and Alexander Yanov, they yearned for the Wilsonian utopia of worldwide democratic brotherhood, above the fray of national or ethnic divisions. The mere mention of Russia, of Russian statehood with its particular interests, grated on the ears of some of them with a disturbing nationalist dissonance.

For Yeltsin and his associates, this tacit refusal of their most famous fellow travelers in the democratic movement to run for the RSFSR parliament was an engraved invitation to uncontested leadership in the race. They viewed the revolutionary path adopted by Sakharov, Afanasiev, labor leaders, and others as too unpredictable and costly, needlessly risking the support of those segments of the nomenklatura and traditionalist groups that Yeltsin had already secured. Yeltsin's own instincts compelled him to seek power through existing institutions, even if that implied the possible fragmentation of the Union. Besides, having inherited the arrogant vanguard mentality of their Bolshevik predecessors, Yeltsin and his circle viewed popular grassroots movements not as the protagonists of history but, rather, as mere vehicles to be commandeered with a determined iron will. On top of that, they had already shown themselves to be at ease with Russian nationalism, despite its close association at that time with ethnic intolerance.

To Yeltsin's benefit, the run-up to the RSFSR elections was marked by a qualitatively new trend within the democratic movement—the coalescence of a new group of democratic activists, most of them young academics or professionals who had already tasted the fruits of governmental impotence under Gorbachev and who favored a stronger authority, provided it could pass the test of democratic legitimation. Bewildered by the anti-Russian virulence of the former allies of the democratic movement in the non-Russian republics, these younger activists sought to protect their identity as Russians and to prove to the world that Russia could become a democratic, Western-type nation, based on the rule of law. Some of them resented the embarrassed reticence about national identity displayed by Sakharov's followers, but they abhorred much more the chauvinism of Pamyat' and thought of themselves as civic, not ethnic, nationalists. This variegated assortment of Russian would-be Young Turks included future parliamentary leaders Oleg Rumyantsev, Mikhail Astafiev, and Viktor Aksiuchits from Moscow; Ilya Konstantinov and Marina Salye from Leningrad; Sergei Baburin from Omsk; Sergei Shakhrai from Rostov; Bela Denisenko from the Kuzbass labor movement; and many others. This democratic-nationalist wave provided dozens of recruits for Yeltsin's electoral slate and enabled him to execute a smooth shift to the right without breaking with his democratic and populist companions. A number of democrats and populists joined Yeltsin's slate either by conviction or for lack of a better choice, but the Young Turks comprised its ideological core. As a sign of their preponderance, the name proposed for Yeltsin's electoral list by the Union of Constitutional Democrats' Mikhail Astafiev was *Democratic Russia,* which sounded impermissibly nationalistic to some of the democrats, but was approved by a general assembly of candidates with a burst of enthusiasm.[115]

Because the CPSU did not have a Russian division that could have served as a vehicle for this election campaign, the only ideological alternative was presented by the traditional, conservative Russian nationalists, and it was clear that they had no chance against Yeltsin's democratic-nationalist coalition. Moreover, the efforts of the conservatives to portray themselves as the genuine, or more radical, nationalists backfired on a regular basis. The conservative camp began preparing for the elections as early as October 1989, when more than fifty deputies of the USSR Congress who had been elected in the RSFSR convened in Tyumen to discuss their electoral strategy.[116] After a heated discussion, only twenty-eight of them managed to agree on a program, which was published a month later in a nationalist magazine. The document contained radical demands for special protection for ethnic Russians throughout the Soviet Union, plus the establishment of separate Russian Academy of Sciences, media and publishing houses for the Russians, and a clause that all Union revenues collected in the RSFSR should also be spent there.[117] A somewhat different group of prospective candidates set up the Russia Club, chaired by the leader of the United Workers' Front, Veniamin Yarin, and featuring *Nash sovremennik* editor-in-chief Stanislav Kunyayev, a notable conservative and CPSU member, and economics columnist Anatoly Salutski as its main ideologues. The two groups backed a joint list of candidates that called itself the Bloc of Public Patriotic Organizations of Russia. Its program, made public on New Year's Eve 1990, larded the already drastic elements of the Tyumen declaration with such demands as a cutoff of federal budget subsidies to the Union republics; the payment of rent by the Union to Russia for hosting USSR institutions; the transfer of the Union capital away from Moscow; the revision of the borders of any constituent republic that tried to secede from the Union; the creation of the Russian Communist Party; and a special law on public morality, including a ban on pornography in the media.[118]

Signatories of this remarkable manifesto who nowadays like to blame the democrats for the collapse of the USSR might re-read this text whenever they are tempted to do so. Their foolhardy attempt to counter secessionism in the republics with an even more virulent and divisive ethnocratic agenda was a sure-fire recipe for speeding up the destruction of the Soviet Union; their demands came down to economic autarky and dismantling the institutional foundations of the USSR. Compared with this irrational and destructive isolationism, the electoral platform of Democratic Russia, which called for a renovated Union Treaty among the republics, impressed voters as remarkably moderate and evenhanded toward the non-Russian citizens of the Union.[119] No wonder the backward-looking manifesto of the right elicited so little support from the conservative Soviet establishment. The Union-level elite factions that had a stake in the outcome of these elections, including Gorbachev himself, favored Yeltsin and his supporters—by now predictable pragmatists—over the desperate and reckless right-wingers whose victory would doom every attempt to cool the interethnic and interrepublican passions that were already threatening the extinction of the USSR.

The election results confirmed public expectations. The conservative-nationalist slate won only a handful of seats across the country and was a fiasco in the major cities. In one of the most spectacular cases in Moscow, Stanislav Kunyayev lost by a margin of nine-to-one to Mikhail Astafiev. (Only two years later, these two were to be brought together by the whirlwind of history as members of the National Salvation Front, the anti-Yeltsin coalition of democratic and undemocratic nationalists to be discussed in chapter 6.) Overall, Democratic Russia and its sympathizers garnered more than a third of the seats in the RSFSR Congress of People's Deputies, emerging as the largest organized political force both inside and outside the parliament.

Among those scholars who view Russian nationalism with some sympathy, John Dunlop blames the procommunist (or, in Russian historical parlance, "National Bolshevik") trend within the conservative-nationalist coalition for its "humiliating defeat."[120] Apparently, he believes that a calibrated dose of anti-communism in their election propaganda would have imparted new magic to the demands listed earlier for an ethnic-based Academy of Sciences, or moving the capital of the USSR away from Moscow. As we have seen, however, the mood of public protest was directed against the ruling establishment, not against communist ideology or rank-and-file Communists. On the contrary, it seems to us that what doomed the conservative opponents of Yeltsin was their immoderate nationalism. No less compelling was a diffuse perception by the Russian educated middle class that the historical trend all over Eastern Europe favored democratic-nationalist modernizers who looked toward the West. Denying victory to their Russian counterparts would violate the Zeitgeist, the ineluctable logic of history, and freeze Russia into a permanent estrangement from its European neighbors. Only a middle-of-the-road force, shunning both the gloom and defeatism of ethnocratic isolationists as well as overconfident global ambition, seemed able to ensure the peaceful preservation of the Union by moving Russia together with other Soviet Bloc nations into what many at that time imagined to be a brotherhood of selfless and benevolent democratic nations.

On the election day of March 4, 1990, an overwhelming majority of voters in major urban centers cast their votes for the candidates fielded by Democratic Russia as the only force that embodied these promises.

4

FROM RUSSIAN SOVEREIGNTY TO THE AUGUST COUP: A MISSED CHANCE FOR A DEMOCRATIC REVOLUTION

It seemed we were all acting like robots,
  not looking at one another or understanding
what was happening.

  —*Valery Boldin, one of the coup plotters,*
    commenting on their return from their meeting
    with Gorbachev on August 18, 1991

D URING THE TWENTY MONTHS between February 1990 and October 1991, the vast territories of what had until recently been the Soviet Bloc of countries went through rapid and far-reaching change. With the benefit of hindsight, it is easy to assert that a comprehensive but relatively peaceful self-destruction of the Soviet state was inevitable, but at the beginning of this period such an outcome appeared to most observers to be one of the least likely among the possible alternatives.[1] Mikhail Gorbachev, at the peak of his worldwide glamour, seemed firmly in the saddle. Significant parts of the political landscape were defined by the mass-based anti-nomenklatura movement and increasingly militant labor unions, whose advocacy of social justice and political participation broadly coincided with the declared purposes of perestroika itself, and even with the original promises of socialism in their most universal, non-Bolshevik form. In most of Eastern Europe, democratic revolutions had brought noncommunist governments into power, but none of them was as yet overtly unfriendly to Moscow.

It seemed to some observers as if the Soviet Union would be able to retain at least some control over this democratic transformation and thus secure for itself a new and more legitimate sphere of moral and political influence in the international system. Few expected Soviet influence in Eastern Europe to decline as quickly as it did. Few observers either in the West or in the East could imagine that the Soviet ruling elite would allow the Warsaw Pact and the Soviet Union itself to fall apart without resorting to an all-out crackdown, perhaps followed by a civil war with a large number of casualties. Likewise, few observers would have believed at the time that, after seven decades of advertising its system as a comprehensive alternative to the market allocation of goods, the Soviet elite would abandon so fully this unique legitimizing teleology and embrace with such buoyant radicalism—as Russia did in October 1991—the Washington Consensus shock therapy doctrine of economic deregulation, privatization, and free trade without giving serious thought to alternative strategies.

Yet by the end of 1991, this seemingly improbable scenario had materialized in full—with a few partial exceptions like Turkmenistan and Ukraine. By then, the internationalist idealism of the Russian democrats had been shaken, the labor movement had subsided, the anti-nomenklatura coalition had been torn apart by conflicting ideologies and interests, a portion of Eastern Europe and several of the former Soviet republics had been severely jolted by vindictive ethnic hostilities, and Mikhail Gorbachev had turned into a political shadow. Against this disarray, the figure of Boris Yeltsin, recently dismissed as a populist, a poser, an opportunist, a simpleton, and a drunkard, rose to unchallenged prominence in Russian politics. After being elected as speaker of the Russian parliament on the third ballot with a tiny four-vote majority, he repeatedly obtained from the parliament special, extraconstitutional powers for himself. By November 1991, he had reduced the parliament to the role of a weak, if critical and sometimes rowdy, spectator of the ensuing economic revolution from above. Within the Soviet body politic, Yeltsin had created for himself a previously nonexistent institution, the presidency of the largest constituent republic of the Union, and built a full-fledged state around it by ruthlessly cutting off or destroying those elements of the Soviet system—like the Communist Party—that he did not need. The speed of these changes bore a striking similarity to the period between February 1917 and July 1918, which witnessed a transition from a decadent but still almost unlimited autocracy, through a series of shaky semi-revolutionary governments, to Bolshevik one-party rule. Yet another similarity lay in the fact that in both cases the ultimate winners emerged from a prolonged period of so-called dual power.

In the saga of Yeltsin's ascendancy, the three-day quasi-coup of August 19–21, 1991, played a pivotal role as the denouement of one of the most breathtaking shifts in modern world history. For a short while, most people sincerely believed that a heroic resistance to the coup by the Russian leaders and by the democratic movement that they claimed to represent, culminating in the defense of the parliamentary headquarters (the Russian White House) by the people of Moscow, had staved off a totalitarian restoration. Thus in the eyes of many Russians and their Western sympathizers, Yeltsin's postcommunist and seemingly democratic Russia acquired for the first time since 1917 the powerful legitimacy of a progressive, revolutionary state. Within a year, however, this myth had been thoroughly dismantled. The revolutionary legitimacy of the new regime had evaporated, with August 1991 becoming a symbol for the opportunities squandered by apparently genuine and progressive reformers. The causes and outcomes of the so-called hard-line coup and of Yeltsin's countercoup are not of some distant historical interest for our analysis. Rather, they shed light on the social and political roots of what has come to be known in Russia as "the August regime"—the period of tense cohabitation between the self-described democrats and the self-described market reformers, which lasted from August 1991 to October 1993—and, more broadly, of Yeltsin's system of rule. In particular, the analysis of events surrounding the coup helps to reveal the unspoken (or at least unpublicized) bargains within the Soviet ruling elite, bargains that laid the foundation for the present social order in Russia.

THE SYSTEM OF DUAL POWER: GORBACHEV AND YELTSIN

Confirmation that the Soviet Union's eventual demise was a realistic possibility became evident in late February–early March 1990. For this period, the electoral timetable prescribed elections for the parliaments of the Union's constituent republics. The run-up to these elections narrowed the scope of public debate from the all-Union democratic agenda to regional, ethnic, and local concerns. The fact that the elections in the tumultuous Baltics were the first on the schedule had far-reaching implications for the fate of the Union. On February 27, the

Lithuanians were the first to vote for their new parliament. The tallying of votes was barely finished when, on the night of March 11, the first session of the Lithuanian parliament, dominated by a secessionist majority, announced the restoration of the Lithuanian Republic (which had been created in 1918 at the end of the German military occupation of territories that previously belonged to the Russian Empire and had been liquidated in 1940 under the Molotov-Ribbentrop Pact).[2] On March 30 and May 4, respectively, the Estonians and Latvians cautiously followed the Lithuanian lead. This new situation had a strong impact on the electoral and postelectoral agenda in other republics. It shifted the focus away from the unionwide socioeconomic change demanded by Russia's anti-establishment movement toward cooperation between republican oligarchies and radical nationalists, in which the former traded some of their political power to the latter for wealth and respectability as fellow founding fathers of national independence.

Meanwhile in Moscow, the Inter-Regional Deputies' Group and the electoral slate of Democratic Russia (with most of its supporters still believing in Russia's leadership of a major revolution in Eurasia) staged a powerful rally of half a million people in the Union's capital, demanding the abolition of Article 6 of the Soviet Constitution, which designated the CPSU as the "leading and directing force of Soviet society." Evidence suggests that Gorbachev and Lukyanov covertly encouraged the organizers of this rally because—as they accurately foresaw—such pressure might scare the recalcitrant Soviet parliament into approving the constitutional amendments required for the establishment of the Soviet presidency.[3] On March 13–15, 1990, the Third Congress of People's Deputies abrogated Article 6, instituted the office of the presidency, and hastily had the president elected by the Congress—not by popular vote—Gorbachev being the only candidate. With an unimpressive 59 percent of the votes in his favor, Gorbachev did formally secure a five-year term, but the procedure was a costly one in terms of his broader legitimacy and democratic credentials. While he and his operatives argued that a fast-track election had been required to counter centrifugal tendencies in the country, the lack of a popularly elected Union president was soon to become a major vulnerability for advocates of the USSR's integrity.

Worse still, Gorbachev's newly enhanced position endowed him with no magic powers for dealing with secessionism. Having avoided decisive actions in the crucial months before the elections in the Baltics, he could now fight for Union integrity only by offering the Balts some vision of economic and social change more appealing than just nationalism. But he had already pulled all the rabbits out of his hat. As could have been expected, his threatened, then imposed, economic sanctions against Lithuania in March–April only boosted the cause of the parliament in Vilnius and elicited sympathy for the Lithuanians among Russian democrats and the world at large. In addition, Yeltsin started cautiously down the fateful but politically rewarding path toward Russian independence, first floating the balloon of secessionism: "Russia, as a union republic, is also entitled to leave the Union, and this is not only a formal right."[4]

Meanwhile, the elections to the RSFSR Congress of People's Deputies were a rather limited success for the democrats. In their battle for Russia, they did not pay due attention to Stalin's canny dictum that "cadres decide everything." Thus many stalwarts of the democratic movement who could have easily won seats did not run because they were distracted by Union-level or local-level activities. When the Russian Congress convened on May 25, 1990, Democratic Russia, although the largest organized political group among the deputies, nevertheless constituted a minority (some 400 members and unregistered supporters among 1,060 deputies). Worse still, Democratic Russia included very few nationally recognizable faces apart from Yeltsin. The majority of the parliament consisted of "the swamp" of regional Communist Party bosses, economic managers, bureaucrats of various levels with either deeply hidden or nonexistent beliefs, and simply ambitious people with connections who happened to be close to politics.

In this unstable environment, a gaping void replaced the Communist Party's constitutional authority. With only a vague sense of who was now in charge, rank-and-file deputies from the Russian heartland, many of whom had never seen Moscow before, were looking for a firm hand to lead the Congress, give it a sense of purpose and relevance, and insulate it from the unionwide turbulence. What was needed, in short, was a decisive and aggressive politician who would show no scruples in defending the collective interests of the Congress as an institution. The only visible candidate for this role was Boris Yeltsin.

Yeltsin and his associates had done their homework. Before the opening of the Congress, they held informal sessions with rank-and-file deputies, within and outside of Democratic Russia. They put special efforts into cultivating "the swamp" because, unlike the fractious democrats with their sometimes oversized egos, regional bosses often controlled the votes of entire regional delegations and could reliably deliver them *en bloc* in exchange for tangible benefits. Yeltsin's ambitious Young Turks, primarily Sergei Shakhrai and Oleg Rumyantsev, drafted a Declaration of Sovereignty for the RSFSR, which in practice gave the Congress institutional autonomy and special status as the most legitimate embodiment of the RSFSR's anticipated statehood.[5] An important clause in the declaration, and a concomitant amendment to the RSFSR constitution, authorized the Congress to make final decisions "on any issues in Russia's jurisdiction."

The institutional advantages of such sovereignty for the deputies themselves were plain to see. The rallying cry of Russian sovereignty furnished a perfect substitute for the program of comprehensive economic and social change that the Yeltsinites so far had been unable to offer. Furthermore, many would-be nationalists among Yeltsin's supporters, concerned about the integrity of the Union, welcomed the declaration as a sign that Russia was ready to take responsibility for, and leadership in, the reconstruction of the Union on a democratic basis, something that the Gorbachev Kremlin was manifestly unable to offer. As for Yeltsin, he was already considering the parliament as a springboard for the nationally elected presidency of the RSFSR, which he openly advocated, although few deputies would have been ready at the time to support such far-reaching institutional changes.

On May 29, despite Gorbachev's hidden and overt attempts to impede Yeltsin's election (and at least partly *because of* such attempts), the Russian Congress, by a margin of four votes, elected Yeltsin as the chairman of its Supreme Soviet, after three stalemated rounds fought against faceless and uninspiring apparatchiks. On June 12, an overwhelming majority ratified the Declaration of Sovereignty drafted by Rumyantsev and Shakhrai without the slightest objection. Probably only a few of those present in the hall sensed its explosive potential for Soviet statehood, in spite of Yeltsin's rhetorical and perhaps sincere allegiance to the idea of a new Union Treaty to preserve and strengthen the federation. Yeltsin may still have had the prime goal of succeeding Gorbachev as president of the Union.

Thus in a way not so different from February 1917, Russia ushered in an era of dual power. Unlike the separation of powers and checks and balances that are characteristic of Western constitutions, the recurrent phenomenon of dual power in Russian history typically implies the simultaneous existence of two institutions without clearly delineated spheres of authority, but with conflicting claims on the same sources of legitimacy. In Russia, with its dismissive attitude toward legalistic pedantry, the prevailing strategy for aspiring politicians has been to seize control of at least one governmental institution (whichever is most accessible) and then to redefine its purpose and expand its authority on a unilateral basis. From June 1990 on, Russia's development was largely dependent on the balance of power and morale between Gorbachev and Yeltsin, rather than on the various vaguely defined and continuously reinterpreted constitutional and legal norms.

THE HEYDAY OF THE DEMOCRATS AND THE ORGANIZATIONAL TRAP

As we have seen, the electoral coalition of the democrats was only a part of the forces that stood behind Yeltsin's ascendancy.[6] This became clear immediately during the election of his deputies, when some of his most prominent followers, such as Shakhrai and Tatyana Koryagina, were voted down. Behind this drama lay the twilight struggle of contending interest groups over Yeltsin's future political agenda. Aware of that struggle, Yeltsin carefully balanced these groups against one another without indicating a clear preference for anyone's particular vision regarding the nature of his emerging rule. This was his trademark political style. Over time, it became clear that it was also largely the substance of his policies.

In this contest, the democrats' key assets were their unrivaled ability to mobilize huge crowds, their command of the radical media, and their apparently solid support in the West. Theirs was "a movement of several million," as two observers reported.[7] Their vulnerability was the lack of organizational and, more important, programmatic cohesion. Over the past seventy years, the notion of a political party had acquired negative connotations, and most democrats, despite all their abstract support for a multiparty system, were unwilling to bind themselves to any disciplined organization. In fact, a majority of them valued organization and program only as vehicles in an electoral campaign, but were loath to extend their commitments beyond that. More than four hundred deputies had ridden to victory on the Democratic Russia electoral slate, but only sixty-six of them registered as members of the Democratic Russia group at the First Congress. As a result, even though Democratic Russia had won de facto a plurality of votes, it was strikingly unclear exactly what it meant to be a democrat and who, if anyone, could legitimately claim leadership in the movement.

Thus, paradoxically enough—and in a sharp contrast to their East European counterparts—Russian democrats did not establish a single nationwide party until after the multiparty system had been legalized under their pressure in March 1990. Even after that, few of them wanted or could afford to indulge in organization building, which was left by default to a narrow circle of self-appointed cadres. They possibly could have built on the first self-proclaimed party, the Democratic Union of former dissidents, but the elitist vanguard mentality and aggressive overconfidence that characterized its activists had alienated the populist anti-nomenklatura base of the democratic movement. More important, the Democratic Union had not sought a place among Yeltsin's supporters (not least because it viewed Yeltsin as a skillful demagogue promoted by a section of the ruling elite) and had opted out of the republic-level campaign, which it saw as tainted by nationalist overtones. As a result, the wave of democratic organizers gravitating toward the new RSFSR parliament (to lobby, form caucuses, and so forth) started from scratch, discarding the experience and insights of their immediate predecessors. The latter were branded as utopian idealists—traditionally a venerable identification in Russian culture, but one that now suddenly acquired the overtones of a pejorative label in the rapidly shifting cultural and ideological atmosphere of early 1990.

The emergence of professional party managers and a crop of their dedicated followers was the major novelty in the political landscape. Yet many rank-and-file supporters and even prominent spokesmen of the vaguely defined democratic cause were not eager to join in. Many of them simply believed that the integrity of their moral and spiritual resistance to the system would be debased by entering a self-serving struggle for power. Hence, there were a number of marked incongruities between these newborn parties and the fluid grassroots base of the populist anti-nomenklatura movement. Most important, groups and individuals socially and culturally identified with the establishment assumed a disproportionate role in these organizational endeavors, in full accordance with Robert Michels's "iron law of oligarchy."[8] Some of them, such as Nikolai Travkin, Vladimir Lysenko, and others, had tried in vain to engineer an ideological split within the CPSU to introduce the formal features of a multiparty system without dismantling the well-established "transmission belts" of administrative and patron-client loyalty. With the emergence of a new political infrastructure centered on the RSFSR, they had to speed up their efforts in order to secure their position in the new elite.

Thus party building became yet another arena of contest between the ideologically repackaged nomenklatura and the discontented citizenry.[9] On both sides, the end products of party-building activities were markedly different. Parties set up and dominated by prominent ex-members of the CPSU, such as Travkin's Democratic Party of Russia (or DPR, the largest of these parties, with some thirty thousand members at the peak of its influence) and the Republican Party of Lysenko and Vyacheslav Shostakovsky, having recruited members within the CPSU on a wholesale basis, tended to be more numerous and ideologically diffuse. Organizations created by semi-dissident intellectuals, with little or no input from the establishment, such as the Russian Christian Democratic Movement (RCDM) led by Viktor Aksiuchits, or the Socialist Party of Boris Kagarlitsky, defined themselves more clearly in the international spectrum of ideologies, but typically had fewer members and a meager material base. Even within generally nonestablishment organizations, leadership was predominantly captured by former members of the CPSU, such as Aksyuchits (a member in 1971–79) or Marina Salye, the leader of the Free Democratic Party (FDP), whose outlook and "operational code" had been shaped at least partly by their previous attempts to pursue public careers according to the Soviet-era rules of the game.

An important ideological innovation that was carried over by the fresh defectors from the CPSU into the democratic movement was their ferocious hostility not only to Communist doctrine and to the various shades of Marxism, but often to the entire legacy of progressive social thought—a reflection of the intensity of the ideological battles they had lost within the CPSU. Travkin, a recent member of the CPSU Central Committee, made virulent anticommunism one of his party's central ideological tenets. Needless to say, this animus was different in subtle but decisive ways from basic aspects of the original movement of popular discontent, which attributed the principal failures of the Soviet system to the deficit of legitimacy in the system's oligarchical distribution of power rather than to the original rallying cry of the system's denial of a just and equitable society. In other words, for this new democratic elite, the core nature of the Soviet inadequacy was neither socioeconomic nor cultural but primarily ideological.

Psychologically, this particular focus partly resulted from the fact that many of the new party managers had embraced their new views not because of a lifelong confrontation with Soviet realities and a critical reassessment of the pluses and minuses of the system but, rather, because of the impact of some outside influence, typically the demonstration effects of Western consumer culture. Thus Travkin, one of the foremost leaders of this new organizational wave, once explained that he had lost his faith in socialism during a trip to a Swedish supermarket while he was visiting that country as part of a CPSU delegation. This type of cultural shock had such an explosive effect on a previously held set of rigorously interconnected beliefs that, instead of undergoing a rational reevaluation, they were instantaneously replaced *in toto* by what was thought to be their diametrical opposite. In some cases, the impact on the individual cognitive map was so strong that fundamental beliefs inherent not only in Soviet, but also in centuries-old mainstream Russian culture, along with the common heritage of post-Enlightenment Western culture, were systematically negated. Among those self-described democrats who had undergone this conversion, some became skeptical about the ability of the Russian people to act rationally, some assigned the blame for the decline of the work ethic to the poor and dispossessed (for whom they reserved the pejorative Marxist label of the *Lumpen*), others lambasted the dangerously utopian intelligentsia for their concern about social justice (which had allegedly doomed the country to Stalin's atrocities), and still others extolled Pinochet as a role model for economic reformers.

To illustrate some features of this evolution, let us quote here from the program of the Social Democratic Party of Russia (SDPR), "The Road to Progress and Social Democracy," adopted by the party's second (programmatic) congress in October 1990. The SDPR (one of whose leaders, Oleg Rumyantsev, coauthored not only the above-mentioned Declaration of Sovereignty, but also a draft constitution later used in 1993 as the basis for the Yeltsin constitution) was a medium-size party that steered a middle course between the visceral anticommunism of such CPSU converts as Travkin or Salye and the liberal-progressive worldview of someone like Yuri Afanasiev. Its programmatic statements, therefore, can be viewed as typical of the new, Young Turk mainstream of Yeltsin's supporters in the parliament. In its overview of Soviet history, the SDPR program stated that "the negative by-products of the painful course of modernization . . . resulted in the rapid swelling of the mass of *Lumpen* and in the growth of antihumanistic, parasitical attitudes."

According to this document, the Bolshevik success in seizing power was attributable to their "unabashed demagogy, which tapped into the vile instincts of the crowd." But their liberal opponents at the beginning of the century were no better, because they "egotistically" engaged in "flirtation with the people." In a similar vein, the authors of the program observed that "the historical disaster of the millions who placed their faith in Bolshevism was their low level of education and culture, the underdevelopment of self-government, and their disrespect for individual rights and freedoms." This comprehensive indictment of the Russian people was matched by the wholesale rejection of the Soviet experience, including the characteristically sweeping claim that the Soviet Union's transformation into an industrial power "was not to the benefit, but rather to the detriment of its citizens, because the growth of their living standards lagged behind the consolidation of the regime."[10]

It was a bitter irony that people so imbued with elitist disdain for whole strata and entire generations of Russians were able to claim the role of ideological vanguard in a movement that had originated in widespread resentment against the arrogance and complacency of the Soviet rulers. It is also a telling fact that in September 1991, one of the SDPR ideologists, Moscow State University professor of economics Aleksandr Shokhin, was appointed RSFSR Minister of Labor (in an agreement between Yeltsin and the SDPR) and thus became one of the leading members of the shock therapy team.[11]

In retrospect, the major dilemma of the 1990–91 period and of the democrats' illusory victory in the August coup appears to be this: At the time when the democratic movement came as close as it ever to did to influencing, if not controlling, the course of events in Russia, the ex-CPSU operatives and ideologues who were becoming the movement's leaders by default undertook a drastic revision of its original social agenda, wiped out or redefined its most revolutionary ingredients, and initiated a revision of some historically embedded elements of continuity in Russian and Soviet culture—such as the intelligentsia's sense of indebtedness to the people and the ideal norms of distributive justice and social welfare. This cognitive revolution among the democratic elite is in itself amenable to rational explanation, but it is clear that such a drastic change in the tenets of their ideology was bound to result in the alienation of their grassroots supporters, who had not been exposed to similar experiences of foreign trips and cultural shocks, nor to such a comprehensive indoctrination in economic determinism (as was required for CPSU cadres). For ordinary people, such an all-out revision of their basic cultural values was painfully shocking. No wonder that none of the so-called democratic parties of the 1990 wave—either separately or in coalition—ever managed to secure support from more than a tiny fraction of the anti-nomenklatura base that constituted the original democratic movement.

However, the irreparable blows to the democratic parties of 1990 vintage would come with the advent of the Yeltsin-Gaidar economic reforms. Whatever the composition of their leadership, these parties had relied on the unprivileged strata, particularly on the middle class, for their supply of followers. With the rapid mass impoverishment and deprofessionalization of the Soviet middle class, all these parties went into eclipse and lost most of their original members. By 1993, only the DPR was able to field a list of candidates for the Duma and muddle through with 5.5 percent of the votes cast; by the next elections, however, the DPR had fragmented and failed to win any seats at all. The remaining members of some parties, such as the SDPR, gravitated into the orbit of Grigori Yavlinsky's Yabloko, while others, such as the Constitutional Democrats, dissolved into the nationalist opposition. By 1998, a tiny minority of the original democratic activists (namely, Chernichenko's Peasant Party and Lysenko's Republican

Party) finally registered their support for the regime they had helped to create. The only political party formed at the peak of the democrats' popularity in 1990 that swelled its ranks under the Yeltsin reforms and managed to secure a permanent place in the Russian political elite is the famously misnamed Liberal Democratic Party of Vladimir Zhirinovsky.

YELTSIN EVOLVES RIGHTWARD

Meanwhile, during the 1990 election campaign and especially during his fight for the parliamentary speakership, Yeltsin began turning his back on the radical-utopian reformism of his grassroots supporters. He skillfully learned to play some partners in his coalition against others. In particular, he used the growing Russophile sentiment in the Young Turk group of professional and pragmatically minded technocrats aspiring to stable and predictable political careers (who formed the core of the Democratic Russia caucus) to offset the pressure from his populist support base. He also looked around for a new ideology to fill the void created by his abandonment of democratic populism. By that time, Yeltsin had become sick of radicals, leftists, and social reformers of all kinds, partly because of the intellectual pretensions and cultural sensitivities of their leaders, and partly because their Western counterparts, who were devoted to Gorbachev, had unceremoniously snubbed him during his Western trips. Accordingly, the talk about social justice and redistribution of property away from the nomenklatura was quickly replaced by vague phraseology about a "Russian national rebirth," an idea surrounded with pre-1917 symbolism and an aura that was intensely anticommunist and infused with a sense of nostalgia and national restoration. The majority of the Russian Congress, and of the new political class coalescing around it, responded with considerable enthusiasm because this nationalist tilt helped such people further rationalize the separate identity of the RSFSR and its institutions.

Thus in 1990, liberal and not-so-liberal nationalisms were shaping up as the dominant political and intellectual currents. State building, nation building, and nostalgic themes from Russia's "organic" imperial past became the top issues of the day, and they were promptly reflected in such works as the film by Stanislav Govorukhin, *The Russia That We Lost*. The unresolved question was the relationship between the Soviet Union and this previously nonexistent nation-state that was being created by political fiat around the institutions of the RSFSR. On this crucial point, neither Yeltsin nor Democratic Russia had a satisfactory response.

From his seclusion in Vermont, Aleksandr Solzhenitsyn was the first who dared to put forward, in September 1990, a specific set of proposals. In his widely published and quoted essay, "How We Should Put Russia in Order" (published in the West as *Rebuilding Russia*), he suggested that the Russian public accept the inevitable disintegration of the Union as a multiethnic entity; in this eventuality, he believed, the Eastern Slavs—Russia, Ukraine, Byelorussia, and the Slavic majority of northern Kazakhstan—would be able to stay together, thanks to the "organic" force of their ethnic and cultural ties.[12] Solzhenitsyn's program was a nebulous and completely ahistorical attempt to resurrect nineteenth-century Romantic Pan-Slavism. As such, it was poorly grounded in late Soviet reality, where ethnic consciousness of this type existed only at the margins of society and was almost completely alien to the Soviet elites, whose attitude toward national sovereignty and federalism was pragmatically defined by their institutional affiliations. At a deeper level, it neglected the Eurasian dimension of Russian ethnicity and the realities of ethnocultural development elsewhere in the Union, which made the western Ukrainians secessionist and hostile to Russia, and the non-Slavic ethnic groups in Central Asia and their administrative elites intensely committed to the Union's preservation. Coming from an authoritative and representative source in the Russian dissident movement, Solzhenitsyn's proposals evoked considerable support, and such support attested to the extent to which the democrats had become detached from the real situation in the country.

Solzhenitsyn's vision of a new nation based on the USSR's Slavic core was accepted *uncritically* by the liberal-nationalist wing of both the Russian parliament and the democratic movement (in other words, by the circles that we described above as the Young Turks). Thus the "Pan-Russian Union," the provisional title given by Solzhenitsyn to his proposed federation, was soon chosen as the name for a major parliamentary group uniting a radical, markedly anticommunist group of prominent Democratic Russia deputies. Their Pan-Slavist ideal and the process of its realization were so amorphous that the group was doomed to fall apart, which it did in late 1991 during the rapid demise of the Union. The final chapter came when some of its members (Lev Ponomarev, Gleb Yakunin, Bela Denisenko, Marina Salye, Vladimir Varov) supported the Belaya Vezha Agreements, which formally dissolved the USSR, while a sizeable group of its founders (Ilya Konstantinov, Mikhail Astafiev, Viktor Aksiuchits) moved into irreconcilable opposition to the Yeltsin regime.[13]

Alongside this Romantic Slavophile utopianism and the Western ideological approach to nation building, a third distinctive trend was shaping up at this time: The slogan of "Russian national rebirth" was being reformulated in an authoritarian vein reminiscent of Byzantium and the tradition of religious Orthodoxy. This more irrational and illiberal approach originated with Sergei Shakhrai, a young lawyer and deputy of the Russian Congress who was extremely well-versed in legal and constitutional controversies but devoid of any identifiable convictions.[14] Shakhrai, as mentioned, played a key role in the team that drafted Russia's Declaration of Sovereignty and amendments to the RSFSR constitution. His versatile procedural thinking made him a key member of Yeltsin's brain trust, where he managed to stay, despite all the ups and downs of his career, until June 1998 (longer than anybody else except Yeltsin's ghostwriter,

Valentin Yumashev, who survived to the end). Although Shakhrai associated himself with Democratic Russia during his election campaign in early 1990, he was primarily identified with Yeltsin's inner circle of advisers; probably for that reason, he failed to be elected by the Congress as Yeltsin's deputy chairman, despite Yeltsin's repeated nominations of him.

Having grown up in Rostov, historically a Cossack region and the Slavic frontier with the restive Caucasus, Shakhrai brought to Yeltsin's inner circle the peculiar psychology of a survivor from a besieged fortress. Shakhrai and his associates had an outlook that was characterized by an almost mystical admiration for the physical display of power and for imperial pageantry; a reclusive and conspiratorial mode of operation; and cultural intolerance, particularly regarding the non-Russian peoples of the Caucasus. In the initial stage, Shakhrai was the mastermind behind Yeltsin's policies aimed at the resurrection of the Cossacks as both an ethnocultural group and a professional military institution. Among the diverse and mushrooming Cossack organizations and groups, Shakhrai picked out those that were most anticommunist and oriented toward the imperial traditions of absolute power. These groups received financial support from the Yeltsin government and were considered in the early 1990s as a basis for a prospective praetorian guard, whose mission would have been to ward off or crush the radical grassroots discontent with the authoritarian and the promarket shift of Yeltsin's political course.[15]

Yeltsin and his immediate advisers quickly appreciated Shakhrai's sensitivity to hitherto unexploited sources of legitimation of their power—sources that lay deep in the Russian historical mentality and were fundamentally different from the ideas the airy democratic theorizers could offer. To preserve and widen their base of support in society (most of all in the nomenklatura), Yeltsin and his team already felt the need to distance themselves from the liberal internationalists of the Sakharov circle. Yet he could not repudiate them completely (for example, by publicly identifying himself with the ethnic Russian cause) because liberal internationalists controlled the strategically important proreform mass media. For that reason, Yeltsin did not at this stage openly embrace Shakhrai's autocratic, Byzantine notion of state power, but instead continued to maneuver skillfully among the liberal-reformist groups of various shades and the nonideological corporate interests that operated behind the scenes.

The cultivation of nationalist and restorationist pageantry borrowed from the pre-1917 period, in both the democratic and the authoritarian veins, reflected the developing crisis of ideals and values within the original radical-reformist ("democratic") movement at large. By the fall of 1990, the self-described democrats in the Russian parliament were seen both as an integral part of the new ruling elite (because of Yeltsin's association, however ambiguous, with Democratic Russia) and as a source of instability, legal chaos, and frightening uncertainty about the future. The democratic populists and the principled idealists of the Sakharov type were but a negligible minority within the new parliamentary elite, although both groups together still held a majority at the level of the rank and file. The parliamentary democrats had no clear program of action to offer either to the populist base that got them elected or to society at large. The anti-nomenklatura and distributive justice rhetoric began to be phased out as soon as the democratic politicians started to identify themselves as part of the new establishment. Those few members of parliament who stayed loyal to the initial values of democratic populism, like radical economist Tatyana Koryagina, were viewed with suspicion or (following the well-known pattern in Russian history) treated as mentally deranged. But the new nationalism of the "Yeltsin Republic" did not work either because few people outside the RSFSR bureaucracy had developed an emotional attachment to its newborn institutions with their uncertain future. This RSFSR nationalism remained an abstraction, and whatever popular sentiment it harnessed was easily outweighed by stronger affinities either with the Soviet state or the ethnic Russian communities beyond the RSFSR's borders.

The search for a proper ideological framework was directly related to the social and economic content of the new Russian government's policies. It was clear from the outset that all factions were in agreement that the command economy was not working any more and that some kind of market mechanism was required. They also agreed that the transition would inevitably involve a large-scale de jure redistribution of national property (which in fact was already being covertly privatized). However, all this constituted only a very vague blueprint. How and in what sequence would the deregulation proceed? Who would be the beneficiaries of the redistribution of property? How legitimate would the guidelines be? Would illegally seized property be expropriated from the nomenklatura and the Mafiya, as advocated by democratic populists at the grassroots? Or, on the other hand, would the creeping de facto privatization of property by the ruling elite and the criminals be tolerated or even legalized? Would the unprivileged classes have some claim on the redistribution process? If so, would it involve all social groups outside the ruling elite, or only some of them, at the discretion of the reformers?

The answers to these questions clearly depended on the social and professional identity of the reformers themselves. While the government certainly needed a team of competent economists, the latter inevitably would have a hard time getting the managerial elite to carry out their decisions and abide by their authority. The factory managers had their deeply ingrained contempt for the intelligentsia, whom they were accustomed to order around as their subordinates. The most influential team of economists in Moscow were the authors of the so-called "400 Days" program (which was rewritten in June 1990 as the "500 Days" program). The driving force in this rather diverse group was Grigori Yavlinsky, a labor economist who had served for a number of years in the Soviet State Committee on Labor and now worked for Leonid Abalkin on the Soviet government's Commission on Economic Reform. Their first blueprint had been compiled in February 1990 at the request of Mikhail Gorbachev, but soon they saw the Russian parliament as a source of more legitimate authority and offered their services to the future Yeltsin government that was in the process of being formed.[16] However, for the reasons mentioned above, they could not aspire for dominance at the decision-making level in this government. The contest for the premiership was fought out in June between the more conservative and the more commercialized wings of the industrial enterprise managers.

The candidate of the business-oriented group was Mikhail Bocharov, who was supported by the Young Turks and who ran explicitly on the 500 Days platform. But Yeltsin, who needed to win over the executives of the largest industrial enterprises, tacitly switched his support to their candidate, Ivan Silayev, who was soon elected premier of the new Russian government. However, because the 500 Days document was the only available program of comprehensive economic reform and was widely viewed as an important asset for the Yeltsin camp in their dealings with prospective Western interlocutors, Yeltsin and Silayev both endorsed it and appointed Yavlinsky as deputy prime minister in charge of economic reform. Yeltsin then offered the program to Gorbachev for implementation by both of them. Gorbachev accepted, and in late July a group headed by Stanislav Shatalin and Yavlinsky was assigned to make the program operational for unionwide application.[17]

Yavlinsky's presence in the Russian government was counterbalanced by quite different forces: The post of another deputy prime minister went to Yuri Skokov, who described himself as a technocrat with no political affiliation; had an extensive background in the military-industrial complex; and was close to the higher echelons of the nomenklatura, including the intelligence services and the leadership of the Russian Communist Party. On top of that, his record included a dubious victory in an electoral campaign in which prominent reformers had been kept off the ballot.[18] His surprising appointment evoked a murmur of discontent from the Young Turks and drew open protests from the parliamentary floor by Mikhail Astafiev.[19] However, as we shall see, Skokov turned out to play a key role in Yeltsin's back-channel compromise with the Soviet managerial elite and became a long-lasting Yeltsin ally, while the democrat Astafiev and his likes soon found themselves in opposition and were evicted from the political stage in October 1993.

Boris Yeltsin, the prodigal son of the nomenklatura, quietly had started to return to it as both the commander and the tamer of the popular protest against the nomenklatura's rule. What he needed now was to commandeer the industrial, raw materials, and financial resources of Gorbachev's decrepit central government. For that reason it was necessary to convince the groups from which he was seeking support—the directors of enterprises nominally owned by the state—that his attacks on the elite's privileges and the shadow economy, as well as the fiery redistributive rhetoric of his electoral machine, reflected not his actual intentions but, rather, his negotiating position for intra-elite bargaining. Some of the theorizers about Soviet economic reform in the West argued at the time for a reassertion of real government control over Soviet enterprises and the eviction of the inefficient managerial bureaucracy before any privatization would make sense. Instead, Yeltsin's team (widely—but wrongly—believed to be at the forefront of the economic reform) was busy co-opting the managers, people like Silayev and Skokov, to demonstrate that a prospective Russian takeover of the Soviet enterprises portended stability for the existing cadres and opened up new prospects for their business and political careers.

THE INTERNATIONAL DIMENSIONS OF THE DUAL-POWER RIVALRY

The Gorbachev-Yeltsin rivalry did not develop only in the domestic Soviet context. To be sure, the history of this period is inextricably bound up with the USSR's relations with its old Cold War adversaries, especially the United States, the German Federal Republic, and the NATO coalition in general. The later years of the USSR were marked by growing dependency on the Western world in economic, cultural, and psychological terms. Therefore, it is not surprising that Western views and actions had an impact on the course of Soviet events. Most important, for our purposes, Western prescriptions for Soviet economic reform, colored as they were by the dominant economic paradigm of the "Washington Consensus" and Reagan-Thatcher deregulation policies, ran counter to one of the basic premises and aspirations of the Russian democratic movement, which was the most principled and committed social base for the prospective reforms. However, as discussed in the previous chapter, few of the movement's activists were able to discern these fundamental philosophical contradictions. The idealistic Westernizers who predominated in the democratic movement had a utopian vision of the West, a vision patterned along the memories of U.S. assistance to the Soviet Union under the Lend-Lease Program in World War II. Indeed, many of them believed that the West would quickly come to their support in what they saw as a common war against Bolshevik totalitarianism, in which they were positioned at the forefront of democratic civilization. Instead, even though many in the West shared this view, Russia's drive for a democratic reform was soon confronted with Kissingerian geopolitics and with "one-size-fits-all" economic prescriptions and "conditionalities."

One of the plausible explanations for this drama was that the Russian cycle of reforms was out of sync with the political cycle in major Western countries. Gorbachev's counterparts in the West were mostly leaders of conservative governments, with little sympathy for social change generated from below. Indeed, many Western leaders, while eager to resort to anticommunist rhetoric in a Cold War propaganda campaign, harbored mistrust of any social revolution, even one directed against the Soviet nomenklatura. Thus in the U.S. government, a number of key officials (including Secretary of Defense Richard Cheney,

CIA Director Robert Gates, and Vice President Dan Quayle) believed that the U.S. national interest would be better served by the breakup of the Soviet Union, especially if it were controlled and without too much open warfare. As early as April 1989, when the newly formed Bush administration was officially conducting its policy review and avoiding official contacts with the Soviet leadership, Cheney volunteered his opinion to CNN, predicting that Gorbachev would "ultimately fail." Others were more sanguine about Gorbachev's prospects, such as Secretary of State James Baker and National Security Adviser Brent Scowcroft (an ex-partner in Kissinger Associates), and viewed the Soviet reforms and unprecedented openness in a mainly instrumental way, as a means to lock in U.S. military advantage and to give their administration an aura of statesmanship in world affairs.

President Bush himself became committed to his personal rapport with Gorbachev at a very early stage, and once described to Gorbachev those in the U.S. establishment who criticized his reforms as "marginal intellectual thugs." Symptomatically, when Soviet troops killed nineteen people and wounded two hundred while dispersing a demonstration in Tbilisi in April 1989, Scowcroft ordered a bland response and pressured the Voice of America to downplay the incident. He summed up his views at a May 31, 1991, national security briefing: "Our goal is to keep Gorby in power for as long as possible, while doing what we can to help head [the Soviets] in the right direction—and doing what is best for us in foreign policy."[20] This echoed the advice given to Bush by Henry Kissinger in December 1988: to end the Cold War by way of a secret deal with the Soviet government so as to keep the transition under control.[21] Following this pattern of reasoning, Baker stated in a December 1989 television interview that the United States would have no objection to a Warsaw Pact intervention in Romania to put an end to the popular uprising there.[22]

At the same time, however, the Bush administration maintained a slow pace in dealing with Gorbachev until the systemic crisis in the Soviet Union was already plain to see. Seemingly, this restraint reflected both different views among various agencies in the U.S. national security establishment and the market wisdom that postpones purchases when prices are falling: Why deal today when the other party will be weaker tomorrow? In this way, the United States was able to exact concessions from Gorbachev on conventional forces in Europe and on the interpretation of the Anti-Ballistic Missile Treaty before yielding to what Gorbachev thought he needed most—support for perestroika and a bilateral summit with Bush. Only in late November 1989, when the Soviet world was already falling apart, did Bush finally endorse perestroika and agree to meet Gorbachev on the island of Malta.

In Malta, Bush concluded that Gorbachev was a solid establishment figure, more to his liking than rabble-rousers like Lech Walesa or Boris Yeltsin. Bush and Quayle had dropped in on Scowcroft's meeting with Yeltsin at the White House in September 1989, before Bush met with Gorbachev as president.

Yeltsin had promised to set aside 15 percent of the Soviet economy for Western investors, but Scowcroft fell asleep during their meeting and later sniped at Yeltsin as being "devious" and a "two-bit headline grabber." Baker thought Yeltsin was simply "a flake" who made Gorbachev look good by comparison.[23]

Pro-Western Soviet and Russian democrats had little understanding of what their dealings with the Western establishment had in store for them, and were generally ignorant even of the relatively public differences of opinion within Western publics and governments. In their tragic naiveté, the Russian democrats simply assumed that the United States and other Western governments were not only both democratic (with all the idealistic overtones this implied for them) and meritocratic, but also to a considerable extent monolithic in their adherence to the values they professed. They thus imagined that dealing with political leaders was the same thing as a dialogue with Western societies as a whole. Therefore, there was no need to seek out minority or opposition views, and certainly none to cultivate contacts outside of what the mass media defined as the mainstream of opinion. Ironically, this distorted concept of the West was reciprocated by the U.S. government in its dealings with late Soviet society, which were marked by a failure to open channels of communication with politicians and public figures outside the narrow Gorbachev circle, even though these outsiders might have proved more effective at preserving the integrity of the USSR, which the Bush administration and other Western governments usually claimed to support. At the time, there was no government or political force in the West with the vision needed to find a common language with the new breed of nonestablishment Russian Westernizers and to come to terms with their purposes and expectations.

At the June 1989 Group of Seven summit in Paris, Gorbachev (who attended as a guest) asserted firmly that the USSR neither wanted nor needed direct Western aid. Within less than a year, the Soviet position shifted radically. In May 1990, Foreign Minister Eduard Shevardnadze gave Baker the estimate that a Soviet transition to a "regulated market economy" (Gorbachev's slogan of the moment) would require about $20 billion in loans and foreign aid from the West.[24] It was also reported that someone in the Soviet government offered to permit Lithuanian secession from the USSR in return for an indemnity of $34 billion.[25] At the June 1990 Bush-Gorbachev summit in Washington, Gorbachev pleaded with the U.S. side that Western economic aid was "really needed" and that the moment had come to show by concrete action that the Americans wanted perestroika to succeed. At Camp David, Gorbachev adviser Yevgeny Primakov told Baker's aide Dennis Ross that the USSR would need $20 billion per year for the next three years to solve its economic crisis. Yet only "most-favored-nation" trade status was offered, and this only at the last minute.[26] As a result, Gorbachev turned his eyes toward West Germany, seeing it eager to pay dearly for reunification, and soon gave a green light both to this and to reunited Germany's continued membership in NATO, a move that paved the way for future

NATO expansion to the east. At this time, in June 1990, Gorbachev also sent a letter to Bush, Thatcher, François Mitterrand, Toshiki Kaifu, Giulio Andreotti, and the other Western leaders asking for significant long-term financing and other assistance. "Without this radical step, a further renewal of our society will be impossible," Gorbachev confided.[27] West German foreign minister Hans-Dietrich Genscher urged Chancellor Helmut Kohl to act quickly, noting that "History does not repeat its offers."[28] Kohl informed his allies that he was going to provide the USSR with up to $15 billion in assistance.

The next month, the Group of Seven met in Houston, with Bush as host. Bush, Thatcher, and Kaifu saw significant aid as impossible, while Kohl, Mitterrand, and Canada's Brian Mulroney were talking about $15–$20 billion, most of which would clearly come from the Germans. Bush tried to paper over this split by offering a program of visiting experts and by commissioning a study by the IMF and the other international financial institutions on how the Soviet economy might be reformed.[29] This proposal, whatever its immediate tactical motivation, marked an important turning point. The Soviet case was handed off to the IMF by the G-7 governments. Decisions about the Soviet and Russian future would henceforth be made not by the leading Western national governments, representing at least ideally the democratic will of their respective nations, but by an international financial bureaucracy.

All in all, between 1989 and 1991, Germany provided a total of about $33 billion in assistance to the USSR, as Russian foreign minister Andrei Kozyrev later confirmed to the State Department.[30] These funds, if they had ever been invested in actual development projects, could have gone far toward renewing the Soviet housing stock or transportation infrastructure. In any case, the willingness of the Germans to pay for quick reunification and the expeditious repatriation of Soviet troops before the "dark forces" could renege on the bargain may have suggested to Gorbachev that the same ploy could work even in regard to the United States, Japan, France, and the United Kingdom, whose budgetary resources were strained because of an economic recession at the time. Perhaps, he seems to have thought, these countries' fear of a coup by Soviet diehards would at last open their purses.

THE ABANDONMENT OF THE 500 DAYS PLAN AND THE DRIFT TOWARD AUTHORITARIANISM

In the fall of 1990, the obvious stalemate between the Russian and Soviet governments inclined both sides toward peaceful coexistence and seemed to promise a prolonged period of dual rule. It was then that the 500 Days program (widely known as the Shatalin-Yavlinsky plan) was approved in principle by an overwhelming majority in the Russian Supreme Soviet on September 11, 1990, the same day that Gorbachev supported it in the USSR Supreme Soviet, and it seemingly became a basis for cooperation between the two heads of the dual power system of government. However, the program evoked a lukewarm attitude from potential Western supporters, and especially from the IMF—apart from its substantive reservations, the fund risked losing a plum assignment if reforms in the Soviet Union were to be implemented along the lines of a domestically generated strategy.

The USSR's radical-liberal press maintained that Western investors favored the Shatalin-Yavlinsky plan because of its consistent radicalism. By contrast, Gorbachev was reproached for his indecisiveness and reluctance to break with the nomenklatura, an accusation that was partly true. However, as is now known (and already then was known to the Soviet leadership), another important reality was that the Bush administration was not keen on committing U.S. Treasury funds (in the middle of a politically dangerous recession) to rescue the collapsing Soviet system, even if the latter were run by reformers and Westernizers; it believed that the 500 Days plan was naively idealistic, while all other reform projects were too conservative.[31]

The IMF and related Western interests involved in Russian reform played an important role in derailing the 500 Days program. In Washington, the program was criticized on two counts: First, it appeared to grant too large a role in reform to the unprivileged classes of society and to local governments. Second, as the program of a single Union republic's government, it worried those who were most concerned about the repayment of foreign debts contracted by the USSR. In late September 1990, at the IMF and World Bank annual meetings attended by the 500 Days team, the program was subjected to fierce criticism on these two points. For example, IMF consulting economist Janos Kornai attacked the indexation of wages and incomes recommended by the program, holding that it would lead to an inflationary explosion. An American economist who had served in the Carter administration found fault with giving too much economic power to local soviets when it came to issues of social welfare. (In so doing, he made clear that Washington's economic thinking ran counter to the basic premises of democratic reform as it was understood in Russia.) Another participant was George Soros, who spoke against the contemplated safety net for socially vulnerable groups, saying that it would create a nonmarket atmosphere.[32] In sum, the discussion made clear that the 500 Days program, because of its residual elements of democratic populism that gave it legitimacy in the Russian political context, did not inspire much confidence in Washington. Therefore, it could not elicit the one thing that Yeltsin and Gorbachev had foremost in their minds when they commissioned the program and hired its authors: Western financial assistance. The West, and primarily the IMF, was willing to lend only in exchange for a program of fiscal austerity.

In the USSR, meanwhile, the 500 Days plan, which emphasized mass privatization and the restructuring of the economy, evoked the economic elite's bitter opposition because it called for the state to halt the nomenklatura's

ongoing clandestine privatization of national property and to conduct privatization on a fair basis.[33] By contrast, immediate price deregulation in advance
of legal privatization (as advocated by Valentin Pavlov and later introduced by
Gaidar) essentially promised a regime of uncontrolled price fixing by quasi-state
monopolies. Many members of the nomenklatura welcomed this project because
they wanted to become the new capitalist owners of the nation's assets. However,
many of them also believed that this scenario would lead to a bloody social explosion unless price deregulation were carried out by a legitimate and popular
national leader. As a result, plans for economic reform looked rather like a massive "double-or-nothing" gamble: A leader who took the initiative in starting
reforms could hope to seize power in the country if they succeeded quickly; but
if they failed, he might become their first political victim.

This awareness caused both Gorbachev and Yeltsin to distance themselves
from the 500 Days approach. Accordingly, the plan was shelved and Yavlinsky
resigned from the Russian government after only three months in office. Under
pressure from the IMF and the G-7 governments, Gorbachev's team decided to
begin with a confiscatory currency reform and price reforms to remove the
"monetary overhang" and tried to protect itself in advance against the possible
consequences. In early January 1991, Gorbachev radically revamped the executive branch. He replaced the Council of Ministers (previously formed with
Supreme Soviet involvement) with a cabinet directly subordinated to himself,
and appointed as his prime minister Valentin Pavlov, his ex-minister of finance
and a fervent believer in financial austerity and the deregulation of prices.
Politically, this implied a shift to the right—the use of authoritarian methods
for subduing public protest.

This right turn, begun in October, resonated with those foes of Democratic
Russia, who had been slumbering since the spring defeat of the conservative
forces, and brought them out of their lethargy. On the political scene, new forces
took center stage with powerful declarations threatening to roll back reform,
crush the Balts, and oust Gorbachev. These included Ivan Polozkov's Russian
Communist Party and the "Union" coalition of USSR deputies, led by the "black
Colonels" Viktor Alksnis and Nikolai Petrushenko and created with the covert
involvement of Anatoly Lukyanov and Vladimir Zhirinovsky's misnamed Centrist Bloc. All this led Shevardnadze to resign in December and Gorbachev to
sanction tougher military measures against Baltic secessionism. In early January,
these measures caused a worldwide uproar when Lithuanians and then Latvians
were killed by Soviet troops as they successfully defended their parliaments
against forcible dissolution.[34]

Meanwhile, the overall situation in the country became ever more strained.
Both Soviet and Russian authorities increasingly feared a popular revolution
or at least a wave of uncoordinated uprisings. In 1990, the Soviet GNP had
contracted by 4 percent, while it shrank by 5 percent in the Russian Federation, more than in most of the other constituent republics of the Union.[35] In

search of short-term solutions for saturating the market with consumer goods, members of the Russian government resorted to a large-scale speculative ruble-dollar exchange, which later resulted in a major scandal involving Mafiya-type figures and the resignation of Vice Premier Gennadi Filshin and inflicted significant moral damage on Yeltsin's team.[36] It seemed that both wings of the ruling elite, federal and Russian, were competing over how to make themselves unpopular.

Throughout the fall and winter of 1990–91, Yeltsin's fissiparous camp was experiencing a dire crisis. Embarrassment in the economic sphere and an absence of other strategies stimulated not only increased opposition activity against him among deputies of the Russian parliament (such as the Rossiya group, led by Sergei Baburin), but also conflicts inside Yeltsin's own parliamentary coalition. Many of its participants were dissatisfied because of Yeltsin's increasing authoritarianism; the cliquishness of his circle; the unjustified ambitions of Shakhrai and Vice Premier Gennadi Burbulis to claim the status of *éminences grises;* and the disregard for procedural norms and deputies' rights of Vice Speaker Ruslan Khasbulatov, who increasingly presided over parliament in Yeltsin's stead. Additionally, Moscow deputies unsuccessfully tried to draw attention to the glaring reality of corruption in the leadership of the Moscow City Council, headed by Mayor Gavriil Popov. Additionally, the tense atmosphere in which the October 1990 founding congress of the Democratic Russia movement was held revealed the numerous rifts in the very core of the radical-reformist movement.[37]

THE IMF PLAN FOR THE USSR, DECEMBER 1990

In early January 1991, in the same days that Pavlov became prime minister and the first blood was spilled in the streets of Vilnius, the International Monetary Fund, the World Bank, the Organization for Economic Cooperation and Development, and the European Bank for Reconstruction and Development issued a multivolume analysis of the Soviet economy and its prospects for reform. Commissioned by the July 1990 Houston summit of the Group of Seven, the report was heavily informed by the Washington Consensus approach to reform, which favors monetarism and unrestricted capital flows—elements that characterized these international financial institutions at the close of the twentieth century.

The organizations contributing to the report acknowledged divergent views about what to do, but they emphatically recommended a radical approach to decontrolling prices and to privatization. They were explicitly willing to accept a sharp fall in output and a rapid increase in prices, and they expected a recovery to follow after two years.[38] These organizations also wanted a single economic space among the republics of the USSR, perhaps partly because it would be easier to collect the USSR's foreign debt from one debtor rather than fifteen or more. They recommended tight money, high interest rates, and "hard budget constraints." They also saw wage increases as a danger and wanted the government pension system (the equivalent of Social Security) to "remain on a pay-as-you-go basis without budgetary support"—a wholly unworkable notion.[39] The report focused repeatedly on what it called "excess liquidity," the "stock problem," and the monetary (or ruble) "overhang," with a concern that Russian companies and households possessed cash holdings estimated at 250 billion rubles (households accounting for two-thirds of this total). In economic reality, this cash represented largely consumer market basket purchases that families had been forced to defer because of the shortages of so many basic goods.

To the report's authors, the "absorption" or wiping out of family savings loomed as a "priority of monetary policy." These organizations failed to distinguish among the different groups in Soviet society and thus added to the momentum building toward the virtual expropriation of the most vulnerable strata. The report contemplated three ways of dealing with the ruble overhang: first, "a monetary reform, which would confiscate or freeze a part of financial assets held by households and enterprises"; second, "letting the real value of existing financial assets be reduced by price increases" (the hyperinflationary path subsequently followed by Gaidar); or third, by letting the ruble holders purchase government property or bonds.[40] Of these alternatives, the report liked confiscation best, viewing a monetary reform as "the most sure and effective instrument," but also obliquely admitted that this method might have explosive political consequences. Precisely this type of confiscation of family savings was attempted by the Pavlov government, which declared certain ruble notes as valueless soon after the report was issued. Pavlov postured as an opponent of foreign *diktat* in economic reform, yet here he seemed to be aggressively bidding for IMF support.

Concerning the other alternatives, the report was hostile to worker ownership of former state-owned companies. It also opposed privatization measures that would give large numbers of citizens a real stake in ownership, because that would "result in widely scattered ownership" and "ineffective monitoring and control of enterprise managers."[41] (Because the separation of ownership from management is typical of many American corporations, this reasoning is hard to follow.) That led to the report's conclusion that "early price reform is of paramount importance."[42] The authors' eyebrows went up over the fact that rents had remained unchanged since 1928 and were absorbing less than 3 percent of household income, only one-tenth of the market economy norm. Here they wanted a transition to market-determined rents. Beyond this, their prescriptions had a strong postindustrial bent, noting that employment in the manufacturing sector was "higher in the USSR than in some market economies"—although it was not as great as in West Germany. For manufacturing sectors like steel, petro-chemicals, and machine tools—the sinews of a modern industrial economy—the report unflinchingly recommended the "downsizing or liquidation" of plants.[43] For the oil, coal, and gas sectors, the report suggested "an internationally agreed investment regime with international arbitration" (in other words, extraterritorial courts to which foreign oil companies might appeal), surely a measure that even the weakest government would not readily accept.

The 1991 maneuvering over economic reform in the USSR may be seen mainly as a bidding war among various political factions to establish which one was the most plausible enforcer of the recommendations from the IMF-led group. Also, the long economic depression, which sharply deteriorated late in 1991, can only be seen as a direct consequence of the IMF's neomonetarist nostrums.[44] Western economists Jeffrey Sachs, Anders Aslund, and other advisers to the Russian government never departed from the essentials of the policy embodied in the Soviet economy report, including the wiping out of private savings by price reform before formal privatization had even begun. Later mutual recriminations between the IMF and the advisers present in Moscow simply amounted to buck-passing. In economics, as in war, prosperity and victory have many fathers, but depression and defeat are orphans.

Early in 1991, a serious East-West effort began to revive the main principles of the 500 Days program and to integrate into it elements of financial assistance and Soviet-Western strategic interaction. A joint team organized by Harvard University and Moscow's Center for Economic and Political Research and led by Graham Allison and Grigori Yavlinsky had been working on the proposed joint program for only a short time when Gorbachev asked to be briefed about it. As a result, he sent Yavlinsky and Primakov to Washington in May as part of his final attempt to obtain major strategic economic assistance from the G-7. Top-level meetings with Bush, Baker, and others produced intense interest. When the new program was finished and sent to the G-7 capitals in mid-June, it was in Allison's words, "widely read at the highest levels of each of the governments. Separately and together, Yavlinsky and I spent many hours discussing the ideas . . . with Presidents Gorbachev and Yeltsin and top-level officials in all the G-7 governments. . . . We discussed not just the general concepts . . . but the specific details."

As Allison relates, the G-7 members had "sharp differences of opinion" in preparing for their summit. Germany and Italy, eventually joined by France, "were eager to do more sooner." The other countries "wanted to do less . . . motivated principally by domestic issues external to their strategic stakes in Soviet reform." To sweeten the atmosphere at the G-7 summit, Gorbachev convinced the Soviet military to let him yield to U.S. pressures regarding one of the obstacles (the so-called downloading issue) to signing the START II treaty. However, as Allison writes, "In the end, Gorbachev proved unwilling, or unable, to adopt a coherent economic reform program. Instead, he sent a letter to the leaders of the G-7 governments with his own program. . . . As a result, Yavlinsky decided not to go to London with the Gorbachev team." Moreover, "given Gorbachev's submission, the G-7 governments found it rather easy to agree on a response" when they gathered on July 17. They recommended him to work with the IMF and the World Bank "to prepare a coherent economic reform program, along the lines of the one outlined in our Joint Program," and gave the USSR "special association" status in the two organizations.[45]

Despite Gorbachev's arms control concession, he obtained neither a rescheduling of Soviet foreign debt nor a hard-currency fund to support the ruble during the planned transition to convertibility. Even a lifting of the Cocom restrictions on advanced technology proved beyond his reach.[46] The Soviet leader was ridiculed as a beggar and a pauper by the world press and was lectured on sound market economics in his bilateral meetings. The result was a big humiliation for him on the international scene. President Bush commented that Gorbachev had "bombed" in London.

During the last two days of July 1991, Bush was in Moscow for a summit meeting. Gorbachev and Primakov pressed him for specific pledges on economic assistance and investments, but the most that Bush was willing to offer was to send to the Senate the 1990 U.S.-USSR trade treaty, which did nothing more than normalize trade relations between the two countries by granting the Soviets most-favored-nation status. Bush's concept of supporting Gorbachev amounted largely to verbally opposing the breakup of the USSR. On August 1, after his talks in Moscow, Bush flew on to Kiev with USSR vice president Gennadi Yanayev as his guest aboard Air Force One. In the Ukrainian capital, Bush delivered the speech that the *New York Times'* William Safire later dubbed his "Chicken Kiev" oration. Bush rejected as false the choice between "supporting President Gorbachev and supporting independence-minded leaders throughout the USSR." "Freedom," he lectured the Ukrainians, "is not the same as independence."[47]

The Gorbachev regime had made sweeping concessions to the Bush administration: It had dropped all objections to the continued NATO membership of reunified Germany. It had agreed in principle to liberalize the Soviet economy. It had refrained from using its veto in the UN Security Council to block actions desired by the United States and United Kingdom against Iraq, a traditional Arab client of the USSR—a humiliating exercise for a foreign policy establishment that had spent decades building relationships with radical Arab regimes like those in Egypt and Syria. It had agreed to the State Department's proposals on the START treaty. It had discussed Soviet internal affairs in the Baltics and elsewhere with the Americans in ways that would have been unthinkable just a few years earlier. It had even liquidated Comecon and the Warsaw Pact.

After making all these concessions, Gorbachev expected a response to his repeated calls for economic assistance, food aid, and large-scale foreign investment—in short, for a modified Marshall Plan for the USSR. But he received little of this, despite the fact that his American and other partners knew full well how precarious his political position had become. They felt that communism and the Soviet Union were disintegrating and decided—perhaps wrongly in retrospect—that they should not slow down the process at this late hour.[48]

After the G-7 meeting in London and the subsequent Bush visit to Moscow, it was clear to all that Gorbachev's fabled prestige in the Western world no longer had any cash value. Some two weeks after this point had been so convincingly demonstrated, the remaining Soviet die-hards made their final desperate attempt to reverse the Union's accelerating collapse.

YELTSIN'S SPRING 1991 OFFENSIVE AND THE NOVO-OGAREVO PACT

In early 1991, amid the scandal over the Filshin scam, Yeltsin was forced to abandon his inactivity and seize the political initiative to safeguard his fragmenting coalition. Gorbachev himself gave Yeltsin the means to do so through his clumsy and doomed attempt to use force against the parliaments of the Baltic republics in January 1991. The bloodshed in Vilnius and Riga was an extreme sign of Gorbachev's rightward evolution, and Yeltsin did not fail to take advantage of this opportunity. In the heat of events, while Gorbachev was squirming to evade responsibility for the bloodshed, Yeltsin flew to Estonia. On behalf of Russia, he expressed his support on January 13 for the peoples and parliaments of the Baltic states and called on the troops not to shed any more blood. This elicited elation from Democratic Russia and vitriol from the right—including the pro-Union Baltic Russian groups, the Union group in the USSR parliament, Zhirinovsky, and others who wanted to preserve the USSR. Yeltsin, who at this time was in regular contact with KGB chief Vladimir Kryuchkov, then made a sensational announcement about the possibility of creating a Russian army (which subsequently he had to disavow partially).[49]

On February 19, just as public outrage over the Filshin affair was at its height, Yeltsin was finally permitted to appear in a live television broadcast in which he bluntly called for Gorbachev's resignation. This watershed demand, though striking, was by now well within the bounds of the possible. In this intense atmosphere, both Democratic Russia and an overwhelming majority of the Russian deputies once again closed ranks behind the man they saw as their leader. Yeltsin established the pattern for his later comebacks, portraying himself as the last hope of the democrats by staging the confrontation on an ideological, not a social, basis. One thing was clear, though: Yeltsin's defeat in this head-on clash with his foe would mean the end of his political career. On March 9, Yeltsin, who until then had carefully kept his distance from Democratic Russia, appeared at a large meeting of its members and called for their support for his candidacy and for Gorbachev's resignation. Yeltsin's popularity once again skyrocketed. When a small group of leaders of the Russian Congress (Vladimir Isakov, Svetlana Goryacheva, and others) condemned Yeltsin's confrontational course of action, they were hissed by the majority of deputies, who had become Yeltsin's faithful fans.

On March 17, a referendum was held on the preservation of the USSR. However, the legitimacy of its results in the most turbulent areas of the Union was bound to be limited: six out of fifteen constituent republics—the Baltics, Georgia, Armenia, and Moldova—boycotted the voting. In the rest of the country, 76 percent of the voters (including 71 percent in Russia) favored preserving the Union. Voters in the RSFSR were also asked to pass judgment on whether to institute the post of a nationally elected president; 70 percent of the voters supported it. The divergences in the responses to the Union-level and the associated republic-level referenda across the RSFSR regions was conspicuous. In the predominantly pro-Yeltsin regions, where support for the institution of a presidency was particularly high, the number of those who voted for the preservation of the Union was low: In Yeltsin's bailiwick of Sverdlovsk, for example, the majority voted against the preservation of the USSR. Despite Yeltsin's assurances that he supported the signing of a Union Treaty, it became clear that the contest between the Russian and Soviet leaderships had degenerated into a zero-sum game and that the survival of the USSR was at stake. Still, the potential for the development from below of a national democratic opposition focused on the preservation of the Union remained a great threat to the nomenklatura; the main hope of much of the latter had become the breakup of the Union. As they wrapped themselves in the flag of their local nationalisms, they could hope to preserve their power and assets only by turning the social revolution into a nationalist one.

THE SPIRIT OF NOVO-OGAREVO

On March 28, 1991, the opening day of the third emergency session of the Russian Congress of People's Deputies, the presence of military and Interior Ministry detachments on the Moscow streets was noticeable and imposing. Participants at numerous democratic rallies made appeals to march on the Kremlin. Many thought that Gorbachev, whose influence had been weakened after the events in the Baltics, would not resort to force in Moscow, even to put down a revolution. But Yeltsin did not need a revolution. He had taken advantage of the favorable atmosphere and was easily granted almost unlimited emergency powers by the Congress. Additionally, the office of a popularly elected president of the RSFSR was established, in accordance with the referendum results, and Yeltsin prepared to campaign for it.[50]

Gorbachev's last chances to take action were running out. Radical economic steps, notable for their similarity to some of the IMF's recipes, were approved by the Soviet leadership and carried out by Pavlov, including a January 1991 confiscatory currency reform and an increase in prices the following April. These measures evoked a wave of resentment from the most diverse segments of society, a resentment that Democratic Russia skillfully used to its own advantage. Sensing defeat, Gorbachev met with Yeltsin and signaled a desire to cooperate. Forced to confront an emerging democratic-nationalist opposition in the Russian parliament (led by Baburin and Isakov) and a liberal one within Democratic Russia (led by Yuri Afanasiev), as well as the pressing demands of his allies in the managerial establishment, Yeltsin met Gorbachev half way. He agreed with Gorbachev's arguments that Western financial support, so crucial for conducting reforms, demanded some sort of agreement among the elites to address both the preservation of the USSR and the emasculation of the populists and radical democrats. In exchange for the Russian leadership's agreement to abandon its policy of fostering a democratic revolution, Gorbachev and the moderate reformers around him promised not to block Yeltsin's bid for the Russian presidency.

On April 23, the agreement was sealed at a meeting attended by Gorbachev, Yeltsin, and leaders of eight other republics at the Novo-Ogarevo country estate near Moscow. The published document made many democratic Yeltsin supporters shudder. In particular, one of its points addressed the need to outlaw strikes and proposed a moratorium on labor protests in general. Several members of Yeltsin's team felt that the upcoming election campaign would be their last: Yeltsin had achieved victory over his main opponents and had already positioned himself as the virtual leader of the "party of power" (that is, the ruling group within the country's political establishment). He would no longer need the services of a mass movement. Moreover, such a movement would become a burden and a political liability for him, especially in the eyes of the West. Despite this evidence, those democrats who understood and foresaw this tendency had neither the resources nor the will either to impose stringent conditions on Yeltsin or to put forward an alternative candidate.

MENACE ON THE FAR RIGHT: THE "BROWN SCARE"

Yeltsin himself, meanwhile, had been worrying about the emergence of new types of right-wing opposition. These groups were, in fact, a matter of immediate concern for all parts of the ruling elite, including both self-styled conservatives and democrats. This concern can be seen clearly from Yeltsin's later reminiscences about early 1991: He saw a looming new force, "for which both Yeltsin and Gorbachev, the left opposition, and the powers-that-be were all undifferentiated 'agents of imperialism'. . . . This, in essence, was the embryo of the future National Salvation Front—mobilizing disenchanted Russians in the Baltics, Polozkov's new Communist Party [of Russia], unofficial groups of 'new communists,' reactionary labor unions, 'blackshirts,' et al."[51]

At first glance, it remains to be explained just how and why these groups could ever hope to represent a real danger for those who held power during the early months of 1991. All of them had absolutely no—or, in the case of the

Russian Communist Party, almost no—direct political leverage in the state institutions. They existed outside of the establishment, outside of a nomenklatura that abhorred both democrats and nationalists with equal fervor. All key positions—in the parliament, in the government, in the security apparatus, at the republic level—were firmly controlled either by Gorbachevians (such as Lukyanov, Kryuchkov, and others) or by fairly moderate elements of the usually self-appointed liberal democratic elite. Yet this was precisely why the emerging third force did matter: It was the first immediate challenge to Yeltsin and the democrats from the realm that was the source of their charismatic legitimation—the grassroots. It was all the more relevant because in the eyes of public opinion Yeltsin was already at the top of the state hierarchy, sharing with Gorbachev many attributes of power and responsibility, yet thus far without a reliable mechanism for putting into practice his own (still embryonic) political agenda. As it became increasingly evident that the early mass-based democratic movement was being torn apart by its factions and was losing ground in society without gaining operational command over the decision-making centers, the far right had a chance to fill the void by incorporating the populist, anti-nomenklatura, primordial drives of the 1980s democratic constituency.

Moreover, by late 1990 the new Russian right was no longer limited to marginal, exotic groupings. It was becoming possible to distinguish within it populist nationalists, nomenklatura nationalists, and a moderate camp of democratic nationalists exemplified by Baburin and Astafiev. Its leaders were actively searching for new channels to influence the key decision-making structures at the Union level. The most appropriate structures for organized discontent and aggressive pressure on the Kremlin proved to be the groups of military deputies in the Supreme Soviet and the Congress of People's Deputies, as well as in the regional and local legislatures. Thus, on November 13, 1990, a meeting was held by Gorbachev at the headquarters of the Soviet army's theater in Moscow. Here, an excited crowd of eleven hundred officer-legislators had assembled. A series of angry pro-Union outbursts by officers stationed in secessionist regions and republics forced the president into a defensive position. To his credit, Gorbachev responded with stern rebuttals. Although, as we shall see, he had already embarked on a bureaucratic-authoritarian course, he was apparently anxious not to encourage any independent political activity on the part of the radical right, which quite explicitly despised and hated him.

Yet on the next day, November 14, coordinated pressure tactics continued on the floor of the Soviet Congress of People's Deputies. The deputies (now, to Gorbachev's surprise and anxiety, under the skillful guidance of Speaker Lukyanov) voted down the prearranged schedule of the session and peremptorily demanded to discuss "the critically dangerous situation in the country." In essence, they were asking for Gorbachev's report and his explanation for his inaction in the face of the country's incipient fragmentation. The Latvian Colonel Alksnis, spokesman for the embattled Soviet military in the Baltics, expressed in the crudest way how disappointed the officers were with Gorbachev's lack of responsiveness. At the previous day's meeting, Alksnis exclaimed, "The President of the country found himself without his Armed Forces. . . . We had a conversation of the deaf with the blind. . . . If the required measures are not taken, people will take up arms and go in the streets. . . . The military will defend their rights."[52]

Since November 1990, a group of radical nationalist intellectuals, headed by the well-known "nightingale of the Soviet General Staff," Aleksandr Prokhanov, had been publishing a newspaper of "the spiritual opposition" called *Den'* (The Day), a name that recalled the vehemently nationalist nineteenth-century paper put out by the Slavophile Aksakov brothers. The newspaper was actively engaged in the search for an alternative, nondemocratic, and anti-Western strategy for independent national development, and some of its essays displayed acquaintance with and intellectual affinity to Huntington's authoritarian modernization argument. In sharp contrast with the plaintive and defensive posture of many nostalgic conservatives, *Den'* was always there to storm the frontier of political correctness, trying to establish new and previously unthinkable norms of public debate. Since early 1991, virtually every issue of *Den'* had been filled with unabashed appeals and incitements to the military, which Prokhanov and his associates envisaged as the backbone of an imminent conservative backlash. Thus Prokhanov and Shamil Sultanov wrote in one issue of *Den'*, "Only a strong authoritarian power based on national consent, which puts an end to fruitless parliamentarism . . . will become the engineering center that will offer the people a strategic plan during the transition period."[53]

Later, Sultanov, complaining about the inaction and loss of vigilance on the part of the security structures, claimed that the close relations of the KGB directorates at the republic and regional levels with the corresponding Party structures were leading to their simultaneous decline:

[I]n these circumstances, the political role of the military is expanding . . . on a purely legal basis. . . . There is a growing influence of the armed forces upon the operations of a number of civilian agencies, primarily the Ministry of Interior. . . . The military become more and more aware that the army is the only force capable of averting the final destruction of the Union. . . . [O]ur only hope is with the intellectual capabilities of the military-industrial complex. . . . Finally, as we see the discrediting of Communist ideology, only the defense complex is able of generating a unifying national ideology . . . of security, stability, and development.[54]

In the same issue, Yevgeny Pashentsev, while rejecting the use of a "strong hand" to set up either a bureaucratic, pseudosocialist restoration or Mafiya capitalism, called for what he defined as a "progressive military regime": "[I]f the democratic institutions are merely formal and work in the interests of specific strata . . . then it is the right and duty of the progressive military circles to take the political initiative."

The spring of 1991 was also marked by the considerable success of the far right in its attempts to establish a dialogue with potential supporters in the Kremlin. Oleg Baklanov, deputy chairman of the USSR Security Council (and Gorbachev's immediate assistant in charge of the military-industrial complex), finally responded to persistent wooing on the part of the *Den'*. This is not to say that Baklanov ever looked like a dove in comparison with the rest of Gorbachev's team. Yet as late as February 1991, in a dialogue with Prokhanov published in *Den'*, he still sounded extremely reluctant to criticize the basic assumptions of Gorbachev's policy and anxiously interrupted Prokhanov's tirades against perestroika.[55] But in a front-page conversation with him and others in the May issue of the newspaper (published for the anniversary of the Soviet V-E Day of May 9, 1945), Baklanov's utterances were quite different—aggressively anti-Gorbachevian in their very substance, though not in favor of military dictatorship: "Wailing and gnashing of teeth reign in the defense companies. The bones of the defense industry are breaking . . . . If not the commitment to ideas, to the Party, to the army, to the people itself—what else can protect the country from chaos?" To this, Prokhanov ruminated: "Maybe, indeed, to avert civil war, the demise of a great country, one should spit upon the legal technicalities and impose a dictatorship? . . . Our army lacks political will. . . . Through all these years, a group of patriotically minded Russian writers has been defending the army, while the army itself kept silent." Baklanov, without reacting to the putschist appeals of his interlocutor, inserted a note of caution concerning the army's capabilities: "The army, if it should be compelled to assume the management of the economy, transportation, the entire society, will be able to sustain this management only for a limited time, and at an extremely low level. The army will be interested in transferring this management to civilians promptly."[56]

On July 23, 1991, a conservative Communist daily *(Sovetskaya Rossiya)* and a centrist one *(Moskovskaya pravda)* published "A Call to the People."[57] The text was unprecedented not only as a landmark appeal for mass political action to halt the dismemberment of the Soviet Union, but also as the first sketch of a national-conservative political program. Signed by radical Russophile journalists *and* high-level government officials, the most significant names on the list were those of Deputy Defense Minister General Valentin Varennikov and Deputy Minister of Interior General Boris Gromov (although Gromov later claimed that he had not signed it), both leading figures in the Afghan War. The appeal was also signed by the defense industrialist Aleksandr Tiziakov and the conservative agricultural official Vasily Starodubtsev (both members of the August putsch); by a secretary of the Russian Communist Party, Gennadi Zyuganov; by the leader of the national-patriotic parliamentary "Union" faction, Yuri Blokhin; and by a group of nationalist writers and artists—Yuri Bondarev, Eduard Volodin, Lyudmila Zykina, Fyodor Klykov, Prokhanov, and Valentin Rasputin.[58]

Perhaps the most remarkable feature of this document was its straightforward appeal to core Russophile values and institutions couched within a general message about the preservation of the Soviet Union. This was one of the first times that the Soviet Union had been explicitly depicted as the Russian state *tout court* by serious politicians. Its authors called on "the workers and peasants," the engineers and scientists, the army and the Orthodox Church to unite and mobilize themselves in an attempt to prevent the demise of the country.

Yeltsin Becomes President of Russia

The June election for president of the Russian Federation, which was held the month before the publication of "A Call to the People," fully legitimated Yeltsin's rise to power; simultaneously, it marked an important stage in the strengthening of the radical right as a tangible alternative to both the liberal and the radical-democratic wings of the party of power. Alongside Yeltsin and two colorless Gorbachevites, three right-wing candidates ran in these elections: the chairman of the Liberal Democratic Party, Vladimir Zhirinovsky; the speaker of the regional soviet in the coal-rich region of Siberia, Aman Tuleyev; and the commander of the Urals Military District, General Albert Makashov. In his memoirs, Yeltsin portrays them as having been "vehemently against the whole democratic idea, against Gorbachev's perestroika, against Gorbachev and Yeltsin personally, and in favor of imposing order with an iron hand." They were, Yeltsin wrote, "quite modern (that is, harsh, determined, aggressive) and savage."[59] Curiously, Yeltsin himself was often praised for these same qualities. Although the predictable result of the elections turned out to be a landslide for Yeltsin, with 57 percent of the votes against six candidates, the combined votes for Zhirinovsky, Tuleyev, and Makashov totaled 18.4 percent (14.6 million supporters), which put the radical right overall in second place and ahead of Yeltsin's main opponent, the moderate conservative of Gorbachevian vintage, Nikolai Ryzhkov. Still more important, with his respectable third-place finish, Zhirinovsky, the only candidate from outside the nomenklatura, defied all the unspoken taboos of political correctness and rose to the status of a nationwide political figure. His campaign lasted only twenty days, but he still got six million votes, or 8 percent.

Vladimir Zhirinovsky: New Spokesman for the Enraged Middle Class

From the outset, the press coverage of the Liberal Democratic Party of the Soviet Union focused on its leader, Vladimir Volfovich Zhirinovsky. The attention to his personality has ebbed and flowed, with high points after his success in the 1991 presidential elections, his triumph in the December 1993 Duma elections, and his impressive second place in the 1995 Duma elections. Through it all, Zhirinovsky has been a prominent fixture in the Russian political establishment of the 1990s, even if most people at first regarded him as a clown. Seemingly achieving the impossible, he became the only one among the leaders of dozens of small and not-so-small parties created in the 1990 heyday of Russian multiparty politics to secure for his party a permanent, stable, and important place in the post-1993 Duma. His sensational antics have also attracted considerable attention in the Western media.[60]

Zhirinovsky's cleverly calculated ability to outrage and affront foreigners has been his stock in trade and the indispensable ingredient in his domestic success. His incendiary statements, sometimes physically violent gestures, and hooliganism at home and abroad have drawn upon him a barrage of epithets such as demagogue, racist, fascist, jingoist, warmonger, and extremist. While these accusations have often been well deserved, it is also important to note that, from the point of view of Russian domestic politics, the Zhirinovsky phenomenon must be seen as a vital element of the Yeltsin-era system—if not its heart, then at least its spleen. He was frequently a harbinger of coming attractions in the movie house of Yeltsin-era government, especially regarding the regime's resort to authoritarianism, jingoistic nationalism, and demagogic attacks on the West by the financial elite. From 1993 on, as we shall explore in more detail later, Zhirinovsky gradually became Yeltsin's essential and most reliable ally in the Duma.

From the very beginning, Yeltsin's strategy of pursuing Russian sovereignty in the guise of a new state limited to the highly artificial borders of the RSFSR generated a vast pool of resentment among those citizens who saw the USSR, and not the RSFSR, as the state to which they owed their allegiance. Since 1990–91, Zhirinovsky has tailored his demagogy (with generous help from the controlled media at decisive moments) to middle-class frustration. From late 1990 to early 1991, he functioned as a link between the die-hard authoritarian wing of the nomenklatura and those strata of formerly democratic populists who were turning toward nationalism. As such, Zhirinovsky might have become the man of destiny needed by the August putschists, if they had ever been willing to adopt a national-populist strategy on a broader basis than that of a mere palace coup.

Who voted for Zhirinovsky in the 1991 elections? Quite simply, his support came from those people for whom their Soviet identity was paramount, people who mourned the collapse of their government and viewed the Yeltsin ideology of democratic Russian nationalism with a deep skepticism that, as time would show, was for the most part justified. Despite the attempts of some researchers to explain Zhirinovsky in terms of class, it seems that cultural-ethnic consciousness, more than social status, was the dominant factor generating his support.

Still, the social factor did play a role. Voters were constantly reminded that of the six presidential candidates, only Zhirinovsky had not occupied a single nomenklatura post during the Soviet era. Of course, even he had traces of an establishment background, such as his study at the Institute of Asia and Africa, his service in military intelligence in the Transcaucasus, plus his jobs at the Soviet Committee in Defense of Peace, in an upper-level trade union school, in a law office, and in the department of legal services in the Mir publishing house.[61] His résumé presumed high-level connections, including good relations with nomenklatura leaders and with the KGB. Yet even if Zhirinovsky had belonged to the CPSU (he was allegedly denied admission), he had had practically no chance of occupying a Party or government post during the Soviet era. For an intellectual or professional man of Zhirinovsky's type, virtually the only path into the nomenklatura would have been through the Marxist social sciences, and Zhirinovsky did not go that route (although the Institute of Asia and Africa had in principle offered such an opportunity).

Zhirinovsky struck a chord with many people by his consistent reminders about his non-nomenklatura past as a "simple Soviet employee." The gap between the new self-proclaimed democratic elite and the mass anti-elite movement that it had generated was growing rapidly larger. Activists and supporters of the earlier democratic movement were increasingly realizing that the leaders of the new institutions of political power consisted of recycled second-echelon nomenklatura. For this new elite, the democratic movement served merely as cannon fodder for election purposes and as extras to swell the ranks of Yeltsin's street rallies when a show of force was needed. An average member of the intelligentsia like Zhirinovsky had practically no place in the new political order. Most of them remained mere faces in the crowd or else became clients of the new nomenklatura. Those who had become disillusioned with the new elite saw in Zhirinovsky's influence the long-awaited rise of the Gogolesque "little person" who refused to be a pawn in the big power games of the world. For that reason, a significant number of former Yeltsin supporters who by now felt betrayed threw their weight behind Zhirinovsky in the 1991 vote.

Indeed, of all the candidates, only Zhirinovsky could hope to gain the support of part of Yeltsin's electorate. The remaining contenders represented four varieties of the vanishing Soviet past: the administrative-managerial nomenklatura (Ryzhkov); the regional nomenklatura (Tuleyev); the military-industrial complex, which became radical because of its powerlessness (Makashov); and a small segment of Gorbachev's perestroika aristocracy (Viktor Bakatin). Zhirinovsky himself stood somewhere between these four and Yeltsin; for that reason, his claims to occupy a centrist niche appeared substantiated, if only in the narrow sense that his supporters did tend to be drawn from the déclassé remnants of the old Soviet middle class. He was an extremist in ideology, but staked his claim as a centrist on the fact that he was socially and culturally an expression of the angry, disoriented petty bourgeoisie. His platform called for a multiparty system and other attributes of Western democracy.

Moreover, like a genuine liberal, Zhirinovsky supported private property and privatization, and in so doing claimed the role of political spokesman for present and future small businessmen, the representatives of the non-nomenklatura business world. In this capacity, he appeared to stand on the ideological middle ground between the past and the future Yeltsin—that is, between the Yeltsin of the anti-nomenklatura battle for social justice and the later Yeltsin of shock therapy (whose contours had already become discernible by May 1991). The only issues in Zhirinovsky's platform that were congenial to conservatives were the demand for preservation of the Soviet Union, the defense of Russian speakers' rights in the Union republics, and the strengthening of the army and state authority. But these issues in some form also found their place in Yeltsin's revamped image as a liberal nationalist. Because Zhirinovsky's centrist profile threatened to erode Yeltsin's electoral base, the radical-reformist press eagerly assailed Zhirinovsky as an extremist, a fascist, and even a populist, the same accusation the Gorbachev press had furiously leveled at Yeltsin several years before. These press attacks backfired, by virtue of a subconscious association between Zhirinovsky and the original Yeltsin. In addition to his other assets, Zhirinovsky acquired the aura of a victim, thereby securing the votes of those who felt contempt for the pro-Yeltsin lockstep of the reformist press.

During the last twenty days of the campaign, Zhirinovsky was able to score a real breakthrough, thanks to his image as a Soviet citizen; as a politician prepared to articulate the fears, resentments, and yearnings of the embattled middle class; as a man who was not a part of the ruling elite; as a moderate liberal and vociferous patriot; and as a supporter of reforms, but one who was critical of the Yeltsin of the moment. Of course, this image did not fully jibe with reality, but as has been wisely remarked in various ways on different occasions, "In politics, facts play a minor role. Politics is about perceptions."[62] Many facts testifying to Zhirinovsky's close ties with the Kremlin and with other institutions of political power were simply unknown to the wider public, while the innuendoes of the pro-Yeltsin media were poorly substantiated and lacked credibility. Still, those who had followed the history of the Liberal Democratic Party (LDP) of the Soviet Union could easily surmise high-level connections with the old Soviet nomenklatura and the security services even before Zhirinovsky had appeared in the political campaign.

On April 1, 1990, the national press covered the founding convention of Zhirinovsky's party in warmly affirmative tones. Commentators noted that the LDP was the only party formed that spring that was not oriented toward the Russian parliament, but emphatically planned to play the all-Union field. In fact, the first press conference after Zhirinovsky's convention was conducted in the CPSU's Oktyabrskaya luxury hotel.[63] Soon thereafter, in June 1990, Zhirinovsky's name once again appeared in the mass media, this time when the self-styled Centrist Bloc of moderate-radical forces was formed with support from the Committee in Defense of Peace (one of Zhirinovsky's former employers). About forty other organizations in addition to the LDP registered as members of the bloc, including Moscow parties that existed primarily on paper or had only a handful of members, but also some more sizable organizations consisting of ethnic minorities from regions experiencing the most severe national conflicts.[64]

In the fall of 1990, at the height of the country's political crisis, a rapprochement took place between the Centrists and the Union faction of radical anti-Gorbachev deputies in the Soviet parliament. The latter group, created in February 1990, was composed of persons who identified themselves as Soviet citizens and who resented being relegated to the status of an ethnic minority, both in the republics that were striving for secession and independence and in Yeltsin's Russia. The Union faction converged with Zhirinovsky in their consternation about their fast-disappearing Soviet national identity. Among the Union faction leaders were the previously mentioned Colonel Viktor Alksnis, the son of a Latvian Bolshevik and an outspoken opponent of Latvian secessionism; a soldier from Moldova named Yuri Blokhin; the Ukrainian Colonel Petrushenko from Kazakhstan; and Estonian Interfront leader Yevgeny Kogan. The pro-Yeltsin press liked to refer to this faction as the "black colonels," who were supported by the army generals and those people whose military-industrial interests were being systematically appropriated in the republics.

In October 1990, the Union faction announced it was joining Zhirinovsky's Centrist Bloc; apparently, it counted on using the bloc's participant organizations, including the LDP, to create its own local structures across the country. The rapprochement between Zhirinovsky and the Union group was sponsored by Supreme Soviet Speaker Lukyanov, who was desperately fighting to preserve the USSR. After a series of meetings within this narrow circle, the Centrists were then allowed to conduct their own roundtables and public relations in the Supreme Soviet building and were invited to participate in drawing up a draft Union Treaty in private meetings with parliamentary officials. The chairman of the Union parliament's Soviet of Nationalities, Boris Oleinik, displayed a particular affection for the Centrists; the press even claimed that his chamber had affiliated itself with the Centrist Bloc as an official observer.[65]

On November 7, 1990, Zhirinovsky, together with his Centrist Bloc associates, was invited to the Kremlin for the celebration of the October Revolution anniversary. He was joined there by Andrei Zavidiya, one of the USSR's first legal millionaires, who was a former employee of Intourist, the state-run travel agency that had also branched out to create a semilegal foreign trade network. After less than a year, in May 1991, Zavidiya would become Zhirinovsky's running mate as vice-presidential candidate. As later became known through reports confirmed by Ivan Polozkov, the leader of the Russian Communist Party, Zavidiya's company had received three million rubles in interest-free loans (considering the rate of inflation, essentially a gift) from the administrative bureau of the CPSU Central Committee shortly before Zhirinovsky picked Zavidiya as his running mate. This money would eventually defray Zhirinovsky's and Zavidiya's campaign expenses.[66]

During Gorbachev's rightward evolution, the threat of a military coup seemed to loom over the country. Nearly every week, the Centrist Bloc and the black colonels from the Union faction were organizing public meetings, rallies, press conferences, roundtables, and marches in the most conspicuous Moscow locales. The participants appealed for presidential rule across the entire country, the dissolution of the secessionist parliaments of the Baltics and Russia, the creation of committees of national salvation, and the transfer of full political power to the people under the aegis of the Union faction and the Centrist Bloc. By February 1991, it seemed that Zhirinovsky had forgotten about maintaining his centrist and liberal image as he joined in the fray, attending a conference organized by the Russian Communist Party under the slogan "For a Great and United Russia." By the beginning of the spring of 1991, however, the rightward shift in the Soviet nomenklatura had petered out. Yeltsin had launched a powerful counteroffensive that altered the situation in his favor, and was now presenting himself as the only viable candidate for the role of authoritarian modernizer.

In this new situation, with the reformist wing of the Union faction in the ascendant and forcing through momentous decisions regarding the future of the country, the activity of the Centrist Bloc and the Union deputies had become a political liability for its original backers. Zhirinovsky urgently needed to refurbish his image to be able to present himself as a legitimate, independent political force. Five days after the referendum in which the issue of creating the Russian presidency was resolved, the new LDP platform, written by Andrei Zagorodnikov (an ex-lecturer in Marxism) and full of liberal mantras, came off the presses at the Krasnyi Proletarii (Red Proletarian) government printing house. Less than a week later, fifty thousand copies of the platform bearing the stamp of the Politizdat state publishing house were distributed throughout the country. Meanwhile, the LDP's registration documents, which had been submitted by Zhirinovsky to the Ministry of Justice at the end of January, were returned on April 3 with the explanation that they did not satisfy the legal requirements for registration. Yet on April 12, after parliament speaker Lukyanov had made a personal call to Justice Minister Sergei Lushchikov, the LDP was nevertheless registered as the second all-Union party (the CPSU had been registered only one day earlier).[67]

The next day, the breakup of the Centrist Bloc and Zhirinovsky's nomination as presidential candidate were the two leading events at an LDP convention. But the nomination did not meet the legal requirements, because only Russian organizations by law could nominate candidates. In order to surmount this obstacle, a constituent congress of the Russian branch of LDP was held on May 10 at the Lenin collective farm just outside of Moscow. Here, twenty-five participants officially constituted the organization that would legally nominate Zhirinovsky.

Still, twenty-five supporters were not sufficient to place a candidate on the Russian presidential ballot. Either one hundred thousand signatures or the support of 20 percent of the deputies in the Russian CPD (213 deputies) needed to be obtained. Because the first option was known to be unrealistic, Zhirinovsky (by what means we can only guess) won an uphill battle to be allowed to address the Russian parliament with an appeal for support. On May 22, after a buoyantly self-confident appearance before the Congress, replete with his typical well-calculated antics (at the end of the speech, he even addressed the deputies in Turkish), Zhirinovsky received no fewer than 477 votes (more than 40 percent of the Russian CPD).[68] Just three weeks later, Zhirinovsky would be able to boast, "An entire country numerically equal to Switzerland has voted for me."[69]

PRE-COUP RUMBLINGS

The second half of this chapter will look in some detail at the buildup to the short-lived hard-line coup attempt of August 1991, its key features, and its aftermath. Our aim is not just to present our interpretation of broad events that form the background for our analysis—namely, the decline and demise of Gorbachev and the USSR, and the birth of independent Russia. These events also provide evidence for key strands in our analysis, such as Yeltsin's instinctive primary reliance on his intra-elite ties, his suddenly fertile relations with the U.S. government, and his resort to mass-based support only when there was no substitute for it. The events also show how the Bush administration, having been initially chilly toward Yeltsin, turned to viewing him almost uncritically after his election as Russia's president and—during the coup—giving him a remarkable degree of support. Here lay the seeds of the future American betrayal—albeit unintended—of Russian democracy.

From the autumn of 1990 on, the possibility of a coup in Moscow became an open secret. Successful coups require secrecy, and palace coups in the Byzantine manner work best if they are kept totally confidential until they are over. But the Soviet coup of 1991 had been an international talking point for many months before it was carried out. This was because the forces backing the coup never made up their minds as to what they intended to do. They were unable to decide the nature of their own plan because they were a leaderless group of high nomenklatura officials of mediocre ability looking for a charismatic leader. Many of them by now were demoralized and believed in nothing. Some, like Pavlov, wanted the specter of a coup rather than the coup itself, because they hoped that the danger of a return to the Cold War would induce Western donors and lenders to open their purses. Others, like Soviet vice president Gennadi Yanayev, seem to have wanted a traditional 1964-style palace coup, but could not grasp that the changes in Soviet society during the Gorbachev era, above all the emergence of the middle-class democratic movement, had made the methods of a palace coup obsolete and unworkable. Such a coup was also made impractical by the fact that there was already a dual-power situation pitting Gorbachev against Yeltsin, and because the latter had secured for himself an official residency in the Kremlin after his election as Russian president, the two presidents shared a single palace (even though Yeltsin's major support base remained in the Russian White House, the parliamentary headquarters).

By contrast, both the competing Soviet and Russian power centers of the nomenklatura—in principle—could have been swept aside by a populist, revolutionary coup capable of generating wide mass mobilization and mass support. However, there were no mass political organizations to carry it out, and Yeltsin was in any case the only leader who knew how to play the populist card. Elements of the Soviet General Staff might have welcomed a coup along the lines of Prague 1948, Budapest 1956, Prague 1968, Kabul 1979, or Warsaw 1981, but in the age of CNN this put them at odds with those who saw the entire exercise as a means of procuring cash. The Soviet army was also more reluctant to move against Russian civilians than it had been to act abroad, and it had been badly shaken by the defeat in Afghanistan. Over many months, the coup backers sought to conjure up Western fears of a return to Stalinism with a series of dress rehearsals for their final action. These practice sessions included the troop movements around Moscow in September 1990, the repressive military actions in the Baltic republics in January 1991, the military and police mobilization for Yeltsin's March 28 demonstration in Moscow, and an attempted parliamentary coup by Pavlov in June 1991. But dress rehearsals are incompatible with the goals any coup, and to reassure his Western admirers, Gorbachev's public repudiation of each rehearsal convinced the officers and officials who were expected to carry out the coup that they would be betrayed and dumped by the coup leaders even more quickly than Marshal Zhukov had been after Khrushchev's nonviolent countercoup in 1957. The dress rehearsals thus served to fragment and dismantle, rather than assemble, the network needed for a coup.

Shevardnadze had spoken to his U.S. counterpart, James Baker, about a possible coup in the USSR as early as July 1989. The conversation came after the violent repression in Tbilisi in April and after the strike of the Kuzbass coal miners in July. Such flare-ups could now occur anywhere at any time, and they could become more serious. "In time, there could be danger of civil war and dictatorship," Shevardnadze forecast.[70] During early 1989, Bush often asked his CIA briefers for evaluations about the likelihood that Gorbachev might be pushed aside by the KGB, the military, or Party forces. The answer came back each time that this was not probable for the moment.[71]

On November 27, 1990, Soviet defense minister Marshal Dmitri Yazov announced a seven-point presidential order giving wide scope for the use of force to prevent a "breakdown" of public order in the USSR. Troops were authorized to use lethal force in their own self-defense and in defending military equipment seized from rebels. The military was henceforth permitted to seize food stocks and electric power facilities if any local government attempted to interfere with their normal operation. On November 30, 1990, Gorbachev signed a decree setting up workers' committees to fight theft and speculation in the food distribution system. These committees harkened back to the bodies of experienced military officers set up in Poland in the autumn of 1981—that is, shortly before the coup in that country—with the announced mission of preparing the Polish economy for the rigors of winter. That action created part of the infrastructure for the declaration of martial law in Poland in December 1981, a power play more serious than the Soviet coup turned out to be.

On December 11, 1990, the television news program *Vremya* carried a statement by KGB chief Kryuchkov that reviewed a climate of "extremely radical political movements," national chauvinism, organized crime, economic sabotage, corruption, and related phenomena. For Kryuchkov, all this raised the threat of "the final breakdown of our society and state, and the liquidation of the Soviet government." Kryuchkov then moved toward his ominous conclusion: "All KGB members believe it is their duty to stop any and all foreign special services from interfering in the country's internal affairs. . . ." He urged "all honest citizens" to report suspicious actions to the KGB. Kryuchkov underlined that he was not acting on his own, but rather "at the president's request." These remarks were widely seen more as an attempt to intimidate the democratic movement than to address the abuses that Kryuchkov claimed to be concerned about.[72]

One prominent public warning that a coup was in the air came from Shevardnadze, who surprised the USSR Congress of People's Deputies by announcing his resignation as Soviet foreign minister on December 20, 1990. The basic reason for his resignation was that he was increasingly being held responsible for the wholesale collapse of the Soviet position in the world. He was also resentful at being upstaged by Primakov's pro-Arab shuttle diplomacy during the Gulf War. However, Shevardnadze portrayed his resignation as a protest against the weakening of perestroika and the authoritarian reaction looming over the country: "A dictatorship is approaching—I tell you that with full responsibility. No one knows what this dictatorship will be like, what kind of dictator will come to power, and what order will be established."[73] The dictatorship of which Shevardnadze warned turned out to be the coup leaders of August 1991.

Two days later, KGB chief Kryuchkov addressed the CPD. He assailed "destructive elements" who were scheming to introduce new forms of property ownership at the people's expense. In his view, law and order now had to be defended by the use of force. He accused the Western powers of stimulating the brain drain so as to pillage the USSR's scientific and technological manpower base. These same powers, said Kryuchkov, were shipping to the USSR grain that was adulterated by chemical additives or even by radioactivity: "Almost 40 percent of all the grain we receive is substandard," he said. Above all, Kryuchkov focused on currency manipulation. First, he noted that organized crime groups were hoarding huge caches of paper rubles, which they planned to use to buy up great chunks of the national wealth once the mooted privatization began. His most dramatic charge was that Western financiers had amassed some twelve billion rubles in Swiss bank accounts, which they planned to dump onto the

Soviet market to ignite a hyperinflationary chaos. Liberal journalists scoffed at Kryuchkov as a self-serving, totalitarian paranoid. But the Filshin affair, which became public knowledge the next month, confirmed much of his charge. Kryuchkov demanded measures "to restore the old order of things in the country's economic life—something foreseen in the president's decree. This is a temporary, but necessary, measure."[74]

On December 27, Gorbachev nominated Yanayev as vice president of the USSR. Yanayev was a colorless apparatchik who had made his career in the Central Council of Trade Unions before moving up to the Politburo; he had the personal reputation of a time-server and philistine. Other possible candidates for this post had included Kazakhstan president Nursultan Nazarbayev or Shevardnadze. The fact that Yanayev had been preferred was another symptom of Gorbachev's authoritarian turn in the deepening gloom. According to some accounts, Gorbachev did offer to make Shevardnadze vice president, but he declined because he knew that as vice president in charge of domestic affairs he would only compound his great unpopularity and possibly would have to assume the role of villain in a coming authoritarian crackdown.[75]

According to David Remnick, during the coup Yanayev kept on his desk a list of precepts entitled "Regarding Certain Axioms of the Extraordinary Situation." This was a kind of *Poor Richard's Almanack* for the apparatchik, including points like no negotiations with the public, no tolerance of manifestations of disloyalty like protest meetings or hunger strikes, and no hesitation in dishing the dirt about political opponents. But Yanayev's axioms also reflected the putschists' understanding of popular aspirations: "Do not be ashamed of resorting to clearly expressed populism," said point three, clearly tailored to encourage the demagogy of die-hard elitists. "This is the law of winning support from the masses. Immediately introduce economic measures that are understandable to all—lowering of prices, easing up on alcohol laws, etc.—and the appearance of even a limited variety of products in popular demand. In this situation do not think of economic integrity, the inflation rate, or other consequences."[76] These instructions illuminate how the late Soviet nomenklatura understood the tactic of masquerading as a populist. However, Yanayev had no credibility in the role of a populist, no matter what decrees he issued.

On the same day that Yanayev was chosen (he fell short of the required majority on his first attempt but squeaked through on a second ballot, after pleading from Gorbachev), the Congress of People's Deputies also approved a series of constitutional changes with a decidedly authoritarian flavor. All executive structures in the central government were made directly answerable to the Soviet president. This amounted to endowing Gorbachev with considerable emergency powers to rule by decree. In January 1991, Gorbachev gave the KGB the authority to raid and search companies that were thought to be guilty of economic crimes such as hoarding, speculation, and charging exorbitant prices. This might have been a throwback to Andropov's anti-Mafiya program, but by now the KGB could no longer be taken seriously as a force against organized crime.

In early February 1991, Kozyrev told Baker in Washington that if attempts at domestic repression succeeded, conservative forces would gain the upper hand and the USSR might "return to aggressive behavior internationally."[77] During this phase, Director of Central Intelligence William Webster, George Kolt, and other CIA officials began vigorously endorsing Yeltsin in the councils of the U.S. government. Ambassador Jack Matlock also urged more attention for Yeltsin, as did Richard Nixon when he reported to Bush on returning from one of his Moscow trips. On March 16, 1991, Baker dined with Shevardnadze at his Moscow apartment. Shevardnadze stressed "the danger of chaos and dictatorship" and confided in Baker that he now viewed Gorbachev as a transitional figure who very possibly might be toppled by a coup.[78] On the eve of Yeltsin's large March 28 demonstration in Moscow calling on Gorbachev to step down, Interior Minister Boris Pugo warned the Soviet president that unless the demonstration was vigorously repressed, he might be ousted in a "coup d'état by mob violence."[79]

March 28 proved to be yet another large-scale dress rehearsal for a coup. Yeltsin had called the Moscow demonstration as a showing of his own strength, but Prime Minister Pavlov had refused to issue a permit for the gathering. At least one hundred thousand Yeltsin supporters turned out near the Kremlin, and fifty thousand troops and police were massed at nearby Mayakovsky Square, the site of the demonstration; there were no major incidents. Even Western reporters could see that Gorbachev was trying to intimidate the democratic movement of Russia. Gorbachev's spin doctors were soon out in force, claiming to foreign journalists and visiting U.S. congressmen that Pavlov and Interior Minister Pugo, not Gorbachev, had called out the troops. During the late spring of 1991, Gorbachev created a new institution, the Soviet Security Council, which included Primakov, Foreign Minister Aleksandr Bessmertnykh, Yazov, Kryuchkov, Pugo, Pavlov, Yanayev, and former interior minister Viktor Bakatin. As it turned out, this new body's membership was virtually identical to the later coup plotters; the only clear exceptions were Primakov and Bakatin.

In late April 1991, the CIA sent Bush a study entitled "The Soviet Cauldron," which included a detailed analysis of how a coup against Gorbachev might occur. The CIA speculated that Yazov, Pugo, Kryuchkov, and other high officials might constitute themselves as a committee of national salvation, oust Gorbachev in a putsch, and set up a dictatorship. The policy recommendation that went with this analysis was that Bush had to do more to build up Yeltsin.[80]

On June 17, Prime Minister Pavlov went before the USSR Supreme Soviet and asked to be invested with the emergency powers that had been granted to Gorbachev earlier. Members of the Supreme Soviet described this maneuver to reporters as "a constitutional coup d'état." Pavlov's speech attacked foreign aid and market reforms as part of a Western conspiracy. Here, Pavlov for the first time cited Gorbachev's exhaustion and overwork as a reason why the prime minister ought to take over, in particular, economic policy. The Supreme Soviet debated Pavlov's request behind closed doors, with Kryuchkov, Yazov, and Pugo all taking the floor to urge that Pavlov be given the emergency powers he was requesting. Kryuchkov attacked the Allison-Yavlinsky economic reform plan as anti-Soviet. "Among the conditions," he told the Supreme Soviet, "is the implementation of fundamental reforms in the country, not as they are envisioned by us, but as they are dreamed up across the ocean." The KGB leader voiced his opinion that many top Kremlin officials were moles planted by foreign intelligence agencies. He added that Gorbachev had chosen to ignore the evidence of hostile foreign intent, refusing to face facts in the same way that Stalin had disregarded reports of an imminent German attack in June 1941. Ambassador Matlock was concerned enough to ask Gorbachev's aide, Anatoly Chernyayev, if he thought top officials were readying unconstitutional measures against Gorbachev.[81]

Matlock was visited on the morning of June 20 at Spaso House (the U.S. ambassador's residence) by Moscow Mayor Popov, a Yeltsin stalwart, who conveyed a warning that a coup was being organized to remove Gorbachev. Because of his fear of KGB electronic surveillance, Popov wrote the names of the plotters on a note pad. Matlock watched as the names Pavlov, Kryuchkov, Yazov, and Lukyanov appeared under Popov's pen. "We must get word to Boris Nikolayevich," Popov scrawled. He wanted the Americans to get word to Yeltsin, who was then visiting the United States. Popov then insisted on tearing the paper into small pieces.[82] So much melodrama to denounce a group of *golpisti* who had just attempted to seize power via the parliament in the bright of day and who had so far not even had their feathers ruffled!

Matlock sent his message to Secretary Baker as a top secret, eyes-only "flash" cable (generally reserved for the outbreak of wars or violent attacks on U.S. embassies). Baker forwarded the message to Yeltsin and also to Gorbachev, who promptly saw Matlock.[83] Gorbachev's reaction to the American ambassador's breathless warning was blasé. He thanked the United States for its friendly concern, conceded that Pavlov had been misbehaving in the Supreme Soviet, but told Matlock there was nothing to worry about. The next day Gorbachev asked the Supreme Soviet to reject Pavlov's bid for emergency powers and prevailed in the voting by 262 to 24. But neither Pavlov nor any of his supporters was given the sack. Instead, at the end of the session the Soviet president demonstratively fraternized with Pavlov, Kryuchkov, and Pugo. "The coup is over," said Gorbachev to the press.[84]

Former CIA director Robert Gates, who was the deputy national security adviser in the Bush administration at the time, commented on this affair: "CIA had been warning us about such a coup attempt for weeks, and we took Popov's warning very seriously."[85] This was one of three formal coup warnings that the Bush administration communicated to Gorbachev from June 1991 on.[86] While

Yeltsin was in Washington, he was asked privately by an important U.S. senator whether he thought the U.S. government was overly concerned about the risk of a coup. Yeltsin replied, "Absolutely not! There will be a coup before the end of the calendar year. Gorbachev doesn't believe it, but I'm preparing for it."[87] One is entitled to wonder in retrospect just what form those preparations took.

THE DEBUT OF THE EMERGENCY COMMITTEE

At 6 A.M. on Monday, August 19, 1991, Soviet radio and television announced that, because of "the inability of President Gorbachev to carry out his duties," Vice President Yanayev was assuming the responsibilities of acting president of the USSR. Simultaneously, it was declared that a state of emergency had been imposed in "certain regions" of the USSR and that the State Committee on the State of Emergency had taken over as the supreme governing body.

Who were the members of this committee, soon to be labeled "the junta" by Yeltsin and his fellow democrats? Two of its eight members—Vice President (now Acting President) Yanayev and Premier Valentin Pavlov—occupied top-level positions but had only eight months' experience in them. Three members —KGB Chairman Vladimir Kryuchkov, Defense Minister Dmitri Yazov, and Interior Minister Boris Pugo—were Gorbachev's appointees in command of the so-called power ministries. These figures had been thoroughly discredited by a wave of exposés and were vilified by the democrats and despised by the broader public. Also, the committee included Gorbachev's deputy in the USSR Supreme Defense Council, Oleg Baklanov, and two persons outside the top governmental structures—the military industrialist Aleksandr Tiziakov and the conservative agricultural administrator Vasily Starodubtsev.

The case of the latter two obviously stemmed from the old Soviet tradition of including token representatives of key branches of the economy in every significant political initiative. The subsequent investigation of the plot revealed that Starodubtsev, at least, had been co-opted on the eve of the coup and had learned about his inclusion in the new governing body from radio reports he monitored while traveling to Moscow from his collective farm, located in the far-off Tula region. Although both Tiziakov and Starodubtsev were relatively well-known and outspoken hard-liners, their political leverage and operational ability to mobilize resources in support of the coup was close to nil.

On the other hand, it was evident from the beginning that some really influential figures on the conservative side had not been enlisted in the junta. This was especially the case with Anatoly Lukyanov, the speaker of parliament (his formal title was chairman of the USSR Supreme Soviet). Lukyanov was the only Union-level official whose position was constitutionally independent of Gorbachev. Together with the decrees and appeals of the committee, the leading newspapers published his separate statement, with a sharply negative assessment of the Gorbachev-Yeltsin draft for a new Union Treaty. Yet Lukyanov's remarks were dated August 16, two days before the junta had stepped forward, which suggested that he was not an integral part of the coup. Also, the junta included none of the powerful leaders from the republics—not even the distinctly conservative Nazarbayev, who had often expressed his unhappiness with the ongoing disintegration of the Soviet Union. All six state officials enlisted in the Emergency Committee were Gorbachev's immediate subordinates, with rather limited constitutional and informal authority.

On the morning of August 19, a TASS wire dispatch carried the political statement of the committee under the title, "Appeal to the Soviet People." In the view of the junta, the predicament of the USSR was now one of "mortal danger"; Gorbachev's reforms had proven to be "a blind alley," and they had made the country "ungovernable." Appealing to citizens fed up with Gorbachev's endless loquacity, the coup committee criticized the "torrents of words and mountains of declarations and promises" whose net effect had been deleterious for the country and its citizens. The committee warned against "extremist forces that have embarked on a course toward liquidating the Soviet Union, ruining the state and seizing power at any cost. . . ." The threat included the "dismembering of the Soviet Union" and even "international supervision of particular facilities and regions of the country." Much of this was true enough, although it would have been more convincing to specify that the "extremist forces" (Gorbachev et al.) were part of the Communist nomenklatura.

According to the Emergency Committee, second only to the crisis of the state came the economic situation, where the committee saw the "catastrophic effects" of political upheaval that had led to the "destruction of the integrated national economic mechanism that had taken shape over decades." "The result includes sharp drops in the living standards of the vast majority of the Soviet people and the blossoming of profiteering and the shadow economy." The junta warned that "hunger and another spiral of impoverishment are imminent in the near future," and that "only irresponsible people can bank on some sort of aid from abroad." That was a fair assessment of the economic outlook in summer 1991, but it was news to no one in Russia. Further, the committee demanded "urgent and decisive measures" to deal with the economic collapse, but the vagueness of this prescription did not inspire confidence.

The junta also spoke of a moral crisis in Soviet society: "Never before in national history has the propaganda of sex and violence assumed such a scale, threatening the health and lives of future generations." The committee promised "to restore law and order straight away, end bloodshed, and declare war without mercy on the criminal world. . . ." Later, there were some indications that the junta had considered empowering the police to carry out instant summary executions of thieves and hooligans. In this regard, the "Appeal" stated, "We shall clean the streets of criminal elements. . . ." The declaration also addressed the humiliation of the USSR in the world, pledging that the pride and honor of the

Soviet people would be "restored in full" and that "all attempts to talk the language of *diktat* to our country, no matter where they come from, will be resolutely suppressed."

Some passages of the "Appeal" on economic expectations make interesting reading today, from across the great shock therapy divide:

> The country's development must not be built on declining living standards for the people. A consistent rise in the living standards of all citizens will become the norm in a healthy society, without reduction of efforts to strengthen and protect the interests of the widest layers of the population, those hardest hit by inflation, production disorganization, corruption, and crime. By developing the many-tiered character of the national economy, we shall support private enterprise, granting it necessary opportunities for the development of production and services. Our prime concern is the solution of the food and housing problems. All available forces will be mobilized to meet these, the most essential needs of the people. We call upon the workers, peasants, working intelligentsia, all Soviet people to restore labor discipline within the briefest period of time in order resolutely to march ahead.[88]

The ideology of the coup was neither Marxist nor socialist, but can perhaps best be described as National Bolshevik; there was no explicit defense of socialism or socialist institutions.[89]

The insoluble predicament of the committee members was that they were Gorbachev's own team and were calling for a repudiation of the failed policies they themselves had been carrying out. Solicitude about the standard of living of the Soviet people coming from a committee that featured Valentin Pavlov, the nomenklatura insider who had so recently looted the savings accounts of working people with his so-called currency reform, was simply not credible. What is significant about the declaration is that it listed things the junta sincerely thought the Soviet people wanted to hear and might support. In this sense, the August 19 "Appeal" ironically may be a useful reflection of some of the aspirations of the Soviet people at the end of the Soviet era.

THE WORLD REACTS

Bush's initial reaction to the coup was one of the few happy events for the plotters during the early hours of their adventure. Scowcroft had informed him of the first CNN reports and told him that history suggested the coup would succeed. Thus it would be a mistake for the United States to burn its bridges to the junta. Bush held a press conference. The events in Moscow were "extraconstitutional," he said. Concerning the new titular head of state, Yanayev, Bush commented that his "gut instinct is that he has a certain commitment to reform." "Coups can fail," Bush pointed out, but his position was to watch the situation unfold and "see where matters go." Questioned about Yeltsin's call for a general strike, he offered a half-hearted endorsement. Bush was indignant at the suggestion that he should be using the hot line to talk to Moscow because that might "over-excite" the public.[90] His tone was similar to that of Mitterrand, who seemed to accept the coup as a *fait accompli*. For Mitterrand on the morning of August 19, Yanayev and his associates were "the men in charge," and any talk of sanctions against the USSR was "premature."[91] It was only during the night between Tuesday, August 20, and Wednesday, August 21, that French foreign minister Roland Dumas issued an official condemnation of the coup. Bush's initial reaction as inspired by Scowcroft was widely criticized, recalling Bush's conciliatory remarks on Sino-American relations in the wake of the Tiananmen crackdown in China two years before. Kozyrev, traveling in western Europe, issued a statement calling the Western response to the coup disappointing, and spoke of appeasement—always a sore point for Bush.

U.S. chargé d'affaires James Collins met with Yeltsin on the morning of August 19 and passed on the Russian president's urgent request that Bush demand the restoration of the legal government, thus reaffirming that Gorbachev remained the head of the USSR. By now, the CIA had noticed that there had been no dragnet of political opponents of the junta and that the troops who had appeared in Moscow were purely decorative, with no specific mission. Compared to the imposition of martial law in Poland in 1981, this was an amateurish and improvised action. The CIA estimated the possible tenure in office of the Emergency Committee as a matter of months. Soon the intelligence bulletins began reflecting the impression that the junta was "a bunch of losers" and that their coup was destined to flop. By late afternoon, Bush was calling the coup "unconstitutional" and "illegal." On the morning of August 20, Bush telephoned Yeltsin to express his solidarity.[92]

The U.S. intelligence community, already favorable to Yeltsin, provided valuable assistance to the Russian leader during the coup. During the spring of 1991, U.S. intelligence agencies began helping Yeltsin to improve his personal security arrangements and the security of his communications system. During the coup, an American communications specialist attached to the U.S. embassy in Moscow was ordered to proceed to the embattled Russian White House with the portable telephone equipment necessary to allow Yeltsin to make secure phone calls to military commanders and others. Yeltsin reportedly used this equipment to urge key military figures not to open channels to the junta. Bush also ordered the National Security Agency (NSA) to make available to Yeltsin real-time reports of calls made by Kryuchkov, Yazov, and others on their special government telephones. While this information was vital for Yeltsin, it also revealed that the NSA was fully able to monitor traffic on the Kremlin's most sensitive phones. The NSA, in fact, opposed sharing these intercepts with Yeltsin, because such sharing would undoubtedly impel the Russian government to take countermeasures in the future.[93]

Mysteries Wrapped in Enigmas

Despite the abundance of factual sources on the coup, most of the writings are surprisingly short on analysis.[94] Yet the most intriguing riddles of the story cannot be resolved by the available empirical evidence and thus require an analytical approach. Even the following enumeration of these riddles is far from complete:

1. To what degree was President Gorbachev involved in the preparation of the coup? To what extent was he denied communications during the coup? Why did the plotters want so badly to meet him after the coup's collapse?

2. Why was Boris Yeltsin not arrested upon his arrival in Moscow on the evening of August 18? Why was he not arrested at his dacha on the first morning of the coup, even after he started his telephone negotiations with the military? Why did the putschists permit him to proceed to the parliament building?

3. Was there an order to storm the Russian White House? If so, who disobeyed the order and why?

On August 21, the *Washington Post* sent a reporter to the Russian community at Brighton Beach in Brooklyn, New York. Here, in the neighborhood known as Little Odessa, the owner of a restaurant commented that "maybe it's Gorbachev's idea to have a coup." A young Russian woman who had departed from the USSR three months before to be free of KGB harassment characterized the coup as "staged" and "vaudeville." This Brighton Beach perspective on those August days may also suggest what the silent majority of ordinary Russians, in their collective farms and nondescript cities, thought about the events that shook the world.[95]

On the question of Gorbachev's complicity, the two existing versions of what transpired naturally reflect the interests of their authors. The plotters asserted that Gorbachev was the driving force behind the coup, and that he pretended to be cut off from the world in order to wait and see which way events would go. Gorbachev, not surprisingly, rejected this as slander. The official version of events endorsed by the victorious politicians has tended to shift. In December 1991, Prosecutor General Valentin Stepankov hinted at Gorbachev's complicity; yet several months later, in the widely publicized book that represented the final official account, he and Yevgeny Lisov accused the Emergency Committee's members, primarily Tiziakov, of concocting the whole story of Gorbachev's collusion in order to provide themselves with a legal defense.[96]

Yet there is some factual evidence that has never been discussed in any of the official accounts. First, just a day before his departure for vacation in Ukraine's Crimean Peninsula, at a session of the government's presidium, the USSR president uttered words that can easily be considered as a direct incitement for the future putschists: "Emergency measures are needed. . . . [I]n emergency situations, all states act and will act accordingly. . . . Tomorrow I will leave for vacation, with your permission, [so as] not to impede your work."[97]

Second, KGB telephone and travel logs show that the main delegation of the plotters, which went to the Crimea on August 18 in an attempt to convince Gorbachev to proclaim a state of emergency, was not the only one: KGB Chairman Kryuchkov and Defense Minister Yazov also traveled to Gorbachev's Crimean dacha in Foros the same day, while Lukyanov and Pugo were both in the Crimea and thus close by.[98] There are no accounts of a meeting by any of these few with Gorbachev, if they had one. More specifically, hard facts contradict the official story about the alleged cutoff of Gorbachev's communications during the putsch. First, two calls made by him to Moscow, both to the chairman of the Scientific Industrial Union, Arkady Volsky, were reported to have been during the hours when Gorbachev was allegedly being held incommunicado. Second, shortly after the coup a senior Ukrainian KGB officer denied the reports that Gorbachev was held in isolation.[99]

YELTSIN AND THE EMERGENCY COMMITTEE

The second question—why the putschists failed to move against Yeltsin—is even more controversial. Stepankov and Lisov claimed that there had been no order to arrest Yeltsin; Yeltsin's own account emphasized that an order in fact had been issued but was later rescinded by Kryuchkov. The commander of the KGB's special Alpha team, Viktor Karpukhin, later claimed credit for not having arrested Yeltsin on the first morning of the coup, when his unit was deployed in the forest around Yeltsin's dacha: "I did everything I could to do nothing."[100] In his book, Dunlop has correctly dismissed the possibility that such flagrant violation of orders could have gone unnoticed by Karpukhin's boss Kryuchkov; following Gosset and Fedorovski, Dunlop assumed that the insubordination had taken place at a lower level. Yet this version makes even more inexplicable Kryuchkov's apparent reliance on the Alpha team for another critical mission later in the coup, on August 20–21. Thus apparently we have to assume that at the beginning of the coup, the KGB deliberately decided to allow Yeltsin to remain at large. This becomes even more intriguing in the light of evidence suggesting that Yeltsin had advance information about the plot. He himself speaks in his book of "a premonition"; yet the premonition happened to be so strong that it compelled him to order changes in the itinerary of his flight from Alma-Ata to Moscow and to land at Vnukovo airport—instead of the Chkalovskaia military air base, where the Alpha unit was waiting for him. All this suggests that the plotters had—or thought they had—specific reasons not to be concerned about Yeltsin's behavior, at least after they failed to capture him at the airport.[101]

The last of the questions—the failure of the putschists to storm the Russian White House, the focus of the Yeltsin government's resistance—is essentially a continuation of the second. Karpukhin and Boris Beskov, commanders of the KGB's Alpha and Beta units, respectively, claimed to be the ones who took the final decision not to attack on the evening of August 21, and the official version of the Russian state prosecutors apparently accepted their account.[102] But two lower-ranking Alpha team officers say that the crucial decision to disregard orders and spare the White House from attack was made by them.[103] A major-general who commanded a special KGB paratrooper force is another defiant officer demanding inclusion in the list of heroes for his refusal to attack the White House on August 21.[104] One could argue, though, that at this stage of the coup (that is, by August 20) wait-and-see was the only sound strategy for anyone in the security forces who cared about his own reputation and security. It would indeed be foolish to carry out the orders of a vacillating group that had already initiated and lost the propaganda war and was plagued by visible disarray. By that time, the purported figurehead of the coup, Yanayev, had not only ruled out an assault but also, in a public speech made at an enlarged Emergency Committee session, urged caution to those who might be contemplating military action.[105]

Also, the split in the General Staff and the emergence of a cohesive anti-junta group (Marshals Pavel Grachev, Yevgeny Shaposhnikov, and Boris Gromov) were already evident. Although some troops continued to arrive in Moscow until the early morning of August 21, these troop movements were carried out in an aimless and uncoordinated manner. Essentially, the enigmatic failure to seize the White House can be explained by our answers to the first two riddles. Our tentative conclusion, growing out of the evidence available thus far, would be that an unexpected convergence of Gorbachev's and Yeltsin's negative reactions to specific aspects of the coup sharply disappointed the initial expectations of the putsch committee, leaving it disoriented and lacking an agreed plan on how to proceed. The putschists evidently felt that Gorbachev and possibly Yeltsin had let them down and left them in the lurch. Apparently, the coup unraveled because of the lack of an appropriate strategy to meet this unexpected and improbable turn of events.

Throughout the coup, Yeltsin was in telephone contact with Kryuchkov, negotiating with him and asking among other things for proof that Gorbachev was physically incapacitated.[106] Therefore, Kryuchkov's decision to go to the Crimea may have been at least in part induced by his talks with Yeltsin. One can only guess that the content of these conversations was not in tune with Yeltsin's simultaneous public labeling of the junta members as "criminals"; otherwise, Yeltsin would not have needed to spend so much time on the telephone with Kryuchkov.

MAJOR INGREDIENTS IN THE PLOT

Concerning the preparation of the coup, we must make an important distinction between two series of interrelated developments. The first is Gorbachev's own rightward drift in 1990–91 and his abortive attempts to break the democratic opposition and the secessionist republican governments—an effort he apparently abandoned in March–April 1991. The other is the indications of a conspiracy against Gorbachev, which had been emanating since early 1991 from the KGB and from the office of Premier Valentin Pavlov.

Thus on March 25, 1991, when Dmitri Simes was handed a message for former U.S. president Richard Nixon from Kryuchkov saying that Gorbachev might soon be ousted through a parliamentary maneuver initiated by Lukyanov with support from the military and the KGB, this seemingly represented Kryuchkov's self-exposure as a coup plotter—at a time when fear of personal responsibility for any radical move, and also of becoming a scapegoat, pervaded Moscow's political elite.[107] Also remarkable was Kryuchkov's apparently personal initiative in establishing a back channel to the U.S. government via Nixon. However, an educated guess would be that it was Gorbachev himself who stood behind this message. In March, the Soviet president was simultaneously engaged in a fierce confrontation with Yeltsin and in desperate haggling for Western aid. The signal via Simes could have been Gorbachev's playing the KGB coup gambit to extort funds from an increasingly tight-fisted group of donor nations. Yet one may also speculate that if Gorbachev did indeed tell Kryuchkov to assume the roll of villain in the eyes of Western "Gorbophiles," the Soviet president also might have antagonized ipso facto his most confident associate and triggered (or further stimulated) autonomous activity by him.

It is important to stress that, in our view, the KGB perception of the global strategic situation and of the USSR's position vis-à-vis the Western powers is crucial to understanding the KGB's behavior during the coup—just as it was crucial to the KGB's earlier planning and support for the Gorbachev Revolution. In fact, this powerful and reputedly most cohesive of Soviet institutions approached August 1991 overburdened and almost incapacitated by its own far-flung global interests and concerns. The evidence suggests that the KGB foreign intelligence directorate held deeply pessimistic views about Soviet capabilities vis-à-vis the West and about Soviet prospects in general. Institutionally speaking, parts of the KGB were quickly evolving into a cartel of business interests heavily dependent on its dealings with Western concerns. Analysis of Kryuchkov's own public pronouncements indicates that he perceived Soviet society as irremediably hemmed in by global capital and Western strategic initiatives.

Gorbachev's closely interrelated foreign and domestic policies, all heavily influenced by the KGB's analyses, were based on the premise that the United States, both as a nation and as the center of global capital, could and would deliberately intervene in Russian domestic affairs in support of Gorbachev. This mindset (which was part and parcel of Gorbachev's vision of global interdependence) became even more pervasive after Kryuchkov's assumption of the KGB chairmanship.[108] The KGB believed that the Soviet Union could develop only if protected by the status of junior but privileged partner of the major world powers. This perception accounted for the KGB's support of Gorbachev's international activities from 1984 on—and for the KGB's profound sense of strategic failure after it became evident that this special status was not being granted.

The KGB's top brass was getting visibly nervous. The Soviet Union was disintegrating, but nobody was intervening to save it. Through Kryuchkov's public warnings and his seeming satisfaction with the thunderings of the hard-liners, the KGB was indirectly threatening the West with an antiliberal coup, but the West preferred to react to hard events rather than simple warnings about them. As Amy Knight has pointed out, Kryuchkov had been an early and ardent supporter of Gorbachev's perestroika, even advocating in 1989–90 the abolition of the Soviet Constitution's Article 6 and the creation of a multiparty system. She suggests that Kryuchkov's desire to turn the clock back may have been influenced by the fact that institutions like the East German Ministerium für Staatssicherheit and other secret police organizations in Eastern Europe had tended to fare poorly after the dismantling of the communist regimes in their respective countries, thus raising the possibility that the KGB also would be broken up. Kryuchkov was not happy with the new Union Treaty, but his dissatisfaction centered on those provisions he saw as infringing on the prerogatives of the KGB.[109] Lacking a coherent strategy, the KGB had to be more and more concerned about its own institutional survival, especially considering the fact that many of its officers had started to drop out by taking jobs with private companies. The February 1991 departure to Vladimir Gusinsky's MOST Bank group of the prudent and farsighted KGB deputy chairman Filip Bobkov became an ominous sign of the security agency's internal decomposition.

Most analyses and investigations concur that the coup was essentially orchestrated by the KGB and assign to Kryuchkov the major role in initiating and consolidating the junta. In fact, the scenario for imposing a nationwide state of emergency, as well as drafts of all documents of the future Emergency Committee, had already been compiled by the KGB by August 4, the day of Gorbachev's departure to Foros.[110] It was only on the next day, August 5, that Kryuchkov brought together for the first time those figures who had been assigned key functions in his plan. That day, Defense Minister Yazov and Defense Council Deputy Chairman Baklanov, along with a secretary of the CPSU Central Committee, Oleg Shenin, and Gorbachev's chief of staff, Valery Boldin, convened in a suite at the ABC Hotel, which belonged to the KGB foreign intelligence directorate. As a result of this encounter, Kryuchkov and Yazov set up a joint KGB/Defense Ministry experts' group, with the task of assessing the optimal strategy and possible consequences of declaring a state of emergency. The experts' group was coordinated on the Defense Ministry side by the commander-in-chief of the Airborne Paratrooper Forces, Lieutenant General Pavel Grachev, who later defected to the Yeltsin camp.

The last appointment proved to be a fatal one, as Grachev was later to play a decisive role in the defeat of the coup. Grachev's involvement in the plan at this preliminary stage must be viewed in light of his earlier record of behavior in emergency situations. In January 1991, at Gorbachev's order, he had directed the deployment of paratroopers in the Baltics, as well as in the other three rebellious republics of Georgia, Armenia, and Moldavia, under the formal pretext of enforcing military conscription. In fact, this was Gorbachev's first serious attempt (in full coordination with future putschists) at the military intimidation of secessionist republic governments. But Grachev, upon arriving in the Baltic area, made a rather sober evaluation of the situation and issued a statement that he would not involve his troops in political conflicts. He was immediately summoned back to Moscow and replaced by the more belligerent General Vladislav Achalov. This experience of Grachev definitely gave him the reputation of being a dove within the military establishment, in comparison with such hawks as Yazov's other two deputies, Ground Troops Commander Varennikov and Achalov.[111] One can only speculate that Grachev's early involvement in the strategic planning of the coup can be explained by Kryuchkov and Yazov's need for a careful and realistic assessment of their chances in the light of their ignominious failure in January 1991 in the Baltics.

If this was indeed Kryuchkov's intention, he made the right choice. The task force produced a carefully hedged "strategic prognosis," emphasizing the dangers that might arise if the unfolding of the coup were to get out of control. The memo, remarkably insightful in its forecasts, envisioned two most unwelcome developments.[112] One was the possibility of a leftist countercoup by the self-proclaimed democratic leaders—in some sense, what actually happened—accompanied by an anticommunist witch-hunt and the dismantling of Soviet-era institutions. Yet the other side of the forecast was also ominous for the putschists, because it included what the experts labeled "an abrupt rightward shift" (in other words, a "brown terror" in the course of which "all those who had collaborated with Gorbachev would be deemed guilty"). This warning directly implied a threat to all the initiators of the plot, a threat from far-right political forces that might dethrone Gorbachev and then purge his appointees. The memo concluded with the discouraging observation that the overall situation in the country was not yet ripe for the majority of the population to accept the toppling of Gorbachev and an abrupt change of political course.

That Kryuchkov may have paused for a time to ponder the reasoning and conclusions of this study may be deduced from the fact that during the next week, from August 7 to August 14, no known significant moves were initiated by the plotters. In retrospect, it looks as though the whole project was, if not canceled, at least suspended. Its apparent resurrection was most likely provoked by the appearance of the final draft of the Union Treaty. This document, surrounded by a veil of secrecy, was distributed to members of the USSR Security Council on Monday, August 12—only a week before the planned August 20 signing by Gorbachev and the republican leaders.

The content of the Union Treaty, as well as the hasty and secretive style of its preparation, infuriated Premier Pavlov, who had just returned to Moscow from a trip around the country. Through his assistants, he arranged the publication of the draft on August 15 by the weekly *Moskovskie novosti* and by other major newspapers around the country. This action, undertaken without Gorbachev's knowledge and, reportedly, against his vehement wishes, was apparently intended not so much to expose the draft to public criticism as to stir up and activate those latent forces at the Union level whose survival was directly endangered by it.

One top KGB officer, A. Yegorov, later testified to investigators that on August 14, Kryuchkov summoned him and some of his other associates and informed them that a state of emergency was to be announced in the next few days. Speaking about Gorbachev, Kryuchkov allegedly said that the president was unable to assess the situation properly and was most likely suffering from a mental disorder. Apparently, it was at this moment and in this place (Kryuchkov's office at KGB headquarters) that the official junta allegation about Gorbachev's illness was born.

Two days later, on August 16, Kryuchkov invited Baklanov for a ninety-minute meeting at KGB headquarters. Thus far, no records of this encounter have become available. Yet the very fact of Kryuchkov's one-on-one meeting with the reactionary spokesman for the military-industrial complex implies that the circumspect KGB boss, after reading the draft of the Union Treaty, was leaning to the most radical, military-backed, anti-Gorbachev scenario of the plot. What implicitly confirms this hypothesis is that immediately afterward, at 2 P.M. the same day, Kryuchkov ordered his deputy to set up a group of communications experts who later went to Foros to sever Gorbachev's lines of communication with the outside world. Again on the same day, August 16—a mere two days before the plotters came out into the open—Yazov informed his most militant colleagues, Varennikov and Achalov, about the forthcoming imposition of a state of emergency.

WHY GORBACHEV NEEDED A COUP

Throughout 1990–91, as we have seen, Gorbachev's overarching concern was securing a substantial package of direct financial assistance from the leading Western economies. The major assumption of his strategy was his belief in the inability of the Soviet command economy to bottom out smoothly without such assistance. This assumption made him fear the collapse of the system and his own personal authority—recalling the December 1989 events in Romania—if Western material and political support were withheld. In Gorbachev's mind, his unprecedented concessions to the West in the 1988–90 period represented his part of a grand bargain, which presupposed Western payments in return. After Soviet acceptance of German reunification, with Germany remaining a member of NATO while the Warsaw Pact was dissolved, Gorbachev strongly believed the time had come for the West to pay its share of the price for the end of four decades of confrontation in central Europe.

Yet all his calculations turned to nothing at the July 1991 G-7 summit in London, where the great industrial powers declined to shoulder the burden. This failure was anticipated and welcomed by Gorbachev's radical opponents, primarily Boris Yeltsin. From a strategic point of view, the outcome signified the de facto end of Gorbachev's internal political relevance. In this sense, both the August coup and the ensuing allegedly democratic countercoup staged by Yeltsin were foreshadowed by the negative results of the London summit.

For Gorbachev, the options were now reduced to two: either quietly contemplating the slow evaporation of the Soviet Union as "president of the liquidation committee" or making a last desperate attempt to reverse the collapse. As usual in such situations, Gorbachev tried to embrace both options without regard to their mutual contradictions. He made a significant move in the first direction at a closed meeting with Yeltsin and Nazarbayev by agreeing to an amended draft of the Union Treaty that eliminated most of the Union administration and made the remains of it dependent upon charity donations from the republic budgets. Simultaneously, he was scheming to stave off the ultimate disintegration of the Union.

The one coup that theoretically made sense for Gorbachev, the removal of the Russian leadership and the suppression of the democratic movement, was neither feasible nor compatible with his political identity; most likely it would have caused his instant collapse. Gorbachev's greatest need was to come up with some dreadful and destabilizing threat, some decisive argument, some new leverage in his bargaining for Western financial aid. One plausible way do this, of course, was to stage a semicoup or pseudocoup, frightening enough to confront the West with the specter of a revanchist USSR, nuclear and unstable, yet controlled and kept within pre-established limits so as not to endanger his hoped-for role as white knight and mediator; otherwise, he would also endanger his guarantee of stability to the West and foreign loans to the republics.[113] Essentially, Gorbachev needed someone important to fall on his sword in public for the sake of his own political survival as the Union's president. The problem was that he had no such team of devoted followers; Kremlin politics was plagued with mutual mistrust and freeloading. Those who surrounded him ex officio were more and more alienated and unreliable (such as Lukyanov and Pavlov) or simply too limited and self-centered (Yanayev); others were excessively obedient (Yazov and Pugo). The sad fact was that none of his courtiers (with the possible exception of the slavishly loyal Boldin) was prepared to stage a coup on his own as a propaganda ploy for Western consumption. Nor was Gorbachev eager to fake a coup on his own, because any hint of his personal involvement in such plans might preclude his peaceful and dignified descent from power and probably would endanger his physical security.

CENTRIFUGAL FORCES WITHIN THE JUNTA

Basing our account on the evidence described above, we can now retrospectively summarize the pre-history of the August coup, which consisted of several disparate strands. One—perhaps the most vociferous but the least influential—was the radical right-wing opposition to Gorbachev's policies, which was entrenched in the military and the military-industrial complex and represented by such people as Baklanov, Varennikov, and Tiziakov. (Their temporary ally in the Ministry of Interior, General Gromov, had drifted away from the putsch planners after signing "A Call to the People.") The radicals strongly believed that they would find powerful support for their agenda at all levels of the USSR state hierarchy, particularly in the officer corps. In addition, they had a number of outspoken allies in public life—from Colonel Alksnis and General Makashov to the "Union" caucus of deputies, Prokhanov's *Den'*, and Vladimir Zhirinovsky. Yet it was precisely these people's propensity for "rabble-rousing" that compromised them in the corridors of Kremlin intrigue.

The radicals, such as Baklanov and Varennikov, were thus let in on the plot at a very late hour. Their late notification, as well as the KGB's perception of a danger that the coup might evolve in an uncontrollable way and be taken over by the far right, is very revealing. As we have noted, Kryuchkov had reason to fear that a conservative shift might be carried along by its own momentum in ways that he personally might find most unpalatable and that radical right-wing populists might prevail in this process. In this case Kryuchkov, who had the public reputation of a faithful Gorbachev man, would face a grim political future.

Another strand of the future plot was initiated by Mikhail Gorbachev, using his perennial ally, the KGB. Perhaps Gorbachev's chief of staff, Valery Boldin, was most heavily involved in this particular gambit. Because of the loyalty of Ministers Yazov and Pugo (the latter a former KGB officer), the Gorbachev-Kryuchkov tandem held a tight control over the Ministries of Defense and Interior, and thereby over such Soviet stalwarts as Deputy Ministers Varennikov and Gromov. Through the president's confidant Arkady Volsky, Gorbachev and Kryuchkov also controlled the activities of Tiziakov, who was Volsky's deputy in the Scientific Industrial Union.

Sandwiched between these two major groups, Premier Pavlov and Speaker Lukyanov pursued relatively separate goals of their own. Each had a shallow political base within the traditional institutions (Party, army, KGB, and Council of Ministers). Both were in charge of fragile, more-or-less democratically accountable structures. And both resented the exclusion of the Soviet Council of Ministers and parliament from the negotiations concerning the new Union Treaty. In addition, from the very beginning of his tenure in January 1991, Pavlov had been deliberately made a scapegoat for previously planned unpopular economic measures. In March, Gorbachev also induced him to take responsibility for the unsuccessful prohibition of the democrats' March 28 demonstration.

Forced to play bad cop while still constitutionally subordinate to Gorbachev, Pavlov was a chronic candidate for dismissal, first in line for the chopping block in case Gorbachev were to decide to reverse himself and move back toward the left. The uncertainty about Pavlov stimulated behind-the-scenes competition among aspiring successors, with Tiziakov as the candidate of the far right and Vice Premiers Vladimir Shcherbakov and Vitaly Doguzhiev as contenders with a reformist label, drawing support from within the cabinet itself and from officials in the republics. After Gorbachev renewed his flirtation with the republics in April 1991, Pavlov found himself in a frontal and hopeless confrontation with the president on a number of issues and, by all accounts, was more than eager for an alliance with the far right.

Lukyanov enjoyed greater prestige. As speaker of the Supreme Soviet, he was in effect (given the traditional weakness of the Russian judiciary) the only high-level Union official with a constitutional position independent of the president. He had room to maneuver and made full use of it in his back-room deals and intricate games with democrats, centrists, and the far right. Yet both constitutional norms and the spirit of the semidemocratic legislature imposed on him a constraining mindset, the tenets of which he had to follow to maintain his image and the support of his constituency in the Congress; such a mindset thus gave him a degree of legitimacy. Also, the carefully crafted Gorbachevian amendments to the 1977 Soviet Constitution immobilized the oversized parliament (with 2,250 deputies) and left little room for independent policies on the part of Lukyanov, to say nothing of any legal, parliamentary moves against the president.

Not fully committed to any one of these groups was a secretary of the CPSU Central Committee, Oleg Shenin. A parochial apparatchik, he had just assumed his once powerful post in 1990, when the Party apparatus began to turn to sawdust under his feet. Indebted for his career to Gorbachev and his followers, and still largely dependent on them, he was simultaneously weaving his own web of relationships with the far right in the military-industrial complex.

Each of these clusters of individuals had its specific agenda for the August coup. The Soviet die-hards obviously aspired to an all-but-complete revision of Gorbachev's policies. Baklanov, in the draft of an undelivered speech for the April 1991 Party Plenum that came to light later, called for a return to the pre-1985 status quo.[114] The die-hards believed in a program of authoritarian modernization à la Huntington-Migranyan, or in some vaguer form, but with a distinctly Andropovian flavor. Some others, including Shenin and perhaps Yazov, were firm believers in what they saw as the undistorted ideology of early perestroika: As Shenin himself later specified, Gorbachev's best phase had ended somewhere in 1989. Still others, like Lukyanov, Kryuchkov, and, not least, Gorbachev himself, were scheming to emasculate the Union Treaty without creating a drastic upheaval, because it was clear that the draft treaty would make the USSR into a rather loose confederation, an eventuality that would have made their functions superfluous.

Further, each of the putschists had his own specific ontology, his personal as well as institutionally indoctrinated worldviews, that governed his methods of analysis and constrained the array of alternative solutions available to him. These deeply embedded cognitive dissonances were capably detected and portrayed by Yeltsin in his retrospective analysis of the coup's major components. His account helps to identify the divergent military-industrial and KGB scenarios shaping the coup, scenarios driven by their respective perceptions of the Western reaction and, correspondingly, by two different political-psychological strategies: "What the [military-industrial complex] needed was a real full-fledged, full-throated putsch that would force the world to believe in the might of the Soviet tank once again. The KGB, however, needed as clean and sophisticated a transfer of power as possible. . . . It had hoped to extract victory with merely the rumble of tanks and perhaps a warning cannon shot or two."[115] The KGB, like Yeltsin, expected polite Western cooperation if the new regime were to prove internally stable. Thus Kryuchkov was reportedly terrified by the prospect of bloodshed and, after the coup began, was filled with consternation by reports of casualties.[116] By contrast, the military-industrial side was thinking more in terms of understated but unmistakable nuclear blackmail and extortion.

The two strategies resulted from radically different perceptions by the KGB and the military-industrial group of the USSR's relations with the outside world during the late Gorbachev era. Clearly, the two approaches were fundamentally contradictory, yet their initiators were drawn together by the rapidity of events and the scarcity of suitable resources for a coup. At the decisive moment, they showed themselves incapable of making a binding commitment to a single, clearly defined scenario. Their incapacity was rooted in the leaderless, oligarchic-bureaucratic character of the coup and in the resulting inability of the putschists to put aside oblique Byzantine ambiguity and bluntly define the available options. Because of the lack of clear direction, several scenarios were operating simultaneously within the coup.

PIRANDELLO IN THE KREMLIN: EIGHT PUTSCHISTS IN SEARCH OF A LEADER

An important moment in the junta's debacle was its international news conference, held at the Foreign Ministry's press center in the early evening of August 19. Attention focused on Yanayev, the new head of state. But Yanayev had the sniffles, and his hands trembled as if with palsy. Was he inebriated? A twenty-four-year-old reporter from *Nezavisimaya gazeta* was bold enough to ask whether the coup was being modeled on 1917 or on 1964. The *Corriere della Sera* reporter wanted to know if the committee had used Chile's General Pinochet as a consultant. In short, the press corps made the junta an object of derision. Marshal Yazov's wife, watching the proceedings on television with her husband, broke into tears and urged her husband to defect from the coup.[117]

After Pavlov physically collapsed from hard drinking on the first night of the coup, the Emergency Committee's course was determined by a nervous co-existence between the Kryuchkov group (with the temporary support of Yazov and Pugo) and the more militant military-industrial group of Baklanov and Tiziakov. Yeltsin, with his superior skills in psychological warfare, precisely identified the plotters' vulnerability: "They had no leader."[118] This was a crucial flaw in the highly personalized politics of the late USSR, where individual prestige and charisma were becoming the strongest public assets amid the decay of most institutions. A committee of bickering nomenklatura oligarchs, events showed, was not a suitable vehicle for the seizure of power.

Can we believe that the coup participants were not aware of this? It is more credible that the KGB strategy—until the last moment and even beyond—was predicated on the expectation that Gorbachev would save the coup by playing the role of *deus ex machina*. After Gorbachev had gotten cold feet, the lack of viable KGB fallback options, coupled with Kryuchkov's unwillingness to let Baklanov and the military take over Moscow with the help of a Napoleonic whiff of grapeshot, created a bureaucratic stalemate within the Emergency Committee itself. (Kryuchkov and the committee, unlike Barras and the French Directory in the crisis of 13 Vendémiaire, could find no ruthless young officer like Napoleon Bonaparte willing to court destiny by firing into the crowds.) The surprising cancellation of Yeltsin's arrest warrant by Kryuchkov suggests that, after Gorbachev refused to join in, the KGB chief was exploring the possibility of recruiting Yeltsin as the Emergency Committee's chairman.[119] These machinations reveal the deeply ingrained pessimism of the KGB about the ability of the plotters to act without the support of a higher, more legitimate authority. To be sure, the KGB was demoralized by its own lack of legitimacy. Its own plan was failing, but Kryuchkov lacked the courage to recognize it. Instead, he was trying to score public relations points for restraining the Soviet military-industrial die-hards.

The latter were far from happy, of course. Stuck in Kiev, Varennikov was bombarding the Kremlin with telegrams demanding "decisive measures" to "eliminate the adventurist group of Yeltsin"; he hinted at his troubles in dealing with the Ukrainian authorities, who had received "no explanation . . . for the amorphous state of affairs in Moscow." Varennikov's fury was clearly directed against Kryuchkov and his cothinkers, especially when he condemned the "idealistic talk about 'democracy' and 'legitimacy'" that "may lead us to collapse with personal consequences for every member of the [Emergency Committee] and their supporters."[120] In Moscow, Baklanov was threatening to walk out. (During a later search, investigators found his unfinished draft resignation from the Emergency Committee "due to its inability to stabilize the situation in the country."[121]) Yeltsin's subsequent account, hypothetically speculating on how the coup might have succeeded, suggested that putting a determined new face like Baklanov in overall command might have made the Emergency Committee far more effective. Yet this was precisely what Kryuchkov and his lieutenants would not allow.

In retrospect, it was this stalemate, produced by mutual distrust between the two main groups of plotters, that accelerated the collapse of the junta. The true intentions and covert intrigues of each of its members were the object of the suspicions of all the others. The KGB, which tried to play the consolidating role in the plot, was itself a rumor mill churning out mistrust and paranoia. The Kryuchkov group, in its ambiguous reports sent through Boldin to Gorbachev two months before the coup, tried to convey to him the "danger" emanating from Pavlov and offered the KGB's services in helping him to neutralize this threat.[122] As we know today, even during the coup the KGB was busily wiretapping the conversations of its fellow travelers Pavlov, Lukyanov, Yanayev, and CPSU Central Committee Secretary Dzasokhov. This pervasive mistrust and lack of reliable information about each other's purposes help reduce the problem of the Emergency Committee's erratic behavior to the well-known psychological dynamics of a leaderless group, thoroughly explored as the "Prisoners' Dilemma" in game theory.

Indeed, the collapse of the August coup is a classic failure of collective action in the absence of information and external authority. At the early stage of the coup, each plotter looked to his partners to make the decisive moves, but no one had any confidence that his fellow putschists would support his actions, rather than appropriate the fruits of his daring while seeking to jettison him as a scapegoat. As the coup unfolded, this feeling spread down the institutional hierarchy. The erosion of the Soviet nomenklatura's collective sense of identity, morale, and elementary solidarity is documented in dramatic fashion by the fact that these high officials, who had worked together for years if not decades, staked their destiny on a risky coup d'état that required total cooperation to succeed; nevertheless, they felt compelled by mutual distrust and suspicion to treat each other as adversary players in a game theory exercise.

THE CRUCIAL PROBLEM: AN OLIGARCHICAL COUP

Within almost any coup, the following functional elements can be identified as analytically separate: legitimation, the transmission of directives through institutions and social structures, and enforcement. Any of these elements may become dominant, depending on the locus of the resources needed for a specific part of the conspiracy—in legitimate political institutions, in administrative chains of command or social transmission belts, or in the coercive structures. In August 1991, the failures occurred consecutively on all three levels of implementation.

From the very beginning, the coup's emphasis was on legitimation, and it was on this level that its performance was poorest. The lack of a clear endorsement from Lukyanov and the sorry figure cut by Yanayev did irreparable damage to the legitimation scenario. Powerful resources were concentrated at the transmission level: in the government presided over by Pavlov and in the military and all heavy industry, supposedly controlled by Baklanov and Tiziakov. Yet there was no serious attempt to mobilize these assets. As noted, Pavlov was in a drunken stupor, and Kryuchkov was too terrified to unleash the destructive energy of the radical right.

In retrospect, it seems that this reluctance to activate the potential support for the coup in social institutions and at the grassroots level outside Moscow reduced the playing field to the capital alone, thus yielding an incalculable strategic advantage to the anticoup forces.[123] Among Yeltsin's winning strategic moves in the confrontation with the Emergency Committee, one of the most important was his success in forcing the putschists to accept Moscow, rather than all of Russia or even the entire USSR, as the decisive political and psychological arena. He achieved this by calling Muscovites into the streets to defend the White House. CNN's camera crews and those of other foreign networks were in Moscow, not in Gorki or Volgograd, and Yeltsin's ability to mobilize telegenic crowds of young people in Moscow gave him an incomparable series of photo opportunities that contrasted favorably with Yanayev's haggard countenance. If Yeltsin had counted on mustering support from the rest of Russia or the USSR, he certainly would have failed.[124] The overwhelming majority of regional officials within Russia accepted the junta regime—some enthusiastically, most with their traditional apathy. As Yeltsin himself admitted in his memoirs, the habitual obedience to a rigid vertical chain of command worked in favor of the Emergency Committee all over Russia.[125]

Finally, on the evening of August 20, when the emphasis switched to the enforcement level, the failures that had accumulated on the other two levels were already too obvious, and the rift in the military too deep, to permit the implementation of a full-scale enforcement plan.

An intriguing issue is what the social and political course of the post-Gorbachev regime would have been in the eventuality that the Emergency Committee had successfully seized power. Analytically speaking, the junta would have had three strategic options.

The first was an attempt to turn the clock back by restoring some version of the pre-perestroika system as it had existed under Andropov. An example of what this would have meant is offered by the draft of the speech Oleg Baklanov prepared but never delivered at the April 1991 CPSU Central Committee Plenum.

Another choice would have been the freezing of the 1991 status quo. This probably would have entailed Gorbachev's reemergence with clean hands after the dirty work of the coup had been done, perhaps allied with Yeltsin (who could have been rewarded by the suppression of all rival candidacies for the RSFSR presidency in the future), and the elimination of the democratic movement by a consolidated elite. Shenin accurately represented the general reasoning of this "status quo faction" when writing from his imprisonment that he had "always fully supported the course of April 1985" but opposed that of April 1991, meaning the concessions made by Gorbachev to the republican elites in the Novo-Ogarevo agreement.[126]

Yet another option would have been a comprehensive, non-Western, alternative developmental strategy, perhaps as expressed by Prokhanov's *Den'* in its praise for the "authoritarian modernization" model.

In reality, of course, these three options were not so clearly distinct in the putschists' minds. One could argue that it was precisely because of this lack of anything more than an extremely vague legitimating developmental formula that the coup took on a hopelessly regressive, reactionary appearance, as if it were trying to move the country backwards against the "natural flow" of history.

Yeltsin's Countercoup: The Army

John Dunlop's analysis accurately emphasizes that "a critical split . . . within the Soviet military . . . was a major reason for the collapse of the putsch." He appears to believe, though, that "serious opposition to the coup did not appear to have crystallized within the military until the evening of the twentieth."[127] Yeltsin himself, along with most Russian sources, believes that the decisive factor in splitting the military was his phone call to Paratroop Commander Pavel Grachev in the early morning of August 19, immediately after the decrees of the Emergency Committee had been made public. As Yeltsin reminisces, the call was made "to exactly the right person," because it was Grachev who was in command of troop deployments in the Moscow area. Yeltsin reminded Grachev about their meeting at the barracks of the Tula Paratroop Division, which Yeltsin had visited in May while campaigning for the presidency. There, he says, Grachev privately pledged to defend the legitimate Russian authorities in case of a "threat to the constitutional order." After Yeltsin had invoked this episode on the morning of the putsch, Grachev took a long pause and said, "I will send a company of my soldiers to your dacha." As Yeltsin writes in his memoirs, he interpreted this as a sign of support. His cultivation of key officials within the power ministries was now paying off. As for Grachev, his behavior at this critical point had been clearly foreshadowed by his precoup profile.[128]

A careful analysis of the roles of Grachev and his paratroopers in the defeat of the junta and in Yeltsin's countercoup provides us with remarkable insights into both civil-military relations and institutional controversies within the armed forces during the final period of Soviet history. The position of the paratroops within the military establishment was anomalous; they were not considered a separate armed service, but were subordinated to the Commander of the Ground Forces and therefore had no representative of their own in the Collegium of the Ministry of Defense. Meanwhile, they were widely viewed as an elite force, with the highest professional qualities and a superior morale, and, despite widespread public disgust with the army as a whole, were held in high regard by much of the population. The paratroops' reputation was boosted during the Afghan War, in which airborne infantry and helicopter crews, although few in numbers, performed the most difficult tasks and received a disproportionately high number of citations, including that of Hero of the Soviet Union. The rest of the Soviet ground troops proved ineffective, demoralized, and unfit for guerrilla war.[129]

From 1988 to 1991, the Kremlin repeatedly involved the paratroops in areas of interethnic clashes and secessionist republics, apparently calculating that their popularity would facilitate the task. Some officers resented what they saw as political exploitation of the paratroops, correctly suspecting that the political leadership might use them as scapegoats for some future atrocity. In retrospect, it seems that the discouraging experience of confronting popular resistance both in Afghanistan and in domestic hot spots had by 1991 made the paratroop officer corps one of the most dovish and reform-minded in the military establishment.

In addition, paratroop officers had every reason to be uneasy about their relationships with the General Staff and their outsiders' position vis-à-vis the key centers of command and control, such as the Defense Ministry Collegium and the General Staff. One can only speculate that the December 1990 decision to appoint Paratroop Commander Achalov a deputy minister of defense—the first paratrooper to get such a high promotion—was an attempt to deal with this discontent. Yet although his function was clearly to be a transmission belt between the High Command and the paratroops, Achalov did not occupy this post in his capacity as paratroop commander, which would have been tantamount to the withdrawal of the paratroops from General Varennikov's Ground Forces command. Instead, Achalov assumed the specially created post of deputy defense minister for emergency situations. Meanwhile, Lieutenant General Grachev, who replaced Achalov at paratroop headquarters, inaugurated his command with a political speech that clearly identified him as a dove: "My opinion on the issue of using the paratroopers for managing ethnic conflicts is negative. This is a job for the troops of the KGB and the Ministry of Interior."[130] This statement by Grachev contained an unambiguous hint at yet another rift within the security forces. The military had every reason to suspect that the KGB—and, implicitly, Gorbachev's inner circle—were trying to use the army as a convenient tool for solving their political problems.[131]

Such was the state of mind of some key military commanders at the time the coup began. Nonetheless, an analytical reconstruction of the outlooks and intentions of other forces is required to explain some bewildering oddities in the military component of the coup. For example, if the coup perpetrators were indeed, in Dunlop's words, "serious men with ruthless intentions," why did they pick Grachev to command military deployments in and around the capital?[132] Neither his dovish record nor his earlier contact with Yeltsin should have been unknown to Kryuchkov and his associates. It also should have been clear that Grachev's deputy, the popular Major General Aleksandr Lebed, who was in direct command of the troops in Moscow, was not likely to be very aggressive. Lebed had had an unpleasant involvement in the highly publicized and politically motivated "potato maneuvers" (dispatching troops allegedly to help with the harvest, but actually to hint at a coming crackdown) around Moscow in September 1990.[133]

The Baklanov-Varennikov axis, which constituted the radical right wing of the coup, had the potential to upset the KGB plan for a controlled semicoup relatively devoid of disturbing media images. Our previous analysis suggests that Varennikov was sent far away from the main battlefield by Defense Minister Yazov, who concurred with Kryuchkov's strategy for a velvet coup—a contest over legitimacy rather than crude force. This strategy required more popular and more flexible officers in charge, commanders able to combine military moves with public relations and psychological warfare.

With hindsight, it must be acknowledged that Yeltsin proved a better analyst and diplomat than the KGB leaders. It is hard to guess whether he would have imposed a strategic constraint on his further options by defying the coup if he had not previously won a psychological game of mutual deception and counterdeception, identifying in the process the locus of a possible rift within the armed forces. Much of the credit for this realization should no doubt be given to those who served as his liaison to the military and the KGB—Skokov, Korzhakov, and others. Yeltsin's own retrospective reasoning only corroborates our argument: "[A]t that moment there were really two armies. One . . . was made up of the highly professional combat units that had served in Afghanistan, an army of the highest world standard. The other was the huge 'truck gardening,' self-serving army. . . . An internal conflict was brewing between . . . the 'lean' generals who had seen action and the 'fat' armchair generals."[134] Gromov, Grachev, and Lebed were from the Afghan school, and all three were definitely lean at the time.

THE HIGH COMMAND DESERTS THE COUP

In the aftermath of the coup's collapse, several important figures in the High Command claimed to have opposed military involvement in the Emergency Committee's gamble and to have pressured Yazov to repudiate the coup. Naturally, given the lack of factual evidence, and taking into account the human tendency to embellish one's deeds post hoc, the concept of opposition should be modified in accordance with the Soviet Army's institutional rites and constraints. For most of the later claimants, opposition to the coup during its first two days generally amounted to not taking initiatives and to the soldier's knack of disappearing from the sight of a commander when the latter is likely to give an unwelcome order.

The only conspicuous evidence on this issue is the postcoup tally of officers cashiered compared to the number of jobs retained and promotions garnered. Out of seventeen members of the High Command, nine were dismissed after the coup by Gorbachev's decrees. Of those who retained their posts, Air Force Commander Shaposhnikov, Yeltsin's hand-picked candidate, was nominated USSR minister of defense after General Mikhail Moiseyev had held that office for one day. This indicates that Yeltsin and Gorbachev viewed Shaposhnikov as someone who had actually opposed the coup, although this officer's post hoc claims to have conferred with Grachev about scrambling his MiG fighter-bombers to strafe the plotters in the Kremlin looked like the product of an overheated imagination, and he soon expressed unwillingness to reminisce on this topic.[135]

The real credit for not giving the necessary orders to go through with the putsch should go to those men who were part of the chain of command over the tank and paratroop units actually deployed in Moscow—Yazov, Grachev, Lebed, and to some extent even Achalov. The roles of others became crucial on the morning of August 21, when, after a night of continued stalemate marked by the first civilian deaths, a decision about what to do was on the Defense Ministry's agenda.

At the lower levels of the military hierarchy, the natural unwillingness to be tricked into uselessly killing Russian civilians activated a traditional Russian skill: resented orders from above were carried out in a way that usually precluded the expected results. In addition, a large number of tanks and other vehicles began to experience sudden mechanical difficulties. Troops ordered to take up positions inside Moscow moved much more slowly than expected, and detachments that had been ordered to converge on certain points failed to do so. This was, perhaps, the most effective resistance to the coup at the grassroots level.

If we had to name the single person whose actions did most to doom the coup to failure, it would be, ironically, Yazov. Early on the morning of August 21, he declined Kryuchkov's insistent invitations to attend one more session of the Emergency Committee. Instead, he summoned the fifteen-member Collegium of the Defense Ministry. Between eight and nine o'clock that morning, the Collegium—with only one member, Varennikov, absent—issued an order directing all troops to leave Moscow at once. By that time, Yazov was not answering persistent phone calls from his fellow junta members. Later, some of the putschists—Kryuchkov, Baklanov, and others—arrived in person at the main building of the Ministry of Defense. They wanted to persuade Yazov to rescind the withdrawal order. Kryuchkov urged Yazov to continue the struggle while other members of the junta lapsed into hysterics. Moscow CPSU committee chairman Yuri Prokofiev reportedly begged for a gun to shoot himself. In response, Yazov advised his colleagues to go to the Crimea and pay a visit to President Gorbachev.

A Pyrrhic Victory for the Democratic Movement

What was the role of the democratic movement and, more broadly, of the embryonic civic society, which at that time overwhelmingly endorsed Yeltsin, democracy, and reform? How much credit should be assigned to the democratic movement for defeating the coup?

The movement exhibited great regional variations, but on the whole it probably peaked some time in 1990 and was already losing steam in 1991, partly because much of its energy and some of its activists were now being siphoned off by the Yeltsin political machine; but the movement was an important factor on the scene. The changes it had wrought in mass psychology, especially in the cities of Russia, were one of the most important structural factors that prevented anything resembling a palace coup of the type that ousted Khrushchev in 1964. In that year, Mikhail Suslov and his confederates did not have to take public opinion into account in any way; they could be certain that the masses of Soviet citizens would do as they were told. By 1991, that certainty had been replaced by another one: the certainty of mass protest, at least in large cities, if the nomenklatura attempted to reassert the old forms of repression. The presence of the democratic movement, along with foreign television cameras ready to send the images of its protests around the world, had come to weight heavily in the calculations of Gorbachev, Yeltsin, and the members of the future junta.

In Russia, few people believe in the romantic myth that in August 1991 the masses, led by the democrats, rushed onto the streets of Moscow and Leningrad and thwarted the reactionary forces. However, Dunlop partially buys into this democratic story. He speculates that if Yeltsin had been arrested, "large-scale resistance," "civil insurrection," and the "Romanian variant" would have been possible. And he quotes without comment Konstantin Kobets's opinion that if the Russian White House had been taken by assault, "then that would have been the beginning of a civil war."[136]

On the other hand, the official version of the Russian post-August regime has gradually de-emphasized the democratic myth. In their book, Stepankov and Lisov cast serious doubts on the relevance of public resistance to the putsch. For them, on the first day of the coup "the ranks of defenders [of the Russian White House] were disappointingly thin. One could have gotten the impression that Russia had betrayed its president."[137] (We leave aside the bitter irony of recriminations against the Russian people for not being quick enough to put their lives on the line to save the political career of the man who was already impoverishing them by his economic policies.) According to this account, it was only later, on August 20, that "it seemed that all Moscow responded to the appeal to come to the defense of the White House."[138]

Yeltsin's own account represents an even more serious challenge to the democratic story. He depicts the main battle as taking place behind the scenes:

The corridors of power were the crucial theater of operations, and it was in this penumbra that his associates and allies—Skokov, Grachev, Korzhakov, and others—waged their struggle. Not only does Yeltsin ascribe no significant role to the democratic movement, he does not even mention the names of any democratic leaders except for those who were ex officio members of his own entourage, such as Anatoly Sobchak. The very spirit of Yeltsin's account suggests that the democratic public and its leaders were merely stooges, supernumeraries in yet another edition of the old Kremlin power game.

Yuri Skokov and Gavriil Popov have provided accounts that are in tune with much of Yeltsin's account. Skokov said that in January 1991, Yeltsin instructed him to act thenceforth as his liaison with the army, the KGB, and the military-industrial complex, and that during the putsch he negotiated on Yeltsin's behalf with Grachev.[139] Popov put this in a wider context, pointing repeatedly to political debts that Yeltsin presumably acquired in these and earlier negotiations. One such debt was paid off through his postcoup promotions of Grachev, culminating in his appointment as minister of defense in May 1992. "The future will show," Popov adds, "how many other negotiations there were of this sort." In general, he noted that Yeltsin had "greatly strengthened his links" with the state apparatus, including the military-industrial complex, since May 1990. Even with Popov's admonishment that the connection is "a delicate theme, . . . a matter for the future" and that "the time to discuss it has not yet come," he attributes victory against the putschists in part to "Yeltsin's complicated and detailed negotiations with the army and the security organs, and with local apparatchiks." Again, Popov stresses, "Only in the future will it become clear how important were these negotiations and the debts that Yeltsin incurred."[140]

With the benefit of hindsight, however, we should note here that practically the only state organizations with which Yeltsin maintained good relations during the years after the coup were the security organs, notably the Interior Ministry police, the secret police, foreign intelligence, and the Federal Agency for Government Communications and Information. As for the democrats, Popov accurately pointed out that Yeltsin had worked with them before and during the coup, but that he had done so "without incurring any formal debts to the democratic organizations" regarding, for example, "personnel appointments or draft laws." Thus, if the democrats were to make unwelcome political demands of him in the future, "I think Yeltsin would simply end his cooperation with them."[141]

Among foreign authors, Mark Galeotti has pointed to the "lack of resistance to the coup outside the politicized journalists and politicians of Moscow and a few urban crowds." His reasoning supports the now pervasive belief that the coup was ruined not by its opponents but, rather, by its planners and their bungled course of action: "The uncaring lesson of history is that crowds do not prevail over soldiers prepared to use their weapons. . . . [T]he mob succeeds when it is pitted against a force unwilling to resist or already convinced it will fail."[142]

This issue requires a more detailed consideration than we can provide here. Briefly, though, an analytical distinction should be made between, on the one hand, the ordinary people who risked their lives by going into the streets of Moscow, Leningrad, Kazan, and other cities to protest against the junta and, on the other hand, that part of the political elite that claimed to represent an organized democratic movement. When it comes to ordinary citizens, it is surprising how many people rushed out to support the legitimate government, despite the mass impoverishment and bitter disappointments of the Gorbachev period. We note that whatever maneuvers may have gone on behind the scenes, it was, in the last analysis, the crowds in the streets of Moscow and the putschists' fear of mass bloodshed that finally ruled out any serious attempt to storm the Russian parliament.

As far as the political organizations within the democratic movement are concerned, they failed to reap the fruits of both the popular mobilization and the collapse of the putsch. In the crucial months before and after the coup, they proved incapable of providing their huge constituency with firm leadership, programmatic vision, or a coherent strategy for capturing the institutions of power. Faced with the legitimacy crisis of the old social order and with the challenges posed by the economic, moral, and psychological collapse of Soviet society, they responded with posturing, or at best with ideas for administrative reform. In those three days of August, the general staff of the democratic movement (that is, the Coordinating Council of Democratic Russia) remained in total disarray. Its leader, Yuri Afanasiev, happened to be in France on the first day. Its other leaders immersed themselves in the crowd scene and generally remained out of touch with political decision making. A fortunate few of them were invited at the last moment to appear as extras in some symbolic photo opportunities: The leader of the Republican Party, Vladimir Lysenko, was picked up for the delegation that went to Gorbachev's dacha on the afternoon of August 21.

Yet by August 1991, the chances of any significant success for the democratic movement as such were already almost nonexistent. By 1990, the lack of any strategy for comprehensive social change, along with endless petty tactical bickering, had already thrown Democratic Russia into the embrace of Boris Yeltsin, where it was destined to be strangled within a year after the August triumph. With the self-destruction of the democratic movement between late 1991 and early 1992, hopes for social justice, which had been rekindled in August 1991, disappeared for the time being. In the words of a leading democratic intellectual, Yuri Burtin, "the August revolution did not expire by itself but, rather, was deliberately extinguished by those whom we saw as its leaders."[143]

WHY YELTSIN NEEDED A COUP

As it turned out, the great beneficiaries of the junta debacle were Boris Yeltsin and his cronies. Had it not been for the coup, Yeltsin's drive for personal political aggrandizement probably would have slowed during the summer and fall of 1991. His turn from populism to the cultivation of the nomenklatura was beginning to erode his base in the democratic movement. After a few months, his loss of momentum—always a danger in a dual-power situation—might have become obvious, and then irreversible.

The abortive coup did him the inestimable favor of lumping together all the military-industrial, bureaucratic, Russophile, pro-Soviet, Communist, and other forces that were disposed to defend certain features of the old order or even the old order *in toto*. The coup portrayed these forces in the worst possible light. They could be readily depicted—and were so—as cowards, hypocrites, drunks, bunglers, reactionaries, goons, and potential mass murderers. But worst of all, they were objects of ridicule, buffoons who failed to intimidate anyone. Whatever their intentions might have been, they had wrapped up the entire cause of conservative Soviet oligarchy in one neat package and deposited it in the proverbial dustbin of history.

The Emergency Committee drove most of the politically active elements of Soviet society into Yeltsin's net. Yeltsin's tank-climbing number, repeated for weeks on end by CNN and a hundred other television networks around the world, also made the Russian president the darling of the international public. How telegenic was this bluff and hearty figure in comparison with the scared, shaking Yanayev! For Gorbachev, these events were the denouement. Within months, Yeltsin inherited his remaining power and, along with it, the mantle of a world celebrity.

THE OUTCOME OF THE COUP

Between August and December 1991, all institutional embodiments of uncompromising anti-Western, antidemocratic, and antimarket thinking seemingly collapsed, together with the construct of "the Soviet people." The Communist Party, in its previous form, ceased to exist. The power ministries, or what journalists liked to call the "hard-line" institutions—the army, the KGB, the Ministry of Interior—were rapidly torn apart by the elites in the republics and simultaneously underwent a series of internal reorganizations and personnel purges, mostly in the upper echelons. The KGB as it had hitherto existed was dismantled. There was a brief spate of rumors about a KGB coup plot, but these were exploited to accelerate the USSR's demise.[144] The headquarters building of the Russian Union of Writers—the intellectual incubator of the new Russian right —was occupied and nearly razed to the ground by a self-proclaimed revolutionary assault carried out by democratic and liberal functionaries. All existing or potential institutional leverage for antidemocratic politics seemed irreparably destroyed. Yet, as soon became evident, the resurgence of such politics was programmed into the very nature and spirit of the August regime that was taking shape in the new, post-Soviet Russia.

During the months that followed August 1991, the invocation of the coup and its defeat served as a vital source of a charismatic, revolutionary legitimacy for the new Russian rulers. Yet as early as August 1992, Stanislav Govorukhin, the famous filmmaker and a prominent figure of the national-democratic wing of the anti-establishment movement, commemorated the first anniversary of the coup with the following words: "We suffered a victory. In those three days, on the barricades, I dreamed of a different Russia than we have today." From the radical liberal side, this opinion was echoed by Valeria Novodvorskaya: "The new August revolution gave us the same thing as the old October one: the looting of the people, their enslavement, the falsehoods of the official press, . . . all this with the servile complicity of the people."[145] Yeltsin himself, speaking on the first anniversary of the coup (August 19, 1992), was above all concerned to rationalize his betrayal of the mass movement that had brought him to power:

> Following the putsch, Russia came to face a most complex choice—the very situation again pushed the country toward a revolution. I was then firmly convinced, and remain so now, that this path would have been tantamount to a very great political error, and that it would have ruined Russia altogether.
>
> Our people are well aware of what a revolution is, of how great its temptations, and most important, how tragic its results. In Russian conditions, the revolutionary option inevitably would have got out of control and led to colossal contradictions and conflicts. . . . If this storm had begun, no one—not just in our country but anywhere else in the world—would have been able to halt it. In September and October we were literally teetering on the brink, but we were able to save Russia from revolution, and mankind from its disastrous consequences.

Two years later, he made this reluctant and evasive confession: "It must be acknowledged that the opportunities which opened up for Russia in August 1991 were by no means exploited to the full."[146]

The official process of re-evaluating the August coup and its main actors was placed on a new legal basis when, on February 23, 1994, the lower house of the Russian parliament (the State Duma) issued a decree of amnesty that covered all defendants in the trial of the junta. In compliance with this decree, on May 10 the military collegium of the Supreme Court vacated the lingering criminal case against all the defendants. While most of them accepted the amnesty, General Varennikov defied the authorities and decided to fight in court for a full acquittal, a battle that he won handily to the admiration of Yeltsin's radical opponents. Although Varennikov's role in the planning and implementation of the coup was rather marginal (he mostly carried out the orders of Defense Minister Yazov), the verdict of acquittal had a far-reaching symbolic meaning as a legal reappraisal of the Emergency Committee's role and intentions. In a sense, the blanket amnesty, coupled with the acquittal of Varennikov, represented a most serious joint assault by the legislative and judicial branches on the very sources of the Yeltsin regime's legitimacy. Still, the moral and political rehabilitation of the Emergency Committee proceeded further. Among its members,

Baklanov and Starodubtsev remained active in politics, the former as a prominent activist of the Russian All-People's Union, and the latter as governor of the Tula region. Among their closest associates, several were elected to the parliament; in the 1995–99 Duma, Anatoly Lukyanov served as chairman of the pivotal Legislative Committee, and Valentin Varennikov headed the Subcommittee on Veterans.

OBITUARY FOR THE SOVIET-ERA NATIONAL-CONSERVATIVES

The Union of Soviet Socialist Republics, one of the most notable political constructs of the twentieth century and the modern era, will shortly disappear from our narrative. For more than seven decades, this gigantic state was hated and feared by many, and idolized by many others, in a way that few other nations have ever been. The USSR had carried out one of the most sweeping industrial modernizations in all of human history, and it had withstood the assault of Hitler's Germany and its allies. To speak of the unusual power of this state, though, is to say simply that its very existence divided the world into two camps.

For nearly half a century, the Soviet Union resisted the combined political and economic power of the United States, the British Empire, NATO, and their allies in Asia, Africa, and Latin America. It made the planet tremble with a fifty-four-megaton hydrogen bomb, the biggest man-made explosion in history. It was the first country to put a man into space, and it contended for world leadership in many areas of science. In short, it expressed some of the very best and the very worst of modern humanity. The USSR was accused by its many adversaries of megalomania, paranoia, brutality, aggression, inhumanity, and tyranny, but it was seldom suspected of weakness. In the end, though, it was a colossus with feet of clay. When this great Leviathan suddenly disappeared beneath the waves of history, it left behind a sense of bewilderment in the minds of many. Before moving on, then, let us briefly consider the collapse of that stratum of the Soviet polity that had been determined to preserve the old order in whole or in part—a group we can dub the "national-conservatives."

In March 1985, when Gorbachev came to power, national-conservative public figures and groups (both advocates of the "native soil" movement and neo-Stalinists), seemed still to possess enough resources to constitute a significant force. They were supported by influential corporate interests in the agricultural-industrial complex, the military-industrial complex, and the Soviet ideology industry (the closest Communist counterpart to Madison Avenue). Because of their influence and resources, they had considerable control over some widely distributed journals, occupied most of the important leadership posts in state cultural institutions, and dominated many outlets of the official mass media. Consequently, they also influenced the struggles going on within the nomenklatura, including within the CPSU Central Committee. However, over the next six years, the national conservatives suffered a number of humiliating defeats; by the summer of 1991, it seemed they had practically ceased to exist.

How can this phenomenon be explained? If we remain within the framework of a purely political analysis, the argument might go like this: The balance of forces that emerged from 1985 turned out to be lethal for the national conservatives. Among their opponents were such powerful groups as the overwhelming majority of the reformist press, that segment of the nomenklatura that advocated an economic opening to the West, the democratic voters of the big cities, the Western allies of the radical reformists, and the dominant political leaders—first Gorbachev, then Yeltsin. These groups stifled the national conservatives with their own powerful preponderance.

However, the facts contradict such an explanation. In 1985, radical Westernizers were, as a rule, inmates of jails and gulags, or had emigrated or been sent into exile. Even in 1991, they comprised a minority both in the Russian parliament and in the parliaments of the republics. The official press, right up until 1989–90, remained for the most part moderately centrist. Among the economic elite (not to mention average citizens), those who had lost out by the USSR's being cast into the globalized world market were far more numerous than those who had gained. Among ex-Soviet citizens in the West, both the opponents and the potential allies and fellow travelers of the Russian nationalists were active. Approximately the same distribution existed in the CPSU Central Committee. As we have seen, Gorbachev in the first years of his rule repeatedly courted both the conservatives and the Russophiles with whom he had been forced to reckon earlier during his years in the agrarian sector. This was his political rationale for conducting an anti-alcohol campaign, opposing the redirection of the northern rivers, and celebrating the millennium of the Orthodox faith in Russia.

We should face some facts: The events of 1985–91 show how small groups of people eventually led by Yeltsin, with few resources and no instruments of coercion, were able to direct a country's development so that it resulted in the dissolution of the former system and its government, as well as in a radical recasting of the geopolitical world map that markedly diminished the danger of thermonuclear holocaust. The numerically superior participants in the political process who possessed powerful advantages and tried to impede this development proved powerless in the end and were relegated to the sidelines.

It is beyond the scope of this chapter to present a detailed analysis of the causes for these developments. However, it is already clear that the key to understanding these causes must be sought not in the realm of formal politics, but in the sphere of social psychology and the clash of ideas. Soviet life was characterized by three important factors: a nearly universal distaste for politics, a tradition of fatalism in public affairs, and the absence of a competent political class. As a result of Soviet rule, 99 percent of the citizens of the USSR had no real power in political affairs. This also applied to the national conservatives, who found themselves strategically unprepared to make the transition from debates in the media and behind-the-scenes intrigues in the corridors of power to an open fight for real participation in official decision making. Because they perceived political power as a given, and because they had been conditioned by history either to serve authority or to rebel against it, Russian nationalists—like the majority of Russian people in general—could not imagine what it might be like to assume power themselves. In the end, only a relative handful of people from across the political spectrum were prepared to become politicians: members of the second echelon of the Party elite, scholarly consultants (sociologists and ideologues) in the CPSU Central Committee, and several former dissidents who were inspired by Andrei Sakharov's example.[147]

These persons, by using the networks and ideologies they possessed, were able to formulate and elaborate a set of material and ideological goals that mobilized several decades of enormous public dissatisfaction with and opposition to the injustices of the Soviet system and the lies and exploitation of the nomenklatura elite. They were able to direct a potentially highly destructive force, which might have taken virtually any form, and channel it toward political and economic change, methodically driving their adversaries from the field or paralyzing their opposition. Morally unprepared to abandon their collective vested interests within the old institutional framework, the army, the KGB, the military-industrial complex, the agricultural complex, cultural institutions, and pundits all lost face, fragmenting into groups that were motivated by all-consuming personal interest and the need to fight for survival. As Galeotti points out, the Soviet Old Order was afflicted by a lack of will.[148]

As events after 1991 proved beyond a doubt, to be a democrat was one thing, to be a radical liberal freemarketeer was another. The radical reformists (soon to be known as "shock therapists") had a strategic advantage in that the public debate taking place in the press, parliament, and the country's leadership developed within the dichotomy between regime and opposition that they themselves had done much to establish. In this framework they relied first of all on the Manichean perception that is characteristic of mass psychological reactions to new situations and problems. They also relied on the realization that fundamental reforms of the social system were a necessity. Every institution was divided into supporters and opponents of reforms. Among the opponents were all those people who at one point or another, on one issue or another, went against the "general line" of the radical-reformist group. This strategy of polarization succeeded mainly because the opponents of the radicals (including the neo-Stalinists, Russophiles, social-democrats, moderate reformists, and representatives of the economic and Party-state elite) for the most part were not prepared for politics to be a fight for power and accepted the logic of the debate that was offered to them, which meant they were drawn into an ideological war with the radicals on all fronts simultaneously. Instead of discussing trends, priorities, consistency, and the human factor involved in the reforms that were so necessary for the country and the people, instead of asserting and coordinating legitimate interests, the opposition voluntarily accepted the role of the villain in a fairy tale about a fight between the absolute forces of Good and Evil, a fairy tale in which the bad guys are inevitably defeated.

The opposition lost, but its ideas, factions, and potential electorate did not disappear. With Yeltsin's rise to power in the RSFSR, the fever pitch of the former polarization began to wane imperceptibly, and the ideological camps of the radical reformists and the national conservatives started to disintegrate into separate and at times conflicting components. On the one hand, Yeltsin and his closest allies, having lost their dire need for the democratic movement and having quietly renounced their former anti-nomenklatura platform, were no longer betting everything on a Russian national state with significant elements of authoritarianism in politics and statism in economics. On the other hand, the feeling of betrayal and disappointment among the rank-and-file participants in the radical-reformist movement with what now passed for serious politics, and the despair of many Soviet citizens (including many Russians) who were rapidly becoming stateless as the USSR moved toward fragmentation, gave rise to the Zhirinovsky phenomenon. His program paradoxically combined an imperial version of the national idea that rejected ethnic borders with Western forms of political democracy and an unbridled quest for riches amidst the growing economic chaos. It is not surprising that Yeltsin's and Zhirinovsky's political visions, even as they increasingly converged in some respects, collided head-on in the 1991 presidential contest on the issue of preserving the Union.

Just when the traditional opposition lay morally prostrate, both Yeltsin and Zhirinovsky emerged as victors—victors, of course, in different senses of the word. In subsequent years, their increasing collaboration would initiate the so-called second wave of conservatism, which would return former antidemocratic ideas and methods to the center stage of Russian political development. Meanwhile, the August coup cleared the way for not only the final demise of the Union, but also Yeltsin's embrace of "shock therapy" and the definitive fragmentation of the democratic movement. The latter two themes form the core of the next two chapters, respectively.

5

CATCHING UP WITH THE PAST: THE POLITICAL ECONOMY OF SHOCK THERAPY

A one-time changeover to market prices is a
  difficult and forced measure but a necessary one.
For approximately six months, things will be worse
  for everyone, but then prices will fall, the
consumer market will be filled with goods,
  and by the autumn of 1992 there will be
  economic stabilization and a gradual improvement
in people's lives.

—*Boris Yeltsin, Speech to the RSFSR Congress of
People's Deputies, October 28, 1991*

AFTER THE AUGUST 1991 COUP, Russia entered a truly critical period of two months, in which its fate for the foreseeable future was decided. The USSR was collapsing too suddenly for a smooth transition to democracy and free markets to be possible. Only the developing embryo of a new, market-oriented order existed beneath the surface, ready to step forward and replace the old order. Russian civil society was vigorous but still in its infancy—there were no mature political parties, no commercial code, no politically neutral bureaucracy, very little of the infrastructure needed for a market economy, and few professionals trained to function in market conditions. Nonetheless, the International Monetary Fund, with the blessing of the world's richest countries and the help of Yegor Gaidar and other young Russian economists, convinced President Yeltsin that economic shock therapy should be applied to his country forthwith, and that if he exercised strong political will, a regular market economy soon could be created. By mid-October, with virtually no public discussion, Yeltsin and his closest associates had opted for a top-down revolution in the economy and for a relatively mild—and unacknowledged—political authoritarianism as the means of implementing it.

In the form advocated by its proponents for the post-Soviet states, the theory of shock therapy holds that strong political leadership can, in three to four years, transform state socialism into a market economy.[1] To achieve these goals, the main requirements are the political will to liberalize prices, drastically cut public spending, and privatize the state's economic assets—in addition to acquiring large-scale financial assistance and know-how from abroad. The theory had been developed in relation to the postcommunist countries with the support and sponsorship of such bodies as the IMF and the World Bank. Although the theory's advocates did not normally discuss the political means needed for its implementation, its most visible proponents and vocal supporters implied that shock therapy could be accomplished in Russia by purely democratic means, and that it could—simultaneously with economic reform—create the basis of a democratic political system.[2] Later, when Yeltsin's authoritarian drift became too obvious, they publicly deplored it, as if completely unaware of any causal links between this political trend and the economic policies that they had advocated.[3]

The immediate model for emulation by the theory's Russian followers was Poland, the only country where this drastic model of transition from a centrally planned economy had ever been applied. Shock therapists' excitement over Poland ignored the fact that by 1991 their recipes had provoked a profound political and moral crisis in that country, which later led to the crushing defeat of the reformers at the hands of the renamed Communist Party in the 1993 elections—even though, by all standards, Poland had far better institutional and cultural preconditions than Russia for a rapid transition to the market.[4] Later, in the mid-1990s, these preconditions and some non-IMF policies facilitated Poland's delayed but rather successful transition.[5]

YELTSIN'S OCTOBER 1991 SPEECH: SHOCK THERAPY PROCLAIMED

On October 28, 1991, two months after his victorious countercoup, Boris Yeltsin appeared before the deputies of the Russian Congress and declared the launching of radical economic reforms. His enumeration of the specific policy steps that would go into the history books under the heading of "shock therapy" took only a few paragraphs in his lengthy speech. Some of his declared measures, notably the deregulation of prices, were actually implemented in the final shock therapy package. Others, such as the reduction of monopolies' power and production-stimulating tax reform, have not been seriously attempted to this day.

First in the presidential program came macroeconomic and especially financial stabilization. Within its framework, the crucial and, as Yeltsin promised, "the most painful" measure was to be the "drastic one-shot unfreezing of prices." Permeating the entire speech was an almost religious faith in the universal efficacy of Western market equilibrium models and their instantaneous applicability on Russian soil: "Free prices," said Yeltsin, "must become the means to achieve a growth in production, and this will in the future set a limit to price increases." "The liberalization of prices," he promised, "will put everything in its right place."[6]

How did Yeltsin link the radical reforms to the broader context of the social-economic transformation that was under way? Price deregulation and the privatization of government property, he said, were already happening, but they were happening in an "elemental," "wild," "ugly" way and "frequently on a criminal basis." The task of the government under these conditions was to "seize the initiative" and to introduce organization, order, and rationality into these processes. The contradiction between this goal and the essence of the measures set forth, which promised the speedy and almost wholesale withdrawal of the government from the economic sphere, could not have been more glaring. Was Yeltsin himself aware of how explosive this contradiction was? Did anyone believe that Yeltsin, a man who by nature and temperament always tried to leap into the saddle and corral chaotic developments, would now embrace the doctrinaire ideology of his advisers and cast aside, one by one, the tools of economic governance? Whatever the answers, this deep, unacknowledged contradiction in his October speech casts a tragic light on Yeltsin's role as the father of shock therapy.

ON THE USE OF THE TERM "SHOCK THERAPY"

In this book, we use the term "shock therapy" to describe the drastic economic measures undertaken by the government of Yeltsin and Deputy Prime Minister Yegor Gaidar in the winter and spring of 1992. Moreover, we contend that, despite numerous tactical maneuvers and retreats, the doctrine of shock therapy guided the economic thinking and policies of Yeltsin and his radical reformers right up to the latter's demise in August–September 1998 and even beyond— except for brief periods of confusion caused by electoral or parliamentary defeats. It thus made good sense that most Western and Russian observers viewed the appointment in March 1997 of the Russian "Dream Team" of reformers (led by Anatoly Chubais and Boris Nemtsov) as the second shock therapy offensive (see chapter 9).

This interpretation differs from the assertions of many Western proponents of shock therapy who argue that its Russian version was gradually phased out during 1992, or that it was never fully applied in its original design. Thus, in one of his postmortems on the failed stabilization effort, Jeffrey Sachs provides a list of six basic elements of "genuine" shock therapy that were missing or belated in the Russian case.[7] Some of these pertain to the scale and direction of Western support for currency stabilization, budget deficit financing, and debt rescheduling. Yet it is hard to believe that such an astute observer of Soviet-Western financial negotiations as Sachs would have still harbored hopes for large-scale Western financial aid to Russia after Gorbachev, with all his international leverage, had been rebuffed at the July 1991 G-7 summit. A sober look at the international landscape and the intellectual vision of Western leaders in the fall of 1991 showed that a Marshall Plan for Russia was not on the horizon. Indeed, the record suggests that Sachs was realistic in this regard, yet was nonetheless vigorously pushing Yeltsin forward. At a Washington meeting in January 1992, Sachs reportedly said, "Shock therapy has a chance of success, but only if the West provides significant aid, especially for a ruble stabilization fund. Unfortunately, the West is not likely to mobilize such aid." Asked how he could, then, advocate a policy that was so dependent on Western aid, he replied testily: "Whether or not the Russian government succeeds with this strategy, it is the only correct strategy."[8]

Similarly, on the domestic front, it was inevitable that the abstract scheme of shock therapy would have to accommodate Russian political realities. Indeed, while ruthlessly pursuing price deregulation and a de facto confiscatory policy toward private savings, the Yeltsin-Gaidar government was remarkably permissive in its credit policy, letting the Central Bank issue nonproductive, inflationary paper credits at low or symbolic interest rates to the old Soviet managers in agriculture and industry. Yet the social analysis of the "reform coalition" outlined below suggests that it could not have been otherwise: The government simply could not afford to antagonize both the middle class and the traditional managerial elite. Thus, the "medium tough" credit policies were a logical consequence of the political slant of Yeltsin's reforms toward company managers and other layers of the economic nomenklatura. To these people, the Yeltsin-Gaidar reforms gave "neither therapy, nor even a genuine shock"—and apparently were not intended to.[9] From the beginning, the strategic alliance of the reformers with the old Soviet managers aimed at safeguarding the regime, which was haunted by a deep fear of revolution, against any serious protest by the lower classes. This is why shock therapy proved to be so lenient toward the old Soviet economic elite, while it was carried out with a remarkable consistency and obstinacy against the majority of ordinary Russians.

The behavior of the ex-Soviet ruling class in post-Soviet Russia recalled in some ways the United States of the 1920s, with the same mixture of frenetic hedonism and high-profile conspicuous consumption. The reformers' ambition was to preside over a new, Russian Jazz Age, benevolently encouraging well-positioned Russians to get rich quick. The new climate in the Russian elite has also been culturally similar to that of Germany's Weimar Republic, as evoked for example by Stefan Zweig's memoir *Die Welt von Gestern,* in which he describes the "witches' sabbath" of nouveaux riches speculators and swindlers cavorting in sleazy Berlin cabarets.

The argument about whether the term "shock therapy" is actually applicable to policy choices made by Yeltsin and Gaidar in late 1991–early 1992 is bound to go on for decades. In many ways, it resembles the debate on whether the order established by Lenin and his comrades after their October 1917 coup had anything in common with pure Marxist theory. In both cases, the precepts of Western teachers had to be modified according to indigenous realities; the resulting "liberalism" in the first case and "communism" in the second were bound to have a peculiar Russian flavor. Similarly, just as we often conveniently label the Soviet system as "communist," it is likely that Yeltsin's economic strategy will be known to history as "shock therapy," whatever the objections of its founding fathers might be. Under the circumstances, Yeltsin's policies were the closest feasible approximation to Sachs's and the IMF's original intentions, and in this sense the present perverted form of Russian robber baron "capitalism" is the unavoidable product of the economic recipes purveyed by the shock therapists.

WHY DID SHOCK THERAPY LAST FOR SEVEN YEARS?

A growing number of independent Western experts (not including the group of foreign former advisers to the Russian government and the ideologues of shock therapy) consider the economic policy of the Yeltsin era at best a tragic error, and at worst a deliberate plundering of the national economy in the service of short-term personal and corporate interests. At the same time, though, as we will see later in the chapter, fundamental criticism of this policy and its Russian and Western sponsors has just started to emanate from the circles of these sponsors, echoing our own criticisms.

In this and subsequent chapters, we will attempt to answer the following fundamental questions:

- Why, despite an array of alternative programs and repeated warnings about the dangers of shock therapy, did the group around Yeltsin choose this specific strategy for economic reform in the fall of 1991?

- Why did this strategy enjoy such an active sponsorship from the governments of the United States and Western Europe, and from the international financial institutions—a combination that, in the eyes of Russian policymakers and ordinary citizens, seemed to represent "the West" unambiguously?
- Why, despite the failure of the program according to Yeltsin's own criteria (a failure that had become evident by the fall of 1992), and despite the removal of Gaidar and some of his associates, has the Kremlin not abandoned the basic premises of shock therapy even today?
- Finally, why was the regime of the radical freemarketeers able to enjoy such enviable longevity compared with those of similar regimes in other ex-communist countries (such as Poland and Albania), despite its policies' heavy economic, social, and cultural costs, despite the dramatic decline in the value of human life and human dignity in Yeltsin's Russia, and despite the proliferation of opposition parties and movements?

These are the questions we will address. We will not, however, assess Yeltsin's reforms from the perspective of economic theory as such. Such a goal would be redundant, given the already exhaustive economic analyses of Russian reform by both its advocates and its critics.[10] More important, the phenomenon of shock therapy by its nature and scope transcends the boundaries of economics. It is the combination and interaction of shock therapy's economic and (mostly implied) noneconomic aspects that is the essence of market bolshevism but has been inadequately studied. In this book, we view market bolshevism as an inclusive political, social, economic, cultural, and ideological strategy of stabilization for the ruling group that came to power on the crest of the wave of democratic revolution—a ruling group that was itself neither democratic nor genuinely reformist, and that had a morbid fear of a grassroots revolution that might escape from its control. The market bolsheviks never possessed a coherent, detailed economic program or rigorous economic strategy. Rather, they improvised their program as they went along, adapting it to political developments. Their ruling passion was political pragmatism, informed by their fear of the "populist" mood of the unprivileged classes that had been aroused by Gorbachev's perestroika and Yeltsin's electoral promises. In this light, the sequence and logic of their economic policies are important for us not so much in themselves, but rather as a reflection of their overall strategy. This strategy was deeply rooted in the cultural experience and worldview of the individuals who most directly devised and implemented the strategy.

THE PROVENANCE AND CREED OF THE "RADICAL REFORMERS"

The group of economists and administrators who entered the government in November 1991 as the "Gaidar team," as well as their cothinkers who stayed out of the government to organize media support for shock therapy, shared a number of similar social traits. Most of them were born in either Moscow or St. Petersburg in well-to-do families of nomenklatura background.[11] All of them had earned graduate degrees in institutions designed for the Soviet establishment, which inevitably required them to display their loyalty to official pseudo-Marxist dogmas of "real socialism," as well as to the existing social order and their individual patrons in the upper echelons of the nomenklatura. They proved themselves to be talented acolytes of the Party who were gradually designated for foreign travel and the chance to familiarize themselves with Western academia. They presented themselves to their counterparts in the Western establishment as enlightened liberals and Westernizers, almost dissidents, as people who were miraculously able to exist within the ruling elite and to withstand the pressure from the hard-liners.

As time went on, their Western contacts became increasingly excited about the "Soviet liberals," who often spoke good English, played with Western concepts and theoretical models, and were well-dressed, polished, and always smiling—in sharp contrast to the sad, exhausted faces of ordinary Russians. For the new generation of the Soviet nomenklatura, establishing credibility with Western elites was a vital necessity. After all, they were preparing to get rid of the last remnants of their Soviet and "socialist" identity and to merge themselves into the global economic order. The "young liberals'" preferential access to foreign goods and contacts placed some of them in the lucrative role of middlemen for import-oriented urban elites, currency speculators, and the voracious black market. No wonder many Russians viewed—and continue to view—them as covert lobbyists for these groups and their trading interests, tightly linked with global commercial and financial markets. Most of these future radical reformers were particularly attracted by the writings of University of Chicago economist Milton Friedman and by the laissez-faire economic policies of Thatcher and Reagan. Hence, these reformers were known in Russia as "the Chicago boys."[12]

They were also attracted to the closely related Washington Consensus doctrine, which applies Friedman's ideas to the world economy and has underpinned most of the work of the IMF and the World Bank in the 1990s. While he was chief economist of the World Bank, Lawrence Summers expressed the core and the fervor of this doctrine when he proclaimed in 1991, "Spread the truth—the laws of economics are like the laws of engineering. One set of laws works everywhere."[13]

While being part and parcel of the late-Soviet oligarchy, this social group was in some important aspects different from the oligarchy's other layers—such as the Communist Party functionaries, the managerial class, or the military-industrial complex (even though all these were so often intertwined by their interests and family links as to make any differences between them fairly obscure to outside observers). By their career paths, most of the future radical reformers belonged to the *institutchiki* stratum (members of social science research institutes, such as the Central Mathematical Economics Institute, the Institute of

State and Law, and so forth)—the younger, privileged group, whom the *appa-ratchiki* often viewed with a degree of suspicion as being overeducated, cosmopolitan, individualistic, and having little real-life experience. Thus, being denied power positions that required political responsibility, the *institutchiki* had to satisfy their ambitions through the petty politics of intra-academic intrigues, competing among themselves for foreign trips with hard currency allowances. Still, they remained at the service of the Party, grinding out analytical memos, draft speeches, and policy advice, most often for the Central Committee's Economic Department.

As a result, these reformers felt little in common with the conservative core of the Soviet oligarchy, but they were even more alienated from the unprivileged strata of society, whom most "liberals" despised as being too lazy, servile, and ignorant to deserve to taste the pleasures of life that were readily available to Western consumers. They also believed in the primacy of individualistic motivations, looking with scorn at the "utopian" social goals of the early 1960s and of the dissident movement. For this social layer, Dostoevsky's depiction of the nineteenth-century Russian liberals was in many ways apposite: They were uprooted from the national soil, felt skeptical about almost every coherent system of values, and harbored bold and abstract dreams of experiments in "social engineering" that would make Russia more comfortable *for them* (that is, closer to their image of affluent Western economies). Yet some of the Soviet liberals' beliefs about their country and the world set them somewhat apart from their predecessors in Russian history:

Market fetishism. All the reform programs compiled by "liberals" in the late 1980s and early 1990s stressed as their short-term as well as ultimate goal the "construction of a market economy." Among all the features of modern capitalism, it was the market that most captivated them. Strikingly, increased production of consumer and producer goods, or the creation of a modern infrastructure for energy, transportation, telecommunications, health services, and education, or the development of a strong and prosperous middle class, were neglected or ignored. As James Millar has pointed out, shock therapy assumes that "if monetary problems can be solved, production will be restored; that is, if one gets retail and wholesale prices right, money wages right, the interest rate right, and the exchange rate right, production will take care of itself."[14] Indeed, any prescription for Russia's problems that required increased commodity production as a necessary part of their solution tended to be indignantly rejected. Production quotas were the obsession of communist commissars, and the reformers wanted no part of them. Their ideal was the postindustrial society, dominated by free markets and a large service sector.[15]

Belief in simplistic behaviorism. This replacement of goals (economic success) by means (the market) led the liberal reformers to obscure the fact that some "market" economies had turned out to be less efficient in terms of production than planned or semiplanned economies (such as Japan, South Korea, or Taiwan in the 1970s, as compared with contemporary Britain). Consequently, in the reformers' "building the market" (even the phrase recalls Stalin's "building socialism"), virtually all elements of planning and control were to be abolished, while the government itself was seen not as a supreme arbiter responsible for national development, but as just another bargaining unit in the operation of "free market forces."

The obsession with the market was to a large extent linked to the liberal reformers' belief in simplistic behavioral explanations of the Soviet economic decline. Pointing to the sharply deteriorating work ethic of the population and the inefficiency of state-owned enterprises, they attributed these tendencies to the lack of "market stimuli," such as the threat of unemployment for labor and constraints on the demand side for enterprises. Once in place, "market stimuli" would impose "rational" patterns of behavior. The reformers' reductionist creed precluded them from considering possible political, social, and moral explanations, including the legitimacy crisis of the establishment, the growing disparities and alienation between elites and the masses (which more thoughtful observers among writers and thinkers in, for example, Andrei Sakharov's circles had pointed to since the early 1960s). After shock therapy had been partially implemented and the "market stimuli" had not resulted in the expected behavioral changes, the free-market reformers predictably turned to blame Russian culture—which, they implied, invariably produced losers.[16]

Inverted Marxism. It follows naturally from the above that the liberal reformers, imbued since childhood with the Marxist dogmas of Brezhnev-style "real socialism," were hard-core economic determinists. No wonder they later espoused the most reductionist and deterministic of Western neoclassical economic doctrines. Essentially, they accepted the Marxian idea of unavoidable historical stages, yet without Marx's optimistic belief in a better society of the future. Accordingly, they viewed the primitive and unregulated paleocapitalism of nineteenth-century Europe, as described by Marx, as the universal stage of development that Russia had failed to achieve on time. Hence, to get "back to civilization," Russians were advised to adopt the ethic of "primitive accumulation" exemplified (though this was not usually spelled out) by the eighteenth-century British stockjobbers or the nineteenth-century American robber barons.[17] In this catching up with the past, any moral brakes would only be an impediment to progress.

Moral relativism. A favorite slogan of the radical reformers went like this: "Everything that is economically efficient is morally acceptable." It was put into circulation in the late 1980s by Nikolai Shmelev, who in other respects was a moderate freemarketeer of the Gorbachev vintage.[18] This view gradually became part of a shared culture of many radical reformers and was widely popularized in the media as evidence of "enlightenment." It is worth noting that many of the newly bred ideologues of this moral relativism were—and are—presented as intellectual luminaries and attained the unofficial rank of court thinkers and writers in the Yeltsin regime. Some of them preached "postmodernism" (in their interpretation). Others embraced Nietzsche, with his ideal of the Superman free from any moral inhibitions.

New class struggle, ideological warfare, and cultural revolution. In Russia, this moral relativism logically implied a decisive and radical rupture with the cultural traditions of Russia's older generation (which was assumed to consist of "natural" Communist sympathizers) and particularly with those of Russia's traditional intelligentsia, including first and foremost its moral imperative of always siding with the weak and the oppressed. In the 1990s, a vast amount of media coverage was devoted to the reformers' ideological warfare against the traditional intelligentsia for its "socialist" proclivity to "worship the people." "The 'people' does not exist," proclaimed one of the favorite postmodern writers of the new elite, Sergei Gandlevsky, "there are only individuals."[19] In one of his recent essays, Gaidar himself attributes the European revolutions of the nineteenth century and the invention of Marxism to nothing more than the radical intelligentsia's lack of respect for property and its unwillingness to adapt to "progress."[20]

The most striking feature of this campaign of social hatred (in some ways a version—if a much milder one—of Mao's Cultural Revolution) was the fact that its most ardent activists themselves appeared to belong to the intelligentsia, at least to judge by their educational and professional careers. Therefore, in many cases the anti-intelligentsia rhetoric involved an unabashed renunciation of their own previous experience and family background.[21] A cutting and credible account of this mass apostasy, welcomed and often promoted by the new oligarchic elite, is found in the posthumous book of Andrei Sinyavsky.[22]

Contempt for or indifference to public opinion. The instant ascent of the Gaidar group was due to backstage court maneuvering, not to a public debate about what form the reform program should take. Neither Gaidar nor his associates belonged to the democratic movement, which made them deeply apprehensive about their acceptance by society, nor were they among Yeltsin's supporters during his "populist" campaigns of 1988–90. Until early 1991, Gaidar himself was a leading economic columnist of mainstream Soviet publications, such as *Pravda* and *Kommunist,* where his often well-argued articles repeatedly warned the public about the threats of market radicalism.

In September–October 1991, Gaidar obtained privileged access to Yeltsin's ear through the president's closest associate, Gennadi Burbulis, a former teacher of Marxism and a vain man intensely disliked by the public. Gaidar's appointment served Burbulis's purpose, because it ensured that Yeltsin would not appoint someone who was either more popular than Burbulis (such as Yavlinsky or Svyatoslav Fyodorov) or more influential with Yeltsin (such as Yuri Skokov and Oleg Lobov), thus endangering Burbulis's position at court. One of Yeltsin's reasons for picking Gaidar for the job of "leading reformer" was that his bland and aloof manner in public made him an unlikely future contender for elective office, even if his reform package were to turn out to be successful and popular. Thus Yeltsin would not risk any future upstaging.

Beyond all this, not only did the government's Gaidar reform team not possess even a semblance of legitimacy (either electoral or in terms of national traditions and culture), it did not even bother to acquire such legitimacy. Instead, it took an aggressively confrontational posture toward the beliefs and ways of life, as well as the opinions, of ordinary citizens. As we will see, two election defeats in 1993 and 1995 did not stop the "liberal reformers" from keeping or quickly regaining dominant positions in the government, nor from launching a second round of shock therapy in March 1997.

This account of the "liberal reformers'" fundamental beliefs and modes of operation should make it obvious that the shock therapy carried out in 1992 was far from being an isolated set of purely economic measures and has to be judged by standards other than those that apply to economic theory alone. In line with this logic, we cannot limit our review of alternatives to shock therapy to questions such as whether the Russian government had a better option than the deregulation of prices on January 2, 1992. At this point, we will just say briefly that, in our view, Yeltsin would have served Russia much better by appointing a team that was very different from the shock therapists as a social and political group. We believe that even a similar set of drastic economic changes, had it been carried out within a different sociopolitical and ideological framework, probably would have resulted in a much less disastrous outcome, and that Russians would have accepted some of the inevitable suffering with much greater understanding and tolerance. In other words, part of the problem from 1992 to 1998 was the personal profiles and worldview of the reformers, which were alien and obnoxious to the majority of everyday citizens.

THE COALITION BEHIND SHOCK THERAPY

How did the exact recipe for Russian-style shock therapy come into being? In the fall of 1991, several powerful groups of players converged to put intense pressure on Boris Yeltsin and his inner circle of advisers. On the domestic side, these were:

1. The movement of "several million"—according to McFaul and Markov—of Russia's discontented and unprivileged, which had been Yeltsin's grassroots base in the democratic movement and now demanded the rapid fulfillment of his democratic reform promises.[23]

2. Influential urban elites, including the "golden youth" of the Soviet ruling class and their clients, who were engaged in private business and a frenetic race of speculative capital accumulation, and who pressed Yeltsin to open the domestic market to foreign goods and to remove all regulations on their "gray market" transactions in currency, finance, and commodities.

3. The Soviet-era monopolistic trade networks, intertwined with the shadow economy and the black market, which were eager to seize the function of price-setting from the weakening hands of the government and whose supporters waged a media campaign for the deregulation of prices. To back up their bargaining with the new authorities of post-Soviet Russia, these trade networks staged large-scale and socially explosive shortages of basic goods, especially in the provinces.

4. The old directors of state-owned "company towns," who feared that a comprehensive reform might lead to their removal, but simultaneously hoped to benefit from any privatization that would effectively make them company owners —provided foreign capital and the domestic middle class stayed out of the game and labor remained safely under control. This group constituted a sort of managerial class known in Russian as *direktorskii korpus* (directors' corps), but in many ways it was not homogeneous. Directors of the lucrative raw materials sector were already well adapted to the market, while many in heavy and military industries faced much bleaker prospects.

The second, third, and fourth groups described above had all put strong pressure on the Communist leadership to facilitate the achievement of their goals, and the leadership responded—through openly promulgated reforms discussed later in this chapter, through secret actions and internal memos,[24] and through the proceeds of covert official gold sales to selected Party, KGB, and Komsomol figures—and their firms and banks—in the USSR and abroad.[25] As General Aleksandr Lebed commented in 1995, he did not know of any party officials who would now support communism, because "They all retreated to their previously prepared commercial positions. They are all once again in positions of power."[26]

The major foreign actors in the process included:

1. Yeltsin's radical economic advisers (many of them from Harvard). These were the utopian crusaders of "marketization," who apparently believed that the fast imposition of Reaganesque capitalist rules of the game could be accomplished in Russia by peaceful and democratic means, without regard to national values, traditions, and culture.

2. The bureaucracy of the International Monetary Fund, which indirectly represented foreign creditors and was anxious to bind the Russian government with "conditionalities" designed to produce budget austerity. Thus the IMF pushed the Kremlin to spend less and save more in order to speed up repayment of the Soviet-era debt caused by the previous rulers' irresponsible appetite for foreign loans and imports.

3. The governments of the G-7 countries, which sought strategic stability at any price, in particular the securing of Soviet nuclear weapons, while also pressing to open up the former Soviet economic space to their goods, partly with the goal of cushioning themselves against possible economic downturns in the West.

It was from these players that Yeltsin and his team had to choose in forging their "coalition of reforms." As we shall see, Yeltsin's skillful maneuvering and reform strategy allowed him to bring virtually all these interest groups on board: urban elites, trade monopolies, and industrial directors, as well as the Western players. Only one group was marked for exclusion and soon became the major loser from the attempt at radical reforms: the unprivileged classes—Yeltsin's former democratic base. They were the most numerous—and yet the weakest in terms of their material resources.

In the autumn of 1991, the real choice for the Yeltsin team and for Russia as a whole was not about whether to move from socialism to capitalism; this choice had already been made. The real choice was about defining the place and role of state power in relation to the "Big Grab"—the furtive privatization of Soviet state assets.[27] Yeltsin had to choose between fostering unbridled nomenklatura capitalism or using the nonprivileged classes and the emerging civil society to create the political, legal, institutional, and moral counterweights to the new nomenklatura capitalists. The latter choice implied the risk of an open confrontation with nomenklatura capital, somewhat along the lines of the conflict between President Franklin D. Roosevelt and the complex of interests that opposed the New Deal, or President Kennedy's successful confrontation with American steel industry executives in 1962 over the issue of price increases in violation of an earlier pledge of restraint.

In hindsight, Yeltsin's decision to implement shock therapy can be seen as a unilateral repudiation of his social contract with the majority of Russians, a contract forged during his populist, anti-establishment campaigns of 1988–91 and sealed by the joint victory in the August coup. When many prices were freed in January 1992, the savings of the middle class in Soviet bank accounts rapidly depreciated and in most cases were reduced to nothing. Thus shock therapy and the ensuing hyperinflation were used by the government as confiscatory tools in the struggle against the monetary "overhang." They swallowed up the people's savings, which under a different set of policies could have been channeled into productive investment, as was done in postwar Japan. This inflationary confiscation of savings from the weakest and most numerous part of society created a huge psychological and moral gap between the Yeltsin regime and the Russian populace that subsequent twists and turns of economic policy have proved unable to close.

YELTSIN'S "SEESAW" SYSTEM: A SUBSTITUTE FOR THE SEPARATION OF POWERS

Meanwhile, in place of the old social contract, a new one (or, one could say, an antisocial one) was gradually put in place. The parties to this contract were the new and the old generations of the Soviet establishment—ideologically positioned as "radical reformers" and "conservative directors," respectively. The former relied on a social base of post-Soviet trade networks and import and financial lobbies; the latter, primarily on the rich exporters of raw materials and the agrarian lobby.[28] The new elite coalition, whose guarantor was Boris Yeltsin, was then sealed at the governmental level in May 1992 with Viktor Chernomyrdin's appointment as deputy prime minister in the Gaidar government. This cartel of elites permitted Yeltsin, with his powerful instinct for maintaining a balance within his government, to install a "seesaw" system in the executive branch. In this arrangement, the "conservative" nomenklatura and "liberal" reformers (exemplified from 1992 by, respectively, Chernomyrdin and Chubais) occupied the opposite ends of the seesaw, permitting the president to position himself safely above the fulcrum, in the center of the new political spectrum that took shape after the demise of the democratic movement. The seesaw's constant up and down movement, representing the country's fluctuating political circumstances and continuous balancing adjustments by Yeltsin and his team, has summed up most of the logic of Kremlin political struggles and explains the zigzags of economic policy throughout the entirety of Yeltsin's reign.

Clearly, the model of a cartel of elites presented above does not depict exactly what happened. A fair number of Soviet-era managers failed to adapt, while some members of the unprivileged classes carved out prosperous careers for themselves in the course of Russia's "transition to the market." For a few people, standards of living markedly improved. We should note that most people received some benefits, but they were often of ambiguous value. They could usually privatize their apartments at little or no cost, but they then faced soaring taxes and utility bills. Also, if you had enough money, you had a much wider selection of goods to choose from. However, for the majority of Russians, living standards fell to a level unprecedented since the country recovered from the devastation of World War II.

More important, though, the strategy that emerged from the coalition of elites proved to be a disaster for Russia as a nation. Specifically, the years since the launching of shock therapy have

- led to devastating consequences for the Russian economy and society in terms of their productive capacities, human capital, health, demographic indicators, culture and education, as well as in terms of people's mutual trust and the nation's psychological self-confidence;
- undermined the initial social base of systemic legitimacy possessed by the postcommunist order and, more specifically, by Yeltsin's rule;
- drastically weakened the incipient civil society, blocked most opportunities for democratic participation in politics, and doomed the Russian body politic to alternate between oligarchy and authoritarianism for the foreseeable future.

The Liquidation of the Soviet Union: Precondition for Shock Therapy

Yeltsin's choice of shock therapy had one regrettable consequence that is not often discussed. By 1991, the breakup of the Soviet Union was probably inevitable, but widely differing views existed about the desirable timing and mechanics of the breakup. In practice, it came about in an abrupt, clandestine, and undemocratic way, and the newly independent states that emerged have continued to bear the scars caused by what in about half the cases was a sudden, painful, and premature birth. This is an important issue because a more gradual and democratic process of separation might have created more politically viable Soviet successor states. We must also carefully distinguish between factors that were merely present in the time leading up to the breakup and factors that can be considered its decisive causes.

The basic forces that started to dismember the Soviet Union right after the August 1991 coup were not so much the avowedly separatist movements (which had the support of only a small minority in all the republics except the Baltic states and Georgia) but, rather, the old Communist leaders of the republics themselves.[29] Most of these leaders had vehemently opposed the democratic movement and had openly or covertly supported the August coup. After Yeltsin and, seemingly, the democrats had triumphed in Moscow, the leaders in the republics (led by such figures as Leonid Kravchuk in Ukraine, Islam Karimov in Uzbekistan, and Ayaz Mutalibov in Azerbaijan) were afraid that the seizure of Soviet institutions by forces seemingly dominated by democrats, and the revolutionary situation that had emerged in the large urban centers of Russia, might spill over into their republics. In that case, these leaders might have faced court proceedings for their roles in supporting the coup. This possibility led them to seize the chance to hang on to power by declaring the independence of their republics during the first days after the coup, even though they had earlier attacked Yeltsin and the democrats fiercely for allegedly wanting to destroy the USSR.

This argument, in our opinion, suggests that the way the disintegration of the USSR actually took place was not the result of a straightforward "national liberation struggle of colonies against the empire," even though such a struggle did indeed take place in some of the republics.[30] One reason the USSR was so brusquely liquidated was the absence of a leadership figure of the first magnitude who was willing to champion the cause of a more orderly transition. After an interval of democratic discussion and calm reflection, such a transition might have led to plebiscites that might well have mandated the continued existence of the USSR minus the Baltic and Caucasian republics, but possibly with all or most of the Central Asian ones. How Ukraine might have responded is hard to say, but we suggest that even here separation was not preordained. Byelorussia (Belarus) would have almost certainly chosen to remain in the Union. Tragically, there was no visible leader who filled the bill. The Democratic Party's Travkin was too weak and confused. Kazakhstan's Nursultan Nazarbayev, though intelligent, was too closely identified with the communist past. Grigori Yavlinsky might have been the most realistic candidate, but at the time he was not yet sufficiently established as a politician. So the fateful decision was left in the hands of Yeltsin and his inner circle, and when he decided to liquidate the Union, the Soviet era came to an end.

Was there a possibility between August and December 1991 of avoiding the disintegration of the Union, notwithstanding the republican Party secretaries who had transformed themselves overnight into fervent partisans of national independence? The evidence suggests that there was such an alternative, and that the key to it did not lie with the military, the security services, or some other elite institution but, rather, with the leaders of the democratic movement in Russia and the republics. The real barrier to the republican nomenklaturas' impulse to dismember the USSR would have been a comprehensive democratic transformation across the entire country. If, as Yeltsin had acknowledged, the survival of the Soviet Union depended on Ukraine's loyalty, the surest way to keep the USSR intact through such an anti-nomenklatura revolution would have begun with an early pro-Union mobilization of central and eastern Ukraine, using its strong democratic movement, coupled with a public airing of Kravchuk's tacit participation in the August coup. A prominent role for Yeltsin himself in such a pro-Union movement would have been counterproductive of course, but had he wanted to, he could have strongly influenced the behavior of the democratic forces in republics other than Georgia and the Baltics, including through the interrepublican association of reformist movements and parties called the Democratic Congress (DC).[31]

Yeltsin's announcement of shock therapy on October 28 was in itself a major factor in the dismembering of the USSR, primarily because none of the other ten republics that might have stayed in it planned to adopt shock therapy. The announcement also undermined Yavlinsky, who had been laboring to obtain the signatures of republican leaders on an all-Union agreement for economic cooperation. It was clear that the Gaidar team was more than willing to break with the non-Russian republics that were the most loyal to the USSR but that Gaidar considered too backward to accept shock therapy (the Central Asian republics in particular).

Thus the start of shock therapy and the appointment of Gaidar were fatal blows to the Union. On December 1, 1991, Ukrainian voters, 75 percent of whom had voted to stay in the USSR in a referendum held eight months earlier, went for independence by the landslide margin of 90 percent. A week later, on December 8, the leaders of Ukraine, Russia, and Byelorussia, meeting under a veil of secrecy at a remote Byelorussian hunting resort called Belaya Vezha, proclaimed in the name of their citizens that the Soviet Union had ceased to exist. After the transfer of power from Gorbachev to Yeltsin and the New Year celebrations, on January 2, 1992, the Russian government implemented a sweeping deregulation of prices.

SHOCK THERAPY IS LAUNCHED

Gaidar and his group proceeded from the monetarism of Milton Friedman, a more radical monetarist than figures like von Hayek, who had been the spiritus rector of Britain's Thatcher government. Gaidar's house ideologue, Sergei Vasiliev, professed his monetarism in the following terms: "The government must limit its activity in the economic sphere to the maximum extent possible and let the market, money, and entrepreneurs work."[32] Given this ideology, Gaidar's first priority was the removal of price controls (that is, carrying on the effort begun by Valentin Pavlov in early 1991). Price deregulation was announced in Yeltsin's decree of December 3, 1991, entitled "Measures to Liberalize Prices," which in principle provided for the freeing of prices on 80 percent of producers' goods and 90 percent of consumer items.

In the short term, a simple administrative decree increased most prices for producers' goods by 500 percent, and for essential household goods (such as food) by 300 percent. During the one-month interval between the announcement and the actual deregulation, "tremendous fear" reigned among the Russian population.[33] Gaidar predicted that prices would rise by 100 percent per month in January and February. In the event, prices rose 250 percent as soon as controls were removed. Andrei Nechayev, Gaidar's deputy finance minister, was brutally candid about the problem: "Let's be frank: Incomes will lag behind price increases. As the standard of living declines, the problem of low-income, socially vulnerable groups will arise. In this regard, a very strict distribution system will have to be organized—direct assistance in kind to specific people."[34] In fact, this was never done.

To institutionalize "free trade" throughout Russia, Yeltsin issued a decree on January 29, 1992 that specifically empowered anyone to sell anything at virtually any time, with no permit. With this decree, a kind of distressed merchandise bazaar became ubiquitous and permanent. Suddenly, hawkers and peddlers were everywhere. Wealthier traders soon had pushcarts and kiosks. Many of the sellers were middle-class people whose incomes and savings had been wiped out by the hyperinflation and who were now grimly accepting the humiliation of taking to the streets to sell some family heirloom for a pittance. When the German middle class similarly had hawked its belongings in the hyperinflation of 1923, it was recognized as a tragedy. In the Russia of 1992, the same phenomenon was hailed as the coming of the market and an "efficient allocation of goods."[35] But was it efficient for aspiring young academics and schoolteachers to be put to work as security guards and janitors? The street selling was a symptom of social breakdown, and it quickly became a threat to public order.

Organized crime became the dominant force in the bazaar, and it thrived by paying off officials, who cut their bosses in on the deals. Aslund commented that the "crucial missing factor is the will of Russian leaders to clamp down on top officials who are evidently corrupt."[36]

Nineteen ninety-two was also the year when privatization was launched. In Yeltsin's speech on the first anniversary of the August 1991 coup, he announced a plan to use vouchers as a key part of his privatization strategy. He tried to sound like a populist, telling Russians that "we need millions of owners rather than a handful of millionaires. . . . [T]he privatization voucher is a ticket for each of us to a free economy."[37] Each Russian citizen was assigned a privatization check or voucher with the nominal value of ten thousand rubles (equivalent to $20 at the time of issue). The vouchers could be sold, exchanged for shares of stock in privatized state companies, or invested in one of some 650 voucher funds that quickly sprang up. Most of these funds failed to pay dividends, and many of them turned out to be pyramid schemes, much like the notorious MMM Company, which soon went bankrupt. Most Russians got little or nothing for their vouchers, and the promised "people's capitalism" never materialized.

By the end of December 1992, almost 47,000 state companies had been privatized, and this figure reached almost 90,000 by the end of December 1993. Fewer than 14 percent of these companies were privatized by a public auction or by a public tender offer for stock. Most privatizations were carried out through backroom deals among insiders, with company managers and the nomenklatura the most frequent beneficiaries. All of these proceedings bore the unmistakable imprint of the chairman of the State Property Management Committee, Anatoly Chubais. The Chubais privatization and its aftermath had the effect of making the government appear in the popular mind as the fountainhead of corruption in the entire society.

Along with price deregulation and privatization, the shock therapists touted what they called macroeconomic stabilization. Gaidar was so emphatic about this that he embarrassed his boss, who later complained that "Gaidar as an inexperienced politician promised immediate stabilization. I had to do the same, whether I liked it or not."[38] But Yeltsin was disingenuous, since he himself also promised immediate stabilization much later, well after Gaidar had left the government. The plain fact is that Russia did not achieve macroeconomic stabilization until 1999—and even then, it was a fragile condition.

In response to a report about the desperate condition of small business, which he should have been busily promoting, Gaidar is reported to have blurted out, "So what? One who is dying deserves to die."[39] This was Gaidar's version of "Let them eat cake." During his polemics with Stalin during the 1920s, Trotsky developed the theory of the permanent revolution. The Gaidar team, and especially Chubais, seemed to believe in a policy of permanent privatization. For them, the Russian state was an inexhaustible garage sale of valuable property that they could sell off indefinitely to meet current expenses. Adam Smith noted long ago that "there is a lot of ruin in a nation," but Chubais and his friends seem to have forgotten that this does not mean infinite ruin, and that sooner or later even the largest quantity of booty will be exhausted.

THE GREAT LEAP TO THE MARKET

The words of Yeltsin's October speech promising lower prices within half a year from January 1992, a guaranteed economic recovery by the fall, and a subsequent improvement in living standards can only evoke bitter irony today. Although financial stabilization, the reduction of inflation, and the shrinking of the budget deficit were finally achieved by 1997, no lasting stabilization of the leading indicators for a productive economy occurred. After the ruble collapse and government default of August 1998, inflation rose sharply and financial instability returned. Despite the almost boundless optimism of the ideologues of top-down reform and their Western advisers over eight years, the real economic indicators testified to a large-scale and unprecedented collapse of the economy of one of the major industrial powers of the modern world—a collapse that bottomed out only in 1999.

According to the rather conservative Russian Statistics Committee (Goskomstat), during the period 1992–1998, the country's GDP declined by about 44 percent. Only a small part of this decline reflected the nonproduction of unwanted goods, and was therefore welcome.[40] (By comparison, Soviet GDP during World War II shrank by 24 percent. During the Great Depression of 1929–1933, the United States lost 30.5 percent of its GDP.[41]) The collapse of industrial production was even larger, amounting to a 56 percent decline for the years 1992–1998.[42] An important statistic that illustrates the main cause of this decline is the investment crisis: Capital investment in the Russian economy, including all foreign investment, had fallen by 1998 to 20 percent of the level of eight years before.

HYPERINFLATION AND DEPRESSION

During the first year of the shock treatment, consumer prices rose at an average annual rate of 1,354 percent over the whole year, and were rising at a rate of 2,318 percent by the end of December. By any definition, this was hyperinflation. After that, inflation gradually subsided, averaging 896 percent during the whole of 1993, 220 percent during 1994, 190 percent during 1995, and 48 percent during 1996. This devastating inflation effectively wiped out the savings of the middle class.

Yavlinsky has argued that Russian inflation is institutional rather than monetary in character and is thus relatively impervious to monetarist countermeasures like controlling the money supply.[43] By contrast, monetarists always argue that inflation is a monetary phenomenon. However, in the Russian case the main cause of inflation is the collapse of production, which cannot be chalked up to the "creative destruction" suggested by Schumpeter.

Inflation also eroded the real wages of working Russians, which dropped by a cumulative total of 25 percent during the years 1992–1996, then held roughly steady before falling by a massive 42 percent in the year from March 1998 to March 1999 (during which real incomes fell by 25 percent). But statistics on real wages became increasingly unreal in these years because they reflected the projected salary bill, not the actual one. The problem in Russia was that a large part of the national payroll was paid out very late (up to a year) or not at all. Real incomes, as Hedlund and Sundström point out, may give a better idea of the disposable income of households. Thus during the first year of shock therapy in 1992, real wages fell by 7 percent, but real incomes fell by 46 percent, although they later rebounded.[44]

As for the government's budget deficit, it was more than 30 percent of GDP during the last year of the Soviet Union, but it fell sharply under shock therapy and measured 4.8 percent at the end of 1998, primarily because of frequent impoundment and sequestration of planned expenditures by the executive branch. This represented nothing less than a default on the government's domestic payment obligations, including those due to pensioners and to the work force in the public sector.

The only sector of the economy that was able to boast comparative success was foreign trade. In 1995, Russia had chalked up a foreign trade surplus of $20 billion, with exports equaling 20 percent of GDP, but the surplus declined to $13.2 billion in 1998 before rising with world oil prices in 1999. Given the predominance of raw materials among these exports, the figures also indicate the economy's high degree of dependency on the unstable conditions in world raw materials markets, particularly in the energy sector. We note in passing that imported goods accounted for about half of all merchandise sold on the Russian market, though this figure drastically declined in the wake of the 1998 ruble collapse, as some healthy import substitution occurred.

THE TRAGEDY OF RURAL RUSSIA

Even in the general economic shipwreck, rural Russia experienced a special tragedy all its own. In 1993, the grain harvest came in at 99.1 million tons. In 1994 it dropped to 81.3 million tons, a fall of almost one-fifth. The 1995 harvest of only 63.5 million tons was the worst result in more than thirty years. In 1996, grain production remained alarmingly depressed at 69.3 million tons, only to rise sharply to 88.6 million in 1997, but then plunge disastrously to 47.8 in 1998, far below figures for the years before World War I. At the close of 1994, total Russian production of all kinds of food was estimated to be about half of the 1986–1990 average, and still had far to fall. There was also a dramatic fall in Russian tractor production, which went from 214,000 units in 1990 to fewer than 29,000 in 1994, a collapse of 87 percent.

The Yeltsin government came under attack for failure to provide investments in rural infrastructure, credit for private farm development, and subsidies to offset terms of trade that are stacked against the farmer. The latter are typified by the estimate of the Agrarian Union's Vasily Starodubtsev that between 1991 and 1994, industrial prices paid by the Russian farmer rose by a factor of 2,042, while agricultural prices paid to the farmer went up by a factor of only 368. Small wonder that during the fourth quarter of 1994, for every 100 new private farms launched, 103 went bankrupt.[45] This state of affairs reflected, among other things, the general hostility of the Yeltsin administration toward rural Russia, which it considered a bulwark of incorrigible communists and antireform forces. By 1999, little had improved in Russian agriculture. Indeed, the Red Cross called for increased international food aid so the country could avoid deaths from starvation in its Far East region.[46]

THE BORROWING BINGE AND THE DEBT ECONOMY

Russia's growing external dependency has been worsened by the country's huge debt obligations. As Chernomyrdin told the State Duma in August 1996, the aggregate of Russian foreign debt was $130 billion, meaning that it was more than half of that year's GDP, thus making Russia a rival of Brazil for the dubious honor of being the country with the world's biggest foreign debt in relation to its own economy. By November 1998, foreign debt had risen to $160 billion.[47] Since then, the Kremlin has not taken on major new debts. Although the nominal debts owed to Russia by other countries (primarily former Soviet allies in the Third World) amount to some $140 billion, the rates of exchange according to which this figure is calculated are still a matter of disagreement. In any case, it is highly doubtful that Russia will collect any sizable share of the debts of these states in the foreseeable future. (In what was clearly an attempt to collect from these former Third World allies, Russia joined the Paris Club of leading creditor nations in 1997, but the prospects that this will lead to the settlement of these debts remain questionable, especially since debtor states like Cuba, Libya, Vietnam, Iraq, and North Korea seem to have neither the means nor the intention of paying.)

During the first years of reform, Yegor Gaidar vaunted as his greatest achievement the fact that the alleged bridling of inflation had allowed companies to switch from barter deals to payments in money; therefore, "the ruble had started to work." Yet the dynamics of the next few years produced a growing "barterization" of the Russian economy, as well as an increased reliance on local scrip, or surrogate money. All this pointed to the resistance of the economy to tough monetarist austerity and the departure of many economic players from the ruble sphere of exchange. Furthermore, the government's unrealistically

tough monetary policies have directly fostered the fragmentation and feudalization of the economy. As such, the government's ability to define and implement
an economic policy at the national level becomes highly questionable. Only following a slight increase in monetary emissions in late 1998 did barter decline and
cash circulation increase the next year.

Clearly, the Yeltsin-Gaidar shock therapy failed to achieve its announced
goals—economic stabilization, the growth of industrial production, the establishment of clear-cut property relations, and an increase in the well-being of the
population. In addition, the economic strategy chosen by the ruling elite has led to
the destruction of vital components of Russian industry, rampant social entropy,
the erosion of a sense of national identity, and the moral and cultural barbari-
zation of society. Beneath the high-sounding rhetoric about liberal modernization
and a return to the community of advanced nations, Russia has been rolled back
to an earlier stage of economic development, erasing many of the achievements
of the modernizations conducted between 1928 and the 1970s.

Underneath the triumphant gloating of Moscow nomenklatura intellectuals
about "the victory over totalitarianism," heavy economic and moral blows were
administered to the cultural, scientific, and educational achievements that had
once made the country a world leader and that had been Russia's most substantial contribution to world civilization. The Russian intelligentsia, the only social
force consciously interested in genuine and comprehensive reform, and a permanent threat to despotic regimes throughout Russia's modern history, was finally
—to the great satisfaction of the old and new nomenklatura—virtually ejected
from public life through massive, targeted budget cuts.

One of the biggest apparent paradoxes of the shock therapy era in Russia has
been the lack of serious, organized social protest commensurate with the decline
of the economy and society. Here we need to underline one specifically economic
reason for the resigned and stoic attitude of the Russian population. Russian working people are totally dependent on the paternalistic industrial structures inherited from the Soviet economy. The core of such structures was the quasi-feudal
company town in which social infrastructure was provided by the company.
The workers became virtual industrial serfs, attached to their jobs as the peasant
serfs were bound to the land. Wage-earners were—and often still are—dependent on managers, not just for wages but for all social services as well. This situation has contributed heavily to the weakness of labor unions and has usually
ensured their subordination to the managers.[48]

WERE THERE ALTERNATIVES TO SHOCK THERAPY?

Alexander Yanov poses the question, "Did Yeltsin make a mistake by launching
market reforms in 1991? Or was he merely following the logic of the circumstances
that prevailed in that decisive autumn? More concisely, did the president have

any choice at that particular moment?" For Yanov the question is of course rhetorical. For him as well as his fellow thinkers, despite their subjective worship of freedom, the deterministic view of history, like implacable fate in Aeschylus's tragedies, serves as the universal weapon in debate. "It is clear," continues Yanov, "that in the fall of 1991 the country could not avoid shock therapy."[49] The intellectual pedigree of this determinism, which allows one to escape the burden of responsible choice, is clear. It takes us back to the main ethical tenet of Soviet Marxism, which defined freedom as nothing but "recognized necessity."

Yet despite what Yanov and others may believe, the initiators of shock therapy did not succumb to this policy blindfolded or like lambs led to the slaughter by the invisible hand of Providence. Their own confessions testify to an acute and realistic perception of the possibilities and limits of strategic choice that defined Russia's societal landscape in the fall of 1991. In essence, the most clear-cut and realistic alternative to the Yeltsin-Gaidar reforms was the continuation and development of the grassroots anti-nomenklatura upsurge, which had been percolating throughout the 1970s and 1980s and which by the fall of 1991 had taken many of the levers of legislative power out of the hands of the ruling class through elections. It was on the crest of this democratic revolutionary wave that the new elite had been carried into the halls of the Kremlin and into the spacious, empty offices of the now banned Communist Party. Gavriil Popov formulated Yeltsin's basic choice very clearly. There were two alternative paths: "Property can be divided among all members of society, or the best pieces can be given to the leaders. The land can be privatized so that it remains in the hands of today's big enterprises, or all who want to become farmers can be given what they need. In a word, there's the democratic approach, and there's the nomenklatura, apparatchik approach." However, in Popov's establishment view, it was "unrealistic to think that in the USSR a revolution 'from below' was feasible." So "reformers from the nomenklatura and the (state) apparatus" had to "carry out the transformations."[50]

In our view, however, it was the fear of further change from below—which might veer out of the Yeltsinites' control and sweep them off the bridge of the ship of state—that pushed the Yeltsin group toward a strategic alliance with the nomenklatura and Mafiya capitalists. It was the alleged specter of a "bloody, irreversible" revolution (though there is no evidence for the word "bloody") that Gaidar writes about in otherwise frank and perceptive words: "In 1990–1991, there was such a threat, but we managed to avoid it. A genuine . . . revolution happily did not happen then."

Gaidar also noted that

> this "prophylactic scare" loomed in 1988–1991 over the consciousness of the radical intelligentsia, who, although they were fanning the general discontent with the regime, were always cautious: In all those cases when the intelligentsia of the early twentieth century stepped on the gas, their grandchildren were quick to step on the brakes. . . . One should also give credit to the political responsibility

of B. N. Yeltsin, who was able to become the leader of the movement and to firmly keep it within bounds, never allowing it to develop into an uprising, and to accomplish the change of regime *in a civilized manner: as a revolution in form, as a compromise in essence.*"[51]

Yeltsin himself remarked in his second volume of memoirs, "I had before my eyes the specter of October [1917]. . . . I could transform August [1991] into another October 1917 with a wave of my hand, with one signature. But I decided not to do this. . . . I saw the continuity between the society of the Khrushchev-Brezhnev period and the new Russia."[52]

Gaidar later noted that the nomenklatura had long "been groping its way forward, step by step, . . . obeying its deepest instincts. It went for the scent of property, as a predator goes for his loot." It was content to "exchange power for property." Moreover, "Nobody fired any managers of state companies or ministerial bureaucrats, nobody seized their bank accounts, nobody confiscated their commercial correspondence, and they were allowed to keep their status, their wealth, and their connections."[53] Here Gaidar was indirectly describing what a real democratic revolution might actually have done to oust the old managerial elite whose incompetence and corruption had undermined the Soviet economy. Instead, Gaidar and his allies in the old elite proceeded to transform the failed managers of state-owned companies into private owners who would now command the companies that they themselves had mismanaged. Gaidar asserted that the government was impotent to salvage these companies and therefore should not interfere with them.

In seeking to head off a democratic revolution, the ruling oligarchy definitely held a winning hand. But the question is whether Russia itself was also a winner. Those who frightened and continue to frighten Russia with greater or lesser bloodlettings (and we should recall that before the 1996 presidential elections the leading tycoon, Boris Berezovsky, threatened the entire country with civil war if it did not choose the right candidate) hinted at the possibility of large-scale human losses if another all-Russian brawl were ever to take place. Doubtless this would have been a heavy price to pay for the removal of the oligarchical regime. However, if one counts all those who have perished since 1992 in the cruel fight over the carving up of national property—businessmen who became the targets of contract killers, elderly owners of privatized apartments who were murdered for their property, the defenders of the White House in October 1993, tens of thousands of Russians and Chechens killed in a war that was partly about oil, and the sharply declining birthrate and diminishing life expectancy—one can also estimate the human costs of the oligarchs' continuing to stay in power.

The vision of a bloody conflict between the nomenklatura and the democratic movement was largely, perhaps completely, unfounded. This was partly because the nomenklatura (as the August coup showed) no longer had firm control over the army and the security services, and partly because Yeltsin's power was unchallengeable in practice and would have permitted him—especially if he had held parliamentary elections in late 1991—to implement the democratic program without massive opposition. The issue is now moot but lives on in rhetoric.

One of the leading Western critics of shock therapy, Peter Murrell, suggests that this economic policy was itself revolutionary and that gradual reforms would have been better. Our analysis, which is sympathetic to his version of gradual reforms, puts forward a somewhat different perspective. Unlike "gradualists" in both the West and Russia, we interpret shock therapy—in light of the analytical framework of Russia's historical cycles developed in chapter 1— as a politically conservative counterreform designed by its principal strategists to weaken the potential for the continuation of the democratic revolution.[54]

In addition to Murrell, there have of course been many economists, in both Russia and the West, who opposed shock therapy from the start (sometimes, like Murrell, offering their own preferred model) or warned that it was working badly and needed to be changed or dropped completely. Their views, of course, varied widely. Until the financial crash of August 1998, most of them were decisively ignored by shock therapy's proponents, who tended to think that listening to criticism was beneath them or a waste of time, or both.

Although this book refers on occasion to critics like Marshall Goldman, Grigori Yavlinsky, James Millar, and Tatyana Koryagina, a review of the work of these regrettably neglected economists is beyond our scope. Nonetheless, we will mention here other notable Russian critics, including Nikolai Petrakov, Oleg Bogomolov, Leonid Abalkin, Stanislav Shatalin, Stanislav Menshikov, Larisa Piyasheva, Vladimir Gel'man, and Sergei Glaziev. Other notable Western critics have included Wassily Leontief, Kenneth Arrow, Robert Solow, James Tobin, Lawrence Klein, Igor Birman, Barry Ickes and Randi Ryterman, David Kotz, Stephen Moody, Michael Intriligator, Robert McIntyre, John Simmons, and Marshall Pomer.[55]

However, we do not plan to ignore the vital issue of alternative economic policies. The shock therapists have advanced various arguments to support their assertion that in the fall of 1991 there were no serious alternatives to Gaidar's recipe of deregulating prices.[56] To consider this matter requires an excursion into the history of the Soviet economic demise. As we shall see, the array of choices in the realm of economic strategy had been progressively narrowed, though not eliminated, by mistakes committed during Gorbachev's perestroika and then by Yeltsin's mindless policy of financial subversion of the central Soviet government. It is to this historical perspective that we now turn.

BACK TO THE ROOTS: SOVIET ECONOMIC DECLINE

The immediate cause of the Gorbachev reforms, which brought on the destruction of the Soviet order, is usually considered to be the economic stagnation of the USSR during the 1970s and 1980s. Indeed, since the early 1970s, the visible slowdown of economic growth had caused widespread concern and insecurity among the ruling elite; by the end of the 1980s, this had evolved into a genuine panic. In due course, broader and broader layers of the Soviet nomenklatura became afflicted by something like a national inferiority complex concerning their country and their social system. By the mid-1980s, the "understanding" that the Soviet economic system was inefficient in principle and unable to compete with the Western system had become a badge of "enlightenment" and "progressiveness" in the new generation of the ruling oligarchy.

How well did this view reflect reality? In the course of the national self-flagellation, one fact was left out of the picture—namely, that the rates of economic growth at the beginning of the 1970s were slowing down virtually worldwide, especially in the most industrially advanced countries. What was referred to as the "socialist world system" (that is, the USSR and the group of its satellite states that were members of Comecon) was nothing more than a somewhat isolated subsector of the global economic system. Global interdependence is widely misused as a political slogan, but it is an indisputable economic fact. Twentieth-century dictators, Stalin and Mussolini among them, have indeed made attempts at autarky, but these efforts have always broken down in the face of severe practical problems. George Kennan had good reasons to predict in 1947 that "in international economic matters, Soviet policy will really be dominated by pursuit of autarky for the Soviet Union and Soviet-dominated adjacent areas taken together."[57] But this striving for autarky, although it could keep the USSR outside the postwar Bretton Woods system of international financial institutions, could never succeed in taking the USSR out of the world economy completely.

Slowdown in Global Economic Growth

Since 1971, the problem of a global slowdown in economic growth has been the subject of many technical and policy-related discussions in the West, but the notion still remains controversial. Yet the majority of researchers concur that the energy crisis of 1973–74 was not the underlying cause but merely aggravated unfavorable trends in the global economy that manifested themselves in the U.S. economic scene as "stagflation" during the Ford-Carter years. Among the immediate factors contributing to the slowdown of growth, the most often mentioned fall under the rubric of "the postindustrial era," marked by a worldwide decline in the productivity of labor and capital, and the end of a period of major technological innovations.[58]

Yet one of the major causes was also the demise of the Bretton Woods system, which featured fixed currency exchange rates and the guaranteed convertibility of the U.S. dollar into gold at $35 per ounce, giving other currencies an indirect gold parity as well. In August 1971, President Nixon terminated this system by closing the U.S. Treasury's gold window and by allowing the dollar's exchange rate to float, which meant that all other currencies' exchange rates would float as well. Citing an inflation rate of 4 percent, Nixon also imposed an import surtax and wage and price controls. Attempts to re-establish a new regime of fixed currency exchange rates were soon abandoned, and a chaotic "nonsystem" of deregulated international monetary relations has persisted to this day.

In 1994, the Bretton Woods Commission, composed of forty-seven influential bankers and economists under the chairmanship of former Federal Reserve Chairman Paul Volcker, offered this evaluation of the impact of floating rates on the world economy: "Since the early 1970s, long-term growth in the major industrial countries has been cut in half, from about 5 percent a year to about 2.5 percent a year. Although many factors contributed to this decline in different countries at different times, low growth has been an international problem, and the loss of exchange rate discipline has played a part."[59]

The importance of the 1971 turning point readily can be seen in the rapid decline in the economic performance of the USSR's rival superpower, especially in the critical area of living standards. In the 1950s and 1960s, U.S. median family income expressed in constant dollars rose by 37 percent per decade. By contrast, between 1970 and 1995, median family income barely managed to eke out a 5.7 percent increase over the quarter-century.

Other advanced industrial countries were entering a similar period of stagnation, and the Soviet Union shared their fate, just as during the 1950s and 1960s it had shared with them the rapid tempo of postwar economic growth. These high rates of growth were achieved in both West and East thanks to an unprecedented concentration of economic power, and thanks to capabilities of mass mobilization that were put at the service of the state during the 1930s and 1940s, be it the Roosevelt-Keynes "welfare state," fascist and communist regimes in Europe, or Japanese military-industrial corporatism. The differences in the forms of ownership of the means of production did not determine any basic divergence in the indicators of economic growth or of their subsequent downturn. Besides, the obsolete ideological boundaries between capitalism and socialism often obscure clear thinking. Take for example Japanese "private capitalism," in which state control over leading corporations through the omnipotent Ministry of International Trade and Industry (MITI) was sometimes more direct and efficient than the Soviet system of managing state enterprises through sectoral ministries, with their multiple and often conflicting bureaucratic interests.

Our attention to these economic trends is designed to counteract the exaggerated view of the Soviet system's exceptional character, which allegedly set the country apart from worldwide historical developments. Yet fundamental differences between the Soviet Union and the Western industrial countries clearly existed. In particular, although the rate of growth in the Soviet Union sometimes equaled or even outstripped that of the capitalist powers, the starting points were quite different. Unlike the United States, Russia suffered two world wars and one civil war on its own territory in the twentieth century. As a result, its industrial potential was twice brought to the brink of annihilation. (One should also add to this Stalin's terror against the peasantry, from which Russian agriculture has never fully recovered.) Unlike postwar Western Europe, the Soviet Union was not a participant in the Bretton Woods system or the Marshall Plan, so the reconstruction of the Soviet economy was conducted under conditions of severe economic isolation.[60]

Finally, in contrast to defeated and occupied Japan, the Soviet Union lacked a talented and highly organized aristocratic elite capable of (1) channeling the wartime resources of labor mobilization and technology into the civilian economy and (2) sublimating military defeat by isolating the domestic market, stressing exports and investment rather than consumerism, and achieving rapid economic growth. The Soviet nomenklatura, who considered themselves the leaders of a victorious world superpower, contented themselves with economic expansion into the countries of Eastern Europe and never set themselves on the task of playing a major role in world markets for industrial goods. The Soviet leaders—especially those who replaced Khrushchev in 1964—considered, not altogether wrongly, that their people were tired of incessant mobilization and that the satisfaction of their immediate consumer demands was long overdue.

Circumstances specific to the Soviet Union that contributed to economic stagnation included the following:

The USSR's one-sided integration into the global economy. The short-sighted emphasis on the export of raw materials and energy hindered the development of high-technology sectors that during the 1960s and 1970s could have aspired to be competitive on global markets. The USSR also got itself excluded from the world market by the 1973 Jackson-Vanik amendment and by Cocom rules, which amounted to a technological blockade against the communist world. By the beginning of perestroika, the experts were openly speaking about the "backward, one could say colonial" structure of Soviet exports to the West, four-fifths of which consisted of energy, mostly oil.[61]

This high degree of external dependency of the Soviet economy became evident in 1984–86, when the fall of world energy prices led to a 40 percent decline in the income earned by Soviet exports to the advanced industrial democracies. On top of this, the demand for consumer goods by the Soviet oligarchy and its clients among the urban professional elites was totally import-oriented, a fact that had a depressing effect on those sectors of industry that were potentially import-competitive. In the late 1980s, even such an orthodox liberal economist as Aslund (a future adviser to Gaidar's government) warned about the "dependency threat" to the USSR because of Western imports. The effect of imitating the consumption patterns of Western elites, when the vast majority of the Soviet citizenry came to believe the myths about "universal prosperity" in the capitalist countries, contributed to a degeneration of morale and national self-confidence in Soviet society.

The oligarchical culture that had taken root in Moscow well before the advent of the Bolsheviks. In the tsarist past, the rulers of Russia were often foreigners who, feeling alienated from the life and culture of the Russian population, attempted to govern the country from their seclusion in the Kremlin, as if from a besieged fortress. This oligarchic culture, accentuated in the Soviet period by the Bolsheviks' paranoia and their constant need to combat "enemies of the revolution," provided fertile soil for the rapid decay and mutation of the Bolshevik revolutionary elite into the nomenklatura—a conservative and privileged ruling class isolated from society.[62]

The rise of an embryonic market and a shadow economy, as described in chapter 3 and also later in this chapter, where we discuss the theories of Mancur Olson.

THE COMMAND ECONOMY

The Soviet command economy had its origins in Stalin's Five Year Plans, which gave top priority to military production and the kind of heavy-industry inputs required to build tanks and planes. Because of its importance for state policy, Soviet military production always came first in the assignment of resources, and it remained competitive in most respects with the best efforts of the United States and other NATO countries. But the Soviet civilian economy, especially its consumer goods production, remained inferior. The production targets developed by Gosplan (the state planning committee) seldom emphasized infrastructure, and when they did it was infrastructure that lent itself to military uses, such as pipelines and rail lines leading to possible future combat fronts, rather than to urban and agricultural areas in the country's interior. As a result, the USSR was left with no highway system worthy of the name, a deficient health care system, and obsolete railroads and telecommunications.

A tragically large part of the Soviet grain harvest (often as much as 30 percent) and other agricultural products were lost every year through spoilage because of the lack of suitable grain elevators, refrigerated storage facilities, food processing plants, and an effective transportation system between the countryside and the cities. Therefore, from the early 1970s on, the USSR became dependent on grain imports, including from the United States.

THE MASSIVE MILITARY BURDEN

The Soviet economy also developed massive distortions as a result of the Cold War. The Soviet military posture featured heavy preponderance over NATO in manpower-intensive land forces and a vigorous nuclear rearmament through the mid-1980s. In the late Brezhnev-Andropov era, the USSR devoted some 20 percent of its GNP and perhaps as much as 60 percent of its national budget to military spending, compared with 5 percent and 17.5 percent, respectively, for the United States under Reagan. In 1984, the Soviet military establishment had over 5.4 million active-duty personnel. However necessary it might have appeared to Kremlin planners, the large-scale Soviet military buildup during the Carter-Reagan era contributed heavily to the depletion and exhaustion of the civilian economy, which in turn set the stage for the Soviet collapse.

THE LIMITATIONS OF GOSPLAN

The Gosplan system of central planning, which attempted to program the economy down to the last bolt, contained numerous irrational features that could have been avoided by a looser system of indicative planning (that is, the setting of broad national priorities as practiced until recently in Japan, France, Taiwan, and other successful modern economies).

Gosplan methods encouraged production in existing modes, but never succeeded in encouraging high rates of technological innovation through the acquisition of new capital equipment or through improvements developed by workers on the shop floor. Soviet factory managers learned never to disclose the true production capacity of their plants to the central planners and never to exceed their plan quotas by more than 1 or 2 percent, lest their quotas be raised for the following years. Managers became adept in "beating down the plan"—convincing the ministry to lower their quotas. Individual workers learned never to produce too much, lest their performance norms be revised upward. Soviet factories often developed a "manic-depressive cycle" that corresponded to the monthly phases of "storming the plan": Little was produced during the first week of the month because of the exhaustion of workers and materials, and the products turned out in the last days of the month were likely to be defective because they were thrown together in a mad rush to meet the plan's quota.

The rate of technological modernization of the society as a whole was also slowed by the almost complete absence of small and medium industry. Because of the legal prohibitions dictated by communist ideology, there were no small engineering or machine-tool businesses built around inventions and new technologies that could have turned the discoveries of Soviet laboratories into cutting-edge capital equipment ready to be installed on the assembly lines of giant factories. Partly because of this lack of small and medium firms, the USSR lagged behind the United States in its ability to spin off new technologies originally developed in the military sector and put them to work in profitable civilian production.

THE "STATIONARY BANDIT" MODEL OF SOVIET SOCIETY

Let us now move from description to analysis in our attempt to understand the decline of the economy, to which Yeltsin was to apply shock therapy. Starting with Anthony Downs's *The Economic Theory of Democracy,* the extrapolation of "market" models to other spheres of social reality sometimes quite distant from economics became one of the dominant trends in American social theory.[63] This approach is based on an ideological belief in the universal applicability of the Western economic model for explaining virtually every phenomenon of human life.

One of the most prominent representatives of this kind of market analysis was Mancur Olson, the intellectual father of the "theory of collective action."[64] The theory's basic contention, which Olson developed over two decades, asserts that small groups have a greater capability and disposition to organize themselves to defend their own interests than do broad masses, because personal benefit from collective action is much more real and tangible in a small group that has limited goals. Therefore, according to Olson, common sense should lead people to be more active in the defense of their private or group interests than in the defense of overarching national goals, to say nothing of global goals.

In one of his recent works, Olson uses elements of Western economic psychology in an attempt to explain the nature of Mafiya structures and the personal and group interests that emerged from the decaying Soviet system.[65] According to Olson's model, a country lacking markets and democracy must inevitably choose between a "stationary bandit" and a "roving bandit." Unlike the dangerous, unpredictable roving bandit, the stationary bandit labors to maximize his tax revenue from his dependents, is economically interested in stability and productivity on his territory, and gladly provides security and other public services. He becomes the most reliable supporter of the collective interest.

In Olson's view, the metaphor of the stationary bandit describes the organizing principle of a Stalinist society. Devastated institutions, expropriations, purges, and political terror were the necessary conditions for the affirmation of collective over private interests. However, postwar stability revitalized narrow group interests, leading to the fall of social productivity and the stagnation of the system. Thus, in post-Stalinist society "bureaucratic competition" in the struggle for perks was replaced by "bureaucratic cartels," from the elite down to the factory level. In a society of the Soviet type, where the rules of the game were originally established without regard to markets, private cartels inevitably led to violations of law on a mass scale. Hence the flourishing of the shadow economy, organized crime, and the Mafiya to which the Soviet Union ultimately succumbed.

As usual, Olson's analysis is impressive for its wit and the paradoxical nature of his analogies and conclusions. But it demonstrates, in our opinion, the limits of any purely economic modeling of complex historical phenomena. For example, he does not recognize any differences between a "stationary bandit" and an authoritarian ruler of the Bolshevik type. He also misses the factor of the legitimation of power, a quality that does not yield to purely economic analysis. At the distance of half a century, anyone can consider Stalin a stationary bandit, but the problem with Olson's model is that while the peasants and many other groups disliked or hated him, many of Stalin's other subjects saw him in quite a different light. For them, even including some of the prisoners in the concentration camps, his regime had unchallengeable legitimacy. This legitimacy was located, at least in part, in a sincere and materially disinterested faith in the possibility and historical necessity of building the most just society in history, and it was buttressed not only by the economic progress of the 1940s and 1950s, but most of all by the victory over Nazi Germany in World War II, despite the colossal price paid in the process. But for Olson, ideology as an extra-economic category is not worth attention and has no inner causality.[66]

This dismissal of ideological causality is characteristic of the nonreflective attitude of most Western economic theorists toward their own intellectual product, because in the final analysis, market "rationality" of the Western type, which is the ideal and the standard of neoclassical economics, is in itself only a form of ideological consciousness. Predictably enough, the uncritical transposition of "Made in USA" models of social behavior and motivational mechanisms to a different cultural and psychological reality imbues the brightest and wittiest analysis with a cold sheen of schematicism. Therefore, we cannot follow Olson in considering the decay of the system Stalin made merely as the unleashing of underground corporate and egoistic interests caused by the decrepitude of the "stationary bandit." The emergence of these interests was the consequence of the gradual loss of legitimacy of the whole system.

Above all, Khrushchev's attempt to marry Marxist-Leninist ideology to Western consumer values proved to be fatal for communist doctrine. Khrushchev's slogan was to catch up and overtake America in the production of "meat, milk, and butter" per capita. This dairy-based version of communism, permeated with archaic peasant psychology, tore away the ascetic veil of individual self-restraint that was perhaps the necessary condition for the survival of the communist idea on Russia's cultural soil. This doctrinal shift, it appears, in large measure precipitated the crisis of the system, which could neither ensure the achievement of its original ideals nor satisfy the explosion of consumer expectations Khrushchev provoked, because it had not been built for that purpose; hence the spread of private and group interests, the fast-track accumulation of wealth, the criminalization of the nomenklatura, and the draining of any genuine passion from communist rhetoric.[67] The consequences were a nationwide awareness of the duplicity of the system, the loss of any remaining trust between the elite and the rest of society, and the emergence in the USSR of an ideological and ethical void.

The insufficiency of a narrowly economic approach gives rise to the onesidedness of the recommendations that follow from Olson's theoretical constructs. If the emergence of the Mafiya and the shadow economy in the 1970s had been accounted for by the antimarket rules of the game, the sweeping changes in the legal system in favor of private business and the curtailing of state participation in the economy in the 1990s should have led directly to the disappearance of criminal capitalism. (In Russia, this point of view is represented by Lev Timofeyev, who has campaigned for the wholesale legalization of criminal capital and the shadow economy.[68]) This recipe is not appropriate, among other things because the Mafiya is far from being simply the product of excessive state regulation. In a number of cases it performs state—not market —functions that the government itself has too hastily abandoned. The State Statistics Committee has estimated that the "shadow" economy comprised 18 percent of Russian GDP in 1995 and rose by early 1997 to 23–25 percent.[69] In these cases, the Mafiya is fulfilling the unsatisfied demand for collective security, protection of self and property, and the creation and preservation of a specific moral code, thus creating criminal surrogates for that institutional framework without which a genuine market is unthinkable. If we were to agree that all this is included under the heading of the general welfare, should not the state, according to Olson's theory, simply evaporate by voluntarily ceding its place to one of the "stationary bandits"?

The Soviet social-political system degenerated partly because the ruling elite either could not or did not want to remain faithful to the ideological basis on which its unlimited power had been built at the cost of enormous sacrifices and suffering. The Yeltsin state, having changed almost all long-standing ideological labels into their opposites, inherited from the Soviet system its social structure and lack of legitimacy—aggravated by the fact that to the unfulfilled promises of the communist nomenklatura were now added the unfulfilled promises of the anticommunist nomenklatura. Such phenomena as mass tax evasion, draft dodging, and honest people dropping out of political life are evidence that, for a substantial number of Russians, state institutions have become synonymous with the "roving bandit"—who, unlike the "stationary bandit," does not care about stability or high productivity among those he preys upon. Therefore, every additional retreat of government from the economy leads not to the decline of shadow activity but, rather, to the further strengthening of clan and Mafiya structures, which are eager to seize functions that have historically belonged to the state. This process will continue until the legally constituted authorities make a serious effort to restore the legitimate basis and traditional role of the state in Russian culture.

ECONOMIC PERESTROIKA AND INCIPIENT COLLAPSE

Gorbachev's first slogan in the field of economic policy consisted of one word: "acceleration"— a renewal of policies planned and initiated under Andropov two years before by his top economic adviser Abel Aganbegyan. One of the basic themes of this phase was an attempt to achieve a breakthrough in the Soviet machine tool industry. The initiative produced an upward spike of economic growth in 1986 but was subsequently undermined by the sharp fall that year in raw materials prices, especially oil, on the world market. As we discussed in chapter 3, Gorbachev wanted his country to join the global economy, but he also wanted local economic autonomy and control. He wanted quality goods that could compete on the world market, but he wanted them produced by units operating in economic conditions of near anarchy.

Obviously, a contradiction existed between Gorbachev's quest for maximum integration with the world economy and his pursuit at home of maximum disintegration of state planning and distribution bodies. At one point, he encouraged the Estonian republic to function as an independent economic and accounting unit. This contradiction exploded when Comecon moved to abandon the use of the ruble in intrabloc trade accounting and replace it with world market prices. In practice, that action meant the introduction of dollar prices and, ultimately, the dollarization of East European trade. It also sounded the death knell for Comecon.

The economic setbacks of 1986 had led Gorbachev to shift his economic strategy toward what he called "perestroika." The substance of this shift was the de-emphasis on government intervention and strategic planning in favor of stimulating more initiatives by lower-level economic players—that is, first and foremost, by factory managers as well as economic bureaucrats at the level of the republics and the regions.

Important measures applied during the perestroika period included the following:

- A November 1986 law governing employment of individuals that for the first time legalized private business, albeit on a very limited scale and under a large tax burden.
- A law on state-owned companies, launched in January 1988, whose main thrust was to empower the managers of state-owned companies, giving them much greater latitude in setting wages for themselves and their employees. Most analysts would now agree that this "Magna Carta" for state enterprises contributed heavily to the explosion of consumer demand and the growth of an inflationary spiral. We would add that it also exacerbated income disparity between managers and workers (even though theoretically the latter were supposed to elect the former), and thus increased social tensions.

  These outcomes were probably a surprise for Gorbachev himself, who was evidently thinking in terms of fostering self-management in state enterprises and was hoping to get society moving by energizing basic industrial units and using them as grassroots pressure against the conservative Party bureaucracy that opposed his reforms. But Gorbachev was unaware of the alienation and mistrust that impelled workers and managers to pursue divergent private interests.
- The May 1988 law on cooperatives (that is, nonstate businesses), which partially legalized private business activity. The problematic feature of this

reform was that most investment capital was already in the hands of the nomenklatura and the forces of the shadow economy. Accordingly, it was the latter who created the first cooperatives and managed to get rich. Almost no cooperatives were engaged in production; most were focused on trading, especially the reselling of imported goods. State-owned import firms used public money to make purchases abroad, but these commodities were then appropriated by Mafiya elements that had infiltrated the trading companies and were then sold on the domestic market for several times their original price. The impact of the growth in cooperatives was to feed price inflation and to escalate social tensions. Several grassroots protest movements that emerged at this time made attacks on the new cooperatives one of their central themes.

In his 1995 book *Is the Chance Lost?* Valentin Pavlov describes how journalists fomented inflationary expectations during the waning years of perestroika by bemoaning price increases and playing to a "populist" audience.[70] Another inflationary factor was the fact that after 1987, Gorbachev felt forced to import more and more consumer goods. Aslund sums up the various stages of macroeconomic destabilization as follows, with a few of our own comments added:

1. The growth of the budget deficit in 1986–87, caused by several factors: the huge investments in machine tools made in 1985; the loss of export income from the drop in raw materials prices on the world market during 1986; and the loss of income caused by Ligachev's anti-alcoholism campaign.

2. The rapid growth of salaries and wages resulting from Gorbachev's 1988 "Magna Carta" for state-owned companies, which also included tax cuts and increased government subsidies for these firms.

3. The increase in social benefits by 25 percent in 1990. This welfare hike derived from the increased power of the parliaments of the fifteen constituent republics, as they embarked on the so-called "parade of sovereignties," aggressively asserting their autonomy from Moscow. Gorbachev and the republican leaders (primarily Yeltsin) reacted by attempting to outbid each other in buying popular support. Aslund believes, and seemingly with good reason, that the summer of 1990 was the "last time the Soviet financial crisis could have been averted."

4. The financial collapse of the USSR, beginning in 1991.[71]

Yeltsin's 1990–91 policy of weakening the institutions of the USSR and especially the Soviet tax base became the biggest driving force of financial collapse. The major move in this regard was the regulation promulgated by the RSFSR's Supreme Soviet in July 1990, which declared the creation of a separate Russian system of credit and finance (*raschetno-kassovye tsentry,* or RKTs), and was a kind of Russian clearing-house interbank payment system independent of the Soviet central bank. This was a clear step toward the financial dismemberment of the USSR.

The next move, prompted by Yeltsin's presidential campaign, was the transfer of Soviet state companies on Russian territory to Russian jurisdiction. These state companies were incited by the Russian Supreme Soviet to declare themselves Russian with the inducement of lower tax rates and a greater availability of credit. By the spring of 1991, the companies that had provided most of the USSR's budget revenues had become "Russian" and had ceased paying taxes to anybody at all, forcing Gorbachev to start negotiations with Yeltsin in Novo Ogarevo.[72] Meanwhile, the erosion of the tax base of both the USSR and Russia, along with the resulting growth in the budget deficit and exploding social demands, led the USSR State Bank and the Russian central bank into a wild race to print money, both for wages and for loans to companies, which were often granted at no interest (or even, with inflation factored in, at a negative interest). All this brought the USSR to the brink of hyperinflation. In the words of the ultraliberal economist Andrei Illarionov,

> the populist macro-economic policy of the Russian leadership dealt a fatal blow to the financial and monetary system of the USSR. . . . [F]rom an economic point of view, the USSR ceased to exist not in December 1991 but earlier, in April of that year, when Yeltsin used the weapon of financial destabilization against the USSR government. . . . The successful use of the battering ram of financial destabilization by Russia led to economic and political devastation, not only in the USSR but in Russia itself and in practice to the complete loss of governability in the economy.[73]

Nomenklatura Privatization

The fate of Soviet state property during the period when Gorbachev and Yeltsin operated a system of dual power (Soviet and Russian) can be best described as "shadow" or "back-door" privatization. Traditionally in the USSR, the means of industrial and agricultural production were the property of the state. Soviet industrial plant and equipment had been created through the blood, sweat, and tears of the workers who were heavily exploited in Stalin's breakneck industrialization of the 1930s. The idea that a tiny stratum of insiders from the old communist-era elite would arrogate this vast property to themselves seemed a scandalous injustice to the majority of those who believed in democracy and reform, and were following Yeltsin and the democrats in their assault on the old system. Yet this is roughly what happened under Gorbachev and then Yeltsin. As Gaidar writes in an eloquent (if somewhat exaggerated) passage, the years 1988–91 were "the most 'golden' period for the elite politico-economic groups." This was when "the foundations of most of the big fortunes and firms . . . were laid." Indeed, "the system of 1990–91 . . . was seemingly (or in reality?) created" so that "the nomenklatura could, with nothing to fear, with no scruples, get rich." Gaidar then exaggerates greatly when he claims that by early 1992, "the nomenklatura had privatized virtually the entire economy, not legally but in terms of the control over property and the extraction of revenue."[74]

One of the leading ideologues of this nomenklatura privatization was Gavriil Popov. When Yeltsin started his career, Popov was one of his harshest opponents.

In fact, when Gorbachev ousted Yeltsin as first secretary of the Moscow city Communist Party committee, Popov's article denouncing Yeltsin as a "populist" and "revolutionary" was one of the most prominent official attacks on Yeltsin.[75] And yet, in 1989–90, Popov emerged as one of the leaders of the Inter-Regional Deputies' Group and then of Yeltsin's election coalition, Democratic Russia. In 1990, Popov was elected chairman of the Mossoviet (the Moscow city council), and in June 1991 he was elected mayor of Moscow.

Here is how Popov interpreted the differences inside the democratic movement:

> On the one side are those who have a social-democratic orientation, including the ultraradicals who rely heavily on populism. . . . The other wing . . . is that of the entrepreneurs. . . . At present, no clear dividing line can be drawn between these two wings. Some entrepreneurs attach importance to the ideals of social democracy, and many within the social democrats are wholehearted supporters of free enterprise. . . . Populism is a threat to the whole . . . transition to market economy. . . . If the populist democrats who are opposed to a rapid transition to a free enterprise society gain the upper hand, the whole of Russia will come to a sudden standstill . . . . The paralysis that it brings with it prepares the way for the chauvinists.[76]

These views derive from the fact that Popov's Moscow became famous for its role as the vanguard of nomenklatura and Mafiya privatization, and for the cooperation of its bureaucrats with the criminal underworld. Popov was also the leading theoretician of "unbridled capitalism" who became well known for arguing in the media that bribery should be legalized because there was no other way to adequately remunerate poorly paid government officials. He resigned as co-chairman of Democratic Russia after he became mayor of Moscow, but a number of his subordinates remained in DR's leadership, allowing Popov to manipulate its internal decision making—a process that quickly led to its virtual demise in 1992 (as the following chapter will show).

SOCIALISM VS. THE FREE MARKET?

Today in the West, one can find a growing number of radically critical theories that explain the collapse of the Soviet system as a betrayal on the part of the ruling elite. Such an analysis is offered by David Kotz and Fred Weir, many of whose arguments add up to a summary of the ideas of Russian democratic socialists.[77] In the Kotz and Weir version, the ruling party-state elite of the USSR, desiring to achieve the prosperity of its Western counterparts, became the nucleus of a "procapitalist" coalition headed by Yeltsin. Against the will of the majority of the population, this coalition rejected the idea of reforming socialism and, instead, destroyed the Soviet Union and led Russia onto the path of capitalist development.

Though we agree with much of this critique, we still believe that considering Soviet economic collapse in terms of the struggle between capitalism and socialism impedes a genuine understanding of the tragedy of these events. That socialism in the rigorous Marxist sense of the word ever existed in the USSR is sure to be the subject of eternal debate, but the "capitalist" market (or even the entire spectrum of separate markets in Katsenelinboigen's classification[78]) was an inherent feature of Soviet reality, at least since the early 1970s. By the beginning of the Gorbachev reforms, even Stalinist methods probably would have been insufficient to exterminate this shadow reality—and besides, not one of the major social groups in the Soviet Union was either ideologically or morally prepared for such a turn of events.

Kotz and Weir's concept of a "procapitalist coalition" standing behind Yeltsin is misleading because there was no prosocialist coalition of any significance arrayed against it—not just in the rarefied atmosphere of the moribund Ideological Department of the CPSU Central Committee, but also in socioeconomic reality. In fact, the real struggle was waged not around the abstract issue of capitalism versus socialism, but around the issue of which social forces would become the protagonists of capitalist development and which rules of the game would apply. By this time in political life, there were only procapitalist forces of different types (although they usually used the word "market," not "capitalism").

It is in this sense that we speak here and elsewhere about the two coalitions that struggled in 1990–92 to influence Yeltsin and to define his socioeconomic policies: the "democratic" coalition (pejoratively labeled by its opponents as "populist") and the oligarchical nomenklatura coalition.[79] The democratic coalition that constituted the majority of deputies in the Russian parliament and regional soviets campaigned more or less consistently on behalf of middle-class participation in the economic transition and especially in the denationalization of industry. The democratic program that stressed the need for a level playing field in the privatization process would have required strong and active government intervention to reduce existing inequalities between ordinary Soviet citizens on the one hand and the ruling nomenklatura, trade Mafiya, privileged Komsomol companies, and the managers of industrial firms on the other.

The other group of forces acted less visibly, but proved to be much more efficient as it worked toward the preservation of the status quo in the distribution of privileges that had taken shape by the beginning of the Gorbachev reforms. This coalition was made up of people who had managed to amass huge fortunes by illegal means by operating either in the high echelons of the ruling elite or among lower-level bureaucrats and black marketeers. It was for them that the genuine democratic revolution, which presupposed the redistribution of property, was the most immediate threat. Therefore, it is not surprising that the ideology of the "Chicago boys" and their allies in Soviet society (who were looking for an oligarchical scenario for the transition to the market) became the radical one of a government retreat from the economy, while their political strategy became the weakening and discrediting of democratically elected parliaments and soviets. The major ideological slur used by the oligarchs in their fight against democrats was the term "populism," the same word that the Gorbachev group had hurled against Yeltsin. Now the same slur was used to alienate committed democrats from Yeltsin.

THE ECONOMIC REFORM DEBATE

Between 1988 and 1991, a competition took place among alternative programs for the reform of the Soviet economy. Although there were many programs, two general orientations within the reform movement soon emerged. First were the "1960s democrats," whose basic inspiration was the 1968 Prague Spring in Czechoslovakia and who, as exponents of "socialism with a human face," believed in the convergence of the world's economic systems—a belief that Andrei Sakharov originally shared.[80] Second were the freemarketeers, whose Western inspiration was the Thatcher-Reagan revolutions. Their domestic social and cultural base was the "golden youth" of the nomenklatura during the Brezhnev "era of stagnation," characterized by an opportunistic and consumerist mentality. The freemarketeers favored the almost complete dismantling of government economic controls.

In all, Marshall Goldman counts twelve plans for economic reform.[81] The multitude of competing reform proposals created the public impression of a "Tower of Babel," to use the term of Leonid Grigoriev, one of the coauthors of the 500 Days program.

Underlying these plans, however, we see seven distinct "ideologies," which differed in their goals and means for economic reform but whose fundamental tenets and assumptions divided along the two basic orientations described above. The seven ideologies are listed here with the officials with which they are associated:[82]

1. Conservative and oriented toward industrial sectors (Ryzhkov).

2. Technocratic "Keynesianism" (Abalkin Commission, October 1989). Abalkin emerged as a public figure during the Nineteenth CPSU Conference in May 1988, when he criticized the policies of the Gorbachev-Ryzhkov government and predicted an inflationary spiral, falling revenues, and declining production. Gorbachev responded with a harsh attack, and Abalkin became a maverick, at least temporarily. After a few months, with crisis symptoms multiplying, he was appointed to the Gorbachev government's own commission for economic reform.

3. Monetarism (Pavlov, Gaidar, B. Fyodorov). Pavlov believed that there was only one major problem in the Soviet economy: the disproportion in prices—wholesale prices were too high and retail prices too low. This view reflected the frustration of state-owned monopolistic trading companies that were forced by strict government price controls to keep their retail prices for basic consumer goods low, leaving them with profits they considered insufficient.

Pavlov criticized the Gorbachev leadership for its fear and reluctance to raise retail prices, a fear rooted in the traumatic memory of the bloody 1962 Novocherkassk revolt. This uprising had been set off by Khrushchev's increases in the prices of meat and clothing, which set the stage for his later ouster. The conflict between industrialists like Ryzhkov and monetarist supporters of trading companies like Pavlov was one of the central themes in the economic history of perestroika. In December 1990, Gorbachev removed Ryzhkov as prime minister and replaced him with Pavlov, thus accentuating the authoritarian drift of that period.

4. Nomenklatura privatizers (Popov, Volsky). Advocates of this ideology favored the transfer of state assets to the existing enterprise directors.

5. Revolutionary, liberal-democratic (Shatalin, Yavlinsky, Yevgeny Saburov). This plan was an attempt (described in some detail below) to blend a Gorbachevian belief in "socialism with a human face" with the revolutionary anticommunist mood that was growing in the nonelite sectors of society.

6. Speculative-anarchic "wild capitalism" (Tarasov, Bocharov). Artyom Tarasov was one of the founders of the cooperative movement, where he amassed a considerable fortune. Mikhail Bocharov was an adventurous construction boss who came close to being named prime minister of Russia in Yeltsin's 1990 cabinet.[83]

7. Social-populist and egalitarian-democratic (Koryagina). The economist Tatyana Koryagina was an early leader of the democratic movement and a close associate of Yeltsin who later became one of the first to break with him. She developed a critique of the shadow economy, explained the role of Mafiya groups in deliberately creating socially explosive shortages of consumer goods, and recommended measures to fight organized crime. She has always remained a maverick and was criticized for envisioning the possibility of an honest, noncorrupt, and activist administration that, her opponents pointed out, was at odds with reality.[84]

THE 500 DAYS PROGRAM (REDUX)

The program entitled "500 Days: Transition to the Market," which we discussed briefly in chapter 4 and which expresses ideology number five above, deserves special attention. The origins of the 500 Days program are found in an August 1990 working group created by a joint decision of Gorbachev and Yeltsin. They took this decision during a brief interlude of cooperation between the two, and their joint backing gave a broad public legitimacy to the program.[85] In its spirit and in many specific elements, the program was the most immediate precursor to Gaidar's shock therapy, but at the same time, there were fundamental differences in philosophy and specific recommendations.

The most obvious and often mentioned difference was the priority given to privatization and price deregulation. The 500 Days program put privatization ahead of freeing prices, which was an important contrast to Gaidar, who proceeded in the reverse order. In the logic of the 500 Days program, privatization was intended to create a framework of competition, as well as to give the middle class the chance for property ownership before their assets were devalued by price deregulation. By contrast, Gaidar's approach destroyed the savings of the middle class overnight, leaving them with no means of acquiring what was to be privatized later. The ambiguity of the 500 Days program, which, though it was never carried out, heavily influenced all subsequent debates and decisions on economic reform, was reflected in the later political careers of its authors. Some of them, such as Yavlinsky, Shatalin, and Petrakov, became rather consistent opponents of the Yeltsin-Gaidar-Chernomyrdin line of shock therapy. Others, such as Boris Fyodorov, Yevgeny Yasin, and Andrei Vavilov, later joined the government and were among the most active and aggressive advocates of Gaidar's program.

The announced goals of the 500 Days program included economic freedom, the well-being of the citizen, and catching up with the more advanced industrial countries. "Human society has never created a more efficient system than the market economy," says the program's precis, and therefore the transition to "the economic system based on market relationships" is the only way to solve the problems facing the country. The program called for replacing the USSR with an "Economic Union of Sovereign Republics."

During the first hundred days, the program called for the denationalization of land and housing, with the reorganization of large companies as corporations. There was also to be some small-scale privatization under the plan, with some housing and real estate ceded to private owners, auctions of state-owned motor vehicles, and an initial public offering of stock in fifty to sixty state companies. The plan also advocated an amnesty for those convicted of economic crimes (a highly controversial measure strongly advocated by the Mafiya and operatives of the shadow economy). The executive would use emergency powers to carry out financial and monetary reform. The mandated goals included cutting the government budget deficit and stopping inflation by shutting down the printing of paper money. The authors of the program wanted to abolish all subsidies to state-owned companies by January 1, 1991. Because most of these subsidies flowed into the pockets of the company managers, this represented a revolutionary measure which Gaidar stopped short of implementing.

The 500 Days program stressed the defense of the ruble and the outlawing of foreign currency trading. (This was another sharp contrast to Gaidar, who in February 1991 published a lengthy article in *Kommunist,* in which he defended the dollarization of the economy as being good for Russia, arguing that the Russian government should not and could not oppose the circulation of dollars.) The purpose of the first hundred days' measures was "to mobilize the reserves of the state to finance the transition to the market."

From Day 100 to Day 250, the program emphasized price deregulation and the fight against inflation. It prescribed an attempt to reduce the budget deficit to zero while stopping the growth of the money supply. The program envisioned the fall of production in certain industries, as well as a reduction of investment caused by financial and credit austerity, but these were viewed as not necessarily negative phenomena because they would contribute to badly needed "structural shifts" in the Soviet economy.

Between Days 250 and 400, the watchword became the "stabilization of the market." According to Yavlinsky and Shatalin, this was the suitable time for antitrust measures, leading to the possible breakup of monopoly cartels. The government would support small business to help create jobs. Social infrastructure (schools, hospitals, vacation facilities, day care, and so forth) would be transferred from companies to local soviets. (The prominent role of local governments in the 500 Days program was again in sharp contrast to the Yeltsin-Gaidar tendency to mistrust local administrations, which were excluded from the redistribution of property under Gaidar and were finally abolished by the October 1993 coup.)

By Day 400, the government was assumed to have deregulated 70 to 80 percent of all prices, while maintaining price ceilings for fuel, energy, metals, and basic consumer goods. (By contrast, Gaidar abruptly deregulated 90 percent of all prices on the first day of his reform program, including those of basic consumer goods, but not those of fuel and energy.)

Between Days 400 and 500, the plan forecast the beginning of growth. During this phase, the government would reform the housing market, with the aim of increasing the mobility of the work force.

In general, the program called for a strong and active government. Measures to sustain stable levels of production over the short term pending the stabilization of prices included maintaining government contracts with companies, demonopolizing and privatizing wholesale and retail trade, selling off government commodity stocks as a form of government intervention in the consumer market, shutting down nomenklatura distribution points for imported luxury goods and using the inventories to finance state interventions in the consumer market, and empowering local elected officials and worker delegates to conduct surveillance of consumer goods inventories to stop Mafiya hoarding.

On November 20, 1990, Yavlinsky resigned his briefly held post as Russian deputy prime minister in protest over what he called the refusal of both Gorbachev and Yeltsin to carry out the 500 Days program. Yeltsin's motive was his reluctance to go ahead with the plan because it might have prolonged the survival of the USSR and thus Gorbachev's power base. For his part, Gorbachev feared that the success of a program developed by Yeltsin's Russian government would increase his rival's popularity.

The same program re-emerged in a different form in June 1991 as the "Grand Bargain" program of Yavlinsky and Graham Allison of Harvard University's John F. Kennedy School of Government.[86] Yavlinsky and Allison hoped that Gorbachev would accept the program and take it with him to the July 1991

G-7 summit in London, where it might attract financial backing along the lines of the Marshall Plan. In reality, both Gorbachev and Bush considered the program to be utopian, revolutionary, and unrealistic. Gorbachev arrived at the summit bearing the Pavlov program for price hikes, for which he was unable to garner any financial support.

Here the role of Soviet prime minister Valentin Pavlov as the immediate precursor to Gaidar needs to be emphasized. The main difference between Pavlov and Gaidar was that Pavlov lacked any popular legitimacy and was considered a reactionary, while Gaidar benefited from Yeltsin's current popularity and legitimacy as the first democratically elected leader in the history of Russia. In January 1991, Pavlov deregulated wholesale prices, and in April he proceeded to deregulate a significant number of consumer prices. The latter action stirred up a storm of criticism, both from the democratic movement and from Yeltsin and his team of future shock therapists. Pavlov was forced to supplement price deregulation with wage increases and social subsidies, which only deepened the threat of hyperinflation.

THE SUBVERSION OF THE RUBLE

Prime Minister Pavlov, whom the radical press had already transformed into the "evil genius" of perestroika, also shocked progressive circles in early 1991 by publicly stating that foreign financial forces were engineering an organized attack to subvert the Soviet ruble. According to Pavlov, there were signs of a massive cross-border infusion of ruble notes into the USSR in order to unleash hyperinflation and undermine the regime.[87] The media, gripped at the time by reformist euphoria, ridiculed Pavlov's statement as one more example of conservative-nationalist paranoia. It took three years for Pavlov's allegations to be confirmed by a reliable independent source.

In her book *Thieves' World,* the American journalist Claire Sterling was the first to provide well-documented research on the Russian criminal revolution, and she assembled evidence of a carefully planned assault against the ruble in 1989–1991; the credibility of her research was somewhat cautiously conceded by Marshall Goldman.[88] In 1990–91, the police and security services of several Western countries recorded "traces of an apparently senseless traffic in rubles." Trucks and railway cars full of ruble notes were seen on the roads and railway lines of France, Belgium, Holland, Germany, Switzerland, Italy, and Poland. In one case, recounted by Sterling's source in the Italian police, a truck carrying millions of rubles drove from Avignon through Marseilles to Turin under KGB escort. As the prefect of Bologna told Sterling, the Soviet embassy in Rome was actively involved in the transportation and sale of these bank notes.

At the same time, investigators traced the active purchase of rubles by the Sicilian Mafia and the Colombian cocaine cartels. On March 16, 1992, a report by the committee of the Italian parliament investigating the Mafia cited height-ened financial activity by the criminal underworld in southern Italy and Sicily involving the laundering of criminal money into rubles. Already in 1989 (a year before the Soviet financial collapse), one of the leading Mafia clans, the San Lorenzo of Palermo, obtained 500 million rubles in cash. In early 1990, a promi-nent Italian drug baron, Santo Pasquale Morabito, struck a deal to buy 70 billion rubles in cash for a total price of $4.6 billion, which was fifteen times less than the official exchange rate. The judge who had ordered the arrest of Morabito's representatives soon freed them. "I just couldn't believe that anybody in his right mind would swap narcodollars for rubles that nobody can spend," said the judge in explaining his decision.[89]

Sterling's research describes a worldwide operation by currency speculators and professional money launderers involving several Western banks. The most obvious goal of this operation was to make big profits (for themselves and wealthy Russians) through currency speculation by sharply driving down the ruble's rate of exchange. One of her sources—someone personally involved in the operation—described in detail the whole scheme, which, during the summer of 1990 alone, brought about a lowering of the ruble exchange rate on the black market from 10 rubles per dollar to 18.

By the fall of 1990, 70 to 80 billion rubles had already been offered for sale on Western foreign exchange markets. This was the equivalent of half of the ruble notes in circulation at that time. (These data were later confirmed by Gen-nadi Chebotaryov, a senior official of the Russian Interior Ministry.[90]) In Ster-ling's opinion, "the ability of three or four largely unknown characters to mount such a planetwide operation . . . and their singular immunity from beginning to end suggests the guiding hand of not just one but several intelligence agencies."[91]

In that light, we must ask, Were there wider purposes behind this ruble specu-lation? Anyone interested in the breakup of the Soviet Union would have also had a keen interest in subverting the Soviet currency. This could have included both domestic and international political forces who realized that a collapsing ruble would exacerbate any and all centrifugal tendencies. Some may have dreamed of creating chaos and profits by cornering the market in rubles in the way the Hunt brothers tried to corner the world market in silver about a decade before.

The USSR was a leading producer of a variety of valuable and strategic minerals, going well beyond the obvious choices like gold, diamonds, and plat-inum; during the early 1990s, a great deal of Soviet aluminum was dumped on the world market. In his book *The Great Criminal Revolution,* Stanislav Gov-orukhin describes in fascinating detail the contraband trade in highly sensitive strategic raw materials and rare-earth elements, including gallium, cesium, tanta-lum, zirconium, vanadium, and indium. Authorities in Pskov confiscated radio-active isotopes that Mafiya elements intended to smuggle out of the country.[92] During these years, Soviet uranium and plutonium, sometimes of weapons grade, began to turn up on the black markets of the world. A number of governments, terrorist organizations, and other interests may have been involved in this traffic. There was also lively interest in certain quarters in acquiring the services of Soviet scientists, many of whom were no longer being paid regularly by their laboratories and research institutes in the USSR's "science cities."

Certainly it could be argued that many of these purchases could have been made using dollars, but it is also probable there would have been instances in which paying in rubles would have been more discreet and convenient, and harder to trace. Other economic interests, expecting the privatization of factories, mines, real estate, communications, and other important assets in the ruble zone, were perhaps hoarding rubles with a view to entering the market, perhaps using Russian front men. These operations could have been part of schemes to launder dollars coming from the international narcotics traffic and other illegal activities into property in the USSR and, later, Russia.

One of the dealers involved in these multimillion-dollar transactions was Roberto Coppola, the bearer of forged papers bearing the name of the Sovereign Military Order of Malta and of eighteen genuine letters of accreditation to assist his work as a special ambassador of various governments, ranging from Equatorial Guinea to the Soviet republics of Georgia, Byelorussia, and even the Leningrad region. One of these letters—issued on behalf of the Russian Federation on October 16, 1990—carried the signatures of Yeltsin and Foreign Minister Kozyrev. This document empowered Coppola to represent Russian interests anywhere in the world. In January 1991, after this scandalous information was publicized by *Komsomol'skaya pravda,* the document issued to Coppola was voided. Yet on January 28, after the Russian leadership had distanced itself from this "Knight of Malta," Coppola, in a telephone conversation wiretapped by the Italian police, informed one of his confederates that the Russian embassy in Rome was looking for a buyer for two thousand tons of gold. The selling price on the world market that day for that much gold was $22 billion, and the broker's commission on this deal, as Coppola's conversation also indicated, was 1 percent.[93]

THE FILSHIN SCAM REVISITED

In those same crisis days of January 1991, which to a large extent predetermined the collapse of the USSR, Russia was roiled by the now-forgotten Filshin affair, to which we referred briefly in chapter 4. In Sterling's words of 1994,

> it took an effort of will to believe that the Russian government had made a deal with a bunch of international con men to swap all the rubles in circulation for black market dollars. The story seemed preposterous. Politicians claimed it was a frame-up; nobody went to jail for it; the foreign press largely ignored it. . . . But the story was true. Exposure was not the end of it, either. Negotiations were resumed and new deals were struck—and are still being struck. The same "businessmen" are running fabulous joint ventures in Moscow to this day.

Sterling evaluated this entire affair as an "almost indecipherable conspiracy in which elements of the KGB, in collusion with the international underworld, set out deliberately to destabilize the Soviet Union's currency, almost certainly with the tacit consent if not active participation of the Western intelligence community."[94] For our purposes, the case illuminates much about Russian and Soviet politics in 1990–91.

What were the basic facts about the Filshin affair? On January 23, 1991, the day when Pavlov abruptly announced that all large-denomination ruble notes would be withdrawn from circulation within three days, the Soviet police arrested British citizen Paul Pearson as he was preparing to depart from Sheremetyevo Airport on an international flight. Pearson had with him a contract signed on behalf of the RSFSR government for the sale of 140 billion rubles for a total price of $7.8 billion. At that moment, 140 billion rubles constituted the sum total of ruble cash in circulation on Russian territory; the official value of these rubles at the so-called commercial exchange rate would have been $224 billion, or about $10 billion on the black market.

This deal, under which the Russian government agreed to sell off at a huge discount its entire extant paper money circulation, appeared to outside observers to be bizarre, with big downsides for both parties. "Who in his right mind was prepared to part with a fortune in solid U.S. dollars for bales of colored paper?" asked *Washington Times* reporter Holman Jenkins.[95] As Sterling correctly observes, most people in Russia and elsewhere were at that time completely ignorant of the turbulent explosion of demand for the depreciating Russian ruble from international criminal syndicates.

On February 15, 1991, the committee formed by the Russian Supreme Soviet to investigate the Filshin affair (headed by a faithful Yeltsinite, Aleksandr Pochinok) published the preliminary report of its investigation. The committee's finding was that since the summer of 1990 (meaning since the first days in office of Ivan Silayev, the RSFSR prime minister from June 1990 to September 1991), the Russian cabinet had received similar offers for a large-scale ruble-dollar deal from the same group of people on three separate occasions. One of the men behind this offer happened to be a former Ukrainian citizen (and twice-imprisoned ex-convict), Yan Zubok, who had emigrated to the United States and acquired the ownership of a condom-producing company. Another businessman, Leo Emil Wanta, who came very close to obtaining the approval of Yeltsin, Silayev, and Burbulis for the opening of a 140 billion ruble credit line for "investments" in the Russian economy, was himself wanted by U.S. authorities for credit card fraud. Only the information supplied by the United States averted the signing of this contract at the last moment. After Wanta had disappeared, the same offer was made to the Russian government by a certain Colin Gibbons, who later turned out to have been Wanta's partner. An arrest warrant for Gibbons had been issued by Interpol in July 1984 (for smuggling high-speed video cameras into the USSR, apparently with the help of the KGB, in violation of the Western technology embargo).[96]

On January 11, 1991, Gibbons obtained a written guarantee from Russian deputy prime minister Gennadi Filshin that 140 billion rubles from the Russian state budget would be paid out to the middleman in the deal, who was a member of parliament from Cheliabinsk named A. A. Sviridov. The committee came to the conclusion that the deal was a plot "that could set in motion uncontrollable financial developments," including the takeover of Russian companies and other national resources at bargain basement prices.

Filshin's written commitment to sell was a glaring violation of the articles of the criminal code, which, however, did not lead to arrests or court hearings. By that time, the efforts of the radical reformist media and proponents of the deregulated market had imbued the very concept of "economic crime" with positive—and even sometimes heroic—overtones in the distorted perception of the public. Although Filshin was fired from his office as deputy prime minister, he was compensated with the post of minister of foreign trade and in the fall of 1991 received a lucrative appointment as Russian trade envoy in Vienna. "We will preserve Filshin for the sake of Russia," promised Yeltsin.[97]

To understand the political and psychological context of the Filshin affair, it is important to examine the explanations offered by its central figure in his testimony before the Russian parliament. In Filshin's words, the deal was nothing less than a new Marshall Plan because the rubles to be paid to Gibbons were intended to saturate the Russian market with food imports. The conjecture of a well-informed London newspaper seems more credible: "Gennadi Filshin's program of fantastic currency transfers was a substitute for all programs and reforms of the Russian government, until it collapsed with a crash."[98] But even if we give Filshin the benefit of the doubt and stipulate that he was acting in good faith, we must note that what he was doing cannot be compared with the Marshall Plan. The Marshall Plan served first and foremost to finance a wave of American capital goods and machine tool exports to Western Europe. These were used to re-equip ruined factories, while other Marshall Plan credits were used as foreign exchange to buy raw materials and semifinished commodities. In this way, the Marshall Plan relaunched Western Europe's output of producer and consumer goods.

The Filshin affair was a predictable result of the mania for dollars and imported goods that permeated both the Soviet and the Russian leaderships and to a large degree fueled the unleashing of the inflationary spiral in 1990–91. The feverish race between Gorbachev and Yeltsin to import the largest possible quantities of foreign goods and to extract economic assistance from the West reflected the extreme reluctance of the elite to uncover the real causes of unfulfilled consumer demand. The core of the problem was not a shortage of basic commodities in the country but, rather, the lack of an open, socially accountable, and genuinely competitive system of distribution.

Consumer goods shortages—in their most extreme and socially explosive forms—were the result of the monopolistic practices of the half-bureaucratic, half-criminal trade Mafiya and of the existence of multiple-level closed systems for the distribution of goods to privileged groups. The voices of the few economists who openly spoke and wrote about this issue (such as Tatyana Koryagina[99]) were drowned out by the noisy assertions of the many journalists who treated the transition to the market as identical to the legalization of shadowy nomenklatura-Mafiya capital. For the new reformist elite, the very issue of trade and distribution monopolies was more and more off-limits—not least because the assets of the commercial nomenklatura were playing a crucial role in the election and propaganda campaigns of the new rulers. Hence the double-edged strategy of Russia's "liberal" reformers: During the struggle for power and its consolidation, they waged a campaign for unlimited imports. Afterward, in the face of exhausted budget resources, they turned to shock therapy and the decontrol of consumer prices in favor of the trading monopolies.

Food shortages plagued the final months of the USSR's existence. In November 1990, Gorbachev directed a desperate plea to the international community to provide food assistance. This was the subject of Foreign Minister Shevardnadze's last mission to Washington in search of large cash grants for purchases of U.S. food stocks. Shevardnadze secured about $1 billion in commodity credits, but this was a disappointment, given the scale of the artificially induced problem. In December, Tatyana Zaslavskaya, the president of the sociologists' association, declared that the conservative camp was "using all possible means to make the economic situation worse and blame the democrats for the misery."[100] Producers' hoarding of food during this period can be partly explained in terms of the classic monopolistic impulse to drive up prices in order to realize a bigger profit through scarcity later on. However, it seems that certain trading elites were also playing a longer-term political game to blackmail the government. Deregulate prices, they said in effect, if you want to see these food stocks back on the market. In any case, even if the causes of food scarcity were artificial, the shortages that tens of millions of families faced were very real.

WHY DID YELTSIN PICK THE GAIDAR TEAM?

After the August coup, the unstable balance of power among Gorbachev, Yeltsin, and the leaders of the republics, coupled with the unclear prospects for the new Union Treaty, prevented the formation of a new Soviet government. Instead, Gorbachev and his "Federation Council" of republican leaders set up a temporary body to run the economy under the chairmanship of Russian prime minister Silayev. Yet because he had no credibility as an economic reformer, Silayev was already on his way out and functioned mainly as a figurehead. Three key players soon emerged in the council: Yavlinsky, Volsky, and Yuri Luzhkov (the last as the new deputy mayor of Moscow after Popov's reorganization of the city's government). Among these, Gorbachev selected Yavlinsky to be his closest collaborator, partly because of Yavlinsky's reputation in the West as a reformer and also because Yavlinsky was personally committed to the survival of the USSR. However, it had become almost impossible to carry out any policy at the USSR level, mainly because the government had run out of cash.

The fatal blow was the discovery that most of the Soviet gold reserves had been sold off. On September 29, 1991, Yavlinsky announced on television that the Kremlin's reserves had been reduced to 240 tons, the equivalent of less than one year's domestic production. This was about one-fifth of the prevailing estimate of Soviet gold stocks among Western experts at the time. The remaining reserves now had a world market value of only $3 billion, which meant that the payment of external debt had become practically impossible and that the Soviet government was on the brink of bankruptcy. Yavlinsky also stated that two-thirds of the Soviet gold reserves had been liquidated during the single year of 1990 to finance imports and service foreign debt. Then, on November 16, 1991, Viktor Gerashchenko, the chairman of the USSR State Bank, shocked the West—but doubtless not the above-mentioned middleman for gold sales, Roberto Coppola —by announcing that no gold whatsoever remained in the government's vaults.

The depleted Soviet stocks were a surprise to the Russian public, but they were far less of a surprise to Western financial insiders. By late 1991, it was an open secret among European bankers and traders that just about every week a Soviet air transport landed in Switzerland with a cargo of gold, which was discreetly turned into hard currency. However, by the last days of the USSR, all the proceeds had disappeared or been spent—there was simply no cash left. When Gorbachev went to Madrid in November 1991 for the Middle East peace conference, he and his retinue had to abscond without paying their hotel bill.

After the August 1991 coup attempt, Yeltsin disappeared from Moscow for two months. The official explanation was that he was simply vacationing in Sochi on the Black Sea coast. But during his absence, political circles in Moscow grew increasingly irritated and demanded his return—most people thought the country was falling apart and that the Gorbachev regime was rapidly becoming irrelevant. When Yeltsin finally returned to public view, he brought his shock therapy speech of October 28, 1991, which we analyzed at the beginning of this chapter. For the Russian parliament, unsophisticated in economics, the confident tone and the reassuring promises relieved some of their main worries. Thus on November 1, 1991, they voted to grant Yeltsin additional powers for one year to carry out urgent reforms and allowed him to combine the posts of president and prime minister. Then, on November 6, after an apparent last-minute idea of Yeltsin's to put bureaucrats into key economic positions had been dropped, the list of his cabinet appointments was announced.[101] It featured two deputy prime ministers: Gennadi Burbulis, responsible for political affairs and Yeltsin's liaison with the reform team that was led by the other deputy prime minister, Yegor Gaidar.

During the two months of seclusion in Sochi, Yeltsin had picked Gaidar's strategy of shock therapy because it attracted him in several different ways. Its economic determinism and supposedly short duration enticed his Bolshevik mind. Its alleged virtual painlessness appealed to his weak, but politically sensitive, democratic impulses. Its use of big capital flows from bodies like the IMF gratified his love of buying support with handouts. And Gaidar's unthreatening lack of personal charisma appealed to Yeltsin's constant concern that no one challenge his power.

WHAT WAS TO BE DONE?

A more promising path to the modernization of the Soviet economy might have proven to be capitalist dirigisme in the tradition of the German Historical school of political economy, founded by Friedrich List. A prominent example of postwar dirigisme is French president Charles de Gaulle's economic reforms after 1958. In his memoirs, de Gaulle described his approach:

> For us . . . the task of the State was not to force the nation under a yoke, but to guide its progress. However, though freedom remained an essential lever in economic action, this action was nonetheless collective, it directly controlled the nation's destiny, and it continually involved social relations. It thus required an impetus, a harmonizing influence, a set of rules, which could only emanate from the State.

This classic example of dirigiste reform was based partly on Jean Monnet's theory of indicative planning, which had been important for the European administration of the Marshall Plan. France had introduced a Commissariat du Plan to carry out planning that would establish broad national priorities, rather than micro-management of the Gosplan type. As de Gaulle later wrote,

> [I]n practical terms, what it primarily amounted to was drawing up the national plan, in other words deciding on the goals, the priorities, the rates of growth and the conditions that must be observed by the national economy, and determining the fields of development in which it must intervene, and the laws and its budgets. It is within this framework that the State increases or reduces taxation, eases or restricts credit, regulates customs duties; that it develops the national infrastructure—roads, railways, waterways, harbors, airports, communications, new towns, housing, etc.; harnesses the sources of energy—electricity, gas, coal, oil, atomic power; initiates research in the public sector and fosters it in the private; that it encourages the rational distribution of economic activity over the whole country, and by means of social security, education, and vocational training, facilitates the changes of employment forced by many Frenchmen by modernization. In order that our country's structures should be remolded and its appearance rejuvenated, my government, fortified by the newfound stability of the State, was to engage in manifold and vigorous interventions.[102]

Some of the fruits of this dirigisme are still visible: The French aerospace industry is one of the most competitive in the world, the French railroad system boasts the fastest trains in Europe, and the French electrical power grid derives a greater proportion of its energy from modern nuclear reactors than that of any other country. In our view, the tradition of étatisme and centralized government common to Russia and France, as well as de Gaulle's stress on national pride, could have been used to make dirigisme *à la Russe* culturally, politically, and economically attractive for Russia.

Gorbachev also could have chosen to rely on the Japanese approach, the most spectacular economic success story of the entire postwar period. The post-1962 economic miracle was decisively promoted by MITI, which elaborated a national development strategy and encouraged private companies to act in harmony with the priorities it set. The leading American authority on MITI offered the following evaluation of Japanese dirigisme:

> [T]he Japanese case differs from the Western market economies, the communist dictatorships of development, or the new states of the postwar world. The most significant difference is that in Japan the state's role in the economy is shared with the private sector, and both the public and private sectors have perfected means to make the market work for developmental goals. This pattern has proved to be the most successful strategy of intentional development among the historical cases. It is being repeated today in newly industrializing states of East Asia—Taiwan and South Korea—and in Singapore and other South and Southeast Asian countries. . . . [T]he Japanese pattern has proved incomparably more successful than the purely state-dominated command economies of the communist world.[103]

What were Russia's specific needs at this critical moment in its history? Some of the suggestions that follow are, we admit, the fruit of hindsight. On the other hand, we are on record as having opposed shock therapy for Russia even before Yeltsin adopted it.[104] Later, in July 1992, one of us noted, "in Russia's present desperate situation . . . a strong case can be made for a . . . radical change of course. . . . [T]he G-7 and the International Monetary Fund will need to have ready a response with more intellectual weight than the shock therapy they pushed that set Russia off on the wrong track last year."[105] Now, as then, we believe that alternative policies existed that would have given Russia a better chance of a good outcome than it has today, in the wake of Yeltsin's ill-considered course since 1991. The "valley of tears" that Jeffrey Sachs said it was "easy to get lost in" if countries did not pursue his policies boldly enough was by no means foreordained.[106]

Our starting point is the fact that in dealing with the legacy of seventy-four years of communism, Russia faced truly daunting challenges. Strong political forces and instruments were essential for dealing with them—a mixture of firm, thoughtful leadership; a representative, democratic, forward-looking parliament of the sort that probably would have been elected if the grassroots democratic movement had been supported by Yeltsin and elections had been held in late 1991; and an extensive array of committed supporters at all levels of society, united in a party or movement. Yeltsin and his colleagues needed to project to the entire Russian populace a powerful, unchanging core message along these lines: "The road to lasting national revival will be long and tough. National solidarity and social justice are crucially important. The government will strive constantly to achieve as equal a degree of hardship as possible for all citizens. It will ensure the maximum possible level of political freedom. And it will expand the range of economic freedom by shifting steadily but not too quickly to a market system, while retaining a social safety net."[107]

This approach would have emphasized the critical importance of a longer-term perspective for development, instead of the utopian belief that the major changes could be carried out in a few years; a strong political base for the government; strengthening and creating vitally needed institutions and using foreign assistance to train a politically neutral civil service; seeking a modified Marshall Plan for the former Soviet republics to get help in restoring—and creating anew —domestic production facilities, to obtain foreign support for macroeconomic stabilization for a limited period, and to facilitate economic cooperation among the recipient countries; not making a fetish of rapid privatization or preventing inflation; and maintaining government legitimacy and national cohesion by pursuing social justice, by making it possible for voters to change the government, by preserving a social-safety net, by spreading the pain of economic dislocation, and by mobilizing popular support to help the police to fight crime and maintain law and order. Effective economic measures certainly involve dislocations that may be painful to those caught up in them. In our view, however, a competent economic recovery program need not be a long, drawn-out agony for most of the population. Reform in Russia needed to bring improvement, and with a different program this would have been feasible.

In the social sphere, the first priority for the government should have been to reassure the nation that while the dimensions of the welfare state would have to be somewhat reduced, they would definitely be maintained at a humane level. More specifically, this approach would apply to the national health system and the education system. At the same time, the government would strongly encourage the development of civil society, assist it, work with it, but also allow it the maximum of freedom from government control.

In the economy, the government would play an important but gradually declining role. Indicative planning would be based on a perspective of twenty to thirty years. Government would be the main shaper of economic policy. With foreign assistance, it would participate in the gradual building of the infrastructure needed for a market economy and would sell off most of the state's assets over a long period of time—for example, as the British government has done over the past two decades. It would also provide the above-mentioned social-safety net. Revenues would come mainly from the profits of Russia's lucrative raw material industries—most of which would remain nationalized for some time—and from taxes and tariffs, which would mostly be kept low to stimulate the private sector's development and competitiveness. Over time, the sale of state assets would bring in substantial additional revenue (much more than came in from the knockdown prices charged during the privatization that has been carried out since 1994). Also, for a strictly limited period, support for the currency stabilization should come from foreign governments, somewhat on the pattern of the Marshall Plan.

Protectionism would be virtually banned regarding trade with communist and former communist countries (that is, with Russia's traditional trading partners), but would play a somewhat greater role regarding advanced industrial countries. Levels of protectionism would be steadily reduced over time. The export of capital would be severely restricted to the extent possible—as it was by West European governments during the Marshall Plan. Monopolies would be broken up (except those such as gas and electricity), with the government helping the private sector to compete against state-owned corporations.

On matters of direct importance to citizens, prices would be made economically more realistic and steadily freed over time as market prices became more bearable to consumers. Apartments would be privatized at little or no cost to their occupants—as the Yeltsin administration has done—but without the concomitant imposition of unreasonably high levels of property taxes and direct payments to bureaucrats. Central, regional, and city governments would provide incentives through a regulated commercial banking system for individuals to use their savings and obtain loans for setting up small businesses, cooperatives, smallholdings, and farms. At first, limits would be placed on buying and selling land to make it easier for peasants to acquire their own holdings. With foreign assistance, courses to train individuals in the skills needed to run small businesses of all kinds would be conducted throughout Russia.[108] These courses would also assist workers laid off from loss-making and overstaffed industries like mining—industries that would steadily be reduced in size and eventually sold off to the private sector. Additional surplus labor would be used for public works projects, such as new roads and other needed infrastructure.

Such are the ideas in programmatic form that, ideally, should have been adopetd in 1991. We shall now discuss some of our themes more discursively.

There is a growing school of thought that favors a more activist role for the Russian government in the area of industrial policy. Yavlinsky, the economist and the leader of Yabloko, has often advocated that "the government should play an active role in determining priority industries and shaping future industrial structure."[109] An industrial policy for Russia can count on a series of important assets that the nation, at least for the moment, continues to hold. The greatest of these assets is Russia's human capital, as expressed in the high levels of education and training that still prevail. Russia also enjoys an enviable geographic position, linking the two greatest concentrations of the world's population in Europe and Asia. It is therefore an obvious candidate for infrastructural development on a massive scale. Russia also still possesses a formidable, if eroding, industrial capacity. A Russian development strategy should use these assets.

A central point in any reconstruction program is the capacity of the national government to channel credit for productive investment and working capital into areas that require revival and renewal. With the credit conditions that prevail in Russia, development credits that are specifically subsidized by the government often represent the only way to finance outlays for new plant and equipment. Such subsidized credits could have low interest rates and long repayment schedules, as required by specific development priorities. However, the refinance rate paid by the Russian Central Bank during 1995 averaged some 180 percent, setting a real interest rate that was far too high to permit productive investment by firms that had to pay even higher interest rates than the Central Bank did. In 1998, the refinance rate peaked at 150 percent. Because of chronic inflation, Russian bank loans tend to have very short repayment schedules, often a maximum of three months. Under these circumstances, it is not surprising that new investment in Russia's productive capacities remains severely depressed. As Keith Bush acknowledged in 1999, "The most disturbing factors in respect to growth prospects are that most industrial plant, equipment, and infrastructure are obsolete or obsolescent, and that investment has dropped faster than output and continues to fall."[110]

Thus the recovery of Russia's depressed economy requires the urgent restarting of productive investment. The private sector has been given an opportunity to tackle this problem, but since it has not done so, government intervention is the only remaining alternative. Further encouragement can be provided through tax incentives in the form of enterprise zones or investment tax credits. Some of these loans would be devoted to the conversion of military industries. Although much redirection of military capacity into civilian production is clearly necessary, this needs to be done in such a way as to maintain the integrity of high-technology networks and assembly lines that need to be preserved so their skilled employees can be retrained and reassigned. Credit is also required for the modernization of the energy sector, particularly oil and mining. This modernization should be done in the framework of redirecting more crude oil and minerals toward high-value-added domestic processing, rather than using them preponderantly for export, as is the case at present.

The upgrading and modernizing of infrastructure could be financed with such subsidized credits. In the areas of "soft" (or human) infrastructure, Russia could make a priority commitment to preserving the quality of its educational system, particularly in science and mathematics. This system could be declared a vital national asset and, as such, receive strong governmental support for the jobs and salaries of teachers and professors, as well as for the maintenance of physical plant, laboratories, and libraries—from the Russian Academy of Sciences in Moscow and St. Petersburg down to the last village schoolhouse in Siberia. Housing is another area for urgent intervention. A shortage of apartments was recognized as a key factor inhibiting the formation and maintenance of families, thus contributing to the demographic decline during the Soviet era. The housing crisis has now been exacerbated in many areas by the repatriation and demobilization of numerous units of the Soviet army. The need to address the housing crisis is stressed by three Russian economists, who also note that,

> housing construction, as an anticrisis locomotive, will pull along a train of related manufactures: construction materials, machinery, lumber, furniture, sanitation equipment, electrical appliances, household equipment, and other durable goods. All that opens wide prospects for industry. . . . A considerable part of this production could be done at converted enterprises of the industrial-military complex. This would provide for its most efficient restructuring, under market conditions.[111]

These specific measures would be possible only in the context of the Russian government's recognition that the laissez-faire approach to economic development has now been attempted and found wanting. What is now needed is a government partnership with private contractors, with the government setting the goals of general welfare and providing the credit, and the private sector furnishing know-how and labor. For this to happen, the Russian government must have a development strategy in the form of an economic recovery program. As Millar writes,

> The government must place a bet on certain existing industries and develop them for domestic and/or export purposes. They will not develop spontaneously, as the current policy presupposes. The Marshall Plan differed from shock therapy precisely because it focused on production and international economic integration as well as on stabilization. It put the burden of organizing investment, production, and distribution on the shoulders of the potential beneficiaries, and it discouraged a mercantilist or beggar-thy-neighbor approach by beneficiaries.[112]

The state should re-enter the economic arena with tools such as indicative planning, subsidized credits, tax incentives for productive investment, effective labor standards (including a real minimum wage), exchange controls, measures to impede capital flight, and increased regulation of the economy. Such are the components of a comprehensive economic recovery program the likes of which many Russian economists and policymakers have only read about—if even that. But as one observer correctly asserts, "successful reform will require a degree of state intervention that most reformers neither contemplate nor comprehend."[113]

Critics may object that our guidelines give too prominent a role to the state and the government, which were excessively powerful under communism and needed to be cut down to size in 1991. As we have indicated, much cutting was certainly required, and this was bound to be politically very difficult. Yet shock therapy as it was implemented in Russia did not cut the number of bureaucratic sinecures inherited from the Soviet era; rather, according to some estimates, it increased the number. More to the point, we believe that the combination of a president elected in June 1991 and new parliaments elected at central and regional levels in late 1991, plus a commitment from Yeltsin and other leaders to reduce the role of government over time, would have made a stronger governmental role in the shorter term acceptable to most Russians. After all, under communism Russians had no experience of taking extensive responsibility for their own lives, and it was not reasonable to expect them to change their psychology and way of life almost overnight. The West Europeans, with long traditions of self-reliance, wanted strong states after World War II and have only gradually reduced the power of their governments over the past three decades.

Some have argued that the Russian state was already so weak that it had no choice but to withdraw from the economy by pursuing a laissez-faire policy. But can we really speak of a collapse of the Russian state at the end of 1991? Government institutions had definitely been weakened by the power struggle between Gorbachev and Yeltsin, but there was one major institution that retained enormous power: the Russian presidency, or, more precisely, Yeltsin himself. The Russian president enjoyed an extremely high level of legitimacy and personal loyalty across most of the political spectrum, as well as grassroots public support. He did have to face resistance and sabotage by some layers of the bureaucracy and the economic elite, but he possessed extensive resources for this struggle. The greatest of his resources was the mass democratic movement of the Russian middle class (whose structural core, linking the movement to the government, despite all its evident weaknesses, was Democratic Russia).

The formation of "civic committees" had been proposed earlier by the radical wing of Democratic Russia, specifically by Leonid Batkin and Yuri Burtin, right after the August coup. As we discuss further in chapter 6, their purpose was to promote economic reform at the grassroots level, secure a fair distribution of state property in the privatization process, expose the excesses of the nomenklatura and the Mafiya, and serve as watchdogs for the proper execution of central government decisions at the regional and local levels. However, the Gaidar team felt no need for dialogue with the public and did not seriously seek public support. Their initial view was that the public was too stupid to understand and accept shock therapy. As even their committed ally, Anders Aslund, admitted, "The prevailing mood was elitist and technocratic, implying considerable contempt for the Russian people as being ignorant and irrelevant."[114]

ALTERNATIVE PERSONNEL CHOICES

So much for alternative policies. What about alternative leaders? In terms of personality as well as substance, the most realistic alternative to the appointment of Gaidar would have been Grigori Yavlinsky. Eloquent testimony to this fact is found in Yeltsin's memoirs, in which he acknowledges that Yavlinsky was "by that time the most popular economist in the country." Yet this encomium also explains why the Yavlinsky candidacy was categorically unacceptable to Yeltsin and his entourage. Yavlinsky's independence and international standing threatened to transform the cabinet into an autonomous center of power.

Against the background of Yavlinsky's personal magnetism, the inflated reputations of such uninspiring courtiers as Burbulis and Shakhrai would have popped like soap bubbles. The potential success of a reform program carrying Yavlinsky's name ultimately could have become a source of political risk for Yeltsin himself, who might have been upstaged by the young reformer.

In addition, Yavlinsky was hurt by his closeness to Gorbachev and by his principled commitment to the preservation of the Soviet economic space. This latter fact can also explain the lack of contact and mutual understanding between Yavlinsky and the leaders of the socially oriented left wing of the democratic movement who were pushing for the dismantling of the USSR.[115] This distance proved to be fatal for the future of Russia's reforms. In this case, short-term political conflicts obscured the fact that it was Yavlinsky's approach, with its emphasis on antimonopoly measures and the creation of a middle class, that best reflected the radical spirit of democratic egalitarianism among the rank-and-file members of the reform movement.

Another potential candidate was Yevgeny Saburov, the Russian economics minister who was Gaidar's predecessor and who drafted the first privatization laws. (Saburov would later become the main economic program writer for Arkady Volsky's Civic Union.) One more candidate from the democratic camp was Svyatoslav Fyodorov, the famous eye surgeon.[116] As the head of his own biotechnology company, he was one of the first successful businessmen in the USSR and had enlightened labor-management ideas, inspired by the American employee stock ownership plan (ESOP) profit-sharing system for workers. However, despite his accomplishments in the corporate world, his ability to chart a course for the Russian economy as a whole remained uncertain. Nonetheless, in hindsight his nomination would have offered a more attractive alternative than Gaidar and his shock therapy.

Yet another candidate mentioned in the press, Yuri Skokov, was Yeltsin's closest confidant and his liaison to the military-industrial complex and intelligence community. Skokov was a quintessential nomenklatura functionary, wholly loyal to Yeltsin personally and favored by Yeltsin on that account. As an apparatchik, though, he led a Byzantine life in trying to avoid publicity, and he became an easy target for a media campaign inspired by Gaidar's backers, who depicted him as a "dark force." Skokov had many shortcomings, but his instincts were those of a statist and dirigiste government official, and this fact might have allowed him to attract a team of economic thinkers capable of elaborating an alternative to shock therapy that Skokov himself could not produce. Later, when named by Yeltsin in April 1992 to be the secretary of the Security Council, he did manage to provide a certain healthy counterweight to the ambitions of the radical reformers. As a result, he became popular with the opposition majority of anti–shock therapy members of parliament and won first place in the December 1992 parliamentary voting for prime minister. However, Yeltsin then proceeded to name Chernomyrdin, even though he had come second. In

March 1993, when Yeltsin made his first unsuccessful attempt to disband the parliament, Skokov refused to go along, would not sign the order declaring a state of emergency, and was soon sacked.

COUNTERING THE REVOLUTION SCARE: SHOCK THERAPISTS' ALLIANCE WITH THE DIRECTORS

By April 1992, it became clear that stabilization had failed, and the situation deteriorated sharply. The statistics indeed were grim: Inflation was headed toward its peak of 2,650 percent. Industrial production was contracting rapidly, headed for a 19 percent fall that year. (This was a decline on the order of magnitude of the Great Depression; for comparison, we recall that during the first full depression year of 1930, the United States lost about 25 percent of its industrial production. Russia was now suddenly in the same ballpark.) Farm production was headed for a 9 percent decline. Russia's gross domestic product was in the process of falling by 14.5 percent that year.

As a result, the government faced two kinds of opposition to its economic policy, one from the radical democratic wing of the parliament and the other from the directors' corps—the managerial class of the state-owned sector lobbying for themselves in the parliament as well as through the government. These factory and company bosses, now free from their dependence on Gosplan and ministerial orders, were important regional and local figures whose collective influence was quite formidable.

Under these circumstances, the government chose to make a series of concessions to the directors, which we look at in more detail in chapter 6. These concessions consisted mostly of state-subsidized loans to industrial and agricultural managers and of personnel appointments, the most important being that of Viktor Chernomyrdin, a long-time administrator of the oil and gas industry, to a vice-premiership.

These personnel changes sealed the alliance between Yeltsin and the old economic elite, and Gaidar was an active participant in every step of the process. A good explanation of Gaidar's motives is given by Aslund, who writes,

> Gaidar harbored a certain fear of populism . . . [and] saw the strong trade unions in Poland as cause for concern. . . . [I]t was argued that the Gaidar team should forge an alliance with progressive "industrialists" and split the managers' ranks. This notion was a confused *mixture of quasi-Marxist class thinking and elitism.* . . . During late 1992 his associates believed Gaidar would accept any compromise to be confirmed as premier.[117]

Aslund apparently sees Gaidar's behavior as a renunciation of some of the basic goals of the reform program and believes the program could be carried out by democratic means with the workers and the Soviet-era middle class as Gaidar's allies. If this is so, he misses the central point: From the beginning, the Gaidar team never intended to conduct reforms by means of public dialogue and was well aware of the undemocratic implications of its own policies.[118] Hence, the compromise with the managerial class was not antithetical to the program of shock therapy but, rather, was a crucial component from the start. It is not by chance that in the first days after Yeltsin's October 1991 speech, Arkady Volsky—the leader of the conservative industrial lobby—fervently endorsed its basic proposals. In a certain sense Volsky, the spokesman of that wing of the managerial class that had gone farthest along the capitalist road to riches, was from the outset a shadow member of Gaidar's government. True, at the beginning of the Gaidar government it would have been impossible to embrace figures like Volsky and Chernomyrdin. The public posture of the Gaidar regime was that of liberal pro-Western reformers. To bring in Volsky would have blown Gaidar's radical cover, because the directors, who constituted the political base of Volsky and Chernomyrdin, were in some ways the most visible face of the old order. Only when the democratic movement had been marginalized as a result of shock therapy could these men become more prominent in or near the government.

Let us also note that during the entire period of the Gaidar "reformist offensive" (from November 1991 to April 1992), Volsky never voiced any strong opposition. His first programmatic speeches and political moves toward the creation of the Civic Union alliance coincided precisely with the first signs of the Gaidar team's loss of momentum, caused by the sharply deteriorating situation and the first massive attacks on shock therapy from the democratic opposition in the parliament and the media. Then, in the spring and summer of 1992, Volsky and the managers backing him seized the initiative from the democrats and presented themselves as the major alternative to the Gaidar team.[119] Thus Volsky's group became the first in a long series of "political insurance policies" for the shock therapists.[120] His quasi-opposition activity had the aim of undercutting the growth of truly radical opposition forces.

It is not hard to see why Volsky's group had a keen interest in the sequence and logic of the reforms that Gaidar chose: price deregulation first, and privatization afterward. Shifting the power to set prices away from the government and into the hands of semigovernmental monopolies, with the resulting hyperinflation and the disappearance of middle-class savings, was a way of sharply narrowing the array of potential contenders for a sizable chunk of state property when privatization finally took place. In the same vein as this "social contract among the elite" was the Chubais privatization program, which in practice was so conservative that it practically ruled out any replacement of top managers in the course of privatization. It is not by chance that Chubais's June 1992 promotion to be a vice-premier at a time when he had a reputation as one of the most radical Gaidarist "reformers" coincided with the industrial lobby's offensive and the appointment of Chernomyrdin as another vice-premier. It is ironic that before too long, Chernomyrdin and Chubais were presented to the Russian public as counterweights to each other. The first was portrayed as conservative and procommunist and the second as a radical Westernizer, even though their personal backgrounds and subsequent behavior showed that they had much more in common than is usually assumed.

Gaidar's reform strategy placed the emphasis on the creation of "privatization coalitions," which, as he later said, had the purpose of integrating into the process "the interests of these social groups and political forces which were capable of blocking it." In his view, it was clear that "optimal economic decisions were practically impossible to achieve. In the long-term view, what is today most socially acceptable and stable should turn out to be the best economically."[121] This was "the essence of the privatization program." Thus speaks Gaidar the conservative politician, who sounds here very much like a Brezhnev-era economic consultant to the CPSU Central Committee.

In December 1992, Gaidar was forced out of office by the opposition, much to Yeltsin's dismay.

THE WEST'S PROMOTION OF SHOCK THERAPY

The degree of the West's involvement in the tragic failure of the Russian reform effort is a sore point in debates on both sides of the Atlantic. In Russia, the exaggerated hopes of the ruling elite that massive Western subsidies would ensure its own political survival have been replaced on occasion by its demonization of the West. This sentiment reflects not so much the growth of national self-awareness among the nomenklatura's ranks as its desire to shift the lion's share of the moral responsibility for what has happened onto foreigners. On the other hand, in the United States, the increasingly numerous critics of Yeltsin's regime have sometimes dodged the issue of U.S. involvement in the shaping and execution of shock therapy. Surprisingly, some of those who manage to give an objective assessment of the criminal and inhuman features of today's Russian capitalism suggest that the required medicine is an even harsher application of the basic tenets of the Washington Consensus.

On January 9, 1997, in his address to leading Russian and American businessmen and Russian government officials at a conference held at Harvard, Deputy Secretary of the Treasury Lawrence Summers was the first high-level Western official to make some forthright criticisms of the sluggishness of Russian reforms.[122] Having correctly pointed out that "successful transition does not end with the creation of markets," Summers called on the Russian government to do more to create a favorable investment climate—primarily through a revamping of the tax system to ensure fiscal support for the budget—and to combat crime and corruption with greater determination. If, as we assume, these calls were made in good faith, they reflect a lack of understanding of the direct links between corruption, crime, and mass tax evasion, on the one hand, and the path of economic transformation chosen in 1991 by the Yeltsin regime with Western approval on the other. This lack of understanding is typical of many Western economists, but is regrettable in a high government official who decides to offer advice to Russian leaders. Ironically, one of the Russian listeners whom Summers urged to escalate the fight against crime and corruption was Boris Berezovsky —the man alleged by leading Russian and Western media to be closely linked to the criminal world and whose membership in Yeltsin's conclave of Russian oligarchs was undoubtedly a major obstacle to any serious fight against economic crime.[123]

A full analysis of the Western role in the Russian tragedy would require many volumes of research. In this book, we limit ourselves to some brief observations. In chapter 4, we examined why the G-7 leaders, notably President Bush and Chancellor Kohl, in 1991 rejected both Gorbachev's conservative reform package and the radical "Grand Bargain" of Allison and Yavlinsky. The key reasons were that the United States was mired in a deep economic recession and a vulnerable Bush was approaching the 1992 presidential election with a second liability: the charge that his excessive concentration on foreign policy was preventing him from seriously addressing the domestic economy. Also significant was the fact that West Germany had compensated the USSR very handsomely in cash for allowing Germany to be reunited, and the cash had been embezzled. As the Russian deputy finance minister admitted in 1991, "A gigantic sum was received . . . from Germany—64 billion Deutsche marks [about $30 billion]— and it all slipped through our fingers."[124] Seemingly ignorant of the domestic constraints on his Western partners, Yeltsin still thought in April 1992 that "the only hope was the promises of the Group of Seven quickly to grant us large sums of financial aid."[125]

This quote reveals the thinking of a regional secretary whose traditional role was squeezing subsidies out of Communist Party headquarters in Moscow, using the real or imagined threat of social and political disorder as blackmail. Both Gorbachev and Yeltsin became national leaders after many years as regional Party secretaries, and as each got in trouble he turned instinctively to the only available patron, which was now the leaders of the West. Janine Wedel arrived at a similar conclusion when she wrote in a well-received book that for the architects of Russian economic reform, "The communist concept of a planned economy was simply replaced by a capitalist one, in which the Western donor filled the gap left by the Communist Party."[126]

We should note here in passing that one of the leading industrial powers, Japan, was constrained by intellectual objections as well as domestic politics. It therefore had a markedly cautious attitude toward Russian reforms. Although in Russia, Japan's stance was usually seen as narrowly linked to the issue of the Kurile Islands, in reality the views of Japanese experts suggest a serious effort to make an objective critique of Russia's reform program.[127] Shock therapy was so diametrically opposed to the principles on which the postwar Japanese economic miracle was founded (principles discussed earlier in this chapter, such as a high degree of government protectionism, administrative coordination, social responsibility of the elite, and solidarity among different strata of society) that it found little credibility with the Japanese. They found their own postwar model more suitable for economic recovery.

The United States, although content that the G-7 passed the responsibility for stabilizing the Soviet economy (and post-Soviet economies) to the IMF, eventually developed a bilateral aid program for Russia, based on the Freedom Support Act of 1992. Characteristic of this program was the U.S. fixation on specific Russian politicians and elite groups (rather than appealing to broad layers of the population and relying on social solidarity and democratic development). In particular, the partisan U.S. support for the clique of Anatoly Chubais had results that were deeply detrimental to long-term understanding between the United States and Russia. The antidemocratic nature of this support is persuasively demonstrated by Wedel in her book.[128] One of the results is that Chubais, the most tenacious survivor among the various members of Gaidar's team, earned the hatred of the expropriated Soviet middle class, which resented his style and methods. His cold-blooded mode of operation recalled Baltic Germans, such as Biron and Nesselrode, who were brought into the government by the Russian tsars and tsarinas from the mid-eighteenth century onward and became deeply unpopular for their brutal imposition of foreign ways.

Of all the nomenklatura intellectuals who advanced to high government posts, Chubais is the least burdened by any illusions about the democratic character of Russia's reforms. His ostentatious elitism and contempt for what he calls the "lumpens" (subproletarians) and "marginals" who populate Russia are the hallmark of his political style. Given the existing rules of the game, which make lack of moral scruples the key to success, his aggressive self-promotion and outspoken scorn for the weak have endowed him with the aura of someone who will always land on his feet. In 1997, he threatened the Duma with dissolution if it failed to do what he wanted, and he repeatedly declared that the government would pursue its own economic policy, no matter what the Duma said.[129]

THE IMF BEHIND THE SCENES

From the outset, Yeltsin's economic strategy included an explicit acceptance of the conditions imposed by the International Monetary Fund in exchange for financing.[130] In his October 1991 speech, Yeltsin proclaimed, "We turn officially to the IMF, the World Bank, and the European Bank for Reconstruction and Development, and invite them to elaborate detailed plans for cooperation and participation in the economic reforms."[131] By the end of 1991, the USSR was an international economic derelict. In December, it defaulted on its international debt payments, and all foreign credit was cut off. Comecon had formally disbanded on July 1, 1991 and, partly as a result, Russian imports fell by almost half in 1991 from 1990, as traditional trade flows in Eastern Europe declined sharply.

As for the IMF conditionalities, their implications tended to be politically undemocratic and economically counterproductive. The first detailed statement of Russian economic policy issued by the Yeltsin-Gaidar government was addressed not to the Russian people but to the IMF in Washington. This was the "Economic Policy Memorandum" of February 27, 1992.[132] From that point on, Russia was bound by IMF conditions and by the encroachments on national sovereignty that they implied. With this document, as Nelson and Kuzes say, "the Russian government was acknowledging the West's leading role as a participant in Russian reform planning. The Western approach had prevailed in the Kremlin."[133] Because the IMF was recommending fast-track privatizations, the Russian memorandum stressed that the privatization process would be "considerably speeded up." Gaidar's priority was clearly to obtain foreign financial support, not domestic political backing. But even this task was not successfully fulfilled, since what Russia got in early 1992 was IMF conditions in exchange for (at least initially) no money.

The leitmotifs of IMF interventions from 1992 to 1998 were austerity, budget cuts, and deflation, with little regard for the social consequences. If Keynes proposed inflation as a cure for depression, the IMF seemed to prescribe Keynes in reverse, with depression favored as the final cure for inflation. Despite their later criticism of the IMF, Aslund and Sachs shared these priorities. According to Aslund, apart from freeing many prices, Gaidar's chief short-term goal in January 1992 was the "balancing of the consolidated state budget," a singular priority in such a chaotic situation.[134] The Yeltsin government had been enticed by tantalizing promises of IMF largesse that were issued by the Group of Seven. In April 1992, Bush and Kohl promised $24 billion in loans; later, even larger sums were mentioned.

Russia was formally inducted into the IMF on April 27, 1992, but many months would pass before the country had anything to show for it. Membership gave the right to apply for an IMF standby loan, and after difficult negotiations the IMF granted one for $4 billion in early July. However, only a first tranche of $1 billion could be disbursed immediately. Moreover, Russia was forbidden to spend the money, which had to be kept in virtual escrow as a reserve fund. (The World Bank also lent Russia about $600 million.) The IMF position was now a circular one: Russia had to achieve currency stabilization before a stabilization fund (designed to shore up the currency) could be created.

There was a further complication. Russia received $12.5 billion in commodity credits during 1992, even though many experts denied that these were needed. They had to be used to buy farm products from various Western countries, which wanted to sell off their farm surpluses to Russia. The IMF, which had encouraged the credits, now declared that Russia had disqualified itself from receiving a stabilization credit because it already had such large food credits. The IMF also complained that because of the food credits, Russia was running an "enlarged fiscal deficit" equal to 25.3 percent of GDP during the first quarter of 1992, even though the government claimed that it was running a surplus.[135]

There is also some question about what finally happened to the foreign loans Russia received during the second half of 1992. A Russian observer has concluded that "their scale, as well as the total absence of any form of public control over their granting, objectively strengthens the point of view, according to which the reasons for seeking this loan were political and even criminal. It was precisely during this period of unlimited credit expansion that the financial foundations for many of the large Russian banks were laid."[136] Nevertheless, in May 1993, the IMF created a Systemic Transformation Facility for Russia, with the promise that loans could now be given under conditions more lenient than those of a standby agreement.

The IMF also gave support to Yeltsin's autumn 1993 offensive against the Russian parliament. In August, the fund sponsored a conference in Moscow at which IMF officials criticized the budget bill that enjoyed wide support in the Russian parliament because it included a higher budget deficit than the IMF wanted. The officials made it clear that IMF aid for Russia would cease if Yeltsin were to approve deficit spending. In mid-September, the organization warned the Russian government that it would not disburse a promised loan tranche until Russia "returned to the path of economic reform." In other words, the IMF and its closest U.S. associates saw the actions of the Russian parliament as an obstacle to their priorities and policies that had to be circumvented.

In early September, then–Under Secretary of the Treasury Summers told the Senate Foreign Relations Committee, "The battle for economic reform in Russia has now entered a new and critical phase in which many of Russia's accomplishments on the economic front are being put at risk. The momentum for Russian reform must be reinvigorated and intensified to ensure sustained multilateral support."[137] The Russian government got the message. On September 16, Yeltsin brought Gaidar back as first deputy prime minister responsible for the economy. Within a few days, the IMF made clear that, because of the high inflation rate and the allegedly slow pace of overall reform, talks on a new $1.5 billion loan to Russia could not go forward. Speaking off the record, an IMF official stated that his organization "was unhappy with Russia's backtracking on reforms during the summer."[138] On the day after these remarks were printed, Yeltsin went on television to announce that he was dissolving the parliament.

The $1.5 billion IMF loan remained in doubt through the spring of 1994. In mid-April the Chernomyrdin government, acting in the spirit of Prince Potemkin, secured passage through the Duma of a smoke-and-mirrors budget that included a deficit low enough to placate the IMF. Partly because Zhirinovsky had shocked the West by his party's triumph in the December 1993 elections, the IMF was now ready to turn over this modest sum in exchange for Russian promises of lower inflation and reduced budget deficits. By early autumn 1994, the IMF was once again demanding lower inflation, this time pressing the government to set a target of 1 percent per month to be attained by the beginning of 1996. At the IMF annual meeting in Madrid in October 1994, Russia's request for an increased borrowing limit was turned down. But in 1995, in the wake of the $50 billion bailout of Mexico, the IMF became willing to grant somewhat larger loans.

The Yeltsin government, fighting a savage and expensive war in its southern republic of Chechnya, was eager to borrow. The IMF, seemingly indifferent to the inevitable perception that it was financing a major war that ended up with some one hundred thousand people dead, granted a standby loan of $6.8 billion, with repayment at 7 percent and a three-year grace period. The conditions accepted by the Russian government were again deflationary, and they included its promises to reduce inflation to 1 percent per month during the second half of 1995; to bar any Central Bank lending to the government; to liberalize foreign trade and investment in the petroleum industry; and, a secret promise, to have economic policy run by Chubais in 1995.[139] Although the inflation and tariff targets were not attained, the IMF put pressure on the Kremlin by disbursing the loan in a series of monthly tranches, the last coming in February 1996.

However, increased lending brought the opposite of the stability the IMF desired. Earlier, the "Black Tuesday" crisis of October 1994 in the Moscow interbank market brought the country's entire banking system close to a meltdown. Now, in January 1996, the Central Bank spent $1.7 billion of its hard currency reserves in a futile defense of the ruble, which had come under heavy speculative attack. Over the next three months, the ruble lost about a quarter of its value. At this point, the IMF offered yet another loan, this time with the transparent political goal of saving Yeltsin from looming defeat in the presidential elections. On March 26, 1996, the IMF Executive Board approved an Extended Fund Facility of $10.1 billion to be paid out over three years. Now the conditions included the reduction of the budget deficit to 3.85 percent of GDP during 1996, the reduction of inflation to 1 percent per month by the end of 1996, more privatization, more rigorous tax collection, the abolition of export tariffs on gas and oil, and the abolition of Gazprom's tax-free stabilization fund.

Reportedly, there were also secret conditions on the new loan, one of which was the return of Chubais to the administration soon after the June presidential election. Yeltsin brought Chubais back, but on July 22, 1996, the IMF claimed that important data on the economy were being withheld from its team in Moscow and announced that the scheduled July disbursement of $330 million would be delayed accordingly. The IMF said it was willing to live with a budget deficit of 5.25 percent of GDP, but still delayed the August, October, November, and December tranches, citing low revenue receipts, the persistence of protective tariffs, and restrictions on Treasury bill purchases by foreign investors.

During 1997, disbursements returned to the normal schedule for a time, but by autumn the IMF once again resorted to withholding, this time delaying a $700 million installment with the demand that Russian authorities stop accepting tax payments in kind and accept only cash. By this time, Russia was thoroughly addicted to loans and was groaning under its debt service payments.

Despite the attempts of Chubais, Chernomyrdin, and Western managers of Russian mutual funds in fall 1997 to popularize the notion that Russia had turned the corner, the country's prospects remained grim. In addition to the domestic problems, there were now the uncertainties deriving from the volatility of global financial markets, to which the country was now fully exposed. After the Russian stock market had risen 150 percent during the first nine months of 1997, Asian financial turbulence reached a crescendo with the Hong Kong crisis of October 1997, which gave world stock markets their biggest shock in many years. The Asian jitters helped undermine prices for Russian shares: The Russian Trading System index peaked on October 6 with a close of 571.6, but by mid-November it had declined by about a third. If a crisis in Hong Kong could cause a fall of this magnitude, what might be the fallout from possible negative events in South Korea, Brazil, or Japan? The best Chubais could manage was a lame pledge: "I think that we will be able to survive November and December, which are going to be difficult months."[140] Here was the pathos of a hand-to-mouth existence.

Because of the limited cash the U.S. government intended to commit to supporting Russian reforms, Washington generally treated aid for Russia as a multilateral task to be shared by the G-7, the Organization for Economic Cooperation and Development, the IMF, and the World Bank. Thus the United States could minimize both its financial outlays for Russia and its responsibility for the impact of the reforms. However, this policy was punctuated by fitful interludes of intense preoccupation with Russian events, triggered by sudden deteriorations in economic and, above all, political conditions. In March 1993, the Clinton administration was suddenly alarmed that Yeltsin might lose power as a result of the spring referendum on serious political and economic issues. Secretary of the Treasury Lloyd Bentsen warned the IMF that it was not feasible to treat Russia like a banana republic. But this brief anxiety apparently did not influence the IMF and did not lead to a change of policy. In December 1993, the sudden ascendancy of Zhirinovsky after the elections for the State Duma once again attracted Washington's concern. Clinton's friend and adviser on Russian affairs, Strobe Talbott, number two at the State Department, announced that the United States wanted "less shock and more therapy for the Russian people." But soon Washington's worries quieted down, and the IMF continued on its implacable course.

One of the reasons Yeltsin submitted to the IMF's demands was that the organization's seal of approval is regarded as a necessary precondition for attracting foreign investment and loans. From the beginning of shock therapy, there was a general expectation that Western investments would be forthcoming and that they would play a key role in revitalizing the economy. But such investments have not been made. As of 1996, foreign investment represented 2.7 percent of total investment in the Russian economy. In 1997, 70 percent of foreign investment was concentrated in Moscow. Only 28 percent of all foreign investment during the first half of 1996 was direct investment, a figure repeated in 1998.[141] Even the Communist rulers of Vietnam have a much better track record than the Yeltsin team when it came to attracting foreign investors: By 1996, foreigners had committed $8 billion in direct investment to Vietnam, compared with just $2 billion to Russia. By the end of 1998, the Russian figure had risen to about $9 billion. Even in the good year of 1997, Russia had the lowest foreign direct investment of all the former Soviet republics in the Commonwealth of Independent States (CIS) when measured in relation to GDP—that is, 0.8 percent.[142]

The IMF's official interventions in Russian affairs are controversial enough. However, in addition to these, persistent reports suggest even more far-reaching IMF and U.S. control over the Russian economy than is admitted in public. The Spanish newspaper *El Pais* reported that, while working as an advisor to the Russian government, Jeffrey Sachs personally edited Yeltsin's decrees.[143] A U.S.-funded institute and the young American lawyer Jonathan Hay drafted numerous Russian laws and regulations.[144] Summers, who had now risen to deputy secretary of the U.S. Treasury, sent Chubais letters virtually instructing him on how to conduct Russia's economic policy, causing great consternation about Russia's humiliation and loss of sovereignty.[145] Such sentiment deepened, first when similar letters to Prime Minister Chernomyrdin from the heads of the IMF and the World Bank were leaked to the media and published verbatim, and second, when a leaked government report to the IMF showed signs of having been drafted by the IMF's Moscow office and then meekly signed by Prime Minister Sergei Kirienko.[146] Also, former minister Boris Fyodorov stated that an article contributed by Prime Minister Chernomyrdin to the *Financial Times* was actually drafted at IMF headquarters.[147]

Actions of this sort were generated and facilitated by special organizations set up in Moscow by Americans using U.S. aid money; the organizations were largely staffed by Russians. As a political anthropologist, Wedel analyzes these hybrid entities and makes the disturbing conclusion that they "had a chameleon-like quality: They were situated somewhere in the twilight zone between state and private, between the Russian government and Western donors, and between Western and Russian allegiance and orientation. They were sometimes private, sometimes state, sometimes pro-Western, sometimes pro-Russian."[148] They were also an ethical swamp, especially when some of the foreigners, who had a certain influence on Russian financial policy, started investing in stocks and government bonds, which yielded up to 200 percent annually.[149]

Such close Western involvement in Russia's economic reform has certainly contributed to the current anti-Western and anti-American sentiment in the

Russian populace, partly as a spontaneous reaction to Western actions and to economic hardship, and partly as a result of manipulations of public opinion by the nomenklatura, who are understandably anxious to pass the buck for the country's economic failure.

SHOCK THERAPY AND ITS DENIALS

However, passing the buck became more difficult in early 1999. A few shock therapists in Russia and the West began to recant, most of them partially and grudgingly, but in two cases quite radically. Pyotr Aven was a Gaidar adherent and the minister of foreign economic relations in 1991–92. He left the government along with Gaidar, worked in Gaidar's institute, then in 1994 became president of Alfa Bank. In January 1999, soon after Russia's 1998 financial collapse had seen the last of his former colleagues leave the Kremlin, Aven (with unclear motives) made a root-and-branch critique of himself and them. He scathingly lambasted the reformers' personalities and personal principles, their dishonesty, their betrayals of liberalism, their large-scale expropriations of the Russian people's savings, their major contribution to the emasculation of the state, and their failure to build a rule of law. He also indicted the role of the IMF.

Here is what Aven says about the personalities of the Gaidar-Chubais team: "Their identification of themselves with God, which flowed naturally from their belief in their all-round superiority, was, unfortunately, typical of our reformers." He also notes something that characterized Lenin and the Bolsheviks, namely that "many of the reformers combined in a remarkable way a love of mankind with an absence of love and respect for individual people." Thus the mission of carrying out "liberal reforms" fell to those

> who were actually far from liberalism: superior, self-confident, with no respect for other people's opinions, . . . people who arrogated to themselves the right to make up stories and lies. Lies about achievements, including about issues the reformers themselves considered important. . . . The hostility to criticism meshes with another fundamental characteristic of our reformers—their absolute inability to admit it when they make a mistake. They are right always and in everything, even if the negative result is obvious to everyone.

Aven then addresses the issue of overall competence:

> A weak understanding of life's realities quickly showed, of course, making the reformers seem like the economic leaders of the last phase of the USSR. . . . Thus, in contrast to a widespread view, we did not have a financial stabilization. . . . We did not have a strict monetary policy. . . . We had an irresponsible and professionally incompetent policy of supporting the ruble by using up the foreign currency reserves of the Central Bank. . . . We did not have the respect for private property that is crucial for a liberal economy. If we had, there would have been no confiscation of the population's savings in 1992, or of the capital of the banks in 1998.

Regarding Chubais's loans-for-shares scheme of 1995, which was a bonanza for the oligarchs, Aven says, "The behind-the-scenes distribution of the most attractive pieces of state property (on the basis of state goals that were not clear) was a mockery of liberalism."

The future, Aven concludes, looks bleak. "It is a long time since the Russian state was so weak. It has weakened under the flag of liberal reforms. And in large measure because 'liberal democrats' struck an extremely strong (though not the first) blow at the Soviet state machine, which was exceptionally well coordinated and effective (for achieving 'its own' goals)." As a result, "The level of competency of today's officials and their organizations cannot be compared with what we had before the reforms." As for his own future, Aven states, "I'd like to see Russia become great again. But I fear that unless a strong state and a free economy appear in the next few years, and. . . the last elements of our scientific and technological potential are saved from destruction, and a new—and this time fatal—wave of emigration is avoided, I won't live long enough."

Finally, Aven does not spare the IMF, with which he earlier dealt as a minister. In his view, "The maniacal obsession of the IMF with budgetary and monetary policy, and its absolutely superficial and formal attitude to everything else, . . . played not a small role in what happened."[150]

Later, Konstantin Kagalovsky, another "young reformer" who during 1992–95 was Russia's representative at the IMF before joining Menatep Bank and then the oil company Yukos, recanted in similar vein. "In 1991 and into 1992," he said, "we were still in our romantic period." Some of the Gaidarists' views were "childish, it seems now. . . . After the 1996 elections, things changed fundamentally." What Chubais did to get Yeltsin re-elected was to say, "'The aim is good—anything goes.' Everyone closed their eyes." On reflection, Kagalovsky says, "We now see such simple truths: that . . . the end does not justify the means. After 1996, corruption . . . went to the core of the new Russian state."

Finally, Kagalovsky expressed a thought by way of conclusion, with which we can only agree : "If the Communists had won in 1996, I'm not sure we would be in a worse situation than now."[151]

It is instructive to compare the self-critical reflections of Kagalovsky and Aven with the confused musings of the most Bolshevik-minded of all the "reformers," Anatoly Chubais. In an interview with a sympathetic journalist, Chubais combines strong self-justification and his characteristic refusal to apologize for anything or admit mistakes with an admission that post-Soviet Russian culture did create some special problems. These, he said, resembled the frustrations met by Count Witte when he tried to modernize Russia a century earlier. Chubais also hints that he wanted but was not able to use authoritarian methods to reform the economy. He advances some rather tortured arguments about how the democratically elected legislature stopped him from implementing economic reforms.

"In Russia," Chubais says,

> basic human values—freedom, private property, the rule of law—are regarded in a more ambiguous way than in Holland or Great Britain. . . . With us, in the Slavic countries, reform is a tougher proposition. . . . It's completely clear that democracy in Russia played a very malicious joke on the process not just of economic, but also of political reform. . . . Legislative organs were elected at all levels. After which, these elected organs consistently, determinedly, often maliciously fought against democracy and the reforms. . . . The reformist president forms an executive power that's in opposition to the representative power. . . . This means that the creation of a legislative basis for moving forward is impossible. In this sense, authoritarian rule, or . . . "a strong hand plus the market," is undoubtedly technically much more attractive. In that way, one could move forward more simply, with fewer losses, in ways less painful to society. But life is how it is.[152]

This "lament of an authoritarian" is revealing. The elected president and the executive, but not the elected parliament, represent "democracy"; Chubais, not the parliament, knows what sort of reforms Russia needs at this stage; and Chubais knows that his own authoritarianism—if only he could find some way of imposing it on the benighted Russian people—would definitely be less painful to them than the present system. He has done the math, we are tempted to surmise, and knows for certain that his policies would succeed and bring prosperity for all, and that in the process he would have to dispose of a smaller number of oppositionists than the number of people currently dying premature deaths from stagnation-induced poverty. Quod erat demonstrandum. Theorem proved!

By comparison with Russia's ex-reformers Aven and Kagalovsky, the U.S. government has so far done no reappraisal, at least in public, of its eight-year position that the Washington Consensus and the Russian "reformers" were just what Russia needed. In a series of similar speeches in the fall of 1998, Secretary of State Madeleine Albright, Deputy Secretary of State Strobe Talbott, and Deputy Treasury Secretary Lawrence Summers held that Russia's reformers—and the self-evidently correct policies of the G-7 and the IMF—had unfortunately been defeated by oligarchs, crony capitalists, and a "retrograde" parliament.[153] In other words, Russia's August 1998 financial collapse was wholly the fault of the Russians, not of anyone one else.

Later, however, as critiques of the West's role multiplied, Summers's deputy David Lipton, who had recently left the government, partially and grudgingly recanted. While basically singing his former boss's song, he nonetheless admitted that although Russian privatization was a great achievement, it "did give too much to insiders." More important, he said of U.S. policy, "It wasn't going to be a sure thing, whatever we did. The key thing was the Russians themselves—the lack of people who knew what to do, the absence of a consensus on a Russian national identity. Poland wanted to be in Europe. Russia had no such consensus."[154]

Here again, as with Kagalovsky and Chubais, the heretical idea creeps in that culture and Russian identity were relevant factors in the perversion of the reforms—an idea always denounced by shock therapists like Aslund. In his 1995 book, for example, Aslund uses a whole page to mock such "populist and socialist critiques." Among these is the view that, for cultural reasons, the Polish experience in 1990–91 was not a relevant guide for Russia. He also derides Nikolai Petrakov's group for believing in 1992 that "our situation is special. It cannot be described by general rules"—a position that, seven years later, the likes of Lipton, Kagalovsky, and Chubais find intriguing or even persuasive. This is how Aslund, in his characteristic tone, summed up his polemic: "The purported uniqueness of Russia was typically presented as the ultimate argument for why normal reasoning did not apply to Russia."[155] Four years later, Aslund was just as sure of himself, holding that the 1998 collapse occurred because the West did not help enough at the right time; the reforms "were too slow and partial"; corrupt businessmen, politicians, and officials conspired against them; and "reformers never had enough power to overrule these avaricious interests."[156] Aslund's article contained no word about culture, no hint of self-criticism, not even a few doubts like those of his hero Chubais.[157]

Finally, we turn to the international institutions, particularly to the financial ones.[158] To date, they have a highly uneven record regarding a frank reappraisal of their role in Russia's collapse. The IMF held an international seminar in November 1998, at which it invited both its supporters and its critics (including one of the authors) to discuss the subject, but it asked participants not to report the substance of the event (except for their own speeches) to the media.[159] Separately, the IMF's number two official, Stanley Fischer, gave a briefing in which he justified the organization's policies, called the collapse only a bump (if a "rather large" one) on the road of IMF-Russia relations, and criticized some of the economy's weaknesses that had contributed to it. He also said, "I am often asked if it was a mistake to move Russia so quickly toward a market economy. I do not believe this strategy was wrong, although there were problems in its implementation, particularly from a structural viewpoint. Specifically, we needed to reduce aggregate government spending."[160]

Here the pronoun "we" is worth noting. It is characteristic of the language sometimes used in the Russian context by officials like Fischer, Summers, and Talbott.[161] In our view, it betrays an unhealthy degree of involvement in the internal affairs of another country and indicates a mindset in which "we" (that is, the IMF or the U.S. government) are "reducing the aggregate spending of the Russian government," to take Fischer's case—something that clearly should be a sovereign decision of the Russians. It was this sort of language that contributed greatly to the public consternation in Russia when letters by Summers and the heads of the IMF and the World Bank were leaked and published in the Russian press.

After a time, other IMF (and also World Bank) officials were ready to go further than Fischer, but only on an anonymous basis. Some of them told of "the anguish they felt when money disappeared and public silk purses had to be made out of private sows' ears." They also knew that the G-7 had been afraid that communism might make a comeback in Russia and had pressed the IMF to lend against its better judgment. Said one official, "The IMF should have shown more guts in resisting political pressure. The big mistake was not realizing soon enough that the reformers lacked the levers of power to do what they had agreed, and to keep on lending. We should have been tougher."[162]

Certainly, these anonymous officials had taken heart from the one major rebellion in their ranks, that of the World Bank's chief economist, Joseph Stiglitz. First in a short article, then in a major paper for a World Bank conference in April 1999, and then in a media interview, Stiglitz escalated his fundamental critique of the Washington Consensus and especially of how it was applied in Russia. In the interview, Stiglitz assailed two of the biggest names involved: "Sachs and Summers were right," he declared,

> when they said that you can't live with hyperinflation—though even the fight against inflation can be taken too far. But those who thought that macroeconomic changes alone were sufficient were wrong. And those who put privatization above all else were clearly wrong. Summers and Sachs and others thought that you had to pursue privatization, and infrastructural change would follow. They thought that the new owners of private property would demand that this happen. But instead they took their money out.[163]

In his article, Stiglitz developed the same argument in a slightly different way: "A huge increase in inequality" occurred during the 1990s, as "living standards collapsed." "All too late, it was recognized that without the right institutional infrastructure, the profit motive—combined with full capital market liberalization—could fail to provide incentives for wealth creation, and could, instead, spark a drive to strip assets and ship wealth abroad."[164]

In his heavily documented paper, which addresses mostly the Russian collapse, Stiglitz analyzes the major issues involved and criticizes, directly or indirectly, some obvious targets and also Shleifer and Vishny, and Parker and Layard.[165] Only a few of the issues can be mentioned here, but Stiglitz emphasizes from the start the enormity of the problem when he points out that in the past decade, China's GDP has nearly doubled, while Russia's has almost halved. Especially important, in Stiglitz's view, "the level of gross fixed investment . . . has fallen dramatically" in Russia. In the same period, social inequality has almost doubled, and the number of people living in poverty (defined as having income of $4 a day or less) rose from two million in 1989 to sixty million by 1995—the latter figure amounting to 40 percent of the population.[166]

Why the failures? This is Stiglitz's central question, and he argues that the causes lie much deeper than the answers to such queries as how much the IMF's prescriptions were or were not followed. Rather, he believes, the causes of the policies' failures lie in their authors' "misunderstanding of the very foundations of a market economy, as well as a failure to grasp the fundamentals of reform processes." Another problem was that "many of the political forecasts of those involved in the reform process were far from clairvoyant: Many worries seem, by and large, not to have materialized, while political developments which should have been of concern were not anticipated." Also, reform recommendations were made without regard to how likely they were to be implemented—in the tangible political, economic, and cultural circumstances. In an apparent criticism of irresponsibility on the part of Sachs, Aslund, and others, Stiglitz admonishes the advisers that they should not just hope for the best about such critical questions; they should ponder them carefully before deciding whether or not to make the recommendations in the first place.

On the massive problem of capital flight, Stiglitz makes the critical point that "the 'reform' advisers facilitated this process by encouraging—in some cases even insisting on—the opening of capital accounts. Thus the failure of privatization to provide the basis of a market economy was not an accident, but a predictable consequence of the manner in which privatization occurred."[167] He reinforces this conclusion by referring to a paper that "argues forcefully that the closed capital accounts in China played a critical role in [China's] success, not only enabling the financial system to provide a major source of income for the government (which it could not have done with full openness), but also in limiting the incentives and scope for asset stripping."[168]

Stiglitz's rich paper, which emphasizes gradualness, popular welfare, social justice, the priority of institution building, and the need for strong bottom-up elements if reform is to succeed, will surely resonate for some time. We hope the debates it provokes will draw on the unjustly neglected research and writings by "alternative" economists, some of whose work we discussed previously. Our only major reservation about his paper is that it does not discuss the one specific thing that could have provided the main basis on which social justice and strong bottom-up reform could have developed. This would have been a strategic decision by Yeltsin to let the grassroots revolution of 1988–91 proceed further than he and his nomenklatura allies in fact allowed, and thus release many thousands of fresh new people into public life and facilitate some redistribution of assets in favor of ordinary Russians. As we argued earlier, we believe that this course would have brought—along with inevitable social conflict —a healthy and fundamental rejuvenation of public life. With skillful national leadership, such a rejuvenation should not have led to civil war.

Instead, however, Yeltsin pursued policies that weakened the state and alienated ordinary people. In so doing, he created conditions in which criminality was sure to flourish.

THE CRIMINAL REVOLUTION

The Mafiya and organized crime have been tolerated by Russia's government because they have functioned as safety valves to divert energy that otherwise might have been expressed as political protest. In this context, David Hoffman writes about "the deepening and corrosive threat to Russia's young democracy and free-market economy: the breakdown of law enforcement and the proliferation of private armies and protection rackets prone to ruthless gangland tactics. . . . In practice, there is a growing sense that Russian police have all but given up trying to protect property and capital." He quotes Olga Kryshtanovskaya, one of Russia's leading social analysts: "The state thinks that private capital should be defended by those who have it. It's a completely conscious policy of the law enforcement authorities to remove themselves from defending private capital."[169]

In fact, the Russian government has had a dual policy with respect to crime and the wealthy. On the one hand, energy that might otherwise be expressed in political protest needs to be channeled into crime, while on the other hand, the capitalists are allowed to maintain their private security armies. As a result, the "security business" has become the only form of employment for thousands of young people who have no chance to fulfill themselves in productive, creative jobs. The legalization and in certain ways the encouragement of criminal gangs on the part of the architects of Russian capitalism have turned out to be the real "Grand Bargain" that ensured loyalty to the Yeltsin regime of the first generation of Russians in seventy years to be denied free universal public education. Any systematic attempt to fight organized crime among youth and to disband private security armies—both desirable goals—may have the perverse side effect of denying many young Russians their only means of survival and their source of social status. In this case, the hatred and aggression of a defrauded generation would inevitably turn against the regime. As early as 1994, a reflective, out-of-office Gaidar could focus on the profound threat posed by the Mafiya, concluding that, "The top priority job for the state today is to tackle . . . the Mafiya, which in many ways shapes the economic development of the country, and negates the invisible hand of the market."[170]

The main reason this "priority job" has still not been tackled is cogently explained by Yuri Boldyrev. In 1992–93, Boldyrev was chief state inspector in the Presidential Administration—Yeltsin's chief corruption fighter. He took the job seriously but soon found that the president would not support him. In March 1993, Yeltsin fired him from his post "in connection with its abolition." In Boldyrev's view, Yeltsin's economic policies by that time had incurred such a loss of public support for him that he had to turn to the state bureaucracy and make it his main political base. Since much of the bureaucracy had by now been corrupted, he could not afford to combat corruption. If he did, he would have immediately alienated his prime political constituency. As Boldyrev put it, the bureaucracy was "simply blackmailing [Yeltsin], forcing him to shut his eyes to certain of their activities—in return for their giving him their political support." Boldyrev then arrives at the logical conclusion: "If you let officials indulge themselves in corruption, then you don't control them any more:

They'll tolerate you for exactly as long as you let them go on getting fat. The longer it all lasts, the more they'll demand. And as soon as you try to take even one step in the direction of limiting their appetites, they'll simply remove you."[171]

This insight goes a long way toward explaining why, many years later, still not a single senior politician, bureaucrat, businessman, or member of the "power ministries" has been arrested, sentenced, and jailed in Russia. Meanwhile, all the charges aired in the media since 1991 suggest that in fact several thousand such figures warrant serving long, long terms.

The Russian Mafiya has expanded its power on such a scale that it no longer represents a national problem for Russia alone. On October 1, 1997, Federal Bureau of Investigation Director Louis J. Freeh told the House Committee on International Relations that approximately thirty organized-crime syndicates headquartered in Russia were operating in the United States and were active in narcotics trafficking, prostitution, and fraud. In an earlier appearance before Congress, Freeh had spoken of the alarming growth of the Mafiya inside Russia. Now he felt obliged to claim that these groups were powerful enough to threaten the United States.[172]

At about the same time, the Center for Strategic and International Studies published its study of the international threat posed by Russian organized crime. The study emphasized the problem of criminal capital flight from Russia, noting that the country had been "plundered since the Soviet Union imploded, and tens of billions of dollars have been moved to safe havens in offshore banking centers." The study also held that a threat of nuclear attacks on U.S. targets now came from the Russian Mafiya: "Russian organized crime constitutes a direct threat to the national security interests of the United States by fostering instability in a nuclear power."[173]

Shock therapy has thus boomeranged on its American supporters: A policy of economic reform that was sold as a way to enhance U.S. security through the creation of a democratic market economy has now produced a threat that in some crucial respects may become greater than the threat of a nuclear war in the decades of Soviet-American rivalry.

In 1990–92, Russia seemingly made a big leap from socialism to capitalism, from a planned and regulated economy to a system of free markets. Indeed, the majority of Russian companies no longer belong to the state. Almost all prices are no longer set by the state but, rather, by independent economic players. Legal limitations on all kinds of economic activities, including those outlawed in most other countries, have either been abolished or are practically ignored. The role of the state as the supreme arbiter speaking on behalf of the economic interests of the majority of citizens—of the public interest—has been reduced to a negligible minimum, far below what prevails in the advanced capitalist countries. This is unprecedented in the history of Russia, with its powerful cultural tradition of a strong role for the state. Yet even the most incorrigible optimists, in both

West and East, must acknowledge that the treatment applied with unswerving and cold-blooded persistence since 1992 has not led to the healing of the patient. Instead, the Russian economy and society are slowly succumbing to shock therapy's sequelae while the world watches. For the first time in the history of modern civilization, one of the world's major industrial powers has fallen to the level of the poorest European states in less than a decade, retrogressing to a stage of historical development it passed long ago.

Does this mean, as some orthodox communists assert, that the rejection of the planned economy and the transition to capitalism were historical blunders? Our analysis of what has happened renders the issue of "choosing" a socio-economic system almost irrelevant. This proposition is no longer a novelty in today's Russia. Of much greater concern is a different way of framing Russia's condition, espoused by Gaidar. Imitating the cultural determinism of Huntington, he interprets the Russian tragedy in the framework of the East-West divide. Gaidar believes that Russian cultural inferiority is to blame, and that Russians could not have done any better.[174] This is merely a variation on the well-known lament of the "progressive" elite: "The problem is our people." (Arkady Volsky once satirized this idea by saying that the Swedish model is the best for Russia, but the problem is that Russia has too few Swedes.) The revulsion felt by the nomenklatura reformers in regard to the Oriental and "Scythian" nature of the Russian people is the mirror image of the anti-Western xenophobia of some extreme Russian nationalists.

Since 1991, as at the beginning of the twentieth century, Russia has turned out to be "the weakest link in the chain" of the world order—or at least one of the weakest links. It was the Soviet nomenklatura that first became disillusioned by the ideology that brought it to power and inspired its social contract with the people. Aslund's assertion that Russia "became a market economy" thanks to Gaidar's reforms is evidence of an inattentive reading of Soviet history: In a narrow, distorted, and oligarchical sense, Russia had become a market economy long before Yeltsin and Gaidar. But it was only with the advent to power of these two that this nomenklatura-criminal market was legalized in its primordial form. The state, which served as the only remaining counterweight to this market, stepped forward as its de facto ally and defender under shock therapy, making a mockery of Yeltsin's rhetoric about fighting corruption, crime, and nomenklatura abuse.

The appearance of Soviet oligarchs mimicked in chameleon-like fashion the colors of the market, and the liquidation of the Soviet system and the Soviet state without any resistance worth mentioning were so abrupt and successful *because the democratic transformation of society lagged behind the capitalist transformation of the ruling elite.* From the 1960s to the 1980s, the Soviet nomenklatura, while fostering the growth of the shadow market, was at the same time violently suppressing all attempts to create grassroots social and political organizations. However, it could not suppress the *aspirations* of an increasing number of people to create these things. Only from 1986–87 did these aspirations have a chance to become reality.

THE DEMISE OF THE SOVIET MIDDLE CLASS

Cold War critics of the Soviet system pointed out that the USSR had a social structure of the imperial type, with a tiny elite (the nomenklatura) commanding a mass of workers and peasants, and not much in between. But in late Soviet society it turned out that something very important had been emerging in between: This "something" was the Russian middle class: the scientists, teachers, professors, academicians, and intellectuals of the research and education sector.

The Russian middle class of the nineteenth century consisted of independent farmers, small businessmen and shopkeepers, lawyers and doctors, and commercial middlemen. The Russian middle class of the late twentieth century were employees of the government-sponsored education, culture, and research establishment, and thus were largely different in occupation. But their self-conception, sense of personal identity, career aspirations, and way of life were those of a modern middle class. They were often independent, and they resisted repression. Andrei Sakharov, nuclear physicist and political dissident, became their best-known representative to the world. This middle class was not as numerous or as widespread as its counterparts in Western Europe or the United States, but it was an important new presence in Russian history.

The rise of such a middle class in Russia during the latter half of the twentieth century was a remarkable achievement in itself: Orthodox Marxist theory had nothing but contempt for the petty bourgeoisie, the *Kleinbuerger*. Stalin's totalitarian state was everything, and the sphere of the individual was reduced to the simple biological dimensions of the human organism. But the political spokesmen of the Russian middle class advocated respect for the inalienable rights of the individual, secured by a democratic republic with representative government. And they advocated more. In the space between the restored individual and private family life on the one hand and a constitutional state restrained by the rule of law on the other, they wanted to create that sphere of autonomous action inhabited by political parties, businesses, cultural associations, churches, firms, professional societies, neighborhood meetings, clubs, chambers of commerce, trade associations, lobbies, advocacy groups—all separate from the government—that constitute civil society and that are characteristically the self-expression of the middle class. The Russian middle class had always been broadly pro-Western, but by 1990 conditions were ripe for it to lead the entire country in turning away from the Byzantine and autocratic past and embracing the best that the West had to offer. Shock therapy destroyed this moment, and its brutal effects have largely destroyed the best elements of the middle class as well.[175]

IMPLICATIONS FOR THE DEMOCRATS AND DEMOCRACY

Before the beginning of shock therapy, Yeltsin and his associates possessed a number of alternative possibilities for leading Russian society out of its historical impasse. The effect of shock therapy has been to complicate or even to foreclose those alternatives. Alternative economic policies might still be attractive and viable, but not if they are advanced by leaders in the mold of Yeltsin's regime. As the Chinese might say, the regime had lost the mandate of heaven, and no economic policies could hope to succeed until new political leaders could be found who would enjoy the confidence of the Russian people and launch a new political and economic strategy. In other words, a government with much stronger legitimacy was now required before any purely economic recipes for recovery could be successful.

If Yeltsin's regime had been sincere in its occasional brief acknowledgments that strategic mistakes were made in economic policy, its first step would have been some official recognition that the opposition was right to criticize the reform strategy. This would have implied the opening of a dialogue with the opposition, along with a readiness to share power (especially the levers of economic policy) with those leaders of the opposition who have proved to be justified in their critiques, be they Yavlinsky, Sergei Glaziev, Abalkin, Petrakov, or even Tatyana Koryagina. Instead, as we shall see in the following chapters, the ruling regime opted for a strategy based on behind-the-scenes manipulation designed to weaken and fragment the opposition. This strategy acted as a sharp brake on the development of civil society and democratic institutions. In 2000, President Putin applied the brake even more sharply, while at the same time pursuing economic policies that coincided in most, but not all, respects with IMF recipes. The sum of these decisions added up to what the Russians call a "Pinochet strategy." However, there were disturbing indications early on in the new administration that elements in Putin's camp had little faith in the chosen economic program and, at the right moment, would favor a political-economic strategy that was more mobilizational and more repressive, combining the "rationalization" and adjustments of the country's market relations with a fairly systemic crackdown on political dissent.

Neither strategy, of course, would bode well for democracy and Russia's democrats.

6

YELTSIN AND THE OPPOSITION: THE ART OF CO-OPTATION AND MARGINALIZATION 1991–1993

"Democratic Russia" has departed this world.

—Nezavisimaya gazeta, *March 17, 1992*

E
VEN AS DISMAY, especially over shock therapy and Yeltsin's desertion of the movement that brought him to power, moved various parts of the political spectrum into opposition, the regime soon co-opted—in full or in part—most opposition leaders and almost every group that wielded substantial economic power. In early 1993, only the parliamentary majority was still a serious opponent. Before long, though, the Yeltsinites managed to bypass it—through the April referendum of that year and the Constitutional Conference in the summer. In this way, the regime weakened the opposition to the point where Yeltsin felt able to risk a sharp change in his tactics: from co-optation and marginalization to frontal assault, a story told in chapter 7. Meanwhile, everyday Russians, who had already lost their savings to hyperinflation, lost their leaders too. Fighting for economic survival, and with no funds to organize themselves, they were politically marginalized.

This chapter examines the rapid rise of opposition to the Yeltsin regime in 1991–92 and the ways in which the regime moved to co-opt or marginalize it. More particularly, we show how Yeltsin's camp discarded the support of all democrats except those who were ready to do his will obediently. We discuss how the same parliament that in November 1991 had granted him special powers to implement his economic strategy by decree progressively turned against him in 1992, when the strategy went into effect.

We see how Yeltsin turned to corporatism in the spring, in the hope that this would satisfy the country's big employers, keep their workers quiet, and make it possible to ride out the daunting, increasingly nationalistic opposition in parliament. We demonstrate how the factory directors tried to dictate their terms to Yeltsin by allying themselves with this opposition, and how the alliance forced him into numerous concessions.

We tell how Yeltsin fought back by getting parliament's reluctant agreement to the April referendum, which essentially would ask the Russian people which side it liked (or disliked) more—himself or parliament. We hold that the outcome, though more favorable to Yeltsin than the legislature, did not resolve the basic conflicts in the country's young political system.

Finally, we suggest why corporatism did not work, and investigate the reasons that nationalism—contrary to what some expected—not only failed to serve as a unifying banner for the opposition to rally around, but also failed to legitimate Yeltsin's rule in the years from 1993 onward.

Aided and abetted by pliant mass media, the Yeltsin government's myth-making machine continuously spoke of a permanent struggle between the "reformist" government and the "conservative" ("reactionary," "antimarket," "red-brown") opposition—a struggle resembling the eternal Manichaean duel between light and darkness, good and evil. Like any myth, it contains a grain of truth—or, rather, one of several possible versions of the truth. Indeed, opposition to one or another aspect of Yeltsin's policy—and to Yeltsin personally—arose almost from the moment he assumed real power following the August coup. After the

USSR was abolished and the first course of shock therapy began in January 1992, influential groups of parliamentarians and several high-ranking officials in the government (beginning with Vice President Rutskoi)—not to mention numerous parties and movements, unions, and business associations—loudly opposed the policies of the president and the government.

From mid-1992, the majority of the deputies in the Russian parliament, who had given Yeltsin power in 1990, moved toward an open and at times uncompromising opposition to his political and economic course. In March 1993, 617 (out of 1,060) members of the Congress of People's Deputies—only 72 short of the required two-thirds majority—voted to impeach the head of state. A month later, almost half the Russian citizens participating in a nationwide referendum said no to the economic policies of Yeltsin's government. In December 1993, two months after his bloody coup d'état against the parliament, Yeltsin and his associates managed to push through his draft constitution with a bare majority—and this thanks only to the apparently large-scale falsification of the results that we discuss in chapters 7 and 8. At the same time, the pro-Yeltsin and progovernment groups experienced a crushing defeat in the elections for a new parliament—the State Duma, a body that the new constitution did not intend to exercise much real authority.

After two years of smoldering confrontations between the branches of power, public sympathy moved even more clearly to the side of the opposition during the 1995 Duma elections, and the popular approval rating of the regime's leaders—Yeltsin and Chernomyrdin—fell to around 5 percent. In June 1996, 65 percent—and in the second round, 45 percent (or 34 million)—of the Russians who took part in the presidential elections voted against Yeltsin. At the beginning of Yeltsin's second presidential term, people who had traditionally been implacable opponents of his regime and its policies were voted in as governors in a significant number of regions, and the percentage of Russians expressing strong trust in Yeltsin fell to 10 percent.[1] Opinion polls attested to a widespread and steady decline in support for his regime among a large proportion of the Russian people.[2]

However, it was equally apparent that the activities of the anti-Yeltsin opposition—its frequent creation of political organizations; its steady domination of the Congress of People's Deputies, the Supreme Soviet, and then the State Duma; and the strong showing of the main candidates it supported in the first round of the presidential elections in 1996—did not lead to any significant changes in the Kremlin's strategy, despite the government's numerous tactical vacillations and maneuvers. The measure of everything the opposition did in these years was the second round of shock therapy introduced by the government in early 1997. Even more significant was the peaceful accommodation—at times scarcely perceptible to the untrained eye—of the various opposition groups with the government. Individuals who had once presided over antigovernment meetings (Volsky, Travkin, Rybkin, Tuleyev, Aksiuchits) now submissively accepted the positions offered them in various government agencies, and so did entire corporations and political organizations, including the State Duma, whose "opposition" majority approved Chernomyrdin for a new term as prime minister without a murmur in August 1996.

Thus, as far as the declared goals of the opposition were concerned—that is, putting an end to: the plundering of the country, the destruction of its industrial capabilities, the decline in production, the widespread impoverishment of the Russian people and the extreme stratification of wealth, the debasement of governmental authority, and the continued weakening of Russia's international status—the final results of its efforts were, judging by objective criteria, close to zero. Nonetheless, the opposition played a significant if sad role in Russia's tragic fate, a role we can document by using a different set of criteria. In our opinion, it has been the unique nature of the anti-Yeltsin opposition and the story of its moral and ideological decay that in many ways explain why and how the "reform" policies adopted by the Yeltsin regime turned out to be so destructive and long-lasting for Russia, inflicting obvious material and moral damage on the great majority of Russian citizens. Without the presence of this kind of "opposition," no government in the world could have succeeded in putting into effect these kinds of "reforms."

Much evidence points to the fact that the ideology, organizational structure, and composition of the opposition's leadership were shaped by the influence and, in many respects, by the direct actions of the ruling elite.[3] At the same time, the character, convictions, and especially the social and corporate interests of the opposition groups as they evolved in Russia became one of the defining factors in shaping the strategy and tactics of the governing regime. The consequences of this intimate relationship—with each side influencing and penetrating the other—are as paradoxical to the detached observer as they are lamentable for the fate of Russian democracy and civil society. The ruling elite and the opposition elite, regardless of their diametrically opposed slogans and platforms, have been closer, more comprehensible, and more predictable to each other than to the Russian populace. In our view, this is what explains the major enigma of the Yeltsin regime: the absence of any well-planned or coordinated attempts on the part of its many enemies to replace it, despite the steadily deteriorating condition of the country and the development of more than one situation that was potentially revolutionary in character.

THE COLORS AND SHADES IN THE OPPOSITION'S SPECTRUM: A SEARCH FOR THE APPROPRIATE PALETTE

The governing regime and the mass media it controlled attempted from the beginning to portray the relations between the government and the opposition in ideological colors that favored the former. Common labels the media used to characterize the numerically strongest trend in the opposition, the Communists, were the phrases "communist-patriots" or even "communist-fascists." The existence of another, ideologically distinct line of opposition—the so-called "democratic alternative"—was acknowledged by the authorities and the press very unwillingly and only after one of its leading representatives, Grigori Yavlinsky, became the leader of a faction in the State Duma (and, later, a contender for the presidency). Such a grudging acknowledgement came despite the fact that the noncommunist and nonconservative, patriotic opposition to which Yavlinsky belonged (in other words, the opposition that questioned the legitimacy of Yeltsin's regime in light of Yeltsin's professed goals) began to speak out early in the months immediately following August 1991. At this time, the deputies belonging to the communist faction in parliament—under the spell of Speaker Khasbulatov's magic wand—were still obediently voting for Yeltsin's "reforms."

Not surprisingly, the swirl of political epithets the Russian media used to characterize the opposition did not help analysts to understand the opposition's ideology. As we argue in detail at the end of this chapter, fascism has never been influential in Russian politics. Members of Yeltsin's regime much exaggerated its contemporary influence to enflame elite passions and frighten the Russian and Western publics, and—not least—to justify the funding requests of a new coterie of professional "fascism fighters." The division of the opposition into a "communist-patriotic" camp and a "democratic" camp had a certain logic to it, but the logic concerned only the origin, history, and traditional symbolism of the various groups, not the major ideological differences between them. In the past, the leaders of today's Communists comprised a core group of ideological activists in the CPSU Central Committee, and they inherited the committee's rituals along with its base of support in Russian society. However, the ideology adopted by the Zyuganov leadership in the CPRF and by the People's Patriotic Union departs dramatically in its most fundamental positions from communist teachings—classical Marxism as well as Leninism and other variations.[4]

Likewise, discontinuities existed on the "democratic" side, too. Some of the founders of Yabloko and other democratic opposition groups (namely, those led by Yuri Boldyrev and Svyatoslav Fyodorov) were formerly prominent figures in the anti-nomenklatura movement of 1988–91, including the original Democratic Russia in particular. However, the "democratic" opposition was not a direct philosophical or ideological descendant of that movement, and it was not the only master of the democratic "rules of the game." These rules were confined to a strictly procedural, Schumpeterian understanding of democracy, and they were quickly learned by almost all the major players in Russian politics, even Yabloko showing only a limited desire to broaden this understanding.[5] Thus, if one applies the criteria of a "democracy of participation" in the spirit of the radical, populist, and anti-elitist mood that prevailed during the grassroots protest on the eve of the failed revolution of August

1991, then one must conclude that there were almost no true democrats left in Russian politics.

To end this brief discussion of ideology (the significance of which in Russian politics has been exaggerated by the media), we can best define the two major opposition movements—the CPRF and Yabloko—as, respectively, "conservative-traditionalist" (or "national-communist") and "social-reformist." Zyuganov's leadership of the CPRF was—in terms of the global political spectrum—closest in its spirit not to Western communists, but to Western conservatism or, more precisely, to its fundamentalist religious wing, which takes traditionalist and moralistic positions against what it views as the excessive influence of commercial and materialistic values on politics and society. By contrast, the "radical reformists" who were in the government from 1992 to 1998 were not considered conservatives on the Russian political spectrum; rather, Russians believed their extreme form of "free market" values constituted radical change.

However, viewed against the ideological spectrum of world politics, the national-communists and the shock therapists corresponded to two wings of contemporary conservatism—social conservatives and proponents of free markets. In the United States, these wings coexist more or less adequately within the Republican Party. Meanwhile, Russia's social-reformist opposition, in terms of its value system, was close to Western liberal reformism and social democracy. Despite all the inevitable limitations of such analogies, they enable us to better understand why the Russian social reformists were far removed in their views and principles from—and, naturally, opposed to—the government and the conservative opposition and their chief representatives, Yeltsin and Zyuganov, respectively.

For all the indisputable significance of the various political figures' ideologies (a topic to which we shall return), the history and fate of the Russian opposition were determined to a much greater extent by factors of quite a different kind. We believe that one of the major factors was the gulf between the social and cultural outlook of the leading opposition groups, including their leaders, and that of post-Soviet society as a whole. This gulf, which was only slightly less wide than the abyss between the Yeltsin regime and the population, derives from *the elitist or even caste-like features of social development in Russia* in the late Soviet and post-Soviet periods. Vacillating and ever-changing, not definable with formal criteria, although always present in the public consciousness as a decisive factor, the division between the nomenklatura and all other social groups and classes led to a schism within the pro-Yeltsin and pro-reform "party," as well as within the various parties of the opposition. Starting in 1991–92, most of the non-nomenklatura elements of all these groups fell away and experienced varying degrees of alienation from them and from the political system as a whole. In the final analysis, it is this factor that has turned out to be a more universal key to understanding the course of Russian politics than any ideological, philosophical, or political differences.

Within the broad coalition of groups that brought Yeltsin's team (which called itself progressive and antitotalitarian—that is, the so-called "August bloc") to power and shaped the general ideology of reform, there were nomenklatura groups (the coalition's most flexible and unprincipled) as well as extra- and anti-nomenklatura groups, the latter composed primarily of democrats of various social backgrounds. As we argued in earlier chapters, although the voices of the latter, such as Tel'man Gdlyan's, were more loudly heard, the opinions and wishes of the former carried more weight in critical situations. The division of labor took this form: Representatives of the middle class, mostly democrats, figured in the political scene as major organizers, popular leaders, and generators of ideas and platforms, while the fruits of their unrelenting labors were invariably harvested by the groups and factions of the nomenklatura, who skillfully directed the "revolutionary process" from behind the scenes. Both components of the coalition lost members to the anti-Yeltsin opposition that formed soon after the initiation of reforms.

Characteristically present in both resulting camps was, first, the sectarian zeal with which—in the Russian tradition—the factions and groups from various parts of the political spectrum (but mainly assorted democrats from the middle class) jostled and competed with one another. Second, by contrast, the representatives of the various nomenklatura groups that supported them showed a striking kinship of souls and a calm, imperturbable ability to agree with one another. Moreover, the main indicator of the close kinship of the elite groups was not so much the wealth and property owned by the different individuals, which varied widely depending on how successfully acquisitive they had been since 1987 (a Chernomyrdin could be super-rich, while Yeltsin aide Lev Sukhanov could live quite modestly); rather, it was the groups' common culture of "process management" and social manipulation. To outsiders, this culture was almost invisible and in many ways esoteric, but it permitted those who mastered it to exploit the human material at hand and then, by well-designed methods, get rid of it. If one filters out everything that was accidental, atypical, and transient in the history of the relationship between the government and the opposition, the "bare bones" of what remains is as clear and unequivocal as it is depressing: Both the "reformist" and the opposition camps experienced the purging and marginalization of their nonelite elements, factions, and political leaders, along with the seizure of key positions by representatives of the "old" and "new" nomenklatura.

These last two epithets are evoked here to remind the reader that the make-up of the nomenklatura underwent substantial changes during the years of reform, as new elements from other layers of society acceded to it, while some of its former components forfeited much of their privileged status.[6] However, the traditional Russian dividing lines—social, cultural, and moral—separating the rulers from their subjects were not only preserved, but in a number of cases significantly strengthened. It was as if the internal party history of the Russian reformists and their opponents was destined from the very beginning to become one more empirical confirmation of the "iron law of oligarchy," which was formulated in 1915 by the disenchanted idealist Robert Michels, one of the originators of the theory of elites.[7]

This classical playing-out of Michels's theory was, in our opinion, one of the main reasons the majority of Russians—sometimes even in the earliest stages of the democratic reforms—lost faith in the effectiveness and possibility of any far-reaching reforms, as well as in the general idea of any kind of social actions that would defend their interests, not to mention their ideals and values. The widespread disillusionment and demoralization, and the collapse of civil society that Russia experienced in the 1990s, are in many ways linked to the fact that the original goal of reform for most of its rank-and-file supporters was not the "building of capitalism," "pluralism," or other such empty abstractions, but the possibility that "ordinary people" could have a real role in determining the fate of their country—that is, overcoming the oligarchic paradigm that had dominated Russian history for so many centuries.

It was the depressing reemergence of this paradigm across the entire political spectrum and the manipulative dismantling of the reformist groups and the opposition that created a situation in which, as a result of the reforms, a fatalistic or cyclical perception of history and the individual's place in it prevailed in Russia, while in the public consciousness, feelings of cynicism and a craving for personal enrichment gained a firm foothold.

Of course, throughout most of history, the business of politics—in almost all its elements—has belonged to the elite. The problem lies not in the existence of this elite, nor even in its social privileges, but in the character of the elite, in the principles underlying its formation, its relations with society, and the origins and degree of its legitimacy. One of the most important components of a democratic and enlightened consciousness has always been, and still remains, the meritocratic notion that the pathway to the elite is in principle open to all members of society, regardless of their origins, views, or personal connections. In Russian history, this idea was not foreign either to the generation of revolutionary romantics of the 1920s or to the rank-and-file intelligentsia of the Khrushchevian "epoch of the Twentieth Party Congress"—undoubtedly the two most creative and productive periods in Soviet history.

Nonetheless, however eloquently the idea was expressed by writers like Dudintsev, it was always mercilessly debunked by officialdom and made limited impact on Russia's traditional and mystically conceived symbols of absolute power. Thus Russia's historical traditions and political norms continue to be defined mainly by the caste-like, oligarchic nature of the elite's relationship to society at large—an elite that is closed, self-sufficient, arrogant, conceited, predisposed to might over right, and therefore contemptuous and merciless toward the Russian people, while turning cowardly and obsequious when confronted with external authority or superiority.

This social, cultural, moral, and psychological gulf, which has long divided Russia into two halves that are alien and in many ways hostile to each other, does much to explain the amorphous condition that has characterized the major institutions of Russian society in the 1990s—the government bureaucracy, the army, the church, the trade unions, the political parties and movements, and the entrepreneurial class. The stratification of wealth and status existed within each of these institutions long before the advent of shock therapy; yet when the "therapy" began, the stratification became more obvious and sharp, and it naturally increased tensions. This differentiation within the vertical hierarchies of post-Soviet Russia's societal institutions became a more powerful factor than common institutional interests and a spirit of "corporate" unity, which, even in the Soviet era, were barely alive, having been suppressed by the efforts of the Communist Party to impose uniformity and subordinate all institutions strictly to itself. In such a light, it is hardly surprising that, regardless of sporadic speeches made by various groups and individuals, Russia has not seen the growth of any systematic, corporate opposition based on, for example, the army, the church, the ministries, or the trade unions. This distinguishes Russia from countries where public institutions, when threatened, call for organized resistance throughout their entire hierarchy, from the leaders to the rank and file. Examples are the Catholic Church in Poland or the labor unions in Great Britain or France.

To make these points about the central role of a multifaceted nomenklatura in Russia's political history, and about its all-encompassing, oligarchic power, does not mean that the nonelite elements of society (that is, nine-tenths of Russia's population) can simply be dropped from consideration when analyzing Russia's recent history and its possible alternative futures. A widespread grassroots opposition to the oligarchy existed throughout the Yeltsin era, and its existence was recognized by the more sober-minded leaders of the ruling class, forcing them to maneuver constantly, always to be devising new ways to prolong the wished-for "stability." Sometimes this opposition even compelled the leaders to yield, for example, by sending a trainload of cash to pacify the miners of the Kuzbass or Vorkuta. Of course, in the drawn-out power struggle between the public and the oligarchy, the nonelite elements of society, having failed to obtain representation that could influence the government, have been unable to replace the existing regime or to accomplish any major change in its political and economic policies. At the same time, however, the ruling class's lack of roots in society means that it has been unable either to provide genuine social stability or—until Putin's advent—to get the populace's support for its policies. Without the latter, a solid economic recovery is impossible. Without economic recovery, moreover, the oligarchy's foreign policy goal of playing a major role on the world stage—whether in ex-Yugoslavia or the Middle East—has been unattainable as well.

This horizontal cleavage in Russian society, which for all practical purposes made it impossible to mobilize its vertical institutional structures for any significant period of time, determined the fate of the great majority of opposition movements and parties. On the one hand, the ones that were attempting to express the interests of the nonelite elements of society—and were not sponsored by nomenklatura factions—were banished to the periphery of public life, or sank into oblivion simply because they lacked financial resources and—even more important—the powerful contacts necessary for success. Such a fate befell the Independent Civic Initiative—the first association formed by the democratic reformist opposition—as well as the bloc People's Accord, discussed below; numerous organizations of the "new left"; the People's Alliance; the Democratic Party of Russia under the leadership of Sergei Glaziev and Stanislav Govorukhin; and many other organizations. The unexpected entry into the Duma of the moderate but generally anti-oligarchic opposition group Yabloko in December 1993 can be explained to a significant degree by its leaders' relations with Moscow mayor Luzhkov's faction of the oligarchy, which at that time provided Yabloko with support that complemented the sympathetic attention it received from the media outlets of MOST Bank.

On the other hand, the "opposition" organizations openly created by the nomenklatura and nomenklatura-affiliated activists and groups—such as the Russian Union of Industrialists and Businessmen, Obnovleniye (Renewal), and the Civic Union (all three led by Arkady Volsky), Yu. Gekht's Industrial Union, Sterligov's Russian National Assembly, and, finally, Rogozin and Skokov's Congress of Russian Communities—either dissolved or became marginalized just as quickly and completely, despite the information and propaganda networks they set in motion to promote themselves. The reasons for this were the presence of a "nomenklatura aura"—so easily recognizable by the politically active public—and the public's resulting distrust of the leaders of these groups. In addition, the groups lacked an attractive ideological focus, and their more active participants faded away as soon as they had satisfied their short-term interests—individual or factional, material or otherwise.

By the middle of 1997, one could count on the fingers of one hand the number of groups claiming to belong to the "opposition" that were in any way influential. These included, first of all, Zyuganov's Communist Party of the Russian Federation and the People's Patriotic Union, which the CPRF headed. These groups—not without the help of Yeltsin's regime—took over a privileged political niche offering the main (if not the only) real alternative to shock therapy. Second, beginning in late 1993 and continuing to 1998–99, the Yabloko movement was the leading force in the social-reformist opposition (which, on a number of issues, was more radical and uncompromising than the generally conservative CPRF leadership). Beyond these three groups, but of much lesser importance, were several radical communist organizations symbolized by the militant figure of Anpilov; the Russian All-People's Union of Baburin, Alksnis, and Konstantinov, which consolidated parts of the conservative, patriotic intelligentsia; and the Republican People's Party of Russia led by

Aleksandr Lebed, whose charismatic myth quickly faded and whose chances for political survival were unclear. In the late 1990s, one could not seriously talk about any other opponents of the regime as organized groups with a promising future.

The disarray in the opposition groups and the changeability of their principles (which harbored the potential for unpredictable developments) cannot, however, be understood on their own terms. To understand better the Yeltsin regime's ability to emasculate such groups, and the groups' tendency to assist this process through their own disunity, we must analyze more closely the figures who created the opposition in its earliest stages. These people laid the foundations of its ideologies, political strategies, and tactics, and then later—for one reason or another—their groups vanished into the shadows.

A PORTENT OF THINGS TO COME: DEMOCRATIC OPPOSITION IN THE MOSCOW SOVIET

One of the few links between Gorbachev's perestroika and the grassroots democratic movement was the revolutionary slogan "All power to the soviets!" After seven decades of Communist Party dictatorship, the soviets were the only government institution that could potentially serve as the foundation for a democratic state. The strong showing of the radical-democratic ("populist") groups in the 1990 elections for the soviets in large cities provided a legitimate route to power for those who were then still perceived as closely associated with Democratic Russia—people like Popov and Sobchak. When these soviets quickly won independence from the CPSU and wielded genuine power, a real opportunity appeared for the first time in Russian history to build a new government hierarchy from the bottom up, a hierarchy in which local self-government and grassroots citizens' groups would have a crucial creative role.

At the same time, however, nomenklatura elements within the Yeltsin camp saw the problem of grassroots democracy's incompatibility with the top-down redistribution of state property that they planned. The 1991 putsch complicated things further. To limit the authority of the soviets would now look like a radical departure from the basic principles of the "August democratic revolution." Thus the Yeltsin government needed an experimental proving ground that, with a little manipulation, would show the country, particularly the "democratic" electorate, that it was necessary to abolish the soviets on a national scale. The city of Moscow became this proving ground. The experiment worked well enough that by late 1992 the Yeltsin camp had effectively opted for a course of abolishing the soviets, depriving local self-government of any attributes of state power, and strictly limiting the authority of the new representative organs of local government that would be created to replace the soviets. Indeed, the consistent erosion of representative democracy, of which this soon became part, was the condition that made it possible to institute reforms forcibly by administrative methods, as was done with shock therapy.

The rapid redistribution of power and property, as well as the elimination of the "populist" democratic threat in Moscow, were strategically significant for the stabilization of Yeltsin's regime. In Russia, where central government traditionally dominated regional government, securing the voluntary or coerced loyalty of Moscow—especially the business and intellectual groups inside the city's Ring Road—was a necessary condition for gaining and holding power on a national scale. Given the bifurcation of power between Yeltsin and Gorbachev that prevailed in 1990–91, it was the active support of these groups and the friendly position adopted by the Moscow soviet that enabled Yeltsin to emerge as the victor at every turn in his conflict with the unionist center. However, a bitter struggle was already going on in the democratic movement itself over who should control the Moscow soviet and the city's other governmental institutions, and over the forms and direction the reforms should take in other cities.[8]

The majority of the 292 deputies who joined the Democratic Russia faction after being elected to the 472-strong Moscow soviet in March 1990 were representatives of the intelligentsia who did not have managerial or government experience but believed strongly in the vaguely formulated program of radical reform: elimination of the nomenklatura's privileges; rapprochement with the West; building an effective, honest, and just market system; and so forth.[9] The thought occurred to few of them that some of these goals might turn out to be incompatible with one another in the context of Russia's current conditions. Therefore, the breakdown within the Moscow soviet into freemarketeers and democrats ("right" vs. "left," and "pragmatists" vs. "radical idealists") occurred spontaneously and in reaction to events like insider privatization. Understandably, it did not acquire any organizational underpinnings.

However, the two wings clashed with each other as early as during the elections for the soviet leadership. Two nationally known politicians, deputies in the USSR Supreme Soviet, were the leading candidates for the chairmanship of the Moscow soviet: the "moderate populist" Sergei Stankevich (supported by the social-democrats in the Moscow People's Front) and Gavriil Popov, a strict pragmatist with strong nomenklatura affiliations (nominated by Democratic Russia and backed by the less ideological Moscow Voters' Association, which was bent primarily on gaining power). After some behind-the-scenes bargaining, Stankevich bowed out; Popov then won easily, and Stankevich became his first deputy.[10]

Popov and his entourage from the Moscow Voters' Association quickly and firmly took control of the city's government agencies, but as the Moscow soviet's new popularly elected chairman, Popov did not conduct a purge of the old soviet executive committee. The position of executive committee chairman (effectively, the head of the city government), which some prominent democrats were already trying on for size, was left in the hands of interim holder Yuri

Luzhkov, a food supply official who appeared to be devoid of political ambition. Popov reasoned that, given the increasing chaos swirling around Russia's institutions and legal system, only old nomenklatura personnel who were linked together by solid personal and clan relationships could provide the kind of crisis-free municipal government that was so necessary for the consolidation of his power in Moscow.[11]

As was to be expected, it was a personnel issue that gave rise to the first big conflict between the soviet's radicals and pragmatists. The faction supporting personnel changes in the Moscow government was headed by Yuri Sedykh-Bondarenko, the chairman of the soviet's Committee for Law and Order. It purposely decided to begin with the law-enforcement agencies, and in January 1991 convinced a majority of deputies to approve General Vyacheslav Komissarov as the new head of the city's Department of Internal Affairs, bypassing Luzhkov and ignoring his threats to resign. The appointment of Komissarov—an uncompromising radical democrat—portended a possible politicization of law enforcement and also sharp conflict over how seriously to fight corruption. In any case, he had broken through the web of informal ties that had been woven over the years by the Moscow city government oligarchy.

Notwithstanding the soviet's decision—which should have been binding—Popov and Luzhkov did not permit Komissarov to assume his duties.[12] This insubordination by the executive to the elected soviet served as an ominous precedent for the subsequent actions of Yeltsin and his government, and became the first in a long chain of constitutional and legal violations that eventually produced the constitutional crisis of 1993. From this point on, the unifying slogan for the proponents of radical democratic reform became "observance of the law," while the proponents of an accelerated adoption of capitalism called for "expediency" and "effectiveness"—in whose cause, they asserted, it was not a sin to ignore the letter of the law.

Fearing accusations of having entered into a secret alliance with the nomenklatura, which could have ruined his chances of winning future elections, Popov soon staged an effective diversion: He appointed as head of the Moscow police Arkady Murashev, a well-known liberal politician who, unlike Komissarov, was a complete novice at police work and possessed few resources with which to become an independent political force. (He was dismissed a year later.) In protest against Popov's violation of the law, a group of deputies headed by Sedykh-Bondarenko went on a hunger strike. As a result, the national minister of internal affairs, Viktor Barannikov, issued a decree confirming Komissarov's authority as the lawfully appointed police chief. Popov, however, took advantage of the country's bifurcated power structure, in addition to his personal influence in the Gorbachev and Yeltsin camps, and successfully refused to comply. With this act, any possibility that the Moscow soviet could use its legal powers to control the law-enforcement agencies—or any of the other institutions of power—was irretrievably lost.[13]

Against the background of Yeltsin's struggle to set up a presidency in Russia during the spring of 1991, Popov began his own campaign to introduce the office of Moscow mayor. His circle of supporters, who occupied key positions in Democratic Russia and the reformist press, had no difficulty convincing the Moscow democrats that the election of a mayor was nothing more than a logical step toward the distribution of government responsibilities and the consolidation of power in the hands of "their party"—as a means of achieving a more effective opposition to the communists. The majority of the Moscow soviet deputies did not oppose this reform, yet they tried to legislate their own version of a "just" division of responsibilities between the soviet and the mayor. A legislative draft titled "Statutes Concerning the Mayor" was approved by the soviet and introduced in Russia's Supreme Soviet as a legislative initiative—only for the "moderates" there, led by first deputy speaker Khasbulatov and pressured by Popov, to block discussion of it. In the end, the Supreme Soviet approved the draft that Popov put forward, which granted the Moscow mayor extremely wide powers.[14]

Immediately after his election as mayor in June 1991, Popov—not one to put things off—set out to eliminate thirty-three borough soviets by redrawing the administrative map of the city and creating prefectures that were under the supervision of his own appointees. At this stage, the opposition—made up of deputies and a significant portion of the voting public—assumed an organized form for the first time: On July 29, an "anti-Popov" public committee was established whose members included not only deputies from the city and borough soviets but also representatives from most of the democratic parties. The committee was led by the physicist and radical democrat Aleksandr Krasnov, who, as the head of the Krasnaya Presnya borough soviet, adopted a relatively moderate position. Acknowledging that the borough soviets were much too big and too politicized, and that the separation of powers at the local level should be implemented in a more orderly fashion, he asked only that the city government observe the law in carrying out reforms—that it cooperate with the deputies and democratic parties over their implementation.[15]

However, with his supporters in Democratic Russia eagerly awaiting a rich new source of patronage appointments, Popov opted for a unilateral and forcibly imposed redrawing of the political-administrative map of Moscow. Instead of attempting to have a dialogue with the deputies, they organized a press campaign in loyal newspapers, labeling the soviets as "reactionary" and "a Bolshevik legacy" (although in fact it was the Bolsheviks who seventy years earlier had deprived the soviets of their political power). Exploiting the increasing discontent of the impoverished lower orders, the media supporting Popov continued to lump together as enemies the radical Anpilov communists and the anticommunist, democratically elected deputies. This led to the political isolation and impotence of the Moscow soviet, which assisted the process of decline with its incessant internal feuding.[16]

THE COLLAPSE OF DEMOCRATIC RUSSIA AND THE BIRTH OF THE DEMOCRATIC OPPOSITION

By chance, the fading of the Moscow deputies' opposition occurred around the time of the August 1991 putsch, after which Yeltsin banned the Soviet Communist Party. Democratic Russia (DR), which consisted of about three hundred thousand active members and had several million supporters, thus became the largest and most influential political organization in the country. (Nikolai Travkin's Democratic Party of Russia claimed to have more than fifty thousand members, but many of them were not active; many were also DR members.[17]) In November 1991, the second DR congress was covered by the mass media as the most important event in the life of the first and only organization that could claim the status of being a ruling party in Yeltsin's Russia; however, the Yeltsinites now aspired to tame DR and to use whatever methods were needed to bring it under their control. On top of this, in November and later in January 1992, DR was shaken by two powerful schisms, and by the summer of 1992 it had practically disappeared from the political scene.[18] What remained was folded into Democratic Choice—an amorphous collection of organizations (for the most part obscure) that were loyal to the president. In the following pages, we look at the two schisms: first, between the "radical democrats" and the "pragmatists" and, second, the simultaneous schism between these two groups on the one hand and the "democratic statists" on the other.

Democratic Russia's collapse and the conflicts that accompanied it point to some paradoxical conclusions. Not one of the leading representatives of DR who engaged in the public debates of 1991–92 obtained a high-level position in the political elite. Afanasiev, Ponomarev, Yakunin, Aksiuchits, Astafiev, Konstantinov, Salye, Batkin, Zaslavsky, and Bokser—all of them, regardless of what group they later joined, either more or less willingly left the public political arena, were unceremoniously pushed out in bureaucratic battles within the reformist camp, or contented themselves with the position of rank-and-file deputies in parliament. The explanation for this was that each member of this bright galaxy of indisputably outstanding but highly disparate personalities had the quintessential features of a strongly idealistic intellectual—the very qualities that were socially and culturally inimical to the new generation of the nomenklatura elite. Although this type of politician was doomed to virtual extinction, however, the problems discussed in 1991–92 in the democratic camp and the proposed philosophical and social solutions to them in many ways defined the content of subsequent public debates, especially those about the Yeltsin regime's legitimacy.

As we have seen, by the middle of 1991, several currents of opinion representing a wide spectrum of views had crystallized within Democratic Russia. Behind the barrage of secondary disagreements, it was not always possible to discern the main issue: Could—for some people, even *should*—the democratic movement be preserved as the leading unifying force in civil society? A number of influential officials on Democratic Russia's staff (Ilya Zaslavsky, Vladimir Bokser, Mikhail Shneider, Kirill Ignatiev) convinced their supporters that Democratic Russia's main historical mission—the overthrow of the communist regime—had been accomplished, and that from now on their only function as "democrats" was to secure the public's support for the new authorities and their policies.

Most of the people with this view had come to Democratic Russia from the Moscow Voters' Association (MVA) and regarded the movement in an instrumental way—as a well-oiled machine to be used for pre-election mobilization. These people—not without a touch of pride—called themselves "pragmatists," and almost all of them joined the inner circle of Moscow's leader, Gavriil Popov. Popov, who had used MVA and Democratic Russia to gain control over the Moscow soviet and also during his campaign for mayor in June 1991, had by now distanced himself from the movement. Indeed, three weeks after his election, together with other representatives of the liberal nomenklatura, he announced the creation of a new party—the Movement for Democratic Reforms.[19]

From Popov's point of view, the anti-nomenklatura radicalism of the majority of Democratic Russia members had outlived its usefulness and now represented a potential threat to his own policies. As we have seen previously, these included a firm, authoritarian reorganization of the government in Moscow, restriction of the rights of the elective organs in favor of the executive, abolition of the borough soviets, and a nomenklatura- and bureaucracy-led "privatization" of municipal property. First, Popov tried to take over DR in July to give his new party a countrywide support base, just as Travkin had tried the same ploy for his party, but these tactics failed.[20] Accordingly, although he had left the movement's leadership in early 1991, Popov consistently pursued a policy of putting an end to DR's autonomous political activity through his subordinates and trusted contacts on DR's staff.

The most influential opponent of the pragmatists within the leadership of DR was its co-chairman, who was one of the most popular politicians of the first democratic wave—the scholar and historian Yuri Afanasiev, president of the Historical Archives Institute (which had just been transformed into the Russian State University for the Humanities). The only democrat of such high rank who was not clearly competing for a government post, Afanasiev by nature would have been more suited to the role of "philosopher king" than leader of a popular mass movement in a revolutionary epoch. His views were influenced by the historical and philosophical ideas of Mikhail Gefter, the French sociological school known as "Annales," and Western democratic thinkers of the 1960s.[21] What links these different schools of thought is their focus on the concept of civil society as a system of horizontal relationships among its members that is largely independent from the government and other forms of power.[22] Afanasiev's devotion to the radical, romantic ideal of a rational and just state order (undoubtedly linked with the many years he spent studying the French Revolution and with his stay at the Sorbonne) was combined with an uncompromising rejection of Russia's imperial and great-power tradition.[23]

By the middle of 1991, a diverse group of intellectuals and prominent leaders of the movement had rallied around Afanasiev within the leadership of Democratic Russia. This created a basis at the national level for the same sort of radical/pragmatist schism that we analyzed in the Moscow soviet. Besides Afanasiev, the intellectual core of the group included Leonid Batkin, a Renaissance historian, and Yuri Burtin, a prominent editor and columnist of *Novy mir* from the 1960s.[24] The majority of the group's members shared to a greater or lesser degree the rebellious, anti-elite, "populist" spirit of the early democratic movement (which in its day had provided Democratic Russia and Yeltsin with triumphant marches and demonstrations for all his electoral campaigns).

They also understood that from the moment Yeltsin achieved de facto status as co-ruler with Gorbachev, the real government policies had been made not by democratic parties and movements, or by parliamentary speeches, but by backroom negotiations and deal-making among various elite groups. The events of the spring and summer of 1991—the Novo-Ogarevo agreements with their ban on strikes, the authoritarian redistribution of power and property in Moscow by Popov's administration and his creation of the elitist Movement for Democratic Reforms, and, finally, the weakness of the nomenklatura's opposition to Yeltsin's election as Russian president—told the radical democrats a lot. They showed that Democratic Russia—with its mass meetings and powerful mechanisms for electoral mobilization—was virtually Russia's ruling party, yet it was unintentionally legitimizing a behind-the-scenes regime run by elements that were alien to it. Recognizing this, the movement's radical wing decided to distance itself from the new government and enter into a critical dialogue with other trends in the movement. It also decided to try to mobilize DR's rank and file and to transform the movement into an equal partner—and, when necessary, an opponent—of Yeltsin's regime.

The radical democrats set about this task in the days after the August putsch after launching one fruitless initiative earlier that month. Afanasiev, Batkin, and their supporters severely criticized the leaders of DR's bureaucracy and "pragmatic" wing, claiming it was their fault that at the decisive moment DR as a whole ended up on the sidelines.[25] The radicals made active preparations for DR's second congress, which assembled 1,298 delegates on November 11–12, 1991, and obtained a considerable majority in decisive votes. In the Council of Representatives, DR's policymaking forum, the radicals gained a clear advantage over the "pragmatists": The top ten people elected included, apart from Afanasiev and Batkin, such authoritative radicals as Bela Denisenko, a leader of the Kuznetsk coal miners' movement; Tel'man Gdlyan, famous for his investigation of criminal cases involving corruption in high places; and Marina Salye, an outstanding public tribune from Leningrad.[26]

In addition, the radicals attempted to take back the Democratic Russia foundation, which they nominally controlled, but which by that time had become the de facto financial and organizational base for the progovernment bureaucrats of the "moderate-pragmatic" wing. Finally, the radicals' most important strategic move was their launching of Leonid Batkin's idea to create an all-Russian organization of "citizen committees" to implement reforms at the local level. As conceived by their creators, these "citizen committees" were tasked with providing a vertical link between the government and the public, and counterbalancing the top-heavy nomenklatura character of the Yeltsin-Gaidar reforms. These bodies would prevent the reforms from turning into the imposition of the oligarchs' will, in tune with Russia's tradition of bureaucratic, officially mandated programs of top-down reform.

However, the plan to radicalize DR, which threatened to pose a real problem for the new nomenklatura regime, was defeated by the joint efforts of Popov's Moscow administration and Yeltsin's inner circle. The chaotic leadership of the Afanasiev wing of DR and its inability to mobilize efficiently its supporters in the provinces made its opponents' job significantly easier. The "moderates" succeeded in putting off for two months—until January 1992—a plenary session of the Council of Representatives, at which the movement's leadership was to be elected. During this time, they seized Batkin's idea of "citizen committees"; obtained financing for them from the newly formed government, which would have denied funds to the radicals; and held a constituent assembly in December, on the very eve of the deregulation of prices.

From this assembly, they formed a new organization called the Public Committee for Russian Reforms, which was fundamentally different from Batkin's original concept in its functions, its structure, and the composition of its leadership. Instead of being equal partners of the government, working out with it the various elements of reform policy and thus gaining legitimacy, the regional Committees for Reforms turned out to be Soviet-style "transmission belts." The government gave them offices, communications equipment, and operating funds.[27] In return, the committees provided friendly advance approval and support from below for the "reform policy" directives launched from above. Ironically, but logically from the government's viewpoint, the leader of the organization was a prominent member of DR's "moderate" wing, Lev Ponomarev.[28] Kremlin co-optation was moving apace.

The plenary session of DR's Council of Representatives took place after the beginning of shock therapy—on January 18–19, 1992. Given the growing opposition to the Kremlin of parliamentary leaders and Russia's underprivileged, the government's most vital task was now to prevent the radical democrats from gaining control of DR. If they did, DR could become the leading force in a mass opposition movement supported by much of the intelligentsia and the middle class. Therefore, the "moderate-pragmatic" wing, which controlled DR's bureaucracy, ensured that most of the regional delegates were its supporters and also engineered the election of its own man as chairman of the finance committee. For purposes of intimidation, the hall where the session took place was cordoned off by security guards who worked for one of the leading "pragmatists," Ilya Zaslavsky.

The Yeltsin government, which had always harbored a certain distrust of DR and, when it was not using it, often tried to push it into the political background, now decided to humiliate the organization. Whereas a few months earlier Yeltsin had appeared at a plenum to ask for the democrats' support, this time the government's top leaders declined to come, sending instead Anatoly Chubais, who merely chaired the State Property Committee. Chubais's speech met a barrage of critical questions, and he quickly departed.

Realizing that the Kremlin now aimed to put an end to DR as an independent social force, Afanasiev and his supporters sharply attacked the "pragmatic" wing and called for DR to take a position of constructive opposition to Yeltsin and his "shock therapy" government. In response, leaders of the bureaucratic, pro-government wing of DR—according to a number of the plenum's participants —resorted to falsifying the results of the leadership elections.[29] Several leaders of the radical wing who enjoyed wide popularity and had received strong support during the November congress—Batkin, Denisenko, and Gdlyan—now received a suspiciously small number of votes.

By contrast, some individuals whose popularity at the congress had been extremely low (particularly Ponomarev, who was known more as an office bureaucrat than a public politician), suddenly got enough votes to become DR co-chairs. As a result, the division among the five co-chairs was three to two in favor of the "pragmatists." The only radicals elected as co-chairs were Afanasiev himself (the bureaucrats would have wholly exposed their manipulations if they had falsified his support) and Marina Salye, whose position at the time was in many respects halfway between the two wings. Meanwhile, in the vote for members of the Coordinating Council (DR's executive board)—the body that made the movement's day-to-day decisions—the number of radicals elected mysteriously sank to zero.

The triumph of those who backed the government, however, turned out to be in many ways a Pyrrhic victory. Afanasiev would not accept the demeaning figurehead role that was offered him. Several days after the plenum, he, Batkin, and three others issued a statement about the nonlegitimacy of DR's new leadership and resigned from the governing bodies.[30] Other resignations followed: Salye (unwillingly and with noticeable detours) and the St. Petersburg group of her supporters; then five parties that were collective members of DR and had formed the social-democratic bloc New Russia. Soon, the largest regional organizations in the movement split in two, roughly mirroring the radical-pragmatist divide. Some of the Russian media, for whom the contrast between the government's inflated claims of DR's support for it and the actual status of DR had long been a subject of irony, now described the schism that had befallen

Democratic Russia as fatal. After the March plenum in St. Petersburg, during which open debates between the opposing sides led nowhere, *Nezavisimaya gazeta* proclaimed that Democratic Russia was dead.[31]

The "pragmatists," who were often more interested in personal enrichment and constructing their own futures than in public policy, did not succeed in preventing DR's sudden collapse. They did, however, manage to squelch Afanasiev's attempts to rebuild the democratic movement on a new foundation. In July 1992, for example, its most tenacious elements—a reradicalized Marina Salye and the Moscow regional organization—tried to hold an alternate DR congress. However, without government funds, they were unable to assemble a quorum of delegates. Now, instead of splitting into two independent and functioning parts, most of Democratic Russia crumbled like dead wood.[32] With the swift departure of the activists, the "pragmatic" leaders of DR, Ponomarev and Zaslavsky—on orders from the Kremlin—attached the remaining rump of DR to Democratic Choice (DC), a weak conglomerate of progovernment organizations and clubs founded in November. This grouping later helped Yeltsin by campaigning for him prior to the April referendum, an event we discuss later in this chapter.

In the fall of 1993, the rump of Democratic Russia joined the ranks of Russia's Choice, the progovernment electoral bloc created by Yegor Gaidar and illegally funded by the government, according to the findings of an official investigation.[33] DC's leader, Lev Ponomarev, after a bitter behind-the-scenes struggle, managed to capture only sixty-seventh place on the bloc's "party list" of candidates and thus did not gain a Duma seat in December. The whole experience was humiliating for DR and showed what a wide gulf existed between the market bolsheviks of Russia's Choice—who were mostly elitist and, at best, marginally democratic—and the ambitious and power-oriented but still democratically inclined activists of DR, some of whom were alienated by their new partners and drifted away to other parties or into passivity.[34]

The unenviable fate of Democratic Russia at first glance seems to resemble that of analogous mass movements in the countries of Eastern Europe—Poland's Solidarity movement, the Czech Citizens' Forum, Lithuania's Sajudis, and the People's Fronts of Latvia and Estonia. All of them—once they had fulfilled their revolutionary role—lost their salient positions or sank into near oblivion. However, they had provided the nucleus of the new political class. The leaders and parties that emerged from their ranks continued to be defining forces in public life. With the collapse of DR, however, Russia's emerging *independent* political class suddenly lost its organizational base. The values of a radical, idealistic restructuring of society that it preached were quickly and purposefully discredited, and its place in politics was largely swallowed up by the old and new nomenklatura.

Democratic Russia's disappearance from the political map as an independent group suited the nomenklatura's vital interests. The shock therapists, who covertly preached an elitist contempt for the benighted masses, were at last freed from the threatening prospect of having to deal with a mass opposition movement led by the democratic intelligentsia. The latter, which for historical reasons enjoyed a high degree of legitimacy, potentially constituted a more serious threat to the government than the communists or the "national patriots." For the conservative, anti-Yeltsin segments of the nomenklatura, the collapse of DR and the failure of the program of *democratic opposition* gave them some breathing space. Furthermore, it allowed them to take advantage of the despair and confusion of the intelligentsia—alienated as it was from the Yeltsin camp—in order to create their own antireformist program of *conservative opposition*. To this opposition we now turn to investigate why it, too, failed to capitalize on the unpopularity of the Yeltsin regime.

THE RUSSIAN-AMERICAN UNIVERSITY: AN INCUBATOR OF NATIONALIST CONSERVATISM

Looking at the history of Russia's national-conservative (or "national-patriotic" in Russian parlance) opposition in the 1990s, one is struck by the abundance of parties and movements, of groups and factions, and even of individuals whose public influence was often greater than that of some parties. However, regardless of the kaleidoscopic changes within this part of the political spectrum (as in all others), one can discern in most of it a certain consistent core—in ideology, in the principles used for selecting officials, and in its political style and methods. Regardless of the makeup and configuration of the current political groups, this continuity points to the existence of a stable analytical and even, to some extent, organizational center, within whose gravitational field the clashes, dissolution, and emergence of new opposition groups occur. Since at least mid-1991, this role has been played by the Russian-American University (RAU), which subsequently became a joint stock company, the RAU Corporation, led from the beginning by Aleksei Podberezkin.[35]

Despite RAU's active and highly visible presence on the political stage for a number of years, information about its origins and activities is rather scanty and unreliable. This can be explained to a large degree by the RAU leaders' close association with the intelligence services, the army, and the military-industrial complex, and sometimes by the conspiritorial character of its activities. The name "Russian-American University" is itself misleading. In the first place, RAU has never concerned itself with teaching in the usual sense of the word and has functioned only as an analytical research center. In the second place, there is nothing "American" about RAU—in fact, its intellectual product has a radical, nationalistic, and strongly anti-American flavor.

RAU was created in June 1990, when most of the Soviet nomenklatura was becoming confused and even panicked by the chaos and disintegration fostered by Gorbachev's reforms. Younger, more farsighted conservatives saw the urgent need for contingency planning and for exploiting the new freedoms to further conservatives' political and business interests. RAU's stated purpose was "research and educational work." Its head, Podberezkin, and his deputy, Dmitri Rogozin, were closely linked and mutually complementary figures. Both had family ties to senior officials in the intelligence services and thus belonged to the best informed corporate circles of the nomenklatura elite.[36] Both worked during the 1980s on the USSR Committee on Youth Organizations, a division of the Komsomol and the intelligence services that handled a wide variety of issues, ranging from international political and economic relations and the creation of financial organizations abroad with CPSU, Komsomol, and KGB capital, to the cultivation of new, "informal" political and cultural currents of a semi-underground type. (The head of the committee at that time was Gennadi Yanayev, the future Soviet vice president and ill-fated leader of the August coup.)

The creation of RAU was aided by the patronage and material assistance of another participant in the future coup, Anatoly Lukyanov, who at that time chaired the USSR Supreme Soviet. The financial strength of the groups supporting RAU is shown by the fact that in 1990–91 there were twenty-five hundred permanent employees (for the most part former officials from the Ministry of Defense, KGB, CPSU Central Committee, Ministry of Foreign Affairs, and Committee on Youth Organizations), and their wages ($400–$500 per month) were equal to those at their previous place of employment. According to Podberezkin, RAU's permanent staff during that period included "six members and five candidate members of the Politburo, and eighty-six generals. But on the whole you couldn't get any sense out of them. . . . They were good people, but bad workers. However, I couldn't refuse my friends."[37] Nonetheless, in 1993–94 RAU's journal *Obozrevatel'* was one hundred to two hundred pages long and came out every two weeks. RAU's stated budget in summer 1994 was 546.4 million rubles, or about half a million U.S. dollars at the time, a sum that must have put it among the wealthiest nongovernmental think tanks in Russia.[38] By 1996, however, the journal had become a monthly of only fifty to sixty pages.

When RAU was created, Podberezkin directed its analytical and scholarly work (he had a correspondence degree from Moscow's Institute of International Relations—a training ground for the Soviet elite—as a specialist in U.S. military policy and had worked as a senior researcher at that institute and at the Diplomatic Academy). Rogozin, younger and more inclined toward public activity, was responsible for developing a network of personal contacts with prominent or promising political figures both in Russia and abroad. (Previously, in 1985, he had spent six months in Cuba doing research for his graduation thesis with assistance from the KGB.[39]) In May 1990, he organized an exclusive club of young politicians called "Forum-90," which had ties to well-known democratic movement leaders like Oleg Rumyantsev, the founder of the Social

Democratic Party and later the main author of Russia's draft constitution, and to such wild cards as Vladimir Zhirinovsky.

The members of "Forum-90" received from Rogozin and his friends in the Komsomol Central Committee prized opportunities for travel abroad, as well as contacts with Western politicians. They also got office space, printing equipment, and coverage in the Komsomol press and on television—all of which were essential to aspiring politicians. In exchange for this, the latter came to RAU as the central gathering point for information on the democratic movement's current and long-range plans, its financial capabilities, job openings, and personal relationships among its leading members.

In 1990–91, the two RAU leaders and several of their associates tried to gain entry to the Yeltsin camp and create within it a "national-patriotic" bloc to drive out some of the radical reformist groups. As Podberezkin reports, this effort was facilitated by many young people from nomenklatura families with conservative views who came to occupy prominent posts in the Yeltsin administration via the Committee on Youth Organizations. Also in 1990, Podberezkin himself became an adviser to a former colleague, Yeltsin aide Aleksei Tsaregorodtsev. (It was evidently in connection with this appointment that Podberezkin left the Communist Party.) As for subsequent efforts to create a national-conservative axis within the Yeltsin administration, RAU placed its hopes on Yuri Skokov (see chapters 3 and 4), who in the summer of 1990 became a deputy prime minister of Russia, and from the summer of 1991 on Vice President Rutskoi, who became close to RAU.[40] When Rutskoi appointed Tsaregorodtsev to head his office, Podberezkin joined the vice president's inner circle.

RAU's parallel political task was to try to push out of the government radical democrats and shock therapists. In the fall of 1990, Yavlinsky, who had provided a counterbalance to Skokov's influence, left the government feeling discouraged over the administration's scuttling of his moderate, people-oriented program for moving to a market economy. The Yeltsin team now relied less on revolutionary appeals to the grassroots democratic movement and more on a systematic intra-elite struggle for power based on nomenklatura game rules. This made the task of the groups supporting RAU easier. The remaining obstacle was Democratic Russia, a number of whose leaders (as discussed previously) were working in 1990–92 to prevent the Yeltsin regime's degeneration into a nomenklatura and national-conservative stronghold.

THE "DEMOCRATIC STATISTS" AND THE SECOND MAJOR SCHISM IN DEMOCRATIC RUSSIA

In these circumstances, RAU evidently planned to foment a major schism in the democratic movement on the issue of whether or not Russia should develop a strong national state identity within the Soviet Union. This rift ran from the spring of 1991 through early 1992 and was thus roughly simultaneous with the radical-pragmatist schism examined previously. Before analyzing the second schism, it may be helpful to lay out in summary form what we mean by the word "statism" and to show how the concept fits into the political philosophy of very different groups on the contemporary Russian political spectrum.

The national-conservatives, such as those in the RAU, were—and are— heavily statist in the sense that they give the highest priority to building a strong state and a much lower one, if any, to building democratic institutions or promoting individual rights. Imperial "restorationists," such as Aleksandr Prokhanov, are also heavily statist, but because the USSR collapsed, their goal has been to rebuild a strong *Soviet-type* state by persuading as many of the USSR's former republics as possible to join a new union.

Then there are—or were—the "democratic statists," who emerged in the democratic, anti-nomenklatura camp in the spring of 1991, as the threat of the USSR's collapse became obvious. The democratic statists favored two sorts of statism at the same time: They wanted to preserve the USSR as a viable, federal, and increasingly democratic state, and they also wanted the RSFSR to develop vital and independent institutions that expressed its own statehood *within*—as they hoped—such a voluntary union of the USSR. In late 1991, they broke with Democratic Russia and the Yeltsin government because by then both entities clearly wanted to dissolve the union. Promptly, the democratic statists began seeking new alliances with more conservative, less democratic statist groups in the opposition. Of course, this was precisely the outcome the RAU's "political technologists" apparently had been seeking. Not surprisingly, in the democratic statists' new political environment, their statism tended to become more marked than their commitment to democracy.

In the summer and fall of 1990, Rogozin had joined up with the ambitious radical democrat Mikhail Astafiev, who was actively seeking to become a parliamentary leader, and later joined his party.[41] Resources mobilized by RAU and the Committee on Youth Organizations enabled Astafiev to assume leadership of the minuscule Constitutional Democratic Party (known as the "Cadets"), join the inner circle of DR, and chair DR's constituent assembly.[42] During the same period, Astafiev moved away from radical, anti-nomenklatura positions and began to accentuate Russian patriotism and statist themes. Notwithstanding his bitter struggle for a leading role in DR, however, Astafiev did not succeed in obtaining a co-chairmanship. Nonetheless, in April 1991, he successfully initiated the creation of a bloc of three statist-minded democratic parties, called People's Accord. A few months later, this bloc, born with covert assistance from RAU and the Committee on Youth Organizations, instigated a schism that had fatal consequences for Democratic Russia. Indeed, by the beginning of 1992, given the passivity of the demoralized communists, the former democrats Astafiev and Ilya Konstantinov, indirectly sponsored by RAU, were transformed into leaders of the anti-Yeltsin and anti-Gaidar opposition in the

Russian parliament. Let us now examine more closely the schism that had this remarkable result.

For a few months after the defeat of the August 1991 putsch, Yeltsin and his team had practically no opponents among the Russian political elite. In part, this resulted from the dual nature of his status. Although he was in essence the undisputed leader of Russia, authority over the whole of the USSR formally remained in the hands of Gorbachev. Moreover, almost every Russian politician (including those who were not enthusiastic about Yeltsin) could see that, after August 21, the Soviet organizations Gorbachev presided over had lost their power and were hindering "natural" political development. Thus, while Yeltsin was accorded the traditional Russian respect for strongly exercised authority, potential opponents could feel only contempt toward Gorbachev.

In our view, this explains the paradoxical situation whereby the headlong dismantling of the USSR's organs of government between August and December of 1991 met with practically no resistance from the conservative end of the political spectrum: The communists and other logical opponents of the changes, including RAU, did not want to do anything to help Gorbachev remain in power and thus preferred to distance themselves from the struggle between the "federal" and "Russian" camps in the spirit of "a plague on both your houses." As a result, neither the Belaya Vezha agreements on the abolition of the Soviet Union nor the agreements' ratification on December 12 by the Russian Supreme Soviet met with any serious opposition from the "Communists of Russia" or other conservative parliamentary factions.

However, the breakup of the Soviet Union produced a new wave of opposition from the very place where one might have least expected it—within the leadership of Democratic Russia. This was the group of "democratic statists" that had emerged as early as the spring of 1991, and that in the autumn (not long before the Belaya Vezha agreements) broke with the main group of Yeltsin's democratic supporters.

We should emphasize here that up to the last moment, at the beginning of 1992, the democratic statists did not join the opposition to Yeltsin himself. Their drive to assert a Russian national state identity, as distinct from a Union identity, always appeared to coincide with Yeltsin's program, which called for strengthening the political status of the RSFSR government agencies. It was Astafiev who invented the name Democratic Russia—with the emphasis on the second word—despite the fact that until then, the internationally inclined Russian democrats were extremely wary of any leanings toward national self-identification, not wanting to end up in the same camp as the "national imperialists."[43]

The appearance of the "right wing" of democratic statists as an ideological trend in Democratic Russia was linked with the formation in January 1991 of the Democratic Congress—the amorphous conglomeration of noncommunist parties and movements from all over the USSR mentioned in chapter 5. The initiative for creating the congress was provided by an anti-imperialist faction within Democratic Russia's leadership (headed by Afanasiev and Ponomarev) and also by moderate Russian democrats like Vladimir Lysenko who came from the Democratic Platform group in the Soviet Communist Party and regarded the interrepublic ties they had developed at the party-chief level as part of their personal political capital. The goal of the non-Russian members of the congress was to dismantle the empire as quickly as possible, using any means available, while the goal of the Russian democrats was to construct an association of independent states in which they would be able to play some kind of coordinating role.

By the time the congress got going, however, Democratic Russia was itself being torn apart by deep conflicts over organizational and personality issues. Most important were the conflicts between the leaders of the parties that belonged to Democratic Russia and the "no-party" politicians who had become DR officials solely on the basis of their personal stature. Most of the parties were made up of people from Moscow and Leningrad, while the overwhelming majority of those who joined DR in the provinces were not members of any party. The party leaders frequently suspected the nonparty officials of trying to push the parties out of DR, thus creating for themselves a unified, noncoalition organization that would claim to represent the whole democratic movement. These suspicions were far from unfounded, given that six of DR's co-chairs as well as almost all the heads of its various offices were nonparty individuals who often used their local influence to select regional representatives for DR's major gatherings—to the detriment of representatives with party affiliations.[44]

Thus the initiative of Democratic Russia's nonparty leaders in sponsoring the creation of the Democratic Congress became, in essence, an excellent opportunity to build a solid base for their anti-USSR strategy. Arrayed against them, opposing any participation in the "destructive" and "antistatist" activities of the congress, were the party-affiliated leaders who, like Nikolai Travkin of the Democratic Party, disagreed from the beginning with DR's structural principles, or, like the "Cadets'" leader Astafiev and others, had been excluded in the course of the organizational battles from the decision-making process. On April 13, a group of democratic statists sharply criticized the decision of DR's policymaking Council of Representatives to have DR join the congress. And on April 19, a smaller group of leaders from only three parties—Astafiev's Cadets, Travkin's Democratic Party, and Viktor Aksiuchits's Russian Christian Democratic Movement—signed an agreement to form a "constructive democratic bloc," called the People's Accord, within Democratic Russia.

In Russia's democratic circles, this last bloc was ironically nicknamed "the agreement between the elephant, the pug, and the cockroach." Travkin's Democratic Party was, by the standards of that time, a massive organization with branches in most of Russia's regions. Aksiuchits's Russian Christian Democratic Movement was a medium-size party with a regional base of several thousand people. The membership of Astafiev's Constitutional Democratic Party barely reached a total of fifty; nonetheless, thanks to the covert support from RAU, it was this tiny party that became the ideological and organizational engine of the so-called "rightist bloc."

Meanwhile, later in April, Yeltsin changed the tactics of his struggle for power and attended the Novo-Ogarevo negotiations with Gorbachev and other republican leaders to try to conclude a new "Union Treaty" and thus arrest the incipient collapse of the USSR. This turn of events deepened the conflicts within the leadership of DR: As expected, the People's Accord expressed its support, while the anti-union radical democrats sharply criticized the "unprincipled Novo-Ogarevo agreement." The August coup shifted the scales sharply to the side of the radicals and of the moderate DR officials who had a tactical alliance with them. People's Accord was prevented from participating in preparations for DR's second congress in November; and at the congress itself, when key documents concerning strategic and organizational issues were discussed, its members were in the minority.

Characteristically, the reconfigurations taking place within the movement throughout all this political tumult were not initially reflected in the democratic statists' attitude toward the policies and personality of Boris Yeltsin. Along with other DR elements, People's Accord signed an October agreement with Yeltsin on economic reforms. In November, the group agreed to the formation of the Yeltsin-Burbulis-Gaidar government. This position was linked not only with Yeltsin's unconditional authority among the overwhelming majority of democrats at that moment, but also with their hopes to have a real influence on his policies, both through the mechanism of the October agreement and through their personal influence on certain figures in Yeltsin's entourage. Thus, for example, the well-known August 27, 1991 announcement in Yeltsin's name by press secretary Pavel Voshchanov regarding the Russian state's possible revision of the borders of those republics that might refuse to join a new voluntary federation was made following pressure that democratic statists exerted on Voshchanov personally.[45]

In early November 1991, however, the parliament's adoption of Gaidar's reforms made the final disintegration of the USSR politically inevitable. On the eve of DR's November 10–11 congress, Afanasiev and Batkin promoted a slogan that was clearly unacceptable to the democratic statists: "Russia is one —but divisible."[46] Opening at a time when DR could still seriously claim the role of a ruling political force, the congress unambiguously added to the movement's list of goals the building of a Russian statehood that was independent of the Soviet Union. Such a goal reinforced from a different angle Gaidar's de facto sentence of economic death for the USSR. This vote, and also the congress's censure of Yeltsin's decree declaring an emergency in Chechnya-Ingushetiya and sending Russian troops there—a vote initiated by Afanasiev—

led to the protest, then the walk-out of the three "rightist" parties of People's Accord.[47]

This exodus from DR was the beginning of the end for People's Accord. Its parties had been bound together primarily by their rejection of actions taken by DR's real leaders. Once they left DR, they were unable to reach agreement on an independent strategy for future action—or even on the degree of their opposition to Russia's leadership.

With the USSR's collapse and the launching of Gaidar's shock therapy, the democratic statists moved into opposition to Yeltsin and tried to build a coalition with nationalist groups and Rutskoi's party at a Congress of Civic and Patriotic Groups held on February 8–9. The RAU Corporation once again played a major role in organizing and financing the congress, as also the coalition body set up by the smaller groups but spurned by Rutskoi's and Travkin's parties. This body soon withered, as new conflicts arose between the democratic statist leaders. In particular, Viktor Aksiuchits, although prepared to criticize strongly the new Commonwealth of Independent States and the "anti-national" policies of Russia's new leadership, considered himself to be a right-leaning conservative democrat of the West European type—a follower of Ludwig Erhard and Margaret Thatcher—and thus was not inclined to oppose the radical economic policies of Yeltsin's government. Rogozin took the same view.

On the other hand, Astafiev and Aksiuchits's colleague, Ilya Konstantinov, preached a Russian variant of right-wing conservatism and experienced no particular pangs of conscience just because their criticism of the government concurred with the positions of Anpilov and other radical communists. Indeed, these two soon began cooperating openly with the communists and the radical national-patriots. This led to the formation in October of the National Salvation Front (NSF), which we discuss later. Meanwhile, the parties of Astafiev and Aksiuchits fragmented and withered. Neither played a significant role in the events of autumn 1993, nor did they collect enough signatures to take part in the subsequent Duma elections.

Thus by summer 1992, the democratic movement was broken. With generous Kremlin support, the "pragmatists" of Democratic Russia had forced the radicals out and turned the demoralized organization into something little better than a Soviet-style transmission belt for mobilizing ordinary people behind government policy. Most of its several million grassroots supporters became apathetic or alienated.

The democratic statists were mostly now conservatives of various stripes. Travkin's Democratic Party remained centrist but declined in strength, gaining only fifteen seats in the December 1993 parliamentary elections. All the leading democrats except the DR pragmatists had turned against Yeltsin and been cut off from Kremlin subsidies. Partly for financial reasons, they were not able to create viable new parties, except for Yabloko.

YELTSIN'S CORPORATIST STRATEGY

Although in April 1992 the Kremlin had managed to mobilize the still servile neo-communist factions in parliament to get a majority vote supporting shock therapy, the situation had changed by summer. With the communists becoming less obedient, only 20 percent of the deputies were now reliable supporters of the government.

Worse still, the parliament was led by Speaker Khasbulatov, whose ambition for high office impelled him to exploit parliament's opposition for his personal ends. He proceeded to abuse his already inordinate powers to aggrandize himself and to harass Yeltsin and the government aggressively at every turn. Khasbulatov was aided in these efforts by the repeatedly changed constitution, which gave the parliament more powers than the president and could easily be—and frequently was—amended to tilt the balance still more. In addition, Vice President Rutskoi was in tune with the parliamentary opposition, and the chairman of the Constitutional Court, Valery Zorkin, clearly had some sympathy for it.

As for society, the widespread impoverishment of ordinary Russians had facilitated the activation (partly, it seems, by the Kremlin) of radical and proto-fascist groups, notably the communist militants of Anpilov and the neofascists of Barkashov.

In response to all this, the government's propaganda machine responded by trying to impose on the public an artificial choice between two extremes—shock therapy or Anpilov and Barkashov—although the former was, of course, presented not as an extreme, but as a sound strategy for building up Russia. As time went on, many of the country's anti-Yeltsin groups were collectively branded "the irreconcilable opposition" and subtly associated by official propaganda with the extremist groups. In this way, the Kremlin sought to compromise the very idea of a civilized and principled opposition (a "third force") and thus win over to its side the disillusioned, weary, and passive majority of the Russian public.

Meanwhile, the Kremlin was up to its neck in handling tensions among its supporters. These occurred primarily along the fault line between the old nomenklatura (mainly the upper-management personnel of heavy industry) and the young shock-therapy team backed by the new financial interests and powerful, corrupt officials who had jumped on the bandwagon. The only party and managerial elites that had more or less given their approval in fall 1991 for Yeltsin to implement shock therapy now came forward with their claims. The pie was being divided up, and they demanded their share of government property, special privileges in the sphere of foreign trade, and—no less important—key positions in the new government, particularly in the administrative bodies that would define its political course, ideology, and propaganda. Of course, Yeltsin had long sought to appease this potential, sometimes actual, opposition by appointing some of them to high positions: Silayev, Skokov, Lobov, Yuri Petrov, and others. Now on June 2, he appointed three more to the top echelon of the government—Chernomyrdin, Georgi Khizha, and Vladimir Shumeiko.

Arkady Volsky, a former member of the CPSU Central Committee and an influential figure from Gorbachev's circle, had become a symbol of this essentially conservative, on-again-off-again opposition.[48] The economic and political organizations he created one after another—the Russian Union of Industrialists and Businessmen; the Renewal party; and, finally, the Civic Union bloc, formed in the summer of 1992—received powerful media promotion, thereby becoming focal points for the various opposition factions that already existed.[49] However, unlike the democratic opposition, whose main task was to radicalize the changes occurring in the country and give them a clear grassroots, anti-oligarchic character, the nomenklatura opposition did not aspire to make fundamental changes in Yeltsin's policies. Its key goals were to integrate itself advantageously into the reformed ruling class and to form an elite cartel. These goals were achieved in part through the government personnel changes that took place in spring 1992 and during Chubais's privatization program. More was achieved along these lines during the Seventh Congress of the full parliament in December, when Gaidar was replaced by Viktor Chernomyrdin—amidst great rejoicing by almost all the opposition.

Underlying these events was Yeltsin's realization by April 1992 that his economic program was not compatible with the essence of representative democracy, as expressed through an elected parliament. Faced with a restive parliament that was not satisfied with the limited concessions he was ready to make on his economic program, Yeltsin decided to confront the parliament as much as conciliate it. He tried to mitigate the negative effects of such confrontation by developing a form of societal corporatism, which he hoped would appease the country's factory directors and union leaders, head off strikes, keep the wheels of industry turning, and thus undermine the opposition, which was focusing mostly on economic issues.

The means the Kremlin used in this corporatist strategy was a tripartite structure of government ministers, directors of state-owned industrial firms, and labor union heads called the Russian Trilateral Commission for the Regulation of Social and Labor Relations (RTC). Set up in January 1992, the RTC attempted to forge a consensus on Yeltsin's economic policies, with government ministers agreeing to only minor changes to their policies as they tried to co-opt the directors and unions through concessions and favors to key individuals and groups in back-room negotiations.

As Walter Connor has shown in an eloquently argued book, this attempt at societal corporatism worked poorly—in 1992 as also later.[50] None of the three sides in the RTC had any prior experience in such an undertaking, and each came to the table with very limited ability (or, in the Kremlin's case, desire) to implement whatever obligations it agreed to. The government, which was trying to implement monetarist policies that antagonized its two RTC partners, was inclined either to neglect the commission by not showing up for meetings, or to use against its partners a mixture of deceptive diplomacy and *force majeure* (for example, simply not supplying credits or wage increases).[51] The unions were divided and had little control over their own members. Most of the directors were not private owners, but state employees directing run-down factories. In practice, they had little incentive or ability to pursue the Kremlin's goals of a contented workforce and efficient production. Finally, because the directors and the unions were not equipped to move forward on the government's policies and were predisposed to maintain the status quo, they tended to unite and pressure the government jointly, thus turning trilateral relations into bilateral confrontation. Paradoxically, this occurred even though the directors belonged much more to the government than to the private sector.

While Connor argues all this persuasively, let us note that we do not share his premises, which are not always explicit. He hints that Russia's peaceful political revolution of 1986–1991 probably would have become violent if pursued beyond the point where Yeltsin halted it. He also implies that shock therapy was, under the circumstances, an appropriate strategy for Russia. Further, he holds that in 1992 "educated people" were "presumably well disposed toward the government conceptually."[52] Not surprisingly, then, he sees any sort of industrial democracy—a key goal of enlightened societal corporatism—as a chimera. Given his premises, this conclusion is reasonable. But the premises—as we argue in this book—are open to debate, to put it gently.

In a similar vein, Connor plausibly suggests that the Yeltsin regime unconsciously agreed with Adam Przeworski that in transitional economies reforms "can progress under two polar conditions of the organization of political forces: The latter have to be very strong and support the reform program, or they have to be very weak and unable to oppose it effectively." Thus the government's alternatives are "either [to] seek the broadest possible support from unions, opposition parties, and other encompassing and centralized organizations, or [to] work to weaken these organizations and try to make their opposition ineffective." Again not surprisingly, given his premises, Connor suggests that the Russian government had no choice but to take the second course.[53] Almost by definition, though, let us note that this course of "divide and rule" meant deliberately destroying the tenuous social solidarity that had developed in 1988–91, rather than *preserving social solidarity as a top priority*—as Havel, for example, did through the tough years in Czechoslovakia, then the Czech Republic, with good results—even though the economic cost was high.

With all this in mind, let us pick out some key episodes of political conflict in 1992 that illustrate our theoretical discussion. As noted earlier, two different, though frequently intersecting conflicts were raging throughout the year. Yeltsin and the government were jousting with the oppositional directors and unions through the corporatist mechanism of the Russian Trilateral Commission. Simultaneously, they were contesting the constitutional supremacy of the legislature over the executive, and the personal ambitions of Khasbulatov and Rutskoi, in a bare-knuckle fight with parliament over who could grab the biggest share of political power.

The shock therapy policy that took effect on January 2 provoked opposition from many democrats and even more nationalists and communists. In March the latter groups, inspired by Vice President Rutskoi's impassioned denunciation of the policy on February 8, formed the opposition "red-brown" parliamentary bloc Russian Unity. In April, at the Sixth Congress of the full parliament (the Congress of People's Deputies), this bloc had the support of some 40 percent of the deputies, while the government could by now count on only about 25 percent.[54] To counter any defeatism in the latter's ranks, Yeltsin had his trusted hatchetman Burbulis trumpet the Kremlin's implicit contempt for the constitution on the eve of the congress. Should "the socialist position gain the upper hand" at the congress, Burbulis warned, "we will not cry 'help' . . . or be forced up against a wall. Our morality means that we will do what needs to be done in uninvited conditions."[55] The next month, Yeltsin upped the ante by being less elliptical about his readiness to dissolve parliament and rule by decree. He declared straight out: "Presidential rule may be required."[56]

Despite the tough rhetoric, Yeltsin did make concessions at the congress. The industrial directors, unions, and regional governments had voiced their anguish about the impending hyperinflation and the epidemic of nonpayments in the economy caused by the Kremlin's strict limits on the money supply. So Yeltsin's team signaled that more money would be printed, new credits given to industry and agriculture, and three major directors—Chernomyrdin, Shumeiko, and Khizha—would be appointed to the government. Also, on May 20, Yeltsin pleased red-browns and centrists by setting up a Security Council and giving it extensive powers. With Yuri Skokov as its director and Foreign Minister Kozyrev as merely a nonvoting member, the council tried to take foreign and security policy away from Kozyrev and put it into its own hands.[57]

In May and June 1992, moreover, Gaidar and senior ministers devoted increased attention to the administrative, corporatist, and ostensibly nonpolitical forum of the RTC, hoping to assuage the directors' and the unions' rising discontent. However, the government blew hot and cold in the RTC—now cajoling, now dictating, now lamenting its partners' reliance on the Kremlin to put out fires, now accepting a set of joint recommendations from its partners' most powerful organizations, Volsky's Russian Union of Industrialists and Businessmen (RUIB) and the Federation of Independent Trade Unions of Russia (FITUR). FITUR was a reincarnation of the Soviet, establishment-oriented union organization, with a claimed membership of sixty million.[58]

Sensing weakness in the government's concessions and wanting to develop not only administrative but also political clout, the RUIB created a political party, Renewal, in May. The following month, Renewal formed a coalition with non-nomenklatura centrist parties. This coalition, known as the Civic Union, embraced most notably Renewal, Travkin's Democratic Party of Russia, and Rutskoi's People's Party of Free Russia, and claimed to control 40 percent of the votes in the Congress of People's Deputies. It also boldly proclaimed its readiness to form a government and submitted lists of proposed ministers to Yeltsin.[59] Civic Union prospered, though for less than a year, by "claiming to represent the *new* interests of the *old* identities" from Soviet times. It built "a social base comprised of old social groups that were now seeking to defend their newly perceived interests," as McFaul says.[60]

Working in tandem with Civic Union, the RUIB and the union federation FITUR developed a similarly aggressive strategy, seemingly intent on sabotaging the government's attempt at corporatism and certainly showing how it would never be effective. First, in May, RUIB became the co-publisher of FITUR's newspaper. Then, on July 8, the two groups created a joint body, the Russian Assembly of Social Partnership, which promptly denounced the government for its monopolism and disregard of the law. Their newspaper called the government "a traditional autocrat, enriched by Bolshevik experience." And the head of FITUR praised RUIB for its readiness to take responsibility for the country's economy, including its workers.[61] In the autumn of 1992, FITUR joined Civic Union.

Connor sums up RUIB's economic goals this way: "The objective . . . was not the preservation of socialism, and not capitalism, but the preservation of Russia's industrial economy itself, the halting of a slide toward the third world." He then comments: "A statist economic order that defended an industrial Russia at the periphery of the world market and was driven by much the same factors that earlier in the century had driven 'peripheral, delayed-dependent capitalism' toward state corporatism . . . was a possible outcome, if the industrialists' program was actuated."[62] If Connor is right on this point, it is worth pondering whether such a program, even though it was proposed by groups with minimal democratic credentials, might have brought Russia to a less tragic condition than the one it is in today.

In any case, the rapid succession of political and psychological punches landed on the Yeltsin team by Civic Union and its associated groups in June and July shook the Kremlin. Yeltsin decided to shift course. On July 17, Viktor Gerashchenko was appointed acting head of the Central Bank, where he quickly further loosened the monetary policies of early 1992, an action that predictably satisfied Civic Union.[63] Earlier, the industrialists had also been allowed to have a strong influence on the drafting of the 1992 program on privatization and got the "Option 2" procedure added to it. As practice soon showed, this option— giving 51 percent ownership to management and workers—favored directors and was subsequently selected by almost 70 percent of the enterprises that were privatized.[64] Still shifting course, the government set up one consultative body in late October to address the concerns of FITUR and another to address those of the big industrialists.[65] As Shumeiko explained, Yeltsin felt he could afford to neglect Democratic Russia, the nationalists, and the communists, but he needed the support of the forces behind the Civic Union.[66]

The latter's tactics were to pocket Yeltsin's concessions and try to extract more by continuing to play hardball. Thus it supported Khasbulatov's parliamentary power plays against the Kremlin in parliament. Moreover, when the National Salvation Front was set up on October 24 as an extraparliamentary body to organize street rallies on behalf of red-brown forces like parliament's Russian Unity, Civic Union held discussions about possible cooperation with both red-brown groups.

These developments scared Yeltsin, and he made a brief stand: He issued a decree on October 28 banning the NSF. However, the NSF saw that the decree had no teeth and ignored it. Yeltsin also hinted on October 30 that he might dissolve parliament. Although the introduction of presidential rule would violate the constitution, he said, he had sworn a presidential oath to serve, in the first instance, the Russian people (not the constitution).[67] Burbulis proceeded to repeat this threat several times, in more explicit ways.

Almost immediately, however, Yeltsin was back in appeasement mode. On November 3, he had a long meeting with Civic Union leaders, whom he had already met earlier in the fall, and announced that his and their positions were "very close, in excess of his earlier expectations."[68] He also asked them whom they would like removed from the government and whom they would like appointed. The next day, Yeltsin was angry that they had leaked all this to the press, thus creating the (true) impression that he was bargaining with them behind his colleagues' backs.[69] Nonetheless, he instructed Gaidar to draft with them an economic reform plan that would be a compromise between their and the Kremlin's plans. He also gave a speech to Volsky's RUIB on November 14 and completed a round of firings of second-echelon liberal members of his team.[70]

The most specific short-term purpose of all these concessions was to win over enough votes so that at the imminent Seventh CPD Congress he could, in particular, get Gaidar elevated from acting prime minister to prime minister, obtain enough congressional support for an economic program that would not differ too much from the present one, and have his special powers to conduct economic reform by decree extended for another year.

Yeltsin's wooing eventually yielded some results. Civic Union announced that it had declined to support the NSF's plans to have him impeached. On the other hand, the two groups had agreed to seek a vote of no confidence in the government as a way of forcing Yeltsin to remove some key officials whom they especially disliked.[71]

On cue, Yeltsin promptly dismissed three such figures on successive days, November 24 to 26: Yegor Yakovlev, the liberal head of the Ostankino television channel; Mikhail Poltoranin, deputy prime minister and minister for the press; and Gennadi Burbulis, whose post was abolished and who received a lesser post instead—only to lose it two weeks later, when a desperate Yeltsin was using every bargaining chip available to him at the Congress.[72]

Nonetheless, on November 26, Yeltsin's carefully crafted deal with Civic Union threatened to unravel. Although Gaidar and Civic Union leaders had successfully produced a compromise program for the economic reform two days earlier, Gaidar proceeded—without explanation—to present a slightly different program to the Supreme Soviet, which promptly rejected it the next day.[73] Civic Union felt betrayed. Three days later, however, the two sides did reach agreement on a genuine compromise document that was the program presented almost immediately to the CPD—*and approved by it.*[74]

Meanwhile, on November 27, Yeltsin was seeking every possible vote at the Congress that would open on December 1, and he appealed to the long neglected democrats at a special "Congress of the Intelligentsia." The democrats had been highly alarmed by his long string of concessions to the Civic Union centrists, and especially by his dismissals of democrats and the prospect that there might be more to come.[75] He tried to rally them by pointing to the "irreconcilable opposition" of the red-browns and claiming that "the threat of fascism is real."[76] On November 30, Constitutional Court Chairman Valery Zorkin dealt Yeltsin a new blow when he dramatically boosted the morale of the communists, two hundred of whom sat in the CPD. Zorkin announced that the court had ruled certain aspects of Yeltsin's 1991 decree banning the Communist Party to be invalid, notably the ban on the party's regional and local organizations. The communists were elated.[77]

The intricate details of the tense, confrontational, two-week congress—at which agreements were made and unmade, and rules were invented on the spot to facilitate the resolution of complex, unforeseen contingencies—do not concern us here. We will focus only on two episodes that bear on the issue of democracy in Russia. First and foremost, Yeltsin was not able to get Gaidar elected prime minister, despite months of negotiations, concessions, manipulations, and direct pressure from President Bush.[78] Parliament's will prevailed. When Gaidar was rejected by nineteen votes on December 9, Yeltsin locked himself in his bathhouse and may have become suicidal.[79] When Gaidar later finished a weak third in a contested vote, Yeltsin gave up. He took Gaidar's advice and opted for Chernomyrdin as prime minister, even though Skokov had narrowly outpolled him.[80] This choice, however, ended up thwarting the CPD's will. The Congress had voted by a margin of three-to-one for candidates it saw as being opposed to shock therapy. While it judged Skokov correctly, Chernomyrdin eventually found the economic policies of late 1992 acceptable and was able to work with shock therapists like Chubais and Boris Fyodorov.

Overall, however, Russian democracy had shown some resilience. As Michael Ellman writes, the Congress's outcome was "the adoption of a compromise economic policy document, the fall of a prime minister whose policies were very unpopular and had failed, and the coming to office of a new premier . . .

close . . . to the opposition."[81] Nonetheless, the Yeltsin–Civic Union relationship remained uneasy at best. From Civic Union's viewpoint, Chernomyrdin proved rather unreliable; also, Yeltsin dug in his heels and refused to add any of Civic Union's nominees to his cabinet.

In the second important episode at the congress, Yeltsin bargained tenaciously to gain the congress's eventual agreement to the holding of a referendum. This would aim to resolve the gridlock between the presidency and parliament by having Russia's voters serve as judges in a popularity contest between them. Although Yeltsin was fearful that the April referendum might go against him, it turned out to favor him rather more than parliament. [82]

THE RAU CORPORATION

Before we examine the reasons for this lukewarm reaffirmation of Yeltsin and his administration, we should look at the preoccupations of the RAU Corporation through early 1993. To recapitulate, all of RAU's activities, and especially Podberezkin's, focused on two related goals. The first was to make long-term efforts to consolidate as much of the Russian political elite as possible around the ideology of national-conservative statism.[83] This meant converting politicians with other views or, if this could not be done, neutralizing them politically. The second was a more specific, short-term goal—to try to shift Yeltsin's regime toward the same conservative ideology by getting the maximum number of people with such views into his government and entourage so as to directly influence his policies and outlook.

Regarding the democrats, we saw earlier how RAU helped to bring the democratic statists into the conservative camp; yet RAU had additional proselytizing goals. One was to create a variety of national-conservative parties and movements that could convert demoralized Communists, whose party was currently banned, to RAU's ideology. When the ban was partially lifted in November 1992, a related RAU goal was to ensure that the most powerful of the new, restructured communist parties was led by a proponent of national-conservatism.

A third goal of 1992 was to assist Civic Union's skillful efforts, described above, to push Yeltsin into accepting most of its economic program on privatization, monetary policy, and government credits for industry. Success in this endeavor did much to consolidate the politico-economic elite by aligning the directors and the trade union elite with the government.

A key figure in achieving the first two goals was Gennadi Zyuganov. Along with former KGB general Aleksandr Sterligov, Zyuganov was brought to work at RAU in the autumn of 1991 by Rogozin. A top communist ideologist in the Soviet period who was closely tied to Podberezkin, his political confidant and strategist, Zyuganov from late 1991 through October 1992 joined or cofounded a succession of national-conservative groups. Helping him in this regard was

Rogozin, for whom such operations were routine. Indeed, from 1990 to 1994, Rogozin founded or cofounded no fewer than ten such parties or groups, and joined an eleventh.[84] The mechanics and—most important—the precise pay-masters behind this sort of political engineering (or, as Russians say, "political technologies") are a subject for a separate research project. Suffice it to report here our impression that the paymasters probably included RAU, powerful banks, and, directly or indirectly, certain sections of the government. Without a doubt, though, such "technologies" were not cheap. In 1993, for example, just one of Rogozin's organizations, the Union for the Resurrection of Russia, reportedly had a Moscow staff of about forty.[85]

One of the nationalist groups that Zyuganov joined (as co-chair in June 1992) was Sterligov's Russian National Assembly. The main thrust of the Assembly's radically nationalist propaganda was directed against "democrats" of every stripe, including those who, like the former democratic statists Konstantinov and Astafiev, had joined the national-patriotic movement.[86] In so doing, Sterligov succeeded in attracting a significant number of supporters of the parliamentary opposition and, above all, rendering lifeless the grassroots support for the democratic statists. Sterligov's former boss, Vice President Rutskoi, who led the regime's internal opposition to Gaidar's reformists, also began to distance himself from these statists.

In October 1992, however, elements of the populist movement, led by intellectuals (such as Konstantinov and Astafiev) who had turned their back on Yeltsin, acquired their own dynamic and created the red-brown National Salvation Front.[87] Because Zyuganov, too, was a founding leader, it was not surprising that the NSF soon began to look like a mirror image of the fractious—and by now, decaying—coalition Democratic Russia. A hidden conflict began within NSF's ranks between a radical revolutionary wing led by Konstantinov (who was working with the increasingly popular radical communist Anpilov) and Zyuganov's conservative, nomenklatura-affiliated grouping.

It was no accident that this peculiar alliance between former Yeltsin supporters, pro-empire intellectuals, and ultraconservative elements of the "street" opposition from the bottom of the social ladder coincided with the political offensive of the "directors' opposition," described previously. The two developments led to perhaps the most serious crisis of the Yeltsin regime. The potential for coordinated actions by Civic Union and the National Salvation Front—which began to emerge in November 1992—possibly could have led to a peaceful, constitutional removal of the government.

However, the strategic alliance of the old and new elites that Volsky and the directors were seeking was clinched when Chernomyrdin became prime minister in December. This blocked any possibility of a revolutionary turn of events. Having lobbied for Chernomyrdin's nomination, soon most of the Civic Union leaders—Volsky, Vasily Lipitsky, and later even Travkin—proclaimed their loyalty to the new coalition government, while the activities of Civic Union itself as a "moderate opposition" bloc quickly wound down. Of its founders, only Vice President Aleksandr Rutskoi—whose national popularity at the time permitted him to act autonomously with respect to the economic interests of the elite groups—continued to drift in the direction of the radical opposition.

Although the NSF did not fade away, its dynamics were affected by the reemergence of the communists. In February 1993, a congress to create the Communist Party of the Russian Federation was held, at which the proponents of the reformist, trade-unionist, internationalist heritage of Marxism, along with the street radicals and revolutionaries of the Anpilov camp, suffered a crushing defeat.[88] The leadership of the CPRF, which had quickly become the largest and best-funded of the post-Soviet communist parties, was captured by Zyuganov's national-conservative "statist" group, which was closely linked via the RAU with senior elements in the ruling elite and with the Russian intelligence services. Without even joining the CPRF, Podberezkin became one of its leading ideologists, a co-author of its official documents, and the main inspiration behind Zyuganov's speeches and writings.[89]

Simultaneously, even though the CPRF did not join the National Salvation Front, Zyuganov and others began to push aside the more radically inclined intellectuals headed by Konstantinov and Astafiev. Also, in July 1993, an authoritative group of nationalists headed by Sergei Baburin abandoned the NSF. Nonetheless, in August, a well-known analyst calculated that if early elections had been held, the NSF could have received 15 percent of the vote, or even 30 percent if Rutskoi had become its leader.[90]

THE REFERENDUM OF APRIL 1993

Let us return now to the referendum of April 25, 1993. Before we provide details of its outcome, however, it is important to sketch in some context. How much popular support did Yeltsin have in early 1993? A series of nationally representative polls taken by the reputable Center for the Study of Public Opinion gives these figures for January 1993. On the one hand, the poll reported that 5 percent of citizens fully shared Yeltsin's views, 11 percent were "ready to support" him because he was "the leader of the democratic forces," and 6 percent had not liked him much before but hoped that "in the future he will be of use to Russia." Thus 22 percent had some sort of positive feelings for Yeltsin. A further 16 percent supported him, but only "because of a lack of other worthy political leaders." On the other hand, 29 percent had become "disenchanted" with him, 16 percent had "no adherence" to him, and 6 percent would have supported "anyone but Yeltsin." We might summarize these findings by saying that in January, Yeltsin had positive support from 22 percent of the population, reluctant support from 16 percent more, and no support from 51 percent.[91]

To a Western politician, these would be catastrophic figures. However, they were less catastrophic than corresponding figures for the Congress of People's Deputies, not to mention the rock-bottom figures for Speaker Khasbulatov, whose Chechen nationality, unpleasant manner, and persistent abuse of his position to promote his own ambitions had made him one of Russia's most disliked politicians. For these reasons, and because the referendum took place in the politically polarized context of "either Yeltsin *or* the CPD," most Russians had to make a "choice between two evils."

In this situation, and with 64 percent of the electorate voting, 58.7 percent of voters checked "Yes" to the question, "Do you trust the president of Russia B. N. Yeltsin?" For most of these voters, in light of the above polling figures, their check clearly did not signify real trust. Rather, it presumably signified, in most cases, that they trusted Yeltsin *more than the CPD,* or mistrusted him less. Meanwhile, 39.3 percent of the voters checked the "No" box.[92]

To the question, "Do you approve of the socio-economic policy conducted by the president and government of Russia since 1992?" 53 percent said yes and 44.5 percent said no. Again, the polarized context of the referendum made it impossible to interpret these figures with any accuracy.

Finally, neither of the questions asking if voters considered early elections for the presidency and the CPD to be essential received enough votes to be binding.

As to *why* Russians had such a low opinion of both Yeltsin and the CPD, the answer probably lies in large measure in the aggressive, ill-tempered, often dirty war that Yeltsin and the CPD majority had waged against each other since January 1992. We touched on some of the key episodes in 1992 earlier; from January to April 1993, notable episodes included the CPD's abuse of its power to amend the constitution, the extraordinary maneuvering by both sides over the wording and timing of the referendum, and Yeltsin's manipulative, ultimately vain attempt of March 20 to impose a state of emergency on Russia by using cleverly crafted phrases to circumvent constitutional and other legal barriers to his action.[93]

TO WHAT EXTENT DID YELTSIN DEFEAT THE OPPOSITION?

To sum up from the perspective of April 1993, what did the different oppositions achieve over the preceding year? How successfully did Yeltsin co-opt or marginalize them?

The radical democrats were severely marginalized. The democratic statists joined the national-conservatives, but still found themselves on the margin. The industrial directors used a mixture of hardball and bluff (given their lack of electoral clout) to get a lot of what they wanted—that is, co-optation in considerable measure on their own terms.[94] Travkin's Democratic Party made the mistake of allying with Volsky's nomenklatura groups and thus emasculating itself. The leaders of the biggest union group, FITUR, were largely co-opted.

The National Salvation Front was considerably marginalized, but could still see a future for itself as a political force backing Rutskoi and Khasbulatov. Rutskoi himself was impotent within the regime, but showed up strongly in opinion polls.[95]

RAU, a quasi-opposition at most, could be satisfied that it helped to integrate the industrial directors into the regime and also to get the CPRF successfully launched with—from RAU's viewpoint—the best possible ideology and leader. On the other hand, although RAU helped to push Yeltsin toward national-conservatism, he was still oriented to the IMF, and his economic and military policies left much to be desired. Finally, although the parliamentary majority fought Yeltsin to a draw in December, the results of the referendum, while not bringing him victory, gave him a definite opening. Through this opening he might soon be able to push a new constitution that would assign the key powers of government to himself.

Meanwhile, the mass of ordinary Russians were most definitely at or beyond the margin. To a large extent, Russia was again divided horizontally between the holders of power and wealth and the rest of society. Most party and labor leaders had little or no connection to society's grassroots. Power struggles concerned competing groups at the top, and the occasional elections that gave ordinary people a voice seemed a weak tool. Indeed, after Moscow's mini–civil war of October 1993 had further deepened popular alienation from politicians, almost half of the electorate (some 46 percent) declined to vote at all in the December elections. And of those who did vote, 12.4 percent voted "against all candidates" and a further 4.8 percent destroyed their ballots.[96]

As of April 1993, then, Yeltsin had used his formidable skills as an in-fighter and manipulator to neutralize most of the opposition groups that sprang up in early 1992. Through clever co-optation and marginalization, he had avoided excessive compromising of his economic program. And now, because the CPRF had conservative, establishment-oriented leaders, he faced at most only three serious foes: the parliamentary majority (unpopular in the country); Rutskoi (then Russia's most popular politician); and the fissiparous, still-untested National Salvation Front.

On the other hand, the pernicious combination of three things—the Yeltsin regime's promotion of de facto nonrepresentation for ordinary Russians, the "market bolshevism" that was materially impoverishing the same mass of people, and the failure of the opposition leaders to reject co-optation and nomenklatura-style elitism and actually mobilize these people in their towns and villages—was creating a deep-seated sort of passive resistance that could be summed up in one sad word: alienation.

NATIONALISM, CONSERVATISM, AND REFORM

As we have seen, large parts of the opposition to Yeltsin from 1991 to 1993, including most of the communists, were nationalists of one type or another. Yet their often fiery rhetoric did not draw a strong response from the Russian people, and even if organizers had gone to the towns and villages, the result would probably not have been dramatically different. Why was this? Also, why did the Yeltsin regime's steady shift toward more nationalist rhetoric from 1993 on fail to give it legitimacy? In this chapter's concluding sections, we examine both Russian and Western reactions to the ideas of nationalism and conservatism, and consider why their appeal is limited—and the appeal of fascism in Russia even more so.

It has become increasingly common to equate Russian nationalism with conservatism and to place it, along with other phenomena that seem mysterious or unattractive to Westerners, in the category of "hard-line" or "dark" forces opposed to democracy and reform. This kind of thinking—dubious in itself—is even more dubious given the fact that social theory has long viewed nationalism as a progressive force in the context of modernization and nation building, both in nineteenth-century Europe and more recently in Third World countries undergoing decolonization. Similarly, the divisive ethnic passions currently on display in parts of eastern Europe and the former Soviet republics usually enjoy more indulgent treatment in Western academia and politics than Russian nationalism, whatever is implied by this loose term.

Although this stigmatization of Russian nationalism can be easily accounted for by the fact that Russia has historically (and unexceptionally) been an expansionist country, it also owes much to the Russians themselves and their age-old dichotomous vision of national history. According to this image, Russia has been perennially torn apart by an ideological civil war between two irreconcilable forces—the Westernizers (alternatively known in different periods as modernizers, liberals, democrats, freemarketeers, and agents of Western malice) and the nationalists (also known as authoritarians, statists, and advocates of all kinds of retrograde policies). This black-and-white scheme was exported to the West from Russia, where virtually no thinker or writer of any importance could escape taking sides in the contention between the Westernizers and the believers in Russia's uniqueness.

However, beyond the journalistic stereotypes, this bipolar model of Russian politics and culture has always been questionable. Take, for example, the original sides in the debate of the mid-nineteenth century, the Slavophiles and Westernizers. The latter were fairly critical of the West of their time, and their foremost representatives, such as Belinski and Herzen, tended to embrace communal socialism, while savaging the consumerism of the average European philistine. For their part, the Slavophiles were staunch opponents of autocracy and of those policies that would qualify as statism in the parlance of modern economists. Their social ideal was the *mir*, or peasant commune, which they aspired to liberate from the suffocating oppression of the authoritarian state; their political ideal was also in the past, in the direct democracy of the northern city-states of Novgorod and Pskov. Some of them also admired England as an example of organic social development, although they did not see it as an appropriate model for Russia. Essentially, both sides converged as utopian populists, despite their mutual antagonism along the conventional left-right political spectrum.

This left-right, or liberal-conservative, spectrum (an often deceptive product of the French Revolution) is especially misleading in the conditions of contemporary Russia. For one thing, the media image of Yeltsin the progressive reformer fighting against evil reactionaries was deeply flawed. This stereotype failed to account for, on the one hand, the strikingly consistent pro-Yeltsin voting record of Vladimir Zhirinovsky's faction in the Duma and, on the other hand, the trenchant critique of Yeltsin by a leading democrat and Westernizer like Grigori Yavlinsky. It failed to explain why individuals and groups routinely classified as nationalists and conservatives (putatively Yeltsin's irreconcilable opponents)— such as Zyuganov, Rutskoi, Lebed, and Zhirinovsky—found it easier to achieve their goals by cooperating with Yeltsin's government, or parts of it, than by forming an opposition coalition to replace the regime via democratic elections.

Without exploring in depth the peculiar ideological culture of the Russian elite, it is hardly possible to understand why Yeltsin's "reformist" regime not only tolerated but benefited from the services of conservatives like Skokov and Yuri Petrov, and such unabashed nationalists as Boris Mironov and Nikolai Yegorov, while at the same time scaring the electorate with the threat of a civil war if a moderate conservative like Gennadi Zyuganov were to win the Russian presidency in the 1996 elections. It is equally difficult to see why people like Yegor Gaidar and Anatoly Chubais, who would qualify as radical right-wingers on the Western political scale and exhibited much affinity for conservative and antidemocratic "revolutionaries from above" in Russian history, were persistently touted as "democrats" and "reformers."[97]

Let us spell out again our understanding of the great divides of contemporary Russian politics. We are not convinced by those who assert that Russian society has been divided between advocates and opponents of reform—although for many participants in the debate, this bipolar framing of the public debate is convenient and even indispensable so that their confrontational rhetoric can be taken at face value. If one factors out the most exotic variants on the radical flanks, all the leading politicians and spokesmen for major sociopolitical currents —Yeltsin, Zyuganov, Luzhkov, Primakov, Yavlinsky, Glaziev, Zhirinovsky, Chubais, Gorbachev, Solzhenitsyn—argue for change in some form. They differ about the direction of reform, its targets and priorities, and *what exactly* in the national experience must be overcome or transformed, and what should serve as the foundation for future development. Each of these individuals symbolizes a particular combination of conservative and reformist views, as well as a specific agenda targeted toward select social and cultural groups.

Yet none of these first-rank politicians is—compared to the others—a pure reformer or revolutionary. The competition between them is for conservative support as each tries to frame his rival as a revolutionary in disguise while reassuring the public that he himself advocates change that will facilitate a return to one or another tradition of the past from the unbearable present. Such competition stems partly from the fact that the main audience for the radical-reformist rhetoric of Chubais-type leaders is to be found among Western creditors and aid-givers, and their leverage in Russian politics has drastically declined. At the elite level, the obscurantist belief (shared by a broad spectrum of politicians, from Zhirinovsky and Zyuganov all the way to the radical Yeltsinites) that every impulse for revolution or reform comes from abroad and invariably reflects Western commercial or security interests, operates as a brake on any genuinely reformist intentions. No wonder those who have tried to claim the mantle of reformist opposition, thereby exposing the conservative nature of the Yeltsin regime (as have Grigori Yavlinsky and Svyatoslav Fyodorov) usually faced hostility from the regime and the media establishment, while the conservative opposition was provided ample opportunity to multiply and prosper.

The great majority of Russians have seen the very notion of reforms discredited as early as 1991–92, since the ascent of the self-styled reformers was marked by painful disruptions, the wiping out of the defenseless citizenry's savings, and a sharp decline in living standards. The Union was dismantled overnight in conspiratorial style, and shock therapy seemed to fulfill the old Chinese curse, "May you live in interesting times." The unhinging experience of Yeltsin's revolution from above has created willy-nilly a societal base for a mass conservatism that is instinctual and fatalistic, not some masochistic satisfaction with the disastrous state of the country. To put it simply, nobody wants to part with the bad, lest something much worse replace it. It will take a qualitatively different kind of revolutionary or reformist ideology to shake up this bedrock conservative consensus, which helps President Putin and sometimes shades unabashedly into reaction.

This visceral and pervasive conservative sentiment, based on uncertainty and fear, obscures the profound cultural differences among the diverse historical brands of Russian conservatism and nationalism that, in turn, reflect the "multicultural" character of Russian society. The lack of agreement about what constituted the essence of Russian conservatism sheds light on the inability or unwillingness of Yeltsin's conservative opponents to build an effective coalition to replace his regime. The potential participants in such a coalition suspected one another of being agents of antagonistic forces and thus tended to cooperate with those factions of the ruling elite that they saw as more genuinely conservative than their fellow members of the opposition camp.

Thus, for example, the largest group in the anti-Yeltsin opposition, the Communists, have been convincingly categorized as *left-wing conservatives:* they regard distributive justice and economic paternalism as the core of the national tradition.[98] Thus they have more in common with the early twentieth-century agrarian populists of the Socialist Revolutionary party than with the Westward-looking and growth-oriented Marxists of the same period. For their part, nationalists such as Zhirinovsky and Lebed represent the *right-wing* brand of conservatism, focused on authoritarianism and the cult of military force. Theirs is a more modern and Western type of conservatism, but more aggressive and intolerant than the Communists regarding ethnic minorities and the intelligentsia; essentially, it is a product of the USSR's collapse and the failed Americanization of Russia through shock therapy, and it still has a visible tinge of foreignness.

Although both brands of conservatism have sometimes been lumped together as one big red-brown bogeyman, they converge only on a limited range of issues, such as a vaguely nostalgic attitude toward the Soviet Union and a yearning for a government that really protects its subjects. At the critical turning points of the Yeltsin era, as we have shown earlier and will show in later chapters, each group tended to ally with a faction of the ruling elite: the Communists with the managerial nomenklatura of the raw materials and agrarian sectors led by ex-premier Chernomyrdin; Zhirinovsky with the military and police establishment; and Lebed with the financial-bureaucratic oligarchy personified by Berezovsky, Potanin, and Chubais. In addition, all of them have had a congenital affinity for the Soviet and post-Soviet intelligence agencies.

A third and more promising version of Russian conservatism is represented by Baburin and Glaziev, among others. First, it made few compromises with the Yeltsin regime, which brings it closer to the progressive opposition represented by Yavlinsky and Svyatoslav Fyodorov. Second, its leaders argue for a strong dirigiste government, somewhat along the lines of postwar Japan or de Gaulle's France, with obligations centered on growth and development rather than on distribution and with enhanced constitutional authority for parliament. Despite their weighty intellectual input in the public debate, their broader political prospects still remain to be seen. They have not yet found political organizers capable of building a serious party for them.

In addition, despite the preponderance in the CPRF of Zyuganov's nationalist and backward-looking group, democratic internationalists in the communist movement can also find common ground with advocates of liberal reformism, as was evident from their cooperation with Yabloko during the protests against the first Chechnya war and in the 1995 parliamentary elections. This track record lays the groundwork for a potential new coalition of social-democratic reformers, dirigistes, and moderate nationalists that could provide a viable alternative to Yeltsin's oligarchical conservatism disguised as reform. No wonder Kremlin strategists were badly scared by the specter of a CPRF-Yabloko electoral coalition in 1995 and early 1996 and, as we will see in chapter 8, worked with tenacity and eventual success to pit the two leading opposition parties against each other.

RUSSIAN NATIONALISM IN THE CRYSTAL BALL OF SOVIETOLOGY

Let us turn now to recent discussion of Russian nationalism in the West. Back in the days when the Sovietology establishment in the West was still fixated on personnel changes in the Kremlin, a handful of maverick scholars was laboring to explore the deeper trends in Soviet society. Yet even among these few, virtually none expected a radical-democratic or a radical-capitalist revolution: It was Russian nationalism that aroused the most passion, seen either as a credible alternative to Soviet supranational imperialism or as a looming threat to the prospects of liberalization. Writing in the early 1980s, John Dunlop was among the first to approach Russian nationalism with empathy. His seminal works treated the early, dissident version of nationalism as a progressive rival to the Leninist ideology of global expansion. This was a daring and provocative approach at a time when many non-Russian ethnic groups—both within the Soviet Union and within its sphere of influence—had already acquired powerful advocates in the Western establishment and an aura of victimization by the Soviet "evil empire."

While the wisdom of Kremlinology now belongs largely to the past, Dunlop's work deserves much credit for forecasting the growing relevance of Russian nationalism. Having said that, we find that he tended to exaggerate the similarities between old-fashioned Russian nationalists and modern Western conservatives. In short, Dunlop harbored unrealistic hopes about the "liberal patriots" (represented by the *Novy mir* of the 1980s under Sergei Zalygin, Christian Democratic protoparties, and the like) that looked potentially more attractive to the corresponding Western audience, and even saw them coming to power after a brief rule by the "National Bolsheviks."[99] Yet he also favored a dialogue with the nationalist "center" (such as the *Nash sovremennik* authors and even Pamyat') that, in his view, "could potentially be educated and morally improved."[100]

An opposite view was advanced with conviction and persistence by Alexander Yanov. Yanov was one of the few Soviet dissidents who emigrated and set out to secure himself a position in Western academia that would enable him to mobilize public opinion and governments behind the dissidents' cause and to shift Western policies toward the USSR in the desired direction—away from detailed concern about the Kremlin elite and toward concern with Russian society in all its complexity. In addition, he tried to instill in American Sovietology a long-range historical perspective on Soviet Russia. Seeing himself as a spiritual heir of the nineteenth-century Westernizers, Yanov conceptualized obscure academic arguments in Soviet periodicals as a new cycle of the perennial

Russian debate between Slavophiles and Westernizers. As a spokesman of the liberal-democratic wing of the dissident spectrum, he also had to compete with nationalist thinking (as represented by Aleksandr Solzhenitsyn, among others) for the tiny Western audience that was paying attention to Soviet dissidents.

With much foresight, Yanov expected the Western elites to emerge as a key, or even *the* key arbiter of the domestic debates of post-Soviet Russia, and aspired to obtain their support for Russian Westernizers outside the Soviet establishment. For this purpose, he played up the ugliest outbursts of Russian nationalism in the USSR, depicting them as typical of the modern-day nationalists who were allegedly set to claim power after the fall of the CPSU regime. In his opinion, only determined and unequivocal backing for the Russian Westernizers from the West would stave off a reactionary nationalist backlash that, according to Yanov, would have catastrophic implications on a global scale.[101]

As Yanov later had to admit, his ambitious attempt to revolutionize Sovietology and alter the premises of U.S. policy toward the USSR fell on sterile ground.[102] The Sovietology establishment treated him as an alien force with an obscure and impractical agenda.[103] Yanov's writings were "sanitized" by forewords written by heavyweights of the discipline—not unlike the Soviet editions of Western social thinkers that were sanitized by critical introductions, lest the reader by some chance accept the erroneous conclusions of the author.[104] With the benefit of hindsight, the mistrust of Yanov appears to have been a defensive reaction to the methodological novelty and scope of his generalizations, which went beyond the narrow disciplinary purview of Sovietologists concerned with the here and now. The importance of Yanov's case lies in the fact that it revealed a certain disconnect between nonestablishment Russian Westernizers and Western elites.

Let us start with the viewpoint of the latter. Starting in 1968, the West woke up to the fact that democratic idealism was far from dead in Eastern Europe and the USSR. In particular, the Prague Spring and the emergence of a democratic movement in major Soviet cities caught the West's imagination. Journalists began to report on these developments, radio stations broadcast to the East the *samizdat* texts that dissidents smuggled abroad, and Western publishers issued dissidents' works and translated classical Western books into Russian, Czech, and Polish, so that travelers and students could quietly give them to dissidents during visits.

At the same time, however, although Western governments played a considerable role in these activities and supported dissidents publicly from the early 1970s, they continued to focus *primarily* on perceived threats from Soviet Third World expansion and the USSR's military power. In the 1970s, Afghanistan, Angola, Ethiopia, and Mozambique were taken over by Soviet-supported Marxist regimes. Between 1956 and 1979, the USSR invaded Hungary, Czechoslovakia, and Afghanistan to suppress opposition. And the Brezhnev regime repeatedly insisted that America's defeat in Vietnam had caused the "world correlation of forces" to change decisively in favor of communism. From 1979 to 1984, however, the West protested strongly as the KGB sharply increased its arrest rate of Soviet dissidents; brought emigration to a virtual halt; and closed down, with a couple of unusual exceptions, every dissenting group in the country. In retaliation for this and for the Afghan invasion, Western governments cut off trade credits and imposed grain and technology embargoes. In 1984, it seemed as though the USSR's fragile democratic movement had been virtually wiped out and would not revive for many years. Western support for Soviet dissidents continued through radio broadcasts and other means, but much of it was concerned not with prodemocracy activity as such, but with moral and material help to the imprisoned dissidents and their families.[105]

Thus the West was not prepared for Gorbachev. When it did start negotiating with him in 1985–86, the main focus was arms control, not support for democracy. Although the latter soon followed, it was usually subordinated to security, foreign policy, and economic concerns.

Let us switch now to the perspective of prodemocracy, pro-Western intellectuals in Russia in the late 1980s. For them, Yanov's writings were influential. The picture they got of the West was one of a community that had failed to study Soviet society and Russian history seriously, had responded grudgingly to dissidents' efforts to open a dialogue between Russian intellectuals and the West, mistook Soviet decline and defensiveness (as over Afghanistan) for expansionism, and was not geared up to make a strong commitment to the democrats in their inevitable struggle with the anti-Western nationalists when the time came to compete over who would succeed the Communists.

None of this prevented the democratic idealism of the dissidents in the sixties and seventies from reviving and flourishing mightily in the late 1980s. But it was a warning that began to resonate when, as we discussed in chapters 3 and 4, the West seemed to be too narrowly concerned with security issues; reluctant to invest serious resources in Gorbachev, then in Russia; and too ready to practice *Realpolitik* when the Kremlin made concessions and was too weak or confused to insist on reasonable quid pro quos. And the warning resonated even more when the West was an active partner in the tragedy of Yeltsin's reforms.

All this makes a reading of Yanov's work useful for those who feel surprised by the deep disillusionment of today's Russian Westernizers with today's West and by the erosion of the cultural and political base for Westernization among the progressive-minded Russian intelligentsia.

Yanov's superiority as a prophet over his critics, who derided the very idea of a systemic crisis and collapse of the Soviet political system, and who denied the relevance of the pre-1917 ideological and cultural legacy for Soviet society, was borne out by history. On the other hand, his portrayal of Russian nationalism was conditioned by his Westernizer's bias and the pre-emigration attacks on his writings, and it often served rhetorical rather than scholarly purposes. His key assertion that any brand of nationalism was inherently prone to ally itself with the ruling elite against the liberal-democratic opposition and degenerate into fascism was not proven—and could not have been. He savaged Solzhenitsyn as an alleged spokesman of the "new Russian right," based on a biased selection of quotations dating back to a transitory period in the complex evolution of this remarkable writer. On top of that, Yanov's metaphysical and anti-evolutionary theory, postulating the circular development of a never-changing "Russian nationalist idea," lacked the insight of a deeper historicism such as we briefly attempted in chapter 1.[106]

In reality, the worldview of Russian nationalism (if we assume such a thing exists as an integral whole) consists of a vast array of diverse ingredients whose intricate mixtures with one another and with non-nationalist beliefs produce political entities with qualitatively different agendas and modes of action. Thus the notorious inability of the leading nationalists of the Yeltsin-era to unite has been caused by not merely their overgrown egos but just as much by the profound cultural, social, and ideological differences among them. Although a loose set of nationalist beliefs inherited from the Slavophiles permeates Russian politics, any attempt to portray Zyuganov, Zhirinovsky, and Lebed as adherents of a single ideology, or as heirs to the Black Hundred, is beyond the pale, even in the heat of parliamentary or journalistic debate, to say nothing of academic analysis. In addition to all this, the Western world itself, which in the 1970s both Yanov and the Westernizers, along with the nationalists in Russia, treated as a stationary and monolithic given, confused Russians after 1985 by turning out to be a repository of contradictions and unfolding potentialities with uncertain outcomes.

Walter Laqueur's book on Russian nationalism aimed to sum up the debate by computing an "arithmetic mean" of the existing approaches. Like Yanov, he emphasized the cultural-historical dimension of nationalism, placing it in the broader comparative context of European history. He likewise treated "the Russian idea" as an indivisible, if developing, entity and ignored or discounted the tensions among its various brands and incarnations. Thus he tended not to draw strong enough distinctions between the European-educated Slavophiles of the 1840s (inspired by Herder and Schelling) and the Black Hundred pogromists of 1905–07, Solzhenitsyn and Pamyat', and Orthodox clerics and the democratic dirigistes of the 1990s. As a consequence, Laqueur's book neglects qualitative differences, except for differences in temperament and levels of activism, between "extreme" nationalists and "moderate" patriots. No wonder that for all his detailed historical analysis, he did not account for the structural disunity among Russia's self-described national-patriots (national-conservatives) and hardly explained their limited political influence.

To understand the fragmentation of Russian conservatism that has enabled the Yeltsin regime to divide and co-opt the conservative opposition, a graphic representation may be useful. The schema in the following figure is based on a situational analysis of conservative attitudes as contrasted with the attitudes and beliefs of the self-styled radical reformers on the three decisive issues of (1) democracy, (2) the IMF's laissez-faire model of a deregulated market economy, and (3) a pro-Western or cosmopolitan ("McWorld") cultural orientation.

Let us elaborate on this picture with brief examples and some analysis.

1. Once the ideals and values of a forward-looking democracy had been tarnished by the Yeltsinites and shock therapists posturing as democrats, the pro-Kremlin media tended to restrict the range of political models on view to either bureaucratic authoritarianism or oligarchic leadership by the nomenklatura. In a nutshell, Russian citizens were offered a choice between a regime of unaccountable, impersonal, and usually corrupt apparatchiks on the one hand, and a regime backed by the often arbitrary coercion of the power ministries and private security services on the other. Yeltsin himself did much to sustain this Scylla and Charybdis framework: In March 1995, when faced with public outrage over corruption and crime, he made his critics shudder by suggesting that the police might be given the right to execute "bandits" on the spot, without trial.

Because his regime included both authoritarian and oligarchical components and oscillated between the two, depending on the circumstances, the conservative opposition tended to split between those who, like Zyuganov and other CPRF leaders, drew close to the Kremlin oligarchs for fear of a repressive dictatorship, and the mainstream nationalists, who gravitated toward an Iron Hand as the antidote to unaccountable collegial rule by a Mafiya-establishment alliance. Representing this split were a large Communist faction in parliament, besieged by special interests and led by colorless functionaries, and a gaggle of prospective authoritarian leaders like Rutskoi, Lebed, and Luzhkov, each endowed with charisma and ruthlessness but lacking both a mass organization and roots in society.

Meanwhile, the camp of the progressive opposition has been a small one because the forward-looking elements in the CPRF, whom Urban and Solovei call Marxist reformers and see as potential social-democrats, have not been able to drag their party into that camp.[107] The CPRF's Duma leaders came to the rescue of Chernomyrdin's cabinet almost every time that Glaziev, Yavlinsky, Baburin, or other non-Communist opponents of the regime came close to obtaining a vote of no confidence in Chernomyrdin and thus to creating a cabinet crisis that might have compelled Yeltsin to share power with the progressive opposition. The informal justification offered for this practice by the Zyuganovites was that if Chernomyrdin were ousted, Yeltsin might appoint Chubais in his place, disband the Duma, and install a full-blown dictatorship. They also feared that if they tried to oust Yeltsin, it could easily split the Russian elite and lead to a civil war from which only the West would benefit. This demoralizing logic of fear attests to the degree of fatalistic resignation on the part of Zyuganov and his comrades, who have gradually come to believe that their opposition is doomed to defeat by some incomprehensible forces of history.

2. On the issue of economic policies, Yeltsin's opponents again imagined that they were facing Scylla and Charybdis: either a wholesale retreat of the

Figure 2. Major ingredients of Russian conservative ideology.

1. Antidemocratic attitudes

*variants:*_____

- a. Bureaucratic authoritarianism:
  - Kremlin version: Chubais, Korzhakov, Putin; leading early theorist: Migranyan
  - Opposition version: Lebed, Zhirinovsky
- b. Nomenklatura oligarchy
  - Kremlin version: Chernomyrdin, Berezovsky
  - Opposition version: Zyuganov

2. Rejection of the IMF or Reagan-Thatcher free market

*variants:*_____

- a. Dirigiste statism in the style of Roosevelt or de Gaulle;
  - Kremlin version: Soskovets, 1993–96; potentially Luzhkov
  - Opposition version: Glaziev
- b. Corporatism: government, business, and (occasionally) labor coordination in policymaking
  - Kremlin version: nonexistent since weak attempt in 1992–93
  - Other versions: Volsky, the Zyuganov group in the CPRF, Chernomyrdin, Berezovsky
- c. Liberal or social-democratic welfare state*
  - Kremlin version: none
  - Opposition version: Yavlinsky and moderate wing of CPRF
- d. Communist egalitarianism (Anpilov et al.)

3. Resentment toward excessive Westernization
- a. Nationalism in a narrow sense

*variants:*_____

- i. Ethnocentric Russian (*russkii*) chauvinism
  - Kremlin version: the 1994–96 Chechnya "War party" (Korzhakov, Yegorov), Putin
  - Opposition version: Sterligov, Barkashov; milder, quasi-opposition version: Rogozin

*Not part of conservative ideology, but included here to assist comparisons.

Figure 2. (continued)

  ii. Statism, or *rossiiskii* patriotism
   ● Kremlin version designed by Shakhrai and Stankevich in 1991;
    nowadays: Primakov, Luzhkov
   ● Opposition version designed by Travkin, Aksiuchits, Baburin, and
    Astafiev in 1991; has merged with the official version
  iii. "People's patriotism": basically supra-ethnic, with emphasis on
   the people and the land, not on the state; implies that the Russian
   Federation is not the authentic Russian state, thus leaving an open
   door to the possibility of the USSR's restoration
   ● Opposition version: People's Patriotic Union—Zyuganov, Pod-
    berezkin, Govorukhin, N. Ryzhkov, Tuleyev, Lapshin
  iv. Cultural patriotism of the "compatriots" (diaspora Russians); often
   merges with ethnic or "people's patriotism" (emigrants), or nostalgic Soviet patriotism (nonethnic Russians in the "near abroad")
  v. Nostalgic Soviet restorationism
   ● Kremlin version: not known
   ● Opposition version: Zhirinovsky, Alksnis, Belarusian president
    Aleksandr Lukashenko

 b. Explicitly supranational forms of non- or anti-Westernism

*variants:*_____

  i. Pan-Slavism (Solzhenitsyn, Aksiuchits, and Astafiev in 1990–91);
   nowadays: Lukashenko and some supporters of Serbia
  ii. Eurasianism
   ● Establishment version: Kazakhstan president Nursultan
    Nazarbayev, Shakhrai, Stankevich, Migranyan; virtually no
    proponents nowadays
   ● Opposition version: Dugin, Sergei Kurginyan, Geidar
    Dzhemal
  iii. Global messianism (a pervasive stream in Russian culture, from
   Filofei of Pskov, Bakunin, and Solovyov to Lenin and Gorky);
   currently, no proponents known

government from its historical obligations to society under the banner of a free market revolution, or collusion between the government bureaucracy and the traditional economic elites to maintain state distribution of goods and paternalistic control, while blocking the development of an independent private sector. Within the Yeltsin coalition of 1991–1998, the former trend was epitomized by Gaidar's shock therapy and Chubais's privatization, and the latter by Chernomyrdin's so-called stabilization policies, which protected monopolistic interests in the traditional sectors of the economy. Both were inimical to progressive social reform, in which an activist developmental state with a democratic government—using a model somewhat like that of the British government in the three decades after World War II—would set the priorities of national economic development. At the same time, such a developmental state would maintain an extensive social safety net, distance itself as much as possible from special interests, and pursue both a moral agenda and fiscal policies to promote small and medium industry and thus empower the Russian middle class.

This social reformist option failed to materialize, precisely because the Yeltsin regime managed to split the opposition: Most of the latter's reform-minded wing remained more or less allied with the Kremlin shock therapists in their largely imaginary struggle against the Chernomyrdin dinosaurs, while the Communists formed a bloc with the dinosaurs, pronouncing them the lesser evil as compared to shock therapy, IMF conditionalities, and foreign economic penetration fostered by Chubais. This false choice—imposed with considerable success from above—prevented, for example, a broad-based electoral alliance among the opponents of the Yeltsin regime in the 1996 elections, despite the fact that all the major potential partners in such a coalition—the CPRF, Yabloko, the Democratic Party of Russia, and the Party for Working People's Self-Management—concurred in the demand for a strong and socially responsible state.

In reality, however, the alleged split in the establishment was a fake: Chernomyrdin and his corporate allies in the traditional industries, who often postured as hidden allies of the conservative opposition, benefited handsomely from shock therapy, lining their pockets in Chubais-administered privatization deals and profiting from foreign financial support. For their part, Gaidar, Chubais, and their associates, posing as freemarketeers, were as assiduous as Chernomyrdin in advancing the monopolistic special interests of their cronies by arbitrary interventions in the market, most notably in the financial and banking sector. They were implicated in corrupt deals with private financiers and in outright scams, which, as we shall see in chapter 9, became the stuff of explosive political scandals during the second round of shock therapy in 1997.

3. The question of whether or not Russian nationalism is a viable opposition ideology begs critical assessment. The West's interest in Russian nationalism has been fueled by two major assumptions—that communism has failed and that the democrats (erroneously identified with Yeltsin, Gaidar, and Chubais) have proved unable to lead the Russian people down the shining path to a capitalist

future. In reality, though, Yeltsin and his retainers could no more be called democrats than the corrupt nomenklatura of the late Soviet period can be identified with the heroes of Marxian historical prophecies. In other words, a sober understanding that neither democracy nor socialism has ever been given a fair chance in Russia might make those concerned with Russia's ills less eager for a nationalist alternative.

Any attempt to choose nationalism as the rallying ideology of the anti-Yeltsin opposition would be highly risky. In the multiethnic and multicultural Russian Federation, it is difficult to come up with a noncontroversial definition of Russian nationalism (although Putin is trying). As discussed in chapter 2, Russians historically have shown marked variations in their identities as ethnic group, civic nation, and cultural nation. There are several reasons for this.

Despite the numerical predominance of ethnic Russians (*russkie*), the non-Russian ethnic groups have invariably played a critical, defining role in Russian culture and politics. Russia's claim to a unique status in European (or, for that matter, Eurasian) civilization has been based on its supra-ethnic identity as a commonwealth of ethnic groups, languages, and cultures, "countries within a country," inhabited by *rossiyane,* or peoples of the Russian land.[108] The very term *natsionalizm* is negatively colored in Russian, because it historically refers to ethnicity and is therefore divisive. The Soviet leadership from the 1950s to the 1980s, while encouraging state patriotism and sometimes even anti-Semitism, censured Russian *natsionalizm,* anticipating its corrosive effects on the cohesion of the Union. The assertion by the prominent Russian ethnocrat Aleksandr Barkashov that "*russkie* constitute 85 percent of Russia's population, and only the remaining 15 percent are *rossiyane*" is a semantic fraud: *russkie* are as much *rossiyane* as all other Russian citizens. Moreover, every attempt by nationalists to compartmentalize ethnic groups within Russia, as in Chechnya and Tatarstan, has eventually led to claims for separate statehood, with Russian national identity shrinking in the process.

Such confusion was the result of Stalin's ill-conceived partitioning of the Russian Federation into constituent republics artificially carved out along ethnic lines, which nobody thought would ever become the borders of national statehood. In addition, the Stalin regime aspired to create a special Soviet nation by mass relocations of ethnic groups within the USSR. This was an inconclusive venture, and by the end of the Soviet era, a sizable group of persons who identified themselves in cultural and civic terms as Soviet people coexisted with the traditional ethnic groups, thereby making the ethnocultural mosaic even more complex than in the past. In addition, the mass political emigrations from Russia in the twentieth century have created a separate entity, sometimes defined as *"people of Russian culture,"* or *"compatriots"*—native Russians, regardless of ethnicity, who for some reason have lacked the country's citizenship or were so hostile to the existing Soviet/Russian state that they preferred to identify themselves with the country and its people, but not with its statehood.[109]

Even this cursory overview of the problem should make it clear why a nationalism of the traditional Western type, grounded in the reality of a nation-state, has not emerged in Russia as a *mentalité,* to say nothing of a coherent political ideology. Suffice it to compare the official Orthodox-autocratic nationalism of Count Uvarov or Ober-Procurator Pobedonostsev with the radically oppositionist nationalism of the early Slavophiles or the Populists. Although on the eve of the perestroika period, tensions between ethnocratic nationalism (as exemplified by the "village prose" writers and the *Nash sovremennik* group) and Soviet imperialism (represented by the "military writers" such as Bondarev, Prokhanov, and the journal *Molodaya gvardiya*) were mostly muted, the explosion of nationalisms of the nation-state category along the Soviet periphery two years later drastically complicated the picture.[110]

The Russian parliament's Declaration of Sovereignty in June 1990 led to the emergence of a new type of Russian nationalism, identified with Yeltsin's RSFSR —an ideology virtually everybody considered artificial, because the RSFSR borders were viewed as arbitrary. Nonetheless, it was widely exploited as an ingenious device for subverting Gorbachev's central authority. This effort was also assisted—if unwittingly—by ethnic Russian nationalists of the anti-Yeltsin camp who clumsily defended the Union on behalf of ethnic Russians, rather than defending it as a multiethnic and multicultural state whose preservation would have benefited its non-Russian constituents. As soon as Yeltsin and his antidemocratic enemies managed to sideline all the democratic and reform-minded politicians operating at the Union level, the fate of the Soviet Union was sealed. Before long, Yeltsin's economic policies and his urging that the RSFSR's administrative units, including nationally defined ones, should take as much sovereignty as they wanted exacerbated regional and social conflicts. These conflicts then blocked the development of a genuine civic nationalism as a unifying ideology of the new Russian state. Since then, advocates of each brand of nationalism—ethnic, statist, cultural, "people's patriotism," and nostalgic Soviet restorationism— have been scattered across the political spectrum, and frequently squeezed into mutually antagonistic coalitions.[111]

The experience of Yeltsin's rule provides ample evidence to suggest that nationalism in Russian politics remains a divisive, not unifying, force. When efforts were made to exploit it, the result was a whipsaw effect across the entire society that weakened both the Yeltsin regime and the opposition camp. The very first attempt to set up an opposition to Yeltsin over the issue of his conspiratorial dissolution of the Union was marred by a clash between the democratic statists (Astafiev and Aksiuchits), who initiated the venture, and the ethnocrats of Pamyat', who lashed out at them for trying to steal the nationalist banner. In October 1993, the Yeltsin camp gained a strategic advantage over its parliamentary opponents holed up in the Russian White House by playing the nationalist card. The strategy helped it to infiltrate the White House with extreme ethnocrats and then to exploit Rutskoi's blunders to frame him as one of them.

The result was that on October 3–4, the Yeltsinites could mobilize the cosmopolitan intelligentsia of the big cities to fight the red-brown bogeyman. The strategy also provided additional pretexts for the CPRF leaders and Zhirinovsky, who felt uneasy about ethnic nationalism pure and simple, to avoid siding with the White House. At the same time, the Kremlin capitalized on the Chechen ethnicity of parliamentary speaker Ruslan Khasbulatov in the period before the confrontation to run a media campaign alerting ethnic nationalists to the danger of a Chechen at the helm of the Russian state, thereby attracting some of them to Yeltsin's side and aggravating the cultural cleavages within the opposition camp.

Perhaps the designers of the nationalist-authoritarian spin in Yeltsin's propaganda war against his erstwhile parliamentary supporters were confident enough to believe that the Kremlin itself would remain immune from aggressive nationalism. If so, this was dangerous self-delusion. After the elimination of the parliament, the tinge of ethnic intolerance in Yeltsin's inner circle grew increasingly pronounced. By late 1994, with the help of such figures as Korzhakov, Yegorov, Barsukov, and others, the country was sliding toward militant chauvinism. Again, as in 1987–91, *natsionalizm* predictably accomplished its destructive work by igniting the Chechnya war and thus, as we shall see in chapter 8, lopping off another slice of Russian territory.

Another by-product of this nationalist drift was the overwhelmingly anti-Yeltsin vote of the non-Russian ethnic groups, particularly Muslims, in the December 1995 elections to the Duma, who instead gave their support to the CPRF and Yabloko. It was only by mid-1996 that the antiwar movement engulfing society and the desperate need to prevail in the presidential elections forced Yeltsin to dump such dyed-in-the-wool ethnocrats as Yegorov and Barsukov from his government.

From then until the fall of 1999, Russia was spared major flare-ups of ethnic intolerance. The appointment of Ramazan Abdulatipov (an academic and parliamentarian from Dagestan, as well as a periodic critic of Yeltsin since 1990) as minister of nationalities in the fall of 1997 amounted to a recognition of the fact that the Kremlin's attempts to use Russian nationalism as a vehicle for nation building and an ideological counterweight to the left-wing opposition had run into a dead end. The Yeltsin regime, having discarded both statist and ethnocratic nationalism, and being devoid of any democratic or reformist credibility, found itself in an ideological void. This void was filled by pervasive anti-Americanism. Thanks to U.S. support for the much-hated Chubais, for NATO expansion, and for NATO's war against Orthodox Serbia, this anti-Americanism affected even the most liberal and Western-minded circles of Russian society. The government hardly needed to devise a national-patriotic ideology of its own, because it could credibly dismiss all Western criticism of the Russian Mafiya or Yeltsin's oligarchical rule as yet another attempt to victimize Russia as a nation. What may be decisive in the future is whether or not a more sophisticated policy can be developed by the United States and its allies that would dispel this Russian mistrust and help Russians to focus more sharply on the grave domestic problems that made Russia's international stature so shaky in the first place.

To sum up, every attempt to rally a progressive anti–shock therapy and anti-oligarchical coalition under the banner of Russian nationalism has so far been a failure. The Yeltsin regime was skillful enough to co-opt even the most extreme nationalists, who were much closer to the regime's Byzantine worldview than was the democratic left. At the same time, by inflating the significance of chauvinists and xenophobes, the Yeltsin regime drove its potential and actual critics from the center into a dead end, where they were forced to choose between various evils: either to acquiesce to a corrupt and incompetent administration whose economic policies had made many of them more destitute than under the Soviets, or to be hanged on a street lamp by some Barkashov, or to prepare to be dispatched by a future Generalissimo Vladimir Zhirinovsky to "wash their feet in the Indian Ocean."

This critical assessment of the role that Russian nationalism has played so far in post-Soviet Russia does not imply that Russians might not, after Putin, develop a creative and viable blueprint for a broadly inclusive national identity. It appears likely that such a vision would be not inward looking but outward oriented, and it would project a message of global significance. Such a turn of events would restore the main line of the Russian cultural tradition, which Russia's foremost patriots, such as Fyodor Dostoevsky, saw in its universal openness and empathy for even the remotest of human cultures.[112]

FASCISM IN RUSSIA: A BOGEYMAN OR A REAL THREAT?

Over the past decade, accusations of "fascism" have been leveled in Russia with such frequency as to make this one of the most common terms of daily political and journalistic usage. In the confrontational rhetoric that has been the hallmark of the domestic cold war between Russia's shock therapists and their opponents, allegations about "fascist" and "Nazi" beliefs (these terms being used as substitutes) have been advanced by self-styled democrats, without scruples about terminological accuracy, against whomever they wanted to stigmatize as the consummate evil. Predictably, the ploy has worked well, given the strong humanitarian tradition in Russian culture that is antagonistic to fascism and thanks to vivid memories of the Soviet victory over German fascism in 1945. Since 1988, abundant financial and human resources from Russia and abroad have been pumped into the creation of numerous self-styled antifascist centers and fronts, as well as research and intelligence facilities to investigate the activities of any politician or group that the new leaders decided to frame as fascists. In the early 1990s, research topics involving the "fight against fascism" and related issues became a good career move for Kremlin-loyal academics and would-be politicians in the same way that the "struggle against Zionism" was fashionable over the preceding two decades.[113]

The use of "fascist," "red-brown," and similar labels for the purposes of witch-hunting has been made easier by the elusive nature of fascism, which has no clear and uncontradictory definition, and by the fact that only a handful of Russians, however dispossessed and hostile to the plutocratic establishment they might be, have a positive view of fascism. Although fascism is not a major theme of this book, some basic commonsense clarification about what fascism is and how it can be identified should be helpful. Is fascism inextricably linked with the traditional Russian beliefs that are routinely vilified by the radical reformers, such as nationalism, statism, socialism, egalitarianism, and the like? Is there any basis to Alexander Yanov's provocative claim that any brand of Russian nationalism, even the most highbrow and culturally refined, is doomed to degenerate into fascism? Given that fascism is not an ordinary political label, but contains an uncompromising value judgment, is there enough rigorous evidence to single out any Russian politicians in the opposition (or, for that matter, in Yeltsin's or Putin's government) as full-fledged or potential fascists?

Fascism is a very modern phenomenon; it was only in the spring of 1919 that the word was used for the first time.[114] In Italy, as elsewhere in Europe, fascism was a product of the great upheaval of World War I and its accompanying economic and ethnocultural dislocations. Like Nazism, it started off as a violent anti-establishment movement of mass protest that fought its way up in street battles. This habitual use of violence had a formative impact on the movement as it matured.

Thus fascism is much younger than other social currents with which it has been rather indiscriminately lumped together: nationalism, which reflected in the writings of Herder and Rousseau the first disenchantment with the cosmopolitan ideals of the Enlightenment; racism, which was used to justify the reintroduction of slavery no later than in the age of the Great Geographic Discoveries; and anti-Semitism, which dates back to the times of Holy Writ. While these three did contribute the necessary ingredients of fascism, the fascist whole has clearly been more than merely a sum of its parts. Suffice it to recall American Know-Nothings or the Confederates: both movements featured elements of sectionalism, racism, and anti-Semitism, yet neither of them can be put in one category with Hitler and Mussolini without violating the historical method.

Another prominent element of fascism was its promise to re-create human beings by restoring their pristine and allegedly genuine nature. This notion of rebirth, or palingenesis, was elevated to the central feature, or "mythic core," of fascism in the thorough analytical work of Roger Griffin, who defined fascism as a "palingenetic (revolutionary) form of populist ultranationalism."[115] Griffin convincingly emphasized the centrality of the fascist belief in the purification of humans from the sin of culture, achieved by a pure act of will as a breakthrough toward a new, more perfect, and authentic form of life. Yet the idea of palingenesis, however important, fails to "individualize" fascism, because themes of rebirth and renewal recur in many religions and social teachings worldwide, as well as in the reformist and revolutionary utopianism of various ages and cultures.[116]

As noted, both as ideology and as political practice, fascism belongs entirely to the twentieth century, an age that has emphasized structural inequities among nations resulting from the unevenness or reversal of modernization, and from the emergence of the global economy, while the mass-media explosion has made these inequities much more conspicuous and painful to endure. The *Encyclopedia Britannica* attaches special significance to the fact that "fascism rejected the main philosophical trends of the eighteenth and nineteenth centuries . . . with their emphasis on individual liberty and on the equality of men and races."[117] Thus, in a sharp contrast to conservative, religious, liberal, or socialist responses to modernity that assumed liberty, justice, morality, and national sovereignty to be norms that had been temporarily violated and needed to be restored, fascism has been, in the lexicon of Russian politics, an ideology of radical reform, or even a revolutionary doctrine. It discards the notions of liberty, justice, and sovereignty as shams designed to weaken or paralyze the human will to action. By renouncing any moral or cultural limitations on self-fulfillment, fascists aspired to re-create human beings by a violent return to their alleged roots *in their animal nature.*

This type of palingenesis is qualitatively different from others in that it radically negates history and culture rather than trying to slow down or speed up social development in order to eliminate history's unevennesses. The fascist's acute desire to get rid of the past (together with the burdensome sense of guilt embedded in it) reveals itself in his intense hostility to two social groups that embody a nation's memory: its intellectuals and its elderly. In its denial of both liberal and socialist claims about freedom and justice, fascism takes its inspiration from Social Darwinism, an influential current of late–nineteenth century thought that is linked with the name of Herbert Spencer and influenced the thinking of Gaetano Mosca and Vilfredo Pareto. In its essence, fascism is a neo-pagan outlook on human nature and on history. Hitler hated Christianity as much as he did Judaism.[118]

Can fascism be found in Russia today? The perennially vague and divisive character of Russian nationalism discussed above suggests that it lacks one of the central components of typical European fascism from 1918 to 1945. Although some variations of ethnic Russian nationalism are congenial to fascism, fascism by its very nature cannot tolerate a rival definition of nationalism—and we have seen many competing visions of Russian nationalism. Racism has been historically alien to Russia, which, unlike the maritime empires, has had no hands-on experience with offshore colonial slavery. That said, one should note that the 1990s have witnessed in Russia, for the first time since the Russo-Japanese War of 1905, explicit and quite widespread hostility toward other races and religions, such as Muslims, peoples of the Caucasus, and Third World nations, who have been used as scapegoats for mass economic deprivation.[119] While anti-Semitism undoubtedly has been an element of Russian ethnic nationalism, it has not enjoyed mass appeal in the post-Soviet age, judging by electoral data and opinion polls.[120]

On the other hand, cognitive elements of Social Darwinism and Mosca-Pareto elite theory are a highly visible presence in contemporary Russian politics. However, these are pervasive ingredients of Russia's "postmodern" political culture and can hardly be identified with any specific political current, be it in the opposition or in the Yeltsin camp. Social Darwinian arguments were abundantly used by advocates of Gaidar-Chubais shock therapy, as well as by such radical market theorists as Vitaly Naishul' and Lev Timofeyev. These and similar authors have tended to view their brand of economics as a branch of quasi-Newtonian natural science and have implicitly portrayed the survival of the fittest as the only universal model for economic development.[121] While they may boastfully claim to be star pupils of Adam Smith, David Ricardo, and modern liberal economists, the Russian shock therapists radically depart from the classical British school's belief in the natural harmony of interests that may eventually lead to the equalization of socioeconomic disparities as the "invisible hand" of the market is allowed to work.

In contrast, the scholars and politicians from the Soviet nomenklatura who dominated the Russian debate about the market economy generally discard the normative notion of economic justice and equality as a red-brown ploy and an obsession of perennial losers. In addition, most of the media, controlled as they are by ambitious plutocrats, have adopted an aggressively anti-intellectual and anti-elderly stance that betrays a protofascist craving for the renunciation of the cultural memory of past generations. The Freudian slip of the tongue by Deputy Prime Minister Boris Nemtsov, who said in 1997 that Russia must enter the twenty-first century "only with young people, including its national leadership,"[122] uncomfortably evokes a theme of classical fascism that, as noted in the *Encyclopedia Britannica,* "regarded itself as representing youth against senility" and also, if distantly, of Mao's Cultural Revolution and Pol Pot's promise of power to adolescents.

We may conclude therefore that the Russian cultural climate is fortunately not propitious for the transmutation of the currently dominant elite mindset into full-scale fascism, which would require the merger of Social Darwinism with some kind of nationalist ideology. Although the Kremlin conservative establishment, disguised as radical reformers, has sometimes tried to forge an alliance with would-be nationalist-authoritarian strongmen like Zhirinovsky or Lebed on the basis of a common Social Darwinist and elitist outlook, the ultimate success of such an enterprise seems dubious. The first Chechnya venture, which might, had it succeeded, have paved the way for a fascist regime in Russia, failed precisely because the rank and file of the Russian army turned a deaf ear to the subliminal protofascist message of government propaganda. The second Chechnya venture may eventually end the same way. Overall, fascism appears to be too subversive of the humanistic legacy of traditional Russian culture to succeed. It cannot easily be merged with the national-conservative mainstream—unless and until the new ideological indoctrination pursued by Russia's current elite, coupled with the progressive lumpenization of many ordinary Russians, should eventually lead some Führer or group to radically reframe the substance of Russian national identity.

In the next chapter, we examine how nationalism failed to unite the opposition when the climax eventually came, in the fall of 1993, to its long tussle for power with the Yeltsin regime. In chapter 8, we look at the failure of the latter's attempt to mobilize nationalism in the service of two goals: crushing the Chechens and moving Russia to a more authoritarian system of rule. These two failures hold, we believe, some useful lessons about nationalism for Russia's political class.

7

TANKS AS THE VEHICLE OF REFORM: THE 1993 COUP AND THE IMPOSITION OF THE NEW ORDER

If Yeltsin suspends an antidemocratic parliament,
  it is not necessarily an antidemocratic act.
If he suspends an antidemocratic parliament and
  throws a lot of people in jail, and troops sympathetic
to Yeltsin spill blood, that's a different situation.

—*A senior U.S. official,* New York Times,
March 13, 1993

AT 8 P.M. ON SEPTEMBER 21, 1993, Boris Yeltsin appeared on Russian national television to inform the populace that he had just signed Decree No. 1400 disbanding the parliament, suspending a number of articles in the constitution, and imposing presidential rule. As the president himself admitted in his address to the nation, this decree violated the country's Basic Law—the constitution upon which he took the oath of office in July 1991 and vowed to be its guarantor. It was by continually amending this constitution with support of the parliament that he had been able to consolidate power and initiate shock therapy. He defended his action by reference to the constitution's outdated "Soviet" and "Communist" pedigree. Nonetheless, according to Article 121-6 of the constitution, the action warranted the president's removal from office. Therefore, within a few hours, acting with concurrence of the Constitutional Court, the legislature found Boris Yeltsin guilty of a coup d'état and revoked his presidential powers. By midnight, Vice President Aleksandr Rutskoi was sworn in as Russia's acting president.

Over the next two weeks, an intense confrontation unfolded between the Russian president and the country's legislature. But the resources on each side were sharply unequal: The Congress of People's Deputies relied on the letter and the spirit of the constitution and on its interpretation by the majority of judges on the Constitutional Court, as well as on the support of the regional and local legislatures. There was also some vague hope on the part of the democratic ideal-ists in the parliament that "the West" would not accept such a violent destruction of constitutional order and representative institutions in Russia, even for the sake of "the reforms." But these factors turned out to be almost entirely incon-sequential. The deeply ingrained culture of military subordination to executive authority ruled out the army's support for the parliament (though, as we will see, it also complicated Yeltsin's task). Paramilitary brigades supplied by ultra-nationalists were of little use, except for discrediting the democratic elements in the parliament; moreover, some of them apparently acted as agents provo-cateurs for the Kremlin's security services.

For their part, Yeltsin and his associates enjoyed virtually undisputed control over key tools of economic power, including the state budget, the Central Bank and quasi-privatized corporations, as well as Western financial aid. With these tools, they had an overwhelming control over the mass media. In addition, the Kremlin could mobilize the repressive power of major law enforcement agen-cies, especially that of the Interior Ministry, which for decades had the worst record regarding corruption and latent privatization of the state and was there-fore a natural power base for the market bolsheviks—the top-down economic reformers in the government who, in tandem with new businessmen, criminal elements, corrupted officials, and factory directors from the communist nomen-klatura, were imposing unattractive forms of capitalism and democracy on a largely helpless Russian populace.

To these Kremlin assets, one should add the submissiveness of the regional administrators (most of them appointed by the president and often complicit in violations of the law) and the zealous loyalty of, and support from, the privileged metropolitan strata, anxious to protect their privileged lifestyle and the advantages of being middlemen between "backward Russia" and "the advanced West." Yet of all these resources, open and implicit support for the Kremlin from key officials in major Western governments and financial institutions would turn out to be the decisive factor. As for the mass of average Russians, subsequent events demonstrated that neither the Kremlin nor the parliament enjoyed broad popular support. As in the final scene of Pushkin's *Boris Godunov,* the Russian people kept their silence.

The fateful fortnight after September 21 witnessed mutual threats and outbursts of violence, alongside an uphill struggle on the part of the advocates of a peaceful compromise. Yet the efforts of various actors—Constitutional Court Chairman Valery Zorkin, a number of centrist politicians, and some of the regional leaders—to negotiate a solution (which gravitated around simultaneous early elections for both the parliament and the presidency, with a redistribution of powers in favor of the cabinet) failed to satisfy Yeltsin's and his associates' desire to define the country's future unilaterally. On October 3, when the forces of compromise were coming dangerously close to success and the Kremlin was on the verge of political defeat, Yeltsin's security strategists skillfully used a group of extraparliamentary radicals under red banners to ignite violence on the streets of Moscow by attacking the office of Mayor Luzhkov—the point man of the centrists who held the balance in the struggle.

Thus political conflict was turned into a contest of physical strength that was more familiar and advantageous for the Kremlin than a legal and constitutional dispute. Early on October 4, Yeltsin and his hard-liners (including such notable figures as then–prime minister Viktor Chernomyrdin and his deputy Anatoly Chubais), having secured the support or acquiescence of the centrists, ordered the attack on the Russian White House with heavy artillery and special commando units. Within a few hours, the lines of defense had been broken, the parliament's headquarters had been shelled and seized, and the leaders of the Congress were thrown in jail. Estimates of the total number of dead range from 140 (the government's figure) to 1,500 (according to the defenders of the parliament), with the human rights group Memorial estimating several hundred.

With the first cannon blast on that October morning, the three-year-old Russian experiment in the democratic separation of powers had come to an end.

RUSSIAN THERMIDOR

The 1993 coup and the subsequent imposition of the Yeltsin constitution marked a key turning point in modern Russian history. For a detached outsider, the 1993 events may have been just a rather big splash on the surface of Russia's perennial "instability." Yet for many Russians, this was the dénouement of Russia's third unsuccessful democratic revolution since 1905. Although the revolution itself had already been blocked with the start of shock therapy, the October coup removed its only institutional base—the federal, regional, and local legislatures—whose continuing operation left some opportunities for the participation of broader strata of Russian society in various levels of government.

From a macrohistorical perspective, the internal logic of the 1993 coup is broadly comparable to landmark events that signaled the onset of reaction after similar revolutionary periods in a variety of countries: the taming of the British Parliament and the establishment of autocratic rule by Oliver Cromwell in 1653; the disbanding of the French Constituent Assembly by Louis Napoleon in 1849; the disbanding of the Second State Duma by Tsar Nicholas II and Prime Minister Pyotr Stolypin after the coup of 1907; and—in a very different context—the dispersal of the Constituent Assembly in January 1918 by Lenin's Bolsheviks (who had promised to transfer power to this very Assembly). On the surface, all these traumatic events represented the revenge of the bureaucratic establishment and the privileged layers of society over weaker and less organized opponents from below. This pattern easily may be interpreted as a vindication of the skeptical views of such scholars as Theda Skocpol regarding the potential of social revolutions. While we leave the weighting of similarities and differences between these events to historians, let us single out three key features that sharply differentiate the 1993 coup from some of its typologically comparable predecessors.

First, unlike all the above-mentioned suppressors of representative government, Yeltsin and the reformers went for a major interruption of historical continuity. They doggedly pursued the elimination of the system of soviets that, despite communist deformations, had seventy-six years of history behind it, enjoyed a traditional legitimacy among three generations of Russians, and was, for better or worse, an established element of national political culture. Thus the October coup was a classic case of autocratic Russian "modernizers" assaulting well-entrenched institutions that had provided participation in governance, however limited, for the lower classes, whom the "reformers" viewed as hopelessly retrograde and ignorant of the genuine needs of the country.

Second, Russia's increasingly burdensome obligations to Western governments and financial institutions (similar to its obligations in 1917, but on a much larger scale) and, more broadly, the acute financial and psychological dependence of the Yeltsinites on "the West" were the defining background factors of the 1993 coup. Hence, the constitutional conflict between Yeltsin and the parliament was not just about legality and justice or democracy and reform. For many opponents of the Kremlin and the intrusive globalism of its Western associates, it was first and foremost about national sovereignty. The Kremlin's propaganda subtly emphasized this theme and managed to persuade statist groups in the bureaucracy that it had better chances to bail Russia out of the debt trap if it courted personal friendships with Western leaders and presented a strong authoritarian bulwark against all who might infringe on Russia's sovereignty.

However, the parliamentary opposition was not convinced. And since the parliament's forcible dissolution, the Kremlin's defeat in an internal conflict with tiny Chechnya, Russia's international defeats in the debate over NATO expansion and in Kosovo, and, finally, Russia's de facto multiple default on its debts have provided ample evidence to buttress the opposition's case.

Third, in the revolutionary conflicts of the past, at least one side, and often more than one, identified itself as the bearer of this or that progressive, developmental idea. In the peculiarly "postmodern" situation of Russia in the early 1990s, with the very notion of linear progress discredited by the Bolsheviks and a widespread sense that the country was in the downward phase of the historical cycle, neither the Kremlin nor the parliament nor any major political force was able or even willing to advance a forward-looking developmental vision to the citizens. On the contrary, as we shall see, most groups tied themselves to images of the national past, sometimes explicitly medieval and feudal in nature. Implicitly, the groups promised to protect these images against the destructive advance of social atomization and entropy.

BEYOND THE DEMONIZATION OF THE PARLIAMENT

To describe the dissolved parliament and lower-level soviets as the institutional base of participatory democracy may raise some eyebrows among Western readers. For, from 1992 on, mainstream Western media, established Russia analysts, and government officials, echoing the consensus among Russian "reformers" and other Kremlin supporters, consistently portrayed the parliament as an anachronistic conclave of die-hard communists and nationalists who were hostile to reform and democracy. In the view of a *New York Times* editorialist, the deputies were people "with a Soviet mentality—suspicious of reform, ignorant of democracy, disdainful of intellectuals or 'democrats.'"[1] The Russian White House prior to Yeltsin's assault was "a theme park of oddities, a Disneyland of paranoia, a Jurassic Park of menace," wrote Lee Hockstader of the *Washington Post.*[2] According to observers like Richard Pipes, the parliament's resistance to the Kremlin was merely "an attempt by the old Communist nomenklatura, or ruling class, to recapture power and the privileges that went with it, while using the parlous state of the economy as a pretext. . . . It is the president who has been democratically elected, while the Congress is a largely self-appointed body dating to the Soviet Union."[3]

The media-establishment consensus is hard to dispel, even when, as in this case, it is far from historical truth. Yet it is helpful to remember that as recently as 1937, many Western media and opinion makers were impressed by Soviet economic success under Stalin's leadership, dismissed rumors about labor camps as reactionary slander, and took at face value the accusations of treason leveled against prominent Soviet leaders at the Moscow show trials.

To dispel these impressions, let us turn to the hard facts of recent history, which show that the majority of deputies in the parliament had been Yeltsin's loyal allies in his power struggle against Gorbachev and the institutions of the Union, and that they also shared responsibility for the initial economic policies of his government, including the launching of shock therapy. True, more than 80 percent of the 1,041 members of the Congress of People's Deputies elected in March 1990 were members of the CPSU, but in Yeltsin's cabinets the record of past CPSU membership was closer to 100 percent. As every student of Soviet history knows, the CPSU was not a conventional party in the Western sense; rather, it was the pivotal institution of government, membership in which was unavoidable for every career-oriented Soviet citizen, whatever his or her ideological convictions, if any, might have been. As we also know, by the late 1980s very few members of the CPSU and almost no one in its top leadership remained loyal to the idea of social justice and public welfare, let alone to communist ideology. Soon after the CPSU crumbled as a government institution, the number of registered members of the communist deputies' group in the Congress shrank to about 6 percent, comprising 67 deputies at the time of the Fifth Congress in October 1991.

The internal political dynamic of the Congress between its election and the start of shock therapy was defined by the steady growth of support for Yeltsin and his policy of separating many RSFSR institutions from the Union. In May and June 1990, 536 deputies of the Congress voted for Yeltsin's election as their chairman, and 907 endorsed his declaration of sovereignty for the RSFSR, which in retrospect can be seen as a major step toward the dismemberment of the Soviet federation. Moreover, in December 1991, all but six members of the Supreme Soviet voted to ratify the Belaya Vezha Agreements. In October and November 1991, 787 members of the CPD voted for the package of measures known as shock therapy and for the temporary assumption of extraconstitutional powers by the president, such as the right to appoint his representatives to the regions and to name cabinet members without parliamentary confirmation. Also, a solid majority of the Congress at last supported Yeltsin's unpopular nominee, Ruslan Khasbulatov, as the new chairman of the Supreme Soviet. Khasbulatov, disliked by many for his manipulative style of leadership, fuzzy political views, and shallow but vainglorious character, was voted in, at Yeltsin's insistence, after five rounds of voting that took place between July and October—with passive support from the marginalized communists and against the wishes of both flanks of Democratic Russia. Being neither a democrat nor a marketeer nor a communist, Khasbulatov was a quintessential representative of the Congress's career-oriented "swamp" and an early member of Yeltsin's inner circle of loyalists.

All this helps to explain the character of Khasbulatov's leadership of the future parliamentary opposition, which he helped lead to a speedy and comprehensive defeat. The most stubborn opposition to his election in 1991 consisted of the nationally minded democrats, who put forward two candidates—one who had already broken with Democratic Russia, Sergei Baburin, and another from Democratic Russia's moderate patriotic flank, Vladimir Lukin. But the promotion of independent and forward-looking parliamentary leaders from among his recent allies, especially the younger ones, was unacceptable to Yeltsin and his entourage. In July 1991, Sergei Baburin, who had campaigned for the speakership by championing the disenchanted intelligentsia and ethnic Slavs mistreated by authorities in the splintering Soviet republics, came dangerously close to winning with a plurality of 485 votes. Later, however, his support declined, as many Communists, intimidated by the August ban on their party, were persuaded to switch their votes to Yeltsin's candidate Khasbulatov.

To sum up, until early 1992 the political position of the parliamentary majority, including the largely reticent communist faction, was hard to differentiate in practice from that of Yeltsin and his entourage. By their political pedigree and culture, as well as by their understanding of democracy, patriotism, and other slogans of the time, the majority of deputies were no better and no worse than the majority of Yeltsinites in the executive branch and the members of his reform team. One major difference, however, was that the deputies of the Congress, or at least those not elected through nomenklatura pressure, were broadly representative of Russian society at large, with its unfocused discontent with the establishment, its desire for justice, its hopes, its illusions, and its weaknesses, while Boris Yeltsin's elitist entourage had very little in common with the majority of Russians.

Another substantial difference was the deputies' collective institutional interest in safeguarding their sphere of competence against encroachments by the executive. Thus the historical mission of the 1990–93 Russian parliament, for which it will rightly be remembered, was that it provided the only realistic institutional counterweight to the autocratic instincts of Yeltsin and his market bolsheviks. Even though most of its members did not have enough skills and experience to fulfill this mission consistently and effectively, they had powerful legal arguments on their side, as well as the legitimacy rooted in the revolutionary expectations of Russia's democratic populism. On key occasions, moreover, they managed to use these resources to block Kremlin violations of the law that would have had bad consequences (such as Yeltsin's attempt in late 1991 to merge the country's main security agencies into a single Ministry of Security and Interior, or his efforts to impose Yegor Gaidar as prime minister in the fall of 1992). Admittedly, their successors in the Duma have been somewhat more experienced and better organized, but having so obviously benefited from the unconstitutional destruction of the Congress, they have never enjoyed a comparable legitimacy in society, and their attempts to check and balance the Yeltsin executive were blocked from the start by the heavily presidential constitution of 1993.

The existence of a consistent ideological opposition to Yeltsin's rule within the 1990–93 legislature is not to be denied, but contrary to the assertions of pro-Yeltsin propaganda and its Western consumers, the origins of this opposition were not in the Soviet-era communist establishment. The principled parliamentary opposition to Russia's so-called reforms came primarily from the ranks of the democratic intelligentsia—the Young Turks, who were Yeltsin's recent allies. Some of them, like Ilya Konstantinov and Viktor Aksiuchits, were diehard anticommunists and semidissidents in the Soviet era; others, like Mikhail Chelnokov, were radical grassroots democrats of socialist tendency; while still others, more sophisticated politicians like Sergei Baburin, were mid-level reformers within the CPSU.

These individuals tried before the August coup to build bridges to the statist elements in the populist anti-nomenklatura movement who had already become disillusioned with the new Yeltsin regime in the RSFSR. This opposition constituted an intellectually advanced minority within the parliament and remained in the minority even after they found opportunistic allies among communists who had been emboldened by the failures and corruption of the "reformers." As we saw in chapter 6, this loose coalition called Russian Unity succeeded in blocking Gaidar's confirmation as prime minister but did not prevent the confirmation of the gas magnate Viktor Chernomyrdin.

DUAL POWER REVISITED

Thus, even though Kremlin propaganda tried to link the parliamentary opposition with the specter of neocommunist revanchism, in reality its principal leaders came from the close-knit group of comrades-in-arms who took power as a result of Boris Yeltsin's countercoup in August 1991. The confrontation between the Yeltsin and Khasbulatov camps was at times painfully reminiscent of the factional struggles in the 1920s among the leadership of the Bolshevik Party. There was, however, an essential difference: In the early 1990s, the fracture in the ruling elite developed not so much along ideological lines as along institutional ones. The political forces loyal to the president grouped themselves inside and around the agencies of the executive branch. Yeltsin's opponents were either concentrated in the Supreme Soviet or affiliated with it. As time went on, those politicians who placed their bets on a parliamentary career or went too far in seeking support among the deputies began to be viewed with suspicion by the hard-line core of the Yeltsin camp and lost their positions in the stronghold of the market bolsheviks, the executive. This was the case, for example, with Yuri Skokov, whose victory in the Congress's advisory vote on the premiership in December 1992 prepared the ground for his ouster four months later from his directorship of the Security Council.

The same was true in reverse—the deputies willing to cooperate with the Yeltsinites in the executive branch were squeezed out of the Supreme Soviet. Thus Sergei Filatov, a moderate and rather faceless parliamentary leader of the liberal Coalition of Reforms, lost his position as deputy speaker of the Supreme Soviet and moved to serve on Yeltsin's staff.

In such a fashion, the executive and representative branches were transformed into mutually exclusive, insular, partisan institutions. Moreover, most of the executive and a large number of legislators were united mostly by their personal loyalties to, respectively, Boris Yeltsin and the parliamentary leadership.

We can suggest several reasons for this phenomenon. In the first place, given the weak condition of civil society and the concentration of economic power in the hands of government bureaucrats with privileged access to the Treasury, the harsh competition among different factions for political influence encouraged them to affiliate with one or another of the existing power structures. The destruction of the middle class had eliminated the otherwise realistic hope that genuinely independent civil-society institutions would emerge. Meanwhile, the endless multiplication of parties and cliques in the steadily shrinking arena of politically involved Russians gave rise to a whole cohort of public figures whose activity had only one attainable goal: to influence the government from behind the scenes so as to further their own personal and small-group interests. By 1993 there had formed around both poles—the president's administration and the leadership of the Supreme Soviet—extensive groups of political clients and claques made up of business-oriented individuals eager to advance their private interests by gaining access to the state budget. For this stratum of society, actions that played the two sides against each other and thus intensified the confrontation between them became their daily bread.

By this time, it was clear that in the concrete socio-economic conditions of Russia, the very concept of a separation of powers, borrowed from Western political theory and specifically from the U.S. Constitution, became utopian and unattainable. The overwhelming concentration of economic power and wealth in the hands of the executive and its nomenklatura allies prevented the establishment of a real separation of powers in the political sphere. Instead, what existed briefly was a type of "dual power" regime, recalling the government-soviets regime of February–July 1917 and the Gorbachev-Yeltsin cohabitation of 1990–91. Under this regime, the relations between the opposing forces constituted a zero-sum game in which the only possible outcome was the complete removal of one of the sides from the political scene. As a foreign observer noted aptly, "between 1991 and 1992, Yeltsin issued about 1,200 decrees and orders, of which strictly speaking 50 percent were illegal. For his part, Speaker Khasbulatov exercised executive powers without any embarrassment."[4]

Regardless of officials' daily rhetoric about the separation of powers, in practice the Yeltsin and Khasbulatov camps both focused on the archaic, feudal question: Who is Number One? Each side worked to bring together in one person ultimate constitutional authority over the military and the police, and operational control over public property and the country's finances. Yeltsin's later remark on the way to overcome anarchy in Russia sheds light on the seizure of the mechanisms of power by the new regime: ". . . everything must be subordinated to one clearly designated principle, law, or precept. To put it bluntly, someone in the country has to be the boss."[5] With these words, which essentially nullified the separation of powers, he justified one-man rule as a basic principle of government.

THE CONTEST OVER LEGITIMACY AS MUTUALLY ASSURED DESTRUCTION

According to the officially accepted concept of the rule of law and the formal post–August 1991 norms of political behavior, the answer to the question of who was the boss should have been found in the constitutional sphere. And here the trump cards were in the hands of the legislature. Article 104 of the constitution—approved in the CPD by Yeltsin's own supporters as part of their legal basis for opposing Gorbachev's center—stated that the Congress could consider any question affecting the interests of the Russian Federation. Given the conditions prevailing in 1993, one such question at any moment might have been the removal of Yeltsin from the presidency. Indeed, an unsuccessful attempt to do this was made by Khasbulatov at the Ninth Congress in March 1993. The president, however, in order to legitimize his de facto control over the state's material resources, urgently needed a new constitution that would clip parliament's wings.

However, the moderately presidential constitution, drafted in 1991–92 by a congressional commission under the titular chairmanship of Yeltsin and the actual leadership of Oleg Rumyantsev, no longer pleased anybody by 1993. It allotted too much power to the president to suit the parliament, while for the Yeltsin camp, the draft gave too little power to the executive. Yet another problem was that the existing Brezhnev-era constitution of 1978 failed to stipulate the means for adopting a new one. This allowed the parliamentary leadership to delay repeatedly the process of constitutional reform by sticking to the familiar path of patchwork amendments to the existing constitution.

Confronted with the impossibility of finding a rational and legal justification for its pursuit of unlimited power, the Yeltsin team unleashed a propaganda campaign. This campaign aimed to deprive the constitution and parliament of their sources of legitimacy and clear the space for new rules of the game that would suit Yeltsin and his inner circle. The constitution and the Soviet system of representative governing organs were declared to be products of the communist era, which in the public mind was associated with lawlessness. According to this interpretation, the 1978 constitution adopted by the Supreme Soviet of the RSFSR was illegitimate because the very establishment of Soviet power had been the result of a "criminal" Bolshevik coup.

This frontal attack on the legitimacy of the Congress did not take into account the fact that from 1988 to 1993 the soviets as a particular type of legislature had undergone structural and functional changes that, to a significant degree, had moved them closer to contemporary Western models of representative government. In addition, the campaign undermined the legitimacy of the institution of the presidency, which, along with the extensive array of special powers assigned to Yeltsin, owed its existence to specific laws and resolutions voted on by the Congress and the Supreme Soviet. Even from a purely logical point of view (not to mention the cultural and psychological aspects), the president of Russia belonged to the communist past no less than did the constitution and the deputies who were so hateful to him. The realization of this fact propelled the ideologists of the presidential party beyond the bounds of rational, legal arguments and toward more primordial sources of legitimacy.

According to the arguments of the radical Yeltsinites, the prerogatives of the president were based on the following: (1) his election by the public in 1991 and the positive results of the nationwide referendum in April 1993 confirming the public's trust in the president and support for his policies; (2) his leadership role and teleological mission in the historical struggle between the forces of progress (the democrats and the reformists) and the forces of evil (the so-called communist-fascists); and (3) finally—and this last argument was used openly only in small circles of ideologically trained supporters—a regime of presidential power would answer the national need for a paternalistic, autocratic system of power and social order. Such power resembled the political and cultural archetype of the iron hand, a traditional source of authority for Russia.

These three components of the market bolsheviks' new legitimizing doctrine represented a classic set of arguments for a postrevolutionary bureaucratic Bonapartism. Yet, to the detriment of its logic, neither in 1991 nor in 1993 did the people voting for Yeltsin have the chance to respond to any questions posed about the nature of a desirable political system—not to mention questions concerning the possible dissolution of parliament and the destruction of the system of soviets. Moreover, the April 1993 referendum did not endorse the holding of presidential elections—or parliamentary elections—ahead of schedule, because less than half of the entire electorate voted in favor. Questions about the people's faith or lack of faith in the legislative branch were not brought up in the referendum.

The weakness of the second argument (based on the well-known Bolshevik principle of "revolutionary"—or in Yeltsin's case, "reformist"—expediency) was its incompatibility with the political realities of the moment. By 1993, a significant number of democrats and advocates of reform (especially at the grassroots level) had irrevocably broken from the president's circle. And influential groups of the old communist nomenklatura—especially supporters of Chernomyrdin who were leaders in the oil, gas, and mining industries, as well as people from the national-patriotic camp who opposed democracy—had rallied to the Yeltsin regime, a fact fully revealed later by the October events.

Only the third argument was difficult to challenge from a rational point of view. Indeed, appealing to an authoritarian, despotic tradition always had the chance of evoking elemental, irrational impulses in the public, and was not subject to logical debate.

THE CONSTITUENT ASSEMBLY: A REJECTED DEMOCRATIC ALTERNATIVE

The efforts of the presidential and parliamentary camps to achieve their mutual legal and moral delegitimation exacerbated a latent crisis involving the very foundations of post-Soviet society—a crisis over the legitimacy of state authority as such. The relative lack of legitimacy on both sides of the constitutional conflict was partly the result of frequent interruptions in the continuity of state authority beginning in February 1917 and lasting until December 1991. After seven-and-a-half decades of what was billed as a revolutionary order, no social institutions—present or past—possessed sufficient legitimacy to fill the political and legal vacuum. The only potential exceptions were the monarchy and the Constituent Assembly, the latter being the first government organ to be democratically elected after the 1917 Revolution and broken up by the Bolsheviks after its opening session on January 5, 1918.

A political platform promoting a Constituent Assembly as a legitimate mechanism for creating a new state from scratch was put forward by the Democratic Union in 1988 and was briefly supported by the president's entourage (the Democratic Russia party included it in its political program in 1992). Later, when the concept of the charismatic, election-based legitimization of the president's regime was adopted and put into practice by the Yeltsin camp, the idea of a Constituent Assembly was retired as being politically inopportune because it allowed less room for a constitutional victory by Yeltsin's team.

Only when it acquired an independent, seemingly nonparty overtone in 1992 did the idea become a basis for the consolidation of a number of centrist forces. The Constituent Assembly platform was supported primarily by groups from the democratic opposition, who unsuccessfully tried to form a third force to counterbalance the Yeltsin and Khasbulatov camps (such as the Independent Civic Initiative led by Yuri Afanasiev, the Social Democratic Party and its coalition of allies called New Russia, and the Christian Democratic Movement led by Viktor Aksiuchits). In 1993, these groups tried to create a powerful coalition to back the assembly idea, but the presidential administration quickly rebuffed them. The Public Committee to Support a Constituent Assembly, formed in January 1993, was swallowed up by a larger organization, the Public Committee of Russia's Democratic Organizations, which, after a brief struggle, was taken over by Yeltsin's supporters and became one more political asset of the market bolsheviks.

Having discarded the Constituent Assembly idea, the Yeltsinites actively flirted with the idea of a monarchy.[6] The mayors of Moscow and Saint Petersburg, Luzhkov and Sobchak, whose views were especially antiparliamentary, became the pacesetters in this nostalgic campaign to support imperial rule—each in turn putting on gala receptions for the family of one of the pretenders to the Romanov throne, the adolescent Prince Georgi.[7] Public statements about the desirability of a future restoration of the monarchy in Russia were made by such prominent representatives of the president's camp as Vice Premier Vladimir Shumeiko and the former radical democrat Bela Denisenko. The Moscow Noblemen's Union launched a campaign to popularize the idea of legitimizing Yeltsin's power by proclaiming him regent for the young Prince Georgi. This offered an easy solution to the problem of the parliamentary opposition and ensured the prolongation of Yeltsin's rule. The self-styled Party of the Majority, which had been created by influential businessmen with the support of the Moscow mayor's office, announced its intention to hold a referendum on the issue of returning to the house of the Romanovs. The plan was never carried out, however, and the Party of the Majority disappeared immediately after the murder of its chairman, Vyacheslav Grechnev, a businessman with shady connections in the criminal world.

Even for the uninitiated, it was obvious that the monarchist propaganda in the government-controlled press did not come from the Romanovs themselves. The campaign was at most a trial balloon and did not have the serious backing of either the public or the ruling elite—although it did, as we will see in chapter 9, resurface with official backing in 1997. Its real purpose was to provide a new source of legitimacy for some aspects of Yeltsin's regime and to make possible a strategic propaganda breakthrough in the regime's drawn-out trench warfare with parliament by going beyond the smokescreen of normal constitutional discourse. Certain restoration symbols were used in the president's draft constitution presented to the constitutional convention of June–July 1993. For example, the lower house of the future parliament was called the State Duma. Developing this theme further, the government-controlled press began referring to the future duma as the Fifth Duma, thus suggesting the new parliament's direct succession to the four state dumas of 1905–17 (three of which were dissolved by the tsar before their terms were up).

As a result of this dalliance with monarchy, the Yeltsinites' fundamentally contradictory ideology took on a schizoid character. Advancing the combination of conservative-monarchist and democratic-reformist platforms in a way that was not contradictory required a sophisticated logic that neither Shumeiko, nor Poltoranin, nor Burbulis possessed. In the terminology of the Russian political elite, with its cultural tradition of conspiratorial and oligarchic Byzantinism, monarchy and democracy were polar opposites. The examples most favored in pro-monarchist propaganda—England, Japan, and the monarchies of continental Europe—served only to expose more clearly the fundamental differences between these examples and Yeltsin's monarchism. Whereas constitutional monarchy in these countries is widely viewed as being closely linked with parliamentary democracy, in Russia the playing of the monarchist and traditionalist card was part of a strategy to *delegitimize* the parliament as a political equal to the executive and to disarm the democratic leaders and groups that were based in the legislature. Thus it was possible to provide a rational explanation for the coexistence of these polar opposites within the presidential camp's propaganda arsenal only by admitting that Yeltsin's liberal-democratic platform had by 1993 drifted away from the essence of democratic values as traditionally understood by Russians as well as the nations of the West.

Indeed, by 1993 the concept of reform was being used to describe the essentially conservative, stabilizing measures taken by Chernomyrdin's government to preserve the oligarchic social structure. In the new political lexicon, the term "democracy" became more and more a synonym for a regime in which almost limitless power was possessed by groups of people who had the money and the mechanisms to get what they needed by manipulating formal democratic procedures. The monarchist-autocratic elements in its propaganda campaign only served to highlight the perverted nature of the government's democratic and reformist rhetoric. Proof of the superficiality of this rhetoric became apparent in the spring of 1993, when the Kremlin, through proxies as well as directly, became friendly with such individuals as Vladimir Zhirinovsky and ex-KGB general Aleksandr Sterligov, the head of the Russian National Assembly, whom we discussed in chapter 6.

However, we should note that Khasbulatov's attempts to strengthen the legitimacy of parliament looked just as peculiar. His persistent efforts to find parliamentary traditions in Russia's feudal past looked at times like a mirror image of the ideological distortions of Yeltsin's supporters. Thus he attempted to identify certain metaphysical origins of Russian parliamentarism in the medieval concepts of "togetherness, popular sovereignty, republican *'veche'* traditions, and the *zemstvo* and cossack forms of self-government." Not stopping at this, he saw a direct link between the Supreme Soviet and the Supreme Privy Council established by the Russian court aristocracy and government bureaucracy in 1720 for the purpose of limiting imperial power. And he expressed dismay over the subsequent dissolution, in the 1720s, of what he now called "Russia's first Supreme Soviet," thus unconsciously revealing his intuitive conception of the parliament headed by himself as a corporate-oligarchic institution representing class interests.[8]

REGIONAL BARONIES SEEK FURTHER AUTONOMY

Another prominent element in the all-encompassing crisis of the Russian state was the increase in centrifugal forces at the regional level. This trend was not so much a manifestation of deliberate separatism on the part of the local governments (with the exception of Chechnya) as it was a by-product of Moscow's constitutional-political conflict. At the regional level, the possibilities for a "dual power" relationship between the president and the soviets were inherent in the fact that the vertical system of soviets already coexisted with the president's representatives and his appointed administrative chiefs in the regions. In some of the Russian Federation's eighty-nine regions and republics, this coexistence was almost conflict-free. In others, however, as a result of power struggles over who would be the boss, only one of the two sides possessed any real power, while the other, though maintaining the external attributes of authority, turned into a stronghold of powerless and partisan opposition.[9] In some cases (as, for example, in the Kemerovo region) the power struggle was continuous and did not permit either side to gain a decisive advantage over the other.

This fluctuating situation, combined with weak communication between the regions and Moscow, left room for subjective assessments by Moscow politicians regarding the actual alignment of power in the Russian hinterland. Both the Yeltsin and Khasbulatov camps had illusory ideas about the amount of support and resources they could rely on in the provinces. Meanwhile, each of the two branches of power tried to mobilize its subordinate departments throughout the country so they could put on a show of force and intimidate the opposing party. This is how the pro-presidential Chamber of Regions was formed under the chairmanship of Sergei Shakhrai as part of the constitutional convention. It was this informal organization that was later—on the third attempt—reorganized as the Federation Council.

A natural result of these activities was the patchwork character of the federal administrative framework and the fragmentation of legal jurisdiction in Russia. In regions where the executive branch was uppermost, the laws and decrees of the parliament were frequently sabotaged or openly disobeyed (the clearest examples being Moscow and St. Petersburg). And wherever real control was in the hands of the regional soviets, presidential decrees and government decisions were often powerless. In everyday life, either legal chaos or arbitrary rule reigned at the local level. In response to Moscow's requests for political support, the regional governments demanded more and more new powers and privileges, even to the point of being given a free hand over their territory, while at the same time they were preparing to act as a collective arbitrator in the Moscow constitutional standoff. This situation threatened to lead to the further transformation of the Russian state into a confederation of semifeudal petty principalities.

At the same time, the regional governments' involvement in the Moscow constitutional conflict exacerbated the rifts at the provincial level—especially between the governors of the sixty-six regions (most of whom were at the time personally appointed by Yeltsin) and the elected chief officials of the twenty-one autonomous republics and the two "federal cities" of Moscow and

St. Petersburg. From the early Soviet period, the RSFSR's republics enjoyed broad constitutional privileges, even if they remained largely on paper until 1986. The republics' role grew even greater in 1990–91, when Gorbachev's federal government tried to counter Yeltsin's push toward "the sovereignty of Russia" by promoting an analogous push by the communist leaderships in Tatarstan, Bashkiria, and other republics within Russia itself. Most of the rulers of the autonomous republics supported the August putsch, but, unlike the rulers of the regions, they could not be replaced by the federal authorities. However, the relative loyalty of the republics' leaders was purchased by the March 1992 signing of the Federation Treaty, which legally guaranteed the special status of the autonomous republics.

Nonetheless, in 1993 the leaders of the republics made their support of the new constitution conditional on the inclusion in it of the Federation Treaty as a preamble. This amendment transformed Russia from a constitutional to a treaty-based federation similar to the USSR—thereby threatening a repetition of the Soviet Union's fate. (However, not only the leaders of Chechnya, which had already proclaimed its independence, but also the president of Tatarstan abstained from putting their signatures on the Federation Treaty.)

From Institutions to the Depths of Society: Conflict and Fragmentation

The deepest and most basic element in the overall conflict was the latent cold war between the Russian elite and the general public—a phenomenon that had become deep-rooted in the Brezhnev era and deepened further after the dramatic failure of shock therapy. An anti-oligarchic, anti-nomenklatura mood characterized the grassroots democratic movement of the 1980s and early 1990s, and it was precisely through populist slogans calling for a fight against corruption and privilege that Boris Yeltsin began his ascent to power. In the public's consciousness, his reforms were at first understood as a means of implementing this program. In the reality of a monopolistic economy, however, shock therapy's deregulation of prices handed over the ostensibly commercial (but actually feudal and bureaucratic) reins of power to the political and economic elite. This led to the sharp and swift impoverishment of the middle class—the only source of political support for genuinely democratic reforms. The voucher privatization implemented by Chubais completed a series of measures that drastically widened the gap between the haves and the have-nots by turning the Soviet-era bureaucrats and commercial elites into de facto owners of former state enterprises. The millions of ordinary Russians who had been lured by Yeltsin's anti-nomenklatura posturing felt cruelly deceived.

Why was it that a third force—potentially consisting of patriotic business leaders and officials, the independent democratic intelligentsia, progressive elements in the officer corps—was unable to form a viable political center and offer an alternative strategy of national development? A partial explanation of this failure lies in the internal contradictions and stratification of the social and ideological demarcations in Russian society. Political sociologist Seymour Martin Lipset has argued that the crosscutting nature of social conflicts ("crosscutting cleavages") can cause a weak sense of political identity and demobilize the social forces that in other circumstances would clash head on.[10] When applied to the Russian situation, this theory provides a convincing explanation for the social passivity and fragility of these groups, when they could have formed a progressive opposition against both of the opposing camps of the post–August 1991 regime.

The result of this social fragmentation and endless conflict was the uncontrolled breakup of the political landscape and a failure to find appropriate political and ideological forms for the expression of the major societal division—between the commercialized ruling class and the rest of Russian society. The potential constituency for the proponents of social democracy, communitarian values, and the organization of civil society at the grassroots level was reduced to a minimum. Public figures outside the ruling elite who supported left-wing, democratic ideas were forced either to refrain from voicing their own views—staying on as a small faction of doubters within the president's camp—or to cross over and join the mostly communist and nationalist opposition. Thus, for example, New Russia, a liberal and social-democratic coalition that in late 1992 and early 1993 had the best chance of becoming a focal point for the consolidation of the critics of market bolshevism from within the democratic movement, was swallowed up by pro-Kremlin organizations and in the end was destroyed. Meanwhile, Civil Society—a group of Congress deputies led by Mikhail Chelnokov, a radical democrat with socialist views—was ousted from the ranks of parliament's democratic factions and dissolved helplessly in the Russian Unity bloc dominated by communists and hard-line nationalists.

The artificial narrowing of the ideological parameters of public discussion prevented any serious development of alternative programs of economic reform by a majority in the Congress of People's Deputies. The intellectual ramblings of the parliamentary opposition began to look more and more like a vicious circle, bounded on the one hand by total opposition to the Yeltsin-Gaidar reforms and on the other by a strict ideological taboo against the restoration of a Soviet communist regime. One can only agree with Yeltsin's assertion that although the parliamentary opposition had "people with good brains who thought actively" about policy issues, "during the years of Khasbulatov's speakership they . . . could not promote their ideas for the development of Russia. Khasbulatov somehow put a lid on the opposition for two whole years, so that only steam escaped, i.e., people who could either scream or speak frightening words with a glassy stare."[11] Meanwhile, the feeble reaction of the proregime democrats to the massive popular rejection of nomenklatura reforms exposed the intellectual poverty of Gaidarism. The ideological workshops of the presidential camp, like the inner workings of parliament, produced no concept of reform that could have replaced Gaidar's shock therapy.

THE HYPERINFLATION CRISIS OF 1992–93

The prelude for the political crisis of 1993 was a bout of hyperinflation that ranks as one of the most severe experienced by a large industrial nation since the great inflation Germany went through in 1922–23. At the start of 1993, Russia was indisputably in the throes of hyperinflation, with prices rising by about 10 percent a week. The new prime minister, Viktor Chernomyrdin, said on January 5 that his government's goal was to "brake, and then halt" the industrial collapse in Russia. Price controls on basic food and medicine items—welcomed by beleaguered Russians but anathema to the IMF—were imposed by Chernomyrdin, but then suddenly lifted. Finance Minister Boris Fyodorov offered the explanation that these controls had been a "bureaucratic mistake." On January 20, Fyodorov and Chubais announced that after "heated debate," the cabinet had approved a crisis program of financial stabilization and tight money to fight hyperinflation. They warned that the January inflation rate might exceed 50 percent per month, which would fulfill even their definition of hyperinflation. Within a few days, the ruble fell 13 percent to a new record low of 568 to the dollar. At the end of the month, Chernomyrdin attended the yearly winter meeting of international financiers at Davos, Switzerland, where he warned that Russia was "on the verge of hyperinflation."

Despite the evident mass impoverishment, the government raised prices for natural gas and telephone calls. At this point, it was estimated that inflation was running at about 2 percent per day. Michel Camdessus, the IMF's managing director, criticized the Yeltsin regime for its failure to hold inflation in check. "Many democracies in the world have been killed by hyperinflation," said Camdessus ominously on February 3. "Hyperinflation must be stopped at all costs."[12] By the middle of the month, the international solvency of Russia was raising serious doubts because the government was now estimated to have only $2.5 billion in cash set aside to pay the $13 billion in debt service and principal due that year on the USSR's foreign debt of $86 billion. In this dire situation, a feud broke out between Finance Minister Fyodorov and Central Bank Chairman Gerashchenko on the question of the money supply. Gerashchenko had excited the ire of the international financiers by his propensity to expand the money supply beyond the IMF's targets. Although the hyperinflation slowly subsided as the year progressed, its political impact was deep.

TOWARD THE SPRING CONFRONTATION

A number of the legal and constitutional issues that would divide Russian political forces during the tumultuous year of 1993 had arisen during the December 1992–January 1993 session of the parliament. Here, as discussed in chapter 6, Yeltsin's desire to make himself virtually immune to control by parliament collided with the determination of Khasbulatov and his supporters to exploit the grave economic crisis to enhance their own power at Yeltsin's expense. On December 6, the Russian government narrowly escaped being toppled by the Seventh Congress of People's Deputies, which rejected anti-Yeltsin changes in the constitution by only a small majority and forced out Gaidar as acting prime minister. As part of this transaction, Yeltsin and Khasbulatov agreed to the April 1993 nationwide referendum to try to settle the conflict over the relative authority of parliament and presidency.

However, this did not bring even a temporary end to the hostilities. On January 29, 1993, the Congress scheduled early elections for both the presidency and the legislature to be held in the fall of 1994. On February 5, 1993, while meeting with Swedish premier Carl Bildt, Khasbulatov attacked Yeltsin for "failing to cope with his duties" and repeated his demand that the cabinet be brought under the control of parliament. During February, Yeltsin's rivalry with Khasbulatov remained at center stage.

THE "ZERO OPTION"

In Russia's political jargon, the "zero option" referred to the above-mentioned plan for simultaneous early elections of both the president and the parliament. Of all the solutions proposed for the constitutional deadlock between the branches of power, this one was the most appealing to common sense and the most popular across Russia's political spectrum. The term itself came from the Euromissile debate from 1978 to 1983, designating an arms control proposal that was largely favorable to NATO and was ultimately imposed on Andropov by the Reagan administration.

The zero option was unrelated to the idea of a Constituent Assembly, but the two were not incompatible. While the Constituent Assembly was a recipe for properly legitimizing the future constitutional order, the zero option addressed the problem of resolving the ongoing conflict between the president and the parliament. The zero option had a broad, nonpartisan support base and was advocated by a wide range of active politicians, as well as by outside analysts and specialists in conflict resolution. It would have enabled the country to express its will without veering into the Bonapartist world of plebiscites and referenda. Most important, simultaneous early elections would have resulted in the turnover of Russia's postcommunist elite and paved the way for a new generation of politicians. It also may have represented the last viable opportunity in a long time for the Russian people to choose freely among alternative courses of reform. This would have afforded the democratic movement that had overthrown the communist regime the opportunity to institutionalize its presence in various branches of government. The only groups that had much to lose from the zero option and resisted it in various ways were, predictably, Yeltsin and his entourage, and also the parliamentary leadership.

ENTER THE UNITED STATES: ROOKIES IN THE WHITE HOUSE

Although the subject of this book is Russia, we must now treat a complex of Russian events that cannot be discussed apart from the international context in which they occurred and that largely determined the array of choices available to Russians, whatever their political persuasion. For by 1993, the logic of the Kremlin's policies had relegated Russia to the status of an economic and political dependency of international financial institutions, such as the IMF, and of major aid dispensers, including the U.S. Treasury. Logically, then, Yeltsin's position of dependency was a primary influence on his behavior. To illustrate this, we examine the West's involvement in some detail.

The final months of the struggle between Yeltsin and the Russian parliament coincided with the first year in office of the new Democratic president of the United States, Bill Clinton, and his team. For various reasons, the early months of the Clinton administration were not an auspicious time for clear thinking on American foreign policy. Part of the public resentment that contributed to the defeat of George Bush came from the perception that Bush was not interested in the domestic economy, but only in international grand strategy. Among Clinton's campaign advisers, some of whom stayed with him during his initial period in the White House, none had a strong background in foreign affairs. Clinton's own expertise in the international arena at the start of his term was very limited. The chief foreign policy appointments in the new administration were used partly to pay off political debts incurred during the election campaign. The appointees hardly could be counted as members of Clinton's trusted inner circle, with the exception of Strobe Talbott, his old Oxford roommate who had since made a career as the diplomatic correspondent for *Time* magazine and whom the president put in charge of Russian affairs. Talbott had been one of the key American journalists to lionize Gorbachev, and now he encouraged Clinton to make Yeltsin as an individual the focus of America's relationship with Russia.

In foreign policy, Clinton was buffeted by crisis and failure. During the first week of October, at about the time Yeltsin was ordering tanks to attack the Russian White House, forces loyal to a Somali warlord killed eighteen U.S.

peacekeeping troops and wounded scores of others in an ambush in Somalia. The body of one of the soldiers was dragged through the streets. Clinton announced that the United States would have to end its participation in the Somalian relief operation. Had the country returned to the weakness of the Carter era? Clinton was subjected to sharply partisan attacks. A year after the Somalia debacle, William Safire told his readers that "Clinton has lost control of his foreign policy."[13] *U.S. News & World Report* wrote that by the fall of 1994, U.S. military operations had to be planned so that they could, if necessary, be called off at the last minute because of "Bill Clinton's indecisiveness."[14]

THE U.S. DEBATE ON RUSSIA AND THE TALBOTT "SUPERCOMMITTEE"

On January 2, 1993, Yeltsin had his last official meeting with outgoing U.S. president George Bush in Moscow, at which the two signed the START II nuclear arms reduction treaty. After snubbing Yeltsin during the Gorbachev era, Bush had already met with Yeltsin in February 1992 at Camp David and in June 1992 in Washington, D.C.[15] However, the political by-products of shock therapy had produced a new crop of Yeltsin skeptics in the U.S. intelligence community. On February 3, George Kolt, the National Intelligence Officer for Russia and Eurasia, told Sam Nunn's Senate Armed Services Committee about differences of opinion in the intelligence community regarding the outlook for Russia. Kolt said there was disagreement as to whether Yeltsin "should push for a breakthrough" by calling new elections and establishing a new constitution or pursue a "policy of compromise" in political affairs.

In economic policy, Kolt portrayed a clash between analysts who believed that "shock therapy is the only way to reform" Russia's economy, and others who thought that shock therapy was "too disruptive" and preferred a gradual transition under state auspices. Also on the economic front, Kolt spoke of those who shared his own view that inflation "is the greatest danger," while others were willing to accept inflation only if unemployment could be controlled. Kolt declined to endorse Yeltsin as "our best hope" and pointed to the existence of other reformers and industrialists who could also be important.[16] As Jerry Hough commented in 1994, "The greatest risk to the administration—because it poses the greatest risks for Russia—comes from the fact [the United States] is pushing an economic policy that has produced a depression with a decrease of production of some 50 percent since January 1991."[17]

Soon after the inauguration in January 1993, the Clinton administration announced the creation of a so-called "Supercommittee," an interagency group under the auspices of the State Department, set up for the purpose of shaping a unified strategy toward Russia and the other former Soviet republics. The chairman was Strobe Talbott, and a key member was the influential Lawrence

Summers, Treasury's undersecretary for international affairs. Talbott was billed by the *New York Times* as cautious on economic aid but an advocate of "an aggressive diplomatic campaign to promote reform." A later press account accurately characterized him as "the architect of a policy that would tolerate moves by Mr. Yeltsin to reach beyond Russia's constitution to promote democracy."[18] Until further memoirs and inside accounts of these events emerge, it is a good working assumption that Talbott was the person most responsible for leading Clinton out on the limb of an uncritical pro-Yeltsin policy during the first year of his presidency.[19]

In our view, Talbott and the Supercommittee failed to elaborate a coherent, farsighted, and successful U.S. policy toward Russia. As Hough later commented,

> the administration has a policy of strategic partnership, pushed by Strobe Talbott of the State Department; one of economic reform based on shock therapy, determined within the Treasury Department largely by Undersecretary Lawrence Summers; and one of promoting democracy defined as plebiscitary presidential rule, associated with National Security Adviser Anthony Lake. Unfortunately, these policies are not fully consistent with each other. . . . If a major change of policy or regime occurs in Russia, there is obviously danger of a reaction against the foreign country that has been strongly advocating and financing the economic and political policies being rejected. . . . Thus a big change in Russia might well endanger the geostrategic relationship the United States has been attempting to build up.[20]

A large part of the problem was that the Clinton administration took over the "standard macroeconomic program of the International Monetary Fund and, to a lesser extent, the World Bank," with ingredients like "a dramatic reduction in the deficit, a tight money policy, price liberalization, aggressive privatization of state-owned enterprises, a sharp reduction in subsidies to industry and agriculture, and an end to import tariffs and other restrictions on imports."[21] Another person who sensed early on that this recipe was not working was former U.S. president Richard Nixon, who visited Moscow in March 1994 as part of his campaign for aid to Russia. "I'm an anticommunist but a pro-Russian," said Nixon.[22] When Nixon returned to America, Clinton talked with him by telephone and then invited him to the White House to discuss his proposals for increased aid to Russia. Despite these efforts, U.S. policy remained an echo of the IMF creed as expounded by the U.S. Treasury and the Federal Reserve.

THE PARLIAMENT'S BID TO REIN IN YELTSIN

In the middle of February 1993, Yeltsin canceled his schedule and retreated to his dacha for what was announced as a twelve-day vacation. A day later, Yeltsin and Khasbulatov—by now united only by their mutual desire to avoid a referendum—agreed to a joint constitutional commission to draft a power-sharing agreement. This commission was to wrap up its work in ten days. Yeltsin warned that if it could not agree, he would go ahead with the referendum. The commission's first meeting turned into a stalemate, with each side accusing the other of rigidity. Yeltsin implicitly attacked the parliament by warning the armed forces against being dragged into politics by "foul and irresponsible" groups.[23] On February 24, a Moscow street demonstration by veterans and pensioners denounced Yeltsin as an "agent of America." On March 3, Yeltsin issued the first of many warnings of "extreme measures" if parliament were to reject his ideas on the separation of powers, adding: "I didn't swear to uphold a constitution which included the amendments of the Sixth and Seventh Congresses."[24]

The confrontation between Yeltsin and the parliament escalated on March 10–12. When he entered the Russian White House to argue his case for sweeping presidential powers, Yeltsin ostentatiously shook hands first with the "power ministers," the chiefs of defense, security, and the interior. On March 12, rejecting Yeltsin's demands, the parliament voted 656 to 184 to end the December 1992 "legislative truce" with Yeltsin, which Khasbulatov now denounced as the "work of the devil." The parliament voted to strip Yeltsin of his power to issue decrees that would immediately take effect. Parliament could now, if it wished, submit his decrees to the Constitutional Court to rule on their legality. Yeltsin replied by stomping out of the parliament. He immediately invoked special emergency powers and set an April 25 date for the constitutional referendum. This led to his final split with Rutskoi. A parliamentary vote on a motion to impeach Yeltsin was narrowly averted. Chernomyrdin was given the power to submit legislation to parliament without the permission of the president. Reportedly, Washington viewed these events as a "humiliating political defeat that would strip [Yeltsin] of much of his authority."[25]

On March 13, a Congress of People's Deputies resolution opposed the general course of shock therapy and called for a slower transition to the market. On the same day, the CPD approved a motion condemning Yeltsin for "adventurism." The Supreme Soviet was instructed by the larger body to consider other limits on the power of the president, to examine the question of early elections, and to address the issue of the parliament's control over the mass media. Yeltsin responded the next day by saying that there was now a "very, very serious threat hanging over democracy and reforms" in Russia. The situation seemed serious enough to Yeltsin to warrant reassuring the United States government that he was still in control in Moscow. This was accomplished by way of a message delivered by Foreign Minister Kozyrev to Secretary of State Christopher in a telephone call. "He told me that the efforts of President Yeltsin at reconciliation with the Congress have not yet succeeded, but he assured me that President Yeltsin was going to continue with his desire to have a democratic referendum as a best way to get an expression of the people of Russia," said Christopher.[26]

THE DEMONIZING OF THE PARLIAMENTARY OPPOSITION

At this juncture, it is worth recalling that the Russian Congress of People's Deputies had 1,041 members who had been elected in March 1990, and whose terms were due to expire in 1995. Of these, about four hundred deputies belonged to the "irreconcilable opposition"; about two hundred could be classed as Yeltsin loyalists; and, as Remnick aptly says, "the rest were members in good standing of the *boloto,* the swamp."[27] Anti-Yeltsin motions could routinely garner five hundred or more votes, meaning that Yeltsin had no working majority. The Western press tended to accept uncritically the Kremlin's propaganda that stressed Soviet-era nostalgia, rather than hyperinflationary depression and mass hardship, as the motive force behind the parliament's challenge to the president.

Western journalists tended to show little sympathy for suggestions like that of Andrei Golovin of the Change–New Politics group that Yeltsin was an American puppet: "If you want to know what Yeltsin is going to do, ask the president of the United States. We happen to know that Yeltsin's behavior is determined by the opinion of the G-7 and the instructions he gets from them," said Golovin.[28] Exaggerated though this view may have been, the pervasive identification of Yeltsin with U.S. policy that was consolidated by the events of 1993 would come back to haunt world politics some years later in the form of general anti-American sentiment among Russians. This tendency was evident to a senior Western diplomat who remarked a few months later that "in some very predictable ways, this American effort to help Yeltsin has backfired. Of course the conservatives have distorted it. But foreigners can't tell Russians what their national interests are."[29]

An example of the demonization of the Russian opposition appeared in an op-ed piece in the *New York Times* written by Richard Pipes, who denied that economic hardship was the principal source of Russia's unrest. "Contrary to conventional wisdom, the economy has not caused this crisis; . . . nobody is starving. . . ," he wrote. In another passage, Pipes held that, "It is Boris Yeltsin who represents the nation. . . . He makes no secret that he has been laying the groundwork for the imposition of emergency rule, which would enable him to continue political and economic reforms. His repeated warnings to this effect are no bluff." Pipes also pushed Clinton to climb further out on the limb with Yeltsin:

> The most helpful thing the West can do is to throw the full weight of its support behind Mr. Yeltsin. . . . It is a welcome sign that after initial hesitation, Washington seems to have realized that the success of democracy in Russia may require resort to methods that in the West would be unacceptable. It should persist in this course and not allow itself to be misled by the putschists' professions that they are fighting for the cause of representative government against a would-be dictator.

Exactly like the Bolsheviks of 1917, they are exploiting populist slogans to camouflage a bid for authoritarian rule.[30]

YELTSIN'S TRIAL BALLOON AND THE REACTION FROM WESTERN POWERS

On February 28, German chancellor Helmut Kohl, on a visit to Japan, issued a plea for more aid to Russia. During his trip home, on March 3, Kohl stopped in Moscow for talks with Yeltsin. It was on this occasion that Yeltsin issued his first known request for international support for extraconstitutional measures against the Russian opposition. He reportedly told Kohl "that he might dissolve the Russian parliament and assume emergency powers to defeat his political opponents," and asked him "whether the United States and the other major industrialized nations would support him if he were forced to take extraconstitutional action." Kohl, who was dependent on Russian cooperation over the repatriation of the sizable Russian military forces still in his country, thereupon wrote letters to Clinton and other G-7 leaders informing them of Yeltsin's request and urging full backing for him. Probably, some officials of the G-7 governments were embarrassed by the prospect of the dissolution of the Russian parliament, but these inhibitions did not last for long. The G-7 finance ministers were immediately assigned to use their March 13–14 meeting in Hong Kong to begin developing an emergency aid program for Russia in consultation with Russian deputy prime minister Boris Fyodorov, who also attended.[31]

On March 5, before Yeltsin's confrontation with parliament exploded, Clinton had said that he was considering "some innovative solutions" for aiding Russia, which he would discuss with the Russian president at their upcoming Vancouver summit. Clinton soon endorsed the idea of an emergency meeting of the G-7 devoted to the Russian crisis, to be held well in advance of the usual summer G-7 summit.

Between March 11 and 13, Clinton responded to the parliament's show of resistance by issuing a series of enthusiastic daily endorsements of Yeltsin. "I intend to do what I can . . . to be supportive of [Yeltsin] while he serves as president of Russia," said Clinton on March 11.[32] On the following day, Clinton again endorsed Yeltsin, saying, "I support democracy in Russia and the movement to a market economy and Boris Yeltsin as the elected president of Russia. He represents that reform." Clinton said that the measures just approved by parliament to limit Yeltsin's powers represented "a parliamentary dispute" that was "within the bounds of legal authority." And he added, "I hope whatever is done in Russia is consistent with that."[33]

However, Clinton also came under pressure not to stake the entire bilateral relationship on Yeltsin personally, which was especially telling because Clinton had faulted Bush for putting too much reliance personally on Gorbachev.

The *New York Times* quoted a "senior administration official" as commenting: "Obviously the previous administration got into some trouble for overpersonalizing the relationship, and a lot of people have made invidious comparisons between Bush's support for Gorbachev and Clinton's support for Yeltsin . . . [but] there is no way you can divorce Yeltsin as a personality from the state and future of reform in Russia."[34] On March 16, Yeltsin was joined at a joint press conference by French president François Mitterrand, who was visiting Moscow to express Western solidarity with Yeltsin. Mitterrand's line was that if the West were forced to choose among the factions in Russia, it would choose the grouping most committed to the reform process. In these talks, Yeltsin again bruited a possible crackdown on the opposition. According to French foreign minister Roland Dumas, "Yeltsin told President Mitterrand in Moscow . . . that he might have to take strong measures."[35]

But how would the United States react to a crackdown by Yeltsin that went beyond the bounds of Russian constitutional law? The answer was given by "a senior administration official" who explained that Washington would not oppose moves by Yeltsin to liquidate the Russian parliament and constitution, but would draw the line at mass arrests and a bloodbath. In the official's words, "If Yeltsin suspends an antidemocratic parliament, it is not necessarily an antidemocratic act." But, "If he suspends an antidemocratic parliament and throws a lot of people in jail, and troops sympathetic to Yeltsin spill blood, that's a different situation. We want what is peaceful and orderly in the furtherance of democratization." Marshall Goldman of Harvard University's Russian Research Center promptly condemned this statement, saying, "It is absolutely the wrong signal, a very shortsighted position. . . . The means become the end, and you get sucked in."[36] When October brought both mass arrests and a bloodbath, Goldman's analysis was borne out.

On March 13, Clinton refused to comment on what he would do if Yeltsin used military force against his opponents.[37] A few days later, Kohl issued a public statement saying that the political survival of Yeltsin was vital to both Germany and a peaceful world order.

By contrast, a former State Department official, Leslie Gelb, summed up the case of the Yeltsin skeptics in a cogent and well-informed way:

> Mr. Clinton is right to promote Boris Yeltsin, but wrong to join him in a war against the Russian parliament. This body has not been a reformer's delight, but it's not dominated by a bunch of right-wing crazies. . . . About one-fifth of the deputies are hard-line nationalists. A roughly equal number are Yeltsin loyalists. The diverse center group stretches from conservatives to industrial managers to former Yeltsin backers. . . . A solid majority of this parliament would pursue reforms more slowly than Mr. Yeltsin, but would not dream of reverting to Communism. It would also be far less friendly to the U.S., but not anti-American. . . . The White House should not be burning bridges with this power-to-be. But that's

exactly what it did in saying it would not oppose Mr. Yeltsin if he moved to suspend parliament.[38]

In the same article, Gelb accurately predicted what the Washington bureaucracy would tend to do with this problem: ". . . facing hard sells, Washington officialdom generally resorts to wrapping its efforts in standard foreign policy baloney. . . . Friends are turned into gods and adversaries into devils."

March 20: Yeltsin Asserts Emergency Powers

Given the chorus of international governmental encouragement, it is hardly surprising that Yeltsin concluded he had carte blanche, quickly put aside any serious attempt to compromise with parliament over the legitimate issues of economic policy and the separation of powers, and prepared to confront the legislative branch.

On March 20, he declared emergency rule, invoking precisely the powers the Congress had voted to abrogate. Yeltsin said he had "signed a decree on special rule until the crisis of power is concluded." According to the decree, "any decisions [by the Supreme Soviet] that would suspend decrees of the president and the government would have no juridical force." Within an hour of Yeltsin's address, both Vice President Rutskoi and Constitutional Court Chairman Zorkin declared that Yeltsin's decree was unconstitutional, and it was clear that they had a strong legal case. Rutskoi criticized Yeltsin for having uttered eighteen constitutional violations in the course of his televised address. Thus began four days of alarm and uncertainty.

On March 21, Khasbulatov convoked an emergency session of the Supreme Soviet and denounced Yeltsin's speech as an "attempt to usurp power cloaked in anticommunist rhetoric." The Supreme Soviet approved a resolution assailing Yeltsin's moves as "an assault on the constitutional foundations of Russia's statehood," and asked for a ruling from the Constitutional Court as to whether Yeltsin was acting legally. Chief Justice Zorkin was already on record with his opinion that Yeltsin's actions were a violation of the constitution, but that this was not yet the definitive verdict. Justice Minister Nikolai Fyodorov, breaking with Yeltsin, resigned his post; other ministers and officials, including Skokov and Glaziev, distanced themselves from Yeltsin.

On March 23, the Constitutional Court passed by a vote 10 to 3 a ruling that Yeltsin had violated nine provisions of the constitution. The justices found that Yeltsin had no right to hold a plebiscite on the question of whether the president or the parliament should have more power. The court also noted that Yeltsin did have emergency powers, but that their use required the justification of extraordinary circumstances, which currently did not exist. In addition, the court ruled that Yeltsin had not followed the necessary procedures in invoking emergency powers. On March 26, acting now as a political mediator, Justice Zorkin proposed a compromise that would give the president more power and spell out the division of labor between president and parliament, in exchange for the zero option—early elections of both president and parliament during the fall of 1993.

Khasbulatov, for his part, was trying to get Yeltsin impeached. On March 28, the issue was put to a vote and failed by a narrow margin; the motion received 617 votes, 72 votes short of the necessary two-thirds majority of 689. A motion to oust Khasbulatov got 339 votes, short of the simple majority of 517 votes needed to force him out as Speaker. Khasbulatov's position had been weakened by his attempt to make a private deal with Yeltsin the night before, in which Yeltsin would have dropped his demand for a referendum in exchange for the suspension of the Congress and would have accepted early elections for both president and a numerically reduced legislature. Thus Khasbulatov, too, had tried to secure a modus vivendi based on the zero option, but he had been rebuffed. On March 29, the parliament passed an omnibus resolution that terminated Yeltsin's power to rule by decree and rejected his claim to primacy over the legislative branch.

Robert Legvold of Columbia University described Yeltsin's move as "a significant misstep" and suggested that few Russians outside of Yeltsin's own grouping would be in favor of emergency rule. "He's in a very deep hole and I don't think he can pull himself out by this means," said Legvold.[39] Dimitri Simes of the Carnegie Endowment for International Peace commented more ambiguously: "If what Yeltsin is trying to do will work out, if it will prove to be fast, bloodless, and efficient and leads to free elections, then it should not worry the U.S. too much. If blood is spilled and the regions go their separate ways, the chances for Western aid would be very, very seriously jeopardized."[40]

Here, if ever, was a moment when Western governments should have counseled restraint. They failed to do so, in large part because the Khasbulatov-Rutskoi forces were not votaries of the IMF's shock therapy economics. Forced to choose between constitutional legality and shock therapy, the United States and its G-7 allies chose—against the well-informed advice of Gelb, Goldman, and others—shock therapy. Napoleon and Hitler were among the dictators who had used referenda without restraint, while the framers of the U.S. Constitution had made no provision for them. But history and prudence were now thrown out the window in the rush to support Yeltsin and his shock therapy policies. On the day of Yeltsin's power grab, a statement issued by the Clinton administration observed that "President Yeltsin has proposed to break that political impasse by taking it to the people. That is appropriate in democracies. . . . As Russia's only democratically elected national leader, he has our support, as do his reform government and all reformers throughout the Russian federation. What matters most is that Russia is, and remains, a democratic country moving toward a market economy—that is the basis for a continued

U.S.-Russian partnership and for a better and more prosperous future for the Russian people."

The statement stopped short of endorsing further measures Yeltsin might take in his struggle for power with the parliament, and also implied that the United States would support any other Russian officials who supported democracy and free markets. Clinton also made clear that the Vancouver summit would go forward as scheduled.[41] Obviously, neither he nor any other Western leader was able or willing to perceive the complex historical conflict between the radical, absolutist formulations of these two goals—democracy and the market—that was playing out on Russian soil. Yet a notable dissent came from former secretary of state Henry Kissinger, who pointed out

> Once again, American policy toward Russia is being presented largely in terms of supporting a particular Russian leader. First it was Mikhail Gorbachev; now it is Boris Yeltsin. Failure to extend him aid, it is said, will bring into power sinister Communist holdouts and Cold War policies that will cost us more than any conceivable aid program. I questioned then and doubt now whether it is wise to gear American policy so totally to any individual, whatever his merits. How would Americans react if a Russian leader were to announce that he is backing the president in a dispute with Congress?

In Kissinger's view, there was definitely common ground between Yeltsin and the parliament on economic questions, implying the possibility of compromise: "On economic policy, the major controversy concerns the pace, not the direction, of reform. No significant group wants to return to the centrally planned system." Kissinger was also wary of referenda as such: "To be sure, a referendum is an appeal to the people. But historically it has smoothed the way to dictatorship more frequently than to democracy." The heart of Kissinger's argument, though, concerned the separate, but actually closely connected, point that superpower geopolitics must take precedence over the issue of Russia's economic regime: ". . . the ultimate test of America's engagement with Russia, whether in aid or diplomacy, should be how it contributes to a restrained Russian foreign policy. . . . Russia must not be tempted to substitute vague slogans of partnership for geopolitical necessities. . . . Above all, the United States must not tie itself to any one leader or any one government in Russia."[42]

YELTSIN'S REFERENDUM CAMPAIGN: CASHING IN ON THE WEST'S RED SCARE

The immediate governmental crisis in Russia ended on March 24: Yeltsin's decree was published, but without the provocative provisions he had described four days earlier. Clinton received Kozyrev, who asked him to help Russia economically and to back its bid for membership in the G-7. Kozyrev also tried to portray Yeltsin as a leader reaching out for compromise, telling reporters that "the president is always open to compromise with those political forces who are not out to just reverse the reform." That evening Clinton offered the American people the disingenuous image of a conciliatory Russian president: "He's a very resilient fellow, you know. He's like all of us in public life. He is not perfect. I'm not perfect. We all have our problems. But he is a genuinely courageous man, genuinely committed to freedom and democracy, genuinely committed to reform, and I think now he is more open perhaps than in the past to try and work out some kind of accommodation with others who would negotiate with him to keep reform going even though they may have some different ideas."[43]

With the April 25 referendum fast approaching, the G-7 governments now mobilized to shore up Yeltsin with demonstrative economic assistance. Strenuous efforts were made to impress Russian voters with the West's politically motivated generosity. On April 1, Britain announced it would double its aid to Russia to $180 million. The next day, Russia and its sovereign creditors in the Paris Club agreed to reschedule three-quarters of Russia's foreign debt, including $15 billion of $20 billion in principal and interest due in 1993; this was to be stretched out over ten years. The deal was signed by Deputy Premier Shokhin, who hoped it would be the prelude to an accord with the private creditors of the London Club. On April 4, Clinton met with Yeltsin in Vancouver for the long-awaited two-day summit and pledged an immediate $1.6 billion in cash. The United States also promised to provide $894 million in food aid credits and grants, especially financing for grain shipments. U.S. shipments were now to resume after having been halted in November 1992, when Russia defaulted on its payments. As for Yeltsin, he began referring to the U.S. president as "my friend Bill."

The April 15 emergency session of the G-7 in Tokyo was wholly devoted to showing political and economic support for Yeltsin. Secretary of State Christopher underlined this purpose, telling reporters, "We simply could not wait for our annual summit in July to act decisively on behalf of the reform government in Moscow." He added that if the Yeltsin regime were defeated, "we would face increased instability" and "the necessity to continue to invest dollars in defense, and not in the urgent domestic needs of our own people." The Japanese government was now resigned to financing Yeltsin. Premier Kiichi Miyazawa pointed out that Russia is at a "critical juncture, with the reform efforts under the leadership of President Yeltsin facing tremendous challenges both politically and economically." It was therefore "incumbent upon the international community to send a clear message that it expects Russia's reforms to be pursued irreversibly."

The G-7 countries unveiled a $28.4 billion aid package, including $18 billion from the IMF, the World Bank, and the European Bank for Reconstruction and Development (EBRD). Three billion dollars was earmarked for privatization, and another $3 billion was a fast-track loan to be extended if the Russian central bank adopted policies to fight hyperinflation. The United States and Japan each offered Russia $1.8 billion bilaterally. The U.S. funds were billed as being in addition to what Clinton had promised Yeltsin in Vancouver on April 4.

It soon turned out, though, that $23 billion of the $28.4 billion was money already promised but not delivered because Russia had failed to meet policy and performance criteria. Part of the funds had already figured in the $24 billion aid package announced in April 1992. Only half of what was promised then had been disbursed so far. Then, on April 20, the IMF announced further details of its own program. Summing up, the G-7 communiqué stated, "Russia has embarked on a far-reaching transformation process with the aim of building a democratic society, establishing a market economy, and improving the welfare of its people under the leadership of President Yeltsin." Further: "Russian reform and progress toward democratization are essential to world peace." Finally, the ministers assured the Russian people of the G-7's "support in coping with the inevitable hardships of the transition period."

On April 25, as discussed in the last chapter, the referendum gave more comfort to Yeltsin than to the parliament: 64 percent of voters turned out, and 58.7 percent reportedly expressed confidence in Yeltsin; 53 percent said they approved of his and the government's social and economic policies. However, because only 43 percent of the total electorate (not of voters) voted for early elections for parliament, and 31.7 percent wanted early elections for the presidency, such elections were rejected.

LESSONS OF THE MARCH–APRIL CRISIS

During the spring crisis, President Clinton was a consistent and vehement supporter of Yeltsin. But the U.S. foreign policy establishment and, we may conclude, the foreign policy bureaucracy, continued to show a measure of skepticism. The strongest support for Yeltsin came from Cold War veterans on the right flank, such as William Safire and Richard Pipes. Former president Nixon diverged from this group with his evident desire to help Russia and not just the Yeltsin regime. Leslie Gelb represented a left-of-center grouping that was also reluctant to bet the ranch on Boris Yeltsin, and the arguments he advanced were sensible. A group of Yeltsin skeptics on the right had a spokesman in Henry Kissinger, who predictably emphasized the need to focus on policy issues, not individuals.

Clinton's energetic support of Yeltsin seemed, for the moment, to be coupled with a caveat: no massive arrests or political crackdown, and above all no bloodbath for the television cameras to project into American homes. And these turned out to be limits that Yeltsin, for the moment, obediently accepted.

Yeltsin's qualified victory in the April 25 referendum, facilitated by both actual Western money and promises of more money in the future, began to convince official Washington that he was not about to lose the Kremlin. By the end of the summer, he had jettisoned a number of ministers and officials who were reluctant to back a crackdown and replaced them with others who were ready for the kind of action he wanted.

The events of March–April left the Russian parliament defeated at the polls. The greatest single factor in the decline in the Russian parliament's position that was visible by September was, however, the implacable international campaign of demonization directed against it by most of the mass media in the G-7 countries. The American wire services now routinely prefixed their references to the parliament with damning epithets like "hard-line," "hostile," and "holdover." The parliament was "packed with former communist apparatchiks"; it had been elected "under Soviet rule" and was "still dominated by former communists." The reporters pretended not to notice that many of these smears applied just as well or better to Yeltsin himself. The parliament was a "rump" and its members "die-hards." The constitution was "a relic" from the Brezhnev era and had been amended too much.

This effective campaign of demonization, combined with the parliament's own ineptitude, decisively weakened the institution. Western reluctance to support strong-arm methods against it was dwindling. The IMF became an important factor with its demand for a new round of shock therapy measures, strongly backed by the U.S. Treasury. Because carrying out more shock therapy meant removing the domestic opposition, by September Yeltsin was being pushed toward a crackdown by his international patrons, rather than being restrained by them. In the final phase, the quality of the parliament's leadership had degenerated to such an extent that Yeltsin could convince at least some people by offering a choice between himself on the one hand and chaos and ungovernability on the other.

The Political Background of the September–October Coup

The immediate background against which the planning of the September–October events took place was the strained and complicated state of relations among the various corporations and government agencies run by the ruling elite. During the summer and early autumn of 1993, several interrelated political intrigues attracted attention.

The first was the investigation of charges of corruption and questionable financial activities, the main targets being Deputy Prime Ministers Vladimir Shumeiko and Mikhail Poltoranin, Gennadi Burbulis, Deputy Defense Minister General Konstantin Kobets, and also State Security Minister Viktor Barannikov and Vice President Aleksandr Rutskoi.

Then there were the ideology-based conflicts among the various groups within the president's camp, the clearest example being the conflict between the radical, highly politicized, free-market wing (Boris Fyodorov, Anatoly Chubais, Poltoranin, and Poltoranin's ally Shumeiko) and the moderately conservative statist officials. Although the latter did not form a distinct group, the following were affiliated in varying degrees: First Deputy Prime Minister Oleg Lobov; Deputy Prime Minister Oleg Soskovets; Sergei Glaziev, the minister for foreign economic relations; and three other ministers: Aleksandr Zaveryukha, Aleksandr Shokhin, and Sergei Shakhrai.

In addition, there were the contradictory and unsuccessful attempts of the president's entourage to form parallel, quasi-representative organs of government that could take over some or all the functions of the hated parliament. The first such attempt was the Constitutional Convention; a second and more serious one was the Federation Council. Furthermore, there was the constant competition for influence over Moscow among the regional elites within Russia, Yeltsin's and Khasbulatov's struggle to increase their personal influence in the nations of the Commonwealth of Independent States, and attempts to encourage and direct unification processes among these nations.

Complicating the whole picture was the accelerating fragmentation of the two intransigent poles on the political spectrum—Democratic Russia and the National Salvation Front—and also of the conservative quasi-opposition of commercialized industrial directors represented by the Civic Union. The same period also saw the growing influence of self-organized, pragmatic, reform-oriented centrists, operating as an independent third force both within parliament and outside it. This led to a crystallization of political and intellectual forces around Grigori Yavlinsky and other relatively independent public figures.

Let us address each of these themes in turn.

THE CORRUPTION ISSUE

By the beginning of 1993, the problem of corruption within government and the close links of government officials with criminal capital became an object of official concern and heightened activity on the part of most groups in the ruling elite. Support grew for a coordinated effort by a range of figures against corruption. Thus on February 12, Yeltsin and Rutskoi jointly addressed a big conference on the problems of organized crime and corruption. Shortly before this, with Yeltsin's approval, a Security Council Interagency Commission on Crime (SCICC), headed by Rutskoi, had been formed.

Only two months later, however, the campaign against corruption had turned into a breeding ground of political conflicts at the highest levels of government. The ultimate sources of various sensational exposés were two representatives of the nomenklatura business world who had close ties with international finance, as well as with Russian and foreign intelligence services: Dmitri Yakubovsky and Boris Birshtein. The war that these exposés unleashed turned the majority of Russia's leaders into objects of suspicion or personally interested participants in the investigation. Thus any possibility of a strategic opposition to corruption at the government level was effectively blocked, while the moral legitimacy of the ruling elite was undermined.[44]

According to reports, the Kremlin received in early 1993 an extensive array of compromising material on prominent figures in the radical wing of the president's entourage from Yakubovsky and from Birshtein. These documents were, in turn, handed over to Rutskoi. However, at some point the interests of Yakubovsky and Birshtein sharply diverged. State Security Minister Barannikov evidently had extensive documents given to him by Birshtein that compromised Shumeiko and shed light on the activities of Yakubovsky. These documents, among others, were made public by Rutskoi in his sensational report on corruption at the April 16 session of the Supreme Soviet. From this moment, Yakubovsky became vitally interested in delivering a counterblow against the positions taken by Birshtein, as well as by Barannikov and Rutskoi. He tried to compromise them with the assistance of Prosecutor General Stepankov, but the latter declined to cooperate with him. At that time, Yakubovsky had entered into a close relationship with Andrei Makarov, an acquaintance from the Moscow Bar Association. Yakubovsky's promises—delivered via Makarov—to provide compromising material against Rutskoi had an effect: On June 30, by Yeltsin's decree, Makarov was appointed to head the operations department of the SCICC over Rutskoi's head.

The direct result of this exchange of information among Yakubovsky, Makarov, and Yeltsin's entourage was the fall of Barannikov, whose financial ties with Birshtein were exposed, along with the fact that he had provided the prosecutor general's office with materials compromising the Yeltsin camp. Yakubovsky, however, was cut off from his sources of information after his conflict with Birshtein and was unable to fulfill his promise: in the final analysis, the documents he provided turned out to be forgeries. As a result, the widely publicized accusations made by Andrei Makarov's department against Rutskoi threatened to boomerang and strike the accusers, while Shumeiko, Poltoranin, and Burbulis remained under a cloud of suspicion. The presence of these people in Yeltsin's entourage became a growing political liability for him—a fact that the Korzhakov and Chernomyrdin factions did not let him forget.

Another consequence of the failure of Makarov's department was the public's increased confidence in Rutskoi's denunciations of the government. In such circumstances, the only weapon left in the battle for public opinion—for both the radical democrats and Yeltsin himself—was to orchestrate a large-scale crisis that would divert the public's attention from moral and legal issues to political problems, thus obscuring the issue of corruption. It was not by chance that the primary figures interested in this outcome—Shumeiko, Poltoranin, Burbulis, Kobets, Makarov, and Yakubovsky—played leading roles in mobilizing pressure groups and instigating Yeltsin to carry out a government coup.

At this point, a chronology of events should be helpful.

April 16—Rutskoi delivered his speech to the Supreme Soviet, announcing that he had eleven suitcases of explosive information on the activities of Burbulis, Poltoranin, Shumeiko, and the leaders of the Russian army's Western Command (headquartered in Germany until 1994).

April 28—The Supreme Soviet directed that a special commission be formed in the prosecutor general's office and headed by Nikolai Makarov (no relation to Andrei) to examine Rutskoi's accusations, which concerned, in particular, the corrupt disposal of Russian property by commanders of the Western Command.

June 22—Nikolai Makarov's commission initiated a criminal case dealing with "large-scale embezzlement," based on the documents implicating Shumeiko. The next day, Prosecutor General Stepankov confirmed the authenticity of other information provided by Rutskoi, including the charges against Burbulis and Poltoranin.[45]

In particular, Burbulis was accused of drawing up a secret presidential decree dated February 21, 1992, which was revoked in an equally secret way on March 20, 1993. This decree granted to the Yekaterinburg branch of a company called Promekologiya, headed by a certain Oleg Sadykov, a monopoly on the manufacture and export of what was purported to be "red mercury"—a substance that, in the opinion of scientists, did not in fact exist but was the object of financial speculation.[46] According to information from business circles, this mythical substance was supposedly synthesized in the USSR at secret military bases and used in the production of nuclear weapons and in other strategic fields. As a result of either intentional disinformation or the ignorance of Russia's fledgling businessmen, the price of red mercury on the black market varied from $320 to $380 per gram.

According to intelligence information, "red mercury business deals served as a cover for a large-scale international scheme, whereby 'shipments' from the CIS were used to 'launder' criminally acquired capital by Western operators (drug dealers) as well as by Russian criminal organizations. Thus, as has been documented, there were a number of cases where strategic materials were exported from Russia in the guise of red mercury: precious and rare metals (platinum, gold, iridium, uranium, and others) were shipped abroad."[47] As Burbulis himself subsequently attempted to explain, his endorsement of the Promekologiya licensing was done in the "interest of the state," after he indirectly received an "expert opinion" that red mercury actually did exist. Although Gaidar was also involved, the main roles in this tragicomic spectacle were played by three men from Sverdlovsk—Yeltsin, Burbulis, and Sadykov. The episode shed new light on the nature of political clans and the unlimited opportunities available to such cliques and cabals in the new Russia ruled by "the reformers."

June 24—The Supreme Soviet was addressed by Nikolai Makarov, Stepankov's deputy.[48] His report had the effect of a political bomb. He presented the results of an examination of the fifty-five charges included in Rutskoi's April report. In addition to a significant number of confirmed instances of corruption at the middle and lower levels of the bureaucratic ladder, several of Makarov's reports implicated politicians. The accusations against Shumeiko, for example, confirmed that he had sanctioned the transfer of $14.5 million—allegedly for the purchase of baby food—to the account of a private Swiss trading company. This was a violation of a presidential decree regarding Russia's foreign currency reserves. Makarov ended by proposing that the Supreme Soviet demand that Yeltsin dismiss his favorites, Shumeiko and Poltoranin, who were also antiparliamentary zealots, "for actions harmful to Russia." After an emotional and unanimous discussion, parliament voted in favor of their removal.[49]

July 22—A search was conducted in Poltoranin's office by employees of Stepankov and Barannikov. The next day, Yakubovsky was brought back to Russia from Canada on a special plane. On the same plane was a group from the SSICC, headed by Andrei Makarov. Later, in response to a question about Rutskoi's accusations, Yakubovsky parried with an argument of limited juridical force: "Communists are communists, even in Africa. But when they joined ranks with the fascists, they became, of course, even more insolent."[50]

July 27—Yeltsin removed Security Minister Barannikov "for ethical reasons." *Nezavisimaya gazeta* linked this with the role ministry employees had played in the search of Poltoranin's office. It was also believed that "Barannikov had in his possession documents exposing scandalous 'unethical acts' on the part of the president's supporters as well as his opponents, both in the government and in parliament. In some way, the manner in which these documents were to be handled depended on Barannikov personally."[51] Viktor Ilyukhin, a communist deputy, responded by noting that Barannikov's ministry "had not participated in the punitive actions taken against the peaceful demonstrations on either February 23 or May 1." Ilyukhin's plausible hypothesis was that Barannikov's dismissal was revenge for the information on Vladimir Shumeiko that he had turned over to the prosecutor general's office.[52]

July 28—The Supreme Soviet declared that Yeltsin's decree dismissing Barannikov lacked legal authority. It violated the constitution and the law on the Council of Ministers, and had not been presented to the Supreme Soviet or discussed by the government. Vice President Rutskoi called Barannikov "a man of high moral standing."

A RIFT WITHIN THE EXECUTIVE: MORE SHOCKS, OR GOING FOR THE "NEW DEAL"?

In the summer of 1993, the Russian government was confronted with the urgent need to produce a strategy for economic development that could replace the failed strategy of shock therapy and financial stabilization. The selection of such a strategy became the subject of bitter conflicts within the executive branch. These

Figure 3. The triangular structure of power in the Russian government, 1993

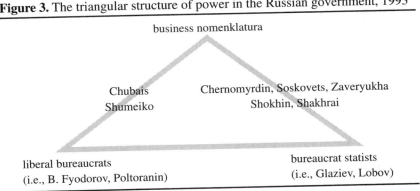

business nomenklatura

Chubais
Shumeiko

Chernomyrdin, Soskovets, Zaveryukha
Shokhin, Shakhrai

liberal bureaucrats
(i.e., B. Fyodorov, Poltoranin)

bureaucrat statists
(i.e., Glaziev, Lobov)

conflicts highlighted the instability of the Russian government, which, ever since the early summer of 1992, had not been a coalition of political platforms or a unified team of political managers but, rather, a motley and disorganized conglomerate of chairmen of various nomenklatura corporations with conflicting interests.

"The present government is essentially a coalition government," Deputy Prime Minister Shokhin asserted in an interview. However, on the basis of official ministry papers, as he noted frankly, "one can put together the programs of all the many and various parts of the political spectrum." His conclusion: "This coalition has no political foundation."[53]

Regardless of the chaotic nature and multiple orientations of the nomenklatura's actions and interests, the conflict among social and corporate interests within the government led to the formation of three roughly defined centers of power, each of which was attempting to strengthen its political position and build a rational ideological foundation for its political claims. At the root of the conflict was, above all, the functional opposition between the capitalized business elite (whose interests were clearly and consistently championed by Prime Minister Chernomyrdin) and the traditional state bureaucracy, which was entrusted with political functions. Within the latter group, in turn, conflicts arose between the now tarnished ideology of the radical reformers (their economic wing was at that time headed by Boris Fyodorov and Chubais, and their political wing by Shumeiko and Poltoranin) and a growing group of statists who supported a protectionist industrial policy (particularly First Deputy Prime Minister and Minister of Economics Oleg Lobov and Foreign Economic Relations Minister Sergei Glaziev, a former Gaidar supporter who was steadily evolving in the dirigiste direction). Relations within the government took on the characteristics of a peculiar triangle of power centers, as shown in the figure above.

The main development within the government during 1993 was the strengthening of Chernomyrdin's faction. On the one hand, Chernomyrdin was able to present himself as continuing Gaidar's policy of financial stabilization, while on the other hand, he was able to turn his economic policy away from the confrontational radicalism of drastic cuts in state subsidies to industry and agriculture and toward an open partnership with the old managerial nomenklatura. The nomenklatura thus became more fully a strategic ally of the government. Thanks to Chubais's privatization, the nomenklatura was able to legitimize its control over state property, while Chernomyrdin's handling of internal politics and decision making gave it access to the mechanisms for lobbying inside the government.

Chernomyrdin's position in the government was strengthened not only as a result of the appointment of such close associates as Soskovets and Aleksandr Zaveryukha to deputy prime minister posts but also as a result of the political evolution of politicians like Shokhin and Shakhrai, who were formerly radical supporters of the Yeltsin-Gaidar camp. Their inclusion in the Chernomyrdin faction had special value because Shokhin at that time had consolidated his control over government channels to Western financial institutions, including negotiations with the Paris and London Clubs over Russia's debts. Shakhrai, it was assumed, would control the strategically important levers of influence affecting the provincial elites.

In reality, however, the key role these figures played in the prime minister's entourage during 1993 was their formulation of a conservatively tinged centrist ideology that would serve as a basis for the political ambitions of the political and business nomenklatura. The March events constituted the key moment in the consolidation of the centrists, when Shokhin and Shakhrai publicly expressed doubts about the wisdom of Yeltsin's attempt to introduce "a special regime for ruling the country." With great reluctance, Yeltsin accepted their advice, thus retreating in a humiliating way from the decisive course that he and antiparliament radicals like Shumeiko and Poltoranin had set their hearts on. During this same period, Shokhin, in accordance with his more activist and politicized role as a member of the government, entered into open conflict with Poltoranin and Shumeiko—figures who had long since provoked the enmity of Chernomyrdin. Shokhin stirred up discussion of a scandal involving Poltoranin precisely when Chernomyrdin was covertly counteracting the attempts of the president's entourage to move Poltoranin into the position of minister for information and the press (while also serving as deputy prime minister).

In August, Shokhin tried to provide the centrist position of Chernomyrdin's faction with an ideological foundation. He defended the necessity of including "conservatism within the framework of the democratic movement" and also of "broadening the social base of reform" by joining forces with "the new property owners." As an example, he mentioned the prime minister: ". . . not for nothing was Chernomyrdin the first to transform his ministry into a business concern."[54]

The practice of seeking compromises and refusing to take drastic steps—which Chernomyrdin's faction adopted as part of its political arsenal—at times looked like weakness. On the other hand, Chernomyrdin took part in a roundtable discussion of economic policy organized by the Supreme Soviet, which elicited a sharp reaction among the radical members of the Yeltsin camp. In reality, the groups supporting the new centrism (which, besides Chernomyrdin and his cohorts in the government, also embraced—to varying degrees— Volsky, Gorbachev, and Konstantin Zatulin's Businessmen for a New Russia) were interested in weakening as much as possible both the presidential and the parliamentary camps, the tactics of which included the anticorruption campaign. The dramatic weakening of the radical reformers' positions in the government because of the compromising of Poltoranin and Shumeiko significantly strengthened the position of Chernomyrdin's supporters. However, they found themselves faced with a new, growing threat from the statist and dirigiste wing of the bureaucracy, whose principal ideologist was First Deputy Prime Minister Lobov.

The basic texts through which the public could judge the activities of this statist wing included: an internal government document titled "Concepts and Methods of Putting into Effect an Industrial Policy," presented by Oleg Soskovets; the draft of a presidential decree prepared by Lobov's economics ministry titled "Urgent Measures to Stabilize the Economy"; and a special "Note to the President" sent in Lobov's name, whose sensational text was published on September 16.[55] The programmatic content of these documents consisted of a strategic revision of the liberal concept of reform and a transition to active support of the country's business sector—in accordance with the Japanese model— with large-scale state intervention through the mechanism of indicative planning. Concrete measures proposed by Lobov included an "industrial policy" of picking winners among nomenklatura allies and manipulating the ruble exchange rate by raising the prices of the vouchers and stocks of privatized companies, while at the same time increasing the value of capital assets. He rejected Chubais's model of privatization and his policy of selling state property as a means of increasing the state's revenue.

Lobov also wanted to ban the use of the dollar as a method of payment and to strengthen state control over exporters. In one of his rare public statements, Lobov supported Volsky's Russian Union of Industrialists and Businessmen, stating that it could play a key role in "defining the strategy and tactics for the most important areas of the economy." To himself he assigned the "role of coordinating and unifying the countries of the CIS." He also called for the transformation of the Ministry of Economics into an organ to provide "leadership and direction" in indicative planning and industrial policy, much like Japan's MITI.[56] When discussing the corruption issue, Lobov consistently viewed Rutskoi's disclosures as an unseemly struggle for power, and stated that "in the given situation, support of the president amounts to support of Russian statehood."[57]

The strategic revision of the government's economic policy proposed by the Lobov-Glaziev-Soskovets group won the sympathy of a significant portion of both the old and the new bureaucracy. The strength of Lobov's position lay in the fact that although the group remained within the framework of the current government, their views and actions were perceived as being highly conservative. The solid support of Lobov's position from such politicians as Volsky and Skokov, and his firm refusal to ally himself with Khasbulatov's party, made Lobov's program into the conceptual basis for the political center's consolidation. In the process, Lobov's close relations with the president made him one of the most obvious potential candidates to replace Chernomyrdin.

The problem was, however, that any revisions of Gaidar's postulates in the direction of statism were firmly linked in the public's mind with the ideology of parliament's counterreform movement and with the unpopular Khasbulatov. Thus even though the parliament's economic proposals were markedly weaker and more amorphous than Lobov's, the latter were unfairly tarred with the brush of the former. Yet the increase in support for Lobov's program that nonetheless occurred in mid-summer presented Yeltsin's entourage with an insoluble dilemma: The strategic interests of state security and the self-preservation of the elite required a transition from a failed policy of financial stabilization to an active industrial policy. Yet such a change in course, coming as it did from governmental and parliamentary circles opposed to market bolshevism, threatened to undermine the ideological foundations of the president's camp and affect the stability of his regime.

Therefore, destroying the parliamentary opposition and securing the full loyalty of the government became for Yeltsin and his entourage necessary preconditions for putting Lobov's program into effect in more than the initial way that he apparently did at the end of August.[58] However, this required the close cooperation of the radical reformist and Chernomyrdin factions in the government. Yet the former could see their ideology being rejected, while the latter saw an end to the gravy train for privileged exporters who were their clients and, in effect, business partners. So, in late summer 1993, a tactical coalition of radicals and Chernomyrdin supporters organized a national campaign demanding the resignation of the "counterreformist" Lobov, while the rump remains of Democratic Russia, together with the liberal press, followed the traditional route and took a still more militant position.

Under these and IMF pressures, Yeltsin decided he had to prevent parliament from exploiting Lobov's program and seizing the ideological initiative. He decided to remove Lobov from the government.[59] However, the ouster of this proponent of the new statism looked more like a promotion than a disgrace: Lobov was appointed director of the Security Council, a post previously occupied by his ally Skokov. Four months later, the Yeltsin camp again would find Lobov's theories attractive during the rather comprehensive revision of economic strategy it attempted following the Duma election disaster.

On June 5, 1993, the Constitutional Assembly began. It had been conceived by the Presidential Administration under Sergei Filatov as a forum to revise the administration's draft constitution. In the opinion of the Kremlin's experts, Yeltsin's alleged victory in the national referendum gave him the right to circumvent the current constitution and to initiate the adoption of a new one. The principal task of the assembly was to legitimize the Kremlin's actions by involving in the rewriting process the regional governments and representatives of society at large—that is, parties and political movements, religious groups, and business representatives. Later, when federal and regional legislators walked out in protest, the assembly consisted largely of Yeltsin loyalists.

The constitutional and political legitimacy of the assembly was highly questionable from the start. Yet the real vulnerability of this conclave, which amounted to a parallel parliament, was the fundamental conflict on several issues among the group of regional leaders presided over by Shakhrai, only a few of which can be discussed here.[60] While the leaders of the autonomous republics (who depended on grants from the central government but could not, according to constitutional law, be replaced by it) insisted on strengthening their special status by including the Federation Treaty as a preamble to the constitution, the representatives of the regions wanted the status of the federation's subjects—republics and regions—to be made equal. Yeltsin's inner circle (in particular Leonid Smirnyagin, his adviser on nationalities issues) was unequivocally on the side of the latter.

This debate revealed Yeltsin's distrust of the autonomous republics (where his support was tenuous, among both the elite and the voting public), as well as the increasingly strong leanings toward strong-state policies within the Yeltsin camp. Indeed, it was at this stage that a covert coalition became evident between Yeltsin's supporters and Zhirinovsky, who alone among the nonregional speakers unambiguously advocated the equalization of the regions and republics—and even the elimination of the republics altogether.[61]

However, Shakhrai's pro-republic positions complicated things for Yeltsin's pro-equalization advisers, who embarked on complex manipulations of the assembly that tended to boomerang. On June 30, for example, representatives of forty regions announced the conditions under which they would ratify the draft constitution. These included: equal status for all federation subjects, exclusion of the Federation Treaty from the new constitution, a ban on seceding from Russia, and equal representation of all federation subjects in the upper house of parliament.[62] The next day, on the initiative of Eduard Rossel, chief executive of the Sverdlovsk region and a close associate of Yeltsin, an announcement was made in Yekaterinburg—presumably with Yeltsin's tacit agreement—proclaiming the "Urals Republic." The Vologda region had done the same thing in May. During the same period, two leaders from the republic of Tatarstan, as if setting an example for others, announced their withdrawal from the assembly. This regions-republics impasse could not be resolved, and although 74 percent of assembly members voted for a draft constitution on July 12, the assembly then adjourned.

The obvious failure of the assembly and the intensification of these conflicts —provoked in part by Moscow—prompted the Yeltsin camp to devise a new kind of parallel pseudoparliament that might in due course displace the Supreme Soviet while at the same time securing support for the regime from a critical majority of the regional elites. The plan was to create a Federation Council (which had already figured in the presidential draft of the constitution as the upper house of the future parliament). The plan's architects were convinced that the equal representation of all subjects in the Federation Council would compensate for the slightly greater autonomy of the republics, while the legislative functions allotted to the council's members would make it possible to lure most of the regional elites to the side of the president. In exchange for the creation of a loyal Federation Council, which solved the power issue that was so crucial for Yeltsin's supporters, part of the president's inner circle wanted to put off the immediate adoption of the full text of a new constitution, which would have aroused the opposition of the regional and especially the republican leaders.

On August 13, Yeltsin arrived in Petrozavodsk to attend a meeting of the Council of Republic Heads, which had been expanded to include the leaders of the eight interregional associations. Marking a significant step forward in the Kremlin's general political line, he proposed creating the Federation Council and adopting not a full constitution but part of the draft as a "law [establishing] the federal organs of power for a transitional period." This law would replace the main part of the current constitution. Yeltsin's approach was the so-called "little constitution" tactic that was being promoted by Shakhrai and representatives of the autonomous republics. This proposal was for the most part supported by the Council of Republic Heads, although it got quite a cool reception from the leaders of the regions.[63]

One of the obstacles to the creation of the Federation Council was the fact that an organ with the same name and similar functions already existed. A Federation Council had been created as a coordinating and consultative body on January 30, 1991, by a Supreme Soviet edict signed by Speaker Yeltsin. (During that period the intended role of the council was to counteract Gorbachev's attempts to encourage demands for sovereignty from the RSFSR's republics.) However, Yeltsin had been unable to find a common language with the council members, and after two sessions he called the meetings off. Beginning in the latter half of 1993, the council's activities were reactivated—this time under the leadership of Speaker Khasbulatov. On August 1, four days after Yeltsin's much-touted proposal to create the Federation Council, there was a meeting of the Khasbulatov-led Federation Council. On September 17, Khasbulatov's deputy, Yuri Voronin, referred to the existence of the "old" Federation Council and, as a gesture of compromise, mentioned the "possibility" of including in its membership the heads of the local administrations, though only those elected by the public or confirmed by regional soviets, not those appointed by the central government.[64] It was clear that this method of selection barred membership for the great majority of regional chief executives.

In essence, the only difference between the new and old Federation Councils was the legislative functions of the former, functions that most of the regional and republic leaders opposed. Of the major regional leaders, only the chief executive of the Sakha-Yakutia republic, Mikhail Nikolayev, a staunch friend of the Kremlin, supported the idea of turning the Federation Council into the upper house of the future parliament. The others wanted to preserve it with only consultative functions. On September 15, supporters of the Kremlin line had "still not obtained even the two-thirds of the votes needed to sign the agreement."[65]

A few days later, the progovernment newspaper *Izvestiya* confirmed the failure of the missions of both the extraconstitutional organs—the Constitutional Assembly and the new Federation Council. About the latter, it said that the Federation Council "could not become the instrument needed to resolve the dual-authority situation."[66]

THE STRUGGLE FOR CONTROL OF INTEGRATION PROCESSES IN THE CIS

By mid-1993, the goal of reunifying most of the former Soviet Union under Russia's leadership was becoming a strategic goal of both Yeltsin and Khasbulatov. (This represented a basic departure from the positions they took in 1990–91, when they played a leading role in the destruction of the Soviet Union.) Khasbulatov acted impetuously—burning the bridges that linked him with his former allies—and joined ranks with the radically nationalist populists in parliament on foreign policy issues. This move permitted him to take a strategically advantageous position vis-à-vis the Yeltsin camp, although he was also threatened by tactical traps he was unable to avoid.

On September 16, in his capacity as chairman of the CIS's interparliamentary assembly, Khasbulatov sent a sensational memorandum to the parliamentary leaders of the commonwealth's member states, advocating the creation of a "political, economic, and social union for 'defense,' . . . possibly a Eurasian union." As a first step, he proposed forming a single parliament based on the CIS assembly and holding elections for it. The boundaries of authority between the "supranational" and "national" organs of government would be demarcated by a special "constitutional act."[67] All too obvious was the hasty nature of the proposed schedule: The memorandum's ideas were to be considered on September 25 at the assembly's session in St. Petersburg, and a "congress of people's deputies" from all the CIS parliaments was to be held by the end of 1993.

Characteristically, Khasbulatov undertook this step personally, and he had the memorandum read aloud at the Supreme Soviet the next day. In response, the progovernment journalist Otto Latsis—through clenched teeth—praised Khasbulatov's "political resourcefulness" and "instincts": "[O]ne is impressed by his determination to add to his armory a theme which has long been monopolized by the national-communists." In Latsis's opinion, this course of action should have been a "disturbing symbol" for Yeltsin, for it underlined the "absence of any policy on the near abroad [that is, the CIS]" in the president's team—in a climate where there was a "growing consciousness in society of a need" for a new union.[68]

With this ploy, the conflict within the Russian power structure spread to other CIS countries. The parliaments themselves were to be given the leading role in the partial re-creation of the union proposed by Khasbulatov. Behind this, one could see a transparent attempt to mobilize the members of the CIS parliaments who supported integration and to win them over to Khasbulatov's side in the conflict with Yeltsin. The plan, however, was based on a serious miscalculation.

Many of the CIS countries had by this time developed authoritarian presidential regimes, in which the parliaments either had a mainly decorative function or were helpless and ineffective in their attempts to counterbalance the executive branch. These authoritarian regimes, which had gained strength on a wave of nationalism, had an ambivalent attitude toward the idea of a partially re-integrated union. On the one hand, they regarded it as economically desirable, but, on the other hand, it threatened to undermine the political and ideological basis of their legitimacy. However, the prospect of activating their own parliaments and reproducing the Russian "dual power" constellation in their own countries turned the CIS leaders into unanimous opponents of the Khasbulatov initiative. This was true even of the president of Kazakhstan, Nursultan Nazarbayev, who was the most consistent supporter of a Eurasian Union and who had earlier offered his services as a mediator between Yeltsin and Khasbulatov. As a result, at a September 24 session of CIS heads of state, they formed a united front supporting Yeltsin and the decisive actions he had taken three days earlier to abolish the Russian parliament.

The Groups within the Opposition

By the time of the September–October crisis, the opposition had experienced yet another schism. Above all, this involved relations between the by now traditional opposition (the communists) and the nationalist-minded conservative democrats, many of whom had previously been radical supporters of the Yeltsin regime and who in many ways retained their reservations about the old nomenklatura even after the communists had joined them in opposition to the Kremlin. A decisive stage in their uneasy relationship occurred at the second congress of the National Salvation Front, which took place on July 24–25, 1993.[69] During the congress, Sergei Baburin's Russian All-People's Union, a leading group of "democratic nationalists" (that is, statists with an above-average concern for democracy), announced its departure from the NSF (followed by smaller factions of extreme Russian ethnocrats and anticommunists led by Valery Skurlatov and Nikolai Lysenko). Although after the congress the NSF still remained an umbrella organization for a range of parties and groups of different size, it could not resolve hidden conflicts within its leadership—first and foremost between the CPRF bosses (with Zyuganov on top) and the disparate group of intellectual democratic populists (such as Konstantinov and Astafiev) with their tiny personal factions.

These conflicts reflected not least the sociocultural gap between the nomenklatura and the intelligentsia. The CPRF apparatchiks were in a strange position. They were faceless leaders of a party that did not even formally belong to the NSF, and although it was the only mass party in the country, it was based on the inertia of subordination and obedience. Yet it claimed to personify almost the entire opposition to Yeltsin and his policies. As was aptly stated by one of its fellow-travelers and critics, Sergei Baburin, throughout the Yeltsin era the CPRF had been fighting not so much for political power as for hegemony within the opposition.

Yet in the ranks of the NSF, the spirit of democratic parliamentarism and factionalism prevailed at the expense of subordination, much as in its opposite twin, Democratic Russia. This resulted in the NSF's acquiring no less than seventeen co-chairs at the congress, most of whom were more closely allied to Konstantinov than to Zyuganov and his cohorts. In addition, Konstantinov, the leader of the democratic-nationalist faction of the NSF, showed a proclivity for campaigning among workers, which complicated the CPRF's already difficult position regarding this social group. He also staged street actions jointly with Viktor Anpilov's Working Russia, the CPRF's chief rival in the struggle to lead the most discontented and radicalized groups. The predictable consequence of all this was that the CPRF's leaders gradually distanced themselves from the NSF, a maneuver that later played a crucial role in the defeat of the parliament. This was when Zyuganov announced on October 2 that the members and followers of his party should refrain from participating in street actions in support of the legislature.

A no less significant role in the breakup and self-destruction of the opposition was played by the distinct brand of centrism peddled by Zhirinovsky. While embracing the public's dissatisfaction with the regime's economic policies, he also supported Yeltsin's autocratic tendencies and his desire to abolish the parliament. The effect of this position was all the more powerful and demoralizing in that for many of the Russian White House's defenders, the values of democracy and parliamentarism were alien. As nondemocrats, for them the struggle against Yeltsin was simply a fight against a pro-Western authoritarianism they found repugnant.

The Crisis Escalates

Now that we have analyzed the key conflicts of the summer of 1993, we can focus on the immediate buildup to Yeltsin's September 21 showdown with the parliament.

On June 5, Khasbulatov walked out of the first session of the Constitutional Assembly called by Yeltsin. Zorkin commented that Yeltsin's entourage was "a court that is making a king." On July 12, the assembly—backed by Yeltsin but boycotted by the parliament—approved the draft of a new constitution, which included a bicameral legislature. On July 21, according to the Kremlin, "Vice President Rutskoi . . . called on troops in the [Russian] Far East to support him in his political struggle against the president [in the upcoming election]."[70]

On September 14, Yeltsin opened a meeting of his advisory Presidential Council with a resolute announcement about the necessity of "bringing to an end the country's dual-government system" in the near future. However, a serious disappointment awaited Yeltsin at this meeting, which assembled a specific group of pro-Kremlin intellectuals whose attitudes on the country's future political system were rather confused. They mostly supported radical reformism but opposed the use of force, and they were rather poorly informed about the strategic plans of the president's inner circle. Most of them, including the keynote speaker Georgi Satarov, agreed that it was impossible to hold new elections in 1993 while simultaneously adopting a new constitution. Instead, they proposed to Yeltsin that any action be limited to having the Supreme Soviet "pass a temporary constitutional law on governmental authority." For Yeltsin, who was by now ready to put the machinery of a government coup into motion, such advice was totally unacceptable. "I expected more support from them," he later admitted in his memoirs.[71]

The West and the IMF Back a Crackdown
on the Parliament

Yeltsin's propensity to terminate the political impasse by going outside of the Russian constitution was encouraged by a series of interventions in Russia's internal affairs by the International Monetary Fund and the U.S. Treasury. In August 1993, the IMF sponsored a conference in Moscow at which its officials criticized the budget bill currently under consideration by the Supreme Soviet. This bill enjoyed wide support in the parliament, but it included a budget deficit that exceeded what the IMF was willing to accept.[72] In early September, U.S. Treasury Undersecretary Summers testified before the Senate Foreign Relations Committee. He viewed the recent developments in Moscow with alarm: "The battle for economic reform in Russia has entered a new and critical phase in which many of Russia's accomplishments on the economic front are being put at risk. The momentum for Russian reform must be invigorated and intensified to ensure sustained multilateral support." The IMF, as later press leaks revealed, was "unhappy with Russia's backtracking on reforms during the summer." An IMF official said off the record, "Important measures in the budget field have not been taken, and credit discipline has been relaxed. This has put their reform program off track."[73] Later, after the crackdown, William Safire highlighted Yeltsin's pre-approval from the West:

> Last week, the confrontation between the reform executive and the red legislature came to a head over—of all things—the budget. Parliament proposed a foolhardy deficit of 25 percent of GNP, which it was ready to pass over Yeltsin's veto. . . . With his Red Army and KGB and Dzerzhinsky [Division] ducks all in a row, and his personal relationship with Washington secure, the Russian leader —assured that no Clinton bet on him would be hedged—made his move. This is a calculated power-play, long-planned and extra-constitutional, that is likely to put too much power into the hands of the Russian chief executive.[74]

Yeltsin had used the summer planning for a new round of confrontations. In his methodical preparations, he recalled an axiom from his Soviet-era political training: "Cadres are everything." On July 27, as noted earlier, he strengthened his political-administrative machine by firing Barannikov as security minister and replacing him with Nikolai Golushko, a longtime KGB officer in the directorate charged with suppressing dissent.[75]

An overt signal of the looming upheaval came on September 1, when Yeltsin suspended Rutskoi as vice president. Yeltsin based this move on the allegations of corruption made against him. Perhaps to preserve an impression of fairness, First Deputy Prime Minister Vladimir Shumeiko was also suspended "due to damage inflicted on state authority as a result of reciprocal accusations of corruption." The next day, Rutskoi accused Yeltsin of "preparing a dictatorship." On September 3, the parliament picked up the gauntlet, voting by a large majority to declare Yeltsin's suspension of Rutskoi null and void.

As a Western observer recounts, "slowly, Yeltsin brought more of his aides into the picture: first, Yuri Baturin, his legal counselor, and then the leading ministers, Grachev, Kozyrev, Viktor Yerin of the Interior Ministry Police, and Golushko. On September 11, they all met at a government dacha outside Moscow and Yeltsin informed them of his plan. . . ."[76] The final task was to convey information to Yeltsin's Western patrons, in anticipation of their much-needed support.

Kozyrev informed the Americans on September 15. As the *New York Times* reported a week later,

> Mr. Christopher received the first hint of today's actions last week, when Russia's Foreign Minister, Andrei V. Kozyrev . . . suggested that there might be a political

showdown in Moscow within a matter of days. . . . Mr. Kozyrev . . . did not tell Mr. Christopher directly that Mr. Yeltsin would dissolve the Parliament. . . . 'It was a cryptic reference, not specific enough to know for certain something was going to happen,' the senior official said. 'Clearly, in retrospect, Kozyrev was trying to give the Secretary a signal.'. . . One senior Administration official who closely follows Russia said it was assumed within the Administration that Mr. Yeltsin would give the Russian Parliament an ultimatum, but it was not expected that he would dissolve it.[77]

Historians will be able to judge later from the archives whether the United States got more specific information from other sources and how far it gave Yeltsin advance approval for his actions.

At the IMF's Urging: Gaidar in, Lobov out

On September 16, Yeltsin visited the Dzerzhinsky Division of the Interior Ministry at its base outside Moscow and was photographed brandishing a machine gun. In this setting, he announced that Yegor Gaidar would return to the government as first deputy prime minister in charge of all economic matters. Yeltsin made this announcement unexpectedly while he was answering questions. He remarked that part of Gaidar's mission would be to resolve the conflict between Lobov and Boris Fyodorov. As noted earlier, Lobov's position was already weak: Two days later, when Gaidar was formally appointed, Lobov was dismissed. Western sources attributed the reappointment of Gaidar to direct prodding from the IMF, saying that "Yeltsin acted under considerable pressure from the United States and international lending institutions like the International Monetary Fund." U.S. officials were reportedly interceding for Yeltsin,

> pushing the Fund to be as understanding as possible with Russia. . . . The next few weeks would be crucial, the senior [U.S.] official said, amidst higher inflation than many hoped and "disturbing signs of further credit growth." Russia's most important task was to limit its budget deficit, he said. Almost as important was to control new credits from the Central Bank. The West also wants significant progress in structural reform, he said, and a reduction of export controls, to enable Russia to earn more hard currency.[78]

On September 19, the IMF made public its decision to delay indefinitely the disbursement of the $1.5 billion loan to Russia. The IMF complained that Russia had not made promised budget cuts and had not reined in credit to industry. Accordingly, the money would not be forthcoming unless and until Russia "returned to the path of economic reform."[79] The World Bank also delayed a planned $600 million loan for Russia. A senior Clinton administration official said, "We're very encouraged by Gaidar's return and by indications from the

Russian government that they now see the need for a rapid turn toward stabilization and reform." After visiting Moscow on September 14–15, Treasury Undersecretary Summers said that the Russian situation had improved since mid-summer: "The recent inflation has been too high, but I am encouraged by Russia's official plans to get financial conditions back under control. It is crucial that these plans be implemented as a basis for economic growth in Russia and for the full effectiveness of Western support."[80] The Summers visit was critically important. As Hough commented later,

> Just before Yeltsin's dissolution of the Congress September 21, the administration sent . . . Summers to Moscow to talk about the conditions for impending IMF aid. . . . Gaidar was immediately brought back as first deputy prime minister, and for the first time he really applied the shock therapy the IMF had been demanding. Bread prices were raised to the point where the daily minimum wage was roughly equal to the price of a loaf of bread in Moscow, and Gaidar promised a vigorous reduction of subsidies to industry beginning January 1 of [1994].[81]

Yeltsin was now prepared to launch his coup. During the September weekend before the storm broke, history provided an ironic counterpoint in a neighboring country to the events that would soon rivet the world's attention on Moscow. On September 19, Poland's former Communist Party took a strong lead in parliamentary elections, emerging as the largest single party with almost 21 percent of the popular vote. Even U.S. mainstream press accounts underlined that "the returns signaled widespread discontent with the market reforms."[82] The post-1989 program of shock therapy, masterminded by none other than Jeffrey Sachs, had set the stage for the ex-Communists to prevail in a free election in a deeply Catholic country in which communism had often been viewed as a foreign body imposed by the now-defunct Warsaw Pact and the bayonets of the Red Army. A political movement sponsored by President Lech Walesa received just 5.4 percent of the votes.

The potential parallels between Russia and its western neighbor Poland were striking. Undoubtedly some officials sitting in the Kremlin, and even perhaps some at IMF headquarters in Washington, now surmised that Russia's disastrous experiment with shock therapy might be dooming the regime that had promoted it, and that Yeltsin and Chernomyrdin might be ousted by leftists or social-democrats promising a market with a "human face," as leftist political leader (and future president) Aleksandr Kwasniewski had put it in his campaign for the Polish Sejm. The impact of the Polish election was a factor seldom mentioned in analyses of Yeltsin's September–October strategy, but its importance should not be underestimated, especially given the fondness of Russian politicians for examining foreign developments with a view to forecasting events at home.

THE STANDOFF BETWEEN YELTSIN AND PARLIAMENT BEGINS

On September 21, Yeltsin decreed the dissolution of the Russian parliament, telling Russia and the world: "In keeping with the president's decree, which has already been signed, as of today the implementation of legislative, executive and supervisory functions of the Congress of People's Deputies and the Supreme Soviet of the Russian Federation ceases."[83] Yeltsin called elections for a new parliament for December 12.

The Supreme Soviet immediately convened and passed a motion impeaching Yeltsin, which was confirmed by the CPD on September 23 by 636 votes to 2.[84] Rutskoi was sworn in as acting president late on September 21. He named Vladislav Achalov (a veteran of the August 1991 coup attempt) as defense minister; the recently fired Viktor Barannikov as security minister; Andrei Dunayev as interior minister; and Iona Andronov, a longstanding KGB associate in the world of international journalism, as his representative abroad. (Rutskoi's appointments were hasty and ill-advised because they had the effect of alienating Defense Minister Grachev and Security Minister Golushko and of driving them squarely into the Yeltsin camp.) Rutskoi also issued a decree annulling the one signed by Yeltsin.

Yeltsin retaliated in kind, issuing decrees to cancel those by Rutskoi. The president was soon endorsed by heads of all the republics of the old USSR, most of whom were themselves authoritarians. Rutskoi and Khasbulatov immediately began issuing calls for civil disobedience and a general strike, but these had little effect; however, the parliamentary security guards were issued weapons. Speaker Khasbulatov and then the Supreme Soviet called on foreign nations for support against Yeltsin, but got no response.

It was clear that the decisive question was the attitude of the G-7 governments, above all the United States. According to media accounts, the United States was officially informed of Yeltsin's intent to dissolve the parliament about an hour before his television speech. Later, Clinton spoke on the telephone with Yeltsin for seventeen minutes and then proclaimed, "I support him fully. . . . He told me that it is of the utmost importance that the elections he has called be organized and held on a democratic and free basis." Clinton said that Yeltsin would act in a way "that insures peace, stability, and an open political process this autumn. . . . There is no question that President Yeltsin acted in response to a constitutional crisis that had reached a critical impasse and had paralyzed the political process." According to a White House background briefing, Yeltsin assured Clinton twice that he would do things that "will quicken the pace of reform." After talking with Yeltsin, Clinton telephoned Kohl, as media accounts put it, "to help drum up support for Mr. Yeltsin." As the administration's background briefing put it, "There are uncertainties and risks associated with this course. I don't think anyone would deny it. I don't think President Yeltsin would deny it."

Secretary Christopher justified further U.S. backing for Yeltsin against the parliament as "an investment in the national security of the United States." He had no comment when questioned as to whether Yeltsin was acting illegally.[85] Within a couple of days, the U.S. Senate passed the 1994 foreign aid bill 88-10, with $2.5 billion for Yeltsin's Russia and other Soviet successor states. This appropriation was signed into law by Clinton on September 30, with the stand-off in Moscow still going on, as part of the $13 billion foreign operations appropriations bill. Of this amount, $1.6 billion was money already appropriated in the previous fiscal year. Clinton signed the bill just a few hours after it had been voted on by the House, remarking that "recent events in Moscow highlight the urgency of helping the momentum of democratic and economic reform." In the Russian context, when everybody looked to the West for the role of final arbiter, this move clearly provided one-sided support to Yeltsin's camp in Russia's civil confrontation.

Other Western governments outdid each other in endorsing Yeltsin; concerns about violations of constitutional law were virtually absent. Belgian foreign minister Willy Claes, speaking on behalf of the European Union, was an exception. He stated that the EU supported Yeltsin but also conceded that what Yeltsin had done was unconstitutional. China made clear that it was neutral, supporting neither Yeltsin nor his rivals, but hoped as a "neighboring country" for "a peaceful solution to the crisis." Statements of support for Yeltsin came from President Lech Walesa of Poland, President Vaclav Havel of the Czech Republic, Secretary General Manfred Woerner of NATO, and the government spokesman in Japan. Rutskoi, appearing on ABC's *Nightline,* deplored Clinton's support for Yeltsin's "unconstitutional actions." "I am very deeply disappointed that the president of the United States is supporting these anticonstitutional actions. If he sees these measures as being reform-like, he is deeply mistaken in that."[86] Rutskoi's response to the chorus of foreign approval for his adversary was: "It's not surprising that the countries which supported the destruction of this country support Yeltsin."[87]

Few observers from the political mainstream of the Western establishment expressed concern about the ethical side of the West's support for the coup. The *Washington Post* was only briefly embarrassed by the "political and philosophical delicacy of having the United States endorse the forced dissolution of a foreign parliament."[88] However, a useful overview of the problematic aspects of Yeltsin's course of action was the *New York Times* op-ed piece titled "Yeltsin's No Jefferson. More Like Pinochet," by Robert Daniels of the University of Vermont. Daniels asked:

> Does election give [Yeltsin] the right, any more than President Clinton, say, to rule by decree and dispense with the democratically elected legislature? Mr. Yeltsin's defenders claim that parliament is a Communist holdover based on a Communist constitution. Nonsense. No parliament had any power before Mikhail Gorbachev's reforms. All the essentials of Russian government today are based on

constitutional amendments enacted since 1989. The present parliament was elected in 1990 without any setting aside of seats for the Communist Party [as had been done, for example, in Poland in 1989]. It gave Mr. Yeltsin everything he wanted at first. Its chairman, Ruslan Khasbulatov, was Mr. Yeltsin's right-hand man when they defied the hard-line coup attempt in August 1991. Mr. Yeltsin's opponents are no more or less communist than he, the former top-level apparatchik. . . . Members of parliament were chagrined over Mr. Yeltsin's peremptory dissolution of the Soviet Union and his embrace of economic shock therapy. As the economy plummeted and corruption mounted, they tried to put on the brakes (a position perhaps vindicated by the recent election in Poland). . . . Mr. Yeltsin has shown that he cannot tolerate legislative opposition. . . . Let us not forget that it was Napoleon Bonaparte who made "plebiscite" a household word. To advance his own conception of reform and to assure his own power, Mr. Yeltsin is well on his way to becoming his own Augusto Pinochet. . . . A reasonable compromise would involve the simultaneous early election of both president and parliament this winter—three years early in Mr. Yeltsin's case, two years early in parliament's.[89]

Like other thoughtful observers, Daniels thus concluded that the zero option was the only platform for a peaceful and democratic solution of the conflict.

There was also an awareness in some Western circles—and even in the major news organizations—that much of the political opposition to Yeltsin was perfectly legitimate and came from reasonable people who were in no way extremists. *Newsweek* quoted political analyst Andrei Kortunov: "Yeltsin has failed to build consensus in this society. The message is, either you support Yeltsin or you go toward violent means of resistance."[90]

In the meantime, the standoff in Moscow dragged on, becoming uglier by the day. On September 23, the ruble reached a new all-time low of 1,299 to the dollar at Moscow Interbank Currency Exchange. On the previous day, Defense Minister Grachev demonstratively went for a public promenade with Yeltsin on a Moscow street. The Constitutional Court upheld the parliament's decision to oust Yeltsin. But the Khasbulatov-Rutskoi camp was rapidly succumbing to the suicidal dynamic of self-isolation. Khasbulatov declared that "Anybody who gives up weapons to the Yeltsin people is committing treason against the Fatherland."[91] Also, as the press reported, "For the Congress of People's Deputies by Thursday evening [September 23] 631 deputies had showed up. That meant that the necessary quorum of 689 was not present. The parliament [Supreme Soviet] nevertheless approved a new law, according to which 'miscreant' members of Parliament lose their seats. Rutskoi again 'called on the citizens for civil disobedience and a general strike.'"[92]

Among those present in the Russian White House by now were several hundred armed soldiers from the "Dniester Republic" in Moldova and from Stanislav Terekhov's Union of Officers. Also present was an armed contingent of supporters of Aleksandr Barkashov, the leader of the ultranationalist and ethnocratic Russian National Unity, which was overtly hostile to democracy and democrats of every shade (that is, to the crucial segment—in this context—of the anti-Yeltsin opposition within the parliament).[93] Yeltsin supporters had a field day with this piece of news, playing up the well-known facts that "Barkashov first became known in Moscow as a bodyguard and 'physical education instructor' for the head of the anti-Semitic group Pamyat' and the partner of a neofascist who dreamed of creating a Nazi-Russian superstate."[94]

At the opening of the Congress of People's Deputies, Aman Tuleyev presented the keynote speech, reading aloud a proposal signed by twenty-six leaders of federation subjects: Yeltsin should repeal Decree No. 1400, and the Congress should vote for the holding of concurrent presidential and parliamentary elections ahead of schedule and should adopt an election law within two weeks. If these demands were not met by September 28, the federation subjects would take "decisive measures," including organizing a general political strike, suspending the transfer of taxes to the federal budget, blocking the export of oil and gas, and blocking railroads and highways. Tuleyev accused the Congress leaders of having no plan of action. It was necessary to collect the weapons from the occupiers of the White House so as not to provide any grounds for provocation, set a date for the elections, transfer the functions of the Congress to the Supreme Soviet, and then leave for the regions, where a solution to the political conflict would be found.[95]

Tuleyev's speech was notable for its blunt endorsement of the zero option. His power lay in his personal authority not only as a leader of the Kemerovo region but also as a long-standing major opponent of Yeltsin; thus his position on most issues was backed to a significant degree by the CPRF. However, the more radical deputies were unwilling to heed Tuleyev's appeal for moderation. Probably this was one of the factors significantly reducing the CPRF leadership's eagerness to support the parliament by means of street actions.

In the ensuing discussion on holding concurrent elections ahead of schedule, only the tiny centrist minority (Aksiuchits, Rumyantsev, and their supporters) backed Tuleyev. As Aksiuchits noted, the weakness of the majority's position lay precisely in the fact that the deputies had opened themselves up to accusations that they were unwilling to hold new elections. Rumyantsev expressed himself even more clearly: "Today the majority of the population certainly does not support us." In his opinion, it was not possible to give in to the extremism of the NSF, which, with its "bull-headedness," had already led the Congress to the unfavorable outcome of the April referendum.[96]

At that critical moment, however, the floor was increasingly controlled by a radical populist group consisting of Baburin, Nikolai Pavlov, Konstantinov, Astafiev, Chelnokov, and their likes. Baburin asserted it was "shameful" to make a decision about elections when surrounded by riot police. The internal logic of the radicals (who chose the glory and moral satisfaction of political martyrdom instead of the hard-nosed realism of power players) was revealed in the words of Pavlov. After throwing out several radical appeals to the Congress (including the demand for Chernomyrdin's resignation and the appointment of a new prime minister) and citing the results of the referendum as an argument against holding early elections, he simultaneously remarked that "life would not come to an end with the death of the Supreme Soviet."[97] In other words, the dissolution of parliament was entirely possible, but it was not the worst thing that could happen.

Khasbulatov's position in the debate appeared to be either ambivalent or nonexistent. However, at a certain point he began to slip in support for the Tuleyev-Rumyantsev line: "What will we gain if we make no decision? The [federation subjects] have given up on us." Once, he tried to put the election issue to a vote as "the Rumyantsev plan." As a result, the Congress adopted a vague and noncommittal resolution calling for simultaneous early elections "no later than March," and tasked the Supreme Soviet to prepare an election law "within a month's time"—a timespan the besieged parliament clearly did not have.[98]

The situation deteriorated sharply on September 24, when pro-Yeltsin Moscow city officials of Mayor Luzhkov shut off the electricity, heat, and telephones in the Russian parliament's White House. In a countermove, the Union of Officers' Terekhov led an armed desperado attack on the military headquarters of the CIS in which one woman was killed by a random shot. His aim was apparently to gain access to military communications and call on units of the armed forces for support. On September 26, supporters of Yeltsin and of Rutskoi held rival demonstrations in Moscow. These coincided with a St. Petersburg meeting of the leaders of forty regional councils, who called for simultaneous new elections for parliament and president. Constitutional Court Chairman Zorkin's proposal for the zero option provided the basis of the final document. This entailed rescinding Yeltsin's Decree No. 1400 (that dissolved parliament) and calling early parliamentary elections in December. The Supreme Soviet and the Congress would then cancel their resolutions creating a counterexecutive, thus restoring the status quo ante. Yeltsin's envoy Shakhrai said he personally favored simultaneous elections.[99]

On September 27, however, Yeltsin rejected the demand for simultaneous parliamentary and presidential elections, citing the danger of a power vacuum that might lead to chaos. "Dual power is dangerous, but a power vacuum is twice as dangerous," said the president.[100] The next day, Yeltsin ordered security forces to cordon off the White House. In addition, to demonstrate its militancy in another respect, the government announced that the price of bread would be decontrolled as of October 15. It also announced that rents would rise and that credit for industry would be strictly limited. These were concrete steps in the direction demanded by the IMF.

On September 29, the Kremlin and Mayor Luzhkov issued a joint ultimatum, ordering the deputies to vacate the White House building no later than October 4. In an ironic counterpoint (reported later), when Clinton met with Kozyrev in Washington the same day, "American officials expressed confidence that Mr. Yeltsin had no intention of using the military to resolve the crisis."[101] On

September 30, Yeltsin had a rather formal meeting with Russian Orthodox Patriarch Aleksei II, who had offered his good offices as mediator; Yeltsin designated two officials to represent him in talks. Meanwhile, to undermine the parliament, Yeltsin's staff was now systematically—at five different locations —offering jobs, cash payments, and immunity from future prosecution to those deputies who were willing to resign from the parliament and come over to him.[102]

Although most Western media portrayed the parliament as totally isolated, the reality was more complicated. On September 28, a Yeltsin spokesman had to admit that "70 percent of the regional soviets have spoken out against Boris Yeltsin's decrees."[103] Numerous acts of defiance and many statements of support for the parliament were reported from all over Russia, along with statements in Yeltsin's support (mostly from executive branch officials).

On October 1, the prospect of a peaceful solution seemed to be at hand. Representatives of Yeltsin and the parliament, meeting with Mayor Luzhkov, agreed to a phased lifting of the White House siege. Electricity, heat, and some telephones would be restored, while the weapons carried by occupants of the building would be put in storage. Then the siege lines around the White House would be replaced by a joint force made up of the usual parliamentary security guards and the police. However, this agreement was quickly rejected by the parliamentary leaders amidst all-round aggressive recriminations.[104] In a related development, Yeltsin and the parliament did agree to negotiations beginning at the Danilov Monastery in Moscow under the mediation of Patriarch Aleksei II. These negotiations, like some earlier initiatives by public-spirited individuals and groups that deserve further research, showed promise. But they were overtaken by events.[105]

Later, Prosecutor General Aleksei Kazannik reproached the Yeltsin team for not having negotiated with the parliamentary leaders on the terms of their surrender (rather than about possible arrangements for elections, and so on). He said his investigators had found no evidence of any attempt to conduct such negotiations, and this fact suggested that storming the Russian White House may have been, in legal terms, a crime. This action would have been legally justified, Kazannik reasonably maintained, only if such negotiations had been tried and had broken down.[106]

BLOODY SUNDAY

On Sunday, October 3, a march of between five thousand and ten thousand conservative, communist, monarchist, and other extraparliamentary forces opposed to the Kremlin broke through lines of riot police attempting to block their march from October Square to the Russian White House. The riot was led by the radical communist Anpilov, whose fringe organization, Working Russia, had no representation in the parliament, and who had long been viewed with suspicion by many opposition deputies as a possible government provocateur. Some demonstrating rioters seized a truck and reached the White House. Soon afterward, Rutskoi appeared on a balcony and urged the crowd to seize the mayor's office (the former Comecon building), the Kremlin, and the Ostankino Television center. St. Petersburg journalist and eyewitness Konstantin Cheremnykh later wrote:

> If Rutskoi had given a different instruction, if he had for example called on the crowd to stay at the White House and to put up defensive barricades rather than going on the attack—events might have taken a different turn. Surely it would have been more difficult today to accuse the deputies of a 'communist putsch against the state.' If they had remained on the defensive, then perhaps those in power would not have dared to attack, and President Yeltsin might have agreed to a compromise in spite of everything. But Rutskoi decided otherwise, and now there was no turning back.[107]

The lower floors of the mayor's skyscraper office were seized after a brief gun battle. Various accounts suggest that the line of security forces was deliberately weakened by the regime in order to let the demonstrators in.[108] There are also indications that the groups marching on Ostankino could have been deflected earlier but were deliberately allowed to proceed several miles through Moscow to reach their target in order to maximize the drama of the incident. One of the leaders of the march that broke through the police lines to the White House was Colonel Vitaly Urazhtsev, a member of parliament and founder of the Shield group of anticommunist military officers.[109] Urazhtsev later recounted that the march that reached the White House on October 3 was organized by "The People's Assembly" and the group Working Moscow. Urazhtsev's account stressed the presence of infiltrated agents provocateurs among the demonstrators on October Square at 2 P.M., and at the Crimea Bridge a little later. Urazhtsev claimed that the marchers were peppered with sniper fire by agents provocateurs holed up in Moscow City Hall. In response, said Urazhtsev, unarmed demonstrators stormed City Hall and captured a member of Luzhkov's staff.[110]

At 4 P.M., Yeltsin declared a state of emergency in Moscow. At Ostankino, Albert Makashov delivered a harangue to the progovernment forces guarding the building. At 7:20 P.M., the attackers fired a rocket-propelled grenade at the main entrance door, and a gun battle ensued. A news broadcast was cut off, but within half an hour transmissions resumed from another, older transmitter located elsewhere in Moscow. Ostankino was defended by "special commando units" renowned for their cruelty in dispersing previous rallies. The government was later criticized for its ineptitude in letting the demonstrators reach the Ostankino building, but it is likely the government thought that bloody incidents at Ostankino would be politically advantageous.

When he received reports of the assault, Khasbulatov reportedly began raving, "Ostankino has been taken. Today we must seize the Kremlin!"[111] For his part, a pro-Yeltsin television announcer went on the air to intone: "Today the fate of Russia and the fate of our children is being decided. The forces of civil war will not succeed. We will triumph."[112] Yeltsin's spokesman Kostikov called for "no concessions to Red Soviets, no concessions to Stalinists and fascists."[113] Gaidar went on television to urge Yeltsin supporters to march to the headquarters of the Moscow City Council. Despite the state of emergency, fifteen thousand did march, putting up barricades in Tverskaya Street in front of the council building.

Eyewitnesses reported the pro-Yeltsin marchers to be heavily armed. They broke into the council building and drove the members of the city council out onto the streets. The demonstrators then began chanting that the council had been abolished. This decision was officially confirmed by Yeltsin. (The decree dissolving the council was also confirmed by Mayor Luzhkov on October 5.) Yeltsin even found time on October 3 to disband the Moscow regional council as well; his supporters cited the pretext that the members of the local soviets were products of the communist era. The city council president, Yuri Sedykh-Bondarenko, his colleague Viktor Bulgakov, and the activist deputy chair of the human rights committee, Viktor Kuzin, were all arrested—and later released.

U.S. OFFICIALS ENDORSE YELTSIN

Eight time zones away, Clinton reacted to the events of October 3 by saying that Yeltsin had "bent over backwards" to avoid violence. Clinton remained adamant in his backing of Yeltsin: "We cannot afford to be in the position of wavering at this moment, or backing off or giving any encouragement to people who clearly want to derail the election process and are not committed to reform." In Clinton's view, Yeltsin had "no other choice than to try to restore order." "I think the United States should support Yeltsin as long as he is the person who embodies a commitment to democracy and to letting the Russian people chart their own course. And he does."[114] A "senior American official" stated bluntly: "We want to see this end as quickly and as peacefully as possible, and we want to see Boris Yeltsin prevail." Pro-Yeltsin troops, in the U.S. view, had orders "not to initiate fire, but only to return fire if fired upon."[115] In all of official Washington, there was not a breath of criticism of Yeltsin's role in what was now becoming a bloodbath.

According to Strobe Talbott, the blame was entirely on the shoulders of Rutskoi and Khasbulatov, who had "sent mobs into the street to attack people."[116] Yet Senator Robert Dole, interviewed on CNN on the day of the violence, suggested the United States should consider whether it was wise to urge countries like Russia to impose economic shock therapies that carried the danger of such a powerful political backlash. Meanwhile, *Newsweek* quoted U.S. officials as saying, "Washington . . . would have supported Yeltsin even if his response had been more violent than it was."[117]

Support for Yeltsin had proved to be a slippery moral slope for the U.S. administration. First, the American position had been acceptance of emergency rule, but rejection of televised carnage. Then, suddenly, a small amount of bloodshed had seemed a price worth paying, and potentially even a little more would be alright.

OCTOBER 4: THE TANK ASSAULT

The final decision to storm the Russian White House was made at a meeting of the Security Council on October 4 from 1:30 to 3:40 A.M. in Grachev's office on the second floor of the Ministry of Defense.[118] The degree to which Yeltsin participated in this meeting and in making the fatal decision remains unclear. According to the testimony of Baburin, who together with General Viktor Filatov tried to go to the defense ministry before the meeting in order to make contact with senior officials, Yeltsin was brought to the building at 1:30 A.M. The pseudonymous "Ivanov" alleges—in his minutely detailed account—that Yeltsin was in an incapacitated state: "His drunken retinue . . . propped him up against a wall in one of the ministry's lounges [off Grachev's office] and gave practically no one access to him."[119] At 1:45 A.M., Chernomyrdin arrived at Grachev's office. The meeting began as a small group of the highest-ranking officials (Chernomyrdin, Luzhkov, Sergei Filatov) and police and military leaders (Grachev, Yerin) and then continued with the addition of high army officials. Yeltsin did not put in an appearance, although, as Ivanov's words indicate, intense communication was maintained between the two offices, possibly with Korzhakov acting as a go-between.

According to Yeltsin's own version of the evening, he arrived at the ministry after 2:30 A.M., when the meeting of his colleagues under the chairmanship of Chernomyrdin was at its height, and he "took a seat to one side and asked them to continue their discussion."[120] In an attempt to move things forward, Korzhakov laid out an aggressive action plan worked out by his assistant: an attack involving tanks, missiles, airborne troops, and commando units. However, the biggest problem for the participants was how to talk the top army command, headed by Grachev, into using tanks without a written order from the president.

Yeltsin's obvious desire to avoid responsibility for launching an operation that would inevitably lead to much bloodshed produced tension between the country's leaders and the military. As in August 1991, Grachev and his colleagues were extremely reluctant to get involved. At the same time, understanding that the army's participation in the planned bloodshed was unavoidable, Grachev decided to bargain. According to Ivanov, Yeltsin "in some unknown way quickly managed to snag Grachev." Although information about the circumstances of the deal understandably remain secret, it is widely believed that Yeltsin paid for the army's participation by promising to strengthen Grachev's position in the political leadership of the country.[121] This view is indirectly supported by the job security Grachev enjoyed through 1994 and 1995, when he remained unscathed by the debacles of the Chechnya crisis, which badly damaged his professional reputation. By contrast, Yeltsin got rid of Yerin—who had demonstrated unconditional loyalty throughout the events of 1993—at the first opportunity, which came during a crisis in the Chechnya war.

On the morning of October 4, a few minutes before 9 A.M., a T-80 tank of the Kantemir Division began shelling the upper floors of the White House. As a result, the central section of the building's upper floors was engulfed in flames, blackening the façade. Some saw parallels to the Berlin Reichstag fire of 1933, the last time that the parliament building of a major country had been set ablaze. After several hours of fighting, commandos entered the White House and arrested Khasbulatov, Rutskoi, Barannikov, Achalov, Dunayev, and others.

Charles Blitzer, chief economist on Russia for the World Bank, said "I've never had so much fun in my life." A jubilant Western economist working closely with the government was quoted in the press as explaining: "With parliament out of the way, this is a great time for reform. . . . The economists around here were pretty depressed. Now we're working day and night."[122]

A few comments on the behavior of the military and security forces are relevant. Richard Pipes noted, "Some fraternization between the internal security forces and the rioters on Sunday gave cause for concern. Nevertheless, in the end the officer corps proved true to Russia's tradition of obeying legitimate authority, and routed the armed rebels."[123] One of the present authors, who witnessed firsthand the shelling of the White House, wrote that "small-scale mutinies by elements supporting the parliament occurred on October 3 and 4, and military commanders, in particular, reportedly hesitated before supporting Mr. Yeltsin."[124] As both Yeltsin and Ivanov recount, the Alfa and Vympel elite military units refused to storm the parliament building, disobeying Yeltsin's direct order. Later, Alfa troops were lured into a dangerous locale, and when one of them was killed by a sniper, they reluctantly took part in the operation.[125]

Before October 4 was over, an 11 P.M. to 5 A.M. curfew had been announced; all newspapers, even pro-Kremlin ones, were subjected to pervasive censorship. Reports of snipers persisted in Moscow for several days; according to some, these were government provocateurs masquerading as die-hard "dark forces." A few days later, the police announced that 187 people had been killed in the October violence, including "76 noncombatants." Estimates of the number of wounded diverged from the official figure of 437; *Time* magazine's estimate was 900 wounded. By any reckoning, it was a far greater human toll than had been exacted by the putschists in August 1991. The Interior Ministry announced that during the mopping-up operations in and around the White House, 1,700 persons had been arrested, and 11 weapons seized. Some of the arrested were interned in a sports stadium, recalling the procedures used by Pinochet after the 1973 coup in Chile.

The events of October 4 were qualitatively different from those of the previous days, but the tone of the international kudos for Yeltsin varied but little. Clinton thought that Yeltsin had "no other alternative but to try and restore order." "As long as he goes forward with the new constitution, genuinely democratic elections for the parliament, genuinely democratic elections for the president, then he is doing what he said he would do." (A little later, Yeltsin would break his promise and postpone the presidential elections for two years without a peep of protest from Washington.) British Prime Minister John Major said in his statement: "There should be no doubt that [Yeltsin] has our total and unequivocal support for the action that he has taken." The European Union foreign ministers, meeting in Luxembourg, blamed "elements hostile to the democratization process" and expressed their continued support for Yeltsin "and the process of reform." In the opinion of Vaclav Havel, the Moscow bloodbath represented "a clash between those who seek democracy and those who have decided to fight under the red flag and at the cost of bloodshed and victims to reinstall the old order." The lone exception was once again China, which still declined to back either side.[126]

Diverging from many of these views, one of the present authors offered the following analysis in a contribution to the *New York Times* of October 10, filed from Moscow:

> Now that a precedent has been set, other authoritarian actions will not be hard for Mr. Yeltsin or any future (perhaps much worse) president to rationalize, in the name of preserving stability. President Yeltsin has not been slow to make his powers dictatorial. On October 4, bombardment of the White House finally disposed of the parliament. [On October 6], Mr. Yeltsin urged the regional councils, Russia's equivalent of America's state legislatures, to disband. (Yesterday, he abolished local councils.) He reinforced the message by outlawing the Moscow legislature, probably wanting to prevent it from becoming an increasingly threatening focal point of opposition. On Thursday, he suspended the Constitutional Court, the top judicial body, until a new constitution is approved, the old one being defunct. The same day, he banned the political parties and groups that had supported the parliament's defiant stand, outlawed their publications, introduced censorship for the rest of the press, only to conditionally withdraw it, and tightened the government's grip on television channels. In Moscow, the police began going beyond their powers under the city's temporary emergency rule, detaining and beating people without cause. Meanwhile, the one body Mr. Yeltsin has preserved in the hope of distinguishing his rule from dictatorship, the embryonic Federation Council, found that the October 9 session he had called had been indefinitely postponed. . . . Stormy weather lies ahead.[127]

We should stress that none of our criticism of Yeltsin implies that a military victory by the White House forces would have set Russia on a better path than it in fact took. That seems most improbable. Our aim, rather, is to emphasize the enormity of the damage done to Russian democracy by two decisions that

Yeltsin made: first, to eschew serious negotiations with the opposition in the summer of 1993 that could have focused on the zero option and even could have involved foreign mediators; and, second, to violate the constitution, dissolve the legislature, and again refuse to negotiate in earnest, thus provoking the fatefully destructive confrontation with parliament.

YELTSIN'S ONE HUNDRED DAYS OF DICTATORSHIP, OCTOBER 1993–JANUARY 1994

From October 4, 1993 until January 10, 1994, when the new parliament convened, Yeltsin operated an unlimited dictatorship. He had broken up the parliament by armed force and promptly suspended the Constitutional Court. The old constitution was inoperative, and the new one did not come into force until December, so the country was ruled exclusively by presidential decrees. Over these three months, with a cascade of edicts, Yeltsin swept away the soviets—the most promising institutions of mass participatory democracy in Russian history —and set in motion the creation of a new political order that suited his authoritarian instincts and goals. This political institutionalization of market bolshevism has since provided the kind of "stability" that the Russian robber barons from the Soviet nomenklatura and the Mafiya needed so as to proceed more easily with the far-reaching privatization of the national government and the treasury.

Yeltsin proceeded swiftly to consolidate his regime of personal and arbitrary rule in the name of reforms. On October 5, he fired Prosecutor General Valentin Stepankov, who had on occasion taken the parliament's side. On October 6, heavy pressure from the Kremlin finally succeeded in forcing the resignation of Valery Zorkin, the chairman of the Constitutional Court and a major advocate of the zero option, who had worked hard to avoid bloodshed through mediation. "I consider it impossible to carry out my duties in the current situation," Zorkin wrote in a bitter address to the other constitutional judges.[128] But this was not enough, because the majority of the court's members had found Decree No. 1400 to be unconstitutional. So, the next day, without diplomatic niceties, Yeltsin decreed that the activities of the Constitutional Court would be suspended until the new constitution was adopted. He later pushed through the new parliament a law that substantially reduced the court's powers vis-à-vis the executive. As a result, the new version of the court did not hold its first public session until March 1995.[129]

Yeltsin also struck on a broad front. The first meeting of the "new" Federation Council was canceled because Yeltsin knew that many regional leaders would still favor the zero option—a compromise that would have defeated the very purpose of Yeltsin's coup, which was the destruction of Russia's parliamentarism for the sake of increasing his personal power. He also sacked without exception all the defectors from the ranks of the executive who had publicly criticized his decree dissolving parliament. Thus on October 5, he fired the governors of the Amur and Novosibirsk regions, his own appointees, for siding with the parliament. On October 8, he decreed that regional governors every-where would be appointed from Moscow and not elected locally (one of the few decisions of this period that failed to endure for long, though it was rein-stated a year later). On October 9, he decreed that all the regional soviets or legislatures must disband—and started by formally dissolving the Moscow city soviet and Moscow's borough soviets, the strongholds of the democratic oppo-sition that had vigorously attacked the corruption and the privatization of the state treasury by both the Kremlin and Moscow's mayor. Two days after that, he dissolved Russia's town and district soviets. And on November 9, he dis-banded the rebellious regional soviet in his bailiwick of Sverdlovsk. Of all the big reforms undertaken by Yeltsin in the Hundred Days of his dictatorship, the abo-lition of regional and local soviets was the most destructive action that negated decades of Russia's institutional development in the direction of mass political participation in the lower-level bodies of government.

Already on the day of parliament's demise, October 4, Yeltsin's Ministry of Justice outlawed eight leading opposition organizations—the NSF, three groups on the far left (the Russian Communist Workers' Party, Working Russia, and the Young Communist League), Russian National Unity, the United Toilers' Front, and the Union of Officers, as well as one group of Yeltsin's former cheerleaders who had turned against his policies by the time of the coup—Shield, the previously mentioned league of socialist-minded army officers. An arrest warrant was issued for its chairman, Colonel Urazhtsev. On October 6, the authorities briefly suspended but soon reinstated the CPRF and Rutskoi's former party, the two largest opposition organizations that by their wavering and calculated caution had in fact assisted Yeltsin's victory. In addition, the stiff requirement that parties collect at least one hundred thousand signatures in a few weeks in order to qualify for the new parliamentary elections wiped out the hopes of the democratic nationalist parties, such as Baburin's Russian All-People's Union, the Russian Christian Democratic Movement, and the Consti-tutional Democratic Party, as well as those of the left-of-center opposition, such as the Socialist Workers' Party. To scare the opposition groups as a whole, on October 21, the key figures of the White House resistance—Rutskoi and Khas-bulatov; Rutskoi's "power" ministers Barannikov, Achalov, and Dunayev; as well as Ilya Konstantinov and General Albert Makashov—were indicted for "instigating mass disorders." Organized labor, though already very weak and despite its earlier conformism, was also put in its place. On October 11, the head of the Federation of Independent Trade Unions, Igor Klochkov, who had rebelled by denouncing Yeltsin's Decree No. 1400 and calling for a general strike, was forced out of office.

As for the media, on October 14, Yeltsin ordered fifteen newspapers to cease publication, including the militant *Den'*, *Sovetskaya Rossiya,* and the relatively moderate *Pravda,* but also such clearly innocuous publications as *Put'* of the Russian Christian Democratic Movement, an irregular periodical of highbrow intellectuals. In addition, he intimidated the entire Russian media by introducing general censorship. Even though this censorship was conditionally withdrawn after two days, a powerful chilling effect lingered for quite a while. *Pravda* and *Sovetskaya Rossiya* were given an ultimatum to fire their editors and change their names if they wanted to be legalized again. In other censorship measures, *600 Seconds,* a highly popular opposition program on St. Petersburg television, was permanently banned. (Its producer, Aleksandr Nevzorov, later returned to national television after switching to Yeltsin's side and lavishly praising the Kremlin's operations in Chechnya.)

By now it was clear that there would be no Clinton-Yeltsin summit before the end of 1993. Instead, Clinton sent Secretary Christopher on a goodwill mission to Russia. On October 23, Christopher chose to give his speech at the Academy for the National Economy, a governmental institution with a highly partisan pro-Kremlin profile. With Yegor Gaidar nodding approval from a corner of the dais, Christopher told an audience of Russian politicians and intellectuals: "The United States does not easily support the suspension of parliaments. But these are extraordinary times. The steps taken by President Yeltsin responded to exceptional circumstances. . . . The parliament and the constitution were vestiges of the Soviet Communist past, blocking movement to democratic reform."[130] Yeltsin was euphoric in thanking Christopher for continued U.S. backing, saying, "Of all the leaders of the world, President Clinton . . . always supports Russia . . . most steadily in all situations."[131]

On November 7, Clinton again endorsed Yeltsin, despite the Russian president's having just reneged on the pledge of early presidential elections in 1994, which had underpinned Clinton's litany of support on October 4. Now Clinton left out the point about presidential elections: "As long as he is promoting democracy, as long as he's promoting human rights, as long as he's promoting reform, I think the United States should support him. He has been brave and consistent." However, "administration officials said they were unsure of the Russian leader's motive in announcing his intention to cancel an early presidential election in June."[132]

YELTSIN STACKS THE DECK FOR THE DECEMBER ELECTIONS

Yeltsin also moved fast on a new constitution. On October 15, he decreed that a constitutional referendum would be held simultaneously with parliamentary elections on December 12. On November 10, the proposed draft of the new constitution was published. Yeltsin and his advisers had amended it unilaterally, in private, in ways that strengthened—still more than in the draft of the summer—the powers of the presidency vis-à-vis the legislature and the regions. Most important, provisions in the new version would enable Yeltsin to legally disregard his promise to hold early presidential elections on June 12, 1994. The Kremlin also changed the existing regulations on the conduct of referendums, so that only 50 percent of those casting votes, not 50 percent of all those registered to vote, would be needed for adoption of the proposed constitution.[133] Two weeks later, on November 26, Yeltsin expressed anger that the text was being widely criticized. Violating the rules and procedures he himself had set up for the ratification process, he threatened that parties campaigning against his draft would be barred from using their allotted time on television. He also tried to censor press criticism of his proposed text.[134] Meanwhile, he made repeated public appeals for its adoption.

By all indications, the constitution did not gain the necessary minimum of voter support, but the authorities nonetheless declared that it had been approved. The gap was seemingly closed by government vote fraud. According to subsequent research on all the voting on December 12 by an independent group set up by Yeltsin's Presidential Administration under Aleksandr Sobyanin of the progovernment party Russia's Choice—research that was not convincingly contested by the Central Election Commission (CEC)—the constitution was approved by only 46.1 percent of those who voted in the referendum, when the prescribed minimum was 50 percent.[135] However, the official figures claimed that 54.4 percent of the electorate had voted in the referendum, and that 58.4 percent had voted for the constitution.

Legally speaking, the official vote counts had to be presented within a month of December 12. However, the CEC took more than two months to produce them, and then they were much less detailed than expected. Ever since, there has been a broad consensus among analysts that the results of the vote were tampered with, even though there have been disagreements about the overall effect of this manipulation. While "the Sobyanin group" of liberal defectors from the Presidential Administration claimed (on the basis of a highly questionable methodology) that vote fraud favored Zhirinovsky's party (and the constitution), but actually decreased the final showing of Gaidar's Russia's Choice, Stephen White and his coauthors reached the conclusion that "insofar as false reporting occurred, the official results are likely to have overestimated support for the governing parties and understated opposition."[136]

In practical terms, the new Duma was designed as a classic rubber-stamp legislature that had little defense in the constitution against Yeltsin's ruling largely by decree if he wished. The Duma could not veto his appointments of ministers. It could reject the president's nominee for prime minister, but if it did so three times, then Yeltsin had the right to dissolve it and call new elections. Thus the new Russian parliament had hardly more constitutional authority than the Duma that had existed under the last Russian autocrat, Nicholas II.[137]

Yeltsin had also weakened the future Duma by decreeing on October 11 that the parliament should include an elected upper house, the Federation Council, and that elections for this body should also be held on December 12. To guarantee that the Federation Council would be a largely progovernment body, Yeltsin set up election rules that tended to ensure that members of the provincial nomen-klatura, like regional governors and factory directors, would have the best chances of being elected. The most effective of these rules was one requiring would-be candidates to collect signatures from at least 3 percent of all registered voters in their districts—a daunting task that was far beyond the means of all but the richest and most powerful candidates.

As we have seen, the initial strategy of the Yeltsin team in the wake of the October 3–4 bloodshed was based on several assumptions: that much of public opinion would be either apathetic or hostile to the government, that obtaining a supportive Duma would therefore be difficult, and that the Duma should therefore be given very limited powers. Thus in preparing for the parliamentary elections of December 12, Yeltsin and his team took measures to ensure a cosmetically presentable result. To guard against a low turnout, they reduced the minimum turnout required in each constituency from 50 percent to 25 percent of registered voters. To woo voters, they raised the minimum wage by 90 percent and handed out promises of financial favors. And they manipulated the media with only minimal restraint. A study conducted during the first part of the campaign found that the main Ostankino Television channel, in a thirteen-day period, had given Yegor Gaidar twenty-four minutes of air time, while the communist leader Gennadi Zyuganov was given six minutes, and Grigori Yavlinsky just ten seconds.[138]

In addition, frightened that too many people might exercise their right to vote against all candidates, the Yeltsin team decided at the last moment to change the election rules again. Previously they had said that if the total votes against all candidates in a constituency exceeded the number of votes won by the candidate who finished first, then no one would be elected. This rule was now dropped in a move that probably reduced the number of electors who went to the polls by depriving some people of an attractive incentive to do so. Despite this disincentive, however, 16 percent of all the electors who voted still felt alienated enough—either in general or because the party they favored had been banned —to turn out and vote for "none of the above," and a further 7.3 percent invalidated their ballots. Consequently, the results showed that, even with a probably reduced turnout, as many as 29 out of the 224 eventual winners in the single-mandate districts would not have been elected if the rule had not been dropped.[139] In view of these facts, and also of the low turnout of 54.4 percent (down from 74.7 percent in the presidential election of 1991, and 64.6 percent in the April 1993 referendum) and the large number of candidates in most of the constituencies, the candidates elected received only 29.2 percent of the valid votes cast; and they were voted for by only 14.8 percent of the total number of registered voters.

Thus the directly elected deputies were far from being representative of public opinion, and the mood of the country was considerably more hostile to the government than the Duma was. Even the half of the deputies who were elected by proportional representation from party lists did not accurately represent public opinion. As noted earlier, some parties had been banned from taking part in the election. Of those citizens who voted, 7.5 percent either invalidated their ballots or voted against all the listed parties, while 9 percent of those who did vote for a participating party were disenfranchised (regarding this half of the Duma) by the fact that their party failed to clear the 5 percent hurdle, so that no candidates from its party list won seats in the new parliament.

Primarily because of the extreme difficulty of getting candidates on the ballot, the elections to the Federation Council produced a broadly progovernment body that was even less representative of public opinion than the Duma. Here the rule that the winning candidate had to get more votes than the number cast against all candidates was *not* dropped. However, when in one constituency the "against all" tally came in first, scoring 30.2 percent of the vote, this rule was simply ignored and the top candidate was illegally declared elected.[140]

In party terms, the main results of the Duma elections were the poor showing of the progovernment parties and the unexpected and stunning victory for Zhirinovsky's Liberal Democratic Party. The LDP had benefited from the ban on the democratic nationalist and conservative parties decreed by Yeltsin in October. The fact that Zhirinovsky had been allowed to practice his dazzling demagogy on television amounted to open assistance from the Yeltsin camp. All this was done because Zhirinovsky cleverly performed the most important service for Yeltsin and his team—he debased parliamentary politics and successfully fostered the alienation of parts of the discontented populace from the only institution that potentially could have represented its interests, the Duma. By contrast, Russia's Choice, the leading establishment party headed by Gaidar and Chubais, which had forecast its share of votes as 30 to 40 percent, received just 15.4 percent. Such a thumping defeat of the market bolsheviks despite their unchallenged control of the national media and Yeltsin's intimidation of the populace in October was a serious moral and political setback for the Kremlin camp. It was also a humiliation for the market bolsheviks' patrons and sponsors in the G-7 governments and the IMF.

In the next chapter, we examine Yeltsin's consolidation of his authoritarian rule, the continuation of the West's uncritical support, and the negative effects of all this on Russian democracy and on the lives of average Russians.

8

THE IMPERIAL PRESIDENCY IN A PRIVATIZED STATE: 1994–1996

KORZHAKOV [retelling his stern lecture to the Communists earlier]: "You ruled for seventy years—so now let us rule for seventy years. If we don't succeed over this period, then we'll hand over power."

CHERNOMYRDIN: "No, we won't hand it over."

KORZHAKOV: "Well, I didn't mean that literally."

> — *From Aleksandr Korzhakov's tape-recorded conversation with Viktor Chernomyrdin in his* Boris Yeltsin: Ot rassveta do zakata (Boris Yeltsin: From Sunrise to Sunset)

BEFORE YELTSIN'S TANK ASSAULT on the democratically elected parliament, condoned by his allies in East and West, he promised the Russians years of calm and an economic upsurge, once the "dark forces" opposed to shock therapy had been removed from the scene. Yet over the subsequent years of his semi-authoritarian rule, Russia continued to lurch from crisis to crisis, big and small, one of them a brutal, draining, two-year civil war.

Whereas in the "dual-power" period of 1992–93 the stakes in the political fight were high for most Russians, the intramural scuffling under Yeltsin's imperial presidency had little to no impact on the plight of the nation or the lives of ordinary citizens, most of whom only sank deeper into poverty and despair as the Western-backed regime stubbornly pursued its economic policies. While the Kremlin and the usually rubber-stamp parliament postured and maneuvered, the single major fact about this period was that Russia continued on its slippery slope of decline; most notably, the assets and powers of the state passed almost continuously into private hands.

Meanwhile, all opportunities for meaningful change that would have enabled Russia to reverse its course were closed off until the presidential elections of June 1996. Yet at that decisive point, when Yeltsin had to wage an uphill battle for a once unthinkable second term in office, the disorientation of society, the skillful ruthlessness of his campaign, and the glaring inadequacy of his opponents resulted in his victory. This enabled him to preside without too much trouble over another period of stagnation and decline. In the meantime, democracy and the rule of law decayed, while crime and oligarchy prospered. And the gulf between the powerful and the powerless, the wealthy and the poor, widened inexorably. Such is the story of this chapter.

THE OCTOBER 1993 REGIME: STABILITY WITHOUT LEGITIMACY

As noted earlier, the legitimacy of the post–October 1993 regime was shaky from the very beginning. The rules for the referendum on the new constitution, as set forth in Yeltsin's decree of October 15, 1993, contradicted not only the still operative "old" constitution (thus violating constitutional continuity, just as in 1917) but also the still valid Russian statute on referendums of October 1990, which had created the legal basis for instituting the presidency. If this statute had been obeyed, the Yeltsin constitution would have been rejected by the referendum vote in December 1993: even according to the official tally, only 31 percent of the electorate voted "yes" for the constitution (the statute required at least 50 percent), and a meager 54.4 percent of the voters turned out at the polls. Moreover, support for the new constitution fell 13 million short of the number of votes cast for Yeltsin two years earlier as president of Russia, on the basis of the old constitution. Among the eighty-nine administrative units of the Russian

Federation, Chechnya did not take part in the voting, the turnout in Tatarstan was only 13.4 percent, and eighteen other territories voted against (with negative results as high as 79 percent in the North Caucasian republic of Dagestan).[1]

More doubt about the validity of the vote was cast by suspicious variations in the electoral count: 107.3 million in the April 1993 referendum, 105.2 million according to the Electoral Commission publications in December, and then 106.2 million in the final results of the poll publicized in February. Local deviations were even more glaring, with 1,604 votes tallied on the Solovki Islands, where only 434 voters had been registered. In Amur region, a member of the electoral commission and of Democratic Russia resigned from both organizations after describing in detail the falsification of the vote.[2] In Moscow, a precinct election official committed suicide, leaving a written confession that he had "grossly deceived the people." On top of all this, lower-level reports to the Electoral Commission were destroyed soon after the official results had been published.[3] One can only agree with White and his colleagues that the way the constitution was rammed through "prejudiced its long-term future."[4] To put it simply, it is a Yeltsin constitution very much as the 1936 Basic Law was a Stalin constitution, but it has less authority than Stalin's and is unlikely to survive for long in the post-Yeltsin era.

Among the eight parties that crossed the 5 percent threshold for the Duma, four (Yabloko, the Democratic Party, the Agrarians, and the Communists) had either strongly criticized the Yeltsin constitution or directly called on their followers to vote against it. Therefore, it is highly significant that, as mentioned earlier, after their election to the new parliament all of them acquiesced in the adoption of the constitution and did not challenge its dubious claim to legitimacy. True, doing this would have been self-defeating in one sense, as it would have ipso facto undercut the legitimacy of the Duma itself and perhaps opened the door to even worse alternatives, including a return to Yeltsin's rule by decree, unchecked in any way by a legislature. In a more realistic scenario, though, such a move simply would have failed because the opposition was a minority in a fragmented parliament populated by parochial lobbyists with fluid or nonexistent political affiliations.

Nonetheless, whatever can be said in its defense, the opposition's acceptance of the rigged rules of the game was a decisive triumph for the Kremlin and the first step toward integrating its parliamentary critics into the political machinery of Yeltsin's rule. Zyuganov soon had to admit with visible regret that the opposition found itself trapped in the walls of the new parliament; however, its unenviable predicament had been conditioned by the behavior of its leaders, in particular Zyuganov's, in the September–October 1993 events. At that time, they took a neutral stand during Yeltsin's military crackdown on his erstwhile democratic allies, and they accepted electoral rules drafted by the executive that enabled them to run for the new parliament while other opposition groups were outlawed or otherwise kept out of the race.

YELTSIN'S LONG-TERM STRATEGY

Between the elections of 1993 and the amnesty crisis of late February 1994, the Yeltsin team worked out its new medium-term strategy. What transpired was, in most respects, a more determined and consolidated version of the improvised strategy of October–December, discussed in the previous chapter. Ten days after the traumas of December 12, at his postelection news conference, Yeltsin drew the conclusion that what the voters really wanted was national reconciliation to heal the traumas and a stronger government that would tighten up on law and order. He also planned to form a presidential political party.[5] At about the same time, David Remnick had conversations with four of Yeltsin's aides:

> All of them admitted that their hopes for a smooth, swift transfer from a communist dictatorship to a free-market democracy were now shattered. . . . Now the talk was of a transitional regime of 'enlightened authoritarianism' or "administrative democracy" or some such hybrid that made no secret of the need for a prolonged concentration of power in the presidency. Yeltsin was known to be drinking more and becoming a creature of a tight circle of antireform aides. . . .[6]

A few weeks later, Gaidar picked up on Yeltsin's intention to form a new party. Speaking as though he were a veteran democrat (not a new and self-declared one), he said: "Unless the democratic movement is consolidated, the slide toward fascism . . . will become reality." "At present our state cannot be considered democratic," said Gaidar. "Once again the ossification of the bureaucracy is taking place. Once again the alienation of the people from the state and its apparatus has been intensified. . . . The nomenklatura largely remains as it was before." All this was leading to an alliance between the bureaucracy and corrupt capital, producing "a closed, rotten, truly 'Weimar' atmosphere in which the terrible homunculi of fascism are born." Unfortunately, the democrats did not have a "new, powerful, integrating idea." Such an idea was urgently needed for use against the powerful appeal of the fascists.[7] So spoke Gaidar after his own president had done something almost analogous to the Nazis' burning down of the Reichstag and then blaming it on Germany's communists.

However, the plan to form a presidential party quickly proved unfeasible. It became clear that the shock therapists were deeply divided over personalities, how best to proceed, and whether to continue their conditional support for Yeltsin when most of them were strongly criticizing Chernomyrdin's government for its change of course on economic reform. True, at Yeltsin's behest several people apart from Gaidar tried to sell the plan for a presidential party, Burbulis being the leading proponent.[8] But there were too few takers, and the idea was reluctantly abandoned until the summer of 1995. The main problem was that Yeltsin was now relying heavily on his chief bodyguard, Aleksandr Korzhakov, and others of an authoritarian outlook who had little interest in sharing their influence with the leaders of a presidential party. Thus the failure to form such a party demonstrated very clearly that the watershed in Russian politics did not run between democrats and antidemocrats. The Yeltsin camp contained a few democrats but a larger number of authoritarians of various stripes, notably shock therapists and people of the Korzhakov type.

Yeltsin's first statement on long-term strategy came in an address to the State Duma on February 24, 1994, in which an implied need for continued authoritarianism (of the "mild" or *"myagkii"* type) was featured, even as the blackened hulk of the parliamentary White House was being whitewashed and refurbished to become the headquarters of the government.[9] Yeltsin's coded approval of authoritarianism came out in his emphasis on "the need to strengthen the state." This intent was reiterated in slightly different ways throughout the speech.

As for his integrating "national idea," this could be summed up in the word "patriotism," which, he held, should permeate both domestic and foreign policy. Other key themes were the need to tackle "Russia's serious illnesses" by building up national solidarity and cooperation; combating crime and corruption; strengthening cohesion between the central government and the regions; and continuing economic reform, although in somewhat different, more state-oriented ways than before.

Notable for their absence or only perfunctory mention in the speech were such themes as the need to strengthen democracy; to respect the will of the people as expressed through the Duma; to reverse the general decline in the nation's education, research capacity, culture, and health system; and to provide specific assistance to the mass of ordinary people who were struggling to survive through the fourth year of a severe economic depression. Yeltsin's tacit rejection of democratic deliberation on these and related issues was one of the fatal flaws in the overall "New Deal" that he was prescribing for the Russian people on the basis of the new constitution.

Beneath a veneer of rhetoric about national reconciliation, then, Yeltsin claimed to be focused on "strengthening the state." However, what really concerned him was strengthening his own grip on power. As soon became clear, achieving this *real* goal had the effect of negating the *advertised* goal. While he was busy creating special institutions and mechanisms to secure his personal rule, the essential institutions of a legitimate state stagnated and decayed: the health service, the education system, the advanced research institutes, the political parties, the parliament, the regional parliaments, the state bureaucracy, the armed forces, the fiscal institutions to support a stable currency, and the whole structure of law enforcement and the courts.

Instead of nurturing these basic institutions of a strong state, Yeltsin applied most of his energies to tasks more reminiscent of Byzantium and the Borgias. He removed most of the limits on his own power. He created his personal KGB. He undermined the state bureaucracy by inflating his Presidential Administration and having the two bodies work in tension-ridden tandem. He gave the parliament minimal powers and kept it in perpetual fear of dissolution. He oversaw the creation of regional institutions that mirrored the federal ones, thus facilitating the rise of a new set of boyars, or regional tsars, as governors. He created or adapted institutions that would produce streams of revenue for his own slush funds and report only to himself. He bought the support of key institutions, bankers, and businessmen so as to exploit their media outlets and tap their funds at critical junctures (such as elections). He also demonized a seemingly vulnerable opponent, the Chechens, and sent his army to crush them—only for the whole venture to collapse in blood, recrimination, and humiliating failure. Why? Because the state had been weakened and, given Yeltsin's style of rule, could not conduct war efficiently.

At each turn, Yeltsin sold off the state's assets and powers, buying enough political support to see him through his next crisis. He privatized not just assets that sooner or later it was wise to sell off, but also those essential attributes of a state, such as its financial integrity and its power to enforce the law. After six years of Russia's society and polity trying to turn the rule of men—the members of the CPSU Politburo—into the rule of law, Yeltsin and his cronies deliberately reversed the process.

Let us look, then, at some key elements in this sorry operation.

"THE ARMY OF OFFICIALDOM"

First there was Yeltsin's manipulation of the strongest parties and of parliament as a whole. A prime Kremlin goal in this regard was to convince the cocky parties of Zhirinovsky, Zyuganov, and Yavlinsky that their election successes did not mean very much. Yeltsin was still the boss; he would not be pushed around by public opinion, and after making a few concessions, he would emasculate the Duma. To this end, the Kremlin opted early for a "good cop, bad cop" routine. Yeltsin usually played the bad cop, sometimes hinting—personally or through a surrogate—that he would not hesitate to close down the Duma permanently, if need be.[10] Ten days after the election, he declared defiantly, "Gaidar will stay, and so will his policies."[11] Later, he violated the spirit of the constitution by ignoring the Duma's adamant opposition to Chubais's cash privatization program. When the Duma voted 186 to 91 against it on July 13, 1994, Chubais threatened the people's representatives with an authoritarian riposte. And so, on July 24, Tsar Boris told the people what he thought of them: he imposed the program by presidential decree.

Likewise, when another such edict suddenly widened the police's powers, enabling them to hold suspects for thirty days without charge, the Duma, which had not been consulted, voted on June 22 to repeal it. The vote was 246 to 6. The deputies argued persuasively that the edict violated both the constitution and the criminal code. On November 13, they reiterated their stand. But the tsar paid no heed. His edict remained in effect.

Meanwhile, good cop Chernomyrdin, using his close personal relationship to Zyuganov, tried to placate the opposition. As early as December 18, he criticized Gaidar and Chubais, charging that "defeat in the elections shows how the people evaluated [their] performance." Suddenly sounding quite reasonable, he rejected shock therapy and stressed the need to invest in industry to reverse the falls in production.[12] Then, during the opening of the Duma on January 10, he denounced "market romanticism" and declared that shock therapy would be dropped because the "prerequisites for moving on to a new stage of economic reforms have appeared."[13] When Gaidar, Pamfilova, and Fyodorov resigned in protest the same month over the changes in economic policy, the Duma majority applauded. Yet Chubais, who got support from Chernomyrdin as well as unofficial help from the Gaidar group, remained in office as privatization chief, partly as a guarantee to "the West" that, in reality, IMF-type reform would continue.

By contrast, the regime usually avoided showing its bad cop face to the Federation Council. In fact, it was solicitous toward the upper house: Yeltsin needed the support of the regional barons who constituted it. On January 10, for example, he stressed the need to cooperate with regional representatives within the framework of the council. Such cooperation would help to neutralize the opposition of the "communist and profascist" forces.

If Yeltsin's edicts were to be obeyed, the Kremlin needed to strengthen the executive branch of government at all levels. And because the core of the Soviet state—the hierarchy of the old Communist Party—had simply disappeared in August 1991, and parts of the ministerial structure had been dismantled between 1991 and 1993, there was much to be done. Also, because the new legislatures created in Moscow and the regions in late 1993 had been deliberately designed to have few powers, and because civil society had been so undermined by shock therapy as to be unable to provide much input, legislation would have to be generated primarily by the executive.

In addition, officials of the executive branch could argue that the economy still needed much attention from the regional administrations. The invisible hand of the market had been much too weak to replace the planning and supply functions previously provided by the CPSU apparatus and Soviet industrial ministries. Although dirigiste and regulatory intervention by the government was thus required to develop a modern market, such intervention had not been forthcoming. The executive, Yeltsin concluded, had to be increased in size. In particular, the Presidential Administration and the analogous personal staffs of the country's governors and mayors had to be expanded so that they could supervise, monitor, and, where necessary, direct the sluggish old bureaucrats of the surviving ministries and the revamped regional administrations (which had absorbed the staffs of the old soviet executive committees, or *ispolkomy*). They also had to supervise the economy in general, the legislatures, the judicial system, civil society—including parties, unions, and the media—the military, the police, and the various security agencies. In other words, the governmental administrations had to carry out many of the functions of the old CPSU apparatus!

To knit things together nationally, the Presidential Administration tried to recreate the vertical chain of command and subordination that had constituted the skeleton and muscles of the CPSU apparatus. Now the chain of command was simply called "the vertical of executive power" (*vertikal' ispol'nitel'noi vlasti*), and the Yeltsin administration began to call—frequently and often desperately, as it did to the bitter end—for this vertical chain of command to be strengthened. At the same time, the cash-starved Kremlin devolved some of its powers and obligations to the regions, partly because communism had greatly overcentralized the state, and partly in an effort (unavailing until recently) to balance the federal budget. In 1997, for example, federal revenues amounted to only 11.3 percent of GDP, creating a budget deficit of 6.1 percent.[14] This made Russia's central government one of the most weakly funded among the industrialized nations of the world, and dangerously dependent on foreign subsidies.

Even though Yeltsin in his programmatic speech deplored the fact that "the army of officialdom is growing rapidly," in practice he did not hesitate to beef up his own administration, and the mayors and regional governors did the same. In December 1993, Yeltsin's staff was reported to number 3,500 officials (*otvetstvennye rabotniki*), compared to the slightly more than 200 who had served Gorbachev as president of the USSR.[15] Before long, though, the figure reportedly rose to 5,500 officials who were in charge of 21,500 subordinates.[16] (Many of the latter apparently belonged to the Main Protective Administration and the Presidential Security Service.) As for government bodies more generally, Prime Minister Sergei Kirienko told the Duma on April 10, 1998, that the staff they employed in Moscow and the regions increased by 1.2 million from 1992 to 1997. In 1997, the cost of maintaining these bodies increased by 62 percent over 1996.

Yeltsin also moved to magnify his personal power in some direct and immediate ways. In December 1993, with Decree No. 2288, he quietly rescinded the existing law "On the President of the RFSFR," which had significantly limited his powers, and did not have it replaced by a new law.[17] This meant that he was henceforth constrained only by a few articles of the new constitution that concerned things like treason.[18] The same month, he announced that he would not, after all, run for re-election in June 1994, as he had promised, but only in June 1996.[19]

Along with arbitrarily expanding and prolonging his own powers, Yeltsin also had told Korzhakov the previous month: "I want you to set up a small KGB. My personal mini-KGB." So, by a decree of November 13, 1993, which was designated "secret" and not published, the Presidential Security Service became an independent federal organ. Unacknowledged by the constitution and unregulated by any law, the service nonetheless received a flowery letter of gratitude from Yeltsin on its first anniversary. He thanked his "dear friends" for enduring "constant tension" in their "not easy work that is full of risk."[20] Korzhakov had already set up large secret police and analytical divisions, and even planned to create a mobile, four-thousand-strong National Guard that would suppress political opposition in any part of the country. However, when the main planning document leaked to the press, Yeltsin evidently decided not to implement the idea.[21]

In order to have at his control all the firepower of Russia—except for the armories of the Mafiya bosses and the private security firms—Yeltsin also subordinated to himself personally, rather than to the prime minister, the so-called power ministries, or *silovye ministerstva,* along with the Ministry of Foreign Affairs.[22] The power ministries included the Interior Ministry (MVD); the Federal Counter-Intelligence Service (FSK); the Foreign Intelligence Service (SVR); and the Federal Agency for Government Communications (FAPSI), the organization for electronic espionage equivalent to the U.S. National Security Agency. On top of this, Yeltsin boosted the executive's sense of privilege and invulnerability by giving the heads of thirty-eight ministries and agencies the right to classify as secret any information they possessed.[23] This action reversed the democratizing trend of the previous few years, which had sought to bring some transparency and accountability into government.

An especially negative aspect of creating a large Presidential Administration and giving it functions not so different from those of the old CPSU Central Committee apparatus was that some key governmental functions were duplicated, reflecting the competing baronies within the regime. As a result, the Presidential Administration and the Cabinet of Ministers clashed as often as they cooperated, causing confusion, delays, and inertia.[24] The picture was similar at the regional level.

At the same time, building up bloated personal staffs—and maintaining the regular governmental administrations—had attractive advantages for chief executives of an authoritarian bent who wanted to hold on to power. It gave them extensive powers of patronage, with which (as with the privatization process) they could reward their friends, buy the political support of key people, and co-opt opponents. It allowed these functionaries to administer innumerable regulatory, taxing, price-setting, housing, legislative, research, police, recreational, health-care, educational, transportation, welfare, and licensing functions, many of which helped to line these officials' pockets as well as to finance government. It also created a critical mass of loyal employees and their families who had a powerful interest in maintaining the political status quo by quietly accommodating organized crime and intimidating would-be troublemakers among the labor force or the citizenry.

At the federal level—and at other levels as well—the president built up his power in less orthodox ways, which later gave rise to major scandals. In November–December 1993, Yeltsin quietly issued a number of decrees granting favors to organizations whose support he wanted to procure. Two decrees gave an extraordinary range of financial privileges to four disabled veterans' organizations and certain sports associations. They were exempted from various taxes, allowed to draw on government funds, and permitted to import and export goods related to their activities and purposes without paying customs duties or excise taxes.[25] The groups whose leaders apparently benefited most were the National Sports Foundation, run by Yeltsin's friend and tennis coach, Shamil Tarpishchev, which reportedly caused the state losses of $1.8 billion in the early 1990s and even more later, and the Russian Foundation for Invalids of the War in Afghanistan.[26] Similar privileges were given to the Russian Orthodox Church, which was thus rewarded for its support of Yeltsin during the October 1993 crisis, despite the opposition of many of its communicants.[27] Yeltsin also set up the Rosvooruzhenie Company as the main channel for the export of Russian arms, and appointed its director, who was answerable only to Yeltsin (that is, in practice, to Korzhakov).[28]

The ability of these organizations to make large sums of money at the state's expense tied them to Yeltsin and made them sources of funds and political support when he needed such help. Similar operations were conducted with the huge state gas monopoly Gazprom, to which Chernomyrdin was closely tied. In late 1993, attempts to break its monopoly by splitting it up, and to bar all oil- and gas-producing companies from owning pipeline companies, were defeated, presumably on Yeltsin's orders. Instead, in 1994, Soskovets signed a secret agreement "allowing the Gazprom management to take over the government's shares in the company after three years—a deal worth tens of billions of dollars." Later, in 1997, the government revoked this bribe—perhaps the biggest in history—and signed a new agreement under which Gazprom's chairman, Rem Vyakhirev, would still manage the government's 35 percent stake, but would receive as compensation only 2 percent of the dividends—not, as previously specified, 45 percent.[29]

In 1993–94, sweetheart arrangements of various types were made with the state's property organization under Yeltsin's crony Pavel Borodin, which owns hundreds of valuable pieces of real estate, and with other organizations.[30] Several special studies are needed to marshal and analyze all the evidence now available on these intricate and deeply corrupt operations.

Strengthening the state also meant trying to restore morale and discipline in the badly shaken army and MVD. The depth of the problem was obvious to the Yeltsinites. Yeltsin's personal intervention had failed to quell the mutiny of the elite Alpha and Vympel security forces on October 4.[31] Thereafter, the especially recalcitrant Vympel had even refused to be transferred to the MVD and had to be decommissioned.[32] The immediate cause of such attitudes was the corrosive effect of Yeltsin's having used the army, against its will, to suppress the old parliament; but deeper causes existed, too. One view came from the assistant head of Yeltsin's analytical center, who concluded that a majority of the military had voted for Zhirinovsky's party. They did so, he said, partly because army educators had "reshaped the communist doctrine into a national socialist ideology," and partly because troops were not receiving their pay on time. With "no presidential or governmental capacity to monitor the army," he warned, "the growing influence of national-socialist ideas on the Armed Forces poses a real threat to the security of Russia and the development of democracy."[33] Statements like this, of course, must be taken with caution and viewed in the context of the regime's efforts to smear any opposition with its all-purpose red-brown brush.

To restore some morale after October 4, Yeltsin pleased the military—the very next day—by having the document "The Basic Principles of Military Doctrine" approved, after he had long resisted doing so.[34] He appeared in photographs "with a machine-gun in hand" and promised that "there will be no more concessions to the West."[35] Also, the armed forces were given permission to campaign for troop and support personnel levels much higher than the previously authorized 1.5 million.[36] Nonetheless, this change was not implemented in the following months, and, partly as a result, military morale remained dangerously low. The Duma opposition repeatedly protested about governmental neglect of the military, but Yeltsin paid little heed and stuck to a policy that enriched top military commanders and the MVD establishment and neglected enlisted men.

A "SEARCH FOR NATIONAL SOLIDARITY AND COOPERATION"

A second major theme of Yeltsin's speech on February 24 was the urgent need for national solidarity, cooperation, and reconciliation. "The basis for social accord," he said, "is the constitution," and added that it was important for the bitter opponents of autumn 1993 to come together in "the common cause" of reviving Russia. Later, this line led Yeltsin to spend much time and energy promoting an "Agreement on Civic Accord," which bound its signatories to eschew calling for early elections and to put forward constitutional amendments only if they were based on broad societal consensus. This document was signed with much pomp on April 28 by the leaders of the federal government and of many regions, parties, labor unions, religious confessions, and social movements. As we will see, some key opposition leaders were not among them.

However, while the whole exercise seemed rather empty and redundant, it contributed to Yeltsin's efforts to isolate significant political forces that ignored it and embarked on hostile activity outside the established system. Three such attempts were made in 1994, and all failed quite badly. These involved the coalition "Accord for the Sake of Russia"; Rutskoi's Derzhava movement; and the "triple entente" of Luzhkov, Yabloko, and Gusinsky.[37]

Yeltsin's phrase "civic accord" suggests an image of respectable politics within one big tent. Even the nationalist/communist opposition (except for Derzhava and Accord for the Sake of Russia), although nursing deep grievances against the regime, decided not to make any serious attempt to mobilize the extensive popular discontent around the country. They gave no thought to trying to overcome the vertical division in society (described in chapter 6). Instead, they ended up doing things that were less demanding: to become a loyal, tame opposition to the government; to operate mainly within the Moscow-based political elite, with its familiar cast of characters and material perks; and to resign themselves to their own lack of independent funding and almost negligible access to the more powerful media. If some elements of this opposition had somehow won the presidency in 1996, they would have posed no threat to the West because the opposition was by now not just tame but housebroken as well. As noted previously, Zyuganov admitted early in the year that the opposition was "trapped" by its election to the Duma, which in his view prevented it from mounting a serious challenge to the Yeltsin constitution.

THE NEW DISTRIBUTION OF FORCES

As most participants of the democratic and nationalist rallies of 1988 to 1992 saw their hopes betrayed and progressively sank into poverty and often apathy, the rowdy era of mass public activism receded into the past. From 1994 to 1996, Russia's civil society contracted and for the most part retreated from politics. No political force with the exception of radical communists was able to muster more than a few thousand supporters for a street rally. Opposition politics became heavily concentrated in the parliament, especially in the Duma, which from now on served as the opposition's main institutional base.

Meanwhile, the upper house, or Federation Council, was largely a synod of regional barons and company bosses, who pursued their special interests and displayed only marginal political differentiation on issues of nationwide concern. It was a major success of Yeltsin's new regime that the Duma, the only body with politicians able to supply strategic alternatives to the Kremlin's policies, had little constitutional power. It could not, for example, dismiss the cabinet or individual members and had virtually no powers to supervise the executive. Its major prerogatives were to enact the state budget and to declare amnesties. A third privilege was to vote on the candidacy of a prime minister nominated by the president. However, if the Duma rejected the nominee three times, Yeltsin had the right to dissolve it and call new elections—a powerful deterrent for backbenchers who were chiefly concerned with lobbying the government and who might, after a dissolution, lose the chance to finish their transactions or to settle permanently in the comfortable surrounds of Moscow.

Most of the divisions of the previous parliament were reproduced in the new Duma: a huge "swamp" of apolitical deputies squarely standing for their special interests (which, in most cases, compelled them to support the executive branch) and a politicized minority divided into supporters and opponents of the regime. In the new parliament, as had been generally the case since the launching of shock therapy, the old script about the "democrats" opposed to the "reds-and-browns" (used by official propaganda and by the dwindling cohorts of Yegor Gaidar to split their opponents along artificial lines) was out of touch with reality. The antagonism between the pro-Kremlin and the anti-Kremlin forces, most pronounced on issues of economic policy, cut across ideological divisions, with many independent democrats and pro-Western liberals attacking the regime as the communists did, while a solid number of dyed-in-the-wool xenophobes and authoritarians voted with the shock therapists from Russia's Choice.

To show the new distribution of forces and how it changed from December 1993 to October 1995 to January 1996, we have compiled the table on the next two pages from a variety of sources; two caveats are needed, however. First, only the larger parties (those clearing the 5 percent hurdle) are listed. Second, the categories "swing deputies" and "opposition" inevitably give a misleadingly precise impression. As we emphasize at various points in this book, the LDP ("swing deputies") has almost always come to the government's aid at critical moments, and the CPRF ("opposition") has often done so as well.

GAIDAR AND ZHIRINOVSKY: THE DOUBLE FACE OF MARKET BOLSHEVISM

Given that the pro-Western liberals were deeply split, Gaidar and his associates in Russia's Choice found themselves, as the table shows, with only 15 percent of the popular vote. Moreover, they exposed themselves as victims of delusion when they claimed the mantle of leadership in a "democratic camp" that had long ceased to exist. The very term "democrat" was not only discredited and worn out, but had ceased to have the clear meaning that it had before 1992. Because all deputies, including Communists, were playing by the parliamentary rules of the game and accepted, at least in rhetoric, the supreme authority of the ballot box (even if sometimes for lack of a better alternative), they were all now democrats in the narrowly procedural, Schumpeterian sense. However, the democratic credentials of any single party did not reach far beyond this minimum; the label "democratic" was even less suitable for the Yeltsinists and Gaidarists in the parliament, who had demanded enthusiastic support for the tank assault on the parliament as the price of admission to their "democratic club."

At the same time, Gaidar and those of his associates who had left the heights of executive power for the parliament had doomed themselves to political irrelevance. The real winners of the October showdown—Yeltsin, the security police, and the military establishment—resented the shock therapists for having provoked the crisis and, worse, for having proved unable (with the partial exception of Chubais) to sway low-level and regional bureaucrats to their side or to deliver solid grassroots support for the coup, even among the Moscow intelligentsia,

Table 1. Political Spectrum in the State Duma, 1993–1996

FACTIONS AND GROUPS*	presence in the Congress of People's Deputies and Supreme Soviet, 1990–1993	vote for the party list in December 1993	deputies joining after the election	total membership/ % of seats in January 1994	total membership in October 1995	change	vote for the party list in December 1995	deputies joining after the election	total membership/ % of seats in January 1996
Progovernment									
Russia's Choice (Gaidar)	*nonexistent*	15.5% (40 seats)	36	76	49	−27	3.9% (0 seats)	9	9
Party of Russian Unity and Accord (Shakhrai)	*nonexistent*	6.8% (18 seats)	12	30	13	−17	0.4% (0 seats)	1 (Shakhrai)	1
Women of Russia (Lakhova)	*nonexistent*	8.1% (21 seats)	2	23	20	−3	4.6% (0 seats)	3	3
Our Home Is Russia (Chernomyrdin, Shokhin)	*nonexistent*				37 ("Stability" group)	+37	10.1% (45 seats)	21	66
Total		30.4 % (79 seats)	50	129 (28.7%)	119 (26.4%)	−10	19% (45 seats)	34	79 (17.6%)

Swing deputies

Party									
Liberal Democrats (Zhirinovsky)	*not in parliament*	22.9% (59 seats)	5	64	55	−9	11.2% (50 seats)	1	51
Agrarians (Lapshin)	*from 183 to 130 in CPD; 13 in SS*	8% (21 seats)	34	55	51	−4	3.8% (0 seats)	20	37[†]
INDEPENDENTS				47	57	+10			23
Total		**30.9% (80 seats)**	**39**	**166 (36.9%)**	**163**	**−3**	**15% (50 seats)**	**21**	**111 (24.7%)**

Opposition

Party									
Communist (Zyuganov)	*from 355 to 67 in CPD; 17 in SS*	12.4% (32 seats)	13	45	47	+2	22.3% (99 seats)	58	147[†]
Yabloko (Yavlinsky)	*nonexistent*	7.9% (20 seats)	7	27	27	0	6.9% (31 seats)	15	46
Democratic Party (Travkin, Glaziev, Govorukhin)	*marginal*	5.5% (14 seats)	1	15	11	−4	*split before the election*		
Total		**25.8% (66 seats)**	**21**	**87 (19.3%)**	**85**	**−2**	**29.2% (130 seats)**	**73**	**193 (42.9%)**

* The Duma consists of 225 deputies elected on party slates and 225 deputies elected on a plurality basis in single-member districts. Factions are formed on the basis of parties that have crossed the 5 percent electoral threshold. Independent deputies from single-member districts can form "groups," which get registered and obtain a seat in the Duma Council and a share of committee positions, but a group must have at least 35 members.

† A number of Communist deputies were "yielded" by the CPRF faction to the Agrarians, so that the latter were able to register their group in the Duma and sit on the Duma Council.

which had now become profoundly divided. During the final stage of the electoral campaign, the "power ministries" had quietly promoted Zhirinovsky's LDP across the country, hoping it would oust self-anointed reformers.

Furthermore, signs of ambivalence on the part of some Western leaders after the coup undercut the credentials of Gaidar and his ilk as middlemen to the West who were always capable of delivering its financial and ideological endorsement for free-market authoritarianism. In December, Strobe Talbott offered good advice—"less shock, more therapy"—which caused bewilderment among Russian politicians across the spectrum, most of whom believed that "shock without therapy" had been a deliberate and coordinated long-term policy on the part of "the West" as a whole.[38] Hard-liners in the power ministries took the admonishment as a sudden case of American jitters—shock therapists, as betrayal. "We were stabbed in the back," exclaimed Finance Minister Boris Fyodorov, seeing the handwriting on the wall for himself and his colleagues. On January 16, 24, and 26, Gaidar, Labor and Welfare Minister Ella Pamfilova, and, finally, Fyodorov himself offered their resignations. They were accepted without delay, much to the delight of the Duma majority. Talbott, meanwhile, back-pedaled hard. On January 5, U.S. officials said his words had been misunderstood, and three weeks later a reporter summarized him as having said in Moscow that "Slowing the pace of reform and propping up inefficient, communist-era industries would only prolong the suffering."[39]

From now on, as the table indicates, the major theme in the pro-regime camp of the Duma was fragmentation and decay. Gaidar's party, which had banked on the continuation of Yeltsin's support and had failed at the polls, often blamed the Party of Russian Unity and Accord (PRUA) for siphoning away votes. PRUA was the tiny elitist party led by Sergei Shakhrai and Aleksandr Shokhin that managed to keep its four high-profile slots in the cabinet because of its informal alliance with Chernomyrdin and its farsighted restraint during the October events.

Early 1994 became the heyday of PRUA influence: Shakhrai, a craftsman of parliamentary intrigue, brokered a deal between the opposition and the cabinet that opened the door for a major political amnesty, and Shokhin, having replaced Gaidar as the major economic policymaker in the cabinet, administered Yeltsin's new economic policy, which worked badly. In the fall of 1994, when the regime was precipitously sliding into a semiauthoritarian nationalism, Shakhrai's party seemed to be Yeltsin's last bastion of support in parliament (Zhirinovsky excepted), with Russia's Choice starting to carve itself a niche next to the opposition.

Yet in the longer term, both these pro-regime parties were on a slippery slope: during their two-year stay in the Duma, Russia's Choice lost no less than a third of its members, and PRUA more than half. Their disarray was exacerbated by competition from groups of parliamentary deputies-cum-lobbyists without any purely political agenda (such as the faction New Regional Policy, headed by the oil magnate Vladimir Medvedev) that were created and dissolved at the government's discretion. By the end of 1995, both parties imploded and failed to pass the 5 percent barrier in the new elections. Some of their prominent members, such as Stepan Sulakshin from Russia's Choice and Konstantin Zatulin from PRUA joined the opposition camp; others were absorbed by Chernomyrdin's Our Home Is Russia, a rag-tag "party of power" that represented the pro-regime forces in the post-1995 Duma.

Against this background, the political stock of Vladimir Zhirinovsky and his well-disciplined cohorts steadily rose. By tirelessly lambasting the self-styled "democrats" and "reformers," while extending equally consistent support for every Kremlin move that smacked of a "strong hand," Zhirinovsky skillfully assisted Yeltsin in recasting his political image. On the Russian political stage, Zhirinovsky became the twin brother of Yegor Gaidar: both of them were strong supporters of the new regime and the Yeltsin constitution. For both of them, such a comparison would have sounded like sacrilege, for they supported two Yeltsins who seemed to be radically different: Gaidar praised Yeltsin the free-market reformer, and Zhirinovsky embraced Yeltsin the authoritarian. Yet, bewildering as it seemed to many Russians, these were merely the two main profiles of the same Yeltsin, the Bolshevik modernizer. By 1994, this fusion of reform and authoritarianism had become so evident and yet so embarrassing to acknowledge, particularly for the shock therapy camp, that Gaidar and Zhirinovsky ended up as irreconcilable rivals, each advancing his own vision of the new, post-October regime.

Their competition erupted publicly in the of spring 1994, when Gaidar published a major article in *Izvestiya* that labeled Zhirinovsky a fascist, and the latter responded by suing him in a case he eventually won.[40] This duel of words did not help dispel the impression of growing ideological convergence between the two; the most vivid testimony was their standing next to each other at the head of the Kremlin table to which loyal politicians had been summoned to sign the Agreement on Civic Accord, a document that imposed on its signatories such obligations as not to call for early elections and not to initiate constitutional amendments. By contrast, both the democratic reformer Yavlinsky and the "red-and-brown" Zyuganov abstained from signing it.

In the view of Kremlin strategists, Zhirinovsky's Liberal Democrats were a much more valuable asset than Gaidar's weak platoons. This was true, even though most of Russia's nationalists denounced the LDP, using epithets like "puppet of the government" and, even though over the next few years, leaders and deputies defected from the party in a steady trickle. Observers concluded that the government retained much of the control over the LDP—especially through funding—that the Soviet regime and the KGB had possessed in abundance when they launched Zhirinovsky into serious politics with large-scale financial and logistical support in 1990–91.[41] As a result, popular support for Zhirinovsky and the LDP proceeded to decline steadily over the next few years. Zhirinovsky's entertaining, exhibitionistic vulgarity lost its novelty for many of his supporters, and his party's failures and vices became ever more transparent.[42] The LDP gave no serious support to the mass of impoverished and unrepresented Russians; it constantly split the opposition to the government; it rescued the government at critical moments, making people rightly suspect hidden and treacherous loyalties; and it was deeply involved in self-serving criminal activities, as witnessed by the contract killings of a couple of dozen LDP deputies, deputies' assistants, and their business associates from 1995 on. We briefly discuss this phenomenon later in the chapter, when we turn to the problem of crime.

The denizens of "the swamp" included the Agrarian Party and Women of Russia. The Agrarian Party tended to exhibit a rhetorical convergence with the CPRF, but it also made lucrative deals with the government whenever its votes were seriously in demand. This allowed it to exercise considerable influence on the budget process and to install one of its leaders, Aleksandr Nazarchuk, as minister of agriculture and deputy prime minister. However, as we will see, these tactics proved costly. Both the Agrarian Party and Women of Russia, which pursued similar opportunistic tactics, failed to clear the 5 percent hurdle in the 1995 elections.

We now turn our attention to the opposition, which in 1994 included Yabloko, the CPRF, and the Democratic Party of Russia (DPR). Yet even the label "opposition" must be qualified, at least as far as many members of these parties were concerned. The parties' common denominator was that, while they were all rhetorically and theoretically opposed to Yeltsin's authoritarianism, they had also meekly accepted the limits on their actions that Yeltsin sought to impose—and the CPRF and the DPR did this well before the contest between the Kremlin and the Russian White House was resolved. In 1994, both the CPRF and Yabloko were fundamentally different from the kind of political opposition groupings that had existed as recently as 1992–93.

While the earlier opposition had been made up mostly of middle-class populist democrats, the CPRF and Yabloko leaderships had backgrounds in the Soviet-era ruling elite, the nomenklatura. They differed from the earlier opposition less in ideology than in their style and methods. But style and methods mattered much more. The CPRF and Yabloko could not help but accept the October coup, albeit reluctantly; such servility was natural, at least to the CPRF. They found it difficult to coexist in an opposition camp where there were grassroots, anti-establishment democrats, the kind of people they found unsettling or wanted to get rid of. It had been necessary for the pre-1994 opposition to vacate the anti-regime space before the new, tamer opposition of these two parties could occupy it. However, because radical-sounding anti-establishment politicians were still in popular demand, and the vast majority of the CPRF and Yabloko rank and file had not belonged to the nomenklatura, both parties (and Yabloko in particular) never closed the door to a more radical, anti-oligarchical stance—in tactics, if not in their strategy.

Turning now to the evolution of the Democratic Party of Russia, we note that this party, given the intellectual function it had exercised in the earlier opposition, highlighted some broad political trends in the Russian political scene at the time. The DPR was important not because of its political clout, which was by now minimal, but because it was the only party that figured in the pre-1991 democratic movement and managed to survive shock therapy and get into the parliament. With fifteen deputies, it constituted the smallest faction; by 1995, it had fallen apart.

The fate of the DPR is closely linked to the failure of Russian centrism, the path that its founder, Travkin, had striven hard to follow. Centrism failed again because there was in practice no ideological middle ground between the regime and the opposition, just as there was no common cultural or social terrain to be shared by the nomenklatura and the rest of society. Thus the DPR slate of candidates featured not their centrist politicians but, rather, a mixture of apologists for and enemies of the status quo who never succeeded in finding a common language. Travkin himself soon defected to the government and was quickly rewarded in June 1994 with the hollow title of minister without portfolio. The DPR deputies' faction in the Duma promptly split between the followers of Travkin and the anti-Kremlin group of Glaziev and Govorukhin. The latter got the upper hand and finally ousted Travkin, who had to quit his own faction in December 1994.

Yeltsin's Techniques for Outmaneuvering the Opposition

How then, despite its manifest incompetence in managing the country—particularly in Chechnya and other Russian regions—and despite one debacle after another in economic policy and its relations with the West, did the Yeltsin regime succeed in disorganizing the opposition and achieving a certain political stability? A number of strategies were used, the most effective of which we will review.

1. *Disguising the seesaw machine as a coalition government.* As we saw earlier, the pro-Kremlin media persistently fed the Russian and foreign publics with a line about a purported rift within the executive, namely between "reformers" and "hard-liners." In this manner, the acute antagonisms that ran through Russian society were radically reframed: *It was no longer the case of supporters of the Yeltsin regime versus its critics but, rather, that of good guys versus bad guys within the regime itself.* The demarcation between these two camps was, in reality, blurred and inconsistent, and the tensions between them were nonexistent or muted; they well understood their appointed roles as different but complementary faces of the regime.

Nonetheless, the pro-Kremlin liberal media constructed these misleading pictures: In the second half of 1992, when Gaidar was carrying the banner of "liberal reform" (read: shock therapy), the camp of the evil hard-liners included his deputy prime ministers Chernomyrdin and Shumeiko. In 1993, the latter two were extolled as reformers, with Oleg Lobov and Sergei Glaziev labeled as reactionaries. In 1994–96, it was the progressives Chubais and Chernomyrdin against Korzhakov and Soskovets, the dark forces of reaction. In 1997–98, it was Chernomyrdin the conservative oligarch against Nemtsov the liberal revolutionary, with Chubais in the middle. Yet this constant fluctuation, which one would expect to cast doubt on the authenticity of the alleged antagonism within the regime, did not prevent observers in West and East, including the anti-Yeltsin opposition, from being captivated by the intramural maneuverings and realignments of the Kremlin insiders. The attention of these observers was thus diverted from the much deeper divide between the establishment and the rest of society.

In this way, a mere competition of bureaucratic and commercial interests within the ruling establishment was mistaken for profound ideological differences. In reality, there were neither reformers nor hard-liners within the executive, but merely an assembly of clans that exercised monopolistic control over their sectors of the shrinking national economy: raw materials traders operating under Chernomyrdin's patronage; privileged bankers and bureaucrats allied with the IMF and the flocks of Western consultants (a clan dominated from 1993 almost exclusively by Anatoly Chubais); arms traders led by the unsteady trio of Soskovets, Grachev, and Korzhakov; a dissonant chorus of collective farm managers that postured as the "agrarian lobby," trying to keep urban speculators, financiers, and bureaucratic "modernizers" from infringing on their rural baronies; and, last but not least, outright lobbyists for the criminal underworld, who preferred to act within each of the established clans on an individual basis.

While each of these groups had its own peculiar approach and a different avenue by which to plunder the Russian economy, they displayed a remarkable degree of unity over central issues of national and foreign policy. At every turning point, the clans closed ranks behind several bedrock principles: never yield decision-making positions to aspiring politicians from outside the nomenklatura, be they loyal or disloyal to the Kremlin; block and neutralize all those who would question the legitimacy of the constitution or propose amendments to it; and extort funding from every Western source available, either by pleasing the West or by scaring it, but never let the Westerners compete as equal partners on the nomenklatura's home turf or unite with the establishment's domestic opponents.

2. *Fomenting ideological antagonisms within the opposition and involving it in the operation of the seesaw.* As discussed previously, while the nomenklatura had progressed rapidly along the path of "capitalist" accumulation of money and property but preserved its retrograde outlook on politics, Russia's civil society had developed a Western-type ideological spectrum. Therefore, the real opposition to nomenklatura capitalism was divided, forming virtually irreconcilable nationalist, socialist, liberal, and other variations. Yeltsin's skillful operation of the seesaw created the mechanism known among Western social scientists as a

system of cross-cutting cleavages:[43] the partly natural, partly imposed "vertical" and "horizontal" divisions produced a segmented society, where no unprivileged group could ally with a congenial branch of the establishment to implement its agenda, nor could an across-the-spectrum, "populist," anti-nomenklatura coalition be formed.

Because the ideological divisions within society were much more pronounced than the divergences of sectoral and institutional interests within the ruling establishment, the latter possessed much more capacity for concerted action. This elite structure was designed primarily to keep out of power those self-made politicians and political groups that did not buy into its conspiratorial culture. In an unspoken agreement, clans positioned themselves along the seesaw so that each could control (or "graze on," to use a characteristic Russian expression) an ideological segment of the opposition—absorbing its analytical or programmatic products for the benefit of the regime, mobilizing members of the grassroots opposition on one side of the seesaw to score points in bureaucratic or commercial feuds with other clans, and wrecking any initiative by an across-the-spectrum anti-Yeltsin alliance before it could gain momentum.

To depict this situation graphically, if one end of the seesaw was going down, its occupants quickly found much in common with the corresponding segment of societal opposition. Thus at every threat of restructuring or demonopolization in the raw materials sector, the "natural monopoly" barons ignited the Duma's Communist backbenchers into radical action, while the chiefs of the power ministries tried to rebalance the seesaw in 1995 after their setback in Chechnya by mobilizing the nationalist opposition behind their military venture. On strategic issues, however, the clans that propped up the regime always developed a mutual understanding among themselves without involving the opposition outsiders. Thus a "radical reformer" like Chubais felt perfectly comfortable with Korzhakov or Soskovets on the other end of the executive seesaw, while at the same time laboring hard to prevent democratic politicians from Yabloko or DPR from joining the government. The same was true about the Kremlin hard-liners, who always found it preferable to deal with the shock therapists rather than rock the unsteady boat of the oligarchy by letting Communists or democratic nationalists like Sergei Baburin join the cabinet.

Those rare cases in which civic-minded politicians uncongenial to the clans were installed in high-level executive positions were "the exceptions that prove the rule." They were summoned for a short-term assignment, to perform a scavenger job in the government that no one else wanted to do, or to split an opposition group that had gained too much strength, and they never survived beyond the task at hand without joining a clan. This was the case with Aleksei Kazannik, a famous democrat of the first wave, who was hired as prosecutor general to sort out the legal mess that arose from the October 1993 coup and whom the Kremlin soon squeezed out of office by forcing him to choose between compliance with the law and obedience to the president. Among nationalists, the same was true of Boris Mironov and Vladimir Polevanov, each of whom was hired to a controversial office (the former as minister of the press, the latter as head of the Committee on State Property) and encouraged to act as scarecrows for the West and for the semiloyal democratic intelligentsia—only to be sacked after the necessary degree of support from the latter two groups for "their" pro-Western side of the executive seesaw had been extorted. In another example beyond the chronological scope of this chapter, Mikhail Zadornov, a defector from Yabloko, was hired as minister of finance in November 1997 to breed disarray in the ranks of the democratic opposition.

3. *Engineering a pro-Yeltsin consensus in the West and an anti-Western consensus in the opposition to prevent domestic and foreign opponents of the regime from cooperating.* From early on, this tactic became a crucial part of the game in which Kremlin propagandists at home and abroad were heavily engaged. Russia's ruling class learned well the lessons of the 1980s, when the anti-nomenklatura opposition in the Soviet Union cooperated with anticommunist groups in the West, with the result that not only did the Soviet Union collapse, but even rule over the successor states by former communist bosses was potentially threatened. Mindful of this bitter experience, the Yeltsin regime labored hard to drive a wedge between international opinion and Yeltsin's domestic opponents.

The key to this game was manipulating information and the mutual perceptions of discontented Russians and Western groups so that each side would see the other as more unpleasant or threatening than the Yeltsin administration. For discontented Russians, the Kremlin needed to equate "the West" with the IMF conditionalities, with aggressive advertisement of Western luxury, and with the most boorish intrusions of Western mass culture. For the Western groups, the Kremlin tried hard to identify all opposition to Yeltsin with the "red-and-brown" extremists. This game also required Yeltsin to be presented as a double-faced Janus: to the Westerners and Russia's Western-minded urban intelligentsia as a democrat and later as the lesser evil compared to the communist-cum-nationalist alternative, and to Russian patriots as their clandestine ally whose authoritarianism was the last bastion shielding the country against much worse scenarios that might be imposed from the West.

In a nutshell, this game involved the same seesaw mode of balancing but this time projected onto the international stage. It created yet another misleading ideological antagonism, this time between "pro-Western" and "anti-Western" forces. It also obscured contentions over specific policies, in which anti-Yeltsin opposition groups could have found both friends and foes in the West. In pursuing this course, the Kremlin found its most valuable, if unwilling, allies in Zyuganov and Podberezkin, who were promoted in various artificial ways to become leaders—Podberezkin in a de facto, not formal, sense—of the resurrected Communist Party (even though both of them, as ardent proponents of geopolitics and Huntington's precepts, would qualify in any other country of the world as strong right-wingers rather than spiritual heirs to Marx).

Obviously, to make this dichotomous scheme work (both at home and abroad), the Kremlin's actual policies on crucial matters needed to remain murky so that everybody would hope that they were closer to "the right side" of the seesaw and nobody from "the wrong side" would be provoked into opposing them. It also required the emasculation of all opposition parties that were not virulently anti-Western (such as Yabloko, Glaziev's DPR, or Svyatoslav Fyodorov's Party for Working People's Self-Management); the promotion of the most intensely xenophobic opposition members, such as Zhirinovsky and Barkashov; and the blocking of all foreign voices that supported—directly or indirectly—the anti-Yeltsin opposition.

The latter imperative sheds light on the reasons behind the oligarchs' heightened nervousness about every exposure of their misdeeds coming from the West. Thus a low-key diplomatic scandal erupted over an article by Thomas Graham, a high-ranking U.S. embassy official in Moscow, that appeared in *Nezavisimaya gazeta* on the eve of the 1995 parliamentary election.[44] The article depicted the Russian political elite as a lot of self-interested clans, none of which was committed to democracy but all of which manifested, with shades of ideological difference, their common desire to keep power and property in the country under their tight control.

What resulted from the combination of these and other intricate strategies was constant frustration for genuine opponents of the regime, who let themselves be mired in conflicts that were either imaginary and exaggerated or had little to do with their real strategic goal: replacing the rulers who were so manifestly mismanaging the country. Before long, the leading opposition parties seemingly discarded this goal from their agenda and tacitly resigned themselves to waiting until power just dropped into their hands, perhaps after some major crisis or, more likely, after Yeltsin's physical exit, which appeared imminent from 1994 on. The resulting standoff explains better than anything else the paradox that the Yeltsin regime presided over relative political stability despite—to judge by opinion polls and the scant respect for the constitution and the law from the state bureaucracy and the general public—its very low degree of legitimacy.

YELTSIN'S "NEW DEAL": ECONOMIC DIRIGISME AND POLITICAL RECONCILIATION

As briefly mentioned earlier, the resounding defeat of the pro-Kremlin parties in the parliamentary elections of December 1993 prompted Yeltsin's team to re-evaluate some aspects of economic policy. The economic reform strategy was not working as expected. The economy showed no signs of stabilization, and the majority of the population had clearly rejected the government's policies as being too painful in purely economic terms, as well as too destructive for society. Yeltsin was in a quandary. His immediate circle, supported by Chernomyrdin, favored some alterations in the economic course. This group talked about slowing privatization, restoring a degree of government regulation and control, instituting measures to halt the flight of capital, pursuing an industrial policy with neocorporatist or state capitalist overtones, restoring subsidies for the farm sector and heavy industry, and embarking on a reflationary monetary policy. It was not worried about a dose of inflation, apparently even if it meant a cutoff of IMF funds.[45] The political side of this strategy included more authoritarianism and nationalism, repression of any serious opposition, and an all-out effort to gain the support of three main constituencies—nationalists, capitalists willing to cooperate with government agencies, and the chief executives of Russia's regions and cities.

Yeltsin had no principled objections to this approach; his preoccupations concerned whether it was practical. Would the power ministries and the police be prepared to arrest opponents of the new authoritarianism without hesitation? Would the government be capable of stanching capital flight? Could the Treasury still meet the government payroll without effective policies to raise revenue if there were no more IMF loans and no foreign investment? Could reliable new allies be found if the West abandoned Russia, as it might do before long? Would the new strategy produce enough popular support for the Kremlin to make Russia governable?

Russia's demoralized leaders were far from sure they could answer these questions in the affirmative. By mid-1994, they seemed to have opted for a compromise strategy, halfway between the original shock therapy and the proposed authoritarian-corporatist variant. They sought at all costs to keep the support of the IMF and the G-7 through the substance of their policies, while at the same time making a public show of curbing a few excesses of the free market and also burnishing their credentials as nationalists. The New Deal of Franklin D. Roosevelt became the all-purpose grab bag for slogans and symbols for this new Potemkin façade.

As for the potential threat from political opponents, there were, of course, the groups led by Zyuganov, Yavlinsky, Rutskoi, Glaziev, Lebed, and Baburin; all these men were available as alternatives to Yeltsin. In our opinion, had a coalition of any of the possible permutations of their groups assumed power, no disaster would have befallen Russia. Rather, the opposite: They presented no serious threat of turning the economic clock back to the days of Gosplan and posed no danger to Russia's Western partners. However, for the reasons adduced in the previous section, these groups were, in actions though not in rhetoric, remarkably uncritical of the establishment. This fact helps to explain their record of impotence, and it certainly explains why the Kremlin had decided that, at least for now, it could safely eschew more militant brands of authoritarianism.

This, then, was the strategy that, despite characteristic wobbles, became Yeltsin's revamped new look for 1994. Thus repackaged, Yeltsin was able to serve out his first term without major difficulty. But few of Russia's problems were solved, many were exacerbated, and public confidence in the regime came out of this period lower than it was at the beginning.

Emblematic of this paradox of economic and political failures prefacing electoral success were the political effects of the war in Chechnya. Russia's stunning military defeats had created by the time of the mid-1995 Budennovsk crisis what might have become a revolutionary situation. Given the precedents of the Crimean, Russo-Japanese, First World, and Afghan Wars, this new humiliation could have led to radical changes in the balance of social forces and the political system. Such an outcome was seemingly foreshadowed by the opposition's crushing defeat of the party of power in the Duma elections of December 1995. In reality, however, the Chechnya crisis prevented neither the re-election of Yeltsin in July 1996, nor the further consolidation of the oligarchic system that he and his confidants had built up around him. One can also argue, as does Lilia Shevtsova, that even if Yeltsin had been clearly defeated at the polls in the 1996 election, he would not have left the Kremlin, except possibly in response to overwhelming Western pressure.[46]

CONFLICT WITH THE DUMA

The social and cultural fragmentation of the opposition manifested itself in the election in January 1994 of the new speaker of the Duma. None of the pro-Kremlin candidates, such as Sergei Filatov of Russia's Choice, had the slightest chance of winning. The two leading opposition candidates were Yuri Vlasov and Ivan Rybkin. Rybkin's victory with the support of the pro-Yeltsin deputies surprised many observers because he had been a hard-line communist. The explanation was simple. The Kremlin helped Rybkin become speaker because he was a typical workhorse of the nomenklatura, whereas Vlasov had been a staunch anti-nomenklatura democrat with considerable oratorical ability and a record of principled behavior. As an independent intellectual who loathed nomenklatura culture, Vlasov would have been a loose cannon outside the ruling coalition's control. So the pro-Kremlin deputies voted for Rybkin, who had opposed Yeltsin, and snubbed Vlasov, who had supported the president in his initial struggle for power.

The choice of a speaker for the Federation Council was also a turbulent process. Even here, several ballots, much arm-twisting by the government, and the bribing of some deputies were required before Vladimir Shumeiko, a member of Yeltsin's innermost circle, could prevail.

Soon, however, two legislative initiatives the government dreaded began to gather support. The first demanded an amnesty for the indicted putschists of August 1991 and also for the imprisoned leaders of the parliamentary resistance of autumn 1993. The second, which passed by a large majority on February 9, authorized the Duma to launch a major investigation into the facts of and polit-ical responsibility for the assault on the parliament. This bombshell for the Yelt-sin camp forced the president to make some hard choices, the circumstances and nature of which are still not wholly clear. He wanted to derail the Duma in-vestigation before it began, to bar the proposed amnesty, and to treat the Duma in the spirit of "I make the decisions, you ratify them."[47] At the same time, he wanted to broaden his support in the Duma and promote a general atmosphere of goodwill between himself and the opposition. Clearly, all these goals could not be pursued at once, especially because the Russia's Choice faction in parlia-ment began losing interest in vigorously supporting Yeltsin, given his removal from the government of the proponents of shock therapy, discussed below. So the Yeltsin camp had to figure out how to mobilize its dwindling support to achieve its top priority—derailing the Duma investigation, which had the potential to further discredit the president, to undermine his U.S. and G-7 support, and—theoretically, at least—to force him out of office and even into jail. As it turned out, the Yeltsinites had their hand forced in two ways, both of which seemed to take them by surprise.

First, Shakhrai and his pro-government PRUA group in the Duma (perhaps encouraged by Chernomyrdin, who was already wooing the moderate opposi-tion forces) decided to switch from opposing the amnesty to supporting it. They justified the switch by including the amnesty—along with the dropping of the Duma investigation—in a bundle of resolutions that the Duma voted on as a package and approved by 252 to 67 on February 23. Also included were amnes-ties for economic and other common criminals, favored by Yeltsin and urged by Zhirinovsky, plus a "Memorandum on Accord" passed by both houses of parliament to promote national reconciliation, another initiative that Yeltsin strongly supported.[48] The language of the new law specified that it was to take effect immediately, and the new prosecutor general, Aleksei Kazannik, firmly stated that he had no choice but to implement the amnesty at once. However, Kazannik received an indirect and legally questionable order from Yeltsin to delay or prevent the carrying out of the amnesty, and on February 26 he resigned in protest.[49] The same day, the prisoners were released nonetheless.

It is still not at all clear whether Yeltsin's publicly expressed resistance to these dramatic events was sincere. It is more than possible that to some extent he only went through the motions of resisting and protesting because he secretly thought the political amnesty, though repugnant to him, was in his interest po-litically.[50] Certainly, trials of the prisoners would have been embarrassing for Yeltsin, and he did get a priceless concession from the Duma: its agreement to drop its planned investigation of the fall 1993 events in return for his acquies-cence in the amnesty.

On the other hand, Russia's Choice was upset because it desired more open confrontation between the radical Yeltsinites (that is, itself) and the "dark forces," without which its political stock tended to decline. If Yeltsin had not offered some simulacrum of resistance, many of his supporters would have been even more confused, angry, and frightened than they in fact became. Gaidar, Chubais, Sobchak, and others immediately saw an acute danger of physical revenge and a breakdown of law and order as their bitter enemies walked out of jail unpunished.[51] Amid a variety of stern warnings to the released prisoners to behave peacefully, Yeltsin's mouthpiece, Shumeiko, called on February 24 for the imposition of martial law as a precaution. It was not in fact needed.

By contrast, though, some democrats saw benefits in the amnesty. Viktor Sheinis of Yabloko, for example, saw it as "a boon for the president and the whole democratic camp." It prevented the parliamentary die-hards, who probably "would never have been indicted anyway," from acquiring the aura of martyrs. And it meant that Rutskoi, who was now likely to run in the next presidential election (and declared his candidacy on March 1), would split the nationalist vote with Zhirinovsky, thus preserving the chance of victory for a democratic candidate.[52] Some democrats, like Boldyrev of Yabloko, believed that Yeltsin deserved to be put on trial for his use of violence just as much as Rutskoi did.

A singular role in the amnesty crisis, as noted earlier, was played by Kazannik, who had been a celebrated democrat of the first wave and who was brought out of oblivion and given his important post on October 5, 1993, in the context of Yeltsin's efforts to rally the democratic forces behind his tank attack on the White House the previous day. Kazannik's position on the amnesty was a severe blow to Gaidar's people, who had wanted to parade their solidarity with the veterans of the democratic movement. Yet Kazannik made a principled decision to act according to law rather than according to any pro-Yeltsin impulses or anti–red-brown phobias. The result was a trauma for the Gaidar camp. After resigning, Kazannik did not join any of the parties of the Duma opposition, but severed his ties with the Moscow establishment and later, much to the consternation of the Gaidarists, joined the opposition party of Svyatoslav Fyodorov. He also revealed that Yeltsin's team put enormous pressure on him in October 1993 to conduct a three-or-four-day investigation of the armed clashes and charge the prisoners with grave crimes, after which they would be sentenced to death in a two-or-three-day trial.[53]

THE DEMOCRATIC NATIONALISM OF SERGEI GLAZIEV

Apart from Kazannik, the only prominent supporter of Yeltsin who quit the presidential camp on his own initiative and went over to the opposition was Sergei Glaziev. Glaziev immediately became a key leader of the opposition because he was one of its very few well-qualified economists. The opposition parties (with the partial exception of Yabloko) had considerable need for his expertise and experience. At the same time, Glaziev was by no means an irreconcilable opponent of the Kremlin, but tried constantly to influence Yeltsin's policies with speeches, memos, and other initiatives.[54] A number of the Yabloko economists more or less agreed with Glaziev's thinking but were not ready to stick their necks out as far as he.

With Glaziev as its chairman, the Duma's Committee for Economic Policy began to publish statistics and documentation that showed the severity of the ongoing economic collapse. The committee also became a forum for expert advice, thus constituting what was probably the most important single intellectual contribution to the Russian political debate of these years. The platform elaborated by the Committee for Economic Policy is also a landmark because it combines valid planks suggested by both democrats and nationalists, thus providing a rare synthesis of the ideas of political forces that were seldom able to cooperate, yet whose interaction was generally fruitful in intellectual terms, as we try to show throughout this book.[55] As part of his experiment in rolling back communism, Glaziev at one point attempted to restore a state company to its rightful pre-1917 owners, who had been expropriated by the Bolsheviks, but the Gaidar forces promptly allied themselves with the CPRF to frustrate his attempt.

The efforts of Glaziev and others to shift Kremlin economic policies into directions more favorable to Russian national interests met with mixed success at best. Glaziev and the economic policy committee did their best to cooperate with the Kremlin on practical matters. A number of measures he favored were in fact included in the "New Deal" package touted by Yeltsin in his February economic policy address. One important problem with Glaziev's proposals was that they—just like Gaidar's original shock therapy—were not approved following a full plenary debate in the parliament. The cabinet was not restructured to reflect the new parliamentary majority, and the same discredited officials were simply given new directives and targets. The government worked to recruit fickle opposition deputies one by one to its side. This was the method employed in the cases of most members of the Agrarian Party, and also of Valentin Kovalev, Travkin, Nazarchuk, and, regarding regional matters, Vladimir Lysenko. The lesson was plain: if you sat quietly in the Duma and voted on cue, you could get a cushy post in the government.

A major point made by Glaziev and others—one that the establishment either deliberately or unconsciously neglected—was that, under the conditions then prevailing in Russian society, the personnel executing the policies had become more important than the policies themselves.[56] The government's clever tactic of co-opting some of the opposition's most valid programmatic points, while at the same time adamantly refusing to share power, became a foolproof way of discrediting good ideas while lowering the credibility of both government and opposition.

A good illustration is the case of the Financial-Industrial Groups, or FIGs, an idea that came out of the Lobov Economics Ministry's interest in Japanese-style dirigisme (see chapter 5) during 1993. The idea had been supported by the opposition and was launched by a Yeltsin decree in December 1993. The FIGs were supposed to channel capital into productive investment, but they were taken over by decidedly nonproductive bankers who looted them financially and did little for their commercial success. The bankers used the FIGs to split up industrial plants and get control of the profitable parts, without making any capital investment of their own in return.

While economic analysis may suggest many reasons for such a transformation, we will point out only that the FIGs failed because of a pattern of collusion between the officials of government agencies that were supposed to supervise the FIGs and the banking and financial operators involved, all to the serious detriment of the productive sector.[57] These officials had little interest in monitoring the bankers running the FIGs; they were focused rather on stock kickbacks, bribes, loans for their own businesses, seats on company boards, and political contributions. A strong oversight and enforcement role for the Duma opposition probably would have been the only way to prevent this collusion, at least in the short term. Yet any such role for the opposition was out of the question as long as Yeltsin remained in power.

THE DRIFT TO AUTHORITARIANISM MAKES RECONCILIATION IMPOSSIBLE

Yeltsin's abortive New Deal was very much conditioned by the new attitude of the United States, which, while far from antagonistic, now had elements of reserve. True, on January 14, 1994, Clinton and Yeltsin signed a statement hailing "a new phase" in their relations, which they called "a mature strategic partnership," and money continued to flow through the IMF and other channels. But tensions over, for example, Bosnia policy and espionage issues meant that the ideological and political support Yeltsin badly needed was not always forthcoming.[58]

Yeltsin was stunned by the visit to Moscow in March 1994 of former U.S. president Richard Nixon, because Nixon was perceived not as a self-starter with his own agenda but as an emissary of Clinton. (Reality probably lay somewhere in the middle.) Nixon, acting on the advice of his Russian affairs adviser Dimitri Simes and with the White House's concurrence, met with a broad array of opposition figures, including Rutskoi, who had just been released from prison. Meeting with these figures was widely interpreted in Moscow as a snub from Clinton to Yeltsin in retaliation for the cancellation of the presidential elections scheduled for June 1994. Yeltsin counterpunched by angrily canceling his own meeting with Nixon. These developments contributed to the appearance of an economic and political shift by Yeltsin, with a temporary de-emphasis of shock therapy and less fraternization with Clinton.

Nixon, meanwhile, stuck firmly to the well-considered line he had developed during his visit to Russia a year earlier. His central theses differed widely from Clinton's. The Russians, he said, should not believe the "myths" that "American democracy can be exported to other nations" and that "all economic problems can be solved by adopting free-market policies." Also, although "Generally Russian interests are the same as those of the United States, . . . Russia must avoid appearing to be in lockstep with the United States in a way that disserves Russia's interests." This would only help opponents of reform.[59]

One of the first elements of Yeltsin's New Deal had been his above-mentioned *ukaz* on creation of the FIGs, which had been launched as a well-meaning but poorly researched Glaziev-Lobov coproduction. The problem with this, as with all of Yeltsin's dirigiste innovations during this phase, was that the president saw them as political maneuvers, not as real policy changes. Whatever the policies and whatever their announced rationale, the real motivation was always to enhance Yeltsin's political power. When Yeltsin and his cohorts said they wanted to strengthen the role of the government in the economy, what they really meant was increasing their influence as power brokers and arbitrageurs. They failed to see that any economic policies, even eminently reasonable ones, were impossible to carry out because of the government's legitimacy gap. In a government apparatus where personal—and often pecuniary—interests relentlessly prevailed over institutional loyalties, increased economic intervention by a government that lacked popular confidence and support at every level of the bureaucratic chain of command could only yield a greedy parody of Gaullism. Instead of an economic miracle, it produced the miraculous enrichment of a few corrupt bureaucrats. The Yeltsinites were aware of the problem. This may be why they linked the notion of a New Deal with gestures toward political reconciliation.

Perhaps Yeltsin was being candid when he said he wanted to unite all the members of the new informal statist consensus around his New Deal. But he was still unwilling to accept any responsibility for the failure of shock therapy or for courting the confrontation that had killed many people and nearly detonated a civil war. This is presumably why Yeltsin's Agreement on Civic Accord prohibited any calls for early elections or constitutional amendments: they might have unleashed conflicts dangerous to the regime. It was thus quite natural that no sizable opposition force that was still capable of imagining a future for itself beyond the short term proved willing to sign Yeltsin's political armistice. As mentioned earlier, Yavlinsky and Zyuganov, and Rutskoi and Baburin, all declined to subscribe. The vast majority of the signatures came from minor parties and groups, most of them fated to dissolve quickly in the warm embrace of the establishment. The refusal of the more formidable opponents to sign attested to the failure of this tactic.

October and November 1994 witnessed a new burst of radicalized opposition, stimulated in particular by the "Black Tuesday" collapse of the ruble and by the murder—apparently with government involvement—of an anticorruption journalist. This opposition had a number of centers, including Yuri Luzhkov's Moscow City Hall; financial interests around Vladimir Gusinsky's MOST

Bank; and the new pro-Western Duma opposition, best exemplified by Yavlinsky. This was an unusual convergence of forces, with each participant—apart from wanting to curb or oust Yeltsin—pursuing separate goals. The most powerful participant was Luzhkov, who was seeking a tactical advantage in a struggle with Korzhakov over economic assets in Moscow. The other two were not attacking Korzhakov; they had wider goals. Gusinsky was closely linked to financial circles in London and was the most thoroughly globalized of the new tycoons. He sought to derail Yeltsin's New Deal. Yeltsin, he thought, had been doing just fine with his imitation of Pinochet. Why switch to aping Roosevelt? Gusinsky and his associates were also concerned about the antiminority animus of Yeltsin's new look, which contained at least an implicit dose of anti-Semitism.[60] And some of their interests were threatened by Yeltsin's trend toward dollarizing the economy.

The third participant was Yavlinsky, whose popularity at this time suggested that he could possibly become the next president and gave an aura of legitimacy to the threesome's attacks on Yeltsin. Yavlinsky's private polls told him that Yabloko had attracted the support of many populist democrats of the 1988–91 period who had become disillusioned with Yeltsin. The explanation for this was that, strangely enough, the moderate liberal Yavlinsky had turned out—in certain respects—to represent the farthest left force present in the Duma. Yavlinsky's mentality did not predispose him to firebrand radicalism, but he nevertheless understood that his vote-getting power depended very much on winning the support of the dispossessed and radicalized former middle class.

As someone who had at least cooperated with the democratic movement in 1990–91, he had a more valid claim to the allegiance of these strata than did his competitors, the communists. Therefore, in the fall of 1994 Yavlinsky became more active and, above all, more radical. From this point onward, he called repeatedly for Yeltsin's resignation. He asserted that democracy had no prospects under Yeltsin's rule. His economic program also became vaguer, partly as a result of his evolution from market romantic to social-democrat, and also because of his need to cater to the interests and aspirations of a more diverse group of allies and supporters.[61] However, this lack of specificity brought an advantage: Yavlinsky made clear that his contest with the Kremlin was not just a matter of economic policy, but also had vital political and moral dimensions. Yavlinsky also thought it politic not to publish a detailed economic strategy. Parts of it might have been purloined by the Kremlin and discredited through incompetent application.

Black Tuesday, October 11, 1994, when the ruble declined by 27 percent against the dollar and an upheaval occurred in the Moscow interbank clearing system, gave the "triple alliance" its chance.[62] In the wake of Black Tuesday, if the alliance's members had acted more forcefully, rather than just launching or facilitating press attacks on Yeltsin and his cronies, Yavlinsky, Gusinsky, and Luzhkov might have obliged Yeltsin to restore confidence by announcing, like

Lyndon Johnson in 1968, that he would neither seek nor accept nomination for another presidential term.

   This was even more clear when, on October 17, a suitcase bomb killed Dmitri Kholodov, a popular investigative journalist for the pro-Luzhkov *Moskovskii komsomolets* newspaper, who had been probing corruption in the Russian army units stationed in Germany. Kholodov's muckraking exposés were viewed by Yeltsin as an attempt to weaken the power ministries, and the Russian president was now facing a real opposition that, although it was ideologically more moderate than Zyuganov or Rutskoi, was potentially much more dangerous. Unlike Khasbulatov and Rutskoi, the triple alliance was potentially formidable because it commanded far more financial resources—enough to enable it to influence financial markets and impact the prices and interest rates of government securities. In addition, the triple alliance had some support in the West, which Yeltsin's foes of 1993 had never possessed.

   The murder of Kholodov was interpreted by most observers as an attempt to terrorize the opposition, perhaps even as a direct riposte to Black Tuesday.[63] However, maybe to the surprise of the crime's authors, the bombing had the effect of generating support for the triple alliance among the mass media because other journalists sympathized with Kholodov personally in his tragic fate. October and November of 1994 were thus marked by heavy media attacks from across the political spectrum on the Kremlin and on Yeltsin's stalwarts.[64] Although this campaign does not seem to have been orchestrated by the triple alliance, having a largely spontaneous dynamic all its own, it was seen by the Kremlin as a coordinated action of the power-hungry Yavlinsky, Gusinsky, and Luzhkov. This perception was created in large part by the magnate and unrivaled master of political intrigue Boris Berezovsky, as vividly described by Korzhakov.[65]

   The spontaneous dynamic did have roots, of course. Black Tuesday and Kholodov's murder were both symptoms of the Yeltsin system's vices and also catalysts that unleashed resentments that had long been building up in various quarters—for example, in the Duma. Most of the deputies deeply resented the cavalier, even contemptuous treatment they usually got from Yeltsin and the government. Floods of indignant rhetoric poured forth, seeking in particular the head of Chernomyrdin on a platter. When Yeltsin sent the prime minister into the lion's den to try to stem the tide, his feeble attempts to appease the legislators had no effect. His defensive, lackluster speech seems to have convinced no one that the government knew how to turn the economy around; his hollow, generalized answers to a slew of sharp questions were even weaker.[66] Nonetheless, Yeltsin had been bribing key opposition groups in the Duma ahead of time; so, while the vote of no confidence in the government passed by 194 to 54, it was 32 votes short of the number needed for it to take effect. Most notably, Yeltsin had just appointed an Agrarian as minister of agriculture; in accordance with their secret deal, some of his party's deputies abstained in the vote.

In any case, most deputies ultimately did not want to dismiss the government because they were not ready with an alternative government and an alternative program to propose. To save face, the next day they passed, by 335 votes to 54, a resolution stating that the government's work was "unsatisfactory" and had not met "the expectations of most of the population."[67]

The Duma's Yabloko faction was less mealymouthed. Referring to Yeltsin in a statement, it threw down the gauntlet in an unprecedentedly explicit way, calling for early presidential elections, to be held together with the Duma elections a year hence, and bluntly declaring of the president: "We, the democratic opposition, regard his mission as completed and his reform potential as exhausted."[68] Clearly they hoped to be rid of Yeltsin and Korzhakov before too long, and they saw the slackening of U.S. support for Yeltsin as auspicious: Maybe Yavlinsky could procure this support for himself as he prepared to run for the presidency.

In this atmosphere, the ranks of the democratic opposition grew rapidly. Among the groups moving over was Democratic Russia, which formally declared: "Democracy in Russia is under threat." Its co-leader, Galina Starovoitova, noted that not one of its members now figured in the government and said that Yeltsin had lost the voters' trust and was "close to exhausting his resources."[69] The former minister Boris Fyodorov took his "December 12" Duma group into opposition and called on all democrats to follow so that they could definitively not be blamed for the government's failing policies. They had to unite and select a new presidential candidate. "Democracy in Russia is under threat," he wrote, "because of attempts to postpone elections, violations of the Constitution, the legal free-for-all, the diktat of regional princelings in the regions, and the breakdown of our statehood through the treaties with the republics. . . . To continue to support the government in these conditions means betraying the interests of democracy, of the electors, and of the state."[70] On this issue, Gaidar and Russia's Choice, whom Fyodorov included in the democratic camp, went halfway by deciding to give the Kremlin only conditional support.

By calling for early presidential elections, Yabloko had brought itself into line with Zyuganov's Communists, who had already been collecting signatures in support of this move for two months. Addressing a big rally on November 7, Zyuganov pressed his case and announced that two million signatures had been gathered to date.[71]

On issues of law and order, crime and corruption, the Yeltsin administration also found itself under siege. The editor of Kholodov's paper charged Defense Minister Grachev with responsibility for the young reporter's murder, as well as with personal corruption, and evoked a sympathetic response from much of the media.[72] Yeltsin proceeded to make a small concession on November 1, by firing one of the main objects of Kholodov's corruption charges, Deputy Defense Minister General Matvei Burlakov. Grachev promptly gave him another senior job in the ministry, however, thus prompting even greater outrage.

Meanwhile, *Izvestiya* ran five heavily researched articles about the rise of the Mafiya as a dangerous political and criminal force that was infiltrating government structures, and on November 5, a communist Duma deputy was assassinated. Earlier, other disturbing events had occurred: Justice Minister Yuri Kalmykov had resigned in protest at current legal trends, the liberal *Kommersant-Daily* commenting bitterly: "in a country where law as such does not exist, there is no need to have a strong ministry of justice";[73] the Federation Council had refused once again to confirm Yeltsin's nomination of Aleksei Ilyushenko as prosecutor general on the grounds that he had reportedly helped build the trumped-up case against Vice President Rutskoi in 1993; and Yeltsin had been accused of delaying the passage of a law on parliament's new watchdog on the executive, the Accounting Office (Schetnaya Palata), and of insisting on limiting its powers.[74]

In addition, commentators deplored the reappearance of some Soviet-type features in the government. For example, a prominent editor complained that "For more than a year now, Russia has been ruled by the decrees of one person. Without doubt, extralegal use of the repressive apparatus and certain special services is increasing. . . . Almost all of Moscow's politicians have stopped conducting frank conversations on government phones, and even on phones in their offices and apartments, because no one doubts that these phones are being tapped."[75]

Finally, all these negative trends for the Kremlin took place against a background of rising public criticism of Yeltsin's personal antics. These focused mainly on his embarrassing drunken behavior during visits to Germany and Ireland. (In the first country, he grabbed a conductor's baton and tried to lead an orchestra. In the second, he failed to come out of his plane to meet the waiting Irish prime minister.) Several of his aides wrote a private letter to him about this problem; a leading communist legislator called for an international medical commission to examine him; and a chief editor and former presidential media adviser, Yegor Yakovlev, wrote a sharply worded article that detailed various shameful episodes. Particularly worrying was Yakovlev's plausible belief, later confirmed by Korzhakov, that because Yeltsin's aides knew a great deal about such episodes, they could blackmail him into signing documents that promoted their personal interests.[76]

In response to this six-week barrage of setbacks and political attacks, Yeltsin at first reacted fairly cautiously. He did fire—or persuaded to resign—three centrists who were assigned major blame for Black Tuesday. He replaced Aleksandr Shokhin, first deputy prime minister in charge of the economy, with the more doctrinaire market bolshevik Anatoly Chubais. Then he replaced Central Bank Chairman Gerashchenko with his deputy, and replaced Acting Finance Minister Sergei Dubinin with a little-known, more conservative official. Lower-level appointments tended to be definitely antagonistic to the market bolsheviks, especially the new head of the State Property Management Committee, Vladimir Polevanov, whom we discuss later, and the new foreign trade minister, Oleg

Davydov, who (like Polevanov) had protectionist tendencies.[77] Thus the overall outcome of the reshuffle was a certain shift economically in the conservative direction, but with Chubais's appointment balancing this shift to some extent.

Yeltsin also appears to have considered replacing Chernomyrdin and thus may have wanted him to be humiliated by the Duma on October 27, as indeed he was. In this connection, Andranik Migranyan, a publicist whom Yeltsin appointed at this time to his Presidential Council of policy-oriented intellectuals, argued passionately for a more authoritarian "government of national salvation" headed by a new premier.[78] On the other hand, the fact that the triple alliance and its supporters in the press were also anti-Chernomyrdin probably made Yeltsin less inclined to sacrifice him. The situation was made more complex by the rivalry between Korzhakov and Chernomyrdin, the former favoring Soskovets for premier and accusing the prime minister of being soft on Yeltsin's internal opponents and also of yielding to World Bank pressures that would result in benefits for foreign oil companies.[79]

Nonetheless, strategic analysts with close ties to the Kremlin saw a very real chance that Chernomyrdin would be forced out and Yuri Skokov appointed in his place. Such a move indeed could have happened: The party of power was seriously divided, the new cabinet had no unity, the opposition had consolidated, and Black Tuesday had produced a serious financial crisis.[80] Somewhat similarly, another analyst believed that the most likely scenario was a frontal assault by Yeltsin against the opposition: Yeltsin would provoke a budget crisis, dissolve the Duma and rule without it for a lengthy period, and in the interim appoint Skokov as premier.[81] In retrospect, these analyses had excellent insights and might have been closer to the mark if the Chechnya war had not gone badly wrong and pushed Yeltsin into his most defensive and stubborn pattern of behavior.

On November 19, Yeltsin's strategy became somewhat clearer when an anonymous article appeared with the arresting subtitle "Will the President and the Government Fall?" It charged that anti-Kremlin plotting was afoot, and that Luzhkov and Gusinsky should be brought to heel. The tipoff regarding the article's source was that it was printed not in the opposition press, but in the government's own paper.[82] Later it became clear that its real author was Yeltsin's "mini-KGB" headed by Korzhakov. The article claimed that "a group of Moscow bankers and businessmen has begun a struggle aimed at putting their own man in the presidency." They had considered Yavlinsky, then General Lebed; now they had chosen Luzhkov and were promoting him through their media outlets in every possible way. They had engineered both Black Tuesday, from which they had made handsome profits, and the subsequent shortage of gasoline in Moscow. They had also, the article claimed, deftly spread false rumors about Chernomyrdin's resignation.

Further, the group was centered around Gusinsky and his MOST holdings, and Luzhkov and the assets of Moscow city. MOST had profited from enormous financial favors it obtained in recent years from Luzhkov, Boris Fyodorov, and

Sergei Dubinin, and it was now trying to gain control of a second national television channel and of a major St. Petersburg channel. It used strong-arm methods in business and probably had ties to Mafiya structures. While Russia's interests were not identical to the West's, MOST was emphatically pro-West.

The paper's government editors added a short postscript calling somewhat obliquely for Luzhkov to be barred from the presidential race for having launched his candidacy too early.

YELTSIN AND KORZHAKOV COUNTERATTACK: BANKERS FACE-DOWN IN THE SNOW

Yeltsin's defensive strategy was cunning. Experience under both him and Gorbachev showed that the most effective way of dealing with a rising threat from the opposition was not with the velvet glove of cajolery or temporizing but, rather, with the mailed fist. Who would back down first? A political cold war was on, with both sides escalating and each side convinced that it would be doomed if it made concessions. Yeltsin may have concluded that he could extort more from the United States by shifting to a belligerent stance, by threatening to burn his bridges to the West. So, perceiving Gusinsky's hostile media attacks and alleged involvement in engineering Black Tuesday as Western financial blackmail of Russia, he pulled out more stops in his nationalist register. Among other things, he shocked the West by observing that a period of "cold peace" between Russia and the West might be at hand.[83] When Clinton began to talk more about NATO expansion, Yeltsin, having initially said Poland was free to join, even gained some popularity inside Russia by turning against expansion and thus putting himself in tune with the anti-NATO backlash at home.

Closer to home, the Kremlin still had little direct financial control over the media at this time, so rather than respond with a propaganda campaign of its own, it chose the path of intimidation. On December 2, a group of armed *oprichniks*, or security men, loyal to Korzhakov raided the Moscow headquarters of MOST Bank, the key asset of Vladimir Gusinsky. During the operation, some of Gusinsky's executives were forced to lie face down in the snow on the sidewalk, while agents carted off loads of documents. Gusinsky was taken by surprise. He had long been worried about his own security and had taken care to set up a large private security force staffed by former KGB officers and directed by Filip Bobkov, the former head of the KGB's Fifth Directorate, which handled the repression of internal dissent. Gusinsky may have thought that Korzhakov, who had never risen above the level of a modest KGB apparatchik, would never dare to challenge his own prestigious former superior. If that was indeed what Gusinsky thought, it was a miscalculation.

Although the raid was not followed by any indictments, had no legal consequences for MOST Bank, and was itself probably illegal, it proved a remarkably effective exercise in intimidation. MOST Bank pulled in its horns and sharply reduced its activity in the Moscow financial markets. Gusinsky's media empire temporarily toned down its criticism of the Yeltsin regime, and Gusinsky himself fled to London with his family for five months.[84] Upon his return, he was so anxious to regain Yeltsin's goodwill that he more or less voluntarily became a secret informer for Korzhakov.[85]

Luzhkov met with Yeltsin and opted for a cease-fire. He had been badly rattled by a series of rapid blows: the raid on MOST Bank; the instant firing of the head of the federal intelligence service for Moscow city, who was close to Gusinsky and his allies; the arrest on December 20 of the high-flying young political manipulator Dmitri Yakubovsky ("General Dima"), who had "provided services to the mayor's team" and also to MOST and the Moscow city police (and who reportedly gave compromising evidence in prison against Luzhkov's wife);[86] and the strong and ultimately successful pressure on him to concur in the firing of an ally, General Pankratov, the corrupt Moscow police chief.[87] But Yeltsin's position was still precarious. His prestige had been permanently tarnished by the media attacks of the autumn. It was urgent to distract public attention from the corruption scandal engulfing the army and the Defense Ministry. More drastic measures, Yeltsin judged, were still needed.

THE WAR PARTY AND THE CHECHNYA DEBACLE

"War party" is the appropriate term, coined by John Dunlop, for that section of the ruling elite that pushed Russia into the quagmire of the Chechnya war. The most important activist of the war party, and the person most responsible for the invasion, was indeed Boris Yeltsin. Supporting him most strongly in getting the pro-war decision adopted were Soskovets and Korzhakov. Reluctant about war until the decision to proceed gave him no choice, Defense Minister Grachev laid out a battle plan that quite wrongly foresaw complete victory within a matter of days. Thus, when things went badly wrong, he soon incurred the war party's anger and disdain. His two accomplices, who made their own contributions to the disaster, were Federal Counterintelligence Service boss Sergei Stepashin and Interior Minister Viktor Yerin. Over the previous few months, these two had antagonized the Chechen leadership around Dzhokhar Dudayev by mounting several bungled attempts to oust or liquidate him with the help of the scattered and impotent opposition within Chechnya.

Paradoxically, the Chechen dictator Dudayev had achieved power in October 1991 through the efforts of Yeltsin's lieutenants. Later, Dudayev had voiced enthusiastic support for Yeltsin's suppression of the parliament, but by 1994 he was bitterly at odds with the Kremlin. An aggravating factor here was the growing streak of ethnic chauvinism among the Yeltsinites. This tendency had become visible by 1993 in the pronouncements of ethnic nationalist Russophiles on Yeltsin's staff, including Shakhrai, Shumeiko, Poltoranin, and above all, Mironov.

This racist undertone was accentuated by the Zhirinovsky factor. Because Yeltsin had lost his original support among the old democratic activists, the Zhirinovsky voters had become an indispensable part of the regime's social and ideological base. The chauvinist mood was clearly reflected in the summer 1994 appointment of Nikolai Yegorov as minister of nationalities and regional affairs, and in his elevation soon after to be a deputy prime minister. A political protégé of Vladimir Shumeiko and a former governor of the Krasnodar region, Yegorov came from a Cossack background and had typically Cossack views. In particular, he reflected the historic Cossack hostility toward non-Russian populations in the ethnic labyrinth of the North Caucasus. Thus Yegorov's appointment constituted a warning to the Northern Caucasians as well as to the Moscow opposition. The Cossacks had been the tsar's favorite shock troops for putting down uprisings, and so, predictably, Yegorov belonged to the most committed group in the war party.

Finally, Sergei Filatov, head of the Presidential Administration, and Foreign Minister Kozyrev also deserve mention for their roles in loyally supporting the war party,[88] as does Oleg Lobov, director of the Security Council. Unconsciously echoing Interior Minister Plehve's influential words of 1904 that Russia needed "a small victorious war to avert revolution," Lobov justified the Chechnya invasion by saying "The president needs a small victorious war, like the USA had in Haiti."[89]

On November 29, 1994, after the failure of its latest attempt to overthrow Dudayev—this time by a proxy group led by Umar Avtorkhanov—the Russian Security Council decided to eliminate Dudayev and seize direct control over Chechnya by military means. It was just a month short of the fifteenth anniversary of Brezhnev's December 1979 invasion of Afghanistan.

The first days of December 1994 were devoted to a jingoistic media campaign designed to whip up nationalist passions for the imminent invasion. On December 1, Kozyrev assailed NATO's eastward expansion and threatened to withdraw from its U.S.-inspired Partnership for Peace. On December 2, to applause from many Russian patriots, Russia vetoed a UN Security Council resolution to embargo arms shipments to the former Yugoslavia. Then on December 4, as mentioned earlier, Yeltsin spoke ominously of the coming of a "cold peace" and reiterated Kozyrev's assault on NATO expansion. Playing to his domestic audience, Yeltsin tried to strike the pose of being a bulwark against a new round of U.S. global hegemonism. But just like Brezhnev's long debacle in Afghanistan, the Chechnya adventure launched on December 9 led to a catastrophic weakening of Russia's great power status—this time, though, with the world and the Russian public watching on television.

A detailed analysis of the first Chechnya war is beyond the scope of the present study.[90] In some ways, the jury is still out on the roles of both Yeltsin and Dudayev, but it is scarcely necessary to point out that Dudayev was no democrat and that he skillfully used Yeltsin's blunders to stoke anti-Russian hatred among his people, just as the nomenklatura oligarchs of the old Soviet republics exploited the national democratic movements of 1991 to seize power for themselves. We will limit ourselves to the Russian side of the process. Given the severity of the Russian military defeat that was to come, and the consequent damage to Russia's prestige in the world, there is no doubt that the Chechnya adventure was an exercise in unintended self-destruction.

Among other things, the Chechnya intervention did not deter U.S. support for NATO expansion, contrary to the hopes of Yeltsin's deluded gaggle of geopoliticians. Instead, the Chechnya war soured Russia's relations with its Muslim neighbors and stirred up ethnic tension inside Russia. The Yeltsin die-hards and their ethnic chauvinist supporters outside the government thus repeated the failure of their predecessors of the Gorbachev era, who had chanted the slogan "Russia First!" without fathoming the backlash they were courting along the southern belt of union republics. Even after the extinction of the Soviet Union, Russia has remained structurally organized in such a way that the alienation of the non-Russian ethnic minorities, however modest their numbers may be, is bound to have a devastating impact on Russia's historic identity as a multi-ethnic state. Thus any Russian nationalism based on ethnic criteria contains the seeds of Russia's own destruction, as we argued in chapter 3.

Russia's stature in the world and its ethnic cohesion were severely damaged in the Chechnya debacle, but strangely enough Yeltsin himself got away with it in terms of his personal power and the stability of his regime. Future chroniclers will no doubt offer their own explanations of Yeltsin's tenacity in office in the face of stunning military defeat and the strenuous efforts of the opposition to topple him. In brief, though, the Chechnya crisis shattered the parliamentary opposition, pitting democrats against nationalists and nationalist hawks against nationalist doves. Perhaps the only institution that could have overthrown Yeltsin at this stage was the army, and he may well have feared a military coup far more than the machinations of Duma politicians, which recalled what Lenin had once dismissed under the heading of "parliamentary cretinism." Indeed, Yeltsin may have been diabolical enough to pursue the war knowing that the casualty list would include the army's coup-making potential for as far as the eye could see.

THE U.S. RESPONSE: BE NICE TO BORIS

We have suggested that Yeltsin must in many ways be considered a satrap of the United States and the world financial powers represented by the International Monetary Fund. It follows that his ability to shake off the Chechnya fiasco so comfortably stemmed from this status. In contrast with the naïve and obsolete geopolitical axioms that guided orthodox Russian policymakers, the

Western response to Yeltsin's episodes of authoritarianism and militarism showed that, from the U.S. point of view, economic considerations dwarfed any residual concerns about Russia's relations with its neighbors or about Yeltsin's treatment of his domestic adversaries. The issue of maintaining laissez-faire economic policies loomed far larger for American officials than either the Chechnya war or Moscow's oppressive political atmosphere, in which the Kremlin could be widely suspected of having an inconvenient journalist murdered.

This mindset produced the following comment from Andrei Sakharov's friend and successor, Sergei Kovalev: "If Kohl and Clinton had taken a different stand" on Chechnya, "a principled, uncompromising, honest stand, the war would not have gone on like it did. But they were thinking of Yeltsin's prestige, they were afraid of political chaos in Russia. This lack of principles was paid for with tens of thousands of human lives."[91]

POLEVANOV AND RENATIONALIZATION

American attention was fixed not on Chechnya but, rather, on the celebrated Vladimir Polevanov. Polevanov, the little-known former governor of the Amur region, located next to China in eastern Siberia, was appointed head of the State Property Management Committee (SPMC) in November 1994. Supported by Korzhakov, this appointment was part of Yeltsin's reaction to Black Tuesday, which had loosened the policy grip of both the Chubais shock therapists who were still in the government and the dovish group of raw materials oligarchs around Chernomyrdin. Polevanov's promotion reflected the temporary ascendancy of the nationalist group of economic dirigistes and statists headed by Deputy Prime Minister Oleg Soskovets. Soskovets was a known defender of the legitimate interests of the productive industrial sector of the Russian economy, which had been decimated by financial austerity. However, much more than Soskovets and other Kremlin dirigistes, Polevanov brought to his job at the SPMC some special qualities that might have made him an influential politician. It was clear that he did not belong to the golden youth of the nomenklatura. Rather, he was a typical, bearded, articulate, outspoken member of the provincial intelligentsia who quickly made the Moscow political elite feel threatened by his statements about the possible need to renationalize some of the state property that the elites had been appropriating.[92]

Renationalization! That kind of talk was clearly beyond the pale of political correctness, even among many communists.[93] Polevanov was the first official to conduct a systematic analysis of issues that had disturbed many people: First, there was the fact that many of the privatizations, especially those of pre-1992 vintage, were highly questionable from a legal point of view. It had also become painfully obvious that privatization had brought few advantages for the privatized companies, which had continued to decline under private ownership, sometimes even more rapidly than before. In fact, Polevanov's careful analysis, backed by input from a variety of state agencies, led him to conclude that of the seven officially declared goals of the privatization program, five were almost complete failures. He recommended that the privatization program be reviewed and that Soskovets replace Chubais as its political overseer.[94] The implication was that the renationalization of some strategically important companies had to be considered.

Such renationalization, especially if it had held open the option of later reprivatization under more legitimate and transparent auspices—with more access for domestic and foreign interests, and not just monopolists—would by no means spell the end of Russian capitalism and a return to the command economy, as Chubais and his retainers claimed. Yet the mere mention of renationalization caused hysteria not just among the new venture capitalists but also among senior figures in the Communist Party, who depended on the financial and political support of certain bankers and ex-nomenklatura robber barons who had taken over the oil and gas sector.[95]

As for Polevanov's presumed backers among the statist circles of the regime, such as Soskovets, their attitude toward renationalization would have depended on whether former state firms now controlled by themselves or their associates were among the targets. Polevanov's moves never posed a major threat of expropriating Western economic assets because, apart from a limited group of oil and metallurgy companies, Western investors had not purchased shares in Russian companies during privatization. Nevertheless, Polevanov's initiatives antagonized the West because they were seen as part of the emerging pattern of challenges issued by the disgruntled satrap Yeltsin.

More specifically, an important threshold was crossed by Korzhakov's November 30, 1994 letter to Chernomyrdin, which was leaked to the foreign press.[96] In contrast to what Polevanov was doing, Korzhakov's letter contained more tangible threats to Western interests in Russia. Korzhakov attacked Chernomyrdin for liberalizing oil exports and making the raw materials sector too dependent on foreign capital. He also sought to interfere with Chernomyrdin's proprietary industrial base by asking him to set up a group of outside experts on oil policy under Korzhakov's ally, Soskovets. The fact that a former KGB bodyguard was trying to change the economic policy of the country was a scandal and provided further evidence that Yeltsin's authoritarian turn was rendering constitutional provisions regarding relations between the organs of government increasingly irrelevant. The G-7 governments began to wonder which officials and which ministries were in charge.

The anxiety of European, especially German, public opinion over the Chechnya war and Russia's bellicose policies reached its height in early 1995. At this time, Polevanov issued an order banning foreign consultants with contracts from the U.S. Agency for International Development from entering the offices of the SPMC. This stemmed from a series of exposés in opposition newspapers, including *Sovetskaya Rossiya,* about insider privatization deals that were turning out to be bonanzas for Western consultants but net losses for Russia. Polevanov's suspicions of graft were later confirmed when AID terminated some of its own Harvard-based contractors, such as Shleifer and Hay, referring to "activities for personal gain by personnel placed in a position of trust."[97] In the climate of January 1995, however, declaring the SPMC building off-limits to such Americans was seen as a shocking display of anti-Western xenophobia, worse than Yeltsin's line about the "cold peace." Polevanov's nemesis, Chubais, whom he had replaced as manager of the SPMC, was nonetheless still a deputy prime minister and thus his bureaucratic superior. One day after Polevanov's order was issued, Chubais directed the SPMC to lift the ban on foreign consultants on its premises.[98] Once again, Chubais had delivered the goods for his IMF backers.

Polevanov was a newcomer to the government whose position was far from entrenched. Hence it is striking that he so openly courted defeat by an apparently foolhardy frontal assault on the Kremlin's economic policy, precisely the area where the influence of Chubais and his foreign networks was paramount. It is likely that Polevanov's order was not just his own idea but was coordinated with senior statist officials like Soskovets and Korzhakov. Indeed, the order may have been favored by Yeltsin himself as a ploy in his haggling with the United States. Evidently, Polevanov had been cast to play two roles—first as a bogeyman to frighten the West, and then as the fall guy to be sacked after his xenophobic order was canceled. His handling by his nomenklatura patrons Soskovets and Korzhakov is instructive about the style of much Russian politics. Seemingly, they gave him an overly optimistic picture of the correlation of forces in the government and promised their support in a final showdown with Chubais. Then they broke their promise to protect their own interests. A victorious Polevanov, having successfully driven the American money-changers out of the SPMC temple, might have attracted wide enough support to disrupt overall nomenklatura control of the government, thus upsetting the interests of all the establishment's clans.

Polevanov's downfall was abrupt and total. On January 12, Chernomyrdin issued an order placing the SPMC and Polevanov under Chubais's authority. Characteristically, the order was not issued by Yeltsin, which doubtless made clear to Polevanov later that he had been deserted by his own protectors. Polevanov hoped to hang on and tried to defend himself: On January 18, he forwarded his scathingly critical analytical report on the outcome of privatization. This gave Yeltsin a pretext to step in and arbitrate the brawl: On January 24, Polevanov was fired by presidential decree. This also ensured that the badly needed public debate on the future of privatization, for which Polevanov's findings were an ideal springboard, would soon fizzle out. The Chubais camp had gained Yeltsin's support and was not going to budge.

Intense exchanges took place between the Kremlin and the G-7 governments before Polevanov was dismissed, but these have not yet become public.

Until they do, any evaluation of the Polevanov affair must be based on speculation. He himself said that three bodies insisted on his dismissal: the IMF, the Ministry of Foreign Affairs (under Kozyrev), and Ambassador Yuli Vorontsov in Washington, who "literally bombarded the government with coded messages saying 'Remove Polevanov, the Americans are dissatisfied with him.'"[99]

Just after Polevanov's ouster, Chubais vigorously reasserted his primacy as Russia's point man in economic dealings with the West by procuring a $6.4 billion loan from the International Monetary Fund. One of the loan's preconditions, exacted behind the scenes by the IMF, was that henceforth Chubais must function as the undisputed chief of Russian economic policy.[100] Chubais was more powerful than ever, and this was the end of Yeltsin's 1994 attempt to disguise himself with the rhetoric of Roosevelt's New Deal or the dirigisme of de Gaulle.

Chubais now dominated Russian foreign policy as well; he had proven to Yeltsin that he was a better strategist than Korzhakov, Grachev, and others of their ilk. These men were guided by a simplistic picture of policymaking that mixed together unrelated issues, combining ethnic nationalism, an anti-Western animus, and hostility to foreign investment in a doctrinaire way that permitted little pragmatic maneuvering and made it easy to portray them to the West as the classic "dark forces." Chubais's modus operandi was more discriminating, more cynical, and more complex.

As a bright student in the school of U.S. policymaking, Chubais had learned to compartmentalize issues. In the great divide between hawks and doves on the Chechnya issue, when Chubais cronies such as Gaidar strongly condemned the war, collaborated with the Communists,[101] and even briefly declared themselves in opposition to Yeltsin, Chubais demonstrated a cold-blooded restraint. Whatever Russian losses there might be, they were irrelevant to Chubais's sphere of influence. Chubais was not about to assail Korzhakov on matters that were indifferent to him, and this meant that Chubais later had what the statists conceded was a legitimate claim to protect his own turf in the Polevanov affair. In the long run, Chubais had more in common with Korzhakov and the other nomenklatura statists than he did with democratic opponents of the war. His economic strategy depended on a strong bureaucratic and police apparatus to enforce it. Especially important were the security forces of Korzhakov and Mikhail Barsukov's Main Protective Administration, and Yerin's Interior Ministry.

PERMANENT PRIVATIZATION AND THE NEW FINANCIAL OLIGARCHS

It was during the years 1994 to 1996 that the emergence of oligarchical government in Russia became widely acknowledged. The country, which had suffered under tsars who preened themselves on being autocratic and absolute rulers, and which had endured the terrifying dictatorship of Stalin, now found itself ruled by a self-appointed clique. This group was described by the press as the "Big Seven" oligarchs and held meetings in foreign countries to decide who should be the next president of Russia.

Oligarchy is described in Plato's *Republic* as "a constitution teeming with many evils" (544c). Oligarchy is a government "based on a property qualification . . . wherein the rich hold office and the poor man is excluded" (550d). Under oligarchy, writes Plato, nearly all are beggars, "except the ruling class" (552d). In his *Politics,* Aristotle wrote of "oligarchy, where the supreme power of the state is lodged with the rich" (1279b). This is the form of government against which Madison warned in Federalist No. 57 because it involved "the elevation of the few on the ruins of the many."

These definitions certainly fit Yeltsin's Russia, as the Russian elite itself has acknowledged on occasion. In the aftermath of the December 1993 elections, for example, the Interaction Club of Moscow heard an address by its president, Yegor Gaidar, and concluded after a discussion that "Russia is not yet ready for pure liberal democracy of the Western type." Because the country "lacks democratic traditions" and shows little promise of developing a middle class in the near future, the only way of preventing a fascist coup is to turn to "enlightened authoritarianism." This, the Interaction Club believed, "should be based on a deliberately cultivated oligarchy—a political and economic elite advocating liberal democratic positions" and consisting of senior businessmen, company directors, and reform-minded leaders of the military and police.[102]

In his address to the State Duma delivered on October 28, 1994, Aleksandr Solzhenitsyn, Nobel laureate and the leading Russian author of our age, formally pronounced his verdict that the Russian state was an oligarchy. "It's not democracy," he said. "Let us admit that it's an oligarchy, . . . the power of a restricted group of individuals." Real power remained with the old Soviet nomenklatura, now posing as democrats.[103]

Grigori Yavlinsky, speaking at George Washington University on September 25, 1997, recounted the details of a telephone call he had recently received from Boris Berezovsky, who had tried to issue directives, informing Yavlinsky of policies that "we, the oligarchs" had decided to impose. Likewise, in 1995 the then-oligarch Oleg Boiko, speaking in the name of his fellow financial chieftains, demanded the postponement of the upcoming parliamentary and presidential elections prescribed by the constitution.[104]

Needless to say, the triumph of oligarchy is ominous for the future of Russia. Oligarchy often turns out to be a worse blind alley than autocracy. Of all the forms of government known to Plato, he considered oligarchy the hardest to reform in a positive direction: "oligarchy . . . only admits of such a development with the greatest difficulty, for there the number of persons of influence is greatest" (*Laws,* 710e). And indeed, autocrats can sometimes take advice: Dionysius of Sicily listened for a time to Plato, and Louis XIV to Colbert. But the

Venetian oligarchy turned a deaf ear to Renaissance sages like Dante, Petrarch, and Erasmus.

While the economic aspects of cash privatization are addressed in chapter 5, here we need to discuss the economic innovations directly associated with Chubais, some of which date back to 1992–93 and involve enough of a redistribution of political power by economic means to impact the political process. Previously, the key forces acting on economic policy had been the theoreticians of shock therapy, backed up by Yeltsin's power and by the support of the United States and the IMF, as well as the former socialist factory managers who had rushed to transform themselves into private owners. Now a new and powerful factor emerged: the two earlier groups—the radical freemarketeers in the government and the nomenklatura capitalists in the former state companies —became dependent on financing from a small group of bankers who described themselves as the "New Russian Oligarchs." These parvenu Russian Morgans and Rockefellers were the creatures of Chubais, who naturally became the spiritus rector of the new system. The huge concentration of financial resources that he had helped to place in the hands of the new oligarchs allowed this group to close ranks and pull up the ladder, effectively excluding potential newcomers from the largely ruined middle class, which the elite always regarded as a threat to its stability.

Where did this oligarchy have its roots? The period from 1991 to 1993 was the heyday of commodity speculators on Russia's new securities and commodities exchanges, where clever operators had a chance to amass considerable fortunes in short order. A few of these speculators, such as Konstantin Borovoi and Valery Neverov, joined the ranks of the nouveaux riches.[105] By 1993, however, the restricted group of bankers who handled government deposits, government disbursements, and Treasury securities had already accumulated financial assets that were much greater than those amassed by the nouveaux riches brokers. The commodity exchanges soon became both unprofitable and unfashionable, and the fortunes of figures like Borovoi were soon at a low ebb.

As the exchanges yielded their dominance to the government-backed banks, many commodity brokers and middlemen who had briefly enjoyed spectacular careers were ruined. Some of these speculators tried to keep up with the times by improvising financial empires of their own, but they were often eliminated in the process. Notorious cases included that of Boiko, the head of OLBI Concern and National Credit Bank, and of Ilya Medkov, an up-and-coming twenty-five-year-old broker-turned-banker who was torn to pieces by a bomb explosion in the center of Moscow.[106] Thus was the space cleared for the self-styled financial oligarchs. The rise of the oligarchy is often considered the joint achievement of Chubais and Chernomyrdin, but the key masterminds behind the strategy were probably Chubais and Gaidar.[107]

The rise of the oligarchy was accelerated by the activities of Russia's check investment funds, or *chify,* which took in individual privatization vouchers from the population and promised unrealistically high rates of return. However, very little money was ever paid out in the way of dividends. Most of the *chify* fund managers were bureaucrats in the orbit of the SCP, along with their relatives, which meant that Chubais's power base became wealthy. The Russian press compared the *chify* to infamous pyramid schemes, the MMM and Tibet investment companies, the main difference being that the latter dealt in cash rather than vouchers and, unlike the *chify*, were not backed by the government.

The most striking development of this phase was the rapid accumulation of finance capital by the privileged banks that did large-scale business with and for the government. The cold fact is that when millions of people were receiving their wages and pensions with up to a year of delay, the banks were using the government funds appropriated for these purposes to speculate in short-term Treasury bonds (GKOs, in the Russian abbreviation) and other securities. The GKOs were traded on a restricted market, where foreigners were not allowed to buy at first. Later, foreigners were allowed to purchase them, but only at a severe interest rate disadvantage: the GKOs paid 80 percent interest to Russians, but only 18 percent to foreign holders. Soon the debt service and rollover needs of the GKOs became a major drain on the Russian Treasury.

In 1995, Deputy Prime Minister Chubais presided over an unorthodox fund-raising scheme known as "loans for shares," whose ostensible aim was to raise badly needed revenue for the budget. In theory, the government would auction off its shares in large state enterprises undergoing privatization, the banks would bid freely for shares, and winners would pay the Treasury in the form of loans. When Russia's independent Accounting Office later investigated the operation, however, it uncovered massive fraud. Not only were the assets greatly undervalued and the winners predetermined, but the government had actually deposited its own funds into the banks that won the auctions. The banks in turn loaned back what were the deposited government funds.

For the Kremlin, the whole transaction was a net loss, not a major infusion of cash. The assets remained instead in the hands of the predetermined winners, among them the Stolichny Bank, owned by Aleksandr Smolensky, one of the new oligarchs.[108] At the time, Chubais swept aside criticism of the operation as completely unfounded. In January 1996, however, when Yeltsin dropped Chubais from the government in another of his seesaw maneuvers, Yeltsin exclaimed: "How those auctions were fouled up—our enterprises were sold for next to nothing!" The powerful mayor of Moscow, Yuri Luzhkov, went further. He declared that the conduct of privatization under Chubais was so dubious that it required a criminal investigation. He also demanded the deprivatization of companies whose shares had been handed over at rock bottom prices.[109]

Because Chubais had helped to create the new banking empires, and because of his close association with the new financial oligarchs, he acquired an inordinate influence over the mass media that the oligarchs increasingly came to acquire. This influence became one of Chubais's key strategic assets in the struggle for power. The media felt free to snipe at Yeltsin during this period, but any principled critique of the fundamentals of economic policy, or of Chubais's activities as a power broker, was—except in a few small-circulation publications—strictly taboo. This self-censorship became a serious handicap for many of Chubais's opponents, above all the economist Sergei Glaziev, whom the media shunned despite the fact that he was a leader of the Congress of Russian Communities and the best-known economist and politician calling for an alternative economic course in the midst of a depression.

Yeltsin and his courtiers were more and more impressed by Chubais's ability to dictate the tone and content of media coverage, especially when they found that the degree of derogatory coverage to which they themselves were subjected seemed to depend on whether their own relations to Chubais were cordial or hostile. At a certain point, Chubais was even able to convince Gusinsky to mute criticism of Yeltsin by the media outlets he controlled.

Another source of power for Chubais was his pragmatic readiness to help expedite the business deals and swindles carried on by government officials of different ideologies, such as the Chechnya hawks. Chubais formulated Yeltsin's economic policy and drafted the president's economic decrees, but he also did not block the government contracts or special tax breaks sought by companies created or controlled by such figures as Korzhakov, Soskovets, and Grachev.

ORGANIZED CRIME: IF YOU CAN'T BEAT 'EM, JOIN 'EM

The disarray and demoralization of the Yeltsin regime in early 1995 are hard to exaggerate. By late 1993, it had alienated at least half of the population for good through its brutally monetarist "wager on the strong" and its violent dissolution of the parliament. In October 1994, "Black Tuesday" proved that financial earthquakes could still strike at any time and depress living standards yet more. Between August and November, the security services and the army humiliated Russia before the world through the incompetence with which they tried in vain to overthrow Dudayev's regime in Chechnya using small-scale and covert action and sending many people to their deaths.[110] In December and January, they dramatically escalated the deaths and deepened the humiliation by having a full-scale invasion fail equally badly.

At the same time, much of the political spectrum united in vociferous protest against the war, raising the specter of a potential alliance between the only two solid and relatively independent opposition parties, the CPRF and Yabloko—a specter that could not be dispelled for months and that deserves further scholarly research. The specter also pointed up the fact that the Kremlin was totally unprepared for the upcoming Duma elections in December.

Finally, Yeltsin went into a major funk over the war, so that by February 1995, only 8 percent of the population still had full faith in him, and only 31 percent had some faith. True, the IMF came through in March with the $6.4 billion loan, despite opposition from a few lone voices.[111] Nonetheless, by April many Russian analysts agreed that "Boris Yeltsin appears to be a political corpse whose activity and reputation have gone into an irreversible tailspin."[112]

A further contribution to this collapse of confidence in the regime was a major defeat in a sphere we have so far touched on only lightly—crime. By early 1995, it was clear that the Kremlin's 1994 effort to recoup some popular support by launching a war on organized crime and official corruption had been, by a variety of means, overwhelmingly defeated. By contrast, the Mafiya, the Berezovskys, the corrupt generals, and the bribe-taking bureaucrats and ministers had decisively won.

Since Russia became independent, high-level campaigns against crime and corruption have occurred roughly on an annual basis. In an early example, Yeltsin declared all-out war in a major speech on February 12, 1993, saying: "Organized crime has become the number one threat to Russia's strategic interests and national security. Corruption in the organs of government and administration is literally corroding the state body of Russia from top to bottom."[113]

Yeltsin's desire to show the criminal world and his foreign and domestic constituencies that he could restore public order in Russia found support from another quarter: the businessmen who had done best in the previous few years and now needed to protect their riches from violent rivals and mobsters. In early 1993, for example, as the oligarch and banker Aleksandr Smolensky reported, ten bankers were assassinated. This led him and six other bankers to send an urgent request for action to Yeltsin in July 1993, arguing that "criminals have resorted to outright physical reprisals against those who refuse to yield to their threats and bribery."[114] In a similar vein, Berezovsky urged the business world in 1993–94 to agree to a categorical ban on contract killings.[115] On November 17, 1993, no doubt partially in response to the bankers' appeal and after the parliament's demise had signaled a turn toward authoritarianism, Yeltsin announced a broad package of anticrime measures, including expanded police powers and tough new visa restrictions.

However, the criminals were not deterred by such announcements, and skeptical voices could already be heard. A high-level Moscow official, for example, said the city was not concerned about whether it received "party, Mafiya, or clean money" because "life shows that it is impossible to organize a successful fight against the Mafiya at the present stage."[116]

It was only Yeltsin's humiliation and Zhirinovsky's triumph in the Duma elections that prompted the Kremlin to become more serious about crime. Yeltsin's research service issued a sobering, hard-hitting report that spelled out its fears that "actual policy" might soon "be determined not by the government or the parliament, but by organized crime." The latter was already "compiling detailed dossiers on all important officials and politicians." These conditions could help Zhirinovsky to mobilize "tens of millions of Russian citizens" behind his LDP. Indeed, "Failure to take resolute measures to remove the economic roots of crime" and to pass laws for combating organized criminal gangs "could bring the national-socialists to power in the 1996 presidential election."[117]

Sensing that a trial of strength was imminent, the Mafiya became more violent than ever in order to intimidate the authorities and make sure that measures taken against it would consist more of words than of substance. Most significantly, it blew apart a member of the parliament who had campaigned against organized crime.[118] Also, in the first five months of 1994, homicides in Moscow rose by 41 percent over the same period in 1993. And in the first two weeks of June 1994, Moscow experienced fifty-two murders, many of them involving organized crime.[119] Not surprisingly, a nationwide poll found 51 percent of respondents saying that the fight against crime should be the government's top priority.[120] One measure of the failure of the 1994 and subsequent anticrime campaigns is the available statistics on killings. Smolensky offers plausible figures in one narrow sphere for the years 1993 through 1997: In 116 attempts on the lives of bankers, 79 were killed and 36 wounded.[121] Figures for a wider spectrum of victims that includes bankers, businessmen, and government personnel show 219 killings for the two-year period July 1995 to July 1997.[122]

The measures the Mafiya had been expecting came in June. First, on the eleventh of that month, the heads of all the law enforcement agencies held a joint news conference to announce a wide range of anticrime programs. The price tag—$2.5 billion—was impressive, but the government expected to collect at least $5 billion in lost revenue by getting tough on financial crimes.[123] Four days later, Yeltsin's previously mentioned decree on urgent measures to combat organized crime was published—to widespread applause, as well as strong criticism from civil libertarians and others.[124] The following week, the acting prosecutor general, Aleksei Ilyushenko, went to the heart of the issue: "Who is going to force whom to his knees? Will the state prevail over the Mafiya, or the Mafiya over the state?"[125]

On July 4, FBI Director Louis Freeh, who had come to Moscow to support Yeltsin and open a branch office that would work with its Russian counterparts to catch international criminals, praised (with a few caveats) Yeltsin's decrees and the Russian anticrime programs. He also signed a U.S.-Russian protocol laying out plans for extensive mutual cooperation in the fight against international crime.[126] During Freeh's visit, he gave a list of highly placed Russians to a senior Yeltsin aide. These individuals—who, according to the Russian press, included Chubais, Luzhkov, Grachev, and other Yeltsin supporters—were said to hold funds in American banks that came from criminal operations. On July 28, the Federation Council, the upper house of the Russian parliament, discussed the list and dispatched an appeal to the U.S. Senate, asking it to send over an actual copy. Shortly thereafter, council members took part in meetings on crime cooperation in Washington as part of a Russian delegation of parliamentarians and officials. They had meetings with senior U.S. law enforcement officers and members of Congress.

A major topic of conversation and of subsequent press coverage in Russia was the list. The Americans said they would send another copy, provided the Russian government formally requested one.[127] At this point, presumably because no such request was issued, the story apparently died, but only after revealing the delicacy of the whole subject. Not before 1999 did hard evidence surface to show that, indeed, many high-level Russian officials and businessmen held U.S. bank accounts. However, without the Kremlin's cooperation it was hard to know, for example, which of the accounts were legal and which contained the proceeds of crimes.

In any case, the murders and bombings continued in Russia through 1994 and beyond—among them, the murder of the journalist investigating military corruption, which we discussed earlier.[128] The fact that two of the people murdered were Americans may well have been a warning by the Mafiya to the United States to stop interfering in its affairs, at least in Russia.[129] Most important, though, thoughtful Russians and Westerners concluded that all the police and the programs, the $2.5 billion to pay for them, the Yeltsin decrees, the planned Duma legislation, the U.S. and Russian visits, and the institutionalization of FBI cooperation with the Kremlin, were ultimately worth very little.

An exceptionally well-informed study of Russian crime by a team of officials and *Izvestiya* reporters concluded that the situation was "tragic": "People are ceasing to believe in the power of the democratic state. . . . Already they are seriously asking: who will defeat whom?" True, "criminals create their empires, not states. . . . But criminal groups are capable of fragmenting and weakening a state after they have put it in the hands of political con-men. Doesn't today's Russia face such a prospect?"[130]

Certainly the Russian press was contemptuous of the first big police effort to implement Yeltsin's June decree. A week after the decree's publication, no less than twenty thousand police and MVD troops, armed to the teeth, swooped down on dozens of Mafiya-run casinos, restaurants, and hotels. But the Mafiya bosses had been tipped off. The fruits of the operation were "practically zero."[131] Yeltsin's former anticorruption chief, Yuri Boldyrev, provided a cogent political judgment on why the Mafiya had won. "The root of the problem," he held, "is that the deliberate policy of our entire present executive, including the head of state and everyone who supported and continues to support him, is to concentrate in their hands the full panoply of absolutely uncontrolled power, allegedly for the sake of the reforms. But such power inevitably becomes Mafiya power, and that is already obvious."[132]

If the government needed a more tangible excuse for a broad regime of repression, it could always rely on the rebellious Chechen republic. Clearly, the Kremlin proponents of the Chechnya war hoped that a quick decisive victory would facilitate Yeltsin's adoption of more authoritarian ways that would please much of the population. But Boldyrev's view casts doubt on their calculation. In any case, the gross incompetence of Yeltsin and the other politicians running the war excluded the possibility of such an outcome. Instead, the authorities were so politically weakened by the hostility of most of the population to the war that in 1995–96 the Committee of Soldiers' Mothers, through their brave and resolute actions, could regularly embarrass the Kremlin with impunity, and sometimes actually extract their sons from the conflict without incurring penalties.

By now, the Russian state had deeply authoritarian instincts but little capacity to suppress its opponents and none at all to suppress the criminal and semi-criminal groups with which it had virtually merged. This meant that ultimately no one was secure, not even top officials. Moscow's Mayor Luzhkov admitted as much when he confessed in early 1995: "We live in times when the toughest people are broken. I, too, could most likely be broken."[133] Smolensky expressed similar thoughts when he said: "Unfortunately, the only lawyer in this country is the Kalashnikov [rifle]. People mostly solve their problems in this way." Bribery, of course, was also needed because government officials "practically have a price list hanging on the office wall."[134]

In subsequent years, it became increasingly clear that, indeed, the whole governmental system was too corrupt to tackle crime effectively. As a Russian friend who occasionally talks with Yeltsin told the authors in 1997, by then, if not earlier, the president had fatalistically accepted this to be the case. Significantly, from 1991 right up to the present, not a single one of the thousands of highly placed politicians, generals, and businessmen on whom the police have lengthy dossiers has been sentenced and jailed; and even figures of lower rank have met this fate in only a few cases.

However, 1994 did witness one positive step to combat crime, even if it had no *immediate* effect and only a very limited, longer-term consequence. This was the creation of the Accounting Office, modeled on the U.S. General Accounting Office. Following the mandate of Article 101.5 of the 1993 constitution, Yeltsin signed the law governing its operation in November 1994, although only after he had insisted at the last minute on limiting its powers.[135] The law stipulates that the chamber is an independent body charged with monitoring federal expenditures and is formed jointly by the two houses of parliament, which each nominates six auditors to run it. This ensures that the auditors reflect the political composition of the legislature. The office's most prominent leaders have been Yuri Boldyrev, Yeltsin's corruption watchdog in 1992–93, whom we discussed earlier, and Veniamin Sokolov, a scientist who chaired the Council of the Union in the parliament of 1990–93. The basic problem with the Accounting Office has been that, although it has done extensive work documenting crime and corruption in government, its reports have been effectively ignored by the office of the prosecutor general, the mainstream media, and the government; as a result, they have had little direct impact. We will discuss a case in point later in this chapter.

BUDENNOVSK

In June 1995, five days after Yeltsin had reassured the Russian people that the economy was improving, the Chechnya war was approaching its end, and the Duma elections would be held on time, a political earthquake hit not only the southern city of Budennovsk, but the whole Russian political firmament. A group of a hundred Chechen guerrillas traveled north and took a thousand Russians hostage in a hospital. Yeltsin promptly left the country for a G-7 meeting in Canada, but the military actions he had approved failed badly, resulting in the death of many troops and hostages. Chernomyrdin then negotiated the release of the hostages and safe passage home for the Chechens.

This profoundly humiliating episode unleashed a torrent of public anger at the Kremlin's incompetence, especially Yeltsin's. This fired up the Duma opposition, and while it failed to impeach the president, it voted no confidence in the government by 241 to 70 and forced Yeltsin to preempt further potentially revolutionary moves by entering into serious negotiations. In return for dropping these moves, the Duma was rewarded with the firing of security director Stepashin and Interior Minister Yerin, plus Yeltsin's promise to end the war and allow the deputies extra powers regarding the 1996 budget. Yeltsin had chosen the lesser of two evils. His popular approval rating sank to record lows, but his impeachment was, for now, removed from the agenda, and the chances of the pro-Kremlin parties in the upcoming elections were saved from complete destruction.[136]

MANUFACTURING THE FUTURE PARLIAMENT: A HUNDRED FLOWERS IN THE BUREAUCRATIC HOTHOUSE

As the December 1995 Duma elections approached, the executive branch displayed remarkable ingenuity in creating a wide assortment of political parties, electoral blocs, alliances, and fronts. However, the cynical desire to splinter the Duma deliberately and divert votes that otherwise might go to the opposition was only one reason for this exercise. Many of the new creations were more or less authentic, expressing the uncontrollable growth of factions and rivalries within the Yeltsin camp. Yeltsin's electoral engineering seemed to be inspired by Chairman Mao's 1956–57 slogan, "Let a hundred flowers bloom. Let a hundred schools of thought contend."

The principal government product was Our Home Is Russia (OHR), the party led by Premier Chernomyrdin.[137] Although the original idea was to have the key members of the cabinet as candidates, the final candidates' list contained largely junior figures: Minister of Graduate Education Kinelev, Minister of Culture Sidorov, and Minister without Portfolio Travkin. Foreign Minister Kozyrev ran under the banner of OHR, but in a single-member district rather than on the candidates' list. In a last-minute attempt to consolidate the OHR as the "party of power," Chernomyrdin also managed to get important endorsements from Mayor Luzhkov and from Defense Minister Grachev.[138] The party's chief slogan was "stability" (that is, the status quo), not democracy or liberal economic reform.

However, OHR was undercut by an extraordinary series of high-level charges during May–July that Chernomyrdin was deeply corrupt.[139] Adding to the damage was the fact that his attempt to rebut the charges apparently convinced no one, and that Yeltsin did nothing to defend him.[140] Indeed, Yeltsin's instructions probably stood behind the clear orchestrator of the charges, Korzhakov. Yeltsin was clearly irritated by Chernomyrdin's unsanctioned presidential ambitions and wanted to make sure that his popular approval ratings remained low; in this, he succeeded. Even though Chernomyrdin's stock rose a little following his negotiation of the Budennovsk crisis, an authoritative poll found that when asked whom they favored as president—first in late May and then in late June (after the crisis) —Russians' support of him had increased only from 3 percent to 3.4 percent.[141]

The corruption charges came from various well-informed sources. First, former finance minister Boris Fyodorov alleged that when Gazprom had been privatized in late 1992, the prime minister had received 1 percent of the stock— worth about a billion dollars in 1995.[142] Although Fyodorov produced no evidence, no one challenged him, and Chernomyrdin did not sue him for libel.[143]

Then, former deputy prime minister Vladimir Polevanov claimed that members of the government had been enriched by Gazprom's profits and that Chernomyrdin had also facilitated a scam involving imported Cuban sugar.[144] And then Yuri Skokov, who held high Kremlin posts from 1990 to 1993, called the prime minister "the chief mafioso of the country." He reiterated and added to the earlier charges concerning Gazprom and then claimed that Chernomyrdin "has a personal plane ready to take him to the West at any moment." But the escape plan would not save him, according to Skokov: "No one will be able to escape the retribution of the people; all the plunderers of Russia will face their Nuremberg trial."[145] Neither Polevanov nor Skokov was sued. The *New York Times* also carried reports of Chernomyrdin's corruption.[146]

Next, a Russian newspaper published a lengthy interview with a man it called Vladimir, who claimed to represent a group of intelligence officers. Under the screaming headline "We'll Murder Chernomyrdin!"—a threat the paper seemed to take seriously—Vladimir said that unless the regime took decisive measures against official corruption and the disintegration of the state in the near future, his group would assassinate the prime minister and others whom it held responsible. This was followed by another newspaper's six-thousand-word analysis of the cooperation of corrupt politicians with organized crime, an article that prominently featured Chernomyrdin.[147] Chernomyrdin was not assassinated. Nine months later, however, his personal doctor was. Press comment recalled Vladimir's interview.[148]

These episodes clearly discredited not just the prime minister personally, but also the party he led, Our Home Is Russia. What about other parties?

The Agrarian Party, despite its strident procommunist rhetoric, was also in reality a government party, listing among its candidates Deputy Premier Zaveryukha and Agriculture Minister Nazarchuk, as well as an impressive number of regional-level agriculture bureaucrats and ministers of Russia's republics.[149] This party's hunger for power went well beyond its vote-getting ability when its leaders, before the election, staked out a claim for additional top posts, including those at the State Property Management Committee and the Ministry of Finance.[150]

The Party of Russian Unity and Accord (PRUA) was once again led into the fray by the deputy prime minister for nationalities affairs Sergei Shakhrai. In the 1993 elections, this party, advocating a mixture of economic liberalism, political conservatism, and regional special interests, was widely considered an electoral proxy for Chernomyrdin; it received 6.7 percent of the vote. In 1995, Shakhrai first joined Chernomyrdin's OHR and then walked out—reportedly in response to tensions between Yeltsin and Chernomyrdin and to the growing influence of anti-Chernomyrdin elements.[151]

The Presidential Administration, managed by Sergei Filatov, was heavily represented in Ivan Rybkin's Agrarian bloc. Here the candidates' list included both Yeltsin's director for administration, Pavel Borodin, and deputy head of the regional policy directorate, Vadim Pechenev. Also, several top business executives close to the administration and the government ran on this ticket, among them Imperial Bank owner Sergei Rodionov and the boss of the Germes trading group, Valery Neverov.[152] The Presidential Administration also spun off two splinter parties of Duma backbenchers, called Stable Russia and Duma '96, apparently with the intent of combining them with other pro-regime groups; but these parties ended up campaigning on their own. The Presidential Administration was also very close to the Women of Russia slate, one of whose leaders, Yekaterina Lakhova, had served as Yeltsin's adviser on family issues.[153]

The statist wing of the Kremlin establishment placed most of its bets on the Congress of Russian Communities (CRC), led by Yuri Skokov. Skokov allied himself with General Lebed, who had been feuding for several years with Defense Minister Grachev, and this caused friction between Skokov and Grachev.[154] The CRC was founded in 1993 by Dmitri Rogozin, a "master of political technologies" and founder of many parties and groups, whom we discussed in chapter 6. Rogozin's purposes in 1994–95 were several. First, he needed to provide a bloc—the "CRC Association"—in which two highly ambitious, statist, law-and-order politicians could be persuaded to coexist. Second, the less experienced, more nationalist, more covertly pro-Kremlin, and much more charismatic of the two, Lebed, required political training and exposure as a future candidate for high office. Third, Sergei Glaziev, who joined CRC more or less as an individual and thus broke up the Democratic Party (half of which joined Svyatoslav Fyodorov's party) needed to become well acquainted with Lebed so that they could cooperate in the future. And fourth, with covert government support, CRC had to campaign hard to draw votes away from nationalist parties not controlled by the Kremlin, like those of Rutskoi and Baburin.[155]

At the last minute, a group of individuals, including military officers and veterans, hastily set up their own election bloc bearing the name "For the Motherland!" and featuring prominent figures like paratroop commander Yevgeny Podkolzin; Admiral Eduard Baltin, the commander of the Black Sea Fleet; and Vladimir Polevanov, whose brief tenure as head of the State Property Management Committee we discussed earlier in this chapter. The bloc was apparently inspired by Korzhakov.[156] Meanwhile, Grachev played in other political arenas, cultivating a personal friendship with Zhirinovsky.

The LDP candidates' list included the head of Voenkombank (the Military Commercial Bank), Aleksandr Zhukovsky, and the former editor of the Defense Ministry's most hawkish periodical, General Viktor Filatov, who had also been a contributor to *Zavtra*. The LDP was now, in reality, a Kremlin ally. It had supported the Chechnya war consistently and voted against Yeltsin's impeachment. Zhirinovsky and Chernomyrdin had discussed cooperation, and key LDP members kept in close touch with top members of Yeltsin's entourage. As Zhirinovsky's number two, Aleksandr Vengerovsky, told Dimitri Simes, "Yeltsin's people like to use us as bogeymen in public, but in private we work together on many issues and have normal personal relations."[157]

The Kremlin hawks, who for a time had seemed to be gaining in power, were weakened and discredited by the ignominious failures of the Chechnya adventure. In local elections in Volgograd, held before the Duma voting, all military candidates were defeated by Communists. This suggested that the real challenge to the Yeltsin regime came not from the manageable right but, rather, from the antisystem left. This state of affairs favored Chernomyrdin in the final analysis, and was a factor forcing Grachev to publicly pledge the army's support to Chernomyrdin's election efforts. In addition, because Rybkin's bloc hardly got off the ground, and there was growing discord within the Congress of Russian Communities, and Zhirinovsky continued to decline, Chernomyrdin and OHR won in the informal primary elections for the principal "party of power," elections that were held not in voting booths but in the corridors of the Kremlin.

Another election association that received support from Yeltsin's circle was Transformation of the Fatherland, headed by Eduard Rossel, the governor of Yeltsin's native Sverdlovsk region, where voter support for Yeltsin and his policies had always been high. Rossel himself was popular only in his own region, where he had just won back the governorship in a duel with a rival backed by Chernomyrdin. The "invisible hand" behind Rossel was assumed to be Vladimir Shumeiko, who combined strong military-industrial connections with an outspoken profession of monarchism. Shumeiko planned a postelection convergence with Rossel as well as with Polevanov, a leader of For the Motherland! who had become disillusioned with Grachev's ministry.

If all these election-year creations had managed to enter the Duma, the result would have been a very fragmented parliament. The fighting among them would also have reverberated within the Kremlin, worsening the rifts inside the executive branch. Let us recall that for party-list candidates to get into the Duma, a party had to clear the 5 percent hurdle. This was required by the election law that was based almost completely on Yeltsin's decrees of October–November 1993. However, when contenders like Rybkin and Rossel began to lag in the polls, they raised doubts about the constitutional legitimacy of this 5 percent threshold, pointing out that under certain circumstances, it could lead to the partial disenfranchisement of a majority of voters. These claims were vehemently supported by officials of the Presidential Administration, such as Filatov and Satarov.[158]

This last-minute attempt to muddy the waters was predictable because a poor showing by their political clients was likely to speed the demotion of the patrons. But it was remarkable when Yeltsin began to express concerns about the election law that he himself had virtually dictated. His aim was to reduce the democratic legitimacy of the Duma compared to that of the upper house, the Federation Council, which consisted largely of Yeltsin's appointees and clients and which, after much legislative wrangling, would henceforth not be directly elected, but would have ex-officio membership.[159] The Federation Council also figured prominently in pre-election speculation about how the Yeltsin camp might respond to the emergence of an antiwar, anti–shock therapy majority coalition in the Duma. In that case, the "party of the Security Council" might have contemplated an extraconstitutional solution, leaning heavily on the Federation Council as the stronghold of "stability" and of regional interests.

THE ELECTION RETURNS AND THE CRISIS OF THE PRESIDENCY

In party terms, the elections turned out to be a striking victory for the left, a bad defeat for the nationalists, and a crushing defeat for the government.[160]

The chief pro-Kremlin party, OHR, for which Chernomyrdin had predicted "120 to 140 seats" out of 450, actually obtained 55. Its share of the party vote was a mere 10.2 percent—despite its massive use of Gazprom funds, which violated the legal spending limit by a wide margin.[161] Its supporters were mainly people tied to government by their jobs and soldiers who were pressured hard by some officers to vote for OHR.

All the other government-oriented parties, except for the special case of the LDP, failed to break the 5 percent barrier. The Congress of Russian Communities got 4.3 percent, evidently because its heavy spending induced the suspicion among voters that it was a covert Kremlin party and also because the archetypical nomenklatura official Skokov jealously insisted that Lebed play second fiddle to him throughout the campaign.

The Women of Russia party likewise looked too close to the government and, at 4.6 percent, almost halved its vote. The Agrarians suffered a similar decline—down to 3.8 percent. The United Democrats led by Gaidar and Chubais plummeted; their domination of the Kremlin's economic policy since 1991 was the key factor that reduced their share of the vote from 14.5 percent in 1993 to a mere 3.9 percent. Rybkin's and Shakhrai's parties got 1.48 percent between them.

Meanwhile, Zhirinovsky's LDP, a party that was not wholly predictable except when the Kremlin (or someone else) rewarded it financially for its support, as it often did, suffered badly for this pattern of behavior. Its vote was almost halved—down to 11.6 percent.

Even if one classifies the LDP and CRC conventionally as nationalist parties, the seven such parties taken together won only 19.6 percent—and only 67 seats. Nationalism, we conclude, had been widely debased, perhaps in large part because it had been espoused by most of the establishment and used to justify the unpopular war in Chechnya.

By contrast with the government and nationalist parties, the left did well. This was true whether they were center-left (Yabloko, S. Fyodorov's party), broad left (CPRF), or hard left (Anpilov's party). Yabloko's vote went down slightly, to 6.9 percent, but because it did well in single-member districts, its number of Duma seats went up from 27 to 46.[162] Fyodorov's social-democratic party polled remarkably strongly for a minimally funded group, getting 4.0 percent. The CPRF doubled its 1993 vote to take first place, with 22.3 percent, reflecting the fact that its relatively strong organization and a swing in public opinion more than made up for its notable lack of funds.[163] Finally, Anpilov's party benefited from Zyuganov's taking the CPRF in a more moderate and nationalistic direction to poll a strong 4.5 percent. However, because it did not quite reach 5 percent, it ended up, like Fyodorov's party, with only one seat.

These results produced a new crisis of the presidency just six months after the previous one. Turnout among the electorate was 64.6 percent—and the voters delivered a stinging rebuke. Yeltsin had even less support in the new Duma than he had had in the previous one. Could he possibly win reelection in June 1996? To many close observers, including Korzhakov, it seemed impossible. However, certain powerful bankers with plenty of cash and even more chutzpah thought otherwise.

RUSSIAN OLIGARCHS ON THE MAGIC MOUNTAIN

The defining moment of the New Russian Oligarchy came in the form of the celebrated Davos Pact. Davos is the Swiss Alpine resort depicted in the celebrated novel by Thomas Mann, *The Magic Mountain.* Here the finance potentates of the globalization era gather each year to discuss the world situation and their strategies. And here a cabal of seven leading Russian bankers met on January 30, 1996.[164] On foreign soil, the seven concluded that the private interests they represented made imperative the re-election of Boris Yeltsin as president of Russia that year.

Earlier, we examined briefly the concept of oligarchy, but we must ask what is meant exactly in Russia by the term "oligarch"? Where did these seven men, and others of similar power, come from? What forces turned them into oligarchs?

To answer these questions, we will both summarize and extend some arguments made elsewhere in this book. In brief, the years 1992 to 1995 saw the Kremlin lose the support of most of the Russian people, most of the intelligentsia, and most of the military. Although it retained the backing of the police, the secret police, and the West, this was not sufficient. True, the West would swallow many things, including Yeltsin's forcible dispersal of parliament in 1993, but it would probably not swallow the sort of sharp undermining of Russia's fragile democracy that Yeltsin, his cronies, and most of the country's top businessmen instinctively favored. In other words, while the West could tolerate the creeping, unspoken victory of market bolshevism over democracy, it would probably not go along with a clear-cut, *explicit* victory by the antidemocratic forces. Otherwise, it might cut off the loans, grants, and political support to which the Yeltsinites were unhealthily addicted.

This meant that the Kremlin still had to win elections. And, given its unpopularity, this meant that it needed substantial flows of extra cash and control of the key media. Where could these commodities be found? Only among the new class of property owners created by Chubais's privatization, for there was no new middle class of any size to call on. The twin banes of capital flight and the investment drought had ensured this. Instead, at different times and in various ways, the "Seven Bankers," the heads of the main oil and gas companies, and other top businessmen were able to buy a share of political power by providing the Kremlin with cash and media support when called upon. In this way, Yeltsin could still win elections and enjoy the backing of the West. And also in this way, new "financial oligarchs" were born and interacted with "crony oligarchs" around Yeltsin—people like Korzhakov, Yumashev, and the president's daughter Tatyana—and also with other oligarchs such as Chernomyrdin, Chubais, and Luzhkov. At the regional level, we should note, a similar process took place, mirroring Moscow's oligarchic structures.

Of course, like most authoritarian rulers, Yeltsin hoped to give up only minimal power in return for the new oligarchs' support. To this end, he used Korzhakov's Presidential Security Service (PSS) as his main instrument. Its goals were to help the president implement his divide-and-rule strategy toward the oligarchs and also to stop them from plundering too blatantly the state's assets.

In both respects, it strove mightily and with guile. However, given Yeltsin's political enfeeblement, its task was impossible. Rarely did the president act forcefully on Korzhakov's recommendations, and Korzhakov was up against some operators as wily as himself. Eventually, in June 1996, these oligarchs brought him and his allies down. Without much exaggeration, his deputy Valery Streletsky commented later on this episode that the PSS had been "the only buffer between political power and big business." And now, with the PSS emasculated, "the state works not for the people. The huge machine of political power serves a small gang of persons who are robbing the people."[165]

Interestingly, Chubais in a 1998 interview implied his agreement with Streletsky's point about the lack of a buffer. Commenting on Berezovsky's famous boast of November 1, 1996, that the Seven Bankers owned half the economy, he said bitterly that "No civilized power has ever allowed itself to be turned into a servant of big business." Commenting in turn on Chubais's statement, the columnist Andrei Piontkovsky noted Chubais's central role in the emergence of the new oligarchs, and criticized his long-standing failure to address the issue. Regarding the 1996 election, Piontkovsky felt that "Berezovsky was largely right when he said: 'We hired Chubais. We secured Yeltsin's election victory. Now it's time to enjoy the fruits of our victory.'"[166] Thus Yeltsin failed to keep the power of the financial oligarchs within bounds. In addition, as we shall see, he failed equally badly in his second goal: to keep their plundering of the state treasury within bounds.

On the political side, the oligarchs, or groups of them, were capable of highly effective collective action in many circumstances. They could get themselves or their associates appointed to key political positions—Berezovsky as deputy head of the Security Council in 1996–97, and as executive director of the CIS in 1998–99; the head of Oneksim Bank, Vladimir Potanin, as a senior government minister in 1996–97; and a raft of them, including Chubais, Chernomyrdin, Smolensky, and Gusinsky's associate Igor Malashenko, as executives in Yeltsin's re-election campaign of 1996.

The oligarchs could also—by choosing the right moment in June 1996—insist that Yeltsin dismiss the trusted Korzhakov and his allies. As Korzhakov recounts, Chubais "presented the demand of 'the oligarchs' to Yeltsin as an ultimatum." And Yeltsin agreed because they were "the 'money-bags' who had financed the president's campaign, whom he had received in the Kremlin and in Novo-Ogarevo, and with whom he had dined." Furthermore, "he had promised them after his election all sorts of favors and privileges." In these circumstances, Korzhakov says, he "quickly got rid of us."[167]

The oligarchs also had great influence on the government's privatization policies. In this regard, the American diplomat Thomas Graham got a useful insight from the horse's mouth: "One day in the summer of 1997," he writes, "I remember asking a certain 'oligarch' . . . whether he didn't think it was time to stop fleecing the country and start creating wealth. 'No,' he replied firmly, 'we still have to divide up all the property.' This task would take more time, he said. Russia is a large country."[168]

BORIS BEREZOVSKY

To put some flesh on the skeleton of these generalizations, we now look more closely at the modus operandi of the boldest and wiliest of all the oligarchs, Boris Berezovsky. This world-class operator combines guile, nerve, and sheer evil in ways that rival the Renaissance princes of Italy. Without him, the fortunes of the other financial oligarchs would have been smaller. In six years spent near the summit of Russian power, Berezovsky has pulled off coup after coup. Since the financial earthquake of August 1998, he has fended off blows that would have felled a less resourceful man. By always planning strategically—several steps ahead of his many ill-wishers—he has, for now, remained a player of the first rank.

The sketch that follows can provide only highlights from the postcommunist career of a man of many complex parts. Among the skills the media have reported him as having acquired are the ability:

- to appropriate revenue flows of state-owned assets;
- to launder revenues through domestic and foreign channels;
- to acquire ownership of state assets at minimal cost;
- to pay minimal taxes;
- to purchase the favors of politicians, journalists, and others with lavish gifts and good salaries;
- to acquire compromising material (*kompromat* in Russian) on a wide range of politicians and businessmen so as to exploit it directly or trade it for favors; and
- to use Mafiya methods to intimidate or kill individuals who stand in his way.

Significantly, Berezovsky has not thought it worth his while to sue the many publications and individuals who have detailed his activities under all these headings, with the exception of one so far unresolved suit against *Forbes* magazine for an article published in 1996.[169] When he responds at all, it is usually to his chief tormentor, Korzhakov. Typical was a response that called a Korzhakov statement "an uncontrolled stream of consciousness" and claimed there was "no sense in analyzing the actions of an idiot."[170]

Until he started in business in the late 1980s, Berezovsky, born in 1946, was a mathematical researcher. According to Nemtsov, he made his first big breakthrough in 1991, when he contracted with the car manufacturer Avtovaz to be the exclusive distributor of its Zhiguli model. He took out a loan before the August putsch to clinch the deal. "He received the cars after the putsch, when Gaidar had become a minister and Berezovsky knew that price controls would soon be lifted. Berezovsky bought the cars for two hundred dollars each, using the official exchange rate for the ruble at the time, and sold them for $5,000 after the leap in prices, thus getting $120 million at one go."[171]

As widely reported, and as Moscow police sources told Berezovsky's biographer Paul Klebnikov, Russia's largest car dealer "built his business under the protection of various Chechen gangs operating in Moscow."[172] This close Chechen tie was to endure, as we shall see.

Berezovsky's car distributorship Logovaz grew out of his close association in the 1980s with Vladimir Kadannikov, the general director of the giant car manufacturer Avtovaz in Tolyatti. In return for help with the plant's automation systems, Kadannikov helped Berezovsky found Logovaz in 1989 as a highly favored distributor for Avtovaz products. Evidently using Kadannikov's links to Gaidar and his Kremlin associates, Logovaz was granted tax and tariff breaks in 1993–94 to help it develop a new Russian car.[173] Although the project did not prosper, Berezovsky himself came out of it well.[174]

Berezovsky also made his political breakthrough during this time—thanks to the young journalist Valentin Yumashev. Like Korzhakov, Yumashev was one of a handful of people who had befriended Yeltsin when he became a political outcast in the autumn of 1987. A year later, Yumashev worked for Yeltsin's election to the USSR Supreme Soviet and made a campaign film about him. In 1990, he helped Yeltsin write his first book of memoirs, and in 1993, they finished a sequel. By this time, the magazine *Ogonek,* for which Yumashev had worked since 1987, had been bought by Berezovsky, and Yumashev had been appointed director of the Ogonek publishing house, presumably by Berezovsky or with his approval.

Thus it was logical that Yumashev should ask his new boss to put up the money to publish the second book. Berezovsky agreed, taking Kadannikov as a partner for the purpose. Yumashev introduced Berezovsky to Korzhakov in late 1993, and in the spring the expensively produced book appeared from Ogonek with ninety-six pages of color photos.[175]

More important, Berezovsky orchestrated an advance to Yeltsin—according to Korzhakov—of $3 million. Deposited in Barclays Bank in London, Korzhakov said, the advance generated $16,000 a month in interest, which Yumashev would regularly bring in cash to Yeltsin's office and put in his safe.[176] To give him a rationale for accepting the advance and the resulting flow of cash, his associates told him—untruthfully—that the book was a best-seller in many countries.

Four years later, Korzhakov announced: "I know the number of the account in a foreign bank in which Yeltsin keeps his 'savings.' His 'secret nest egg' *(zanachka)* . . . amounts today to more than five million dollars." In commercial terms, Korzhakov said that for his book, Yeltsin "was due to receive about 100 thousand dollars." Later, his American publisher reportedly said that "Yeltsin's book was excellent—and that the American edition never made a penny."[177] As on other occasions, Korzhakov made clear without saying in so many words his view that the difference between the real book payment and the original $3 million was a straightforward bribe.[178] On no occasion did Yeltsin or his representatives deny such statements, or sue Korzhakov for them, or threaten to sue him.

In summer 1994, just after Berezovsky had survived an assassination attempt that decapitated his driver, he was inducted into the President's Club, an exclusive social meeting place for Yeltsin's friends and associates. He arrived with his face burned and his arm in a sling.[179] This access enabled him through Yumashev to meet Yeltsin's daughter, Tatyana, to whom he soon started to give presents—jewelry, then a customized sports utility vehicle, then a Chevrolet Blazer.[180] Later, when he threw a party for the international jet set, he contrived for the invitations to go out in the name of President Yeltsin.[181]

Berezovsky had cemented his relationship with Korzhakov, as the latter admits, by providing him with the products of another of Berezovsky's enterprises—the acquisition of *kompromat* on powerful people.[182] To this end, Berezovsky employed former detectives and secret policemen, and also the services of a notorious partner, Pyotr Listerman. The latter ran a high-class international "escort" service designed to generate *kompromat* on senior politicians and businessmen.[183] Korzhakov was clearly glad to receive such material and sometimes, as his book suggests, to use it.

Also in late 1994, the government decided to raise badly needed cash by privatizing 49 percent of the main state television company, which was now renamed Public Russian Television (PRT). Through Logovaz and his United Bank, Berezovsky bought a 16-percent share in PRT for the artificially low price of $320,000, and also persuaded other new owners to let him manage their shares.[184] Named deputy chairman of the board, he soon exerted a powerful influence on PRT's editorial line, partly by paying supplementary salaries to key figures. Again, Korzhakov admits that he facilitated all this on the grounds that Yeltsin needed to have the country's biggest television company both solvent and strongly committed to him politically.[185]

To make sure that Berezovsky did not use PRT against Yeltsin in the future, Korzhakov masterminded a complex scheme. For three years from December 1994, 26 percent of PRT's shares were formally transferred to the temporary ownership of the Yeltsin family so that, if necessary, the voting power of these shares could be added to that of the state's 51 percent to prevent any anti-Yeltsin maneuvers. The 26 percent was made up of Berezovsky's two holdings plus two smaller ones. The revelation of this arrangement caused a big scandal in November 1998, but Yeltsin's annulment in 1993 of the old law on the presidency and his failure to have a new one drawn up meant that he had not violated the law. It did not become clear if his family had received dividend payments on the television company's stock.[186]

In any case, the family apparently was a passive owner because Berezovsky managed the shares in their interest. However, having gained considerable political power through his effective control of 26 percent of PRT's voting shares, Berezovsky reportedly also wanted to direct the network's advertising revenues to one of his cronies. To understand this episode as a representative part of Berezovsky's activities, it helps to examine the founding of PRT in more detail.

In Korzhakov's plausible account, the main television channels in 1994 were largely unfriendly to Yeltsin. Then Yumashev introduced Berezovsky into Kremlin circles as someone who "could swing a whole channel behind the president." Korzhakov, whose duties included the promotion of Yeltsin's public image, at once showed interest. As he recounts, "Berezovsky suggested bringing Listiev in. Who could oppose the chance to have such a famous person expressing positions sympathetic to the president's?"[187]

Vladimir Listiev, an enormously popular television talk-show host, first recommended the semiprivatization that quickly went ahead. Then, in early 1995, he was appointed PRT's first head and decided to halt all on-air advertising until the corrupt middleman agencies that supplied the ads—and often failed to pay the channel—could be cleaned up or dispensed with. The most notorious of these was Sergei Lisovsky's Premier SV agency, which, according to police information, featured leading Mafiya figures from Moscow's Solntsevo gang among its key personnel. As Klebnikov concluded from his careful 1996 investigation, Premier effectively monopolized a very lucrative market: "To buy time on any of the top five Russian TV channels, you must go through Lisovsky or an allied company."[188]

On February 20, 1995, Listiev announced the end of the monopoly. PRT, he said, needed to draw up new "ethical standards." Shortly afterward, he told his friends that Lisovsky had promptly demanded $100 million in compensatory damages. Listiev had agreed and recruited Berezovsky as the transfer agent. Berezovsky had taken the cash, but then told Lisovsky he would get it only in three months' time. On March 7, Listiev—evidently wrongly suspected of a double-cross—was gunned down by hit men.

At this point, Berezovsky asked Korzhakov to sanction Lisovsky's appointment as PRT's sole agent for its advertising.[189] Despite Korzhakov's hesitations, Berezovsky and Lisovsky got their way. Meanwhile, both men were regarded by the police as prime suspects regarding Listiev's assassination and had their offices searched.[190] Five years later, however, still no one has been charged. As of 1996, according to an official report, Lisovsky's agency had a monthly turnover of $60–80 million, of which he gave "not more than 3 percent" to Berezovsky "for his silence."[191]

We should note here that Berezovsky has largely ignored numerous public allegations and reports about his proximity to various murders or attempted murders and about his inciting others to murder. Some of these cases have concerned his enemies—namely, Gusinsky and Luzhkov—whom he knew to be angering the Kremlin in 1994–95 by opposition activities described earlier in this chapter. At that time, according to Korzhakov and Streletsky, he repeatedly incited Korzhakov to murder these two men, and also Luzhkov's adviser, the singer Iosif Kobzon (who is barred from entry into the United States because of his Mafiya connections).[192] Asked by one interviewer when Berezovsky had asked him to kill Gusinsky, Korzhakov replied: "Many times. And the expressions he used were right out of the underworld. Gusinsky had to be 'rubbed out': 'You zapped him, but now he's returned from London, and again he's working against the president.' . . . He always tried to provoke me by saying, 'I see that your outfit is pretty weak.'"[193]

Among shooting and bombing episodes, some relate to Berezovsky's car business. As Klebnikov explains, Berezovsky's car dealerships, of which Logovaz was the biggest, devised a ruthlessly efficient way of bleeding the car manufacturer Avtovaz—to their own enormous profit: "The carrot: an envelope full of cash to car executives. The stick: a bullet in the head." As mentioned earlier, Berezovsky had long used a Chechen Mafiya gang as his "protection." In 1994, however, the Solntsevo gang challenged the Chechen gang. In the ensuing shootout in central Moscow, six Chechens and four Russians were killed. Shortly after, Berezovsky himself narrowly escaped death in a related car bombing, as mentioned earlier, and one of his two banks was bombed.[194]

In the same period, Berezovsky's net worth was growing by a new order of magnitude. Having formed the All-Russian Automobile Alliance (known by the Russian acronym AVVA) in 1993, he sold bonds worth $50 million to investors, promising to pay each of them back with a car of new design. Only in 1996, however, did he begin to do this. Meanwhile, he had used the $50 million skillfully, in a time of raging inflation, and amassed $300 million worth of real estate in Moscow and St. Petersburg. He had also, among other things, bought two publications and invested in PRT.[195] By 1997, his fortune was estimated by *Forbes* magazine at $3 billion, considerably larger than that of any other Russian.

The purpose of summarizing the above episodes from Berezovsky's early years is to convey something of the texture of life among Russia's senior ruling elites. By the mid-1990s, this texture was one in which private, usually corrupt, interests had eroded any serious consideration of the national interest. Rather, most of the infighting among the country's elites focused on who could plunder the assets of the state the quickest and on the largest scale. Regarding Berezovsky's role, his sheer aggressiveness and access to the top echelons of state power suggest that many detailed examinations of this archetypical Russian oligarch and his methods of obtaining power will eventually appear.[196] Here, we round out our sketch of his modus operandi only in the most summary fashion.

In the fall of 1995, Berezovsky—along with other top oligarchs—benefited handsomely from Chubais's loans-for-shares scheme.[197] Berezovsky gained access to this bonanza by persuading Korzhakov that only his control of the richly endowed Sibneft oil company could save the crumbling finances of PRT and turn the television channel into a powerful pro-Yeltsin tool. In this way, he had his equally manipulative insider colleague, Roman Abramovich, obtain one of Russia's major energy firms for nothing.[198] Soon they took the chance to give a good job to Yeltsin's son-in-law Aleksei (formally, Leonid) Dyachenko, husband of Yeltsin's daughter Tatyana. They made him head of East Coast Petroleum, a company selling oil products from Sibneft's refinery, a position that appears to have made him rich.[199]

Although Berezovsky was to clash fiercely with Chubais several times, as we shall see, he never forgot his debt to him. On one occasion, he spoke his oft-quoted words about the oligarchs: "We are all children of Chubais," and on another he explained: "I am a product of privatization. That is why I am so close to Chubais's mentality." Later, he defended Chubais against the financier-philanthropist George Soros, who had charged Chubais with promoting "bandit capitalism." Berezovsky called the attack unfair and tactless, and noted that Chubais had managed to distribute the state's assets without incurring bloodshed. At the same time, Berezovsky called on Russian businessmen to help create a middle class. The number of people living in poverty had to be reduced "so that they don't hang us." He omitted to add that his own looting of the state's assets was helping the poverty level to rise.[200]

His widely alleged looting of the state airline Aeroflot—to the tune of hundreds of millions of dollars—has been one of the few cases to get him into serious trouble with the law that he has not been able to quickly brush aside. In the fall of 1998, when the generally "anti-oligarch" Yevgeny Primakov was prime minister, Moscow detectives raided Berezovsky's Sibneft offices and his *"kompromat* factory," which housed eavesdropping equipment they said was used to spy on Yeltsin's family. A criminal case was opened against him.[201] In reply—to pressure Yeltsin into fighting Primakov and getting the case closed—Berezovsky appears to have caused evidence of some of the financial shenanigans of Yeltsin and his family to be made public.[202] The tactic apparently worked: the Yeltsin family was alarmed; in April 1999, Primakov was fired and the case was apparently closed. Later, however, it was revived.[203]

That Berezovsky may have had numerous ways of blackmailing the Yeltsin family is not surprising. As we have seen, Korzhakov's information that he gave lavish presents to Tatyana, provided handsome jobs to her husband and also to Yeltsin's other son-in-law as the director-general of Aeroflot, and organized the oligarchs jointly to give Yeltsin $3 million in "book royalties" that he had mostly not earned, remains uncontested.[204] Beyond that, according to Korzhakov, Berezovsky—"the family's treasurer"—repeated the last exercise in 1997, but to a different end. Noting that Berezovsky "likes to pay, but not with his own money," Korzhakov says that he "scares the 'money bags' with his ties to the president and forces them to pay particular sums for particular purposes. In this way, they bought a mansion in Nice for [Tatyana] Dyachenko for 25 million francs [about $4 million]."[205] The mansion was the Château de la Garope on the Cap d'Antibes. However, it was purchased not in the name of Dyachenko, but in that of a company. Who stands behind the company is not yet clear.

A somewhat similar pattern emerges from the detailed account of a journalist who sought out an imposing mansion in Garmisch-Partenkirchen in the Bavarian Alps. The local people believed this to have been bought by Tatyana Dyachenko in the fall of 1997, but its purchase is in the name of a firm in Liechtenstein. The locals also described visits to the mansion by Dyachenko and her Russian companions.[206] It would not be surprising if the oligarchs have some connection to the purchase of this house.

Finally, as regards real estate, the same applies to the land that Yeltsin purchased in April 1995 in an exclusive district near Moscow, and to the country house of some five thousand square feet that he then built on it. According to an official document obtained by Russian journalists who carried out a careful investigation, Yeltsin bought the land through the local district council. However, he paid a so-called "normative price" of about $15,500 (80 million rubles), even though its market value was about $2 million. The journalists did not discover the cost of building the house.[207]

Of course, this was Yeltsin's private house, in contrast to the thirteen official country houses that were at his disposal during his presidency. This figure was reported by Boris Nemtsov, a senior member of the government during the time it made a complete inventory of the president's official property.[208]

Now even if the country house and the German mansion should turn out to have had nothing to do with the oligarchs, the leverage that the other items gave Berezovsky and his associates over Yeltsin was clearly substantial. That leverage gave them the confidence to call openly in spring 1996 for the presidential election to be postponed and, when that did not work, to throw their weight around in Yeltsin's election campaign as if there were few restraints.

Korzhakov recalls Berezovsky giving a lecture at this time to Korzhakov's friend Mikhail Barsukov, who ran the Main Protective Administration. "If you don't understand that we've come to power, we'll simply remove you," the oligarch admonished. "You will have to serve our money, our capital."[209] After Yeltsin's re-election and during his long illness, Berezovsky became even more explicit. During a well-known interview with the *Financial Times* on November 1, 1996, he explained how he and six other oligarchs were saving Russia by funding and organizing Yeltsin's election campaign, by co-opting Dyachenko as "the most effective channel to inform the president," by later getting Chubais appointed to run the Presidential Administration, by placing two of their own number in the government, and by meeting weekly to collaborate closely with Chubais on government policies. According to Berezovsky's grandiose imagination, the seven men even controlled about half of the Russian economy.

THE LOOTING OF YELTSIN'S RE-ELECTION WAR CHEST

What Berezovsky did not say, however, was that the election campaign had provided another fine opportunity—perhaps on the scale of "loans for shares" —to embezzle money and send it abroad. Presumably because the election law allowed each candidate to spend no more than the equivalent of $2.9 million, Berezovsky told the *Financial Times* interviewer that the oligarchs jointly had given Yeltsin "about $3 million." Apparently, he overlooked the direct inference that either no one else in Russia contributed anything at all or the campaign had broken the law.

However, future historians will have to try to determine three key figures: how much money flowed into Yeltsin's campaign, how much of it was spent on his election expenses, and how much was embezzled by the individuals running or assisting the campaign. The first figure was very large—probably well over a billion dollars—because contributions were required from not only the oligarchs and their companies, but also all the bodies, as we saw earlier, to which Yeltsin granted financial and other privileges, mostly in 1993–94: among others, Gazprom; Aeroflot; the National Sports Foundation; the arms export agency Rosvooruzhenie; the Russian Orthodox Church; the Afghan War veterans' organizations; the presidential property agency run by Pavel Borodin; and perhaps the investment company FIMACO in the Channel Islands, which secretly speculated with state budget funds in 1996 and, when this was revealed later, greatly angered the IMF.[210] Even Korzhakov was expected to raise funds. In December 1995, he negotiated in Milan with an American, Roger Tamraz, who wanted to gain Russian support for a proposed oil pipeline through Central Asia. Reportedly, Korzhakov offered to obtain this in return for a donation of $100 million to Yeltsin's campaign.[211]

Here we should note two important points. First, some big contributors used the campaign fund for money laundering.[212] Second, it is not clear how much of their *own* money companies like Gazprom contributed. An unchallenged press report based on leaked documents revealed that in 1995–96, Gazprom, working closely with the National Reserve Bank, operated complex laundering schemes to obtain government cash from the Ministry of Finance. In two of these, sums of about $20 million and $200 million became available to Gazprom for financing Chernomyrdin's political party and Yeltsin's re-election.[213]

On April 16, 1996, Chernomyrdin and Korzhakov had the previously mentioned six-hour chat that the latter secretly recorded and then—even though parts of it reflect badly on him—printed in his book. At one point they turn to discussing Yeltsin's new campaign team, the leadership of which had been switched a month earlier from Soskovets to Chubais. Chernomyrdin and the banker Aleksandr Smolensky had the job of handling the money. During the chat, Chernomyrdin tells Korzhakov that he is getting things organized and that, because "colossal sums are flowing," all documents will be checked and analyzed. Yet there are problems with the people on the team: "They're such an unreliable lot—it would be better to get rid of these swine at once. . . . Now even Smolensky has started to worry. . . . He doesn't know where the money is going." Korzhakov agrees, commenting that Chubais decides which programs to adopt and how much to pay for each. Chernomyrdin: "And they cost four million, five, seven, fifteen. . . . Big sums. You can do a lot with 200 million, and it's all in hard foreign cash [U.S. dollars]." Korzhakov: "A lot of it can get stolen." Chernomyrdin: "Whatever happens, they'll steal; the question is: how much?"[214]

With this and other evidence in hand, Korzhakov and his associate Streletsky now launched an investigation. On June 10, they were ready to escalate it, and Korzhakov went to tell Yeltsin how corrupt and chaotic his campaign team had become. Yeltsin acceded to his request that all the campaign's financial records and documents be immediately turned over to Korzhakov for investigation and safe keeping. On Korzhakov's written request Yeltsin wrote a note by hand: "To V. S. Chernomyrdin and A. P. Smolensky. Hand over everything. 10/VI. (signature) B. N. Yeltsin." He underlined the word "everything" four times. He also instructed Korzhakov: "Investigate, then report back."[215]

On the evening of June 18, as Streletsky recounts, his men surreptitiously opened the campaign's safe and found $1.5 million in cash, money transfer forms, and other financial documents that showed "the true expenditures of the campaign. For example, on May 23 over 300 million dollars was disbursed for various purposes." Regarding money sent abroad, the documents indicated that campaign officials dispatched, "at a minimum," $115 million.

This scam was "extremely simple: using documents with made-up information, they transfer it [the money] abroad to the accounts of particular firms, then it is divided up and transferred to their personal accounts." In his book, Streletsky reproduces facsimile copies of six typical forms that transferred a total of $28 million during the week of May 24–30.[216] Four of them are for "graphic printing services," two for "advertising services." All are in suspiciously round figures—either $4 million or $5 million.

In each case, the money followed a circuitous route, crossing the Atlantic twice: from a Moscow bank (Oneksim, Menatep, and Alfa were used); to the Republican Bank of New York; to Aizkraukles Bank in Riga, Latvia. At this point, the instructions were to put it in an account of a mysterious firm, "Atlanta-Direct," incorporated in Delaware. The instructions trail then ends—though not, presumably, the passage of the money. Perhaps it crossed the Atlantic a third time—to land in Atlanta or Delaware and then be transferred to the oligarchs' personal accounts? Whatever the truth on this score, Streletsky reasonably dismisses the theoretical possibility that the payments were for genuine campaign expenses.

Some of the documents are campaign accounts. One of them lists ninety-five individuals, media outlets, and political organizations, with the sums to be paid to each. By June 6, 1996, 741,734 million rubles (roughly $148,347,000) had been paid out—some fifty-one times the legal maximum. And further hefty payments had been contracted for.[217] Also, there was one further, climactic month of the campaign still to go, which certainly incurred heavy additional expenses. Published as well were Chubais's credit card statements—showing that between mid-April and early August 1996, he received payments of $277,555 —and a letter to Yeltsin from Duma deputies asking that Chubais be investigated for failing to pay tax on this income.[218]

At about the same time, Barsukov reported to Yeltsin on Gusinsky's financial activities in the campaign. Gusinsky was working with Smolensky, "whose bank has been actively investing state budget money, so that it can give some of the profits to the president's campaign fund. Some of the income has been ending up in accounts of firms belonging to Gusinsky. According to various estimates, and what Gusinsky himself has said, before he flew to Spain . . . his personal 'cut' totaled 3–5 million dollars."[219] Here we should note, first, that this sum exceeds the total that Berezovsky said his whole group had donated and, second, that Barsukov appears to condemn Gusinsky's, but not Smolensky's, allegedly illegal use of government cash to benefit Yeltsin. Apparently, Yeltsin sanctioned such use.

Finally, and not surprisingly, the man who appears to have profited the most from the campaign's feeding trough was Berezovsky. According to Korzhakov's uncontested testimony, he received $169 million from the campaign to use for PRT programming. But "according to my information," says Korzhakov, "PRT received only $32 million. Where's the rest?" The remaining $137 million could "only have been stolen. . . . The Procuracy has this information."[220]

How much money, then, was collected by Yeltsin's campaign, how much was spent on the campaign, and how much was embezzled? Chernomyrdin says that $200 million had been collected by mid-April; Streletsky that $300 million was disbursed on May 23 alone; and $115 million, at a minimum, was sent abroad, all of it apparently stolen. From these figures, readers must form their own impressions. However, a careful study of leaked campaign documents that was published later showed that the oligarchs had actually received from the campaign (through complex schemes described by the study's researchers) monetary benefits amounting to no less than $6.3 billion. According to the study, the architects of the most brilliant schemes were a junior oligarch, Aleksandr Mamut, head of Project Financing Company; and Mikhail Kasyanov, a senior Finance Ministry official who became Russia's prime minister in 2000.[221]

OTHER OLIGARCHS

Among the oligarchs, we have focused mainly on Berezovsky—he is outspoken, attracts attention, and has been the most politically powerful of them. However, solid material of a largely similar nature can be assembled on most of the other twenty-five to thirty men who can reasonably be called senior oligarchs. Here we will mention only three.

Smolensky, an Austrian citizen, has been less visible and flamboyant, but has long been close to key politicians.[222] Roman Abramovich, born in 1966 and a close associate of Berezovsky, shuns publicity and remained wholly in the shadows until 1998, even though he has exploited political openings with skill.[223] Anatoly Chubais, long a favorite in the West, received an unflattering portrait from one of this work's authors, who noted his organizational skills, economic dogmatism, authoritarian ways, dubious integrity about money, and his propensity to lie his way out of trouble.[224] In 1998, Chubais became a full-blown oligarch when he assumed leadership of Russia's national electricity grid.

THE EAGER LOSER: GENNADI ZYUGANOV AND HIS ARCHAIC QUASI-POPULISM

Even if the oligarchs had not thrown the entire weight of their power behind Yeltsin, or if the Kremlin had not succeeded in its relentless efforts to coerce or intimidate the undecided majority, Yeltsin and his supporters still had a unique asset on their side: a covert, reluctant, but still real advocate of the president's reelection—none other than the leading opposition candidate, Gennadi Andreyevich Zyuganov.

Zyuganov's background and creed warrant particular attention, given the fact that since 1993 he has been a major Russian leader, standing at the helm of the opposition majority and running ahead of most other politicians in opinion polls.

Born in 1944 in a small village of the Orel region, Zyuganov is a typical first-generation urbanite from Russia's agrarian heartland, with a heavily pronounced communitarian-populist outlook. This does not mean, however, that his mindset was rigidly determined by this provenance, which has produced politicians of diverse stripes. His urban affiliations were of primary importance; of these, we should note his connection, first, with the intelligence community, which dated back to his military service in East Germany and, second, with the agricultural lobby and the village writers' group in the pre-perestroika and early Gorbachev periods. He shared Gorbachev's grim and fatalistic view about the downside of progress—the fear of an impending environmental disaster and misgivings about economic growth. These views were reinforced by quite legitimate and sincere bitterness about Stalin's crushing assault on the peasants that resulted in the depopulation of the countryside.

An ardent believer in the tenets of the 1985 Gorbachev-Ligachev quasi-populist platform, Zyuganov became severely alienated by the policies of Aleksandr Yakovlev, which represented a competing stream of populism that embraced a wholesale dissolution of Russia's uniqueness in the bright new world order under American hegemony. Zyuganov, already a prominent but faceless functionary of the Russian Communist Party, acquired some name recognition in 1991 with his bitter invectives against Yakovlev, and then as a cosigner of the "A Call to the People," the harbinger of the August coup that we discussed in chapter 4. He spent his last formative period before entering big-time politics as an associate of Aleksei Podberezkin, a man with close ties to Russian intelligence organizations and a distinguished Americanologist. Zyuganov drafted papers for Podberezkin's secretive multipurpose intelligence and business venture, the RAU Corporation, whose activity we examined in chapter 6.

Zyuganov's picture of the world, and of Russia's place in it, is presented in a succession of his books and one doctoral dissertation; however, these works mostly repeat themselves, with only minor variations.[225] The doctrine of "Zyuganovism" (a term used by Joan Urban and Valery Solovei, who, like Robert Otto, have extensively analyzed this peculiar ideology) can be easily disassembled into autonomous elements reflecting the ideas of different circles in which Zyuganov moved at earlier stages of his career.[226]

There is a reclusive, backward-looking, rhetorical nationalism in Zyuganov's writings, congenial to the "village prose" writers, but fluctuating widely between assertions of ethnic exclusivity and vague talk about Russia as a supra-ethnic civilization of its own. There is geopolitics, the Byzantine creed of parts of the security establishment, which have locked themselves in an imaginary fortress besieged by alien and incomprehensible forces. Finally, there is the neo-Malthusian idea of a worldwide zero-sum fight for scarce resources, intertwined with a pervasive fear of an impending global catastrophe. This latter set of beliefs originates in the millenarian doomsday fears that permeated the early Gorbachev period and reveals Zyuganovism as nothing more than an extremist variation of a widespread mode of thinking about the world that has been highly influential in the late Soviet and post-Soviet establishment; such thinking has been personified by, among others, the former foreign minister and prime minister Yevgeny Primakov, a member of the Club of Rome since 1986.[227]

Judging by his books, Zyuganov is anxious to find intellectual allies both in Russia and abroad. But the list of "classics" he mentions in deferential ways is rather unorthodox for the leader of a self-described Communist Party. In the Russian cultural tradition, the objects of his fascination include Filofei of Pskov, the author of the famous dictum, "Moscow Is the Third Rome"; Count Uvarov, Nicholas I's ideologist, notorious for his formula "Autocracy, Orthodoxy, Popular Spirit"; conservative-populist thinkers Lavrov and Mikhailovsky; the grim crusader for Russian uniqueness, Nikolai Danilevsky; the court theologian Konstantin Pobedonostsev, renowned for his advice to Alexander III to "freeze Russia"; the mystical-autocratic brand of Russian philosophy personified by Konstantin Leontiev and Ivan Ilyin; and a fashionable theorist of ethnopsychological exclusivity, Lev Gumilev.[228]

Among Western authors, Zyuganov cites with much fascination Karl Haushofer and Halford Mackinder, Oswald Spengler and Arnold Toynbee, Samuel

Huntington, and Lyndon LaRouche. In his 1996 book, a summary of Hunting-ton goes on for four pages, even though Zyuganov hurries to distance himself somewhat from the controversial political scientist by admitting, in the muddy jargon of Soviet agitprop, that "under certain conditions the existing contradic-tions can be overcome in a nonconfrontational way."[229]

This simple enumeration of Zyuganov's intellectual allies suffices to show that the major alternative to Yeltsin's oligarchical regime in the 1996 elections was not a progressive force, but one that was profoundly conservative and, in many ways, neomedieval. Zyuganov has never paid more than lip service to tra-ditional leftist slogans, and he certainly does not consider any of the leftist politicians, intellectuals, or labor movements worldwide as potential allies of the Russian opposition; indeed, these forces are hidden from him in the impercep-tible "black boxes" of alien and thoroughly hostile civilizations that surround Russia. Moreover, he even harbors a subliminal mistrust for the Western left, which—not unlike the Russian dissidents and democrats—is prone to under-mine the autarkic cohesion of "civilizations" and the balance of power that is the ultimate paradigm of Zyuganov's foreign policy mindset.[230] Viewed in such a way, the leaders of the Christian Right and politicians like Patrick Buchanan, as we suggested in chapter 6, are closer analogues to Zyuganov than any of the associations or parties of the American left.

In the Soviet past, Zyuganov's next-to-ideal society is postwar Stalinism. These were years replete with campaigns of hatred and obscurantism, mysteri-ous murders, and violent harassment of the intelligentsia and the Jews. In char-acteristically Aesopian language, Zyuganov credits the late Stalin era, in fact, for the transformation of Soviet Communism from a revolutionary-international-ist to a hard-line imperialist ideology, aligned with the statist traditions of the Orthodox Church. (This was the time when the Moscow authorities had just shut down the Socialist Third International and downgraded the anticapitalist movements worldwide from Soviet allies in the struggle for a common cause to national subdivisions of the Soviet intelligence empire.) In no uncertain terms, Zyuganov reveals himself as a neo-Stalinist; understandably, though, his neo-Stalinism is not looking forward to conquering the world but, rather, looking backward in a profoundly pessimistic and defeatist way to the security of an insulated and self-sufficient peasant community.

However scary and seemingly confrontational in its rhetoric, Zyuganovism is not threatening in any way to the existing distribution of forces worldwide—in fact, it is thoroughly harmless because its scope for maneuver is remarkably limited. A communist party under different leadership—perhaps more moder-ate in rhetoric, shunning both nationalist and quasi-communist pageantry, but eager and skillful enough to build alliances with co-thinkers across "civiliza-tional" borders—might have had more impact on the global balance of forces. Instead, in the crucial struggle to get the international public to condemn Yelt-sin's rule, a struggle that in an increasingly globalized milieu has been one of the major forums in the presidential contests of 1996 and 2000, Zyuganov disarmed himself by his autarkic approach to national problems.

That is not to say that he gave up all attempts to win over foreign constituencies, but he tried to do so in an inept and self-defeating way. Instead of engaging the international left, he zealously courted the multinational corporate establishment at the January 1996 Davos Forum, an obsession that betrayed his lack of confidence in the power of the ballot box. When prompted to write an article for the *New York Times,* rather than reaching out to influential American audiences across the spectrum by addressing international issues of concern to both sides, he wasted this rare opportunity by indulging in geopolitical ruminations and pathetic muscle-flexing that smacked of an adolescent inferiority complex.[231]

Likewise, despite his rhetorical sympathies for the Third World, he never gave support to its demands for a fair share of the global economic pie. On the contrary, his 1996 book contains an admonition to the developing countries *never even to try* to achieve the living standards of the leading industrial nations:

> The path of development that had been taken by rich Western countries, whose inhabitants constitute the "golden billion" of the super-affluent consumers, is unacceptable and unfeasible for the rest (that is, for the overwhelming majority) of the world. Attempts to move along this path may aggravate the situation and speed up the denouement, because the biosphere of the Earth will simply not sustain this kind of pressure from energy and technology.[232]

It is difficult to regard as anything but neoconservative fantasy the belief that poorer countries would voluntarily abandon their aspirations to catch up with the developed world in terms of production. Although the term preferred by Zyuganovites is "sustainable development," in its essence, Zyuganovism is a plea for arrested development.

Equally unrealistic is Zyuganov's neo-Stalinist belief that a country like Russia can be effectively insulated from outside influences. While denying that he advocates "economic autarchy," Zyuganov writes, "It is extremely important for Russia to avoid integrating itself too much into 'the world economic system' and 'the international division of labor,' because this can create a dangerous dependence on external factors." Russia's human and natural resources "give us a unique possibility to achieve the maximum of economic autonomy . . . and allow us, so to speak, to 'avoid involvement' in the arena of today's main social-economic divide [between rich and poor countries]."[233]

In this sense, Zyuganov's mirage of economic autarky is a striking parallel to the utopian faith in the global harmony of interests characteristic of the early Russian democrats, and it is just as impractical. However, unlike the democrats' utopianism, Zyuganov's is an ideology of Brezhnev-style decline and stagnation. It is one of the utmost expressions of the Russian tragedy that in 1996, amidst an economic collapse that surpassed the American Great Depression and summoned an agenda for Russia's revival and growth along the lines of

Roosevelt's New Deal,[234] the second round of Russia's presidential race came down to a choice between continuing the destruction and returning to the stagnation that had provoked it.

One can only wonder how someone as imbued with historical pessimism and archaism as Zyuganov could propel himself to the leadership of the self-described Russian left, and what kind of appeal this particularistic vision of humanity could have for the only mass-based political party in Russia, a nation whose historical identity and self-esteem had hinged on its ability to absorb and integrate more than a hundred dissimilar languages and cultures. To be sure, few tenets of Zyuganov's idiosyncratic worldview have found their place in the CPRF's official doctrine. Indeed, some of them are hardly compatible either with the Marxist conceptual core or with the incipient elements of modern social reformism in the party's program. Within the CPRF leadership, Zyuganov and a reclusive crew of his fellow thinkers coexist with people of different mindsets, such as the social-reformist wing represented by Gennadi Seleznev and Valentin Kuptsov, a revolutionary-populist branch typified by Tengiz Avaliani, the Leninist Platform of Richard Kosolapov, and the statist-dirigiste nationalism of Viktor Ilyukhin, to name but a few. Although the Zyuganovites prudently have not constituted themselves as a faction and therefore have not registered their supporters, one may doubt whether their neo-Malthusian, isolationist, and almost clerical outlook commands more than a handful of enthusiasts among the rank and file of the party.

It is highly plausible that Zyuganov's domination of the CPRF owes nothing to his ideology and a lot to extraneous factors. In 1991–92, he was singled out among the communist leaders and put in the limelight by the Kremlin-loyal media, apparently because his sectarian and extravagant views simplified the task of demonizing the left as a whole. His appearances at high-profile sessions of extremist ethnic-nationalist groups, such as Aleksandr Sterligov's Russian National Assembly, fit neatly into the familiar script about an evil red-brown coalition. While radical Yeltsinists and freemarketeers were eager to inflate Zyuganov as an easier target than the more enlightened and popular democratic leftists, the rising cohorts of the nomenklatura privatizers, fearing both foreign competition and popular revolt, appreciated his eagerness to put ethnicity above class politics. His recurrent overtures to "nationally conscious entrepreneurs," as well as his gloomy preachings about the looming exhaustion of the world's supply of raw materials, did not go unrewarded: a steady flow of private and corporate funds from extractive industries, facilitated by Sterligov's and RAU's proxy financial ventures, kept Zyuganov in the public eye during the public hearings in the Constitutional Court that led to the lifting of Yeltsin's ban on the Communist Party.

Meanwhile, Zyuganov returned their favors in December 1992, laboring hard behind the scenes of the Congress of People's Deputies to muster support among the disoriented and demoralized Communist and Agrarian deputies for

Chernomyrdin's candidacy as prime minister. Then he used the breathing space created by the Yeltsin-Chernomyrdin unstable equilibrium and the generous funding from the new establishment to resurrect the Russian Communist Party (RCP). His cash-starved comrades had neither the guts nor the resources to oppose his leadership. The CPRF's legal status as the heir of the banned RCP enabled Zyuganov to claim some of its vast property, while the inordinate attention to him on the part of the widely distrusted pro-Kremlin media helped him to eclipse other potential leaders of the communist and socialist camp, such as Aman Tuleyev, Viktor Tyulkin, Aleksei Prigarin, and Lyudmila Vartazarova.[235]

The presence of Zyuganov's nomenklatura-style Communist Party in the opposition camp virtually guaranteed the continued rift within the opposition along social, cultural, and ideological lines that manifested itself at crucial turning points. It was Zyuganov's abrupt withdrawal of his support from the cause of the democratic nationalists in the Russian White House in October 1993 that immobilized the only mass-scale opposition movement, the National Salvation Front, and thus left the parliament prey to the tank assault. By knocking out his democratic fellow travelers, the October coup enabled Zyuganov to emerge as the uncontested leader of the leftist and nationalist anti-Yeltsin forces.

Still, it would be unfair to treat Zyuganov as a completely manipulable entity. Once his party got into the Duma and gained a momentum of its own, Zyuganov often showed himself a sophisticated and determined opponent of the regime (even though he did this by following not his congenital caution but, rather, the impetus from radicalized members of his faction). He was one of only two (together with Yavlinsky) out of eight parliamentary leaders to snub Yeltsin's 1994 agreement on accord, and he showed remarkable flexibility and acumen by spearheading the CPRF's leftward turn in the fall of 1994, a shift that propelled his party to the leadership, alongside Yabloko, of the nationwide campaign against the Chechnya war and earned it first place in the 1995 Duma elections.

If Zyuganov had run in the presidential race as the leader of the traditional left—on either his party's platform or that of a bloc of communist and socialist organizations, rather than under his personal conservative-nationalist agenda—then, in the wake of the Chechnya debacle and the left's gains in the Duma vote, the odds would have been markedly in his favor. Yet such a prospect spelled trouble for the Kremlin, as well as for the reclusive clique of ethnocultural populists, psychics, and intelligence operatives surrounding Zyuganov and the raw materials' magnates who had invested in his political and academic career. His presidential campaign was launched with much haste by Podberezkin's Spiritual Heritage group, well before the party's cumbersome apparatus got moving—most probably to pre-empt the CPRF's influence on Zyuganov's electoral agenda or even the nomination of alternative candidates from within the party. The campaign's coalition-building was limited to pompous assemblies and collective appeals signed by conservative, ethnocratic, religious, and monarchical organizations, most of which had no nationwide standing and some of which later turned out to exist primarily on paper. Foremost among Zyuganov's supporters were notorious losers from the conservative camp, such as ex–vice president Rutskoi and ex–Soviet prime minister Nikolai Ryzhkov, and leaders of special-interest lobbies, such as the Agrarian Party. No attempt was made to reach out to more influential forces on the left, such as the radical part of Yabloko and Svyatoslav Fyodorov's Party of Labor Self-Management—presumably because, being a new vintage of democrats and internationalists, these parties were suspected by Podberezkin to be agents of an alien civilization.

These sectarian tactics, suitable for a would-be opposition primary, were entirely misplaced in the run-up to a nationwide election. As mentioned earlier, they prompted Sergei Baburin, one of Zyuganov's few democratic-nationalist fellow travelers in the presidential campaign, to remark appositely afterward that the Zyuganovites "keep fighting not for real power in the country, but rather for their leadership in the opposition camp."[236]

What was behind this seemingly counterrational behavior? It is plausible that Zyuganov and Podberezkin took as a given that the majority of voters would support anyone who acted and sounded anti-Yeltsin, so all they needed to do in the campaign was to surpass all other contenders for that role. At the same time, they never fully placed their trust in the ballot box and viewed the Kremlin's behind-the-scenes power game as the determinant variable in the equation. The intricate maneuvers of the intelligence cabal in Yeltsin's inner circle and the accurate belief that the election might easily be canceled because Korzhakov's group and Chernomyrdin favored it certainly helped to substantiate this perception. Until very late in the game, some of Zyuganov's strategists were in fact bargaining with Korzhakov about a postponement of the election, something that Korzhakov wanted the communists, not Yeltsin, to propose. Korzhakov reports: "I conducted negotiations with the communists. They, too, agreed to the postponement." As we shall see, however, Yeltsin could not persuade his cabinet to implement a postponement.[237]

Other Zyuganov strategists speculated whether the CPRF leader might be allowed to win at the polls if he displayed moderation and struck a last-minute deal with the current ruler, as Yeltsin did in April 1991. Thus they shared the belief of the demoralized majority that any radical or revolutionary jolt from the elections had been ruled out in advance. This belief manifested itself in the paradoxical results of opinion polls, which showed from the start a belief in Yeltsin's imminent victory, even as the majority of respondents expressed their preference for Zyuganov.

Much to the Kremlin's benefit, Zyuganov's fatalistic belief that he would lose was atmospherically transmitted to his actual and potential voters and acted as self-fulfilling prophecy, steadily decreasing the level of his active support. In Russia, as elsewhere, people do not like to identify with self-designated losers, so many of Yeltsin's dyed-in-the-wool enemies simply turned their backs on pollsters and the ballot box. This is the most plausible explanation for the fact that Yeltsin, who had registered a meager 6 percent of support in January polls, overtook Zyuganov among respondents as the preferable candidate by the end of April in a would-be runoff, and by mid-May in the first round. From this time on, Zyuganov's campaign stalled. His advisers publicly engaged in soul-searching and complaining about the people's unresponsiveness, while Aleksei Podberezkin, the mastermind of the game, instructed the Communists to "be morally prepared for a defeat" two weeks before the first round.[238]

With the benefit of hindsight, we note that the Yeltsin campaign strategists took advantage in the most skillful ways of Zyuganov and his associates' initial naïveté and subsequent defeatism. The Yeltsin camp exploited Zyuganov's initial overconfidence about not needing to cooperate with other opposition candidates by co-opting or neutralizing them itself. Also, by creating suspense about whether the election would be held at all, it enticed Zyuganov into conciliatory talk and self-defeating maneuvers that made it seem as if he were selling out to Yeltsin for future cabinet portfolios. Finally, the Kremlin managed to isolate Zyuganov from the constituencies beyond the hard core of his followers and forced him to run as a lone wolf—a crucial outcome for the Kremlin because his continued participation in the game gave some legitimacy to its rigged outcome. After all, they could be sure that Zyuganov would not make a successful fuss about fraud on the Kremlin's part and would not be able to engage Western observers across the "civilizational" barriers that he himself had constructed.

THE UPHILL BATTLE FOR A "THIRD FORCE"

One of the major worries of all Yeltsin's supporters in the first three months of 1996 was the efforts of Yavlinsky, Lebed, and the eye surgeon Svyatoslav Fyodorov to stitch together a political "third force." This would rally forces across quite a wide section of the political spectrum not occupied by the Kremlin-loyal groups, the communists, and the nationalists. However, the dirty tricks department of the Yeltsin campaign worked intensively to derail the embryonic third force.

One of the evil geniuses of this department was the brilliant scholar and publicist Gleb Pavlovsky, who after the election talked and wrote about his sins at some length. Summarizing these sources, Julia Wishnevsky concludes that Pavlovsky was "busy inventing deliberate lies aimed at blackening Yeltsin's rivals."[239] Regarding the third force, a favorite trick of the Yeltsin camp was to put out phony opinion polls to confuse the opponents. One Yeltsinite was frank about this when he said: "None of these polls are accurate. . . . We have put them out to influence Yavlinsky and Lebed. They may still decide to continue their own campaigns, but we're confident now that at least they won't combine into a third-force coalition that could knock the President out of the box in the . . . first round . . . ."[240]

THE STOLEN VICTORY

The most surprising and perhaps the only positive fact about the 1996 election was that it took place on time. In September 1993, Yeltsin had felt compelled to promise Russians and his foreign audience an early presidential election to be held in June 1994—though he soon broke that promise. In 1996, he stood for re-election, but as late as forty days before the first round, Korzhakov publicly suggested that the vote be postponed.[241] Not until all the major polls registered Yeltsin ahead of all other contenders was it certain that the election would take place as scheduled. Even after that, few observers believed that Yeltsin was ready to accept an adverse outcome if the government-funded pollsters turned out to be wrong. The headline of the previously mentioned article by the influential analyst Lilia Shevtsova—"Yeltsin Will Stay, Even If He Is Defeated"—caused no dispute, because it captured the prevailing mood of resignation in the country.[242] Unlike in 1993, there was no force in sight (except, perhaps, the opinion of Western creditors and investors—but certainly no force to speak of within Russia) that would have been able to compel Yeltsin to hold the election on time if he had not been prepared to accept the possibility of defeat.

There is little doubt that Yeltsin and his court would not have taken the risk unless they had powerful weapons that virtually guaranteed their victory. For instance, the hard-line faction in Yeltsin's entourage, which was widely held responsible for the Chechnya ordeal and had largely alienated Yeltsin's Western patrons, the media, and the financial elite, was far from sure about Yeltsin's chances for success. On February 27, Oleg Soskovets, who was briefly in charge of Yeltsin's re-election campaign until the reemergence of Chubais, told his American advisers: "One of your tasks is to advise us, a month from the election, about whether we should call it off if you determine that we're going to lose."[243]

By March, Soskovets and Korzhakov had persuaded Yeltsin to postpone the election, shut down the Duma, and ban the CPRF. At the time, a few sketchy articles in the opposition press reported this, along with the news that Yeltsin had then been prevented from executing his plan. Minister of Internal Affairs Anatoly Kulikov had said that if the plan went ahead he could not guarantee public order or the loyalty of his own police and troops. Three years later, Kulikov gave a vivid, detailed, two-thousand-word account of what happened, which none of the participants has questioned.[244]

To summarize: On March 17, Yeltsin summoned individually the ministers who would have to carry out his orders. Kulikov found the president "in a fired-up, self-confident mood." With reference to the Duma's renunciation two days before of the agreement that dismembered the USSR, Yeltsin declared: "'I've taken the decision to dissolve the Duma, because it's exceeded its powers. . . . I need two years.' (He repeated several times: 'I need two years.') 'It's necessary to postpone the election, we must ban the Communist Party, and I've taken this decision. This afternoon, you'll get the decree.'"[245]

Kulikov reacted with cautiously expressed skepticism and said he would think it all through and report back with "my suggestions" at 5 P.M. He believed that "society would react extremely negatively. We knew the political moods of the citizens. At the time the prestige of the Communist Party was rather high, and I, frankly speaking, was simply afraid of a social explosion in the country." Compared to October 1993, "popular trust in the president was completely different."

Kulikov went to consult with Prosecutor General Yuri Skuratov and Constitutional Court Chairman Vladimir Tumanov about questions of legality. Tumanov quickly revealed Yeltsin's method: "The president told me that Kulikov had agreed, Barsukov had agreed, and the prosecutor general had agreed. How could I tell him that his plan was impermissible?" Kulikov's comment: "It turned out, as was later confirmed, that everyone who saw the president was told by him that the others had agreed."

Yeltsin's capacity to tell big lies became clear early in his rule. Sometimes they were fairly harmless, as when he claimed to have personally written the text of the famous Decree No. 1400 of September 1993 that dissolved the parliament.[246] But this time, his lies were aggressively manipulative and came close to causing tumult and, potentially, civil war.

At five o'clock, the three men told an angry Yeltsin why they advised against his plan. Yeltsin interrupted Kulikov with the words, "I'm dissatisfied with you, minister. The decree is coming, go and get ready to carry it out."

On leaving, they met Ilyushin and the other aides who were drafting the decree. Kulikov repeated his speech and implored them to halt their work. They, too, had been reassured by Yeltsin that Kulikov and the other ministers had agreed to the plan.

It then turned out that neither Chernomyrdin nor Defense Minister Grachev knew anything about Yeltsin's intentions. Kulikov spoke with both of them and explained his position.

At 6 A.M. the next day, March 18, a glowering Yeltsin conducted a meeting of selected officials in the style of an autocratic principal handling naughty schoolboys. He was especially rude to Kulikov, who felt sure he was about to be fired. It turned out that the plan included arresting the members of the CPRF's Central Committee, and that the Moscow MVD had lined up police and troop units totaling sixteen thousand men, but needed ten to twelve thousand more. Again Kulikov led the opposition, and again Yeltsin refused to budge: "Yes, of course they must be dissolved. I need two more years."

However, at 8 A.M., the Duma, which had been sealed shut, was reopened. Thanks to Kulikov, Yeltsin had at last seen sense. Without him, it probably would have been different. Contrary to all the wishful thinking in the West about Russian democracy, "Tsar Boris" had no qualms about throwing the constitution out the window—something that not even the enemies of his rival Zyuganov would seriously charge against the Communist leader. Even now, many in the Yeltsin camp did not give up their efforts to violate democracy. On April 16, Korzhakov conspired at length with Chernomyrdin to this end.[247]

And on April 27, when Yeltsin had already caught up with Zyuganov in the government-funded opinion polls, a group of thirteen business tycoons, including most of the participants in the Davos Pact with Chubais, produced an open letter calling for a deal between Yeltsin and the Communists, which tacitly implied canceling the elections. The letter was reprinted in full by all the major newspapers, indicating a level of attention unmatched even by Yeltsin decrees and bringing to mind the Soviet media's obligation to publish in full the CPSU's resolutions. As bluntly explained by one of its signatories, Boris Berezovsky, the Yeltsin-Zyuganov contest concerned a choice between two socioeconomic systems, and "[a] question like this cannot be decided by voting; it can be decided only by civil war."[248] Throughout the entire campaign, this was the most unabashed call for violence if the Communists were to win and attempt to implement their program. Berezovsky apparently forgot that seventy years earlier a civil war had been fought on this issue, and it ended badly for Russia's semi-medieval oligarchy—as well as for the rest of the country.

As it happened, however, the new oligarchy's supreme arbiter, Boris Yeltsin, opted for the ballot box instead of the heavy artillery. For the first time in Russia's millennial history, the sitting head of state was putting his fate in the hands of the public. Thus, as compared with 1993 and 1995, when relatively free elections were held for a relatively inconsequential parliament, Russia in 1996 passed a more stringent test regarding minimal democratic legitimacy. This miraculous achievement predictably obscured the fact that the presidential campaign was widely seen in Russia (though not in the West) as neither free nor fair, and therefore did little to reinvigorate the much-discredited notion of democracy, or to bolster the already shaky legitimacy of the political system.

The race was marked by spectacular violations of the law on the part of the incumbent. First, even according to Yeltsin's campaign staff, the expenses of his campaign ran about $100 million, thirty times above the legal spending limit of $2.9 million.[249] As we saw earlier, the real expenses probably surpassed $100 million by a wide margin. Second, Yeltsin opened wide the coffers of the state budget for an aggressive clearance sale of government favors and services. On April 1, he decreed a pension raise for retired bureaucrats, and on April 17 for the rest of the country's pensioners; on April 16, he offered tax breaks and a cash infusion for the numerous institutions of the Academy of Sciences, where his support had been at a very low ebb; on May 10, a presidential decree granted extra funds for military industries; on June 8, he ordered a raise in benefits for single mothers and large families; on June 10, another decree extended government funding to garden owners and small-scale farmers. In addition, most of Yeltsin's campaign trips to the provinces were marked by the granting of government credits and tax breaks, and by outright giveaways of money. Thus, facing a disgruntled audience in Yaroslavl, Yeltsin promised $2 million for a military college, $700,000 for Afghan War veterans, $20,000 for a Muslim cultural center, and $10,000 for an Orthodox convent.[250] In another case, at the request of a miner, Yeltsin ordered his escorts to provide him with a brand new car as a gift.

This lavish spending was intended to make clear which side in the electoral contest controlled the nation's resources and was therefore able to deliver the goods. It made a magic impression on average citizens, most of whom had been driven to misery by the invisible hand of the Russian-style free market. As estimated by *The Economist,* this profligacy cost the Russian Treasury some $10 billion, a sum equal to the three-year IMF loan given in March 1996 to plug the gaping holes in the state budget. This figure was also almost twice as much as outstanding wage arrears, which, despite Yeltsin's generous promises, totaled $5.8 billion in the last week of the campaign.[251] Evidently, his campaign manager, Anatoly Chubais, who had won admiration in the West as a crusader for fiscal austerity amid the greatest depression in modern world history, had no second thoughts about digging into the budget to rescue his and his confederates' political and financial fortunes.[252] The better-informed minority of Russians could reach their own conclusions as to how far the privatization of the Treasury had progressed under the rule of the freemarketeers. Not only did this aggressive giveaway dwarf the promises of all the other contenders, it also sowed desperation about the chances of any of them to renationalize or reprivatize the expropriated national resources without a bloody fight. In a pathetic twist, the parliament, supposedly dominated by the opposition, voted on the eve of the first round to support the transfer of $1 billion from the Central Bank to the Treasury in order to help pay for Yeltsin's promises.[253]

Besides the Treasury funds, the most powerful weapon in Yeltsin's hands was the electronic media. All of Russia's television channels were either owned or funded by financial magnates who owed their fortunes to their privileged access to the state budget; their fear and greed made them the most zealous activists at Yeltsin's campaign headquarters. Thus the director of the Gusinsky-owned "Independent TV" (NTV), Igor Malashenko, the proud name of his company notwithstanding, joined Yeltsin's campaign team as a full member.

The brazen violations of the law in the television coverage of the campaign were summarized in a well-documented report by the European Institute for the Media. According to the report, between May 6 and July 3, the three nationwide television channels allocated 53 percent of their prime-time coverage to candidate Yeltsin, compared to 18 percent to Zyuganov and 11 percent to all other candidates combined. Within the overall coverage, there were 492 more positive than negative comments about Yeltsin. For Zyuganov, the picture was the reverse: he was mentioned 313 more times in a negative than in a positive context. The Yeltsin camp did not even feel the need to distance itself from this government-orchestrated campaign of defamation. Valery Kucher, the director of the president's Department of Information and Propaganda, told his foreign guests without blinking: "We are not going to give the communists equal time or conditions. They don't deserve it. They are an unconstitutional party."[254]

The "Red Scare" theme (developed under the guidance of a low-profile team of campaign advisers who had been dispatched at Yeltsin's request by California governor Pete Wilson) dominated the pro-Yeltsin campaign in the media. It often took outrageous forms, as in the case of a ten-million-copy, full-color tabloid newspaper, *God Forbid,* that even compelled the unapologetic Kremlin spokespersons to state emphatically that the Yeltsin team had nothing to do with its production. *Time* magazine discovered this denial to be an outright lie.[255] Even the most unbiased observers were struck by the cartoons and leaflets that "portrayed Communists as the cause of starvation, theft, oppression, and murder" and stigmatized Zyuganov by comparing him to Hitler. Similarly notable were the pro-Kremlin tabloids that coined the greeting *Zyug Heil!* allegedly—but not in reality—used by Zyuganov's followers. Campaign videos presented viewers with lists of communist crimes, which included even ecological disasters and the 1986 explosion at the Chernobyl nuclear station.[256] The print media presented a somewhat more differentiated picture, with a few openly supporting either Zyuganov or Yavlinsky. Yet they had only 10 percent of television's audience, and most of the articles reached the voters, if at all, only through filtered television press reviews that emphasized anticommunist publications. One of these, a week before the elections, ran a manufactured story about a coup allegedly planned by the Communists—in cooperation with Chechen guerilla commanders.[257]

THE LEBED MYTH: HOW TO ENGINEER A POLITICAL MIRACLE

In the course of the campaign, the most valuable acquisition for Yeltsin's camp was General Aleksandr Lebed. Having told Korzhakov his ultimate plan was to run jointly with Yeltsin, having asked Korzhakov for money and political support, and having eventually received it, Lebed entered the race on April 30 (a month and a half before the first round) as a complete rookie.[258] He had no party of his own—the Congress of Russian Communities had fragmented in the wake of its defeat in the Duma elections—and no affiliation in the parliament. He had briefly joined the mildly leftist and nationalist Popular Power group, but earned little credit as a parliamentarian and quietly left the group after its leaders, Ryzhkov and Baburin, tied their political fortunes to Zyuganov's campaign. He looked pathetically inexperienced for any executive office outside the military and polled behind all major candidates, including his would-be companions in the abortive "third force." In early May, six weeks from the first round, a poll showed Lebed at 6 percent support, lagging behind Yavlinsky and Svyatoslav Fyodorov, as well as Zhirinovsky.[259]

Yet on the day after his registration as a candidate, Lebed was granted a high-profile audience with none other than Yeltsin—ahead of the more popular candidates. This was a telling signal to both the elites and society that Lebed was part of a larger game and ought to be taken seriously. After his encounter with Candidate No. 1, his campaign took off smoothly, benefiting from generous donations from the privileged banks, such as Potanin's Oneksim, and reveling in the limelight of the dominant media. Also, he was conspicuously exempt from any of the demeaning attacks that the Kremlin team used to undermine Zyuganov, Yavlinsky, and Fyodorov.[260] Unlike these three, who were subtly induced to negotiate publicly with Yeltsin over policies and cabinet slots, Lebed did not put forward any conditions and consistently spoke on his own behalf, which made him appear more principled and self-sufficient than the others. This image was boosted by well-orchestrated leaks, such as a purportedly off-the-record session at Lebed's electoral headquarters, where he vowed "not to bring the votes of his supporters to the marketplace" and predicted that the other candidates would provoke people's rage by their open bargaining in front of the television cameras.[261]

In reality, this cavalier attitude, so attractive to a public that had grown weary of conspiracies and bargains struck at its expense, resulted from a simple fact: politically, Lebed was a blank slate. He was ready to be filled with whatever message would make him popular among key constituencies that the Kremlin needed to sway to its side. He had not identified himself with any clear-cut ideology or program, he had no specific obligations to his followers, he was not tied to any identifiable group in the electorate, and so he bore no responsibility for the consequences of his actions. In personal terms, his position was not so good: stripped of his post as commander of Russia's army in Transdniestria and discharged from the military for his widely publicized criticisms of Defense Minister Grachev, Lebed had become a virtually unemployed Duma backbencher whose most valuable personal asset was constantly being in the spotlight of the pro-Kremlin media. Playing on this vulnerability, the skillfully calculated actions of the Kremlin strategists forced Lebed to rely on these appearances as his major source of income and self-esteem. In this way, the shock therapists and the Seven Bankers' group that dominated the media gained enough leverage to subtly guide Lebed's behavior and shape his image and pronouncements.

The message of Lebed's campaign was seductively simple, having been crafted with much sophistication under the supervision of a highly experienced spin doctor of the Gaidar-Chubais clan, Aleksei Golovkov.[262] The secret of Lebed's success was his ability to appeal to the powerful anti-nomenklatura anger that pervaded Russian society, the most enduring leftover of the now extinct populist-democratic movement that had propelled Yeltsin to power. The Yeltsin strategists thought—accurately—like this: The pro-Kremlin media, in tandem with the Communists, had persuaded a large stratum of society that the democratic anti-nomenklatura rhetoric had been hopelessly discredited and would backfire if used by any opposition member who aspired to be taken seriously. Yet the strategists themselves, people like Golovkov and Yeltsin's senior aide Viktor Ilyushin, knew very well that the unfulfilled aspirations of the anti-oligarchical movement were alive and vibrant—and so, in fact, an electoral "miracle" *could* be produced by tapping into them. This had been the case with Zhirinovsky in 1993 and, to a large extent, with the disparate leftist parties that had won a landslide in 1995 when they ran under anti-establishment banners. So, not bound by the elitist conventions of the Moscow punditry, Lebed walked confidently in the footsteps of his predecessors: He adopted the catchwords the democratic left had used to stigmatize the Yeltsin regime—"nomenklatura capitalism" and "nomenklatura democracy"—while of course also using the scavenger habits of Russian politics, that is, making no reference to Yuri Burtin and Grigori Vodolazov, who had put these terms into circulation. By lashing out at the nomenklatura, Lebed reaped success on Yavlinsky's home turf, while the latter campaigned ineptly, indulging in pointless negotiations with the Kremlin via television and the press.[263]

At the same time, Lebed's friendly relations with Russian ethnocrats, his occasional anti-Semitism, and his acerbic vitriol against "the democrats" (now widely understood as the Gaidar-Chubais forces) earned him support from the scattered nationalist constituency that had lost faith in Zhirinovsky, mistrusted the ballot box, and saw the ideological conversion of the Yeltsin regime as the only way to achieve its goals. This clever catch-all strategy enabled Lebed to retrace Zhirinovsky's path of December 1993: After several weeks of an aggressive media campaign, he overtook both Yavlinsky and Zhirinovsky in the polls, a breakthrough that became public only late in the game, leaving the other contenders for the bronze medal no time to come up with an adequate response. As Zhirinovsky complained, "Lebed stole my act and he stole my votes. I should take him to court."[264] Lebed's third-place tally was 14.5 percent. Yavlinsky came in fourth with 7.3 percent.

Another message incorporated into Lebed's campaign by strategists and speechwriters lent to him by the Kremlin was his promise of a tough stance on crime. While probably sincere, this campaign theme was designed for undecided foreign constituencies at least as much as for domestic consumption: In Russia proper, few were prone to believe that a maverick general who had popped up out of the blue and who lacked a credible economic strategy and a nationwide organization of supporters would ever be able to mount a challenge to what had effectively become a criminal state. One can safely assume that the single-issue anticrime voters were overwhelmingly swayed to Zyuganov's side. Yet influential Russia-watchers in America and Europe were looking for a semiauthoritarian leader—harsh on crime yet cooperative with the West. They were appalled at the transnational explosion of Russian organized crime and rightly doubted Yeltsin's determination to combat the Mafiya that had benefited from his economic policies and become an important part of his power base. Some of them sincerely believed that enforcing compliance with the laws was a matter of political will and personal integrity, rather than a profound economic and psychological problem hinging on the legitimacy of the existing order. They pressed hard on Western governments and public opinion to withhold support from Yeltsin.

The Kremlin sensed the weight of this international anti-Mafiya constituency keenly in January 1996 in Davos, where Yeltsin's envoy Chubais found his primitive anticommunist bluster a hard sell, while Zyuganov and Yavlinsky enjoyed more attention. (Lebed was still in political limbo as a result of CRC's December debacle.) Yet as the Russian election drew near, those Westerners concerned with curbing Russian crime grew more and more uneasy at the prospect of a Zyuganov presidency and, because they were poorly informed, worried about a "revolutionary" outcome. From their point of view, the best solution would be for Yeltsin to strike a deal with one of his more principled and resolute, yet not anti-Western, opponents and make him an informal crown prince who would take over presidential responsibilities gradually and without upheaval. It was at this crucial point that Lebed became Yeltsin's most valuable asset.

Thus Lebed's marketability in the West was a major factor in his political promotion. His natural bluntness, self-confidence, and humor tapped into the longing of desperate people for basic integrity in a Russian politician. But the expectations Westerners placed on Lebed in the 1996 campaign were as vague and diffuse as his own political agenda: Some sincerely viewed him as the last hope for the resurrection of Russia's self-esteem and at least a regional role for it as a power balancer; others imagined him to be Russia's future de Gaulle—or perhaps an Ataturk, able to put the country's house in order and to reconcile the nation with the sudden loss of its empire. Still others dreamed about a real Russian Pinochet, called upon to steer Russia with a firm hand into the iron embrace of the IMF and the global world order designed by the freemarketeers. (Lebed himself praised Pinochet for restoring order and salvaging the Chilean economy while killing "no more than three thousand people."[265]) Most of this wishful thinking neglected such basic facts as Russians' historical aversion to military rule and the impossibility for anyone to make the prostrate institutions of a privatized government function properly without either a merciless secret police with emergency powers or enthusiastic populist support at the grassroots.[266]

This transient benevolence toward Russian authoritarianism worked in favor of the Yeltsin regime. For the Kremlin strategists, to inflate Lebed's stature through a calibrated media campaign and then to strike a deal with him that would look like the creation of a coalition of major political forces was easy. As mentioned previously, unlike Zyuganov, Yavlinsky, and even Fyodorov, Lebed carried no political baggage and had no institutional roots in the system, so he could be elevated to any prestigious office and then dumped without ceremony as soon as his role in a Potemkin coalition had been exhausted.

After the Kremlin skillfully dragged Yavlinsky into public bargaining (and thus tarnished his opposition credentials), the potential Yeltsin-Lebed alliance became the major theme of the campaign. The Kremlin strategists showed sophistication by going public with their relationship well before anyone could accuse Lebed of selling out to Yeltsin, and at a time when hardly anyone expected Lebed to finish third. Just as Zyuganov's stock depreciated because his supporters were induced to believe that his victory, however desirable per se, was impossible in light of some ineluctable forces of history, so Lebed's standing in the polls was raised by virtue of the establishment's conspicuous treatment of him as the bearer of some mysterious mandate of heaven. As early as May 21, Boris Nemtsov publicly stated that a Yeltsin-Lebed alliance was required for Yeltsin to stay in power, adding that Yavlinsky might be welcome as a third partner.[267] Of course, this preferential treatment came at some cost: Lebed was subtly made to disengage from his closest associate, Sergei Glaziev, whose dirigiste economic strategy was unacceptable to the Kremlin; instead, he was supplied with a radical free-market, Pinochet-style economic platform that won approval from the Moscow branch of the conservative U.S.-based Heritage Foundation.[268]

The most outspoken of the newly bred financial oligarchs did not conceal their joy at Lebed's third place in the first round. Some of them even hurried to explain to the public (and, inadvertently, to Lebed himself) that his dizzying success had been paid for with their money. Therefore, when Yeltsin appeared in public the day after the first round with Lebed at his side to announce their coalition and Lebed's appointment as executive director of the Security Council and presidential adviser on national security, this was the predictable denouement of the most intricate maneuver in the campaign. In passing, Yeltsin fired Defense Minister Grachev, who had long been discredited by the Chechnya debacle, but whose earlier firing would have been interpreted as kowtowing to the democratic opposition.

THE REAL WINNERS TAKE THE FIELD: CHUBAIS AND THE OLIGARCHS

Yeltsin's plurality of 35 percent in the first round and Lebed's vow to save the Kremlin abruptly shifted the balance of forces in yet another behind-the-scenes conflict that was no less important than the election itself: the struggle for influence over Yeltsin and his second-term agenda that was being waged within his own team. For the sake of simplicity, the opposing camps in this struggle could be labeled the "warriors" and the "merchants" (the same two blocs of interests that had coexisted within the Soviet-era establishment and had also propped up Yeltsin's regime throughout his first term in office).

The "warriors" were defined by their affiliations with the intelligence community and led by Korzhakov (in alliance with Deputy Prime Minister Oleg Soskovets, the patron of the big industrial plants that had been most badly damaged by shock therapy). The "merchants" rallied around Anatoly Chubais and the oligarchs. Although sharing their vital interest in the survival of the

Yeltsin regime at any cost, the two groups differed on the best method to this end. While Korzhakov and Soskovets, mistrustful of the ballot box on principle, advocated canceling the election and striking a deal with the Zyuganovites regarding a coalition government and some policy changes, the oligarch faction persuaded Yeltsin and his family that it had enough money to buy votes and that he should turn his attention away from the opposition camp and toward the kingpins of the financial empires as his most crucial constituency.

The magic wand of the Chubais group that conferred overwhelming advantage on Yeltsin's camp over his opponents was the shock therapists' virtual monopoly on the "Western-style" techniques of aggressive marketing that they used to psychologically manipulate the voters.[269] In particular, the flurry of pro-Yeltsin propaganda in the media owned by the oligarchs targeted the urban "golden youth" that disdained the traditional industries, as well as professionals in education and science who were clients of the oligarchical upper class in the nonproductive sectors of the economy, such as trade, finance, entertainment, tourism, personal security, and so forth. After Chubais replaced Soskovets as the point man of Yeltsin's re-election campaign (with support from Yeltsin's younger daughter, Tatyana) intensive indoctrination of the "first capitalist generation" was assigned top priority.

The subliminal message of this campaign, which spilled over to other segments of the population, was that the presidential race ought to be perceived as an "organic" struggle between the young and the old whose outcome was preordained by "the natural order of things." Thus much of the campaign was tinted with a generational chauvinism that smeared the older generation as Zyuganovite and retrograde. It was also marked by ruthless covert warfare and dirty tricks against Yeltsin's opponents, as detailed in a secret strategy document that categorized tactics under headings like "Measures to destroy [each] opponent's resources" and "Separation of opponents from their funding sources and media access."[270]

Pursuing the generational theme and aided by generous funding from the banks, Chubais and his team recruited scores of young pop artists and singers who toured the country to perform in huge stadiums, dance clubs, bars, and elsewhere.[271] Although sources of funding were, predictably, not disclosed, information leaks and intelligence research (performed by Korzhakov and his associates, among others) indicated that the money—in blatant violation of the law—came partly from American and Russian corporations and right-wing political groups, and partly from the government Treasury (at the expense of millions of government employees and pensioners who typically waited months for their payments). Among the campaign officials who administered the cash flow, Korzhakov's intelligence singled out—apart from the previously mentioned Smolensky and Gusinsky—Chubais's associate Arkady Yevstafiev, and also Sergei Lisovsky, the young television advertising magnate we discussed earlier.

In the Kremlin court, the outcome of the first round was seen as vindicating Chubais's strategy of manipulating voter sentiment through commercial advertising. At this point, Korzhakov and his team felt they had to rein in Chubais or else risk sliding into irrelevance and political limbo. On the evening of June 19, Korzhakov's men detected Lisovsky and Yevstafiev carrying a suspiciously large Xerox-paper box out of the government's White House. They were apprehended at the gate and, after a brief argument, forced to display the box's contents—$538,000 in crisp bills, fresh from the Treasury coffers, to which the two men had no legal connection.[272]

Shortly after they had been escorted to Korzhakov's headquarters and their interrogation began, cell phones rang in the offices of Chubais and key oligarchs to notify them about the impending crisis.[273] Immediately they mounted a hysterical media campaign that within hours would persuade Yeltsin to dump Korzhakov, Soskovets, and their associates. In the middle of the night, an entertainment program featuring naked models on Gusinsky's NTV channel was abruptly cut off, and in its place appeared the talking head of Yevgeny Kiselev, NTV's chief commentator and propagandist, who warned the audience about a looming coup masterminded by unspecified plotters in the intelligence agencies. At 4:20 A.M., Lebed appeared on the screen, showing little understanding of what had happened, but predictably boastful about his readiness to crush without mercy "those who want to throw the country into the abyss of bloody chaos."

Early in the morning, amid continuing uproar in the media and after a protracted visit from Chubais, Yeltsin emerged before the cameras to announce the dismissal of his decade-long bodyguard and lately also domestic intelligence chief Korzhakov, along with Soskovets, and their buddy and ally Mikhail Barsukov, chairman of the Main Protective Administration and an organizer of the 1993 bloody assault on the rebellious parliament. "They took too much upon themselves, but delivered little in return," was Yeltsin's stern farewell to three of his most faithful lieutenants.

An old ploy worked again. Skillful types of manipulation allowed the perpetrators of the only successful coups (Yeltsin himself in 1993, and Chubais in the present case) to disguise their actions as resistance to a coup devised by their opponents. Later, the claims of Chubais and his associates were exposed as lies when a secretly made recording of a meeting between him and three others on June 22 was published. In April 1997, the tape was pronounced authentic by the prosecutor general.[274] On February 2, 2000, the latter declared that he had been pressured earlier by the Yeltsin family to stop investigating the Xerox-box case and to declare that it had been impossible to establish to whom the $538,000 belonged.

The triumph of Chubais, the hard-line enforcer of the IMF's conditionalities, relegated the whole issue of the presidential elections' second round to the back burner. The sheer display of power and resolve by Yeltsin, Lebed, and the oligarchs had a demoralizing effect on the hardcore anti-Yeltsin voters. On top of that, the manifestly pro-Yeltsin Electoral Commission moved the second round to an earlier date, eleven days after the official results of the first round were made public. Additionally, as an imperial gesture of benevolence to his subjects, Yeltsin made the July 3 election day a public holiday; this decision reduced the second round to a mere formality. The inability or unwillingness of the Zyuganov camp to oppose such forceful tactics attested to the virtual paralysis in his headquarters. His public appearances became bland and repetitive, but even these were carefully filtered by the media.

Zyuganov's Achilles' heel in campaigning during the remaining days was his inability to activate and muster the anti-Yeltsin votes of the democratic left, which included a significant part of the urban intelligentsia. Recasting himself as a fighter against the repressive authoritarianism that had become more pronounced in the Kremlin because of the Yeltsin-Lebed alliance was perhaps Zyuganov's last chance to reach beyond his partisan hard core of Communist and nationalist supporters. But his inflexible nomenklatura style compelled him to go along with the schedule preprogrammed by Podberezkin's team, which featured a stereotypical high-profile congress of his staunchest ideological allies.

The congress was dominated by ethnocrats and the religious right, whose speeches projected powerless rage and desperation. Zyuganov, apparently swayed by the mood of his audience, resorted to a risky comparison of Gorbachev and Yeltsin as the two beasts of the Apocalypse, one with a mark on his head and the other marked on his hand (an implicit reference to Gorbachev's birthmark on his pate and to Yeltsin's two missing fingers). Once again, what might have been suitable at a party congress was clearly misplaced at the last stage of a campaign that should have targeted undecided voters. However, when Zyuganov tried to use his allotment of paid television time on the last day of his campaign for an address by Stanislav Govorukhin, a powerful and rational speaker with broad appeal outside the "red-and-brown" constituencies, the television executives flatly denied him access to the screen, in violation of the law.

All this relieved the Kremlin of the unwelcome prospect of a challenge from the progressive opposition on the left—the major fear that had dogged the Kremlin strategists ever since the December 1995 election. The voters thus faced a choice between two brands of the Russian right, both equally conspiratorial and elitist. To a majority of them, the Yeltsin-Lebed team looked less confused and unsure of itself than the other.

LEBED'S BRIEF TENURE IN THE KREMLIN

Of the 13.5 million voters who switched to Yeltsin's side between June 16 and July 3, about 7 million—more than half, or about 10 percent of the voter turnout —had cast their ballots for Lebed in the first round. Presumably, they believed in a full-scale alliance between the two, which would have enabled Lebed to implement the most crucial parts of his electoral agenda: initiating an all-out war on crime, reforming nomenklatura capitalism, and luring back to the country tens of billions of dollars of Russian capital flight. If so, these 7 million people soon discovered they had been fooled: The regime they had helped to sustain in power did not intend to consult their opinion any more than the opinion of those 33.7 million (45 percent of the turnout) who voted against Yeltsin in the second round.

Meanwhile, many observers East and West had applauded Lebed's appointment either as a genuine power-sharing arrangement with the opposition, or, on the contrary, as a guarantee of a more ruthless pursuit of radical free-market policies. Others saw Lebed's position from the outset as extremely precarious.[275] First and foremost, Lebed's new position in the executive had no independent constitutional or legal base and was not guaranteed by a clear-cut agreement with Yeltsin; essentially, he was attached to the president, who did not need anybody's permission to fire him. Likewise, Lebed commanded no institutionalized support outside the executive—no party, no parliamentary faction, no interest group or wealthy clan inside the ruling oligarchy—and his Duma mandate had technically expired once he accepted his executive post. His only associate of any political significance, Sergei Glaziev, was a committed member of the opposition unacceptable to the Kremlin. As shown earlier, Lebed's political orphanage was one of the main reasons the Kremlin strategists picked him over all other candidates as Yeltsin's most secure and manipulable coalition ally.

As a consequence, Lebed had no political leverage to implement the agenda for which he received a mandate from his voters. Moreover, any serious attempt to fulfill his promises to crack down on the Mafiya and organized crime would have had revolutionary consequences and thus entailed a de-facto revision of the election results. However, it was clear that Yeltsin's re-election (and, to a large extent, Lebed's miraculous rise) had been engineered by the Mafiya-linked clans that controlled the media and had benefited most from Yeltsin's economic policies. Their aggressive crusading for Yeltsin had made it clear that their paramount concern was the security of the assets they had acquired in their furtive carving up of the economy. While most of the newly bred oligarchs would have been happy to see Lebed in the role of Augusto Pinochet, they were prepared to get rid of him without hesitation were he to infringe on their interests and backroom privileges.

For Lebed himself, the options boiled down to either playing the role assigned to him, with the risk of losing the support of his voters, or trying to push ahead despite the likelihood of being curbed or even dumped as a troublemaker. After weighing the circumstances, Lebed took the second path. His decision was influenced in part by Yeltsin's serious illness and withdrawal into the background in anticipation of heart surgery, which fueled a widespread belief that another presidential campaign was already in the making. Lebed acted on this belief and psychologically stayed on the campaign trail. This turned out to be a strategic miscalculation.

Simultaneously, he labored to create his own autonomous chain of command within the executive by expanding the authority and staff of the Security

Council and by setting up specialized directorates that duplicated or triplicated key ministries and also departments in the Presidential Administration; a presidential decree to this effect, drafted in Lebed's office, was signed by Yeltsin on July 11—obviously as a reward for his electoral assistance—but without much enthusiasm. In addition, Lebed even toyed with a plan to dispatch his own representatives to the regions to monitor the implementation of the Security Council's resolutions—clearly a prerogative of a co-ruler rather than of the presidential apparatchik that he in fact was.

From his first days as Yeltsin's openly declared partner, Lebed behaved so as to antagonize the real winners of the electoral race—Chubais and the financial oligarchy. Instead of acting by the script as a free-market authoritarian, he made overtures to both the economic dirigistes and the democratic opposition. Thus as early as June 29, he published his platform on Russia's economic security, written by Glaziev, which predictably clashed with the economic policies of Chubais and Chernomyrdin and with the informal obligations of the Yeltsin regime to both the IMF and the oligarchs.[276] The paper highlighted the threat of Russia's growing dependence on global financial centers "amid the growing instability of the dollar-based world financial system." Among other items, the document advocated price controls in the public sector, governmental planning and financial support for science and technology, government-paid contracts for agricultural producers, and the establishment of a property tax and rent on natural resources to boost government revenues. It also proposed the establishment of a special group attached to the Security Council for tracking illegal capital flight and devising means for its repatriation.

The Lebed-Glaziev economic platform was a forthright attempt to reverse Russia's financial and political dependency on the IMF and steer the national economy toward the type of mercantilist and protectionist regime that had proved beneficial for every major country making the transition to modern capitalism—for Britain before the repeal of the Corn Laws, for the United States in the first half of the nineteenth century, for Germany under Bismarck and his successors, for France under de Gaulle, for Japan and the Asian Tigers in the postwar period, and so on. As such, the plan was a significant document for post-Soviet Russia's economic development. No less significant, though, was the fact that the implementation of the Lebed-Glaziev plan would have dealt a serious blow to the Mafiya-nomenklatura clans that had come to dominate the Russian economy, and whose covert activities had emerged as a major threat to international economic stability.

In spite of the manifest displeasure of most of the Kremlin court and the financial oligarchy, Lebed created an Economic Security Directorate within the Security Council. He wanted the new agency to be headed by Glaziev, who was finally appointed on August 20 after several rebukes from Yeltsin. This move implied a serious challenge to the cabinet's conduct of economic policy. In less than ten days after Glaziev's appointment, Lebed and Glaziev addressed a letter to Yeltsin with a sharp critique of the draft 1997 budget, which, they claimed, violated the requirements of Russia's economic security. On September 20, they demanded that the government revise the rules of the loans-for-shares auctions—a swindle that had already become the sacrosanct base of the Kremlin's alliance with the financial empires. Lebed and Glaziev proposed a system of strict oversight over the use of the stock shares that had been given to banks as collateral for their loans to the government. Yeltsin's response was to follow his balancing instincts and to commission Lebed and Chernomyrdin to work on parallel tracks to resolve the issue; yet his simultaneous designation of Chubais as arbiter between the two made it clear that the Security Council's initiative was in fact a nonstarter.

However daring, the economic activities of the Security Council were no more than advisory opinions or declarations of intent: Lebed had no legal means to force Chernomyrdin's cabinet or the Presidential Administration headed by Chubais to follow his proposals. Yet even in this capacity they were too disturbing for Russia's ruling elite because they broke strict taboos about Kremlin-level discussion of economic policies. Undoubtedly, this was sufficient reason for the real winners of the election, such as Chubais and Berezovsky, to get scared and start pressing Yeltsin for Lebed's ouster. Even if Lebed and his associates had not created any more controversy, their dismissal from the executive was now merely a matter of time. However, the core conflict between Lebed and the oligarchs over economic policy was soon driven into the background by more dramatic and spectacular events.

On the eve of Yeltsin's inauguration for his second term, Chechen guerillas resumed fighting after two months of relative tranquillity (apparently, they had promised the Kremlin not to act up until after Yeltsin's re-election, and they had kept their promise). On August 9, when Yeltsin was slurring his presidential oath in the Kremlin's Palace of Congresses, the rebel army led by an erstwhile Soviet officer, now Chechen commander-in-chief Aslan Maskhadov, recaptured Grozny. As confusion and embarrassment over the latest debacle grew in Moscow's corridors of power, and as Russian commander Lieutenant General Pulikovsky threatened to shell the city with heavy artillery, Lebed stepped in. Without advance notice, he traveled to Chechnya and met with the rebel leaders to negotiate a cease-fire.

On August 13, the Kremlin made an ambiguous move. A Yeltsin decree, apparently drafted by Chubais, conferred on Lebed the authority he badly needed to broker a settlement—the powers of presidential representative in Chechnya. But the decree also contained a hawkish and unrealistic assignment to "restore the order that existed in Chechnya on August 5" (that is, before the resumption of hostilities and the recapture of Grozny). As soon became known, Yeltsin himself did not sign the order; from the first days of his second term, he had entrusted Chubais, his new Iron Chancellor, with putting a presidential facsimile signature on decrees.

Lebed reacted to his unexpected predicament with insight, saying that "someone is straining hard to make me break my neck while working on this task."[277] Having neither the army nor the police nor the security services under his command, he had no other means to proceed except to negotiate with the Chechens. This is what he did, and the results came quickly: On August 23, a preliminary truce was concluded by Lebed and Maskhadov, followed within a week by a more detailed agreement signed in Khasavyurt. Notwithstanding the Kremlin's earlier order, the agreements between Lebed and the Chechen leaders were essentially based on acceptance of the status quo that emerged after the guerrillas had by several bold advances re-established control over the territory of the republic. As for the legal and political issue of Chechnya's independence, according to the Khasavyurt agreement, its resolution was postponed for five years—which essentially meant that the Chechens promised not to assert unconditionally their claims to full independence, and the Russians promised not to deny them, in advance of 2001.

Back in Moscow, Lebed's unsanctioned activities raised an uproar—within both the ruling establishment and the radical nationalist camp. In the parliamentary hearings that followed on October 2, no one gave Lebed any support except for Yavlinsky's Yabloko. Yabloko had long ago been on the front line of the anti-war movement, and its most experienced negotiator and lawmaker, Vladimir Lukin, had been summoned by Lebed to help draft the Khasavyurt agreement. Zhirinovsky, Baburin, and some radical communists assailed Lebed with accusations of surrendering Russian territory to the enemy. Lebed, seconded by Yavlinsky, pointed to the fact that the Russian military and interior forces stationed in Chechnya—underpaid, underfed, and undertrained—were in no condition to resist the determination and fervor of the rebels in defense of their homeland.

Because the Ministry of Defense would have been an awkward target for blame shortly after the dismissal of Grachev and the appointment of Igor Rodionov (for which Lebed had lobbied personally), Lebed directed his public attacks against the powerful interior minister, Anatoly Kulikov, criticizing him for the inadequacy of the MVD troops that had become a more important presence in Chechnya after the first pullbacks of the army in the spring of 1996. Lebed's indictment of Kulikov was poorly thought out: Kulikov was politically well entrenched, one of the few ministers in Yeltsin's government who had no track record of corruption or conspicuous enrichment and who, on top of that, enjoyed broad support in the parliament. Before long, the clash between Lebed and Kulikov acquired excessively personal dimensions, and both used the front pages of the major newspapers to appeal for Yeltsin to step in as arbiter.

Yeltsin's attitude was not easy to gauge, especially since he had disappeared from public sight for much of the time since June and was secluded mostly in his Barvikha resort to prepare for quintuple-bypass surgery. Even though Chernomyrdin was appointed acting president for the day of Yeltsin's surgery, the increasingly erratic president was still calling the shots, and the oligarchs were anxious to see him in charge, because no one else was prepared to relieve him of the responsibility for managing Russia's steadily deepening decline. Yeltsin seemed to vacillate between those who kept reminding him that Lebed had rescued his re-election and gave some legitimacy to his rule both in Russia and abroad, and those who lobbied for Lebed to be dumped for overstepping the limits of decency.

Reportedly, Lebed found his strongest defender not inside the ruling establishment (whose lukewarm or hostile attitudes to the ambitious parvenu were predictable), but from German chancellor Kohl, who visited Yeltsin on September 7. Two weeks later, the popular daily *Komsomol'skaya pravda,* moderately nationalist but loyal to the Kremlin, published a leaked transcript of one of the summit's sessions, at which Kohl bluntly asked Yeltsin not to undermine Lebed. Kohl said attacks and reprisals against him would tarnish Yeltsin's reputation in the West.[278] In light of this, it was apparently no coincidence that the October 3 encounter between Yeltsin and Lebed on the eve of the latter's dismissal, when Lebed won rare praise from the president and his resignation offer was turned down, was followed by a Yeltsin phone call to Kohl.

Whatever the case, if any "pro-German" tilt was discernible in the Kremlin in the brief period of Yeltsin's uneasy cohabitation with Lebed, it soon yielded to the unchallenged predominance of the pro-IMF party. Chubais and the oligarchs were the ones who wielded the real power in the country, and while some of them were unhappy with the statist bent in the economic proposals of the Security Council, others like Boris Berezovsky had their geopolitical stakes in the ongoing conflict in Chechnya, a possible transit point for Caspian oil flowing to the West, and were infuriated by Lebed's unsolicited intrusion on their turf. Once, Berezovsky came to Lebed and brazenly complained: "Oh, Aleksandr Ivanovich, Aleksandr Ivanovich, you have destroyed such a good little business, everything was going so well. Okay, there may have been a bit of killing, but there is always killing going on somewhere—and there always will be."[279]

Another factor was that Chubais and the bankers had made an alliance that would seem most unlikely to outside observers but that merely confirmed the Byzantine patterns of Russia's post-Soviet politics. They found support in Zyuganov's camp, which now enjoyed the status of one of the two leading forces in what they claimed to be a bipartisan system. Because this status was the most valuable acquisition of the Communists during their inept presidential race, they were eager to cooperate with the anti-Lebed forces in the Kremlin so as to destroy his claim to be a leading third force. All this explains why the escalation of embarrassing allegations against Lebed by Anatoly Kulikov found tacit support both in the Presidential Administration and in the ranks of the Duma majority.[280]

On October 7, when Lebed was granted a high-profile reception at the Brussels headquarters of NATO, Kulikov unexpectedly resumed his attacks on Lebed: He publicly alleged that one of Lebed's associates, recently hired at the Security

Council, was a convicted criminal. Lebed and his spokesmen promptly denied the allegations. Within a few days, Yeltsin was back in the news, expressing his worries about the growing conflict between the two men, but Kulikov must have been secretly given a green light for his campaign. This is the only plausible explanation for the fact that on the day after Yeltsin's comments, he accused Lebed of engineering a "creeping coup" in cooperation with the Chechens. The next morning, on October 17, Gusinsky's *Segodnya* published the most improbable report that Lebed, Glaziev, and their supporters had been setting up cells of an embryonic political organization right in the Ministry of Defense—which would have been a clear violation of the law. Before the end of the day, and before the claims could be substantiated or refuted by facts, Yeltsin re-emerged from his seclusion; after turning down Lebed's plea for a personal meeting, he announced his ouster. The last stage of the re-election spectacle, dubbed "the coalition," ended as abruptly as it began, without leaving any imprint on Russia's oligarchical system of governance.

CHOOSING THE LESSER EVIL

Would it have made any difference for Russia if Zyuganov had had enough courage to wage an offensive electoral campaign and win the presidency? It seems to us that, even given his defeatist mindset and nomenklatura-style quasi-populism, a Zyuganov victory would still have been marginally better for Russia than Yeltsin's reelection. The second round was a contest between the virtually unchecked personal power of the incumbent and an opponent who was almost a nonentity if viewed apart from his party and the broad and variegated coalition that joined its protest against Yeltsin's misrule.

However whimsical and archaic Zyuganov's personal ideology was, once elected, he was doomed to rule by coalition if he wanted his orders to be implemented against determined resistance from the Yeltsin-bred oligarchy. Because the Communist Party's top political goal was to curb presidential powers, Zyuganov certainly would have had to renounce many of Yeltsin's prerogatives, which could only have been beneficial to Russia's democratic development. Given the impractical character of Zyuganov's own program, he would have had to give key governmental positions to forward-looking and growth-oriented professionals, such as Glaziev, Petrakov, or even perhaps Yavlinsky. Thus if the democrats and nationalists with a progressive agenda in Zyuganov's coalition would have managed to minimize the clout of the Byzantine and backward-looking intelligence groups in his inner circle, his election might have opened the door to socially oriented reformers and potentially could have led to Russia's economic recovery. It goes without saying that all these opportunities, however uncertain, were unequivocally ruled out in the event of a Yeltsin-Chubais victory —a proposition that events quickly proved to be true.

We should note, finally, that Korzhakov asserts, without producing evidence, that Zyuganov got more votes than Yeltsin, but the returns were falsified.[281]

Whatever the validity of these speculations, we believe that the dominant reaction in the West to the election was profoundly wrong. President Clinton set the tone by calling the result "a triumph for democracy" that showed "just how far Russia's political reform has come over the last five years." Among academics, Michael McFaul called the outcome a "tremendous victory for democracy and democrats," adding that "Russians overwhelmingly opted to continue the present course of reform." On the conduct of the election, Strobe Talbott praised "what everyone acknowledges has been a free and fair election."[282]

This chapter has laid out some of the evidence for considering these judgments to be misleading or wrong. Unfortunately, such judgments created or reinforced illusions in the West about Russia's course. They also encouraged the camp of Yeltsin, his cronies, and the oligarchs to believe that the West *approved* of their constant cheating, unscrupulous manipulation of public opinion, and ruthless plundering of the state. In chapter 9, we show how these patterns of behavior, with minor exceptions, became steadily more entrenched and thus made inevitable the financial crash and political realignment that eventually came in August–September 1998.

9

MARKET BOLSHEVISM IN ACTION: THE DREAM TEAM, SHOCK THERAPY II, AND YELTSIN'S SEARCH FOR A SUCCESSOR

A former president of the Russian Federation . . . possesses immunity . . . [and] cannot be held criminally or administratively liable, detained, arrested, searched or interrogated, or body-searched.

> —*The first decree of Acting President Putin, December 31, 1999*

ERE, WE COVER THE PERIOD from July 1996 through early 2000, a time
of dramatic events, climaxing in Yeltsin's sudden resignation on the eve of the
new millennium and the subsequent election of a new president. In so doing, we
illustrate and develop in this chapter several of the book's main arguments. We
show the depths of Yeltsin's obsession with his own power, even as he became
incapable of ruling Russia more than intermittently. We show the inability of a
system lacking legitimacy and permeated with cronyism to tackle Russia's severe
underlying problems, even when crises struck repeatedly. And we shows how
deeply that system has undermined Russia's civil society. As Yeltsin faded in the
fall of 1999, many Russians could see hope in a shapeless party hastily cobbled
together by the Kremlin, in a manufactured and destructive new war against
Russia's Chechens, and in an unknown new leader subtly imposed on them by
a president they despised.

First, we examine the aftermath of Yeltsin's re-election to the presidency in
1996. His second term was marked by the distribution of rewards to the oligarchs
for organizing his campaign, by a major cash-flow crisis for a treasury depleted
by campaign expenses and handouts, and by the continued deterioration in the
president's health. As the regime drifted, both the Yeltsin clique and its Western
sponsors grew fearful. Popular discontent was growing in tandem with the arrears
in wages and pensions, and the government had no realistic strategy for boosting
its revenues.

As the anti-Kremlin demonstrations planned for March 27, 1997 approached,
Yeltsin's advisers and the IMF agreed that shock therapy should not be abandoned, but relaunched. The president assigned a new and vigorous team to reverse the trends toward cronyism, monopolism, and government insolvency,
and to end, at last, the depression that had reduced Russia's GDP by almost
50 percent. While the team of Chubais and Nemtsov embraced the old method of
simply not paying out sums specified in the budget, it also embarked on new
initiatives. The most promising of these were plans to tackle inefficient state
monopolies, reduce the number and severity of the officially prescribed taxes, and
increase real tax revenues with the help of a new tax code. Other plans to reform
pensions, housing subsidies, and utility payments were, while rational in theory,
politically explosive, because they would reduce most people's already depressed
living standards. Finally, yet another anticorruption campaign was prepared.

On March 27, the popular protests failed to achieve political traction. In the
spring, the new government program did likewise. Meanwhile, a military opposition movement was gaining strength. The Kremlin began to panic, turning
for its salvation to half-baked schemes to control the media and resurrect historical symbols and imagery that could possibly supply the kind of legitimacy
and national purpose that the regime lacked. It also decided to raise desperately
needed cash by auctioning off valuable state assets. In so doing, it set the oligarchs
at each other's throats. In October 1997, the weakened economy caught the
Asian financial flu.

At this point, we review Yeltsin's ineffective responses to the mounting crises of his regime: He fires some of his government; allows Chernomyrdin, Chubais, and Boris Nemtsov—the politically balanced "Dream Team"—to conduct a new round of economic shock therapy; and seeks a degree of national unity on a second front by promoting, with the West's inadvertent help, an anti-Western consensus in Russian society. We also review the reasons that the fragmented opposition failed to capitalize on the Kremlin's disarray.

Finally, we analyze the last agony of Yeltsin's regime in 1998–99. The key to understanding this period—marked by a succession of replacements for Chernomyrdin as premier and, ultimately, the election of a new president, as well as by a mysterious series of events that returned the regime to the Chechen front —is the president's obsessive concern for his own power and security, his legacy, and his immunity from likely prosecutions over brewing financial scandals.

THE BIG DRIFT: JULY 1996 TO MARCH 1997

At a closed gathering in Moscow on August 10, 1996, a sick old man with an uncertain gait and a wooden stare appeared before a select audience of high-ranking officials. He stepped onto a dais in the Kremlin and, pronouncing his words with a slow slur, recited the presidential oath of office. Then, dragging his feet, he retreated behind a curtain. Thus began the second term of Boris Yeltsin's rule.

The onlookers kept a reverent silence, once again living through the mystical ecstasy of being physically close to Power. At the same time, they experienced a profound feeling of relief: Having spent exorbitant resources to prevail over the common foe in the elections, Power, like the man who embodied it, now appeared feeble, passive, and pliable to those who had ensured its survival— bankers, media moguls, television personalities, traders, and the new cultural elite. Now the time had come to reap the dividends from the frail body of Power, without being afraid of its threatening growls.

They also may have had some contradictory feelings. On the one hand, never since August 1991 had the rout of their rivals been so crushing, and never had the position of the regime been so firm. Zyuganov and Yavlinsky had chosen not to challenge the official election results, while Lebed became a full member of the Kremlin court without insisting on any policy commitments in return. The parliamentary opposition, without much grumbling, confirmed Chernomyrdin as head of the "new" cabinet and was unable to block the appointment of Chubais as the head of the Presidential Administration. Forty million votes in support of someone who in five years had sent the national economy into a spiral, started a war with a part of his own country (then lost the war), and who was in questionable physical and mental health persuaded the majority of the ruling class that the power of media propaganda and the gullibility of the Russian people seemingly knew no bounds.

On the other hand, it was becoming more and more clear that the two-stage election, having solved the short-term problem of how to hang on to power, had created new and no less difficult problems. An election that required the bribing of journalists, regional authorities, and businessmen had depleted the state budget, fueled a massive growth of government debt, and made the state bureaucracy and Yeltsin's inner circle distressingly dependent on the IMF and the so-called oligarchs. The economically active part of society voted for Yeltsin largely because of the media-induced "Red Scare," and it was in no hurry to refill government coffers now that the political wars were over.

Production and investment continued their free fall, and short-term speculation—notably in the government's high-interest GKOs—remained the principal form of economic activity. Huge amounts of liquidity were either hiding in the shadows or fleeing abroad. Tax evasion by regional authorities and major corporations assumed major proportions during the elections, just as it had during the struggle between Yeltsin and Gorbachev five years earlier. During this fifth year of the monetarist "struggle against inflation," consumer prices had increased by 30 percent over twelve months, according to nongovernmental estimates, and the GDP deflator (that is, the price increase across the entire spectrum of goods and services produced) amounted to between 43 and 45 percent. Moreover, the prices of specific goods in certain regions had been jumping by 15 to 30 percent per month, just as they had during the last year of Gorbachev's rule. Epicenters of economic growth in Russia had not crystallized, while the boom in luxury housing construction in the wealthiest cities had deflated, with the number of housing units completed decreasing by 20 percent. The fiscal pyramid of GKOs and related promissory notes had continued to grow; by the end of 1996, the sum total of this pyramid was approximately equal to the country's M2 money supply, while debt service expenditures were consuming about one-third of state budget outlays.[1]

The situation was growing increasingly intolerable. Now that the elections were over, payment of people's meager wages and pensions could be safely delayed, but the shrinking ability of the Treasury to satisfy the demands of the bureaucracy (and especially the power ministries) transformed the Kremlin into one of the weakest players on the field of power. The poverty of the Russian state made the Kremlin's inhabitants the object of growing contempt and mockery on the part of financial elites in Russia and the West. Although much of the economy had already been in ruins for six years, it was only the fiscal crisis of 1996 that compelled the rulers to recognize the seriousness of the situation.

Thus in the fall of 1996, Yeltsin's comrades in arms began to publicly assert the urgency of strengthening the government's role in the economy. This was not a sign of any sudden enlightenment on their part, nor of any understanding by them that the economic strategy they had pursued since 1991 had brought them to a dead end. Chubais and his ilk in top bureaucratic posts viewed state intervention in the economy primarily as a power play to squeeze revenue out of the indecently obese raw material and financial sectors. So it was not by chance that the campaign for increased government intervention in the economy started in the fall of 1996 not by stimulating production or working out a reasonable industrial policy, but by creating the "Cheka," or Emergency Commission, devoted to the collection of tax arrears and headed by Chernomyrdin and Chubais.

The Cheka was established under pressure from the IMF, which made rigid tax collection policy a condition for the continued disbursement of loans. It was the ultimate tool in the arsenal used by the IMF to solve the short-term fiscal crisis without changing the overall framework of monetarist austerity. The terrifying acronym of the commission—the same as that of Feliks Dzerzhinsky's infamous secret police, the precursor of the later KGB—was designed to intimidate Russia's largest corporations and showed the readiness of the bureaucratic wing of the oligarchy to use the most severe measures in the struggle for a share of the economic spoils. The need for such aggressive symbolism betrayed the loss of mutual confidence between the Kremlin, on the one hand, and the oligarchs and enterprise directors, on the other.

"Share the wealth!"—this appeal to the economic elites from Aleksandr Livshits, the minister of finance in 1996–97, contains the gist of the entire government tactic of threats, incantations, and cajolery that filled the autumn of 1996. Yet the parasitic layer of new capitalists nurtured by government subsidies, the exploitation of inflation, and various types of privatization since 1988 were inured to appeals of this type that were not backed up by government action. For the Kremlin's intentions to be taken seriously, the emergence of an acute crisis situation and a mobilization against a common foe were necessary. This would unite the economic elite's oligarchs and enterprise directors around the Kremlin and motivate it to demand harsh measures by the authorities. A development of this kind was predictable, and it crystallized during the winter of 1996–97 as a result of Yeltsin's almost continuous absence from the scene between late June 1996 and early March 1997 because of chronic bad health, his recent bypass surgery, and the heightened activity of the estranged Lebed. With his almost weekly forecasts of new presidential elections and his own coming to power, Lebed united the rest of the establishment against him.

The worsening political climate compelled the Kremlin to announce in early 1997 the creation of a consultative quartet composed of Chernomyrdin, Chubais, Stroyev, and Seleznev. It was the first time in a long while that parliamentary leaders were allowed to take part in the Yeltsinites' discussion of impending political decisions. Sensing the growing senility of the regime, the radical wing of the communists began to behave more boldly, disregarding the compromise policies of the party leadership. The turning point was the attempt initiated by Viktor Ilyukhin in January 1997 to have the Duma vote to remove Yeltsin from office because of his often incapacitating health. In addition, other opposition leaders, including Zyuganov himself, started in various ways to mock Yeltsin, wounding his pride and irresponsibly provoking his retaliation, but not laying any credible claims to take over power.

The Kremlin's plight was further aggravated by gubernatorial elections in most of Russia's regions, which brought Communists and even a member of Zhirinovsky's party into the Federation Council and allowed the return to the political stage of once-terrifying figures such as Aleksandr Rutskoi, who was certified as a gubernatorial candidate three days before the elections in his native region of Kursk and then amassed 80 percent of the votes. Chernomyrdin and leading oligarchs were also unnerved by Korzhakov's election to the Duma from the Tula region. The campaign of the former presidential bodyguard and confidant had been ostentatiously endorsed by Lebed, and Korzhakov's book documenting the dubious activities of his erstwhile colleagues soon caused a sensation. Although Korzhakov had no prospect of becoming anything more than a backbencher in the Duma, his wealth of compromising information collected during his years in power, his close ties to the official and shadow-economy security agencies (the "black market of violence"), and the mere fact of his return to the political stage caused anxiety among many prominent businessmen and government officials. The latter also could not rest easy in the presence of the growing political authority of Interior Minister Kulikov, who spoke in favor of renationalizing some recently privatized companies and was promoted to deputy prime minister in January 1997.

In the same series of developments, one could list the alarming speeches of Defense Minister Rodionov about the progressive breakdown of the army. Although not necessarily very accurate in Russia, opinion polls supported Rodionov's concern: According to the Public Opinion Foundation, if presidential elections had been held in January 1997, Yeltsin would have received only 7 percent of the first-round votes and would have lost a second round with 24 percent, against 38 percent for Zyuganov. These results reflected Russians' overall loss of confidence in their government, which had lost control of the situation in the country, according to 66 percent of those queried.[2] Against this backdrop, the authorities were filled with anxiety by the impending protest actions that had been scheduled for March 27 by the Federation of Independent Trade Unions against the nonpayment of salaries and pensions.

In the winter of 1996–97, the mounting panic of the ruling elite erupted onto the pages of leading newspapers, which hitherto had been known for their optimism and unshakable loyalty to the regime. "Russia is looking into the abyss of a total national crisis," announced *Finansovye izvestiya* with banner headlines on December 10, 1996. "Never before during the years of reform has Russia been moving so markedly toward the degradation of her intellectual and industrial potentials, a bacchanalia of financial despotism, the triumph of criminalized elites, and the economic and political autarky of the regions. . . . Opposition to the authorities is assuming overwhelming dimensions." Only a few months before, similar expressions would have been considered pre-election agitation in favor of Zyuganov.

On February 21, 1997, *Nezavisimaya gazeta,* reflecting the interests of the Berezovsky financial group, printed an alarmist manifesto by its editor Vitaly Tretiakov, expressing the views of many Moscow elites:

> Never in Russia since August 1991 has the political crisis been so deep and comprehensive, and never has the threat of sliding or precipitously stumbling into a coup or a civil conflict been so evident. . . . Today state power is lying on the ground and any adventurer who is brazen enough can pick it up.
>
> The political elite of the capital is demoralized by internal squabbles, by the awareness of its own complete ignorance of how to rule the country, and paralyzed by the fear of tomorrow, when decisions will have to be made.
>
> People try not to think about the future, because the problems of today are nothing compared with the catastrophic outline of what is expected.
>
> The highest government officials, like sleepwalkers, carry out their ritual activities designed either to demonstrate general stability to the public, or to hypnotize the participants in these rituals themselves. . . . The paralysis of will is truly total.

This suggested a collective nervous breakdown among Russia's political and financial leaders, especially among the country's leading oligarchs. It read like an unambiguous appeal to Yeltsin and Chubais to take tough authoritarian measures to avoid the regime's collapse—even if this required a temporary bridling of the raw material and financial cartels for the sake of the country's—and thus their own—survival.

CHUBAIS, THE IMF, AND THE PREPARATION OF THE NEW SHOCK THERAPY

By contrast, in the fall of 1996 the U.S. government had been ebullient about the Russian economy. The retiring American ambassador in Moscow, Thomas Pickering, expressed his views in a series of talks in Moscow and then in Washington. In October, he told a Moscow audience that by the autumn of 1999, the Russian Far East would be as vibrant as the rest of the Pacific Rim economies, Russian tax laws and accounting standards would "approach Western norms," and that Russia would be "one of America's top trading partners."[3] Soon, however, the progressive paralysis of the Yeltsin regime and the possibility of popular upheavals in Russia caused increasing concern among Western officials. In response, the United States in particular sought to avoid a weakening of the Chubais clan, because this could have led to decreased American leverage over events in Russia and the reversal or revision of some of the windfall privatization deals. Hence Washington began to actively push Chubais toward a political counteroffensive to restore the balance of forces that existed before Yeltsin's re-election. It was precisely in this vein that Russian observers perceived the reproaches about "the delay of reforms" that resounded in U.S. Treasury Deputy Secretary Summers's January 1997 Harvard speech.

Against the background of a general spinelessness and lack of qualified and reliable personnel in both the elite and the mainstream opposition in Russia, Chubais undoubtedly looked like the most ruthless and goal-oriented politician on the scene and, at the same time, the best choice for the global financial community. So from the beginning, the Western establishment saw him as the main battering ram for the "reform" counteroffensive. He was not afraid to assume responsibility for widely detested policies, and he did not hide his indifference to the opinions of the majority of the population who hated him and whom he dismissed as unenlightened. Moreover, the experience of a long line of Bolsheviks suggested to him that in Russia an unyielding will in the implementation of even the most insane policies transforms public discontent within a few years into a feeling of impotence and resignation in the face of Power—Power that is seen as Fate and that turns discontent into a mute prostration before its incomprehensible wisdom.[4]

At the same time, it was clearly understood in both Moscow and Washington that Chubais's counteroffensive could not be a simple repetition of the original shock therapy project with which Gaidar and Chubais entered the political arena in 1991. Not only would such a restoration have had no support in Russia, but also, and more significantly, it would have looked like an anachronism in the international context that always served as an essential weathervane for the Moscow elite. In this connection, the advance of leftist parties in Europe, especially the election victory of the Socialists in France, as well as the frighteningly anarchic upheavals in Albania and Zaire, were discussed anxiously in the Moscow media and created unfavorable conditions for the introduction of another bout of right-wing economic policy in Russia.

In addition, under the impact of these developments, a leftist and "revolutionary" phraseology started to enter the mainstream political lexicon, thus undermining many years of effort on the part of the regime and a number of opposition leaders to talk society into the idea that "Russia had used up its allowance of revolutions." From the fall of 1996, the possibility of an "anticomprador revolution"—long canvassed by left and right extremists—was raised by Sergei Baburin, the veteran leader of the nationalist opposition in the parliament. Anticipating the nationwide demonstration against the nonpayment of wages and pensions scheduled for March 27, 1997, many journalists and politicians seemed to seriously entertain the possibility of an Albanian-type scenario. Was this scenario inflated for political purposes? "Russians, Study Albanian!" was the inflammatory headline that appeared in the nationalist *Zavtra,* which for once was only a little outside the mainstream.[5]

In such an anxious period, Chubais and his Western advisers worked out a qualitatively new strategy to achieve their goals. First, a propaganda campaign was staged to deflate the revolutionary rhetoric of the opposition and persuade the radically minded population of Russia's industrial cities that the "liberal revolution" engineered by the IMF and Chubais was the appropriate response to the above-mentioned anti-establishment trends in Europe and beyond. Second, as during the election campaign, the most popular ideas and slogans of their opponents were borrowed—primarily those of Lebed (in the sphere of restoring order) and Yavlinsky (in that of social policies). Third, as in 1996, the new campaign again claimed that the regime was better equipped to carry out the program of its irreconcilable opponents than were the opponents themselves.

February 1997 became a month of intensive preparation by Chubais and his Western allies of Yeltsin's address to parliament that would spark the government reshuffle. The preparatory propaganda barrage, which extended to the regional level, included rumors that radical personnel changes and a full-scale return to shock therapy were imminent. The goal was to deter any resistance by the opposition. Thus on February 27, in Tambov (whose mayor Valery Koval' was closely linked to Chubais), all the regional newspapers, clearly by coordinated command, published an appeal to Yeltsin to dismiss Chernomyrdin and appoint in his place none other than Gaidar.[6]

YELTSIN'S MARCH APPEARANCE: THIRD REVOLUTION FROM ABOVE

Yeltsin's speech before both chambers of the parliament on March 6, 1997, prompted a Western journalist to write: "Yeltsin Rises Again From Political Grave."[7] For the first time after an absence of seven months, punctuated by a brief return of a week at the New Year, the president made an attempt to explain himself—if not to society, then at least to the country's political elite. His appearance looked like a bid to board the train just as it was pulling out of the station. The atmosphere in the hall betrayed a total lack of the traditional fear and idolatry of power: the speech was accompanied by laughter, catcalls, and open mockery.[8]

Probably in expectation of such a response from the deputies, the organizers barred Russian journalists from the speech. (Only foreigners were allowed to attend!) The following day, *Nezavisimaya gazeta* ostentatiously carried a blank frame on the front page where a photo of the president standing before parliament should have been.

In terms of the program it laid out (which was never fully implemented), the March speech could be compared with two other historical addresses by the president: the October speech of 1991, which proclaimed the beginning of shock therapy, and the February 1994 speech, which promised the country national reconciliation. This time, though, there was no trace of the heroic radicalism of 1991, nor of the 1994 spirit of compromise born of the bitter lessons from the attack on parliament four months earlier. The March speech was offensive and cantankerous in its tone and deeply conservative in substance. The mismatch between the steps proposed and Russia's real situation was pointed out most starkly by Western observers: the *Chicago Tribune* compared Yeltsin's speech to the "rearranging of deck chairs on the sinking Titanic."[9]

Between the lines of Yeltsin's speech, one could read genuine alarm that the upcoming March protests might develop along Albanian lines (as soon became clear, this alarm was greatly overblown). Trying to look as if he were directing events, Yeltsin called the planned protest "largely justified" and a sign that "people's patience has reached its limit."[10]

As expected, Yeltsin appropriated the major themes of the leading opposition forces and placed them at the center of the speech. Lebed's slogans were recited in a single breath: "It is time to restore order," Yeltsin declared—"first and foremost in the government. And I will do that." It was slightly more difficult for the president to appropriate the moral and social critique of the authorities by the democratic opposition: Their target was Yeltsin's regime itself. Clearly, an open admission of guilt would strongly suggest the need to share power, which for Yeltsin and Chubais was out of the question.

An escape hatch was found in the form of a peculiar turn of phrase: Sounding like Brezhnev in his last few years, the president spoke about the government as something completely alien to him. "A lack of backbone and indifference, a lack of responsibility, and incompetence in solving national problems —this is how the Russian government is viewed. . . . It fusses around, rather than governing, it pretends to act, rather than acting. . . . The government is getting fat." Similar pronouncements by a head of state, which in other countries might suggest a split personality, were in this case a skillful tool for manipulating the archetypes of the Russian national mentality, according to which the tsar is always benevolent but is always hampered by faceless members of his entourage. Thus the promise to correct the mistakes of an impersonal government not only allowed, but even presupposed, the further concentration of personal power in Yeltsin's hands.

It was in this spirit that Yeltsin's speechwriters crafted their critique of the cabinet in particular. "I am not happy with the cabinet," announced Yeltsin, promising to change both its structure and its composition: "Competent and energetic people will be brought in." But much harsher opprobrium was directed against the parliament. Yeltsin viewed the Duma as a center of subversion, and he planned to quell it in the traditional way: by humiliating it in public. He branded its work as "altogether lacking any system" and reprimanded it for passing laws that were lobbied for by "special interest groups" and were impossible to enforce. In a peremptory tone, he ordered "the immediate approval" of a number of laws, simultaneously promising to use his veto "without the slightest hesitation."

The true target of these attacks was the recent parliamentary attempts to amend the constitution in order to reduce Yeltsin's monarchical powers and to restore at least in part the legislature's oversight of the executive. It was constitutional reform that Yeltsin and Chubais perceived, not wholly without grounds, as the major threat capable of ultimately triggering a domino effect of democratic upheaval, possibly leading to the downfall of the regime. Sensitive to the explo-siveness of this issue, Yeltsin feigned nonchalance, warning in passing against any "excessive haste" in amending the constitution. At the same time, he found it necessary to recall twice in his short speech that his term in office "will end at the turn of the century" and that the next elections would take place no ear-lier than the year 2000—thus quelling gossip about the possibility of his vol-untary resignation.

The positive part of Yeltsin's program was built wholly around the chronic worry of Russia's oligarchs: the shortage of budget revenues. As we have seen, the aggravation of this crisis in 1996, as in 1991, was caused by a massive abuse of power by Yeltsin and top officials, who had distributed chunks of state property, government money, and tax exemptions to privileged corporations and entire regions during the election campaign. Just like five years before, the budget deficit would now be reduced first of all by a drastic slashing of outlays, primarily by cutting the government's traditional obligations toward its citizens. In particular, Yeltsin announced the following plans:

1. *Tax reform,* including the adoption of a new tax code—this was "the key economic task of this year, whose solution will be under permanent presiden-tial supervision."

2. *Control over "natural monopolies"* (in other words, the fuel and energy sector and the railways), which had set "unjustified" prices. The point was not to freeze prices and help citizens, but to extort revenue payments from big companies to fill the gaps in the budget.

3. *The reform of the pension system* by gradually replacing government pen-sions by private pension funds. Aware of the explosive nature of this project (given the wiping out of most Russians' personal savings), Yeltsin hastened to reassure his audience that the reform would be implemented step by step and would not impact people already receiving pensions.

4. *The reform of housing and public utilities,* the ideological justification for which lay in a misguided comparison of Russia with the West that persuaded shock therapists that the percentage of Russians' disposable income spent on housing and public utilities was too small. Hence, government subsidies should be abolished. The absurdity of this reasoning in a country where the average wage was $150 per month, while urban prices roughly equaled those of New York City, was obvious enough.

5. *Military reform,* which meant primarily speeding the transition from con-scription to a volunteer force, a measure that was always unrealistic because of the inadequate budget resources that were actually committed to this task.

At the conclusion of his speech, Yeltsin promised to ensure GDP growth of at least 2 percent. At the same time, he declared his intention to ram through a more feasible budget for the coming year and pointed out that "it will be very difficult" to comply with the existing budget law, which sounded like a thinly veiled hint that the budget would again be sequestered.

The Seesaw and the Triangle: Chubais and Chernomyrdin in Search of a Third Force

Yeltsin's speech was prepared by the old guard of shock therapists—Anatoly Chubais and Yegor Gaidar—with the help of American advisers. On March 7, the day after he spoke, Yeltsin appointed Chubais to the post of first deputy premier. This decision was typical of Yeltsin—a confrontational challenge to the opposition. "Yeltsin's appointee is surrounded by hatred," remarked London's *Sunday Times*.[11] The appointment conspicuously ignored media reports about Chubais's dubious earnings during his tenure as the head of Yeltsin's re-election campaign.[12] As for Gaidar, he remained outside the government for tactical reasons, but nonetheless functioned as its leading economic adviser, as he regularly boasted to the press. In this way, by the will of the Tsar and with the support of Western governments, power over Russia's economy was given to a political party that had won fewer than 4 percent of the votes in the last elections.

We must acknowledge the openness of these men, who did not try to wrap their ascent to the heights of power in a democratic veil. On the contrary, Yeltsin gave them power in full view of the silent masses, displaying his crude strength, while they impassively confirmed their own unpopularity in the same way that a weatherman delivers the forecast for a rainy weekend. "Our political base is very weak," admitted Gaidar, the leader of Russia's Democratic Choice. "We are perfectly aware of this. But the necessity to conduct liberal reforms is enormous."[13]

The potential for such an assumption of power by an aggressive minority—on the eve of mass protests against the results of its earlier policies—was built into the weakly democratic constitution of 1993 and was also embedded in the centuries-long tradition of Bolshevism. This tradition holds that government is not generated by society but, rather, represents political spoils claimed by the most cold-blooded contender. On the other hand, the lack of an alternative to Chubais was interpreted by critics as a sign of a profound personnel crisis in the Kremlin, a vacuum of ideas and political will up and down the line. Hence, "Chubais seized power because it was up for grabs. He was the only one who showed a real will to power," conceded his opponents in the pages of *Moskovskii komsomolets*.[14]

We should note that Chubais had in fact exercised probably an equal amount of power in his previous job. However, for the tasks Yeltsin now planned, a top government job was necessary. Indeed, the scope of responsibilities of the new first deputy premier was very broad, and was clarified stage by stage in Yeltsin's further decrees. Soon, Chubais became minister of finance, official mediator in Russia's relations with international economic institutions and the G-7 governments (a de facto foreign minister on the Western front), supervisor (or "curator") of the mass media, and the informal patron of intellectuals loyal to the Kremlin. Later, he managed to subordinate the Ministry of Culture to his authority by installing as minister there an associate from his St. Petersburg power base. In this way, he concentrated in his hands a degree of power in the sphere of propaganda and ideology that was unprecedented since the days of the Ideological Department of the CPSU Central Committee.

By dint of both his position and his zeal in performing these functions, Chubais emerged as the direct heir of the unforgettable Soviet ideologist Mikhail Suslov, although the weapons he wielded were of course weaker than Suslov's. Yet even broader comparisons are not out of place: According to James Millar, thinking about Chubais's appointment and the scope of his responsibilities, "one instantly remembers Albert Speer, who received economic carte blanche from Hitler toward the end of the Second World War. If in the United States similar powers were given to the Secretary of the Treasury, it would be considered a threat to democracy."[15]

Chubais's ascendancy elicited gossip about the future weakening or even resignation of Chernomyrdin, especially among Duma politicians and in the Western media. These rumors were based on the myth that the actually quite manageable differences between Chubais and Chernomyrdin amounted to a serious feud, a myth that was assiduously cultivated.[16] Yet, as described in previous chapters, from mid-1992 until 1998, Chubais and Chernomyrdin cooperated closely within the parameters of a joint strategic scenario, and their rivalry rarely went beyond the bounds of routine bureaucratic competition. Some of their differences were matters of political style: Chubais's was more autocratic, Chernomyrdin's more oligarchical. The cyclical ebbs and flows of their respective influence conformed to the seesaw principle that enabled Yeltsin to preserve the coalition behind shock therapy for almost seven years. He catered to the West and the pro-regime intelligentsia with radical reforms, while firmly relying on the plutocratic nomenklatura in whose interests the reforms had been carried out.

Chernomyrdin's retreat into the shadows during the spring of 1997 was a "conscious necessity" on his part: Unlike Chubais, he was not equipped to lead a tough political offensive to rescue the Yeltsin regime. Instead, he protected the rear echelon of the entire team by functioning as an effective middleman between the Kremlin and the parliamentary opposition, especially the numerically dominant Communists, and between the Kremlin and the raw materials export barons. The rumors concerning a mooted resignation of the prime minister may have been circulated with his consent—in order to reduce any communist militancy on the eve of their demonstrations and to procure more funding for the budget from the "natural monopolies."

In the crisis atmosphere of 1997, when both Chubais and Chernomyrdin were viewed by society as conservative forces, the regime had an acute need for an additional leg to stand on. To have some basis for asserting that a fundamentally new team was now in charge, the regime had to secure its left flank, purloin the social-democratic slogans about a third force, and include in the government a visible public figure not spattered with the mud of the previous reform effort. All three tasks were related, but the third was vital to the regime's survival during these crisis days. The new man would have to raise the popularity of the regime without interfering with the rules of the game. The search for a suitable person to fill the critical post of second first-deputy premier was assigned to Chubais.

Chubais's task was arduous, given the personnel crisis. The confrontational logic of the zero-sum game had led to a situation in which politicians and economists of the most diverse brands who still had a reputation for independence believed that joining the cabinet might not only undermine their reputation but even complicate their lives and political careers in post-Yeltsin Russia. In particular, Sergei Glaziev declined a Kremlin feeler offering cooperation and perhaps a job. Ella Pamfilova also rejected an offer of a deputy prime ministership.[17]

From the Kremlin's point of view, the best candidate would have been Grigori Yavlinsky; he, too, had been sounded out long before Yeltsin's address to the parliament. The Kremlin was attracted by his relatively high popularity, and, among all the opposition leaders, he would have been the most predictable partner. Yet he constantly avoided cooperating with the Yeltsin regime (despite views on some economic issues that were not radically antagonistic to those of the government)—among other reasons, because he clearly understood the impossibility of implementing successful reforms under a regime so lacking in legitimacy. In Yavlinsky's own words, the reasons for the failure of reforms were to be found "in the reputation of the majority of the present government, which most Russians view as corrupt."[18]

Yavlinsky also understood that he would have joined the government not as an equal coalition partner to work out a strategic program, but as a player in someone else's game that had been rigged in advance. Probably he was cautioned against joining by Moscow mayor Yuri Luzhkov. The pro-Luzhkov newspaper *Moskovskii komsomolets* asserted that if he did this, "only two political forces would be left—the Communists and Lebed; there would be no more democrats at all because Yabloko, after cohabitation with the government, would melt away like the dirty spring snow."[19]

A few hours before Yeltsin's address, the Kremlin made a last desperate attempt to solve its personnel problem at Yabloko's expense. On March 6 at 2 A.M., a meeting between Chubais and Yavlinsky took place in the Kremlin. According to a leak to the media, Chubais expressed deep concern about the upcoming protests of March 27 and their possible "Albanianization," complained about a government made up of consummate thieves, and asked Yavlinsky to strengthen the cabinet with his associates from Yabloko's faction in the Duma. Chubais handed Yavlinsky a list of Yabloko candidates whom he wanted for the government, which consisted of progovernment members like Mikhail Zadornov.[20] Chubais's list was, in effect, a thinly veiled attempt to split Yabloko.

Yavlinsky hesitated. He was definitely coming under psychological pressure not only from the self-styled democratic circles in Moscow (who had long ago denounced him as a traitor), but also from those members of his own party who were tired of waiting for government posts and were now ready to accept them, even at the price of abandoning the political and moral principles of their movement. On the eve of his meeting with Chubais, Yavlinsky told the media: "Despite everything, we have a tiny hope that some positive changes will begin." A bit earlier, on March 4, Yavlinsky's deputy, Vyacheslav Igrunov, informed journalists that Yabloko would agree to join the cabinet only if it were offered some real political power.[21]

In his negotiations with the Kremlin, Yavlinsky put forward the following conditions: a radical change of economic strategy, a role for Yabloko in choosing the cabinet as a whole, and a publicized agreement between Yabloko and the president or the prime minister. When he learned about the appointment of Chubais to the government, Yavlinsky denounced it. On March 9, he forwarded to Yeltsin his draft of an anticrisis pact between the president and Yabloko, including principles for the formation of the government.[22] Behind the scenes in the Kremlin, however, a different decision had already been made. On March 17, Boris Nemtsov, the governor of Nizhny Novgorod, was appointed as the second first-deputy premier.

THE PINCH HITTER TAKES THE FIELD

The media and official image-makers bent over backwards to portray the choice of Nemtsov as creating a broad coalition, almost as a change of government. In contrast to the laconic decree about Chubais's appointment, Nemtsov was publicly and politely invited to join the government and was enticed with broad, though vague, personnel responsibilities. Yeltsin's official welcome to Nemtsov, published by the media, was composed in a manner uncharacteristic for the president, using courtly and even ingratiating tones: "This is a very interesting opportunity: you and Anatoly Chubais in the cabinet can create a fresh young team practically from scratch. You have all the assets you need for that—experience, authority, and skill." At the same time, reportedly secret information was leaked to the media that Nemtsov had had to be convinced to enter the government and that Yeltsin's daughter, Tatyana Dyachenko, and Boris Berezovsky had visited Nizhny Novgorod for that purpose.[23]

The crux of the matter was that for a large segment of public opinion, Nemtsov was closely tied to Yavlinsky, who in 1992 had briefly served as Nemtsov's economic adviser and had worked out a special program of regional economic reforms for Nizhny Novgorod. Nemtsov's appointment was designed as a surrogate for the alliance with Yabloko, which had been made impossible by Yavlinsky's stubborn maintenance of his principles and his insistence on firm guarantees from the regime. After Nemtsov's appointment, Gaidar and other members of Yeltsin's team hurried to proclaim that their long-term goal of "uniting all democrats" around the Kremlin had finally been achieved. In reality, this was nothing but an illusion: Nemtsov had no relation to Yabloko and had never belonged to the opposition. Although he collected a million signatures to protest against the Chechnya war, he had never seriously criticized Yeltsin; in 1996, he had supported Yeltsin's re-election with vigor and also commented skeptically about Yavlinsky's candidacy. While Yavlinsky had broadly social-democratic views (with elements of Gaullism), Nemtsov was in most respects (if sometimes not in rhetoric) a radical free-market ideologist of the Anglo-American stripe.

Yet unlike most members of the ruling elite, Nemtsov also had a utopian belief in the possibility of using top-down administrative methods to reshape Russia's monopolistic and heavily criminalized market to accord with Western standards. Right before his appointment in December 1996, Nemtsov reportedly had a long meeting with Margaret Thatcher to discuss ways to reform the Russian "natural monopolies"; this suggested an analogy with Gorbachev, whose promotion to the post of CPSU general secretary also received preliminary approval from the grande dame of the conservative revolution. Yet it took a while for Russian observers to figure out this trick: "There is a strong suspicion that the Nemtsov reforms are simply a direct continuation of the Gaidar and Chubais reforms," remarked Marina Shakina.[24]

In other respects, Nemtsov was also introduced to the public as a different person than he was in reality. Supposedly, he had the duty to bring Chernomyrdin's raw materials lobby in the cabinet to heel; however, he had maintained a long and intimate relation with Chernomyrdin. In 1992, in the wake of Chernomyrdin's election as premier, rumors had circulated in the media about the possible appointment of Nemtsov as economics minister.[25] In 1993, both Nemtsov and Chernomyrdin endorsed Yeltsin's creation of the original Federation Council —an unelected, oligarchic, and extraconstitutional body designed to politically marginalize the Supreme Soviet and usurp some of its constitutional powers.[26] Chernomyrdin had visited Nizhny Novgorod several times to express his support for Nemtsov, and the latter in return once declared that Chernomyrdin would not make a bad president.[27] Thus Nemtsov was by no means a new figure; he had been waiting on the bench for his chance for a long time, and his appointment had been carefully prepared.[28] This explains the extreme moderation of his demands in comparison with Yavlinsky's: not asking for any institutional guarantees, he merely requested the ability to maintain constant personal contact with Yeltsin and to retain his gubernatorial powers in Nizhny Novgorod for two years. (The latter was illegal and soon forgotten.)

Nemtsov was also recruited by Yeltsin because, unlike Yavlinsky, he believes in the salutary role of authoritarian institutions for Russia, be they monarchical or presidential. This view is evident from Nemtsov's book, in which Yeltsin is depicted as "a genuine Russian tsar."[29] Therefore, the political deployment of Nemtsov was viewed by Yeltsin as an extra guarantee against any amendment of the antiparliamentary constitution of 1993—an effort firmly supported by most of the Communists and Yabloko. "For Russia, the weakening of presidential power would be extremely deleterious," Nemtsov argued. "Those who insist on transforming Russia into a parliamentary republic are consciously or unconsciously pushing the country toward chaos."[30]

Nemtsov's nomination had three major goals: to calm or split the democratic opposition, to temper the governors' discontent in the Federation Council by showing them they might get promoted for good behavior, and to regain the support of those Western elites and publics who had become to varying degrees disenchanted with Yeltsin. As already alluded to, in the first case, the calculation was based not on any congruence of political views between Nemtsov and Yabloko but, rather, on psychological issues: The clan mentality suggested to the Kremlin spin doctors that Yavlinsky would undoubtedly support his old buddy Nemtsov, with whom he had once worked. This calculation was only partially confirmed: Yavlinsky cautiously approved Nemtsov's nomination and wished him success in his new office.[31] After meeting with Nemtsov, Yavlinsky said that "the rationale described to me by Boris [for accepting the nomination] didn't seem persuasive, but I accepted it."[32]

Simultaneously, the game of attracting members of the democratic opposition one by one into the government went on: Chernomyrdin announced that he had commissioned Nemtsov to "research the possibility" of including "serious professionals" from Yabloko in the government (which, in the coded language of the Russian elite, meant that giving policymaking positions to Yabloko had already been ruled out). A March 22 meeting between Nemtsov and Yavlinsky produced a vague agreement on "political, economic, and intellectual support" by Yabloko for Nemtsov's activities in the cabinet, but without any Yabloko members joining the cabinet.[33] In addition, Nemtsov managed to garner support from smaller groups of opposition democrats not related to Yabloko. Thus Viktor Aksiuchits, the democratic statist who was influential among the nationalist, traditionalist intelligentsia, became one of Nemtsov's assistants.

Nemtsov's trump card was his attractive and persuasive manner on television. He had no rivals among Russian politicians in this regard, with the exception of Zhirinovsky and, sometimes, Yeltsin. The general faith in the omnipotence of television created by Yeltsin's 1996 victory allowed a number of leading newspapers to declare Nemtsov the most promising candidate of the "party of power." The strength of Nemtsov's image lay in his spontaneity, his provincial naïveté, and his skill at playing the Holy Fool, an inspired builder of castles in the air. Attuned to the mood of the age, he hinted in his speeches and pronouncements at a need to go back to the basics of democratic reforms in their authentic sense and to realize at least some elements of Yeltsin's 1989 antinomenklatura program.

Indeed, Nemtsov's first moves recalled the populism of the early Yeltsin: He proposed to strip all government officials of their foreign-made cars and replace them with Russian ones. The press immediately derided this moderately protectionist measure as Nemtsov's lobbying for the interests of the Volga automobile plant in Nizhny Novgorod; these accusations gained him sympathy in significant parts of society. Meanwhile, the summer of 1997 witnessed a barrage of petty and inconclusive personal accusations against Nemtsov that had little connection with the substance of his policies.[34] The high point of this campaign was the ridiculous statement by the usually pro-Kremlin Zhirinovsky that Nemtsov had put out a contract for his assassination.

The final composition of the three-headed cabinet was announced at a joint press conference given by Chernomyrdin, Chubais, and Nemtsov on the eve of the March 27 protest. The cabinet's ideology clearly pointed to a second round of shock therapy, or, as the official commentators enthused, "the Second Liberal Revolution."[35] In his role as a public relations man for the government, Gaidar publicized this ideology in the media. His favorite formula was "either oligarchical capitalism or liberal reforms," despite the obvious evidence that liberal reforms themselves, under his guidance, had legalized and strengthened the emerging oligarchical capitalism of the late Gorbachev era. Among those who had access to television broadcasts, only Solzhenitsyn expressed no admiration for the new cabinet.[36] In the laudatory choir of Western commentators, the tone was set by officials of the U.S. government: Deputy Treasury Secretary Lawrence Summers, who apparently had played an insider role in its formation, called the new cabinet a "dream team."[37] More cautious observers remarked that the second shock therapy "may turn out to be Yeltsin's last great gamble" in the political game.[38]

THE MARCH PROTESTS: THE REVOLUTIONARIES DIDN'T SHOW UP—REVOLUTION POSTPONED

As March 27 drew near, the alarm of the authorities seemed to rise. On March 18, Chernomyrdin called on the executives of Russia's regions to "immediately engage in a negotiation process with the labor unions" and urged them to pay all wage arrears as soon as possible.[39] The Gaidar-Chubais party appealed to citizens to give the cabinet one hundred days to carry out its program and to refrain from strikes for this period. At the same time, newspapers published reports about possibly including organizers of the mass protest in the cabinet— among them, the leaders of the Federation of Independent Trade Unions of Russia (FITUR), headed by Mikhail Shmakov.[40] As the French press commented, the gyrations of the Russian cabinet seemingly showed the fear of a possible repetition on a Russian scale of the upheavals that had recently shaken Albania.[41]

The labor union leaders and the communists threatened to bring thirty million to forty million people into the streets (a calculation apparently based on the number of votes received by Zyuganov in 1996).[42] The organizers of the protest were joined by Lebed's party, Yabloko, and other opposition forces. Nonetheless, the number of demonstrators turned out to be substantially less than planned. FITUR's major ideologue, Andrei Isaev, insisted that 20 million people took part, while the Interior Ministry's figures stated that only 1.8 million had demonstrated in all of Russia.[43] The figure of 7.5 million given by the head of the CPRF demonstration headquarters may have been only slightly inflated.[44]

More important, though, the March protests did not project the mood of boiling rage and rebellion for which the protests of February 1992 and May 1993 had been remarkable. "Russians rebel in a harmonious and calm way," noted the progovernment paper *Segodnya*.[45] Another paper summed it up: "The March strike was a victory for the authorities. . . . The great upheavals that were scheduled for March 27 did not occur. People assembled. They marched in protest. They spoke to the authorities in tough language, but without an Albanian accent."[46] Perhaps the authorities had deliberately exaggerated the danger.

In any case, Russian civil society once again turned out to be weaker and more helpless than those in power had feared. As the *Wall Street Journal* said, the explanation lay in such factors as "a weak union movement whose leaders remain close to the government, an ideologically bankrupt and politically divided opposition, . . . and widespread skepticism about the effectiveness of the protest."[47]

Over the years of the CPSU's dictatorship, the organizational and cultural skills needed for mass protest had atrophied among the unprivileged layers of society and, most important, among the workers of the industrial sector. The labor unions, which had lost their independence in the early 1920s, proved unable to regain it seventy years later. Guided by pragmatic considerations, as shown in chapter 6, their leaders moved toward corporatism, agreeing to play the role of weak sister in the tripartite commissions of government officials, corporate managers, and union representatives—all meeting for the purpose of mutual appeasement. In this triple alliance, the regional and local officials had the final say: they were able to haggle with both industrialists and labor leaders using tax exemptions, debt restructurings, office facilities, foreign trips, patronage, and the symbols and pageantry of power. With the slowdown of production and the collapse of economic and moral incentives for work, it was access to the nomenklatura's power resources at the local level that was most in demand. This is what the regional elites repeatedly doled out at moments when social tension was about to explode. In particular, it was the governors who deserved the credit for cooling off the passions of March 1997, as was emphasized by Speaker of the Federation Council Yegor Stroyev.[48]

NEW REFORMS, OLD AGENDA

REFORM OF THE "NATURAL MONOPOLIES"

With the March 27 protests safely behind them, Nemtsov and Chubais could focus their attention more fully on the "natural monopolies." The major problem of these monopolies in Russia was (and is) political. It lay in the merger between the CEOs of raw materials, fuel, and energy companies and the state apparatus, primarily in the person of the long-term patron and lobbyist for these sectors, Viktor Chernomyrdin (as well as other state officials who were large shareholders and board members in such companies as Gazprom and United Energy Systems of Russia). This state of affairs was and continues to be the primary source of corruption and unfair privileges—including tax exemptions —that the Council of Ministers had generously granted to the natural monopolists over the years. This is why first Glaziev and then Yavlinsky, from 1994 on, continuously demanded the resignation of the prime minister. Yet all the competing clans in Yeltsin's environment were remarkably united in favor of keeping Chernomyrdin in place. One of the major reasons for their support was that the system of shadow agreements between the premier and the CPRF top brass served as a comfortable surrogate for a legitimate democratic parliamentary process, according to which the cabinet is formed on the basis of a legislative majority.

As for economic solutions to the problem, Yabloko diverged from the other major opposition forces and saw them in terms of encouraging competition from foreign corporations. The government could grant them privileged access to raw materials, along the lines of the NEP concessions to Western investors of the 1920s. This was the intention of a bill on production-sharing agreements that caused a number of sharp exchanges in the Duma between Yabloko and the pro-Chernomyrdin communists. Among the active lobbyists for the adoption of this law were Western corporations, George Soros, and the U.S. government (as shown in the "instructional" letter from Summers to Anatoly Chubais).[49] This is why Westerners pressed both Chubais and Yavlinsky to make a deal and create a joint cabinet, despite their irreconcilable political positions. Some Western consultants even insisted on the breakup of the natural monopolies, which, unless carried out gradually and with extreme care, would have led to a price explosion and caused grave economic damage, especially given the scope of destruction in other economic sectors caused by shock therapy.[50]

The program of encouraging competition from Western firms was by and large unfeasible, given the growing anti-Western mood in society and the joint resistance from Chernomyrdin and the Communists. In these political conditions, the Yeltsinites did not allow free debate about a price freeze or administrative price controls for the natural monopolies. Such a debate would have meant a wholesale revision of the economic and social strategy of Yeltsin's reign. In reality, by announcing an impending reform of the natural monopolies, Chubais and Nemtsov were addressing rather limited and mostly fiscal purposes. As premier, Chernomyrdin undoubtedly agreed with the necessity of extracting more funds for the state budget from these large corporations. But the necessary political tool for procuring this revenue under Russian conditions was simple intimidation—namely, rumors about the weakening, or even the resignation, of the premier and about far-reaching plans for restructuring and even dismembering the monopolies.

The Moscow media were full of these rumors during the first weeks of the new cabinet. In April came Nemtsov's appointment as minister of fuel and energy, replacing Chernomyrdin's protégé Pyotr Rodionov—a purely political appointment because Nemtsov had no experience for the job. (He relinquished it after a few months.) In early May, Nemtsov was also appointed chairman of the governmental directors' caucus on the Gazprom board of directors.

The proof of these tactics' effectiveness was evident in the panic of Gazprom boss Rem Vyakhirev, who showed up in the Duma on April 9 and called on the Communists to block the plans of Nemtsov and Western companies to dismantle the natural monopolies.[51] Such anxiety ignored the personal ties between Nemtsov and Chernomyrdin, as well as the remarkable moderation of Nemtsov's reformism. The proof was soon forthcoming: As soon as back taxes from natural monopolies began reaching the state Treasury, the subtle assault on the monopolies began to wind down. On August 6, Yeltsin hosted Vyakhirev in the Kremlin and gave him a ringing endorsement. The interests of the Western and Russian proponents of breaking up the natural monopolies were checkmated, but the urgent political problem posed by the alliance of corporations and top bureaucrats received no attention.

HOUSING AND PUBLIC UTILITIES REFORMS

The proposals on housing and utilities that Yeltsin had put forward to further reduce state obligations and expenditures evoked outraged resistance in Russian society. The struggle against Nemtsov's draft plan for these reforms (which aimed at bringing the individual citizen's housing and public utilities bill up to "global" levels without taking structural features and the accumulated decay of the national economy into account) was headed by Moscow mayor Luzhkov, who published a blunt critique of the reform plan three days before Yeltsin signed the relevant decree on April 28.[52] Public support for Luzhkov's protest was so imposing that on May 6, Yeltsin invited the mayor to the Kremlin and announced that he was granting the city of Moscow a special waiver enabling the city to conduct housing and utilities reform according to its own plan, "without shock therapy."[53]

PENSION REFORM

A related plan for pension reform—the most unpopular measure of all—was prepared in secrecy under the personal supervision of Chubais. Despite the precautions, the main outlines of a draft of the plan were leaked to the media, and devastating attacks followed. One of the draft versions envisioned raising the retirement age for men from 65 to 70, even though the average male life expectancy in Russia declined during the Yeltsin era, reaching a low of 58 in 1997. The irony was captured by an editorial writer for *Kommersant-Daily*, who titled an article on pension reform: "The Average Russian Male Will Start To Get His Pension Thirteen Years After His Death."[54]

CORRUPTION

The authorities made much fanfare about yet another declaration of war on corruption by Yeltsin on April 10. As observers noted, however, this was the sixth time that total war on corruption had been declared during the five years of Yeltsin's rule. Each time, the hydra heads of graft and embezzlement that supposedly had been severed quickly grew back, a process assisted by the ideology of shock therapy, above all by its doctrine of primitive accumulation at any cost. Yet the main factor behind the growth of corruption was and remains the non-accountability of ruling elites to society in the form of effective representative institutions. This lack of accountability, inherited from the Soviet era, was codified in the Yeltsin constitution. The scale and impunity of the financial abuses of the regime is evident from the fact that Yeltsin's daughter, Tatyana Dyachenko, received by official rescript an allowance of $25,000 of government money for a one-week trip to France, while the standard per diem allowance for state officials on such foreign trips amounted to about $20.[55]

The Yeltsin administration needed a show trial to convince society of its seriousness in the new anticorruption campaign, a trial that would neither hit any top officials, nor require a major rethinking of the ideology and economic strategy undergirding Yeltsin's rule. Obviously, the target of such a trial would have to be a former high official among those ex-comrades of Yeltsin's who had fallen from favor. The first unsuccessful attempt to take action targeted Sergei Stankevich, Yeltsin's former adviser and once-leading democrat, who hid out in Poland because of accusations that he had embezzled $10,000—a ridiculous sum when measured against the presidential daughter's expense account. Well-informed observers immediately identified Stankevich as a potential scapegoat.[56] Soon afterward, more serious charges of graft were used to request an arrest warrant against former St. Petersburg mayor Anatoly Sobchak, who managed to find refuge in France because of his medical condition.

Finally, one of the key demands of the left-democratic opposition was carried out by the Kremlin: Yeltsin's decree of May 15 compelled government officials to file disclosure statements covering their property and income. As usual, however, no efforts were made to secure genuine compliance with the decree. Nonetheless, given the moral anomie of the ruling elite, the very raising of this issue at the national level was a significant step forward, caused in the final analysis by fear of Western opinion. Apparently, the catalyst for the decree was an article that revived the revelations about Chernomyrdin's allegedly enormous and ill-gotten wealth (see chapter 8). The appearance of the decree created a new psychological atmosphere in which regular exposures of financial abuses in the opposition media could no longer be ignored by the authorities. Although they did not become an independent political factor, such revelations became a powerful tool in the growing internecine feud among the clans at the Kremlin court. Thus in November 1997, a radio report by Aleksandr Minkin on the $90,000 fees collected by five leading free-market reformers from their banker pals for an unpublished book accelerated the weakening of the Chubais group by contributing to Yeltsin's decision to dismiss the four who remained in high government posts—although Chubais lost only his post as finance minister; soon, though, he lost his deputy premiership as well.[57]

BUDGET SEQUESTRATION

The 1997 budget law had been passed by the Duma before Chubais joined the government and in the absence of a realistic program for raising the required budget revenues. The budget passed despite tough opposition from Yabloko deputies, who forecast that the cabinet would not comply with the budget law and would again take the path of summarily impounding authorized expenditures. In previous years, sequestration frequently had been imposed by the cabinet without consulting the parliament, which was illegal. According to an official of the Accounting Office, budget allocations were routinely made not according to law but by uncoordinated ministerial orders, decrees, letters, and telegrams.[58] The Duma majority traditionally winked at this practice, thus protecting its special relationship with Chernomyrdin (despite the fact that, even under the Yeltsin constitution, any contravention of the budget law was grounds for dismissing the cabinet).[59] But Chubais, who became responsible for budget compliance issues in 1997, could not count on such indulgent treatment either from the Duma or—a more sensitive matter—from the Federation Council. In addition, Chubais's character predisposed him to act decisively and put the sequestration issue on the table for public discussion, despite the risk of yet another confrontation between the Kremlin and the parliament. Besides, he apparently expected that such procedural propriety and publicity would enable him to bring order into the decentralized and messy appropriations system—that is, to concentrate it in his own hands at the Finance Ministry.

On April 17, Chubais addressed the Federation Council and indicated the existence of a "monstrous budget crisis." "We must acknowledge that the budget law approved by parliament cannot be fulfilled," he declared. As he asserted, the revenues in the current budget forecast were a minimum of 100 trillion rubles above the realistic level.[60] In Chubais's view, which was parroted by the progovernment media, the new "team" assembled in March should not be bound by budget parameters approved by the "old" cabinet. The media, under the control of the oligarchs, immediately blamed ex–finance minister Livshits, Chernomyrdin, and the leaders of the Duma majority for the "predictably unrealistic" budget that allegedly represented a smokescreen for delaying radical spending cuts during Yeltsin's long illness of 1996–97. (Few cared to remember that at that time, Chubais himself had been the omnipotent chief of the Presidential Administration, without whom no budget could have been delivered to Yeltsin for his signature.)

Chubais's proposal, as well as his tactics of circumventing the Duma by appealing to the upper house, ran into stiff opposition from democrats and nationalists in the Duma, who believed that the leaders of the cabinet should be personally responsible for any failure to comply with the budget law. On May 5, the sequestration bill was placed before the Duma, but Chubais was already headed for a confrontation and intended to achieve his goals through coercion: He announced that if the bill were voted down, sequestration would be carried out by cabinet orders—again, in violation of the constitution.

As usual, the role of the good cop was played by Chernomyrdin, who on May 21 delivered a conciliatory report to the Duma. On the eve of his speech, the Yabloko faction, in alliance with a part of the People's Power group of deputies headed by Sergei Baburin, tried to bring a no-confidence resolution to the floor in order to force the resignation of Chernomyrdin and Chubais. But the joint action by Yavlinsky and Baburin was not endorsed by the Communists or the Agrarians: the leaders of the Duma majority were apparently afraid of losing their man at the head of the cabinet and suspected that Yabloko would have promoted Nemtsov for the premiership. They also wished to avoid a confrontation with Yeltsin, which might have provoked the dissolution of the Duma and early elections. Judging by the polls, the newspaper *Trud* argued, such a move would have allowed the more principled opposition groups, such as Yabloko, to enlarge substantially their representation in the parliament at the expense of the Communists, who had discredited themselves by making excessive concessions to the Kremlin.[61] But neither was Chernomyrdin able to change the mood of the Duma majority, which wanted to solve the budget impasse by their traditional method of printing more money. As a result, the Duma made no coherent rebuttal to the premier's report.

What was worse, the cabinet not only failed to get support from the parliamentary majority, but even started to lose backing among its own followers. Thus on May 25, General Rokhlin, a prominent member of Chernomyrdin's faction and the chairman of the Duma Defense Committee, published a sharp attack on the sequestration proposal, remarking that any further cuts in military spending would lead to the final loss of the country's ability to defend itself.[62]

After the Duma had rebuked Chernomyrdin, the pro-Chubais media spread rumors about its possible dissolution if it were to reject the sequestration bill. At the same time, the leading Communist newspaper published a "leak" from the cabinet that foresaw a long-term closing of the Duma. The headline recalled the Bolshevik methods for dealing with the Constituent Assembly of 1918: "Duma To Be Put Under Lock and Key."[63] The cabinet did not denounce the publication of this "working paper"; on the contrary, the impression grew that the leak had been deliberately planted to intimidate the Duma. During this period, at a closed session with insider reporters, a Chubais associate who preferred to remain anonymous confirmed the possibility that the Duma might be shut down.[64] Duma Speaker Seleznev replied with dignity: "I would recommend not indulging in blackmail and not provoking the Duma. There are no nervous Nellies here."[65] The situation heated up to such a degree that a majority in the Federation Council (which usually disdained the Duma) decided to oppose the threat to dissolve it. Their unprecedented statement of support, published by *Sovetskaya Rossiya* on June 17, 1997, went unreported in all other media, presumably because Chubais gave the appropriate orders.

In reality, both the "Dream Team" and many Duma members were aware that the threat of dissolving the lower house was almost certainly a bluff aimed at sowing panic. Early elections did not really appeal to the Kremlin because, according to all the polls, they would return to the parliament a similar or more radical opposition. This was publicly stressed by veteran Yeltsinists such as Georgi Satarov, who noted that disbanding the Duma "would not pay."[66] On the other hand, there was no doubt that even without dissolving the parliament, an extraconstitutional sequestration would not represent any risk for the cabinet. For the deputies, however, this would have been a very bad outcome, denying them the chance to lobby and excluding them from any real role in the budget process. The awareness of such a danger impacted the Duma hearings on the sequestration bill, as a result of which the Duma created a Reconciliation Committee to work with the cabinet on the bill—thus agreeing in principle that sequestration would occur.[67]

By the summer of 1997, it had become clear that open and covert resistance to the second shock therapy had succeeded in blocking the ambitious efforts of the "Dream Team" to carry out its maximal program. The anticipation of acute crisis and the urgent necessity for short-term crisis management compelled the reformers to revamp their own program. On May 19, the media published a new government program, from which certain points in Yeltsin's March speech had been expunged, their place filled by rather desperate populist promises designed to boost the appeal of the "Dream Team."[68] The seven goals consisted of: (1) paying out wage arrears; (2) providing social support for the indigent;

(3) producing an industrial upswing during the current year; (4) supporting local initiatives; (5) escalating the war on corruption; (6) cutting the state bureaucracy; and (7) delivering on a murky promise to start a "dialogue with society" (an oblique acknowledgement that the reproaches of the democratic opposition to the Kremlin were justified).

According to well-informed sources—and in visible contradiction with point number seven—the new cabinet program also included secret plans that were not intended for public knowledge. Among them was an attempt to amend the country's election law in order to reduce or, if possible, eliminate the use of proportional representation. Such an attempt was aimed at an electoral method (widely used throughout Europe) that, in Russia's case, favored political parties that were, unlike the LDP, more resistant to manipulation from the Kremlin than deputies directly elected by plurality in individual election districts, who tended to act as parochial-minded lobbyists for their own precincts. The same sources suggested that the cabinet planned to launch an amendment to the constitution via the Communist majority (in connection with the forthcoming Russia-Belarus pact) that would allow Yeltsin to run for a third term as president.[69]

We should also note certain successes scored by the "Dream Team," which, however, remained limited to foreign policy and the financial sector and were, in some cases, mixed blessings. As mentioned previously, support from the U.S. government and from a narrow circle of Western financiers enabled Chubais to obtain a restructuring of Russia's foreign debt from the London Club of private creditors. In addition, because of Chubais's efforts, Russia was allowed to join the Paris Club of government creditors. The behavior of the Moscow stock market also reflected optimism and confidence in the cabinet. Here, however, one can speak about only a narrow and extremely politicized group of players who were more closely connected to the government bureaucracy than to everyday Russians' experiences with the new economy. Furthermore, the rise in Russian companies' stock prices did not help to reverse the ongoing slump in capital goods investment.

As we have remarked, skillfully calculated political pressure on the natural monopolies permitted an improvement in tax revenues, allowing the reformers to report to Yeltsin that back payments on pensions had been completed on schedule by July 1. Spearheaded by Nemtsov's appointments of government bureaucrats to the boards of monopolistic corporations, "the role of state management was restored" in the energy sector—particularly in Gazprom—and in rail transportation.[70] Finally, the decree on property and income disclosure, which originated solely from the pressure of the democratic opposition, was a step forward, even though it contained massive loopholes that, for example, allowed officials to conceal ownership of assets by putting them in their spouse's name. Despite these measures' serious intent, however, the much-desired expansion of a regular and sustainable revenue base for the budget was still nowhere to be seen. A fair summary of these months appeared in *Itogi:* "The Chubais-

Nemtsov group scored impressive bureaucratic victories. We still have to wait for economic triumphs."[71]

PERMANENT PRIVATIZATION AND THE BANKERS' FEUD: LOSING OLIGARCHS INVOKE DEMOCRATIC PRINCIPLES

For the Russian oligarchy, the major economic problem was not the decade-long decline in industrial production, not the glaring social inequality, and not the rampant unemployment—all of which it accepted as the norm—but, rather, the chronic shortfall of budget revenue. In the framework of shock therapy, the permanent privatization carried out by Chubais and his comrades in arms (in spirit, not unlike Trotsky's "permanent revolution") always constituted the major tool for combating this crisis. The distribution of vouchers and buying them up from the impoverished majority, the workings of the fly-by-night voucher investment companies, the loans-for-shares scheme, stock auctions based on promises of capital infusion ("investment auctions")—these and other mechanisms were repeatedly used by the Chubais group for a continuous redistribution of current and former state property. This technique allowed the extraction of more and more revenue for the Treasury and more and more bribes for the functionaries involved. It thus served as a surrogate for a regular tax system, for a real struggle against the shadow economy's oligarchs, for parliamentary control of appropriations, and so on.

It was this old program for the redistribution of property and wealth that the "Dream Team" inscribed on its banner. However, in 1997, significant revenues could be obtained only from the privatization of politically potent chunks of state property—or, to put it simply, from selling some key levers of political power.[72] This strategy entailed a commensurate political risk. The blind alley of political privatization became suddenly visible in the summer of 1997, during the scandal surrounding the sale of shares in the telecommunication company Sviazinvest—a scandal that reflected a rift among the winners of the previous year's presidential election.

The political worth of Sviazinvest was defined by the fact that this predominantly government-held firm regulated the use of the electromagnetic spectrum used by Russia's television and computer networks, cellular telephones, and other communications systems. With Sviazinvest on the auction block, the winner could thus obtain a strategic advantage over the contending oligarchic factions in the fight for control of the media. In light of the 1996 campaign, the country's elites saw such control as the crucial tool for seizing and keeping power—and possibly for dominating the entire system of communications in Russia. Therefore, all those involved in the under-the-table fight for Sviazinvest pursued political goals from the outset; their haste and aggressiveness suggested that both bankers and bureaucrats were well informed about Yeltsin's deteriorating health and were urgently preparing a springboard for early presidential elections.

The principal block of Sviazinvest shares was won by a proxy company based in Cyprus that represented the interests of Vladimir Potanin, the head of Oneksimbank, a member of the cartel that had backed the Yeltsin-Chubais presidential campaign, and former deputy premier. He had amassed his fortune thanks in part to several years at the USSR Foreign Economic Relations Ministry and was well known for his close ties with the old Soviet security services. The block's selling price was 10 trillion rubles (the equivalent of $1.8 billion), but it was obvious to most observers that neither Oneksimbank nor any other leading Russian bank that had stayed afloat for years thanks only to short-term Treasury bill speculation and by being a privileged bank for the deposit of government funds possessed resources of this magnitude. Thus it was not surprising that more than half of the bid for Sviazinvest (almost $1 billion) came from a foreign buyer—namely, George Soros.[73] The Russian media of all political colorations regarded Soros's move as open interference by a global financier in the incipient struggle for primacy in post-Yeltsin Russia. *Zavtra* opined that the sale of the Sviazinvest shares to the Potanin-Soros group would lead to "the establishment of total American control over telephone communications in Russia."[74]

The Sviazinvest sale had a brief but stormy prelude. From the moment the auction was scheduled, all major newspaper and television magnates entered the political squabble over the rules by which the auction would be conducted. During the night of July 24, Chubais, who was vacationing in France, was visited by Potanin, Berezovsky, and Gusinsky. A heated discussion over the auction rules took place, in which Potanin prevailed with the support of Chubais. Prior to the meeting, Berezovsky had taken the trouble to make the long flight to Beijing, where he tried to obtain the support of Chernomyrdin, who was there on a state visit.[75] Meanwhile, back in Moscow, Nemtsov and Valentin Yumashev, Yeltsin's young ghost-writer who had recently become presidential chief of staff, met with Yeltsin and secured his personal agreement for the transfer of the shares to Potanin's control. This intensive behind-the-scenes haggling, with Yeltsin and his closest courtiers fully involved, reveals the hypocrisy of later assertions by Chubais and Nemtsov that the Sviazinvest sale was an example of the allegedly new and fair rules of the game that had put an end to the privileges of the financial oligarchy.

On July 30, Yeltsin received Chubais after the minister's return from abroad and expressed satisfaction with the results of the investment tender. Television reported the words of the happy president, who said that the sale had respected all the rules and was "legally clever." Only after Yeltsin's approval for the deal had been delivered on television was the formal contract finally signed. After meeting Yeltsin, Chubais told the press that the Sviazinvest deal had already procured half of the Treasury revenue from privatization that was planned for the second half of 1997.[76]

The Sviazinvest deal will most likely enter the textbooks of Russian history in the same category with loans-for-shares as a classic example of the privatization of the state. Oneksimbank invested in the deal using speculative profits made possible by Treasury deposits entrusted to the bank for the purpose of issuing government payments. Because of such speculative operations, millions of government workers were deprived of their wages and pensions for months, or became an unpaid work force. Like ancient Egyptian slaves, in exchange for mere subsistence, they had to build the pyramids—of Russian criminal capitalism in this case. As a result of the Sviazinvest deal, the bank paid the Treasury with the Treasury's own money, thus allowing the government to pay a part of its own debt to citizens—but in exchange for a monopolistic position for Oneksimbank in the country's communications sphere. In this way, the money that Oneksimbank received thanks to oligarchical access to political power was spent to buy new and more effective levers of power for itself.

One can only guess why George Soros—who had long been an active player in the Russian communications field—decided to join forces with Potanin rather than Berezovsky or Gusinsky. Some observers hinted that a group of Western financiers and policymakers saw Potanin—who had family ties with the old nomenklatura and security services, was prone to nationalism, and had invested heavily in Lebed's presidential campaign—as a promising promoter of authoritarian centralization whose ascendancy would increase the predictability of Russian political developments. From this point of view, Potanin had advantages over Berezovsky and Gusinsky, who owed their rise to political and financial adventurism in the Gaidar era. On top of that, some believed that further strengthening of them might have provoked an explosion of mass anti-Semitism in Russia.

In any case, Potanin and Chubais now filled part of the political niche that Lebed had left behind—that of "Iron Chancellor," the tough pacifier of public unrest. (Lebed also had a second image, we should note, as a critic of Chubais's privatization program.) Judging from some evidence, Chubais was keen to capture Lebed's tough-guy image and voters, and was thus vitally interested in dropping his alliance with a group of bankers with Jewish names who were becoming a political liability for him. The outcome of the auction was reasonably interpreted by the Russian media as the opening shot in a behind-the-scenes race for the presidency and as favoring either Chubais or Potanin.[77]

By giving the Chubais-Potanin group a strategic advantage in the communications market, the Sviazinvest deal triggered the rage of other leading bankers, who used their media outlets to unleash vicious attacks on the winners. The deal was a grave blow to Berezovsky, who thus far had been considered the top oligarch, primarily because he was the paymaster, sponsor, and financial manager of the Yeltsin family. His panic was acted out in a hysterically threatening television appearance by his mouthpiece, Sergei Dorenko, on PRT. "Because of Oneksimbank, a revolution will occur in the country," opined Dorenko in another statement.[78] In response to Dorenko's incendiary tirades, the chairman of the State Property Management Committee (SPMC), Chubais appointee Alfred Kokh, ordered an investigation into the legality of PRT's statute. This smacked of political blackmail.

Some observers saw the eruption of this conflict as "the breakdown of the Davos Pact," which had been concluded between Chubais and the oligarchs in January 1996 to ensure the victory of their candidate in the presidential elections and the subsequent redistribution of power.[79] This view, of course, was exaggerated: Despite all the noise the deal provoked, the Chubais group was still so closely allied with the leading oligarchs and their banks through political-financial interests that only a full and final disappearance of any opposition (for example, a sudden extinction of millions of Communist voters and the disintegration of Yabloko) would allow the feuding oligarchical clans to become genuinely irreconcilable enemies in their war for political primacy.

The Kremlin's Chubais-Nemtsov group tried to portray these events as a kind of struggle between the state and big finance. Nemtsov went the furthest by presenting the sale of the communications monopoly to an insider bank as "Russia's choice of direction" between "bandit capitalism" and the rule of law. It is hard to believe in such an interpretation; after all, the highest-ranking Russian officials were themselves inseparably linked to the oligarchy. Moreover, Chubais and his ilk had not only generated the financial tycoons through their reform policies but were themselves to become tycoons much like Berezovsky.[80] Similarly, Potanin belonged to the upper crust of the "financial oligarchy" mentioned by Nemtsov, which had now—allegedly—surrendered in the war with the legitimate political authorities.[81]

The Berezovsky-Gusinsky group tried to regain lost ground by using its influence with the prime minister. On August 1, Chernomyrdin responded by issuing an order to the State Anti-Monopoly Committee, the Ministry of Justice, and the Federal Currency and Export Control Service to investigate the legality of the Sviazinvest auction.[82] No sooner had he done this, though, than another big firm came up for auction.

Norilsk Nikkel is the world's largest producer of nonferrous metals and the owner of 35 percent of the world's known nickel reserves. In this sale, which featured 38 percent of the stock, the main rivals were none other than Berezovsky and Potanin. Chernomyrdin issued an urgent directive to block the sale of shares in Norilsk Nikkel and "to bring auction conditions into conformity with existing laws."[83] But the next day, despite a clear directive from the prime minister, the Norilsk Nikkel sale took place. There was a loophole in Chernomyrdin's directive: Formally speaking, the seller of the shares was not the government, but Potanin himself. Using government funds, he had taken control of the stock in April 1996 under the loans-for-shares program. As was to be expected, Potanin also became the successful bidder in this auction, thus turning the shares he had received as collateral for a loan to the government into the property of his own company. Berezovsky's *Nezavisimaya gazeta* described Potanin's aggressiveness as "economic totalitarianism" whose goal was "to monopolize not only the economy, but also political power."[84]

The main victim of this affair was Chernomyrdin's reputation: This open flouting of at least the spirit of his instructions—not only by the bank chaired by his own former deputy, but also by the State Property Management Committee, which was responsible for supervising these dealings—revealed the illusory quality and institutional weakness of even the premiership in a semi-privatized government. However, because an excessive weakening of the premier might have fomented disobedience on the part of the Duma majority, all key members of the ruling elite were interested in restoring the balance of power. On August 15, Yeltsin's decree ousted Alfred Kokh, the head of the SPMC and Chubais's closest ally, who had overseen the Sviazinvest and Norilsk Nikkel sales. The reasons for the ouster were given rather inarticulately by Yeltsin himself. In his words, "certain banks" turned out "to be closer than others to the heart of Kokh," who, in Yeltsin's strange phraseology, "had them as more his than other banks."[85] Kokh's place was given to Maksim Boiko, deputy head of the Presidential Administration and also a member of the Chubais clan.[86] Boiko's appointment implied that throwing Kokh to the wolves had been a symbolic action to appease Chernomyrdin. The premier did not put his own man as head of the SPMC, however, and apparently did not intend to do so because of the unspoken agreement among Russia's political and economic elites that strictly assigned privatization issues to the Chubais group. The lack of fundamental change was evident from Boiko's first statements, which made it clear that the latest auctions were final and not subject to revision.

Kokh's dismissal consoled at least some of those who had figured in the summer auctions as direct or indirect losers. Thus Gusinsky, an experienced and crafty guardian of the elite's political balance, staged a press conference of reconciliation. Apparently, after assessing the situation, competing elite clans accepted Chubais's new role and his emergency tactics for stocking up the Treasury as a necessity and as the best way to sustain the regime. Perhaps the only one who did not accept defeat was Boris Berezovsky. On August 18, in Chubais's political bailiwick of St. Petersburg, a killing occurred that the government media blamed on Berezovsky. The victim was Mikhail Manevich, deputy governor of the city, head of its Committee on State Property, Chubais's close associate, and a prominent leader of the city's Jewish community. Manevich's funeral became a demonstration of solidarity by the Chubais clan, its allies, and its clients in business and the intelligentsia. The powerful pressure of these forces created a wave of intense hostility around Berezovsky and, apparently, in the final reckoning, outweighed the financial considerations and other private interests of the Yeltsin family. On November 5, Berezovsky was fired by presidential decree from his post as deputy director of the Security Council.

In the view of Russian observers, the scandal that surrounded the Sviazin-vest auction demonstrated "the inability of the executive to create basic order in the denationalization of state property . . . and its impotence as regards forcing the participants in the process to comply with the rules of the game."[87] As Lyudmila Telen' aptly remarked, the outcome of the bankers' war revealed "first and foremost that all talk about stability having been achieved in the country is nothing but a myth. Looking forward to the next elections, the government and the financial groups close to it have begun yet another redrawing of spheres of influence." Meanwhile "the newspapers and television channels have spoken out aggressively, each on the side of its owner, thus demonstrating . . . how much freedom of speech Russian-style is worth."[88]

DREAM-TEAM POLITICS AND SOCIAL RESISTANCE

In addition to their attempts to solve budget and fiscal problems, the Chubais-Nemtsov duo tried some unusual methods for tackling the perennial issues of ensuring an orderly Kremlin succession and legitimizing the regime's usurped power.

THE PLAN FOR A "VELVET" MONARCHICAL RESTORATION

Nurtured by various circles of the ruling elite at least since 1993 (see chapter 7), this plan was once again placed on the agenda with Boris Nemtsov's accession to the cabinet. Nemtsov, who had repeatedly and publicly expressed his monarchical sympathies, hired for this project Viktor Aksiuchits, an Orthodox Christian monarchist and the leader of a minor party to which Nemtsov belonged for a time in 1990. At their joint initiative, Nemtsov obtained an official commission from the Kremlin to prepare a draft decree recognizing the official governmental status of the Romanov imperial house.[89] One journalist later opined that in April–June 1997 "we were as close to a monarchical restoration as we have ever been."[90] As was perceptively noted, the restoration project (which, in reality, probably never came close to implementation) reflected mainly the interests of those parvenu establishment figures who particularly felt the flimsiness of the status they had obtained over the reform years and were striving to legitimize their power with the aid of some rather outmoded traditions.[91]

Among the factors that blocked the realization of this project were the fractiousness of the small promonarchy movement and the absence of genuinely legitimate contenders for the role of dynastic head, or of anyone who could be sold as such to the public by the progovernment media. The best-known contender was the adolescent Prince Georgi, who lived in Paris and had already been courted by the Russian authorities. However, his candidacy evoked the harsh protests of many monarchists inside Russia, who pointed out that the prince by his education was alien to Russian culture, really belonged to the Prussian House of Hohenzollern, and came from a family branch that had lost its succession rights because of illegitimate marriages.

News about the impending ceremony to invest Prince Georgi as the head of the imperial family in the city of Kostroma caused a public outcry by eight editors of progovernment newspapers; by a number of nationalist leaders;[92] and by the Kostroma authorities, who declared their support for republicanism. Apparently, even Aksiuchits, who was not devoid of democratic convictions and who at any rate was not aiming at a restoration of autocratic tsarism, felt uncomfortable in the preposterous role of choreographer for a monarchical restoration in which the oligarchs wanted to cast him. He publicly issued a warning against attempts at top-down monarchical restoration without first convoking a *zemsky sobor*, or constituent assembly.[93] Soon afterward, the ignominious collapse of an analogous attempt to restore monarchy in Albania compelled Nemtsov himself publicly and unconvincingly to recant his monarchical views.[94]

THE FIGHT OVER POLITICAL SYMBOLS

The bizarre scheme of restoring the tsar was only a part of the long-term strategy of the Yeltsin regime, which had kept power partly by means of an artificial polarization of society over historical symbols that were seemingly unconnected with everyday life. In the spring of 1997, Yeltsin's entourage launched two additional and equally confrontational initiatives: an official plan to re-inter the remains of Tsar Nicholas II amidst great pomp and, at the same time, to transfer Lenin's mummified body from his mausoleum in Moscow to a cemetery in St. Petersburg. (The latter plan was a thinly veiled proposal to demolish the Red Square mausoleum, which had always been an object of worship for the Communists.)

Yeltsin presented this proposal on June 9 in St. Petersburg, where he arrived escorted by Chubais for a session of the Culture and Arts Council that had been packed with his loyal supporters. The president called for a national referendum on reburying Lenin "according to Christian customs," ignoring the fact that Lenin was a militant atheist. This appeal to the "Christian feelings of the population" was aimed at the nationalistic audience that Yeltsin had long tried to co-opt with little success in his struggle with the Communists and the democratic opposition. To be sure, the reaction of the radical forces in society to this dangerous game of political symbology had already occurred: In April 1997, after the first rumors about a possible restoration of the monarchy, a bomb exploded under the monument to Nicholas II in the village of Taininskoe.[95]

Yeltsin's announcement of his proposal to transfer Nicholas's relics was followed by another alarming event: An unexploded bomb was found under the monument to Peter the Great. The responsibility for this action was later claimed by an underground leftist group, the Revolutionary Military Council. Perhaps sensing his inability to control a possible wave of terrorist actions around the country, Yeltsin and his inner circle signaled the media to soft-pedal further discussion of their reburial project.

THE FEUDALIZATION OF THE PRESIDENCY

At this time, the Yeltsin regime took on some features that were typical of feudalism, involving archaic symbolism, nepotism, cronyism, and a trend toward autocracy. The regime's recourse to medieval symbols in the struggle with its own recent past can be largely explained by the need to legitimize the increasingly authoritarian and paternalistic character of its rule over the country. Access to Yeltsin was the main lever of political influence, and the autocratic principle "I am the State" was reflected in many articles of the Yeltsin constitution. Despite this, Yeltsin had refrained from appointing members of his family to government positions in his first term.

In 1997, these scruples came to an end. In March, Yeltsin's son-in-law Andrei Okulov was appointed head of Aeroflot. (His other son-in-law got a job from an oil industry oligarch closely allied with Boris Berezovsky.) As a leading national newspaper remarked, "Sons-in-law have not flown at ministerial altitude in our fatherland since the age of Leonid Ilyich [Brezhnev] and a direct parallel between today and those times is inevitable."[96] As mentioned in the previous chapter, financial control over the still formally semigovernmental aviation empire Aeroflot was in the hands of Berezovsky, casting a light on the special relationship of Russia's first family with the leading financial tycoon and again on subsequent assertions by the reformers about their intention to fight the "financial oligarchy" for the sake of fair rules of the game.

The next step on the path to introducing autocracy by fait accompli was the appointment of Yeltsin's personal ghost-writer Valentin Yumashev as chief of the Presidential Administration. Finally, on June 30, Yeltsin's daughter Tatyana Dyachenko was formally appointed presidential adviser (although she had been informally taking part in making important decisions at least since the 1996 election campaign). In Moscow, traditionally the city most loyal to Yeltsin (after Ekaterinburg), 48.5 percent of survey respondents condemned this appointment—it was approved only by 15.7 percent.[97]

Giving high government posts to close relatives and personal friends was a sign of the profound disease of the regime. The mass exodus of highly qualified professionals from public service, a growing brain drain through emigration, and the unwillingness of competent candidates to enter the ranks of the Yeltsin bureaucracy increasingly compelled the Kremlin to conduct governmental personnel policy as a family affair and to design it along clan and dynastic lines.

THE REGIME TRIES TO BECOME MORE DOCTRINAIRE

As the stakes in the struggle around historical symbols grew, the Kremlin decided to revert to the Bolshevik practice of providing official interpretations of Russian history and culture. One of the first and unavoidably comic harbingers of this trend was Yeltsin's authoring his own preface—ghost-written no doubt—to the complete works of Aleksandr Pushkin.[98] Potentially more detrimental consequences for intellectual freedom lurked in the bureaucracy's search for a "Russian National Idea," which was undertaken by ideologues on the Kremlin payroll after Yeltsin officially dubbed the idea indispensable.[99] Several competing teams of court theorists delivered lengthy and mutually contradictory projects for such a new ideology. Recurring rumors that Yeltsin had already made his choice and was about to proclaim the approved National Idea caused waves of panic in various intellectual circles close to the Kremlin that had placed bets on particular projects. As the media reported, Yumashev and Aksiuchits could not agree on its essence, and Yeltsin was still waiting for a text to approve.[100] As things turned out, he never approved one; instead, his regime reverted to its more familiar ideological opportunism.

CHUBAIS AS THE POLICEMAN OF THE MASS MEDIA

The official principle of government supervision over the mass media became the institutional mechanism for the ideological control described above. The fact that Chubais combined this censor-like role with his post as minister of finance was bluntly presented to the public as the pragmatic measure that made possible "an efficient solution to the problem of financing the media." Certainly it was quite evident that Chubais could use his power of the purse to influence the media's editorial positions.[101] Yegor Gaidar, the leader of Russia's Democratic Choice (a name that was just as much a misnomer as that of Zhirinovsky's Liberal Democratic Party), openly told the press: "I will advise Chubais to consider this his key field of responsibility." Such an institutionalization of patronage and censorship of the media in the hands of a top government official with a clear authoritarian bent caused a murmur even in the outlets most loyal to the regime. As an *Izvestiya* writer noted, "This is yet another obvious sign of our backwardness and lack of democracy. It is also a manifestation of the viciousness of the rulers, who in their attitude to the media, have never gotten beyond the unforgettable [Soviet-era] Agitprop."[102]

Yet *Izvestiya's* discontent was belated: Although the office of media supervisor was being set up for the first time, Chubais in his capacity as presidential chief of staff, and Burbulis, Poltoranin, Shumeiko, and others before him, had been carrying out these functions informally for a long time. In one of his meetings with top editors during the fall of 1996, Chubais bluntly told an editor to obey the orders of the paper's majority stockholder; otherwise, as Chubais put it, "bones will break."[103] The self-styled liberal media themselves had from 1991 on offered a fertile soil for this evolution by sometimes yielding freedoms they had won during the Gorbachev period under pressure from the "reformers."

The results of this supervision were soon clear enough. Chubais introduced the practice of regular lunches with the chief editors of the leading newspapers.

During these sessions, he graded recent editions and gave out guidelines for media coverage of government activities. Vivid evidence on this practice came from Chubais's political ally, Oleg Poptsov, the longtime head of the State Television and Radio Company. Said Poptsov:

> Chubais is a bright, clever, talented person, but with his own neocommunist style. That's a fact. The way he's conducted meetings with editors should not be a surprise to anyone. The government is now ours, but it behaves like the previous [Soviet] one. There's no difference in the way such meetings are conducted. The Party Central Committee used to summon a larger group, whereas now a narrower group is called in. But the methods are the same.[104]

Yet the shortage of budget resources narrowed the possibilities for direct manipulation of the media using the Treasury. Therefore, at Chubais's initiative, leading bankers and major corporations hurried to buy up the majority of media outlets.

The most impressive event in this "clearance sale of the media"[105] was the financial takeover of the major national newspaper *Izvestiya* by the Chernomyrdin and Chubais cartels. The first capital infusion to bail out the faltering newspaper was made by the Lukoil Corporation, a company closely affiliated with the prime minister. Although it was one of the biggest single debtors to the Treasury, Lukoil nevertheless managed to plunk down a large sum for the *Izvestiya* stock. However, after *Izvestiya* reprinted an article from *Le Monde* on Chernomyrdin's exorbitant wealth, Lukoil said it was freezing any further investment and was considering canceling the original agreement to purchase the shares.

Sergei Agafonov, the famous *Izvestiya* columnist, saw these punitive measures as "political censorship carried out by methods of economic blackmail."[106] Soon Vagit Alekperov, the head of Lukoil, summoned Igor Golembiovsky, the long-serving editor of *Izvestiya,* and pressured him to step aside in favor of a new editor to be selected by the oil barons. Alekperov made no attempt to hide the fact that he was acting in accordance with Chernomyrdin's wishes. As the newspaper commented, "the mass media (and *Izvestiya* is not the first case) are equated with simple merchandise—such as oil or gas, and this . . . is used to restore political censorship in CPSU style, since in our country big business itself is extremely dependent on the government."[107]

The *Izvestiya* editorial board tried to counterbalance the influence of Lukoil by selling a large block of shares to Potanin, who, as an ally of Chubais, was considered likely to defend *Izvestiya* against the assault from the Chernomyrdin camp. But the widespread belief in a Chubais-Chernomyrdin feud based on the conflicts between the financial and raw-materials sectors turned out to be an illusion: Having bought the *Izvestiya* stock, Potanin joined the Lukoil management in demanding the dismissal of the chief editor and a purge of the editorial board. As Lebed remarked about all this, "The executive branch has finished devouring the fourth estate with much crunching and gusto."[108] *Izvestiya* tried to mobilize Moscow intellectuals in its defense, but it was a futile effort.[109] After a short resistance, Golembiovsky was removed as chief editor, followed by the ouster or semivoluntary exit of the majority of the editorial board and the paper's most famous journalists.

Within a few short years, *Izvestiya* paid for its fervent support of the Yeltsin regime in 1991–93, which went on to increase its political and financial control over the media. Back then, the paper's editors and authors had apparently believed that such repressive measures would be limited to communist and nationalist publications and would never strike the organs of the liberal intelligentsia loyal to the regime. As in the early Bolshevik period, the weapon of "temporary" censorship was, before long, turned against its own creators.

The supervision of less prominent publications was carried out with less of a struggle. Chubais simply shut down the government magazine *Rossiiskaya federatsiya,* whose editor, Yuri Khrenov, had gone so far as to publish articles about popular discontent with the reforms and a critique of the World Bank. In May 1997, after the magazine published an article by recently elected Duma deputy Dmitri Rogozin, whom Chubais disliked, the finance minister summoned Khrenov, dressed him down, and gave him twenty-four hours in which to resign or be sacked.[110] When Khrenov stood his ground, a governmental order went out on June 9 to shut the magazine down.[111] (It was revived later as a publication of the parliament.)

Apparently, a major lesson the ruling elite learned from the 1992–97 history of its dealings with the society at large, particularly from the 1996 election campaign, was that the propaganda machinery inherited from the Soviet era remained a potentially strong tool in Russia, capable of transforming a deeply discredited person into the favorite in an election race. This lesson was evident in the media campaign to promote Chubais as a contender for heir to the throne.[112] Thus Fyodor Shelov-Kovedyaev, Chubais's party comrade (but posturing as an independent political scientist), publicly called on the democrats "to stop dilly-dallying" and nominate Chubais for the presidency. British and American consultants were hired to build up Chubais's image as a future presidential candidate, and $4 million was transferred for this purpose from certain American banks to a well-known British public relations firm.[113] However, these efforts did not succeed—nor ultimately did Chubais's attempts to cow the freethinking media; the government was too unpopular.

THE CONFRONTATIONAL TACTICS OF THE KREMLIN AGAINST PARLIAMENT AND OPPOSITION

As outlined in Yeltsin's March address, these tactics were an integral part of his Bolshevik-style strategy to keep the elite polarized and prevent the emergence of a truly independent third force. Yeltsin repeatedly addressed the parliament with crude and humiliating harangues, provocatively displaying his superior power. The publication of his reprimands to the parliament in the official press routinely included demeaning headlines (for example, "An Example of Pretending to Legislate").[114] Meanwhile, the parliament itself, lacking its own financial base, was dependent on the executive and mainly on its most brazen antagonist, Finance Minister Chubais, who sometimes withheld payments to it.[115] The special ire of Yeltsin was excited by anything that seemed to him an encroachment on his authority, which the Kremlin interpreted as broadly as possible, sometimes even denying the Duma any right of political initiative. In one of his letters to Duma Speaker Seleznev, Yeltsin took the Duma to task for passing resolutions on issues of foreign and domestic policy, which, in his opinion, belonged to the exclusive competence of the president.[116]

An even sterner rebuke from the Kremlin was evoked by any attempts to amend the constitution, which all major opposition parties were correctly suspected of wanting to do. In June 1997, Yeltsin rudely rejected a Duma bill concerning the possible calling of a constitutional assembly.[117] On May 13, he presumed to warn Speakers Stroyev and Seleznev that the parliament had no right to pass laws without consulting cabinet ministers.[118] Meanwhile, Yeltsin himself unhesitatingly made decisions on his own that legally required consultation with the parliament—such as the August 1997 decision to revalue the ruble by a factor of one thousand.[119]

Despite all the bullying of its opponents, however, the ruling elite itself borrowed more and more of their terminology to describe current realities—an implicit admission that the opposition had been right on many issues. After Berezovsky's ouster from the Security Council in November 1997, he and Chubais exchanged blunt accusations about aiding and abetting the creation of criminal-oligarchical capitalism in Russia. In this respect, the situation was strikingly similar to that of the Gorbachev era, when the nomenklatura, while continuing to vilify the opposition and block its access to real power, rapidly appropriated its phraseology and even tried to carry out parts of its program in ways that would benefit the establishment.

While using every chance to humiliate the Duma, Yeltsin skillfully flirted with the upper house and with selected regional barons among its members.[120] The attempt to win over the loyalty of the regions often took the shape of bribe-like inducements to the regional rulers. For example, Yeltsin made a phone call on June 9 to the mayor of Cheliabinsk and granted the city's tractor plant two years of total tax exemption. Such generosity was always at the expense of the state budget, thus undermining the credibility of the allegedly tough fiscal policies.

The Kremlin's conciliatory line toward the regions had a simple explanation: If the parties in the Duma lacked the resources to resist its bullying, Yeltsin's autocratic behavior often failed to overcome public resistance in the provinces. A characteristic example was the Kremlin's handling of elections in the Kemerovo region (comprising the coal-mining area of Kuzbass)—one of the few Russian regions with a well-developed civil society, especially in the realm of labor activity. The recurrent strikes in the Kuzbass, which once helped propel Yeltsin to the heights of power, were often openly anti-Yeltsin and anti–shock therapy from 1991 on. The odds-on favorite in the 1997 regional elections was Aman Tuleyev—Yeltsin's longtime adversary who was close to the Communist leadership and who had garnered 6 percent of the vote in the 1991 presidential elections. Yeltsin had sized up the situation; on the eve of the elections, he fired the notoriously corrupt and authoritarian Mikhail Kisliuk, the incumbent governor whom he had appointed and who was deeply disliked by the local population. Yeltsin then appointed Tuleyev in his place before the election. Soon after arriving in the Kuzbass, Tuleyev adopted tough measures to tamp down the strikes and then was elected in a landslide with the benevolent neutrality, if not direct backing, of the Kremlin. The media's assessment: "Moscow and Tuleyev struck a cynical bargain: power for Tuleyev in exchange for his calming down the Kuzbass."[121]

However, the new members of the Federation Council, regional governors elected in the fall of 1996, were, as noted above, more radical and less susceptible to Yeltsin's usual enticements. In the summer of 1997, it was the Federation Council (under such leaders as Stroyev, Luzhkov, and Eduard Rossel') that boldly challenged the "Dream Team's" offensive. The economic ideologist of the governors' opposition was Sergei Glaziev, who, after his split with Lebed, became head of the Information and Analysis Directorate of the parliament's upper house. On June 10, when a draft resolution prepared by Glaziev (entitled "On Urgent Measures to Increase the Government Role in Regulating the Market Economy") was brought to the floor of the Federation Council, some observers viewed it as a projected revolutionary shift away from shock therapy.[122] The uproar it caused occasioned a quick appearance in the council by Chubais, who gave a speech trying to persuade the governors that he himself favored the government's regaining its lost economic functions and was ready to lead such an effort. The council thus exhibited a level of radicalism that had no precedent. Its more typical conformism stemmed from the governors' need to have viable relations with the Kremlin to obtain government funds.

THE EMERGENCE OF ORGANIZED MILITARY OPPOSITION

On the heels of a personnel shake-up in the Defense Ministry, dissent within the ranks of the Russian army became perhaps the most serious nonelite challenge of 1997 to the second round of shock therapy. On May 22, Yeltsin removed Defense Minister Rodionov, appointing in his place the commander of the Strategic Rocket Forces, Igor Sergeyev. This action had been preceded by a session of the Defense Council, which was broadcast live on television. Before the eyes of millions of Russians, Yeltsin staged a high-profile dressing down of the defense minister for his sluggishness in carrying out military reform (meaning personnel cuts and budget reductions) and did not allow him to speak in his own defense.

Yeltsin's furious tirade, even measured against his well-known record of violent mood swings, looked like a sudden loss of self-control. In any case, the far-reaching consequences of the broadcast had not been calculated in advance. Many observers viewed Yeltsin's attacks on Rodionov as unfair: The pace of military reform was hindered by the Treasury's chronic underfunding of the army, which invariably received less than the meager funds authorized. As John Erickson, an expert on the Russian military, commented in this regard, "It is a tried and true Yeltsin technique—blaming others for his own failures."[123] Even without sociological surveys, subsequent events made it clear that the orchestration of Rodionov's ouster helped fuel antigovernment sentiment in the army, a body that already lacked loyalty to Yeltsin, having repeatedly voted for opposition parties.

On June 26, 1997, leading communist and nationalist newspapers (*Sovetskaya Rossiya and Pravda-5*) published an appeal to Yeltsin and the army signed by Lieutenant General Lev Rokhlin, the chairman of the Duma Defense Committee, and twelve of the other eighteen committee members.[124] Its text was largely a mirror image of Yeltsin's indictment of Rodionov; in this case, though, Rokhlin blamed the decay of the army and the wretched situation of the military on the president and supreme commander. In Rokhlin's words, the government's policies had brought the officer corps to the brink of social extinction, demolished military industry, blocked the development of science and technology, and weakened the country's nuclear potential. As for the soldiers and officers, Rokhlin called on them to defend themselves—in a way that was unprecedented for such a high officer: "Organize yourselves, select your leaders as chairmen of officers' assemblies, demand your legal rights."[125] This sounded like an open manifesto of military opposition to the regime.

The appeal was explosive because its author not only had never belonged to the opposition, but also was a prominent member of the government party Our Home is Russia. True, Rokhlin had become known partly for investigating military corruption and partly for publicly declining the highest military decoration as Hero of Russia for his role in the Chechnya war.[126] Yet during the 1996 presidential campaign, he had publicly endorsed Yeltsin's candidacy. Not surprisingly, his letter caused a nervous reaction in Moscow. The day it was published, Yeltsin's press secretary expressed his "concern" about it; the new leadership of the Defense Ministry spoke of a "provocation" designed to undermine military reform; and the de facto leader of the OHR faction in the Duma, Shokhin, said that Rokhlin's letter was a violation of the law, a call to rebellion, and "1917-type Bolshevik agitation."[127]

The journalist who reported these comments remarked that Rokhlin's manifesto "is finding fertile soil in military units." The explanation for this was given by a well-informed military reporter, Aleksandr Zhilin: "Boris Yeltsin's authority in the army is not simply low, . . . the feeling in the military can be defined by one word—antipresidential."[128] According to some sources, Rokhlin's letter received such quick and widespread circulation in army units that the military counterintelligence agency was ordered to conduct a special investigation to identify informal opposition cells in the armed forces.[129] In addition, Rokhlin's supporters collected donations to set up an assembly of officers from all the ranks of the army in Moscow.[130]

Apparently, Rokhlin's action was not just his own personal initiative. It was a natural and predictable response of recently retired senior officers to Rodionov's humiliation; to the financial offensive against a military-industrial complex that already had its back to the wall; and, most immediately, to the Yeltsin administration's arrogant rejection of Duma hearings on the severe problems of Russia's strategic nuclear forces.[131] It cannot be ruled out that Rokhlin's move was also a by-product of the Chernomyrdin-Zyuganov alliance's resentment about the overweening advances of Chubais, Nemtsov, and their retinue of "Young Wolves." This hypothesis is supported by the fact that Chernomyrdin seemed neither quick nor eager to expel Rokhlin from his party and distanced himself from him in a relatively gentle way, calling his letter merely "a grave political mistake."[132] The open support for Rokhlin's movement on the part of Arkady Volsky and Nikolai Travkin probably would not have been possible without the tacit consent or at least neutrality of the premier.

Whatever the case, a more immediate role in the emergence of Rokhlin's letter had been played by the radical wing of the Communist Party and its spokesman, Viktor Ilyukhin, who evidently wanted to end the stagnation and decay of the CPRF by creating a new leader more radical than Zyuganov, one more acceptable to a broad spectrum of the opposition. Even if Chernomyrdin and Zyuganov had at first also been somewhat interested in promoting Rokhlin's initiative, its final form turned out to be too radical for Chernomyrdin and the leaders of the Duma majority. The Duma apparatus blocked an attempt to mail out Rokhlin's statement to military units as an official document of the chairman of the Defense Committee.[133] The media also noticed that other opposition forces at first pretended to ignore the letter—probably in part because they feared provoking the dissolution of the Duma.[134]

Rokhlin also announced the creation of a Movement in Support of the Army and the Defense Industries (MSADI) and published a list of his associates. This action was another sign that his move had been well planned in advance. The MSADI's founding session featured a broad spectrum of politicians, from ultraradicals of the 1991–93 era (Stanislav Terekhov and Vladislav Achalov and the August putschists Valentin Varennikov and Vladimir Kryuchkov) all the way to the Yeltsin loyalist Volsky; the former head of foreign intelligence Leonid Shebarshin; and Aleksandr Shulunov, the head of the League to Help Defense Companies. Yet perhaps the most visible figure in this group was former defense minister Igor Rodionov, who immediately became a de facto leader of the movement on a par with Rokhlin.[135]

Rokhlin and Rodionov formed a carefully crafted balance in the leadership: The statements of the former were more radical, while the latter's were more moderate. On July 9, during a meeting of the organization committee, Rokhlin announced that if officers "rebel and march on Moscow," he was ready to join them.[136] On August 28, at the first gathering of the movement's Moscow chapter, Rokhlin stated that Russia was on the brink of a nationwide catastrophe. Rokhlin's appeals were widely published by the opposition media, and *Sovetskaya Rossiya* put out a special issue with documents from Rokhlin's movement and letters of support from ordinary citizens.[137]

Rodionov's statements were published separately and in different periodicals, and their tone was more restrained; they even denied that the new movement was part of the opposition.[138] Yet these divergences looked like a skillful tactic to broaden the range of potential allies. In a televised address, Rokhlin called on Yeltsin to resign and give either Yavlinsky or Zyuganov a chance to lead the country out of the crisis, while Rodionov courted Moscow mayor Luzhkov, calling him "the presidential candidate who would be most acceptable to the military."[139] However, the careful Luzhkov hastened to answer that Rodionov's implied association with him had "no basis whatsoever" and that he was not in contact with the movement.[140]

The president's reaction came with some delay, which suggested a degree of uncertainty. Only on July 21, in his meeting with Defense Minister Sergeyev, did Yeltsin deliver his verdict in his traditional style: "We will brush these Rokhlins aside."[141] In response, Rokhlin himself boldly stated that he was ready to fight for the resignation of Yeltsin and the entire cabinet and to replace them with "a government of popular trust."[142]

On August 15, in a statement titled "We Will Soon Lose the Right to Call Ourselves Russian Citizens," Rokhlin urged the public to "demand an accounting from the rulers for the whole six years of failed reforms." He went on: "We will push for a peaceful transfer of power in a constitutional way, as occurred in the Czech Republic, Slovenia, Bulgaria, and Yugoslavia, where tens of thousands of people went into the streets to demand the resignation of the ruling regimes."[143] It is worth noting that this was the first time in the post-1992 history of the anti-Yeltsin opposition that one of its leaders had compared his own struggle with the eastern European revolutionary movements of 1989, a point that could not fail to attract considerable sympathy from the democrats of those days.

Rokhlin also called for a broad opposition front and enhanced his legitimacy as a prime mover of such a coalition by firmly stating that he and his movement were not vying for political power for themselves. Rokhlin's other big asset as a politician (differentiating him from Lebed and ultranationalist communist leaders) was his consistent repudiation of ethnic intolerance and xenophobia, even though some extremist elements turned up at his meetings. In the words of Rokhlin, a Jew, his movement had no place "for those who profess the superiority of one nation over another."[144]

An indirect acknowledgment that military discontent was justified and the new movement had to be taken seriously came on August 28 with the ouster of

Yuri Baturin, the secretary of the Defense Council. Baturin was the author of shock therapy projects for military build-down and, according to rumor, the main plotter in the intrigue that led to Rodionov's firing. The exit of Baturin, a Chubais protégé, indicated that a determined and open opposition force that was ready for decisive action could still, in spite of everything, force the Kremlin to take note of its demands. On the other hand, this and other outcomes of Rokhlin's moves strengthened Chernomyrdin's position. In particular during these months, the premier took control of military-industrial policy and was appointed to supervise Rosvooruzhenie, the state-owned arms-trading corporation. After the presidential decree to this effect had been issued, Chernomyrdin removed the corporation's head, Aleksandr Kotelkin, who had in the past been close to Korzhakov and then to Potanin.

In the fall of 1998, Rokhlin was murdered in mysterious circumstances that aroused suspicions of government involvement. His movement, which had already lost momentum, weakened further. It was too threatening to the establishment, so figures like Rodionov faded into the background, and Rokhlin's successor, Ilyukhin, was not able to restore its vigor.[145]

THE 1997 AUTUMN CRISIS: ROLLING BACK THE "YOUNG WOLVES"

By late summer, it became obvious that the institutional mechanisms of the velvet dictatorship so carefully set up by the reformers were working poorly. Despite all the hopes the IMF invested in Chubais, he proved unable to significantly increase tax collections on a regular basis. He also had failed to successfully control the mass media. After the July auction of Sviazinvest, the losing bidders' media outlets persistently hurled muck at him and his team with impunity. Additionally, on July 1, in the twilight of its independent existence, *Izvestiya* had printed an article suggesting that Chubais, in addition to everything else, might be personally corrupt. The article asserted that in February 1996, a month after his sacking from the government, the Stolichny Savings Bank had extended a five-year interest-free loan of $2.9 million to the Center for the Defense of Private Property, which Chubais had just founded. The center had put up no collateral, and Chubais used the loan to speculate in the lucrative market for Treasury bills and then deposit the spectacularly large profits in his personal bank account. *Izvestiya* also claimed that in his capacity as presidential chief of staff, he had helped the same bank to take over a state-owned agricultural bank in November 1996.

Without disputing the facts, Chubais replied on July 5 that the interest-free loan was "absolutely normal" in any democratic country. Yet this hardly convinced anyone that nonprofit bodies in democratic countries could use such loans for short-term speculation in securities markets, or that their officers could legally deposit the profits from such speculation into their personal accounts. In addition, Chubais, who at that time headed Yeltsin's re-election campaign, had been in a position to issue public statements that could directly affect the price of the very government securities in which he was speculating. The whole matter was referred to the prosecutor general's office, which claimed to find nothing illegal in it because, as Streletsky wrote, "the laws are not written" for the likes of Chubais.[146]

In the meantime, Nemtsov had tied himself too closely to Chubais and found that his earlier popularity was declining. Chernomyrdin sensed the shakiness of the young reformers. In July, when Chubais was on vacation, the prime minister reasserted his control over the management of the cabinet, and on July 8, he even criticized Chubais's Finance Ministry for poor control over budget allocations.[147] However, the usual ups and downs of the seesaw no longer had the same effect on the public, which was angry now, according to opinion polls—not toward individual members of the cabinet, but with the government as a whole. As the Kremlin-oriented Public Opinion Foundation reported, in August 1997 only 20 percent of respondents agreed that "government policies are leading to an upswing of production and a bottoming out of the economic crisis"; 67 percent disagreed.[148]

Once again there was the smell of fire in the air, as the Communists and the labor unions promised a hot autumn. Nemtsov's closest associate, Deputy Prime Minister Oleg Sysuyev, issued a sobering statement: "I do feel the wall at my back. Only people who are habituated to the special conditions here in Moscow could fail to feel it."[149] Critical comments came also from people close to Yeltsin. Aleksandr Livshits, Chubais's predecessor as finance minister, found fault with "Chubaisocracy" and called for Keynesian-style changes in economic policy.[150]

The Russian cabinet responded to the acute criticism of its policies by continuing the habit of borrowing the slogans of its rivals. Boris Nemtsov came up with a promise to build a "people's capitalism" in place of the current bandit variety and was not shy about the fact that this slogan had once been put forward by the parliamentary opposition that had been crushed by the Kremlin's tanks—with Nemtsov's support—in October 1993. His speech was written by one of the former leaders of the parliamentary "democratic statists" or "national democrats" (that is, nationalistically inclined democrats), his aforementioned assistant, Aksiuchits.[151]

Changes in the interior design of Yeltsin's court, however, did not alter the substance of its policies. Despite the radical reformers' rhetoric about people's capitalism, the draft budget bill for 1998 did not envision much government effort to support small- and medium-size businesses. Despite promises to restore the government's role in the economy, the draft called for a further shrinking of government investment. Despite the government's assurances to maintain infrastructure and military-industrial plants, the draft budget bill foresaw continued privatizations along the old discredited lines.[152]

In September 1997, the reputation of Chubais and the ruling elite received a new blow: *Nezavisimaya gazeta* printed a document leaked by Boris Berezovsky's informers. It was the previously mentioned April letter from U.S. Deputy Treasury Secretary Summers to "Dear Anatoly" (Chubais). The letter contained peremptory and self-assured recommendations concerning each item on the government agenda, including methods of solving the "Dream Team's" domestic political problems. The content of the missive was aptly expressed by the headline: "The Recommendations of the U.S. Treasury Are Carried Out by Anatoly Chubais Far Better Than the Decrees of the Russian President."[153] Obviously, the letter was embarrassing for Chubais, Yeltsin, and the national pride of the vast majority of Russians.

In October, Moscow was shaken by a stock market crisis. The summer-long East Asian financial meltdown, culminating in the collapse of the Hong Kong stock exchange, triggered severe blows to the Moscow business and political elite. The stock prices of Russian companies went into free fall as Western investors pulled $5 billion of their money out of the Moscow stock and Treasury bill markets.[154] The Central Bank threatened dire sanctions against Russian investors who might be tempted to follow suit.[155] Russian and Western experts were unanimous in judging that this loss of investment had finally made unrealistic not just Yeltsin's March promise of 2 percent growth, but any growth perspective at all. The crisis made starkly obvious the dependency of Russia's vital economic indicators on global market conditions. Again, as at the beginning of the century, Russia looked like one of "the weakest links in the chain" of international finance. The responsibility for this financial defenselessness lay with Anatoly Chubais, the indefatigable fighter for an "open" economy.

In light of all this, it became less and less profitable for Yeltsin to keep Chubais as the locomotive of reform, his chief ideologist, and his envoy to the West. Already in August, there was sufficient reason to expect that Yeltsin would "curb Chubais before long."[156] Therefore, the scandal that plagued the $450,000 book advance to Chubais and his coworkers from Potanin's proxy became a convenient pretext to push the bungling "Dream Team" off center stage. In reality, Chubais's $90,000 cut was a modest sum compared to the financial abuses going on in the country, as we saw in the previous chapter. But it was this scandal—not Chubais's responsibility for damaging the national economy—that was the pretext chosen for the offensive against his clan. With such a pretext, there was no need to change basic economic policy, and Yeltsin might even be able to bring back the Chubais team later, if that were necessary.

Chubais's withdrawal into the shadows was also needed in order to draw qualified opposition experts into cooperation with the government and to broaden the coalition base, while keeping real policy in the same hands. Because he was famous for his Grand Inquisitor intolerance of dissent, Chubais lacked the sophistication required to recruit potentially willing opposition figures. Behind-the-scenes negotiations with potential turncoats from the

CPRF and Yabloko had always produced a visceral resentment against the Chubais clique.

In mid-November, after the book deal scandal had broken, Yeltsin decided that the time had come to act. He issued decrees firing Chubais's coauthors Aleksandr Kazakov, deputy presidential chief of staff and at the same time a member of the Gazprom board; Maksim Boiko, appointed three months before as chief of the State Property Committee; and Pyotr Mostovoi, chairman of the Anti-Monopoly Committee. Alfred Kokh had been dismissed earlier. Chubais himself submitted his resignation from all his posts, but Yeltsin kept him on as first deputy premier, while firing him as finance minister. Nemtsov also suffered losses in the process: He was removed as minister of fuel and energy on the pretext of "an excessive workload." But while Nemtsov was able to transfer this portfolio to his deputy and protégé, Sergei Kirienko, the choice of Chubais's successor as finance minister was a surprise—Mikhail Zadornov, a prominent member of Yabloko and the recent chairman of the Duma Budget and Finance Committee.

Zadornov's appointment resulted from a palace intrigue and went against the wishes of Yavlinsky, who harbored hopes of eventually becoming head of government himself and bringing in an entire team after a weakening or fall of the regime that he considered inevitable. Accordingly, the Yabloko faction in the Duma had voted to bar its own members from joining the government; in response Zadornov quit Yabloko. The operation had been cunningly designed: It demonstrated to the public that not just Communists and Zhirinovsky supporters were eager to abandon the unstable benches of the Duma opposition for plusher seats in ministries or large corporations, but that even the opposition democrats, who had the reputation of being incorruptible intellectuals, were now inclined to accept the Byzantine reality of court politics. Zadornov's exit undoubtedly had a demoralizing effect on Yabloko supporters.

As was to be expected, Prime Minister Chernomyrdin emerged triumphant from the crisis caused by Chubais's failures. Although there had been no feud between them, a certain quiet rivalry sometimes had been apparent. Chernomyrdin had been behind the choice of Zadornov; the latter's authority in the Duma now enabled the premier to enlarge the base of his coalition, and he was also able to add the Finance Ministry to his list of controlled assets. Yet immediately after grabbing the reins of economic management as they fell from Chubais's hands, Chernomyrdin hurried to reassure the ruling elite by declaring that no fundamental changes in economic policy should be expected. Indeed, there was no strong pressure for him to change it. The seesaw machinery typical of Yeltsin's rule required only minor adjustments, and the majority of Russian politicians, even though they mostly resented the system, lacked the will, ideas, organizational resources, and mutual trust that would have enabled them to get rid of Yeltsin, Chernomyrdin, and Chubais.

OPPOSITION DEVELOPMENTS IN 1997

Duma member Boris Fyodorov remarked in June 1997 that the situation reminded him of the years before 1917, when the old monarchy was dying and a modern parliamentary system was unable to take root.[157] Another observer found quite similar the disposition of political forces in mid-1997 and the situation in the spring and summer of 1992: "The same young reformers in the government, the same opposition majority in the parliament, the same recalcitrant governors in the provinces, the same nostalgia for the USSR in the routinized demonstrations. The cast of actors on the stage has changed slightly, but the play is the same."[158] Indeed, despite the illusions of some foreign observers that a torrent of changes had occurred, the political and ideological structure of society had stagnated over the six years of Yeltsin's reforms, especially when compared to the dynamics of the Gorbachev revolution.

The only relatively durable institutional base for opposition activity was the State Duma. The Duma opposition's influence on the feuding among the court clans, and thus on the fluctuation of the regime's policies, was defined not by the opposition's inner force but, rather, by the weakness of the social and political base of the regime itself. The government's faithful followers—the deputies of Chernomyrdin's OHR faction, the Russian Regions group, and the handful of deputies from the Gaidar-Chubais party—made up less than a quarter of the Duma. The largest of these groups, OHR, shaped by bureaucratic and personal loyalty to the premier rather than by any clear-cut political convictions, was in a permanent state of crisis. Its initial loyalty to the government was weakened by the suffocating atmosphere of the parliament, which was constantly humiliated and denied any real power or authority. In the words of one OHR member, "In the present situation, the cabinet has more supporters in the CPRF and [Zhirinovsky's] LDP than among us."[159]

In this ideological void, the OHR faction, lacking authoritative leaders, led a ghostly existence, always teetering on the brink of splits. During the summer of 1997 alone, three of its best known members left: Lev Rokhlin, Nikolai Travkin, and, finally, its caucus chairman, Sergei Belyayev, who quarreled with Chernomyrdin's apparatus. Amidst all this, the Kremlin and the cabinet were compelled to maneuver among the CPRF, Yabloko, and the fragmented nationalists. Such tactics became more and more complicated because in most political sectors, the forces seeking an intraelite compromise were gradually losing ground to radical opponents of the regime.

THE COMMUNISTS

Throughout 1997, the Communists worked hard to preserve a fragile equilibrium among the three major wings of their party—the national conservatives (exemplified primarily by Zyuganov), the radicals (such as Duma deputy

Viktor Ilyukhin), and the social reformers (such as Seleznev)—while continuing to lose rank-and-file members. As acknowledged by the party's number-two man, Valentin Kuptsov, CPRF membership rapidly shrank by half after July 1996—from about 500,000–600,000 to 250,000–280,000 members.[160] Aleksei Podberezkin's RAU Corporation and Spiritual Heritage organization remained the driving force pushing CPRF leaders toward compromise and integration with the ruling elite on the doctrinal basis of a conservative corporatist statism. However, Podberezkin's influence on the party as a whole was gradually declining, and the political ineffectiveness of the People's Patriotic Union of Russia, a CPRF front organization he engineered, was only one of the contributing factors.

The Podberezkin-Zyuganov ideological line was subjected to more and more devastating attacks from both the party's prominent members and the left radical media, especially in the pages of *Pravda-5*. Duma deputy Tatyana Astrakhankina publicly called Podberezkin an "agent of influence" of the government and held him responsible for the CPRF's "ideological crisis."[161] Many Communists saw national-conservative ideology as the cause for Zyuganov's fraternization with the Kremlin camp during the 1996 elections in which he was defeated. While the party expelled some of Zyuganov's most vehement critics, other radicals stayed in the leadership, such as Tamara Pletnyova.[162] The famous Duma deputy from the Kuzbass mining region, Tengiz Avaliani, opposed Zyuganov's re-election as party chairman at the fourth CPRF congress.[163]

The real threat from the left remained in the person of Zyuganov's rivals outside the CPRF, such as Anpilov, who insisted that "the CPRF was and remains a nomenklatura-style party."[164] The attitude of the new generation of dissenters toward Zyuganov was expressed by members of the Communist youth group Yeblom, who pelted him with rotten tomatoes while he was delivering a memorial wreath at the Lenin Mausoleum. One of the participants in this action later turned out to be an assistant to Avaliani.[165]

Not surprisingly, the radicals increasingly dominated the CPRF's large forums. Thus the party's fourth congress largely endorsed the platform of *Pravda-5* and announced the CPRF's transition from "constructive" to "responsible and irreconcilable" opposition.[166] In the corridors of the congress, prominent CPRF members complained to the media that if Zyuganov's course were to be sustained, the party's popularity might be reduced to almost nothing within two or three years.[167] Forced to yield to the radicals, Zyuganov announced his intention to change the constitution by both parliamentary and extraparliamentary methods—but, faithful to himself, he called on his comrades to integrate themselves into the existing power structure.

The general public, however, displayed little confidence in the radical tone of the CPRF congress: 37 percent of those queried believed that the CPRF's opposition would amount to words only and that in reality the party would cooperate with the executive branch.[168] Yavlinsky, whose persistence enabled him to attract some erstwhile CPRF supporters, remarked that the party had maintained "informal and amorphous relationships" with the government. The competition for votes between the CPRF and Yabloko became more obvious and led to mutual distancing, thus making the scenario of a broad opposition front (seen during the Chechnya war) less feasible.

In particular, the dwindling likelihood of such cooperation weakened the social-reformist wing of the CPRF—the party's flank that was ideologically close to Yabloko but not united on the question of possible cooperation with it. Duma Speaker Seleznev remained close to Yabloko; in his words, "They [Yabloko] are for a strong state, for a multiplicity of property forms, for strong social policies, for a level playing field, and we are for the same things."[169] But another party leader of the social-democratic stripe, Valentin Kuptsov, viewed the possibility of such cooperation as an "illusion." He saw Yavlinsky and Svyatoslav Fyodorov as "self-proclaimed social-democrats" and accused them of collusion with Yeltsin during the 1996 election.[170]

The economic ideas and proposals of the Communist faction were limited largely to their traditional goal of expanding the money supply. Not once did the Communists as a party attempt to focus public debate on the issue of returning to the Treasury the enormous national resources illegally moved into the pockets of private and corporate owners since 1987, although the radical Ilyukhin did so repeatedly as an individual deputy in the Duma.

THE DEMOCRATIC OPPOSITION

On the left, as we have noted, the democratic opposition continued to augment its influence as the most intellectually coherent alternative to the old and new oligarchies, while the Kremlin used all available means to co-opt Yabloko members who had the economic expertise that it needed. By 1997, Yabloko had established itself as the first structured political movement of the intelligentsia (in the traditional Russian sense of this word) and Yavlinsky had consolidated his image as the chief political leader of the intelligentsia, as was indicated by opinion surveys. On the other hand, he had personality traits that prevented him from becoming president of Russia: his inability to be brazen, his academic professionalism of judgment, and his moral scruples.

Inside Yabloko, especially in its Moscow leadership, divergences had grown, especially between the supporters of a further leftward drift (such as Vyacheslav Igrunov) and the proponents of a "reformist" coalition with the government (such as Ivan Grachev). These disagreements boiled over with the departure of Zadornov. As in the case of the CPRF's social-democratic wing, Yabloko's left wing suffered from the competition between the two parties, which compelled it to emphasize differences rather than seek civilized cooperation. This emphasis was reflected above all in the struggle for influence over Russia's labor unions. On Igrunov's initiative, Yabloko took part in the March 27 labor protest, displaying typical social-democratic slogans; however, the Communist-influenced FITUR denied Yabloko the right to form a separate column in the demonstration.[171]

Yabloko's leader, who appeared to sympathize with the left wing, inevitably had to hold the balance in the middle, trying to unite his followers around those goals that had the most support. Because the Duma remained the major, if not the only stage for Yabloko's political self-expression, it is not surprising that the party found unity in a drive to obtain more power for parliament by trying to amend the constitution. In particular, Yavlinsky spoke in favor of depriving the president of the ability to issue secret laws and also to issue decrees on economic matters that had the immediate force of law. Such a constitutional reform might have allowed Yavlinsky to accept the position of prime minister under most of the potential presidential candidates because he would have exercised enough authority to implement his program. In Yabloko's stance on economic policies, elements of mercantilism were increasing, which left less and less room for the Communists and national-conservatives to challenge Yabloko as an excessively pro-Western force. Thus Yavlinsky charged the government with failing both to ensure foreign markets for Russian goods and to provide protectionist defense for Russian producers.[172]

Nemtsov's and then Zadornov's arrival in the government posed a serious problem for Yabloko because these changes reflected the stubborn efforts of the Kremlin to disorient Yabloko's voters. Yavlinsky was obliged to work hard at explaining and defending his decision not to participate in the government. Besides the matters of principle involved, he saw in the attempts to entice his team to join the government a desire to eliminate Yabloko from the Duma, after which it would be easy to fire the Yabloko ministers as soon as anything went wrong. In connection with this ploy, Yavlinsky perceptively noted that Aleksandr Lebed's political trajectory—from the Duma to the Kremlin and thence into the wilderness—was not an example to be imitated. Also, friendly relations with Nemtsov did not inhibit Yavlinsky from noticing that, in institutional terms, Nemtsov had feet of clay. In Yavlinsky's words, "Nemtsov's whole existence in the cabinet is built on his personal relations with Yeltsin. Nothing more. As long as Yeltsin picks up the phone when Nemtsov calls, Nemtsov will represent something in the government. When everyone finds out that Yeltsin has stopped answering the phone, then it'll all be over."[173] It was this awareness that the country was ruled not by laws but by personal networks inside the elite that inhibited Yavlinsky and most of his colleagues from joining the executive.

In Yabloko's political neighborhood, some former radical Yeltsinists had moved over to the opposition, often using the organizations and reputation of the old human rights movement as their vehicles. During the summer of 1997, a group of human rights activists announced the founding of a new association called Common Action, whose purpose was "to promote oversight over the state authorities and to oppose the formation of a criminal-oligarchic regime in the country."[174] In this venture, along with the work of such authoritative 1960s dissidents as labor union organizer Lyudmila Alekseyeva, recently converted opponents of shock therapy were highly visible, such as Lev Ponomarev, one of the leaders of the defunct Democratic Russia. In his new role, Ponomarev issued attacks on the cabinet and called on the democrats to unite around Yavlinsky.[175] As Ponomarev rightfully observed, "The present rulers, who can hardly be described as democrats, cut their ties with and roots in the democratic movement three years ago." Meanwhile, Yeltsin, as an "able actor," "skillfully played the role of a fellow traveler" of the democrats.[176]

Having said all that, Ponomarev failed to mention that in 1992 he himself, as a fervent supporter of the regime, had resisted the attempts of independent-minded democrats to transform Democratic Russia into a genuine opposition force, which would have enabled it to survive as a powerful grassroots civic movement (see chapter 6). In October 1993, moreover, Ponomarev had welcomed the violent dissolution of the parliament. His disenchantment with Yeltsin and the Kremlin reformers occurred only after Gaidar and Chubais failed to place him high enough on their list of candidates for him to get into the Duma in December 1993. This served notice to him that the Yeltsin regime had squeezed every possible political advantage out of him and Democratic Russia and that their services were no longer required. In 1997, he moved into outright opposition and was not shy about calling Yeltsin's regime "an alien power," though without quoting the originator of this expression, Yuri Burtin.[177] Burtin was one of the earliest critics of the regime, whom Ponomarev had forced out of the Democratic Russia leadership in 1992 at the behest of the government.[178]

In sum, the Kremlin became aware that the demand of the educated public for the ideas and values of a Yabloko-style democratic opposition was growing and that the latter's links to the dissident legacy of the 1960s conferred historical legitimacy on its aspirations for postcommunist Russia. Having exhausted its means to contain this political force, and believing that the combined effects of Yabloko expansion and CPRF decline posed a potential threat, the Kremlin tried to both entice Yabloko members to defect and also publicize the accession to Yabloko of people whose pedigrees could only disorient the democratic left. This may help to explain the publicity around the return to the political scene of once-fervent Yeltsinists such as Ponomarev and Yeltsin's former propaganda minister Mikhail Poltoranin.[179]

THE SEMI-OPPOSITION OF YURI LUZHKOV

The increasing alienation of the powerful mayor of Moscow from the Kremlin in 1997 represented a development that was complex, significant, and rich in possibilities. The Luzhkov phenomenon could not be fitted neatly into any part of the opposition spectrum, although the mayor's apparent worldview suggested that he was halfway between Yabloko and statist nationalists like Rutskoi. Luzhkov was a controversial figure, viewed askance by traditional long-term oppositionists. From 1990 to 1993, he was one of the most assiduous and un-scrupulous architects of a capitalism oriented to the nomenklatura and criminal elements. By 1997, few journalists still dared to refer publicly to these criminals. An exception was Yevgeniya Albats, who gave her readers some vivid insights into the Mafiya world of two close associates of the mayor, Umar Dzhabrailov and Iosif Kobzon.[180]

According to conventional estimates, four-fifths of all financial flows in Russia found their way to Moscow. Without the skills of a formidable nomenkla-tura capitalist, Luzhkov would have been unable to achieve such an unprece-dented concentration of national resources in the capital. These qualities should have guaranteed Mayor Luzhkov the support of pragmatically minded regional and business elites who, having got their hands on a slice of the pie during the distribution of national assets, were now looking for order and stability, for clear-cut and predictable rules of the game, and for a firm central power capable of safeguarding their lives and property.

However, courage and persistence were not among the mayor's traits. His behavior vacillated markedly, depending on the political climate, and he was not immune to the Kremlin's political mind games. Thus, as the leader of the regional elites, Luzhkov had all the trump cards needed to become the arbiter be-tween Yeltsin and parliament in October 1993, a development that would have helped to avoid bloodshed. However, he was intimidated by a volley of gunfire that hit the Moscow city hall and promptly gave Yeltsin his endorsement, with-out which the president would hardly have dared to shell the White House. In the fall of 1994, Luzhkov, with support from Yavlinsky and MOST Bank, tried to pressure Yeltsin into abandoning his authoritarian scenario for reforms. But after Korzhakov's praetorian guard staged its brutal show of force against MOST, Luzhkov backed down and retreated into the shadows for quite a while. In December 1995, when Kremlin strategists were debating whether Yeltsin should run for a second term, Luzhkov gave a lecture at the Russian State University of the Humanities that contained a devastating critique of government policies, of which the most intransigent social-democrat would have been proud.[181] Yet after Yeltsin had demonstrated in early 1996 his determination to stay in power, Luzhkov put all of Moscow's administrative resources at the disposal of his campaign.

Thanks to his remarkable survival skills, Luzhkov managed to secure sup-port (or, at least, toleration) across a broad political spectrum. Those who might have blamed him for vacillation tended to accept him because of the absence of any realistic alternative. During the June 1996 mayoral election, Luzhkov garnered 89 percent of the Moscow vote—including the majority of those who were voting against Yeltsin on the same day. Although boosted by clever pre-election manipulations, the size of the winning margin gave Luzhkov a legiti-macy greater than that enjoyed by any other Russian politician of similar rank.

From the outset of the second shock therapy, Luzhkov assailed the government's policies so sharply that the media began to acknowledge him as "the new oppositionist-in-chief."[182] Luzhkov flayed Nemtsov's plans for housing and utilities reform, and successfully obtained from Yeltsin an exemption for Moscow.[183] He also won the sympathy of the national-conservatives by his repeated assertions that the Crimean city of Sevastopol should be considered juridically a part of Russia, and by his support for reunion with Belarus (Byelorussia).[184] In addition, he attacked Chubais and Berezovsky for leading the opposition to the union within the Russian leadership.

By becoming one of the founders of the Support Committee for Russian-Byelorussian Union, Luzhkov was bold enough to appear on the same list as such implacable leaders of the opposition as Baburin. As he had before, Luzhkov denounced Chubais-style privatization, demanding an "investigation of the legality" of a number of privatization deals.[185] Here, he was hitting a raw nerve because the prosecutor general had earlier drawn up a long list of crimes committed by Chubais's privatization agency in the early 1990s, only for the Kremlin to veto the idea of prosecutions.[186] He also joined the Yabloko faction in challenging the government's draft tax code, pointing out that it infringed on the interests of the regions and gave priority to revenue gathering over development needs. He also hinted broadly that Chubais represented foreign interests in the government.[187]

The Kremlin's attempt to weaken Luzhkov by sequestering budget funds earmarked for Moscow's special expenses as the national capital provoked a strong response. Speaking in the traditionally anti-Yeltsin city of Krasnodar, Luzhkov blamed the government for discriminating against Moscow and for covertly trying to deny Moscow its highway and subway funds. "The federal authorities are irritated by the independent behavior of the capital, by its own distinctive line on issues of national economic development."[188] He also sided with Yevgeny Nazdratenko, the rebellious Mafiya-connected governor of the Primorski province in the Far East, calling on the Federation Council to demand that Yeltsin cancel the emergency powers of his presidential representative there, General Kondratov of the Federal Security Service.[189] In the end, the pro-Nazdratenko campaign won the day.

Although his criticism was harsh, Luzhkov prudently avoided personal confrontation with Yeltsin and thus grew into a potentially unifying force for a large number of realistically minded opponents of the regime—and into a clear and present danger to the shock therapists. His influence was reflected by the vigorous agitation against him by Gaidar's party and also by the support he received from an influential ideologue of national authoritarianism and erstwhile ally of Lebed, Andranik Migranyan.[190] Open support of Luzhkov (who began his Moscow career as a boss in the agro-industrial complex) came from the Agrarian Party, which promised assistance for Moscow from farm producers in all regions should an open challenge to the regime by Luzhkov result in a food blockade of Moscow by Western suppliers.[191]

To avoid becoming a target for all-round political attack, Luzhkov repeatedly denied that he would bid for the presidency. Although a nationwide organization called "Luzhkov For President" built him up in both the daily media and semiopposition periodicals such as *Novaya Rossiya* (founded with more-or-less overt financial support from the Moscow city government), Luzhkov did not link himself publicly to the campaign and insisted (perhaps sincerely) that the daily power he already wielded as mayor of Moscow satisfied him for the time being.[192]

NATIONALISTS

From 1992 to 1997, the nationalists remained the most fragmented and amorphous of Russia's major political forces. The long-standing and partially successful Kremlin efforts to co-opt the national-conservatives created a situation in which, by 1995, nationalism ceased to be seen as an opposition ideology. In addition, mistrust of Western governments' policies toward Russia (a sentiment akin to nationalism) became a component of the nationwide foreign policy consensus, encompassing even those democratic and liberal circles in society that did not challenge the basic values of Western civilization. In this way, the nationalist idea spread itself thinly across the entire political spectrum. To describe oneself as a pure nationalist—never a widespread phenomenon in Russia—gradually came to seem sectarian.

The main casualty of this process was Lebed, who, throughout Yeltsin's long illness of 1996–97, seemed to be a major threat to the political status quo. As late as March 1997, while on a party-building tour across the country, Lebed confidently stated: "The country is on the road to a social explosion. The president is incapacitated. Power has dropped from his hands and must be picked up. . . ."[193] Opening the first congress of his party on March 14, Lebed felt himself so firmly in the saddle that he rejected cooperation with communists or democrats out of hand and declared that he was moving along a third path. Lebed's party was sponsored in particular by the "aluminum kings," the brothers Lev and Mikhail Chernoi, whose financial backing had ensured the election of Lebed's younger brother as prime minister of aluminum-rich Khakassia in Siberia.[194] Among the largest banks, Lebed still received backing from Potanin's Oneksimbank. Oneksimbank bet on Lebed and Chubais simultaneously, which may help account for Chubais's astute aping of the general's most popular traits—toughness, devotion to ironclad order, and inflexibility in the struggle against his opponents.

By the spring of 1997, however, confidence in Lebed was declining, especially regarding his authenticity as a nationalist leader. In addition to such controversial points in his record as his clandestine bargain with Yeltsin in the spring of 1996, and what were seen as his one-sided concessions to the Chechens at Khasavyurt, there were his too frequent trips to the West and the favorable comments about him by such intensely disliked figures as Henry Kissinger and George Soros, which looked like endorsements.[195] Many opponents on the left viewed him as yet another incarnation of Samuel Huntington's ideal of the pro-Western authoritarian leader and foresaw that the shock therapists might be able to use Lebed as a tough enforcer of their Pinochet-style doctrine. In addition, more enlightened radicals believed that American conservatives were shaping and using Lebed's image to pursue their own purposes. In the words of Eduard Limonov, Lebed "is cherished by American hawks as a political and psychological illustration of the inhuman face of the Russian people, which can be used to increase American taxpayers' support for defense spending."[196]

The extent of mistrust toward Lebed among the opposition became visible during the March 27 protest action of the labor unions, when a hostile crowd shouted him down as he tried to speak from the tribune in Moscow.[197] Even before that, Lebed had been unable to count on support from the same social strata to which the Communists or Yabloko appealed. He inherited his mass following largely from Zhirinovsky and Rutskoi—that is, retail merchants who were used to defending their economic interests by physical force; consequently, they had interactions with the criminal underworld. This social group was defined by world chess champion Gary Kasparov—one of Lebed's few well-known associates and also his "foreign minister." According to Kasparov, Lebed's party was made up of "people between 25 and 45 who have come into fortunes. Let's not specify how they did it."[198] The labor movement, just like the big nomenklatura and bureaucratic capitalists, had every reason to distrust Lebed, while most of the intelligentsia, even if nationalistically minded, viewed him as a clearly hostile force. In the words of Aleksei Podberezkin, Lebed's party is built "around the principle of hatred toward fedoras and eyeglasses."[199]

Lebed's eclipse was in fact preordained. It resulted from his abortive union with Yeltsin's team in 1996, described in the previous chapter. By trading his Duma mandate for an executive office, which he would soon lose unceremoniously, Lebed also lost the only national forum still available in Russia for an opposition figure. Lebed's enemy, Sergei Kurginyan, opined that "Yeltsin not only managed to neutralize Lebed after cynically using him, but also made him permanently harmless."[200] This estimate—accurate except for the word "permanently"—was shared by the progovernment media, which remarked with a slight touch of regret: "Lebed's image as a decisive and efficient politician is being erased from the mass consciousness. His party has not acquired a mass base, and he is losing support in the military."[201] Lebed succeeded in alienating his most reliable and competent associates, such as Sergei Glaziev and Lyudmila Vartazarova, and ended up in political isolation, surrounded by inexperienced and uninspired people. His hopes for an alliance with Korzhakov also failed.

The emergence of Rokhlin's movement (though, strictly speaking, it cannot be classified as nationalist) turned into one more blow for Lebed. In a gesture that smacked of despair, when Lebed met Rokhlin in Tula, he publicly announced that his party was joining Rokhlin's movement, despite the fact that Rokhlin had repeatedly expressed mistrust of Lebed and unwillingness to cooperate with him.[202] Ultimately, Lebed's party was denied admission to the movement—a decision made public by Rokhlin himself.[203]

An alternative center of regrouping for "pure" nationalists remained the Russian All-People's Union (RAPU), headed by Deputy Duma Speaker Sergei Baburin. Baburin enjoyed historical advantages as a long-term, persistent opponent of Yeltsin's policies starting in early 1991, and as someone who could not be suspected of secret collusion. Besides, Baburin was a quintessential parliamentarian: He ran second in the elections for speaker of the Supreme Soviet in 1991, functioned continuously as a leader of various factions and groups of deputies, and became deputy speaker of the Duma in January 1996. He had mastered the Duma's institutional culture and learned to achieve his goals, including those of a nationalistic bent, by democratic means. Unlike Lebed, he was not feared as a potential dictator—which helped him to consolidate national democrats who had become disillusioned with Yeltsin, such as the once-famous Ilya Konstantinov (see chapter 6). Still, the doors of RAPU were not closed to representatives of the traditional elites such as Oleg Baklanov, an August 1991 putschist who served on the RAPU presidium.[204]

Baburin also looked for sponsors and a social base in the metallurgy sector, but, unlike Lebed, he managed to put together a coherent group, not only in Russia, but also in the former Comecon countries. He gave political leadership to an umbrella group of east European metallurgical companies whose owners wanted to advance their interests in the European Union market in response to the Europeans' protectionist antidumping legislation.[205] However, sustained leadership and organization of political groups was never one of Baburin's fortes, so his initiatives tended to lose momentum. He also disturbed some people by his occasional interactions with such radical figures as Stanislav Terekhov.

Baburin's left-leaning outlook was oriented toward urban populations, especially the traditionalist intelligentsia and skilled labor. Beginning in 1993, when the rising influence of the Communists compelled him to take his party out of the National Salvation Front, Baburin repeatedly and emphatically distanced himself from CPRF nomenklatura conservatism, convincingly blaming the Communists for the weakness and indecisiveness of the opposition movement. Unlike Zyuganov, Baburin was not allergic to the word "revolution." Moreover, from autumn 1996 on, he claimed several times that a "revolutionary situation" had developed. In March 1997, despite his intense and long-standing commitment to parliamentarism as the core of democracy, he called for civil disobedience and a shift to extraparliamentary methods of struggle, saying that "the politics of maneuvering and concessions has proved fruitless."[206] Inside the Duma, however, Baburin showed himself more likely to side with Yabloko than with the Communists, especially when it came to spearheading no-confidence votes against the government.

Smaller groupings of national-democratic orientation also preserved their autonomy and remained politically active. Worthy of mention among these was the Democratic Party of Russia. In the spring of 1997, the party set up (with the participation of Baburin's RAPU) a Union of Patriotic and Democratic Forces under the ideological leadership of Glaziev and the political patronage of Yegor Stroyev, the governor of Orel region and speaker of the parliament's upper house.[207] Radical ethnic nationalists also became somewhat stronger during this period, primarily because of the election of Dmitri Rogozin and then Yelena Panina as members of the Duma.[208]

UNDERGROUND SUBVERSIVE MOVEMENTS

The higher profile of subversive groups in 1997, including some with terrorist leanings of the type Jowitt calls "movements of rage,"[209] was an alarming signal of the inadequacy of the legal opposition and its loss of the public's confidence. The most spectacular actions of these new Savinkovs were the bombing of the monument to Nicholas II and the failed attempt to blow up the huge new memorial to Peter the Great in Moscow.[210] Responsibility for the latter attempt was claimed by two near-bankrupt young businessmen, the names of whose underground organizations—the Revolutionary Military Council and the Workers' and Peasants' Red Army—recalled the 1917–21 Bolshevik terror.[211] As they frankly stated, their actions were a response to Yeltsin's launching of a confrontational debate about demolishing the Lenin Mausoleum and were aimed at provoking the many people who still revere the Bolshevik leader. A chronicle of terrorist actions in Russia published by the media suggested that, despite the reassurances of the government and some opposition leaders, political violence had long ceased to be taboo, not only for the rulers (this was evident in October 1993 and the Chechnya war), but also for people caught in despair at the bottom of society.[212]

THE NATURE AND DYNAMICS OF THE ANTI-WESTERN CONSENSUS

As noted earlier, the absence in Russia of a well-organized and influential force of a distinctly nationalistic type has been more than compensated for by the increasingly consensual "anti-Western" mood of public opinion—among both supporters and enemies of the Yeltsin regime, among elites and ordinary citizens. In 1997, the most spectacular manifestations of this consensus (and those most disturbing for the West) included the nationwide campaign against NATO expansion; the Duma law blocking the repatriation of trophy art taken by the Soviets from Germany after World War II; and, finally, the discriminatory bill on freedom of conscience and religious organizations that Yeltsin signed into law on September 19, 1997.[213]

The heated domestic and international debates about the latter bill revealed an ideological alliance between the Kremlin, the national-conservative Duma majority, and the Moscow Orthodox Patriarchate, with substantial support in various strata of Russian society. Seen against the background of increasing regime-society polarization over almost all other issues, mistrust toward the West and the idea that Western and Russian interests could be mutually exclusive gradually emerged as perhaps the main psychological factor holding elite and society loosely together.

A detailed academic investigation of this complicated issue would require a separate work. Instead, we will limit ourselves here to a brief interpretation of this new anti-Westernism, based on analytical points made in this book. In our view, it would be wrong to treat this growing consensus of mistrust as an expression of ideological nationalism—because, as noted in chapters 2 and 6, the Russian national mentality has not been prone to nationalism in the usual sense of the word. One of the reasons for the new anti-Western mood was the growing public awareness of Russia's acutely painful structural dependence on the global economic system and especially on its leading financial centers. Another factor concerned the mutual cultural and psychological misunderstandings, the roots of which lie in the two-sided communications barrier that has divided Russia from the ruling elites of Western nations, above all the United States. Let us begin with this latter point.

As psychologists have shown, in every communication process with a certain degree of complexity (especially collective communication between nation-states), each side tends to perceive the actions of the other as being better organized and more deliberately goal-oriented than its own are—and, also, than the other's actions are in reality. Rational thinking, with its analytical apparatus, should (but often does not) allow us to counteract this predisposition to perceive the other side in this distorted way. For example, during the Cold War period in Russian-American relations, flare-ups were marked by monolithic perceptions of each other, as in the West's rigid totalitarian model of Soviet society. On the other hand, the years of détente provided an opening for a more enlightened and analytical approach, which allowed observers to see the countries of each bloc as complex social organisms with their own internal contradictions.

Yet for the Russian elites who defined perceptions of global politics for their own populace, this rational-analytic faculty of seeing the West in a differentiated way began to erode rapidly late in the Gorbachev era, especially among pro-Western circles of elite and opposition intellectuals. In a nutshell, these Moscow elites went from a monolithic perception of the West as enemy to an equally simplistic view of the West as savior. One of the main reasons for this one-sided way of seeing things was the artificial isolation of most Soviet citizens from the West, which contrasted with the growing Soviet dependency on the world economy. There was also the provincialism of postwar Kremlin leaders, who, by their education and career, lacked the international sophistication of the founders of the Soviet state and their adversaries.

An idealistic perception of the West as one homogeneous unit, together with the uncritical belief in the existence of a universal harmony of interests, were traits shared by the Gorbachev team, by leaders of the democrats and reformers, and by most of their hard-line opponents. Despite much evidence to the contrary, the West was perceived as an undifferentiated and static force, personified by such people as Bush, Baker, Thatcher, Kohl, and later Clinton, who were seen in Russia as spokespeople for a united and purposeful set of interests. This view was not affected by the fact that in reality, during the entire course of the Soviet disintegration, the West had no clear-cut or consensual understanding of its interests as a whole vis-à-vis Russia, to say nothing of a clear and rational strategy. The neoliberal economic doctrine, whose application was thought to have yielded some of the desired results in Britain and the United States in the late 1970s and early 1980s, was uncritically perceived by many Russians as the only correct and universal recipe for economic rejuvenation, one that enjoyed universal and unquestioning support in the West.

In the cacophony of Western commentaries on economic reform in Russia, the voices that came through loudest and clearest to Russians were those that expressed euphoria about the changes and that endorsed not just reforms, but also the individuals who declared themselves most loudly to be reformers. Thus the position of "the Western world" as a whole was interpreted by most Russians as concerted support for a single scenario for their country and, moreover, as the readiness of the Western elites to share responsibility with Russian rulers for that scenario's execution and results. Because that scenario, as we have seen, brought tragic consequences for Russia, it was no surprise when the bulk of the public in the mid-1990s—especially those who had been most eager to entrust their future to the good intentions of the West—now began to charge the West with much of the blame for what occurred.

Which side had the ability to identify and counteract this distorted perception of Western activities in Russia, this harbinger of future disenchantment, mistrust, and, perhaps, even more ominous developments? Certainly Western elites, and especially the U.S. establishment, had devoted far greater resources to analyzing the former enemy and forecasting its behavior than Moscow ever had vis-à-vis the West. Even though the knowledge accumulated by Sovietologists was imperfect, it nonetheless provided fuller and more objective accounts of the cultural and psychological characteristics of Russia than Russians had available about America. However, in 1990–93, the Bush and Clinton administrations neglected most of these resources and chose as the cornerstone of their policies the supposedly universal Washington Consensus, the strategy for economic change that had been developed by economists to fit Russia without reference to the country's unique historical and social contours. In the view of many Russians, this choice linked U.S. policies directly to Yeltsin's harmful reform scenario of shock therapy and also to his authoritarian means for carrying it out. We believe these policies were rooted in weak statesmanship, poor use of available expertise, and sometimes short-term domestic considerations. Yet even if, as we firmly believe, Western policy (often seen in Russia as conscious and deliberate interference) was not intentionally harmful, this does not alleviate its consequences—consequences we see as equally harmful for both sides and also damaging to the future of Russian-Western relations.

Whatever the case, policymakers under Bush and Clinton apparently believed that after the disappearance of the USSR as a strategic adversary, concern about how U.S. policy really appeared to most Russians was secondary. Thus these U.S. officials preferred to prop up by artificial means those self-styled Russian reformers who were most complaisant toward the West—to the detriment of long-term mutual understanding and partnership with those responsible groups in Russian society who were likely to become more influential in the future. Moreover, by uncritically supporting Yeltsin, Gaidar, Chubais, and their associates, U.S. policymakers contributed to an alarming weakening of the Russian intelligentsia, which had historically served as the most solid long-term social and cultural base of pro-Westernism and Westernization in Russia. The economic and related strategies of the reformers not only discredited that part of the Western-minded intelligentsia that had helped Yeltsin come to power but also produced the material improverishment of the intelligentsia, a deep intellectual and moral crisis throughout its ranks, and its marginalization in public life.

All this leads us to view the anti-American consensus in today's Russia as a natural and logical outcome of strategic miscalculations in U.S. policy, as well as in Russian policy. Thus, although the economic and psychological dependency of Russia on the West is a structural phenomenon, accepted by the Kremlin's leaders and exacerbated by their mistakes and weaknesses, this does not change the fact that U.S. policymakers have managed their superior power without the wisdom and foresight they displayed when assisting the destinies of Western Europe and Japan after World War II.

The crisis of 1997 provoked by NATO expansion was an especially serious test of the wisdom and generosity of leaders of the United States, the only remaining superpower. The decision to bring three former Soviet allies into NATO—two of them nations with Slavic culture—was the watershed beyond which Russians' mistrust of U.S. policy became a dominant note in Russia's public consciousness. The decision exacerbated many Russians' regret about their leaders' one-sided concessions to the West of the previous decade, concessions often motivated by idealism and excessive trust. NATO expansion was not just an isolated disappointment, but the biggest in a series of Russian foreign policy failures that marked 1997 and rounded out a full decade of what had become a tradition of retreat for Soviet and Russian diplomacy, starting with the pullout from Afghanistan in 1988.

Besides the NATO controversy, 1997 also saw other foreign policy setbacks, such as the West's de facto snubbing of persistent attempts by the Russian elite to obtain full membership in the Group of Seven. Russia was also hit by the European Union's antidumping measures, which were especially onerous, given that Western insistence on Russia's removal of trade barriers had created a situation in which 54 percent of the country's consumer goods were imported.

In addition, the May 1997 peace treaty between Russia and "the Chechen Republic of Ichkeria" aroused deep, if largely suppressed resentment in some circles, especially those of the power ministries. The treaty stated that the two sides had agreed to build their relations "in accordance with the generally recognized principles and norms of international law" and that these relations would be ones "of equality."[214] Although the treaty was not persistently opposed in public at the time, two years later the level of anger it caused became clear during the launching of a new war against Chechnya, a region that the power ministries and others had always regarded inwardly as being an integral part of Russia.

Many Russians, including traditional Westernizers, viewed the decision to invite Poland, the Czech Republic, and Hungary to join NATO as evidence of U.S. readiness to ignore the fundamental interests—and no less important, the national dignity—of Russia in favor of the alliance's bureaucratic interests and electoral support for Democratic politicians representing overwhelmingly east European constituencies. Even such a moderate member of the proreform elite as Aleksandr Shokhin, the leader of the OHR faction in the Duma, claimed that NATO expansion would trigger the militarization of the Russian economy, while also denying Russia its remaining arms markets in eastern Europe.[215] Grigori Yavlinsky, considered one of the foremost leaders of contemporary pro-Westernism, commented that Russia's giving in to NATO expansion "demonstrates the surrender of our foreign policy."[216] Aleksei Podberezkin, the shadow foreign minister of the conservative opposition majority, stated that both the opposition and the Duma should accept responsibility for the Paris accord that Russia and NATO signed in May 1997—a view that was repudiated by neither the Communists nor the democratic opposition and reflected a stance shared by a wide range of politicians.[217] Finally, the anti-NATO group created among Duma deputies was joined by members of all factions, so that the group's traditional hard-liners found themselves in a minority. The anti-NATO group became the largest association of deputies in the Duma, numbering 254 out of 450 members.

The position of Russia's Westernizers on the whole issue usually derives not from any military threat, which, most of them agree, NATO expansion does not pose. Rather, in NATO expansion they detect Western unwillingness to recognize Russia as a part of European and Western civilization, which they find insulting and painful in the light of their decades of resistance to communism and upholding of Western values. Judging from the entire panoply of U.S. policies toward postcommunist Russia, with NATO expansion at its pinnacle, many of them drew the conclusion that from the start influential forces in the West accepted with equanimity the defeat of genuine Russian democrats and Westernizers, and even preferred to them the authoritarian politicians—such as Chubais and Lebed—to whom they looked for stability without regard to the fate of democracy and civil society. One of the most radical Russian Westernizers, Sergei Kovalev, expressed a widespread opinion when he said that those Western leaders who think that "Russia has nothing to do with Europe" are valuable allies of the Russian nationalists. In Kovalev's view, Western policies, to the extent that they were defined by such leaders, "made a large contribution to the unfortunate developments in Russia that resulted in the Chechnya war. Geopolitical racism, whether emanating from Mr. Zhirinovsky or from his American co-thinkers, can bear only one fruit—Russia transformed into a huge and dangerous source of instability worldwide."[218]

However, it would be too simple to reduce all anti-Western rhetoric by Russian politicians and mass media to the natural reaction of protest against apparently self-interested American behavior and against the repeated demonstrations of Western superiority. There is, of course, another side of the coin. The Russian ruling elite has striven to hang on to power by evading responsibility for the failures of shock therapy, and this has required putting the main responsibility on the West. Clearly, at the outset of the reforms, Yeltsin and his entourage, encouraged by influential Westerners, believed that by dint of their tough and widely resented policies they would earn large-scale Western credits and massive infusions of investment, as well as Western acceptance of Yeltsin's Russia as the legitimate and full heir of the superpower attributes of the USSR, including its sphere of influence. On their side, the Bush and Clinton administrations acted in this spirit at first, offering aid, trade, "strategic partnership," and unconditional support of Yeltsin. However, when things began to go wrong in Russia, the Clinton team and the IMF refused to change their reform strategy. As a result, the situation deteriorated further, and Washington increasingly resorted to blaming the Russians. This mutual misperception gave the Russian ruling elite reason to suspect an American "betrayal." Yeltsin and his court (both the self-styled reformers of the Chubais vintage and the conservatives of the Chernomyrdin camp) were so disappointed with Western unwillingness to waive Soviet-era debts that they would have been happy to put themselves at the head of a nationalist party and blame the West for their own sins, if only such a U-turn on their part could ever have seemed credible to the general public or at least to traditional nationalists.

In this respect, the behavior of Anatoly Chubais was particularly revealing. In the spring of 1997, believing himself to be the master of the Russian economy and the media, he hastened to show that the Yeltsin regime was no longer dependent on the financial and political help of the West. He proudly announced that Russia did not need any more IMF loans and would not ask for new ones when the current payments ended.[219] However, IMF credits were not so generous when tied to the conditionalities Russia had been compelled to accept, so his declaration did not impress most of the public, especially because even after the announcement, IMF money kept flowing into the Treasury through Chubais's hands: a quarterly tranche of $700 million arrived not long after he spoke.

Soon Chubais ostentatiously broke off his relations with the U.S. Agency for International Development, which was portrayed in the pro-Chubais media as a major patriotic move. Yet the real reason behind this decision was that Chubais had become too deeply entangled in a relationship with Harvard University's Institute for International Development, which was in charge of administering U.S. funds to Russia and whose associates were charged by AID with improperly using their insider information to profit from financial speculation in Russia.[220] Thus by quickly canceling the AID contract, Chubais minimized the damage to his reputation among the Americans and among his rivals in Russia. Later the nationalist anti-Western slant in the statements and actions of Chubais and Nemtsov was accentuated under the impact of their alliance with the nationalist-minded banker Potanin. In the course of the ensuing media war regarding the Sviazinvest sale, the pseudo-liberal press controlled by Chubais and Potanin never tired of harping on the Jewish backgrounds of their rivals, Berezovsky and Gusinsky.

There was another factor that reinforced the interest of most elite groups in encouraging the emerging anti-Western consensus. As became clear in 1997, Russian rulers lived in mortal fear of any serious critique of Yeltsin's regime in the Western media. The reprinting of a number of unfavorable articles from the West in Russian periodicals provoked feverish damage control efforts by the Kremlin spin doctors. The anguished yelps of Russian officials and oligarchs— be they Chubais, Chernomyrdin, or Berezovsky—in response to Western revelations about their possible personal corruption were especially thought-provoking in light of the fact that hundreds of similar and equally well-documented accusations had been published inside Russia, starting in the early days of reform, but had been dismissed by the regime as slanders inspired by "dark forces." Russians' extensive documentation of their rulers' violations of legal and moral norms, which we sampled in chapter 8, simply received no substantive reply from the Kremlin.

Why, then, the much greater sensitivity to Western than to domestic criticism? First, of course, the opposition was fragmented and deprived of any stable institutional base from which to challenge the abuses and authoritarianism of the Yeltsin group. Less obviously, Western opinion emerged as an autonomous and quite influential opposition force inside Russia for quite a different reason. Extensive evidence in this book suggests that the Russian rulers would have been happy to dispense with the parliament altogether in 1993 and drive the opposition parties underground had they not risked losing the support of the U.S. government and the IMF under the impact of Western opinion. Thus we see that the effects of globalization and Russian structural dependency (as discussed in chapter 2) cut in two directions: On the one hand, they painfully restricted Russia's ability to choose an autonomous strategy of economic development based on its national interests and also strengthened the position of the Russian oligarchs. On the other hand, they restrained the oligarchy's greed for absolute power by inhibiting its temptation to destroy the parliament and the seeds of civil society. This situation was broadly comparable to the developments of the détente era, when concern about Western public opinion restrained the Soviet oligarchs in their desire to destroy the various dissident movements.

How could the Yeltsinites mitigate their dilemma? They badly needed to engineer such a degree of anti-Western consensus in society that the most dangerous opposition elements could be isolated from the moral and psychological support of the outside world. Unlike in the 1970s, the task of the ruling clique was easier to achieve, primarily because of the West's mistakes in its Russia policy that we have discussed. More specifically, the consensus of mistrust toward the West permitted the Kremlin to maintain a disposition of forces under which the national-conservative leadership of the CPRF preserved its dominant position in the variegated landscape of the opposition. These CPRF leaders and their closest allies in the opposition and in the Kremlin kept insisting (and apparently believed) that any radical, bottom-up transformation of the existing system in the direction of democracy and genuine economic freedom would play into the hands of the West. More important, such a transformation would be detrimental to Russia's unity, because it would lead to the splitting and further debilitation of the ruling elites.

This type of opposition ideology, grounded in historical fatalism and a denial of the ability of new generations to draw lessons from the mistakes of their predecessors, relieved Yeltsin's regime of at least half of its concerns about its own survival and how to prevent the recurring threat of social explosion. Logically, therefore, the CPRF national-conservatives, whom Yeltsin rigorously excluded from economic policymaking, were allowed actively to influence the formation of foreign policy and its ideology. This tended to deter Western political forces from cooperating with the Russian opposition and impeded mutual understanding between the democratic opponents of the Yeltsin oligarchy and their potential Western partners.

To the extent that the Yeltsin-Chernomyrdin-Chubais regime and the cartel of financiers, raw materials barons, and arms traders that propped it up became rhetorically, if not substantively, more intransigent in their relations with the West and with genuine Russian democrats, and increasingly discarded the verbal shell of reformism, their conservatively clannish Byzantine substance became more and more evident to observers.

SHAKY FOUNDATIONS IN THE HOUSE OF YELTSIN: FINANCIAL COLLAPSE AND THE ONSET OF FAMILY ANXIETY

The years 1998 and 1999 witnessed mounting political, financial, and military problems, which remarkably did not destroy Yeltsin's system of rule. They ended with the president's sudden resignation—a present to the Russian people on the very eve of the new millennium. However, the cynically conceived and brilliantly manipulated bequeathing of presidential power to Vladimir Putin, an eight-month process sealed by his election on March 26, 2000, appeared merely to reanimate the essence of Yeltsin's system, if in a slightly different guise. Thus the exponents of market bolshevism triumphed again. While observing the forms of a minimalist, Schumpeterian democracy, they once more manipulated the electoral process in ways that negated democracy's goals. Above all, they negated the Russian populace's right to informed participation in the making of critical decisions, such as launching a new war against the Chechens and the selection of a new president.

The period shows an often physically ill Yeltsin to be heavily obsessed with his personal power and private interests—and therefore unconcerned about the national interest and devoid of new ideas on any topic except how to manipulate people and events for his own ends. A succession of grand and tactical political, economic, and legal bargains made earlier are now showing their severely troubling consequences, and Yeltsin is under intense pressures from many sides: the Duma, certain oligarchs, the miners, the IMF, foreign investors, Swiss prosecutors, Russian prosecutors, militant Muslims, Luzhkov and Primakov, even the Federation Council and the U.S. government. His only possible domestic backers are the oligarchs, as Berezovsky gleefully notes. However, Yeltsin sounds almost pathetic when he helplessly appeals to "the big banks that bought important industrial enterprises during privatization" to invest in the real economy out of gratitude for the privileges he has given them. To enable them to invest, the state has "promoted the concentration of financial and industrial resources." Now, he begs, "society has the right to count on reimbursement."[221] Alternatively, he issues empty threats, telling Berezovsky he may "drive him out of the country" if the oligarch does not stop his intrigues aimed at putting his imprint on a new government.[222]

On other occasions, though, Yeltsin brutally and impulsively wields his presidential power. On March 23, 1998, for example, he suddenly sacks—without giving a reason—his faithful prime minister of the past five years, Viktor Chernomyrdin, and with him the government. Chubais, Nemtsov, and Anatoly Kulikov depart for good. A month earlier, Chernomyrdin had made statements in Washington that implied he might be Russia's next president. These remarks were lèse majesté because Yeltsin had not yet decided whether to run for a third term himself and was still periodically issuing contradictory statements on the subject.[223]

Yeltsin named as acting premier Sergei Kirienko, a man who met two criteria of paramount importance to him: He was a provincial banker and oilman with relatively little national political experience; as such, he would not pose a threat to Yeltsin if the latter ran for re-election. Kirienko also was a "young reformer" who would appeal to the West and thus keep Yeltsin in good standing with his friends Clinton and Kohl. However, Kirienko was a neophyte with no political base; he could not hope to persuade the Duma to vote for IMF-type policies—and therefore would need to subvert democracy even more than his predecessor by having Yeltsin rule through presidential decrees. These factors apparently eluded Yeltsin's calculations on a successor. Moreover, most of the political class registered sharp opposition to the nominee: the Duma ignored Yeltsin's threat to dissolve it and formally rejected Kirienko on April 10. But Yeltsin did not retreat and seek a better candidate. He stubbornly schemed to get his way—at the expense of Russia's being without a confirmed premier for more than a month, and then getting one rammed down its throat.

The Duma's rising anger at Yeltsin was clear enough from the fact that General Rokhlin, head of its Defense Committee, had announced on March 31 that it now possessed enough materials to start impeachment proceedings against the president. Stung by this announcement and by the rejection of Kirienko, Yeltsin decided to renominate the young businessman and this time openly use the weapon of bribery. On April 13, he announced that he had told his lieutenant, Pavel Borodin, who handled perquisites like cars and apartments for deputies, to take care of deputies' needs, providing they showed "a constructive approach" to Kirienko's nomination. He added that he had told Borodin not to deal with deputies' requests before April 17, the date set for debating the nomination. Yeltsin said pointedly that deputies would understand his remarks.[224]

However, the Duma responded by rejecting Kirienko even more forcefully than before, by 271 votes to 115. Only later, when Yeltsin nominated him yet again and the critical third vote neared, did the bribery work its magic, coming on top of deputies' fears of losing their seats if Yeltsin exercised his right to dissolve the Duma. This time, many of the Duma's parliamentarians were absent or abstained, and about forty Communists reportedly broke ranks, taking advantage of the secret ballot and voting "the right way."[225] On April 24, Kirienko's previous crushing defeat suddenly became a crushing victory—by 251 to 25. As the media noted in a variety of derisive formulations, the deputies "saved their apartments and their cars."[226]

In many ways, however, the president's crude use of carrot-and-stick lobbying rendered his eventual victory Pyrrhic. The humiliated Duma refused to cooperate with him, press criticism of him escalated, and Russia's far-flung miners launched myriad protests, including the demand that he resign. Their delegates organized a tent city in the middle of Moscow, where Mayor Luzhkov quietly gave them moral and material support. In addition, Korzhakov ratcheted up to new heights his criticism of his former boss, casting an ironic light on the ceremony in which the two men had once sworn eternal loyalty to each other in their own blood. Yeltsin, he said, "is causing Russia only harm." Part of the reason, he implied, was that the evil genius Berezovsky had suborned the president with a payment of several million dollars in phony "royalties" for his book.[227]

At this moment of political isolation, Yeltsin evidently felt the need to install two strong-minded allies and clan leaders in senior positions, thus restoring some balance to the seesaw. First, he appointed Berezovsky (whom he had fired only five months earlier) to be the executive director of the Commonwealth of Independent States, a position that gave the oligarch plenty of opportunity to combine government business with personal business as he traveled incessantly around his domains. Then, on May 5, with Yeltsin's clear approval, Chubais became a full-blown oligarch himself upon assuming the powerful post of chairman of the board of the electricity monopoly United Energy Systems.

Abroad, Western leaders were increasingly worried by the state of Russia's economy and were pressing the Kremlin for corrective action. On April 1, both U.S. Deputy Treasury Secretary Summers and IMF head Michel Camdessus went further than before in their criticisms, suddenly discovering problems that other observers had been writing about for several years. Camdessus identified a "crony capitalism" in Russia that was similar to the "incestuous relationships" between government and business in the East Asian countries whose financial systems had recently crashed. Summers divined that the challenge for Russia was no longer to make government weaker, but to make it stronger so that it could perform the crucial functions required by an effective state. In his opinion, there could be "no worse news to come out of Russia than that, after years of throwing off one defunct economic model, it was on the verge of entrenching another questionable one."[228] It seemed as though the two men had only just seen through the facade of economic success erected by Russian officials, a facade neatly summed up by an associate of the young reformers when he said: "Under Chernomyrdin, programs were drafted just to be shown to IMF officials. They were, so to speak, an export commodity. Nobody really intended to implement them. . . ."[229]

On the political side, the U.S. government was still operating in full Panglossian mode. Even though Yeltsin's impulsive, vengeful replacement of Chernomyrdin by the unknown Kirienko was causing profound consternation in Moscow, Ambassador-at-Large Stephen Sestanovich considered the event to be

> a small milestone for Russia watchers. It was a turnover in which nobody was accused for disloyalty or treason. It was just said to be time for a change. One has to be impressed with the calm nature by which this constitutional transition has taken place. We should also remember what President Yeltsin said were the reasons for the change: a new government will have a mandate to move quickly and increase the pace of policy making.[230]

Almost immediately, however, financial markets began to signal their lack of faith in the ability of Kirienko's government to maintain the value of the ruble. The Kremlin panicked and sent Chubais—now head of the semiprivatized electricity monopoly UES—on a late May mission to Washington, where he went straight to the homes of Summers and Strobe Talbott. Having trumpeted for a year that Russia had weaned itself off IMF assistance and no longer required it, Chubais begged the two men to press for an emergency loan, a loan that had to be much bigger than any of its predecessors. Promptly, on May 31, President Clinton issued a statement that the United States "endorses additional conditional financial support" for Russia from the IMF and the World Bank.[231]

The subsequent negotiations were long and difficult. As in the past, when Yeltsin feared the loan spigot might at last be turned off, he started proclaiming that Russia was in imminent danger from extremist forces, and that whatever doubts the West might have about him, it should rush to his support nonetheless, lest the extremists take over Russia. However, having long ago house-trained the Communists, he could provide no evidence. The negotiations were definitely not helped along by the arrival in the United States of Veniamin Sokolov, the parliamentary leader who had tried to mediate between the parliament and the government during the crisis of 1993 and had later been chosen as an auditor of the Accounting Office.

As mentioned in the discussion of the loans-for-shares scheme, this independent government body quickly established a track record for careful investigation and honest reporting on numerous cases of incompetence and corruption. It had earned a reputation among close observers as the only official body that could gain access to official documents as it tried to monitor objectively the legality of executive branch operations. Its reward for doing so was a deafening silence about its reports, which received little attention from the justice system and virtually no media coverage except in the small opposition sector of the press.

Abroad, the Western allies of the "young reformers" conducted a campaign of innuendo regarding the Accounting Office, claiming that its work was "unreliable" or "biased." Sometimes they went further; Anders Aslund, for example, dismissed all its work in one sentence, claiming it was "controlled by the communist-dominated parliament."[232] In fact, the auditors are chosen to represent all the main factions in parliament's two houses. When Aslund was challenged on his claim, he did not reply.[233]

During Sokolov's visit, he met with the IMF, the World Bank, and congressional bodies, supplying them with details of the Russian government's financial corruption. He also reported in a *New York Times* op-ed piece that, for example, of $3 billion appropriated by the Russian parliament for Chechnya's reconstruction after the first war, "less than $150 million reached Chechnya." Sokolov also claimed that several years after the World Bank had lent $30 million to compensate victims of Russian bank frauds and pyramid schemes, "audits showed that not one victim had received the money." He also pointed out that fraud and corruption had led to massive state borrowing, which was "strangling the economy. Forty-five percent of state revenue is now used to service that debt."[234]

One would think that these points, made at the right time and place, might have persuaded the IMF not to throw good money after bad. However, the concerns of some of its analysts were swept aside when the U.S. government put heavy pressure on the organization's leadership and persuaded it to give priority to propping up the ruble and helping to ensure that Yeltsin and his cronies stay in power. On July 20 came the announcement that a package of $17.1 billion in new money for Russia had been assembled by the IMF, the World Bank, and the G-7 governments; the IMF's share alone was $11.6 billion, the first tranche of which was hastily transferred a week later.

At this point, the Kremlin apparently tipped off the top oligarchs that it was nonetheless going to devalue soon, prompting them to sell their big holdings of government bonds for rubles, exchange the rubles for the government's new shipment of dollars, and send the dollars abroad to American banks. Three weeks after the tranche transfer, on August 17, the ruble crashed, ending up with a value of about a quarter of its previous worth. The prior warnings of some observers that devaluation was inevitable even if the new loans were granted were thus vindicated.[235] The government also announced a ninety-day moratorium on payments by banks and businesses on overseas debts and a restructuring of the government's massive short-term bond commitments. The latter action meant that, before long, foreign and domestic bond holders would find their securities to be worth only five to ten cents on the dollar. For the population as a whole, the overall outcome was that prices rose sharply and most people suffered another precipitous decline in their standard of living.

After the dust settled, how did the big banks and their small depositors come out of the whole episode? According to a pioneering study by some investigative journalists in the fall of 1999 (prior to the crash), "The Central Bank blew a total of $9 billion in a fruitless attempt to prop up the ruble. Russia's major banks were able to pay six rubles for every dollar." And after the crash:

> the price was nearly twenty rubles. Those banks paid only $1.2 billion on their debt to foreigners. And according to Moscow economist Andrei Illarionov, $2.9 billion of the net hard-currency purchases are effectively unaccounted for. Some of it almost certainly remains in offshore accounts. And some may have gone to help capitalize new "bridge banks" that SBS Agro, Oneksimbank, and Bank Menatep have since set up. Many creditors owed money by the three believe that the new bridge banks now house performing assets that were shifted from the old insolvent banks. If true, those assets are now effectively—and illegally—shielded from stiffed lenders and depositors.

The study's authors also recount how, on August 20, the top oligarchs started to put enormous pressure on the Kremlin to grant them special credits. Before long, the subsequent Primakov government gave in and provided cheap loans worth about $1 billion at the prevailing exchange rate to "a handful of insolvent but politically powerful banks."[236]

The poor judgment of the IMF, the World Bank, and the G-7 governments in granting the new loans may have been induced in part by the apparent fact that Chubais and the Kirienko government expressed confidence that they could avoid a devaluation with the new loans. In any case, Chubais dubiously claimed three weeks after the crash that the lenders had forgiven the Kremlin for whatever deception was involved: "Today in the international financial institutions, despite everything we've done to them—and we cheated them out of $20 billion—there is an understanding that we had no alternative."[237] When these words provoked a storm of controversy, he tried to amend the record, and the effort was tinged with the deceptiveness reminiscent of his lies during the 1996 episode of the intercepted Xerox-paper box containing $538,000. Chubais did not claim that he was misquoted, nor that what he said was an unintentional error. Instead, in the following passage from his letter to the *Moscow Times*, he quoted some of the relevant words and claimed: "I expressed the view that even despite the enormous damage suffered by investors—and we cheated them out of $20 billion (a reference to the moratorium on repayment of $16 billion in loans by Russian banks and $4 billion by other commercial banks—note by A. Chubais), there is an understanding that we had no alternative."[238]

While quoting himself in this passage, Chubais left out the first part of his original sentence: "Today *in the international financial institutions,* despite everything we've done to them" and substituted the phrase quoted above: "even despite the enormous damage suffered *by investors* . . ." (whom he defined as banks).[239] Clearly, he changed the meaning of what he had said without admitting he was doing so. He also lambasted an American newspaper for reporting what in fact he did say.[240]

How did the West's policies in the whole episode appear to ordinary Russians? If the West had declined to make the new loans, Russian coal miners, teachers, health workers, scientists, and other groups that had been striking through the summer would have known the West was listening to them. By indulging Yeltsin, however, it conveyed the opposite message: that it knew nothing of the polls showing, for example, that the percentage of Russians prepared to support anti-Yeltsin demonstrations was growing fast and that Yeltsin's approval rating had fallen to the low single digits, while his negatives had soared to the vicinity of 80 percent.

Predictably, the president reacted to the currency and bond crash by punishing a scapegoat. On August 23, 1998, he sacked Kirienko and appointed as acting premier none other than the man he had fired as prime minister five months earlier, Viktor Chernomyrdin. This time, however, even though Yeltsin defiantly announced on August 28 that he would not resign, his usual battery of carrots and sticks availed him naught. The Duma saw the appointment as a desperate ploy to defend the personal interests of Yeltsin himself and of Berezovsky and other oligarchs; sensing the new public mood, it voted down Chernomyrdin on August 31 and September 9 by wide margins. The Duma had, at last, genuinely rebelled. The Communists had finally concluded that Yeltsin would probably be forced to accept the nominee favored by them and most other Duma factions, Yevgeny Primakov—the foreign minister and former head of the Foreign Intelligence Service—and that Yeltsin probably would not dare to dissolve the Duma and thus deprive them of their cherished perquisites.

They were right. The president saw that he did not have enough support to beat the legislature into submission. Moreover, Yeltsin could tolerate Primakov because, although this prospective premier would surely indulge the Communists too much, he was quietly but firmly opposed to Yeltsin's early retirement; Primakov believed that the polity was too fragile to risk its possible consequences. Thus on September 11, the Duma approved him by the sweeping margin of 317 to 63.

The West, by contrast, tended to disapprove of his appointment at first, labeling Primakov "a former spymaster." Russians, however, remembered that he had got this unenviable job from Gorbachev after the abortive hard-line coup of 1991, partly because he had been one of only two members of the Security Council to oppose the junta. At that time, the intelligence agencies were being dismembered and Russian democrats were at the peak of their influence; had they doubted Primakov's liberal credentials, they could have blocked his appointment.

Yet Primakov's political viability was secondary to the central fact that he was the first Russian leader since 1993 to enjoy broad-based legitimacy; only the Kremlin and Zhirinovsky's ultranationalists had opposed him for the premiership. Given the unpopularity of his predecessors, Primakov's appointment was a major step toward representative democracy. His popular approval ratings had consistently surpassed those of all other Russian politicians, mainly because most Russians viewed him as a statesman who did not put his personal interests above the nation's. He also represented that small, enlightened section of the elite that abstained from participating in the orgy of capital accumulation, thus preserving its independence from the crony capitalists.

Partly for these reasons, partly because Yeltsin reassured President Clinton —in a letter that was subsequently leaked to the media—that Primakov was the man Russia needed, and partly because Primakov maintained his reputation of being a predictable defender of Russia's national interests, the West gradually came to accept him. And this trend suffered no reversal—not even after the famous March 22, 1999 episode in which Primakov ordered his plane to turn around over the Atlantic to protest NATO's air raids on Belgrade while he was en route to visit Clinton. Indeed, that decision deepened the West's respect for him. This respect had become apparent earlier, when U.S. secretary of state Madeleine Albright gave him her conditional blessing and when German chancellor Gerhard Schroeder went further, perceptively noting that, "Stabilizing Russia now means stabilizing Primakov's government."[241]

We should note here that Yeltsin's letter to Clinton was probably leaked by a highly placed official, not because it revealed anything secret (it did not), but because it demonstrated the startling contrast between the way the Russian president conducted foreign policy and the way he acted at home. To his subjects he was the imperious Tsar Boris, who dispensed goodies when his mood was good and cruelly scolded his ministers in public when he needed a scapegoat. By contrast, Yeltsin's behavior toward Clinton, from whom he hoped to receive IMF loans and a seat on the world stage, reverted to the ingratiating style of the servile CPSU secretary from Sverdlovsk that he once was, trying to wheedle extra funds out of Moscow for a new Party sanatorium.[242]

Korzhakov, too, did not pass up the new chance—given Yeltsin's unprecedented political isolation—to torment the man who had abused him in 1996. As we noted earlier, Korzhakov declared that he knew "the number of the foreign bank account in which he [Yeltsin] keeps his 'savings,'" which now amounted to "more than five million dollars" and came from phony royalties on his memoirs.[243] Moreover, according to Korzhakov, the oligarchs had purchased the west European real estate we mentioned earlier for the use of Yeltsin and his family. No one charged Korzhakov with inaccuracy.

Meanwhile, Primakov's government was proving that, while it did not have a coherent economic strategy, it could avoid the financial disasters that many critics had forecast by printing some rubles to get desperately needed cash circulating in the economy and by pursuing cooperative relations with the Duma. Indeed, because of the government's good relations with the parliament, whose political composition it roughly reflected, and because its ultimate goal was creating a humane "social market," it could actually proceed to draft and enact a more IMF-friendly budget for 1999 than had ever been passed before. However, the IMF—badly burned by the August collapse and roundly criticized for this and other sins—did not approve of the budget.[244] Thus future loans to Russia remained problematic. They became even more so a few months later, when an audit by PricewaterhouseCoopers of the Russian Central Bank's dealings with the Channel Islands investment firm FIMACO showed that the Kremlin had committed the serious offense of misrepresenting its currency reserves to the IMF to the tune of about a billion dollars.[245]

The most intriguing feature of Primakov's rule was the tense maneuvering between his government, the president, and the oligarchs. The prime minister understood that to improve Russia's situation in any substantial way, he had to cautiously acquire for the government a measure of the power the president and his oligarch allies possessed. With Yeltsin, he tried to work out a variety of power-sharing agreements, but to little avail. Even when chronically ill, Yeltsin was allergic to signing away any of his power vis-à-vis the government or the Duma. As for the oligarchs, the picture looked more promising, because while only a few of them suffered severely from the August crash (only Vladimir Vinogradov's Inkombank went completely out of business), most of them were set back by it to one degree or another. Nonetheless, as a group, they fought Primakov tooth and nail.

Primakov wanted to change a system in which, as one oligarch had said, "the most profitable business is politics" and, as another had admitted, personal merit was not the key quality.[246] "To become a millionaire in our country," Pyotr Aven of the Alfa group had noted,

> it is not at all necessary to have a good head or specialized knowledge. Often it is enough to have active support in the government, the parliament, local power structures, and law enforcement agencies. One fine day, your insignificant bank is authorized to, for instance, conduct operations with budgetary funds. Or quotas are generously allotted . . . for the export of oil, timber, and gas. In other words, you are appointed a millionaire.[247]

To combat such a system, Primakov had to reduce the support the oligarchs had purchased in the structures Aven listed. To do that, he could try to keep them away from his own government, but it was almost impossible to reduce their easy access to the Presidential Administration. Indeed, Berezovsky had just strengthened his presence in that key institution by having its head—his former employee Valentin Yumashev, a central, pivotal figure in Yeltsin's extended "Family"—hire as a deputy a notoriously shady associate of Berezovsky's, Aleksandr Voloshin.[248] Before long, Voloshin rose further, eventually heading the Presidential Administration himself.

To undermine this nexus of presidential and oligarchic power in the Presidential Administration, Primakov evidently decided that his government had to demonstrate to Yeltsin and the nation the criminal nature of at least one of the top oligarchs. Official actions began in January against both Berezovsky and Smolensky. While the latter soon managed to halt the escalating pressures against him, Prosecutor General Yuri Skuratov opened a criminal investigation against Berezovsky for illegal business dealings. Evidence suggested that, among other things, Berezovsky and a colleague may have illegally appropriated money belonging to the airline Aeroflot. On February 2 and 4, heavily armed Federal Security Service agents raided two companies closely associated with Berezovsky—Aeroflot and the private security firm Atoll—and took away numerous documents.[249]

Starting at this time—the first few weeks of 1999—and ending with Yeltsin's resignation on December 31, Russian politics becomes more intense than at any other time since the country gained independence (except perhaps the fall of 1993). Certainly, it becomes more complex. Here we can present an analysis of only the main threads, some of which run through the whole year:

- The prosecutor general's investigation of Berezovsky.
- The investigation of Pavel Borodin, the Yeltsin family, and others by Swiss and Russian prosecutors in the so-called "Mabetex case," and the attempts by the Yeltsin entourage to get Prosecutor General Skuratov fired and the Mabetex case shut down.
- The joint U.S.-Russian investigation of alleged money-laundering transfers from Russia of tens of billions of dollars to Russians' accounts in the United States, particularly in the Bank of New York.
- Yeltsin's dismissal of two premiers, Primakov and Sergei Stepashin, and appointment of a third, Vladimir Putin.
- The rise and fall of serious political opposition, led by Primakov and Luzhkov, to Yeltsin's extended "Family."
- The Kremlin's secret search for pretexts to launch a new war against the Chechens and the mysteries surrounding the murderous apartment bombings in Russian cities that produce the crucial pretext.
- The cautious prosecution of the new war in Chechnya and neighboring Dagestan.
- The last-minute rise of a new establishment party, and the victory of this party and (despite their political inertia) the Communists in the Duma elections.
- The propulsion of Vladimir Putin toward the presidency.
- The constantly disorienting uncertainty about Yeltsin's health and political intentions, culminating in his sudden resignation and Putin's decree granting him immunity for life from criminal prosecution.

THE YELTSIN INVESTIGATION

In January–February 1999, observers noted that two of these threads came together in the office of Prosecutor General Skuratov. With help from Swiss officials, Skuratov had been investigating numerous cases of corruption that implicated both Berezovsky and, separately, Borodin, the Yeltsin family, and others. The origin of these two investigations apparently lies in the fall of 1997, when Swiss prosecutor general Carla del Ponte was given police reports showing that the Russian Mafiya now controlled more than three hundred firms in Switzerland and that a Swiss businessman of Kosovar Albanian origin, Behgjet Pacolli, who headed the Mabetex construction company, was providing unexplained funds to Yeltsin and his daughters.[250]

In December 1997, del Ponte and Skuratov met. Over the next four months they drew up and signed a memorandum on assisting each other with their investigations. In May 1998, del Ponte asked Skuratov if he would like to receive documents concerning corruption in Yeltsin's entourage. According to Skuratov, he replied that "everyone was equal before the law and that I would look into it." Back in Switzerland, del Ponte was soon visited by Felipe Turover, a man of Russian-Spanish background who had left the USSR in 1983 at age 19 and had recently been working as a debt collector for the Gottardo Bank in Lugano, Switzerland. He had an enormous amount of information that he gave to the Swiss and also, in the fall, to Skuratov's staff.[251] In September, del Ponte's documents reached Skuratov. He could not get an appointment to see Yeltsin about them but informed Prime Minister Primakov, who told him "to go ahead in accordance with the law." By now, Skuratov had details on twenty-three apparently corrupt Kremlin officials and thirty-two Swiss checking accounts in their names.

On January 22, 1999, del Ponte led a search of the Mabetex offices in Lugano, first giving Pacolli a copy of Skuratov's request for Swiss assistance in the case and then interviewing him. He had files of records of credit card payments on behalf of dozens of Russians, including small payments for Yeltsin and much bigger ones for his daughters. (Turover later said that the total for the three of them was "about $600,000."[252]) When del Ponte asked Pacolli to name the beneficiary of a $1 million deposit that moved from his private account to Borodin's account to a bank in Hungary, he answered that the money was "for the president. At that time he was on an official visit to Hungary, and needed money for small expenses." Likewise, the credit card payments for the president and his daughters were for "small expenses."

It also seemed that Pacolli had paid kickbacks to Borodin for construction work contracts on the Kremlin and other buildings. In addition, he did not explain why he had gone on paying large sums to Mercata Trading and Engineering in Geneva, even after Mercata had completed its work as a subcontractor to Mabetex for Kremlin restoration work. Mercata was owned by Viktor Stolpovskikh, a former copresident of Mabetex, an influential but low-profile member of "the Family," and an associate of, in particular, Viktor Chernomyrdin, Russia's prime minister at the time. In the mid-1990s, Stolpovskikh, nicknamed "Moneybags" (he paid $15 million in taxes in 1998 alone), allegedly received a commission of some $8 million from Pacolli, which he may have divided up among a large number of Russian officials. He also reportedly registered in his own name the mansion bought for the Yeltsin family in Garmisch-Partenkirchen.[253]

On January 22, del Ponte called Skuratov to inform him of the results of the Mabetex search and, evidently, Pacolli informed his former Russian clients about it. At about the same time, two other things happened: Skuratov opened his criminal investigation of Berezovsky and prepared for the raids on his two firms. Also, what appears to have been a complex operation to compromise Skuratov came to fruition, apparently masterminded by Federal Security Service director Vladimir Putin with important help from Aleksandr Lebedev, head of the National Reserve Bank.

A man resembling Skuratov was lured into frolicking with two women in a room equipped with a concealed camera. Dyachenko then showed the resulting videotape to her father and was said to have obtained the desired angry reaction. On February 1, the prosecutor general, having created too many powerful enemies, was summoned before the head of the Security Council, Nikolai Bordyuzha, and asked to resign. Without confirming anything about the tape, he wrote a letter offering to resign "on grounds of ill health" but pointed out that only the upper house of parliament, the Federation Council, had the power to remove him. He then admitted himself to a hospital for a week. Before doing so, however, he instructed his deputy to proceed with two politically charged cases: that of former Central Bank head Sergei Dubinin concerning the collapse of the Kremlin's bond market pyramid in August, and that of Berezovsky. The raids on the Berezovsky-connected firms began the next day.

In subsequent weeks, the political temperature in Moscow soared as the Federation Council three times rebuffed Yeltsin's efforts to have it vote Skuratov out of office. This unprecedented rebellion by the normally compliant council showed the extent of its alienation from the president and the rising determination of many of the regional leaders to demonstrate their increased political power both now and also later in the Duma elections in December.

Feeling itself under intense siege, Yeltsin's "Family" decided, after the council refused to dismiss Skuratov for the first time on February 17, that it must reverse course on the matter of the prosecutor general and try something risky. According to a plausible account by a reliable reporter, Leonid Krutakov, the family decided to negotiate secretly with Skuratov, offering to help him prosecute Berezovsky in return for Skuratov's dropping the Mabetex investigation.[254] Proceeding with this plan on March 4, Yeltsin proved his bona fides by dismissing Berezovsky from his position as CIS executive director and berating him for "repeated actions" that exceeded his powers. Two days later, *Kommersant-Daily* reported that the Yeltsin family was angry with Berezovsky for using the Atoll company to record its cellular telephone calls, and that Dyachenko resented press reports about her financial dependence on him.[255]

However, Skuratov dug in his heels and refused to deal. In March, more detailed reports about Mabetex reached him from the Swiss. He ordered them to be checked out by his staff. Later, senior investigator Georgi Chuglazov said that he had done the checking and "At least 90 percent of what has been published is true, and the investigation has all the appropriate documents."[256] As to the scale of Mabetex's bribing of highly placed Russians, Skuratov said that del Ponte's figure of $10 million "seems to be a realistic estimate, although it has to be proved."[257]

Skuratov's stubbornness now forced the family to reverse course once again and go all out to oust him. A few hours after the Federation Council voted again on March 17 to back the prosecutor general, the state television channel RTR showed a videotape of a man by the name of Yura in the intimate company of two prostitutes. Berezovsky had worked hard to have copies of the tape sent to all the bigger television networks, but only RTR agreed to show it.

It is not clear whether Yeltsin had supported this move, because the next day he received Skuratov and Prime Minister Primakov. They proceeded to show him documents received from the Swiss, documents that were frank about the bribery they revealed because Swiss law does not penalize the bribing of foreign officials. Reportedly, Yeltsin was enraged and later dressed down his daughter Tatyana. He also ordered the Security Council to investigate the Mabetex information and the apparent violation of Skuratov's privacy. This appeared to presage the second U-turn on Skuratov within a month, and other members of the Yeltsin family swung into action to counter it. They quickly persuaded the president that the squalid public exploitation of the tape was the fault of Security Council head Bordyuzha. So Yeltsin fired him.

The next day, March 19, the president appointed Vladimir Putin to take Bordyuzha's place and also asked him to remain head of the FSB. Born in 1953, Putin had first been a KGB intelligence officer specializing in Germany. He lived for five years in its eastern half, the German Democratic Republic. As a colonel, he moved in 1991 to St. Petersburg to work for Mayor Anatoly Sobchak and rose to become his principal deputy, mostly handling city development issues and relations with foreign firms. After Sobchak's ouster in 1996, Putin worked in the Presidential Administration on property and then regional matters before being appointed in 1998 to run the FSB, the successor to the secret police divisions of the KGB.

After his further elevation, Putin at once led a new charge to replace Skuratov. On April 2, the Moscow Procuracy started a criminal case against Skuratov, alleging that he was the figure on the videotape and that the services of the women represented illicit payment for professional favors. This decision gave Yeltsin a pretext to suspend Skuratov and appoint an acting prosecutor general. True, on April 6, the Kremlin did not block the issuance of an arrest order against Berezovsky, but this was its last concession. Nine days later, the order was revoked—not coincidentally, perhaps, five days after a major explosion shook the FSB's headquarters. The salient lesson of this whole sordid affair was not lost on tens of millions of ordinary Russians: Once again, the limitless impunity of the upper orders was preserved. But there was more to come.

On the eve of the third vote on Skuratov, Yeltsin personally lobbied members of the Federation Council. Suggesting he was ready to renegotiate the government's power-sharing agreements with many of Russia's regions, he blatantly pandered to their representatives in the council: "I am insisting that you, and not the federal government, have priority, that you come first. So we will give you more independence than is set down in the bilateral agreements we have signed. Let us gradually revise these agreements."

This sale of federal power for governors' votes was doubly contemptible because it directly sabotaged Primakov's active strategy of rebuilding federal power by curbing the long-running power grab by the governors. The next day, April 21, Presidential Administration head Voloshin read aloud an ingratiating letter from Yeltsin to the council before the vote, which expressed certainty that its decision would "calm society and stabilize the political situation in the country," thus removing a weapon from "criminal elements and unscrupulous politicians." But too many of the senators refused to take the bait. In closed session, they listened to Skuratov's report on high-level corruption in the still unpublicized Mabetex case and then supported him by 79 votes to 61. It was a crushing defeat for Yeltsin's clique.[258] As Leonid Krutakov commented, "The fight of 'the family' for the post of [prosecutor general] cost the country its stability."[259]

Motivating this fight, of course, was the real fear of Yeltsin, his family, and many of his associates that an ongoing joint Swiss-Russian investigation of some of their misdeeds could quite conceivably lead to their ostracism from international society, to bans on their entry into certain countries, and even to their trials and prison terms. Getting someone appointed prosecutor general who would cut off the Swiss investigation was imperative.

STEPASHIN AND THE "STORM IN MOSCOW"

For now, though, the thwarted Yeltsinites turned their sights on a more immediate danger, albeit one that was not as acute as the president's legal morass. The long-standing movement in the Duma to impeach the president had gathered momentum, so the regime started threatening to dissolve the Duma and dismiss the government. It also reportedly offered deputies bribes of $5,000 to oppose impeachment, and some sixty to eighty of them accepted.[260]

On May 12, with the critical Duma vote only three days away, Yeltsin fired Primakov and his government, and installed as acting premier the candidate of Chubais's camp, Interior Minister Sergei Stepashin. Both the timing and the choice of Stepashin were clever: Just as they were gearing up to vote, Duma deputies saw that a decisive Yeltsin could remove the premier and standard-bearer of the left at a stroke, and that he intended to replace the center-left government with a center-right one. Centrist deputies of the parliamentary factions Russia's Regions and Our Home Is Russia who had been planning to vote for one or more article of impeachment now had to wonder if they would be destroying a chance of a government job or government favors. If they stuck to their original intention, they might be the swing votes that would be decisive in impeaching the president. Thus only two OHR deputies and only about half the legislators from Russia's Regions voted for one or more articles. The vote failed— even the motion on Yeltsin's indictable responsibility for the Chechnya war received only 283 votes out of a maximum of about 440—and the whole impeachment effort collapsed. Its chief sponsors—the Communists and (on the article regarding Chechnya) Yabloko—looked weak and isolated.[261] It seems probable that most of the Communists did not actually intend impeachment to succeed, but mainly wanted their public opposition to Yeltsin to be noticed and to win them votes in the next election.

Apart from the supreme tactical motive for dismissing Primakov (that is, derailing impeachment), Yeltsin of course had other reasons as well. One, according to an often reliable inside source, was that Primakov, even though he had always opposed impeachment, had refused to promise that if the Duma were to back the initiative, he would resign in protest.[262]

Another was Yeltsin's fear that Primakov might continue to oppose NATO's military actions against Milosevic in Yugoslavia and thus block the deal that Yeltsin wanted to make—and eventually did make—with the United States and the Western alliance. The deal may have included an unpublicized informal agreement that Russia would cooperate with NATO over Kosovo, provided that the NATO powers in return would not criticize too strongly the new war that the Kremlin was already planning against Chechnya.[263]

A longer-term reason, but probably the most important, was that Primakov remained the most popular politician in Russia, and the Yeltsinites emphatically opposed his becoming president, the chances of which would probably increase during one more year of his incumbency as premier. We should also note that Yeltsin's tactics in destabilizing Primakov prior to his dismissal had been unusually aggressive. Apart from sabotaging Primakov's strategy for bringing the regions to heel, he had also encouraged Yabloko to harass the premier. He had met with Yavlinsky, hinted that he might oust Primakov and then bring Yabloko into the government, and gave Yavlinsky the green light to continue accusing Primakov of having appointed certain corrupt individuals to his cabinet.

Up to the very last minute, Yeltsin had reportedly intended to appoint as premier the railways minister Nikolai Aksenenko, a close associate of the oligarch Roman Abramovich and a man also favored by Berezovsky. However, the Chubais camp within Yeltsin's entourage just succeeded in persuading him to change horses and pick Stepashin. This episode strengthened the theory that, especially with Yeltsin in poor health, "the Family" constituted a "collective Yeltsin" that could make decisions in unplanned, chaotic style.[264] (We should also note here, however, our belief that some of the leaks of 1996–99 about Yeltsin's declining health were disinformation designed to see how various politicians and oligarchs would react.) In any case, evidently because the Duma had been made to look foolish by Yeltsin, had also appreciated having good relations with Primakov's government, saw no particular threat in Stepashin, and had no consensus candidate of its own, it quickly confirmed Stepashin on a vote of 301 to 55.

Right before the vote, Stepashin had made a grim, but realistic speech on April 21 about Russia's overwhelming debt mountain, the rising tide of mass poverty, and the drastic decline in industrial production, which made Russia seem like a banana republic, rich only in raw materials. He also claimed that everyone knew there was "a high degree of probability" that (unspecified) criminal groups could come to power if they were not resolutely opposed.

Freed of Primakov's restraints, the resurgent oligarchs almost immediately put in doubt Stepashin's ability to pursue a coherent strategy. By appointing the ex-Yabloko economist Mikhail Zadornov as first deputy premier and promising him the right to choose a new finance minister, the new prime minister had signaled his intention to develop Russia's relations with the IMF in the hopes of getting the loan spigot turned back on. This move angered the Berezovsky camp, which got the ailing Yeltsin to veto the deal three days later, provoking Zadornov to resign. Zadornov said that because he had blocked the oligarchs' attempts to pilfer government accounts, some of them had instantly struck back. A well-connected lobbyist commented, "It's really disgusting. The wolves are out—to get all they can in the time that is left while Yeltsin is in office. And what's worse is that they don't care what anyone else thinks of them."[265] Beyond this, though, because the oligarchs still had no candidate they could count on to win the presidency a year hence, they lost no time spreading rumors that the election should be postponed, possibly in connection with the planned creation of a Russia-Belarus union.[266]

Nonetheless, Stepashin plowed ahead with Chernomyrdin-like policies, quickly reestablishing warm relations with the United States, courting the IMF, and working to create a new pro-Kremlin party that would perform better than Chernomyrdin's OHR so that it could push aside Luzhkov's burgeoning Fatherland movement and the rival regional movement called All Russia. As Stepashin later said, he got support for such a party from about fifty regional leaders, and strategy meetings took place in the Kremlin between himself, Yeltsin, and Voloshin on the one side, and eighteen mostly All Russia–aligned provincial governors on the other. The governors had said, "We're ready to 'fall into line' under Stepashin, but will he be premier for long?" To this question, Voloshin remained silent.[267]

The whole enterprise foundered for two or three months, and it revived only after Stepashin fell victim on August 9 to Yeltsin's compulsive search for the right man who could be counted on to protect him politically and legally from the come-uppances that he and his "Family" so deeply feared. As a result of the delay, All Russia and Fatherland soon merged under the leadership of Luzhkov, whereupon the powerful mayor of Moscow managed to recruit Primakov to lead the new coalition.[268] On August 23 he promised that if Primakov were to run for president, he would step aside and support him.

In the meantime, a number of ominous developments had taken place that help explain why the man "the Family" needed was neither Stepashin nor (despite strong lobbying from Berezovsky) Aleksandr Lebed, and why Russia's fifth premier in seventeen months, Vladimir Putin, probably was. In early summer, "the Family" came to the conclusion that if political life took a normal course over the next year, Russia would probably have a new president—perhaps Primakov or Luzhkov—who would not protect its interests and might even declare war on it. This could mean imprisonment and financial disaster for the Yeltsins and many of the oligarchs.

A president of this sort, with a fresh popular mandate, could hardly be expected not to clean out at least parts of the Augean stables to satisfy popular demand and give his administration momentum. Ergo, there would have to be some events that would drastically disrupt political life and help propel into the presidency a man who had "the Family's" complete trust. Moreover, the disruptions might have to be violent enough to provide a convincing pretext for canceling the elections for both the Duma in December and the presidency in June 2000.

At first, "the Family" hoped that Stepashin might be the one who could help facilitate such events. However, it soon became clear he was not: He started to behave too presidentially, as during a successful visit to the United States in late July. Because he proved quite good at it, his approval rating went steadily up and made Yeltsin jealous. Also, while working to thwart the politically alarming rise of Luzhkov and Primakov, he still behaved normally toward them. More broadly, according to a reliable source, he "categorically rejected all the Kremlin's wild plans involving canceling elections, fabricating compromising material against Luzhkov, and so on. He insisted it was necessary to get out of the existing situation without upheavals that could ignite a civil war."[269] More opaquely, Stepashin said in public that he was sacked because he "could not be bought."[270]

In taking this stance, Stepashin was reacting against a Kremlin plan contained in a document dated June 26 and known among insiders as "Storm in Moscow."[271] On July 2, a copy of the plan was leaked to *Moskovskaya pravda;* according to some reports, the leak was among the reasons a deputy head of the Presidential Administration, Sergei Zverev, was subsequently dismissed. Published on July 22, it laid out an elaborate program to discredit Luzhkov through aggressive and violent actions designed to make life in Moscow unbearable. Listed examples were brazen acts (or attempted acts) of terrorism, kidnappings of public figures and ordinary people by "Chechen guerrillas," a massive media campaign accusing the mayor and his associates of robbing the city blind, and Mafiya-type attacks on businessmen and businesses that supported Luzhkov. The plan also referred to a separate blueprint for provoking an all-out war between rival Mafiya clans, a war that would provide cover for these major acts of terrorism. All this would make it seem reasonable to introduce a state of emergency and cancel elections.

On August 25, the newspaper listed a dozen events in the capital over the previous few weeks that suggested such a scenario was already taking shape: various small-scale bombings, daily shootings, big public campaigns against Vladimir Gusinsky and his media empire, Federal Security Service harassment of the mayor's wife for her business dealings, and so on.[272] In addition, Justice Minister Pavel Krasheninnikov was dismissed on August 17 because, he said, his ministry had been pressed but had failed to find legal grounds for banning the CPRF and preventing Luzhkov's Fatherland movement from registering for the Duma elections.[273] However, the leaking of the Kremlin's plan may have inhibited somewhat its implementers, with the result that the requisite "storm" was not forthcoming. In any case, a second, overlapping plan with the same goal had already come into view. This was a plan to create suitable pretexts for gradually starting something to which the public would at first be strongly opposed—a new war against the Chechens.

"THE RIGHT MAN"

Ever since the first Chechen war had ended with an armistice in 1996 and a treaty in 1997, the two sides remained unreconciled in practice. In Chechnya, the promised Russian aid for reconstruction did not arrive, and the more militant anti-Russian elements, including Muslim fundamentalists from abroad who had fought alongside the Chechens, used the opportunity to create terrorist training camps and to proselytize throughout Russia's Muslim communities. They scored some successes, notably in Dagestan, Tatarstan, Karachayevo-Cherkessia, and the Moscow, Stavropol, and Astrakhan regions, as well as in Chechnya. Moreover, graduating classes from the training camps conducted raids into areas next to Chechnya; in March 1999, Chechens kidnapped an Interior Ministry general and later killed him.

On the Russian side, that abduction changed the nature of the military and Interior Ministry's contingency planning, which had not stopped since 1996. As Stepashin later said, "A plan for military actions in that republic [Chechnya] was worked out, beginning in March. We planned to advance to the Terek River [that is, to occupy the northern third of the country] in August–September. . . . I actively worked on strengthening our positions on Chechnya's borders, preparing to attack. . . . But I would have thought carefully about whether it was wise to cross the Terek and move further south."[274]

On August 5, 1999, a military action began that provoked months of speculation in Russian and Western media. A Muslim force led by the Chechen guerrilla leader Shamil Basayev and Khattab, a guerrilla leader believed to be a Saudi citizen, entered western Dagestan with the goal of sparking an anti-Russian uprising. It found less support and stronger resistance than expected. Stepashin immediately flew down to study the situation for himself. On August 9, he was dismissed, and Vladimir Putin took his place with a quick Duma confirmation. On August 22, the force withdrew back into Chechnya without heavy losses.

To the Russian public, the episode was little more than another nasty scuffle in the North Caucasus. To many close observers, however, it smelled of some degree of official or semiofficial orchestration, the goal of which was to create public pressure for a new Chechnya war. These suspicions were summed up by an unusually persuasive source—the trusted, long-standing editor of Berezovsky's flagship paper *Nezavisimaya gazeta,* Vitaly Tretiakov. Some weeks after the events, he delivered his considered opinion:

It is perfectly obvious that the Chechens were lured into Dagestan . . . in order to provide a legitimate excuse for restoring federal power in the republic and beginning the offensive phase of struggle against the terrorists grouped in Chechnya. Clearly it was an operation by the Russian special services, . . . which was, moreover, politically authorized from the very top.

In light of all this, here is my own personal hypothesis: at worst, Berezovsky may have been used by the Russian special services without his knowledge, or, more than likely, he acted in coordination with them. . . . My hypothesis is far more realistic than the theory that 'Berezovsky set everything up,' which presumes his absolute influence on the two warring sides simultaneously.[275]

Given Tretiakov's close relations with Berezovsky, and the latter's deep and long-standing involvement in the affairs of Chechnya and the North Caucasus, it is hard to believe that his judgment is far wide of the mark, even though he may be shifting some of the blame from the oligarch to the FSB.[276] If it is indeed essentially true, the more elaborate conspiracy theories spelled out by writers like Boris Kagarlitsky have a core of truth to them, even if some of their elements may be wrong.[277] Certainly, for example, Basayev had close links with Russian military intelligence from 1992, when it supervised his military support of the Abkhazians in their separatist war against Georgia. Also, Berezovsky has often confirmed his close ties to Basayev and other Chechen separatists, to whom he has sent valuable material aid. In addition, evidence strongly suggests that from about 1994, Basayev enjoyed some sort of official Russian immunity, at least for several years, from being personally targeted by Russian troops.[278] Finally, the apparent syndrome of August 1999—Basayev gets to wage war and thus reopens his backers' purses, and in return, the Kremlin gets to toughen its authoritarian rule—seems to be a pattern that, in various murky ways, has continued to function since that time. We should also note that the complex interplay of financial, political, military, loyalty-related, nationalist, religious, and other motivations in all these relationships will occupy political analysts and historians for decades to come.

In mid-August, the journalist and retired army colonel Aleksandr Zhilin was able to have rather frank conversations with high-ranking officers in the Russian military's General Staff, the Ministry of Defense, and the Interior Ministry. He reported that they were all "in agreement that the dramatic events in Dagestan are the consequence of initiatives taken by certain forces in Moscow. True, few of the generals dared to name these forces, limiting themselves to meaningful glances at the ceiling. And only one of the General Staff officials said outright that both the first and the second war in the Caucasus have been instruments for use in election campaigns." However, "in the corridors," the people he spoke with "call the present conflict in Dagestan . . . nothing but a second pre-election Caucasian war," referring, of course, to Yeltsin's intention to use the first war to generate support for himself during the long run-up to the election of 1996.[279]

As proof of their views, the officers produced "indirect evidence." For example, a recently retired Federal Security Service (FSB) officer said that the agency had long been well informed about guerrillas preparing armed bases in Dagestan, but that despite the numerous appeals of Dagestani leaders, no action had been taken. Another example, recounted by air traffic control experts, was that for years nothing had been done to regulate the one thousand flights a year into Chechnya. As a result, the terrorists had been able to receive large quantities of armaments and conduct their drug business without constraint.

"In this connection," Zhilin wrote, "all my interlocutors without exception stressed a not unimportant point: the FSB and the Security Council were headed simultaneously by the present head of the government, Vladimir Putin."[280]

As we have indicated, as of about August 25, those forces that were determined to sway public opinion from being hostile to the very idea of starting a new Chechnya war to actually favoring it had made little progress. Russia's North Caucasus was far from the minds of ninety percent of Russians. What could be done? Without a new war, the Kremlin would have to revert to the hitherto ineffective "Storm in Moscow" scenario—and drastically escalate it. A state of emergency could be introduced and, if necessary, the elections could be canceled; then Putin would succeed Yeltsin at an appropriate moment.

Whether deliberately or by chance—it is still far from clear—starting on September 4 or earlier, one element of the scenario *was* drastically escalated, and it worked better than possibly could have been expected.

September Bombings

Between September 4 and 16, 1999, four apartment houses were blown up, one each in Buinaksk (Dagestan) and Volgodonsk (in the Rostov-on-Don region), and two in Moscow. More than three hundred innocent Russians died, and everyone saw the grisly results on television. Immediately, though without proof, the Kremlin blamed the Chechens. Popular anger rose; citizens formed self-defense and vigilante groups; and, at the beginning of October, a creeping invasion of Chechnya began from the north.

Who was behind the bombings? It is not yet clear, and the slow and uncertain handling of the official investigation, led by the FSB, gave extra credibility to conspiracy theories. So did a suspicious episode in Ryazan a week after the last bombing, when local residents were turned out of their apartment block at night in what they suspected was another attempted bombing that evidence strongly suggested had official involvement. Following a long, anxious delay, they were told that the whole thing was just a training exercise. But they were far from convinced.

Initial official statements that the Chechens were responsible for the monstrous crimes gradually gave way to the version propounded to the news agency Interfax in January: there were fourteen suspects, but none of them was a Chechen, and none was in custody. However, the FSB spokesman held that all of them had been trained in camps in Chechnya and that they had escaped to Chechnya after the bombings.[281] In early 2000, the FSB web site listed nine individuals who appeared to have actually placed and detonated the bombs: four Karachais, two Tatars, and three Dagestanis.[282] At the same time, nothing officials said suggested that they had an idea who planned the whole complex operation. Either they really did not know, or they knew but did not want to say.

According to the theory of Boris Kagarlitsky, the Moscow bombings were masterminded by Russian military intelligence, using North Caucasians as the bomb-setters.[283] The financier George Soros believes that a variant of this theory—with Berezovsky in a central role—may be true. He bases his admittedly circumstantial argument mainly on his personal knowledge of Berezovsky, with whom he has had business meetings that give him considerable insight into this oligarch.[284]

Another, perhaps more plausible and overlapping theory is that the Dagestan Liberation Army (DLA), which claimed responsibility for some of the bombings, indeed may have perpetrated them, with or without some official assistance.[285] If this is the case, then the group most likely to lie behind the DLA label were religious conservatives of Karamakhi, Chabanmakhi, and a few other neighboring villages in central Dagestan. A form of Wahhabism—a conservative Islamic movement that has made some inroads in Central Asia and Russia's predominantly Muslim regions—developed a following in this area in the 1990s, leading to major clashes with the police. The villagers used the five hundred vehicles of their up-to-date trucking business to help them proselytize their beliefs in many parts of Russia. The police responded by stopping the trucks and fining the drivers.

In the spring of 1998, the Wahhabis set up organs of self-rule and their own militia; they also declared the area off-limits to the police and other officials, and started fortifying it. In August 1998, a Russian journalist filed an illuminating report from the area, elaborating on these preparations and warning that the authorities under no circumstances should use or threaten to use force against the villagers. If they did, he wrote, there would be all-out war and "everything would burn up in that fire."[286] Shortly thereafter, perhaps in response to his article, Interior Minister Stepashin personally visited Karamakhi and talked with the village's leaders. He promised to deal positively with their grievances; however, nothing came of the promises, and because Moscow vetoed any action—to the intense frustration of the Dagestani officials—the standoff continued.[287]

In mid-August 1999, when Russian-Muslim fighting was raging in western Dagestan, a Finnish reporter traveled from the republic's capital Makhachkala to Karamakhi, where he interviewed some villagers, including their military commander "General Dzherollakh," and wrote a story very similar to that of his Russian colleague a year earlier. Again, the villagers warned of their fierce determination to defend their self-rule. The journalist wrote, "The Wahhabis' trucks go all over Russia. Even one wrong move in Moscow or Makhachkala, they warn, will lead to bombs and bloodshed everywhere. 'If they start bombing us, we know where our bombs will explode.'"[288] In the last days of August, the Russian military launched sustained bombardments against the villages by land and air.[289] After putting up a fierce resistance for three weeks, the survivors escaped.

On September 4, a week after the attack began, the first apartment bombing took place in the Dagestani town of Buinaksk, not far from the Wahhabi-controlled villages. Possibly the villagers had precise contingency plans for their fellow believers of other ethnicities—once the deterrent effect of their explicit threats to all who would listen over the previous year had failed—to set off bombs in revenge in Buinaksk, Moscow, and Volgodonsk. If that is so, then we believe it is impossible that the Moscow authorities did not know about the plans, at least in general terms. Even before Stepashin visited the district a year earlier, they must have been receiving numerous reports from, in particular, the FSB, the Interior Ministry, and probably the eavesdropping agency FAPSI. After all, the villages were the only off-limits area for officialdom, apart from Chechnya, in the whole of Russia.

Thus the possibility arises that the Moscow decision to attack the villages was made with the deliberate intention of provoking a terrorist response that was partly or wholly anticipated. Alternatively, the decision could have been made impulsively, without reviewing the appropriate intelligence about the target. In either case, the officials in Moscow would have had plenty of reason to organize a cover-up. Individuals guilty of negligence or deliberate intent regarding the deaths of three hundred civilians obviously would have much to fear.

A POPULAR WAR

For the Kremlin, the last part of August 1999 was a truly tumultuous time. While its troops were still fighting Basayev in Dagestan, on August 19 the *New York Times* broke the Bank of New York scandal about the billions of dollars of suspicious money that had been sent out of Russia to the United States by criminals and political leaders. Developments in the story ensued almost daily in the world press, while Russian ground and air forces attacked Karamakhi.[290] On August 25, the first detailed report on the Mabetex case appeared in *Corriere della Sera*, quoting Turover's testimony that implicated the Yeltsin family. On August 30, Georgi Chuglazov, a senior Russian prosecutor, whose boss, Skuratov, had had his own apartment and country cottage searched by police on August 8 and 14 to intimidate him regarding this case, announced that he, too, was a victim of reprisal. As we noted earlier, he had studied documents showing that 90 percent of what the press had written about Mabetex was accurate; yet now, because he was about to fly to Switzerland for consultations with Swiss colleagues, he had been forcibly removed from the case.

The same day, Russian officials hit back at the Swiss. Berezovsky's paper *Novye izvestiya* carried a scurrilous attack on Turover, and Borodin told the Geneva *Le Temps* and Radio Free Europe that he was innocent of all charges. Further, according to Borodin, Yeltsin believed that the case was "a plot against him." At the same time, the Kremlin threatened Berezovsky with reprisals for using his media outlets to publicize negative news about Yeltsin. Also, the oligarch was pressuring the Kremlin to take drastic action against Luzhkov, who had supposedly orchestrated the simultaneous launching of the *New York Times* and *Corriere della Sera* stories to embarrass the president.[291] Still on August 30, the IMF announced that it would not give Russia the $640 million it was hoping for because it had failed to produce a promised audit.[292] On top of all this, a major explosion destroyed parts of a new underground shopping mall in Moscow on August 31, though by good fortune no one was killed.

In October, as Russian troops advanced across the northern Chechnya plain toward the Terek River, resistance was relatively light. The war became popular, and its official objectives escalated until the Terek had been crossed and Grozny, after terrible fighting, had fallen. Both sides committed major atrocities. By now, the Kremlin's declared aims had become the physical liquidation of all terrorists, requiring the blanket bombing of entire villages on the grounds that terrorists were hiding in them and most of the villagers must be sheltering them. Enthusiastic supporters of the war, such as television producer Sergei Dorenko, came close to calling for genocide. "Filtration camps" were set up to interrogate all Chechen males and some females physically capable of fighting. At least a quarter of a million refugees fled Chechnya, mostly to neighboring Ingushetia.

Although polls showed a consistent 25 to 30 percent of Russians to be opposed to the war, the majority approved it, and Putin's popularity rose fast. Apart from his purposeful, systematic, and seemingly efficient prosecution of the war, most people were pleased that Yeltsin had retreated into the background and that now they were ruled by a healthy, focused, and businesslike leader who could, perhaps, miraculously extricate Russia from its morass. While Putin remained loyal to Yeltsin, he acted as though he was, and always had been, his own man.

In these hitherto unimaginably favorable circumstances for the Kremlin "Family," it actually became possible to put aside its plans to cancel the two elections. In the last two months before Russians voted for a new Duma, a pro-Kremlin party called Unity was hastily stitched together and excluded only a few of the corrupt and criminal elements that thronged to it. Although Unity had no ideology, the official report said that it took 23 percent of the vote on December 19 (mainly because Putin associated himself with it, if not too strongly), finishing close behind the CPRF, which had 24 percent. Yabloko and other groups lodged numerous charges of electoral fraud.[293] The Communists fared relatively poorly because, as the evil genius of Kremlin strategists Gleb Pavlovsky explained in a penetrating analysis, their potential edge as vote-winners had evaporated in May, when the Duma voted against the impeachment they had long championed. Beyond this issue, which quickly died, they had little to offer: just intellectual stagnation (except for a last minute embrace of more genuinely market-oriented economic principles), a poor track record of providing real help to the impoverished majority of the population, and a weak leader, Zyuganov, with a backward-looking ideology of nationalist conspiracy theories and Soviet-era nostalgia.[294]

Meanwhile, Fatherland–All Russia (FAR)—the object of vicious Kremlin media attacks—received only 13 percent of the vote. But it proceeded to make some impact in the Duma, thanks in part to the leadership provided by Primakov. The LDP's vote, having gone from 23 percent to 12 percent in 1995, halved again to 6 percent. Yabloko's share declined less severely, also to 6 percent, but left it weakly represented in the Duma and open to charges of near-impotence. As an institution, the Duma was likely to be mostly progovernment, and it quickly showed signs of working quite well with Putin.

With the Duma election successfully negotiated, the last piece of the puzzle had fallen into place. After FAR's poor showing, it was most unlikely that Primakov or Luzhkov would run for president (a presumption soon shown to be true), so Putin would have no strong rivals. The Chechnya war had been going quite well; but if the first war was a guide (and it proved to be), the situation might soon deteriorate, and no one could tell how the population would react. Thus everything pointed to the wisdom of Yeltsin's resigning early to make sure that Putin's approval rating would not have time to fall much, and also that no rival would have time to build himself up. In this way, Putin's victory would be assured—and with it, the ultimate goal: Yeltsin's freedom from prosecution.

"The Family" managed with surprising ease to get Yeltsin on board. They assured him that he would continue to be treated like royalty at home and abroad. As a theatrical gesture, he chose the eve of the new millennium for handing over the reins of supreme power. Because the secret was well kept, his grand gesture came as a surprise to the world. The same day, Vladimir Putin was sworn in as acting president. His first official act was to sign a decree, issued at once, that provided generously for the material and security needs of Yeltsin and his family. The decree also stipulated that a former president possessed immunity from prosecution and could not be arrested, searched, interrogated, or subjected to administrative penalty. Similar immunity extended to private and public premises, means of transport and communication, baggage, and so on.[295]

What was so striking about this episode was the unseemly need to issue such a document at all, and for Putin to sign it with such haste as his first presidential act. But the act was emblematic of the essence of Yeltsin's rule.

The presidential election, set for March 26, proved to be a shoo-in. As long as Putin made no major blunders, which he did not, his opponents felt they had no chance. Hence the campaign was largely anticlimactic. Russians had known this man for only seven months, and he had little experience in governing a nation; nonetheless, Putin won with 54 percent. Zyuganov got 30 percent (2 percent less than he got in the first round against Yeltsin in 1996), and Yavlinsky 6 percent. In many regions and also at the federal level, fairness was not the election's central feature. Putin was frank enough to say that Zyuganov had done better than expected, "even though—let's be direct and honest about it—he didn't have many opportunities in the media, especially the electronic media."[296]

Much, much more daunting for Putin was the path ahead. Could he retain the personal and institutional legitimacy the election had given him, even though the Russian people had little idea for whom they had voted? Could he handle Russia's profound problems?

The first, most immediate problem was the war. The generals could and did declare victory, with only policing functions now required. But could this bluff be concealed from the people, when the Chechens were in fact far from beaten? Could Putin find a Chechen of authority with whom to negotiate a settlement? Would the army and the Interior Ministry allow him to negotiate seriously? After all, General Vladimir Shamanov had said in November 1999, "Many officers, including some generals, are ready to resign if military operations are stopped." Any such course would be another "slap in the face" to officers, like that of 1996.[297] Finally, even if he could get a settlement, what defense would it be against the plausible prospect of a long campaign of terror and assassination against the Russian state by international and Russian fundamentalist Muslims? Could such a campaign—which was only made more likely by the initiative in 2000 to ban Wahhabism throughout Russia—even, perhaps, cause Russia to fragment?[298]

The second problem was whether Vladimir Putin could ever acquire the power with which to reform Russia's corrupt economy and polity. He was, after all, a product of this system. He had his own history of corruption, some of which was already on public record.[299] The oligarchs and the governors, the two groups whose enormous power he had to reduce, had at least some of the facts at their fingertips. Possibly they even knew something about a connection between the new president and the apartment bombings, as Berezovsky's threat of January 2000 suggested.[300] In these circumstances, how could Putin build a coalition strong enough to change the status quo, assuming he really wanted to do so? What economic strategy might work? Would he end up, after some tinkering, with a new version of market bolshevism?

The next few months saw the emergence of the outlines of the Putinites' economic strategy. On the one hand, they accepted many of the recommendations of a commission Putin had set up under German Gref, which were in most ways a more radical version of the second shock therapy program unveiled by Chubais and Nemtsov in 1997: pensions, taxes, health care, education, utilities, housing rents, and the "natural monopolies" would all be "modernized" (that is, brought into line with Western practice), and the gigantic bill for these drastic changes was to be paid mainly by ordinary people, who were mostly already living in poverty. On the other hand, the state was to play a greater economic role than before. Hence, a national industrial policy was commissioned for the state sector by the new premier, Mikhail Kasyanov, who had both liberal and statist sympathies. Later, a vice-premier announced that each of the seven federal regions that Putin had set up would devise its own economic plan, whereupon, in a response that revealed the government's disunity, another vice-premier promptly denounced his colleague's policy as unthinkable.[301]

Putin's main contribution to the economic debate was, while supporting both of the somewhat dissonant trends in strategy, to inject a note of urgency. In his address to parliament and the nation on July 8 he started with the shocking statistic that "in fifteen years from now there may be 22 million fewer Russians": that is, the population might decline by one-seventh to 124 million. (Some longer-term projections envisioned a possible decline to 80 million by 2050.) He went on to say that although investment was at last growing, "The fact is that economic growth, as was the case in 1997, is on the brink of collapsing." The helpful effects of the import substitution that resulted from the sharp devaluation of 1998 were fading. Also, "at least a third of budget revenues are spent on the servicing and repayment of foreign debts."

Further alarming statistics were provided by the government and other authorities: 41.2 percent of the population was now living below the official poverty line, defined as income of less than the ruble equivalent of $500 a year. Also, capital flight was continuing at a high rate, and real average monthly pay in 2000 would "constitute only 70 percent of the 1997 level."[302] Adding to the sense of alarm was a widely debated book that argued that Russia could not hope to survive by relying on its extractive industries' exports because— owing to these industries' remote locations—they were being priced out of world markets.[303]

Meanwhile, a group of eighteen prominent Russian and American economists, including three Nobel laureates, put forward in June an agenda for economic reform that was very different from the Kremlin's model of authoritarian modernization.[304] It emphasized the reform of institutions, decriminalization, restructuring and competition, putting the growth of production ahead of keeping inflation near zero, and the need for a social contract that would make the work force believe the government was concerned about social justice. They also emphasized that "not only the quality of Russian life, but also the prospects for economic recovery and growth depend on ensuring civil liberties, a free press, and a democratic system of government."[305]

How could ordinary Russians be made to endure the further sacrifices the Kremlin was planning for them? This became clearer as the Putinites' plans for political reform gradually came into view: emasculating the Duma and the Federation Council, intimidating the opposition (for example, by telling college students they would be expelled if they persisted in supporting Yabloko), tightening police controls in general, sharply reducing the powers of the governors, selectively harassing some oligarchs, and—most important of all—bringing the nationwide media under tight government control.

Elements of media policy, such as the high-profile arrest of Radio Free Europe/Radio Liberty journalist Andrei Babitsky, became visible from April onward. By June, though, journalists and editors were getting leaks on more specific plans for the media that "have been under discussion in an atmosphere of secrecy in certain Kremlin offices." The general plan was to introduce painful economic reforms (Putin's "Great Leap Forward") in the fall, and to have strong media controls in place by then to make sure that the resulting protests and repressive actions would not be publicized.[306]

In July–August, the picture came into sharper focus from leaks of large portions of a detailed planning document commissioned by the Presidential Administration from Gleb Pavlovsky's Foundation for Effective Politics. The document laid out in a monthly timetable how independent journalists and media outlets were to be either bought or silenced, and all the regional and metropolitan media tamed. In this way, no one would learn about whatever might happen in the wake of the draconian economic measures planned for the fall. Beyond this, the media were to start propagating the idea of "mobilizational reforms" of the type introduced in their day by Peter the Great and by Stalin. They were also to stop reporting distressing news and begin printing upbeat stories to inspire readers—in the inimitable style of Soviet Agitprop.

In the field of power politics, the CPRF was to be split through the development of the broad, malleable, leftist party "Russia" under Duma Speaker Seleznev. Other members of the opposition would be intimidated, and the Duma would become a forum dominated by the pro-Kremlin Unity and the tame "Russia." In general, everything would be done to ensure that the legislature and the judiciary were firmly controlled by the executive.

Two days earlier, Pavlovsky, without referring to his foundation's plan, had spelled out the rationale for such a strategy: Russia had been so weakened by Yeltsin's rule and the scheming of the West, he said, that it had to build up its defenses in all fields: military, economic, and informational. Building "informational security" meant ensuring that the West would not be able to exploit any domestic protests against the measures needed to build Russia's economic and military security. Thus, he implied, the protests should not be publicized.[307]

At the same time, Putin held a closed-door meeting with newspaper editors that caused a sensation. For the first time, after many years of ostracism by the Kremlin, the radical imperial nationalists Aleksandr Prokhanov of *Zavtra* and Valentin Chikin of *Sovetskaya Rossiya* were included in such a meeting. Earlier, they had gradually come around to supporting Putin, though with strong reservations about the economic liberalism he avowed, and had written him an open letter asking for a meeting. After the meeting, Prokhanov wrote that Putin had impressed him by the openness and knowledgeability with which he had discussed a wide range of topics with the group.[308]

It was possible, of course, that the leaks about the Kremlin's future plans were designed mainly as psychological warfare against independent media and political groups, and the plans were never intended for thorough implementation. If, however, the plans were real, it still remained to be seen whether such a radical suppression of civil liberties could actually be carried through to completion, and what impact Western protests—seemingly quite effective in the cases of Babitsky and, as discussed below, Vladimir Gusinsky—would have on Putin.

Regarding the governors and selected oligarchs, the Putinites' approach was primarily one of intimidation. Using administrative measures and, where necessary, the threat of legal action, the goal was to induce them to give up some of their powers and their property. In the case of the intermittently oppositionist oligarch Gusinsky, he was subjected to repeated pressure regarding the repayment of large outstanding loans, detained in prison for a few days in June, and then, after lengthy secret negotiations with the authorities, he went abroad. It appeared that a deal may have been made under which some of his media holdings, including his national television station NTV, which the Putinites specially wanted to control, would be sold to a buyer sympathetic to them.[309]

Against the governors, Putin used both intimidation of this sort and also radical structural innovations. On May 31, his official representative in the Duma, Aleksandr Kotenkov, created a storm when he said that as soon as the governors lost their parliamentary immunity, at least sixteen of them would be jailed, to be followed soon by many more.[310] When this law and two related ones were finally passed with various amendments on July 26, it said that the governors' immunity (not unconditional in any case) would last only until they completed their terms, after which they would no longer have seats in the Federation Council.

In addition to this radical structural change, Putin had decreed the formation of seven federal regions (*okrugi*) and had appointed commissioners answerable to himself to run them. Five of the seven were generals from the police, secret police, and military, and debate soon raged about what exactly their powers would be, including, as mentioned above, whether or not they would draw up economic plans for their regions.[311]

Finally, on foreign policy, could Putin develop a viable relationship with the West, whereby he would quietly, behind some nationalist rhetoric, accommodate it on most issues in return for the West's pledge not to interfere while he solved the Chechnya problem and gradually curbed civil liberties?[312] Would not such an agreement, if it were ever reached, contribute heavily to the withering—even the extinction—of Russia's shaky democracy? We attempt to provide some informed speculation on questions of this sort in the epilogue of this book.

EPILOGUE:
MARKET
BOSLSHEVISM,
A HISTORICAL
INTERPRETATION

W<small>E BEGAN THIS BOOK</small> by pondering the elusive meaning of reform in the Russian political tradition. On August 17, 1998, the collapse of the Russian Treasury bills market, the government's default on its debt, and the devaluation of the ruble—all the work of the "young reformers" who had been extolled by Western leaders for seven years—marked the beginning of the end of a short but dramatic era in Russian history, an era in which the grassroots movement for reform from 1987 to 1991 was largely negated by the top-down reforms we have called market bolshevism.

The collapse of the pyramid of government debt that had piled up over years of speculative operations at the expense of the state budget drastically reduced the political influence of the two elite groups that, despite their frequent quarreling with each other over slices of the budgetary pie, had jointly steered Russia through the period of so-called reforms: Gone were the enforcers of the radical marketization by authoritarian means that had been launched in the fall of 1991 under the name of "shock therapy," and so was much of the backroom political influence of the self-described "oligarchs"—the infamous "Seven Bankers" plus chief executives of large semiprivate monopolies in the raw materials sector who had reaped tremendous benefits from the conduct of "reforms" under Prime Minister Viktor Chernomyrdin at the expense of productive, manufacturing industries and of the nation's impoverished majority.

The subsequent appointment of Yevgeny Primakov as premier at the insistence of the parliament and over the heads of the corporate establishment probably will be seen by historians as Russia's most substantive step toward representative democracy since 1991; it altered, if only temporarily, some basic traits of the Yeltsin regime, such as the ever-shifting balance between authoritarian "reformers" and oligarchs, groups that had portrayed themselves as each other's opponents, even as they cooperated within the same governments and switched to and fro between positions in government and major corporations. However, Yeltsin remained president for sixteen more months, ousted Primakov in May 1999 in favor of a more congenial figure, and ultimately installed his chosen successor, Vladimir Putin.

Although some policies have changed under Putin, what is still fundamentally the Yeltsin system of market bolshevism in Russia has not acquired any qualitatively new features. Thus, whatever political jolts Putin engineers, Russia's regional governors and the oligarchs will probably be peripheral to what we expect to be the overarching theme of the coming years: Russians' search for a qualitatively new strategy of national recovery and development that will enable them to transcend the Manichaean antagonism between "reformers" and "antireformers" and similar ideological divisions that have paralyzed Russian society over the last decade.

Russia's elites across the board lack an inspiring vision of the nation's identity and future, and have been unable to steer the country away from decline and bankruptcy. Externally, the image of "the West" as a selfless savior and sponsor has long since waned. The barrenness of these two traditional, fundamental sources of social change means that Russians will have to search for internal civic and cultural resources in the depths of society that will help to pull the nation out of its present troubles. This general understanding was reflected in the billboard posters that appeared all over Moscow in late 1998: "Nobody will help Russia but we ourselves."

Such an internally driven recovery requires a comprehensive analysis of three things: the sociocultural, as well as the political legacy of "the era of reforms"; the transformation of Russia's "social capital" from the state of considerable cohesion and expectation that defined the public mood in the late 1980s to its current state of pervasive mistrust and apathy, tinged only with a desperate popular hope that Putin might perform some miracles; and the series of more promising alternative courses that appeared during the last decade, the ignoring or rejection of which brought Russia to its present plight. In this epilogue, we pick up some of our theoretical points from chapter 2 and outline our understanding of the issues we think essential for an accurate historical interpretation of Russia's experiment with radical marketization of its economy and society. Following that, we conclude with some thoughts about the implications of our interpretation for U.S. and Western policy.

COMPETING VISIONS OF CHANGE IN THE EARLY 1990S: DEMOCRATS VERSUS RADICAL FREEMARKETEERS

Let us examine one of the most widespread and misleading clichés of the Russian and Western press: the assertion that in 1990–91, political power in Russia was seized by "democrats." As we have seen, although this claim was at the least inaccurate, remarkably it was propagated by both wings of the Russian political elite—by the radical freemarketeers and by the Communist opposition. Moreover, support for both "democracy" and "free-market reforms" that were allegedly developing in Russia in frictionless tandem became the favorite mantra of the U.S. government. This position reflected an uncritical projection of the American system —which, as discussed in chapter 2, is based on "peaceful coexistence" between constitutional democracy and the market allocation of goods—onto a nation with a fundamentally different culture and history, notably regarding the history of the relationship between authority and wealth.

It is true that in contemporary Russia, democracy as a set of procedures and a culture has been closely linked in the public consciousness to the notion of the "democratic movement," which between 1987 and 1991 united large numbers of unprivileged Russians from the most diverse social and educational backgrounds. However, the evidence of this book demonstrates that not only did this movement never achieve anything close to administrative power, but, in fact, the program of economic and political reforms that was shaped and carried out by Yeltsin, Yegor Gaidar, Anatoly Chubais, and their Western advisers ran counter to the most basic aspirations and tenets of the movement that had ensured Yeltsin's success in the 1989, 1990, and 1991 elections.

This broad-based nationwide movement, which had its roots in the political underground of the 1960s and 1970s, coalesced and appeared on the political stage as a result of Gorbachev's reforms. As we explained in chapter 3, the movement defined itself in opposition to the political power and economic privileges of the Soviet oligarchy and its Mafiya allies, most often without the ideologically radical anticommunism of the freemarketeers, many of whom belonged to the Soviet establishment. The movement also aspired to broadly conceived democratic values of European as well as native Russian origin, rooted in the Russian ideal of a "people's rule" in national and local government, and to a more just and equitable society than the corrupt system of "developed socialism."[1] Besides these common values and the quintessentially Russian "populist" vision of a body politic without rigid divisions between rulers and ruled, the movement had few clearly defined programmatic goals. It was also organizationally fragmented, encompassing dozens of amorphous groups and protoparties without rigid ideological affiliation, whose creeds ranged from communitarian traditionalism to liberal Marxism.[2] In this regard, it was typologically similar to other protest movements, such as the American civil rights movement in the 1960s or Poland's Solidarity.

On a parallel track, meanwhile, large segments of the Soviet managerial elite, as well as the entrepreneurially minded officials in institutions such as the CPSU, Komsomol, and KGB, were busily engaged in a process of discarding their administrative power (which no one else picked up) and illegally or semilegally privatizing economic property, a process that inevitably weakened the chain of command that had been holding society together, namely the CPSU apparatus. The weakening of the state and the subversion of its revenue base were unopposed and even facilitated by the Gorbachev government and by Yeltsin's a fortiori; this effectively prevented the democrats at the national and local levels from consolidating enough political and administrative power to block and overturn the abuses of the Soviet nomenklatura and the mostly illegal redistribution of public property that was under way.

In addition, the interests of the capitalist-minded nomenklatura were furthered by the historical imbalance between the development of civil society and that of the Soviet ruling class's private economic activity. The era of Brezhnevite "stagnation" had been characterized by many authorities' covert encouragement of the monopolistic black markets created by elite groups in association with the Mafiya, which used opportunities provided by détente to open clandestine channels to Western economies. As for the activities of political opponents of the nomenklatura and other dissenters, they were almost invariably suppressed. As a result, by the time of perestroika, the civic development and self-organization of society lagged far behind the capitalistic development of the nomenklatura.

The allies and admirers of Russia's "market reformers" in the West mostly failed to grasp that by 1991, when the Soviet economy had already been in trouble for more than a decade, the real debate was not between "reformers" and "anti-reformers" but, rather, between the proponents of different methods and directions of change. They were split along political and cultural lines between democrats and radical freemarketeers, populists and elitists, idealists and pragmatic manipulators. Even within the group of resolute Westernizers, some were inspired primarily by Western protest movements of the 1960s and the Prague Spring ideal of "socialism with a human face," while others saw the West through the prism of Thatcher's and Reagan's deregulated capitalism. In any event, the cyclical paradigm of Russian history—in which top-down reformers have clashed with proponents of change from lower social strata—reproduced its zero-sum game: the radical freemarketeers (with support from the IMF and Western governments) won and the democratic movement lost.

The widespread cliché that "Russia has already gone through all the revolutions that history allows her" may be true for administrative revolutions from above (such as Stalin's collectivization and Yeltsin's shock therapy), but hardly so for revolutions from below. To be sure, one—the 1905–07 revolution—deserves this name; and, in the final analysis, it was suppressed. February 1917 was mostly a spontaneous uprising of soldiers and housewives in Petrograd, combined with a plot involving members of the tsar's entourage and the embassies of the Triple Entente powers. This uprising merely pulled the plug on the already incapacitated monarchy.

The events of October 1917 were a conspiratorial coup that certainly led to a far-reaching revolution from above with broad masses of the populace drawn in, but it can hardly be seen as a popular, nationwide rebellion against the old regime, on a par with England's Puritan Revolution of the 1640s or the French Revolution of 1789. Therefore, except for the case of February 1917 (when popular discontent was only one of the factors), no Russian government of modern times has been brought down by protests from below. Likewise, in 1991, the Russian democratic movement was able neither to unseat the rulers, nor to promote the kind of reforms that it desired. In fact, by 1990, it had virtually delegated the representation of its interests to one of the warring factions within the nomenklatura—namely, to Boris Yeltsin and his team.

Pragmatically minded and lacking scruples, this group benefited from the electoral resources of the democrats and the appeal of their anti-establishment rhetoric, and thus acquired a popular legitimacy that was unprecedented for Soviet politicians since the end of World War II. In 1990, however, the Yeltsin team was not particularly interested in using this legitimacy and the support of the democrats for the purpose of social reform and economic development. Instead, it used the democratic movement as a battering ram to destroy the USSR's unionwide institutions, while Yeltsin built his own, previously only embryonic state, the Russian Federation (centered around him personally), and in 1991 chopped off those union republics and institutions that the new state was unable to swallow.

Soon after their success in defeating the August 1991 coup by sections of the old elite, Yeltsin and his allies in the entrepreneurial part of the establishment took firm steps to pre-empt and block the further development of the grassroots democratic movement because it threatened to reduce them to transitional figures who could well be sidelined by the brewing democratic revolution. In particular, Yeltsin, Gavriil Popov, Yuri Luzhkov, and others encouraged successive splits within the movement, discredited its potential leaders with the help of Kremlin-loyal media, and tarnished the leaders' image in the West by squeezing them out of the democratic political mainstream and toward the "red-brown" periphery. Most important, the wiping out by the government of most people's savings (held in frozen bank accounts amidst hyperinflationary conditions) effectively expropriated the middle class, which had constituted the social base of the democratic movement. This expropriation was done even as the reformers repeatedly promised, with little ultimate success, to create a new middle class from those entrepreneurial groups that benefited from the demise of the old one.

By mid-1992, these policies had secured unchallenged domination over the economic and political agenda for an array of oligarchical clans that came mostly from the former Soviet establishment. Having contributed greatly to the collapse of the Soviet system by their ideological disorientation, their mindless wasting of national resources (for example, when helping to wage the Cold War), their attempts to emulate Western elites' consumption patterns, and their conscious neglect of the needs and opinions of the population at large, these clans were now ruling independent Russia.

Fixated as they were on the vicissitudes of power politics in Gorbachev's Kremlin, Western observers failed to notice the decline of the anti-nomenklatura movement. They neglected the evidence showing that Yeltsin and his shock therapists substantially reduced the amount of influence that civil society and democratic institutions had acquired during the years of perestroika and acted contrary to the democrats' aspirations and goals. Thus, instead of pursuing an equitable denationalization of property and a level playing field for law-abiding new entrepreneurs, the regime accelerated Soviet-era elites' and the criminal underworld's rush to conduct what Soviet history textbooks called "the primitive accumulation of capital," something that was supposedly an inevitable stage in the building of a capitalist society.

Instead of promoting the development of democratic institutions and a genuine separation of powers, Yeltsin and his associates disbanded the new post-Soviet parliament by force and emasculated its successor, blocked the development of an independent judicial branch, reduced the power and revenue base of local self-government, and by 1994 had imposed a regime of Byzantine authoritarianism on the country. Thus Russia was thrown backward regarding the development of civil society and is now farther removed from the initial goals of the democratic movement than it was before Yeltsin came to power.

Therefore, the labels of "democrat" and "reformer," often applied to various factions within the Yeltsin-era elite, are misleading. If one takes the values and goals of the popular democratic movement as being what reform initially meant to the unprivileged social groups, then Yeltsin-era policies represented a roll-back of reform, or, in terms of Russia's cyclical paradigm, a counterreform. In fact, it is a striking psychological fact that people like Gaidar and Chubais, whose policies the majority of citizens consistently opposed, managed to appropriate the generic label of "democrats" and were acknowledged as such even by their opponents. As a result, the words "democrat" and "democracy" have acquired pejorative and even obscene connotations for many ordinary Russians.

Government opponents, in their turn, acquired the equally misleading label of "hard-liners." In reality, it was Yeltsin, Chernomyrdin, and Chubais who proved to be the real hard-liners in their implacable drive to impose policies that had little support in society. Among their opponents, some acted as soft-liners, such as influential apparatchiks in the Communist Party of the Russian Federation, never really trying to reverse Yeltsin's antidemocratic policies; in fact, some of the Communist leaders and their allies derived electoral and often direct economic benefits from such policies. Other, more persistent opposition groups were firmly kept at the margins of the political process through the joint efforts of the communist and anticommunist nomenklatura. Among such opposition groups, we have in mind primarily the social-democrats led by Grigori Yavlinsky, as well as the socially conscious nationalists led by Sergei Baburin; the ranks of these groups were recruited mainly from Russia's disillusioned democrats.

Taking a longer historical perspective, we have argued that an appropriate term for Russia's rulers in the 1990s was market bolsheviks. Indeed, in Russian historical parlance, bolshevism long ago acquired the additional meaning of a certain pattern of political culture and behavior that dates back at least to Peter the Great.[3] It is defined by the self-confident, almost messianic vanguard mentality of a self-anointed elite that sees itself entitled to impose "progress" and "development"—according to its own understanding of these terms—on the "backward" majority by wiping away traditional ways of life and the socio-cultural diversity that characterizes Russia's "many-layeredness," or *mnogoukladnost'*. In the 1990s, as in 1917, the bolsheviks of the day framed their struggle against Russia's "backwardness" so as to portray the ultraconservative forces as their main enemies. In reality, however, they often cooperated behind the scenes with leaders of these "dark forces," such as Zhirinovsky and Zyuganov, to oppose grassroots, democratic alternatives that represented a different, more tolerant, and inclusive vision of development and progress.

In our view, the concepts of market bolshevism and history's cyclical development yield a more profound understanding of Russia in the 1990s than the common cliché about "democrats and reformers" struggling against "dark forces." It casts a light on why the intelligentsia and other unprivileged strata (especially in Russia's provinces) that had been the driving force of Russia's democratic movement have in recent years given their votes and intellectual support to all kinds of opposition to market bolshevism; their determination is evident in their support of even the most radical alternatives while they still hold on, as polls indicate, to many of the democratic values of the 1987–91 period.

Finally, the historical framework suggests that Putin's successors, who, we can only hope, will search for indigenous resources for recovery, will eventually have to enter into a dialogue with those sociocultural groups that stood behind the abortive democratic revolution. This will mean reassembling piece by piece the social and human capital of grassroots reformism that has been neglected or destroyed by the market bolsheviks.

MARKET BOLSHEVISM'S BEQUEST TO RUSSIA

If Russia is to transcend the legacy of the market bolsheviks' rule, it is important to identify the basic elements of this legacy that the leaders of post-Yeltsin Russia will have to confront sooner or later. What follows is a short list of the seven features that we see as fundamental to the political and social order that existed in Russia from October 1993 to September 1998. It should be noted that while some of them have become less visible since the end of this period, most have remained fully in force and may become even more deeply entrenched if not addressed, or if some segments of the post-Yeltsin elite find them suitable for their own purposes. For this reason, choosing between the present and the past tense in discussing the Yeltsin legacy is usually not an easy task.

A LEGITIMACY VACUUM

The failure to redistribute power and wealth in the period of "reforms" in a way that would be legitimate by the standards and norms of Russian culture is the most fundamental reason that the present system possesses little legitimacy. This lack of legitimacy corrupts the very foundations of the state and influences the norms of human conduct in society, especially the way the public relates to governmental authority. The basic reason for this pervasive illegitimacy, in our view, is that under Yeltsin the state abrogated its unspoken social contract with the population—a contract that was deeply rooted in the nation's history and culture, at least as an ideal. In particular, government repudiated its responsibility to promote, or at any rate sustain, the welfare of society and to guarantee a subsistence income for its disadvantaged members. Thus it squandered the legitimacy that flowed from the initial democratic aspirations for a more just social order, and it failed to develop any substitute.

The Yeltsin team acknowledged this choice in the 1996 elections, when it declared its candidate to be the "the lesser evil" compared to the Communist contender. As a result, to use Mancur Olson's imagery, Russians saw the government as just another in a seemingly infinite series of "stationary bandits," whose fiscal demands amounted not to the advancement of the public good but simply to an extortion of tribute to enrich the "party of power." Hence the revenue crisis is a derivative problem, which can be resolved after the government's social contract with the nation—and therefore its legitimacy as well—is restored. To Primakov's credit, he acknowledged early on that mistrust of the authorities was the central problem his government had to address.

A PRIVATIZED STATE

It is no wonder that the alienated majority of Russians identifies the Yeltsin-era state with individuals and factions within the establishment, most of whom put their private interests above those of the nation, and some of whom became indistinguishable from organized crime. Since 1993, the shifting balance of forces within this "Mafiya-establishment alliance" has determined most of the country's political and economic fluctuations. In 1996, Giulietto Chiesa remarked with only slight exaggeration that "fighting corruption and crime in Russia would mean no less and no more than changing the political elite of the country."[4]

The Primakov government—whose key members, including Primakov himself, came from traditionally the least corrupt institutions of the establishment, such as the Academy of Sciences—also appeared to understand this axiom and was apparently willing to prosecute some members of the Yeltsin-era elite for economic crimes to the extent possible without disrupting the fragile social peace and the administrative capacity of those government institutions that were still more or less functioning. Meanwhile, the antigovernment campaign unleashed by the Russian media, controlled by such financiers as Boris Berezovsky (widely seen as connected to the criminal world), and the semivoluntary resignation of the country's prosecutor general in February 1999, showed that this would be an arduous task for the Primakov government, and one fraught with serious political danger.

This assessment was borne out when Yeltsin and his associates saw that Berezovsky's prosecution was likely to provoke credible threats to expose their own misdeeds. At the same time, Yeltsin realized that Primakov was well positioned to be elected president in his place; so Yeltsin removed him, and the privatizers of the state breathed easier. In 2000, President Putin reawakened the worries of at least some of them.

MARKET BOLSHEVISM AS AN IDEOLOGICAL DOCTRINE

The Yeltsin regime did not merely pursue a set of policies. Like its predecessors, it had a comprehensive ideology that was shared by most factions within the elite and was propagated by a range of pro-Kremlin media. This ideology consisted of a peculiar blend of three elements: Social Darwinism, which sees survival of the fittest and neglect of the weak as the iron law of social progress;

the "postmodern" cult of the autarkic self, which scorns civic obligations and community values; and traditional Russian fatalism.

The Russian elite used this ideology both explicitly and subliminally to remold society in its own image, calling to mind not only its Bolshevik predecessors, but also certain aspects of China's Cultural Revolution. Thus the descent of the middle class into poverty and its scramble for subsistence were seemingly designed to produce psychological effects similar to, if less drastic than, those of the Maoist policy of "moral re-education" for urbanites consigned to manual labor in impoverished villages.

Beyond this, the mainstream Russian media have often presented the use of brute force and backroom connections as the most rational method of self-advancement. They portray public-sector employees, such as teachers, as people who have been consigned to low wages by their limited skills and lack of initiative, and thus to perpetual but hopeless opposition to the brave new world. Because pensioners and the unprivileged intelligentsia were seen as the most solid and sustainable base of the opposition, the media have also tended to fuel anti-intellectualism and to foster a generation gap by patronizing or even mocking the elderly. At the governmental level, this generational chauvinism was made explicit by the previously quoted statement by the senior politician Boris Nemtsov: "Russia must enter the twenty-first century only with young people, including in its national leadership."[5]

This subtle but sustained brainwashing sought to drag as many Russians as possible into the get-rich-quick operations and schemes of the "casino economy," so that the elite's own abuses would acquire legitimacy in the light of what it projected as a "national norm." As a result of this propaganda campaign, many Russians, especially the young, have gradually accepted the new system as the normal way of life, or at least as a lesser evil. They have descended into the shadow economy after dropping out of the public sector and the education system. There, a rising number succumb to social scourges such as drug abuse.

Impotent Authoritarianism

The Yeltsin regime's persistent attempts to strengthen its grip without addressing the legitimacy problem produced a vicious circle of escalating autocratic centralization of executive powers within a government whose administrative capacity was progressively declining. Thus the buildup of presidential authority from late 1991 on, and the bouts of bureaucratic authoritarianism staged by Yeltsin's string of "iron chancellors" (from Gennadi Burbulis to Chubais), were often counterproductive in terms of administrative efficacy. Fiscal anemia and the rising fetish of market speculation that devalued the work ethic created an environment in which the government's chain of command dissolved (not far below the autocrat himself) into a fluid agglomeration of bureaucratic, private, and corporate interests, where shifting allegiances between patrons and clients prevailed over institutional loyalties.

A PARTISAN CONSTITUTION

Although the 1993 constitution has not been strictly observed, it still remains a major stumbling block to national reconciliation and democratic development. This is not so much because it is superpresidential (although Yeltsin's and Putin's presidential powers have exceeded those of the American and French presidencies combined, and approximate the powers of Tsar Nicholas II under the 1905 quasi-constitutional system) but, rather, because it has never been openly debated and accepted by most of society. As shown in chapter 7, it was drafted as a partisan document tailored to fit the regime and to perpetuate the new distribution of political forces. It was also promulgated under conditions of one-man rule that violated the previous constitution and laws. Moreover, evidence suggests that the referendum approving it was rigged.

With the executive branch subject to few restraints and very little legislative or judicial oversight, Yeltsin and his cabinets had ample room to interpret the constitution in their own favor and to violate it with impunity.[6] Today, even the most moderate parties favor amending it, but because it was designed to be impossible to change without the president's consent, and Yeltsin predictably opposed any change, every move to adjust the constitutional order in his time contained destabilizing and revolutionary potential.

Consider Primakov's cautious attempt of January 1999 to negotiate a pact that would create stable relations among the branches of power. According to the plan, Yeltsin was supposed to renounce his right to dismiss the government and the Duma at his own discretion and to appoint acting cabinets without regard for the parliamentary majority. In exchange, he would receive extensive guarantees of political and legal immunity and material welfare after the completion of his term. Yeltsin's inner circle first turned down the plan and then considerably diluted it with support from opposition members who apparently hoped to gain his favor and join the government. However, nothing came of the plan until, as noted in chapter 9, he and Putin redrafted the provisions on the president's immunity and welfare, and Putin issued them as his first decree on the day Yeltsin resigned.

DEPENDENCY ON THE WEST

Dependency theory was originally developed in the Western school of political economy with regard to Latin American nations. Unlike some Western academics in the 1980s, Soviet scholars and analysts never spoke about Soviet economic dependency; nor is the notion popular in today's Russia, where liberal and nationalistic modes of wishful thinking hold sway. Indeed, Russia still possesses human and technological resources that, in the past, would have guaranteed it a considerable degree of economic self-sufficiency. Today, however, it presents plenty of evidence to support the view that it depends economically on the West.

In our view, dependency has had two distinct elements: first, Russia's "pipeline economy" has had an objective structural dependency on global markets; and, second, both the Soviet- and the Yeltsin-era elites have had a cultural and psychological dependency on the image of "the West," a dependency nurtured by both sides and continuously remolded to suit the interests and phobias of various groups within the post-Soviet establishment. These two elements have developed autonomously, but they are often difficult to separate from each other.

Culturally, dependency stems from the hierarchical vision of the world—characteristic of Russia's bolsheviks old and new—that divides humanity into "the West" and "the Rest." This image of the omnipotent and single-minded West, as well as rumors about the "Western support" being given to this or that faction, have been used as powerful levers in Russian politics. This leverage was particularly visible during the two stormiest confrontations between Kremlin factions—in August 1991 and September–October 1993—when the image of a unified "West" standing behind one of the warring cliques was cleverly employed, with conscious support from powerful Westerners and passive acquiescence from others. The goal was to ensure a winner-take-all victory for one side in the conflict and to lay on "the West" the ultimate responsibility for the consequences of the winner's actions.

As we showed, especially in chapter 5, one particular agent of this dependency, the IMF, has been at the center of debate about Russia since 1991, and we have argued extensively that the IMF's lending to Russia has been harmful to its economy and national interests. By now, few would dispute that the loans, as well as the billions of dollars in Western aid given to the central government in Moscow, were pumped into sustaining the political fortunes of unpopular and inefficient administrators, whose only major success was to make the West coresponsible for the results of their policies in the eyes of the Russian people. For both Russians and Westerners, this was a waste of money and moral capital. However, the degree of the Russian establishment's psychological dependency is clearly demonstrated in the fact that even Putin's psychologically less dependent government has sought continued IMF lending, if only to stretch out debt repayment schedules.

The problem with this approach is that the IMF loans never come without "conditionalities," and these have too often been harmful for the countries that accepted and applied them, as an increasing number of authoritative economists now admit.

Another aspect of the same psychological dependency is the talk since 1998 about the terrible consequences of default on sovereign debt that some view as leading inevitably to Russia's eviction from the world financial system. It is worth remembering that in 1931, Britain and France defaulted on their sovereign debt to the United States, which was incurred during World War I. Of course, Russia's initial position vis-à-vis world financial markets is quite different. Yet both Western lenders and Russian doomsayers should realize that Russia's depression has been much more severe than that of the early 1930s in Europe, and that a significant share of these debts were incurred in pursuit of policies that the IMF and Western financial circles had advocated and that ultimately proved bankrupt. In these circumstances, given that Russia does not have enough revenue to pay its debts without risking social breakdown, the West may eventually find it realistic and sensible, however unprecedented, to write off much of Russia's current debt to the IMF and other bodies rather than lend it more money.

Whether structural or psychological, dependency is part of the reality that Russians currently have to deal with. It carries both advantages and disadvantages for various strata and political interests in Russian society, including, paradoxically, for the less privileged ones and for those that no longer expect anything good from "the West." True, during 1991–93, the dependency factor played a definitive role in the rise of an essentially antidemocratic regime. Yet it also inhibited the Kremlin from destroying some formal elements of democracy, such as comparatively free elections and a parliament, which it otherwise probably would have done away with after October 1993. In 1997–98, the elite's psychological dependency on approval from "influential Western circles" translated into a panicked reaction among Western scholars and mainstream media to revelations of abuses by "oligarchs" like Chubais, Berezovsky, and Alfred Kokh. This reaction contributed ultimately to the eviction of the Chubais clan from the Russian Olympus of politics, if not from the business world.[7] Also, it was the turmoil in global financial markets that in August 1998 triggered Russia's financial crisis and then the anti-oligarchic "velvet revolution" by which the Duma brought Primakov to power. This reaction showed that upheavals in global finance can lead to upheavals in Russian politics more quickly and decisively than any isolated domestic event could do.

Conversely, it is possible that in the future, conservative elites in Russia's financial and extractive sectors will try to rebuild their diminished power with support from the regional and corporate barons in the most autarkic areas of the country and also from the most inward-looking social groups. If this should happen, they are likely to counter proponents of social change by appealing to ethnic Russian nationalism and adopting a protectionist strategy that would help them insulate their power and wealth from the vicissitudes of the global economy.

THE INDISPENSABILITY OF AN AUTOCRAT

While the structural factors defining the Yeltsin regime were essential, the personal role of an autocrat is pivotal in protecting the system of market bolshevism from factional fragmentation, administrative paralysis, and popular upheaval. In fact, such an autocrat seems to be an essential structural element in any bolshevik type of modernization. The Yeltsin-era establishment was fully aware of this necessity; hence its desire to postpone Yeltsin's departure and its tolerance over several years of his aberrant behavior and pronouncements that embarrassed and demeaned Russia (including its oligarchs) on the world stage.

Eventually, some of the financial and administrative elites realized they had to engineer a smooth transition of power to a new potential autocrat, and they sought to select one who would treat them well. In 1999, some former associates of Chernomyrdin and Chubais saw Yuri Luzhkov as their best bet under the circumstances and flocked to his newborn party in droves. This attraction was understandable; after all, in the early 1990s, Luzhkov was among the founders of the present system who played a pioneering role in privatizing the state and shutting down and revamping regional legislatures. All this helped him to install a heavily corporatist system of governance in Moscow, based on the diversion of financial flows from the rest of the country to the capital via Moscow banks. In the summer of 1999, however, he underestimated the ability of the Yeltsin clique to control events and failed to convince the crony capitalists that he wielded enough authority nationwide to become the legitimate arbiter for the entire spectrum of their interests.

For a time, it seemed that Yeltsin's political system might follow its founder off the stage, and some observers prepared for a process of "de-Yeltsinization" (somewhat akin to the de-Stalinization of Soviet society in the 1950s) that might alter significantly the distribution of forces in society. Such a development would have increased the political leverage of opposition parties, the legislature, and civil society in general vis-à-vis the oligarchs and any potential new autocrat. However, as we saw in chapter 9, from August 1999 onward, the Yeltsin camp performed prodigious feats of "political technology," managing to install a new president who could be counted on to protect Yeltsin's immediate family and did not seem too threatening to most of the oligarchs. This managed transfer of power did not necessarily mean, though, that Putin would succeed in assuming the role of autocrat and keeping the Yeltsin system going, if in modified form. That remains an open question.

MISSED ALTERNATIVES TO MARKET BOLSHEVISM

In Russian perceptions of history, deterministic belief in the inevitable has more often than not prevailed over the idea of reasoned choice, whether individual or collective. In the past two decades, the Marxist-Leninist certainty about "scientific regularities of development" (*zakonomernosti*) and pseudo-Marxist economic determinism have been steadily replaced in public consciousness by much simpler notions containing elements of archaic fatalism and manifesting themselves in assertions that Russia's decline and present sociopolitical order are inevitable products of either national culture or global developments beyond

Russia's reach, or both. As for us, we share the view of thinkers who believe that history does present alternative courses of action for both individuals and nations, and that denying their existence suggests a poverty of imagination— or lack of will—in those whose interests and beliefs would favor a different path of development.

Ample evidence indicates that a peaceful democratic alternative to market bolshevism was available to Russian political actors, if they had been willing to struggle for it—in 1989–91, in 1993, and even afterward. The most important chance was missed in the fall of 1990, when economists produced a compromise blueprint for democratic economic reforms that would have required the Soviet government gradually to dismantle central planning but retain a single nationwide economy. This plan fell victim to political feuds and the skepticism of the IMF, which then proceeded to endorse the monetarist, authoritarian approach to reform of Prime Minister Valentin Pavlov. The major responsibility for this failure inside the USSR lay with Boris Yeltsin and his team, who, as discussed in chapter 5, had abandoned the program of economic reforms endorsed by the Russian legislature and embarked on the path of large-scale speculations in foreign currency, as well as fiscal and financial warfare against the USSR government.

Another chance was missed in April 1991, when Yeltsin, troubled by the prospect that the grassroots anti-nomenklatura movement he had encouraged and used in his struggle for power might escape from his control, signed the Novo-Ogarevo agreement with Gorbachev and the presidents of eight other union republics. This agreement effectively transferred power and the fate of the union to a Federation Council consisting of leaders of the nomenklatura in the union republics, most of whom possessed no democratic legitimacy at all. In return for this accretion of powers and the lure of a separate Russian presidency for himself, Yeltsin instructed the coal miners of the Kuzbass, who were among the most powerful forces to initiate a democratic transformation of the country, to stop their political strike; the miners obeyed.

Another chance for democratic reforms was missed in July 1991, at the Group of Seven summit in London, when the leaders of the major industrial countries did not provide the big, long-term aid package that was widely expected in the Soviet Union. This refusal accelerated the transformation of the political struggle among Soviet elites into a zero-sum game, leading to the August coup, as well as Yeltsin's countercoup and his takeover of the institutions of the Soviet central government without regard to the concerns of other union republics. The final outcome was the abrupt dissolution of the USSR, accomplished in a conspiratorial style, without democratic deliberation in Russia and against the verdict of the March 1991 referendum on the preservation of the union.

Two more chances were missed in October–December 1991, when Yeltsin decided against calling new parliamentary elections that would have stimulated the incipient democratic revolution, and when the Russian parliament, dominated by the nomenklatura and Yeltsin loyalists, added one more to Russian history's list of revolutions from above by approving the shock therapy that Yeltsin and the IMF prescribed. It did this without substantive debate. Then, with great fanfare, it handed over a range of its constitutional powers to Yeltsin for a period of one year—but, as events turned out, the transfer was effectively permanent.

Another opportunity for a democratic revolution slipped away in April 1992, when Communists and lobbyists for various industrial sectors in the Russian parliament blocked members of the democratic opposition and advocates of alternative strategies of economic reform in their attempts to force the new government of market bolsheviks to step down. Instead, the legislative majority voted for a "Declaration of Reforms" that enabled Yeltsin to keep his policies in place.

One more chance was missed in December 1992, when public opinion and political momentum were on the side of the democratic nationalists and centrists opposed to Yeltsin, but their internal divisions enabled the Russian president to replace the shock therapy government with a cabinet of lobbyists for the raw materials sector. This cabinet, led by Viktor Chernomyrdin, was inimical to the interests of Russia's manufacturing industries.

Yet another chance was passed up in September–October 1993, when Western leaders both first extended their unconditional support to Yeltsin's extra-constitutional acts, thus frustrating the attempts of influential moderates to hammer out a negotiated solution, and then approved the use of force to disperse the parliament that had brought Yeltsin to power.

Another opportunity was missed in the winter of 1993–94, when the opposition in the newly elected Duma rushed to fill the parliamentary seats vacated by their predecessors and accepted the new constitutional system, despite strong evidence of fraud and legal violations before and during the referendum on the constitution.

Still another opportunity was wasted during the presidential campaign of 1996, when the leading candidates who opposed the system of "nomenklatura capitalism" failed to develop their embryonic tactical alliance and were lured one by one into negotiations with the Kremlin, thus enabling Yeltsin to secure his second term in office.

A further opportunity was discarded in May 1999, when, having triumphantly seized the chance nine months earlier to force Primakov on Yeltsin as premier, the Duma succumbed to Kremlin blandishments and failed to keep Primakov in place. The choice of Primakov had been a clear triumph for the principles of democratic deliberation over those of Byzantine maneuver and intrigue. Only the radicals on the Duma's extreme flanks—the followers of Vladimir Zhirinovsky and those of Anatoly Chubais—voted against Primakov. Thus for the first time since 1993, Russia had acquired a leader who enjoyed broad legitimacy and could play a consolidating rather than a divisive role in Russian society. His removal opened the door to renewed, intensely manipulative, and ultimately successful efforts by the Yeltsinites to propel their last-minute choice as Yeltsin's successor into the presidency.

Today, the United States has a new opportunity to rebuild trust among Russians by holding back and respecting their democratic choices, however imperfect or undesirable these may be from the standpoint of U.S. officials and elites in general. This is the course suggested to us by our critical analysis of transitology in chapter 2. That analysis showed that neither the G-7, nor the IMF, nor the Kremlin seriously considered in 1991 the sort of gradualist strategies for the USSR's economic development that we favored. These organizations were in thrall to the supposedly universal Washington Consensus, with its dangerous economic determinism and its complete unsuitability for countries in Russia's condition. We cannot know today how well or badly a gradualist strategy of the kind we laid out in chapter 5 would have worked then, but clearly no strategy of that type can be applied to Russia today. Just as the Russia of 1991 was in a unique condition not previously studied by social scientists, so it is in a *different* unique condition today.

Again, therefore, existing theories of transitology are of little help. They may be suggestive, as when they identify crime and corruption of, say, a Mexican type to be serious threats to nascent democracies. But they may also be deceptive in the instant case if Russia's special features are not kept clearly in mind. These features are respected in the strategy for Russian development put forward by a group of Russian and American economists in June 2000 and summarized in chapter 9. This strategy, which we support, emphasizes the view that economic recovery depends on preserving democracy and civil liberties, and giving priority to production, social justice, institutional reform, and decriminalization.

By contrast, Russian analysts of the Migranyan school believe that Huntington's model of authoritarian modernization is applicable to Russia. They hold that while Yeltsin was a weak authoritarian who presided over an amorphous system of pluralist autocracy, today Putin has a chance to become what is evidently his dream: a successful Russian Pinochet.[8] This vision will require him to put firmly in their place not only Russia's governors and oligarchs but also the country's formidable bureaucracy—a daunting agenda indeed.[9] We would not be surprised if some Western theorists should soon begin to champion this authoritarian strategy.

However, in our opinion, which is based more on the cyclical theory of Russian history than on transitology, such a scenario is most unlikely to succeed. To ordinary Russians, it will look like a more aggressive continuation of the already delegitimized strategy of the Yeltsin regime. Thus it might fail because it would encounter too much opposition. Alternatively, if pursued with ruthless determination, such a course might "succeed" for a time, but would tend to stimulate the "anarchical absolutism" that we described in chapter 2 (for example, revolution and potentially terrible destruction). In other words, this course would probably bring to a definite end the shock therapy cycle of top-down reform that was launched in 1991. At that point, a critical mass of thought on Russia's future might develop around some new, probably universally oriented vision, out of which would eventually spring a new populist movement for change from below.

If all this were to happen, Russia would probably move for a time to the margins of the international system. Whether it does or not, though, the West should in our opinion discard its lectures about economic development, leave the Russians to debate their own future, take part only if invited, and quietly give aid to Russia's battered civil society—again, if invited. In the long run, such an approach will serve America's interests better than the futile and damaging attempts of recent years to remold Russia in its own image.

Russia's Lost Decade?

It is a remarkable feature of the Russian philosophical and spiritual tradition always to seek a higher, ideally universal meaning that the often violent and self-destructive course taken by Russians at various points in their history may contain for the rest of humanity. We ourselves believe that Russia's recent experience does contain, almost like texts of ancient history, some important lessons for other countries. While the twentieth century opened for Russia with Lenin's rhetorical recycling of Nikolai Chernyshevsky's question, "What Is To Be Done?" most people would probably agree that Russia in the course of this century has convincingly shown other nations what was *not* to be done.

The idea that Russia's history provides graphic warnings about which roads not to take has been expressed by Russian thinkers in the past. In the 1830s, Pyotr Chaadayev, a founding father of Russia's "Westernizing" thinkers, hypothesized that Russians were one of those nations that existed "in order to teach the world an important lesson."[10] A century later, in the middle of the Russian Civil War, the poet and historical thinker Maximilian Voloshin elaborated on Chaadayev's hypothesis by inquiring:

> Might it be our destiny to live out
> Europe's latest dreams,
> So that we can divert it
> From its perilous paths?[11]

As if in accordance with these words, Russia in the twentieth century has demonstrated to the outside world the dehumanizing extremes of two different utopian visions based on economic determinism and designed for global use: first, bureaucratic state bolshevism with a command economy and one-party rule; and now, market bolshevism. The implementation of this new radical doctrine in the 1990s—aimed at a comprehensive "marketization" of the economy, society, and even parts of government—has led to the destruction of Russia's industrial base (built with tremendous effort and sacrifice over many decades), an alarming trend of population decline, and the danger of an irreversible criminalization and privatization of the Russian state. This is likely to serve as a warning about the dangers of a bolshevik-style dismantling—in the name of free-market dogma—of democratically accountable regulation of the economy. If this experience diminishes enthusiasm in other countries for programs that seek to impose "progress" and uniformity from above without broad societal consent, then the lessons for which Russia has paid a heavy toll will at least have served a good purpose for civilization at large.

NOTES

INTRODUCTION

1. Statistics on economic performance are from the March and April 1999 issues of _Russian Economic Trends_ of the Moscow Institute for Macroeconomic Research. The same figures can be derived from the Economist Intelligence Unit's _Country Reports_.

2. _Historical Statistics of the United States from Colonial Times to 1970_ (Washington, D.C.: U.S. Department of Commerce, Bureau of the Census, 1975), 224–25.

3. Stefan Hedlund and Niclas Sundström, "The Russian Economy after Systemic Change," _Europe-Asia Studies_ 48, no. 6 (September 1996). Yuri Petrov, "The Economic Recovery," _Ekonomika i zhizn,_ no. 21 (2000). According to the State Statistics Committee, 41.2 percent of Russians lived below the poverty line, down from 43.6 percent a year earlier; Dow Jones Newswires, June 13, 2000.

4. _Argumenty i fakty,_ no. 50 (1997).

5. Jim Hoagland, _Washington Post,_ January 8, 1998.

6. _Russian Organized Crime: A Report of the Global Organized Crime Task Force_ (Washington, D.C.: Center for Strategic and International Studies, 1997), 7, 67. The findings of this report are criticized as excessively negative in a report compiled by working groups of the semiofficial Council on Foreign and Defense Policy in Moscow and published by Harvard University's John F. Kennedy School of Government under the names of Sergei Karaganov, Igor Malashenko, and others as _Russia: Eliminating Crime_ (Cambridge, Mass.: Strengthening Democratic Institutions Project, John F. Kennedy School of Government, September 1998). However, among the participants in the December 1997 conference from which the report originated was Anatoly Kulikov, who was still Russia's interior minister. On January 30, 1998, ITAR-TASS reported that Prosecutor General Yuri Skuratov had effectively announced that Russia's crime statistics had been "cooked" in recent years, and that the real crime rate was probably three to four times higher than that officially reported. For more details on this issue, see Peter Reddaway's letter in _Johnson's Russia List,_ February 7, 1998.

7. _New York Times,_ November 6, 1997.

8. To name but one, the electronic newsletter _Johnson's Russia List_ (www.cdi.org/russia/johnson) is a major, balanced, and comprehensive source on various aspects of Russian affairs.

9. Public Opinion Foundation, "How Would You Characterize the Economic Situation in Russia This Year?" January 12, 2000.

10. As cited by Vladimir Shlapentokh, "The Four Faces of Russian Society," _Transitions_ 4, no. 5 (October 1997).

11. _Rossiiskaya gazeta,_ March 7, 1997.

12. _Komsomol'skaya pravda,_ July 29, 1997.

13. Yegor Gaidar, _Anomalii ekonomicheskogo rosta_ (Moscow: Evraziia, 1997), 214.

14. _Segodnya,_ July 31, 1997.

15. Thomas Kuhn's _The Structure of Scientific Revolutions_ (Chicago: University of Chicago Press, 1962) is but one of the classic examples of this trend, which dates back at least to Werner Heisenberg.

16. Poll conducted by the market research firm Fessel GPK. See _Johnson's Russia List,_ July 28, 1998.

17. The concept we endorse here, which posits that every stage of history presents us with an array of alternatives, goes back to Leibniz's teachings about infinite potentiality and is exemplified in modern social thought by Jose Ortega-y-Gasset.

18. For this understanding of historicism, we are indebted to a number of Russian writers, including some whose overall approach is not entirely identical to our own. Among these, the writings of Mikhail Gefter, maverick Soviet historian and a founder of an entire dissident school of social thought, are worth particular attention. See Mikhail Gefter, *Iz tekh i etikh let* (Moscow: Progress, 1991).

19. Peter Reddaway, *Uncensored Russia: The Human Rights Movement in the Soviet Union* (London: Cape, 1972).

20. We borrowed this latter insight from Imre Lakatos's interpretation of the cosmological debate between Galileo and the followers of Copernicus. See Imre Lakatos, "Falsification and the Methodology of Scientific Research Programmes," in *Criticism and the Growth of Knowledge*, ed. Imre Lakatos and Alan Musgrave (New York: Cambridge University Press, 1970).

21. For the basic epistemology of the interpretive approach to "theories" and "facts," see Hans Georg Gadamer, *Truth and Method*, trans. and ed. Garrett Barden and John Cumming (London: Sheed & Ward, 1975); and Charles Taylor, *Philosophy and the Human Sciences* (New York: Cambridge University Press, 1985). For an illuminating application of these and similar insights to the study of public opinion, see John Zaller, *The Nature and Origins of Mass Opinion* (New York: Cambridge University Press, 1992).

22. Vladimir Solovyov, *The Crisis of Western Philosophy: Against the Positivists* (Hudson, N.Y.: Lindisfarne Press, 1996).

23. In late 1993, the banner of the democratic opposition was picked up by the newly formed Yabloko faction in the Duma, led by Grigori Yavlinsky. Soon, the extinction of most other groups, barred from parliamentary elections and lacking funds and access to the media, helped to legitimize Yabloko's claim to this role.

1. Reform or Reaction? The Yeltsin Era in a Millennium of Russian History

1. A pessimistic version of the same modernization doctrine is the belief that the most advanced level of development is attainable only by a few "chosen" nations, while most of the world is doomed to remain on the lower rungs of the historical ladder. This outlook, which goes back to such precursors of contemporary racism as Gobineau, has surfaced in a peculiar form among Westernizers in modern Russia, some of whom have suggested since the late 1980s that Russia has become a perpetual laggard behind the world's "advanced" countries. One of the earliest and most passionate critiques of modernization doctrines of all stripes can be found in the classic work by Miguel de Unamuno, *The Tragic Sense of Life* (New York: Dover, 1954 [1921]), which affirmed the right of diverse cultures to establish their own immanent criteria for development and achievement.

2. See, for example, Arthur M. Schlesinger, Jr., *The Cycles of American History* (Boston: Houghton Mifflin, 1986).

3. In one of the earliest comprehensive programs of reform, "Conversations on Governance," compiled in the seventeenth century by a Russian intellectual of Croatian origin, part one begins with a discussion on how to raise state revenues; see Yuri Krizhanich, *Politika* (Moscow: Novyi svet, 1997). Among the major harbingers of the Great Reforms in the 1850s was the alarming unpublished report by Yu. Gagemeister, "On Russia's Finances," first published in *Istoricheskii Arkhiv*, no. 2 (1956).

4. This obsession with the West was ingrained so deeply that even setbacks in the southern and eastern theaters of foreign policy were still perceived in a framework of competition with the West and were followed by the strengthening of the Westernizing trend among elites and in society. Thus the defeats in the Russo-Japanese or Afghan Wars elicited little attention to relevant features of the social order of Japan or the Islamic countries (in both cases, dismissed as "backward," which demonstrates the peculiar ethnocentrism of Russian Westernizers). The growth of Eurasianism in the 1920s had different roots, and its practical influence on subsequent bouts of reform has so far been negligible in comparison with that of the Westernizers.

5. Consider Taranovski's comment that the reformers of the 1860s, in contrast with the Soviet reformers of the 1980s and early 1990s, "possessed a level of national self-confidence and of cultural and psychological distance from the West that permitted them to adopt and adapt creatively." Theodore Taranovski, ed., *Reform in Russian History: Progress or Cycle?* (Washington, D.C.: Woodrow Wilson Center Press, 1995), 18.

6. By "expropriation," we mean here not only the direct confiscation of property but also administrative manipulation of the nominal value of the ruble during the 1920s, in 1947, in 1961, and the attempts to increase government revenues by fostering hidden inflation, most notably in the 1980s, all of which repeatedly decimated the incomes and savings of Soviet citizens.

7. In addition to the major reforms under Lenin's New Economic Policy (NEP) and under Khrushchev and Gorbachev, the limited "thaws" included brief relaxations of control over public life under Stalin (in 1939–40 and in the wake of the victory in World War II in 1944–46) and the partial attempts at economic reform made by Kosygin (1965) and Brezhnev (1979).

8. Moshe Lewin, *The Gorbachev Phenomenon: A Historical Interpretation* (Berkeley: University of California Press, 1988).

9. On this evolution of the middle class in the United States, see C. Wright Mills, *White Collar: The American Middle Classes* (New York: Oxford University Press, 1956); and Max Lerner, *America as a Civilization: Life and Thought in the United States Today* (New York: Simon & Schuster, 1957).

10. The possession of housing and agricultural land—strictly speaking, treated as the rental of government property—had many gradations and, in a large number of cases, came close to private ownership (though in shadow-economy, not legal, terms).

11. Aleksandr Solzhenitsyn's pejorative labeling of those professionals who abandoned the ethos of the intelligentsia and allied themselves with the establishment as "*obrazovantsy*" (degree-grabbers) is evidence of the vitality of the intelligentsia standard as an ideal type.

12. Ludmilla Alexeyeva, *Soviet Dissent: Contemporary Movements for National, Religious, and Human Rights* (Middletown, Conn.: Wesleyan University Press, 1985), 401.

13. Henryk Flakierski, *Income Inequalities in the Former Soviet Union and Its Republics* (Armonk, N.Y. : M. E. Sharpe, 1993), 23.

14. Shock therapy's destructive effects on the middle class were clearly stated in an appeal to Russia's presidential candidates in the 1996 elections, signed by leading economists from the Russian Academy of Sciences and six American Nobel Prize winners in economics (*Nezavisimaya gazeta,* July 1, 1996). The fate of the Soviet middle class was also vividly portrayed in the writings of the late Andrei Fadin.

15. See Lev Timofeyev, *Russia's Secret Rulers* (New York: Alfred A. Knopf, 1992).

16. The Soviet financial system of two separate circuits—cash and credit—was yet another source of the shadow economy, as credit could be converted into cash with the help of backroom connections or for an additional fee.

2. RUSSIAN POSTCOMMUNISM IN THE MIRROR OF SOCIAL THEORY

1. See, for example, Frederic J. Fleron, Jr., and Erik P. Hoffmann, eds., *Post-Communist Studies and Political Science: Methodology and Empirical Theory in Sovietology* (Boulder, Colo.: Westview, 1993); and Abbott Gleason, *Totalitarianism: The Inner History of the Cold War* (New York: Oxford University Press, 1995). For an enlightened conservative critique of Sovietology that makes many of the same points, see Walter Laqueur, *The Dream That Failed: Reflections on the Soviet Union* (New York: Oxford University Press, 1994), chapters 5–6.

2. The classical point of departure for this and most other discussions of the issue is Max Weber, "The Types of Legitimate Domination," in his *Economy and Society: An Outline of Interpretive Sociology*, vol. 1, ed. Guenther Roth and Claus Wittich (New York: Bedminster Press, 1968). Although Weber's taxonomy of modes of legitimation has been maintained as the dominant frame of reference in Western social sciences, much as the writings of Karl Marx were for Soviet sociology, it contains a number of unresolved problems, such as, for example, the legitimation of modes of legitimacy themselves and their potential to clash with one another.

3. Jurgen Habermas, *Legitimation Crisis* (Boston: Beacon Press, 1975). For the history of the debate on legitimacy and a compendium of basic arguments, see William Connolly, ed., *Legitimacy and the State* (New York: New York University Press, 1984).

4. T. H. Rigby and Ferenc Feher, eds., *Political Legitimation in Communist States* (New York: St. Martin's, 1982); and Leslie Holmes, *The End of Communist Power: Anti-Corruption Campaigns and Legitimation Crisis* (New York: Oxford University Press, 1993).

5. For the most recent version of his theory, see Leslie Holmes, *Post-Communism: An Introduction* (Durham, N.C.: Duke University Press, 1997).

6. In the early 1960s, even a theorist like Seymour Martin Lipset clearly distinguished between the concepts of legitimacy and economic effectiveness, which attested to the independent value of noneconomic, ideal-type notions in Western social thought; see Seymour Martin Lipset, *Political Man: The Social Bases of Politics* (Garden City, N.Y.: Doubleday, 1960), 77–83. However, by the late 1970s, the tendency to merge basic structural concepts with economic reductionism was in full view. For example, in Soviet studies, the assumption that economic effectiveness alone could constitute the basis of legitimacy was fairly widespread; see Holmes, *The End of Communist Power,* 15. Some even claimed that the mass belief in the legitimacy of the powers that be is irrelevant as long as the public demand for well-being is satisfied (the "social contract" theory). The crisis of public ideals and the growth of pragmatic tendencies from the 1970s on, at least as reflected in social theory, was influenced not least by the manifest erosion of *telos* in the countries of the Soviet Bloc.

7. Holmes, *The End of Communist Power,* 5.

8. This line of argument is confirmed by polls: A late 1989 survey conducted by the All-Union Center for the Study of Public Opinion (VTsIOM) showed support for political reform that would weaken the Communist Party but not for the "abandonment of socialist principles." This evidence led Western sociologists to a well-grounded conclusion that the failure of the CPSU as an institution "may have been due largely to its unwillingness or inability to service the norm." See A. Finifter and E. Mickiewicz, "Redefining the Political System of the USSR: Mass Support for Political Change," *American Political Science Review* 86, no. 4 (December 1992): 860–61.

9. For the detailed evolution of the so-called August regime of 1991–93 in terms of the erosion of its legitimacy, see Dmitri Glinski, "Legitimizing the Legislature: Russian Parliamentarism in a Struggle for Survival" (paper presented at the Seventh Annual Conference on Legislative Studies, Ohio State University, 1995).

10. Francis Fukuyama, "The End of History?" *The National Interest,* Summer 1989.

11. For a recent rehearsal of this perennial debate, see Fareed Zakaria, "The Rise of Illiberal Democracy," *Foreign Affairs,* November–December 1997; Robert Kaplan, "Was Democracy Just a Moment?" *Atlantic Monthly,* December 1996; Adrian Karatnycky, "Still the Bedrock of a Better World," *Washington Post,* December 29, 1996; and Robert Kaplan, "A Real Look At Democracies," *Washington Post,* January 9, 1997.

12. Joseph A. Schumpeter, *Capitalism, Socialism, and Democracy* (New York: Harper & Brothers, 1942).

13. Talcott Parsons, "Evolutionary Universals in Society," *American Sociological Review* 29 (1964). Jackson Toby, ed., *The Evolution of Societies,* (Englewood Cliff, N.J.: Prentice-Hall, 1977). Seymour Martin Lipset, "Some Social Requisites of Democracy: Economic Development and Political Legitimacy," *American Political Science Review* 53 (1959); *Political Man*; and "The Social Requisites of Democracy Revisited," *American Sociological Review* 59 (1994).

14. Gabriel A. Almond and Sidney Verba, *Civic Culture: Political Attitudes and Democracy in Five Nations* (Princeton, N.J.: Princeton University Press, 1963).

15. J. L. Walker, "A Critique of the Elitist Theory of Democracy," in *Political Elites in a Democracy,* ed. Peter Bachrach (New York: Atherton, 1971).

16. Anthony Downs, *The Economic Theory of Democracy* (New York: Harper, 1957).

17. Michael Mann, "The Social Cohesion of Liberal Democracy," *American Sociological Review* 33 (1970).

18. J. Gibson, "Political Intolerance and Political Repression During the McCarthy Red Scare," *American Political Science Review* 82 (1988).

19. Robert D. Putnam, *Making Democracy Work: Civic Traditions in Modern Italy* (Princeton, N.J.: Princeton University Press, 1993).

20. Peter Berger, "The Uncertain Triumph of Democratic Capitalism," in *Capitalism, Socialism, and Democracy Revisited*, ed. Larry Diamond and Marc F. Plattner (Baltimore, Md.: Johns Hopkins University Press, 1993), 1.

21. Lipset, "The Social Requisites of Democracy Revisited."

22. David Held, *Democracy and the Global Order: From the Modern State to Cosmopolitan Governance* (Stanford, Calif.: Stanford University Press, 1995), 5.

23. See also Sergei Pushkarev, *Self-Government and Freedom in Russia* (Boulder, Colo.: Westview, 1988).

24. Peter Reddaway and Catherine Dale, *The Increasing Attraction of the Russian People to Authoritarian Values: How Far Has It Gone? What Political Implications May It Have?* (Washington, D.C.: National Council for Soviet and East European Research, 1995), 5–6.

25. Milton and Rose Friedman, *Free to Choose, A Personal Statement* (New York: Harcourt Brace Jovanovich, 1980), 21.

26. A comprehensive formulation of this approach is in Charles E. Lindblom, *Politics and Markets: The World's Political Economic Systems* (New York: Basic Books, 1977).

27. Robert A. Dahl, *After the Revolution? Authority in a Good Society* (New Haven, Conn.: Yale University Press, 1990), 83.

28. Held, *Democracy and the Global Order*, 246.

29. Robert A. Dahl and Charles E. Lindblom, *Politics, Economics, and Welfare* (New York: Harper, 1953); Lindblom, *Politics and Markets*; Robert A. Dahl, *Polyarchy; Participation and Opposition* (New Haven, Conn.: Yale University Press, 1971); Robert A. Dahl, *Democracy and Its Critics* (New Haven, Conn.: Yale University Press, 1989). A variation of the polyarchical model, centered on the mutual autonomy of elites, is found in Eva Etzioni-Halevy, *The Elite Connection: Problems and Potential of Western Democracy* (Cambridge, Mass.: Harvard University Press, 1993).

30. Herbert McCloskey and John Zaller, *The American Ethos: Public Attitudes toward Capitalism and Democracy* (Cambridge, Mass.: Harvard University Press, 1984).

31. Finifter and Mickiewicz, "Redefining the Political System of the USSR."

32. John Loewenhardt, *The Reincarnation of Russia: Struggling with the Legacy of Communism, 1990–1994* (Durham, N.C.: Duke University Press, 1995). For a similar analysis, see Harvey Feigenbaum and Jeffrey Henig, "Privatization and Democracy," *Governance: An International Journal of Policy and Administration* (July 1993).

33. Sakharov's *samizdat* essay was first published in the West as *Progress, Coexistence, and Intellectual Freedom* (London: Deutsch, 1968).

34. Ken Jowitt, "Dizzy with Democracy," *Problems of Post-Communism* 43, no. 1 (January–February 1996): 4.

35. Samuel P. Huntington, *Political Order in Changing Societies* (New Haven, Conn.: Yale University Press, 1968).

36. Ibid.

37. In "Pareto and Pluto-Democracy: The Retreat to Galapagos," *American Political Science Review* 62 (1968): 440–450, S. E. Finer defends Pareto against charges that he was protofascist.

38. This alleged potential of the authoritarian regime to evolve in an organic way toward "standard" Western democracy struck a chord with some U.S. policymakers in the late 1970s and 1980s and sounded in tune with the influential distinction between totalitarian and authoritarian systems. This distinction allowed its theoreticians to draw a clear line between (1) the nonmarket "totalitarianism" of Soviet-type regimes that was immanently unreformable and could disappear only by collapse and (2) the market authoritarianism of friendly anticommunist regimes in the Third World that were to be allowed to muddle through toward democracy on their own for an indefinite future; see Carl J. Friedrich and Zbigniew K. Brzezinski, *Totalitarian Dictatorship and Autocracy* (Cambridge, Mass.: Harvard University Press, 1965). The intellectual foundation for the Reagan-era distinction came from the administration's ambassador to the United Nations, Jeane Kirkpatrick, in a November 1979 *Commentary* article, later elaborated in her *Dictatorships and Double Standards* (New York: Simon & Schuster, 1982).

39. A. Migranyan, "Dolgii put' v evropeiskii dom" (A Long Way to the European Home) *Novy mir,* July 1989; (with Igor Klyamkin), "Est' li nuzhda v zheleznoi ruke?" (Is There a Need for an Iron Hand?) *Literaturnaya gazeta,* August 16, 1989; and "Ob avtoritarizme my mozhem tol'ko mechtat'" (We Can Only Dream About Authoritarianism) *Latinskaya Amerika,* January 1990.

40. David Kolb, *The Critique of Pure Modernity* (Chicago: University of Chicago Press, 1986); Jurgen Habermas, *The Philosophical Discourse of Modernity* (Cambridge, Mass.: MIT Press, 1987); and Anthony Giddens, *The Consequences of Modernity* (Stanford, Calif.: Stanford University Press, 1990). The following discussion is indebted for its initial impulse to Holmes, *The End of Communist Power.*

41. Holmes, *The End of Communist Power,* 320.

42. James C. Scott, *The Moral Economy of the Peasant: Rebellion and Subsistence in Southeast Asia* (New Haven, Conn.: Yale University Press, 1976).

43. This view of modernization and development derives from the work of two European philosophers of history, the Spaniard Miguel de Unamuno and the Russian Mikhail Gefter (who have also influenced our discussion on historical cycles in chapter 1). The most far-reaching of the Russian philosophical works on these issues is Aleksandr Panarin, *Revansh istorii: rossiiskaya strategicheskaya initsiativa v 21 veke* (The Revenge of History: Russian Strategic Initiative in the Twenty-First Century) (Moscow: Logos, 1998).

44. This section has benefited from the insightful essay by Andrei Tsygankov, "Western Theories of Comparative Political Science vs. Russian Politics" (George Washington University, Institute for European, Russian, and Eurasian Studies, Washington, D.C., 1995).

45. See the section entitled "The Folly of Transitology" in Jowitt, "Dizzy with Democracy," 5.

46. Giuseppe di Palma, *To Craft Democracies: An Essay on Democratic Transitions* (Berkeley: University of California Press, 1990).

47. Guillermo A. O'Donnell and Phillipe C. Schmitter, *Transitions from Authoritarian Rule: Tentative Conclusions About Uncertain Democracies* (Baltimore, Md.: Johns Hopkins University Press, 1986); Larry Diamond, Juan J. Linz, and Seymour Martin Lipset, eds., *Democracy in Developing Countries,* 4 vols. (Boulder, Colo.: Lynne Rienner, 1988–89); and John Highley and Richard Gunther, eds., *Elites and Democratic*

Consolidation in Latin America and Southern Europe (New York: Cambridge University Press, 1992). For the application of these models to Russia, see Michael McFaul, *Post-Communist Politics: Democratic Prospects in Russia and Eastern Europe* (Washington, D.C.: Center for Strategic and International Studies, 1993).

48. Valerie Bunce, "Should Transitologists Be Grounded?" *Slavic Review* 54, no. 1 (1995); Tsygankov, "Western Theories"; and Jowitt, "Dizzy with Democracy."

49. Loewenhardt, *The Reincarnation of Russia,* 22.

50. Juan Linz, "The Perils of Presidentialism," *Journal of Democracy,* Winter 1990. Linz's influential article was reprinted in early 1994 in the Russian journal *Vek XX i mir,* where it was used by a number of Russian intellectuals as a springboard for one of the most far-reaching assaults on Yeltsin's rule and the Yeltsin constitution.

51. The *Journal of Democracy* debate, featuring Arend Lijphart, Guy Lardeyret, and Quentin Quade, was reprinted in *The Global Resurgence of Democracy,* ed. Larry Diamond and Marc F. Plattner (Baltimore, Md.: Johns Hopkins University Press, 1993). See also Scott Mainwaring, "Presidentialism, Multipartism, and Democracy," in *Issues in Democratic Consolidation: The New South American Democracies in Comparative Perspective,* ed. Scott Mainwaring et al. (Notre Dame, Ind.: University of Notre Dame Press, 1992); and Highley and Gunther, eds., *Elites and Democratic Consolidation.*

52. Loewenhardt, *The Reincarnation of Russia,* 41. See also Igor Klyamkin and Lilya Shevtsova, *Vnesistemnyi rezhim Borisa II: Nekotorye osobennosti politicheskogo razvitiya postsovetskoi Rossii* (Moscow: Moscow Carnegie Center, 1999).

53. On nationalism as a mode of legitimation, see Holmes, *The End of Communist Power.*

54. See also Liah Greenfeld, *Nationalism: Five Roads to Modernity* (Cambridge, Mass.: Harvard University Press, 1992).

55. Ernest Gellner, *Nations and Nationalism* (Ithaca, N.Y.: Cornell University Press, 1983). See also John Hutchinson and Anthony D. Smith, eds., *Nationalism* (New York: Oxford University Press, 1994).

56. The term "Realist," put into circulation by E. H. Carr and Hans Morgenthau, is more often used in the context of international politics.

57. See also Charles Fairbanks, "The Withering of the State," *Uncaptive Minds* 8, no. 2 (1995).

58. One of the major alternatives to Realism, focusing on decision-making units within states, was inaugurated by Graham Allison's *Essence of Decision* (Boston: Little, Brown, 1971). The analysis of global actors, or "the world-system," is often, although not exclusively, associated with structural Marxists, exemplified by Immanuel Wallerstein's *The Modern World-System* (New York: Academic Press, 1974).

59. Hedley Bull, *The Anarchical Society: A Study of Order in World Politics* (New York: Columbia University Press, 1977), 254–55.

60. Jowitt, "Dizzy with Democracy."

61. G. M. Tamas, "Socialism, Capitalism, and Modernity," in Diamond and Plattner, eds., *Capitalism, Socialism, and Democracy Revisited,* 54–58.

62. Peter Alter, *Nationalism* (New York: E. Arnold, 1989).

63. Ernest Renan *Qu'est-ce qu'nne Nation?* (Paris: Imprimerie Nationale, 1996 [1882]), 26–29.

64. Karl Deutsch, *Nationalism and Social Communication* (Cambridge, Mass.: MIT Press, 1953), 96–105.

65. Roland Barthes, *Mythologies* (Paris: Editions du Seuil, 1957), 155–61.

66. Fredrich Meinecke, *Cosmopolitanism and the National State* (Princeton, N.J.: Princeton University Press, 1970 [1907]); and Hans Kohn, *The Idea of Nationalism: A Study in Its Origins and Background* (New York: Macmillan, 1945).

67. See also Hugh Seton-Watson, *Nations and States: An Enquiry into the Origins of Nations and the Politics of Nationalism* (Boulder, Colo.: Westview, 1977).

68. Gellner, *Nations and Nationalism.*

69. Veljko Vujacic, "Historical Legacies, Nationalist Mobilization, and Political Outcomes in Russia and Serbia: A Weberian View," *Theory and Society* 25, no. 6 (December 1996): 766.

70. See, for example, Loewenhardt, *The Reincarnation of Russia.*

71. Vujacic, "Historical Legacies," 771. See also Raymond Aron, *The Century of Total War,* (Garden City, N.Y.: Doubleday, 1954).

72. Marianne Ozernoy, "Neo-Communist Ethnic Politics," *Prism,* January 1996.

73. Vujacic, "Historical Legacies."

74. Theda Skocpol, *States and Social Revolutions: A Comparative Analysis of France, Russia, and China* (Cambridge, Mass.: Harvard University Press, 1979), 23.

75. A major exception is the work of Peter Schweizer in *Victory: The Reagan Administration's Secret Strategy That Hastened the Collapse of the Soviet Union* (New York: Atlantic Monthly Press, 1994), which depicts in graphic terms the purposeful efforts of some elements within the Reagan administration to weaken the Soviet position in the world economy, efforts that effectively derailed the original design of the Gorbachev reforms. Schweizer's work, however, is written more from a journalistic than a social science perspective.

76. See Kenneth N. Waltz, *Man, the State, and War* (New York: Columbia University Press, 1959).

77. The traditional school of geopolitics dates back to the nineteenth century and includes Nikolai Danilevsky, Karl Haushofer, and Sir Halford MacKinder, a European ancestor of modern American Realism who, however, expressed more archaic, parochial, and, in many ways, irrational and fatalistic concepts.

78. Gennadi Zyuganov, *Rossiia—rodina moya. Ideologiya gosudarstvennogo patriotizma* (Moscow: Informpechat', 1996), esp. 122–73; and Aleksandr Dugin, *Osnovy geopolitiki: geopoliticheskoe budushchee Rossii* (Moscow: Arktogeia-tsentr, 1999). See also V. Lukin and A. Utkin, *Rossiya i zapad: Obshchnost' ili otchuzhdenie?* (Moscow: Sampo, 1995). The touting of geopolitics was reflected in the creation in 1993 of a special Duma Committee on Geopolitics, which in many ways duplicated the purpose of the Foreign Affairs Committee.

79. Studies of dependency were connected with traditional Marxism by such bridges as Immanuel Wallerstein's theory of the modern world-system. However, dependency theorists were fundamentally distinguished from all major streams of Marxism by, among other things, their emphasis on the autonomous role of cultures and worldviews, and by a much more skeptical and pessimistic view of the potential for revolutionary transformations on the international or global scale.

80. Johan Galtung, "A Structural Theory of Imperialism," *Journal of Peace Research* 2 (1971): 81–94.

81. Ibid. See also Fernando Enrique Cardoso and Ernesto Faletto, *Dependency and Development in Latin America* (Berkeley: University of California Press, 1979).

82. Kenneth Jowitt, *The Leninist Response to National Dependency*. Research Series no. 37 (Berkeley: University of California, Institute of International Studies, 1978).

83. Robert Keohane, *After Hegemony: Cooperation and Discord in the World Political Economy* (Princeton, N.J.: Princeton University Press, 1984); and David Baldwin, "Interdependence and Power: A Conceptual Analysis," *International Organization* 32 (1978).

84. Held, *Democracy and the Global Order.*

85. David Held, ed., *Prospects for Democracy: North, South, East, West* (Stanford, Calif.: Stanford University Press, 1993).

86. Held, *Democracy and the Global Order*, 21.

87. Ibid., 133.

88. Ibid., 132.

89. George Orwell, "Politics and the English Language," *Horizon*, April 1946.

90. For the broader context of this argument, see Jowitt, "Dizzy with Democracy."

3. Populists, the Establishment, and the Soviet Decline

1. Schweizer, *Victory.*

2. See, for example, the contributions by Stephen Sestanovich and Vladimir Kontorovich to the symposium "The Strange Death of Soviet Communism," *The National Interest*, Spring 1993.

3. Archie Brown, *The Gorbachev Factor* (New York: Oxford University Press, 1996); and Jack Matlock, *Autopsy on an Empire: The American Ambassador's Account of the Collapse of the Soviet Union* (New York: Random House, 1995).

4. Merle Fainsod, *Smolensk Under Soviet Rule* (Cambridge, Mass.: Harvard University Press, 1958), 449.

5. Among the key works in this context were Andrei Amalrik, *Will the USSR Survive Until 1984?* (New York: Harper & Row, 1970); *A Chronicle of Current Events*, 1968–1982 (issues 16–64 published by Amnesty International Publications, London); and Alexeyeva, *Soviet Dissent*. See also Alex Inkeles and Raymond Bauer, *The Soviet Citizen: Daily Life in a Totalitarian Society* (Cambridge, Mass.: Harvard University Press, 1959); James R. Millar, ed., *Politics, Work, and Daily Life in the USSR: A Survey of Former Soviet Citizens* (New York: Cambridge University Press, 1987).

6. This calculation is based on copies of archival documents Peter Reddaway obtained in his research on political prisoners and the dissident movement during the Soviet period: a note from then–KGB chairman Yuri Andropov to the CPSU leadership in December 1975; and a KGB report to the CPSU Central Committee dated May 11, 1987 (ref. no. 6/2140), entitled "Po voprosu o statyakh 70 i 190-1 UK RSFSR" (Concerning Articles 70 and 190-1 of the RSFSR Criminal Code). For the method of calculation see Peter Reddaway, "Sovietology and Dissent: New Sources on Protest," *RFE/RL Research Report*, January 29, 1993.

7. "O nekotorykh itogakh predupreditel'no-profilakticheskoi raboty organov gos-bezopasnosti" (Concerning Certain Results of the Preventative-prophylactic Work of the State Security Agencies), a report by Andropov of October 31, 1975. Peter Reddaway was able to obtain a copy of this archival document in his research on political prisoners and the dissident movement during the Soviet period.

8. Andropov's note to CPSU leadership, December 1975.

9. Reddaway, "Sovietology and Dissent," 15.

10. This misperception was enhanced by some Russians who styled themselves democrats, even as they viewed their foreign trips as visits to important constituencies while campaigning for power positions in Russia.

11. Boris Yeltsin, *The Struggle for Russia,* trans. Catherine A. Fitzpatrick (New York: Belka Publications/Times Books, 1994), 25. This is Yeltsin's second volume of memoirs, whose original, Russian-language version was published as *Zapiski prezidenta* (Moscow: Ogonek, 1994).

12. The argument that the CPSU, at least in the twilight of its history, was not a political party with any identifiable ideology shared by most of its members is supported by opinion polls. The responses to a New Russian Barometer survey show very little difference in political attitudes between rank-and-file members of the CPSU and other citizens, with most of the Party members lacking any positive view of Soviet-type "socialism." See Stephen White, Richard Rose, and Ian McAllister, *How Russia Votes* (Chatham, N.J: Chatham House Publishers, 1997), 44.

13. Alex Inkeles, "Images of Class Relations Among Former Soviet Citizens," *Social Problems* 3, no. 3 (January 1956).

14. Inkeles and Bauer, *The Soviet Citizen.*

15. Ibid.

16. "Demokraticheskii nakaz. Programmnye tezisy po perestroyke politicheskoy sistemy v SSSR. Puti k demokraticheskomu sotsializmu" (Democratic Mandate. Programmatic Theses on the Restructuring of the Political System in the USSR. Roads Toward Democratic Socialism), May 1988, in *Partii, assotsiatsii, soyuzy, kluby: Sbornik dokumentov i materialov,* vol. 9 (Moscow: RAU Press, 1993), 25 (Prilozhenie k analiticheskomu ezhenedel'niku "Obozrevatel'") (Appendix on the analytical weekly *Obozrevatel'*).

17. "Vozzvanie Patrioticheskogo obyedineniya 'Pamyat'' k russkomu narodu, k patriotam vsekh stran i natsiy" (The Call of the Pamyat' Patriotic Association to the Russian People, to the Patriots of All Countries and Nations), December 1987, in *Partii, assotsiatsii, soyuzy, kluby*, vol. 5, 91.

18. "Manifest Mezhregional'noy assotsiatsii demokraticheskikh organizatsiy" (Manifesto of the Inter-Regional Association of Democratic Organizations), October 1989, in *Partii, assotsiatsii, soyuzy, kluby*, vol. 4, 18.

19. "Deklaratsiya" (Declaration), May 1988, in *Partii, assotsiatsii, soyuzy, kluby*, vol. 9, 79.

20. *Vlast'—narodu. Tezisy k programme prakticheskoy deyatel'nosti Mezhregional'noy gruppy narodnykh deputatov SSSR po uglubleniyu i realizatsii perestroiki* (Power to the People. Programmatic Theses for the Practical Activity of the Inter-Regional Group of People's Deputies of the USSR Regarding the Deepening and Implementation of Perestroika), July 1989, in *Partii, assotsiatsii, soyuzy, kluby,* vol. 4, 23.

21. The factual side of this section owes much to the writing of John D. Hicks, in particular to his *The Populist Revolt* (Lincoln: University of Nebraska Press, 1961).

22. Richard Hofstadter, *The Age of Reform: From Bryan to FDR* (New York: Alfred A. Knopf, 1955), 61.

23. Ibid., 4–5.

24. This double-edged nature of original populism, fully emulated by its twentieth-century successors, was pointed out by a sympathetic commentator, Christopher Lasch. In his words, late–twentieth century populism rejects "both the market and the welfare state in pursuit of a third way. . . . [T]hese positions belong to neither the left nor the right, and for that very reason they seem to hold out the best hope of breaking the deadlock of current debate"; Christopher Lasch, *The Revolt of the Elites and the Betrayal of Democracy* (New York: W. W. Norton, 1995), 101. See also Michael Kazin, *The Populist Persuasion: An American History* (New York: Basic Books, 1995).

25. For comprehensive analyses of Russian Populism, see B. S. Itenberg, *Dvizheniye revolyutsionnogo narodnichestva* (Moscow: n.p., 1965); and G. D. Alekseeva, *Narodnichestvo v Rossii v XX v.: ideinaia evoliutsiia* (Moscow: Nauka, 1990). For reliable Western sources, see Oliver Radkey, *The Agrarian Foes of Bolshevism* (New York: Columbia University Press, 1958); and James H. Billington, *Fire in the Minds of Men: Origins of the Revolutionary Faith* (New York: Basic Books, 1980). For a congenial interpretation of agrarian populism as a source of Russia's missed historical opportunities, see V. F. Antonov, "Norodnichestvo v Rossii: utopiya ili otvergnutye vozmozhnosti," *Voprosy istorii,* no. 1 (1991).

26. Scott, *The Moral Economy of the Peasant*; Robert Redfield, *The Little Community: Viewpoints for the Study of a Human Whole* (Chicago: University of Chicago Press, 1955); and Samuel Popkin, *The Rational Peasant: The Political Economy of Rural Society in Vietnam* (Berkeley: University of California Press, 1979).

27. Studies in Soviet social history show that the country shifted from being predominantly agrarian to being predominantly urban within the active lifespan of one generation, between the 1930s and 1960s. While in 1917, urbanites made up 17.9 percent of the total population of Russia, they crossed the 50 percent threshold in the early 1960s. See David Lane, *Soviet Society Under Perestroika* (Boston: Unwin Hyman, 1990), 126.

28. For elaborations of Trotsky's approach, see Bruno Rizzi, *La Bureaucratisation du Monde* (Paris: Editions Champ Libre, 1939); and James Burnham, *The Managerial Revolution* (New York: John Day, 1941).

29. Mikhail Voslensky, *Nomenklatura: The Soviet Ruling Class* (Garden City, N.Y.: Doubleday, 1984).

30. Draft of the "Founding Declaration of the Penza Front in Support of the Perestroika."

31. Gavriil Popov, "S tochki zreniya ekonomista. O romane Aleksandra Beka *Novoye naznacheniye*," *Nauka i zhizn'* 4 (1987).

32. See, for example, Mikhail Bakunin, *Selected Writings*, ed. Arthur Lehning (London: Cape, 1973).

33. Some of the liberal-anarchists converged with the nomenklatura-class theorists to the point where their views became indiscernible. Thus Aleksandr Shubin, blithely ignoring the differences in power and wealth that exist within any bureaucracy, argues that the bureaucracy is a social class in itself ("the oldest class in the world") and that the nomenklatura is merely its "pseudonym." Shubin sees the crisis of the industrial-bureaucratic system in the USSR as similar to the crisis of the welfare state in the West, a point that helps to explain Shubin's convergence on a number of issues with ultraradical free-market economists. Aleksandr Shubin, *Istoki perestroiki, 1978–1984 gg.*, vol. 1 (Moscow: n. p., 1997), 59–61.

34. Leading anarchists later were found in the ranks of both opponents and enforcers of shock therapy. Thus Andrei Isaev has become the most authoritative ideologist of the pro-CPRF labor union (FITUR), while Aleksandr Shubin served in 1997–98 as adviser for "special ideological projects" to Deputy Prime Minister Boris Nemtsov, working under conservative monarchist Viktor Aksiuchits! See *Moskovskii komsomolets*, December 11, 1997. For an exceptionally well-targeted critique of the beginnings of nomenklatura capitalism, see Andrei Isaev, "'Krasnye' kapitalisty," *Obshchina*, no. 47 (1991).

35. Quotations are from Shafarevich's *Russofobiya*, as reprinted in I. R. Shafarevich, *Sochineniya*, vol. 2 (Moscow: Feniks, 1994), passim.

36. See Augustin Cochin, *La crise de l'histoire révolutionnaire* (Paris: H. Champion, 1909).

37. Shafarevich, *Sochineniya*, vol. 2, 142–43.

38. Ibid., 163.

39. This uninterrupted legacy is underscored by the fact that in December 1991, Shafarevich had at least a symbolic part in the foundation of Sergei Baburin's Russian All People's Union, which is now the most visible rallying point for mainstream nationalists.

40. The tradition of conservative elitism was exemplified in 1909 by the famous words of Mikhail Gershenzon, who found in the "bayonets of the government" the only protection for the intelligentsia "from the rage of the people." Boris Shragin and Albert Todd, eds., *Landmarks: A Collection of Essays on the Russian Intelligentsia* (New York: Karz Howard, 1977), 80.

41. Andropov quoted in Dusko Doder, *Shadows and Whispers: Power Politics Inside the Kremlin from Brezhnev to Gorbachev* (New York: Random House, 1986), 122.

42. On the Mafiya's contribution to the collapse of the Soviet Union, see Louise Shelley, "Crime and the Collapse of the Soviet State," in *The Social Legacy of Communism*, ed. James Millar and Sharon Wolchik (New York: Cambridge University Press, 1994).

43. *Blat*, a term apparently derived from the German *Blatt*, meaning a sheet of paper, referred originally to a kind of letter of recommendation drawn up by a group of inmates to certify the underworld reliability of a prisoner being transferred to another jail or colony who could thus reassure his new inmates that he was not an informant. *Blat* gradually evolved into a broader term for solidarity among criminals.

44. In 1905, Bolsheviks, under the supervision of the twenty-six-year-old Joseph Stalin, cooperated with the famous gang of Kamo to organize an armed robbery in Tiflis.

45. Walter Krivitsky, *In Stalin's Secret Service* (Lanham, Md.: University Press of America, 1985), chapter 4.

46. Varlam Shalamov's masterpiece, *Kolyma Tales* (New York: Penguin, 1995), remains a classic testimony on the subculture of Soviet penal colonies.

47. On the symbiosis of government officials and the Mafiya in the Brezhnev era, see Ilya Zemtsov, *La Corruption en Union Soviétique* (Paris: Hachette, 1976); Konstantin Simis, *USSR, The Corrupt Society: The Secret World of Soviet Capitalism* (New York: Simon & Schuster, 1982); Voslensky, *Nomenklatura*, 298–309; Arkady Vaksberg, *The Soviet Mafia* (New York: St. Martin's, 1991); Claire Sterling, *Thieves' World: The Threat of the New Global Network of Organized Crime* (New York: Simon & Schuster, 1994); and Stephen Handelman, *Comrade Criminal: Russia's New Mafiya* (New Haven: Yale University Press, 1994).

48. The MVD also became the main channel for the Mafiya's political influence on the Soviet leadership—not only through Minister Shchelokov, but more effectively through his deputy, who was also Brezhnev's son-in-law, Yuri Churbanov.

49. See Stanislav Govorukhin, *Velikaya kriminal'naya revolyutsiya* (Moscow: Andreevsky flag, 1993).

50. See in particular Shubin, *Istoki perestroiki,* vol. 1, 106–36.

51. Mikhail Gorbachev, *Memoirs* (New York: Doubleday, 1996); Nikolai Ryzhkov, *Perestroika: Istoriya predatel'stv* (Moscow: Novosti, 1992); Yegor Ligachev, *Inside Gorbachev's Kremlin* (New York: Pantheon, 1993); and Vadim Pechenev, *Gorbachev: k vershinam vlasti* (Moscow: Gospodin narod, 1991).

52. Jonathan Steele and Eric Abraham, *Andropov in Power: From Komsomol to Kremlin* (Garden City, N.Y.: Anchor, 1984), 167.

53. Roy Medvedev, *Gensek s Lubyanki; politicheskaia biografiia Yu. V. Andropova* (Moscow: LETA, 1993).

54. Schweizer, *Victory,* 128, with reference to Vladimir Solovyov and Elena Klepikova, *Behind the High Kremlin Walls* (New York: Dodd Mead, 1986).

55. On Ivankov, see Handelman, *Comrade Criminal,* 242–43. For more details on the Andropov campaign and some theoretical analysis, see William A. Clark, *Crime and Punishment in Soviet Officialdom: Combating Corruption in the Political Elite, 1965–1990* (Armonk, N.Y.: M. E. Sharpe, 1993).

56. See Vaksberg, *The Soviet Mafia,* 213–16; and Timothy Colton, *Moscow: Governing the Socialist Metropolis* (Cambridge, Mass.: Belknap Press, 1996), 569–70.

57. For a similar assessment, see Shubin, *Istoki perestroiki,* vol. 1, 146.

58. Tel'man Gdlyan and Yevgeny Dodolev, *Piramida-1* (Moscow: APS, 1990); Tel'man Gdlyan and Nikolai Ivanov, *Kremlyovskoe delo* (Rostov-on-Don: AO Kniga, 1994); and Viktor Ilyukhin, *Vozhdi i oborotni: Prervannoe rassledovanie* (Moscow: Paleya, 1994).

59. Gdlyan and Ivanov, *Kremlyovskoe delo,* 33.

60. Gdlyan and Dodolev, *Piramida-1,* 79.

61. Ibid., 17, 139–40, 219.

62. As was recently revealed in the West, the seeds of Central Asian unrest had been skillfully nurtured by the Reagan administration. See Schweizer, *Victory,* 273–74.

63. For the most extensive and insightful analysis so far of Gorbachev as a classic agrarian administrator who had spent years fighting to adapt related branches of industry to agricultural needs, see Shubin, *Istoki perestroiki,* vol. 1, 112–31, 179–80.

64. Although it does not command armed personnel, the Foreign Affairs Ministry is often included in this category because of its exceptionally high political profile and also because the political culture of the Soviet establishment equated its grip over Russia's "satellite states" with the coercive instruments of domestic political control.

65. This point is explored in more depth by Anders Aslund, *Gorbachev's Struggle for Economic Reform* (Ithaca, N.Y.: Cornell University Press, 1989), 27–36.

66. *Pravda,* February 26, 1987.

67. The present analysis aims to uncover the logic of major developments but does not establish chronological "turning points" because various developments of the Gorbachev era continued on parallel tracks. Thus Gorbachev's populist phase ended no earlier than 1989, after the destabilizing effects of his institutional experiments on law and order had become clear. On some of the themes of this section, see Peter Reddaway, "The Quality of Gorbachev's Leadership," in *Milestones in Glasnost and Perestroyka,* vol. 2, ed. Ed Hewett and Victor Winston (Washington, D.C.: Brookings Institution, 1991).

68. For background on these events, see Vera Tolz, *The USSR's Emerging Multiparty System* (New York: Praeger, 1990), chapters 2 and 3.

69. Aleksandr Yakovlev, *The Fate of Marxism in Russia* (New Haven, Conn.: Yale University Press, 1993), 228.

70. A separate group of authors headed by Fyodor Uglov focused specifically on the anti-alcohol campaign. After prohibition had been quietly repealed, this group fought to reimpose it, creating in the process a new organization called the All-Russian Voluntary Society of Struggle for Sobriety. However, they failed to provide a mass populist base for returning to the initial conservative inspiration of perestroika, and the movement soon petered out. Some of its members joined the ranks of Pamyat'.

71. For background on this episode, see Nikolai Petro, "The Project of the Century," *Studies in Comparative Communism* 20, no. 3/4 (1987).

72. Schweizer, *Victory,* 140–44, 242.

73. On topics covered in this paragraph, see Josephine Woll, "'Glasnost' and Soviet Culture," and Thomas Sherlock, "Politics and History under Gorbachev," in *The Soviet System: From Crisis to Collapse,* ed. Alexander Dallin and Gail Lapidus (Boulder, Colo.: Westview, 1995).

74. For background, see Tolz, *The USSR's Emerging Multiparty System,* chapters 3 and 6; and Steven Fish, "The Emergence of Independent Associations and the Transformation of Russian Political Society," in Dallin and Lapidus, eds., *The Soviet System,* 147–59.

75. About the onset of their political activities, see *Literaturnaya gazeta,* March 9, 1988; and *Literaturnaya Rossiya,* March 27, 1987.

76. Laqueur, *The Dream that Failed,* 204.

77. For background on this section, see ibid., chapter 13; and Semyon Reznik, *The Nazification of Russia* (Washington, D.C.: Challenge Publications, 1996).

78. Yakovlev, *The Fate of Marxism in Russia.*

79. V. D. Solovei, "Evolyutsiya sovremennogo russkogo nationalizma, 1985–1993" (The Evolution of Contemporary Russian Nationalism, 1985–1993), in *Russkii narod: istoricheskaia sud'ba v XX veke,* ed. Yu. S. Kukushkin et al. (Moscow: ANKO, 1993), 283–305. Conceivably, these rumors originated from Pamyat' leaders, who alluded to their protection by the KGB as a form of bragging and a way to intimidate their critics.

80. "A National Town Meeting: President Gorbachev and President Yeltsin Take Questions From Americans," ABC News, transcript, September 5, 1991, as quoted in Reznik, *The Nazification of Russia,* 204.

81. See, for example, V. Kozhinov, "My menyaemsya?" (Are We Changing?), *Nash sovremennik,* no. 10 (1987): 167–72.

82. For evidence that those in American academia who sympathized with Russian nationalists were put on high alert, see John Dunlop, "The Contemporary Russian Nationalist Spectrum," *Radio Liberty Research Bulletin,* December 19, 1988, 7.

83. Boris Yeltsin, *Ispoved' na zadannuyu temu* (Moscow: Ogonek, 1990). The English-language edition of this first volume of memoirs appeared as *Against the Grain,* trans. Michael Glenny (New York: Summit, 1990).

84. Another prominent member of this same group was Prime Minister Nikolai Ryzhkov, but the group was identified overall with Ligachev, who, as the administrator of the Secretariat of the CPSU Central Committee, was the Party's chief day-to-day boss for personnel.

85. In his autobiography, Yeltsin describes "the Moscow syndrome" at some length and admits that he "used to have a prejudiced attitude toward Muscovites" (*Ispoved' na zadannuyu temu,* p. 42; *Against the Grain,* p. 90). The provincial ambivalence toward the capital, as Yeltsin insightfully shows, manifested itself in mistrust of Muscovites but also in a "passionate desire to move to Moscow and become a Muscovite." Such feelings toward capital cities are common in today's world, especially in countries with a "dual economy," where most of the population depends on the capital dwellers for financial flows and access to the outer world.

86. For more details of his assault on the old regime in Moscow, see Colton, *Moscow,* 572–82.

87. John Morrison, *Boris Yeltsin: From Bolshevik to Democrat* (New York: Dutton, 1991), 48.

88. For some details, see the chapter on the media by Vitaly Korotich in *Russian Pluralism—Now Irreversible?* ed. Uri Ra'anan, Keith Armes, and Kate Martin (New York: St. Martin's, 1992).

89. For helpful details about this period, see Morrison, *Boris Yeltsin,* 54–57.

90. For some background, see Tolz, *The USSR's Emerging Multiparty System,* 26–29; and Michael Urban, Vyacheslav Igrunov, and Sergei Mitrokhin, *The Rebirth of Politics in Russia* (New York: Cambridge University Press, 1997), 105–7.

91. Yeltsin, *Ispoved' na zadannuyu temu,* 5–7.

92. Background on this and the other episodes of fall 1987 discussed in the following pages can be found in Morrison, *Boris Yeltsin,* 56–73.

93. Yeltsin, *Ispoved' na zadannuyu temu,* 9–10, 80–81.

94. Ibid., 86 (p. 203 of *Against the Grain*).

95. Ibid., 37, 95 (pp. 75, 222 of *Against the Grain*).

96. For an English translation, see Dallin and Lapidus, eds., *The Soviet System,* chapter 22.

97. Some background on this and subsequent paragraphs can be found in Urban, Igrunov, and Mitrokhin, *The Rebirth of Politics in Russia,* 109–39.

98. For details on Popov, see ibid., 187, 198–200.

99. Alexander Lukin, *Political Culture of Russian Democrats* (New York: Oxford University Press, 2000), 284. These data fit into the pattern of a more or less permanent scale of value priorities among Russians, a pattern that appeared in the emigrant surveys discussed at the beginning of this chapter. However, the present authors do not share Lukin's conclusions, which are permeated by hostility toward Russia's democrats.

100. See Urban, Igrunov, and Mitrokhin, *The Rebirth of Politics in Russia,* 108–14, for an analysis of the activity of the Democratic Union that provides extensive documentation.

101. See also her autobiographical *Nad propastiu vo lzhi* (Moscow: AST, 1998).

102. For more on the groups discussed in this section and below, see Urban, Igrunov, and Mitrokhin, *The Rebirth of Politics in Russia;* Tolz, *The USSR's Emerging Multiparty System*; and Michael McFaul and Sergei Markov, *The Troubled Birth of Russian Democracy: Parties, Personalities, and Programs* (Stanford, Calif.: Hoover Institution Press, 1993).

103. On the nationalists, see John Dunlop, *The Rise of Russia and the Fall of the Soviet Empire* (Princeton, N.J.: Princeton University Press, 1993), chapter 4.

104. Yeltsin, *Ispoved' na zadannuyu temu*, 102.

105. On this episode, see Urban, Igrunov, and Mitrokhin, *The Rebirth of Politics in Russia,* 126–28.

106. Rolf H. W. Theen, ed., *The U.S.S.R. First Congress of People's Deputies: Complete Documents and Records, May 25, 1989–June 10, 1989*, vol. 1 (New York: Paragon House, 1991), 230–33.

107. Details on this episode are provided in Morrison, *Boris Yeltsin,* chapter 8.

108. For an account of the First Congress and its aftermath, see Urban, Igrunov, and Mitrokhin, *The Rebirth of Politics in Russia,* chapter 7.

109. On the IDG, see ibid., 159–68.

110. The Council for Mutual Economic Assistance (CMEA, or "Comecon") was the Soviet-controlled body that coordinated the communist economies of the USSR and Eastern Europe.

111. See Urban, Igrunov, and Mitrokhin, *The Rebirth of Politics in Russia,* 152.

112. For more information on these groups, see ibid., 169–71; and Dunlop, *The Rise of Russia,* chapter 4.

113. On the miners, see Peter Rutland, "Labor Unrest and Movements in 1989 and 1990," *Soviet Economy,* no. 6 (1990).

114. The atmosphere of this period is skillfully evoked in Donald Murray, *A Democracy of Despots* (Boulder, Colo.: Westview, 1996), chapter 6.

115. See Urban, Igrunov, and Mitrokhin, *The Rebirth of Politics in Russia,* 168–69.

116. For the flavor of their debate, see Pavel Yemelin, "Russkii vopros" (The Russian Question), *Literaturnaya Rossiya,* November 17, 1989.

117. *Nash sovremennik,* no. 12 (1989), 3–6.

118. "Za politiku narodnogo soglasiya i rossiiskogo vozrozhdeniya" (For a Policy of National Harmony and Russian Rebirth), *Literaturnaya Rossiya*, December 29, 1989.

119. For more about Democratic Russia's program and electoral campaign, see Urban, Igrunov, and Mitrokhin, *The Rebirth of Politics in Russia*, 182–93.

120. Dunlop, *The Rise of Russia*, 142–43.

4. From Russian Sovereignty to the August Coup: A Missed Chance for a Democratic Revolution

1. An alternative view was expressed by Peter Reddaway, "Is the Soviet Union Drifting toward Anarchy?" *Report on the USSR* 1, no. 34 (August 1989).

2. On Lithuania's return to independence, see the balanced account by the historian Alfred E. Senn, *Gorbachev's Failure in Lithuania* (New York: St. Martin's, 1995).

3. See, for example, Anatoly Sobchak, *Khozhdenie vo vlast': rasskaz o rozhdenii parlamenta* (Moscow: Novosti, 1991), 134–35.

4. *Duma* (Sofia), May 17, 1990, as quoted in Morrison, *Boris Yeltsin*, 142.

5. The original model for this declaration was Andrei Sakharov's draft "Decree on State Power," which had been unsuccessfully proposed to the Union Congress in 1989. For many democrats, this symbolic parallel was enough to ensure their support for the motion. The big difference was that although Sakharov's original decree had intended to claim for the Soviet parliament the powers held by the Communist Party, the Shakhrai-Rumyantsev declaration sought to aggrandize the Russian Congress by gutting the Soviet federal government.

6. "Democrats" henceforth refers to activists and supporters of the 1990 electoral coalition (that is, to Democratic Russia and its organizational offspring).

7. McFaul and Markov, *The Troubled Birth of Russian Democracy*, 138.

8. See Robert Michels, *Political Parties: A Sociological Study of the Oligarchical Tendencies of Modern Democracy* (New York: Hearst International Library, 1915).

9. On this process, see Urban, Igrunov, and Mitrokhin, *The Rebirth of Politics in Russia*, parts II and III; and McFaul and Markov, *The Troubled Birth of Russian Democracy*.

10. "The Road to Progress and Social Democracy." Fundamentals of the SDPR program (provisional version), October 1990, in *Partii, assotsiatsii, soyuzy, kluby*, vol. 9, 16.

11. As of 2000, Aleksandr Shokhin, having displayed a remarkable capacity for political survival by switching sides within the governmental "seesaw" system, was serving as chair of the Duma Committee on Credit and Finance.

12. *Komsomol'skaya pravda*, September 18, 1990.

13. On this issue, see Dunlop, *The Rise of Russia*, 278–79.

14. On Shakhrai's career through 1993, see the detailed information in A. Vasilevsky and V. Pribylovsky, *Kto est' kto v rossiiskoi politike*, vol. 3 (Moscow: Panorama, 1993), 631–34.

15. On the Cossacks, see Peter Reddaway, "Moscow-Krasnoyarsk-Ekaterinburg Diary, October 1994" (Institute for European, Russian, and Eurasian Studies, George Washington University, photocopy), 60–61, 119–21, 144–45.

16. For a detailed description of these events, see Anders Aslund, *How Russia Became a Market Economy* (Washington, D.C.: Brookings Institution, 1995), 36–38.

17. The result was a two-volume, unbound work issued in separate Russian and English versions that was later published in English as Grigori Yavlinsky et al., *500 Days: Transition to the Market* (New York: St. Martin's, 1991).

18. See Urban, Igrunov, and Mitrokhin, *The Rebirth of Politics in Russia,* 126–28.

19. *Sovetskaya Rossiya,* September 12, 1990, 4.

20. Robert Gates, *From the Shadows: The Ultimate Insider's Story of Five Presidents and How They Won the Cold War* (New York: Simon & Schuster, 1996), 502.

21. Michael Beschloss and Strobe Talbott, *At the Highest Levels: The Inside History of the End of the Cold War* (Boston: Little, Brown, 1993), 13.

22. Ibid., 170.

23. Ibid., 104.

24. Ibid., 210. Baker indicated that this sum was unrealistic and that technical cooperation and some American experts were all that could be managed. But in January 1995, the international lending community proved itself capable of assembling a loan package of some $50 billion to stop a run on Mexico's currency and stock market. In late 1997, a similar package of $55 billion was put together for South Korea. Both of these bailout programs were accompanied by stern conditionalities that the USSR of 1991 would have found highly unpalatable (or indeed impossible to fulfill in the short run). Yet the fact remains that sums comparable to what the Soviets were asking for were quickly found when the Western financial community thought its interests were served by doing so.

25. Ibid., 194.

26. Ibid., 223.

27. Ibid., 236.

28. Ibid., 209.

29. Ibid., 237.

30. Ibid., 376.

31. Ibid., 266. Senator Robert Dole seems to have fostered this view. According to Yavlinsky, Dole told him in October 1990 that Yeltsin had asked Dole two weeks earlier if the 500 Days plan might be "politically dangerous," and Dole responded in the affirmative. Yeltsin replied that if that were the case, "I won't adopt it, because I have (presidential) elections coming up in the spring." See Yavlinsky's interview in *Komsomol'skaya pravda,* March 17, 1998.

32. On this conference, see Mikhail Berger, "Nashi reformy i Mezhdunarodnyi Valyutnyi Fond," *Izvestiya,* October 4, 1990, 5.

33. See Yavlinsky et al., *500 Days,* esp. part II, sections 1 and 8.

34. On the swing toward authoritarianism, see Reddaway, "The Quality of Gorbachev's Leadership."

35. Vladimir Isakov, *Predsedatel' Soveta Respubliki: Parlamentskie dnevniki* (Moscow: Paleya, 1996), 277.

36. See chapter 5 and also Sterling, *Thieves' World,* especially part IV, "The Great Ruble Scam."

37. See Urban, Igrunov, and Mitrokhin, *The Rebirth of Politics in Russia,* 226–27.

38. The fatalistic notion that economic reform necessarily brings recession or depression is difficult to understand. The successful economic reform measures of the past, such as the Dawes Plan/Rentenmark policy of Stresemann and Schacht in 1923–24, or the Erhard D-Mark of 1948, produced dramatically positive results in less than a year. Roosevelt's Lend-Lease Program, initiated in March 1941, was dictated by military requirements, but it was the centerpiece of an economic mobilization policy that cut U.S. unemployment in half between January and December 1941. See Broadus Mitchell, *Depression Decade: From New Era through New Deal, 1929–1941* (New York: Rinehart, 1947), 452. The IMF's pessimism may reflect the fact that all but narrowly monetarist and fiscal approaches were excluded a priori.

39. International Monetary Fund, International Bank for Reconstruction and Development/World Bank, Organization for Economic Cooperation and Development, and European Bank for Reconstruction and Development, *A Study of the Soviet Economy,* abridged ed. (Washington, D.C.: International Monetary Fund, 1990), 21.

40. Ibid., 22.

41. Ibid., 26.

42. Ibid., 36.

43. Ibid., 46.

44. We should note here that Western nonmonetarist forces—whether of the social-democratic or other type—never came forward with a serious program of economic reform. Western leftists simply did not understand the reasons for Soviet citizens' rejection of the old economic system.

45. Graham Allison and Grigori Yavlinsky, *Window of Opportunity: The Grand Bargain for Democracy in the Soviet Union* (New York: Pantheon, 1991), ix–x.

46. Cocom (or the "Coordinating Committee") was a special trade regime established by NATO countries to try to prevent advanced technology that could be used for military purposes from reaching communist countries.

47. *New York Times,* August 2, 1991.

48. Dmitri Glinski, in Moscow at the time, felt they had made a serious mistake.

49. On Yeltsin's contacts with Kryuchkov, see the interview with Kryuchkov's first deputy, Viktor Grushko, in *Nezavisimaya gazeta,* April 14, 1994. See also Morrison, *Boris Yeltsin,* 222–31 for more on these events.

50. For details on the March confrontation, see Dunlop, *The Rise of Russia,* 4.

51. Yeltsin, *Zapiski prezidenta,* 39.

52. *Izvestiya,* November 15, 1990.

53. *Den',* no. 6 (March 1991).

54. *Den',* no. 9 (May 1991).

55. *Den',* no. 4 (February 1991).

56. *Den',* no. 9 (May 1991).

57. The literal title was "The Word to the People," with an allusion to the anonymous twelfth-century heroic poem "Slovo o Polku Igoreve," which tells the story of the Russians' major military defeat. A salient aspect of the poem is its appeal for unity among the Russian princes to defend the country against foreign attack.

58. Stylistic analysis of "A Call to the People," as well as some later hints in the media, points to Aleksandr Prokhanov and Eduard Volodin as principal authors (although not necessarily initiators) of the appeal.

59. Yeltsin, *Zapiski prezidenta,* 50.

60. The most thorough analysis to date of the early stage of Zhirinovsky's career (along with an analytical survey of "Zhirinovskyana") can be found in Andreas Umland's "Vladimir Zhirinovsky in Russian Politics. A Case Study in Post-Communist Right-wing Extremism, 1990–93" (1996).

61. On this last job, see Vladimir Kartsev (with Todd Bludeau), *!Zhirinovsky!* (New York: Columbia University Press, 1995), part I.

62. Loewenhardt, *The Reincarnation of Russia,* 76.

63. Vladimir Solovyov and Elena Klepikova, *Zhirinovsky: Russian Fascism and the Making of a Dictator* (Reading, Mass.: Addison-Wesley, 1995), 8.

64. Other groups also joined the bloc. There was the self-styled Sakharov Union of Democratic Forces, headed by Vladimir Voronin, a former apartment broker with an underworld past. This group chose Sakharov's name despite an indignant protest from his widow, Elena Bonner. Also participating were the "Blue Movement," founded by Yuri Bokan, a little-known employee of the CPSU Central Committee's ideological department; the Russian People's Front of Valery Skurlatov, a veteran of the Komsomol Central Committee and author of an explicitly racist "Moral Code" that was widely known in the 1960s; and national societies of Abkhazians and Georgian Turks. Subsequently, Zhirinovsky used the membership lists of these groups to draw up a fake list of his own party members for the purpose of getting registered. Specifically, almost half of his claimed party members, or 2,714 people, were registered in a single region of Abkhazia. See Umland, "Vladimir Zhirinovsky," 32–36 and 43–44.

65. Ibid., 36–38.

66. Ibid., 50–52.

67. On April 22, RSFSR justice minister Nikolai Fedorov launched an investigation of Lushchikov, hinting at the questionable circumstances of the LDP registration. It later became known that Lushchikov had prohibited the transfer of any documents relating to party registrations to Russian government organs. During the fall of 1991, a committee of the Russian Supreme Soviet, while probing the circumstances of the August putsch, revealed that Lukyanov had exerted pressure to secure the LDP's registration. On August 11, 1992, the registration was voided in connection with these irregularities. However, on December 14, 1992 (the day of Chernomyrdin's election as prime minister), the Ministry of Justice reregistered the LDP under the name of the Liberal Democratic Party of Russia. See ibid., 43–46 and 237.

68. Ibid., 46–49.

69. *Literaturnaya Rossiya,* no. 28 (1991), 3.

70. Beschloss and Talbott, *At the Highest Levels,* 95.

71. Michael Duffy and Dan Goodgame, *Marching in Place: The Status Quo Presidency of George Bush* (New York: Simon & Schuster, 1992), 172.

72. See Vladimir Pozner, *Eyewitness: A Personal Account of the Unraveling of the Soviet Union* (New York: Random House, 1992), 129–30. Was Kryuchkov's alarm justified? A former senior U.S. intelligence official later told Seymour Hersh that the CIA did indeed recruit high-level Soviet sources during the twilight years of the USSR. How did the CIA do this? "The answer is by paying them," said the official. "What an incredible position to be in. You can pay men in authority, and you know by technical means who's in control, and by technical means you can monitor what they're doing." See Seymour Hersh, "The Wild East," *Atlantic Monthly,* June 1994.

73. *New York Times,* December 21, 1990.

74. Pozner, *Eyewitness,* 134–36.

75. Beschloss and Talbott, *At the Highest Levels,* 294–95.

76. David Remnick, *Lenin's Tomb: The Last Days of the Soviet Empire* (New York: Random House, 1993), 464.

77. Beschloss and Talbott, *At the Highest Levels,* 348.

78. Ibid., 353.

79. Ibid., 357.

80. Duffy and Goodgame, *Marching in Place,* 172.

81. This paragraph is based on Beschloss and Talbott, *At the Highest Levels,* 393–95.

82. Matlock, *Autopsy on an Empire,* 541.

83. James A. Baker III, *The Politics of Diplomacy: Revolution, War, and Peace, 1989–1992* (New York: Putnam, 1995), 470–71.

84. Beschloss and Talbott, *At the Highest Levels,* 395–401.

85. Gates, *From the Shadows,* 504.

86. Dunlop, *The Rise of Russia,* 194.

87. Hersh, "The Wild East." Hersh does not name the senator.

88. *New York Times,* August 20, 1991.

89. See Mark Galeotti, *The Age of Anxiety: Security and Politics in Soviet and Post-Soviet Russia* (New York: Longman, 1995), 138.

90. Beschloss and Talbott, *At the Highest Levels,* 422, 429–30.

91. *Time,* September 9, 1991.

92. Beschloss and Talbott, *At the Highest Levels,* 424–34.

93. See Hersh, "The Wild East."

94. In the Russian literature, the most thorough and illuminating account (despite, or rather because of, its intrinsic bias) is offered by Yeltsin's *Zapiski prezidenta.* In American scholarship, the benchmark is established by the chapter on the August coup in Dunlop's *The Rise of Russia.* See also chapter 1 of Amy Knight's *Spies without Cloaks: The KGB's Successors* (Princeton, N.J.: Princeton University Press, 1996), and the heated debate between her, Archie Brown, Donald Jensen, and Jack Matlock in *The New York Review of Books,* June 26, 1997. Our own views are close to those of Knight.

95. See *Washington Post,* August 22, 1991.

96. *Sel'skaia zhizn',* December 27, 1991, 1. The evidence consisted of a letter, allegedly compiled by Tiziakov in prison, instructing other Emergency Committee defendants to blame Gorbachev and to transform the whole trial into an attack on Gorbachev's policy. Tiziakov's letter, as published in Valentin Stepankov and Yevgeny Lisov, *Kremlevskii zagovor* (Moscow: Ogonek, 1992), appears to be of doubtful authenticity.

97. Stenographic record of the session quoted in *Sovetskaia Rossiya,* September 3, 1994, 4. See also the report of the Supreme Court verdict in the case of General Valentin Varennikov, *Izvestiya,* August 12, 1994, 5. According to Anatoly Lukyanov, his closing words were, "The people will understand this." See *Narodnaia pravda,* no. 40 (October 1992).

98. Igor Baranovski, "KGB Listened in to Gorbachev and Plotters," *The Times* of London, January 22, 1992. The fact of Yazov's trip to the Crimea on the eve of the coup was also confirmed by U.S. intelligence sources; see *New York Times,* August 25, 1991, 16L.

99. Interviewed in *RFE/RL Daily Report on the USSR,* August 25, 1992, 2.

100. *Korichnevyi putch krasnykh* (Moscow: Tekst, 1991), 32; as quoted in Dunlop, *The Rise of Russia,* 212.

101. Another explanation is that the actions of the putschists were simply poorly planned; see Jonathan Steele, *Eternal Russia: Yeltsin, Gorbachev, and the Mirage of Democracy* (Boston: Faber & Faber, 1994), chapter 4. Yet it is hard to believe that the core group of the plotters—Kryuchkov, Baklanov, Shenin, and Boldin—were just plain bunglers. Kryuchkov, for example, had been a part of overthrowing at least four governments—in Hungary (1956), Czechoslovakia (1968), Afghanistan (1979), and Poland (1981).

102. Karpukhin in *Chernaia noch nad Belym Domom: Dokumenty* (Moscow: Rossiya, 1991), 35; and Stepankov and Lisov, *Kremlevskii zagovor,* 174.

103. *USSR Today,* August 26, 1991, 719/06-07.

104. *Komsomol'skaia pravda,* December 21, 1991, 3.

105. Stepankov and Lisov, *Kremlevskii zagovor,* 165.

106. See, for example, his *Zapiski prezidenta,* 97–98, and interview with Grushko, *Nezavisimaya gazeta.*

107. On Kryuchkov's note to Nixon, see Beschloss and Talbott, *At the Highest Levels,* 356.

108. Kryuchkov's orientation toward the West can partly be accounted for by the fact that he rose through the KGB's First Directorate, the branch responsible for foreign operations. On his and the KGB's views from 1983 to 1991, see his memoirs, *Lichnoe delo,* vol. 1 (Moscow: Olimp/AST, 1996), chapters 4–6. Kryuchkov admits here that as late as September 1988, he was still enthusiastic about Gorbachev's strategy and had "an enormous desire to help him" (p. 332).

109. Amy Knight, "The KGB, Perestroika, and the Collapse of the Soviet Union," in *The Collapse of the Soviet Union,* ed. Mark Kramer (Boulder, Colo.: Westview, in press).

110. After the coup, various sources hinted that a similar plan had existed since the fall of 1990, although nothing more specific was revealed. According to Mark Galeotti, the August coup plan was developed from a Brezhnev-era model called "Operation Snowstorm," designed for use in cases of natural disaster. See Galeotti, *The Age of Anxiety,* 12.

111. In fact, Grachev exposed his dovishness in the very first days after his appointment as APF commander, stating in his first public interview that he was against the use of paratroopers in the "hot spots" of interethnic tensions. See "Dlia etikh tselei sleduet privlekat' voiska KGB i MVD," *Krasnaia zvezda,* January 4, 1991.

112. Stepankov and Lisov, *Kremlevskii zagovor,* 150, passim.

113. Our interpretation echoes the opinion of a Russian democrat in exile, Anatoly Koryagin, as quoted by Aleksandr Podrabinek, "Chto eto bylo?" *Ekspress-Khronika,* August 27, 1991, 10.

114. Stepankov and Lisov, *Kremlevskii zagovor,* 33.

115. Yeltsin, *Zapiski prezidenta,* 96.

116. See Knight, "The KGB, Perestroika, and the Collapse of the Soviet Union."

117. Remnick, *Lenin's Tomb,* 471–72; and Matlock, *Autopsy on an Empire,* 592.

118. Yeltsin, *Zapiski prezidenta,* 96, 101–2.

119. Such a possibility is indirectly confirmed by Yeltsin's own hints that the KGB did not expect him or the democrats to rush to Gorbachev's rescue. See ibid., 75, 101.

120. Ironically, the "decisive" measures suggested by Varennikov and not taken by Kryuchkov—cutting the Russian parliament's electricity, communication and sewage lines, and water supplies—were used without much vacillation by Yeltsin himself in his assault on the Russian parliament in the same building in October 1993.

121. Stepankov and Lisov, *Kremlevskii zagovor,* 149; and Yeltsin, *Zapiski prezidenta,* 115.

122. Stepankov and Lisov, *Kremlevskii zagovor,* 80.

123. A winning strategy for the Soviet putschists would have been to fly into Moscow large numbers of their supporters from the Russian communities in the secessionist republics, from military plants, and so forth for high-profile pro–Emergency Committee demonstrations within range of CNN cameras. This strategy would have been far more effective than deploying tanks. By transporting crowds of supporters to Moscow, the committee might have attempted to create a "people's power" coup of the type staged against the Shah of Iran in 1978–79 and against President Marcos of the Philippines in 1985. In contrast to the passivity and ineptitude of the Emergency Committee, a remarkable example of the successful use of "transmission belts" was presented by the Romanian postcommunist president and party veteran Ion Iliescu. When antigovernment demonstrations in Bucharest threatened his power, he turned to his loyalists in the labor unions to bring to the capital large numbers of miners who helped to crush the protests of the students and the intelligentsia. Another example is Richard Nixon, who in 1970 used construction workers to break up antiwar demonstrations in New York City. However, the fatal weakness of the Emergency Committee was that it feared any attempt to mobilize mass support would soon get out of hand and threaten the status of the nomenklatura as a whole.

124. Looking ahead to October 1993, we must note Yeltsin's learning ability as a coup organizer. When preparing his own coup against the legislature, he carefully seized for himself strategic advantages on the Moscow political scene. At the same time, his opponents' inability to make any use of their powerful resources in the Russian provinces was yet more proof of the regions' historically marginal ability to influence the outcome of a power struggle in Moscow.

125. Yeltsin, *Zapiski prezidenta,* 105.

126. Text in *Den',* no. 19 (September 1991).

127. Dunlop, *The Rise of Russia,* 254.

128. On this episode, see Yeltsin, *Zapiski prezidenta,* 83–85.

129. See Bruce Porter, "The Military Abroad," in *Soldiers and the Soviet State: Civil-Military Relations from Brezhnev to Gorbachev,* ed. Timothy Colton and Thane Gustafson (Princeton, N.J.: Princeton University Press, 1990), 322–23; and Porter's "Heroes of the Soviet Union—Afghanistan," *Jane's Soviet Intelligence Review* 1, no. 3 (March 1989): 111–15. Grachev himself had been named Hero of the Soviet Union, and the paratroopers assumed a sort of corporate authority among Afghan War veterans, whose associations had by 1991 become an important factor in social and political life.

130. Interview in *Krasnaia zvezda,* January 4, 1991. It remains to be explained whether Grachev's appointment to this position was motivated by reluctance to irritate paratroop officers by bypassing him or was a conscious move to promote the doves within the army in order to balance such figures as Varennikov.

131. See the interview with Paratroop Chief of Staff Yevgeny Podkolzin in *Krasnaia zvezda,* September 11, 1991, 1.

132. Dunlop, *The Rise of Russia,* 253.

133. See Lebed's memoirs, *Za derzhavu obidno—* (Moscow: Gregori-Peidzh, 1995), 343–50.

134. Yeltsin, *Zapiski prezidenta,* 81.

135. See the interview with Grachev in *Nezavisimaia gazeta,* September 12, 1991, 8.

136. Dunlop, *The Rise of Russia,* 254–55.

137. As John Dunlop notes, Stepankov and Lisov's book can be viewed as the semi-official account, because they "propagate the authorized view of the Yeltsin leadership." See Dunlop, "The August Coup and Its Impact on Soviet Politics," in Kramer, ed., *The Collapse of the Soviet Union,* 497.

138. Stepankov and Lisov, *Kremlevskii zagovor,* 169.

139. Interview with Skokov on Russian Television, August 22, 1992. In his article "Avgust devyanosto-pervogo" (*Izvestia,* August 21, 1992), Popov reported that Skokov made the claim about the liaison to Grachev in a recent television interview.

140. Gavriil Popov, "Avgust devyanosto-pervogo," *Izvestiya,* August 21, 1992.

141. Ibid.

142. Galeotti, *The Age of Anxiety,* 139.

143. Yuri Burtin, "Chuzhaia vlast'," *Nezavisimaia gazeta,* December 1, 1992, 5.

144. See Knight, "The KGB, Perestroika, and the Collapse of the Soviet Union." For further details on the Soviet collapse, see Dunlop, *The Rise of Russia.*

145. Both in *Nezavisimaia gazeta,* August 19, 1992, 7.

146. *Rossiiskie vesti,* August 23, 1994, 1.

147. Sakharov himself did not live to see this alliance finally come together and contend for power, so we will never know how he would have appraised the political activity of his former allies and colleagues in terms of his own humanitarian values.

148. Mark Galeotti, *Gorbachev and His Revolution* (New York: St. Martin's, 1997), 118–19.

5. Catching up with the Past: The Political Economy of Shock Therapy

1. In chapter 4 and the conclusion of his *Chechnya: Tombstone of Russian Power* (New Haven, Conn.: Yale University Press, 1999), Anatol Lieven puts this revolutionary strategy into the context of Russian history, as we did in chapter 1, and also into that of the history of such revolutions in various countries since the eighteenth century.

2. See, for example, Aslund, *How Russia Became a Market Economy*, 7–12.

3. Jeffrey Sachs, "Why Russia Has Failed to Stabilize," in *Russia's Economic Transformation in the 1990s*, ed. Anders Aslund (Washington, D.C.: Pinter, 1997), 127–34.

4. See Peter Murrell, "What Is Shock Therapy? What Did It Do in Poland and Russia?" *Post-Soviet Affairs* 9, no. 2 (1993): 111–40.

5. On Poland (and other transitional economies), see the major work by Grzegorz Kolodko, *From Shock to Therapy: The Political Economy of Postsocialist Transformation* (New York: Oxford University Press, in press), passim—for example, chapter 4, section 3. Kolodko's analysis of Russia's reforms is broadly in tune with our own.

6. TASS, October 28, 1991.

7. Sachs, "Why Russia Has Failed to Stabilize," 12–28.

8. See Georgi Arbatov, "'Gaidarizm'—eto reaktsiya na svoi sobstvennyi marksizm," *Nezavisimaya gazeta*, March 13, 1992.

9. Grigori Yavlinsky, "Ekonomika Rossii: nasledstvo i vozmozhnosti," *Oktyabr'*, no. 7 (1995), 161.

10. Among the critics, see Marshall Goldman, *Lost Opportunity: Why Economic Reforms in Russia Have Not Worked* (New York: W. W. Norton, 1994). Among the advocates is Aslund, *How Russia Became a Market Economy*.

11. Yegor Gaidar's grandfather was a Bolshevik commissar and writer in the service of the Party. Gaidar's father, who attained the rank of admiral, was an official journalist covering military affairs, including the Soviets' "brilliant victories" in the Afghan War. See Boris Kagarlitsky, *Restoration in Russia: Why Capitalism Failed* (New York: Verso, 1995), 16.

12. Valuable insights into the pedigree of the "Chicago boys" can be found in Peter Stavrakis's essay, *State-Building in Post-Soviet Russia: The Chicago Boys and the Decline of Administrative Capacity*. Occasional Paper, no. 254 (Washington, D.C.: Kennan Institute for Advanced Russian Studies, 1993).

13. Quoted in Stefan Hedlund, *Russia's "Market" Economy: A Bad Case of Predatory Capitalism* (London: UCL Press, 1999), 112.

14. James R. Millar, "The Failure of Shock Therapy," *Problems of Post-Communism* 41, special issue (Fall 1994): 22.

15. See, for example, Vitaly Naishul', "Vysshaya i poslednyaya stadiya sotsializma," in *Pogruzhenie v tryasinu*, ed. T. A. Notkina (Moscow: Progress, 1991), 31–62, esp. 59–62, in which the Russian word for "market" is reverently capitalized.

16. Yegor Gaidar, *Gosudarstvo i evolyutsia* (Moscow: Evraziya, 1995), passim.

17. Ibid., chapter 5.

18. See, for example, his "Avansy i dolgi," *Novy mir,* June 1987.

19. *Obshchaya gazeta,* August 7–13, 1997, 11.

20. Gaidar, *Gosudarstvo i evolyutsia,* chapter 4.

21. This was the case, in particular, of such a leading figure in the "proreform" media as NTV director Igor Malashenko.

22. Andrei Sinyavsky, *The Russian Intelligentsia* (New York: Columbia University Press, 1997).

23. McFaul and Markov, *The Troubled Birth of Russian Democracy,* 138.

24. See, for example, the secret memorandum of August 1990 from CPSU secretary Vladimir Ivashko, in Stepankov and Lisov, *Kremlevskii zagovor,* 302–3. Viktor Gerashchenko has also said that while employed in the USSR State Bank in 1990–91, he was primarily engaged "in the development of the system of commercial banks"; interview with Gerashchenko in *Segodnya,* January 19, 1996.

25. For information on these processes, with special emphasis on the KGB's roles, see Konstantin Borovoi, "Demokratiya v shtatskom," *Moskovskii komsomolets,* December 24, 1998. On the "CPSU money," see Fritz Ermarth, "Seeing Russia Plain: The Russian Crisis and American Intelligence," *The National Interest,* Spring 1999, 10–11.

26. *Literaturnaya gazeta,* May 17, 1995.

27. This expressive phrase (*bolshoi khapok*) was coined by the writer and liberal politician Yuri Chernichenko.

28. The military-industrial complex that once seemed so powerful (especially to foreign observers) was easily pushed to the margins of the establishment and, after the violent demise of the parliament in 1993, was relegated to a peripheral role, almost on a par with the impoverished middle class and the anti-establishment intelligentsia.

29. In Ukraine and Moldova, the leaders of secessionist movements never obtained more than one-third of the votes in elections, while in Byelorussia and especially the Central Asian republics, the supporters of secession from the USSR consisted of small numbers of people. The Armenian All-National Movement, led by Levon Ter-Petrossian, raised the banner of national independence only in the fall of 1991, when the union institutions de facto ceased to function.

30. Goldman, *Lost Opportunity,* 23.

31. In reality, Yeltsin never took the Democratic Congress seriously and did not exploit its potential. Yet it was the DC, where the influence of radical nationalists from the republics was rather limited, that could have become the unionwide political base for democratic elements favorable to maintaining the USSR. Another testament to the shortsightedness and dithering of many politicians was the conduct of those Russian democrats, led by Nikolai Travkin, who had campaigned to preserve the Union but then boycotted the creation of the DC in January 1991.

32. Lynn Nelson and Irina Kuzes, *Radical Reform in Yeltsin's Russia: Political, Economic, and Social Dimensions* (Armonk, N.Y.: M. E. Sharpe, 1995), 96.

33. Aslund, *How Russia Became a Market Economy,* 140.

34. Interview with Andrei Nechayev, *Rossiiskie vesti,* no. 27 (November 1991), 3.

35. Aslund, *How Russia Became a Market Economy,* 142.

36. Ibid., 176.

37. Ibid., 235.

38. Yeltsin, *Zapiski prezidenta,* 255.

39. This comment is quoted by Lynn Nelson and Irina Kuzes, "Privatization and the New Business Class," in *Russia in Transition: Politics, Privatization, and Inequality,* ed. David Lane (London: Longman, 1995), 128–29.

40. Unless otherwise noted, statistics in this chapter are taken from Goskomstat's publications, which are widely quoted by international and Russian agencies—for example, *Russian Economic Trends* of the Moscow Institute for Macroeconomic Research. We have used in particular the March and April 1999 issues of this publication.

41. See *Historical Statistics of the United States,* 224–25.

42. The Great Depression of the early 1930s provides a benchmark for severe industrial contraction. The Federal Reserve's Index of Industrial Production stood at 121 in October 1929 and bottomed out at 56 in July 1932, for a decline of just under 54 percent. Shock therapy, with a 56 percent reduction, has thus been slightly worse for Russia than the Great Depression was for the United States in its impact on industrial output. See Lionel Robbins, *The Great Depression* (London: Macmillan, 1934), 214.

43. Nelson and Kuzes, *Radical Reform,* 94–95.

44. Hedlund and Sundström, "The Russian Economy after Systemic Change," 897.

45. For further discussion of figures in this section, see Stephen K. Wegren, "Rural Politics and Agrarian Reform in Russia," *Problems of Post-Communism* 43, no. 1 (January–February 1996): 23–34.

46. Stephen Wegren, "The Russian Food Problem," *Problems of Post-Communism* 47, no. 1 (January–February 2000): 38–48.

47. *Oxford Analytica Brief,* November 12, 1998.

48. See Lisa Baglione and Carol Clark, "The Challenge of Transforming Russia's Unions," *Problems of Post-Communism* 45, no. 1 (January–February 1998): 43–53.

49. Aleksandr Yanov, *Posle Yeltsina: "Veimarskaya Rossiia"* (Moscow: KRUK, 1995), 57.

50. Popov, "Avgust devyanosto pervogo."

51. Gaidar, *Gosudarstvo i evolyutsia,* 137–39; emphasis added.

52. Yeltsin, *Zapiski prezidenta,* 166.

53. Gaidar, *Gosudarstvo i evolyutsia,* 135, 143–44, 155.

54. See Peter Murrell, "Evolutionary and Radical Approaches to Economic Reform," *Economics of Planning,* no. 25 (1992): 79–95.

55. Selected and abbreviated bibliographic data on these writers follow: Petrakov (with coauthors) and Bogomolov published articles in *Nezavisimaya gazeta* on March 6 and February 7, 1992, respectively; Leonid Abalkin, *V tiskakh krizisa* (Moscow: Institut Ekonomiki, 1994); Abalkin, Shatalin, Bogomolov, Arrow, Leontief, Solow, Tobin, Klein, Intriligator, and others signed "A New Economic Policy for Russia," which appeared in English in *Economic Notes* 25, no. 3 (1996) and *Economics of Transition* 5, no. 1 (April 1997), and in Russian in *Nezavisimaya gazeta,* July 1, 1996. Articles by Piyasheva, Gel'man, and Simmons appeared in *God posle Avgusta: Gorech' i vybor,* ed. Yuri Burtin

(Moscow: Literatura i Politika, 1992); by Birman in *Europe-Asia Studies* 48, no. 5 (1996); Ickes and Ryterman in *Post-Soviet Affairs* 9, no. 3 (1993); and by McIntyre, Kotz, and Menshikov in a key Russian journal of alternative economic thinking, *Problemy teorii i praktiki upravleniya,* for example, in nos. 3 and 5 (1996). Another outlet for such thinking has been the journal *Voprosy ekonomiki.* See also the article by Stephen Moody, "Virtual Meltdown: Russian Industry and Barter in the Aftermath of the August Crash," *The Harriman Review* 11, no. 4 (1998): 15–17.

56. See, for example, Aslund, *How Russia Became a Market Economy,* 139–40.

57. "X" [George Kennan], "The Sources of Soviet Conduct," *Foreign Affairs,* July 1947.

58. "Symposium: The Slowdown in Productivity Growth," *The Journal of Economic Perspectives* 2 (1988): 3–98. For the Carter-Reagan parallels to the Brezhnev stagnation, see Barry Bluestone and Bennett Harrison, *The Deindustrialization of America* (New York: Basic Books, 1982) and *The Great U-Turn* (New York: Basic Books, 1988).

59. William Greider, *One World, Ready or Not: The Manic Logic of Global Capitalism* (New York: Simon & Schuster, 1997), 250.

60. When U.S. secretary of state George C. Marshall gave his celebrated Harvard commencement address of June 5, 1947, proposing what became the European Recovery Program, he left open the possibility of participation by the USSR and the Soviet allies in Eastern Europe. However, within a month, the Soviet leadership decided to withdraw, and Soviet foreign minister Vyacheslav Molotov staged a walkout from the tripartite conference in Paris with the United Kingdom and France. Stalin feared that acceptance of the Marshall Plan might strengthen pro-American elements in the Kremlin, such as former foreign minister Maksim Litvinov. However, Western leaders were apparently also reluctant to include the Soviet Union in the Marshall Plan. William Appleman Williams, in his *The Tragedy of American Diplomacy* (Cleveland: World Publishing Co., 1959), gives a credible account of the relief felt by Western representatives when Molotov walked out.

61. *Literaturnaya gazeta,* October 21, 1987, cited by Aslund, *Gorbachev's Struggle for Economic Reform.*

62. Voslensky, *Nomenklatura.*

63. Downs, *The Economic Theory of Democracy.*

64. Mancur Olson, *The Logic of Collective Action: Public Goods and the Theory of Groups* (Cambridge, Mass.: Harvard University Press, 1965), and *The Rise and Decline of Nations* (New Haven, Conn.: Yale University Press, 1982).

65. Mancur Olson, "The Devolution of Power in Post-Communist Societies: Therapies for Corruption, Fragmentation, and Economic Retardation," in *Russia's Stormy Path to Reform,* ed. Robert Skidelsky (London: Social Market Foundation, 1995), 9–42.

66. Ibid., 21–22.

67. See an eloquent, if sometimes self-serving description of these processes in Gaidar, *Gosudarstvo i evolyutsia,* 121–40.

68. See, for example, Timofeyev's *Chernyi rynok kak politicheskaya sistema* (Moscow: VIMO, 1993).

69. *OECD Economic Surveys, 1997–1998: Russian Federation* (Paris: Organization for Economic Cooperation and Development, 1997), 29. However, the issue of the "shadow economy" is complex and contentious. The Rand Corporation's John Ted-strom conducted a study of what he calls the "informal economy" and concluded that in December 1996, it constituted 49.8 percent of GDP, with similar figures for 1994 and 1995. See his report in *Johnson's Russia List,* June 10, 1998.

70. Valentin Pavlov, *Upushchen li shans?* (Moscow: Terra, 1995), 65.

71. Aslund, *How Russia Became a Market Economy,* 47–49.

72. A key figure in all this was Yuri Skokov, who was Yeltsin's liaison to industri-alists, the KGB, and the old nomenklatura in general.

73. Andrei Illarionov, "Popytki provedeniya politiki finansovoi stabilizatsii v SSSR i v Rossii," *Voprosy ekonomiki,* no. 7 (1995).

74. Gaidar, *Gosudarstvo i evolyutsia,* 150–51, 153.

75. *Moscow News,* no. 51 (December 20, 1987).

76. "Popov Interviewed on Political Situation," *Foreign Broadcast Information Service/Daily Report: Soviet Union,* September 19, 1991.

77. David M. Kotz and Fred Weir, *Revolution From Above: The Demise of the Soviet System* (New York: Routledge, 1997).

78. In the analysis of an astute Soviet émigré economist, this economy could be divided into "black," "gray," and "pink" markets. See the essay "Tsvetnye rynki i sovet-skaya ekonomika" in Aron Katsenelinboigen, *Sovetskaya politika i ekonomika,* vol. 3 (Benson, Vt.: Chalidze Publications, 1988), 5–83.

79. Michael McFaul and Sergei Markov conducted interviews in this period with politicians across the entire spectrum. Only the politically weak Communists and the in-effective communist-sponsored United Workers' Front (UWF) favored a socialist econ-omy. Moreover, they wanted a much more democratic form of socialism than the Soviet type. See *The Troubled Birth of Russian Democracy;* chapter 10 covers the Communists and the UWF.

80. See Sakharov, *Progress, Coexistence, and Intellectual Freedom.*

81. Goldman, *Lost Opportunity,* 76.

82. For more detail on the plans, see ibid., 64–77.

83. See Bocharov's biography in Vasilevsky and Pribylovsky, *Kto est' kto,* vol. 1, 85–86.

84. See Tatyana Koryagina, "Tenevaya ekonomika v SSSR," *Voprosy ekonomiki,* no. 3 (1990): 110–20, and her biography in Vasilevsky and Pribylovsky, *Kto est' kto,* vol. 2, 297–98.

85. Basic tenets of this program were published for the first time by Yavlinsky, Mikhailov, and Zadornov in the newspaper *Delovoi mir* on July 31, 1990. In this ver-sion, the title spoke of "400 Days." For the final version, see Yavlinsky et al., *500 Days.*

86. Allison and Yavlinsky, *Window of Opportunity.*

87. See his interview in *Trud,* February 12, 1991. See also *The Sunday Times* of London, February 19, 1991. For Pavlov's subsequent account, see Pavlov, *Upushchen li shans,* 119–25.

88. See Sterling, *Thieves' World,* part IV; and Goldman, *Lost Opportunity,* 84. Ster-ling's biography makes it impossible that her research was distorted by sympathy for

Soviet conservative forces. Especially during the 1980s, she earned the enmity of the KGB with publications tracing Bulgarian and Soviet connections with the 1981 assassination attempt against Pope John Paul II. See her *The Time of the Assassins* (New York: Simon & Schuster, 1984).

89. Sterling, *Thieves' World,* 170.

90. Ibid., 192.

91. Ibid., 189.

92. Govorukhin, *Velikaya kriminal'naya revolyutsiya,* 6.

93. Sterling, *Thieves' World,* 174–75.

94. Ibid., 176.

95. *Washington Times,* June 17, 1991, as quoted by Sterling, *Thieves' World,* 178.

96. Gibbons's long-term relationship with the Soviet intelligence services suggests the possibility that he was earmarked to play the role of an *agent provocateur* planted to implicate the Russian government (and, even more important, the democratic movement that had identified itself with the government) in a high-profile money scandal. This suspicion is supported by the fact that Kryuchkov's subordinates detained Pearson, the courier who was carrying Filshin's documents, for only a brief time and only long enough to be able to launch the scandal.

97. *Izvestiya,* February 22, 1991.

98. *The Independent* (London), November 6, 1991.

99. See Koryagina, "Tenevaya ekonomika."

100. *Izvestiya,* December 18, 1990.

101. According to Andrei Nechayev, a first-hand observer, "There was an attempt to put old personnel such as Malei and others in charge of economics, and then turn over the ministries to us and say: Well, boys, carry out the economic reform now! All this was just a few days ago. We responded: . . . carry out the reform yourselves." Yeltsin backed down. Nechayev interview, *Rossiiskie vesti,* 3.

102. The quotes from de Gaulle are from his *Memoirs of Hope: Renewal and Endeavor* (New York: Simon & Schuster, 1971), 150–51.

103. Chalmers Johnson, *MITI and the Japanese Miracle* (Stanford, Calif.: Stanford University Press, 1982), viii.

104. In Peter Reddaway's "The End of Empire" (*New York Review of Books,* November 7, 1991), the author attacked Aslund's shock therapy program for Russia.

105. Peter Reddaway, "Next From Russia: 'Shock Therapy' Collapse," *Washington Post,* July 12, 1992.

106. Jeffrey Sachs, "The Economic Transformation of Eastern Europe: The Case of Poland," *Economics of Planning* 25 (1992): 17.

107. See the discussion of Keynes's views on the danger "of sacrificing large numbers of people for a contingent end" and the greater rationality of aiming "for a smaller good with a high probability of attainment than for a larger one with a low probability of attainment," in Robert Skidelsky, *John Maynard Keynes,* vol. 2 (New York: Penguin Press, 1992), 60–62.

108. On the sad plight of small business, see Timothy Frye and Andrei Shleifer, "The Invisible Hand and the Grabbing Hand," *The American Economic Review* 97, no. 2 (May 1997): 354–58. See also the report by the leader of a small business group in *Moskovskie novosti*, October 11–18, 1998. Because of inordinate taxation, venal banks, and the Mafiya, Russia has only one-sixth as many small businesses as Poland on a per capita basis.

109. Grigori Yavlinsky, *Laissez-Faire versus Policy-Led Transformation* (Moscow: Center for Economic and Political Research, 1994), 52.

110. Keith Bush, *The Russian Economy in March 1999* (Washington, D.C.: Center for Strategic and International Studies, 1999), 5.

111. D. L'vov, V. Grebennikov, and V. Dementiev, "The Path of Russian Reforms." Working Paper WP/96/014, TsEMI (Russian Academy of Sciences, Moscow, 1996).

112. Millar, "The Failure of Shock Therapy," 23.

113. L. Taylor, "Pragmatic Gradualism: Reform Strategy for Russia" (Economic Transition Group, Moscow, August 1995).

114. Aslund, *How Russia Became a Market Economy,* 60.

115. We refer especially to leaders of Democratic Russia in the parliament, such as Yuri Afanasiev; to the groups Smena and Novaya Politika; and to the left wing of the Moscow City Council.

116. See the detailed biographies of Saburov and S. Fyodorov in Vasilevsky and Pribylovsky, *Kto est' kto,* vol. 3.

117. Aslund, *How Russia Became a Market Economy,* 96; emphasis added.

118. Jeffrey Sachs, however, was fully in tune with Gaidar's plan to destroy the middle class financially. New York–based journalist and independent scholar Anne Williamson quotes Sachs as saying in 1991, "We intend to create hyperinflation and wipe out all claims [savings]." See Williamson's "Contagion: The Betrayal of Liberty: Russia and the United States in the 1990s" (unpublished ms.), 468.

119. For the most radical programmatic statements of Volsky's Civic Union, see "Trinadtsat' punktov programmy Volskogo," *Izvestiya,* September 30, 1992; and A. Volsky, "Zashchitit' gosudarstvennuyu promyshlennost'," *Ekonomicheskaya gazeta,* November 1992.

120. Other such insurance policies were represented by, in 1995, Yuri Skokov and his Congress of Russian Communities political party, as well as by certain elements in the CPRF leadership.

121. Gaidar, *Gosudarstvo i evolyutsia,* 158–59.

122. See the text of the speech in U.S. Information Agency, press release, January 10, 1997. Berezovsky and others replied indignantly to Summers's criticism in *Nezavisimaya gazeta,* January 11, 1997.

123. See Paul Klebnikov, "Godfather of the Kremlin?" *Forbes,* December 30, 1996.

124. Nechayev interview, *Rossiiskie vesti,* 3.

125. Yeltsin, *Zapiski prezidenta,* 255.

126. See Wedel's "Clique-Run Organizations and U.S. Economic Aid: An Institutional Analysis," *Demokratizatsiya* 4, no. 4 (Fall 1996): 577.

127. See, for example, Fusae Ota, Hiroya Tanikawa, and Tasuke Otani, "Russia's Economic Reform and Japan's Industrial Policy" (MITI Research Institute, Tokyo, March 1992, mimeo.). The paper applies to Russia in an undoctrinaire way the lessons learned from the program Japan used to recover from the "drastic plunge in production from 1945–49" and "a 34 percent loss of national wealth compared with 1934." The paper's judgments and its sharp criticisms of the IMF and Kremlin policy in early 1992 hold up very well almost a decade later.

128. In May 1997, the U.S. Agency for International Development cut off grants to Harvard's Institute for International Development, which played a key role in financing the activities of Chubais's group. The official explanation for this cutoff was "activities of personal gain" on the part of two of the institute's representatives in Russia, Jonathan Hay and Andrei Shleifer. U.S. Agency for International Development, press release, May 20, 1997.

129. See the portrait of Chubais in Peter Reddaway, "Questions about Russia's 'Dream Team,'" *Post-Soviet Prospects,* September 1997.

130. To date, the most detailed study of the IMF's Russian policy appears to have been done by Hedlund in *Russia's "Market" Economy*, passim., and in his *Russia and the IMF: A Sordid Tale of Moral Hazard.* Working Paper 45 (Uppsala, Sweden: Uppsala University, Department of East European Studies, February 1999). For a succinct review, see Peter Reddaway, "The Roots of Russia's Crisis: The Soviet Legacy, IMF/G-7 Policies, and Yeltsin's Authoritarianism," *Russia Business Watch* 6, no. 3 (Fall 1998): 12–15. For valuable papers and testimony by Andrei Illarionov, Boris Kagarlitsky, David Lipton, Peter Reddaway, Yevgeny Saburov, Mark Weisbrot, Curt Weldon, and others, see *An Examination of the Russian Economic Crisis and the International Monetary Fund Aid Package,* hearing before the Subcommittee on General Oversight and Investigation of the Committee on Banking and Financial Services, U.S. House of Representatives, 105th Cong., 2d sess., September 10, 1998 (Washington, D.C.: Government Printing Office, 1998). A review of the early years by an IMF participant is Ernesto Hernandez-Cata's "Russia and the IMF: The Political Economy of Stabilization," *Problems of Post-Communism* 42, no. 3 (May–June 1995): 19–26.

131. *Sovetskaya Rossiia*, October 29, 1991.

132. Published in *Nezavisimaya gazeta,* March 3, 1992.

133. Nelson and Kuzes, *Radical Reform,* 24.

134. Aslund, *How Russia Became a Market Economy,* 187.

135. Ibid., 190.

136. Illarionov, "Popytki provedeniya politiki," 7.

137. Nelson and Kuzes, *Radical Reform,* 148.

138. *New York Times*, September 20, 1993.

139. Anders Aslund, *The Russian Economy: Where Is It Headed?* (Baltimore, Md.: Johns Hopkins University Press, 1997), 10.

140. *Washington Post*, November 12, 1997.

141. G. V. Osipov et al., eds., *Rossiya u kriticheskoi cherty* (Moscow: Respublika, 1997), 26; *Russian Economic Trends,* March 1999.

142. *Russian Economic Trends,* March 1999.

143. *El Pais* (Madrid), January 22, 1997.

144. Janine Wedel, *Collision and Collusion: The Strange Case of Western Aid to Eastern Europe, 1989–98* (New York: St. Martin's, 1998), 145–46.

145. See the full two-thousand-word text of Summers's April 11, 1997 letter, which even offered advice on how to operate tactically in Russian politics, in *Nezavisimaya gazeta,* September 26, 1997.

146. *Nezavisimaya gazeta,* December 18, 1997. See also Vitaly Tretiakov's analysis of Russia's humiliation in the December 19, 1997 edition of the newspaper, and a further analysis by T. Koshkareva and R. Narzikulov criticizing the reaction of Yeltsin's spokesman to the two letters in the December 20, 1997 edition. The spokesman, A. Livshits, is charged with hypocrisy for expressing surprised indignation at the directive tone of the letters, given that the Summers letter had been even more directive, and that Summers did not even have relevant standing as head of the aid-providing IMF or World Bank. The Kirienko-signed report to the IMF was subjected to withering criticism by Yuliya Kalinina, who printed extracts from its list of servile pledges to take measures A and B by April 15, C and D by April 19, and so forth. Her skeptical commentary about the pledges' unlikely fulfillment and the humiliation to Russia of making phony promises to obtain yet another loan—which, like previous loans extracted through similarly empty promises from Chubais, would not achieve its goals—is a polemical tour de force. Yuliya Kalinina, "Sufler dlya prem'era: El'tsinu i Kirienko diktuyut iz-za granitsy," *Moskovskii komsomolets,* April 28, 1998.

147. B. Fyodorov, "Macroeconomic Policy and Stabilization in Russia," in Aslund, ed., *Russia's Economic Transformation in the 1990s,* 119.

148. Ibid., 147.

149. Apart from the previously mentioned Shleifer and Hay, Wedel discusses in this connection Anders Aslund, who had "significant" investments according to the head of the Russian Interior Ministry's Department for Organized Crime, and also advisers to Harvard University's endowment fund. See Wedel, *Collision and Collusion,* 146–49, 152–53, and 159.

150. "Evangelie ot Petra" ("The Gospel According to Peter"), *Kommersant-Daily,* January 27, 1999. See also the intensely approving commentary on this article by Vitaly Tretiakov, *Nezavisimaya gazeta,* January 28, 1999.

151. Interview with Kagalovsky in John Lloyd, "The Russian Devolution," *The New York Times Magazine,* August 15, 1999, 52.

152. Chubais interview by Aleksandr Budberg, *Moskovskii komsomolets,* September 23, 1998.

153. On, respectively, October 2, November 6, and November 9. An expanded version of Talbott's speech appeared in *The Economist,* November 20, 1998. The fourth architect of U.S. policy, Vice President Gore, made no speech on the subject.

154. Lloyd, "The Russian Devolution," 38–39. We should note also that parts of the U.S. government's bureaucracy were anxious to show that they had opposed elements, at least, of government policy and therefore did not deserve blame for the collapse of the country's Russia policy; see p. 52 of the article. See also Ermarth, "Seeing Russia Plain" and James Risen, "Gore Rejected CIA Evidence of Russian Corruption," *New York Times,* November 23, 1998, for charges from the intelligence community that the U.S.

administration was too partisan regarding support of Yeltsin; wanted to hear only good news out of Russia; and deliberately turned a blind eye to the corruption of Russia's leaders, notably that of Chernomyrdin.

155. Aslund, *How Russia Became a Market Economy,* 83.

156. Anders Aslund, "Russia's Collapse," *Foreign Affairs*, September–October 1999, 64–65. Sachs's explanation is very similar; see Lloyd, "The Russian Devolution," 37–38.

157. Here is one example of Aslund's hero-worship: "Anatoly Chubais is an amazing politician who has smoothly done everything right, to an extent that rarely happens. He has combined ideological principles with effective execution of his ideas." Aslund, *How Russia Became a Market Economy,* 315.

158. As this book was in its final stages, reports appeared of a major publication of the United Nations Development Program, written by Anton Kruiderink, which concludes that economic reform and democracy in the formerly communist East have, in most countries, failed badly and produced widespread misery. See Michael Binyon, "Maimed by the Market," *The Times* of London, August 23, 1999.

159. See interview with Peter Reddaway in *Kommersant Daily,* December 3, 1998.

160. "Members' Briefing with Stanley Fischer," *Russia Business Watch* 6, no. 4 (Winter 1998–99): 7–9.

161. On Talbott, see Peter Reddaway, "Visit to a Maelstrom," *New York Times,* January 10, 1994. Reddaway argues that the U.S. administration "has often spoken as if it were making Russia's domestic policies jointly with the Russian government—in some subcommittee of the U.S. Cabinet."

162. Lloyd, "The Russian Devolution," 39.

163. Ibid., 39.

164. Joseph Stiglitz, "Development Based on Participation—A Strategy for Transforming Societies," *Transition* 9, no. 6 (December 1998): 2.

165. Andrei Shleifer and Robert Vishny, *The Grabbing Hand: Government Pathologies and Their Cures* (Cambridge, Mass.: Harvard University Press, 1998); and Richard Layard and John Parker, *The Coming Boom in Russia* (New York: The Free Press, 1996).

166. Joseph Stiglitz, "Whither Reform?: Ten Years of the Transition" (The World Bank, Washington, D.C., April 1999), 1–2. This paper (available on the World Bank's Web site at www.worldbank.org/knowledge/chiefecon) is slated to appear in *Proceedings of the 1999 Annual Bank Conference on Development Economics* (Washington, D.C.: World Bank, forthcoming). The present authors obtained a copy of the paper as this book neared completion. Hence, only a few of its major themes are discussed.

167. The latest responsible estimate of capital flight known to us relates to the five years between 1993 and 1998. Fitch IBCA, the international credit rating agency, concludes that in this period, U.S. $136 billion left Russia. See John Thornhill and Charles Clover, "Russia: The Robbery of Nations," *Financial Times* (London), August 21, 1999.

168. For the above two paragraphs, see Stiglitz, "Whither Reform ?," 3–5.

169. *Washington Post*, May 12, 1997.

170. Gaidar, *Gosudarstvo i evolyutsia,* 189.

171. Yuri Boldyrev, "Oba khuzhe!" *Stolitsa,* no. 20 (May 1993). For an academic treatment of corruption and why it harms economic development, see Andrei Shleifer and Robert Vishny, "Corruption," *The Quarterly Journal of Economics* (August 1993): 599–617. The authors draw examples from contemporary Russia.

172. *Washington Post,* October 2, 1997.

173. Center for Strategic and International Studies, *Russian Organized Crime.*

174. Gaidar, *Gosudarstvo i evolyutsia,* esp. chapter 1; and chapter 4, section 7.

175. For a profound discussion of the rise and fall of the middle class, see the essay by the late Andrei Fadin, "Modernizatsiya cherez katastrofu?" in *Inoe: Khrestomatiya novogo rossiiskogo samosoznaniya,* vol. 1, ed. Sergei Chernyshov (Moscow: Argus, 1995), 322–42.

6. YELTSIN AND THE OPPOSITION: THE ART OF CO-OPTATION AND MARGINALIZATION 1991–1993

1. *Washington Post,* November 13, 1996, citing figures from the All-Union Center for the Study of Public Opinion (VTsIOM).

2. See the series of polls commissioned by the research department of the U.S. Information Agency from the top Russian polling organizations. Also, in the seventh year of Yeltsin's regime, a rank-and-file official in the president's administration cold-bloodedly admitted—as if pronouncing the results of a laboratory science experiment—that in Russia "a civil war is smoldering—in non-violent, quasi-constitutional forms"; *Kommersant,* July 15, 1997, 36.

3. Zhirinovsky's LDP is an extreme case of a government-created opposition, as we showed in chapter 3. See also Aleksandr Zhilin, "Vladimir Zhirinovsky: A Scarecrow in Yeltsin's Garden?" *Prism,* November 3, 1995, 10–11.

4. See Joan Barth Urban and Valery D. Solovei, *Russia's Communists at the Crossroads* (Boulder, Colo.: Westview, 1997); and Robert Otto, "Gennadii Ziuganov: The Reluctant Candidate," *Problems of Post-Communism* 46, no. 5 (September–October 1999).

5. See Schumpeter, *Capitalism, Socialism, and Democracy.*

6. For a good overview of these changes, see Olga Kryshtanovskaya and Stephen White, "From Soviet Nomenklatura to Russian Elite," *Europe-Asia Studies* 48, no. 5 (July 1996): 711–34.

7. See Michels, *Political Parties.*

8. For a good overview of the "deputies' opposition," see Boris Kagarlitsky, *Square Wheels: How Russian Democracy Got Derailed* (New York: Monthly Review Press, 1994) and Andrei Kol'ev, *Myatezh Nomenklatury* (Moscow: Intellekt, 1995).

9. On this election, see Colton, *Moscow,* 604–30.

10. On this election, see ibid., 630; and on the groups that backed Popov and Stankevich, see ibid., 610–18.

11. Ibid., 632.

12. For the tragicomic sequence to the impasse, see ibid., 635.

13. For more on the Komissarov affair, see Kol'ev, *Myatezh Nomenklatury*, 257–61.

14. For a view of this episode that is less critical of Popov, see Colton, *Moscow,* 633 and 668.

15. *Demokraticheskaya gazeta*, September 1991.

16. On this whole episode, see Colton, *Moscow,* 661–68.

17. On this party, see chapter 4 in McFaul and Markov, *The Troubled Birth of Russian Democracy.*

18. On Democratic Russia for the period through 1991, see ibid., chapter 8. For a fuller assessment, see Yitzhak Brudny, "The Dynamics of 'Democratic Russia', 1990–1993," *Post-Soviet Affairs,* no. 2 (1993): 141–70.

19. See McFaul and Markov, *The Troubled Birth of Russian Democracy,* chapter 13.

20. See Brudny, "The Dynamics of 'Democratic Russia,'" 155.

21. See Gefter's article "Est' li vykod?" in the Moscow *samizdat* journal *Poiski,* no. 1 (1978): 215–53, and also his major work, *Iz tekh i etikh let.*

22. In American sociopolitical thought, Harvard philosopher Robert Putnam has developed similar views in his *Making Democracy Work.*

23. Afanasiev edited and contributed to the well-known anthology of topical articles by Russian democrats, *Inogo ne dano* (Moscow: Progress, 1988). He also wrote two articles in Burtin, ed., *God posle Avgusta,* a similar anthology in which most of the twenty-seven authors expressed deep concern at the direction of events in early 1992.

24. For Batkin's biography, see Vasilevsky and Pribylovsky, *Kto est' kto,* vol. 1, 64–65.

25. Ibid., 47.

26. See Vasilevsky and Pribylovsky, *Kto est' kto,* vol. 3, 488.

27. See Brudny, "The Dynamics of 'Democratic Russia,'" 157–58.

28. Predictably, the Committees for Reforms failed in their tasks. Rejected by the majority of democratic activists, they were effectively stillborn from the start. The stratification and polarization of the middle class, after the beginning of the reforms, into strong supporters of the regime and its radical opponents—with the doomed and passive majority neutral—made the task of winning over the "undecided" to the side of the shock therapists impossible.

29. Personal communication to Glinski. Afanasiev singled out Bokser and Ponomarev. See Vasilevsky and Pribylovsky, *Kto est' kto,* vol. 1, 47.

30. See the text in *Megalopolis-Ekspress,* January 30, 1992.

31. March 17, 1992, 2.

32. The definitive departure from DR of Salye and her supporters did not occur until November. See *Nezavisimaya gazeta,* November 17, 1992.

33. Regarding government funding of Russia's Choice, see the interview with Yuri Boldyrev in *Izvestiya,* November 4, 1994. Boldyrev recounts that while he was working as Yeltsin's chief corruption fighter, he discovered through a complex investigation that democratic ministers had illegally given government money in 1992 to the Association of Peasant Holdings and Cooperatives, which later passed the funds on to Russia's

Choice; Yeltsin ignored Boldyrev's report. On DR's subsequent activities in 1992–93, see Brudny, "The Dynamics of 'Democratic Russia.'"

34. This process is traced in some detail by Michael McFaul in "Russia's Choice: The Perils of Revolutionary Democracy," in *Growing Pains: Russian Democracy and the Election of 1993*, ed. Timothy Colton and Jerry Hough (Washington, D.C.: Brookings Institution Press, 1998), 116–19.

35. Sources on RAU's activities include the articles by Ye. Krasnikov, "Tainyi sovetnik mnogikh vozhdei," *Moscow News,* July 27–August 3, 1997; and "Podberezkin: Communist and/or Nationalist," *Moscow News,* August 7–13, 1997. See also Podberezkin's interview in *Nezavisimaya gazeta,* December 28, 1996. For a good look at RAU's public self-image, see appendixes 5 and 6 in its publication (introduced and edited by Podberezkin) *Rossiya segodnya: Real'nyi shans* (Moscow: RAU Korporatsiya, 1994), 506–13.

36. Specifically, Podberezkin's wife is the daughter of Konstantin Rusakov, a secretary of the CPSU Central Committee. Dmitri Rogozin's relative, Georgi Rogozin, was a general in the state security service and later was a close colleague of Yeltsin's bodyguard, Aleksandr Korzhakov, who was the power behind Russia's throne in 1993–96. He was widely known for his research in the field of mysticism and the use of parapsychology as a means of social and political manipulation.

37. Yevgeny Krasnikov in *Nezavisimaya gazeta,* November 18, 1994.

38. Podberezkin, ed., *Rossiya segodnya,* 508–9.

39. See Sergei Parkhomenko, "Merlin's Tower," *Moscow News,* April 28–May 4, 1995. Rogozin interview with Peter Reddaway and Catherine Dale, Moscow, October 21, 1994.

40. *Obozrevatel'* published some of Rutskoi's writings and, in 1994, put out a five-hundred-page special issue consisting entirely of his work.

41. See Astafiev's biography in Vasilevsky and Pribylovsky, *Kto est' kto*, vol. 1, 43–45.

42. Paradoxically, the registration of the "Democratic Russia" movement as a legal political entity marked the beginning of the end for a genuine people's democratic movement—the movement described in chapter 3.

43. It is an irony of history that one of the intellectual creators of the new Russian identity, Mikhail Astafiev, won his mandate to represent Moscow's Dzerzhinsky district while running against the "national-imperialist" Stanislav Kunyayev, with whom he later joined forces in the National Salvation Front.

44. See for example *Dvizheniye "Demokraticheskaya Rossiya,"* information bulletin, special edition no. 1 (1991).

45. Personal communication to Dmitri Glinski.

46. See *Demokraticheskaya Rossiya*, no. 33 (1991), 1.

47. See *DR-Press*, no. 129 (November 10, 1991).

48. For useful analyses of this whole phenomenon, see Gordon Hahn, "Opposition Politics in Russia," *Europe-Asia Studies* 46, no. 2 (1994): 305–35; and Michael McFaul, "Russian Centrism and Revolutionary Transitions," *Post-Soviet Affairs* 9, no. 3 (1993): 196–222.

49. Volsky founded the Russian Union of Industrialists and Businessmen under a slightly different name in June 1991. Later, Mikhail Poltoranin, Yeltsin's press minister, claimed he had read documents found in the CPSU archives showing that it was founded on the Party's initiative and with Party money. See the interview with Poltoranin in *Literaturnaya gazeta*, November 25, 1992, 10.

50. Walter Connor, *Tattered Banners: Labor, Conflict, and Corporatism in Post-communist Russia* (Boulder, Colo.: Westview, 1996), especially chapters 2 and 3.

51. As Adam Przeworski says about transitional governments in Latin America and southern Europe, "They promise consultation, and shock the eventual partners with decrees; they pass decrees, and hope for consensus." Przeworski, *Democracy and the Market* (New York: Cambridge University Press, 1991), 186.

52. Connor, *Tattered Banners,* 11–14, 74.

53. Ibid., 22. The quotations are from Przeworski, *Democracy and the Market,* 180, 182.

54. Urban, Igrunov, and Mitrokhin, *The Rebirth of Politics in Russia,* 273–74.

55. Interview in *Moscow News,* April 5–11, 1992.

56. *Komsomol'skaya pravda,* May 27, 1992.

57. See Peter Stavrakis's analysis of how the fragmentation of policymaking in this field made any coherent policies impossible: "Government Bureaucracies: Transition or Disintegration?" *RFE/RL Research Report* 2, no. 20 (May 1993): 26–33. He illustrates persuasively Samuel Huntington's argument that without coherently operating state institutions, political decay is inevitable.

58. Connor, *Tattered Banners,* 44–46.

59. Urban, Igrunov, and Mitrokhin, *The Rebirth of Politics in Russia,* 274–75.

60. McFaul, "Russian Centrism and Revolutionary Transitions," 207.

61. Connor, *Tattered Banners,* 48. The quotation is from *Rabochaya tribuna,* July 10, 1992.

62. Connor, *Tattered Banners,* 169–70. The quotation is from Philippe Schmitter, "Still the Century of Corporatism?" *Review of Politics* 36, no. 1 (1974): 123.

63. Urban, Igrunov, and Mitrokhin, *The Rebirth of Politics in Russia,* 274.

64. McFaul, "Russian Centrism and Revolutionary Transitions," 206.

65. *Radio Liberty Daily Report*, November 13, 1992, 2.

66. McFaul, "Russian Centrism and Revolutionary Transitions," 209, summarizing Shumeiko's interview in *Pravda,* October 29, 1992.

67. Interfax, October 30, 1992.

68. Interfax, November 3, 1992.

69. For a vivid description of this meeting, see Vyacheslav Kostikov, *Roman s prezidentom* (Moscow: Vagrius, 1997), 136–39.

70. ITAR-TASS, November 14, 1992; and McFaul "Russian Centrism and Revolutionary Transitions," 207. Those fired were Valery Tishkov, Fedor Shelov-Kovedyayev, and Galina Starovoitova.

71. *Izvestiya,* November 23, 1992; and *Nezavisimaya gazeta,* November 24, 1992.

72. ITAR-TASS, November 24, 25, and 26, 1992.

73. McFaul, "Russian Centrism and Revolutionary Transitions," 206–7.

74. See the detailed analysis of the genesis of this document, and of the underlying differences between the Civic Union and the government, in Michael Ellman, "The Economic Program of the Civic Union," *RFE/RL Research Report* 2, no. 11 (March 1993): 34–45. Remarkably, Aslund does not discuss this notable episode in his *How Russia Became a Market Economy.*

75. On this alarm, see Kostikov, *Roman s prezidentom,* 139, 141. Kostikov also reports that a memo written by Yeltsin adviser Sergei Stankevich at this time, advocating a strategic change of course, "created an impression of panic in the family of democrats" (pp. 135–36).

76. ITAR-TASS November 27, 1992.

77. ITAR-TASS November 30, 1992. On this complex case, which helped to keep political passions on the boil in 1992, see Yuri Feofanov, "Russia's Nuremberg" in his and Donald Barry's *Politics and Justice in Russia,* (Armonk, N.Y.: M. E. Sharpe, 1996), chapter 18.

78. On Bush's influence, see Yeltsin, *Zapiski prezidenta,* 299.

79. See his remarkably frank account in ibid., 292–93. Evidently, Yeltsin was so shaken that the next day he made a major blunder through careless preparation. He appealed to the Russian people over the Congress's head, and then called for those deputies who supported him to walk out and paralyze the CPD's work. Only a small percentage walked out. See Kostikov, *Roman s prezidentom,* 149–50.

80. On this episode, Yeltsin has a vivid and seemingly accurate account in *Zapiski prezidenta,* 296–99.

81. Ellman, "The Economic Program of the Civic Union," 44.

82. See Kostikov, *Roman s prezidentom,* 152–53.

83. For a systematic elaboration of this ideology in programmatic form, see Podberezkin, ed., *Rossiya segodnya.*

84. For details on this activity by Rogozin and Zyuganov, see their entries in Vasilevsky and Pribylovsky, *Kto est' kto,* vols. 3 and 2, respectively. Not listed in Rogozin's entry is a group he cofounded in 1994, the Union of the Peoples of Russia.

85. Ibid., vol. 3, 457.

86. On Sterligov and the Assembly, see Nikolai Kotenko, *Aleksandr Sterligov* (Moscow: Paleya, 1992), and Sterligov's *Opal'nyi general svidetel'stvuet* (Moscow: Paleya, 1992).

87. For a good analysis of the Front between fall 1992 and September 1993, see Wendy Slater, "Russia's National Salvation Front 'On the Offensive,'" *RFE/RL Research Report* 2, no. 38 (September 1993): 1–16.

88. On the revival of the communists and the founding of the CPRF, see Urban and Solovei, *Russia's Communists,* chapters 1 and 2.

89. Krasnikov, *Nezavisimaya gazeta.*

90. Vladimir Pribylovsky quoted in Slater, "Russia's National Salvation Front," 6.

91. See the table in Archie Brown, "The October Crisis of 1993," *Post-Soviet Affairs* 3 (1993): 189.

92. For detailed regional results of the referendum and a short commentary, see Michael McFaul and Nikolai Petrov, eds., *The Political Almanac of Russia 1997,* Russian ed., vol. 1, (Moscow: Carnegie Moscow Center, 1998), 177–78 and 382–84.

93. Regarding the CPD's actions, it amended the constitution no fewer than 320 times between April 1992 and March 1993; see Urban, Igrunov, and Mitrokhin, *The Rebirth of Politics in Russia,* 278. On all these episodes see, for example, Loewenhardt, *The Reincarnation of Russia,* 133–35.

94. In January 1993, for example, Volsky touted an opinion poll claiming that Civic Union would win 22 percent of the votes in the next election; the democrats, 4 percent; and the communists, 3 percent. Eleven months later, after Yeltsin's coup had upset the whole political system, Civic Union got 2 percent of the vote; Travkin's party, 5.8 percent; and Rutskoi's party was banned. See "News Brief," p.7, supplement to *RFE/RL Research Report* 2, no. 3 (January 1993).

95. In a detailed ROMIR poll of October 1992 comparing opinions about him and Yeltsin, positive evaluations of Rutskoi outnumbered negative ones by 39 percent to 15 percent, while the figures for Yeltsin were 36 percent and 37 percent. See Amy Corning, "How Russians View Yeltsin and Rutskoi," *RFE/RL Research Report* 2, no. 12 (March 1993): 57–59.

96. McFaul and Petrov, eds., *The Political Almanac of Russia 1997,* 390.

97. In grappling with the elusive nature of Russian conservatism, Andreas Umland divided the anti-Yeltsin opposition into the "conventional" and "unconventional" right; see his "Vladimir Zhirinovsky." It is revealing that virtually all parties and groups Umland categorized as part of the "conventional right" (such as the Russian Christian Democratic Movement of Viktor Aksiuchits) have turned out to be ephemeral and have left the stage, while all the more prominent and durable conservative leaders—Zhirinovsky, Zyuganov, Lebed—fall into the "unconventional right." To date, every attempt to transplant the Western type of conservatism (understood as respect for tradition and patriotism, preference for the private sector, and limited government) to Russian soil has been artificial and has scored no electoral success.

98. A useful analysis of the CPRF's left-wing conservatism has been contributed by Boris Kapustin, "Levyi konservatizm KPRF," *Nezavisimaya gazeta,* March 5, 1996.

99. John Dunlop, *The Faces of Contemporary Russian Nationalism* (Princeton, N.J.: Princeton University Press, 1983), 262; and "The Return of Russian Nationalism," *Journal of Democracy,* Summer 1990. Although these and similar currents had significant intellectual influence on the development of the anti-Yeltsin opposition during the 1990s, their political role remained marginal and was diluted in broader coalitions, such as Yabloko and Baburin's party.

100. Dunlop, "The Contemporary Russian Nationalist Spectrum," 7.

101. Alexander Yanov, *The Russian New Right: Right-Wing Ideologies in the Contemporary USSR.* Research series no. 35 (Berkeley: University of California, Berkeley, Institute of International Studies, 1978), 161–62; and *The Russian Challenge and the Year 2000* (New York: Oxford University Press, 1987), 264–89.

102. Alexander Yanov, "Russian Nationalism as the Ideology of Counter-reform," *Radio Liberty Research Bulletin,* December 19, 1988, 46.

103. George Breslauer, as quoted in Yanov, *The Russian New Right,* 74; Walter Laqueur, *Black Hundred: The Rise of the Extreme Right in Russia* (New York: Harper-Collins, 1993), 165–66.

104. See especially Richard Löwenthal in Yanov, *The Russian New Right,* xiii.

105. On all this, see Peter Reddaway, *Soviet Policies on Dissent and Emigration: The Radical Change of Course since 1979.* Occasional Paper no. 192 (Washington, D.C.: Kennan Institute for Advanced Russian Studies, 1984); and "Dissent in the Soviet Union," *Problems of Communism* 32, no. 6 (November–December 1983): 1–15.

106. In the debate on this topic between Yanov and his opponents, Western scholars' negation of history, which allegedly becomes irrelevant in the face of a radical political change (a view characteristic of mainstream American social science) was countered by the Russians' insistent perception of latent continuity in social change, which mitigates any superficial change. The latter outlook is endemic to the Russian mentality, in both its "Westernizer" and "Slavophile" versions. If the Western view of development tends to emphasize stages, the Russian perception of history is embodied in circular movement—which, however, always contains the possibility of a will-driven messianic breakthrough into the "ultimate future," be it the Orthodox Tsardom of God, a worldwide socialist revolution, or the universal triumph of liberal democracy to which Yanov and his fellow thinkers aspired.

107. Urban and Solovei, *Russia's Communists,* 191–92, for example.

108. All these points are supported by the recent sociological findings of A. G. Zdravomyslov, "Etnopoliticheskie protsessy i dinamika natsional'nogo samosoznaniya rossiyan," *Sotsiologicheskie issledovaniya,* no. 12 (1996): 23–32.

109. To see these self-definitions as mutually exclusive would be another extreme: an ethnic Russian nationalist could well be—or not be—a Soviet patriot at the same time. We argue here that these nationalisms were distinct and potentially contradictory, but not, in practice, ideologically incompatible.

110. See Alain Besançon, "Nationalism and Bolshevism in the USSR," in *The Last Empire,* ed. Robert Conquest (Stanford, Calif.: Hoover Institution Press, 1986), 11.

111. See V. D. Solovei, "Sovremennyi russkii natsionalizm: ideino-politicheskaya klassifikatsiya" (Contemporary Russian Nationalism: An Ideological-Political Classification), *Obshchestvennye nauki i sovremennost',* no. 2 (1992); and "Evolyutsiya sovremennogo russkogo natsionalizma."

112. For an alternative approach, see Tim McDaniel, *The Agony of the Russian Idea* (Princeton, N.J.: Princeton University Press, 1996).

113. For a thorough report on achievements in this recently booming field, see Reznik, *The Nazification of Russia.* After Yegor Gaidar ignominiously lost his court case to Zhirinovsky (whom he had branded a fascist), the wave of antifascist activities somewhat receded.

114. In 1919, Benito Mussolini founded his *Fasci di combattimento,* which emerged as a force on the Italian scene as strikebreakers during the sit-down strikes of August–September 1920, and then captured world attention with the October 1922 March on Rome.

115. Roger Griffin, *The Nature of Fascism* (New York: Routledge, 1993), 38.

116. Andreas Umland faced precisely this problem when he tried to apply Griffin's definition in his analysis of what he saw as fascistic elements in the activities of

Vladimir Zhirinovsky. As Umland rightly observed, the theme of "Russia's rebirth," in various modulations, was central to the ideology of many Russian democrats of the early 1990s and shaped the ideological profile of Boris Yeltsin; see Umland, "Vladimir Zhirinovsky," 170. Umland's witty attempt to draw a semantic distinction between "rebirth" and "new birth" does not help to rescue the palingenetic criterion as a unique marker of fascism.

117. *Encyclopedia Britannica*, 15th ed., s.v. "fascism."

118. In the Russian humanistic tradition, the most profound juxtaposition of Christianity and modern paganism is located in the first pages of Boris Pasternak's *Doctor Zhivago*.

119. See, for example, Yuliya Latynina, "Caucasians are Real Victims of Discrimination," *Moscow News,* November 17, 1998. Also, John Dunlop regards Russian fascism as potentially a strong force; see his "Barkashov and the Russian Power Ministries, 1994–2000" (2000).

120. One authoritative survey showed that only 8 percent of respondents blamed Jews for the economic problems of the country; Centre for the Study of Public Policy/ Paul Lazarsfeld Society, New Russia Barometer III, 1994, as quoted in White, Rose, and McAllister, *How Russia Votes*, 55.

121. Naishul', for example, wrote that the laws of the market are "as independent of our will as the laws of Newton in physics." Naishul', "Vysshaya i poslednyaya stadiya sotsializma," 59.

122. *Izvestiya,* April 23, 1997.

7. Tanks as the Vehicle of Reform: The 1993 Coup and the Imposition of the New Order

1. *New York Times,* March 13, 1993.

2. *Washington Post,* October 1, 1993.

3. *New York Times,* March 14, 1993.

4. *Die Zeit,* September 24, 1993. German press quotations in this chapter are drawn from Willi Steinbacher, *Boris Jeltzin und seine Aera (aus der Sicht der Presse in den Jahren 1993, 1994, und Anfang 1995)* (Frankfurt am Main: H.-A. Herchen Verlag, 1995).

5. See Yeltsin, *Zapiski prezidenta,* 15.

6. For an overview of monarchism in the late USSR and independent Russia, see Ann Robertson, "Kings, Queens, Tsars, and Commissars," *Demokratizatsiya* 4, no. 2 (Spring 1996): 201–22.

7. For Sobchak's views on monarchy, see his *Zhila-byla kommunisticheskaya partiya* (St. Petersburg: Lenizdat, 1995), 220–23.

8. *Pravda,* July 3, 1993.

9. In most respects, the Russian Federation's regions and ethnically designated republics had the same rights and status. However, the republics had some important extra rights—most notably, the fact that Yeltsin could not dismiss their presidents, whereas he could, until 1996, dismiss their counterparts in the regions, the governors.

10. Lipset, *Political Man*, chapter 3.

11. Yeltsin, *Zapiski prezidenta,* 287.

12. *New York Times*, February 4, 1993.

13. *New York Times*, September 22, 1994.

14. *U.S. News and World Report*, October 3, 1994.

15. For background, see Raymond L. Garthoff, "The United States and the New Russia: The First Five Years," *Current History*, October 1997.

16. *New York Times*, February 4, 1993.

17. Jerry F. Hough, "America's Russia Policy: The Triumph of Neglect," *Current History*, October 1994, 308.

18. *New York Times*, October 5, 1993.

19. *New York Times*, February 8, 1993.

20. Hough, "America's Russia Policy," 308–9.

21. Ibid., 311.

22. On Nixon's trip, see his article, "Moscow, March 1994: Chaos and Hope," *New York Times,* March 25, 1994.

23. *Krasnaya zvezda,* February 22, 1993.

24. Vasilevsky and Pribylovsky, *Kto est' kto,* vol. 1, 199.

25. *New York Times*, March 13, 1993.

26. Ibid.

27. Remnick, *Lenin's Tomb,* 48.

28. *New York Times*, March 14, 1993.

29. *New York Times*, August 29, 1993.

30. *New York Times*, March 14, 1993.

31. *New York Times*, March 12, 1993. On March 10, the *Financial Times* (London) had carried a similar report.

32. *New York Times*, March 12, 1993.

33. *New York Times*, March 13, 1993.

34. Ibid.

35. *New York Times*, March 22, 1993.

36. *New York Times*, March 13, 1993.

37. *New York Times*, March 14, 1993.

38. Ibid.

39. *New York Times*, March 21, 1993.

40. Ibid.

41. Ibid.

42. *Washington Post,* March 23, 1993.

43. *New York Times*, March 25, 1993.

44. For a detailed analysis of this complex episode, see Julia Wishnevsky, "Corruption Allegations Undermine Russia's Leaders," *RFE/RL Research Report* 37 (September 1993): 16–22. See also the partisan but highly revealing series of articles by

Iona Andronov, "O chem molchit uznik 'Krestov,'" *Zavtra*, nos. 13–15 (March–April 1996), and the lengthy interview given by Vladimir Shumeiko (in tacit response to Andronov) in *Sobesednik*, no. 5 (May 1996).

45. Interview in *Literaturnaya gazeta*, June 23, 1993.

46. On this episode, see Sterling, *Thieves' World*, 212–15.

47. Quoted in *Moskovskiye novosti*, August 15, 1993, 9. Similar information is found in ibid.

48. An abbreviated text of the report was published in *Rossiiskaya gazeta*, June 26, 1993. See also *Pravda*, June 25, 1993.

49. *Izvestiya*, June 26, 1993. For the deputies' speeches, see *Pravda*, June 26, 1993, and *Rossiiskaya gazeta*, June 29, 1993.

50. Interview in *Moskovskii komsomolets*, August 10, 1993.

51. *Nezavisimaya gazeta*, July 28, 1993.

52. *Pravda*, July 29, 1993.

53. *Obshchaya gazeta*, August 20–26, 1993.

54. Ibid.

55. *Delovoi mir,* September 16, 1993.

56. Lobov's economic strategy had much in common with the MITI approach. See Ota et al., "Russia's Economic Reform and Japan's Industrial Policy."

57. *Rossiya*, June 23–29, 1993.

58. On August 30, Yeltsin issued the directive "On the Simultaneous Indexation of Privatization Checks and Capital Stock," which apparently embodied Lobov's highly revisionist measures for sharply slowing the pace of privatization. However, on September 11, Yeltsin rescinded the directive. For details on this interesting episode, see *Kommersant-Daily,* September 15, 1993; and *RFE/RL Daily Report,* September 16, 1993.

59. See the article by Irina Demchenko in *Izvestiya,* September 14, 1993, which recounted why Yeltsin opted against Lobov's views and which anticipated his removal on September 18.

60. For a pro-Kremlin analysis of the assembly by a participant, see Sobchak *Zhila-byla,* chapter 4.

61. It is quite possible that Zhirinovsky's party was being subsidized by Yeltsin's government, as it had been by Gorbachev's. Certainly it already had plenty of money for foreign travel and numerous publications and meetings.

62. *Rossiiskie vesti*, June 30, 1993.

63. *Rossiiskie vesti,* September 15, 1993.

64. *Rossiiskaya gazeta*, September 17, 1993.

65. *Rossiiskie vesti*, September 15, 1993.

66. *Izvestiya*, September 21, 1993.

67. Reuters, September 17, 1993.

68. *Izvestiya*, September 21, 1993.

69. See *Sovetskaya Rossiya* and *Izvestiya*, July 27, and *Komsomol'skaya pravda,* September 7, 1993.

70. Russian Television program *Vesti,* July 21, 1993, cited by Layard and Parker, *The Coming Boom in Russia,* 189.

71. *Zapiski prezidenta,* 354.

72. Nelson and Kuzes, *Radical Reform,* 148.

73. *New York Times,* September 20, 1993.

74. William Safire, "Yeltsin Planned His Coup," *New York Times,* October 7, 1993.

75. Barannikov evidently had collected compromising material on both Yeltsin's entourage and his opponents. See Yeltsin, *Zapiski prezidenta,* 327–38; Oleg Poptsov, *Khronika vremen Tsarya Borisa* (Berlin: Edition Q Verlags-GmbH, 1995), 346–47 and 487–88; and, for an opposition view, A. Baranov and A. Lyasko, "Spisok seyushchii smert'," *Komsomol'skaya pravda,* August 25, 1995.

76. Remnick, *Lenin's Tomb,* 57–58.

77. *New York Times,* September 22, 1993.

78. *New York Times,* September 18, 1993.

79. Nelson and Kuzes, *Radical Reform,* 148.

80. *New York Times,* September 20, 1993.

81. Hough, "America's Russia Policy," 311; emphasis added.

82. *New York Times,* September 20, 1993.

83. There is still no major analytical study of the extraordinarily complex, often murky events from September 21 through October 4 in English, Russian, or, it seems, any other language. The collections of documents and analysis that we have found most helpful in writing this section are Postfactum Information Agency's compilation *Politicheskii krizis v Rossii, sentyabr'–oktyabr' 1993* (Moscow: Postfactum, 1993); A. Buzgalin and A. Kolganov, *Krovavyi oktyabr' v Moskve,* special issue of *Intervzglyad* (1994); A. P. Surkov, ed., *Moskva. Osen'-93: Khronika protivostoyaniya* (Moscow: Respublika, 1994); Veronika Kutsyllo, *Zapiski iz Belogo Doma, 21 sentyabrya–4 oktyabrya* (Moscow: Kommersant, 1993); R. Khasbulatov, *Velikaya Rossiiskaya tragediya* (Moscow: TOO SIMS, 1994); and Ivan Ivanov (pseud.), *Anafema: Khronika gosudarstvennogo perevorota: zapiski razvedchika* (St. Petersburg: Paleya, 1995). Aleksandr Rutskoi, *Krovavaya osen': Dnevnik sobytii* (St. Petersburg: n.p., 1995) is mostly derivative from the above works.

84. Remnick, *Lenin's Tomb,* 61.

85. See the *New York Times,* September 22, 1993, for statements from the Clinton administration. See also Surkov, ed., *Moskva, Osen'-93,* 67–68, and, for further support from Clinton and Christopher, 172, 239, and 256.

86. *New York Times,* September 22, 1993.

87. Remnick, *Lenin's Tomb,* 61.

88. *Washington Post,* September 23, 1993.

89. *New York Times,* October 2, 1993.

90. *Newsweek,* October 18, 1993.

91. *Der Spiegel,* September 27, 1993.

92. *Frankfurter Allgemeine Zeitung,* September 24, 1993.

93. On the "Dniester Republic" troops, see Vladimir Socor's well-documented article "Dniester Involvement in the Moscow Rebellion," *RFE/RL Research Report* 2, no. 46 (November 1993): 25–32.

94. Remnick, *Lenin's Tomb,* 49.

95. Surkov, ed., *Moskva. Osen'-93,* 132–33.

96. Ibid., 135, 137.

97. Ibid., 138.

98. Ibid., 138–139.

99. Postfactum, *Politicheskii krizis v Rossii,* 62, 64. The Kremlin's nervous response is found on page 64.

100. *Foreign Broadcast Information Service/Daily Report: Eurasia,* September 28, 1993, 1.

101. *New York Times,* October 4, 1993.

102. Postfactum, *Politicheskii krizis v Rossii,* 64, 71, 78. Shumeiko said that each payment would "cost" the government about one million rubles (nearly $1,000 at the time).

103. Ibid., 71.

104. Ibid., 95–97.

105. For these various initiatives—centering mostly around the "zero option" solution —by the Patriarch; a group led by Skokov and Nikolai Fyodorov; Gorbachev and Ilyumzhinov; Zorkin; Glaziev; Ispravnikov; Yavlinsky; Chernomyrdin, V. Sokolov, and Abdulatipov; and the regional group Siberian Agreement, see Postfactum *Politicheskii krizis v Rossii,* 58, 61, 63, 66, 67, 71, 80, 95, 99, 100, 102, 111, 122; Surkov, ed., *Moskva. Osen'-93,* 189–90, 198, 252, 258, 267, 286, 295, 310; Poptsov, *Khronika vremen,* 370 and 391; Sobchak, *Zhila-byla,* 91; and the transcript of the Patriarch-sponsored negotiations, *Tishaishie peregovory* (Moscow: Magisterium, 1993).

106. Interview in *Komsomol'skaya pravda,* March 18, 1994.

107. Konstantin Cheremnykh, "Schicksalsschwere Tage in der russischen Hauptstadt," *Neue Solidarität,* October 13, 1993.

108. The first book entirely dedicated to the October events and claiming to provide a logical explanation of them was Artyom Tarasov's *Provokatsiya* (Moscow: Feniks, 1993). Tarasov concentrated on the events of October 3–4, and systematically analyzed the theories (put forward by various people during the coup) suggesting that the October 3 retreat of the riot police from the street demonstrators' onslaught, which permitted the crowds to force their way to the White House and seize city hall, were a planned provocation on the part of the Kremlin, designed to provoke parliament's supporters into taking violent actions, thus creating an excuse for armed reprisal.

109. For Urazhtsev's biography, see *Kto est' kto,* vol. 3, 565–67.

110. Vitaly Urazhtsev, "Eine Diktatur, die über Leichen geht," *Neue Solidarität,* December 22, 1993.

111. *Newsweek,* October 18, 1993.

112. Surkov, ed., *Moskva. Osen'-93,* 422.

113. *Rossiiskie vesti,* October 5, 1993, 2.

114. *New York Times,* October 4, 1993. See also Surkov, ed., *Moskva. Osen'-93,* 485–86.

115. *New York Times,* October 4, 1993.

116. Ibid.

117. *Newsweek,* October 18, 1993.

118. For descriptions of this meeting, see Yeltsin, *Zapiski prezidenta,* 384–86; Ivanov, *Anafema,* 315–22, quotation at 319.

119. Ivanov, *Anafema,* 315.

120. Yeltsin, *Zapiski prezidenta,* 383–84.

121. Yuri Afanasiev, "Russian Reform Is Dead," *Foreign Affairs,* March–April 1994, argues thus: "The real winner in the October 1993 showdown . . . was the military-industrial complex, acting in unison with the bureaucracy. . . . The very day after the resolution of the parliamentary insurrection, Yeltsin convened a Security Council meeting that had only one item on the agenda: a new military doctrine that expanded Russia's security interests throughout the territory of the former USSR and rescinded the no-first-use nuclear weapons pledge from the Gorbachev era."

122. *Newsweek,* October 18, 1993.

123. *New York Times,* October 5, 1993.

124. Peter Reddaway, "Dictatorial Drift," *New York Times,* October 10, 1993.

125. Yeltsin, *Zapiski prezidenta,* 11–13; Ivanov, *Anafema,* 324–25 and 385–406.

126. *New York Times,* October 5, 1993.

127. Reddaway, "Dictatorial Drift."

128. *Rossiiskie vesti,* October 7, 1993, 1.

129. The law was signed by Yeltsin on July 21, 1994. See Robert Sharlet, "Reinventing the Russian State: Problems of Constitutional Implementation," *The John Marshall Law Review* 28, no. 4 (Summer 1995): 775–86, at 780–81.

130. *New York Times,* October 24, 1993.

131. *RFE/RL Daily Report,* October 25, 1993.

132. *New York Times,* November 8, 1993.

133. Michael McFaul and Nikolai Petrov, eds., *The Political Almanac of Russia 1995.* Russian ed. (Moscow: Carnegie Moscow Center, 1995), 21–22.

134. Loewenhardt, *The Reincarnation of Russia,* 141.

135. A. Sobyanin and V. Sukhovol'sky, *Demokratiya, ogranichennaya falsifikatsiyami: vybory i referendumy v Rossii v 1991–93* (Moscow: Proektnaya gruppa po pravam cheloveka, 1995), 51–119.

136. McFaul and Petrov, eds., *The Political Almanac of Russia 1995,* 22; White, Rose, and McAllister, *How Russia Votes,* 126–29, especially 127.

137. For a wide-ranging collection of coordinated studies on different aspects of the Duma elections and the referendum, see Colton and Hough, eds., *Growing Pains.*

138. Report of the Russian-American Information and Press Center, ITAR-TASS, December 2, 1993, and *Los Angeles Times,* December 4, 1993.

139. Only 219 were elected on December 12, partly because in four constituencies those voting made up less than 25 percent of the electorate, which invalidated the election.

140. For the figures on the elections and the constitutional referendum, see McFaul and Petrov, eds., *The Political Almanac of Russia 1995,* 21 and 658–65.

8. The Imperial Presidency in a Privatized State: 1994–1996

1. *Byulleten' Tsentral'noy izbiratel'noi komissii Rossiiskoi Federatsii* 1, no. 12 (1994), 34–38. For analysis of who voted for and against, see Timothy Colton, "Public Opinion and the Constitutional Referendum," in Colton and Hough, eds., *Growing Pains*.

2. Rimma Korelova, "Ne zabud'te uteret'sya," *Sovetskaya Rossiya,* February 24, 1994, reprinted from *Amurskaya pravda,* February 16 and 19, 1994.

3. For one of the fullest collections of facts challenging the legitimacy of the constitution, see White, Rose, and McAllister, *How Russia Votes,* especially pp. 98–101 and 126–129. As noted earlier, the confusion became even worse when, on May 4, 1994, *Izvestiya* ran a report by Aleksandr Sobyanin, head of a research group in the Presidential Administration and a close associate of Yegor Gaidar, alleging massive falsification of the vote.

4. White, Rose, and McAllister, *How Russia Votes,* 106.

5. ITAR-TASS, December 12, 1993.

6. David Remnick, *Resurrection: The Struggle for a New Russia* (New York: Random House, 1997), 102.

7. *Izvestiya,* January 20, 1994.

8. Nikolai Medvedev, for example, a presidential aide for the regions, said that Yeltsin was ready to form the "Russian Presidential Party of Reformers." An organizing committee had already started operating in Irkutsk. Mayak Radio, February 7, translated in *Foreign Broadcast Information Service/Daily Report: Eurasia,* February 8, 1994, 22.

9. Text of some five thousand words published in *Rossiiskaya gazeta,* February 25, 1994, along with the text of the more formal "Message" of the president to the parliament, titled "On Strengthening the Russian State," which made roughly the same points at three to four times greater length.

10. This became a periodic event, even over issues like approving the budget. See an example in *RFE/RL Daily Report,* December 23, 1994.

11. ITAR-TASS, December 12, 1993.

12. *Trud,* December 18, 1993.

13. ITAR-TASS, January 10, 1994.

14. *Ekonomika i zhizn',* no. 2 (1998), as quoted in *Monitor,* February 3, 1998.

15. *Moskovskie novosti,* December 8, 1993.

16. Peter Reddaway and Catherine Dale's interview with Dmitri Rogozin, Moscow, October 21, 1994. Rogozin read these figures out from a 1994 publication by Dr. Boris Pugachev.

17. *Sobranie aktov prezidenta i pravitel'stva Rossiiskoi Federatsii,* no. 52 (1993), 5751, 5753.

18. See "Yeltsin—aktsioner," *Kommersant-Daily,* November 19, 1998.

19. ITAR-TASS, December 12, 1993.

20. Aleksandr Korzhakov, *Boris Yeltsin—ot rassveta do zakata* (Boris Yeltsin— From Sunrise to Sunset) (Moscow: Interbuk, 1997), 404; Parkhomenko, "Merlin's

Tower." Parkhomenko's remarkable investigative series appeared in this and the next two issues of *Moskovskie novosti* (May 5 and 12). The series focused mainly on the activities of Korzhakov's deputy, KGB General Georgi Rogozin, describing his efforts to create and manipulate quasi-governmental structures. The aims were to build financial support for Yeltsin's 1996 election campaign and to intimidate his opponents, notably through electronic surveillance.

21. The document was published in full in *Nezavisimaya gazeta*, December 15, 1994, and received further coverage in *Izvestiya*, January 24, 1995.

22. Yeltsin signed a decree on February 15 enhancing his control of the executive organs of government.

23. Order No. 506 of February 11, 1994, *Sobranie aktov prezidenta i pravitel'stva Rossiiskoi Federatsii*, no. 7 (1994), as quoted in Pilar Bonet, *Nevozmozhnaya Rossiya: Boris Yeltsin, Provintsial v Kremle*, a book published in full in *Ural*, no. 4 (1994), 1–224 at 195.

24. See Eugene Huskey's careful analysis of these problems, "The State-Legal Administration and the Politics of Redundancy," *Post-Soviet Affairs* 11, no. 2 (1995): 115–43.

25. The decrees on sports associations and disabled veterans' organizations were, respectively, No. 4646 (November 22) and No. 5066 (December 22), published in *Sobranie aktov prezidenta i pravitel'stva Rossiiskoi Federatsii*, no. 48 (November 29, 1993) and no. 52 (December 27, 1993). On the scandals it created, see the articles by N. Gevorkyan in *Moscow News*, April 28, 1995; V. Ivkin in *Profil'*, no. 37 (1997); and S. Lunev in *Prism* 4, no. 3 (February 1998).

26. On the NSF, see Valery Streletsky, *Mrakobesie* (Moscow: Detektiv-Press, 1998), 186–215, especially 204. In December 1998, Yuri Boldyrev of the Accounting Office reported that NSF caused losses of some $7 billion in 1995 alone; *Monitor* 4, no. 236 (December 22, 1998).

27. For some of the ROC scandals involving huge profits on cigarette sales, see articles in *Moskovskii komsomolets*, February 1 and 19, 1997.

28. The director was General V. Samoilov, and the company was created by a decree of mid-November 1993.

29. Interfax, as reported in the *Washington Post*, December 24, 1997, and *RFE/RL Newsline*, December 23, 1997.

30. Valery Kryukov and Arild Moe, *The New Russian Corporatism? A Case Study of Gazprom* (London: Royal Institute of International Affairs, 1996) provides some leads on Gazprom; see pp. 10–11, 13, 16–17, 22. On Borodin's organization, see, for example, *Komsomol'skaya pravda*, June 4, 1998.

31. Yeltsin, *Zapiski prezidenta*, 11–13.

32. Interfax in English, February 22, reprinted in *Foreign Broadcast Information Service/Daily Report: Eurasia*, February 22, 1994, 32. For additional information, see Knight, *Spies Without Cloaks*, 70, 73, 76, and note 102 on p. 270.

33. Vladimir Smirnov, quoted by ITAR-TASS, December 23, 1993.

34. Published in *Izvestiya*, November 18, 1993.

35. Yuri Afanasiev, "Russia's Vicious Circle," *New York Times*, February 28, 1994.

36. See the perceptive analysis of these issues by Stephen Foye, "Updating Russian Civil-Military Relations," *RFE/RL Research Report* 2, no. 46 (November 1993): 44–50.

37. "Accord for the Sake of Russia" somewhat resembled the essentially defunct National Salvation Front; however, it was launched in February 1994, and was moribund by autumn. See *Obshchaya gazeta,* September 16–22, 1994. In articles, media interviews, and a three-hour interview with Peter Reddaway on October 20, 1994, Rutskoi described building Derzhava from the grassroots up. However, his lack of money and of effective means of communication with supporters, his inability to work smoothly with other leaders, and his fixation on numbers of registered members (he claimed to have 672,000 in October 1994, and anticipated having over four million by the time of the Duma elections) resulted in only 2.6 percent of the party list vote in December 1995. See Reddaway, "Moscow-Krasnoiarsk-Ekaterinburg Diary," 137–43. On the "triple entente," see later in this chapter.

38. *Washington Post,* December 23, 1993.

39. *Washington Post,* January 1 and 25, 1994.

40. Yegor Gaidar, "Stavka na negodyaev" (Banking on Scoundrels), *Izvestiya,* May 17, 1994.

41. See Umland, "Vladimir Zhirinovsky," 31–52, for numerous sources regarding 1990–93; and Zhilin, "Vladimir Zhirinovsky: A Scarecrow in Yeltsin's Garden," on 1993–95.

42. Umland analyzes the many faces and complex personality of Zhirinovsky, seeing him in different modes as, inter alia, the centrist, the liberal democrat, the moderate, the provisional autocrat, the anticonservative, the imperialist, the nationalist, the alarmist, the cosmopolitan pacifier, and the geopolitician. Umland, "Vladimir Zhirinovsky," 91–124.

43. Lipset, *Political Man.*

44. "Novyi rossiiskii rezhim," *Nezavisimaya gazeta,* November 23, 1995.

45. On this trend, see Vladimir Mau, "The Ascent of the Inflationists," *Journal of Democracy* 5, no. 2 (April 1994): 32–35.

46. See Shevtsova's article "Yeltsin ostanetsya, dazhe esli proigrayet," *Nezavisimaya gazeta,* April 26, 1996, 5.

47. See Ravil Zaripov's useful analysis of the mounting tensions between Yeltsin and the Duma in *Komsomol'skaya pravda,* February 19, 1994.

48. The amnesty text was published by *Rossiiskaya gazeta* on February 26, 1994, and the Memorandum by ITAR-TASS on February 24.

49. See Kazannik's interview on Russian Television, *Foreign Broadcast Information Service/Daily Report: Eurasia,* March 1, 1994, 19–20.

50. For a persuasive exposition of this view, see Gavriil Popov's article in *Argumenty i fakty,* no. 9–10 (March 1994), 2. For the opposite view, see Tamara Zamyatina's article in *Rossiiskaya gazeta,* March 1, 1994.

51. See, for example, Gaidar's article in *Izvestiya,* March 3, 1994, 4.

52. *Segodnya,* February 24, 1994. A. Ostapchuk and Y. Krasnikov argued in similar fashion in their commentary in *Nezavisimaya gazeta,* March 1, 1994, also speculating that Yeltsin only pretended to resist the amnesty so as to appease his supporters.

53. See *Komsomol'skaya pravda,* April 12, 1994.

54. Sergei Glaziev, *Poltora goda v Dume* (Moscow: Gals Plyus, 1995), chapters 1–4, passim. Glaziev's richly documented book is essential reading if one wants to understand the rigidity of the Yeltsin regime over failed economic policies. Its refusal to listen to the new, more promising approach advocated by Glaziev and his Duma committee is striking.

55. Ibid., chapter 2.

56. For examples, see ibid., 7, 41.

57. On the FIGs, see Juliet Johnson, "Russia's Emerging Financial-Industrial Groups," *Post-Soviet Affairs* 13, no. 4 (October–December 1997): 333–65; and Irina Starodubrovskaia, "Financial-Industrial Groups: Illusions and Realities," *Communist Economies and Economic Transformation* 7, no. 1 (1995): 5–19.

58. The new relationship was well depicted in the *Washington Post,* February 5 and March 1, 1994.

59. Quoted in Dimitri Simes, *After the Collapse: Russia Seeks Its Place as a Great Power* (New York: Simon & Schuster, 1999), 98–99.

60. An especially vivid example of this was Yeltsin's appointment as head of the Russian Press Committee of Boris Mironov, a hard-line nationalist of anti-Semitic tendency. For a portrait of Mironov, see Valery Vyzhutovich, "Sovmestitel'," *Izvestiya,* May 28, 1994.

61. See, for example, "Yavlinsky Views Duma Working, Reform," *Foreign Broadcast Information Service/Daily Report: Eurasia,* November 11, 1994.

62. For an account of this still murky episode, see Aslund, *How Russia Became a Market Economy,* 205–06. For an attempt to blame the commercial banks for it, especially MOST Bank and Imperial Bank, see Anatoly Salutsky, *Zagadka chernogo vtornika* (Moscow: Veteran MP, 1995), 5–6, 32–33. An interim report of the commission Yeltsin set up to investigate the crash appears in Korzhakov, *Boris Yeltsin,* 405–08. The report perceives a conspiracy involving several banks, Gusinsky, Shokhin, Vavilov, B. Fyodorov, Gaidar, Popov, and others.

63. No one was arrested for Kholodov's murder until 1998. See *Zavtra,* July 1, 1998, 2. As of mid-2000, no trial had taken place.

64. See, for example, Galina Starovoitova's interview in *Kuranty,* October 18, 1994, 4; Viktor Loshak, "Vremya gotovit' estafetu," *Moskovskie novosti,* October 23–30, 1994; A. Migranyan, "Prezident dolzhen prinyat' reshenie," *Nezavisimaya gazeta,* November 4, 1994, 1.

65. Korzhakov, *Boris Yeltsin,* 282–85.

66. For the speech and the questions, see *Stenogramma zasedaniya Gosudarstvennoi Dumy, 27 oktyabrya 1994 g.* (official typescript), 5–35 and 35–93, respectively.

67. See the full text in *Sovetskaya Rossiya,* October 29, 1994.

68. The statement was widely published, for example, in *Novaya ezhednevnaya gazeta,* October 28, 1994, under the heading "Democracy in Russia Can Be Built Without Yeltsin."

69. *Kuranty,* October 18, 1994.

70. See his article in *Izvestiya,* November 9, 1994.

71. ITAR-TASS, November 7, 1994.

72. *Moskovskii komsomolets,* November 18, 1994.

73. *Kommersant-Daily,* November 1, 1994.

74. Interview with Yuri Boldyrev, *Izvestiya,* November 4, 1994.

75. Vitaly Tretiakov, "1996-i. Konets Rossii? (5): Dozhret li gosudarstvo obshchestvo?" *Nezavisimaya gazeta,* October 19, 1994.

76. *Obshchaya gazeta,* October 7, 1994. Other material on this theme is presented by Fred Hiatt in the *Washington Post,* October 8, 1994.

77. *Moskovskii komsomolets* picked up very quickly on the protectionist trend, printing on November 19, three days after Polevanov's appointment, a major article by Andrei Pronchik about the undesirable Western invasion of the Russian stock market.

78. Migranyan, "Prezident dolzhen."

79. See *Izvestiya* and the *Financial Times* (London), December 22, 1994, for parts of Korzhakov's leaked letter making the latter charge. For the full text and additional materials, see Korzhakov, *Boris Yeltsin,* 409–12.

80. Aleksandr Golovkov, Sergei Golovkov, and Teimuraz Mamaladze, "Osennii marafon v kuluarakh vlasti," *Izvestiya,* November 16, 1994.

81. Yevgeny Krasnikov in *Nezavisimaya gazeta,* November 18, 1994.

82. "Padaet sneg: upadut li prezident i pravitel'stvo?" *Rossiiskaya gazeta,* November 19, 1994.

83. *Washington Post,* "Yeltsin, Clinton Clash over NATO's Role," December 5, 1994. See also *Washington Post,* "U.S.-Russian Relations Develop Rifts" and "Yeltsin Foresees U.S. Taking Harder Line," November 12 and 14, 1994, respectively.

84. On Gusinsky, see Korzhakov, *Boris Yeltsin,* 282–90, 418–22; and Remnick, *Resurrection,* chapter 6. For information on NTV's rise, see Ellen Mickiewicz, *Changing Channels: Television and the Struggle for Power in Russia* (New York: Oxford University Press, 1997), 222–25.

85. On this revealing episode, see the detailed account in Streletsky, *Mrakobesie,* 115–26.

86. See the third of the remarkable series of investigative reports on Yakubovsky and his numerous shady exploits and associates in Russia, Canada, Israel, and elsewhere by the KGB-connected Iona Andronov, "O chem molchit."

87. On Pankratov, see Streletsky, *Mrakobesie,* 166–68.

88. Korzhakov has tried repeatedly to amend the record by claiming that he was a dove on Chechnya and by painting Grachev in the worst possible light. He has also tried to shield Yeltsin from responsibility by portraying Sergei Filatov as a conscious hawk rather than just an executor of Yeltsin's will, which is probably what he was. See, for example, Korzhakov, *Boris Yeltsin,* 370–72.

89. Lieven, *Chechnya,* 87.

90. For a detailed study of the war, see Carlotta Gall and Thomas de Waal, *Chechnya: A Small Victorious War* (London: Macmillan, 1997). For a study that sets the war in a broad historical and political context, see Lieven, *Chechnya.* On the roots of the conflict, see John Dunlop, *Russia Confronts Chechnya* (New York: Cambridge University Press, 1998).

91. Interview with Kovalev in *The New Presence,* November 1997, 15.

92. For some of these statements, see the *Washington Post,* January 10, 1995.

93. In laying out the CPRF's economic program in a two-hour interview with Peter Reddaway on October 8, 1994, Zyuganov made no mention of any renationalization. Nor do successive versions of the party's program, although the January 1995 version speaks of "emergency measures of government regulation." The CPRF's electoral program of September 1995 does not even mention the word "socialism," let alone "communism." See Urban and Solovei, *Russia's Communists,* 125, 136, and 162–63.

94. This document, an official report to Chernomyrdin, circulated widely in the Duma, and long extracts and commentaries appeared in papers not under Chubais's control, such as *Nezavisimaya gazeta* (January 25, 1995), *Rabochnaya tribuna* and *Pravda* (both January 24, 1995), and *Zavtra,* no. 5 (January 31, 1995).

95. See the pioneering research by Robert Otto on the CPRF's finances in his "Gennadii Ziuganov," 43–44.

96. *Financial Times* (London), December 22, 1994.

97. U.S. Agency for International Development, press release, May 20, 1997.

98. *Washington Post,* January 10, 1995.

99. Interview in *Rossiya,* no. 32 (September 27, 1995), 3. See also subsequent interviews in *Pravda,* November 17, 1995, and *Trud,* October 14, 1998.

100. See Anders Aslund, *The Russian Economy: Where Is It Headed?* (Baltimore: Johns Hopkins University Press, 1997), 10.

101. See Boris Slavin's article in *Pravda,* January 12, 1995.

102. *Segodnya,* December 23, 1993.

103. *Rossiiskaya gazeta,* November 1, 1994.

104. See the interview with Boiko in *Kommersant-Daily,* March 14, 1995.

105. See the colorful autobiography of Borovoi, who also founded the Party of Economic Freedom, *Tsena svobody* (Moscow: Novosti, 1993).

106. On Boiko, see *Russia: Insider Bankers in the Yeltsin Regime* (Washington, D.C.: Federal Broadcast Information Service, 1997), 11–13, 48–49, 53–54; and Streletsky, *Mrakobesie,* 186–225. On Medkov, the president of DIAM Bank, see "The Assassinations of Russian Businessmen Detailed," *Moscow News* 29 (July 22–28, 1994); see also "Osen' oligarkhov," *Sovershenno sekretno* 9 (1998), 6.

107. On Gaidar's thinking, see chapter 5.

108. On all this, see, for example, the interview of Yuri Boldyrev, deputy head of the Accounting Office, in *Moskovskie novosti* 22 (June 1–8, 1997).

109. On these two episodes, see *Monitor,* January 22, 1996, which quotes a January 19 dispatch from Interfax.

110. For an expert analysis of this subject, see Lieven, *Chechnya,* 86–96.

111. Peter Reddaway, "Cancel the IMF Loan to Russia," *Wall Street Journal Europe,* March 9, 1995. See also Boris Fyodorov's article in *Izvestiya,* February 7, 1995.

112. Article by Lev Sedov in *Segodnya,* April 8, 1995, as quoted by Lilia Shevtsova in a telling passage on this topic in her *Yeltsin's Russia: Myths and Realities* (Washington, D.C.: Carnegie Endowment for International Peace, 1999), 121.

113. Yeltsin also said that $2 billion had disappeared in the Ministry of Foreign Trade and that 40 percent of all businessmen and two-thirds of private firms were involved in corrupt activities. His security minister added that criminal elements had penetrated the highest levels of power. *RFE/RL News Briefs* 2, no. 9 (1993), 3.

114. Smolensky quoted in David Hoffman, "Russian Banker Reaches Pinnacle of Capitalism," *Washington Post,* October 17, 1997.

115. Reported by Chubais in a long interview with Yevgenia Al'bats in *Kommersant-Daily,* March 5, 1998.

116. Vladimir Ivanov in *Nezavisimaya gazeta,* July 7, 1993.

117. Summary of the report in *Izvestiya,* January 26, 1994.

118. Andrei Aizderdzis was murdered on April 26, soon after he had published an annotated list of 266 Mafiya bosses in *Kto est' kto,* no. 7 (April 1994). On his murder, see *The Independent* (London), April 28, 1994.

119. *Washington Post,* June 16, 1994. One of the high-profile victims was the colorful "Godfather" figure Otari Kvantrishvili; see *New York Times,* April 14, 1994.

120. *Washington Post,* January 26, 1994.

121. Hoffman, "Russian Banker."

122. This figure is the product of work we developed from detailed information compiled by Robert Otto, mostly from *Kommersant-Daily.* We are grateful to him for generously making this information available to us.

123. Ibid.

124. *Izvestiya,* June 15, 1994.

125. Ilyushenko's address to his staff, quoted in the *Washington Post,* June 24, 1994.

126. *Washington Post,* July 5 and 6, 1994.

127. On all this, see especially Oleg Zhirnov's article in *Obshchaya gazeta,* August 26, 1994; and Viktor Ilyukhin's letter in *Sovetskaya Rossiya,* August 13, 1994.

128. Blair Ruble was prescient to suggest that the bombings of the summer and early fall might be "one of the most pivotal events" of 1994. See Kennan Institute for Advanced Russian Studies, *Annual Report 1994* (Washington, D.C.: Woodrow Wilson International Center for Scholars, 1995), 3.

129. Michael Dasaro and Anthony Riccio were the American victims of murders possibly directed by the Mafiya. See *Washington Post,* November 18, 1993 and September 25, 1994.

130. "Ugolovnaya Rossiya: ot gorodskoi ulitsy do kremlevskogo kabineta," *Izvestiya,* October 18, 1994. See also parts 2–5 of this study, appearing in the October 19–22 editions of the paper, and the interview with one of the study's chief authors, Vladimir Ovchinsky, in *Trud,* October 22, 1994.

131. *Moskovskii komsomolets,* June 23, 1994. *Segodnya* and other papers carried similar reports on the same day.

132. Interview with Boldyrev in *Izvestiya,* November 4, 1994, as translated in *Foreign Broadcast Information Service/Daily Report: Eurasia,* November 4, 1994, 20.

133. *Obshchaya gazeta,* January 26, 1995.

134. Remnick, *Resurrection,* 356.

135. For details, see Yuri Boldyrev's interview in *Izvestiya,* November 4, 1994.

136. For more on the political aspects of this two-week crisis, see Shevtsova, *Yeltsin's Russia,* 123–25. On the military aspects, see Lieven, *Chechnya,* 124–26.

137. For more detailed information on Our Home Is Russia, see McFaul and Petrov, eds., *The Political Almanac of Russia 1995,* 73–79.

138. *OMRI Special Report,* no. 7 (November 17, 1995) and *OMRI Daily Digest,* November 20, 1995.

139. For detailed discussions of the charges and the circumstances and U.S. policy to Russia, see Peter Reddaway, "Better than Whitewater," *Washington Post,* August 20, 1995, C3; and "Is Chernomyrdin a Crook?" *Post-Soviet Prospects* 3, no. 8 (August 1995), 1–4.

140. *Komsomol'skaya pravda,* July 5, 1995.

141. *Kommersant-Daily,* July 7, 1995.

142. *Kommersant-Daily,* May 30, 1995.

143. In an international news conference on June 9, however, Chubais attacked some organizations almost certainly patronized by Korzhakov—including the National Sports Foundation and some veterans' groups—hinting that their leaders had embezzled large sums.

144. Russian Television, May 29, 1995.

145. *Obshchaya gazeta,* June 29, 1995.

146. See the articles in the June 6 and July 3, 1995, editions.

147. *Komsomol'skaya pravda,* July 7, 1995; *Zavtra,* no. 28 (July 11, 1995). See the commentary on these articles by Aleksandr Budberg, "Kto khochet ubit' Chernomyrdina?" *Moskovskii komsomolets,* July 22, 1995.

148. *Moskovskii komsomolets,* May 8, 1996.

149. For more details, see McFaul and Petrov, eds., *The Political Almanac of Russia 1995,* 97–99.

150. *OMRI Special Report,* November 5, 1995.

151. For more details, see McFaul and Petrov, eds. *The Political Almanac of Russia 1995,* 81–83.

152. For more details, see ibid., 83–85.

153. For details, see ibid., 79–81.

154. For more details, see ibid., 108–112.

155. For more details on the Congress of Russian Communities, see ibid., 102–108.

156. For more details, see ibid., 117; and Polevanov's interviews in *Rossiya,* September 27, 1995, and *Pravda Rossii,* November 10, 1995.

157. Dimitri Simes, "Yeltsin Runs the Kremlin: Get Over It," *Washington Post,* March 12, 1995, C4.

158. See *OMRI Daily Digest,* November 16 and November 22, 1995; and Satarov's interview to *Kommersant-Daily* on November 18, 1995.

159. For details of the legislation and the wrangling over Federation Council membership, see White, Rose, and McAllister, *How Russia Votes,* 194–95.

160. Broad analyses of the elections include Stephen White, Matthew Wyman, and Sarah Oates, "Parties and Voters in the 1995 Russian Duma Election," *Europe-Asia Studies* 49, no. 5 (July 1997): 67–99; and Peter Reddaway, "Red Alert," *The New Republic,* January 29, 1996.

161. White, Wyman, and Oates, "Parties and Voters," 77.

162. For a detailed analysis of Yabloko's strengths and weaknesses on election eve, see Dmitri Glinski, "Reformers with Clean Hands: A Challenge to Yeltsinism," *Post-Soviet Prospects* 3, no. 11 (November 1995), 1–4.

163. For an analysis of the CPRF's performance, see Urban and Solovei, *Russia's Communists,* 157–66.

164. Remnick, *Resurrection,* 329–30.

165. Streletsky, *Mrakobesie,* 126.

166. On all this, see Andrei Piontkovsky, "What Was Wrong? Asian Flu or Russian Pneumonia?" *Prism* 5, no. 12 (1998), 9.

167. "Aleksandr Korzhakov: Schitayu, chto prezident dolzhen uiti v otstavku," *Parlamentskaya gazeta,* September 16, 1998.

168. Thomas Graham, "Despite Its Many Problems, Russia Has A Unique Opportunity," *Wall Street Journal–CEER,* October 25, 1999.

169. Klebnikov, "Godfather of the Kremlin?"

170. Leonid Krutakov, "Aleksandr Korzhakov: v posteli s vragom," *Moskovskii komsomolets,* November 3, 1999. Yeltsin's press spokesman has used the same sort of unconvincing defense against Korzhakov's revelations, claiming that he "simply wants to draw attention to himself." See "Korzhakov o FSB," *Kommersant-Daily,* November 27, 1998.

171. Valery Lebedev, "Beseda s Borisom Nemtsovym," http://www.Lebed.com/art 869.htm. This is a lengthy transcript of what Nemtsov said at a meeting in Boston on February 13, 1999.

172. Paul Klebnikov, "Conflagration in Russia," *Forbes,* November 1, 1999, 95.

173. *Kto est' kto v Rossii* (1997), 62–64, 277. Yegor Gaidar, *Days of Defeat and Victory* (Seattle: University of Washington Press, 1999), 196–97.

174. *Obshchaya gazeta,* March 9–15, 1995.

175. *Kto est' kto v Rossii* (1997), 742–43. Krutakov, "Aleksandr Korzhakov"; in this interview, Korzhakov describes with considerable literary flair some of his meetings with Berezovsky, notably the first ones. At these, the financier would open the door of Korzhakov's office slowly: "First his briefcase would jut through, and then gradually Berezovsky would enter, his side toward me. As he approached my desk, he would bow several times, asking in a servile voice, 'May I?'"

176. Paul Klebnikov, "The Day They Raided Aeroflot," *Forbes,* March 22, 1999, 110.

177. Interview by Peter Osnos, *New York Times,* October 7, 1999.

178. Korzhakov interview, *Parlamentskaya gazeta.*

179. Krutakov, "Aleksandr Korzhakov."

180. Klebnikov, "The Day They Raided Aeroflot."

181. Klebnikov, "Godfather of the Kremlin?"

182. Korzhakov, *Boris Yeltsin,* 418.

183. *Sovershenno sekretno,* "Osen' oligarkhov." This article recounts "a series of sensational contract killings with which Listerman's name is linked." It also says that Berezovsky was outraged when the press reported on his "very close relationship with Listerman."

184. *Profil',* November 14, 1996.

185. Klebnikov, "Godfather of the Kremlin?"; *Kommersant-Daily,* "Korzhakov o FSB."

186. *Kommersant-Daily,* November 19 and 27, 1998; *Komsomol'skaya pravda,* November 21, 1998; and *Moskovskaya pravda,* November 19, 1998.

187. Interview with Korzhakov in *Moskovskii komsomolets,* April 22, 1998.

188. The main source for this paragraph is Klebnikov, "Godfather of the Kremlin?" 95–96.

189. Krutakov, "Aleksandr Korzhakov."

190. *Izvestiya,* February 26, 1996. On Lisovsky's proximity to several murders, see Streletsky, *Mrakobesie,* 232–34.

191. Report by M. Barsukov, head of the Main Protective Administration, reprinted in Korzhakov, *Boris Yeltsin,* 436–37.

192. See Korzhakov's interviews in *Parlamentskaya gazeta* and Krutakov, "Aleksandr Korzhakov"; *Corriere della Sera* (Milan), September 1, 1999; Streletsky, *Mrakobesie,* 120 and 123; and Federal Broadcast Information Service, *Russia: Insider Bankers in the Yeltsin Regime,* 8.

193. Krutakov, "Aleksandr Korzhakov."

194. Klebnikov, "Godfather of the Kremlin?" 93–95.

195. Ibid., 94.

196. For example, Paul Klebnikov's masterful study, *Godfather of the Kremlin: Boris Berezovsky and the Looting of Russia* (New York: Harcourt, 2000).

197. On this fateful episode, which launched the term "oligarchs" into wide circulation, see Matt Bivens and Jonas Bernstein, "The Russia You Never Met," *Demokratizatsiya* 6, no. 4 (Fall 1998): 627–29; and interviews by Yuri Boldyrev of the Accounting Office in *Novaya gazeta,* October 28, 1996, and *Moskovskie novosti,* June 1, 1997. Later, one of the oligarch beneficiaries, Pyotr Aven, confirmed that the cash involved belonged to the government; see *Monitor,* February 17, 1999.

198. Krutakov, "Aleksandr Korzhakov"; Vladimir Komov, "Pochemu Berezovskomu vse skhodit s ruk," *Parlamentskaya gazeta,* February 5, 1999.

199. Brian Whitmore, "Yeltsin's Invisible Son-In-Law Surfaces," *Moscow Times,* September 24, 1999.

200. *Financial Times* (London), November 1, 1996; Interfax, January 11, 1998, as quoted in *RFE/RL Newsline,* January 12, 1998. See also his revealing interview in *Nezavisimaya gazeta,* February 3, 1998, on Soros and Western and Russian businessmen.

201. For a particularly thorough analysis of this complex case, see Klebnikov, "The Day They Raided Aeroflot."

202. *Kommersant-Daily,* "Korzhakov o FSB."

203. Other spheres of Berezovsky's murky activity that need much more research concern Chechnya and the National Sports Foundation. Regarding the latter, whose exemption from import tariffs cost the state budget no less than $7 billion in 1995 alone, according to the Accounting Office, see *Monitor,* December 22, 1998; Streletsky, *Mrakobesie,* 186–225; Bivens and Bernstein, "The Russia You Never Met," 624–25; and Klebnikov, "Godfather of the Kremlin?" 96. Regarding Chechnya, where Berezovsky has long had important business interests and has gotten deeply involved in freeing some of the hundreds of kidnap victims through ransom payments that have financed warlords and encouraged further kidnappings, see Klebnikov, "Conflagration in Russia," 90–96. Berezovsky also admitted in this article donating a million dollars in 1998 to Shamil Basayev, one of the most militant Chechen leaders, supposedly for reconstruction work. Berezovsky also told Interfax (December 17, 1997) that he maintained regular contact, both by phone and in person, with Basayev and his fellow first deputy prime minister at the time, Movladi Udugov.

204. On Berezovsky's dealings with Yeltsin's other son-in-law, see Klebnikov, "The Day They Raided Aeroflot," 110.

205. Korzhakov interview, *Parlamentskaya gazeta.* One of the early reports to name this château gave the sale price as 55 million francs; see *Kur'er* (a weekly Russian newspaper published in Los Angeles), November 27, 1997.

206. Aleksandr Fitts, "Tatyana Dyachenko priobrela zamok v Germanii?" *Moskovskii komsomolets,* August 21, 1998.

207. Sergei Pluzhnikov and Sergei Sokolov, "'Malaya zemlya' Borisa Yeltsina," *Kur'er,* July 18, 1997. Evidently, the authors were unable to publish this embarrassing article in Russia, so they decided to do it abroad.

208. Lebedev, "Beseda s Borisom Nemtsovym."

209. Korzhakov, *Boris Yeltsin,* 289.

210. On Aeroflot and campaign contributions, see ibid., 437. On NSF's contribution of $10 million, see Streletsky, *Mrakobesie,* 194. On the presidential property agency, see *Komsomol'skaya pravda,* June 4, 1998, and *The Economist,* September 24, 1999. Run by a Yeltsin crony from 1993, the agency owns property in 78 countries, operates two hundred businesses, and has an annual turnover of $2.5 billion. Its employees increased tenfold from 1993 to 1999, to reach one hundred thousand, reflecting Yeltsin's remarkable opportunities for patronage. On January 24, 2000, the Swiss prosecutor's office issued a warrant for Borodin's arrest, charging him with laundering $14 million of his own money. On FIMACO see, for example, *Monitor,* August 2, 1999, 1–2.

211. *Los Angeles Times,* September 10, 1997.

212. Streletsky, *Mrakobesie,* 193.

213. Leonid Krutakov, "Nash Dom—'Gazprom,'" *Moskovskii komsomolets,* March 6, 1999.

214. Korzhakov, *Boris Yeltsin,* 365–66.

215. Streletsky, *Mrakobesie,* 229. A photograph of the document with Yeltsin's note appears in Korzhakov, *Boris Yeltsin,* 438.

216. Streletsky, *Mrakobesie,* 228, 280–86.

217. For details on these documents and commentary on them, see Viktor Ilyukhin, *Na trone porazit' porok* (Moscow: Federatsiya, 1997), 28–42, 51–52.

218. Ibid., 43–50; *Novaya gazeta,* January 13–19, 1997.

219. Korzhakov, *Boris Yeltsin,* 436. The report was written on about June 20.

220. Krutakov, "Aleksandr Korzhakov."

221. *Novaya gazeta,* March 20, 2000. The newspaper's research team decided to remain anonymous, doubtless for its own safety. The article also reveals similar schemes used to finance Putin's presidential campaign in 2000.

222. Useful starting points on Smolensky are *Sovershenno sekretno,* "Osen' oligark-hov"; and David Hoffman, "Russian Banker."

223. See L. Krutakov, "Abramovich vykhodit iz teni," *Moskovskii komsomolets,* February 6, 1999.

224. See Peter Reddaway, "Beware the Russian Reformer," *Washington Post,* August 24, 1997. Korzhakov has made allegations that Chubais has not disputed that in 1996 the latter profited from a $128 million scheme operated jointly with Deputy Finance Minister Andrei Vavilov and the head of the National Sports Foundation, Boris V. Fyodorov. Reportedly, Fyodorov gave evidence against Chubais; see Korzhakov interview, *Parlamentskaya gazeta.* Streletsky refers to the same case, calling Vavilov—in terms similar to those used by other observers—"the most prodigious, professional, and talented swindler" of the contemporary world; Streletsky, *Mrakobesie,* 192–93.

225. The earliest of these, *Drama vlasti* (Moscow: Paleya) appeared in 1993; a later one is *Rossiya—Rodina moya,* whose English version was published in the United States as *My Russia: The Political Autobiography of Gennady Zyuganov* (Armonk, N.Y.: M. E. Sharpe, 1997) after the presidential elections.

226. Urban and Solovei, *Russia's Communists,* 97–105; and Otto, "Gennadii Ziuganov," 38–41.

227. Founded in Rome in 1968, the Club of Rome is an international group of scientists, economists, businessmen, international civil servants, heads of state, and former heads of state concerned in general with industrial production and technological growth, and its negative effects on population and society. The group's popularity was at its height during the 1970s with its sponsorship of the best-selling *The Limits to Growth* (New York: Universe Books, 1972) and *Mankind at the Turning Point* (New York: Dutton, 1974).

228. One character who is notably missing from this gallery is Grigori Rasputin. This is understandable, given the extensive exposure of his role in the degeneration of the monarchy that led to its overthrow in February 1917.

229. Zyuganov, *Rossiya—Rodina moya,* 115–20.

230. Amusingly, he seems to view himself at the extreme left of his own imaginary spectrum of political correctness, while dismissing virtually every one of his neighbors on the left flank, whether liberals or socialists, as "Trotskyists"—or the "permanent revolutionaries" and, implicitly, agents of hostile civilizations.

231. Gennadi Zyuganov, "Junior Partner? No Way," *New York Times,* February 21, 1996.

232. Zyuganov, *Rossiya—Rodina moya,* 241. Let us note here the recurrent myth about the "super-affluence" of Westerners irrespective of class—a myth born out of deep ignorance about "the West" and nomenklatura envy for the consumption patterns of the upper class in some of the "Western" countries that, as we already discussed, played a formative role for the mindset and agenda of the Russian shock therapists.

233. Gennadi Zyuganov, *Za gorizontom* (Moscow: Informpechat', 1995), 32.

234. See the joint appeal published by several Nobel laureates in economics on the eve of the voting in *Nezavisimaya gazeta*, June 1, 1996.

235. For a detailed account of this period, see Urban and Solovei, *Russia's Communists,* chapters 2 and 3.

236. S. N. Baburin, *Rossiiskii put': utraty i obreteniya* (Moscow: Novator, 1997), 437. On Zyuganov's failed campaign, see Urban and Solovei, *Russia's Communists,* 167–73.

237. On all this, see Korzhakov's long talk with Chernomyrdin on April 16, 1996 in Korzhakov, *Boris Yeltsin,* 367–69; and also his interview in *Moskovskii komsomolets.*

238. *Rossiiskaya gazeta,* May 14, 1996; and *Vechernyaya Moskva,* June 5, 1996.

239. See Julia Wishnevsky, *Russia's Communists* (Washington, D.C.: Jamestown Foundation, 1999), 239.

240. Reuters, May 5, 1996.

241. Ibid. On Korzhakov, see *Izvestiya,* May 6, 1996.

242. *Nezavisimaya gazeta,* April 26, 1996.

243. Michael Kramer, "Rescuing Boris," *Time,* July 15, 1996.

244. "Anatoly Kulikov: Ya v avantiurakh ne uchastvuyu," *Nezavisimaya gazeta,* July 23, 1999. Interestingly, an official, secret U.S. account of a Yeltsin-Clinton meeting on March 13, 1996 gives the impression that, unlike in September 1993, Yeltsin gave Clinton no hint that he was considering taking drastic steps; see Bill Gertz, *Betrayal: How the Clinton Administration Undermined American Security* (Washington, D.C.: Regnery, 1999), 275–76.

245. For Yeltsin's previously unpublished angry letter on this topic to the Council of the Federation, seeking its support against the Duma, see Korzhakov, *Boris Yeltsin,* 440–41.

246. Yeltsin, *Zapiski prezidenta,* 207–8. In fact, Baturin was the main author of the decree.

247. Korzhakov, *Boris Yeltsin,* 362–86.

248. See Chrystia Freeland, "Draped in the Enemy Flag," *Financial Times* (London), May 11, 1996.

249. Lee Hockstader and David Hoffman, "From Tears to Triumph: How Yeltsin Came Back," *International Herald Tribune,* July 8, 1996, 1.

250. *Time,* May 27, 1996.

251. Peter Reddaway, "Russia Heads for Trouble," *New York Times,* July 2, 1996.

252. Other economists who were less enthusiastic about shock therapy, such as Yeltsin's economic adviser Aleksandr Livshits, predicted dire financial consequences from all this.

253. *Washington Post,* June 9, 1996.

254. European Institute for the Media, *Media and the Russian Presidential Elections.*

255. Michael Kramer, "The People Choose," *Time,* May 27, 1996.

256. White, Rose, and McAllister, *How Russia Votes,* 250.

257. *Nezavisimaya gazeta,* June 8, 1996

258. For a description of Lebed's request, which he made prior to April 16, see Korzhakov, *Boris Yeltsin,* 373–75. This source makes clear that Gusinsky and Malashenko had promoted this scenario, using NTV to build Lebed's support, and that Korzhakov was, at least initially, skeptical about it.

259. *Segodnya,* May 15, 1996.

260. As calculated by a team of European observers, Lebed was the only candidate beside Yeltsin who received more positive than negative coverage on television. See European Institute for the Media, *Media and the Russian Presidential Elections,* 7.

261. *Komsomol'skaya pravda,* May 30, 1996.

262. See Golovkov's retrospective description of the campaign in *Itogi,* no. 7 (1996). He claimed that the campaign cost 13 billion rubles (around $2 million) and employed at its height eighty people.

263. Lebed had attracted a certain type of democrat from early on. See, for example, *Kuranty,* August 18, 1994.

264. Remnick, *Resurrection,* 343.

265. Interview with Victor Loupan, *Le Figaro* (Paris), January 21, 1995.

266. For details on Lebed's participation in the election, see White, Rose, and McAllister, *How Russia Votes,* chapters 11 and 12; and Michael McFaul, *Russia's 1996 Presidential Election: The End of Polarized Politics* (Stanford, Calif.: Hoover Institution Press, 1997), chapters 5 and 6.

267. *Segodnya,* May 22, 1996.

268. *Moskovskii komsomolets,* June 25, 1996.

269. See, for example, Chubais's secret, minutely detailed timetable and battle plan for a visit by Yeltsin to Volgograd in Korzhakov, *Boris Yeltsin,* 443–50.

270. Ibid., 433–35.

271. According to a number of the authors' friends and acquaintances who witnessed these shows in Moscow and elsewhere, crowds of adolescents and adults, often high on drugs, were induced by the performers to repeat as a rhythmic incantation slogans of the Yeltsin campaign, such as "Vote, or You Will Lose!" Many of these shows featured discounted tickets, cheap drinks, and drugs—and fees in the thousands of dollars for the performers.

272. On this entire episode and its aftermath, see Streletsky, *Mrakobesie,* 226–89, an often first-hand account that includes thirty-six pages of documents. Reddaway gives a succinct account in "Questions about Russia's 'Dream Team.'"

273. For Lisovsky's brazen explanation of his actions, see Korzhakov, *Boris Yeltsin,* 455–56.

274. On this whole episode, see Reddaway, "Questions about Russia's 'Dream Team,'" 2.

275. Testimony of Peter Reddaway on July 10 before the U.S. Commission on Security and Cooperation in Europe in *Russia's Election: What Does It Mean?* (Washington, D.C.: Government Printing Office, 1996), 22–42.

276. *Nezavisimaya gazeta,* June 29, 1996.

277. See *Rossiiskaya gazeta,* October 9, 1996.

278. *Komsomol'skaya pravda,* September 21, 1996.

279. Episode reported at least twice by Lebed. For this quotation, see Andrei Piontkovsky, "A City Saved by a Righteous Man," *Prism* 5, no. 3 (February 1999).

280. See, for example, the allegations in the official *Rossiiskaya gazeta,* October 9, 1996; and in *Zavtra,* no. 41 (October 1996).

281. Korzhakov interview, *Parlamentskaya gazeta,* 1–2.

282. See the *Washington Post,* July 4, 7, and 5, 1996, respectively.

9. Market Bolshevism in Action: The Dream Team, Shock Therapy II, and Yeltsin's Search for a Successor

1. *Finansovye izvestiya,* December 10, 1996.

2. Poll by VTsIOM, the All-Russian Center for the Study of Public Opinion, in *Literaturnaya gazeta,* no. 10 (1997).

3. See the article by Michael Dobbs and Paul Blustein in the *Washington Post,* September 12, 1999. In fact, in fall 1999, Russia occupied thirtieth place among America's trade partners. See the full text of another of Pickering's talks in *Russia Business Watch* 4, no. 4 (Fall 1996): 46–49.

4. For the historical pattern of Bolshevism, see chapter 1.

5. *Zavtra,* no. 11 (March 1997).

6. *Moskovskii komsomolets,* February 28, 1997

7. *Washington Post,* March 17, 1997.

8. *Kommersant-Daily,* March 7, 1997.

9. Quoted by S. Menshikov, *Pravda* (extra edition), March 14–21, 1997.

10. *Rossiiskaya gazeta,* March 7, 1997.

11. Cited in *Pravda-5,* March 11, 1997

12. See the article by Aleksandr Minkin in *Novaya gazeta,* no. 8 (1997).

13. *Novoe vremya,* no. 9 (1997).

14. *Moskovskii komsomolets,* March 17, 1997.

15. *Sovetskaya Rossiya,* March 29, 1997.

16. See, for example, *Izvestiya,* April 22, 1997.

17. *Kommersant-Daily,* March 18, 1997.

18. *Nezavisimaya gazeta,* June 14, 1997.

19. Yulia Kalinina in *Moskovskii komsomolets,* March 14, 1997.

20. *Obshchaya gazeta,* no. 10 (1997).

21. *Nezavisimaya gazeta,* March 5, 1997.

22. *Izvestiya,* March 14, 1997.

23. *Argumenty i fakty,* no. 13 (1997) and *Sovetskaya Rossiya,* August 9, 1997.

24. *Novoe vremya*, no. 21 (1997).

25. *Moskovskaya pravda*, March 27, 1993.

26. *Nezavisimaya gazeta*, March 30, 1993.

27. *Rossiiskie vesti*, September 27, 1994.

28. See Marina Shakina in *Novoe vremya*, no. 21 (1997).

29. *Provintsial* (Moscow: Vagrius, 1997), 81, for example; on Chernomyrdin, see 88–90.

30. *Moskovskii komsomolets*, August 19, 1997.

31. *Kommersant-Daily*, March 18, 1997.

32. *Sobesednik*, no. 14 (1997).

33. *Segodnya,* March 24, 1997.

34. Perhaps the only serious charge against Nemtsov was his acceptance of a $100,000 fee for the self-promoting book mentioned earlier. The fee came from Sergei Lisovsky, the hero of the 1996 criminal saga of the Xerox-paper box containing $538,000. At the same time, as the press recounted, Nemtsov attempted to delay Yeltsin's signing of the decree on personal financial disclosure statements by government officials so that he had time to include this fee in his own statement; see *Segodnya*, August 5, 1997. Numerous allegations against him appear in some Duma documents (see Korzhakov, *Boris Yeltsin,* 423–26) and in an interview by his former friend and ex-convict Andrei Klimentiev in *Kur'er* (Los Angeles), September 19, 1997.

35. *Nezavisimaya gazeta,* April 10, 1997.

36. The television broadcast "Itogi," March 23, 1997.

37. *Russia Business Watch* 5, no. 2 (Spring 1997): 19.

38. Stefan Hedlund, *The Russian Economy: A Case of Pathological Institutions?* Working Paper no. 35 (Uppsala University, Department of East European Studies, September 1997).

39. *Izvestiya*, March 19, 1997.

40. *Moskovskii komsomolets*, March 24, 1997.

41. Cited in *Trud*, March 29, 1997.

42. *Vechernyaya Moskva*, March 29, 1997.

43. For Isaev's figure, see *Pravda-5*, March 29, 1997. For the government's estimate, see *Kommersant-Daily*, March 28, 1997.

44. *Vechernyaya Moskva*, March 29, 1997.

45. *Segodnya,* March 28, 1997.

46. *Komsomol'skaya pravda,* March 29, 1997.

47. *Wall Street Journal*, April 8, 1997.

48. *Rossiiskaya gazeta*, March 29, 1997.

49. *Nezavisimaya gazeta*, September 24, 1997.

50. As shown by Sergei Glaziev, *Ekonomicheskaya gazeta*, no. 11 (1997).

51. *Delovoi mir*, April 10, 1997.

52. *Nezavisimaya gazeta*, April 26, 1997.

53. *Nezavisimaya gazeta*, May 8, 1997.

54. *Kommersant-Daily*, June 17, 1997.

55. Oleg Rumyantsev, *Sotsialisticheskaya Rossiya,* no. 17 (1997).

56. Stanislav Govorukhin, *Kommersant-Daily*, April 29, 1997; *Pravda-5,* April 24, 1997.

57. Radio Ekho Moskvy, November 13, 1997.

58. *St. Petersburg Times*, April 7–13, 1997.

59. *Moskovskaya pravda*, June 17, 1997.

60. For details of parliament's budget discussion, see *Kommersant-Daily*, April 18, 1997; and *Nezavisimaya gazeta*, April 19, 1997.

61. *Trud*, June 4, 1997.

62. *Nezavisimaya gazeta*, May 25, 1997.

63. *Sovetskaya Rossiya*, June 7, 1997.

64. *Moskovskii komsomolets*, June 14, 1997.

65. *Gudok*, June 10, 1997.

66. *Demokraticheskii vybor*, no. 32 (1997).

67. *Ekonomicheskaya gazeta*, no. 22 (1997).

68. *Rossiiskaya gazeta*, May 19, 1997.

69. *Nezavisimaya gazeta*, May 23, 1997.

70. *Inzhenernaya gazeta*, no. 31 (1997).

71. *Itogi,* no. 24 (1997).

72. This picture is well summarized in Louise Shelley's expression "the privatized state." See chapter 1.

73. *Kommersant-Daily*, July 30, 1997, with reference to *Financial Times*; *Sovetskaya Rossiya*, August 2, 1997.

74. *Zavtra,* no. 31 (August 1997)

75. *Komsomol'skaya pravda*, July 30, 1997.

76. *Rossiiskie vesti*, July 31, 1997.

77. *Novaya gazeta*, no. 31 (1997); see also *Nezavisimaya gazeta*, July 29, 1997.

78. *Novaya gazeta*, no. 31 (1997).

79. *Moskovskie novosti*, no. 31 (August 1997).

80. On June 10, 1997, news agencies reported that Chubais had declared a 1996 income of $296,000, of which only 2 percent was salary for his government work and for his role in managing Yeltsin's re-election campaign.

81. *Segodnya*, July 30, 1997.

82. *Segodnya*, August 2, 1997.

83. *Delovoi mir*, August 5, 1997.

84. *Nezavisimaya gazeta*, August 6, 1997.

85. ITAR-TASS, August 15, 1997.

86. Only three months later, Boiko had to quit this position because of the previously mentioned scandal around a $450,000 book deal in which Chubais and four of his associates, including Boiko, figured as authors of a book about privatization.

87. *Nezavisimaya gazeta*, August 6, 1997.

88. *Moskovskie novosti*, no. 31 (1997).

89. *Russkii vestnik*, nos. 13–14 (1997).

90. *Litsa*, no. 8 (1997).

91. See Yuri Afanasiev's article in *Izvestiya*, June 20, 1997.

92. "The Sacrilege of the Anti-Russian Oligarchy," *Zavtra,* June 25, 1997.

93. The *zemsky sobor,* or the medieval Assembly of the Land, represented the estates and was the first body to elect the Romanovs to the throne in 1613 in Kostroma.

94. *Komsomol'skaya pravda*, July 31, 1997.

95. *Segodnya*, June 24, 1997.

96. *Izvestiya*, March 14, 1997.

97. *Komsomol'skaya pravda*, July 19, 1997.

98. Aleksandr Minkin, "Couldn't he think up something better?" *Novaya gazeta*, no. 20 (1997); *Nezavisimaya gazeta*, June 5, 1997.

99. Like other papers, *Segodnya* (August 9, 1997) mocked the whole enterprise when the first volume of official materials appeared. *Rossiya v poiskakh idei,* ed. Georgi Satarov (Moscow: Gruppa konsul'tantov pri Administratsii Presidenta Rossiiskoi Federatsii, 1997), is a compilation of 162 single-spaced pages with numerous tables and charts.

100. *Russkii telegraf*, September 24, 1997; *Moskovskie novosti*, no. 38 (1997).

101. *Rossiiskaya gazeta*, April 2, 1997.

102. *Izvestiya*, March 28, 1997.

103. Jonas Bernstein, "Requiem for a Reformer," *Moscow Times*, November 22, 1997.

104. *Novaya gazeta,* November 24, 1997.

105. *Novaya gazeta*, no. 15 (1997).

106. *Izvestiya*, April 15, 1997.

107. *Izvestiya*, April 17, 1997.

108. *Izvestiya*, April 19, 1997.

109. An appeal signed by famous authors like Okudzhava, Zhvanetsky, Voinovich, and others that spoke of an "offensive against democracy" appeared in *Izvestiya* on April 19, 1997.

110. *Zavtra*, June 30, 1997.

111. *Pravda-5*, May 21, 1997; *Kommersant-Daily*, May 24, 1997; *Nezavisimaya gazeta*, June 17, 1997.

112. *Megapolis-Kontinent*, nos. 24–25 (1997).

113. See *Sovetskaya Rossiya*, July 10, 1997; and *Moskovskii komsomolets*, July 14 and October 25, 1997.

114. *Rossiiskaya gazeta*, July 4, 1997.

115. *Kommersant-Daily*, April 9, 1997.

116. *Rossiiskie vesti* and *Rossiiskaya gazeta,* April 10, 1997.

117. *Rossiiskaya gazeta,* June 17, 1997.

118. "Without the Cabinet, Laws Are Not to Be Written," *Rossiiskaya gazeta*, June 10, 1997.

119. *Sovetskaya Rossiya*, August 7 and 9, 1997.

120. *Rossiiskaya gazeta*, April 10, 1997.

121. *Nezavisimaya gazeta*, July 30, 1997.

122. *Kommersant-Daily*, June 11, 1997.

123. *Washington Post*, May 23, 1997.

124. For the full text of the letter (dated June 20) and an account of its composition, see Andrei Antipov, *Lev Rokhlin: Zhizn' i smert' generala* (Moscow: EKSMO Press, 1998), 253–54, 362–79. This biography contains 135 pages of documents written by Rokhlin in 1995–98.

125. Ibid., 379.

126. Ibid., 220–22, 229–35.

127. *Nezavisimaya gazeta*, June 26, 1997.

128. Quoted from *Pravda*, July 4–11, 1997.

129. *Zavtra*, no. 26 (1997).

130. *Nezavisimaya gazeta,* June 25, 1997.

131. Antipov, *Lev Rokhlin,* 251–53.

132. *Kommersant-Daily*, July 1, 1997.

133. *Segodnya,* June 25, 1997.

134. *Moskovskaya pravda*, June 26, 1997.

135. As Rodionov later stated, Varennikov and Kryuchkov were in attendance but did not join his organization. They probably were told that their formal participation would make the whole venture too controversial; see *Obshchaya gazeta*, no. 28 (1997). On Rodionov's involvement with MSADI, see *Moskovskii komsomolets*, July 7, 1997.

136. *Kommersant-Daily*, July 10, 1997.

137. "Narodnaya Armiya" ("People's Army"), *Sovetskaya Rossiya*, July 12, 1997.

138. *Nezavisimaya gazeta*, July 18, 1997.

139. *Kommersant-Daily*, July 10, 1997.

140. *Kommersant-Daily*, July 11, 1997.

141. *Kommersant-Daily*, July 22, 1997; Antipov, *Lev Rokhlin,* 255.

142. *Nezavisimaya gazeta*, August 5, 1997.

143. *Kommersant-Daily*, July 12, 1997; see the full text in Antipov, *Lev Rokhlin,* 379–91.

144. *Nezavisimaya gazeta*, August 18, 1997.

145. On MSADI's evolution through 1999, see Sergei Chernyakhovsky, "The Movement in Support of the Army" in *Primer on Russia's 1999 Duma Elections,* ed. Michael McFaul, Nikolai Petrov, and Andrei Ryabov (Moscow: Carnegie Endowment for International Peace, 1999), 125–27.

146. Streletsky, *Mrakobesie,* 231–32.

147. *Izvestiya*, July 10, 1997.

148. *Obshchaya gazeta*, no. 33 (1997).

149. *Moskovskie novosti*, no. 24 (1997).

150. *Izvestiya,* August 28, 1997.

151. *Moskovskie novosti*, no. 28 (1997).

152. *Nezavisimaya gazeta*, August 28, 1997.

153. *Nezavisimaya gazeta*, September 24, 1997.

154. *RFE/RL Newsline*, November 24, 1997.

155. *New York Times,* October 29, 1997.

156. Peter Reddaway in the *Washington Post,* August 24, 1997.

157. *Rossiiskie vesti*, June 17, 1997.

158. *Nezavisimaya gazeta*, June 17, 1997.

159. *Trud,* August 29–September 4, 1997.

160. *Moskovskaya pravda*, March 5, 1997.

161. *Rossiisskaya pravda*, no. 11 (1997).

162. For her revolutionary creed, see *Pravda-5*, April 19, 1997.

163. *Nezavisimaya gazeta*, April 24, 1997.

164. *Moskovskii komsomolets*, April 2, 1997.

165. *Kommersant-Daily*, April 23, 1997; *Sovetskaya Rossiya*, April 24, 1997.

166. *Pravda Rossii*, no. 10 (1997); *Sovetskaya Rossiya*, April 26, 1997.

167. *Moskovskie novosti*, no. 16 (1997).

168. *Segodnya*, May 23, 1997; *Pravda-5*, May 25, 1997.

169. *Vechernyaya Moskva*, no. 30–31 (1997).

170. *Pravda Rossii*, August 15, 1996.

171. *Nezavisimaya gazeta*, March 28, 1997.

172. *Segodnya*, May 31, 1997.

173. *Vechernyaya Moskva*, April 24, 1997.

174. *Literaturnaya gazeta*, no. 21 (1997); *Novaya gazeta*, no. 21 (1997).

175. See Ponomarev, "Ne doveryayu reformatoram," *Nezavisimaya gazeta*, July 2, 1997.

176. *Moskovskii komsomolets*, August 1, 1997.

177. *Novaya gazeta*, October 13, 1997.

178. Yuri Burtin, "Chuzhaya vlast," *Nezavisimaya gazeta*, December 1, 1992.

179. For some of Poltoranin's indictments of the regime, see *Literaturnaya gazeta*, no. 17 (1997).

180. See Albats's articles in *Novaya gazeta—Ponedel'nik,* September 22 and October 6, 1997.

181. Yuri Luzhkov, *Egoizm vlasti* (Moscow: RGGU, 1996). This thirty-six-page booklet contains the text of the lecture and ten pages of questions and answers.

182. *Novoe vremya*, no. 19 (1997).

183. *Nezavisimaya gazeta*, April 26, 1997.

184. Strictly speaking, these assertions do not contradict historical fact. In 1954, the Crimea was transferred from the RSFSR to the Ukrainian SSR by an arbitrary Kremlin

decision that had poor historical and cultural justification. Sevastopol was excluded from this transfer as a special administrative unit under the central government of the USSR. In the course of the USSR's disintegration, Yeltsin made no effort to bring Sevastopol under Russian jurisdiction.

185. *Obshchaya gazeta*, no. 18 (1997). Earlier, Luzhkov had called for criminal investigation of Chubais's conduct of privatization and demanded the deprivatization of companies sold to cronies for rock-bottom prices; see Interfax, January 19, 1996.

186. See the report by Deputy Prosecutor General Oleg Gaidanov, who noted, "We have recently repealed seven unlawful orders issued by Anatoly Chubais." *Krasnaya zvezda*, November 1, 1994.

187. *Rabochaya tribuna*, June 24, 1997.

188. *Moskovskii komsomolets*, May 23, 1997.

189. *Segodnya*, July 4, 1997.

190. *Moya gazeta*, May 7, 1997.

191. *Nezavisimaya gazeta*, August 8, 1997.

192. *Kommersant-Daily*, June 17, 1997.

193. *Kommersant-Daily*, March 4, 1997.

194. On the Chernoi brothers, see "Moya gazeta," supplement in *Moskovskaya pravda*, April 2, 1997. While the Communists possess a political base in agriculture and the raw materials sector, the nationalists of today's Russia, as a rule, enjoy the support of the metallurgy sector. It is not by chance that Oleg Soskovets, the 1994–96 first deputy premier closest to the national-conservatives, was and largely remains the political patron of ferrous and nonferrous metal producers.

195. See, for example, Stanislav Menshikov in *Pravda* (special edition), March 7–14, 1997.

196. *Limonka*, no. 68 (1997).

197. *Segodnya,* March 28, 1997.

198. *Moskovskie novosti*, no. 14 (1997).

199. *Kommersant-Daily*, April 9, 1997.

200. *Zavtra*, no. 27 (1997).

201. *Nezavisimaya gazeta*, August 1, 1997.

202. *Nezavisimaya gazeta*, August 5, 1997.

203. *Komsomol'skaya pravda*, August 27, 1997.

204. *Pravda-5*, August 23, 1997.

205. *Segodnya*, April 8, 1997.

206. *Pravda-5*, July 9, 1997.

207. *Izvestiya,* April 2, 1997.

208. See Rogozin's programmatic statement titled "The Russian State Is for Ethnic Russians," *Pravda-5*, April 25, 1997, which is somewhat more radical than his party's manifesto adopted in May 1996—Dmitri Rogozin, ed., *Manifest vozrozhdeniya Rossii* (St. Petersburg: Glagol, 1996).

209. Kenneth Jowitt, *Notes on National Weakness* (Washington, D.C.: National Council for Soviet and East European Research, 1995), 6–9.

210. *Kommersant-Daily* and *Vechernyaya Moskva*, July 8, 1997.

211. For more details about these organizations, see *Nezavisimaya gazeta*, July 11, 1997.

212. *Moskovskii komsomolets*, August 5, 1997.

213. See the law's full text in *Rossiiskaya gazeta,* October 1, 1997, and an analysis of its genesis and significance in Commission on Security and Cooperation in Europe, *Status of the Russian Religious Law* (Washington, D.C.: CSCE, 1998).

214. See the text of the treaty in *Rossiiskaya gazeta,* May 20, 1997.

215. *Kommersant-Daily*, April 3, 1997.

216. *Nezavisimaya gazeta,* May 20, 1997.

217. *Patriot*, no. 31 (1997).

218. *Obshchaya gazeta*, August 28–September 3, 1997.

219. *Kommersant-Daily*, May 7, 1997.

220. U.S. Agency for International Development, press release, May 20, 1997.

221. See his written address to parliament in ITAR-TASS, February 17, 1999.

222. *RFE/RL Newsline,* April 15, 1998; *Kommersant-Daily,* April 15, 1998.

223. See *Monitor,* March 30, 1998.

224. *RFE/RL Newsline,* April 15, 1998.

225. Independent Television (NTV) report, April 26, 1998.

226. *Moskovskii komsomolets,* April 25, 1998.

227. Interview in *Moskovskii komsomolets,* April 22, 1998.

228. Robert Lyle, "Two Supporters Warn Russia," RFE/RL Report, Washington, D.C., April 2, 1998. Modified texts of Summers's and Camdessus's speeches, bowdlerized to soften the criticism, can be found in *Russia Business Watch* 6, no. 2 (Spring 1998): 14–15 and 19–20, respectively.

229. *Kommersant-Daily,* April 19, 2000.

230. Summers and Camdessus speeches, *Russia Business Watch,* 15.

231. This story was written up in some detail in an article by Michael Dobbs and Paul Blustein in the *Washington Post,* September 12, 1999.

232. See his letter in *The Weekly Standard,* January 19, 1998, 5. The letter is in response to Peter Reddaway's criticism of him in the same issue.

233. See the detailed response to Aslund by Peter Reddaway in *Johnson's Russia List,* February 7, 1998.

234. "The Virus in Russia," *New York Times,* June 1, 1998. See also Sokolov's much lengthier material, "Privatization, Corruption, and Reform in Present Day Russia," *Demokratizatsiya* 6, no. 4 (Fall 1998): 664–75. For valuable material on the misuse of the enormous funds intended for the reconstruction of Chechnya, of which Soskovets and Lobov appear to have been beneficiaries, see John Dunlop, "Sifting Through the Rubble of the Yeltsin Years," *Problems of Post-Communism* 47, no. 1 (January–February 2000): 10–11. For a painstaking and balanced compilation of the corruption charges against the four groups headed by Yeltsin, Chernomyrdin, Chubais, and Nemtsov, see the first in a planned series of five volumes by Aleksei Mukhin on Russian corruption, *Korruptsiya* *i gruppy vliyaniya* (Moscow: Sluzhba politicheskoi informatsii i konsul'tatsii "Tsentr," 1999). Volumes 2–5 are to cover corruption in the top political and judicial structures, the police and special services, the business world, and the regions.

235. The Russian economist Andrei Illarionov warned about this, as did Reddaway and Glinski in an article in the *Los Angeles Times,* July 19, 1998.

236. Yevgenia Albats, Owen Matthews, Bill Powell, and Mark Hosenball, "Where Did Russia's Money Go?" *Newsweek International,* September 30, 1999.

237. See Chubais's interview in *Kommersant-Daily,* September 8, 1998.

238. Chubais's letter in *Moscow Times,* September 16, 1998.

239. Ibid., emphasis added.

240. Ibid.

241. For insightful analysis of U.S.-Russian relations in 1998, see Dimitri K. Simes, "Russia's Crisis, America's Complicity," *The National Interest,* no. 54 (Winter 1998–99): 12–22, and his subsequent exchange with Henry Trofimenko in *The National Interest,* no. 55 (Spring 1999): 118–19. This article later formed part of his book *After the Collapse.*

242. See the full text of the letter dated September 18 in *Zavtra,* no. 41 (October 13, 1998).

243. Interview in *Parlamentskaya gazeta,* September 16, 1998.

244. *Kommersant-Daily,* November 3, 1998.

245. See the useful account by David Hoffman in the *Washington Post,* July 1, 1999.

246. See the portrait of Khodorkovsky in *Nezavisimaya gazeta,* April 8, 1997; article quoted in Bivens and Bernstein, "The Russia You Never Met," 619.

247. See the article by I. Baranovsky in *Moscow News,* July 22–28, 1994, as quoted in Bivens and Bernstein, "The Russia You Never Met," 618–19.

248. On Voloshin's wide range of shady dealings, see Oleg Lurie's article in *Sovershenno sekretno,* no. 8 (1998).

249. For knowledgeable analysis of this episode and its background, see Klebnikov, "The Day They Raided Aeroflot," 106–110.

250. Except where otherwise indicated, the sources for this section on the Swiss involvement come from an article by Carlo Bonini and Giuseppe D'Avanzo in *Corriere della Sera* (Milan), August 25, 1999; and an interview by Skuratov in *La Reppublica* (Rome), September 15, 1999.

251. The fullest account we have seen of Turover's extensive and carefully organized files on numerous individuals is the article by Oleg Lurie in *Novaya gazeta,* December 27, 1999.

252. See his interview in *Moskovskii komsomolets,* September 14, 1999.

253. On the rather shadowy Stolpovskikh (born 1963), see his interviews in *Komsomol'skaya pravda,* December 2, 1998, and *Argumenty i fakty,* no. 36 (August 9, 1999); Bonini and D'Avanzo in *Corriere della Sera;* Leonid Krutakov's revealing article, "Stolpy vlasti," *Moskovskii komsomolets,* June 15, 1999; and an interview with Felipe Turover in ibid., in which Turover claims that Stolpovskikh acquired a house in Lugano worth $15 million. When the *Argumenty i fakty* reporter asked him about the ownership of the mansion in Garmisch-Partenkirchen, she mistakenly placed it in Austria, not Germany. Stolpovskikh simply replied that he did not own any houses in Austria, thus avoiding the question the reporter was trying to ask.

254. Krutakov, "Stolpy vlasti," on which much of this section is based.

255. *Kommersant-Daily,* March 6, 1999. Because the paper is owned by Berezovsky, it cannot be excluded that this report was not accurate and was designed to mislead the public about his relations with Yeltsin.

256. Chuglazov's interview with Interfax, Moscow, August 30, 1999.

257. Krutakov, "Stolpy vlasti."

258. See *Monitor,* April 21 and 22, 1999, for quoted sources and summaries of Russian media reaction. Yeltsin's talk of the agreements can only have reminded the governors of their unrelenting struggle to get the payments due them from Moscow, a struggle routinely requiring them to give 10–20 percent of the payment to extortionate middlemen (*zhuchki*) working hand in glove with the federal bureaucrats. See the remarkable article by Lev Segal, "Shell Games in the Ministry of Finance: Everyone Profits But the Russian Taxpayer," *Prism* 3, no. 10 (June 1997): 8–11.

259. Krutakov, "Stolpy vlasti."

260. This was stated categorically by the businessman and politician Vladimir Semago. See *Novaya gazeta,* July 17, 2000. Semago's claim has not been denied.

261. Most of these arguments are advanced by Vitaly Tretiakov in "Proshchai, Yabloko!" *Nezavisimaya gazeta,* May 18, 1999.

262. Aleksandr Shokhin, as quoted in *Monitor,* May 12, 1999.

263. In the fall of 1999, a Russian diplomat in Washington, D.C., privately alleged that such an agreement had been made.

264. *Kommersant-Vlast',* May 18, 1999.

265. Quoted in the *Washington Post,* May 29, 1999.

266. See, for example, *Kommersant-Daily,* May 21, 1999.

267. See Stepashin's revealing interview in *Nezavisimaya gazeta,* January 14, 2000. It appears that he was building on pioneering work done in April–May by Berezovsky and generously funded by the aluminum magnate and alleged organized crime figure Lev Chernoi. See the report based on Interior Ministry information in *Kommersant-Daily,* May 19, 1999.

268. See his programmatic speech published on August 18 in the Russian press, in which he said that his agreement to lead the coalition did not mean he had joined either of its two main constituents.

269. Aleksandr Zhilin, "Opasnye igry v kremlevskikh zastenkakh," *Moskovskaya pravda,* August 25, 1999, quoting insider sources.

270. Quoted in the editorial "Dizzy With Success," *Moscow Times,* January 18, 2000.

271. Zhilin, "Opasnye igry."

272. Ibid.

273. Interview on Radio Ekho Moskvy, August 17, 1999, as reported in *RFE/RL Newsline,* August 18, 1999.

274. Stepashin interview, *Nezavisimaya gazeta.*

275. See Tretiakov's editorial in *Nezavisimaya gazeta,* October 12, 1999.

276. For a useful analysis of this involvement, including Berezovsky's unfailing compulsion to profit either financially or politically from war and from the Chechens' kidnappings of usually innocent victims, see Klebnikov, "Conflagration in Russia," 90–96. For a broader and documented analysis of this whole episode, see John Dunlop, "Two Incursions into Dagestan and Their Extraordinary Consequences," *Contemporary Caucasus Newsletter,* no. 9 (Spring 2000), 20–24.

277. See Kagarlitsky's analysis, "S terroristami ne razgovarivaem. No pomogaem? Versiya vzryvov v Rossii," *Novaya gazeta,* no. 3 (January 24–30, 2000). A less subtle variation of his thesis is Pyotr Pryanishnikov's article in *Versiya,* February 1–7, 2000. See also *Le Monde,* January 26, 2000, and Pryanishnikov's article in *Versiya,* July 4, 2000. The common thread in these articles is an alleged meeting in June or July in France to set the ground rules for the Dagestan incursion. The meeting was allegedly attended by Basayev, Presidential Administration head Voloshin, and others, and orchestrated by Anton Surikov, a scientist and political analyst connected with Russian military intelligence. An early version of the general theory appeared in *Profil',* September 13, 1999.

278. On these issues see, for example, Klebnikov, "Conflagration in Russia."

279. A. Zhilin, "Vtoraya predvybornaya kavkazskaya voina," *Moskovskaya pravda,* (special section on "Stolichnyi kriminal"), August 25, 1999; emphasis added.

280. Ibid.

281. Interfax, January 25, 2000. For probing analyses of the Ryazan episode, see *Segodnya* and *Nezavisimaya gazeta,* September 25, 1999.

282. www.fsb.ru/search/search.html.

283. See Kagarlitsky, "S terroristami," and also the other articles listed after it.

284. George Soros, "Who Lost Russia?" *New York Review of Books,* April 13, 2000, 10–18. Soros presented a short version of his thesis in *Moscow News,* February 22, 2000.

285. See the details in *Monitor,* September 10, 1999.

286. *Izvestiya,* August 29, 1998.

287. See Stepashin's account of his visit in an interview in *Kommersant-Daily,* September 18, 1999.

288. See the article by Kalle Koponen in *Helsingin Sanomat* (Helsinki), August 22, 1999.

289. *Moscow Times,* August 30, 1999; *Monitor,* August 31, 1999.

290. Six months later, no Russians living in Russia had yet been charged in this case, but two living in the West, Lucy Edwards and Peter Berlin, pleaded guilty to having set up front companies, opened accounts, and facilitated 160,000 electronic bank transfers worth over $7 billion during a four-year period at the behest of figures controlling two Moscow banks. *Washington Post,* February 17, 2000.

291. The Media Ministry warned Public Russian Television, which Berezovsky controlled, that "statements disrespectful to the president" could lead to the revocation of the station's license; Russian Information Agency, August 30, 1999. The same day *Moskovskii komsomolets* reported on the Kremlin's anger with the oligarch. On Luzhkov, see Interfax interview, August 28, 1999, and an article under the pseudonym Nikolai Ulyanov, *Nezavisimaya gazeta,* August 30, 1999.

292. *Moscow Times,* August 31, 1999.

293. For a wide selection of these charges, see Yabloko's web site at www.yabloko.ru.

294. G. Pavlovsky, "Kak nam reorganizovat' KPRF? Kommunisty—vsego lish' mif, sozdannyi antikommunistami," *Nezavisimaya gazeta,* May 27, 1999. For an analysis of the broad political significance of the Duma elections, see the article by Dmitri Glinski Vassiliev in *Moscow Times,* December 30, 1999.

295. ITAR-TASS, December 31, 1999.

296. Quoted in Charles Gati, "The Proof's in the Putin," *Review and Outlook,* 24, no. 4 (April 2000), 4.

297. Interview in *Nezavisimaya gazeta,* November 3, 1999. For further virtual in-subordination by military leaders, see *Moskovskii komsomolets,* November 5, 1999.

298. For intelligent thinking along these lines, see Rajan Menon and Graham Fuller, "Russia's Ruinous Chechen War," *Foreign Affairs,* March–April 2000, 32–44. See also the penetrating insights of French philosopher André Glucksmann following his visit to Chechnya in *Novaya gazeta–Ponedel'nik,* July 10, 2000, and the far-sighted warnings of the chief Mufti of Russia, Ravil Gainutdinov, quoted in Paul Goble, "Russia—Analysis from Washington: Aiming at the Wrong Target," RFE/RL Report, Washington, D.C., July 28, 2000. Gainutdinov's warnings suggested, in summary, that "misplaced official attacks on Wahhabism could have the effect of making it more attractive to those Muslims who for other, political reasons are angry with Russian policies." For evidence that Karachayevo- Cherkessia may be the next North Caucasus republic to follow Chechnya and Dagestan into turmoil, see *Moskovskii komsomolets,* July 17, 2000.

299. See in particular the articles by Oleg Lurie in *Versiya,* August 17–23, 1999, and *Novaya gazeta,* no. 10 (December 27, 1999).

300. Agathe Duparc reported this comment by an "associate of Berezovsky" who was one of those people who "do not hesitate to issue warnings: 'If we had the shadow of a doubt about Putin's loyalty [to Berezovsky], certain things could surface, like his exact role in the murderous bombings of September. Just before they occurred, Putin was directing the FSB, and he probably knew what was in the works," *Le Monde,* January 27, 2000, 6.

301. On the national industrial policy (and new orders for the defense industries), see ITAR-TASS, May 22, 2000. On the regional economic plans announced by Ilya Klebanov, see *Kommersant-Daily,* August 2, 2000. And for Viktor Khristenko's sharp objection to the plans, see *Kommersant-Vlast',* August 15, 2000.

302. Goskomstat figures reported by Dow Jones Newswires, June 13, 2000, and an article by Yuri Petrov in *Ekonomika i zhizn',* no. 21 (May 2000).

303. The debate erupted in July 2000. See Andrei Parshev, *Pochemu Rossiya ne Amerika: Kniga dlya tekh, kto ostaetsya zdes'* (Moscow: Krymskii Most-9D, 2000).

304. For an early analysis of this mode!, see Dmitri Glinski Vassiliev, "To Join or Not to Join? NATO and Russia's Ruling Class" (http://www.antiwar.com/), March 29, 2000.

305. Text in *Johnson's Russia List* and *Nezavisimaya gazeta,* June 9, 2000. The signatories included L. Klein, F. Modigliani, D. North, M. Goldman, L. Abalkin, O. Bogomolov, D. L'vov, and N. Petrakov.

306. Quotations are from the article by A. Porfiriev in *Segodnya,* June 21, 2000.

307. See the anonymous article "Chto gotovit vlast'," *Novaya gazeta,* August 14, 2000, and Pavlovsky's interview in the military newspaper *Krasnaya zvezda,* August 12, 2000.

308. See the Prokhanov-Chikin open letter in *Zavtra,* no. 28 (July 2000); their discussion of Putin's policies and problems in *Sovetskaya Rossiya,* July 18, 2000; and Prokhanov's impressions of the meeting in *Argumenty i fakty,* August 16, 2000.

309. For an incisive analysis of the Gusinsky case, see Boris Kagarlitsky's article from Novosti News Agency, June 28, 2000.

310. Interview with RIA Novosti, May 31, 2000.

311. For Putin's decree, see *Rossiiskaya gazeta,* May 16, 2000. For key issues in the debate, see the interviews by Sergei Samoilov, head of regional affairs in the Presidential Administration, in *Russian Regional Report* 5, no. 30 (August 2, 2000), and by Viktor Khristenko in *Kommersant-Vlast',* August 15, 2000.

312. On this topic, see Vassiliev, "To Join or Not to Join?"

EPILOGUE: MARKET BOSLSHEVISM, A HISTORICAL INTERPRETATION

1. Thus, for example, a poll conducted in April 1988 by Moscow's Perestroika Club among its audience highlighted social justice as a paramount value, supported by 70 percent of its respondents. See Lukin, *Political Culture of Russian Democrats,* 284. These broad aspirations were also supported at the mass level. Thus a 1989 survey by VTsIOM showed support for political reform, but not for the "abandonment of socialist principles." This evidence led Western sociologists to the conclusion that the failure of the CPSU as an institution was not equivalent to the rejection of the norm of social justice and, in fact, "may have been due . . . to its unwillingness or inability to service the norm"; Finifter and Mickiewicz, "Redefining the Political System of the USSR," 860–61. That this is evidence of remarkable continuity in Soviet attitudes about their system is shown by the Soviet émigré participants of the Harvard Project in the 1950s, who also expressed their discontent with the privileges of the Communist elite, along with support for many basic elements of the Soviet economic system, such as government ownership of heavy industry; see Inkeles, "Images of Class Relations."

2. It was only very late, in October 1990, that the better-structured part of the movement, Democratic Russia, became institutionalized as a single political organization. However, it did not represent the full spectrum of the original movement and already by January 1992 had split over such key issues as the disintegration of the Union and shock therapy.

3. Again, consider Maximilian Voloshin's famous line: "Peter the Great was the first Bolshevik."

4. See his "Notes About Corruption in Russia" (talk delivered at the Woodrow Wilson International Center for Scholars, Washington, D.C., September 27, 1996).

5. *Izvestiya,* April 23, 1997.

6. See the article by Viktor Luchin, a member of Russia's Constitutional Court, "Decretal Law," *Yuridicheskaya gazeta,* no. 17 (1997).

7. In trying to counteract these revelations, prominent Russian "reformers" used American aid money for Russia to pay public relations companies, notably Burson

Marsteller in New York. See "Burson Marsteller. Kredity, kotorye my poteryali," *Profil'*, no. 12 (April 1997), 30–31.

8. This sort of thinking is also expounded by the democrat Dmitri Furman. See, for example, his "Oni v svoikh korridorakh: Putin kak 'novyi Andropov,'" *Obshchaya gazeta*, November 18, 1999.

9. Vitaly Tretiakov's insightful pro-Putin article, "Goliath and the Leviathan" (*Nezavisimaya gazeta*, June 1, 2000), emphasizes the difficulty of subduing the bureaucracy.

10. Pyotr Chaadayev, *Polnoe sobranie sochinenii*, vol. 1 (Moscow: Nauka, 1991), 326.

11. Maximilian Voloshin, *Stikhi, stat'i, vospominaniya* (Moscow: Pravda, 1991), 137.

INDEX

Peter Reddaway, a veteran scholar of Soviet and Russian politics, is professor of political science and international affairs at George Washington University in Washington, D.C. He is the author of many articles and books on Soviet political protest, including *Uncensored Russia: The Human Rights Movement in the Soviet Union.* From 1986 to 1989, Professor Reddaway was director of the Kennan Institute for Advanced Russian Studies. He was a distinguished fellow at the U.S. Institute of Peace in 1993–94.

Dmitri Glinski Vassiliev is a senior research associate at the Russian Academy of Sciences' Institute of World Economy and International Relations in Moscow, from which he recently obtained his doctorate in history. He has published several articles on Russian domestic and foreign policy, and was formerly an active member of Russia's democratic movement.

United States Institute of Peace

The United States Institute of Peace is an independent, nonpartisan federal institution created by Congress to promote research, education, and training on the peaceful management and resolution of international conflicts. Established in 1984, the Institute meets its congressional mandate through an array of programs, including research grants, fellowships, professional training, education programs from high school through graduate school, conferences and workshops, library services, and publications. The Institute's Board of Directors is appointed by the President of the United States and confirmed by the Senate.

Chairman of the Board: Chester A. Crocker
Vice Chairman: Max M. Kampelman
President: Richard H. Solomon
Executive Vice President: Harriet Hentges

Jennings Randolph Program
for International Peace

This book is a fine example of the work produced by senior fellows in the Jennings Randolph fellowship program of the United States Institute of Peace. As part of the statute establishing the Institute, Congress envisioned a program that would appoint "scholars and leaders of peace from the United States and abroad to pursue scholarly inquiry and other appropriate forms of communication on international peace and conflict resolution." The program was named after Senator Jennings Randolph of West Virginia, whose efforts over four decades helped to establish the Institute.

Since 1987, the Jennings Randolph Program has played a key role in the Institute's effort to build a national center of research, dialogue, and education on critical problems of conflict and peace. More than a hundred senior fellows from some thirty nations have carried out projects on the sources and nature of violent international conflict and the ways such conflict can be peacefully managed or resolved. Fellows come from a wide variety of academic and other professional backgrounds. They conduct research at the Institute and participate in the Institute's outreach activities to policymakers, the academic community, and the American public.

Each year approximately fifteen senior fellows are in residence at the Institute. Fellowship recipients are selected by the Institute's board of directors in a competitive process. For further information on the program, or to receive an application form, please contact the program staff at (202) 457-1700.

Joseph Klaits
Director

THE TRAGEDY OF RUSSIA'S REFORMS: MARKET BOLSHEVISM AGAINST DEMOCRACY

This book is set in the typeface Times Roman; the display type is Charlemagne. Cover design by Hasten Design Studio, Inc. of Washington, D.C. Interior design by Mike Chase and Marie Marr. Page makeup by Helene Redmond of HYR Graphics. Copyediting and proofreading by EEI Communications, Inc. of Alexandria, Virginia. Peter Pavilionis was the book's editor.